June 23-27, 2014
Vancouver, BC, Canada

I0053423

Association for Computing Machinery

Advancing Computing as a Science & Profession

HPDC'14

Proceedings of the 23rd International Symposium on

High-Performance Parallel and Distributed Computing

Sponsored by:

ACM SIGARCH and The University of Arizona

Supported by:

U.S. Department of Energy, NVIDIA, EMC^2, Indiana University, and COHO Data

Association for
Computing Machinery

Advancing Computing as a Science & Profession

The Association for Computing Machinery
2 Penn Plaza, Suite 701
New York, New York 10121-0701

Notice to Past Authors of ACM-Published Articles
ACM intends to create a complete electronic archive of all articles and/or other material previously published by ACM. If you have written a work that has been previously published by ACM in any journal or conference proceedings prior to 1978, or any SIG Newsletter at any time, and you do NOT want this work to appear in the ACM Digital Library, please inform permissions@acm.org, stating the title of the work, the author(s), and where and when published.

ISBN: 978-1-4503-2748-0 (Digital)

ISBN: 978-1-4503-3093-0 (Print)

Additional copies may be ordered prepaid from:

ACM Order Department
PO Box 30777
New York, NY 10087-0777, USA

Phone: 1-800-342-6626 (USA and Canada)
+1-212-626-0500 (Global)
Fax: +1-212-944-1318
E-mail: acmhelp@acm.org
Hours of Operation: 8:30 am – 4:30 pm ET

Printed in the USA

HPDC 2014 Chairs' Message

Welcome to the *23nd ACM Symposium on High-Performance Parallel and Distributed Computing* (HPDC'14). HPDC'14 follows the tradition of previous versions of the conference by providing a high-quality, single-track forum for presenting new research results on all aspects of the design, implementation, evaluation, and application of parallel and distributed systems for high-end computing. The HPDC'14 program features seven sessions on Checkpointing and Migration, Fault Tolerance, Memory Management, Scheduling and Mapping, BigData and MapReduce, Graph Processing, and Cloud and Virtualization. Additionally, this year the conference has included a number of short papers for presentation in three sessions: Systems, I/O, and Data-Intensive Computing. Professor Krishna Palem of Rice University will give a keynote presentation. This program is complemented by an interesting set of workshops on a range of timely and related systems and application topics.

The conference once again features the presentation of the HPDC Annual Achievement Award, which was started in 2012. The purpose of this award is to recognize individuals who have made long-lasting, influential contributions to the foundations or practice of the field of high-performance parallel and distributed computing, to raise the awareness of these contributions, especially among the younger generation of researchers, and to improve the image and the public relations of the HPDC community. The process of selecting the winner of the award was formalized this year with an open call for nominations. The recipient of the 2014 HPDC Achievement Award is Professor Rich Wolski of the University of California at Santa Barbara, who will give an Achievement Award Talk as a keynote at the conference.

The HPDC'14 call for papers attracted 130 paper submissions. In the review process this year, we followed two established methods that were started in 2012: the two-round review and the author rebuttal. In the first round of review, all papers received three reviews, and based on these reviews, 91 papers went to the second round in which virtually all of them received another two or three reviews. In total, 559 reviews were generated by the 49-member Program Committee along with a number of external reviewers. For many of the 91 second-round papers, the authors submitted rebuttals. Rebuttals were carefully taken into consideration during the Program Committee deliberations as part of the selection process. On March 20-21, the Program Committee met at Northwestern University (Evanston, IL) and made the final selection. Every one of the 130 submissions was discussed at the meeting. At the end of the 1.5-day meeting, the Program Committee accepted 21 full papers, resulting in an acceptance rate of 16.2%. In addition, the committee accepted 13 submissions as short papers. We would like to thank all contributing authors, regardless of the results of their submissions. We are very grateful to the Program Committee members for their hard work and for providing their reviews on time, in what was a very tight review schedule and a very rigorous review process.

HPDC 2014 has been generously sponsored by ACM SIGARCH and The University of Arizona. We would also like to acknowledge the support of the US Department of Energy, the US National Science Foundation, NVIDIA, Indiana University, EMC Corporation, COHO Data and PGI.

Beth Plale
HPDC'14 General Chair

Franck Cappello
HPDC'14 Program Chair

Matei Ripeanu
HPDC'14 General Chair

Dongyan Xu
HPDC'14 Program Chair

Table of Contents

Session: Checkpointing and Migration

Session: Fault Tolerance

Session: Memory Management

Short Paper Session 1: Systems

Session: Scheduling and Mapping

Session: BigData and MapReduce

Session: Graph Processing

Short Paper Session 2: I/O

Session: Cloud and Virtualization

Short Paper Session 3: Data-Intensive Computing

HPDC 2014 Organization

General Chairs: Beth Plale *(Indiana University, USA)*
Matei Ripeanu *(University of British Columbia, CA)*

Program Chairs: Franck Cappello *(Argonne National Lab and INRIA, USA)*
Dongyan Xu *(Purdue University, USA)*

Workshops Chair: Martin Swany *(Indiana University, USA)*

Sponsorship Co-Chairs: Dean Hildebrand *(IBM Almaden, USA)*
Jack Lange *(University of Pittsburgh, USA)*

Poster Chair: Abhishek Chandra *(University of Minnesota, USA)*

Publicity Chair: Ioan Raicu *(Illinois Institute of Technology, USA)*

Publications Chair: Pavan Balaji *(Argonne National Lab, USA)*

Treasurer: Nicole Todd *(Indiana University, USA)*

Webmaster: Abdullah Gharaibeh *(University of British Columbia, CA)*

Program Committee: David Abramson *(University of Queensland, Australia)*
Gabriel Antoniu *(INRIA, France)*
Henri Bal *(Vrije Universiteit, the Netherlands)*
Adam Barker *(University of St Andrews, UK)*
Michela Becchi *(University of Missouri - Columbia, USA)*
Greg Bronevetsky *(Lawrence Livermore National Laboratory, USA)*
Ali Butt *(Virginia Tech, USA)*
Abhishek Chandra *(University of Minnesota, USA)*
Andrew Chien *(University of Chicago and Argonne National Laboratory, USA)*
Paolo Costa *(Microsoft Research Cambridge, UK)*
Dilma Da Silva *(Qualcomm Research Silicon Valley, USA)*
Peter Dinda *(Northwestern University, USA)*
Dick Epema *(Delft and Eindhoven University of Technology, the Netherlands)*
Gilles Fedak *(INRIA, France)*
Wu-chun Feng *(Virginia Tech, USA)*
Renato Figueiredo *(University of Florida, USA)*
Ian Foster *(Argonne National Laboratory, USA)*
Kartik Gopalan *(Binghamton University, USA)*
Haryadi Gunawi *(University of Chicago, USA)*

HPDC 2014 Reviewers

Dulcardo Arteaga

Atilla S. Balkir

Jorge Cabrera

Jin Chao

Straube Christian

Pietro Cicotti

Alexandru Costan

Narayan Desai

Umesh Deshpande

Minh Dinh

Matthieu Dorier

Aiman Fang

Hajime Fujita

Hajime Fujita

Inigo Goiri

Kyle Hale

Benjamin Heintz

Shadi Ibrahim

Ward Jaradat

Gregory Jean-Baptise

Matt Kappel

Kostas Katrinis

Francis Liu

Andre Merzky

Kwangsung Oh

Anne-Cécile Orgerie

Filip Panovski

Ajaykrishna Raghavan

Zachary Rubenstein

Kittisak Sajjapongse

Jason Sonnek

Maciej Swiech

Wei Tang

Rajeev Thakur

Antons Trekalis

Radu Tudoran

Blesson Varghese

Ole Weidner

Justin Wozniak

Yiqi Xu

Fan Yang

Zhao Zhang

HPDC 2014 Sponsors & Supporters

Sponsors:

Arizona's First University.

Supporters:

Snapify: Capturing Snapshots of Offload Applications on Xeon Phi Manycore Processors

Arash Rezaei[1], Giuseppe Coviello[2], Cheng-Hong Li[2], Srimat Chakradhar[2], Frank Mueller[1]

[1] Department of Computer Science, North Carolina State University, Raleigh, NC.
[2] Computing Systems Architecture Department, NEC Laboratories America, Inc., Princeton, NJ.

ABSTRACT

Intel Xeon Phi coprocessors provide excellent performance acceleration for highly parallel applications and have been deployed in several top-ranking supercomputers. One popular approach of programming the Xeon Phi is the *offload* model, where parallel code is executed on the Xeon Phi, while the host system executes the sequential code. However, Xeon Phi's Many Integrated Core Platform Software Stack (MPSS) lacks fault-tolerance support for offload applications. This paper introduces Snapify, a set of extensions to MPSS that provides three novel features for Xeon Phi offload applications: checkpoint and restart, process swapping, and process migration. The core technique of Snapify is to take consistent process snapshots of the communicating offload processes and their host processes. To reduce the PCI latency of storing and retrieving process snapshots, Snapify uses a novel data transfer mechanism based on remote direct memory access (RDMA). Snapify can be used transparently by single-node and MPI applications, or be triggered directly by job schedulers through Snapify's API. Experimental results on OpenMP and MPI offload applications show that Snapify adds a runtime overhead of at most 5%, and this overhead is low enough for most use cases in practice.

Categories and Subject Descriptors

D.4.5 [**Reliability**]: Checkpoint/Restart—*Fault Tolerance*

Keywords

Checkpoint and restart, process swapping, process migration, snapshot, fault tolerance, Xeon Phi, coprocessor, system software

1. INTRODUCTION

A Xeon Phi coprocessor has up to 61 cores, connected by a high-speed on-chip interconnect. Each core supports four hardware threads, and has a 512-bit wide vector unit to execute SIMD instructions. The coprocessor has its own physical memory of 8/16GB, which can be accessed with an aggregate memory bandwidth of 352GB/s. Both the coprocessor and the host system run their own operating systems. The host system and the coprocessor

do not share a common memory space, and the two are physically connected by the PCIe bus.

Xeon Phi's software stack (MPSS) supports two programming models. In the *offload* programming model, highly parallel, code segments are executed on Xeon Phi, while the host system executes the sequential code. On the other hand, the *native* programming model allows users to execute their applications entirely on the Xeon Phi coprocessor. MPSS provides high-level language support and a modified Linux OS on Xeon Phi to facilitate both programming models. As a result of its performance acceleration for highly parallel applications and ease of programming, Xeon Phi coprocessors have been deployed in HPC systems, including several top-ranking supercomputers [14].

Using coprocessors like Xeon Phi in HPC systems, however, compounds the problem of the increasing failure rate due to the system's growing size and complexity [6]. A recent study on a GPU-based supercomputer shows a failure rate of 13 hours on average [32]. It is projected that the mean time between failure of HPC systems will continue to shrink [6, 33]. Therefore programmers must adopt certain fault tolerance mechanism for their applications.

Checkpoint and restart is a fault-tolerance technique widely used in HPC systems. Such a method periodically takes a snapshot of the application state and saves it on persistent storage. In case of an error, the application can be restored to a former saved state. The popular checkpoint and restart tool BLCR provides application-transparent checkpoint and restart support [11]. It can take a snapshot of the entire process state in both the user and the kernel space, with no modification to the application code. It has been integrated with MPI to provide distributed checkpoint and restart for MPI applications running on a cluster [31].

Although Xeon Phi's software stack is designed to ease the programming effort, its support of fault tolerance is inadequate. MPSS uses BLCR to support checkpoint and restart of native applications. BLCR can either save the snapshot of a native process on Xeon Phi to the host's file system through Network File System (NFS), or to Xeon Phi's own local file system. However, both of these two storage choices have limitations. Saving directly to the host file system through NFS incurs high data transfer latency on PCIe bus. And because Xeon-Phi does not have any directly accessible storage and uses a RAM-based file system, a locally saved snapshot on Xeon Phi's own file system competes the physical memory space with active processes, including the native process whose snapshot is to be saved.

A more severe problem is that MPSS has no fault-tolerance support for offload applications. Given the fact that even a single-node offload application involves the participation of a number of host and coprocessor processes that use proprietary communication libraries in MPSS to exchange messages, it is not surprising that none of the existing distributed checkpoint and restart tools like BLCR or DMTCP [1] can be used. This is because these tools do not consider the communication between the coprocessor processes and the host processes.

In addition MPSS also lacks sufficient support for process migration among Xeon Phi coprocessors. When compute nodes are equipped with multiple coprocessors, process migration can benefit coprocessor load balancing and fault resiliency. For example, a job scheduler may decide to migrate an offload or native process from a heavily-loaded coprocessor to a lightly-loaded one to increase job turnaround time [3]. Moreover, by using fault prediction methods [30], it is possible to avoid imminent coprocessor failures by proactively migrating processes to other healthy coprocessors.

The limited physical memory on the Xeon Phi coprocessor also restricts the sharing of the coprocessor among multiple applications. Previous studies have shown that allowing multiple user applications to share coprocessor like GPU or Xeon Phi can significantly benefit system utilization and job turnaround time [3, 5, 25, 29]. However, Xeon Phi OS's own page swapping mechanism is a poor solution to overcome the capacity limit of Xeon Phi's physical memory for multiprocessing. First, as shown by the study in [5], Xeon Phi OS's swap uses the host's file system as its secondary storage. Swapping in and out memory pages between the host and the coprocessor incurs high data transfer latency. Second, many offload applications use pinned memory buffers to allow fast remote direct memory access (RDMA) between the host and the coprocessor's memory. Pinned memory pages cannot be swapped out by OS. As a result, the size of Xeon Phi's physical memory puts a hard limit on the number of processes that can concurrently run on the coprocessor.

Contributions. To address these shortcomings of MPSS, we created Snapify, a set of extensions to MPSS that captures snapshots of offload applications on Xeon Phi. We make the following specific contributions:

- We propose Snapify, an application-transparent, coordinated approach to take *consistent* snapshots of host and coprocessor processes of an offload application. We believe this is the first proposal that correctly and transparently captures a process-level snapshot of offload applications on many-core processors like the Xeon Phi.

- We use Snapify to implement three new capabilities for offload applications: application-transparent checkpoint and restart, process migration, and process swapping. Again, to the best of our knowledge, this is the first proposal that provides such capabilities for offload applications on Xeon Phi.

- We propose a fast, remote file access service based on RDMA that speeds up the storage and retrieval of snapshots (of both offload and native applications) from the host's file system.

- We evaluate Snapify on several OpenMP and MPI benchmarks. Our results show that Snapify imposes negligible overhead in normal execution of offload applications (less than 5%), and the overheads due to the capture of snapshots in checkpoint and restart, process swap, and process migration are small enough to make it practical to use Snapify for a variety of offload applications.

This paper is organized as follows. Section 2 gives a concise background of Xeon Phi's programming model. Section 3 discusses Snapify's design challenges. Section 4 describes Snapify's

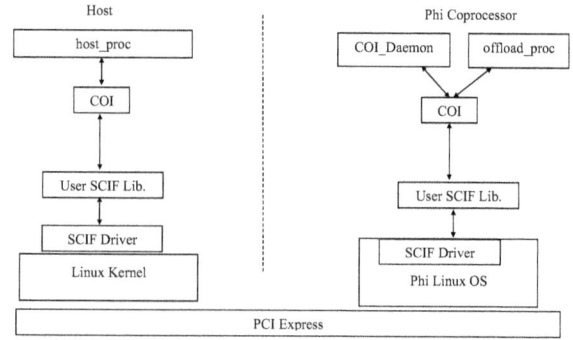

Figure 1: The software architecture of host & Xeon Phi.

internal design and its API. Section 5 shows how Snapify's API can be used to implement checkpoint and restart, process swapping, and process migration. Section 6 introduces our RDMA-based remote file access service for snapshot storage. Section 7 presents the experimental results. Related work is discussed in Section 8.

2. BACKGROUND

In this section we briefly describe the offload programming model and its implementation in MPSS.

Xeon Phi's software stack MPSS consists of a hierarchy of runtime libraries that execute on the host and the coprocessor [17]. These libraries hide complex, low-level communication mechanisms away and present a simple, high-level offload programming semantics to the programmers. The software stack also has a modified Linux OS that is run on Xeon Phi. The Xeon Phi OS has its own file system (built on RAM disk using Xeon Phi's own physical memory), virtual memory management, and an optional page-swap mechanism that uses the host's file system as secondary storage.

To program an offload application a programmer uses special compiler directives to delineate regions of code to be executed on Xeon Phi coprocessors. In particular, the pragma "offlaod" is used to mark an offload region with language-specific scoping constructs (curly braces in C, and "begin" and "end" in Fortran). In particular, the offload pragma can have additional data transfer clauses "in" and "out", specifying the input and output buffers of the offload region. Input buffers specified in the "in" clauses are transferred from the host memory to the Xeon Phi coprocessor through the PCIe bus prior to the execution of the offload region, while output buffers specified in the "out" clauses are transferred back from the Xeon Phi coprocessor to the host memory following the completion of the offload region. More details of Xeon Phi programming can be found in [20].

The Xeon Phi compiler generates one binary for the host processor and one binary for the Xeon Phi coprocessor for an offload application. The host binary is an executable, while the Xeon Phi binary is a dynamically loadable library. The compiler translates each offload region as a function to be executed on the Xeon Phi coprocessor and saves the generated code in the Xeon Phi binary. For each offload region, in the host binary the compiler also generates a function call to the lower-layer runtime libraries, which coordinate the data transfer between the host and the Xeon Phi coprocessor and initiate the "remote" procedure call of the offload function.

The execution of an offload application to be accelerated by Xeon Phi coprocessors involves a minimum of three processes, as reported in Fig. 1. The three processes are a host process (host_proc) running on the host processor, an offload process (offload_proc) running on the Xeon Phi, and a service named Coprocessor Offload

Infrastructure (COI) daemon (`coi_daemon`), also running on the Xeon Phi. After a user launches the application (`host_proc`), the host process requests the COI daemon to launch a process on the Xeon Phi. Then the host process copies the Xeon Phi binary to the coprocessor. The binary contains offload functions to be executed on the coprocessor, and these functions are dynamically loaded into `offload_proc`'s memory space. The execution of an offload function is done by a server thread in the offload process. To execute a function, the host process sends a request to the server thread to run the specified function. Once the function completes on Xeon Phi, the server thread will send the function's returned value back to the host process.

Prior to the execution of an offload function the host process also transfers the input data needed by the offload region to the offload process's memory space. The host process also receives data, if any, that is generated by the offload process.

MPSS provides different levels of abstractions to facilitate the communications between the host process and the processes running on the Xeon Phi. The COI library is an upper level library offering APIs for a host process to perform process control and remote function calls on a Xeon Phi coprocessor [16, 17]. It also allows a host process to create buffers, called COI buffers. The host process can use COI's API to transfer data between the host process and the buffers allocated in the offload process. The COI library in turn uses the lower level Symmetric Communications Interface (SCIF) library to accomplish the real message exchanges and data transfers between the host process and the offload process [18].

The COI library on the Xeon Phi coprocessor manages the memory space used by COI buffers. A COI buffer is composed of one or more files that are memory mapped into a contiguous region. These files are called local store. COI buffers can be created and destroyed through COI functions, while the files created to be used by COI buffers are persistent until the offload process terminates.

SCIF provides two types of APIs that allow two processes in different memory space to communicate. The first type is message-based. The processes use `scif_send()` and `scif_receive()` to send and receive data. The second type offers remote direct memory access (RDMA) functions to speed up the data transfer. To use SCIF's RDMA functions to transfer a buffer, a process first registers the buffer's virtual memory address using `scif_register()` function. The function returns an offset address that can be used in SCIF's RDMA functions: `scif_vreadfrom()`, `scif_readfrom()`, `scif_vwriteto()`, and `scif_writeto()`. In fact, the COI library uses SCIF's RDMA functions to copy data in COI buffers between the host and coprocessors.

Each Xeon Phi device runs one COI daemon process to coordinate the execution of offload processes and the corresponding host processes. The COI daemon maintains SCIF connections with each active host process that uses COI library to offload part of its computation to Xeon Phi. The connections are used to communicate the process control messages between host processes and the COI daemon. For example, the COI daemon launches new offload processes upon requests from applications on the host. If the host process exits, the daemon will terminate the offload process and clean up the temporary files used by the offload process.

3. CHALLENGES

There are several challenges that must be overcome to capture a process-level snapshot of an offload application, and subsequently restart the application from the snapshot. These challenges arise from the distributed nature of an offload application on a Xeon Phi

server, and Xeon Phi's own software stack. Below we summarize these new challenges.

Capturing consistent, distributed snapshots. Since the execution of an offload application on Xeon Phi involves multiple communicating processes that do not share memory or a global clock, it is necessary to ensure that the snapshots of the host and offload processes form a *consistent* global state [7, 22, 31]. In the simplest case, an offload application has three processes: a process on the host and two processes (an offload process, and `coi_daemon` process) on the Xeon Phi. A global state consists of states of the three processes, as well as the state of the communication among these processes. A consistent global state satisfies two properties. First, it is possible to reach this state during the normal operation of the application. Second, it is possible to correctly restart the processes and resume the execution of the application. As a counter example, if the host snapshot is taken before the host process sends a message to the coprocessor, and the snapshot of the offload process is taken after the receipt of the message, then this pair of snapshots does not form a consistent global state, and the global state cannot be applied to resume the application. Due to the distributed nature of Xeon Phi's offload model, snapshots obtained by just using an existing single-process checkpoint tool like BLCR [11] or MTCP [27] cannot form a consistent global state.

The states of communication channels are also part of the global state. Since we cannot take a snapshot of the physical state of a PCIe bus and the internal hardware state of its controllers, we must make sure all communication channels between the involved processes are drained before local snapshots are taken.

Xeon Phi-specific communication libraries. A Xeon Phi offload application uses its own proprietary communication libraries (i.e. COI and SCIF) for inter-process communication. Therefore the existing cluster checkpoint tools designed for applications based on communication libraries like MPI [31] or TCP/IP [1, 19, 28] cannot be applied to Xeon Phi offload applications.

Dealing with distributed states. The states that are distributed among the processes participating in the execution of an offload application may get disturbed by the action of taking a snapshot, swapping out, or restarting the offload process. For example, the COI daemon is responsible for monitoring the status of both the host and the offload process. If an offload process is terminated due to being swapped out or being migrated, the `coi_daemon` will assume that the offload process has crashed and (incorrectly) mark the process as terminated. On the other hand, when an offload process is restarted from a snapshot, the `coi_daemon` needs to be brought into the picture again to monitor the restarted host and offload process.

Storing and retrieving snapshots. The split of Xeon Phi's physical memory between the file system and system memory puts a serious restriction on how the snapshot of an offload process can be stored. A naive solution that saves a snapshot on Xeon Phi's local file system cannot be applied to any process, either native or offload, whose memory footprint exceeds 50% of the Xeon Phi's physical memory.[1] The same restriction also applies when we attempt to restart a process from a snapshot stored on Xeon Phi's local file system. Even if the snapshot and the process fit in the Xeon Phi's physical memory, the memory used to store the snapshot is unavailable to other offload or native applications on the Xeon Phi, resulting in a decrease in the number of applications that can run concurrently or even a crash of some applications due to lack of memory. Therefore, it is desirable to store and retrieve snapshots from the host's file system.

---

[1] The actual limit is less than half, since the system files and the OS use a small portion of the memory.

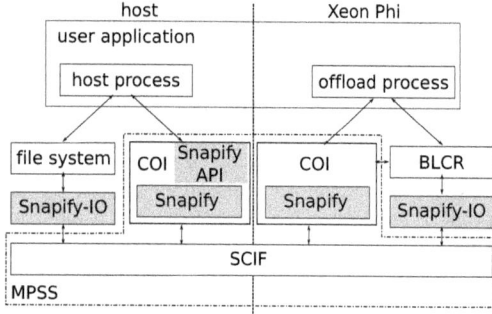

Figure 2: The architecture of Snapify.

```
typedef struct {  char* m_snapshot_path;
                  sem_t m_sem;
                  COIProcess* m_process;
               }snapify_t;

void snapify_pause(snapify_t* snapshot);

void snapify_capture(snapify_t* snapshot,
                bool terminate);

void snapify_wait(snapify_t* snapshot);

void snapify_resume(snapify_t* snapshot);

void snapify_restore(snapify_t* snapshot,
                int device);
```

Table 1: Snapify API.

Saving data private to an offload process. A snapshot of an offload process contains the offload process's own private data. Unlike GPU-based coprocessor systems, an offload process on Xeon Phi is a full-blown Linux process. The offload process has host-allocated COI buffers, and its own private data that may not be visible to the host system (for example, stacks of threads or data regions that are either statically or dynamically allocated through standard system calls like `malloc()` by the functions in the offload process are not visible to the host). The offload-private data may persist across several offload regions. Therefore the strategy of only saving the host-controlled memory regions in a snapshot, as proposed for GPU-accelerated applications in CheCL [34] and CheCUDA [35], is not suitable for Xeon Phi's offload applications.

4. SNAPIFY

Fig. 2 shows the positioning of Snapify technologies in the software stack of the host and the Xeon Phi. Intel's MPSS includes COI (which contains the COI daemon) and SCIF. The file system is part of the Linux OS on the host, and BLCR is the open-source checkpoint and restart framework. Applications offload computations to the Xeon Phi using the COI library, which has a component that executes on the host and a component that executes on the Xeon Phi. Key technologies in Snapify are implemented as modifications to the COI library and the COI daemon, and as an independent user-level library called *Snapify-IO*. The implementation does not change the COI programming interface, and thus is transparent to user applications. Sections 4.1, 4.2, and 4.3 discuss our techniques to create process-level snapshots of the offload application, restore the execution of the application from a snapshot, and resume the application after a snapshot has been taken, respectively. Snapify-IO, to be described in Section 6, is a very efficient

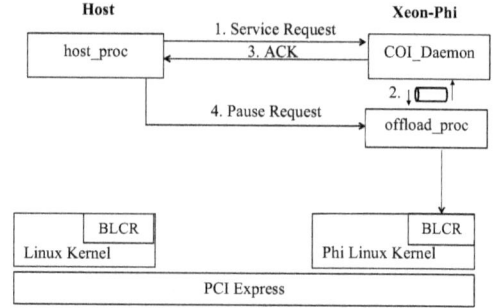

Figure 3: Overview of taking a snapshot.

mechanism that we designed to store and retrieve snapshots from the host file system using SCIF's RDMA functions.

Snapify provides a simple API that is used to capture snapshots of an offload process and restore the offload process from snapshots. The API is summarized in Table 1. Snapify's API defines a C structure and five functions. The functions are called by a host process to capture a snapshot of the offload process (`snapify_pause()` and `snapify_capture()`), to resume the communication and the partially-blocked execution of the host process and the offload process after a snapshot is taken (`snapify_resume()`), to restore an offload process from a snapshot (`snapify_restore()`), and to wait for a non-blocking API function to complete (`snapify_wait()`). All functions except `snapify_capture()` are blocking calls. The structure is used to pass parameters and to receive results of the functions. The API functions are detailed in the rest of this section.

4.1 Taking Snapshots

Taking a snapshot of an offload process involves the host process on the host and the COI daemon and the offload process on each of the coprocessors installed in a Xeon Phi server. Although our approach handles multiple Xeon Phi coprocessors in a server, for simplicity we assume there is only one Xeon Phi coprocessor in the following discussions. Therefore we consider the case of three involved processes: the host process, the COI daemon, and the offload process.

The snapshot process is accomplished in two separate steps. In step one, all of the communications between the host process and the offload process are stopped, and the channels are drained. In step two, a snapshot of the offload process is captured and saved in the file system of the host. These two steps are implemented by `snapify_pause()` and `snapify_capture()`, respectively.

Pause. To pause the communications between the host process and the offload process, the host process calls `snapify_pause()` and passes the handle of the offload process (`COIProcess` in the structure) to `snapify_pause()`. A directory structure in the host's file system for storing the files of a snapshot is also needed by `snapify_pause()` (and `snapify_capture()`). The path to the directory is passed to `snapify_pause()` through the member variable `m_snapshot_path`. In the first step of `snapify_pause()` it saves the copies of the runtime libraries from the host's file system needed by the offload process to the snapshot directory.[2]

Fig. 3 shows the interactions between the host process, the COI daemon, and the offload process that are triggered by

---

[2]MPSS maintains copies of the runtime libraries on the host file system. Therefore as an optimization we do not copy the libraries of the offload process from the coprocessor back to the host system.

snapify_pause(). Function snapify_pause() first sends a snapify-service request to the COI daemon (step 1 in Fig. 3). The daemon then creates a UNIX pipe to the offload process, and writes the pause request to the offload process. Next the daemon signals the offload process, triggering the signal handler in the offload process to the pipe and send an acknowledgement back to the daemon through the pipe (step 2). The daemon then relays the acknowledgement back to the host process (step 3). At this point all parties (the host process, the offload process, and the COI daemon) have agreed to pause the communications and drain the communication channels.

The COI daemon is chosen as the coordinator of Snapify's pause procedure. This is because there is one daemon per coprocessor, and each daemon listens to the same fixed SCIF port number. It services pause requests that may come from different host processes. It also maintains a list of active requests. Upon receiving a new pause request, the daemon adds an entry to the list. The entry is removed after the pause request is serviced.

To avoid any interference with its regular tasks, the daemon uses a dedicated Snapify monitor thread to oversee the progress of the pause procedure. Whenever a request is received and no monitor thread exists, the daemon creates a new monitor thread. The monitor thread keeps polling the pipes to the offload processes on the list of active pause requests for status updates. The monitor thread exits when there is no more active pause request in the list.

Following the initial handshake snapify_pause() sends a pause request to the offload process (step 4 in Fig. 3) to drain the communication channels. The draining needs the collaboration between the host process, the COI daemon, and the offload process, and will be discussed in more detail shortly. It is a necessary step to ensure that the snapshots form a consistent global state (see Section 3). During the draining process some of the threads in the host process and the offload process spawned by the COI library are blocked. The blocking of these threads keeps the SCIF channels from being used until snapify_resume() is called. These threads are responsible for sending and receiving COI commands, COI events, and the COI logs.

After the SCIF channels are quiesced, the offload process will save its local store (memory allocated in the offload process's memory space for storing data in COI buffers) to the host's snapshot directory. This operation does not use any existing SCIF channels between the host process and the offload process. Saving the local store and the snapshot will be discussed in detail in Section 6.

At the end of snapify_pause() all of the SCIF channels between the host process, the COI daemon, and the offload process become empty. To notify the host process that the pause has completed, the offload process sends a message through the pipe to the COI daemon, and the COI daemon informs the host process that the offload process has completed the pause operation. After this the offload process waits on the pipe to wait for the next request from the the host process. The next request is either a capture or a resume request, which will be discussed later.

We now give more details on how snapify_pause() drains the SCIF communication channels. We first classify all SCIF communication use instances in the COI runtime to four different cases.

1. The host process, the offload process, and the COI daemon exchange messages when an offload process is created and before it is destroyed. These messages carry information regarding process creation, confirmation, request for termination, and etc.

2. The host process and the offload process use one SCIF channel to perform RDMA transfers of the data in COI buffers.

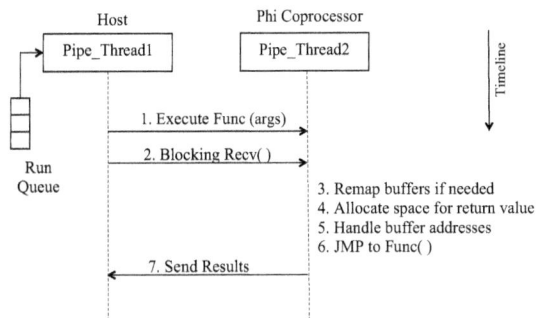

Figure 4: Executing an offload function.

The RDMA transfers are carried out by scif_writeto() and scif_readfrom() functions.

3. The host process, the COI daemon, and the offload process have several pairs of client-server threads. Each server thread serves only one client thread. It handles the incoming commands in a sequential fashion. The commands are sent by the client thread through a dedicated SCIF channel.

4. The execution of an offload function is also implemented by a client-server model. In order to take a snapshot during the execution of an offload function, however, we treat this case separately. Our method handles both synchronous and asynchronous offload executions.

Fig. 4 reports the client-server model that executes offload functions. When a thread *Pipe_Thread1* in the host process enters an offload region, it sends a run function request to the server thread *Pipe_Thread2* in the offload process. After sending this request, *Pipe_Thread1* performs a blocking receive to wait for the result, while *Pipe_Thread2* calls the function and sends the function's return value back to *Pipe_Thread1* of the host process.

For each of the four use cases of SCIF we develop a method to drain the SCIF communication channels. For case 1, we declare the initialization and cleanup code regions of creating and terminating offload processes as critical regions, protected by a mutex lock. When snapify_pause() is called, it will try to acquire the lock. If a thread is executing the code in a critical region, snapify_pause() will be blocked until the thread leaves the critical region. On the other hand, once snapify_pause() holds the lock, any other thread that attempts to enter these critical regions will be blocked.

For case 2 we delay any snapshot attempt when a RDMA transfer is active. Similar to the case above, we protect the call sites of SCIF's RDMA functions with mutex locks.

To handle a SCIF channel in the client-server model of case 3, we take advantage of the sequential nature of the client-server implementation in COI. We added a new "shutdown" request to the server's request handling routine. This request is only issued by snapify_pause(), and is used as a special marker that indicates no more commands will follow until snapify_resume() is called. To send the shutdown request, snapify_pause() first tries to acquire the lock that is used by the client thread to protect the communication channel. After snapify_pause() acquires the lock, the client thread will not be able to send any more requests. The lock that is used by a client thread will only be released in snapify_resume(). After acquiring the lock snapify_pause() sends the shutdown request to the server.

The pause function will not continue until all of the server threads in the host process, the COI daemon, and the offload process receives a shutdown command. This ensures that the SCIF channels used between the client and the server threads stay empty until `snapify_resume()`.

For case 4 to drain the SCIF channel used by *Pipe_Thread1* and *Pipe_Thread2* we made a number of changes to the implementation of the COI pipeline. First we transformed the two send functions in Step 1 and 7 to be blocking calls. We then placed these two send functions in two separate critical regions protected by mutex locks. The thread executing `snapify_pause()` in the host process and in the offload process will acquire these locks. The locks will be released in `snapify_resume()`.

Capture. To capture a snapshot of an offload process the host process calls `snapify_capture()`. Similar to `snapify_pause()`, the caller of `snapify_capture()` passes the handle to the offload process and the path to the directory on the host's file system where the snapshot files should be saved. It also gives a Boolean variable `terminate` to indicate whether the offload process should be terminated after its snapshot is captured. At the beginning `snapify_capture()` sends the capture request first to the COI daemon, which in turn forwards the request to the offload process through the pipe opened in `snapify_pause()`. The snapshot of the offload process can be captured by any application-transparent checkpoint tool.

Our current implementation uses BLCR to capture the snapshot of the offload process. When the offload process receives the capture request from the pipe, it calls BLCR's `cr_request_checkpoint()`. When the snapshot is captured, the offload process sends back the completion message using the pipe to the COI daemon, which in turn informs the host process.

The snapshot of an the offload process is saved on the host file system. The snapshot is written by the checkpoint and restart tool running on the coprocessor. Section 6 details several novel techniques of saving a snapshot "on the fly" from the coprocessor to the host file system.

Notice that `snapify_capture()` is a non-blocking function call. It returns immediately with a semaphore `m_sem` in `snapify_t*` snapshot. The caller can thereafter call `snapify_wait()` with the `snapify_t` structure to wait for the completion of the capturing operation. The semaphore will be signaled when the host process receives the complete message from the COI daemon.

4.2 Resume

To resume the execution of the blocked threads of both the host process and the offload process after a snapshot of the offload process is taken, the host process calls `snapify_resume()` with the handle of the offload process. To resume the host process first sends a resume request to the COI daemon. The daemon then forwards the request to the the offload process through the pipe that is created in `snapify_pause()`. In `snapify_resume()`, both the host process and the offload process release all the locks acquired in the pause operation. Once the locks are released in the offload process, the offload process sends an acknowledgement back to the host process through the COI daemon. After the host process receives the acknowledgement and releases the locks, it returns from `snapify_resume()`.

4.3 Restore

To restore an offload process from its snapshot the host process calls `snapify_restore()` with the path to the snapshot files. Snapify relies on the COI daemon and Xeon Phi's checkpoint and

restart tool (BLCR) that is also used by `snapify_capture()` to restart an offload process. To restore, `snapify_restore()` first sends a restore request to the COI daemon. After receiving the restore request, the COI daemon first copies the local store and the runtime libraries needed by the offload process on the fly to the coprocessor. Then it calls BLCR to restart the offload process from its snapshot. We developed a novel I/O mechanism, called *Snapify-IO*, that allows BLCR to read the snapshot of the offload process "on-the-fly" from the host storage directly without first saving the entire snapshot in the memory file system on Xeon Phi. Snapify-IO will be discussed in detail in Section 6.

After BLCR restores the process image of the offload process, the host process and the offload process will reconnect all of the disconnected SCIF communication channels between them. After SCIF channels are restored, the host process and the offload process re-registers the memory regions used by the COI buffers for RDMA. The re-registration of a buffer may return a new RDMA address different from the original one. Therefore we keep a lookup table of (old, new) address pairs for conversion.

Since the restored offload process is new, `snapify_restore()` returns a new COI process handle (`COIProcess*`) to the offload process. The new handle can be used by the host process in the subsequent COI function calls. Notice that the offload process, though restored, is not fully active after `snapify_restore()` returns. The caller needs to call `snapify_resume()` so that the blocked threads in the host process and the offload process can continue their executions.

5. API USE SCENARIOS

In this section we explain how Snapify's API can be used to implement checkpoint and restart, process swapping and migration.

Checkpoint and restart. To take a checkpoint of an offload application we need to capture both the snapshots of the host process and of the offload process. To capture a snapshot of the host process, we can use an application-transparent checkpoint and restart tool like BLCR on the host. As to the snapshot of the offload process, we use `snapify_pause()` and `snapify_capture()` in Snapify's API.

The sample code in Fig. 5(a) shows how Snapify's API can be combined with the host BLCR to implement checkpoint and restart for offload applications. Fig. 5(b) and 5(c) reports the timing diagrams of the checkpoint and restart. The function `snapify_blcr_callback()` is a callback function that is registered to BLCR on the host. When BLCR receives a checkpoint request, it will call `snapify_blcr_callback()`. Within `snapify_blcr_callback()`, we call BLCR's `cr_checkpoint()` to take a snapshot (a checkpoint) of the host process. Before `cr_checkpoint()`, we call `snapify_pause()` and `snapify_capture()` to take a snapshot of the offload process. Notice that `snapify_capture()` is a non-blocking call. Therefore we need to wait for its return in the "continue" section of the `if` statement after `cr_checkpoint()` returns.

In restarting BLCR first restores the host process. The execution of the restored host process will begin after `cr_checkpoint()` returns with `ret > 0`. The control flow of the execution will go through the "restart" section of the "if" statement. There we call `snapify_restore()` to recreate the offload process. In the sample code the offload process will be restored on a Xeon Phi coprocessor whose device ID is extracted from `COIProcess*` by function `GetDeviceID()`.

Process swapping. Fig. 6 shows sample process swapping-out and swapping-in functions and their timing diagrams. Process-

```
int snapify_blcr_callback(void* args){
    int ret = 0;
    snapify_t* snapshot = (snapify_t*)args;
    snapify_pause(snapshot);
    snapify_capture(snapshot, false);
    ret = cr_checkpoint(0);
    if ( ret > 0 ) { // Restarting.
        snapify_restore(snapshot,
          GetDeviceId(snapshot->m_process));
        snapify_resume(snapshot);
        // Save snapshot.m_process.
    }
    else { // Continue.
        snapify_wait(snapshot);
        snapify_resume(snapshot);
    }
}
```

(a) Sample code.

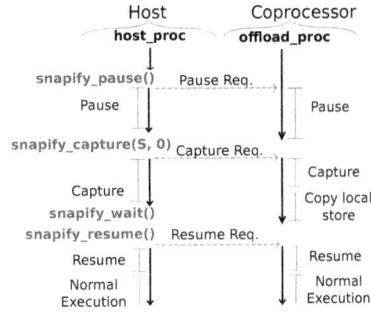

(b) Checkpoint timing diagram.

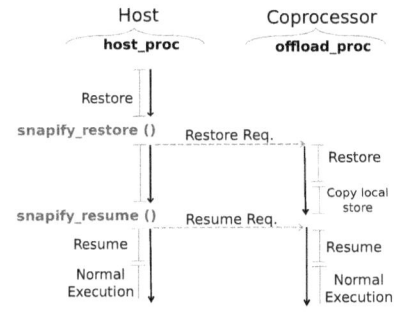

(c) Restart timing diagram.

Figure 5: Using Snapify's API to implement checkpoint and restart.

```
snapify_t* snapify_swapout(const char* path,
        COIProcess* proc){
    snapify_t* snapshot = (snapify_t*)malloc(
        sizeof(snapify_t));
    snapshot->m_snapshot_path = path;
    snapshot->m_process = proc;
    snapify_pause(snapshot);
    snapify_capture(snapshot, true);
    snapify_wait(snapshot);
    return snapshot;
}

COIProcess* snapify_swapin(snapify_t*
        snapshot, int device){
    COIProcess* ret = 0;
    snapify_restore(snapshot, device);
    snapify_resume(snapshot);
    ret = snapshot->m_process;
    free(snapshot);
    return ret;
}
```

(a) Sample code.

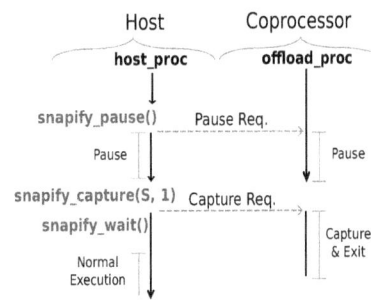

(b) Swapping-out timing diagram.

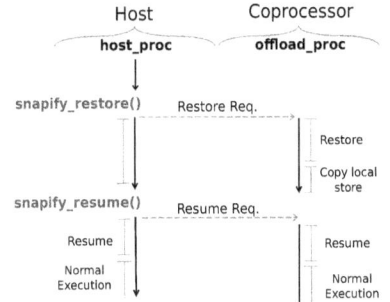

(c) Swapping-in timing diagram

Figure 6: Using Snapify's API to implement process swapping.

swapping can be used, for example, by a job scheduler to swap out one offload process and swap in another based on the scheduler's scheduling and resource management policies. Both of the swapping functions are called in the context of the host process. The caller of `snapify_swapout()` needs to prepare a directory where the snapshot files of the offload process can be stored, and passes the path in parameter `snapshot` to `snapify_swapout()`. The implementation of `snapify_swapout()` is fairly straightforward: we call `snapify_pause()`, `snapify_capture()`, and `snapify_wait()` one by one. Since the offload process is to be swapped out, we set the second parameter of `snapify_capture()` to be true, terminating the offload process after its snapshot is captured and saved. The returned pointer of `snapify_t` structure from `snapify_swapout()` represents a snapshot of the offload process. It can be used to restore the offload process.

The swapping-in of an offload process reverses the effect of swapping-out. In `snapify_swapin()`, we use `snapify_restore()` to restore the offload process. The returned Snapify data structure `snapshot` from `snapify_swapout()` is passed to `snapify_swapin()`,

which uses the path of the snapshot files in `snapshot` to restart the the offload process on the specified Xeon Phi coprocessor (identified by `device_to` parameter). The new handle to the restored offload process is returned at the end of `snapify_swapin()`.

Process migration. Fig. 7 shows the implementation of a process-migration function. Process migration moves an offload process from one coprocessor to another on the same machine. It can be viewed as swapping out the offload process from coprocessor 1 and swapping it in on coprocessor 2. Its implementation simply reuses `snapify_swapout()` and `snapify_swapin()`.

Command-line tools. The offload applications can directly benefit from Snapify without any modifications. Checkpoint and restart can be applied transparently by using BLCR's `cr_checkpoint` command-line tool on the host system. This utility will send a signal to trigger the checkpoint procedure, which calls Snapify's own BLCR callback function as shown in Fig. 5(a). If the MPI runtime supports BLCR, MPI applications using Xeon Phi for offload computation will automatically benefit from Snapify.

In order to provide swapping and migration transparently, we provide a command-line utility named `snapify`. Its arguments are the PID of the host process and a command. The commands include swapping-out, swapping-in, and migration. In case of

7

```
COIProcess* snapify_migration(COIProcess* proc, int
    device_to){
    const char* path = "/tmp";
    snapify_t* snapshot = snapify_swapout(path, proc);
    return snapify_swapin(snapshot, device_to);
}
```

Figure 7: An implementation of process migration.

swapping-in and migration, `snapify` also needs an additional parameter indicates the coprocessor number on which the offload process will be launched. This utility signals the host process and submits the command through a pipe. The signal handler provided by Snapify in the host process then calls one of the three functions in Fig. 6(a) and 7 according to the user-given command.

Remark. Process swapping and migration may lead to resource contentions. E.g., two processes might be swapped into the same Xeon Phi. Such problems are best addressed by a job scheduler like COSMIC in [5], and are beyond the scope of this paper.

6. Snapify-IO

All of the snapshots taken on the host and on a Xeon Phi coprocessor are saved to a file system mounted in the host OS. Snapify provides three novel "on-the-fly" approaches to store and retrieve snapshots between the host and coprocessors. All of these methods use very little Xeon Phi memory for buffering. In the following we will first describe the most efficient approach based on SCIF's RDMA API, called Snapify-IO. Then we will discuss our NFS-based methods.

Snapify-IO. Snapify-IO is a remote file access service that transfers data using RDMA between the host and the Xeon Phi coprocessors on a Xeon Phi server. It provides a simple interface that uses UNIX file descriptors as data access handles. Snapify-IO allows a local process running on a Xeon Phi coprocessor to read from or write to a remote file on the host through standard file I/O functions, as if the file is local. For example, the file descriptor created by Snapify-IO can be directly passed to BLCR for saving and retrieving snapshots. Internally, Snapify-IO transfers the data over the PCIe bus using SCIF's RDMA data transfer functions.

Fig. 8 shows Snapify-IO's architecture. Snapify-IO consists of a user-level library providing a simple I/O interface (Snapify-IO library) and a standalone binary called *Snapify-IO daemon*. The Snapify-IO library is linked to the user code that wants to use Snapify-IO for remote file I/O, while each SCIF node (the host and any of the Xeon Phi coprocessors on a Xeon Phi server) runs a Snapify-IO daemon as a long-running process. The Snapify-IO daemon serves I/O requests from both the local user processes using Snapify-IO library and remote Snapify-IO daemons. It can either receive data from a local process, transfer the data to a remote Snapify-IO daemon, which in turn saves the data into a remote file system. Or it can retrieve data from a local file system, transfer the data to a remote Snapify-IO daemon, which feeds the data into a remote user process.

Snapify-IO library is designed for transparent integration with the standard `read()` and `write()` system calls. Its only API function `snapifyio_open()` returns a standard UNIX file descriptor. It accepts three arguments: a SCIF node ID, a path to a file that is valid on the SCIF node, and a file access mode flag indicating either a read or write mode (but not both). The returned file descriptor represents a file on a (remote) SCIF node as specified by the arguments.

Snapify-IO uses a UNIX socket as the local communication channel between the Snapify-IO library and the Snapify-IO dae-

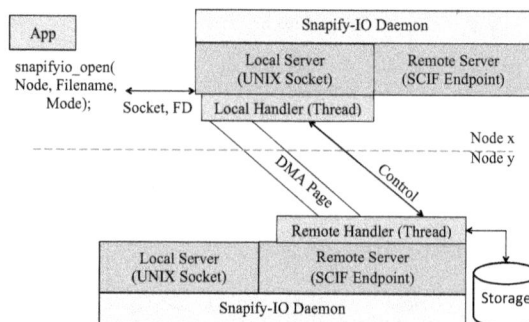

Figure 8: The architecture of Snapify-IO.

mon. When `snapifyio_open()` is called, the Snapify-IO library creates a UNIX socket that connects to the local Snapify-IO daemon. Once the socket is established, `snapifyio_open()` sends the SCIF node ID, the file path, and the access mode to the Snapify-IO daemon. It then returns the file descriptor of the socket to the caller. To serve the local socket connections, the Snapify-IO daemon has a local server thread listening on a designated port. Once the server thread accepts the socket connection from the Snapify-IO library, it spawns a local handler thread to handle further I/O activities coming from the user process, which may either write to or read from the socket, depending on the access mode. Notice that the file descriptor returned by `snapifyio_open()` is a UNIX file descriptor, so the user code can call `close()` to release the resources associated with the file descriptor.

The communication channel between two Snapify-IO daemons is a SCIF connection. After receiving the SCIF node ID, the file path, and the access mode from a local user process, the Snapify-IO daemon's local handler thread will create a new SCIF connection to the Snapify-IO daemon on the specified SCIF node. Once the SCIF connection is established, the local handler thread will forward the path and the access mode of the file to the remote Snapify-IO daemon, and register an internal buffer to the SCIF library for RDMA transfer. The buffer size is configurable. To balance between the requirement of minimizing memory footprint and the need of shorter transfer latency, the buffer size is set at 4MB. To handle incoming SCIF connections, the Snapify-IO daemon employs a remote server thread, which listens to a predetermined SCIF port. Once the remote server thread accepts a SCIF connection from a remote Snapify-IO daemon, it spawns a handler thread to handle communications over the newly established SCIF channel.

Once the communication channels are established, the local handler thread will start to direct the data flow between the user application and the remote file. In write access mode, the local handler will copy the data written to the socket by the user application to the registered RDMA buffer. After the buffer is filled, the local handler will send a SCIF message to notify the remote Snapify-IO daemon (i.e. the daemon's remote handler thread) using `scif_send()`. Subsequently the remote handler thread will use SCIF's RDMA function `scif_vreadfrom()` to read the data from the registered RDMA buffer, and saves the data to the file system at the specified location. After the RDMA completes, the local handler thread will reuse the RDMA buffer and repeat the above process until all data from the user process are saved to the remote file. In the read access mode, the data flow in the reverse direction. The remote handler thread in the remote Snapify-IO daemon will read data from the specified file, and copy the data to the registered RDMA buffer using `scif_vwriteto()`. Once the buffer

Table 2: Characteristics of our Xeon Phi server.

	Host Processor	Coprocessor
CPU	Intel E5-2630 @ 2.30GHz	Intel Xeon Phi 5110P
Cores	6 physical cores (12 threads) per socket	60 physical cores (240 threads) per coprocessor
Memory	32GB	16GB per coprocessor
OS	Linux RHEL 6.2, kernel 2.6.32-220	Linux kernel 2.6.38.8 MPSS 2.1.6720-130
Number	2 CPU sockets	2 coprocessors

Table 3: File copy performance (seconds).

Size	Device to Host			Host to Device		
(MB)	scp	NFS	Snapify-IO	scp	NFS	Snapify-IO
1	0.97	0.01	0.03	0.48	0.01	0.07
64	15.07	3.23	0.43	14.08	1.94	0.53
128	29.88	6.36	0.85	28.30	3.96	1.82
256	57.02	11.81	1.67	55.50	7.95	3.68
512	113.71	20.91	3.34	111.07	16.07	6.17
1024	224.68	40.10	6.76	221.59	31.06	9.57

is filled, it will notify the local handler thread in the local Snapify-IO daemon, which in turn will copy the data from the RDMA buffer to the socket.

Snapify uses Snapify-IO to save and retrieve snapshots. The COI library with Snapify implementations is linked with the Snapify-IO library. To take a snapshot of an offload process, Snapify calls `snapifyio_open()` in write mode in the pre-snapshot phase. The returned file descriptor is then passed to BLCR, which uses it to write the context file. Similarly, to restart an offload process Snapify calls `snapifyio_open()` to open a remote context file in read mode. The returned file descriptor is then used by BLCR to load the process context from the remote file to the local Xeon Phi's memory. Thanks to Snapify-IO, the data transfer between a Xeon Phi coprocessor and the host's file system is completely transparent to BLCR. In addition, the Snapify-IO library does not introduce extra SCIF connections. Therefore it does not complicate the process of taking a snapshot.

NFS. We also implemented two optimizations to speedup NFS-based snapshot storage. In these approaches Snapify uses NFS to mount the host file system on a Xeon Phi coprocessor. A snapshot is stored or retrieved through the NFS. To overcome the problem of high latency of small writes in NFS, we developed two new approaches based on buffering. In the first approach we modified BLCR's kernel module such that it accumulates write data to a larger chunk before the data is written to the file system. Since using a modified BLCR's kernel module may not always be feasible, our second approach uses the same concept but applies it in the user level. In this approach the BLCR writes are redirected to our user-space utility through the standard output and input. This utility buffers data from its standard input and writes out the data in the buffer to NFS at larger granularity.

7. EXPERIMENTAL RESULTS

We used micro benchmarks and a suite of MPI and OpenMP applications to evaluate Snapify-IO and Snapify on a Xeon-Phi cluster. This section reports our experimental results.

Setup. Table 2 shows the hardware and software configuration of our computing system. For Snapify-IO evaluation, we used a single node that has one Xeon Phi (8GB of physical memory). For MPI applications, we used a 4-node cluster, where each node in the cluster has one Xeon Phi many-core processor with 8GB of memory.

Snapify-IO performance. To evaluate the performance of Snapify-IO, we used a micro-benchmark that copies files of various sizes between the host and the Xeon Phi. The micro-benchmark runs natively on the Xeon Phi. We compared the time taken by our Snapify-IO to move files between the host and the Xeon Phi with the time taken by two methods natively supported by Xeon Phi's OS, i.e. `scp` and read/write from NFS mounted directories.

Table 3 shows the time taken to copy files of different sizes (file-size ranged from 1MB to 1GB). We observed that Snapify-IO consistently performs better than NFS and `scp` (except for the 1 MB file-size case, where NFS outperforms others by buffering data). As the file size increases, Snapify-IO's advantage is more pronounced.

For a 1GB file, Snapify-IO has about 6x better write performance and 3x better read performance when compared with NFS. For the same file, Snapify-IO has 30x faster write performance and 22x faster read performance when compared with `scp`. We also observed that transfer of a file from the Xeon Phi to the host by using Snapify-IO is generally faster than moving the same file from the host to Xeon Phi. This is because Snapify-IO daemon on the host flushes the file to the secondary storage asynchronously. Thus the write operation on the host runs parallel to the data transfer.

We also evaluated the impact of using Snapify-IO for storing and restoring BLCR's checkpoints of processes on the Xeon Phi. We ran a second micro-benchmark as a native application on the coprocessor and captured the snapshots using BLCR. Our micro-benchmark performed a `malloc()` call and it had a long loop in an OpenMP region (240 threads). We used different malloc sizes (ranging from 1MB to 4GB) to control the file-size of snapshots. Table 4 compares the performance of Snapify-IO with three variants of read/write from NFS mounted directories, as well as a method (labeled as *Local* in Table 4) that saves the application snapshot in the physical memory of the Xeon Phi. The BLCR checkpoint time in Table 4 is the end-to-end latency of capturing and saving the process snapshot. BLCR restart time is the end-to-end time to read and restore the snapshot. Note that in most cases the snapshot is written to and read from the host file system (except the *Local* case). As expected, storing and restoring snapshots from the physical memory of the Xeon Phi (the *Local* case) takes the least time. However, when the checkpoint file-size increases to 4GB, it is impossible to store the checkpoint file in the physical memory of the Xeon Phi (memory limit on the Xeon Phi card is 8GB, and 4GB is already used by the micro-benchmark). In practice, it is not feasible to save checkpoint files locally because, more often than not, several other processes on the Xeon Phi are already using the limited physical memory on the Xeon Phi.

The performance of all three variants of NFS was poor (when compared with Snapify-IO) for storing checkpoints. BLCR performs multiple small writes before reaching the loop where it actually takes snapshots of the application's memory pages, and these small writes lead to poor performance for the NFS variants. Our method of "NFS-Buffered in kernel" boosts the performance of NFS to a large degree while our buffering in user-space does so to a lesser degree (but it still provides significant improvements). Finally, Snapify-IO performance is a large improvement compared to NFS and NFS-Buffered (both modes).

Note that the buffering solutions do not apply to the cases of restarting or restoring. Again, restarting from checkpoint files in the physical memory of the Xeon Phi is very fast, but this is generally not possible due to the limited physical memory on the Xeon Phi. We observed that Snapify-IO performs 1.4x, 2.6x and 5.9x faster than NFS for 1MB, 256MB and 4GB snapshots, respectively.

Snapify overhead. We evaluated Snapify on 8 OpenMP and 3 NAS MPI benchmarks (LU-MZ, SP-MZ, BT-MZ in [9]). The benchmarks are described in Table 5. All benchmarks were modified to offload computations to the Xeon Phi. All time measurements were made on the host, unless mentioned otherwise.

Table 4: Comparing Snapify-IO with NFS-based I/O in BLCR (seconds).

Size (MB)	Checkpoint time (Snapshot + Write)					Restart Time (Read + Restore)		
	Local (RAM)	NFS	NFS-Buffered (kernel)	NFS-Buffered (user)	Snapify-IO	Local (RAM)	NFS	Snapify-IO
1	2.16	67.64	1.70	2.71	**2.76**	0.577	1.392	**0.979**
64	2.38	71.21	3.25	4.81	**2.28**	0.829	3.547	**1.377**
128	2.62	70.97	4.30	7.64	**3.71**	0.832	5.834	**2.066**
256	3.15	75.67	7.30	12.48	**4.59**	1.255	8.975	**3.397**
512	4.12	80.98	12.60	20.98	**6.44**	2.034	17.613	**4.934**
1024	6.34	87.27	21.44	30.47	**9.94**	3.732	32.550	**7.373**
2048	10.14	118.65	38.48	53.82	**17.41**	6.736	62.217	**13.506**
4096	NA	155.92	93.05	109.06	**32.84**	NA	121.452	**22.935**

Table 5: Description of benchmarks.

Name	Description	Problem Size
MD	Molecular dynamics simulation	25000 particles, 10 time steps
MC	Monte Carlo simulation of N paths and T time steps	N = 32M, T = 2000
SG	A series of matrix-matrix multiplications (SGEMM)	8Kx8K matrices, 10 iterations
SS	Supervised semantic search indexing computing top K for each of the Q queries	256K documents, K=32, Q=512
KM	Computing K-means using Lloyd clustering algorithm	4M points, 3 dimensions, 32 means
LU-MZ	A CFD application using lower-upper Gauss-Seidel solver [2]	Grid: 162x162x162, 250 iterations
BT-MZ	Computation fluid dynamics (CFD) using block tri-diagonal solver [2]	Grid: 162x162x162, 200 iterations
SP-MZ	A CFD application using scalar penta-diagonal solver [2]	Grid: 162x162x162, 400 iterations

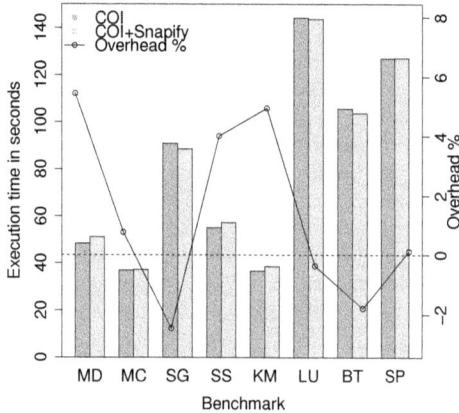

Figure 9: Runtime overhead of Snapify.

Fig. 9 compares the runtime of the normal executions (no snapshot) of the OpenMP benchmarks with and without Snapify support. Each experimental run was repeated 20 times. The average runtime is reported as bars, and the runtime overhead (in percentage) added by Snapify is shown in line graph on the right y-axis. In average Snapify adds a 1.5% overhead to the application runtime, and in the worst case the overhead is less than 5% (MD). We used the Linux command-line tool `time` to measure the end-to-end execution time of an offload application.

Checkpoint and restart. Fig. 10(a) shows the checkpoint time and 10(b) reports the size of the files generated by the checkpoint procedure. As detailed in Section 4.1, during pause the local store (files on Xeon Phi for COI buffers) of the offload process was stored in the snapshot directory on the host system as a file. Thus for benchmarks with a large local store (SS and SG in Fig. 10(b)), the pause is longer. The time that BLCR on the host and BLCR on the coprocessor take to capture and save snapshots are the bars labeled as "Snapshot + Write (host)" and "Snapshot + Write (device)", respectively. The host BLCR finishes early in all cases except for SS and SG. In these two cases, Fig. 10(b) indicates a large host-process snapshot while the offload-process snapshot is fairly small. Thus the offload process finishes early. The checkpoint time ranges from 3 to 21 seconds in time, shorter for small files (8.4 MB) and longer for large ones (1.3 GB).

Fig. 10(c) reports the restart time of the OpenMP benchmarks. The total restart time ranges from 3 to 24 seconds across the bench-

marks. Fig. 10(c) also reports the breakdown of the time spent in each stage of the restart. The host-restart time varies based on the size of the host-process snapshot. Benchmarks SS and SG have larger host snapshots, and thus longer host-restart time. The time of restoring an offload process strongly depends on the size of local store, which is copied from the host to the coprocessor when the offload process is restored.

Process migration. Fig. 10(d) shows the runtime overhead of process migration. The migration time varies from 4.9 seconds (MC) to 31.6 seconds (SS). As expected, it is strongly correlated with the size of the local store and the snapshot of an offload process. In process migration, the offload process copies its local store directly from its current coprocessor to another coprocessor using Snapify-IO. Thus the pause time in process migration is different from the one in the checkpoint procedure. In all but one benchmarks the time of capturing and saving the snapshot of an offload process is shorter than the time of reading the snapshot and restoring the offload process. This is because Snapify-IO is faster when writing to the host from a coprocessor, as explained earlier.

Process swapping. Fig. 10(e) and 10(f) show the runtime of swapping-out and swapping-in, respectively. The time of swapping out the offload processes ranges from 2.1 seconds to 11.8 seconds, and the time of swapping-in takes between 2 seconds and 14.8 seconds. Except in the case of SS and SG, the pause of swapping-out is much shorter than the time of the capturing phase. Again, this is because the local stores of SS and SG are larger than their snapshots.

Checkpoint and restart for MPI. We use three MPI benchmarks LU-MZ, SP-MZ, and BT-MZ, to evaluate checkpoint and restart of MPI applications. For all three benchmarks, we choose the class C input size, and run the benchmarks with 1, 2 and 4 MPI tasks (ranks). Each rank is executed on one node. Fig. 11(a) and 11(b) report the time of taking a checkpoint and restarting from a checkpoint, respectively. Fig. 11(c) shows the checkpoint size of a single rank. We observe that as the number of nodes increases, CR time decreases at various degrees. This is because the checkpoint size of each MPI rank decreases as the total number of MPI ranks increases. CR time ranges between 4 and 14 seconds for a single checkpoint, depending on the respective benchmarks and the number of the MPI ranks. When no checkpoint is performed, the runtime of the benchmarks ranges from 2-3 minutes for the selected

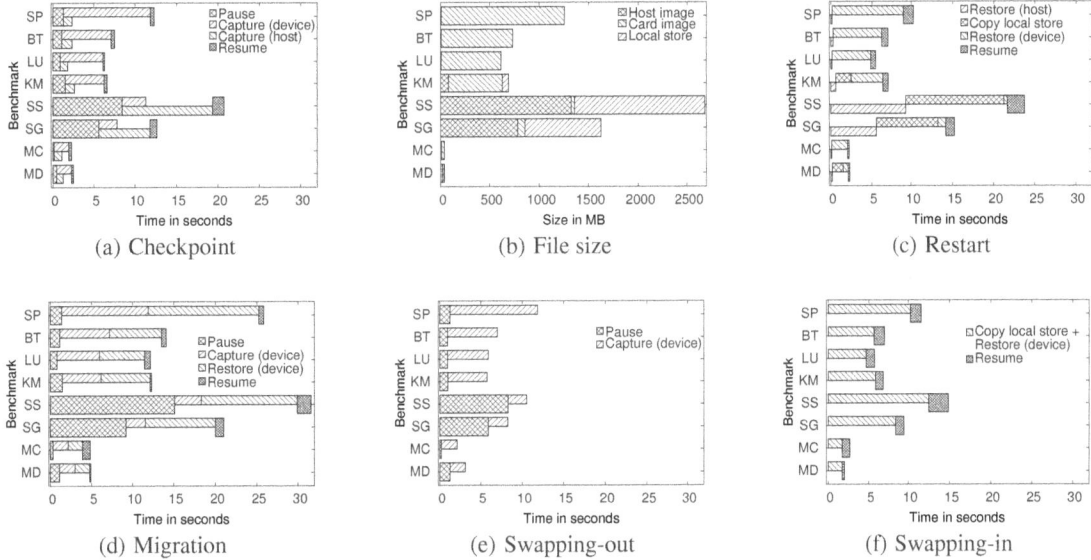

(a) Checkpoint   (b) File size   (c) Restart

(d) Migration   (e) Swapping-out   (f) Swapping-in

Figure 10: Performance evaluation on OpenMP benchmarks.

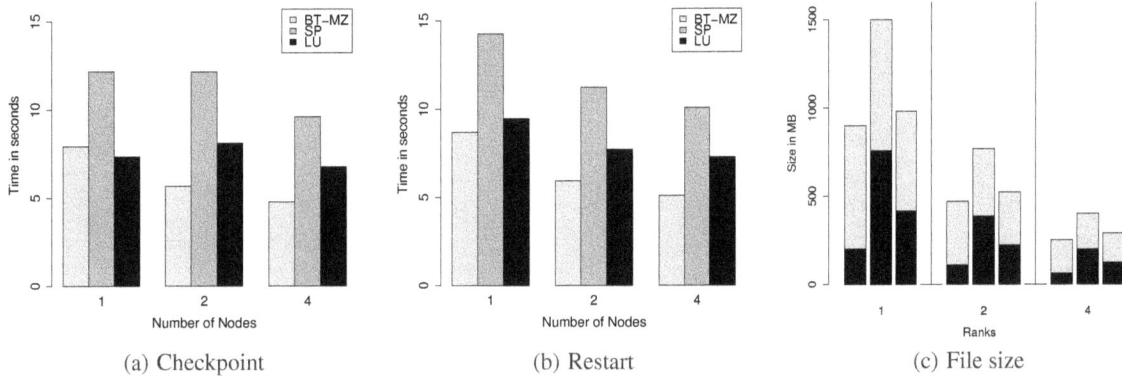

(a) Checkpoint   (b) Restart   (c) File size

Figure 11: Performance evaluation of checkpoint and restart on MPI benchmarks.

input size. This indicates the feasibility to taking frequent checkpoints, particularly for larger inputs and longer runtime.

8. RELATED WORK

Checkpoint and restart (CR) has a long history in computing systems. Libckpt [26] was one of the first UNIX implementations. Condor [36] provides CR and process migration for load balancing. These libraries provide process-level checkpointing. There are also user-level checkpointing libraries [10, 13, 19], and recent studies suggest using nonvolatile memory to improve CR performance [21]. Rollback-recovery protocols in message-passing systems is a classical research field [12]. Multiple MPI libraries, including Open MPI [15] and MPICH-V [4], provide distributed CR for MPI applications.

Several previous studies proposed CR and process migration for GPUs. CheCUDA supports a part of basic CUDA APIs [35]. It copies all the user data from a GPU to the host system during checkpointing. Then it destroys the CUDA context before taking a checkpoint. The data and context are copied back from the host to the GPU at post-checkpoint (restart) time. NVCR keeps a database of the memory allocations in GPUs [23]. Before checkpointing it releases all the memory contents and replays the log at the restart time. The replay is necessary to avoid invalid memory addresses

at restart time. This imposes overhead during restart time and specially normal execution of application. CheCL provides CR and migration for OpenCL [34]. CheCL synchronizes the host and command queues by waiting for all commands to complete. A command queue is used to schedule the execution of kernels and perform memory operations in OpenCL context. CheCL benefits from a proxy mechanism to decouple the process from OpenCL implementation. However, each kernel execution involves an additional step of inter-process communication, incurring extra communication latency.

Process migration has been extensively studied in the past. Zap is a system that performs process-group migration [24], while Wang et al. studied live migration of processes in HPC environment [37]. In addition, live migration of entire virtual machines is a very useful tool for data center and cluster administrations [8].

9. CONCLUSION

To conclude, in this paper we presented Snapify, a set of extensions to Xeon Phi's software stack that captures process snapshots of offload applications. Using Snapify we implemented application-transparent checkpoint and restart, process migration, and process swapping for offload applications. Experimental results on OpenMP and MPI offload applications show that Snapify added negligible runtime overhead (1.5% in average) and is very efficient in taking snapshots and restoring processes.

We also created Snapify-IO, a remote file access service based on RDMA to transfer process snapshots between the host system and coprocessors. Snapify-IO benefits both Snapify *and* the default checkpoint and restart tool for native applications. For native applications our experimental results show that Snapify-IO achieves 4.7x to 8.8x speedup in checkpoint, and 4.4x to 5.3x speedup in restart over NFS, for snapshot size between 1GB to 4GB.

10. REFERENCES

[1] J. Ansel, K. Arya, and G. Cooperman. DMTCP: Transparent checkpointing for cluster computations and the desktop. In *Proc. of Intl. Parallel and Distributed Processing Symposium*, 2009.

[2] D. Bailey et al. The NAS parallel benchmarks. Technical Report RNR-94-007, NASA Advanced Supercomputing Division, Mar. 1994.

[3] M. Becchi, K. Sajjapongse, I. Graves, A. Procter, V. Ravi, and S. Chakradhar. A virtual memory based runtime to support multi-tenancy in clusters with GPUs. In *Proc. of the Intl. Symposium on High-Perf. Parallel and Distributed Computing*, pages 97–108, June 2012.

[4] G. Bosilca et al. MPICH-V: toward a scalable fault tolerant MPI for volatile nodes. In *Proc. of the ACM/IEEE Intl. Conf. for High Perf. Computing, Networking, Storage and Analysis*, 2002.

[5] S. Cadambi, G. Coviello, C.-H. Li, R. Phull, K. Rao, M. Sankaradass, and S. Chakradhar. COSMIC: Middleware for high performance and reliable multiprocessing on Xeon Phi coprocessors. In *Proc. of the Intl. Symposium on High-Perf. Parallel and Distributed Computing*, pages 215–226, June 2013.

[6] F. Cappello, A. Geist, B. Gropp, L. Kale, B. Kramer, and M. Snir. Toward exascale resilience. *Int. J. High Perform. Comput. Appl.*, 23(4):374–388, Nov. 2009.

[7] K. M. Chandy and L. Lamport. Distributed snapshots: Determining global states of distributed systems. *ACM Tran. on Computer Syst.*, 3(1):63–75, Feb. 1985.

[8] C. Clark, K. Fraser, S. Hand, J. G. Hansen, E. Jul, C. Limpach, I. Pratt, and A. Warfield. Live migration of virtual machines. In *Proc. of the USENIX Conf. on Networked Syst. Design and Implementation*, pages 273–286, 2005.

[9] R. F. V. der Wijngaart and H. Jin. NAS parallel benchmarks, multi-zone versions. Technical Report NAS-03-010, NASA Advanced Supercomputing Division, July 2003.

[10] W. R. Dieter. User-level checkpointing for linuxthreads programs. In *USENIX Annual Technical Conf. (FREENIX Track)*, pages 81–92, 2001.

[11] J. Duell. The design and implementation of Berkeley Lab's Linux Checkpoint/Restart. Technical report, Lawrence Berkeley National Laboratory, 2003.

[12] E. N. M. Elnozahy, L. Alvisi, Y.-M. Wang, and D. B. Johnson. A survey of rollback-recovery protocols in message-passing systems. *ACM Comput. Surv.*, 34(3):375–408, Sept. 2002.

[13] http://www.criu.org/.

[14] http://www.top500.org/.

[15] J. Hursey, J. M. Squyres, T. I. Mattox, and A. Lumsdaine. The design and implementation of checkpoint/restart process fault tolerance for Open MPI. In *Proc. of Intl. Parallel and Distributed Processing Symposium*, Mar. 2007.

[16] Intel Corporation. *MIC COI API Reference Manual*, 0.65 edition.

[17] Intel Corporation. *Intel Manycore Platform Software Stack (Intel MPSS): User's Guide*, 2013.

[18] Intel Corporation. *Symmetric Communications Interface (SCIF) for Intel Xeon Phi Product Family Users Guide*, 2013.

[19] G. J. Janakiraman, J. Renato, S. D. Subhraveti, and Y. Turner. Cruz: Application-transparent distributed checkpoint-restart on standard operating systems. In *Dependable Systems and Networks, 2005. DSN 2005. Proceedings. International Conference on*, pages 260–269, June 2005.

[20] J. Jeffers and J. Reindeer. *Intel Xeon Phi Coprocessor High-Performance Programming*. Morgan Kaufmann Publishers, 2013.

[21] S. Kannan, A. Gavrilovska, K. Schwan, and D. Milojicic. Optimizing checkpoints using NVM as virtual memory. *Proc. of Intl. Parallel and Distributed Processing Symposium*, pages 29–40, 2013.

[22] R. Koo and S. Toueg. Checkpointing and rollback-recovery for distributed systems. *IEEE Tran. on Software Engineering*, SE-13(1):23–31, Jan. 1987.

[23] A. Nukada, H. Takizawa, and S. Matsuoka. NVCR: A transparent checkpoint-restart library for NVIDIA CUDA. In *IEEE Intl. Symposium on Parallel and Distributed Processing Workshops and Phd Forum*, pages 104–113, 2011.

[24] S. Osman, D. Subhraveti, G. Su, and J. Nieh. The design and implementation of Zap: A system for migrating computing environments. In *Proc. of the USENIX Conf. on Oper. Syst. Design and Implementation*, pages 361–376, Dec. 2002.

[25] R. Phull, C.-H. Li, K. Rao, H. Cadambi, and S. Chakradhar. Interference-driven resource management for GPU-based heterogeneous clusters. In *Proc. of the Intl. Symposium on High-Perf. Parallel and Distributed Computing*, pages 109–120, June 2012.

[26] J. S. Plank, M. Beck, G. Kingsley, and K. Li. Libckpt: Transparent checkpointing under unix. In *USENIX Technical Conf. Proc.*, 1995.

[27] M. Rieker, J. Ansel, and G. Cooperman. Transparent user-level checkpointing for the native posix thread library for linux. In *Proc. of the Intl. Conf. on Parallel and Distributed Processing Techniques and Applications*, pages 492–498, July 2006.

[28] J. F. Ruscio, M. A. Heffner, and S. Varadarajan. DejaVu: Transparent user-level checkpointing, migration, and recovery for distributed systems. In *Proc. of Intl. Parallel and Distributed Processing Symposium*, Mar. 2007.

[29] K. Sajjapongse, X. Wang, and M. Becchi. A preemption-based runtime to efficiently schedule multi-process applications on heterogeneous clusters with GPUs. In *Proc. of the Intl. Symposium on High-Perf. Parallel and Distributed Computing*, pages 179–190, June 2013.

[30] F. Salfner, M. Lenk, and M. Malek. A survey of online failure prediction methods. *ACM Comput. Surv.*, 42(3), Mar. 2010.

[31] S. Sankaran, J. M. Squyres, B. Barrett, and A. Lumsdaine. The LAM/MPI checkpoint/restart framework: System-initiated checkpointing. In *Proc. of the Symposium of Los Alamos Computer Science Institute*, pages 479–493, 2003.

[32] K. Sato, N. Maruyama, K. Mohror, A. Moody, T. Gamblin, B. R. de Supinski, and S. Matsuoka. Design and modeling of a non-blocking checkpointing system. In *Proc. of the ACM/IEEE Intl. Conf. for High Perf. Computing, Networking, Storage and Analysis*, Nov. 2012.

[33] B. Schroeder and G. A. Gibson. Understanding failures in petascale computers. *J. of Physics: Conf. Series*, 78(1), 2007.

[34] H. Takizawa, K. Koyama, K. Sato, K. Komatsu, and H. Kobayashi. CheCL: Transparent checkpointing and process migration of OpenCL applications. In *Proc. of Intl. Parallel and Distributed Processing Symposium*, pages 864–876, May 2011.

[35] H. Takizawa, K. Sato, K. Komatsu, and H. Kobayashi. CheCUDA: A checkpoint/restart tool for CUDA applications. In *Proc. of the Intl. Conf. on Parallel and Distributed Computing, Applications and Technologies*, pages 408–413, Dec. 2009.

[36] T. Tannenbaum and M. Litzkow. Checkpointing and migration of unix processes in the Condor distributed processing system. *Dr Dobbs Journal*, Feb. 1995.

[37] C. Wang, F. Mueller, C. Engelmann, and S. L. Scott. Proactive process-level live migration in HPC environments. In *Proc. of the ACM/IEEE Intl. Conf. for High Perf. Computing, Networking, Storage and Analysis*, 2008.

Transparent Checkpoint-Restart over InfiniBand

Jiajun Cao*   Gregory Kerr*   Kapil Arya*   Gene Cooperman*
College of Computer and Information Science
Northeastern University
Boston, MA 02115 / USA
jiajun@ccs.neu.edu, kerrgi@gmail.com, kapil@ccs.neu.edu, gene@ccs.neu.edu

ABSTRACT

Transparently saving the state of the InfiniBand network as part of distributed checkpointing has been a long-standing challenge for researchers. The lack of a solution has forced typical MPI implementations to include custom checkpoint-restart services that "tear down" the network, checkpoint each node in isolation, and then re-connect the network again. This work presents the first example of transparent, system-initiated checkpoint-restart that directly supports InfiniBand. The new approach simplifies current practice by avoiding the need for a privileged kernel module. The generality of this approach is demonstrated by applying it both to MPI and to Berkeley UPC (Unified Parallel C), in its native mode (without MPI). Scalability is shown by checkpointing 2,048 MPI processes across 128 nodes (with 16 cores per node). The run-time overhead varies between 0.8% and 1.7%. While checkpoint times dominate, the network-only portion of the implementation is shown to require less than 100 milliseconds (not including the time to locally write application memory to stable storage).

Keywords

checkpoint/restart; InfiniBand; MPI; UPC

Categories and Subject Descriptors

D.4.5 [**Operating Systems**]: Reliability—*checkpoint/restart*

1. INTRODUCTION

InfiniBand is the preferred network for most of high performance computing and for certain Cloud applications, due to its low latency. Historically, transparent (system-initiated) checkpoint-restart has typically been the first technology that one examines in order to provide fault tolerance during long-running computations. *Checkpoint-restart* is the process of saving to stable storage (such as disk or SSD) the state of the processes in a running computation, and later re-starting from stable storage. The checkpoint-restart is *transparent* if no modification of the application is required. This is sometimes called *system-initiated* checkpointing.

Since transparent checkpoint-restart had not previously been available for distributed computations over InfiniBand, support for this important case had been based on: (i) "tearing down" the InfiniBand network connection; (ii) checkpointing the processed on each single computer node in isolation; and (iii) then re-building the network connection. Such schemes are typically implemented within each MPI implementation [15, 16, 25, 26], while using the BLCR kernel module [9, 14] for single-node checkpointing. However, such MPI-based implementations carry the overhead of waiting for completion of pending MPI messages, while blocking the sending of any new messages.

We present a new approach to checkpointing over Infini-Band. This is the first efficient and transparent solution for *direct* checkpoint-restart over the InfiniBand network (without the intermediary of an MPI checkpoint-restart service that is implementation-specific). This also extends to other language implementations over InfiniBand, such as Unified Parallel C (UPC [10]).

The new approach for InfiniBand provides at least three advantages:

1. Resuming after a checkpoint can be faster if there is no need to tear down and re-connect the network. (Section 4.2.2 shows the network-only portion of checkpointing to be two orders of magnitude faster than the older approach of Open MPI/BLCR.)

2. PGAS languages (e.g., UPC) often include two implementations of InfiniBand support: a direct implementation for greater network performance, and a refactoring on top of MPI in order to gain the advantage of MPI-based checkpointing. This work provides checkpoint-restart support in the direct case, thus supporting both speed and fault tolerance within a single implementation.

3. The use of the popular BLCR kernel module implies that the restart cluster must use the same Linux kernel as on the original checkpoint cluster. The new work eliminates this restriction.

The current work is implemented as a plugin on top of DMTCP (Distributed MultiThreaded CheckPointing) [1].

*This work was partially supported by the National Science Foundation under Grants OCI-0960978 and OCI 1229059, and by a grant from Intel Corporation.

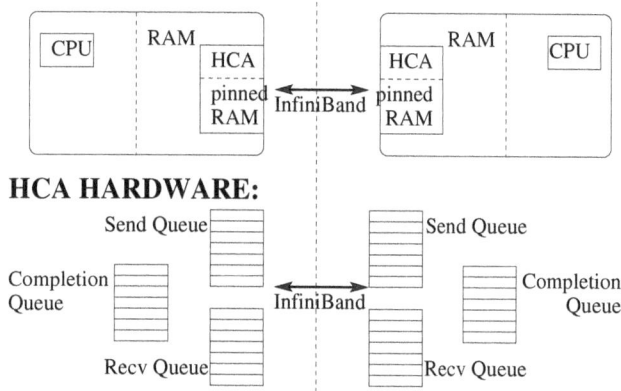

HCA HARDWARE:

Figure 1: InfiniBand Concepts

The experimental evaluation demonstrates DMTCP-based checkpointing of Open MPI for the NAS LU benchmark and others. For 512 processes, checkpointing to a local disk drive, occurs in 232 seconds, whereas it requires 36 seconds when checkpointing to back-end Lustre-based storage. Checkpointing of up to 2,048 MPI processes (128 nodes with 16 cores per node) is shown to have a run-time overhead between 0.8% and 1.7%. This overhead is shown to be a little less than the overhead when using the checkpoint-restart of Open MPI using BLCR. Tests were also carried out on Berkeley UPC [5] over GASNet's ibv conduit [3], with similar results for checkpoint times and run-time overhead.

A particular advantage of the older MPI-based approach using network "tear-down" is the possibility to checkpoint on an InfiniBand network and restart on a TCP network (or vice versa). Such an interconnection-agnostic possibility was presented for the checkpoint-restart service of Open MPI [15]. The InfiniBand plugin design is intended to also be compatible with a future interconnection-agnostic capability for the new approach. An early proof of principle is presented here, showing an additional IB2TCP plugin, capable of checkpointing over InfiniBand and restarting over TCP in the special case of an MPI program over two nodes.

Finally, the number of lines of code of an implementation is a useful indicator of the likely effort required for maintenance. The primary InfiniBand plugin consists of 2,700 lines of code (while the additional IB2TCP plugin comprises 1,000 lines of code).

Organization of Paper.

Section 2 covers the background on the InfiniBand Verbs API and DMTCP. Section 3 provides design principles for checkpointing over InfiniBand. An experimental evaluation is presented in Section 4. Limitations and possible future directions are presented in Section 5. Finally, the related work (Section 6) and conclusions (Section 7) are presented.

2. BACKGROUND

Section 2.1 reviews some concepts of InfiniBand, necessary for understanding the checkpointing approach described in Section 3. Section 2.2 describes the use of plugins in DMTCP.

2.1 InfiniBand Verbs API

In order to understand the algorithm, we review some concepts from the Verbs API of InfiniBand. While there are several references that describe InfiniBand, we recommend one of [19, 2] as a gentle introduction for a general audience.

Recall that the InfiniBand network uses *RDMA* (remote DMA to the RAM of a remote computer). Each computer node must have a Host Channel Adapter (HCA) board with access to the system bus (memory bus). With only two computer nodes, the HCA adapter boards may be connected directly to each other. With three or more nodes, communication must go through an InfiniBand switch in the middle. Note also that the bytes of an InfiniBand message may be delivered out of order.

Figure 1 reviews the basic elements of an InfiniBand network. A hardware host channel adapter (HCA) and the software library and driver together maintain at least one *queue pair* and a *completion queue* on each node. The queue pair consists of a send queue and a receive queue. Sending a message across a queue pair causes an entry to be added to the completion queue on each node. However, it is possible to set a flag when posting a work request to the send queue, such that no entry is added to the completion queue on the "send" side of the connection.

Although not explicitly introduced as a standard, libibverbs (provided by the Linux OFED (OpenFabrics Enterprise Distribution)) is the most commonly used InfiniBand interface library. We will describe the model in terms of the functions prefixed by `ibv_` for the *verbs library* (libibverbs). Many programs also use OFED's convenience functions, prefixed by `rdma_*`. OFED also provides an optional library, librdmacm (RDMA connection manager) for ease of connection set-up and tear-down in conjunction with the verbs interface. Since this applies only to set-up and tear-down, this library does not affect the ability to perform transparent checkpoint-restart.

We assume the reliable connection model (end-to-end context), which is by far the most commonly used model for InfiniBand. There are two models for the communication:

- Send-receive model

- RDMA (remote DMA) model (often employed for efficiency, and serving as the inspiration for the one-sided communication of the MPI-2 standard)

Our InfiniBand plugin supports both models, and a typical MPI implementation can be configured to use either model.

2.1.1 Send-Receive Model

We first describe the steps in processing the send-receive model for InfiniBand connection. It may be useful to examine Figure 1 while reading the steps below.

1. Initialize a hardware context, which causes a buffer in RAM to be allocated. All further operations are with respect to this hardware context.

2. Create a protection domain that sets the permissions to determine which computers may connect to it.

3. Register a memory region, which causes the virtual memory to be pinned to a physical address (so that the operating system will not page that memory out).

4. Create a completion queue for each of the sender and the receiver. This completion queue will be used later.

5. Create a queue pair (a send queue and a receive queue) associated with the completion queue.

6. An end-to-end connection is created between two queue pairs, with each queue pair associated with a port on an HCA adapter. The sender and receiver queue pair information (several ids) is exchanged, typically using either TCP (through a non-InfiniBand side channel), or by using an rdmacm library whose API is transport-neutral.

7. The receiver creates a work request and posts it to the receive queue. (One can post multiple receive buffers in advance.)

8. The sender creates one or more work requests and posts them to the send queue.

9. The application must ensure that a receive buffer has been posted before it posts a work request to the send queue. It is an application error if this is not the case.

10. The transfer of data now takes place between a posted buffer on the send queue and a posted buffer on the receive queue. The posted send and receive buffers have now been used up, and further posts are required for further messages.

11. Upon completion, work completions are generated by the hardware and appended to each of the completion queues, one queue on the sender's node and one queue on the receiver's node.

12. The sender and receiver each poll the completion queue until a work completion is encountered. (A blocking request for work completion also exists as an alternative. A blocking request must be acknowledged on success.)

13. Polling causes the work completion to be removed from the completion queue. Hence, further polling will eventually see further completion events. Both blocking and non-blocking versions of the polling calls exist.

We also remark that a work request (a WQE or Work Queue Entry) points to a list of scatter/gather elements, so that the data of the message need not be contiguous.

2.1.2 RDMA Model

The RDMA model is similar to the send-receive model. However, in this case, one does not post receive buffers. The data is received directly in a memory region. An efficient implementation of MPI's one-sided communication (MPI_Put, MPI_Get, MPI_Accumulate), when implemented over InfiniBand, will typically employ the RDMA model [18].

As a consequence, Step 9 of Section 2.1.1 does not appear in the RDMA model. Similarly, Steps 11 and 12 are modified in the RDMA model to refer to completion and polling solely for the send end of the end-to-end connection.

Other variations exist, which are supported in our work, but not explicitly discussed here. In one example, an InfiniBand application may choose to send several messages without requesting a work completion in the completion queue. In these cases, an application-specific algorithm will follow this sequence with a message that includes a work completion. In a second example, an RDMA-based work request may request an immediate mode, in which the work completion is placed only in the remote completion queue and not in the local completion queue.

2.2 DMTCP and Plugins

DMTCP is a transparent, checkpoint-restart package that supports third-party plugins. The current work on Infini-Band support was implemented as a DMTCP plugin [8]. The plugin is used here to virtualize the InfiniBand resources exposed to the end user, such as the queue pair struct (ibv_qp) (see Figure 1). This is needed since upon restart from a checkpoint image, the plugin will need to create a new queue pair for communication. As a result, the InfiniBand driver will create a new queue pair struct at a new address in user space, with new ids.

Plugins provide three core features to support virtualization:

1. wrapper functions around functions of the InfiniBand library: these wrappers translate between virtual resources (seen by the target application) and real resources (seen within the InfiniBand library, driver and hardware). The wrapper function also records changes to the queue pair and other resources for later replay during restart.

2. event hooks: these hooks are functions within the plugin that DMTCP will call at the time of checkpoint and restart. Hence, the plugin is notified at the time of checkpoint and restart, so as to update the virtual-to-real translations, to recreate the network connection upon restarting from a checkpoint image, and to replay some information from the logs.

3. a publish/subscribe facility: to exchange ids among plugins running on the different computer nodes whenever new device connections are created. Examples of such ids are local and remote queue pair numbers and remote keys of memory regions.

3. DESIGN PRINCIPLES

The InfiniBand completion queue is the most complex of the subsystems being checkpointed. The key difficulty here is that at the time of checkpoint, the plugin needs to "drain" the notifications in the InfiniBand completion queue, and then re-insert those notifications at the time of resume or restart.

In this section, we will describe two orthogonal issues. First, Section 3.1 describes some important principles needed for draining the completion queue. Understanding of those underlying principles will be more enlightening than pseudo-code for a detailed implementation of an algorithm for draining the queue.

Second, Section 3.2 describes how the DMTCP plugin virtualizes the InfiniBand ids (e.g., rkey, qp_num, lid, pd). This is a key issue since the ids are shared among distributed processes. InfiniBand will typically assign new ids, when DMTCP restarts from a checkpoint image. Since the Infini-Band library and application code may have already cached the pre-checkpoint ids, the plugin uses its wrapper functions to interpose and pass on only virtual ids to the application and libraries. The plugin maintains an internal table of virtual and real ids. This table must be consistently updated across all processes on restart.

Figure 2 presents an overview of the virtualization of a queue pair. Observe that the DMTCP plugin library interposes between most calls from the target application to the InfiniBand ibverbs library. This allows the DMTCP Infini-Band plugin to intercept the creation of a queue pair by the

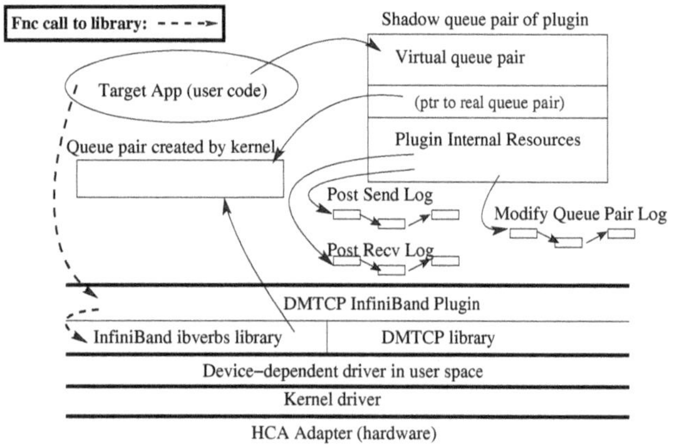

Figure 2: Queue pair resources and their virtualization. (The plugin keeps a log of calls to post to or to modify the queue pair.)

InfiniBand kernel driver, and to create a shadow queue pair. The target application is passed a pointer only to the virtual queue pair created by the plugin. Thus, any further ibverbs calls to manipulate the queue pair will be intercepted by the plugin, and appropriate fields in the queue pair structure can be appropriately virtualized before the real ibverbs call.

Similarly, any ibverbs calls to post to the send or receive queue, or to modify the queue pair, are intercepted and saved in a log. This log is used for internal bookkeeping by the plugin, to appropriately model work requests as they evolve into the completion queue.

Note also a subtle corner case: a call to ibv_post_send may request that no work completion entry be entered for that one call. The log must account for this through later calls that provide a completion entry, similarly to typical application code that works with InfiniBand.

In this work, we always use the three terms checkpoint, resume and restart as follows. *Checkpoint* refers to saving the state, *resume* refers to the original process resuming the computation, and *restart* refers to launching a new process that will restart from stable storage.

3.1 Draining the Completion Queue

As the user base code makes calls to the verbs library, we will use DMTCP plugin wrapper functions around these library functions to interpose. Hence the user call is first received by our DMTCP plugin library. We then extract parameters describing how the resources were created, before passing on the call to the verbs library, and later passing back the return value. This allows us to recreate semantically equivalent copies of those same resources on restart *even if we restart on a new computer*. In particular, we record any calls to `modify_qp` and to `modify_srq`. On restart, those calls are replayed in order to place the corresponding data structures in a semantically equivalent state to pre-checkpoint.

While the description above appears simple, several subtleties arise, encapsulated in the following principles.

Principle 1: Never let the user see a pointer to the actual InfiniBand resource.

A verbs call that creates a new InfiniBand resource will typically create a struct, and return a pointer to that struct. We will call this struct created by the verbs library a *real*

struct. If the end user code creates an InfiniBand resource, we interpose to copy that struct to a a new *shadow struct*, and then pass back to the end user the pointer to this shadow struct. Some examples of InfiniBand resources for which this is done are: a context, a protection domain, a memory region, and a queue pair.

The reason for this is that many implementations of InfiniBand libraries contain additional undocumented fields in these structs, in addition to those documented by the corresponding "man page". When we restart after checkpoint, we cannot pass the original pre-checkpoint struct to the verbs library. The undocumented (hidden) fields would not match the current state of the InfiniBand hardware on restart. (New device-dependent ids will be in use after restart.)

So, on restart, we create an entirely new InfiniBand resource (using the same parameters as the original). This new struct should be semantically equivalent to the pre-checkpoint original, and the hidden fields will correspond to the post-restart state of the hardware.

This is a form of virtualization. The user is passed a pointer to a *virtual struct*, the shadow struct. The verbs library knows only about the *real struct*. So, we will guarantee that the verbs library only sees real structs, and that the end user code only sees virtual structs.

To do this, we interpose our DMTCP plugin library function if a verbs library function refers to one of these structs representing InfiniBand resources. If the end user calls a verbs library function that returns a pointer to a real struct, then our interposition will replace this and return a pointer to a corresponding virtual struct. If the user code passes an argument pointing to a virtual struct, we will replace it by a pointer to a real struct before calling the verbs library function.

Remark: In the OFED ibverbs implementation, some of the apparent library calls to the verbs library are in fact inline functions. A DMTCP plugin cannot easily interpose on inline functions. Luckily, these inline functions are often associated with possibly device-dependent functions. However, each of the important OFED inline functions expands to a dispatch through a global function pointer. So, the plugin resets the global function pointer to a plugin function, which wraps a call to the original function pointer.

Principle 2: Carry out bookkeeping on posts of work queue entries to the send and receive queue.

As work requests are entered onto a send queue or receive queue, the wrapper functions of the DMTCP plugin record those work requests (which have now become work queue entries). When the completion queue is polled, if a completion event corresponding to that work queue entry is found, then the DMTCP plugin records that the entry has been destroyed. At the time of checkpoint, there is a log of those work queue entries that have been posted and not yet destroyed. At the time of restart, the send and receive queues will initially be empty. So, those work queue entries are re-posted to their respective queues. (In the case of resume, the send and receive queues continue to hold their work queue entries, and so no special action is necessary.)

Principle 3: At the time of checkpoint, "drain" the completion queue of its completion events.

At the time of checkpoint, and after all user threads have been quiesced, the checkpoint thread polls the completion queue for remaining completion events not yet seen by the end user code. A copy of each completion event seen is saved by the DMTCP plugin. Note that we must drain the completion queue for each of the sender and the receiver. Recall also that the verbs library function for polling the completion queue will also remove the polled completion event from the completion queue as it passes that event to the caller.

Principle 4: At the time of restart or resume, "refill" a virtual completion queue.

At the time of restart or resume and before any user threads have been re-activated, we must somehow refill the completion queue, since the end user has not yet seen the completion events that were drained (see previous principle). To do this, the DMTCP plugin stores the completion events of the previous principle in its own private queue. The DMTCP plugin library then interposes between any end user calls to a completion queue and the corresponding verbs library function. If the end user polls the completion queue, the DMTCP wrapper function passes back to the end user the plugin's private copy of the completion events, and the verbs library function for polling is never called. Only after the private completion queue becomes empty are further polling calls passed on to the verbs library function. Hence, the plugin's private queue becomes part of a *virtual completion queue*.

Principle 5: Any InfiniBand messages still "in flight" can be ignored.

If data from an InfiniBand message is still in flight (has not yet arrived in the receive buffer), then InfiniBand will not generate a completion event. Note that the InfiniBand hardware may continue to transport the data of a message, and even generate a completion event *after all user threads have been quiesced for checkpoint*. Nevertheless, a simple rule operates.

If our checkpoint thread has not seen a completion event that arrived late, then we will not have polled for that completion event. Therefore, our bookkeeping in Principle 2 will not have removed the send or receive post from our log. Further, this implies that the memory buffers will continue to have the complete data, since it was saved on checkpoint and restored on restart. Therefore, upon restart (which implies a fresh, empty completion queue), the checkpoint thread will issue another send or receive post (again following the logic of Principle 2).

Remark: Blocking requests for a completion event (`ibv_get_cq_event`) and for shared receive queues create further issues. While those details add some complication, their solution is straightforward and is not covered here.

3.2 Virtualization of InfiniBand Ids

A number of InfiniBand objects and associated ids will change on restart. All of these must be virtualized. Among these objects and ids are ibv contexts, protection domains, memory regions (the local and remote keys (lkey/rkey) of the memory regions), completion queues, queue pairs (the queue pair number, qp_num), and the local id (lid) of the HCA port being used. Note that the lid of an HCA port will not change if restarting on the same host, but it may change when restarting on a new host, which may have been configured to use a different port.

In all of the above cases, the plugin assigns a virtual id and maintains a translation table between virtual and real id. The application sees only the virtual id. Any InfiniBand calls are processed through the plugin, where virtual ids are translated back to real ids.

On restart, the InfiniBand hardware/driver may assign new real ids for a given InfiniBand object. In this case, the real ids are updated within the translation tables maintained by the plugin.

3.2.1 Virtualization of remote ids: rkey, qp_num and lid

A more difficult issue occurs in the case of remote memory keys (rkey), queue pair numbers (qp_num) and local ids (lid). In all three cases, an InfiniBand application must pass these ids to a remote node for communication with the local node. The remote need will need the qp_num and lid when calling `ibv_modify_qp` to initialize a queue pair that connects to the local node. The remote node will need the rkey when calling `ibv_post_send` to send a message to the local node.

Since the plugin allows the application to see only virtual ids, the application will employ a virtual id when calling `ibv_modify_qp` and `ibv_post_send`. The plugin will first replace the virtual id by the real id, which is known to the InfiniBand hardware. To do this, the plugin within each remote node must contain a virtualization table to translate all virtual ids by real ids.

Next, we recall how a remote node received a virtual id in the first place. The InfiniBand specification solves this bootstrapping problem by requiring the application to pass these three ids to the remote node through some out-of-band mechanism. When the application employs this out-of-band mechanism, the remote node will "see" the virtual ids that the plugin passed back to the application upon completion of an InfiniBand call.

The solution chosen for the InfiniBand plugin is that it assigns a virtual id, which is the same as the real id at the time of the initial creation of the InfiniBand object. After restart, the InfiniBand hardware may assign a new real id. At the time of restart, the plugin uses the DMTCP coordinator and the publish-subscribe feature to exchange the new real ids, associated with a given virtual id. Since the application continues to see only the virtual ids, the plugin can continue to translate between virtual and real ids through any wrapper by which the application communicates to the InfiniBand hardware (see Figure 2). (A subtle issue can arise if a queue pair or memory region is created after restart. This is a rare case. Although we have not seen this in the current work, Section 5 discusses two possible solutions.)

3.2.2 Virtualization of rkeys

Next, the case of rkeys (remote memory region keys) poses a particular problem that does not occur for queue pair numbers or local ids. This is because an rkey is guaranteed unique by InfiniBand only with respect to the protection domain within which it was created. Thus, if a single InfiniBand node has received rkeys from many remote nodes, then the rkeys for two different remote nodes may conflict.

Normally, InfiniBand can resolve this conflict because a queue pair must be specified in order to send or receive a message. The local queue pair number determines a unique queue pair number on the remote node. The remote queue pair number then uniquely determines an associated protection domain *pd*. With the remote *pd*, all rkeys are unique. Hence, the InfiniBand driver on the remote node uses the (*pd*, rkey) pair, to determine a unique memory address on the remote node.

In the case of the InfiniBand plugin, the vrkey (*virtual rkey*) and rkey are identical if no restart has taken place. (It is only after restart that the rkey may change, for a given vrkey). Hence, prior to the first checkpoint, translation from vrkey to rkey is trivial.

After a restart, the InfiniBand plugin must employ a strategy motivated by that of the InfiniBand driver. In a call to `ibv_post_send`, the target application will pass the required parameters, including both a virtual queue pair number and a virtual rkey (vrkey). Unlike InfiniBand, the plugin must translate the vrkey into the real rkey on the local node. However, during a restart, each node has published its locally generated rkey, the corresponding *pd* (as a globally unique id; see above), and the corresponding vrkey. Similarly, each node has published the virtual queue pair number and corresponding *pd* for any queue pair generated on that node. Each node has also subscribed to the above information published by all other nodes.

Hence, the local node is aware of the following through publish-subscribe during restart:

$$(\text{virtualqp\_num}, \text{pd})$$
$$(\text{vrkey}, \text{pd}, \text{realrkey})$$

The call to `ibv_post_send` provides the (local) virtual qp_num, and the vrkey. The previous InfiniBand calls building the connection had provided the corresponding remote virtual qp_num. The first of the publish-subscribe tuples above yields the globally unique *pd*. The *pd* and *vrkey* together are then enough to use the second tuple to derive the necessary rkey, which is used when calling the InfiniBand hardware.

4. EXPERIMENTAL EVALUATION

The experiments are divided into four parts: scalability with more nodes in the case of Open MPI (Section 4.1); comparison between BLCR and DMTCP for MPI-based computations (Section 4.2); tests on Unified Parallel C (UPC) (Section 4.3); and demonstration of migration from InfiniBand to TCP (Section 4.4).

Experimental Configuration.

Two clusters were employed for the experiments described here. For scalability tests with up to 2048 cores, a large cluster was reserved for our sole use (Section 4.1). This was the Massachusetts Green High-Performance Computing Center (MGHPCC), with Intel Xeon E5-2650 CPUs running at 2 GHz. Each node is dual-CPU, for a total of 16 cores per node. It employs Mellanox HCA adapters. In addition to the front-end InfiniBand network, there is a Lustre back-end network. The operating system is RedHat Enterprise Linux 6.4 with Linux kernel version 2.6.32. (Section 4.4 also used this cluster in small tests, not as the sole user.)

Sections 4.2 and 4.3 refer to a cluster at the Center for Computational Research at the University of Buffalo. It uses SLURM as its resource manager, and a common NFS-mounted filesystem. Each node is equipped with either a Mellanox or QLogic (now Intel) HCA, although a given partition under which an experiment was run was always homo-geneous (either all Mellanox or all QLogic). The operating system is RedHat Enterprise Linux 6.1 with Linux kernel version 2.6.32.

In Section 4.2, experiments were run using one core per computer. Hence, the MPI rank was equal to the number of computers, and each MPI process was on a separate computer node. Not all computer nodes were identical. For reproducibility, a uniform memory limit per CPU was set at 3 GB. The CPUs had clock rates ranging from 2.13 GHz to 2.40 GHz.

In all cases, we used Open MPI 1.6, DMTCP 2.1 (or a pre-release version in some cases), and BLCR 0.8.3, respectively. Open MPI was run in its default mode, which used the RDMA model for InfiniBand, rather than the send-receive model. Although DMTCP version 2.1 was used, the plugin included some additional bug fixes appearing after that DMTCP release. For the applications, we used Berkeley UPC (Unified Parallel C) version 2.16.2 and NAS Parallel Benchmark version 3.1.

Tests of BLCR under Open MPI were run by using the Open MPI checkpoint-restart service [15]. Tests of DMTCP for Open MPI did not use the checkpoint-restart service. For DMTCP, all checkpoints are saved to a local disk (local to the given computer node), except as noted. Open MPI/BLCR uses the same strategy, except that it copies each local checkpoint image to a central coordinator process. Unfortunately, this serializes part of the parallel checkpoint. Hence, checkpoint times for BLCR are not directly comparable to those for DMTCP.

In case of DMTCP, the experimental timings reported here did not employ any particular tuning techniques and were run using the default DMTCP parameters. Thus, there are opportunities to reduce the run-time overhead by reducing the copying of buffers.

DMTCP also supports a faster forked checkpointing mode (taking advantage of checkpointing a forked child process under copy-on-write), and a fast restart using mmap to overlap running and reading in the remaining pages. Checkpoint times can also be sped up by omitting the DMTCP default on-the-fly gzip compression. See [12] for experiments exploring these extra options.

4.1 Scalability of InfiniBand Plugin

Table 1, and its graphical representation in Figure 3, present a study of scalability for the InfiniBand plugin. The NAS MPI test for LU is employed. For a given number of processes, each of classes C, D, and E are tested provided that the running time for the test is of reasonable length. The overhead for DMTCP is analyzed further in Table 2.

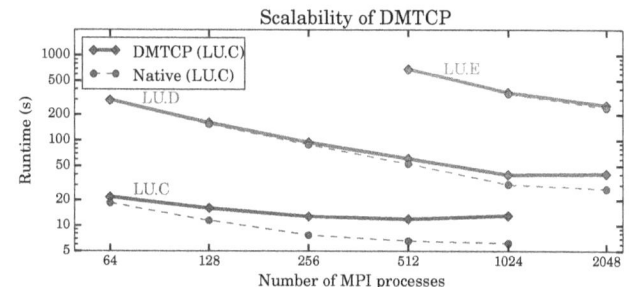

Figure 3: Plot based on Table 1.

NAS benchmark	Num. of processes	Runtime (s) (natively)	Runtime (s) (w/ DMTCP)
LU.C	64	18.5	21.7
LU.C	128	11.5	16.1
LU.C	256	7.7	12.8
LU.C	512	6.6	11.9
LU.C	1024	6.2	13.0
LU.D	64	292.6	298.0
LU.D	128	154.9	161.6
LU.D	256	89.0	94.8
LU.D	512	53.2	61.3
LU.D	1024	30.5	39.6
LU.D	2048	26.9	40.3
LU.E	512	677.2	691.6
LU.E	1024	351.6	364.9
LU.E	2048	239.3	256.4

Table 1: Demonstration of scalability: running times without DMTCP (natively) and with DMTCP; The corresponding plot is in Figure 3.

Table 1 and Figure 3 show runtimes decreasing with more MPI processes. This is because NAS experiments are based on *strong scalability*: each benchmark consists of a fixed amount of work. Hence, the runtime decreases with an increasing number of MPI nodes. The DMTCP plugin shows small overhead compared to native runs, except for cases where the runtime is below about 50 s. In these cases, startup overhead becomes a significant percentage of the total runtime (see Table 2).

# processes (running LU)	NAS classes	Startup overhead (s)	Slope (runtime overhead in %)
64	C, D	3.1	0.8
128	C, D	4.4	1.5
256	C, D	5.0	0.9
512	D, E	7.6	1.0
1024	D, E	8.7	1.3
2048	D, E	12.9	1.7

Table 2: Analysis of Table 1 showing derived breakdown of DMTCP overhead into startup overhead and runtime overhead. (See analysis in text.)

In Table 2, the overhead derived from Table 1 is decomposed into two components: startup overhead and runtime overhead. Given a NAS parallel benchmark, the total overhead is the difference of the runtime with DMTCP and the native runtime (without DMTCP). Consider a fixed number of processes on which two different classes of the same benchmark are run. For example, given the native runtimes for two different classes of the LU benchmark (e.g., t_1 for LU.C and t_2 for LU.D), and the total overhead in each case (o_1 and o_2), one can derive an assumed startup overhead s in seconds and runtime overhead ratio r, based on the formulas:

$$o_1 = s + rn_1$$
$$o_2 = s + rn_2.$$

Table 2 reports the derived startup overhead and runtime overhead using the formula above. In cases where three

NAS benchmark	Number of processes	Ckpt time (s)	Ckpt size (MB)
LU.E	128×4	70.8	350
LU.E	64×8	136.6	356
LU.E	32×16	222.6	355
LU.E	128×16	70.2	117

Table 3: Checkpoint times and image sizes for the same NAS benchmark, under different configurations. The checkpoint image size is for a single MPI process.

classes of the NAS LU benchmark were run for the same number of nodes, the largest two classes were chosen for analysis. This decision was made to ensure that any timing perturbations in the experiment would be a small percentage of the native runtimes.

The runtime overhead shown in Table 2 remains in a narrow range of 0.8% to 1.7%. The startup overhead grows as the cube root of the number of MPI processes.

Table 3 shows the effects on checkpoint time and checkpoint image size under several configurations. Note that the first three tests hold constant the number of MPI processes at 512. In this situation, the checkpoint size remains constant (to within the natural variability of repeated runs). Further, in all cases, the checkpoint time is roughly proportional to the total size of the checkpoint images on a single node. A checkpoint time of between 20 MB/s and 27 MB/s was achieved in writing to local disk, with the faster times occurring for 16 processes per node (on 16 core nodes).

Next, a test was run to compare checkpoint times when using the Lustre back-end storage versus the default checkpoint to a local disk. As expected, Lustre was faster. Specifically, Table 4 shows that checkpoint times were 6.5 times faster with Lustre, although restart times were essentially unchanged. Small differences in checkpoint image sizes and checkpoint times are part of normal variation between runs, and was always limited to less than 5%.

Disk type	Ckpt size (MB)	Ckpt time (s)	Restart time (s)
local disk	356	232.3	11.1
Lustre	365	35.7	10.9

Table 4: Comparison with checkpoints to local disk or Lustre back-end. Each case was run for NAS LU (class E), with 512 processes (32 nodes × 16 cores per node).

Finally, a test was run in which DMTCP was configured not to use its default gzip compression. Table 5 shows that this makes little difference both for the checkpoint image size and the checkpoint time. The checkpoint time is about 5% faster when gzip is not invoked.

Program and processes	Ckpt size (MB)	Ckpt time (s)	Restart time (s)
with gzip	117	70.2	23.5
w/o gzip	116	67.3	23.2

Table 5: Comparison of checkpointing with and without the use of gzip for on-the-fly compression by DMTCP.

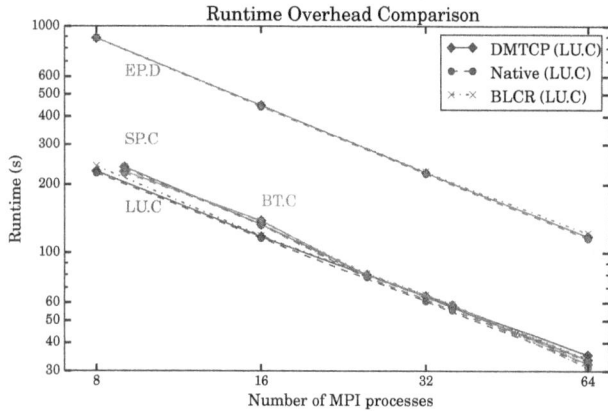

Figure 4: Comparison of running natively or with DMTCP or BLCR

4.2 Comparison between DMTCP and BLCR

The NAS Parallel Benchmarks using Open MPI provide a test of performance across a broad test suite. For the sake of comparability with previous tests on the checkpoint-restart service of Open MPI [15], we emphasize the previously used NAS tests: LU.C, EP.D, BT.C and SP.C. An analysis of the performance must consider both runtime overhead and times for checkpoint and restart.

4.2.1 High-Level overview of DMTCP vs. BLCR

Runtime overhead.

The runtime overhead is the overhead for running a program under a checkpoint-restart package as compared to running natively. No checkpoints are taken when measuring runtime overhead. Figure 4 shows that the overhead of running DMTCP or BLCR is typically only a few per cent, and the runtime performance of the two systems is comparable. (Curves are based on strong scalability: work is held constant as the number of MPI processes varies.) For longer program runs, the total runtime overhead is in the range of 1% to 2%, or 1 to 5 seconds, with 3 seconds being common. Since these overhead times do not correlate with the length of time for which the program was run, we posit that they reflect the constant overhead incurred primarily at the time of program startup (see, for example, Table 2).

Checkpoint/Restart times.

Figure 5 shows checkpoint times. These times are as reported by a central DMTCP coordinator, or by an Open MPI coordinator in the case of BLCR. Open MPI/BLCR does not report restart times. For DMTCP, restart times are approximately between 2 and 3 seconds for LU.C and EP.D, and between 2 and 4 seconds for BT.C and SP.C. Consistent with strong scalability, both checkpoint and restart times were longer when there were fewer MPI processes.

Checkpoint times are particularly important for issues of fault tolerance, since checkpoints are by far the more common operation. In the case of DMTCP, For the BT, SP, and LU benchmarks, the memory footprint decreases with an increasing number of MPI processes, thus accounting for decreasing checkpoint times. The EP *Embarrassingly Parallel* benchmark is an exception, in which the memory foot-

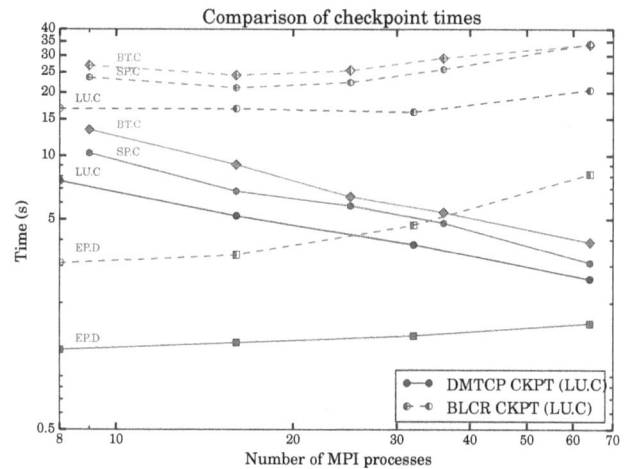

Figure 5: Comparison of checkpoint times

print remains approximately 150 MB, independently of the number of processes.

In contrast, the times for checkpointing with Open MPI/ BLCR are often roughly constant. We estimate this time is dominated by the last phase, in which Open MPI copies the local checkpoint images to a single, central node.

Note that the restart time for DMTCP was typically under 4 seconds, even for larger computations using 64 computer nodes. The Open MPI/BLCR package did not report restart times.

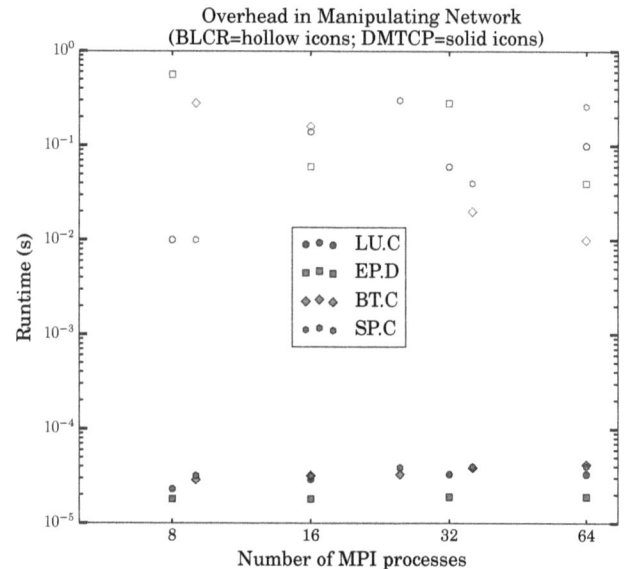

Figure 6: Overhead due to network for DMTCP and for BLCR. For BLCR, three times were measured for each case, and the middle time is reported.

4.2.2 Overhead of Network Management: DMTCP vs. BLCR

Figure 6 has the goal of analyzing the network-only portion of the checkpoint/restart time for both DMTCP and BLCR. For DMTCP, this includes the time of draining all completion queues, as well as the time of saving all Infini-

Band states. For BLCR, this includes all times for BLCR to tear down and rebuild the InfiniBand network. These times are not a bottleneck for the current experiments, when checkpointing to disk. But future technologies promise faster stable storage, which can expose the network-related time as a major cost.

Since Open MPI/BLCR must tear down the InfiniBand network, and re-build it at the time of checkpoint, it incurs a significantly higher network cost, as expected. Two advantages of the current approach are exposed in Figure 6:

1. The DMTCP plugin approach is shown to be over 100 times faster (two orders of magnitude), as compared to BLCR.

2. For any particular NAS benchmark, the DMTCP approach presents a clear and predictable trend, while the times for BLCR vary by an order of magnitude even within the same NAS benchmark and for the same number of MPI processes, under repeated runs.

In the case of BLCR, we speculate that the lack of reproducibility of times is due to some additional component of the Open MPI checkpoint-restart service, which cannot be interrupted by a network tear-down. The seemingly random random delays would be explained by whether a checkpoint is requested near the beginning or end of such a pending operation.

Note also that the times for DMTCP represent the total time spent by DMTCP in the InfiniBand plugin. No other part of the DMTCP code deals with any aspect of Infini-Band.

Number of processes	Runtime natively (s)	Runtime w/ DMTCP (s)	Ckpt (s)	Restart (s)
4	123.5	124.2	27.6	9.7
8	64.2	65.1	21.9	8.9
16	34.2	35.5	16.3	7.0

Table 6: Runtime overhead and Checkpoint-restart times for UPC FT B running under DMTCP

4.3 Checkpointing under UPC: A non-MPI Case Study

The study of checkpointing of Berkeley UPC is based on a port of the NAS parallel benchmarks at George Washington University [13]. Since that did not include a port of the LU benchmark, we switch to considering FT in this section.

The Berkeley UPC package was compiled to run natively over InfiniBand for this experiment, and it did not use MPI at all. The FT B NAS benchmark, as ported to run on UPC, was chosen because the port of NAS to UPC does not support the more communication-intensive LU benchmark. Table 6 shows that the native runtimes for FT B under UPC are comparable to the time for MPI in Figure 4. DMTCP total run-time overhead ranges from 4% down to less than 1%. We posit that the higher overhead of 4% is due to the extremely short running time in the case of 16 processes, and is explained by significant startup overhead, consistent with Table 2.

Note that BLCR could not be tested in this regime, since BLCR depends on the Open MPI checkpoint-restart service for its use in distributed computations.

4.4 Migrating InfiniBand to TCP sockets

Some traditional checkpoint-restart services, such as that of Open MPI [15], offer the ability to checkpoint over one network, and restart on a second network. This section represents an early proof of principle that a similar technology could be implemented as a DMTCP plugin. This capability has the potential to support interactive debugging in a production environment, by copying checkpoint images from an InfiniBand-based production cluster to an Ethernet/TCP-based debug cluster. Note that since DMTCP is a user-space package, it does not require that the Linux kernels on the two clusters be the same.

4.4.1 Ping-pong

The IB2TCP plugin was tested with a communication-intensive ping-pong example InfiniBand program from the OFED distribution. In this case, a smaller development cluster was used, with 6-core Xeon X5650 CPUs and a Mellanox HCA for InfiniBand. Gigabit Ethernet was used for the Ethernet portion. Parameters were set to run over 100,000 iterations.

Environment	Transfer time (s)	Transfer rate (Gigabits/s)
IB (w/o DMTCP)	0.9	7.2
DMTCP/IB (w/o IB2TCP)	1.2	5.7
DMTCP/IB2TCP/IB	1.4	4.6
DMTCP/IB2TCP/Ethernet	65.7	0.1

Table 7: Transfer time variations using two nodes on InfiniBand versus Gigabit Ethernet hardware, with the DMTCP InfiniBand and IB2TCP plugin; 100,000 iterations of ping-pong, for a total transfer size of 819 MB

Table 7 presents the results. This is a worst case, since a typical MPI program is not as communication-intensive as the ping-ping test program. We hypothesize that the full transfer rate for Gigabit Ethernet was not achieved by this hardware/Linux combination.

Environment	Runtime (s)
IB (w/o DMTCP)	26.61
DMTCP/IB (w/o IB2TCP)	27.81
DMTCP/IB2TCP/IB	27.38
DMTCP/IB2TCP/Ethernet (restart on two nodes)	45.75
DMTCP/IB2TCP/Ethernet (restart on a single node)	66.34

Table 8: Runtime variations (no checkpoint-restart) for LU.A.2 using two nodes on InfiniBand versus Gigabit Ethernet hardware, with the InfiniBand and IB2TCP plugin.

4.4.2 NAS LU.A.2 Benchmark

The NAS LU.A benchmark was conducted on the the same MGHPCC cluster that was described in Section 4.1. Table 8 shows times for NAS LU.A.2 (2 MPI nodes) for migrating from InfiniBand to TCP using the IB2TCP plugin. The test is limited to two nodes due to a missing feature in DMTCP, the support for a function wrapper around the "poll" system call, used by Open MPI.

The combined InfiniBand and IB2TCP plugins do not add considerable overhead to the run time of the application at runtime. However, when the process is migrated from Infini-Band to TCP, the runtime increases drastically. A runtime overhead of 67% is seen for the restarted computation on on two TCP nodes. The runtime overhead further increases to 142% when the entire computation is restarted on a single node.

5. LIMITATIONS AND FUTURE WORK

In this section, we discuss some other limitations in the current implementation and our plans to overcome them in future.

5.1 Heterogeneous InfiniBand Architectures

Recall that DMTCP copies and restores all of user-space memory. In reviewing Figure 2, one notes that the user-space memory includes a low-level device-dependent driver in user space. If, for example, one checkpoints on a cluster partition using Intel/QLogic, and if one restarts on a Mellanox partition, then the Mellanox low-level driver will be missing. This presents a restriction for heterogeneous computing centers in the current implementation.

There are two possible alternative implementations as described next. First, it is possible to implement a generic "stub" driver library, which can then dispatch to the appropriate device-dependent library. Second, it is possible to force the InfiniBand library to re-initialize itself by restoring the pre-initialization version of the InfiniBand library data segment, instead of the data segment as it existed just prior to checkpoint. This will cause the InfiniBand library to appear to be uninitialized, and it will re-load the appropriate device-dependent library.

5.2 Out-of-Sync Send/Recv Completions

The InfiniBand hardware may post completions to the sender and receiver at slightly different times. Thus, after draining the completion queue, the plugin waits for a fraction of a second, and then drains the completion queue one more time. This is repeated until no completions are seen in the latest period. Thus, correctness is affected only if the InfiniBand hardware posts corresponding completions relatively far apart in time, which is highly unlikely. (Note that this situation occurs in two cases: InfiniBand send-receive mode; and InfiniBand RDMA mode for the special case of ibv_post_send while setting the immediate data flag.)

In a related issue, when using the immediate data flag or the inline flag in the RDMA model, a completion is posted only on the receiving node. These flags are intended primarily for applications that send small messages. Hence, the current implementation sleeps for a small amount of time to ensure that such messages complete. A future implementation will use the DMTCP coordinator to complete the bookkeeping concerning messages sent and received, and will continue to wait if needed.

5.3 Unreliable Connections

The current implementation does not support unreliable connections (the analog of UDP for TCP/IP). Most target applications do not use this mode, and so this is not considered a priority. For a potential solution, one could add wrappers for InfiniBand functions that provide unreliable connections and adjust the draining logic.

5.4 Virtual Id Conflicts After Restart

In typical MPI implementations, memory region keys (rkey), queue pair numbers (qp_num), and local ids (lid) are all exchanged out-of-band. Since virtualized ids are passed to the target application, it is the virtualized ids that are passed out-of-band. The remote plugin is then responsible for translating the virtual ids to the real ids known to the InfiniBand hardware, on later InfiniBand calls.

The current implementation ensures that this is possible, and that there are no conflicts prior to the first checkpoint, as described in Section 3.2. In typical InfiniBand applications, queue pairs are created only during startup, and so all rkeys, qp_nums and lids will be assigned prior to the first checkpoint. However, it is theoretically possible for an application to create a new queue pair, memory region, or to query its local id after the first restart.

The current implementation assigns the virtual id to be the same as the real id at the time of the initial creation of the InfiniBand object. (After restart, the InfiniBand hardware may assign a different real id, but the virtual id for that object will remain the same.) If an object is created after restart, the real id assigned by InfiniBand may be the same as for an object created prior to checkpoint. This would create a conflict of the corresponding virtual ids.

Two solutions to this problem are possible. The simplest is to use DMTCP's publish-subscribe feature to generate globally unique virtual rkeys, and update a global table of virtual-to-real rkeys. In particular, one could use the existing implementation before the first checkpoint, and then switch to a publish-subscribe implementation after restart. A second solution is to choose the virtual rkeys in a globally unique manner, similarly to the globally unique protection domain ids of the current plugin.

6. RELATED WORK

In the case of distributed computations over TCP (e.g., over Ethernet), several distributed checkpointing approaches have been proposed [7, 17, 22, 21, 27]. Unfortunately, those solutions do not extend to supporting the InfiniBand network. Other solutions for distributed checkpointing are specific to a particular MPI implementation [4, 11, 15, 16, 20, 23, 25, 26]. These MPI-based checkpoint-restart services "tear down" the InfiniBand connection, after which a single-process checkpoint-restart package can be applied.

The implementation described here can be viewed as interposing a shadow device driver between the end user's code and the true device driver. This provides an opportunity to virtualize the fields of the queue pair struct seen by the end user code. Thus, the InfiniBand driver is modelled without the need to understand its internals. This is analogous to the idea of using a shadow kernel device by Swift et al. [28, 29]. In that work, after a catastrophic failure by the kernel device driver, the shadow device driver was able to take over and place the true device driver back in a sane state. In a similar manner, restarting on a new host with a new HCA Adapter can be viewed as a catastrophic failure of the Infini-Band user-space library. Our virtual queue pair along with the log of pending posts and modifications to the queue pair serves as a type of shadow device driver. This allows us to place back into a sane state the HCA hardware, the kernel driver and the device-dependent user-space driver.

This work is based on DMTCP (Distributed MultiThreaded CheckPointing) [1]. The DMTCP project began in 2004 [6, 7]. With the development of DMTCP versions 2.x, it has emphasized the use of plugins [8] for more modular maintainable code.

Currently, BLCR [14] is widely used as one component of an MPI dialect-specific checkpoint-restart service. This design is fundamentally different, since an MPI-specific checkpoint-restart service calls BLCR, whereas DMTCP transparently invokes an arbitrary MPI implementation. Since BLCR is kernel-based, it provides direct support only on one computer node. Most MPI dialects overcome this in their checkpoint-restart service by disconnecting any network connections, delegating to BLCR the task of a single-node checkpoint, and then reconnect the network connection. Among the MPI implementations using BLCR are Open MPI [16] (CRCP coordination protocol), LAM/MPI [25], MPICH-V [4], and MVAPICH2 [11]. Other MPI implementations provide their own analogs [11, 23, 25, 26]. In some cases, an MPI implementation may support an *application-initiated* protocol in combination with BLCR (such as SELF [16, 25]). For application-initiated checkpointing, the application writer guarantees that there are no active messages at the time of calling for a checkpoint.

Some recommended technical reports for further reading on the design of InfiniBand are [2, 19], along with the earlier introduction to the C API [30]. The report [19] was a direct result of the original search for a clean design in checkpointing over InfiniBand, and [20] represents a talk on interim progress.

In addition to DMTCP, there have been several packages for transparent, distributed checkpoint-restart of applications running over TCP sockets [17, 21, 22, 27]. The first two packages ([17] and [22, 21]) are based on the Zap package [24].

The Berkeley language Unified Parallel C (UPC) [10] is an example of a PGAS language (Partitioned Global Address Space). It runs over GASNet [3] and evolved from experience with earlier languages for DSM (Distributed Shared Memory).

7. CONCLUSION

A new approach to distributed transparent checkpoint-restart over InfiniBand has been demonstrated. This direct approach accommodates computations both for MPI and for UPC (Unified Parallel C). The approach uses a mechanism similar to that of a shadow device driver [28, 29]. In tests on the NAS LU parallel benchmark, a run-time overhead of between 0.8% and 1.7% is found on a computation with up to 2,048 MPI processes. Startup overhead is up to 13 seconds, and grows as the cube root of the number of MPI processes. Checkpoint times are roughly proportional to the total size of all checkpoint images on a single computer node. In one example with 512 MPI processes, checkpoint times varied by a factor of 6.5 (from 232 seconds to 36 seconds), depending on whether checkpoint images were written to a local disk or to a faster, Lustre-based back-end. In both cases, there were 16 MPI processes per node, and a total of approximately 5.8 GB per node was written.

The new approach also provides a viable checkpoint-restart mechanism for running UPC natively over InfiniBand — something that previously did not exist. Finally, an IB2TCP plugin was shown for migrating from InfiniBand to TCP, demonstrating that the plugin design is compatible with a an interconnection-agnostic feature, similar to that of the Open MPI checkpoint restart service [15]. Since the DMTCP plugin approach is purely user-space, it has the added benefit of supporting a destination cluster with a different Linux kernel image.

Acknowledgment

We are grateful to facilities provided at several institutions with which to test over a variety of configurations. We would like to thank: L. Shawn Matott (U. of Buffalo, development and benchmarking facilities); Henry Neeman (Oklahoma University, development facilities); Larry Owen and Anthony Skjellum (the University of Alabama at Birmingham, facilities based on NSF grant CNS-1337747); and the Massachusetts Green High Performance Computing Center (facilities for scalability testing). Dotan Barak provided helpful advice on the implementation of OpenFabrics InfiniBand. Jeffrey M. Squyres and Joshua Hursey provided helpful advice on the interaction of Open MPI and InfiniBand. Artem Polyakov provided advice on using the DMTCP batch-queue (resource manager) plugin. We also benefited from valuable comments and feedback from the reviewers. We are also grateful for help from Bogdan Nicolae in shepherding the paper.

8. REFERENCES

[1] J. Ansel, G. Cooperman, and K. Arya. DMTCP: Scalable user-level transparent checkpointing for cluster computations and the desktop. In *Proc. of IEEE International Parallel and Distributed Processing Symposium (IPDPS-09, systems track)*. IEEE Press, 2009. published on CD; version also available at http://arxiv.org/abs/cs.DC/0701037; software available at http://dmtcp.sourceforge.net.

[2] T. Bedeir. Building an RDMA-capable application with IB Verbs. Technical report, http://www.hpcadvisorycouncil.com/, August 2010. http://www.hpcadvisorycouncil.com/pdf/building-an-rdma-capable-application-with-ib-verbs.pdf.

[3] D. Bonachea. GASNet specification, v1.1. Technical report UCB/CSD-02-1207, U. of California, Berkeley, October 2002. http://digitalassets.lib.berkeley.edu/techreports/ucb/text/CSD-02-1207.pdf.

[4] A. Bouteiler, T. Herault, G. Krawezik, P. Lemarinier, and F. Cappello. MPICH-V project: a multiprotocol automatic fault tolerant MPI. *International Journal of High Performance Computing Applications*, 20:319–333, 2006.

[5] W. W. Carlson, J. M. Draper, D. E. Culler, K. Yelick, E. Brooks, and K. Warren. Introduction to UPC and language specification. Technical report CCS-tr-99-157, IDA Center for Computing Sciences, 1999. http://upc.lbl.gov/publications/upctr.pdf.

[6] G. Cooperman, J. Ansel, and X. Ma. Adaptive checkpointing for master-worker style parallelism (extended abstract). In *Proc. of 2005 IEEE Computer Society International Conference on Cluster Computing*. IEEE Press, 2005. conf. proc. on CD.

[7] G. Cooperman, J. Ansel, and X. Ma. Transparent adaptive library-based checkpointing for master-worker style parallelism. In *Proceedings of the 6th IEEE International Symposium on Cluster Computing and the Grid (CCGrid06)*, pages 283–291, Singapore, 2006. IEEE Press.

[8] DMTCP team. Tutorial for DMTCP plugins, accessed Apr., 2014. `http://dmtcp.sourceforge.net/api.html`.

[9] J. Duell, P. Hargrove, and E. Roman. The design and implementation of Berkeley Lab's Linux checkpoint/restart (BLCR). Technical Report LBNL-54941, Lawrence Berkeley National Laboratory, 2003.

[10] T. El-Ghazawi and F. Cantonnet. UPC performance and potential: A NPB experimental study. In *Proc. of the 2002 ACM/IEEE Conference on Supercomputing*, Supercomputing '02, pages 1–26, Los Alamitos, CA, USA, 2002. IEEE Computer Society Press.

[11] Q. Gao, W. Yu, W. Huang, and D. K. Panda. Application-transparent checkpoint/restart for MPI programs over InfiniBand. In *ICPP '06: Proceedings of the 2006 International Conference on Parallel Processing*, pages 471–478, Washington, DC, USA, 2006. IEEE Computer Society.

[12] R. Garg, K. Sodha, Z. Jin, and G. Cooperman. Checkpoint-restart for a network of virtual machines. In *Proc. of 2013 IEEE Computer Society International Conference on Cluster Computing*. IEEE Press, 2013.

[13] GWU High-Performance Computing Laboratory. UPC NAS parallel benchmarks. `http://threads.hpcl.gwu.edu/sites/npb-upc`, accessed Jan., 2014, 2014.

[14] P. Hargrove and J. Duell. Berkeley Lab Checkpoint/Restart (BLCR) for Linux clusters. *Journal of Physics Conference Series*, 46:494–499, Sept. 2006.

[15] J. Hursey, T. I. Mattox, and A. Lumsdaine. Interconnect agnostic checkpoint/restart in Open MPI. In *HPDC '09: Proceedings of the 18th ACM international symposium on High performance distributed computing*, pages 49–58, New York, NY, USA, 2009. ACM.

[16] J. Hursey, J. M. Squyres, T. I. Mattox, and A. Lumsdaine. The design and implementation of checkpoint/restart process fault tolerance for Open MPI. In *Proceedings of the 21st IEEE International Parallel and Distributed Processing Symposium (IPDPS) / 12th IEEE Workshop on Dependable Parallel, Distributed and Network-Centric Systems*. IEEE Computer Society, March 2007.

[17] G. Janakiraman, J. Santos, D. Subhraveti, and Y. Turner. Cruz: Application-transparent distributed checkpoint-restart on standard operating systems. In *Dependable Systems and Networks (DSN-05)*, pages 260–269, 2005.

[18] W. Jiang, J. Liu, H.-W. Jin, D. K. Panda, W. Gropp, and R. Thakur. High performance MPI-2 one-sided communication over InfiniBand. In *CCGRID*, pages 531–538, 2004.

[19] G. Kerr. Dissecting a small InfiniBand application using the Verbs API. arxiv:1105.1827v2 [cs.dc] technical report, arXiv.org, May 2011.

[20] G. Kerr, A. Brick, G. Cooperman, and S. Bratus. Checkpoint-restart: Proprietary hardware and the 'spiderweb API', July 8–10 2011. talk: abstract at `http://recon.cx/2011/schedule/events/112.en.html`; video at `https://archive.org/details/Recon_2011_Checkpoint_Restart`.

[21] O. Laadan and J. Nieh. Transparent checkpoint-restart of multiple processes for commodity clusters. In *2007 USENIX Annual Technical Conference*, pages 323–336, 2007.

[22] O. Laadan, D. Phung, and J. Nieh. Transparent networked checkpoint-restart for commodity clusters. In *2005 IEEE International Conference on Cluster Computing*. IEEE Press, 2005.

[23] P. Lemarinier, A. Bouteillerand, T. Herault, G. Krawezik, and F. Cappello. Improved message logging versus improved coordinated checkpointing for fault tolerant MPI. In *CLUSTER '04: Proceedings of the 2004 IEEE International Conference on Cluster Computing*, pages 115–124, Washington, DC, USA, 2004. IEEE Computer Society.

[24] S. Osman, D. Subhraveti, G. Su, and J. Nieh. The design and implementation of Zap: A system for migrating computing environments. In *Prof. of 5th Symposium on Operating Systems Design and Implementation (OSDI-2002)*, 2002.

[25] S. Sankaran, J. M. Squyres, B. Barrett, V. Sahay, A. Lumsdaine, J. Duell, P. Hargrove, and E. Roman. The LAM/MPI checkpoint/restart framework: System-initiated checkpointing. *International Journal of High Performance Computing Applications*, 19(4):479–493, 2005.

[26] S. Sankaran, J. M. Squyres, B. Barrett, V. Sahay, A. Lumsdaine, J. Duell, P. Hargrove, and E. Roman. The LAM/MPI checkpoint/restart framework: System-initiated checkpointing. *International Journal of High Performance Computing Applications*, 19(4):479–493, 2005.

[27] O. O. Sudakov, I. S. Meshcheriakov, and Y. V. Boyko. CHPOX: Transparent checkpointing system for Linux clusters. In *IEEE Int. Workshop on Intelligent Data Acquisition and Advanced Computing Systems: Technology and Applications*, pages 159–164, 2007.

[28] M. M. Swift, M. Annamalai, B. N. Bershad, and H. M. Levy. Recovering device drivers. In *Proceedings of the 6th conference on Symposium on Operating Systems Design and Implementation*, OSDI'04, Berkeley, CA, USA, 2004. USENIX Association.

[29] M. M. Swift, M. Annamalai, B. N. Bershad, and H. M. Levy. Recovering device drivers. *ACM Trans. Comput. Syst.*, 24(4):333–360, Nov. 2006.

[30] B. Woodruff, S. Hefty, R. Dreier, and H. Rosenstock. Introduction to the InfiniBand core software. In *Proceedings of the Linux Symposium (Volume Two)*, pages 271–282, July 2005.

ConCORD: Easily Exploiting Memory Content Redundancy Through the Content-aware Service Command

Lei Xia
VMware
leix@vmware.com

Kyle Hale
Department of Electrical
Engineering and Computer
Science
Northwestern University
kh@northwestern.edu

Peter Dinda
Department of Electrical
Engineering and Computer
Science
Northwestern University
pdinda@northwestern.edu

ABSTRACT

We argue that memory content-tracking across the nodes of a parallel machine should be factored into a distinct platform service on top of which application services can be built. ConCORD is a proof-of-concept system that we have developed and evaluated to test this claim. Our core insight is that many application services can be described as a query over memory content. This insight leads to a core concept in ConCORD, the content-aware service command architecture, in which an application service is implemented as a parametrization of a single general query that ConCORD knows how to execute well. ConCORD dynamically adapts the execution of the query to the amount of redundancy available and other factors. We show that a complex application service (collective checkpointing) can be implemented in only hundreds of lines of code within ConCORD, while performing well.

1. INTRODUCTION

Memory content redundancy, particularly across a large-scale parallel system, represents an opportunity for new services. For example, copy-on-write mechanisms can reduce memory pressure by keeping only a single copy of each distinct page in memory. Fault tolerance mechanisms that seek to maintain a given level of content redundancy can leverage existing redundancy to reduce their memory pressure. Migration of processes or virtual machines (VMs) can lever-

age identical content at source and destination machines—a single process or VM could be reconstructed using multiple sources. Deduplication of host, VM, process, or application-level snapshots or checkpoints can reduce their storage costs. As far as we are aware, all existing such services integrate the tracking of memory content directly into the service.

We argue that memory content-tracking should be factored out into a separate *platform service* that higher-level *application services*, such as the above, can then be built upon. There are several reasons for this refactoring:

- It will result in having a *single* implementation of memory content-tracking to maintain and enhance.
- There will be no redundant memory content tracking overhead when multiple application services exist.
- The platform service can simplify the creation of application services because their developers will not need to reinvent the wheel.
- The application services benefit as the platform memory content-tracking service is enhanced, for example as new hardware features are leveraged.

To evaluate this concept, we have developed a memory content-tracking platform service called ConCORD. ConCORD is a distributed system that runs across the nodes of a parallel computer, tracks memory content across collections of *entities* (objects that have memory such as hosts, VMs, processes, and applications), and answers queries about this content. In this work we focus our discussion of entities on processes and VMs. The overall ConCORD design and implementation is described in Section 3.

ConCORD has an extensive node-level and collective content-sharing query interface for both memory content and metrics about it, and it is possible to write an application service that uses this interface to make queries. However, we found that many application services could be best understood *as* queries instead of as *users* of queries. For example, a checkpoint of a collection of entities can be thought of as a query for the distinct content they collectively contain. Furthermore, the distributed execution of a collective query in ConCORD already addresses many of the challenges of building an application service, for example, parallelism, scheduling, and synchronization.

The response to these observations is a key concept and contribution of ConCORD and our work, namely the *content-aware service command architecture*. The content-aware service command architecture consists of a carefully designed query template, the content-aware service command, that is parametrized by a set of node-local callback functions that define a specific application service. An analogy can be made

This project is made possible by support from the United States National Science Foundation (NSF) via grant CNS-0709168, the Department of Energy (DOE) via grant DE-SC0005343, and Sandia National Laboratories through the Hobbes Project, which is funded by the 2013 Exascale Operating and Runtime Systems Program under the Office of Advanced Scientific Computing Research in the DOE Office of Science. Sandia National Laboratories is a multi-program laboratory managed and operated by Sandia Corporation, a wholly owned subsidiary of Lockheed Martin Corporation, for the U.S. Department of Energy's National Nuclear Security Administration under contract DE-AC04-94AL85000.

with relational databases: the application service is implemented as a set of stored procedures that are used in a single query, the service command. Although multiple service commands are possible, we have carefully designed the initial service command to be general enough to support a range of application services, including those described above.

Given the very nature of the consensus problem in distributed systems, ConCORD is a best-effort platform service. It is possible that the distributed database's view of the memory content is outdated when a query executes: particular entities may no longer hold certain content hashes, and may hold others that ConCORD is unaware of. This is not an issue for collective query execution, as the service is defined to return best-effort results, but application services are usually not best-effort. To address this, the content-aware service command architecture has a two phase execution model in which the best-effort distributed information is combined with reliable local information. In the first phase, the best effort information is used and inaccuracies are discovered. In the second phase, these inaccuracies are then fed back to be handled using node-local information only. If there is considerable memory content redundancy and few inaccuracies, ConCORD's execution of the content-aware service command implicitly leverages the redundancy without any explicit action on the part of the application service developer. If memory content redundancy is low or there are many inaccuracies due to rapidly changing memory content, ConCORD's execution of the content-aware service command nonetheless remains correct. A single distributed component handles both collective queries and content-aware service commands. Details of the content-aware service command architecture are given in Section 4.

We evaluate ConCORD and the content-aware service command architecture in several ways. First, the small scale and complexity of the ConCORD implementation has bearing on our claim. The bulk of ConCORD consists of ~12,000 lines of user-level C, with the interface code for a given kind of entity being about 3,000-4,000 lines of C. This suggests it is quite feasible to factor out memory content-tracking as a platform service—the resulting service is not inordinately large. The second aspect of our evaluation is the performance of ConCORD, which we do at scales of up to 128 nodes, considering its overhead, update rates, latencies, and the response time of queries and the service command. Section 5 presents these results.

To test the service command architecture, we describe the design, implementation, and evaluation of an application service. *Collective checkpointing*, described in detail in Section 6, saves the memory content of a collection of entities (we specifically study processes) with the goal of saving each distinct memory block exactly once. This service is implemented on top of ConCORD as a service command that comprises a mere *230 lines* of C code and performs well.

The contributions of our paper are as follows.

- We show it is feasible and sensible to factor memory content-tracking into a separate platform service.
- We define the content-aware service command architecture, which can greatly facilitate the creation of application services through the insight that services are often well expressed as queries, and, indeed that perhaps a single, parametrized query, *the* content-aware service command, is sufficient for many of them.

- We design, implement, and evaluate ConCORD, a proof-of-concept memory content-tracking platform service.
- We build and evaluate a complex application service, collective checkpointing, within ConCORD, providing evidence of the effectiveness of the above.

2. RELATED WORK

Content-based memory sharing has been studied for many years with the goal of deduplicating memory pages to reduce memory footprints or communication costs. For example, VMware ESX [19] and Xen [10] use background hashing and page comparison to transparently identify identical pages in VMs on the same node. Potemkin [18] uses flash cloning and delta virtualization to support a large number of mostly-identical VMs on the same node. Satori [14] implements memory sharing in Xen by detecting deduplication opportunities when reading from a block device. Difference Engine [8] demonstrates even higher degrees of content sharing can be obtained by sharing portions of similar pages. Kernel SamePage Merging (KSM) [3] allows the Linux kernel to share identical memory pages amongst different processes. In the context of HPC systems, SBLLmalloc [5] can identify identical memory blocks on the same node and merge them to reduce the memory usage. In the context of cloud computing, Memory Buddies [20] uses memory fingerprint to discover VMs with high sharing potential and then co-locates them on the same node. Live gang migration [7] optimizes the live migration of a group of co-located VMs on the same node by deduplicating the identical memory pages across them before sending them. VMFlock [2] and Shrinker [16] present similar migration services optimized for cross-datacenter transfer.

Our work differs in two ways. First, we factor memory content tracking into a separate service on top of which application services such as these could be built. We believe we are the first to propose and evaluate this idea, producing a proof of concept, ConCORD. Second, we focus on the whole parallel machine, considering *inter-node* as well as intra-node sharing of content. Our earlier paper [23] and the work of others [5, 12] have clearly shown that such content sharing exists in the HPC context. The work we present here illustrates how to leverage it.

A core mechanism in ConCORD is a custom, high-performance, lightweight, zero-hop distributed hash table (DHT) that associates content hashes with sets of entities and their nodes. Many DHT implementations have been developed [17, 6], with most targeted at wide-area distributed systems. More recent work has considered DHTs for more tightly coupled HPC environments, examples including C-MPI [21] and ZHT [13]. ConCORD's DHT is similarly designed for zero-hop routing and low churn. However, it is not a general key-value store, but rather is specialized specifically for the best-effort content hash to entity set mapping problem in ConCORD. A detailed description is available elsewhere [22].

We use checkpointing as an example application service to test ConCORD and our claims of the utility of the content-aware service command architecture. Checkpointing has a large literature. Nicolae and Cappello describe this literature in detail in their paper on their memory access pattern-adaptive incremental checkpointing system, AI-Ckpt [15]. Our collective checkpointing service saves the content of a group of entities (processes, VMs), deduplicating pages that are have shared content. Other than building upon

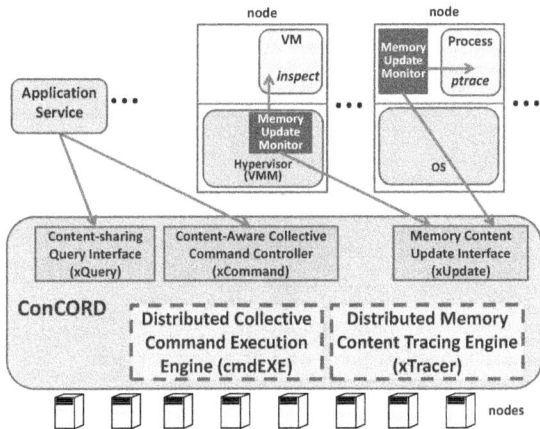

Figure 1: ConCORD's high-level architecture. Dashed boxes represent distributed components.

a general-purpose memory content tracking system and the content-aware service command architecture, we do not claim innovations in checkpointing.

3. DESIGN AND IMPLEMENTATION

The goal of ConCORD's design was to factor scalable memory content tracking across the nodes of a parallel computer into a distinct platform service that would be useful for implementing application services and ease such implementation. It was clear from the outset that this required that ConCORD itself be a distributed system.

Initially, we focused on tracking the content of distributed VMs running in instances of our Palacios VMM [11], but almost all of the concepts involved in building VMM-based application services readily generalize beyond VMs. Consequently, it made the most sense to partition ConCORD into a component that operates over general entities (as described in the introduction). The design evolved into one that is partitioned into an entity-agnostic user-level component (the majority of the system), and node-specific components that handle specific kinds of entities on specific kinds of nodes. The latter comprises little code, and may or may not be user-level.

Our original model was that ConCORD would be a distributed database system that captured a best-effort view of memory content across all the nodes and entities. It would then facilitate the creation of application services by providing a query interface that supported both queries that could be answered using information on a single node, and queries that required information to be integrated across multiple nodes, perhaps all of them. These latter collective queries are the key challenge, both for ConCORD to implement and for an application service to use. The content-aware service command architecture is essentially a carefully designed collective query into which the application service is integrated. Instead of the application service making queries, there is a single query that makes callbacks to the application service.

3.1 High-level architecture

Figure 1 illustrates the high-level architecture of ConCORD, highlighting core components and interfaces.

The core functionality of ConCORD is to track memory content across entities in the site. To do so, ConCORD needs to know when the content of a block of memory[1] changes. Furthermore, the nature of the content of a memory block on any node must be accessible (within a query) from all other nodes. To make this possible, ConCORD has two components: (1) a *memory update monitor* running on each node, and (2) a site-wide *distributed memory content tracing engine* that maintains a scalable, distributed database that, given a content hash, can find nodes and entities that are likely to have copies of the corresponding content.

Several kinds of memory update monitors are possible. The figure illustrates two, a kernel-level/VMM-based monitor that inspects a VM's guest physical memory, and a user-level monitor that inspects a process's address space using ptrace. Memory update monitors produce the heartbeat of ConCORD: discovery of memory content changes. One mode of operation for a memory update monitor is to periodically step through the full memory of the entities being traced, identifying memory blocks that have been updated recently, and then sending memory content hashes for the newly updated blocks to the ConCORD memory tracing engine. We use this mode of operation in this paper. In addition, a memory update monitor maintains a local mapping table that allows ConCORD to efficiently locate a memory block's content from its hash.

Memory update monitors can also operate in a mode where they detect writes by leveraging the paging infrastructure. For example, for Palacios VMs, we can apply a copy-on-write model, temporarily marking shadow or nested page table entries as unwritable. Page faults then indicate writes. We can also exploit the x86's nested page table entry's dirty bit, periodically marking page table entries as clean and then rescanning the entries to see which ones the processor has marked dirty. More details about both of these techniques are given elsewhere [4].

Regardless of its kind or mode, a memory update monitor can also be throttled, limiting the rate at which it produces updates. This makes it possible to limit the load placed on the individual node and on the network, trading off load and precision/accuracy, as we described in earlier work [23].

The distributed memory content tracing engine is a site-wide distributed system that enables ConCORD to locate entities having a copy of a given memory block using its content hash. It also allows ConCORD to find the amount of memory content sharing among nodes . ConCORD employs a custom, high-performance, lightweight, zero-hop distributed hash table (DHT) to store unique memory content hashes and map each content hash to a list of entities and their nodes that have a copy of the corresponding memory block. A detailed description of the design of the engine is given elsewhere [22].

The *memory content update interface* is the interface between memory update monitors and the distributed content tracing engine. It is carefully defined so that new monitors can be created, and so that the engine is not entity-specific.

Application services or other tools can ask questions or issue content-aware service commands that operate over the information stored in the tracing engine. The *content-sharing query interface* makes possible two forms of questions. "Node-wise" queries involve data stored within a single node. Note that because memory block content information is stored in

---

[1] Block size is a configurable parameter, but, as we showed earlier [23], the base page size (4 KB on x64) works very well. We use 4 KB pages throughout the paper.

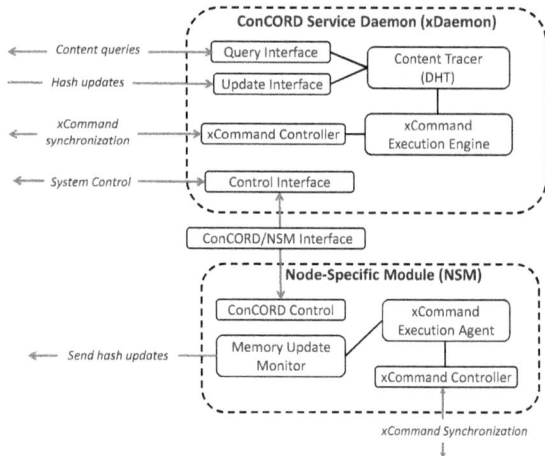

Figure 2: ConCORD's node-level architecture.

a DHT in a node determined by its content hash, the information available in a single node represents a "slice of life" of all the nodes in the system. The query interface also exposes collective queries, which aggregate memory content information across multiple nodes (or all nodes). We describe the query interface (and update interface) in Section 3.3.

The *content-aware collective command controller* provides the interface for both collective queries and content-aware service commands and controls the overall execution of them. The *distributed collective command execution engine* is the most complex distributed component of the system, and is responsible for both these queries and commands. At a high-level, it can be viewed as a purpose-specific map-reduce engine that operates over the data in the tracing engine. We describe these in detail in Section 4.

3.2 Node-level architecture

Figure 2 shows ConCORD's node-level design, which comprises two components and an interface between them.

The *ConCORD service daemon* is a multithreaded user-level component that most importantly includes the local instances of the content-tracing and command execution engines. The daemon exposes multiple interfaces on the network for issuing and responding to queries and updates, synchronizing the execution of collective queries and service commands, and overall system control.

The *node-specific module* (NSM) is responsible for handling particular kinds (e.g., VMs, processes, etc) of entities on the node. We have already seen the most important element of the NSM, namely the memory update monitor, but it also needs to contain some components of the content-aware service command architecture. One aspect of this is how memory is to be accessed for the given kind of entity. Another is the environment in which the callbacks made by the service command need to execute. For example, if we build a checkpointing service for processes, the callback code may run at user-level and use system calls, but if we build the service for VMs, the callback code may run at kernel-level and use VMM-specific mechanisms.

The NSM is also responsible for maintaining a mapping from content hash to the addresses and sizes of memory blocks in the entities it tracks locally. This information is available as a side effect of the memory update monitor.

Node-wise Queries	
number	num_copies(content_hash)
entity_set	entities(content_hash)
Collective Queries	
number	sharing(entity_set)
number	intra_sharing(entity_set)
number	inter_sharing(entity_set)
number	num_shared_content(entity_set, k)
hash_set	shared_content(entity_set, k)
Updates	
void	insert(content_hash, entity)
void	remove(content_hash, entity)

Figure 3: Query and update interfaces.

3.3 Queries and updates

Queries to ConCORD take two forms. *Node-wise queries* depend only on information stored in a single ConCORD instance on a single node, while *collective queries* depend on information spread over instances on multiple nodes, or even all nodes. Application services can issue queries, and NSMs can issue updates through a set of simple C interfaces provided by libraries. Figure 3 shows the query and update interface of ConCORD.

The node-wise queries allow the application service to ask how many copies of the content corresponding to a content hash exist and which set of entities currently have copies of the content. Note that an entity may have more than one copy of given content. An application service can use these queries to find the existing redundancy of particular memory content, and where the replicas are.

The first three collective queries compute the degree of content sharing (redundancy) that exists across a set of entities. Here we are concerned about all the content in these entities, not particular content. We consider two forms of sharing. Intranode sharing is sharing of content across the entities located within a node, while internode sharing is sharing of content across entities in distinct nodes. Either form, or both together can be queried. An application service can use these queries to discover if there is sufficient overall redundancy to make it worthwhile to leverage.

The final two collective queries allow an application service to discover, for a set of entities, the amount of content that is replicated k or more times, and the set of content hashes for which this is true. These "at least k copies" queries allow the application service to find content whose redundancy is particularly useful to leverage due to its many replicas.

Updates simply insert or delete (key, value) pairs, where the key is a content hash and the value is the entity. A hash over the key determines the node and service daemon to which the update is routed. The target daemon maintains a hash table that maps from each content hash it holds to a bitmap representation of the set of entities that currently have the corresponding content. Given this simple mapping, the originator of an update can not only readily determine which node and daemon is the target of the update, but, in principle, also the specific address and bit that will be changed in that node.

3.4 Communication

ConCORD uses two forms of communication. First, reliable 1-to-n broadcast and synchronizing communication is used between client libraries and the shell, and xDaemon and VMM instances. This communication is infrequent, generally only occurring when a query or service command is running. The data size for messages here is small. Unreliable peer-to-peer data communication is used among service daemons and NSMs. Examples include an update being sent from an NSM to a target service daemon, and a content hash exchange among service daemons during the execution of a content-aware service command. The second form of communication, unreliable peer-to-peer communication, forms the bulk of communication in the system, both due to the frequency of such communication and its volume. The motivation for separating these communication paths and their requirements is to eventually facilitate the use of fast, low-level communication primitives for most communication. For example, because the originator of an update in principle knows the target node and address, and because the update is best effort, the originator could send the update via a non-blocking, asynchronous, unreliable RDMA.

In its current implementation, ConCORD uses UDP for network communications in both cases. Unreliable peer-to-peer communication is done using standard UDP socket calls, i.e., "send and forget". Reliable 1-to-n communication is implemented on top of standard UDP, combined with an acknowledgment protocol that allows out-of-order delivery of ConCORD messages. We require the underlying hardware to provide error detection for both reliable and unreliable communication. As we are operating within a single network of a parallel machine, underlying hardware mechanisms like the Ethernet CRC readily do this. Reliable messages may arrive out of order, but they *will* arrive without errors. Unreliable messages may not arrive, but if they do arrive, they have no errors.

4. CONTENT-AWARE SERVICE COMMAND

The goal of the content-aware service command architecture is to ease the construction of application services that build on ConCORD's distributed memory content tracing facility. As we have described so far (Section 3), ConCORD helps the application service developer avoid reinventing one wheel, namely that of memory content tracking and queries. In the design of the content-aware service command architecture, we seek to help the developer avoid reinventing another wheel, the distributed execution of the application service over the relevant memory content.

The developer creates the service by implementing a set of callbacks. The interface of these callbacks and the protocol by which they are invoked form the core of the service command architecture from the developer's perspective. The callbacks parametrize a service command. The parametrized service command is the application service implementation. The execution system in ConCORD in turn is able to automatically parallelize and execute a service command over the nodes of the parallel machine. The execution is driven by the memory content tracked in ConCORD, as well as the "ground truth" memory content information available locally. As a consequence, the service can leverage redundancy while being correct.

4.1 Running example

Consider that we seek to build a "collective checkpointing" service that operates over a set of distributed processes (or VMs), where each process's address space consists of pages. When we execute the service, we require correctness: each page in each process must be recorded so that it can be restored later. We also desire efficiency: The checkpoint should contain few duplicate pages; ideally, each distinct page of content would be recorded exactly once.

A correct implementation would simply record each page in each process. A highly efficient implementation would find each distinct page captured in ConCORD's database, select a replica, and have that replica recorded. However, ConCORD's database is best effort, as described previously, so this implementation would not be correct—it would include pages that no longer exist, and fail to include pages that aren't yet in the database. What the service command architecture allows us to do is combine efficiency (using ConCORD's database) and correctness (using local information). We will describe the design, implementation, and evaluation of this service in detail in Section 6.

4.2 Scope and mode

A service command has a scope, a set of entities over which it will operate. For example, this might be the set of processes or VMs we wish to checkpoint. We refer to these as the set of *service entities* (SEs), or we say that these entities have the service role. Because ConCORD's memory tracking is not specific to any one application service, however, it is likely that there are many other entities being tracked that could contribute to our service. For example, an independent process on a separate node might share a page of content with one of the processes we are checkpointing. If the separate node wrote this page, it would speed up our checkpoint. We refer to entities that will be involved in this way as *participating entities* (PEs), or we say that these entities have the participant role. The scope of the execution of an application service consists of the set of SEs and PEs. The service command uses the memory content in the SEs and PEs to apply the service to the SEs.

A service command can be executed in one of two modes. In *interactive mode*, the application service's callbacks are invoked for each content hash and are expected to immediately apply the relevant transformations. In *batch mode*, the callbacks instead drive the creation of an execution plan by the application service. The application service then executes its plan as a whole. This allows the application service developer to refine and enhance the plan. In this paper we focus on interactive mode.

4.3 Interface and execution

Figure 4 describes the high-level interface of an application service. The detailed C interface is available elsewhere [22, Chapter 7]. The service developer implements the application service by implementing these callbacks. The service command invokes the callbacks in four phases, as shown in the figure. At the heart of execution are the collective phase (which uses the content information in ConCORD's database) and the local phase (which uses node-local content information).

Service initialization passes a service-specific configuration file to be parsed. Within the service_init() function, which is executed on each node holding a service or participating

Service Initialization	
error	service_init(service, config)

Collective Phase	
error	collective_start(entity_role, entity, content_hash_set, private_service_state)
entity	optional_collective_select(content_hash, entity_set, private_service_state)
error	collective_command(entity, content_hash, pointer, size, private_service_state)
error	collective_finalize(entity_role, entity, content_hash_set, private_service_state)

Local Phase	
error	local_start(entity_role, entity, content_hash_set, private_service_state)
error	local_command(entity, content_hash, pointer, size, private_service_state)
error	local_finalize(entity_role, entity, content_hash_set, private_service_state)

Service Teardown	
error	service_deinit(private_service_state)

Figure 4: Content-aware service command callbacks. An application service is created by implementing these callbacks.

entity, the developer can also associate private service state with the service. This is then passed to subsequent callbacks on that node as the private_service_state parameter. This state can grow during the execution of the command.

The collective phase of execution is supported by four callbacks, one of which is optional. The collective_start() function is executed exactly once for each service and participating entity. It indicates what role (service or participating) the entity has and provides a partial set of the content hashes ConCORD believes the entity contains. This partial set is derived using the data available on the local instance of the DHT, and is mostly advisory. collective_start() is usually where the service typically allocates and initializes resources that are outside of the scope of ConCORD. For example, the collective checkpointing service opens its checkpoint files here.

ConCORD synchronizes on collective_start(). After all instances have returned, it will then compute distinct content hashes across all of the service entities, and, for each of them, find the set of service entities and participating entities that appear to have this content. This information will drive callbacks to the PEs and SEs to execute over their content. Because a particular content hash might exist on multiple entities, ConCORD needs to pick one. If the service developer has implemented the optional_collective_select() callback, ConCORD invokes this on some node to allow the service to choose. Alternatively, it chooses one of the entities at random.

Given a content hash and a selected entity, ConCORD invokes the collective_command() callback on the node where the entity resides. In addition to the hash and entity, ConCORD also passes an opaque pointer and data size to the callback. This information is computed by the NSM (Section 3.2). In effect, in the collective phase of execution, ConCORD maps the collective_command() function across unique content hashes that it believes exist in the SEs, selecting for each hash a single entity (and thus node) from the SEs and PEs that it believes contains that hash. A collective_command() invocation may fail because the content is no longer available in the node. When this is detected, or if the collective_command() invocation is taking too long, ConCORD will select a different potential replica and try again. If it is unsuccessful for all replicas, it knows that its information about the content hash is stale.

After exhausting all relevant content hashes in its distributed database, ConCORD invokes the collective_finalize() function for each entity. Here, the service has a chance to reduce and gather results from work that has been done during the collective phase, and clean up and free resources that

are not needed in the local phase. collective_finalize() also acts as a barrier.

ConCORD now invokes local_start() for each SE to allow the service to prepare for the local phase. PEs are not involved in the local phase. ConCORD then invokes the local_command() callback for each memory block (e.g., page) in each service entity. The callback includes the block's hash, as well as the set of all hashes that have been successfully handled by a previous collective_command(). The service can thus easily detect and handle content that ConCORD was unaware of. For example, the collective checkpoint service can save a page that was not previously saved. Further, for content that ConCORD did previously handle, the service can now make use of that fact. For example, the collective checkpoint service can save a file offset for a page that was previously saved. With successive invocations for the process, the collective checkpoint service builds a file of pointers to where the process's page content exists.

The local_finalize() callback is invoked for each service entity to complete the local phase and to synchronize. Here, the service typically does cleanup, for example, closing the checkpoint files.

At the end of service command execution, the service_deinit() function is called on each node with a service or participating entity. This function is responsible for interpreting the final private service state to indicate to ConCORD whether the service was successful or not. For batch mode execution, the service typically builds up a plan in the private service state, driven by collective_command() and local_command() callbacks, and then executes it as part of local_finalize() or service_deinit().

5. GENERAL EVALUATION

We now describe the general evaluation of ConCORD, independent of any application service. The evaluation focuses on ConCORD's overheads and scalability. ConCORD consists of ~19,300 lines of code (~12,000 in the core system, ~3,300 in NSM for processes, ~4,000 in NSM for VMs).

5.1 Testbeds

Our evaluations are done on the following hardware.

Old-cluster is used for most of the general evaluation of this section. It consists of 24 IBM x335 nodes, each having two dual-core Intel Xeon 2.00GHz processors, 1.5 GB RAM, 32 GB disk, and a gigabit NIC connected to a 100 Mbit Cisco 3550 48 port switch, which has the full backplane bandwidth needed to support all of its ports. The nodes run Red Hat

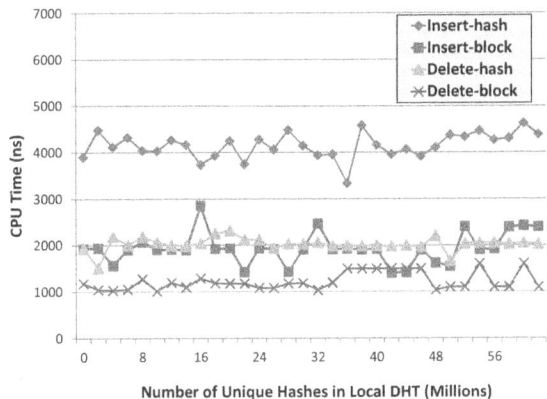

Figure 5: CPU time of DHT updates as a function of number of unique hashes in the local node.

Enterprise 6.2 with a 2.6.30.4 kernel. Note that good performance on such old hardware bodes well for newer hardware.

New-cluster is used for benchmarking the DHT. It consists of 8 Dell R415 machines, where each has two quad-core 2.2 GHz AMD Opteron 4122 processors, 16 GB RAM, 500 GB disk, and a gigabit NIC attached to an HP Procurve 2848 48 port gigabit switch, which has the full backplane bandwidth needed to support all of its ports. The nodes run Fedora 15 with a 2.6.38 kernel.

Big-cluster is used to study high node scaling of the service command and the collective checkpoint service (Section 6). *Big-cluster* is Northwestern's HPC resource, consisting of 824 nodes in three categories. 504 nodes contain two quad-core 2.4 GHz Intel Nehalem processors and 48 GB of RAM, and are connected via an InfiniBand DDR network. Two other machine pools contain nodes with faster processors and similar RAM that are interconnected with QDR InfiniBand (252 nodes) and FDR10 InfiniBand (68 nodes). They run Red Hat 6.4 with a 2.6.32 kernel.

5.2 Distributed memory content tracing

We expect the memory tracing component of ConCORD, which discovers memory content changes and maintains the distributed database of content to have low overhead. Here, we focus in particular on the overheads of the distributed database (the DHT). We do not consider the amount of redundancy that is available within particular environments and how well this can be captured because our previous publication [23] and Xia's dissertation [22] include this. The latter presents a detailed study of redundancy in a range of parallel applications.

Our previous publication also considered the costs and overheads of the memory update monitor, which scans an entity's memory to discover updates. We summarize these results. On our slowest hardware (*Old-cluster*), we found that a memory update monitor that periodically scans a typical process from a range of HPC benchmarks and computes content hashes from its pages exhibits a 6.4% CPU overhead when scanning every 2 seconds, and a 2.6% CPU overhead when scanning every 5 seconds. This is with the MD5 hash function. With the non-cryptographic SuperHash function, these overheads drop to 2.2% and less than 1% for these rates. The updates sent into the network from the memory update monitor typically require about 1% of the outgoing link bandwidth.

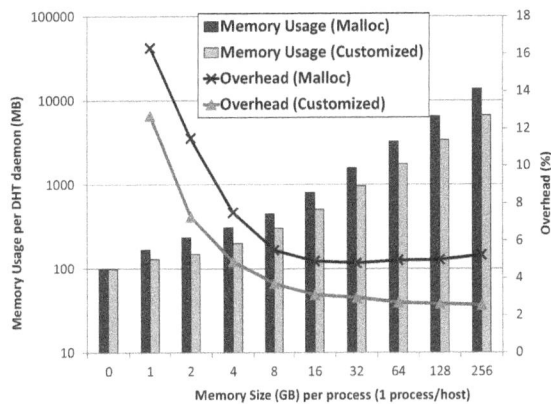

Figure 6: Per-node memory use to store the DHT as a function of the size of entities

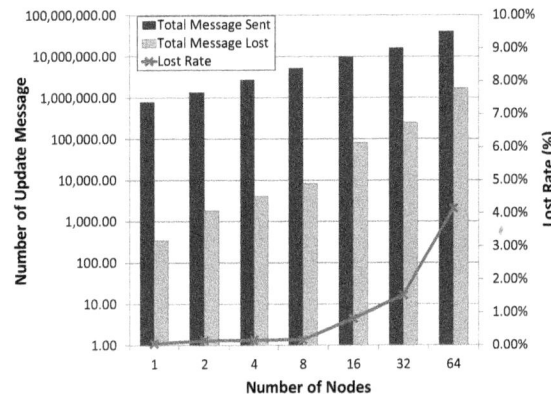

Figure 7: Update message volume and loss rate as a function of the number of nodes on *Big-cluster*.

We now consider the costs of updates to the distributed database, which are measured on *New-cluster*.

One question is the latency of updates, which depends on both the network and local computation. At the network level, the latency of an update is the latency of a UDP packet. In Figure 5, we illustrate the costs of the local computation as a function of the number of hashes stored within the local instance of the DHT. Both inserts and deletes are measured. The block insertion or delete is the cost of updating the local mapping from content hash to block within the entity, while the hash insertions and deletions are the cost of updating the (typically remote) mapping from content hash to entity. The important thing to note is that these costs are independent of how many unique content hashes are stored.

A second question is the memory costs of storing the content of the DHT. Figure 6 shows the memory needed on each node as the entity size grows. Because the allocation units of the DHT are statically known, a custom allocator can improve memory efficiency over the use of GNU malloc. With the custom allocator, at an entity memory size the same as the node's physical memory (16 GB), the additional memory needed is about 8%. Even at 256 GB/entity (achieved using swapping), only about 12.5% more memory is needed to store the DHT content.

Finally, we consider the network load imposed by updates, and how often updates are lost. Here, we use *Big-cluster* to consider a larger number of nodes. Figure 7 shows the results. Here each node contains one entities (4 GB total

31

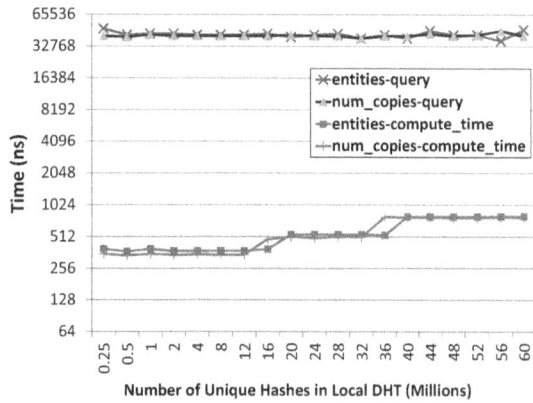

Figure 8: Latency of node-wise queries as a function of unique hashes in the local node.

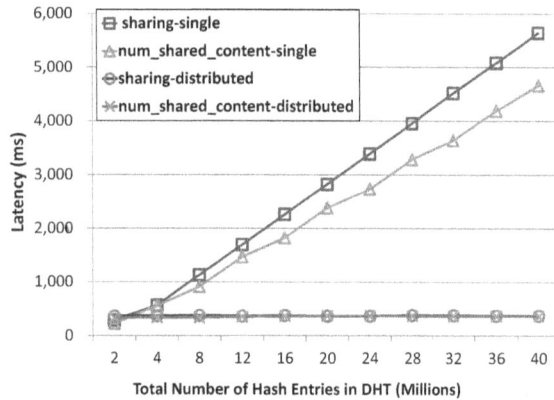

Figure 9: Total latency for collective queries as a function of the number of content hashes.

RAM per entity), and we are considering the initial scan of their memory, that is, each node is sending an update for each page of each entity, which is the worst case. As we scale up the number of nodes the total number of update messages in this scenario of course scales linearly with it. However, so do the number of sources and destinations of these messages, as the DHT itself grows. We are currently trying to understand why the loss rate grows with scale.

Our results suggest that the memory update monitor and updates to the distributed database scale well with the number of nodes and the total size of entities across those nodes, in terms of the update work and network traffic per node.

5.3 Queries

We now consider the performance of queries in ConCORD. Here, *Old-cluster* is used. Our primary focus is on latency as the system expands in terms of amount of memory tracked and number of nodes participating.

We first consider the node-wise queries, those that require only a single node to respond. Figure 8 illustrates the latency for the two node-wise queries. The "query" time includes the communication and computation, while "compute_time" captures the time for the computation at the answering node. The latency is dominated by the communication, which is essentially a ping time. This should come as no surprise as these queries are computed with a local hash table lookup to a bitmap that is then scanned.

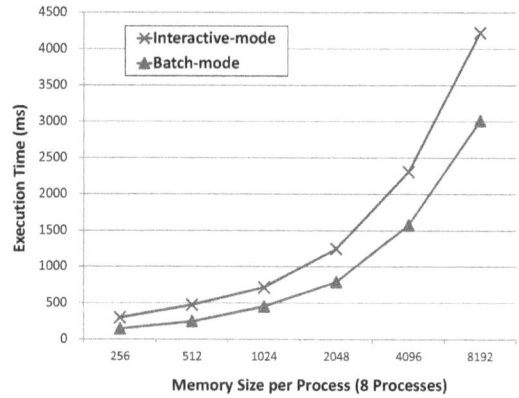

Figure 10: Null service command execution time on a fixed number of SEs and nodes with increasing memory size per process.

When observed from the perspective of a single node, the collective queries perform similarly to the node-wise queries. More important is the latency seen across the machine as communication is used to compose the query results. Figure 9 shows the total latency for the collective queries. For the "distributed" case, the DHT (and thus the query computation and communication) is distributed over the nodes of *Old-cluster*. Here, we scale up the number of nodes used so that the number of content hashes per node is kept constant (at about 2 million hashes per node). For the "single" case, the DHT (and thus the computation) is limited to a single node, which handles more and more hashes. As can be seen from the figure, at around 2-4 million hashes there is a crossover point, and the distributed storage and execution model perform better, giving a constant response time as the system scales.

Under the expected operating model of a system like ConCORD, the maximum possible number of content hashes is limited by the total memory of the parallel machine. As we add more nodes, we add more memory that may need to be tracked and operated over, but we also add more compute and network capability to support tracking and operating over it. The figure makes it clear that the system scales in terms of memory and nodes, providing a stable response time as this happens. On *Old-cluster*, our slowest computational and network hardware, this stable response time for collective queries is about 300 ms.

5.4 Null service command

We now consider the performance of the content-aware service command. Here, we focus on the baseline costs involved for any service command by constructing a "null" service that operates over the data in a set of entities, but does not transform the data in any way. That is, all of the callbacks described in Figure 4 are made, but they do nothing other than touch the memory. We consider this command both in interactive mode and in batch mode. In batch mode, the callbacks record the plan and in the final step the memory is touched. Evaluations of both modes are done on *New-cluster*, while on *Big-cluster*, we study the scaling of interactive mode.

Figure 10 shows the execution times for the null service command for a fixed number of SEs (processes) and nodes as we vary the memory size per SE. As we would hope,

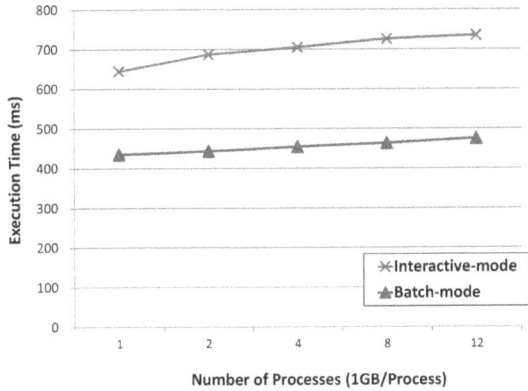

Figure 11: Null service command execution time for an increasing number of SEs and nodes, holding per-SE memory constant.

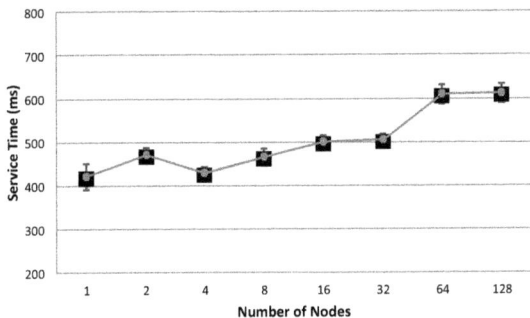

Figure 12: Null service command response time on *Big-cluster*.

the execution time is linear with the total memory size of the SEs. Figure 11 shows the execution time for the null service command as we simultaneously increase the number of SEs (processes) and nodes, while holding the per-process memory constant. This is how we would expect to use the service command architecture in practice—as we scale the number of SEs over which the service command operates, we expect the number of nodes to also scale, as there is a limited amount of memory in each node. In this regime, we see that the execution time stays relatively constant, suggesting the service command architecture scales nicely.

Beyond this scalable execution time, we would also hope to see that the network traffic to execute the null service command scales. As we scale the number of SEs and nodes simultaneously, as we did for Figure 11, the average traffic volume sourced and sinked per node stays constant at about 15 MB. This further lends support to the scalability of the service command architecture under the expected regime.

Figure 12 shows the scaling of the null service command running in interactive mode on *Big-cluster*. As previously, we scale up nodes and total memory simultaneously. The response time is constant, up to 128 nodes, providing further evidence of the scalability of the content-aware service command architecture.

6. COLLECTIVE CHECKPOINTING

We claim that the content-aware service command is sufficient for implementing a range of application services. To evaluate this claim, we considered three services. The first,

collective checkpointing, is described in detail here. The second, collective VM reconstruction, recreates the memory image of a stored VM (the service entity) using the memory content of other VMs currently active (the participating entities). This is described in the first author's dissertation [22, Section 7.2]. The third, collective VM migration, migrates a group of VMs from one set of nodes to another set of nodes, leveraging memory redundancy.

Our focus in collective checkpointing (and for the other two) is in exposing and leveraging memory redundancy. Our work does not extend to, for example, selecting which replica to use for a specific operation. ConCORD, through the optional_collective_select() callback, provides the ability for the service developer to introduce such smarts, however.

The goal of collective checkpointing is to checkpoint the memory of a set of SEs (processes, VMs) such that each replicated memory block (e.g., page) is stored exactly once. For parallel workloads that exhibit considerable redundancy (for example, the Moldy and HPCCG benchmarks we studied in previous work [23]), collective checkpointing will reduce the overall size of the checkpoint and the benefits will grow as the application scales. Such benefits should be clear whether we checkpoint processes or VMs containing them.

The collective checkpointing service is easily built within the content-aware service command architecture. The implementation we use here comprises a total of only 230 lines of user-level C and can be seen in its entirety elsewhere [22, Appendix A]. The developer does not have to consider parallel execution, memory content location, or other factors. The performance of the checkpointing service is also promising. When no redundancy exists, the execution time has only a small overhead over the obvious design of purely local checkpoints for each SE. Furthermore, checkpoint size can be reduced significantly when redundancy exists—considerably more than compression. Finally, the time to checkpoint a set of SEs scales well as the number of entities and nodes increases. These results support our claim.

6.1 Design and implementation

Figure 13 schematically shows the format of the collective checkpoint. Only two SEs are shown for simplicity, although a real checkpoint will have as many as there are processes or VMs. A single shared content file stores the content of most memory blocks that have been found. That is, for each distinct memory block with one or more copies among the SEs, there is ideally exactly one copy stored in the shared content file.

Each SE has a separate checkpoint file that contains an entry for each memory block within the SE. The entry either represents the content of that block or it represents a pointer to the content's location within the shared content file. The reason why content may exist within the SE's checkpoint file is due to the best-effort nature of ConCORD. If an SE contains a memory block whose content is unknown to Con-CORD, it appears in the SE's checkpoint file, otherwise it appears in the shared content file.

The syntax $1 : E : 3$ means that memory block 1 (e.g., page 1) of the SE holds content whose hash is E and which is stored as block 3 of the shared content file. Figure 13 shows four replicated blocks. Each SE has four blocks, three of which are stored as pointers, and one of which is stored as data. In this diagram, a total of 8 blocks (each SE has 4 blocks) is stored using 6 blocks. Ignoring the pointers, this

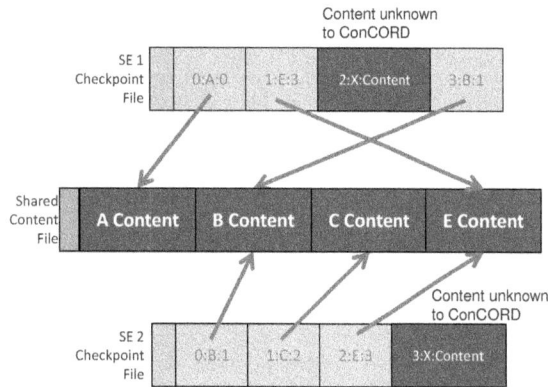

Figure 13: Checkpoint format, showing two SEs.

would yield a *compression ratio* of 75% (6/8) compared to simply saving each SE's blocks independently.

To restore an SE's memory from the checkpoint, we need only walk the SE's checkpoint file, referencing pointers to the shared content file as needed. Our implementation focuses on taking the actual checkpoint. In describing this process, we use Section 4's terminology, in particular the collective and local phases of service command execution.

In the collective phase, ConCORD determines what it believes to be the distinct memory content hashes that exist across the system. It then issues collective_command() callbacks for them. Our handler receives the content hash, as well as an NSM-supplied pointer to the data of the local copy of the content. It then issues an append call to the file system to write the block to shared content file. The file system returns the offset which is stored in a node-local hash table that maps from content hash to offset. It indicates to ConCORD that it has handled the content hash and includes the offset in the private field of its return value. At the end of the collective phase, the shared content file is complete, and each node has its local hash table from which pointers into the shared content file can be derived.

Since these collective commands are happening in parallel across the nodes, we do require that the file system provide atomic append functionality with multiple writers. In effect, we have a log file with multiple writers. This is a well-known problem for other forms of logging on parallel systems and is either a component of the parallel file system or of support software that builds on top of it (e.g., [9]).

In the local phase of execution, ConCORD issues callbacks that cause each SE's memory to be scanned, with a local_command() callback issued for each block. These callbacks write the records of the SE's own checkpoint file. If the callback indicates that the content hash was successfully handled in the collective phase, then the private data field is interpreted as being the offset within the shared content file. The callback can then append a pointer record to the SE's checkpoint file. If the callback indicates that the content hash was not handled during the callback phase, then the block does not exist in the shared content file because ConCORD's DHT was unaware of it. In this case, the callback writes a record that contains the content to the SE's checkpoint file.

After the collective and local phases are done, the full set of files is complete. The assorted callback functions for initialization of the service and the phases are where the files are opened and closed.

6.2 Evaluation

Our evaluation focuses on the overall performance and scalability of the collective checkpointing service. We consider performance on *Old-cluster* and *Big-cluster*, which are described in Section 5.1.

Reducing checkpoint size is an important goal of collective checkpointing, but the degree to which this is possible depends on the workload. In the following, we consider two workloads consisting of SEs that are MPI processes. Moldy [1] is a general purpose molecular dynamics simulation package we identified in our previous paper [23] as exhibiting considerable redundancy at the page granularity, both within SEs and across SEs. In contrast, Nasty is a synthetic workload with no page-level redundancy, although its memory content is not completely random.

We consider four methods for generating the checkpoint. Raw simply has each SE save its content independently. ConCORD is not used. Raw-gzip further concatenates all the per-SE files and compresses them with gzip. ConCORD uses the scheme of Section 6.1. Finally, ConCORD-gzip further compresses the shared content file. The purpose of introducing gzip is to understand how redundancy elimination through compression compares to ConCORD's approach, and how much it can improve the ConCORD approach.

Figure 14 shows the compression ratio for the four strategies, for both Moldy and Nasty, as a function of the number of processes. For Moldy, the measured degree of sharing (the results of the sharing() query of Figure 3 is also shown. These results are measured on *Old-cluster*.

The Moldy results show that when redundancy exists, the collective checkpoint service (ConCORD) is able to exploit it well. Indeed, all the redundancy that ConCORD has detected via its query interface is captured in the service command. The results also show that the redundancy goes well beyond that which can be captured via compression, although compression does slightly increase compression ratio. The Nasty results, in contrast, show that when no page-level redundancy exists, the additional storage overhead of the collective checkpoint service is minuscule.

We measured the response time of the collective checkpoint service and the simple raw service in several ways. In doing so, we factor out the overhead of the file system by writing to a RAM disk. We compare the performance of the raw service with and without gzip with the performance of the interactive ConCORD-based collective checkpoint service as described in Section 6.1. We also consider a batch ConCORD-based collective checkpoint. These results are measured on *Old-cluster*.

In Figure 15 we fix the number of nodes and SEs while we increase the memory size of each SE. This creates more work per node. The response times of all of the checkpointing implementations increase linearly with the amount of memory we are checkpointing, as we would expect.[2] The collective checkpointing service is faster than raw with gzip, but slower than the simple raw service.

Figure 16 shows results for scaling within the expected regime. Here, the amount of memory per SE is kept constant, and the number of nodes grows with the number of SEs. Essentially, the application uses more nodes to tackle a larger problem. In this regime, the response time is inde-

---

[2]The plot is on a log-log scale to make it easier to see the differences, but the curves are, in fact, linear.

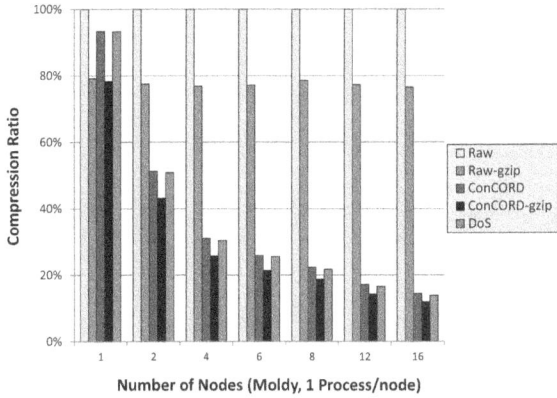

(a) Moldy (considerable redundancy)

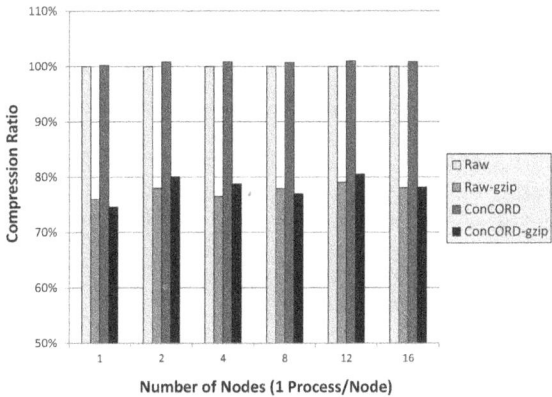

(b) Nasty (no redundancy)

Figure 14: Compression ratios for Moldy and Nasty.

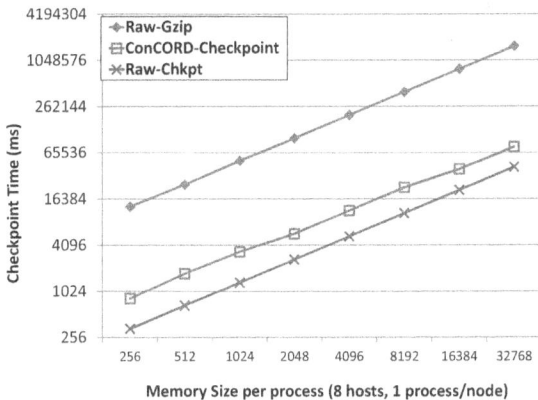

Figure 15: Checkpoint response time for a fixed number of SEs and nodes as the memory size per SE increases.

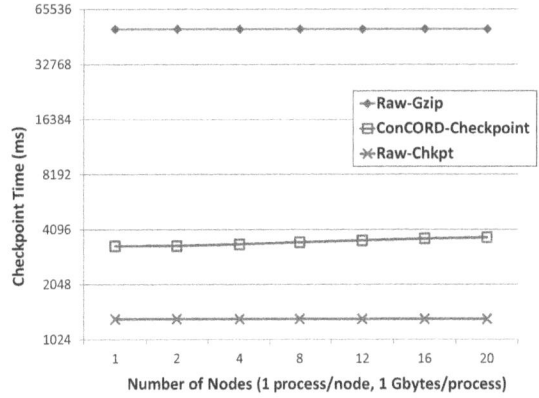

Figure 16: Checkpoint response time as a function of the number of SEs as the number of nodes increases with the memory being checkpointed.

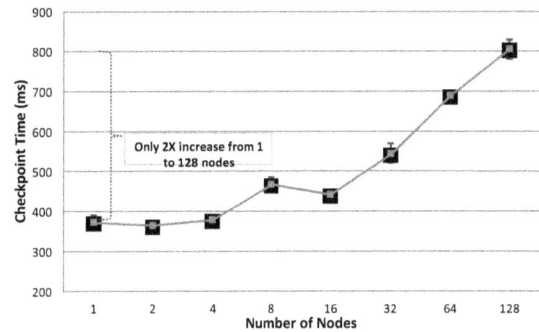

Figure 17: Checkpoint response time on *Big-cluster*.

nodes, supporting the case that a scalable application service can be effectively built on top of the content-aware service command architecture.

7. CONCLUSIONS

We have made the case for factoring out system-wide memory content-tracking into a separate platform service on top of which application services can be built. ConCORD is a proof-of-concept for such a platform service. In building ConCORD, we also developed the content-aware service command architecture, which allows an application service to be readily built as what is effectively a parameterized query in the system. This greatly simplifies the construction and execution of the application service because it allows us to leverage the platform service's existing automatic and adaptive parallel execution model.

8. REFERENCES

[1] MOLDY. http://www.ccp5.ac.uk/moldy/moldy.html.
[2] AL-KISWANY, S., SUBHRAVETI, D., SARKAR, P., AND RIPEANU, M. VMFlock: virtual machine co-migration for the cloud. In *Proceedings of the 20th international symposium on High performance distributed computing (HPDC'11)* (June 2011).
[3] ARCANGELI, A., EIDUS, I., AND WRIGHT, C. Increasing memory density by using KSM. In *Proceedings of the Linux Symposium (OLS'09)* (July 2009).
[4] BAE, C., XIA, L., DINDA, P., AND LANGE, J. Dynamic adaptive virtual core mapping to improve

pendent of the number of nodes. All of the checkpointing approaches scale. Similar to the earlier figure, the response time of the collective checkpointing service is within a constant of the embarrassingly parallel raw checkpointing service. This is evidence that the asymptotic cost to adding awareness and exploitation of memory content redundancy across the whole parallel machine to checkpointing using the content-aware service command is a constant.

Figure 17 shows the scaling of the collective checkpointing service on *Big-cluster*. As previously,we scale up the memory and the number of nodes simultaneously. The response time is virtually constant (within a factor of two) from 1 to 128 power,energy, and performance in multi-socket multicores. In *Proceedings of the 21st ACM Symposium on High-performance Parallel and Distributed Computing (HPDC 2012)* (June 2012).

[5] BISWAS, S., DE SUPINSKI, B. R., SCHULZ, M., FRANKLIN, D., SHERWOOD, T., AND CHONG, F. T. Exploiting data similarity to reduce memory footprints. In *Proceedings of the 25th IEEE International Symposium on Parallel and Distributed Systems (IPDPS'11)* (May 2011).

[6] DABEK, F. *A Distributed Hash Table.* PhD thesis, Massachusetts Institute of Technology, Department of Electrical Engineering and Computer Science, 2005.

[7] DESHPANDE, U., WANG, X., AND GOPALAN, K. Live gang migration of virtual machines. In *Proceedings of the 20th international symposium on High performance distributed computing (HPDC'11)* (June 2011).

[8] GUPTA, D., LEE, S., VRABLE, M., SAVAGE, S., SNOEREN, A. C., VARGHESE, G., VOELKER, G. M., AND VAHDAT, A. Difference engine: Harnessing memory redundancy in virtual machines. In *Proceedings of the 8th USENIX Symposium on Operating Systems Design and Implementation (OSDI '08)* (December 2008).

[9] ILSCHE, T., SCHUCHART, J., COPE, J., KIMPE, D., JONES, T., KNOEPFER, A., ISKRA, K., ROSS, R., NAGEL, W., AND POOLE, S. Enabling event tracing at leadership-class scale through i/o forwarding middleware. In *Proceedings of the 21st ACM International Symposium on High-performance Parallel and Distributed Computing (HPDC'12)* (June 2012).

[10] KLOSTER, J., KRISTENSEN, J., AND MEJLHOLM, A. On the feasibility of memory sharing: Content-based page sharing in the xen virtual machine monitor. Tech. rep., Master Thesis, Department of Computer Science, Aalborg University, 2006.

[11] LANGE, J., PEDRETTI, K., HUDSON, T., DINDA, P., CUI, Z., XIA, L., BRIDGES, P., GOCKE, A., JACONETTE, S., LEVENHAGEN, M., AND BRIGHTWELL, R. Palacios and kitten: New high performance operating systems for scalable virtualized and native supercomputing. In *Proceedings of the 24th IEEE International Parallel and Distributed Processing Symposium (IPDPS'10)* (April 2010).

[12] LEVY, S., FERREIRA, K. B., BRIDGES, P. G., THOMPSON, A. P., AND TROTT, C. An examination of content similarity within the memory of hpc applications. Tech. Rep. SAND2013-0055, Sandia National Laboratory, 2013.

[13] LI, T., ZHOU, X., BRANDSTATTER, K., ZHAO, D., WANG, K., RAJENDRAN, A., ZHANG, Z., AND RAICU, I. ZHT: A light-weight reliable persistent dynamic scalable zero-hop distributed hash table. In *Proceedings of the 27th IEEE International Parallel and Distributed Processing Symposium (IPDPS'13)* (May 2013).

[14] MIŁÓS, G., MURRAY, D. G., HAND, S., AND FETTERMAN, M. A. Satori: Enlightened page sharing. In *Proceedings of the 2009 conference on USENIX Annual technical conference (USENIX'09)* (June 2009).

[15] NICOLAE, B., AND CAPPELLO, F. Ai-ckpt: Leveraging memory access patterns for adaptive asynchronous incremental checkpointing. In *Proceedings of the 22nd ACM International Symposium on High-performance Parallel and Distributed Computing (HPDC'13)* (June 2013).

[16] RITEAU, P., MORIN, C., AND PRIOL, T. Shrinker: Improving Live Migration of Virtual Clusters over WANs with Distributed Data Deduplication and Content-Based Addressing. In *Proceedings of the 17th International European Conference on Parallel and Distributed Computing (EuroPar'11)* (August 2011).

[17] STOICA, I., MORRIS, R., KARGER, D. R., KAASHOEK, M. F., AND BALAKRISHNAN, H. Chord: A scalable peer-to-peer lookup service for internet applications. In *Proceedings of ACM SIGCOMM'01* (August 2001).

[18] VRABLE, M., MA, J., CHEN, J., MOORE, D., VANDEKIEFT, E., SNOEREN, A. C., VOELKER, G. M., AND SAVAGE, S. Scalability, fidelity, and containment in the potemkin virtual honeyfarm. In *Proceedings of the 20th ACM Symposium on Operating Systems Principles (SOSP'05)* (October 2005).

[19] WALDSPURGER, C. A. Memory resource management in vmware esx server. In *Proceedings of the 5th Symposium on Operating Systems Design and Implementation (OSDI'02)* (December 2002).

[20] WOOD, T., TARASUK-LEVIN, G., SHENOY, P. J., DESNOYERS, P., CECCHET, E., AND CORNER, M. D. Memory buddies: exploiting page sharing for smart colocation in virtualized data centers. In *Proceedings of the 5th International Conference on Virtual Execution Environments (VEE'09)* (March 2009).

[21] WOZNIAK, J. M., JACOBS, B., LATHAM, R., LANG, S., SON, S. W., AND ROSS., R. C-mpi: A dht implementation for grid and hpc environments. Tech. Rep. ANL/MCS-P1746-0410, Argonne National Laboratory, 2010.

[22] XIA, L. *ConCORD: Tracking and Exploiting Cross-Node Memory Content Redundancy in Large-Scale Parallel Systems.* PhD thesis, Department of Electrical Engineering and Computer Science, Northwestern University, July 2013. Available as Technical Report NWU-EECS-13-05.

[23] XIA, L., AND DINDA, P. A case for tracking and exploiting memory content sharing in virtualized large-scale parallel systems. In *Proceedings of the 6th International Workshop on Virtualization Technologies in Distributed Computing (VTDC'12)* (June 2012).

Fault Tolerance for Remote Memory Access Programming Models

Maciej Besta[*]
Dept. of Computer Science
ETH Zurich
Universitätstr. 6, 8092 Zurich, Switzerland
maciej.besta@inf.ethz.ch

Torsten Hoefler
Dept. of Computer Science
ETH Zurich
Universitätstr. 6, 8092 Zurich, Switzerland
htor@inf.ethz.ch

ABSTRACT

Remote Memory Access (RMA) is an emerging mechanism for programming high-performance computers and datacenters. However, little work exists on resilience schemes for RMA-based applications and systems. In this paper we analyze fault tolerance for RMA and show that it is fundamentally different from resilience mechanisms targeting the message passing (MP) model. We design a model for reasoning about fault tolerance for RMA, addressing both flat and hierarchical hardware. We use this model to construct several highly-scalable mechanisms that provide efficient low-overhead in-memory checkpointing, transparent logging of remote memory accesses, and a scheme for transparent recovery of failed processes. Our protocols take into account diminishing amounts of memory per core, one of the major features of future exascale machines. The implementation of our fault-tolerance scheme entails negligible additional overheads. Our reliability model shows that in-memory checkpointing and logging provide high resilience. This study enables highly-scalable resilience mechanisms for RMA and fills a research gap between fault tolerance and emerging RMA programming models.

Categories and Subject Descriptors

C.4 [**Computer Systems Organization**]: Performance of systems—*Fault tolerance*

General Terms

Reliability, Performance, Algorithms

1. INTRODUCTION

Partitioned Global Address Space (PGAS), and the wider class of Remote Memory Access (RMA) programming models enable high-performance communications that often outperform Message Passing [19, 34]. RMA utilizes remote direct memory access (RDMA) hardware features to access

memories at remote processes without involving the OS or the remote CPU.

RDMA is offered by most modern HPC networks (Infini-Band, Myrinet, Cray's Gemini and Aries, IBM's Blue Gene, and PERCS) and many Ethernet interconnects that use the RoCE or iWARP protocols. RMA languages and libraries include Unified Parallel C (UPC), Fortran 2008 (formerly known as CAF), MPI-3 One Sided, Cray's SHMEM interface, or Open Fabrics (OFED). Thus, we observe that RMA is quickly emerging to be the programming model of choice for cluster systems, HPC computers, and large datacenters.

Fault tolerance of such systems is important because hardware and software faults are ubiquitous [38]. Two popular resilience schemes used in today's computing environments are coordinated checkpointing (CC) and uncoordinated checkpointing augmented with message logging (UC) [17]. In CC applications regularly synchronize to save their state to memory, local disks, or parallel file system (PFS) [38]; this data is used to restart after a crash. In UC processes take checkpoints independently and use message logging to avoid rollbacks caused by the *domino effect* [37]. There has been considerable research on CC and UC for the message passing (MP) model [6,17]. Still, no work addresses the exact design of these schemes for RMA-based systems.

In this work we develop a generic model for reasoning about resilience in RMA. Then, using this model, we show that CC and UC for RMA fundamentally differ from analogous schemes for MP. We also construct protocols that enable simple checkpointing and logging of remote memory accesses. We *only* use *in-memory* mechanisms to avoid costly I/O flushes and frequent disk and PFS failures [24,38]. We then extend our model to cover two features of today's petascale and future exascale machines: (1) the growing complexity of hardware components and (2) decreasing amounts of memory per core. *With this, our study fills an important knowledge gap between fault-tolerance and emerging RMA programming in large-scale computing systems.*

In detail, we provide the following major contributions:

- We design a model for reasoning about the reliability of RMA systems running on flat and hierarchical hardware with limited memory per core. To our knowledge, this is the first work that addresses these issues.

- We construct schemes for in-memory checkpointing, logging, and recovering RMA-based applications.

- We unify these concepts in a topology-aware diskless protocol and we use real data and an analytic model to show that the protocol can endure concurrent hardware failures.

[*]MB is supported by the 2013 Google European Doctoral Fellowship in Parallel Computing.

	MPI-3 one sided operation	UPC operation	Fortran 2008 operation	Cat.
comm.	MPI_Put, MPI_Accumulate, MPI_Get_accumulate, MPI_Fetch_and_op, MPI_Compare_and_swap	upc_memput, upc_memcpy, upc_memset, assignment (=), all UPC collectives	assignment (=)	PUT
	MPI_Get, MPI_Compare_and_swap, MPI_Get_accumulate, MPI_Fetch_and_op	upc_memget, upc_memcpy, upc_memset, assignment (=), all UPC collectives	assignment (=)	GET
sync.	MPI_Win_lock, MPI_Win_lock_all	upc_lock	lock	LOCK
	MPI_Win_unlock, MPI_Win_unlock_all	upc_unlock	unlock	UNLOCK
	MPI_Win_fence	upc_barrier	sync_all, sync_team, sync_images	GSYNC
	MPI_Win_flush, MPI_Win_flush_all, MPI_Win_sync	upc_fence	sync_memory	FLUSH

Table 1: Categorization of MPI One Sided/UPC/Fortran 2008 operations in our model. Some atomic functions are considered as both PUTs and GETs. In UPC, the collectives, assignments and upc_memset/upc_memcpy behave similarly depending on the values of pointers to shared objects; the same applies to Fortran 2008. We omit MPI's post-start-complete-wait synchronization and request-based RMA operations for simplicity.

- We present the implementation of our protocol, analyze its performance, show it entails negligible overheads, and compare it to other schemes.

2. RMA PROGRAMMING

We now discuss concepts of RMA programming and present a formalization that covers existing RMA/PGAS models with strict or relaxed memory consistency (e.g., UPC or MPI-3 One Sided). In RMA, each process explicitly exposes an area of its local memory as shared. Memory can be shared in different ways (e.g., MPI windows, UPC shared arrays, or Co-Arrays in Fortran 2008); details are outside the scope of this work. Once shared, memory can be accessed with various language-specific operations.

2.1 RMA Operations

We identify two fundamental types of RMA operations: *communication* actions (often called *accesses*; they transfer data between processes), and *synchronization* actions (synchronize processes and guarantee memory consistency). A process p that issues an RMA action targeted at q is called the *active source*, and q is called the *passive target*. We assume p is active and q is passive (unless stated otherwise).

2.1.1 Communication Actions

We denote an action that transfers data from p to q and from q to p as $PUT(p \rightrightarrows q)$ and $GET(p \leftrightarrows q)$, respectively. We use double-arrows to emphasize the asymmetry of the two operations: the upper arrow indicates the direction of data flow and the lower arrow indicates the direction of control flow. The upper part of Table 1 categorizes communication operations in various RMA languages. Some actions (e.g., atomic compare and swap) transfer data in *both* directions and thus fall into the family of PUTs *and* GETs.

We also distinguish between PUTs that "blindly" replace a targeted memory region at q with a new value (e.g., UPC assignment), and PUTs that combine the data moved to q with the data that already resides at q (e.g., MPI_Accumulate). When necessary, we refer to the former type as the *replacing* PUT, and to the latter as the *combining* PUT.

2.1.2 Memory Synchronization Actions

We identify four major categories of memory synchronization actions: $LOCK(p \rightarrow q, str)$ (locks a structure str in q's memory to provide exclusive access), $UNLOCK(p \rightarrow q, str)$ (unlocks str in q's memory and enforces consistency of str), $FLUSH(p \rightarrow q, str)$ (enforces consistency of str in p's and q's memories), and $GSYNC(p \rightarrow \diamond, str)$ (enforces consistency of str); $\diamond$ indicates that the call targets all processes. Arrows indicate the flow of control (synchronization). When we refer to the whole process memory (and not a single structure),

we omit str (e.g., $LOCK(p \rightarrow q)$). The lower part of Table 1 categorizes synchronization calls in various RMA languages.

2.2 Epochs and Consistency Order

RMA's relaxed memory consistency enables non-blocking PUTs and GETs. Issued operations are completed by memory consistency actions (FLUSH, UNLOCK, GSYNC). The period between any two such actions issued by p and targeting the same process q is called an *epoch*. Every $UNLOCK(p \rightarrow q)$ or $FLUSH(p \rightarrow q)$ *closes* p's current epoch and *opens* a new one (i.e., increments p's epoch number denoted as $E(p \rightarrow q)$). p can be in several independent epochs related to each process that it communicates with. As GSYNC is a collective call, it increases epochs at every process.

An important concept related to epochs is the *consistency order* (denoted as $\xrightarrow{co}$). $\xrightarrow{co}$ orders the visibility of actions: $x \xrightarrow{co} y$ means that memory effects of action x are globally visible before action y. Actions issued in different epochs by process p targeting the same process q are always ordered with $\xrightarrow{co}$. Epochs and $\xrightarrow{co}$ are illustrated in Figure 1. $x \parallel_{co} y$ means that actions x and y are *not* ordered with $\xrightarrow{co}$.

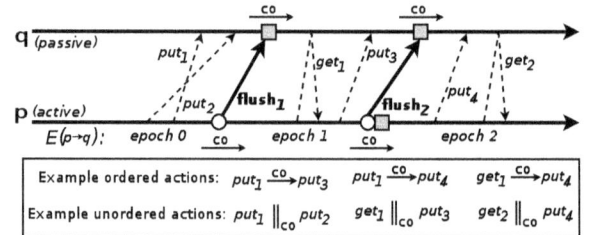

Figure 1: Epochs and the consistency order $\xrightarrow{co}$ (§ 2.2). White circles symbolize synchronization calls (in this case FLUSH). Grey squares show when calls' results become globally visible in q's or p's memory.

2.3 Program, Synchronization, and Happened Before Orders

In addition to $\xrightarrow{co}$ we require three more orders to specify an RMA execution [22]: The *program order* ($\xrightarrow{po}$) specifies the order of actions of a single thread, similarly to the program order in Java [29] ($x \xrightarrow{po} y$ means that x is called before y by some thread). The *synchronization order* ($\xrightarrow{so}$) orders LOCK and UNLOCK and other synchronizing operations. *Happened-before* (HB, $\xrightarrow{hb}$), a relation well-known in message passing [27], is the transitive closure of the union of $\xrightarrow{po}$ and $\xrightarrow{so}$. We abbreviate a *consistent happen-before* as $\xrightarrow{cohb}$: $a \xrightarrow{cohb} b \equiv a \xrightarrow{co} b \wedge a \xrightarrow{hb} b$. To state that actions are *parallel* in an order, we use the symbols $\parallel_{po}, \parallel_{so}, \parallel_{hb}$. We show the orders in Fig. 2; more details can be found in [22].

38

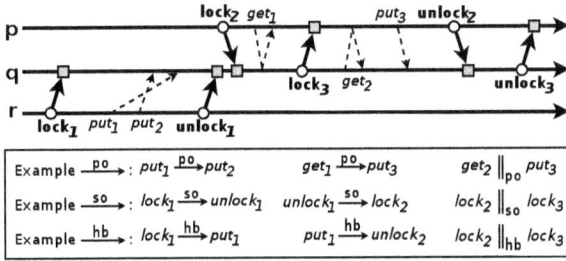

Figure 2: Example RMA orderings $\xrightarrow{po}, \xrightarrow{so}, \xrightarrow{hb}$ (§ 2.3).

2.4 Formal Model

We now combine the various RMA concepts and fault tolerance into a single formal model. We assume fail-stop faults (processes can disappear nondeterministically but behave correctly while being a part of the program). The data communication may happen out of order as specified for most RMA models. Communication channels between non-failed processes are asynchronous, reliable, and error-free. The user code can only communicate and synchronize using RMA functions specified in Section 2.1. Finally, checkpoints and logs are stored in *volatile* memories.

We define a communication action a as a tuple

$$a = \langle type, src, trg, combine, EC, GC, SC, GNC, data \rangle \quad (1)$$

where *type* is either a put or a get, *src* and *trg* specify the source and the target, and *data* is the data carried by a. *Combine* determines if a is a replacing PUT (*combine* = *false*) or a combining PUT (*combine* = *true*). *EC* (*Epoch Counter*) is the epoch number in which a was issued. GC, SC, and GNC are counters required for correct recovery; we discuss them in more detail in Section 4. We combine the notation from Section 2.1 with this definition and write PUT$(p \rightrightarrows q).EC$ to refer to the epoch in which the put happens. We also define a *determinant* of a (denoted as $\#a$, cf. [6]) to be tuple a without *data*:

$$\#a = \langle type, src, trg, combine, EC, GC, SC, GNC \rangle. \quad (2)$$

Similarly, a *synchronization action* b is defined as

$$b = \langle type, src, trg, EC, GC, SC, GNC, str \rangle. \quad (3)$$

Finally, a trace of an RMA program running on a distributed system can be written as the tuple

$$\mathcal{D} = \langle \mathcal{P}, \mathcal{E}, \mathcal{S}, \xrightarrow{po}, \xrightarrow{so}, \xrightarrow{hb}, \xrightarrow{co} \rangle, \quad (4)$$

where

$\mathcal{P}$ is the set of all $\mathcal{P}$rocesses in $\mathcal{D}$ ($|\mathcal{P}| = N$),

$\mathcal{E} = \mathcal{A} \cup \mathcal{I}$ is the set of all $\mathcal{E}$vents:

$\mathcal{A}$ is the set of RMA $\mathcal{A}$ctions,

$\mathcal{I}$ is the set of $\mathcal{I}$nternal actions (reads, writes, checkpoint actions). READ(x, p) loads local variable x and WRITE$(x := val, p)$ assigns val to x (in p's memory). C_p^i is the ith checkpoint action taken by p. Internal events are partially ordered with actions using $\xrightarrow{po}, \xrightarrow{co}$, and $\xrightarrow{hb}$.

$\mathcal{S}$ is the set of all data $\mathcal{S}$tructures used by the program.

3. FAULT-TOLERANCE FOR RMA

We now present schemes that make RMA codes fault tolerant. We start with the simpler CC and then present the protocols for UC.

3.1 Coordinated Checkpointing (CC)

In many CC schemes, the user explicitly calls a function to take a checkpoint. Such protocols may leverage RMA's features (e.g., direct memory access) to improve the performance. However, these schemes have several drawbacks: they complicate the code because they can only be called when the network is quiet [21] and they do not always fit the optimality criteria such as Daly's checkpointing interval [15]. In this section, we first identify how CC in RMA differs from CC in MP and then describe a scheme for RMA codes that performs CC *transparently* to the application. We model a coordinated checkpoint as a set $C = \{C_{p_1}^{i_1}, C_{p_2}^{i_2}, ..., C_{p_N}^{i_N}\} \subseteq \mathcal{I}, p_m \neq p_n$ for any m, n.

3.1.1 RMA vs. MP: Coordinated Checkpointing

In MP, every C has to satisfy a *consistency condition* [21]: $\forall C_p^i, C_q^j \in C : C_p^i \parallel_{hb} C_q^j$. This condition ensures that C does not reflect a system state in which one process received a message that was *not* sent by any other process. We adopt this condition and extend it to cover all RMA semantics:

DEFINITION 1. *C is RMA-consistent iff $\forall C_p^i, C_q^j \in C : C_p^i \parallel_{cohb} C_q^j$.*

We extend $\parallel_{hb}$ to $\parallel_{cohb}$ to guarantee that the system state saved in C does not contain a process affected by a memory access that was *not* issued by any other process. In RMA, unlike in MP, this condition can be easily satisfied because each process can drain the network with a local FLUSH (enforcing consistency at any point is legal [22])

3.1.2 Taking a Coordinated Checkpoint

We now propose two diskless schemes that obey the RMA-consistency condition and target MPI-3 RMA codes. The first ("Gsync") scheme can be used in programs that *only* synchronize with GSYNCs. The other ("Locks") scheme targets codes that *only* synchronize with LOCKs and UNLOCKs. Note that in correct MPI-3 RMA programs GSYNCs and LOCKs/UNLOCKs cannot be mixed [31]. All our schemes assume that a GSYNC may also introduce an additional $\xrightarrow{hb}$ order, which is true in some implementations [31].

The "Gsync" Scheme Every process may take a coordinated checkpoint right after the user calls a GSYNC and before any further RMA calls by: (1) optionally enforcing the global $\xrightarrow{hb}$ order with an operation such as MPI_Barrier (denoted as BAR), and taking the checkpoint. Depending on the application needs, not every GSYNC has to be followed by a checkpoint. We use Daly's formula [15] to compute the best interval between such checkpoints and we take checkpoints after the right GSYNC calls.

THEOREM 3.1. *The Gsync scheme satisfies the RMA-consistency condition and does not deadlock.*

PROOF. We assume correct MPI-3 RMA programs represented by their trace $\mathcal{D}$ [22, 31]. For all $p, q \in \mathcal{P}$, each GSYNC$(p \rightarrow \diamond)$ has a matching GSYNC$(q \rightarrow \diamond)$ such that $[$GSYNC$(p \rightarrow \diamond) \parallel_{hb}$ GSYNC$(q \rightarrow \diamond)]$. Thus, if every process calls BAR right after GSYNC then BAR matching is guaranteed and the program cannot deadlock. In addition, the GSYNC calls introduce a global consistency order $\xrightarrow{co}$ such that the checkpoint is coordinated and consistent. $\square$

The "Locks" Scheme Every process p maintains a local *Lock Counter* LC_p that starts with zero and is incremented after each LOCK and decremented after each UNLOCK. When $LC_p = 0$, process p can perform a checkpoint in three phases: (1) enforce consistency with a FLUSH($p \to \diamond$), (2) call a BAR to provides the global $\xrightarrow{hb}$ order, and (3) take a checkpoint C_p^i. The last phase, the actual checkpoint stage, is performed collectively thus all processes can take the checkpoint C in coordination.

THEOREM 3.2. *The Locks scheme satisfies the RMA-consistency condition and does not deadlock.*

PROOF. The call to FLUSH($p \to \diamond$) in phase 1 guarantees global consistency at each process. The BAR in phase 2 guarantees that all processes are globally consistent before the checkpoint taken in phase 3.

It remains to proof deadlock-freedom. We assume correct MPI-3 RMA programs [22, 31]. A LOCK($p \to q$) can only block waiting for an active lock LOCK($z \to q$) and no BAR can be started at z while the lock is held. In addition, for every LOCK($z \to q$), there is a matching UNLOCK($z \to q$) in the execution such that LOCK($z \to q$) $\xrightarrow{po}$ UNLOCK($z \to q$) (for any $z, p, q \in \mathcal{P}$). Thus, all locks must be released eventually, i.e., $\exists a \in \mathcal{E} : a \xrightarrow{po}$ WRITE($LC_p := 0, p$) for any $p \in \mathcal{P}$. $\square$

The above schemes show that the transparent CC can be achieved much simpler in RMA than in MP. In MP, such protocols usually have to analyze inter-process dependencies due to sent/received messages, and add protocol-specific data to messages [11, 17], which reduces the bandwidth. In RMA this is not necessary.

3.2 Uncoordinated Checkpointing (UC)

Uncoordinated checkpointing augmented with message logging reduces energy consumption and synchronization costs because a single process crash does not force all other processes to revert to the previous checkpoint and recompute [17, 37]. Instead, a failed process fetches its last checkpoint and replays messages logged beyond this checkpoint. However, UC schemes are usually more complex than CC [17]. We now analyze how UC in RMA differs from UC in MP, followed by a discussion of our UC protocols. Data structures for the protocols are shown in Table 2.

3.2.1 RMA vs. MP: Uncoordinated Checkpointing

The first and obvious difference is that we now log not *messages* but *accesses*. Other differences are as follows:

Storing Access Logs In MP, processes exchange messages that *always* flow *from* the sender (process p) *to* the receiver (process q). Messages can be recorded at the sender's side [17,37]. During a recovery, the restored process interacts with other processes to get and reply the logged messages (see Figure 3 (part (1)).

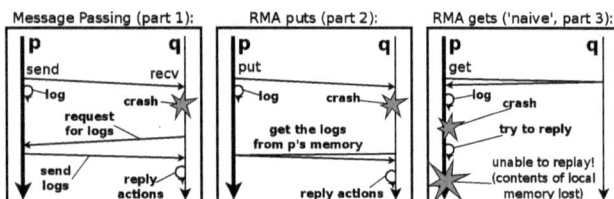

Figure 3: The logging of messages vs. RMA puts and gets (§ 3.1.1).

In RMA, a PUT($p \stackrel{\rightrightarrows}{} q$) changes the state of q, but a GET($p \stackrel{\leftleftarrows}{} q$) modifies the state of p. Thus, PUT($p \stackrel{\rightrightarrows}{} q$) can be logged in p's memory, but GET($p \stackrel{\leftleftarrows}{} q$) cannot because a failure of p would prevent a successful recovery (see Figure 3, part 2 and 3).

Transparency of Schemes In MP, both p and q actively participate in communication. In RMA, q is oblivious to accesses to its memory and thus any recovery or logging performed by p can be *transparent* to (i.e., does not obstruct) q (which is usually *not* the case in MP, cf. [37]).

No Piggybacking Adding some protocol-specific data to messages (e.g., *piggybacking*) is a popular concept in MP [17]. Still, it cannot be used in RMA because PUTS and GETs are accesses, not messages. Yet, issuing additional accesses is cheap in RMA.

Access Determinism Recent works in MP (e.g., [20]) explore *send determinism*: the output of an application run is oblivious to the order of received messages. In our work we identify a similar concept in RMA that we call *access determinism*. For example, in race-free MPI-3 programs the application output does not depend on the order in which two accesses a and b committed to memory if $a \parallel_{co} b$.

Orphan Processes In some MP schemes (called *optimistic*), senders postpone logging messages for performance reasons [17]. Assume q received a message m from p and then sent a message m' to r. If q crashes and m is not logged by p at that time, then q may follow a run in that it *does not* send m'. Thus, r becomes an *orphan*: its state depends on a message m' that was *not* sent [17] (see Figure 4, part 1).

In RMA, a process may also become an orphan. Consider Figure 4 (part 2). First, p modifies a variable x at q. Then, q reads x and conditionally issues a PUT($q \stackrel{\rightrightarrows}{} r$). If q crashes and p postponed logging PUT($p \stackrel{\rightrightarrows}{} q$), then q (while recovering) may follow a run in which it does not issue PUT($q \stackrel{\rightrightarrows}{} r$); thus r becomes an orphan.

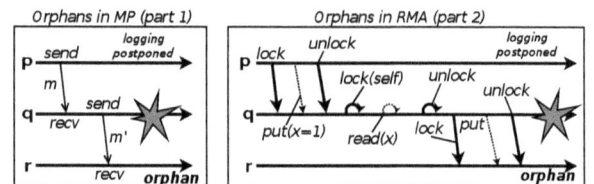

Figure 4: Illustration of orphans in MP and RMA (§ 3.1.1).

3.2.2 Taking an Uncoordinated Checkpoint

We denote the ith uncoordinated checkpoint taken by process p as C_p^i. Taking C_p^i is simple and entails: (1) locking local application data, (2) sending the copy of the data to some remote volatile storage, and (3) unlocking the application data (we defer the discussion on the implementation details until Section 6). After p takes C_p^i, any process q can delete the logs of every PUT($q \stackrel{\rightrightarrows}{} p$) (from $LP_q[p]$) and GET($p \stackrel{\leftleftarrows}{} q$) (from $LG_q[p]$) that committed in p's memory before C_p^i (i.e., PUT($q \stackrel{\rightrightarrows}{} p$) $\xrightarrow{co} C_p^i$ and GET($p \stackrel{\leftleftarrows}{} q$) $\xrightarrow{co} C_p^i$).

We demand that every C_p^i is taken *immediately after* closing/opening an epoch and *before* issuing any new communication operations (we call this the *epoch condition*). This condition is required because, if p issues a GET($p \stackrel{\leftleftarrows}{} q$), the application data is guaranteed to be consistent only after closing the epoch.

40

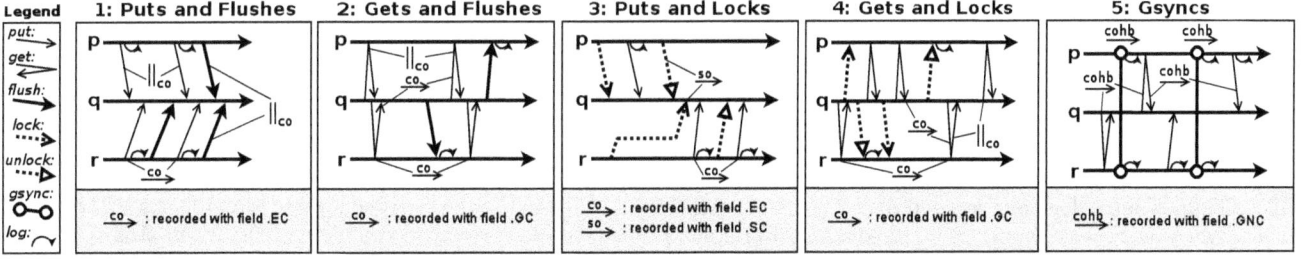

Figure 5: Logging orders $\xrightarrow{so}$, $\xrightarrow{co}$, and $\xrightarrow{hb}$ (§ 4.1). In each figure we illustrate example orderings.

Structure	Description
$LP_p[q] \in \mathcal{S}$	Logs of PUTs issued by p and targeted at q.
$LG_q[p] \in \mathcal{S}$	Logs of GETs targeted at q and issued by p.
$LP_p \in \mathcal{S}$	Logs of PUTs issued and stored by p and targeted at any other process; $LP_p \equiv \bigcup_{r \in \mathcal{P} \wedge r \neq p} LP_p[r]$.
$LG_q \in \mathcal{S}$	Logs of *gets* targeted and stored at q, issued by any other process; $LG_q \equiv \bigcup_{r \in \mathcal{P} \wedge r \neq q} LG_q[r]$.
$Q_p \in \mathcal{S}$	A helper container stored at p, used to temporarily log #GETs issued by p.
$N_q[p] \in \mathcal{S}$	A structure (stored at q) that determines whether or not p issued a non-blocking GET($p \overset{\rightarrow}{\rightarrow} q$) ($N_q[p] = true$ or $false$, respectively)

Table 2: Data structures used in RMA logging (§ 3.2.3). $LP_p[q]$ and LP_p are stored at p. $LG_q[p]$ and LG_q are stored at q.

3.2.3 Transparent Logging of RMA Accesses

We now describe the logging of PUTs and GETs.

Logging Puts To log a PUT($p \overset{\rightarrow}{\rightarrow} q$), p first calls LOCK($p \rightarrow p, LP_p$). Self-locking is necessary because there may be other processes being recovered that may try to read LP_p. Then, the PUT is logged ($LP_p[q] := LP_p[q] \cup \{$PUT($p \overset{\rightarrow}{\rightarrow} q$)$\}$; ":=" denotes the assignment of a new value to a variable or a structure). Finally, p unlocks LP_p. Atomicity between logging and putting is not required because, in the weak consistency memory model, the source memory of the put operation may not be modified until the current epoch ends. If the program modifies it nevertheless, RMA implementations are allowed to return any value, thus the logged value is irrelevant. We log PUT($p \overset{\rightarrow}{\rightarrow} q$) before closing the epoch PUT($p \overset{\rightarrow}{\rightarrow} q$).$EC$. If the PUT is blocking then we log it before issuing, analogously to the *pessimistic* message logging [17].

Logging Gets We log a GET($p \overset{\leftarrow}{\rightarrow} q$) in two phases to retain its asynchronous behavior (see Algorithm 1). First, we record the determinant #GET($p \overset{\leftarrow}{\rightarrow} q$) in Q_p (lines 2-3). We cannot access GET($p \overset{\leftarrow}{\rightarrow} q$).$data$ as the local memory will only be valid after the epoch ends. We avoid issuing an additional blocking FLUSH($p \rightarrow q$), instead we rely on the user's call to end the epoch. Second, when the user ends the epoch, we lock the remote log LG_q, record GET($p \overset{\leftarrow}{\rightarrow} q$), and unlock LG_q (lines 4-7).

Note that if p fails between issuing GET($p \overset{\leftarrow}{\rightarrow} q$) and closing the epoch, it will not be able to replay it consistently. To address this problem, p sets $N_q[p]$ at process q to *true* right before issuing the first GET($p \overset{\rightarrow}{\rightarrow} q$) (line 1), and to *false* after closing the epoch GET($p \overset{\rightarrow}{\rightarrow} q$).$EC$ (line 8). During the recovery, if p notices that any $N_q[p] = true$, it falls back to another resilience mechanism (i.e., the last coordinated checkpoint). If the GET is blocking then we set $N_q[p] = false$ after returning from the call.

Algorithm 1: Logging *gets* (§ 3.2.3)

Input: $get := $ GET($p \overset{\leftarrow}{\rightarrow} q$)
/* Phase 1: starts right before issuing the *get* */
1   $N_q[p] := true$
/* Now we issue the *get* and log the #*get* */
2   issue GET($p \overset{\leftarrow}{\rightarrow} q$)
3   $Q_p \leftarrow Q_p \cup \#get$
/* Phase 2: begins after ending the epoch *get*.EC */
4   LOCK($p \rightarrow q, LG_q$)
5   $LG_q[p] := LG_q[p] \cup get$
6   $Q_p := Q_p \setminus \#get$
7   UNLOCK($p \rightarrow q, LG_q$)
8   $N_q[p] := false$

---

4. CAUSAL RECOVERY FOR UC

We now show how to causally recover a failed process (*causally* means preserving $\xrightarrow{co}$, $\xrightarrow{so}$, and $\xrightarrow{hb}$). This section describes technical details on how to guarantee all orders to ensure a correct access replay. If the reader is not interested in all details, she may proceed to Section 5 without disrupting the flow. A causal process recovery has three phases: (1) fetching uncoordinated checkpoint data, (2) replaying accesses from remote logs, and (3) in case of a problem during the replay, falling back to the last coordinated checkpoint. We first show how we log the respective orderings between accesses (Section 4.1) and how we prevent replaying some accesses twice (Section 4.2). We finish with our recovery scheme (Section 4.3) and a discussion (Section 4.4). Due to space constraints, we include full proofs in the techreport version of the paper[1].

4.1 Logging Order Information

We now show how to record $\xrightarrow{so}$, $\xrightarrow{hb}$, and $\xrightarrow{co}$. For clarity, but without loss of generality, we separately present several scenarios that exhaust possible communication/synchronization patterns in our model. We consider three processes (p, q, r) and we analyze what data is required to replay q. We show each pattern in Figure 5.

A. Puts and Flushes First, p and r issue PUTs and FLUSHes at q. At both p and r, PUTs separated by FLUSHes are ordered with $\xrightarrow{co}$. This order is preserved by recording epoch counters (.EC) with every logged PUT($p \overset{\rightarrow}{\rightarrow} q$). Note that, however, RMA semantics *do not* order calls issued by p and r: [PUT($p \overset{\rightarrow}{\rightarrow} q$) $\|_{co}$ PUT($r \overset{\rightarrow}{\rightarrow} q$)] without additional process synchronization. Here, we assume *access determinism*: the recovery output does not depend on the order in which such PUTs committed in q's memory.

B. Gets and Flushes Next, q issues GETs and FLUSHes targeted at p and r. Again, $\xrightarrow{co}$ has to be logged. However, this time GETs targeted at *different* processes *are* ordered (because they are issued by the same process). To log this

---

[1] http://spcl.inf.ethz.ch/Research/Parallel_Programming/ftRMA

ordering, q maintains a local *Get Counter* GC_q that is incremented each time q issues a FLUSH($q \rightarrow \diamond$) to any other process. The value of this counter is logged with each GET using the field $.GC$ (cf. Section 2.4).

C. Puts and Locks In this scenario p and r issue PUTs at q and synchronize their accesses with LOCKs and UNLOCKs. This pattern requires logging the $\xrightarrow{so}$ order. We achieve this with a *Synchronization Counter* SC_q stored at q. After issuing a LOCK($p \rightarrow q$), p (the same refers to r) fetches the value of SC_q, increments it, updates remote SC_q, and records it with every PUT using the field $.SC$ (cf. Section 2.4). In addition, this scenario requires recording $\xrightarrow{co}$ that we solve with $.EC$, analogously as in the "Puts and Flushes" pattern.

D. Gets and Locks Next, q issues GETs and uses LOCKs targeted at p and r. This pattern is solved analogously to the "Gets and Flushes" pattern.

E. Gsyncs The final pattern are GSYNCs (that may again introduce $\xrightarrow{hb}$) combined with any communication action. Upon a GSYNC, each process q increments its *GsyNc Counter* GNC_q that is logged in an actions' $.GNC$ field (cf. Section 2.4).

Algorithm 2: The causal recovery scheme (§ 4.3, § 4.4).

```
 1  Function recovery()
 2  │   fetch_checkpoint_data()
 3  │   put_logs := {}; get_logs := {}
 4  │   forall the q ∈ P : q ≠ p_new do
 5  │   │   LOCK(p_new → q)
 6  │   │   if N_q[p_f] = 1 ∨ M_q[p_f] = true then
 7  │   │   │   /* Stop the recovery and fall back to the
 8  │   │   │      last coordinated checkpoint          */
 9  │   │   end
 8  │   │   put_logs := put_logs ∪ LP_q[p_f]
 9  │   │   get_logs := get_logs ∪ LG_q[p_f]
10  │   │   UNLOCK(p_new → q)
11  │   end
12  │   while |put_logs| > 0 ∨ |get_logs| > 0 do
13  │   │   gnc_logs := logsWithMinCnt(GNC, put_logs ∪ get_logs)
14  │   │   while |gnc_logs| > 0 do
15  │   │   │   gnc_put_logs := gnc_logs ∩ put_logs
16  │   │   │   gnc_get_logs := gnc_logs ∩ get_logs
17  │   │   │   ec_logs := logsWithMinCnt(EC, gnc_put_logs)
18  │   │   │   gc_logs := logsWithMinCnt(GC, gnc_get_logs)
19  │   │   │   replayEachAction(ec_logs)
20  │   │   │   replayEachAction(gc_logs)
21  │   │   │   gnc_logs := gnc_logs \ (ec_logs ∪ gc_logs)
22  │   │   end
23  │   │   put_logs := put_logs \ gnc_logs
24  │   │   get_logs := get_logs \ gnc_logs
25  │   end
26  │   return
27  Function logsWithMinCnt(Counter, Logs)
    │   /* Return a set with logs from Logs that have the
    │      smallest value of the specified counter (one
    │      of: GNC, EC, GC, SC).                         */
28  Function replayEachAction(Logs)
    │   /* Reply each log from set Logs in any order.    */
29  Function fetchCheckpointData()
    │   /* Fetch the last checkpoint and load into the
    │      memory.                                        */
```

4.2 Preventing Replaying Accesses Twice

Assume that process p issues a PUT($p \rightrightarrows q$) (immediately logged by p in $LP_p[q]$) such that PUT($p \rightrightarrows q$) $\xrightarrow{co} C_q^j$. It means that the state of q recorded in checkpoint C_q^j is affected by PUT($p \rightrightarrows q$). Now assume that q fails and begins to replay the logs. If p did not delete the log of PUT($p \rightrightarrows q$) from $LP_p[q]$ (it was allowed to do it after q took C_q^j), then q replays PUT($p \rightrightarrows q$) and this PUT affects its memory *for the second time*. This is not a problem if

PUT($p \rightrightarrows q$).*combine* $= false$, because such a PUT always overwrites the memory region with the same value. However, if PUT($p \rightrightarrows q$).*combine* $= true$, then q ends up in an inconsistent state (e.g., if this PUT increments a memory cell, this cell will be incremented twice).

To solve this problem, every process p maintains a local structure $M_p[q] \in S$. When p issues and logs a PUT($p \rightrightarrows q$) such that PUT($p \rightrightarrows q$).*combine* $= true$, it sets $M_p[q] := true$. When p deletes PUT($p \rightrightarrows q$) from its logs, it sets $M_p[q] := false$. If q fails, starts to recover, and sees that any $M_p[q] = true$, it stops the recovery and falls back to the coordinated checkpoint. This scheme is valid if access determinism is assumed. Otherwise we set $M_p[q] := true$ regardless of the value of PUT($p \rightrightarrows q$).*combine*; we use the same approach if q can issue WRITEs to the memory regions accessed with remote PUTs parallel in $\|_{co}$ to these WRITEs.

4.3 Recovering a Failed Process

We now describe a protocol for codes that synchronize with GSYNCs; consult the technical report for other schemes. Let us denote the failed process as p_f. We assume an underlying batch system that provides a new process p_{new} in the place of p_f, and that other processes resume their communication with p_{new} after it fully recovers. We illustrate the scheme in Algorithm 2. First, p_{new} fetches the checkpointed data. Second, p_{new} gets the logs of PUTs (put_logs) and GETs (get_logs) related to p_f (lines 3-11). It also checks if any $N_q[p_f] = true$ (see § 3.2.3) or $M_q[p_f] = true$ (see § 4.2), if yes it instructs all processes to roll back to the last coordinated checkpoint. The protocol uses LOCKs (lines 5,10) to prevent data races due to, e.g., concurrent recoveries and log cleanups by q.

The main part (lines 12-26) replays accesses causally. The recovery ends when there are no logs left (line 12; $|logs|$ is the size of the set "logs"). We first get the logs with the smallest $.GNC$ (line 13) to maintain $\xrightarrow{cohb}$ introduced by GSYNCs (see § 4.1 E). Then, within this step, we find the logs with minimum $.EC$ and $.GC$ to preserve $\xrightarrow{co}$ in issued PUTs and GETs, respectively (lines 17-18, see § 4.1 A, B). We replay them in lines 19-20.

4.4 Discussion

Our recovery scheme presents a trade-off between memory efficiency and time to recover. Process p_{new} fetches all related logs and only then begins to replay accesses. Thus, we assume that its memory has capacity to contain put_logs and get_logs; a reasonable assumption if the user program has regular communication patterns (true for most of today's RMA applications [19]). A more memory-efficient scheme fetches logs while recovering. This incurs performance issues as p_{new} has to access remote logs multiple times.

5. EXTENDING THE MODEL FOR MORE RESILIENCE

Our model and in-memory resilience schemes are oblivious to the underlying hardware. However, virtually all of today's systems have a hierarchical hardware layout (e.g., cores reside on a single chip, chips reside in a single node, nodes form a rack, and racks form a cabinet). Multiple elements may be affected by a single failure at a higher level, jeopardizing the safety of our protocols. We now extend our model to cover arbitrary hierarchies and propose *topology-*

aware mechanisms to make our schemes handle concurrent hardware failures. Specifically, we propose three following extensions:

The Hierarchy of Failure Domains A *failure domain* (FD) is an element of a hardware hierarchy that can fail (e.g., a node or a cabinet). FDs constitute an FD hierarchy (FDH) with h levels. An example FDH is shown in Figure 6, $h = 4$. We skip the level of single cores because in practice the smallest FD is a node (e.g., in the TSUBAME2.0 system failure history, there are no core failures [3]). Then, we define $\mathcal{H} = \bigcup_{1 \le j \le h} \left(\bigcup_{1 \le i \le H_j} H_{i,j} \right)$ to be the set of all the FD elements in an FDH. $H_{i,j}$ and H_j are element i of hierarchy level j and the number of such elements at level j, respectively. For example, in Figure 6 $H_{3,2}$ is the third blade (level 2) and $H_2 = 96$.

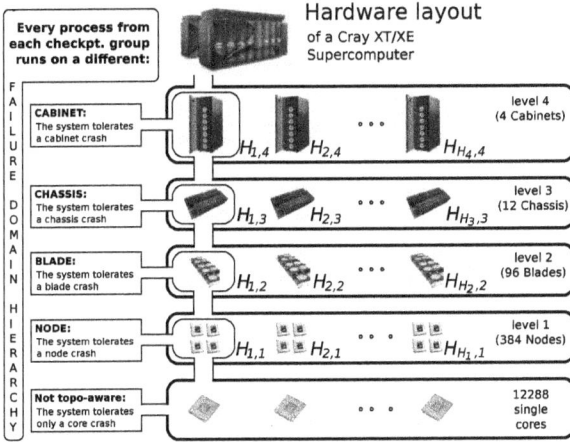

Figure 6: An example hardware layout (Cray XT/XE) and the corresponding FDH (§ 5). In this example, $h = 4$.

Groups of Processes To improve resilience, we split the process set $\mathcal{P}$ into g equally-sized groups G_i and add m *checksum* processes to each group to store checksums of checkpoints taken in each group (using, e.g., the Reed-Solomon [36] coding scheme). Thus, every group can resist m concurrent process crashes. The group size is $|G| = \frac{|\mathcal{P}|}{g} + m$.

New System Definition We now extend the definition of a distributed system $\mathcal{D}$ to cover the additional concepts:

$$\langle \mathcal{P}, \mathcal{E}, \mathcal{S}, \mathcal{H}, \mathcal{G}, \xrightarrow{po}, \xrightarrow{so}, \xrightarrow{hb}, \xrightarrow{co}, \mathcal{M} \rangle. \quad (5)$$

$\mathcal{G} = \{G_1, ..., G_g\}$ is a set of $\mathcal{G}$roups of processes and $\mathcal{M} : \mathcal{P} \times \mathbb{N} \to \mathcal{H}$ is a function that $\mathcal{M}$aps process p to the FD at hierarchy level k where p runs: $\mathcal{M}(p, k) = H_{j,k}$. $\mathcal{M}$ defines how processes are distributed over FDH. For example, if p runs on blade $H_{1,2}$ from Figure 6, then $\mathcal{M}(p, 2) = H_{1,2}$.

5.1 Handling Multiple Hardware Failures

More than m process crashes in any group G_i result in a *catastrophic failure* (CF; we use the name from [8]) that incurs restarting the whole computation. Depending on how $\mathcal{M}$ distributes processes, such a CF may be caused by several (or even one) crashed FDs. To minimize the risk of CFs, $\mathcal{M}$ has to be *topology-aware* (t-aware): for a given level n (called a *t-awareness level*), no more than m processes from the same group can run on the same $H_{i,k}$ at any level $k, k \le n$:

$$\forall p_1, p_2, ..., p_m \in \mathcal{P} \quad \forall G \in \mathcal{G} \quad \forall 1 \le k \le n :$$
$$(p_1 \in G \land ... \land p_m \in G) \Rightarrow (\mathcal{M}(p_1, k) \ne ... \ne \mathcal{M}(p_m, k)) \quad (6)$$

Figure 7 shows an example t-aware process distribution.

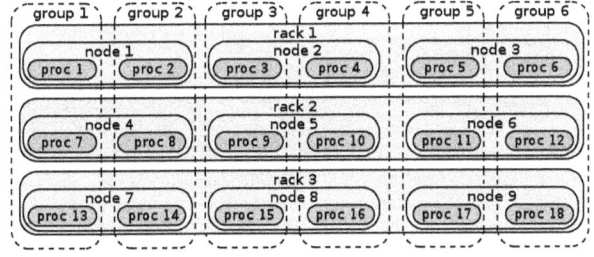

Figure 7: T-aware distribution at the node *and* rack level (§ 5.1).

5.2 Calculating Probability of a CF

We now calculate the probability of a catastrophic failure (P_{cf}) in our model. We later (§ 7.1) use P_{cf} to show that our protocols are resilient on a concrete machine (the TSUMABE2.0 supercomputer [3]). If a reader is not interested in the derivation details, she may proceed to Section 6 where we present the results. We set $m = 1$ and thus use the XOR erasure code, similar to an additional disk in a RAID5 [12]. We assume that failures at different hierarchy levels are independent and that any number x_j of elements from any hierarchy level j ($1 \le x_j \le H_j$, $1 \le j \le h$) can fail. Thus,

$$P_{cf} = \sum_{j=1}^{h} \sum_{x_j=1}^{H_j} P(x_j \cap x_{j,cf}) = \sum_{j=1}^{h} \sum_{x_j=1}^{H_j} P_j(x_j) P_j(x_{j,cf}|x_j). \quad (7)$$

$P(x_j \cap x_{j,cf})$ is the probability that x_j elements of the j hierarchy level will fail *and* result in a catastrophic failure. $P_j(x_j)$ is the probability of the failure of x_j elements from level j of the hierarchy. $P_j(x_{j,cf}|x_j)$ is the probability that x_j given concurrent failures at hierarchy level j are catastrophic to the system. It is difficult to analytically derive $P_j(x_j)$ as it is specific for every machine. For our example study (see Section 7.1) we use the failure rates from the TSUBAME2 failure history [3].

In contrast, $P_j(x_{j,cf}|x_j)$ can be calculated using combinatorial theory. Assume that $\mathcal{M}$ distributes processes in a t-aware way at levels 1 to n of the FDH ($1 \le n \le h$). First, we derive $P_j(x_{j,cf}|x_j)$ for any level j such that $1 \le j \le n$:

$$P_j(x_{j,cf}|x_j) = \frac{D_j \cdot \binom{|G|}{2} \cdot \binom{H_j - 2}{x_j - 2}}{\binom{H_j}{x_j}}. \quad (8)$$

$\binom{|G|}{2}$ is the number of the possible catastrophic failure scenarios *in a single group* ($m = 1$ thus any two process crashes in one group are catastrophic). D_j is the number of such single-group scenarios *at the whole level* j and is equal to $\left\lceil \frac{H_j}{|G|} \right\rceil$ (see Figure 8 for intuitive explanation). $\binom{H_j - 2}{x_j - 2}$ is the number of the remaining possible failure scenarios and $\binom{H_j}{x_j}$ is the total number of the possible failure scenarios. Second, for remaining levels j ($n + 1 \le j \le h$) $\mathcal{M}$ is *not* t-aware and thus in the worst-case scenario any element crash is catastrophic: $P_j(x_{j,cf}|x_j) = 1$. The final formula for P_{cf} is thus

$$P_{cf} = \sum_{j=1}^{n} \sum_{x_j=1}^{H_j} P_j(x_j) \frac{D \cdot \binom{|G|}{2} \cdot \binom{H_j - 2}{x_j - 2}}{\binom{H_j}{x_j}} + \sum_{j=n+1}^{h} \sum_{x_j=1}^{N_j} P_j(x_j). \quad (9)$$

6. HOLISTIC RESILIENCE PROTOCOL

We now describe an example conceptual implementation of holistic fault tolerance for RMA that we developed to understand the tradeoffs between the resilience and performance in RMA-based systems. We implement it as a

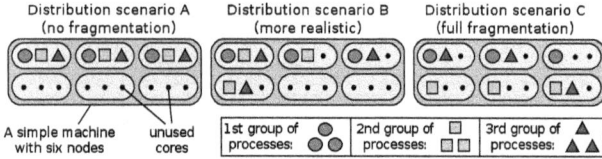

Figure 8: (§ 5.2) Consider three process distribution scenarios by $\mathcal{M}$ (each is t-aware). Optimistically, processes can be distributed contiguously (scenario A) or partially fragmented (scenario B). To get the upper bound for P_{cf} we use the worst-case pattern (scenario C). Now, to get the number of single-group CF scenarios at the whole level j (D_j), we need to obtain the number of the groups of *hardware elements* at j that hold process groups: $\lceil H_j/|G| \rceil$.

portable library (based on C and MPI) called FTRMA. We utilize MPI-3's one sided interface, but any other RMA model enabling relaxed memory consistency could be used instead (e.g., UPC or Fortran 2008). We use the publicly available FOMPI implementation of MPI-3 one sided as MPI library [1] but any other MPI-3 compliant library would be suitable. For simplicity we assume that the user application uses one contiguous region of shared memory of the same size at each process. Still, all the conclusions drawn are valid for any other application pattern based on RMA. Following the MPI-3 specification, we call this shared region of memory at every process a *window*. Finally, we divide user processes (referred to as CoMputing processes, CMs) into groups (as described in Section 5) and add one CHecksum process (denoted as CH) per group ($m = 1$). For any computing process p, we denote the CH in its group as $CH(p)$. CHs store and update XOR checksums of their CMs.

6.1 Protocol Overview

In this section we provide a general overview of the layered protocol implementation (see Figure 9). The first part (layer 1) logs accesses. The second layer takes uncoordinated checkpoints (called *demand* checkpoints) to trim the logs. Layer 3 performs regular coordinated checkpoints. All layers are diskless. Causal recovery replays memory accesses. Finally, our FDH increases resilience of the whole protocol.

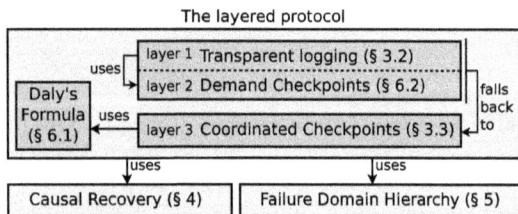

Figure 9: The overview of the protocol (§ 6.1). Layer 1 and 2 constitute the uncoordinated part of the protocol that falls back to the coordinated checkpointing if logging fails or if its overhead is too high.

Daly's Interval Layer 3 uses Daly's formula [15] as the optimum interval between coordinated checkpoints: $\sqrt{2\delta M} \cdot [1 + 1/3\sqrt{\delta/(2M)} + (1/9)(\delta/(2M))] - \delta$ (for $\delta < 2M$), or M (for $\delta \geq 2M$). M is the MTBF (mean time between failures that FTRMA handles with coordinated checkpointing) for the target machine and δ is the time to take a checkpoint. The user provides M while δ is estimated by our protocol.

Interfacing with User Programs and Runtime FTRMA routines are called after each RMA action. This would entail runtime system calls in compiled languages and we use the PMPI profiling interface [31] in our implementation. During window creation the user can specify: (1) the number of CHs, (2) MTBF, (3) whether to use topology-

awareness. After window creation, the protocol divides processes into CMs and CHs. If the user enables t-awareness, groups of processes running on the same FDs are also created. In the current version FTRMA takes into account computing nodes when applying t-awareness.

6.2 Demand Checkpointing

Demand checkpoints address the problem of diminishing amounts of memory per core in today's and future computing centers. If free memory at CM process p is scarce, p selects the process q with the largest $LP_p[q]$ or $LG_p[q]$ and requests a demand checkpoint. First, p sends a *checkpoint request* to $CH(q)$ which, in turn, forces q to checkpoint. This can be done by: closing all the epochs, locking all the relevant data structures, calculating the XOR checksum, and: (1) streaming the result to $CH(q)$ piece by piece or (2) sending the result in one bulk. $CH(q)$ integrates the received checkpoint data into the existing XOR checksum. Variant (1) is memory-efficient, and (2) is less time-consuming. Next, q unlocks all the data structures. Finally, $CH(q)$ sends a confirmation with the epoch number $E(p \to q)$ and respective counters (GNC_q, GC_q, SC_q) to p. Process p can delete logs of actions a where $a.EC < E(p \to q)$, $a.GNC < GNC_q$, $a.GC < GC_q$, $a.SC < SC_q$.

7. TESTING AND EVALUATION

In this section we first analyze the resilience of our protocol using real data from TSUBAME2.0 [3] failure history. Then, we test the performance of FTRMA with a NAS benchmark [14] that computes 3D Fast Fourier Transformation and a distributed key-value store. We denote the number of CHs and CMs as $|CH|$ and $|CM|$, respectively.

7.1 Analysis of Protocol Resilience

Our protocol stores all data in volatile memories to avoid I/O performance penalties and frequent disk and parallel file system failures [24,38]. This brings several questions on whether the scheme is resilient in practical environments. To answer this question, we calculate the probability of a catastrophic failure P_{cf} (using Equations (7) and (9)) of our protocol, applying t-awareness at different levels of FDH.

We first fix model parameters (H_j, h) to reflect the hierarchy of TSUBAME2.0. TSUBAME2.0 FDH has 4 levels [38]: nodes, power supply units (PSUs), edge switches, and racks ($h = 4$) [38]. Then, to get P_{cf}, we calculate distributions $P_j(x_j)$ that determine the probability of x_j concurrent crashes at level j of the TSUBAME FDH. To obtain $P_j(x_j)$ we analyzed 1962 crashes in the history of TSUBAME2.0 failures [3]. Following [8] we decided to use exponential probability distributions, where the argument is the number of concurrent failures x_j. We derived four probability density functions (PDFs) that approximate the failure distributions of nodes ($0.30142 \cdot 10^{-2} e^{-1.3567 x_1}$), PSUs ($1.1836 \cdot 10^{-4} e^{-1.4831 x_2}$), switches ($3.9249 \cdot 10^{-5} e^{-1.5902 x_3}$), and racks ($3.2257 \cdot 10^{-5} e^{-1.5488 x_4}$). The unit is failures per day. Figures 10a and 10b illustrate two PDF plots with histograms. The distributions for PSUs, switches, and racks are based on real data only. For nodes it was not always possible to determine the exact correlation of failures. Thus, we pessimistically assumed (basing on [8]) that single crashes constitute 75% of all node failures, two concurrent crashes constitute 20%, and other values decrease exponentially.

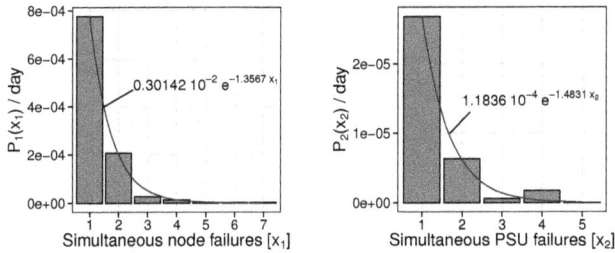

(a) Distribution of node crashes (samples and the fit) (§ 7.1). (b) Distribution of PSU crashes (samples and the fit) (§ 7.1). (c) Probability of a catastrophic failure (§ 7.1.1). (d) NAS FFT (class C) fault-free runs: checkpointing (§ 7.2.1).

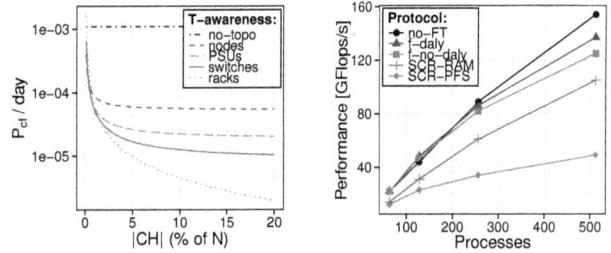

Figure 10: Distribution of PSU & node failures, P_{cf} in TSUBAME2.0 running 4,000 processes, and the performance of NAS 3D FFT.

7.1.1 Comparison of Resilience

Figure 10c shows the resilience of our protocol when using five t-awareness strategies. The number of processes N is 4,000. P_{cf} is normalized to one day period. Without t-awareness (no-topo) a single crash of any FD of TSUBAME2.0 is catastrophic, thus P_{cf} does not depend on $|CH|$. In other scenarios every process from every group runs on a different node (nodes), PSU (PSUs), switch enclosure (switches) and rack (racks). In all cases P_{cf} decreases proportionally to the increasing $|CH|$, however at some point the exponential distributions ($P_j(x_j)$) begin to dominate the results. Topology-awareness at higher hierarchy levels significantly improves the resilience of our protocol. For example, if $CH = 5\%N$, P_{cf} in the switches scenario is ≈4 times lower than in nodes. Furthermore, all t-aware schemes are 1-3 orders of magnitude more resilient than no-topo.

The results show that even a simple scheme (nodes) significantly improves the resilience of our protocol that performs only in-memory checkpointing and logging. We conclude that costly I/O flushes to the parallel file system (PFS) are not required for obtaining a high level of resilience. On the contrary, such flushes may even *increase* the risk of failures. They usually entail stressing the I/O system for significant amounts of time [38], and stable storage is often the element most susceptible to crashes. For example, a Blue Gene/P supercomputer had 4,164 disk fail events in 2011 (for 10,400 total disks) [24], and its PFS failed 77 times, almost two times more often than other hardware [24].

7.2 Analysis of Protocol Performance

We now discuss the performance of our fault tolerance protocol after the integration with two applications: NAS 3D FFT and a distributed key-value store. Both of these applications are characterized by intensive communication patterns, thus they demonstrate worst-case scenarios for our protocol. Integrating FTRMA with the application code was trivial and required minimal code changes resulting in the same code complexity.

Comparison to Scalable Checkpoint/Restart We compare FTRMA to Scalable Checkpoint-Restart (SCR) [2], a popular open-source message passing library that provides checkpoint and restart capability for MPI codes but does not enable logging. We turn on the XOR scheme in SCR and we fix the size of SCR groups [2] so that they match the analogous parameter in FTRMA ($|G|$). To make the comparison fair, we configure SCR to save checkpoints to both in-memory tmpfs (SCR-RAM) and to the PFS (SCR-PFS).

Comparison to Message Logging To compare the logging overheads in MP and RMA we also developed a simple message logging (ML) scheme (basing on the protocol

from [37]) that records accesses. Similarly to [37] we use additional processes to store protocol-specific access logs; the data is stored at the sender's or receiver's side depending on the type of operation.

We execute all benchmarks on the Monte Rosa system and we use Cray XE6 computing nodes. Each node contains four 8-core 2.3 GHz AMD Opterons 6276 (Interlagos) and is connected to a 3D-Torus Gemini network. We use the Cray Programming Environment 4.1.46 to compile the code.

7.2.1 NAS 3D Fast Fourier Transformation

Our version of the NAS 3D FFT [14] benchmark is based on MPI-3 nonblocking PUTs (we exploit the overlap of computation and communication). The benchmark calculates 3D FFT using a 2D decomposition.

Performance of Coordinated Checkpointing We begin with evaluating our checkpointing "Gsync" scheme. Figure 10d illustrates the performance of NAS FFT fault-free runs. We compare: the original application code without any fault-tolerance (no-FT), FTRMA, SCR-RAM, and SCR-PFS. We fix $|CH| = 12.5\%|CM|$. We include two FTRMA scenarios: f-daly (use Daly's formula for coordinated checkpoints), and f-no-daly (fixed frequency of checkpoints without Daly's formula, ≈2.7s for 1024 processes). We use the same t-awareness policy in all codes (nodes). The tested schemes have the respective fault-tolerance overheads over the baseline no-FT: 1-5% (f-daly), 1-15% (f-no-daly), 21-37% (SCR-RAM) and 46-67% (SCR-PFS). The performance of SCR-RAM is lower than f-daly and f-no-daly because FTRMA is based on the Gsync scheme that incurs less synchronization. SCR-PFS entails the highest overheads due to costly I/O flushes.

Performance of Demand Checkpointing We now analyze how the size of the log impacts the number of demand checkpoints and the performance of fault-free runs (see Figure 11a). Dedicating less than 44 MiB of memory for storing logs (per process) triggers demand checkpoint requests to clear the log; checkpoints are taken every ≈0.25s on average (when the size of the log is 36 MiB). This results in performance penalties but leaves more memory available to the user.

Performance of Access Logging As the next step we evaluate our logging scheme. Figure 11b illustrates the performance of fault-free runs. We compare no-FT, FTRMA, and our ML protocol (ML). FTRMA adds only ≈8-9% of overhead to the baseline (no-FT) and consistently outperforms ML by ≈9% due to the smaller amount of protocol-specific interaction between processes.

Varying $|CH|$ and T-Awareness Policies Here, we analyze how $|CH|$ and t-awareness impact the performance of NAS FFT fault-free runs. We set $|CH| = 12.5\%|CM|$ and

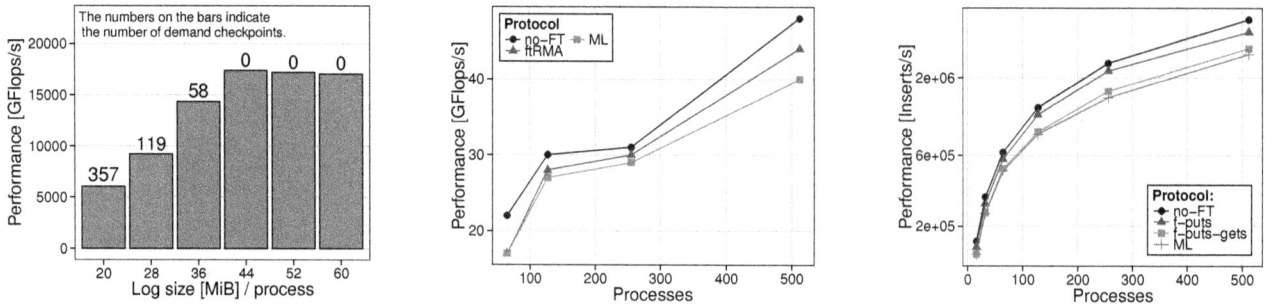

(a) NAS FFT (class A) fault-free runs: demand checkpointing.

(b) NAS FFT (class A) fault-free runs: logging.

(c) Key-value store fault-free runs.

Figure 11: Performance of the NAS FFT code (§ 7.2.1) and the key-value store (§ 7.2.2).

$|CH| = 6.25\%|CM|$, and we use the no-topo and nodes t-awareness policies. The results show that all these schemes differ negligibly from no-FT by 1-5%.

7.2.2 Key-Value Store

Our key-value store is based on a simple distributed hashtable (DHT) that stores 8–Byte integers. The DHT consists of parts called *local volumes* constructed with fixed-sized arrays. Every local volume is managed by a different process. Inserts are based on MPI-3 atomic Compare-And-Swap and Fetch-And-Op functions. Elements after hash collisions are inserted in the overflow heap that is the part of each local volume. To insert an element, a thread atomically updates the pointers to the next free cell and the last element in the local volume. Memory consistency is ensured with flushes. One GET and one PUT are logged if there is no hash collision, otherwise 6 PUTs and 4 GETs are recorded.

Performance of Access Logging We now measure the relative performance penalty of logging PUTs and GETs. During the benchmark, processes insert random elements with random keys. We focus on inserts only as they are perfectly representative for the logging evaluation. To simulate realistic requests, every process waits for a random time after every insert. The function that we use to calculate this interval is based on the exponential probability distribution: $f\delta e^{-\delta x}$, where f is a scaling factor, δ is a rate parameter and $x \in [0; b)$ is a random number. The selected parameter values ensure that every process spends ≈5-10% of the total runtime on inserting elements. For many computation-intense applications this is already a high amount of communication. We again compare no-FT, ML, and two FTRMA scenarios: f-puts (logging only PUTs) and f-puts-gets (logging PUTs and GETs). We fix $|CH| = 12.5\%|CM|$ and use the nodes t-awareness. We skip SCR as it does not enable logging.

We present the results in Figure 11c. For $N = 256$, the logging overhead over the baseline (no-FT) is: ≈12% (f-puts), 33% (f-gets), and 40% (ML). The overhead of logging PUTs is due to the fact that every operation is recorded directly after issuing. Traditional message passing protocols suffer from a similar effect [17]. The overhead generated by logging GETs in f-puts-gets and ML is more significant because, due to RMA's one-sided semantics, every GET has to be recorded remotely. In addition, f-puts-gets suffers from synchronization overheads (caused by concurrent accesses to *LG*), while ML from inter-process protocol-specific communication. Discussed overheads heavily depend on the application type. Our key-value store constitutes a worst-case scenario because it does not allow for long epochs that

could enable, e.g., sending the logs of multiple GETs in a bulk. The performance penalties would be smaller in applications that overlap computation with communication and use non blocking GETs.

8. RELATED WORK

In this section we discuss existing checkpointing and logging schemes (see Figure 12). For excellent surveys, see [6,17,40]. Existing work on fault tolerance in RMA/PGAS is scarce, an example scheme that uses PGAS for data replication can be found in [5].

8.1 Checkpointing Protocols

These schemes are traditionally divided into *uncoordinated*, *coordinated*, and *communication induced*, depending on process coordination scale [17]. There are also *complete* and *incremental* protocols that differ in checkpoint sizes [40].

Uncoordinated Schemes Uncoordinated schemes do not synchronize while checkpointing, but may suffer from the *domino effect* or complex recoveries [17]. Example protocols are based on *dependency* [9] or *checkpoint graphs* [17]. A recent scheme targeting large-scale systems is Ken [41].

Coordinated Schemes Here, processes synchronize to produce consistent global checkpoints. There is no domino effect and recovery is simple but synchronization may incur severe overheads. Coordinated schemes can be *blocking* [17] or *non-blocking* [11]. There are also schemes based on *loosely synchronized clocks* [39] and *minimal coordination* [26].

Communication Induced Schemes Here, senders add scheme-specific data to application messages that receivers use to, e.g., avoid taking useless checkpoints. These schemes can be *index-based* [21] or *model-based* [17,32].

Incremental Checkpointing An incremental checkpoint updates only the data that changed since the previous checkpoint. These protocols are divided into page-based [40] and hash-based [4]. They can reside at the level of an *application*, a *library*, an *OS*, or *hardware* [40]. Other schemes can be *compiler-enhanced* [10] or *adaptive* [4].

Others Recently, *multi-level* checkpointing was introduced [8,30,38]. *Adaptive* checkpointing based on failure prediction is discussed in [28]. [35] presents diskless checkpointing. Other interesting schemes are based on: Reed-Solomon coding [8], cutoff and compression to reduce checkpoint sizes [23], checkpointing on clouds [33], reducing I/O bottlenecks [25], and performant checkpoints to PFS [7].

8.2 Logging Protocols

Logging enables restored processes to replay their execution beyond the most recent checkpoint. Log-based pro-

Logging-based protocols

- Moment of logging: Optimistic [37], Pessimistic [18], Causal [16]
- Addressed comm. model: RMA [this paper], Message-passing [16,18,20,37]
- Place of logs: Receiver-based [17], Sender-based [20,37]

Checkpoint-based protocols

- Scale of coordination: Coordinated [25], Comm.-induced, Uncoordinated [18,20,20,41]
- Moment of checkp.: Index-based [17], Model-based [32]
- Way of recovery: Dep. graph [9], Checkp. graph [17]
- Way of coordination: Blocking [17], Non-blocking [11]
- Other coordinated schemes: Clock-based [39], Min.-coordination [26]
- Other schemes: Multi-level [8,30,38], Diskless [35], Stable storage [7,25], Checkpointing on clouds [33]
- Other inc. schemes: Adaptive [4], Compiler enhanced [10]
- Size of checkpoints: Incremental, Complete
- Place of residence [40]: OS level, Hardware level, Library level, Application level
- Way of detecting changes in data: Page-based [40], Hash-based [4]

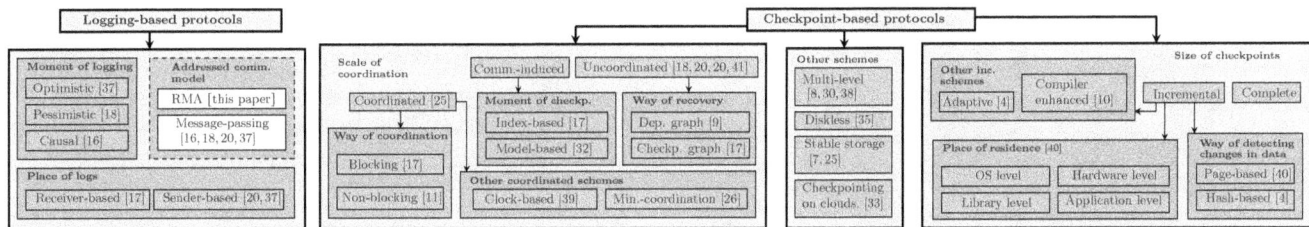

Figure 12: An overview of existing checkpointing and logging schemes (§ 8). A dashed rectangle illustrates a new sub-hierarchy introduced in the paper: dividing the logging protocols with respect to the *communication model* that they address.

tocols are traditionally categorized into: *pessimistic, optimistic, causal* [17]; they can also be *sender-based* [20,37] and *receiver-based* [17] depending on which side logs messages.

Pessimistic Schemes Such protocols log events before they influence the system. This ensures no orphan processes and simpler recovery, but may incur severe overheads during fault-free runs. An example protocol is V-MPICH [18].

Optimistic Schemes Here, processes postpone logging messages to achieve, e.g., better computation-communication overlap. However, the algorithms for recovery are usually more complicated and crashed processes may become orphans [17]. A recent scheme can be found in [37].

Causal Schemes In such schemes processes log and exchange (by piggybacking to messages) dependencies needed for recovery. This ensures no orphans but may reduce bandwidth [17]. An example protocol is discussed in [16].

8.3 Other Important Studies & Discussion

Deriving an optimum checkpointing interval is presented in [15]. Formalizations targeting resilience can be found in [17,32]. *Containment domains* for encapsulating failures within a hierarchical scope are discussed in [13]. Modeling and prediction of failures is addressed in [8,13]. Work on send determinism in MP can be found in [20].

Our study goes beyond the existing research scope presented in this section. First, we develop a fault tolerance model that covers virtually whole rich RMA semantics. Other existing formalizations (e.g., [6,17,32]) target MP only. We then use the model to formally analyze why resilience for RMA differs from MP and to design checkpointing, logging, and recovery protocols for RMA. We identify and propose solutions to several challenges in resilience for RMA that *do not* exist in MP, e.g.: consistency problems caused by the relaxed RMA memory model (§ 3.1, § 3.2.2, § 3.2.3), access non-determinism (§ 4.2), issues due to one-sided RMA communication (§ 3.2.1), logging multiple RMA-specific orders (§ 4.1), etc. Our model enables proving correctness of proposed schemes; all proofs omitted due to space constraints can be found in the technical report. Extending our model for arbitrary hardware hierarchies generalizes the approach from [8] and enables formal reasoning about crashes of hardware elements and process distribution. Finally, our protocol leverages and combines several important concepts and mechanisms (Daly's interval [15], multi-level design [30], etc.) to improve the resilience of RMA systems even further and is the first implementation of holistic fault tolerance for RMA.

9. CONCLUSION

RMA programming models are growing in popularity and importance as they allow for the best utilization of hardware features such as OS-bypass or zero-copy data transfer. Still, little work addresses fault tolerance for RMA.

We established, described, and explored a complete formal model of fault tolerance for RMA and illustrated how to use it to design and reason about resilience protocols running on flat and hierarchical machines. It will play an important role in making emerging RMA programming fault tolerant and can be easily extended to cover, e.g., stable storage.

Our study does not resort to traditional less scalable mechanisms that often rely on costly I/O flushes. The implementation of our holistic protocol adds negligible overheads to the applications runtime, for example 1-5% for in-memory checkpointing and 8% for fully transparent logging of remote memory accesses in the NAS 3D FFT code. Our probability study shows that the protocol offers high resilience. The idea of demand checkpoints will help alleviate the problem of limited memory amounts in today's petascale and future exascale computing centers.

Finally, our work provides the basis for further reasoning about fault-tolerance not only for RMA, but also for all the other models that can be constructed upon it, such as task-based programming models. This will play an important role in complex heterogeneous large-scale systems.

10. REFERENCES

[1] foMPI, 2013. http://spcl.inf.ethz.ch/Research/Parallel_Programming/foMPI.

[2] Scalable Checkpoint / Restart, 2013. http://sourceforge.net/projects/scalablecr/.

[3] TSUBAME2.0: Failure History, April 2013. http://mon.g.gsic.titech.ac.jp/trouble-list/index.htm.

[4] S. Agarwal, R. Garg, M. S. Gupta, and J. E. Moreira. Adaptive incremental checkpointing for massively parallel systems. In *Proc. of the Ann. Intl. Conf. on Supercomp.*, ICS '04, pages 277–286, 2004.

[5] N. Ali, S. Krishnamoorthy, N. Govind, and B. Palmer. A Redundant Communication Approach to Scalable Fault Tolerance in PGAS Programming Models. In *Par., Dist. and Net. Proc. (PDP), the Eur. Intl. Conf. on*, pages 24–31, 2011.

[6] L. Alvisi and K. Marzullo. Message Logging: Pessimistic, Optimistic, Causal, and Optimal. *IEEE Trans. Softw. Eng.*, 24(2):149–159, Feb. 1998.

[7] D. Arteaga and M. Zhao. Towards Scalable Application Checkpointing with Parallel File System Delegation. In *Proc. of the IEEE Intl. Conf. on Net., Arch., and Stor.*, NAS '11, pages 130–139, 2011.

[8] L. Bautista-Gomez, S. Tsuboi, D. Komatitsch, F. Cappello, N. Maruyama, and S. Matsuoka. FTI: high performance Fault Tolerance Interface for hybrid systems. In *Proc. of the ACM/IEEE Supercomputing*, SC '11, pages 32:1–32:32.

[9] B. Bhargava and S.-R. Lian. Independent checkpointing and concurrent rollback for recovery in distributed systems-an optimistic approach. In *Rel. Dist. Syst., 1988. Proc.., Symp. on*, pages 3 –12.

[10] G. Bronevetsky, D. J. Marques, K. K. Pingali, R. Rugina, and S. A. McKee. Compiler-enhanced incremental checkpointing for OpenMP applications. In *Proc. of the ACM SIGPLAN Symp. on Prin. and Prac. of Par. Prog.*, PPoPP '08, pages 275–276.

[11] K. M. Chandy and L. Lamport. Distributed snapshots: determining global states of distributed systems. *ACM Trans. Comput. Syst.*, 3(1):63–75, Feb. 1985.

[12] P. M. Chen, E. K. Lee, G. A. Gibson, R. H. Katz, and D. A. Patterson. RAID: high-performance, reliable secondary storage. *ACM Comput. Surv.*, 26(2):145–185, June 1994.

[13] J. Chung, I. Lee, M. Sullivan, J. H. Ryoo, D. W. Kim, D. H. Yoon, L. Kaplan, and M. Erez. Containment domains: a scalable, efficient, and flexible resilience scheme for exascale systems. In *Proc. of the ACM/IEEE Supercomputing*, SC '12, pages 58:1–58:11.

[14] D. H. Bailey et al. The NAS parallel benchmarks. Technical report, The Intl. J. of Super. App., 1991.

[15] J. T. Daly. A higher order estimate of the optimum checkpoint interval for restart dumps. *Future Gener. Comput. Syst.*, 22(3):303–312, Feb. 2006.

[16] E. Elnozahy and W. Zwaenepoel. Manetho: transparent roll back-recovery with low overhead, limited rollback, and fast output commit. *Comp., IEEE Trans. on*, 41(5):526 –531, 1992.

[17] E. N. M. Elnozahy, L. Alvisi, Y.-M. Wang, and D. B. Johnson. A survey of rollback-recovery protocols in message-passing systems. *ACM Comput. Surv.*, 34(3):375–408, Sept. 2002.

[18] G. Bosilca et al. MPICH-V: Toward a Scalable Fault Tolerant MPI for Volatile Nodes. In *Supercomputing, the ACM/IEEE Conf.*, pages 29–29, 2002.

[19] R. Gerstenberger, M. Besta, and T. Hoefler. Enabling Highly-scalable Remote Memory Access Programming with MPI-3 One Sided. In *Proc. of the ACM/IEEE Supercomputing*, SC '13, pages 53:1–53:12, 2013.

[20] A. Guermouche, T. Ropars, E. Brunet, M. Snir, and F. Cappello. Uncoordinated Checkpointing Without Domino Effect for Send-Deterministic MPI Applications. In *Par. Dist. Proc. Symp., the IEEE Intl.*, pages 989–1000.

[21] J.-M. Helary, A. Mostefaoui, R. Netzer, and M. Raynal. Preventing useless checkpoints in distributed computations. In *Rel. Dist. Sys., 1997. Proc.., the Symp. on*, pages 183 –190, 1997.

[22] T. Hoefler, J. Dinan, R. Thakur, B. Barrett, P. Balaji, W. Gropp, and K. Underwood. Remote Memory Access Programming in MPI-3. *Argonne National Laboratory, Tech. Rep*, 2013.

[23] S. Hogan, J. Hammond, and A. Chien. An evaluation of difference and threshold techniques for efficient checkpoints. In *Dep. Sys. and Net. Work. (DSN-W), IEEE/IFIP Intl. Conf.*, pages 1–6, 2012.

[24] F. Isaila, J. Garcia, J. Carretero, R. Ross, and D. Kimpe. Making the case for reforming the I/O software stack of extreme-scale systems. In *Ex. App. and Soft. Conf. (EASC'13)*, 2013.

[25] H. Jin and K. Hwang. Distributed Checkpointing on Clusters with Dynamic Striping and Staggering. In *Advances in Computing Science - ASIAN 2002*, volume 2550, pages 19–33. 2002.

[26] R. Koo and S. Toueg. Checkpointing and Rollback-Recovery for Distributed Systems. *Soft. Eng., IEEE Trans. on*, SE-13(1):23 – 31, 1987.

[27] L. Lamport. Time, Clocks, and the Ordering of Events in a Distributed System. *Comm. ACM*, 21(7):558–565, 1978.

[28] Y. Li and Z. Lan. Using adaptive fault tolerance to improve application robustness on the Teragrid. *Proc. of TeraGrid*, 322, 2007.

[29] J. Manson, W. Pugh, and S. V. Adve. The Java Memory Model. In *Proc. of ACM Symp. on Prin. of Prog. Lang.*, POPL '05, pages 378–391, 2005.

[30] A. Moody, G. Bronevetsky, K. Mohror, and B. R. d. Supinski. Design, Modeling, and Evaluation of a Scalable Multi-level Checkpointing System. In *Proc. of ACM/IEEE Supercomputing*, SC '10, pages 1–11.

[31] MPI Forum. MPI: A Message-Passing Interface Standard. Version 3, September 2012. available at: http://www.mpi-forum.org (Sep. 2012).

[32] R. Netzer and J. Xu. Necessary and sufficient conditions for consistent global snapshots. *Par. and Dist. Sys., IEEE Trans. on*, 6(2):165 –169, 1995.

[33] B. Nicolae and F. Cappello. BlobCR: efficient checkpoint-restart for HPC applications on IaaS clouds using virtual disk image snapshots. In *Proc. of ACM/IEEE Supercomputing*, SC '11, pages 34:1–34:12.

[34] D. Petrović, O. Shahmirzadi, T. Ropars, and A. Schiper. High-performance RMA-based broadcast on the Intel SCC. In *Proc. of ACM Symp. Par. Alg. Arch.*, SPAA '12, pages 121–130, 2012.

[35] J. Plank, K. Li, and M. Puening. Diskless checkpointing. *Par. and Dist. Sys., IEEE Trans. on*, 9(10):972–986, 1998.

[36] I. S. Reed and G. Solomon. Polynomial codes over certain finite fields. *J. of the Soc. for Indust. & Appl. Math.*, 8(2):300–304, 1960.

[37] R. Riesen, K. Ferreira, D. Da Silva, P. Lemarinier, D. Arnold, and P. G. Bridges. Alleviating scalability issues of checkpointing protocols. In *Proc. of ACM/IEEE Supercomputing*, SC '12, pages 18:1–18:11.

[38] K. Sato, N. Maruyama, K. Mohror, A. Moody, T. Gamblin, B. R. de Supinski, and S. Matsuoka. Design and modeling of a non-blocking checkpointing system. In *Proc. of the ACM/IEEE Supercomputing*, SC '12, pages 19:1–19:10.

[39] Z. Tong, R. Y. Kain, and W. T. Tsai. Rollback Recovery in Distributed Systems Using Loosely Synchronized Clocks. *IEEE Trans. Par. Dist. Sys.*, 3(2):246–251, 1992.

[40] M. Vasavada, F. Mueller, P. H. Hargrove, and E. Roman. Comparing different approaches for incremental checkpointing: The showdown. In *Linux Symposium*, page 69, 2011.

[41] S. Yoo, C. Killian, T. Kelly, H. K. Cho, and S. Plite. Composable Reliability for Asynchronous Systems. In *Proc. of the USENIX Ann. Tech. Conf.*, USENIX

FT-ScaLAPACK: Correcting Soft Errors On-Line for ScaLAPACK Cholesky, QR, and LU Factorization Routines

Panruo Wu
pwu011@cs.ucr.edu

Zizhong Chen
chen@cs.ucr.edu

Department of Computer Science and Engineering
University of California, Riverside
Riverside, CA 92521

ABSTRACT

It is well known that soft errors in linear algebra operations can be detected off-line at the end of the computation using algorithm-based fault tolerance (ABFT). However, traditional ABFT usually cannot correct errors in Cholesky, QR, and LU factorizations because any error in one matrix element will be propagated to many other matrix elements and hence cause too many errors to correct. Although, recently, tremendous progresses have been made to correct errors in LU and QR factorizations, these new techniques correct errors off-line at the end of the computation after errors propagated and accumulated, which significantly complicates the error correction process and introduces at least quadratically increasing overhead as the number of errors increases. In this paper, we present the design and implementation of FT-ScaLAPACK, a fault tolerant version ScaLAPACK that is able to detect, locate, and correct errors in Cholesky, QR, and LU factorizations on-line in the middle of the computation in a timely manner before the errors propagate and accumulate. FT-ScaLAPACK has been validated with thousands of cores on Stampede at the Texas Advanced Computing Center. Experimental results demonstrate that FT-ScaLAPACK is able to achieve comparable performance and scalability with the original ScaLAPACK.

Categories and Subject Descriptors

G.4 [**MATHEMATICAL SOFTWARE**]: Reliability and robustness; G.1.3 [**NUMERICAL ANALYSIS**]: Numerical Linear Algebra—*Linear systems (direct and iterative methods)*

Keywords

Algorithm-Based Fault Tolerance; ABFT; Cholesky Factorization; LU Factorization; QR Factorization; ScaLAPACK

1. INTRODUCTION

The fastest supercomputers in the world are approaching exascale, which brings many challenges including reliability

and resiliency. Exascale machines are expected to experience more hardware faults for shrinking device feature size and operating voltage and increasing number of components. If the trend continues, soon supercomputers are no longer very likely to finish large scale computations without any hardware faults. Because of this, large scale applications are forced to use checkpoint/rollback (C/R) to avoid starting over upon hardware faults. In fact, studies show that, when failure rate is high, the ratio of time spent on computation over on C/R will be so low that only insignificant time is spent on useful work [6, 7, 37, 15, 14, 23].

This scenario however only covers part of the actual faults that cause damages noticeable by hardware, OS, or software monitoring. Some soft errors (also known as silent data corruption) may silently corrupt data rather than disrupt program flow thus escaping any of the conventional fault detectors. Soft errors can be in the form of bit-flips in disk, DRAM, cache, or even processor registers. It has been reported that Jaguar supercomputer saw a double-bit error every 24 hours, and exascale machines are projected to have a double-bit error every 4 minutes [26]. Significant error rates have been observed in a BG/L L1 cache without error-correcting code (ECC) protection [4]. The presence of potentially "continuous" [26] soft errors has to be addressed in order to make exascale computing viable.

Although there are many types of errors and a wide range of applications in today's high performance computing (HPC) environments, this paper restricts its scope to only handling silent soft errors in Cholesky, QR, and LU factorizations which are the core operations of the widely used linear algebra library ScaLAPACK. They have been widely used to solve systems of linear equations, linear least square problems, and eigenvalue and eigenvector problems which are fundamental for today's science engineering. They usually consume the majority of time needed for an application, therefore, protecting these operations can improve the overall application reliability substantially.

While soft errors in today's DRAM and cache can often be effectively protected using ECC, the use of ECC DRAM and cache often introduces considerable performance, energy, and storage overhead [30]. More importantly, soft errors in processor registers and arithmetic logic units (e.g., computing errors such as $1 + 1 = 3$) cannot be protected through the use of ECC DRAM and cache.

It is well known that soft errors in linear algebra operations can be detected efficiently at the end of the computation (i.e., off-line) using algorithm-based fault tolerance (ABFT) [29, 1]. However, the ABFT technique in [29, 1] usually cannot correct even one soft error [18, 16, 34] in Cholesky, QR, and LU factorizations because one error in one matrix element will be propagated to many other matrix elements and hence cause too many errors to correct.

Recently, tremendous progresses have been made to correct soft errors in LU and QR factorizations. In [21], Sherman-Morrison-Woodbury formula was successfully used to correct one soft error in the solutions of linear systems obtained via LU factorization. In [20], Sherman-Morrison-Woodbury formula was extended to correct multiple soft errors. In [22], Spike-Eliminating and QR-Update techniques were used to correct one soft error in QR factorization. In [16], an online technique was designed to correct soft errors in LU factorization of the high-performance Linpack(HPL) benchmark.

1.1 Limitations of the Current State of the Art

Although tremendous progresses have been made to handle soft errors in Cholesky, QR, and LU factorizations recently, the current state-of-the-art ABFT techniques have the following limitations:

- **Cholesky Factorization:** The current state-of-the-art ABFT scheme for Cholesky factorization (i.e., [29, 1]) can detect soft errors effectively with very low overhead. However, it can not correct even one single soft error because one error in one matrix element will be quickly propagated to many other matrix elements during the factorization process.

- **QR Factorization:** While the current state-of-the-art ABFT schemes for QR factorization (i.e., [22]), can correct single soft error during the whole QR factorization off-line at the end of the computation, the overhead to correct multiple errors increases at least quadratically as the number of errors increases. Single error will be propagated to many other places. Multiple errors will not only be propagated but also be accumulated, which significantly complicates the error correction process. No scheme is available to correct errors on-line in the middle of the computation before errors propagate and accumulate.

- **LU Factorization:** The current state-of-the-art ABFT scheme for LU factorization [16] can effectively detect, locate, and correct soft errors on-line in the middle of the computation before errors propagate. However, the recovery of any soft error in any processor involves expensive global communications and synchronizations among all processors. Global checksums need to be created and maintained during computations. Note that [21, 20, 18] are only off-line schemes with the recovery overhead increasing at least quadratically as the number of errors increases.

- **Software Implementation:** Today's HPC applications usually solve linear algebra problems by calling highly optimized library routines. But existing ABFT schemes can not be directly implemented into the widely used linear algebra libraries like LAPACK and ScaLAPACK without modifying the library interfaces. Therefore, today's HPC applications can not benefit from existing ABFT techniques without modifying source codes.

1.2 Our Contributions

In this paper, we present the design and implementation of FT-ScaLAPACK, a fault tolerant version ScaLAPACK that is able to detect, locate, and correct soft errors in Cholesky, QR, and LU factorizations on-line in the middle of the computation in a timely manner before the errors propagate and accumulate. FT-ScaLAPACK has been validated with thousands of cores on Stampede at the Texas Advanced Computing Center. Experimental results demonstrate that FT-ScaLAPACK is able to achieve comparable performance and scalability with the original ScaLAPACK library. More specifically, our contributions include:

- **Cholesky Factorization:** We designed an on-line scheme to correct soft errors in Cholesky factorization before the errors propagate and accumulate, where the existing best schemes [29, 1] cannot correct errors. Existing schemes need to restart the whole computation if any error occurs, therefore, introduces much higher overhead than our on-line scheme.

- **QR Factorization:** We designed an on-line scheme to correct soft errors in QR factorization before the errors propagate and accumulate, where the existing best schemes [22, 18] can only correct errors off-line at the end the computation after the errors propagated and accumulated. While the overhead of the existing off-line schemes increases at least quadratically as the number of errors increases, the overhead of our on-line scheme is much lower and increases only linearly.

- **LU Factorization:** We designed a new on-line scheme to correct soft errors in LU factorization without global communications or synchronizations, where the existing best schemes [16] are on-line, but involve expensive global communications and synchronizations.

- **Software Implementation:** We made the widely used ScaLAPACK library core routines (Cholesky, QR, LU) fault tolerant without modifying the library interfaces. Existing HPC applications that use ScaLAPACK library can now make use of our new FT-ScaLAPACK library to tolerate soft errors by just linking to the new library without any modification on source codes.

The rest of this paper is organized as follows. Section 2 discusses the background. Section 3 illustrates the basic design framework using Cholesky factorization as an example. In section 4, on-line error correction schemes for LU and QR factorization are discussed in detail. Section 5 evaluates the performance and scalability both theoretically and experimentally. Related works are discussed in Section 6.

2. BACKGROUND

This section provides the necessary background required to understand the idea of this paper. At first we give a brief introduction to traditional ABFT (we refer to as off-line ABFT); then in order to describe on-line ABFT we need to have a big picture of the so-called block version of algorithms for dense linear algebra algorithms, which are essential for high performance on modern hierarchical memory systems and distributed memory systems.

2.1 ABFT

ABFT was first introduced by Abraham and Huang [29]. The idea is that, for some matrix (or matrices) operation $P(A, \ldots) = (X, \ldots)$, we first encode the operands into their checksum form, for example $A \xrightarrow{\text{encode}} A^f := \begin{bmatrix} A & Ae \\ e^T A & e^T Ae \end{bmatrix}$ where e is a predefined (column) vector; then apply the operation on the encoded matrix (matrices) and the results are automatically "encoded":

$$P(A^{\text{enc}}, \ldots) = (X^{\text{enc}}, \ldots)$$

An example is the ABFT enabled matrix-matrix multiplication (matmul), in which case the operator P is $P(A, B) = A \times B = X$. The classic way to encode the operands A, B is as follows:

$$A \xrightarrow{\text{encode}} A^c = \begin{bmatrix} A \\ e^T A \end{bmatrix}, \quad B \xrightarrow{\text{encode}} B^r = \begin{bmatrix} B & Be \end{bmatrix}$$

And it can be shown that the result is also in some checksum form:

$$P(A^c, B^r) = X^f, \text{where} X = AB$$

The superscripts c, r, f of the encoded matrices A^c, B^r, X^f stand for "column, row, full" checksum matrices respectively. By definition, column checksums are the (weighted) sums of every columns of matrix A, or mathematically $e^T A$. Row checksums are (weighted) sums of every row in A or mathematically Ae.

Another example is the LU factorization $A = LU$ where L is a unit lower triangular matrix and U is an upper triangular matrix. We may define the LU factorization operation as $P(A) = (L, U)$. To make LU factorization ABFT enabled, we encode the operand A into its full checksum form:

$$A \xrightarrow{\text{encode}} A^f = \begin{bmatrix} A & Ae \\ e^T A & e^T Ae \end{bmatrix}$$

then we apply P on A^f and the results are two automatically checksum encoded matrices:

$$P(A^f) = (L^c, U^r)$$

After the operation on the encoded matrix, we end up with the encoded result that includes our desired output and its checksums. We can verify the result by checking the matrix against its checksums: a match means the operation is carried out correctly and a mismatch indicates a problem. Of course, "match" here means within roundoff error bounds since floating point arithmetics are not exact.

2.2 Block algorithms

Modern dense linear algebra algorithms are arranged in such a way that level 3 BLAS operations (basically matrix-matrix multiplication) are used as much as possible for high performance. This results in block versions of the algorithms that "defer" many lower level BLAS operations and aggregate them together into a single level 3 operation later. It's called "block" because matrices are divided into rectangular blocks which, instead of scalars, are the basic units for the description of block algorithms. For example, the block version of the Cholesky factorization (as implemented in ScaLAPACK [13]) is given as follows.

Cholesky factorization turns a symmetric, positive definite square matrix into the product of a lower triangular matrix

and its transpose: $A = LL^T$. The factorization happens in-place: the result L overwrites the original A. At each iteration, we write the $n \times n$ matrix A as four blocks:

$$\begin{bmatrix} A_{11} & A_{21}^T \\ A_{21} & A_{22} \end{bmatrix} = \begin{bmatrix} L_{11} & 0 \\ L_{21} & L_{22} \end{bmatrix} \begin{bmatrix} L_{11}^T & L_{21}^T \\ 0 & L_{22}^T \end{bmatrix}$$

$$= \begin{bmatrix} L_{11}L_{11}^T & L_{11}L_{21}^T \\ L_{21}L_{11}^T & L_{21}L_{21}^T + L_{22}L_{22}^T \end{bmatrix}$$

The northwest block A_{11} is a $n_b \times n_b$ block; A_{21} is $(n - n_b) \times n_b$ block; A_{22} is $(n - n_b) \times (n - n_b)$ block. It follows that

$$A_{11} = L_{11}L_{11}^T \tag{1}$$

$$A_{21} = L_{21}L_{11}^T \tag{2}$$

$$A_{22} = L_{21}L_{21}^T + L_{22}L_{22}^T \tag{3}$$

If we solve the first Cholesky factorization of a block A_{11} from the first equation using unblocked algorithm we get L_{11}; then from the second equation we can solve L_{21} and from the third we have a new Cholesky factorization problem on a smaller $(n - n_b) \times (n - n_b)$ matrix A':

$$A' := A_{22} - L_{21}L_{21}^T = L_{22}L_{22}^T$$

Note that this step involves a matrix-matrix multiplication. It also turns out that this step accounts for the majority of computations. Repeat the above 3-step procedures, until the the whole matrix is factorized. In summary, each iteration in the block right-looking Cholesky factorization algorithm is a 3-step procedure:

1. xPOTF2: Cholesky factorize the diagonal block A_{11} from (1) and L_{11} overwrites A_{11}.

2. xTRSM: Solve the column panel L_{21} from (2) and L_{21} overwrites A_{21}.

3. xSYRK: Update the trailing matrix from (3) by $A_{22} \leftarrow A_{22} - L_{21}L_{21}^T$

3. ON-LINE ABFT DESIGN FRAMEWORK

Off-line ABFT works regardless of the actual algorithms used to carry out a particular matrix operation. For example, there are quite some different algorithms for matrix-matrix multiplication; off-line ABFT works with any one of them. No matter which algorithm is chosen to do matrix matrix multiplication, the checksums will maintain at the end of the operation. However, the checksums do not necessarily maintain *in the middle* of the multiplication; in fact, Chen etc [9] showed that among the algorithms to do matrix matrix multiplication, only one of them (outer product algorithm) can maintain the checksums *during* the multiplication. This seems to imply that designing on-line ABFT is harder than off-line ABFT since we have to choose a specific algorithm that has the special property to maintain checksums during the operation.

However, in this paper we'll show that it is possible to design on-line ABFT for *any* block algorithms, not only for one particular algorithm. For this we deploy two strategies: 1) we attach checksums to each block instead of to the whole matrix; 2) the checksums are only loosely related to their corresponding blocks but not part of the blocks. We found that these strategies allow us to easily design on-line ABFT checksum schemes for all one-sided factorizations and potentially for any other block algorithms that exhibit similar structures of one-sided factorization.

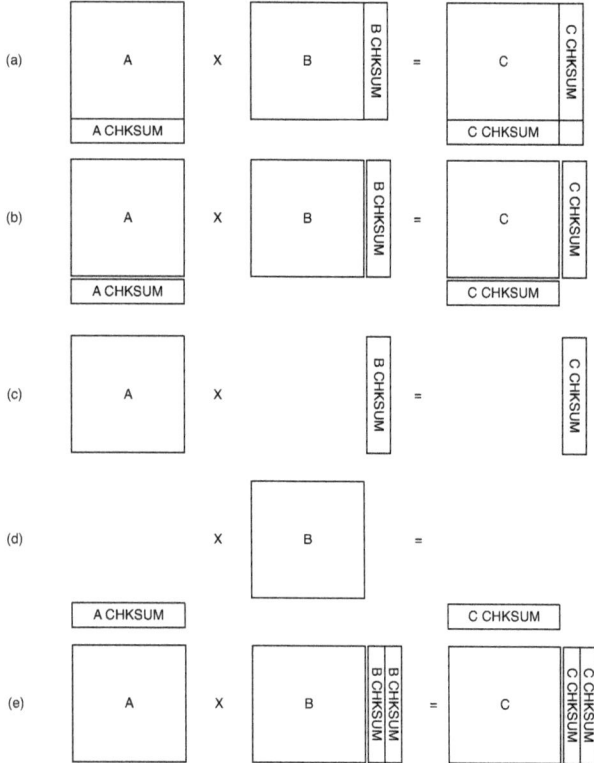

Figure 1: **Traditional ABFT matrix matrix multiplication and the separation of checksums with the matrices**

3.1 A Separation: checksum and matrix

Inspired by this work [27], we develop a different view on ABFT that separates checksums from the matrix. Let us see an example on matrix matrix multiplication. Originally, the idea of ABFT is that the product of two checksum encoded matrices is also a checksum encoded matrix, which is illustrated in Fig 1 (a). In (a), the checksums of A, B, C are parts of the encoded matrices. A different point of view is to separate the checksums from their corresponding matrices, as shown in (b). It follows that the row and column checksums of C can be obtained by multiplying A with the row checksums of B and the column checksums of A with B, shown in (c) and (d). Using this point of view on ABFT, we are no longer relying on the "automatic" update of the checksums as part of the matrix operation on the encoded matrix. Instead, we can manipulate the checksums freely, so long as the checksums are updated to remain consistent with their corresponding matrices at certain points. It then became possible to maintain the consistency of checksums with their corresponding matrix blocks in the middle of the matrix operation instead of only at the end, at the expense of having to manually update the checksums rather than relying on the automatic update by the matrix operation.

3.2 Double checksums

As shown in Figure 1 (a), there are two checksums for C—a row checksum and column checksum. Actually, to detect errors in C, one checksum is sufficient. However, to locate

and correct errors, multiple checksums are required. In fact, to be able to correct m errors, at least $m + 1$ checksums have to be used. In the simplest setting, two checksums can detect errors and correct up to 1 error. And it does not have to a row and column checksum; two row checksums or two column checksums also work for up to 1 error. Fig 1 (e) shows two row checksums for matrix matrix multiplication. We found that two row checksums or two column checksums work best, for reasons that should be clear when the on-line ABFT Cholesky is presented later.

Let us see a simple example on how two checksums can detect and correct up to 1 error in a matrix row or column. In this example we use two checksums with different weights: $e_1 = [1, 1, \ldots, 1]^T, e_2 = [1, 2, \ldots, n]^T$. Assume that a matrix row is $a = [a_1, a_2, \ldots, a_n]$ and it is supposed to have two checksums r_1, r_2 available

$$r_1 = ae_1 = \sum_{i=1}^{n} a_i$$

$$r_2 = ae_2 = \sum_{i=1}^{n} ia_i$$

Now we have a computed $a' = [a'_1, a'_2, \ldots, a'_n]$ with up to 1 erroneous element $a'_j \neq a_j$ where the error position j is unknown to us. We know the error exists if

$$\delta_1 = \sum_{i=1}^{n} a'_i - r_1 = a'_j - a_j \neq 0$$

$$\delta_2 = \sum_{i=1}^{n} ia'_i - r_2 = j(a'_j - a_j) \neq 0$$

And a simple division $\delta_2/\delta_1 = j$ would give us the error position j; further $\delta_1 = a'_j - a_j$ gives us the magnitude of the error from which the correct a_j can be recovered from erroneous computed value a'_j using δ_1 and position j.

Note that this example only shows a single row and its two checksums; the same procedure can be applied to each row of a matrix and its column checksums; therefore with double row checksums we can tolerate up to 1 error per matrix row at a time. After the current error is corrected, the same scheme can be used to correct the next potential error. **Therefore, this scheme can correct multiple errors if errors arrive one after another.**

3.3 An example: on-line ABFT Cholesky factorization

The objective of designing on-line ABFT is to maintain checksum consistency during the matrix operation. Specifically, as shown in Fig 2, we want the checksums of every involved blocks after each step. For example, after the first step that factorizes the block A_{11} into lower triangular block L_{11}, we want to update the checksums of A_{11} (denoted by $R(A_{11})$) to $R(L_{11})$. Similarly, we want to update the checksums involved in the second step and the third step $R(A_{21}), R(A_{22})$ to the checksums of the outputs $R(L_{21}), R(A'_{22})$. Fig 2 illustrates the idea of updating the checksums of the involved blocks at the end of every step in every iteration.

In Fig 2, (a) illustrates the 2nd iteration of the block right looking Cholesky factorization algorithm. Every iteration consists of 3 steps: the first step factorizes the diagonal block A_{11}; the second step updates the panel matrix blocks A_{21}; the third step updates the trailing matrix A_{22}. Subfigures (b), (c), (d) illustrate the three steps that update A_{11}, A_{21}, A_{22} to L_{11}, L_{21}, L_{22} respectively. Note that after updating the blocks, we also need to update their corresponding checksums, as shown in subfigures (b), (c), (d) lower parts. For example, in subfigure (b), we need to somehow update $R(A_{11})$ to $R(L_{11})$ in such a way that if $R(L_{11})$ remains the checksums of L_{11} if and only if the xPOTF2 procedure is carried out correctly.

The method to update of $R(A_{11})$ can be derived by examine the partial unblocked Cholesky factorization (xPOTF2) on matrix $\begin{bmatrix} A_{11} \\ R(A_{11}) \end{bmatrix}$. However, the result is independent of the specific algorithm used in xPOTF2. See the first part of subsection 4.3 for details.

After the update $R(A_{11}) \rightarrow R(L_{11})$, the updated checksum will be consistent with the updated block unless the Cholesky factorization on A_{11} is faulty. This is the basis on which we can use the checksum to check whether the xPOTF2 is carried out without faults.

We further need to do the same thing on the second and third steps. Fortunately, it is easier than the first step.

The second step is to update the panel matrix A_{21} using the result of the first step L_{11}. The triangular solve can be described mathematically:

$$A_{21} \times (L_{11}^T)^{-1} \rightarrow L_{21}$$

The obvious way to update the checksums of the panel matrix A_{21} is

$$R(A_{21}) \times (L_{11}^T)^{-1} \rightarrow R(L_{21})$$

Similarly, the third step is mathematically:

$$A_{22} - L_{21} \times (L_{21})^T \rightarrow L_{22}$$

The checksums of the trailing matrix A_{22} can be updated by

$$R(A_{22}) - R(L_{21}) \times (L_{21})^T \rightarrow R(L_{22})$$

The validity of the updates to the second and third steps can be easily seen and understood, once we note that the checksums of a matrix is just a product of a matrix and checksum vector:

$$R(A) = e^T \times A$$

where e is a predefined (column) vector or a predefined matrix consisting of several (column) vectors.

3.4 A framework to design on-line ABFT for block algorithms

Now that we can update the checksums after each step and we can use the checksums to verify every step in every iteration of the Cholesky factorization, we in effect achieved "on-line" ABFT on this particular Cholesky factorization algorithm. Because the correctness of each step is verified, no error can escape and propagate. In the meantime, simple errors (single error per column) can be effectively corrected by checksums. These two properties of "on-line" ABFT significantly improves the resilience of ABFT approaches. Furthermore, the ability to verify the correctness continuously also provides otherwise missing information for other layers of fault tolerance such as checkpoint/rollback etc.

After examining the right-looking block Cholesky factorization algorithm and the method to maintain checksums,

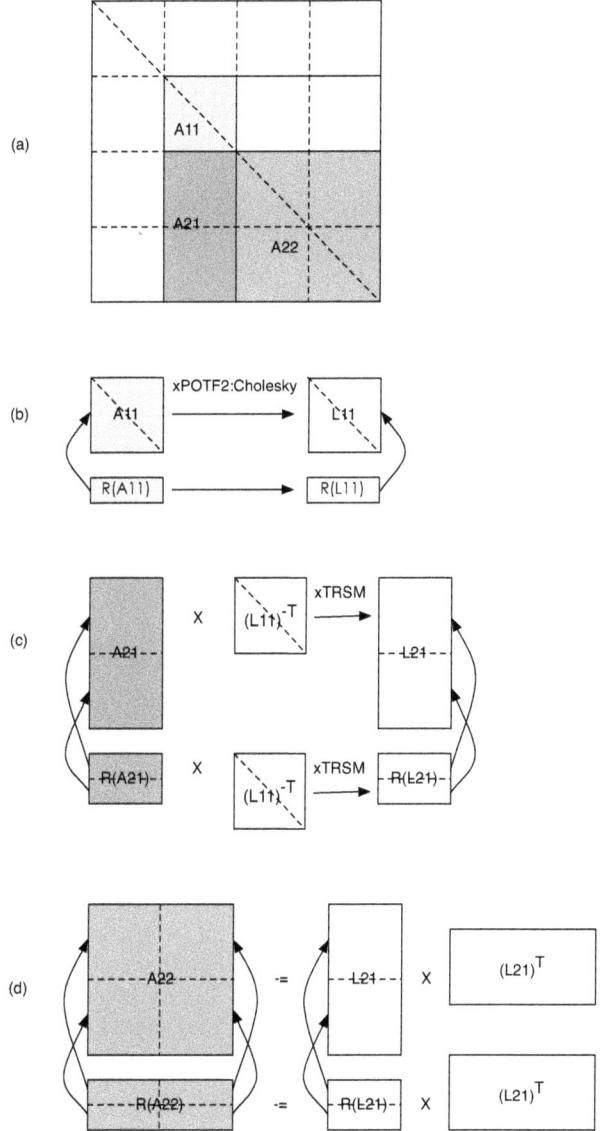

Figure 2: **On-line ABFT Cholesky** (a) the snapshot of the second iteration in a right-looking block Cholesky factorization algorithm. (b) the first step in this iteration is unblocked Cholesky factorization on A_{11}. (c) the second step in this iteration is a triangular solve to update the panel matrix; the checksums can be updated accordingly. (d) the third step is matrix multiplication to update trailing matrix; the checksums can be updated accordingly.

we can summarize a systematic way to derive checksum schemes for potentially many block linear algebra algorithms. First, we look at the description of the block algorithm at the block level; it usually consists of several steps in every iteration. The first step is usually updating the diagonal block (A_{11}) using unblocked factorization. The following steps update the panel matrix (A_{21}) and trailing matrix (A_{22}) using some kind of matrix multiplication. To update the checksums for the first step, we just need to attach the checksums to the block and do a "partial" factorization on them (see subsection 4.3). To update the checksums for the following matrix multiplication steps, we just need to multiply the checksums with proper matrix, as shown in Fig 2 (c) (d).

Using this framework, we can derive "on-line" ABFT for all one-sided factorizations LU, QR, and Cholesky; the details vary but the principles apply. LU usually comes with partial pivoting which involves swapping rows; QR has a more complicated matrix multiplication update step. See section 4 for details on how to customize the checksum scheme for all one-sided factorization.

4. ON-LINE ABFT ENABLED ONE-SIDED FACTORIZATIONS

In this section, additional one-sided factorization LU and QR and their customized "on-line" ABFT checksum schemes are discussed in detail. The missing part on how to update the checksums after the unblocked factorization step will be discussed thoroughly. Note in this section, in order to save space we may also use $[A; B]$ to denote a vertically stacked matrix $\begin{bmatrix} A \\ B \end{bmatrix}$, while $[A, B]$ denotes a horizontally stacked matrix $\begin{bmatrix} A & B \end{bmatrix}$.

4.1 LU

The LU factorization is essentially Gaussian elimination that factorizes a $M \times N$ matrix into $A = PLU$, where A and L is $M \times N$ matrices and U is $N \times N$ matrix. L is unit lower triangular and U is upper triangular; P is permutation matrix, which is stored in a vector IPIV.

The block right-looking LU factorization algorithm follows very similar structure of the Cholesky factorization algorithm described in the previous section. It is a series of iterations, with each iteration processing the trailing matrix of the previous iteration. The second iteration is illustrated in fig 3 (a). Every iteration is a 4-step process which can be described mathematically as follows.

1. xGETF2: Apply the (unblocked) LU factorization on the panel matrix $[A_{11}; A_{21}]$. This results in the upper triangular matrix U_{11} and lower triangular matrix L_{11} and the updated panel matrix blocks L_{21}, as shown in fig 3 (a).

2. xLASWP: Apply row interchanges to the left and right of the panel.

3. xTRSM: Solve the row panel U_{12} by $U_{12} \leftarrow (L_{11})^{-1} A_{12}$.

4. xGEMM: Update the trailing matrix A_{22} by $A'_{22} \leftarrow A_{22} - L_{21} U_{12}$.

Applying the framework described in section 3, we can derive the scheme to update checksums after each step.

The update to the checksums of the first steps can be derived from partial LU factorization on $\begin{bmatrix} A_{11} & R(A_{11}) \\ A_{21} & R(A_{21}) \end{bmatrix}$, which will be discussed in subsection 4.3. This results in the checksums of upper triangular block U_{11} and the lower part U_{21} which is zero.

The second step, not shown in fig 3 is applying row interchanges to the left and right of the panel. If the checksums rows are interchanged according to the matrix rows the checksums will stay consistent after the update.

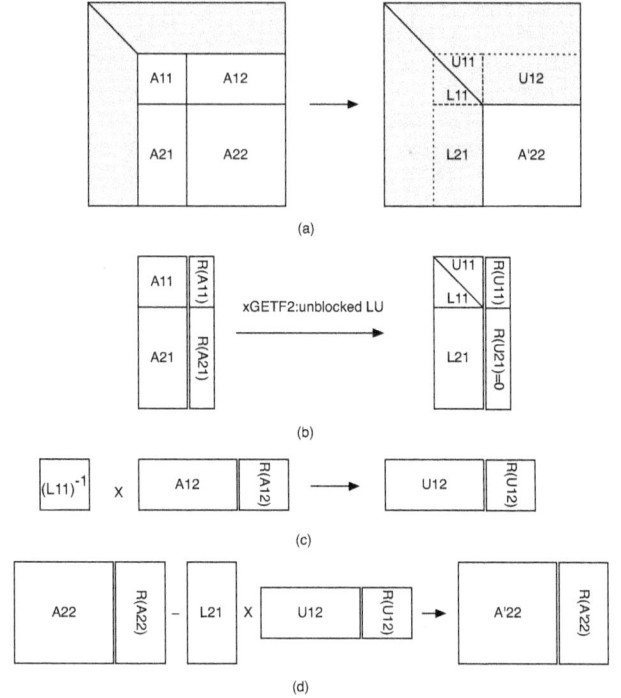

Figure 3: **On-line ABFT LU** (a) a snapshot of one iteration in a right looking block LU factorization algorithm: before and after. (b) the first step in this iteration is to update the column panel matrix by unblocked LU; the checksums are updated to checksums of right factor U_{11}, U_{21}. (c) second step is to update the row panel matrix by triangular solve; the checksums of the panel matrix can be updated accordingly. (d) the third step is matrix multiplication to update the trailing matrix; the checksums of the trailing matrix can be updated accordingly.

The third and fourth steps are essentially matrix multiplications. Again, we update the checksums by multiplying appropriate checksums with matrices, as shown in fig 3 (c) and (d).

4.2 QR

The QR factorization takes a $M \times N$ matrix A and factorizes it into the product $A = QR$ where Q is a $M \times M$ orthogonal matrix and R is upper triangular matrix.

The computation of block QR algorithm can be summarized as three steps in every iteration:

1. xGEQR2: Apply the (unblocked) QR factorization on the panel matrix $[A_{11}; A_{21}]$. This results in the upper triangular matrix R_{11} and the Householder vectors stored in V, as shown in Figure 4 (a).

2. xLARFT: From the Householder vectors a factor matrix T is computed, such that the Householder matrix factor is $Q = V^T \times T \times V$

3. xLARFB: Update the trailing matrix A_{22} by $A'_{22} \leftarrow (I - VT^TV^T)A_{22}$.

Applying the "on-line" ABFT block algorithm framework, we want to update the checksums of the involved blocks

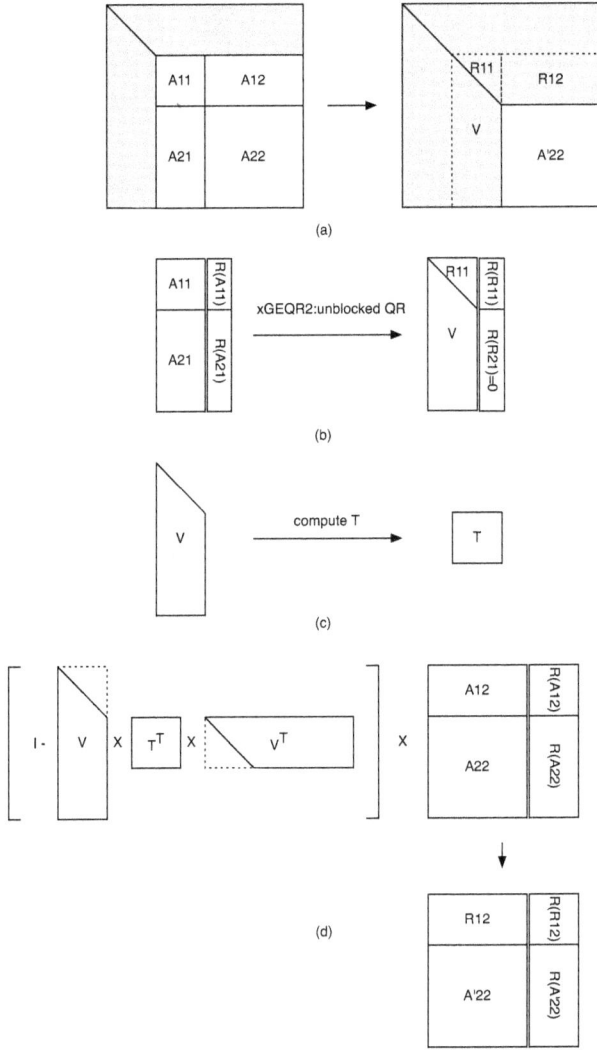

Figure 4: **On-line ABFT QR** (a) a snapshot of one iteration in right-looking block QR algorithm: before and after. (b) first step is updating column panel matrix by unblocked QR; checksums are updated to the checksums of right factor R_{11}, R_{21}. (c) the second step is to derive factor matrix T (d) the third step is to update the trailing matrix by matrix multiplication; the checksums can be updated accordingly.

for every step. Like in the case in LU, the update to the checksums for the first step can be derived by doing partial QR factorization on $\begin{bmatrix} A_{11} & R(A_{11}) \\ A_{21} & R(A_{21}) \end{bmatrix}$ which will result in the checksums of the upper triangular block R_{11} and the lower part R_{21} which is 0.

The second step is computing Householder factor T from Householder vectors in V. This step cannot be protected by checksums; however we could test the orthogonality of $K = I - VT^TV^T$ by verifying the property that orthogonal transformations preserve 2-norm. In other words, for any vector x, we should have $\|Kx\|_2 = \|x\|_2$. To efficiently evaluate Kx we can use the associativity of matrix multiplication to reduce the computation cost by $Kx =$

$(I - VT^TV^T)x = x - V(T^T(V^Tx))$. The runtime overhead for the verification can be shown to be insignificant, and upon failure of the test, we can regenerate T from V.

The third step is essentially matrix multiplication. We update the checksums by multiplying the left factor to the checksums of A_{22} to obtain the checksums of A'_{22}.

4.3 Partial factorization

This subsection will discuss the missing part of the whole scheme—how to do partial factorization and derive the method to update checksums after the first step in LU, QR, and Cholesky factorizations.

First let us take the Cholesky factorization for an example. The (unblocked) Cholesky procedure that factorizes the block A_{11}—xPOTF2—is the outer-product version of Cholesky factorization. It can be described as Algorithm 1:

Algorithm 1 (out product unblocked Cholesky) Given a symmetric positive definite $A \in R^{n \times n}$, the following algorithm computes the L such that $A = LL^T$ and L overwrites the lower triangular part of A.

1: **for** $j = 1 : n$ **do**
2: $A(j, j) \leftarrow \sqrt{A(j, j)}$
3: **if** $j < n$ **then**
4:    $A(j+1 : n, j) \leftarrow A(j+1 : n, j)/A(j, j)$
5:    $A(j+1 : n, j+1 : n) \leftarrow A(j+1 : n, j+1 : n) - A(j+1 : n, j) \cdot A(j+1 : n, j)^T$
6: **end if**
7: **end for**

Suppose before the factorization we have the column checksum of A which we denote as $r := e^TA$. After the above factorization, A is factorized and overwritten by the factor L. We want to update r so that r equals to e^TL and r can be used to check L (apparently we cannot sum L up to get r, in which case r cannot be used to check L). The method to derive such update is to do the above factorization over $[A; r]$ partially instead of over A fully. If we plug in $[A; r]$ into the above algorithm, the last row which is our checksum r will be updated as in algorithm 2.

Algorithm 2 Given a positive definite matrix $A \in \mathbb{R}^{n \times n}$ and its column checksum $r = e^TA$, after Cholesky factorization $A = LL^T$, this algorithm updates the checksum r such that r will be the row checksum of L, i.e $r = e^TL$.

1: **for** $j = 1 : n$ **do**
2: $r(j) \leftarrow r(j)/A(j, j)$ ▷ line 4 in Alg 1
3: $r(j+1 : n) \leftarrow r(j+1 : n) - r(j) \cdot A(j+1 : n, j)^T$ ▷ line 5 in Alg 1
4: **end for**

Because the checksum r is updated as a part in $[A; r]$ and the line 4 and 5 in algorithm 1 are all linear operations, the resulting r will still be checksum of A (which has been overwritten by L) at the end; i.e. $r = e^TL$.

Now let us look at the LU case. As usual, we first write down the outer product unblocked LU factorization as algorithm 3.

Since algorithm 3 involves row swapping, column checksums are hard to maintain. We therefore choose to use a row checksum $r = Ae$. If we swap the rows of checksums

Algorithm 3 (outer product unblocked LU) Given a matrix $A \in \mathbb{R}^{m \times n}$ ($m \geq n$), the following algorithm factorizes A into $A = PLU$ where $L \in \mathbb{R}^{m \times n}$ is a unit lower triangular matrix that overwrites the lower triangular part of A, and $U \in \mathbb{R}^{n \times n}$ is a upper triangular matrix that overwrites the upper triangular part of A. P is permutation matrix stored in a vector $IPIV$

```
1: for j = 1 : n − 1 do
2:     Find the pivot row index i = arg max_{j≤k≤m} |A(k,j)|
3:     IPIV(j) ← i
4:     Swap row i with row j: A(i,:) ↔ A(j,:)
5:     if A(j,j) ≠ 0 then
6:         A(j + 1 : m, j) = A(j + 1 : m, j)/A(j, j)
7:         A(j + 1 : m, j + 1 : n) = A(j + 1 : m, j + 1 :
          n) − A(j + 1 : m, j)A(j, j + 1 : n)
8:     end if
9: end for
```

in accordance with the swapping of matrix A in this algorithm, the row checksum will remain consistent. Similar to the Cholesky case, we apply this algorithm 3 on $[A; r]$ instead of on A; the resulting update procedure is described in algorithm 4.

Algorithm 4 Given a matrix $A \in \mathbb{R}^{m \times n}$ ($m \geq n$) and its column checksum $r = Ae$, after LU factorization $A = PLU$, this algorithm updates the checksum r such that r will become the column checksum of $[U; 0] \in \mathbb{R}^{m \times n}$, i.e. $r = [Ue; 0] \in \mathbb{R}^m$

```
1: for j = 1 : n − 1 do
2:     Swap row j with row IPIV(j): r(j) ↔ r(IPIV(j))
       ▷ line 4 in Alg 3
3:     if A(j,j) ≠ 0 then
4:         r(j + 1 : m) = r(j + 1 : m) − A(j + 1 : m, j)r(j)
           ▷ line 7 in Alg 3
5:     end if
6: end for
```

Again, because the operations in line 4 and 7 in algorithm 3 are all linear, after LU on A and the algorithm 4 on r, the updated A and r will still be consistent in the sense that $r = [U; 0]e$ holds.

The last case of the one-sided factorizations is QR. As usual, we first write down the outer product unblock QR factorization. It will be more complicated than the previous two factorizations, but still the structures are the same the same design can be applied.

We also choose to use row checksum $r = Ae$. Applying algorithm 5 on $[A, r]$ instead of on A we derive the algorithm 6 that updates the checksum r so that $r = [R; 0]e$

After performing algorithm 6 on r, the updated r will become the row checksum of $[R; 0]$ ($r = [R; 0]e$). This concludes our description on how to derive the method to update checksums for the first steps in LU, QR, and Cholesky factorization. Note that this subsection only derives the update methods (algorithms 2, 4, 6) based on but *not* relied on outer product unblocked LU, QR, and Cholesky algorithms (algorithms 1, 3, 5); actually, the update algorithms 2, 4, 6 work with *any* LU, QR, Cholesky factorization algorithms, not only with the out product versions.

Algorithm 5 (outer product unblocked QR) Given a matrix $A \in \mathbb{R}^{m \times n}$ ($m \geq n$), this algorithm finds Householder matrices $H_1, \ldots, H_n$ such that if $Q = H_1 \cdots H_n$, then $A = QR$ where $Q \in \mathbb{R}^{m \times m}$ is an orthogonal matrix and $R \in \mathbb{R}^{n \times n}$ is upper triangular matrix. Householder vectors $H_1, \ldots, H_n$ overwrite the lower triangular part of A and R overwrites the upper triangular part of A.

```
1: for j = 1 : n do
2:     [v, β] ← householder(A(j : m, j))
3:     A(j : m, j : n) ← (I − βvv^T)A(j : m, j : n)
4:     if j < m then
5:         A(j + 1 : m, j) ← v(2 : m − j + 1)
6:     end if
7: end for
```

Algorithm 6 Given a matrix $A \in \mathbb{R}^{m \times n}$ ($m \geq n$) and its column checksum $r = Ae$, after the QR factorization $A = QR$ this algorithm updates the checksum r such that r becomes column checksum of $[R; 0]$, i.e. $r = [R; 0]e$.

```
1: for j = 1 : n do
2:     v ← [    1    ]              ▷ line 5 in Alg 5.
             [A(j+1:m,j)]
3:     r(j : m) ← (I − βvv^T)Ar(j : m)   ▷ line 3 in Alg 5.
4: end for
```

4.4 Duplicate to protect panel blocks

Note in the LU and QR case, after the first step that factorizes the panel matrix $[A_{11}; A_{21}]$ and its row checksums, the checksums will become the checksums of the right factor (U in LU and R in QR) as shown in fig 3 (b) and fig 4 (b); the left factors L and Q will have no checksums to protect them. This means that even though errors in L and Q will be detected as erroneous left factor leads to erroneous right factor, the left factors have no redundant information to correct errors. To be able to tolerate errors in left factors we can duplicate the panel matrix in memory before the first step factorization so that if the first step proves to be faulty, we can rollback using that duplicate to repeat the first step factorization. This procedure only duplicate the current panel matrix A_{11}, A_{21} thus inducing little run time and memory overhead.

5. PERFORMANCE ANALYSIS AND EXPERIMENTAL EVALUATION

In this section we first introduce a model to analyze the overhead of incorporating the proposed on-line ABFT to ScaLAPACK factorizations. We then show the performance of our implementation of "on-line" ABFT enabled LU,QR, and Cholesky on up to 1600 processes.

5.1 Performance and scalability analysis

According to ScaLAPACK user manual [2], ScaLAPACK is "scalable" in the sense that, maintaining constant memory use per process (n^2/P), the overall efficiency should be maintained no matter how many processes are used. We argue that, adding "on-line" fault tolerance as described in this paper into the one-sided factorization subroutines in ScaLAPACK the scalability should remain the same. The overhead should be bounded by a small constant.

Table 1: The meaning of the variables in equation 4, according to [2]

Variable	Description
$C_f n^3$	Total number of floating-point operations
$C_v n^2$	Total number of data items communicated
$C_m n/NB$	Total number of messages
t_f	Time per floating-point operation
t_v	Time per data item communicated
t_m	Time per message
n	Matrix size
P	Number of processes
NB	Data distribution block size

Table 2: The value of the factor C_f, C_v, C_m for LU, QR, and Cholesky factorizations in ScaLAPACK according to [2]

	C_f	C_v	C_m
LU	2/3	$3 + 1/4 \log_2 P$	$NB(6 + \log_2 P)$
Cholesky	1/3	$2 + 1/2 \log_2 P$	$4 + \log_2 P$
QR	4/3	$3 + \log_2 P$	$2(NB \log_2 P + 1)$

A simple model of run time of one-sided factorizations in ScaLAPACK [2] is decomposing the time into computation, message bandwidth, and message latencies. It is not a very accurate model but a good enough first order approximate for the run time ScaLAPACK one-sided factorization subroutines. For our purpose to show the performance and scalability impact of "on-line" ABFT, we list the model here:

$$T(n,P) = \frac{C_f n^3}{P} t_f + \frac{C_v n^2}{\sqrt{P}} t_v + \frac{C_m n}{NB} t_m \qquad (4)$$

where n is the matrix size (assuming the matrix is $n \times n$ square matrix), P the number of processes, C_f, C_v, C_m the computation, message size and message number factors respectively (see table 2), and t_f, t_v, t_m the time per FLOP, interconnection bandwidth and its latency; see table 1.

The parallel efficiency [2] of a one-sided factorization is

$$E(n,P) = (1 + \frac{1}{NB} \frac{C_m t_m}{C_f t_f} \frac{P}{n^2} + \frac{C_v t_v}{C_f t_f} \frac{\sqrt{P}}{n})^{-1} \qquad (5)$$

5.1.1 Overhead for maintaining checksums

In order to correct errors in every row of every block at every iteration, two checksums for each row in each block are needed. After introducing checksums we are actually factorizing a matrix of size $(1 + \frac{2}{NB})n$. Our algorithms behave similar to the original ScaLAPACK subroutines. Therefore, similar to 4, our computation time can be modeled by

$$T'(n,P) = \frac{C'_f n^3}{P} t_f + \frac{C'_v n^2}{\sqrt{P}} t_v + \frac{C'_m n}{NB} t_m \qquad (6)$$

where

$$C'_f = (1 + \frac{4}{NB})C_f, \quad C'_v = (1 + \frac{4}{NB})C_v, \quad C'_m = C_m \qquad (7)$$

Plugging in new C's into equation 5 gives us the efficiency of "on-line" ABFT factorizations:

$$E'(n,P) = (1 + \frac{1}{NB + 4} \frac{C_m t_m}{C_f t_f} \frac{P}{n^2} + \frac{C_v t_v}{C_f t_f} \frac{\sqrt{P}}{n})^{-1} \qquad (8)$$

From the two running time equations 4 and 6, the performance overhead introduced by adding on-line fault tolerance is bounded by a constant factor $\frac{4}{NB}$, which is independent of P and often small because NB is usually in hundreds in today's optimzied library codes. Notice that, the only difference between equations 5 and 8 is the factor before the second term in parentheses. ScaLAPACK is scalable in the sense that, maintaining the local memory usage $\frac{n^2}{P}$ on each process will lead to maintained efficiency; and the larger the local memory usage per process the better efficiency will be. Equation 8 shows that our online ABFT factorizations are also scalable in the same sense as in ScaLAPACK.

5.1.2 Overhead for error detection

In order to detect errors, all elements in the same row of a block need to be added together and then compared to existing checksums maintained in the factorizations. The total number of FLOPs (floating point operations) to verify all checksums for all blocks in any processor is $\frac{n^2}{P}$. Therefore, the overhead for error detection is approximately $\frac{1}{n}$. Even if we verify correctness at every iteration (i.e., approximately every second in our experiments in Section 5.2) of the factorization, the performance overhead is still only $\frac{1}{NB}$, which is independent of P and negligible since NB is usually in hundreds in today's library codes. Hence, the scalability will be the same as the orginal ScaLAPACK

5.1.3 Overhead for error location

After an error is detected, in order to locate the error, the weighted checksum of the faulty row (or column) needs to be calculated. The total number of extra FLOPs to locate an error is NB. Therefore, the performance overhead for error location is approximately $\frac{NB}{n^3/P}$. Even if there is an error on every processor at every iteration of the factorization, the total overhead is only $\frac{P}{n^2}$, which is again negligible because the problem size n is often much larger than the number of processors P in today's supercomputing applications. Furthermore, the total overhead will not incease as the processor P increases if the size of the local matrix $\frac{n}{\sqrt{P}}$ on each processor does not decrease. Therefore, the scalability is not affected.

5.1.4 Overhead for error correction

After an error is located, the error correction is just simply adding the error back to the corrupted matrix element (see Section 3.1 for details), which needs only one FLOPs. Correcting k errors needs only k FLOPs.

5.2 Experimental evaluation

Our FT-ScaLAPACK implementation is based on ScaLAPACK 2.0.2. ScaLAPACK uses the so-called 2D block cyclic matrix distribution [3] to spread matrix and computation onto multiple processes to achieve load balance. The natural strategy to implement the "on-line" checksum scheme is placing the checksum on the same process where its corresponding matrix block resides. In this way checksums are always local to their corresponding blocks and all checking and correcting error procedures can be performed locally without inter process communication. Also, it is convenient to treat the checksums of the matrix blocks as a normal ScaLAPACK distributed matrix so that common operations involving the checksums can be performed using ScaLAPACK infrastructure. However, in order to eliminate extra communications to update checksums, we must aggregate the communication of matrix blocks and their checksums to avoid communicating checksums separately. In this way we can keep the number of messages unchanged but increase the message size a little bit which is reflected in Equation 7.

We implemented the double precision "on-line" ABFT enabled PDGETRF (LU), PDGEQRF (QR), and PDPOTRF (Cholesky) subroutines, indicated with prefix "FT-". We use double checksums for each block which means we can correct an error in every row/column of every bolck at every iterations in every processor. As we can see from section 4, except for Cholesky which has symmetry, checksums for the other two factorizations can only protect one factor of the factorization result: in $A = PLU$ checksums only protect U but not L and in $A = QR$ checksums only protect R. We used duplicates described in subsection 4.4 to tolerate errors in L or Q.

We run both FT-ScaLAPACK and ScaLAPACK subroutines on the Stampede supercomputer at the Texas Advanced Computing Center, which is a 10 PFLOPS Dell Linux cluster ranking #7 at the current TOP500 Supercomputers List. Each node has 2x 8-core Xeon E5 processors, with each core peaking 21.6GFLOPS. The interconnect is FDR 56 Gb/s mellanox switches organized in a fat-tree topology. We use all 16 cores in every node and 1 MPI task per core.

Software side, ScaLAPACK 2.0.2 from netlib is compiled against MKL 13.0.2.146 using Intel compiler 13.1.0 and Intel MPI 4.1.0.030. We only use MKL for its BLAS and LAPACK functions. For each factorization subroutine, we perform weak scaling tests; i.e. we scale the problem size with the number of processes and maintain the memory usage per process. For simplicity, we use square process grids $8 \times 8, 16 \times 16, 24 \times 24, 32 \times 32, 40 \times 40$. Since matrix A is distributed almost evenly on $P \times P$ processes, if we keep the memory use per process fixed at $F \times F$ double precision floats (for QR is $2F \times F$) then the size of matrix A is $(FP) \times (FP)$ (for QR is $(2FP) \times (FP)$). The parameters F, NB, M, N are indicated in the figure headers, where $M \times N$ is the shape of matrix A.

Figure 5 indicates: (1). The fault tolerance overhead fluctuates around 5%, which does not increase with the number of processes P and is not far from the theoretical estimation in subsection 5.1; (2). The total program execution times for both FT-ScaLAPACK and ScaLAPACK routines increase linearly as $\sqrt{P}$ increases, which implies both versions have constant efficiency and hence the same scalability. These experimental results confirmed our theoretical performance and scalability analysis in subsection 5.1.

6. RELATED WORKS

Offline ABFT methods usually can detect errors and correct up to a certain number of errors using some formulas after the operation [32, 35, 34, 29]. Although offline ABFT techniques usually have very small runtime overheads [20], they cannot stop errors from propagation and accumulation. Instead, they try to recover from the mess after the errors propagated and accumulated, which significantly complicates the error correction process and introduces at least

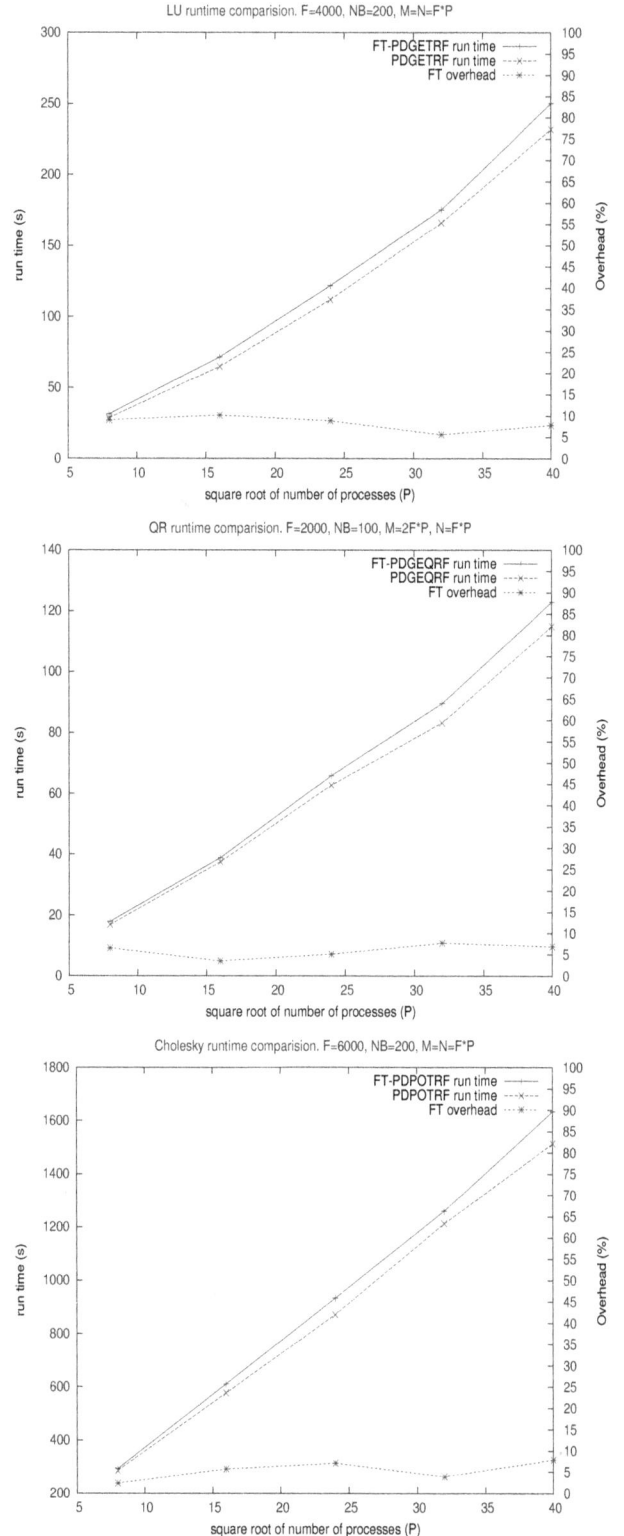

Figure 5: Run time for fault tolerant versions of LU, QR, and Cholesky in FT-ScaLAPACK and their original versions in ScaLAPACK. The fault tolerant versions can detect, locate, and correct one error in every row of every bolck on every processor at every iteration. On average, one iteration takes roughly one seconds in these experiments.

quadratically increasing overhead as the number of errors increases. Our approach on the other hand, tries to contain the errors from propagating and accumulating thus is more powerful in tolerating more errors at less overhead.

The state-of-the-art algorithmic technique for tolerating soft/hard errors are extensively studied in the recent PhD thesies by P. Du [18] and Z. Chen [8]. ABFT based approach to survive hard errors (fail-stop) for matrix multiplication, LU, QR, and Cholesky factorizations was well studied in [19, 17, 28, 10, 12]. But to survive soft errors in the matrix factorization subroutines, the jobs are arguably more difficult. Some study on LU [20] and QR [22] exist to deal with soft errors. The technical report by Du [20] proposes a technique to tolerate soft errors in LU, which is based on a mathematical model of treating soft error during LU factorization as rank-one perturbation to the original matrix and recovering the solution of $Ax = b$ with the Sherman-Morrison [25] formula. Although our one-sided factorizations we are dealing with here and the LU factorization discussed in paper [20] have the same goal, our approach is different in many fundamental aspects. Firstly while their work guarantees the solution x to the linear system $Ax = b$ is correct, we aim at ensuring that the factorization of $A = LL^T, A = LU, A = QR$ is correct. Secondly, their work casts soft errors occur during the factorization process to the original matrix thus avoiding consideration of timing of errors, our work deals directly with errors as they occur, as the factorization proceeds. Thirdly, after making some tradeoffs their works can effectively tolerate two soft errors in each block with minimum overhead, our approach has the potential to tolerate significantly more soft errors at the expense of a little bit more overhead. Lastly, unlike LU decomposition, Cholesky factorization can easily break down if soft errors happen to invalidate the positive definiteness of the matrix, in which case all off-line approaches would fail since the Cholesky factorization would simply not finish.

The pioneering works of on-line ABFT on matrix-matrix multiplication [9, 36] and LU factorization in HPL [16] are the main inspiration of our work. While those works went at length to design, validate, and analyze the checksum schemes for the specific algorithms they aimed at, we used a unified approach guided by a high level framework that we show can make the design, validation, and analysis of on-line ABFT checksum schemes with block linear algebra algorithms almost mechanical. We think this higher level viewpoint helps mitigating the disadvantage of ABFT that major efforts have to be made to design on-line ABFT for each algorithm. By making on-line ABFT design systematic and easier, we hope to see more commonly used algorithms and other fault tolerance techniques such as checkpoint/rollback, ECC [30], and hybrid memory systems using non-volatile memories benefiting more from on-line ABFT.

There are other fault tolerant techniques that can deal with SDCs in high performance computing that have various characteristics in terms of error detection and correction capability, runtime overhead and resources overhead [31, 11, 33, 5]. Among them, we compare our approach to node level TMR (RedMPI [24]). So far the RedMPI approach is the most general and powerful method to detect and tolerate silent (soft) errors. According the paper [24], RedMPI introduces overhead between 20% to 60% for triple redundancy, and 13% to 45% for double redundancy, depending on applications. To detect error at least double redundancy

is required, which means 2x nodes are required while to correct errors by voting at least triple redundancy or 3x nodes are required. Our approach is not as general and requires adaptions for each algorithm considered, but has much less overhead both in run time and node numbers.

7. CONCLUSION

In this paper we proposed a systematic way to design and reason about on-line ABFT that is resilient to soft errors for all three one-sided factorizations LU, QR, and Cholesky. We showed that by following a few principles, it is not hard to obtain correct and efficient on-line checksum schemes for LU, QR, and Cholesky subroutines used in ScaLAPACK and potentially many other block algorithms that share similar structure with them. We also showed that this approach can lead to efficient and easy to use implementations.

Acknowledgements

The authors would like to thank the anonymous reviewers for their valuable suggestions and the TACC for the use of Stampede supercomputer. This research is partly supported by National Science Foundation under grants #CCF-1305622 and #ACI-1305624.

8. REFERENCES

[1] Cynthia J. Anfinson and Franklin T. Luk. A linear algebraic model of algorithm-based fault tolerance. *IEEE Trans. Computers*, 37(12):1599–1604, 1988.

[2] L S Blackford, J. Choi, A Cleary, and E D'Azevedo. ScaLAPACK user's guide. 1997.

[3] L S Blackford, J. Choi, A Cleary, J Demmel, I Dhillon, J Dongarra, S Hammarling, G Henry, A. Petitet, K Stanley, D. Walker, and R C Whaley. ScaLAPACK: A Portable Linear Algebra Library for Distributed Memory Computers - Design Issues and Performance. In *Supercomputing, 1996. Proceedings of the 1996 ACM/IEEE Conference on*, page 5. IEEE Computer Society, 1996.

[4] G. Bronevetsky and A Moody. Scalable I/O systems via node-local storage: Approaching 1 TB/sec file I/O. *Lawrence Livermore National Laboratory Technique Report LLNL-TR-415791*, 2009.

[5] Greg Bronevetsky and Bronis R. de Supinski. Soft error vulnerability of iterative linear algebra methods. In Pin Zhou, editor, *ICS*, pages 155–164. ACM, 2008.

[6] Franck Cappello. Fault tolerance in petascale/ exascale systems: Current knowledge, challenges and research opportunities. *IJHPCA*, 23(3):212–226, 2009.

[7] Franck Cappello, Al Geist, Bill Gropp, Laxmikant V. Kalé, Bill Kramer, and Marc Snir. Toward exascale resilience. *IJHPCA*, 23(4):374–388, 2009.

[8] Z Chen. Scalable Techniques for Fault Tolerant High Performance Computing. Technical report, The University of Tennessee, Knoxville.

[9] Z Chen and J Dongarra. Algorithm-based fault tolerance for fail-stop failures. *IEEE Transactions on Parallel and Distributed Systems*, 19(12):1628–1641, 2008.

[10] Zizhong Chen. Optimal real number codes for fault tolerant matrix operations. In *SC*. ACM, 2009.

[11] Zizhong Chen. Online-abft: an online algorithm based fault tolerance scheme for soft error detection in iterative methods. In Alex Nicolau, Xiaowei Shen, Saman P. Amarasinghe, and Richard Vuduc, editors, *PPOPP*, pages 167–176. ACM, 2013.

[12] Zizhong Chen and Jack Dongarra. Condition numbers of gaussian random matrices. *SIAM J. Matrix Anal. Appl*, 33 (4), 2005.

[13] J. Choi, J.J. Dongarra, L S Ostrouchov, and A.P. Petitet. Design and Implementation of the ScaLAPACK LU, QR, and Cholesky Factorization Routines - Scientific Programming - Volume 5, Number 3 / 1996 - IOS Press. *Scientific . . .* , 1996.

[14] J T Daly. A higher order estimate of the optimum checkpoint interval for restart dumps. *Future Generation Computer Systems*, 22(3):303–312, February 2006.

[15] J T Daly, L S A Pritchett, and S.E. Michalak. Application MTTFE vs. Platform MTBF: A Fresh Perspective on System Reliability and Application Throughput for Computations at Scale. *CCGRID '08*, pages 795–800, 2008.

[16] Teresa Davies and Zizhong Chen. Correcting soft errors online in LU factorization. In *HPDC '13: Proceedings of the 22nd international symposium on High-performance parallel and distributed computing*. ACM Request Permissions, June 2013.

[17] Teresa Davies, Christer Karlsson, Hui Liu, Chong Ding, and Zizhong Chen. High performance linpack benchmark: a fault tolerant implementation without checkpointing. In *Proceedings of the 25th International Conference on Supercomputing, 2011, Tucson, AZ, USA, May 31 - June 04, 2011*, pages 162–171, 2011.

[18] P Du. Hard and Soft Error Resilience for One-sided Dense Linear Algebra Algorithms. Technical report, The University of Tennessee, Knoxville.

[19] Peng Du, Aurelien Bouteiller, George Bosilca, Thomas Herault, and Jack Dongarra. Algorithm-based fault tolerance for dense matrix factorizations. In *Proceedings of the 17th ACM SIGPLAN symposium on Principles and Practice of Parallel Programming*, pages 225–234, New York, NY, USA, 2012. ACM.

[20] Peng Du, P Luszczek, and J Dongarra. High Performance Linear System Solver with Resilience to Multiple Soft Errors. In *UT-CS report (UT-CS-11-683)*, pages 272–280, 2011.

[21] Peng Du, Piotr Luszczek, and Jack Dongarra. High performance dense linear system solver with soft error resilience. In *CLUSTER*, pages 272–280, 2011.

[22] Peng Du, Piotr Luszczek, Stan Tomov, and Jack Dongarra. Soft error resilient QR factorization for hybrid system with GPGPU. *Journal of Computational Science*, March 2013.

[23] K Ferreira, J Stearley, J H Laros, R Oldfield, K Pedretti, R Brightwell, R Riesen, P G Bridges, and D Arnold. Evaluating the viability of process replication reliability for exascale systems. In *High Performance Computing, Networking, Storage and Analysis (SC), 2011 International Conference for*, pages 1–12, 2011.

[24] David Fiala, Frank Mueller, Christian Engelmann, Rolf Riesen, Kurt Ferreira, and Ron Brightwell. Detection and correction of silent data corruption for large-scale high-performance computing. In *SC '12: Proceedings of the International Conference on High Performance Computing, Networking, Storage and Analysis*. IEEE Computer Society Press, November 2012.

[25] P Fitzpatrick and C.C Murphy. Fault tolerant matrix triangularization and solution of linear systems of equations. In *Application Specific Array Processors, 1992. Proceedings of the International Conference on*, pages 469–480, 1992.

[26] Al Geist. WHAT IS THE MONSTER IN THE CLOSET? Technical report, Oak Ridge National Laboratory.

[27] John A Gunnels, Daniel S Katz, Enrique S Quintana-Orti, and R A Van de Gejin. Fault-tolerant high-performance matrix multiplication: Theory and practice. In *Dependable Systems and Networks, 2001. DSN 2001. International Conference on*, pages 47–56. IEEE, 2001.

[28] Douglas Hakkarinen and Zizhong Chen. Algorithmic cholesky factorization fault recovery. In *IPDPS*, pages 1–10. IEEE, 2010.

[29] Kuang-Hua Huang and Abraham. Algorithm-Based Fault Tolerance for Matrix Operations. *IEEE Transactions on Computers*, C-33(6):518–528, June 1984.

[30] D Li, C Zizhong, W Panruo, and S Vetter Jeffrey. Rethinking Algorithm-Based Fault Tolerance with a Cooperative Software-Hardware Approach. *International Conference for High Performance Computing, Networking, Storage and Analysis*, 2013.

[31] Guoming Lu, Ziming Zheng, and Andrew A. Chien. When is multi-version checkpointing needed? In *FTXS*, pages 49–56, 2013.

[32] Franklin T Luk and Haesun Park. An analysis of algorithm-based fault tolerance techniques. *Journal of Parallel and Distributed Computing*, 5(2):172–184, April 1988.

[33] Joseph Sloan, Rakesh Kumar, and Greg Bronevetsky. An algorithmic approach to error localization and partial recomputation for low-overhead fault tolerance. In *DSN*, pages 1–12. IEEE, 2013.

[34] Michael Turmon, Robert Granat, Daniel Katz, and John Lou. Tests and tolerances for high-performance software-implemented fault detection. *IEEE Trans. Computers*, 52(5):579–591, 2003.

[35] Michael J. Turmon, Robert Granat, and Daniel S. Katz. Software-implemented fault detection for high-performance space applications. In *DSN*, pages 107–116. IEEE Computer Society, 2000.

[36] Panruo Wu, Chong Ding, Longxiang Chen, Feng Gao, Teresa Davies, Christer Karlsson, and Zizhong Chen. Fault tolerant matrix-matrix multiplication: correcting soft errors on-line. In *ScalA '11: Proceedings of the second workshop on Scalable algorithms for large-scale systems*. ACM, November 2011.

[37] Ziming Zheng and Zhiling Lan. Reliability-aware scalability models for high performance computing. In *CLUSTER*, pages 1–9, 2009.

When Paxos Meets Erasure Code: Reduce Network and Storage Cost in State Machine Replication

Shuai Mu*, Kang Chen†, Yongwei Wu†, Weimin Zheng†
Tsinghua National Laboratory for Information Science and Technology (TNLIST)
Department of Computer Science and Technology, Tsinghua University, Beijing 100084, China
Research Institute of Tsinghua University in Shenzhen, Shenzhen 518057, China
*shuai@cs.nyu.edu
†{chenkang, wuyw, zwm-dcs}@tsinghua.edu.cn

ABSTRACT

Paxos-based state machine replication is a key technique to build highly reliable and available distributed services, such as lock servers, databases and other data storage systems. Paxos can tolerate any minority number of node crashes in an asynchronous network environment. Traditionally, Paxos is used to perform a full copy replication across all participants. However, full copy is expensive both in term of network and storage cost, especially in wide area with commodity hard drives.

In this paper, we discussed the non-triviality and feasibility of combining erasure code into Paxos protocol, and presented an improved protocol named RS-Paxos (Reed Solomon Paxos). To the best of our knowledge, we are the first to propose such a combination. Compared to Paxos, RS-Paxos requires a limitation on the number of possible failures. If the number of tolerated failures decreases by 1, RS-Paxos can save over 50% of network transmission and disk I/O. To demonstrate the benefits of our protocol, we designed and built a key-value store based on RS-Paxos, and evaluated it on EC2 with various settings. Experiment results show that RS-Paxos achieves at most 2.5x improvement on write throughput and as much as 30% reduction on latency, in common configurations.

Categories and Subject Descriptors

C.2.4 [**Computer-Communication Networks**]: Distributed Systems–client/server; distributed applications; distributed databases; D.4.5 [**Operating Systems**]: Reliability–fault-tolerance; H.3.4 [**Information Storage and Retrieval**]: Systems and Software–distributed systems

Keywords

Paxos, erasure code, asynchronous message passing model, consensus, state machine replication

1. INTRODUCTION

Paxos-based state machine replication (SMR) has proven to be an effective approach to build highly reliable distributed services. For example, Google's Chubby[4] replicates important metadata through a couple of nodes, such as locks and configuration files in a storage system[7][9]. Since Gaios[3], Paxos has been used to replicate all user data instead of only metadata. Furthermore, systems such as MegaStore[2] and Spanner[8] use Paxos to replicate data across datacenters globally.

A key challenge of data replication through Paxos is the cost of network transmission and disk writes that need to be flushed to disk to tolerate crashes. And as the size of data increases, these costs increase. In an optimized Paxos instance, the value is required to be sent to a quorum of nodes at least once. And to tolerate more than minority crashes, all nodes need sync to disk on every acknowledged accept request in the accept phase. Both the network and the I/O costs can be expensive to achieve low latency and high throughput in a distributed system.

Erasure coding[22][18] is a very effective and common technique to reduce storage and network cost in data replication. Erasure coding encodes data objects into a configurable number of data fragments (including both original shares and redundant shares). From any large enough subset of these shares we can rebuild the original data objects. The redundancy rate of erasure coding depends on configuration. It is usually much smaller than making a full copy replication.

Can we extend Paxos to support erasure coding, instead of using the original value in Paxos? A naive approach to combine Paxos and erasure coding is to encode the original value into a majority of original data shares and a minority of redundant shares, and then send one coded data share to each acceptor. Because each share is smaller than the original value, network and disk I/O costs are reduced. However, this simple approach of injecting erasure code into Paxos is incorrect, mainly due to the asynchronous message passing model of Paxos (see details in Section 2.3).

In this paper, we examine the problem and present an improved protocol named RS-Paxos (Reed Solomon Paxos). By redefining the quorum number in each Paxos phase and correlated configuration of erasure coding, RS-Paxos incurs a huge reduction of message sizes, thus largely reducing network and disk I/O costs. A side effect of RS-Paxos is that it tolerates fewer failures than original Paxos in an instance.

But this is acceptable in realistic systems because most failures are one or two nodes. This is also the same assumption in EPaxos[20]. And by automatic reconfiguration of the state machines we can tolerate more failures in practice.

Most real-world Paxos systems takes the leader-follower design[4][8][6]. The leader acts as a distinguished proposer, in order to avoid live lock and save one message roundtrip. Leader serves all write requests and are in charge of proposing values. A follower usually redirects all requests to leader, unless the leader fails and it becomes the new leader. In certain cases, it can also serve read requests with relaxed consistency. RS-Paxos fits this pattern quite well. In RS-Paxos, the leader caches the original value itself, while sending coded shares to the followers. Both leader and follower only need to flush the coded shares into disks. A follower does not have to learn the original value immediately, since it redirects all consistent requests to the leader.

In the remainder of this paper, first we briefly go through the background knowledge and point out the incorrectness of an intuitive approach in Section 2. Next, Section 3 gives details of the design and algorithms of RS-Paxos. Section 4 presents a key-value store based on RS-Paxos. Section 5 is about implementation. We describe our experiments and evaluate the system in Section 6. Section 7 discusses about related work, and Section 8 concludes.

2. BACKGROUND AND PROBLEM

We begin by briefly describing the classic Paxos and erasure code algorithms, and an example showing the incorrectness of directly injecting erasure code into Paxos.

2.1 Paxos and SMR

The consensus problem requires a set of distributed processes[1] to agree on a single value in spite of possible failures. Paxos considers this problem in a partial-asynchronous system (partial-asynchrony is further explained in Section 3.1). Paxos assures that at most one value can be chosen (safety); if there are only a minority of faulty processes, all correct processes can eventually agree on a value (progress). Paxos does not tolerate Byzantine failures: A process may crash or fail to respond for an arbitrary long time; but it cannot respond in an undefined way; message corruption can be excluded by simple techniques such as checksums.

A single Paxos instance is barely useful in real systems. The more practical use is running multiple Paxos instances in a pre-defined order, such as to represent the state transitions of state machine replication (SMR). SMR is a classical approach to model and build a highly reliable and available distributed system. SMR aims to make a set of replicas execute the same commands (or make the same transitions) in the same order. For each state transition, a Paxos instance is run to decide what is the next command. Paxos instances can also run in parallel, as long as the decisions–commands are executed in the same order.

An unoptimized Paxos instance could go as following: When receiving client requests, a replica R picks the next unused Paxos instance, sends prepare messages containing a unique number to all replicas including itself. Upon receiving a majority of promises, R proceeds to send accept messages containing the command to all other replicas. If these messages are also confirmed by a majority of replicas, R then decides the command locally and notify all replicas. The majority rules can be replaced with read and write quorums. Any read quorum and write quorum must have an intersection part.

The canonical Paxos takes at least two roundtrips to commit a value. An important optimization in practice is Multi-Paxos. Multi-Paxos let one replica be the distinguished proposer and prepare a large amounts of instances at once, before the instances are actually used to propose values. This leader-follower variant of Paxos is widely taken in many systems such as Chubby, Spanner, etc.

After optimized, there are still two worth-noticing aspects of cost in Paxos. First, at least a full copy of the value need to sent to each replica, in the accept phase (the value sent in learn phase can be skipped, represented by a value id, assuming the target has received this value before). Second, in order to recover from failures, each replica has to log its decisions to disk whenever it responds to prepare and accept messages. In some cases, this can be avoided if we assume there is always a majority of correct processes (such as each process in a separate datacenter). But if we need to tolerate a majority crash such as in a power failures, this logging is necessary.

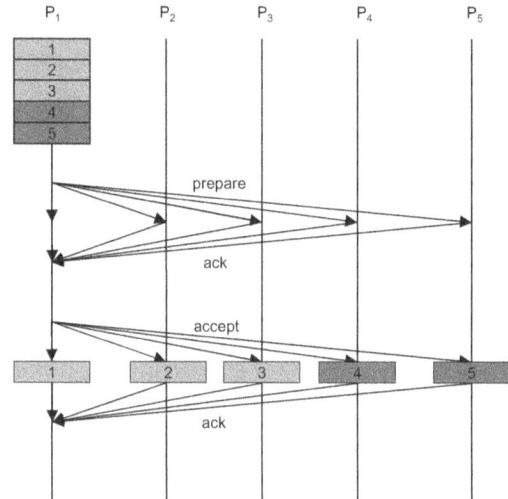

Figure 1: A naive combination of Paxos and erasure code. The configuration of erasure code is $\theta(3,5)$. The original shares (1~3) are colored as blue ; the redundant shares (4~5) are colored as red.

2.2 Erasure Code

Erasure coding is a very mature technique used in storage systems for data striping and fault tolerance. The principle of erasure coding is as follows. A data object is first divided into m equal-sized fragments called original data shares. Then, k parity fragments with the same size as original data shares are computed, called redundant data shares. This will generate a total of $n = m + k$ equal-sized shares. The erasure code algorithm guarantees any arbitrary m shares out of total n shares is sufficient enough to recon-

[1]In following sections we will use terms of *process*, *replica*, and *server* in a mixed manner, depending on context. They are synonyms in this paper.

struct the original data. Both m and k are positive values and configurable by users.[2]

Erasure code can reduce data redundancy in strict replication (full copy). Let r denote the data redundancy rate. For a strict replication with n copies, $r = n/1$. For erasure code, since each share is $1/m$ the size of the original data object, $r = n/m$. For example, if $n = 5$, $m = 3$, $k = 2$, the redundancy rate $r = n/m = 5/3$. The original data can be recovered as long as there are 3 replicas that are not permanently damaged. The space saved compared to full replication is $n - r = 10/3$ size of the original data object.

2.3 Problem with a Naive Approach

Since Paxos and erasure code can both be configured to be tolerant to a minority of failures, is it feasible that we can intuitively merge the two algorithms? The answer is no, it can be shown in a simple example.

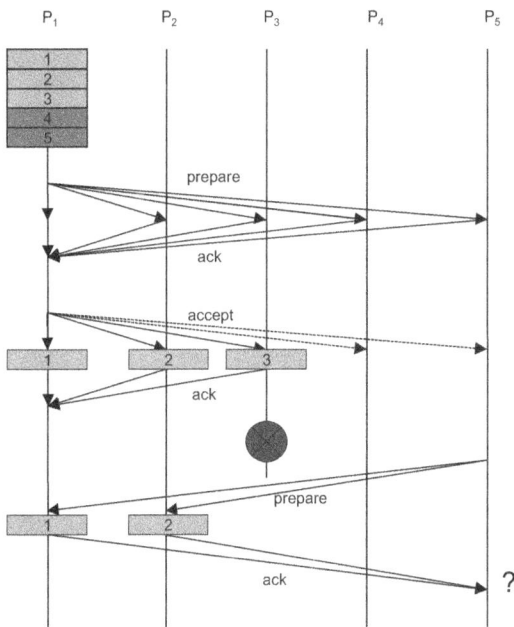

Figure 2: Incorrectness of an intuitive combination of Paxos and erasure code. After P_1 has decided the value, P_3 crashes, and P_5 tries to learn the value by sending prepare requests. The dotted line means the message is delayed or lost.

As shown in Figure 1, suppose there are 5 processes running Paxos (each processes act as proposer, acceptor, and learner at the same time). The Paxos protocol can tolerate any two crashes. The intuitive approach merging Paxos and erasure coding would be to configure erasure code as the same fault tolerant level as Paxos. In this example, say dividing the data into 3 original shares, and computing 2 redundant shares, which can be denoted as $\theta(3,5)$. The original data can be recovered with any 3 pieces of the data shares.

[2]There are many types of erasure codes, mainly in two categories: optimal erasure codes and near optimal erasure codes. In this paper we only refer to Reed Solomon code, a type of optimal erasure code.

However, this intuitive approach won't tolerate two failures as expected. A simple example to reveal this is shown in Figure 2. One proposer P_1 successfully passes phase 1, and goes into phase 2. In phase 2, it sends accept requests to all replicas. Each of these requests contains a coded data share. After a certain amount of time, it receives 3 acknowledgements saying the proposal is accepted. According to Paxos protocol the value is now legally chosen. But here, if one of the replica P_3 fails after this, a learner P_5 would never be able to recover the value, even though it may discover that there was a value accepted. Since it cannot gather enough pieces of coded data shares, it is unable to recover the original value and re-propose it again.

The nature of the problem lies: Paxos is a consensus algorithm used for multiple processes to reach an agreement on the same value, not 5 different values in the above case. This is why we cannot directly use the same fault-tolerant level configured erasure code on the value proposed in Paxos. However, on careful analysis, we will find that the five values are not entirely independent to each other, they are still related. The key observation of this paper is that from any large enough subset of them we can recover the same value, which we will leverage below.

3. RS-PAXOS

We now go through the details of RS-Paxos. First we give a brief summary of the assumptions, models and goals of our protocol. Next the detailed protocol, followed by a brief summary of the proof structure. At last we give an example of RS-Paxos in a common case.

3.1 Preliminaries

The problem is considered in a partial-asynchronous system. The nodes in the system exchange information by sending messages to each other. The messages can be delayed, duplicated, or lost. But if a correct process repeatedly sends a message to another correct process, eventually the message will go through. A more formal definition of "eventually" is that only after an unknown period of time γ, the messages can be delivered within a timeout Δ if the source and the target are both non-faulty processes.

The processes in the system act as the following roles.

- **Proposer** proposes values.

- **Acceptor** votes on values that are proposed by proposers.

- **Learner** learns if a value is chosen based on the votes of acceptors.

These roles are only logical, a process can and usually act as multiple roles. Different systems may have different role assignments. For example, a system may assign clients as proposers and learners, and servers as acceptors and learners. However, in many practical systems such as Chubby, clients do not directly propose values, but ask one of the servers to propose as instead. This is also our model in this paper.

To be correct and useful, RS-Paxos must guarantee the following properties.

- **Non-triviality**: Only proposed value can be chosen.

- **Stability**: Decisions can not be altered.

- **Consistency**: At most one value is chosen.

- **Liveness (Progress)**: Eventually a value is chosen.

The first three guarantees are usually called safety guarantees. Non-triviality is usually trivial. Stability means that for any process, if it decides a value at time t_1, then for any time $t_2 \geq t_1$, it will still decide on the same value. Consistency is the most important guarantee of safety, it means that for any two processes p_1 and p_2, if p_1 decides on a value v_1 and p_2 decides on v_2, v_1 must equal v_2.

The system can only make progress if there are a quorum of non-faulty acceptors, and at least one proposer and one learner that functions correctly.

3.2 Basic Protocol

The key principle of Paxos is that any two different majorities of processes have a non-empty intersection. And from that intersection a process can learn if a value is chosen or might yet be chosen. The insight of RS-Paxos is to increase the size of any intersecting set, so that it is possible to recover data from such intersections. Nevertheless, this approach unavoidably decreases the fault tolerance number of failed nodes.

Let N denote the number of acceptors; let F denote the number of failed acceptors that can be tolerated. Assume that proposers have different ids to identify themselves. Assume each proposer can generate a distinguished value id to identify the value to be proposed.

RS-Paxos shares many similarities with Paxos. The proposal in RS-Paxos includes following: 1) a ballot id, formed with the proposer id and a natural number, making it globally unique 2) a value id, to identify the value, which is also globally unique; 3) a coded data share, and the meta data of erasure code configuration.

RS-Paxos includes two phases:

Phase 1

(a) The proposer chooses a ballot id, sends a prepare request to at least a read quorum (denoted by Q_R) of acceptors.

(b) If an acceptor receives a prepare request with ballot id i greater than that of any prepare request which it has already responded to, then it responds to the request with a promise. The promise reply contains the proposal (if any) with the highest ballot id that it has accepted. The proposal contains a coded piece.

(c) The proposer waits until it collects Q_R promises. If no value is ever found accepted, then the proposer can pick up its own value for next phase. If any already accepted coded piece is found in one of the promises, the proposer then detects whether there are enough pieces in these promises to recover the original value. Next, the proposer picks up the recoverable value with highest ballot, recover it using erasure code and use it for next phase. If no value is recoverable, the proposer may also choose its own value.

Phase 2

(a) Based on the value v picked up in the previous phase, the proposer generates accept requests for at least a write quorum (denoted by Q_W) of acceptors. Every accept request should contain a coded piece of v. The piece is encoded with a configuration of $\theta(X, N)$, meaning that it divides the data into X original data shares, and computes $(N-X)$ redundant shares. After coding, the proposer sends these accept requests to acceptors.

(b) If an acceptor receives an accept request with ballot i, it accepts the proposal unless it has already responded to a prepare request having a ballot j greater than i.

(c) If the proposer receives Q_W of acknowledgements, the value is successfully chosen.

The two phase together with ballot i, we call it *round i*.

RS-Paxos is actually a superset of Paxos. In Paxos, $X = 1$. And if we take the canonical majority approach, $Q_R = Q_W = \lfloor N/2 \rfloor + 1$, $F = \lceil N/2 \rceil - 1$. In RS-Paxos, the size of the value in each accept request is about $1/X$ of the original value size in original Paxos.

The relationship between Q_R, Q_W, X, N is following:

$$Q_R + Q_W - X = N$$

This implies that any read quorum must have a non-empty intersection with any write quorum, which is a key to guarantee safety.

The relationship between Q_R, Q_W, X, F, N is following:

$$F = N - max(Q_R, Q_W) = min(Q_R, Q_W) - X$$

This tells us how to achieve the smallest data redundancy given a fault tolerate level. With a fixed F (then also a fixed $max(Q_R, Q_W)$), we have

$$X = min(Q_R, Q_W) - F$$

To get the maximum X, we need $Q_W=Q_R$ (also common in practice). The larger X is, the smaller the data redundancy will be, the more network and I/O cost we can save.

3.3 Proof Framework

Due to space limitation, this paper only conveys a brief proof framework. But given our proofs here, one can construct a full proof such as in [16] [15].

Non-triviality is straight-forward. Since all values are from proposers in phase 1(a), a value can only be chosen if it has been proposed.

Consistency can be proved by the following proposition.

Proposition 1 For any two rounds with ballot ids i and j, and $j < i$, if a value v has been chosen or might yet be chosen in round j, then no acceptor can accept any code pieces except those of v in round i.

Proposition 1 is equivalent to the following proposition.

Proposition 2 For any two rounds with ballot ids i and j, and $j < i$, if an acceptor has accepted a coded piece of value v in round i, then no coded piece other than those of v has been or might yet be chosen in round j.

To prove Proposition 1, we only need to prove Proposition 2. To prove Proposition 2, we still need to prove another proposition first.

Proposition 3 For any two rounds with ballot ids i and j, and $j < i$, if a value v has been chosen or might yet be chosen in round j, then the value must be recoverable in phase 1(c) in round i.

Proof Sketch for Proposition 3 If a value v is chosen in round j, it means that at least Q_W acceptors have accepted one coded piece of that v. The proposer collects at least Q_R responses after phase 1(b). The intersection part of Q_R and Q_W is X, due to the protocol. It means from the Q_R promises, at least X of them are from the Q_W acceptors those have accepted the coded piece of v. Since the coding configuration is $\theta(X, N)$, it means we only need X part to recover the value. Thus, v must be recoverable in phase 1(c). In the phase 1 of round i, If v is not chosen yet, for it to be chosen there must be at least Q_W of acceptors that will accept the proposal in round j. This means these Q_W of acceptors must see the accept message of round j before the prepare message of round i, otherwise v cannot be chosen. Since Q_R and Q_W have X acceptors in common, the value must be recoverable in round i.

Now we can prove for Proposition 2 and Proposition 1.

Proof Sketch for Proposition 2 If an acceptor A has accepted value v from some proposer P with a round ballot i, there must be a read quorum Q_R of acceptors have promised to P with that ballot id i. If a different value v' is chosen or might yet be chosen in round j, P must be able to recover v' due to Proposition 3. If P recover such value v', it will use v' as the value in the accept phase. Since P proposes v to A, such v' must not exists. Proposition 2 and proposition 1 are proved.

Because acceptors log their states into persistent storage that can survive crash, proposition 1 and 2 also implies **stability**.

Each replica keeps sending message to one another until it gets response. As long as at least a $max(Q_R, Q_W)$ of replicas are non-faulty and messages eventually arrive, **liveness** is ensured.

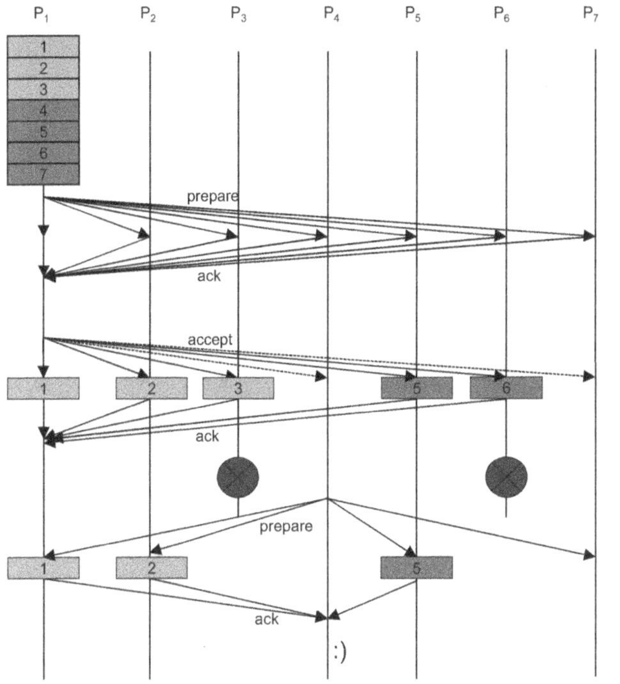

Figure 3: An example of RS-Paxos. $N=7$, $Q_W=Q_R=5$, $X=3$. With two lost accept messages and two replica crashes, the system is still safe.

3.4 An Example

Now we use a simple example to demonstrate the principle of of RS-Paxos. Suppose we have $N=7$ acceptors, and want to tolerate $F=2$ possible failures. Q_W and Q_R are both set to 5.

The procedure is shown in Figure 3. In phase 1, a proposer sends prepare to all acceptors. After it collects $Q_R=5$

N	Q_W	Q_R	X	F
7	4	4	1	3
7	5	3	1	2
7	5	4	2	2
7	5	5	3	2
7	6	2	1	1
7	6	3	2	1
7	6	4	3	1
7	6	5	4	1
7	6	6	5	1

Table 1: Various configurations when N=7. Given a fixed F, the configuration for maximum X is highlighted.

successful acknowledgements. It encodes the data with a coding configuration $\theta(3, 7)$. Each coded data share is $1/3$ size of the original data. Then it sends accept requests to everyone. Within each of these requests is a coded data share. Then it waits for $Q_W=5$ successful acknowledgments, after which the value is considered successfully decided.

After the coded value pieces have been accepted by 5 acceptors, if another proposer tries to propose, it will collect at least 3 coded data shares. From these data shares it can recover the original value and use that to propose again.

Table 1 shows about all possible configurations of RS-Paxos, when $N=7$. When a fault tolerance number F is chosen, there are different choices of Q_R, Q_W, and X. We highlight these lines in table that reaches the maximum X. With a maximum X, smallest amount of data $(1/X)$ is needed to be sent during phase 2.

4. A KEY-VALUE STORE BASED ON RS-PAXOS

In this section we go through our key-value store[3], which is designed to demonstrate the capacity of RS-Paxos. The rationales and techniques we use are mostly taken from previous Paxos-based systems[8][2] . This key-value store can be thought as a minimal functional component of these systems.

4.1 Architecture

The architecture of the key-value store is shown in Figure 4. Each a server has a persistent storage space attached. This storage space could be a local key-value datastore such as LevelDB and Redis. Or it could be distributed key-value storage such as HBase, depending on application requirements. Each server is responsible for one or more particular data shards. Of all the replicas in a shard, there is a *leader* replica which can provide consistent fast read and function as a *distinguished proposer*. Upon a client request (write), a leader start a new instance of Paxos, using it to commit a *write ahead log*. Once the Paxos instance commits, the leader commits the change log to its local persistent storage and returns to client. The Paxos instances of each data shard are committed and executed in a linearizable sequence.

---

[3]The system in this paper may seem closer to an *object store* to some readers. We just use the name of *key-value store* for simplicity.

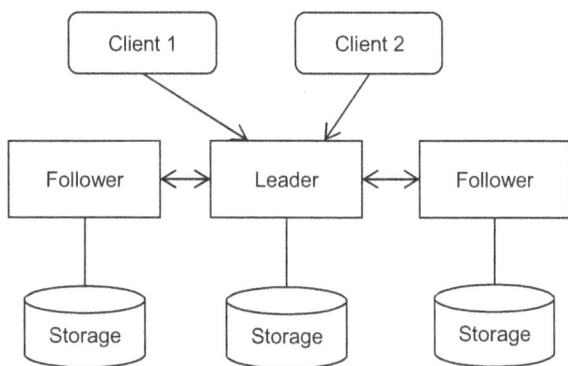

Figure 4: Architecture of the replicated key-value store

4.2 Data Shards and Paxos Groups

To improve throughput, data are partitioned into different shards. Operations on each shard run in a separate Paxos group. This is one common solution to reduce the unnecessary ordering inside a Paxos group, since canonical state machine replication requires all commands committed and executed in order to ensure linearizability.

To simplify, the number of shards are statically configured. The mapping relations of keys into shards is defined by a deterministic mapping function. The granularity of partition is controlled by users by configuring the number of shards and defining a proper mapping function.

4.3 Leader-leases

We use a very simple leader lease mechanism. Suppose the maximum time drift between different servers is δ. The leader maintains a lease which confirms its leadership in next Δ period of time. Each follower can only drops such lease in $\Delta + \delta$ of time.

The above leader lease mechanism can guarantee a solo leadership if all replicas always obey the time drift of δ. Spanner does this by introducing customized hardware (atomic clocks, etc.) and interfaces. In more common systems this is usually done by periodically time synchronization between replicas. Notice that even that leases are broken in rare circumstances and two replicas believe themselves to be leaders, (RS-)Paxos still guarantees safety of the system. But fast read may indeed return inconsistent data in such cases.

4.4 Data Operations

On client startup, it firstly gather the information that which replica is the leader of each data shard, and save this information in its local cache. Clients send their requests to the leaders. On most client requests (except fast read), the leader use RS-Paxos to commit the command as a write ahead log, then modify the actual data in its local storage.

Write. On write requests, the leader commit a log using RS-Paxos, containing operation type, key and value. Only the value are coded into pieces. This is for followers to conveniently tracking which keys are modified. Upon successful commits, the leader (which has the whole value) can write to its local storage, the follower (which only holds part of the value) also write to its local storage, but tag this value as incomplete. Notice that writes to local storage do not have

flush to disks, because we already have a persistent write ahead log committed to disks by RS-Paxos.

Read. There are three kinds of reads. 1) *Fast read.* The leader can return values in its local storage. The results are correct as long as leader leases works correctly. If leader leases are malfunctioning, the results may be inconsistent. For example, if two replica both consider themselves as leaders, one of them may server client requests with outdated data from its local cache. We do not have particular solutions for this, neither do we make the problem worse, and it is not our main concern. 2) *Consistent read.* The leader can invoke a explicit Paxos instance, which works as a mark, to read the value. It returns the value on commit of this instance. This approach always return consistent value in spite of the correctness of leader leases. 3) *Recovery read.* This happens when a new leader comes up to replace the old one. Because the new leader only has a piece of the value, it needs to scan through its RS-Paxos history, find the most recent write to that key, and run an explicit RS-Paxos to gather enough pieces of the value before it returns to client. Recovery read can also function as *snapshot read* if the application requires a snapshot version from a non-leader replica.

Insert. For simplicity, the insert operations can be treated as regular writes.

Delete. Delete operations are treated as *write(key, NULL)*.

4.5 Crash and Recovery

When a follower crashes within the fault tolerance level of the system. The system can still correctly server requests. Actually, the throughput of the system might increase because that fewer messages due to the crash.

If the error is fixed and the crashed server comes back online, it is essential that it is able to recover all its states including all including the maximum ballots it replied to and all the values it accepted. Otherwise the system will misbehave. That's why it needs to log all these decisions into disks before sending out the reply.

On recovery, the server needs to catches up all the chosen values in the instances it has missed. In Paxos, it only needs to ask for any other server that is aware of these values. In RS-Paxos, only the leader is aware of these decisions. Therefore, the leader needs to re-code the data and sends the corresponding fragment to the recovering server.

If a leader crashes, there will be a time window during which the server cannot server any new requests until a new leader takes over. Leader election can be a complex issue. Deciding a new leader is actually also a consensus problem. We simply use another Paxos instance to decide the new leader. After the new leader starts to serve requests in the system, it needs to perform recovery read to rebuild a local cache, in order to server fast read requests from clients. This will affect system performance. Write requests, however, are not influenced by this. When a new write request arrives, the leader can simply issue a new RS-Paxos instance containing the write request, even if it has not observed the previous value of this key.

4.6 Reconfiguration

Our design includes a classical way to reconfigure Paxos-based the state machines, aka *view change*. On adding a new replica or removing a current replica, a special Paxos instance *view change* is proposed, containing the new view

66

of the replicas. Each view change will give the Paxos group a new *epoch* number. Each epoch number represents a distinguished configuration of the system. Each Paxos instance should be attached with a correct epoch number to guarantee the quorum calculation corresponds to a correct view.

The view change also leads to new configuration of erasure coding. For example, the system currently has $N=5$ replicas, quorum $Q=4$, coding configuration $\theta(3,5)$. Now a new replica is added to the system, and the new configuration becomes $N'=6$, $Q'=5$, $\theta'(4,6)$. Strictly, the system needs to issue new RS-Paxos instances to re-code the data with the new configurations.

RS-Paxos contains a few optimization to reduce this cost. First, if the new configuration keeps the same k in the new $\theta(k,m)$, it is unnecessary to resend the original coded fragments again in the new RS-Paxos instances. For example, a previous configuration of $N=5, Q=4, \theta(3,5)$ is changed to $N'=5, Q'=4, \theta'(3,3)$. In this case there is no need to re-spread the data. The system only needs to launch an instance to ensure that every replica has its own data share.

Another important optimization also aims to avoid resending and recoding all data. If the quorum in the new configuration is greater than the number of original shares in old configuration, i.e. $Q' \geq X$, the system only needs to confirm that every server is already holding its data share. For example, with the old configuration $N=5, Q=4, X=3$, and a new configuration $N'=4, Q'=3, X'=2$, the system only needs to confirm every server holds all its data shares correctly when applying a view change. The insight of this optimization is that the fault tolerance level rules that at most $F=N-Q$ errors can be tolerated during an RS-Paxos instance. If the value is chosen at each server and each data share is stored correctly, the actual fault tolerance becomes $N-X$.

5. IMPLEMENTATION

Our prototype is implemented using C and C++. The core RS-Paxos framework is implemented in C. The key-value store part is implemented in C++. Since RS-Paxos is a superset of Paxos, we chose to firstly build a Paxos implementation, and then modified it to adapt RS-Paxos protocol.

RPC. We built an asynchronous RPC module for message passing between processes. It uses TCP as transmission protocol. This layer ensures that common network errors are handled properly, such as occasional packet loss and duplicate. Unit tests showed that it can complete over 1 million batched `ADD` operations in 1 second between two servers (using single CPU core each) in our local clusters.

Paxos. We built a Paxos implementation from scratch. Our Paxos implementation includes common optimization such as: 1) The leader do a batch prepare for a large amount of instances before it actually use the instances; 2) The commit message is delayed and bundled together and sent off the critical path of leader.

Erasure Code. We chose to use Zfec[25] as the erasure coding library, instead of on our own. A recent performance evaluation[21] shows that Zfec performs well and has relatively low cost.

6. EVALUATION

This section presents an experimental evaluation of RS-Paxos as the core protocol in a key-value store. The experiments include a series of micro-benchmark and a dynamic workload, including both intra and inter datacenter situations.

6.1 Setup

To test for how our key-value store functions, we configure the system with 5 replicas within a Paxos group ($N=5$). We have to make a trade-off in choosing the number of replicas inside a Paxos group. The benefits of RS-Paxos is more obvious as the number of replicas increase, but it is impractical in real systems to have a 100-replica Paxos group. If the size is very small, for example a 3-replica Paxos, RS-Paxos has no win over Paxos because it has to set $X=1$ to tolerate a failure, making it no different to Paxos. At last, we chose $N=5$, which is a common configuration in practical systems[4].

Both read and write quorum size $Q=4$, which means $X=3$, theoretically the message size should be about 1/3 about the original size (if the value is large enough). If one replica fails, the system is configured to change to a new quorum $Q=3$, and change to a new erasure coding configuration with $X=2$. This strategy allows the system tolerates two uncorrelated failures, given enough time for view change.

To increase parallelism, the whole key space is partitioned into 100 Paxos groups, following the typical configuration in practical Paxos systems[8]. A replica is configured to be the leader, which is responsible for all client write requests and is able to do fast read. In spite of our configuration, finer granularity of data sharding is totally possible. In real systems there could be thousands of machines and millions Paxos groups, and each server serves a certain number of Paxos groups[8]. But since scalability is not our concern in this paper, our full replication configuration is sufficient to observe the improvements of RS-Paxos to Paxos.

For comparison, we also test for a key-value store based on Paxos. The group size is also set to 5. Although strictly speaking, a 5-node Paxos offers stronger fault-tolerance than RS-Paxos. It can tolerate two concurrent failures, while RS-Paxos can only tolerate one at a time. Another possible configuration is to set up a 3-node Paxos group, which tolerates exactly one failure. Theoretically, the data redundancy of a 3-node Paxos group is 3/1; the data redundancy of a 5-node RS-Paxos group is 5/3. Therefore, a 5-node RS-Paxos is still better than a 3-node Paxos. The transformation from RS-Paxos to Paxos is very easy, simply to configure the quorum to be a simple majority and turn off the erasure coding function. In our evaluation, our major considerations include latency, throughput, computational cost and failure recovery.

Our experiment is run on Amazon EC2 platform. We use the `extra-large` EC2 VM instances in the `us-east-1` region. Each VM has 7GB memory and 8 virtual CPU cores, and connected by a gigabyte Ethernet network. 5 VMs are deployed as servers, and 10 VMs are deployed as clients. Each client VM serves up to 100 logical clients.

The above configuration shows the performance of RS-Paxos compared to Paxos in a local cluster environment. Inspired to see how RS-Paxos performs in various environments, we also emulate a wide-area deployment by adding a 50 ± 10ms delay to the network interface, thus having a

| (a) Local cluster | (b) Wide area |

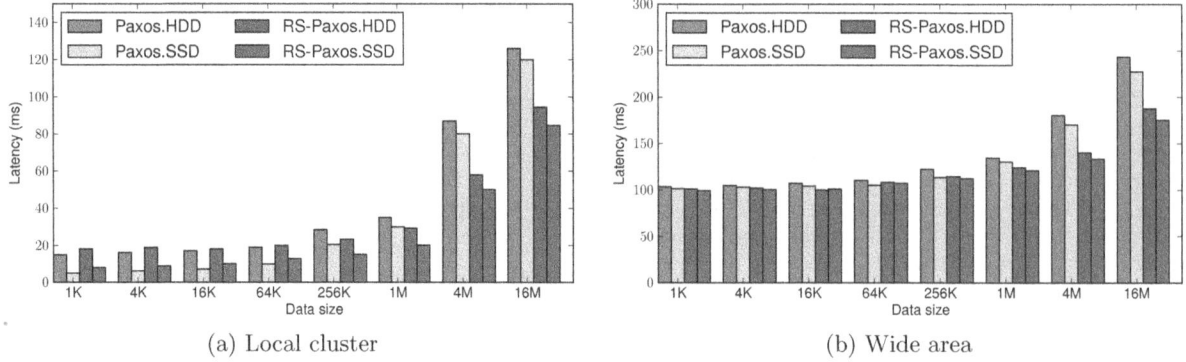

Figure 5: Micro-benchmark: Average Latency

100 ± 20ms latency for a message roundtrip. Also the bandwidth is limited to 500Mbps. We choose this rather than deploy in actual different EC2 datacenters, in order to keep the ability of a large bandwidth, to emulate the private network connecting different datacenters in enterprises.

To evaluate the performance of RS-Paxos in various storage environment, we use two kinds of EBS volumes in our benchmarks. One is regular EBS volume, with around 100 IOPS, representing traditional hard drives; the other is high-performance EBS volume, with over 4,000 IOPS, representing high performance solid-state drives. We will use .HDD and .SSD as postfix to distinguish in the following evaluation, such as RS-Paxos.SSD.

6.2 Micro-Benchmark

Our major concern is the performance of write requests, including the possible encoding overhead and the potential benefits of smaller amount of network transmission and disk flushes. And since we almost have no overhead on read requests compared to Paxos, we should supposedly have similar read performance. Accordingly, in this benchmark we test RS-Paxos with various sized write requests, to its maximum throughput. The value size ranges from 1KB to 16MB. We believe that larger sized data are usually chopped into smaller chunks, such as 16MB each.

6.2.1 Latency

Figure 5 shows the latency of various sized write requests in both local cluster and wide area. When measuring latency for a given size request, there is a fixed cost that the client send the request to the server, and the server reply to client when it finishes. Since this cost is identical for both Paxos and RS-Paxos, we remove it from our results for better comparison of cost that matters.

In the local cluster, when the request size is small (lower than 64KB), latency of both Paxos and RS-Paxos is dominated by file system flushes. Thus SSD can commit within 10ms, while HHD takes 20-30ms. RS-Paxos performs slightly worse than Paxos, due to extra computational time for coding. But for data object larger than 256KB, RS-Paxos has an obvious advantage. It achieves a 20%-50% lower latency, because it reduces the number of network packets and the number of the disk I/Os.

In wide-area deployments, the network becomes the dominating factor in latency. The CPU cost is hardly affecting RS-Paxos. RS-Paxos performs almost the same as Paxos at

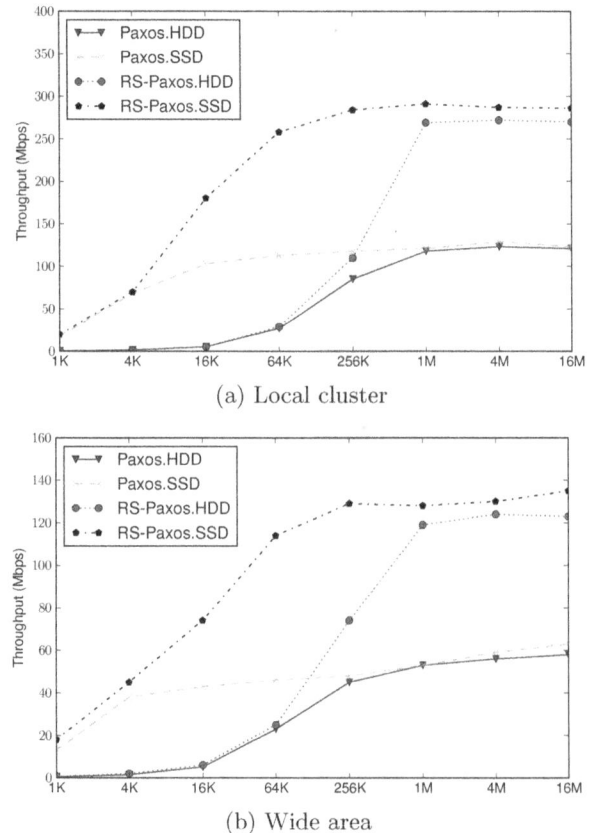

(a) Local cluster

(b) Wide area

Figure 6: Micro-benchmark: Throughput

small size requests. And with larger objects, the advantage of RS-Paxos is more obvious, saving more than 50ms.

6.2.2 Throughput

Since RS-Paxos can largely reduce the amount of data needed to be sent over network and flushed into disk, it is expected to have much better throughput than Paxos, especially for large writes. This is proved in this benchmark. Figure 6 show the write throughput of the system in both local cluster and wide-area.

In any deployment, the system is more disk-bounded for small writes. This is more obvious in HDD than SDD, which

68

is easy to understand because HDD has a much lower capability of handling small writes than SDD. When the data size is small, RS-Paxos performs no better than Paxos because it has the same amount of disk seeking and writing, touching the limit of disk access rates.

For HDD deployment, as data size grows larger than 64KB, the system becomes both network and disk bounded. And disk cost lies mainly on writing, rather than section seeking with small objects. In such case RS-Paxos performs about 2.5x better than Paxos, which is a giant improvement. For SDD deployment, this turning point comes smaller between 4KB and 16KB, due to its better performance with small writes.

6.2.3 CPU Cost

The major CPU cost in the system can be categorized as follows: ① Paxos logic; ② system calls such as epoll; ③ thread switching and synchronization; ④ encoding and decoding; ⑤ marshalling and unmarshalling. The overhead that RS-Paxos has over Paxos is mainly on ①④⑤. We try to measure and compare the CPU cost of the system by periodically sampling the CPU usage in the micro-benchmarks. In different setups, the CPU cost fluctuates around 10~20% per core, and RS-Paxos barely shows an observable overhead compared to Paxos. This is reasonable since such storage system is severely network and disk bounded, rather than CPU bounded. Our observation does not conflict with the fact that erasure coding may cause more overhead in other systems, because the amount of data the system handle per second is far smaller than it can compute in erasure coding. Even with the maximum throughput, the amount of data the system only needs to encode is less than 50MB. Moreover, it proves that it is fair to trade CPU time for a better system throughput in such storage systems.

6.3 Macro-Benchmark

To evaluate the performance of RS-Paxos in various workload, we built a macro-benchmark following Intel's COS-Bench[27]. The benchmark include four dynamic workloads, with different size ranges and kinds of requests.

One dimension to distinguish the workloads is object size:

- SMALL objects. Size range: 1KB~100KB.
- LARGE objects. Size range: 1MB~10MB.

Another dimension is read write ratio:

- WRITE intensive. Read write ratio is 1:9.
- READ intensive. Read write ratio is 9:1.

Each combination of the two dimensions above represents a dynamic workload. Every workload simulates the characteristics of real world workload. For example, the SMALL-READ workload represents a web hosting service, and the LARGE-WRITE workload represents an enterprise backup service.

In this benchmark throughput is our major concern. The results are as shown in Figure 7. In both local cluster and wide area, for small objects, the throughput of SSD is much better than HDD. This is true for both Paxos and RS-Paxos, which proves the same conclusion as in micro-benchmark, that small object size request is mainly disk bounded. Also, for large objects, the difference between HDD and SSD is much less obvious, since it is limited by bandwidth.

In either case, the read performance of RS-Paxos is almost identical to Paxos. This fits our expectation because Paxos

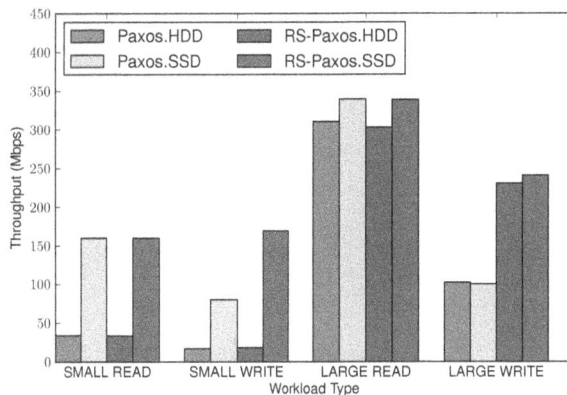

(a) Local cluster

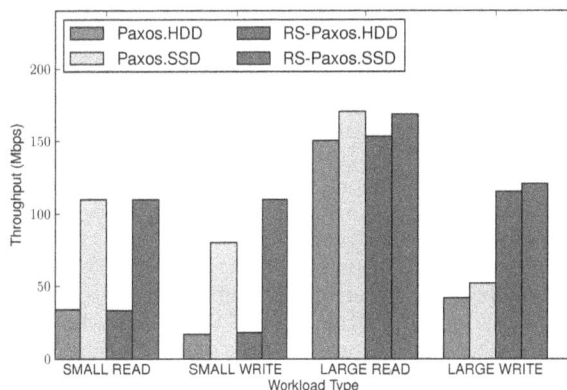

(b) Wide area

Figure 7: Throughput in different dynamic workloads

and RS-Paxos share the same mechanism in reading. Both of them do a fast read from local copy as consistent read, when leader leases holds up.

RS-Paxos performs much better than Paxos in the LARGE-WRITE workload, for both HDD and SSD. It also performs better in SMALL-WRITE workload, for SSD. This case suggests that as the disk performs increases, the advantage of RS-Paxos is more obvious, and the threshold of object size to observe that advantage will decrease, unless another boundary is touched, such as network or CPU.

6.4 Availability

In this part we evaluate the the behavior of RS-Paxos under uncorrelated failures. In our configurations, RS-Paxos can tolerate 2 uncorrelated failures, under the conditions that there is enough time for the system to perform view change between the failures.

To reduce the statistical influences of possible time skew on different machines in our observation, we choose to do this evaluation in the wide-area deployment. The test flow goes as following. Initially we keep the server fully loaded. Next we shut down the leader replica R_1. After a while another replica R_2 should become leader. Then we shut down R_2. During this procedure we keep observing system throughput on the next coming leading replica.

(a) Write intensive workload

(b) Read intensive workload

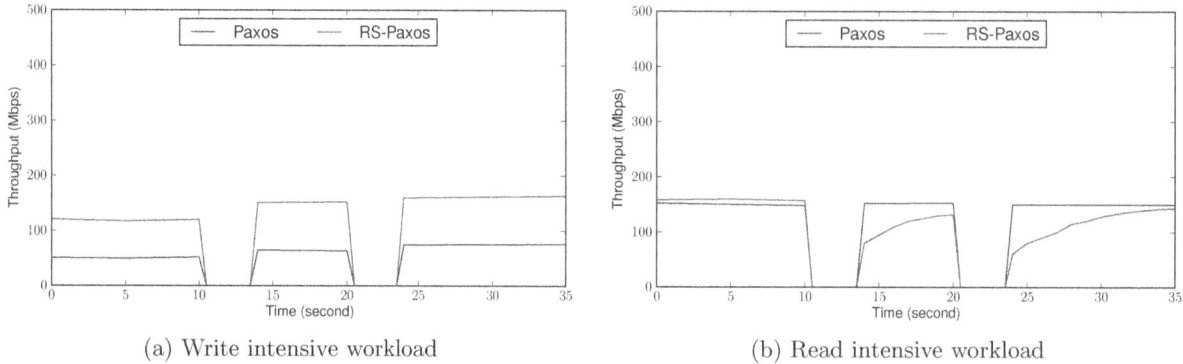

Figure 8: Fail-over time. The first crash is triggered at 10s; the second crash is triggered at 20s.

We are also interested in different kinds of workloads. Because if it is read-intensive workload, a new leader must perform recovery read on client read requests. So the test is done twice, once with write intensive and once with read intensive workload.

Results are as shown in Figure 8. For both RS-Paxos and Paxos, when the current leader is killed, there is a time window where system throughput drop to zero. After the rest replicas wait for the lease to timeout, a new leader will be elected before the system goes back to normal. This time period is the same for RS-Paxos and Paxos, since RS-Paxos does not incur any overhead in design for view change.

After the leader is elected, there is a period during which the system throughput climbs to its maximum. For write intensive workload, RS-Paxos has almost the same recovery time as Paxos because RS-Paxos can directly handle writes without recover the previous value. Notice after each failure, the throughput for write workload actually becomes higher than before. This is because the amount of message to finish a (RS-)Paxos instance decreases with fewer nodes in the system.

For read intensive workload, it takes a longer time for RS-Paxos to climb up to its maximum throughput. This is because the new leader replica does not hold the actual object value in its local storage. So the new leader has to perform a recovery read for every missing object. The cost of a recovery read is similar to a write.

7. RELATED WORK

In the last decade, Paxos[14][13] has become a de facto standard for state machine replication[23]. Many practical systems choose to use Paxos to synchronously replicate their states across multiple nodes. Chubby[4] is one of the earliest industrial implementations of Paxos. It uses Paxos to replicate critical metadata such as configuration files and system views.

Later on, there are more and more systems using Paxos to replicate data, as well as metadata. Many research database systems[1][24][26] use Paxos (at least as an option) to replicate data records, in a single site or across sites. Google has published two systems, MegaStore[2] and Spanner[8]. Both of them use Paxos to replicate data record globally.

Besides database records which are usually of small size, there are also systems using Paxos to replicate larger data, such as files and data objects. This is also currently the target system of RS-Paxos. Gaios[3] presents a design of building a high performance data store using Paxos-based replicated state machines. There are also other file system designs[1] using Paxos as the replication module.

The original Paxos is more of a research theory than a real-system protocol. It is seldom used without any optimization. There are various optimization directing on different dimensions to reduce network messages. The most common optimization is Multi-Paxos[6]. A long-lived leader can act as the distinguished proposer. It can issue prepare requests for next coming Paxos instance before it is executed. RS-Paxos is totally compatible with Multi-Paxos, and we have adopted it in our implementation and evaluation.

Some Paxos-based systems do not take the leader-follower approach, such as Round-robin Paxos, proposed in Mencius[19]. Each participant in the system proposes in an independent set of instances which are pre-defined. On execution, these instances are ordered in a round robin manner. In such case every participant can propose without conflict, getting rid of the leader bottleneck. It is feasible to merge Round-robin Paxos and RS-Paxos together. But a replica may have to issue a recovery read to read the value proposed by other replias.

There are other optimizations those can not be easily combined with RS-Paxos, like Fast Paxos. Fast paxos allows a client directly sends its proposal to each accepter, bypassing the leader. It saves a message trip than sending the proposal to the leader and let leader re-propose it to acceptors. Fast Paxos has a fast quorum and regular quorum. Normally it runs in fast quorum, on conflicts it backs off to a regular quorum. The reason it is hard to combine RS-Paxos and Fast Paxos is that they both modify the quorum definition. It is still possible, but may require cautious work to guarantee the correctness of combination.

The same goes with EPaxos[20]. EPaxos requires client send requests to a nearby server. And it allows every server node to propose value without conflict in common cases. Every proposal is attached with extra dependencies. Based on these dependencies, each server can execute instances in a consistent and efficient manner. It is also not a simple job to combine EPaxos and RS-Paxos, because EPaxos alters the quorum definition as well.

IO batching is also an important engineering technique used in practical Paxos systems and other systems[6], in order to reduce disk and network cost to improve throughput. Usually the server would delay all disk write requests for a small time window (say 10ms), save all the write log in a cache, and then flush them together. This is a good utilization of disk resources, especially when disk performs badly handling small writes. The same batching techniques also goes with RPC, with similar principles. Batching is also an orthogonal optimization to RS-Paxos.

Erasure code[22][18] has been used in many distributed systems such as [12][5][17], in order to reduce storage and network cost. When doing replication, these systems have stronger assumptions about messages passing model and failures. They assumes a more "synchronous" model of the network. If two servers are both healthy, messages must be delivered within a timeout. If the message cannote be delivered within the timeout, the server must have failed. This model does not work properly when there is long message delay or message loss. In another point view, RS-Paxos also points out how to do erasure coding correctly in an asynchronous network.

There are many recent works on erasure coding optimizations[10][11], including reduced the size of data shares, efficient recovery mechanisms, etc. These works have very different perspectives from our work. However, we believe RS-Paxos can benefit from them with careful revisit and combination. On the other hand, rethinking these works in an asynchronous messaging passing model may also lead to promising results.

8. CONCLUSION

In this paper we pointed out a new direction to optimize Paxos protocol. By combining coding techniques into Paxos we can largely save the cost of network transmission and disk flushes. We summarized the possible problems in intuitive approaches, analyzed the requirements for safety guarantees of Paxos in an asynchronous message passing model, and gave an improved protocol RS-Paxos, combing Reed Solomon code with Paxos. We designed and built a key-value store based on RS-Paxos. The experiment results of RS-Paxos is very promising. It shows that RS-Paxos improves throughput by 2.5x in common configurations, with reasonable extra cost and a minor relaxation on fault tolerance level.

9. ACKNOWLEDGEMENTS

The authors are greatly indebted to Jinyang Li, for giving us valuable suggestions and help revise the paper. We thank our shepherd Charles Killian and the anonymous reviewers for their feedback. We also thank Feng Ye, Wenlei Zhu, Pin Gao for their contribution to our Paxos codebase.

This work is supported by National Basic Research (973) Program of China (2011CB302505), Natural Science Foundation of China (61373145, 61170210), National High-Tech R&D (863) Program of China (2012AA012600, 2013AA01A213), Chinese Special Project of Science and Technology (2013zx01039-002-002), Ministry of Education-China Mobile Funding: MCM20123021.

10. REFERENCES

[1] M. K. Aguilera, A. Merchant, M. A. Shah, A. C. Veitch, and C. T. Karamanolis. Sinfonia: a new paradigm for building scalable distributed systems. In *SOSP*, pages 159–174, 2007.

[2] J. Baker, C. Bond, J. C. Corbett, J. J. Furman, A. Khorlin, J. Larson, J.-M. Leon, Y. Li, A. Lloyd, and V. Yushprakh. Megastore: Providing scalable, highly available storage for interactive services. In *CIDR*, pages 223–234, 2011.

[3] W. J. Bolosky, D. Bradshaw, R. B. Haagens, N. P. Kusters, and P. Li. Paxos replicated state machines as the basis of a high-performance data store. In *Proceedings of the 8th USENIX conference on Networked systems design and implementation*, pages 11–11. USENIX Association, 2011.

[4] M. Burrows. The chubby lock service for loosely-coupled distributed systems. In *OSDI*, pages 335–350, 2006.

[5] B. Calder, J. Wang, A. Ogus, N. Nilakantan, A. Skjolsvold, S. McKelvie, Y. Xu, S. Srivastav, J. Wu, H. Simitci, et al. Windows azure storage: a highly available cloud storage service with strong consistency. In *Proceedings of the Twenty-Third ACM Symposium on Operating Systems Principles*, pages 143–157. ACM, 2011.

[6] T. D. Chandra, R. Griesemer, and J. Redstone. Paxos made live: an engineering perspective. In *PODC*, pages 398–407, 2007.

[7] F. Chang, J. Dean, S. Ghemawat, W. C. Hsieh, D. A. Wallach, M. Burrows, T. Chandra, A. Fikes, and R. Gruber. Bigtable: A distributed storage system for structured data (awarded best paper!). In *OSDI*, pages 205–218, 2006.

[8] J. C. Corbett, J. Dean, M. Epstein, A. Fikes, C. Frost, J. J. Furman, S. Ghemawat, A. Gubarev, C. Heiser, P. Hochschild, W. C. Hsieh, S. Kanthak, E. Kogan, H. Li, A. Lloyd, S. Melnik, D. Mwaura, D. Nagle, S. Quinlan, R. Rao, L. Rolig, Y. Saito, M. Szymaniak, C. Taylor, R. Wang, and D. Woodford. Spanner: Google's globally distributed database. *ACM Trans. Comput. Syst.*, 31(3):8, 2013.

[9] S. Ghemawat, H. Gobioff, and S.-T. Leung. The google file system. In *SOSP*, pages 29–43, 2003.

[10] C. Huang, H. Simitci, Y. Xu, A. Ogus, B. Calder, P. Gopalan, J. Li, S. Yekhanin, et al. Erasure coding in windows azure storage. In *USENIX ATC*, volume 12, 2012.

[11] O. Khan, R. Burns, J. Plank, W. Pierce, and C. Huang. Rethinking erasure codes for cloud file systems: Minimizing i/o for recovery and degraded reads. In *USENIX FAST*, 2012.

[12] J. Kubiatowicz, D. Bindel, Y. Chen, S. Czerwinski, P. Eaton, D. Geels, R. Gummadi, S. Rhea, H. Weatherspoon, W. Weimer, et al. Oceanstore: An architecture for global-scale persistent storage. *ACM Sigplan Notices*, 35(11):190–201, 2000.

[13] L. Lamport. The part-time parliament. *ACM Transactions on Computer Systems (TOCS)*, 16(2):133–169, 1998.

[14] L. Lamport. Paxos made simple. *ACM Sigact News*, 32(4):18–25, 2001.

[15] L. Lamport. Generalized consensus and paxos. 2004.

[16] L. Lamport. Fast paxos. *Distributed Computing*, 19(2):79–103, 2006.

[17] J. Li and B. Li. Erasure coding for cloud storage systems: A survey. *Tsinghua Science and Technology*, 18(3):259–272, 2013.

[18] W. Lin, D. M. Chiu, and Y. Lee. Erasure code replication revisited. In *Peer-to-Peer Computing, 2004. Proceedings. Proceedings. Fourth International Conference on*, pages 90–97. IEEE, 2004.

[19] Y. Mao, F. P. Junqueira, and K. Marzullo. Mencius: Building efficient replicated state machine for wans. In *OSDI*, pages 369–384, 2008.

[20] I. Moraru, D. G. Andersen, and M. Kaminsky. There is more consensus in egalitarian parliaments. In *Proceedings of the Twenty-Fourth ACM Symposium on Operating Systems Principles*, pages 358–372. ACM, 2013.

[21] J. S. Plank, J. Luo, C. D. Schuman, L. Xu, Z. Wilcox-O'Hearn, et al. A performance evaluation and examination of open-source erasure coding libraries for storage. In *FAST*, volume 9, pages 253–265, 2009.

[22] L. Rizzo. Effective erasure codes for reliable computer communication protocols. *ACM SIGCOMM Computer Communication Review*, 27(2):24–36, 1997.

[23] F. B. Schneider. The state machine approach: A tutorial. In *Fault-Tolerant Distributed Computing*, pages 18–41, 1986.

[24] A. Thomson, T. Diamond, S.-C. Weng, K. Ren, P. Shao, and D. J. Abadi. Calvin: fast distributed transactions for partitioned database systems. In *Proceedings of the 2012 ACM SIGMOD International Conference on Management of Data*, pages 1–12. ACM, 2012.

[25] Z. WILCOX-OHEARN. Zfec 1.4. 0. *Open source code distribution: http://pypi. python. org/pypi/zfec*, 2008.

[26] Y. Zhang, R. Power, S. Zhou, Y. Sovran, M. K. Aguilera, and J. Li. Transaction chains: achieving serializability with low latency in geo-distributed storage systems. In *Proceedings of the Twenty-Fourth ACM Symposium on Operating Systems Principles*, pages 276–291. ACM, 2013.

[27] Q. Zheng, H. Chen, Y. Wang, J. Zhang, and J. Duan. Cosbench: cloud object storage benchmark. In *ICPE*, pages 199–210, 2013.

CMCP: A Novel Page Replacement Policy for System Level Hierarchical Memory Management on Many-cores

Balazs Gerofi[†], Akio Shimada[‡], Atsushi Hori[‡], Takagi Masamichi[§], Yutaka Ishikawa[†,‡]

[†]Graduate School of Information Science and Technology, The University of Tokyo, JAPAN
[‡]RIKEN Advanced Institute for Computational Science, Kobe, JAPAN
[§]Green Platform Research Lab, NEC Corp., Tokyo, JAPAN

bgerofi@il.is.s.u-tokyo.ac.jp, a-shimada@riken.jp, ahori@riken.jp, m-takagi@ab.jp.nec.com, ishikawa@is.s.u-tokyo.ac.jp

ABSTRACT

The increasing prevalence of co-processors such as the Intel® Xeon Phi™, has been reshaping the high performance computing (HPC) landscape. The Xeon Phi comes with a large number of power efficient CPU cores, but at the same time, it's a highly memory constraint environment leaving the task of memory management entirely up to application developers. To reduce programming complexity, we are focusing on application transparent, operating system (OS) level hierarchical memory management.

In particular, we first show that state of the art page replacement policies, such as approximations of the least recently used (LRU) policy, are not good candidates for massive many-cores due to their inherent cost of remote translation lookaside buffer (TLB) invalidations, which are inevitable for collecting page usage statistics. The price of concurrent remote TLB invalidations grows rapidly with the number of CPU cores in many-core systems and outpace the benefits of the page replacement algorithm itself. Building upon our previous proposal, per-core Partially Separated Page Tables (PSPT), in this paper we propose *Core-Map Count based Priority* (CMCP) page replacement policy, which exploits the auxiliary knowledge of the number of mapping CPU cores of each page and prioritizes them accordingly. In turn, it can avoid TLB invalidations for page usage statistic purposes altogether. Additionally, we *describe and provide an implementation of the experimental 64kB page support* of the Intel Xeon Phi and reveal some intriguing insights regarding its performance. We evaluate our proposal on various applications and find that CMCP can outperform state of the art page replacement policies by up to 38%. We also show that the choice of appropriate page size depends primarily on the degree of memory constraint in the system.

Categories and Subject Descriptors

D.4 [**Operating Systems**]: Storage Management—*Virtual Memory*

Keywords

Page Replacement; Manycore; Xeon Phi

1. INTRODUCTION

Although Moore's Law continues to drive the number of transistors per square mm, the recent stop of frequency and Dennard scaling caused an architectural shift in high-end computing towards hybrid/heterogeneous configurations. At present, a heterogeneous configuration consists of a multicore processor, which implements a handful of complex cores that are optimized for fast single-thread performance, and a manycore unit, which comes with a large number of simpler and slower but much more power-efficient cores that are optimized for throughput-oriented parallel workloads [26].

The Intel® Xeon Phi™ product family, also referred to as Many Integrated Cores (MIC), is Intel's latest design targeted for processing such highly parallel applications. The *Knights Corner* Xeon Phi card, used in this paper, provides a single chip with sixty x86 cores each processor core supporting a multithreading depth of four. Currently, the Intel® Xeon Phi™ comes on a PCI card, and has its own on-board memory, connected to the host memory through PCI DMA operations. The on-board memory is faster than the one in the host, but it is significantly smaller. Only 8 Gigabytes on the card, as opposed to the tens or hundreds of GBs residing in the host machine. This limited on-board memory requires partitioning computational problems into pieces that can fit into the device's RAM and orchestrate data movement along with computation, which at this time is the programmer's responsibility. This architecture with user managed data movement is shown in Figure 1a.

Although current programming models execute applications primarily on the multicore host which in turn offloads highly parallel sections to the co-processor, in the future, focus will shift further towards the manycore unit itself. Intel has already announced details of its next generation Xeon Phi chip, codenamed *Knights Landing*, which will come in a standalone bootable format and will be equipped with multiple levels of memory hierarchy[1][1], called "near" and "far" memory, respectively. Similarly, Nvidia has also argued that additional levels of memory hierarchies will be necessary for future massively parallel chips [18]. Keeping this architectural direction in mind, this paper primarily focuses on the manycore unit itself and investigates how the host memory can be utilized from the co-processor's point of view.

---

[1]The term *multiple levels of memory hierarchy* does not refer to multiple levels of caches in this paper.

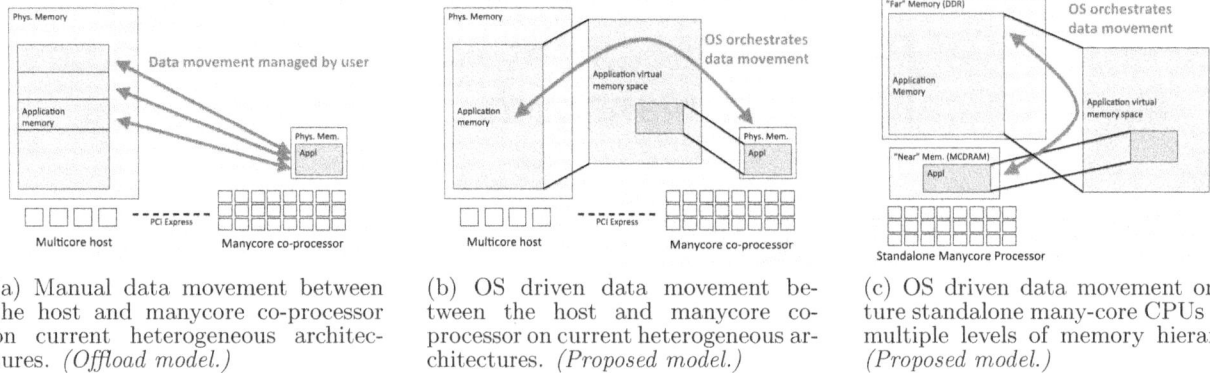

(a) Manual data movement between the host and manycore co-processor on current heterogeneous architectures. *(Offload model.)*

(b) OS driven data movement between the host and manycore co-processor on current heterogeneous architectures. *(Proposed model.)*

(c) OS driven data movement on future standalone many-core CPUs with multiple levels of memory hierarchy. *(Proposed model.)*

Figure 1: Overview of data movement scenarios on current heterogeneous systems and future standalone manycore CPUs with multiple levels of memory hierarchy.

Because the Intel® Xeon Phi™ co-processor features a standard memory management unit (MMU), it is capable to provide much larger virtual memory than that is physically available. The operating system can keep track of the physical memory, manage the mapping from virtual to physical addresses, and move data between the card and the host in an application transparent fashion. This proposed OS level data movement on current heterogeneous architectures and future standalone many-cores is shown in Figure 1b and Figure 1c, respectively.

We emphasize that data movement is *inevitable* in these architectures and we investigate the feasibility of a system level solution. While OS level data movement may sound analogous to swapping in traditional operating systems, the scenario of current manycore co-processor based memory management is considerably different than regular disk based swapping on a multicore CPU. First, data movement between the co-processor's RAM and the host memory, which takes place through the PCI Express bus, is *significantly faster* than accessing a disk in the host. This makes the relative cost of data movement during page fault handling *much lower* than in a disk based setup. Second, the large number of CPU cores on the co-processor renders the cost of remote TLB invalidations using regular page tables (i.e., shared by all cores) much higher than in a multi-core CPU.

We have already proposed per-core *partially separated page tables* (PSPT) to alleviate the TLB problem of frequent address remappings [14]. Further investigating co-processor based hierarchical memory management, we are focusing on page replacement policies in this paper. We show that state of the art replacement algorithms, such as approximations of the least recently used (LRU) policy, are not good candidates for massive many-cores due to their inherent cost of TLB invalidations required for tracking page usage statistics. LRU based algorithms aim at decreasing the number of page faults by keeping the working set of the application close to the CPU in the memory hierarchy [6]. To approximate the working set, however, they rely heavily on the access bit of page table entries which needs to be checked and cleared periodically. Unfortunately, on x86 each time the access bit is cleared in a PTE, the TLB for the corresponding virtual address needs to be invalidated on all affected CPU cores. We find that despite the fact that LRU successfully decreases the number of page faults, the price of frequent

TLB invalidations for monitoring page usage eventually outweighs the benefit of the page replacement algorithm itself.

To address this issue, we propose a novel page replacement policy which relies on the auxiliary knowledge of the number of mapping CPU cores for each address obtained from the per-core page tables. Intuitively, pages that are mapped by a large number of CPU cores are likely more important than those mapped by only a few. Furthermore, swapping out such pages requires TLB invalidations on a large number of CPU cores. Therefore, our algorithm prioritizes victim pages based on the number of mapping CPU cores and in turn it can avoid remote TLB invalidations for page usage statistics altogether. Moreover, we also consider the impact of using different physical page sizes supported by the Xeon Phi. We summarize our contributions as follows:

- Building upon PSPT, we propose a *Core-Map Count based page replacement Policy* (CMCP), which prioritizes victim pages based on the number of mapping CPU cores when pages are moved between the host and the MIC and compare its performance against various page replacement policies.

- We *describe and give an implementation of the experimental 64kB page size feature* of the Xeon Phi (which currently goes unused in Intel's Linux stack [17]) and reveal various insights regarding its performance in the context of OS level hierarchical memory management. To the best of our knowledge, this is the first time the 64kB page support of the Xeon Phi is discussed.

- Additionally, while we presented preliminary results earlier for partially separated page tables on a simple stencil computation kernel using 4kB pages [14], we *further evaluate PSPT (both with and without the CMCP policy) running various NAS Parallel Benchmarks and SCALE*, a climate simulation stencil application developed at RIKEN AICS, including measurements on the *impact of different page sizes*.

We demonstrate that partially separated page tables work well on real applications and provide scalable memory management with the increasing number of CPU cores in contrast to regular page tables, which fail to scale over 24 cores. We also show that the core-map count based replacement policy outperforms both FIFO and LRU on all applications we investigate by up to 38%.

Moreover, we confirm that the optimal page size depends on the degree of memory constraint imposed and demonstrate that under certain circumstances 64kB pages can yield superior performance compared to both 4kB and 2M pages.

The rest of this paper is organized as follows, Section 2 provides background and gives on overview of PSPT, Section 3 discusses the design of core-map count based replacement policy and Section 4 describes the 64kB page support of the Xeon Phi. Section 5 provides experimental results, Section 6 surveys related work, and finally, Section 7 concludes the paper.

2. BACKGROUND

2.1 Interface for Heterogeneous Kernels

The Information Technology Center at the University of Tokyo and RIKEN Advanced Institute of Computational Science (AICS) have been designing and developing a new scalable system software stack for future heterogeneous supercomputers.

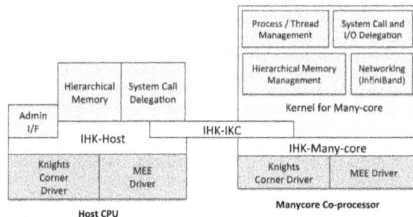

Figure 2: Main components of Interface for Heterogeneous Kernels (IHK) and the manycore kernel.

Figure 2 shows the main components of the current software stack. The *Interface for Heterogeneous Kernels* (IHK) hides hardware-specific functions and provides kernel programming interfaces. One of the main design considerations of IHK is to provide a unified base for rapid prototyping of operating systems targeting future many-core architectures.

IHK on the host is currently implemented as a Linux device driver, while the IHK manycore is a library that needs to be linked against the OS kernel running on the co-processor. Another component of the IHK worth mentioning is the *Inter-Kernel Communication* (IKC) layer that performs data transfer and signal notification between the host and the manycore co-processor.

We have already explored various aspects of a co-processor based system, such as a scalable communication facility with direct data transfer between the co-processors [29], and possible file I/O mechanisms [21]. We are currently developing a lightweight kernel based OS targeting manycore CPUs over the IHK, and at the same time, design considerations of an execution model for future manycore based systems is also undertaken. The minimalistic kernel is built with keeping the following principles in mind. First, on board memory of the co-processor is relatively small, thus, only very necessary services are provided by the kernel. Second, CPU caches are also smaller, therefore, heavy system calls are shipped to and executed on the host. Third, the number of CPU cores on the co-processor board is large so kernel data structures need to be managed in a scalable manner.

2.2 Execution Model

Projections for future exascale configurations suggest that the degree of parallelism inside a node could experience over a hundred fold increase, while the number of nodes in the system will likely grow by at least a factor of ten. In order to realize scalable communication among processes running on such systems, we believe that sharing the address space among multiple CPU cores inside a node, i.e., running a single, multi-threaded process (think of hybrid MPI and OpenMP programming), or at most a few, are the only viable approaches as opposed to assigning separate processes to each core. Thus, our main concern is how to handle a single address space running on a manycore co-processor.

In our current model (shown in Figure 1b) the application executes primarily on the manycore unit (similarly to Intel's native mode execution [16]), but it has transparent access to the memory residing in the host machine, as an additional level in the memory hierarchy. The application virtual address space is primarily maintained by the co-processors and is partially mapped onto the physical memory of the manycore board. However, the rest of the address space is stored in the host memory. The operating system kernel running on the co-processor is responsible for moving data between the host memory and the co-processor's RAM and for updating the virtual address space accordingly. It is worth pointing out that due to the large number of CPU cores the OS needs to be able to handle simultaneously occurring page faults in a scalable manner.

2.3 Per-core Partially Separated Page Tables

In order to provide the basis for further discussion on page replacement policies, this Section will first give a brief overview of our previous proposal, per-core partially separated page tables (PSPT) [14].

With the traditional process model all CPU cores in an address space refer to the same set of page tables and TLB invalidation is done by means of looping through each CPU core and sending an Inter-processor Interrupt (IPI). As we pointed out earlier, the TLB invalidation IPI loop becomes extremely expensive when frequent page faults occur simultaneously on a large number of CPU cores [14].

However, as we will show later in Section 5.2, in many HPC applications the computation area (the memory area on which computation takes place) is divided among CPU cores and only a relatively small part of the memory is utilized for communication. Consequently, CPU cores do not actually access the entire computation area and when an address mapping is modified most of the CPU cores are not affected. However, the information of which cores' TLB have to be invalidated is not available due to the centralized book-keeping of address translations in the address space wise page tables.

In order to overcome this problem we have already proposed per-core *partially separated page tables (PSPT)*, which is shown in Figure 3. In PSPT each core has its own last level page table, i.e., Page Global Directory (PGD). Kernel-space and regular user-space mappings point to the same Page Middle Directories (PMD), and thus, use the same PTEs to define the address space (regular boxes in the top of Figure 3). However, for the computation area per-core private page tables are used (denoted by dashed boxes in Figure 3). There are multiple benefits of such arrangement. First, each CPU core sets up PTEs exclusively for addresses

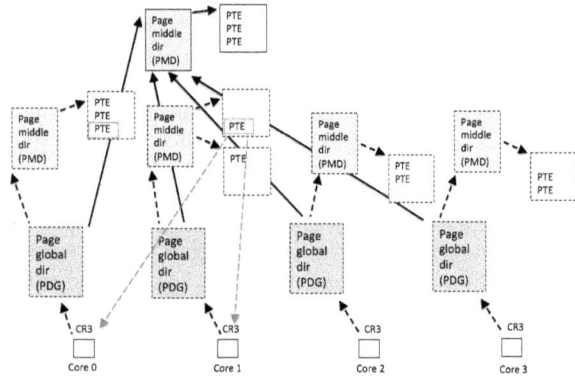

Figure 3: Per-core Partially Separated Page Tables.

that it actually accesses. Second, when a virtual to physical mapping is changed, it can be precisely determined which cores' TLB might be affected, because only the ones which have a valid PTE for the particular address may have cached a translation. Consider the red dashed lines in Figure 3, PTE invalidation in case of regular page tables require sending an IPI for each core, while PSPT invalidates the TLB only on $Core_0$ and $Core_1$. Third, synchronization (particularly, holding the proper locks for page table modifications) is performed only between affected cores, eliminating coarse grained, address space wise locks that are often utilized in traditional operating system kernels [9].

It is also worth pointing out, that the private fashion of PTEs does not imply that mappings are different, namely, private PTEs for the same virtual address on different cores define the same virtual to physical translation. When a page fault occurs, the faulting core first consults other CPU cores' page tables and copies a PTE if there is any valid mapping for the given address. Also, when a virtual address is unmapped, all CPU cores' page table, which map the address, need to be modified accordingly. This requires careful synchronization during page table updates, but the price of such activity is much less than constant address space wise TLB invalidations. For further discussion on PSPT refer to [14].

Note that an alternative solution to the careful software approach could be if the hardware provided the right capability to invalidate TLBs on multiple CPU cores, such as special instructions for altering TLB contents on a set of CPU cores. Thus, although we do provide an OS level solution in this paper, we would encourage hardware vendors to put a stronger focus on TLB invalidation methods for many-core CPUs.

3. CORE-MAP COUNT BASED PAGE REPLACEMENT

State of the art page replacement algorithms, such as approximations of the LRU policy, aim at minimizing the number of page faults during execution by means of estimating the working set of the application and keeping it in RAM [11]. To estimate the working set, the operating system monitors memory references, relying on the access bit of page table entries. Specifically, the OS scans PTEs checking and clearing the accessed bit in a periodic fashion. In case of the x86 architecture, however, every time the accessed bit is cleared, it is also required to invalidate the TLB entry

(on all affected CPU cores) corresponding to the given PTE in order to ensure that the hardware will set the access bit when the page is referenced again.

We have already stated above that the many-core co-processor accessing the host memory setup is significantly different than the multi-core CPU based host machine accessing a regular disk configuration. First, the PCI Express bus is orders of magnitude faster (we measured up to 6GB/s bandwidth between the host and the MIC) than accessing a regular disk, which makes the relative price of data transfer during page fault handling less expensive compared to the disk based scenario. Second, as we pointed out previously, the large number of CPU cores on the co-processor renders the price of remote TLB invalidations much higher, when frequent page faults occur simultaneously in multiple threads [14].

As we will demonstrate through quantitative measurements in Section 5, LRU can successfully decrease the number of page faults (compared to the basic FIFO policy), but the price of frequent TLB invalidations for obtaining page usage statistics outweighs the benefits of the algorithm itself, rendering the performance of LRU lower than FIFO. We emphasize that the problem with LRU on manycore CPUs is not the original policy how victim pages are chosen. It is the *overhead of collecting information* so that the policy can be realized.

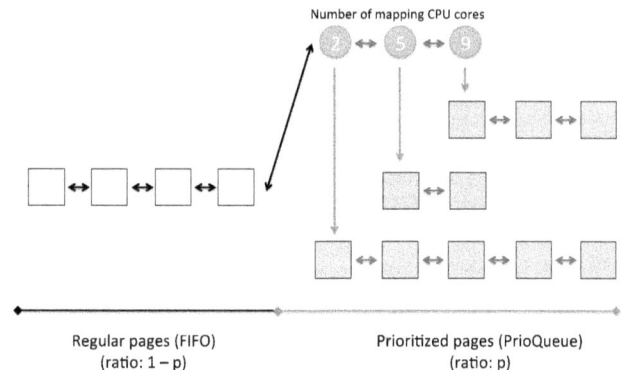

Figure 4: Core-Map Count based Priority Replacement. *The ratio of prioritized pages is defined by* p, *where* $0 <= p <= 1$.

In order to overcome the aforementioned issue, we propose a novel page replacement policy that exploits the auxiliary knowledge of the number of mapping CPU cores of each memory page, which we gather from the per-core partially separated page tables. Note that such information cannot be obtained from regular page tables due to their centralized book keeping of address mappings. As an example, in Figure 3 one can see that the page corresponding to the red circled PTE is mapped by two CPU cores. Intuitively, pages that are mapped by a large number of CPU cores (and thus have been accessed by them) are likely more important than per-core local data. Furthermore, remapping a page that has been referenced by a large number threads requires TLB invalidations on all the mapping CPU cores, while pages that are per-core private (or mapped by only a few cores) imply less time spent on TLB invalidation.

The high level design of the algorithm, which we call *Core Map Count based Priority replacement* (CMCP), is shown in Figure 4. Physical pages are separated into two groups, regular pages (left side of the Figure) are maintained on a simple FIFO list, while the priority pages (shown on the right) are held on a priority queue according to the number of mapping CPU cores for each page. The parameter p of the algorithm defines the ratio of prioritized pages. With p converging to 0, the algorithm falls back to the simple FIFO replacement, while p approaching 1, all pages are ordered by the number of mapping CPU cores. The motivation behind introducing p is to allow an optimization method to discover the appropriate ratio which yields the best performance. In Section 5, we will provide measurements on the effect of varying the ratio.

When a new PTE is set up by a CPU core, it first consults PSPT to retrieve the number of mapping cores for the particular page, and it tries to place the page into the prioritized group. If the ratio of prioritized pages already exceeds p and the number of mapping cores of the new page is larger than that for the lowest priority page in the prioritized group, then the lowest priority page is moved to FIFO and the new page is placed into the priority group. Otherwise, the new page goes to the regular FIFO list. Gradually, pages with the largest number of mapping CPU cores end up in the priority group. In order to enable moving pages to the other direction (i.e., from the prioritized group to the FIFO group), we employ a simple aging method, where all prioritized pages slowly fall back to FIFO. Such mechanism is required so that prioritized pages which are not used any more can also be swapped out, and thus preventing the priority group from being monopolized by such pages.

As for eviction, the algorithm either takes the first page of the regular FIFO list, or if the regular list is empty, the lowest priority page from the prioritized group is removed.

The most important thing to notice is that there are no extra remote TLB invalidations involved in the decision process. Although one could intentionally construct memory access patterns for which this heuristic wouldn't work well, as we will show in Section 5, CMCP consistently outperforms both FIFO and LRU on all applications we have evaluated. It is also worth mentioning, that although we use LRU as the basis of comparison, other algorithms such as the least frequently used (LFU) policy or the clock algorithm also rely on the access bit of the PTEs [6], and thus would suffer from the same issues of extra TLB invalidations.

4. XEON PHI 64KB PAGE SUPPORT

This Section describes the 64kB page support of the Xeon Phi. The MIC features 4kB, 64kB, and 2MB page sizes, although the 64kB support currently goes unused in the Intel modified Linux kernel [17].

The 64kB page extension was originally added to create an intermediate step between 4kB and 2MB pages, so that reducing TLB misses and preserving high granularity can be attained at the same time. Figure 5 illustrates the page table format. Support can be enabled for 64kB pages via a hint bit addition in page table entries for which the hardware mechanism relies upon the operating system manipulating the page tables and address maps correctly. As indicated by $PageFrame_k$ in Figure 5, to set a 64kB mapping, the operating system must initialize 16 regular 4kB page table entries (PTE), which are a series of subsequent 4kB pages of a contiguous 64kB memory region. Furthermore, the first entry of the 16 entries must correspond to a 64kB aligned

virtual address, which in turn must map to a 64kB aligned physical frame. The OS then sets a special bit of the PTE to indicate that CPU cores should cache the PTE using a 64kB entry rather than a series of separate 4kB entries, denoted by the flag 64 on the header of the PTEs in Figure 5.

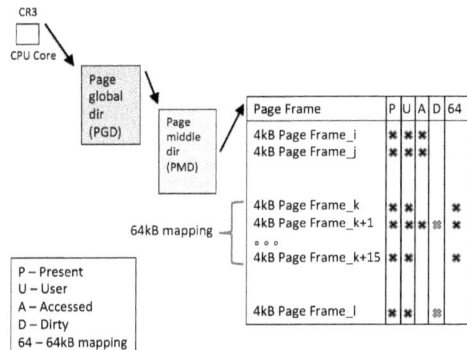

Figure 5: Xeon Phi 64kB page table entry format.

On a TLB miss, the hardware performs the page table walk as usual, and the INVLPG instruction also works as expected. On the contrary, page attributes set by the hardware work in a rather unusual way. For instance, upon the first write instruction in a 64kB mapping the CPU sets the dirty bit of the corresponding 4kB entry (instead of setting it in the first mapping of the subsequent 16 mappings as one might expect). This is indicated by the dirty bit set only for $PageFrame_{k+1}$. The accessed bit works similarly. In consequence, the operating system needs to iterate the 4kB mappings when retrieving statistical information on a 64kB page. One of the advantages of this approach is that there are no restrictions for mixing the page sizes (4kB, 64kB, 2MB) within a single address block (2MB). With respect to OS level hierarchical memory management, 64kB pages also come with multiple benefits. On one hand, they offer lower TLB miss rate compared to 4kB pages, while on the other hand, they allow finer grained memory management than using 2MB large pages. We will provide quantitative results on using 64kB pages below.

5. EVALUATION

5.1 Experimental Setup and Workloads

Throughout our experiments the host machine was an Intel® Xeon® CPU E5-2670, with 64 Gigabytes of RAM. For the manycore co-processor we used the *Knights Corner* Xeon Phi 5110P card, which is connected to the host machine via the PCI Express bus. It provides 8GB of RAM and a single chip with 60 1.053GHz x86 cores, each processor core supporting a multithreading depth of four. The chip includes coherent L1 and L2 caches and the inter-processor network is a bidirectional ring [15].

We use the OpenMP [24] version of three representative algorithms from the *NAS Parallel Benchmarks* [2]. Namely, CG (Conjugate Gradient), LU (Lower-Upper symmetric Gauss-Seidel) and BT (Block Tridiagonal). We chose not to include the other benchmarks from the NAS Parallel set for the following reasons. EP (Embarrassingly Parallel) uses very

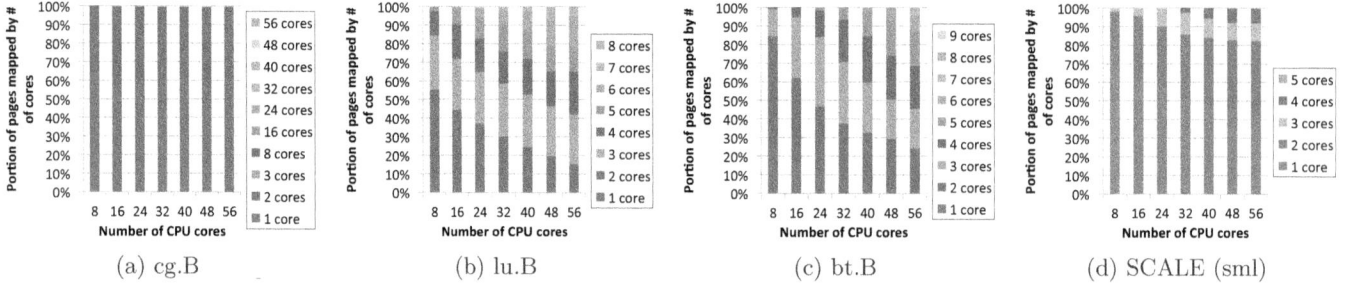

(a) cg.B   (b) lu.B   (c) bt.B   (d) SCALE (sml)

Figure 6: Distribution of pages according to the number of CPU cores mapping them for NPB B class benchmarks and SCALE (512MB).

small amount of memory and thus hierarchical memory management is not necessary. It has been already pointed out by [27] that FT (Fourier-Transformation) and MG (three-dimensional discrete Poisson equation) are highly memory intensive workloads. We found that without algorithmic modifications, such as shown in [30], running these applications in an out-of-core fashion is not feasible. Finally, IS (Integer Sort) doesn't appear to have high importance for our study.

However, we use the *Scalable Computing for Advanced Library and Environment* (SCALE) [3], a stencil computation code for weather and climate modelling developed at RIKEN AICS. SCALE is a complex stencil computation application, which operates on multiple data grids. It is written in Fortran 90 and it also uses OpenMP to exploit thread level parallelism.

For each benchmark we used two configurations with respect to memory usage. Small configuration, i.e., B class NPB benchmarks and 512 megabytes memory requirement for SCALE, which we denote by SCALE (sml) were used for experiments using only 4kB pages, while C class NPB benchmarks and a 1.2GB setup of SCALE, denoted by SCALE (big) were utilized for the comparison on the impact of different page sizes. For all applications we used Intel's compiler with the $-O3$ flag and verified in the compiler log that special vector operations for the Xeon Phi^{TM} were indeed generated. In order to move the computation data into the PSPT memory region we interface a C block with the Fortran code which explicitly memory maps allocations to the desired area. It is also worth mentioning that in all experiments we mapped application threads to separate CPU cores, partially due to the fact that we dedicated some of the hyperthreads to the page usage statistics collection mechanism for LRU.

Regarding the discussion on page replacement policies, we will be comparing our proposal against an LRU approximation, which implements the same algorithm employed by the Linux kernel [22]. It tracks pages on two lists, the *active* and *inactive* queues, where *active* denotes pages which are derived as part of the application's working set, while *inactive* represents the rest of the memory. Pages transit between these two states based on periodic scanning of the access bit of the corresponding PTEs, which is carried out in a timer set for every 10 milliseconds. As briefly mentioned above, we use dedicated hyperthreads for collecting page usage statistics, i.e., the timer interrupts are not delivered to application cores so that interference with the application is minimized.

5.2 Page Sharing among CPU Cores

As we mentioned above, we found that in various HPC applications the footprint of CPU cores accessing pages on the computation area is surprisingly regular. Figure 6 illustrates the result of our analysis, which we obtain from the per-core page tables of PSPT. For each application we show the distribution of pages (in the computation area) according to the number of CPU cores that access them. The key observation is that for all applications listed, regardless the overall number of CPU cores involved, the majority of pages are shared by only a very few cores.

Specifically, in case of both CG and SCALE (stencil computation) over 50% of the pages are core private. Furthermore the remaining pages are mainly shared by only two cores. LU and BT show somewhat less regular pattern, nevertheless, the majority of pages are still mapped by only less than six cores and over half of them are mapped by at most three. This implies that with PSPT, every time when a page is swapped out only a few CPU cores' TLB need to be flushed as opposed to the every CPU scenario that regular page tables require.

5.3 Relative Performance to Memory Constraint

Before moving on to demonstrate scalability of PSPT, as well as the impact of various page replacement policies, we provide measurements on how the degree of memory constraint imposed on various applications affects performance.

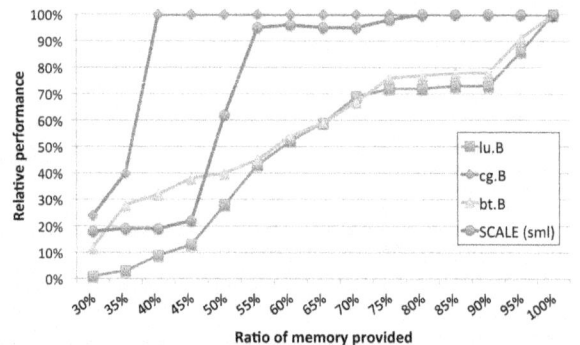

Figure 8: Relative performance with respect to physical memory provided for NPB B class benchmarks and SCALE.

Figure 8 illustrates the measurements for small size benchmarks using PSPT with 4kB pages, 56 CPU cores, and FIFO

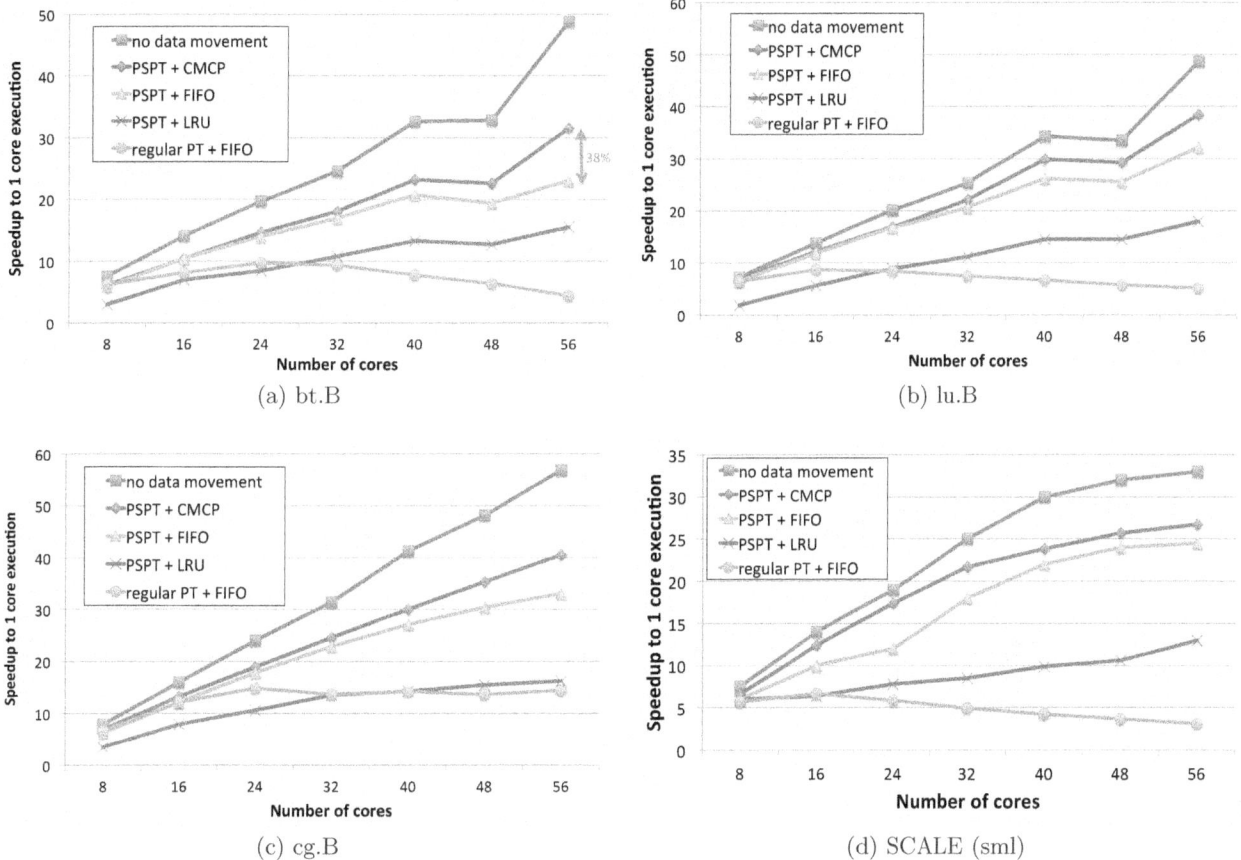

(a) bt.B

(b) lu.B

(c) cg.B

(d) SCALE (sml)

Figure 7: Performance measurements of NAS Parallel benchmarks and SCALE (sml) comparing regular page tables and PSPT using various page replacement policies.

replacement policy. The X axis shows the ratio of memory provided and Y axis represents the relative performance compared to the case where no data movement takes place. As seen, two kinds of behavior can be distinguished. LU and BT shows gradual decrease in performance with respect to the amount of memory provided, which is immediately visible once the physical memory available is less than 100% of the application's requirement.

On the other hand, CG and SCALE doesn't suffer significant performance degradation until approximately 35% and 55%, respectively. We believe this is due to sparse representation of data in these applications. Nevertheless, once the turning point is crossed, performance starts dropping steadily for both of the benchmarks.

In order to stress our kernel's virtual memory subsystem, in the rest of the experiments we set the memory constraint so that relative performance with FIFO replacement results between 50% and 60% for each application.

5.4 PSPT and Page Replacement Policies

We will now provide runtime measurements for the three benchmarks we evaluated from the NAS parallel suite and for RIKEN's SCALE. We are focusing on the benefits of partially separated page tables with the combination of various page replacements policies, as well as on their scalability with the number CPU cores. As it has been discussed be-

fore (and shown in Figure 6), all of these applications have very regular page sharing pattern among the CPU cores, where a large fraction of the pages are mapped by only a few CPU cores, suggesting significant benefits using PSPT. Results are shown in Figure 7.

For each benchmark we ran five configurations. First, using regular page tables and providing sufficient physical memory so that data movement does not occur. This is indicated by the legend *no data movement*. As mentioned above, we limit physical memory so that FIFO replacement using PSPT achieves approximately half of the performance of the *no data movement* configuration. This translates to physical memory limitation of 64% for BT, 66% for LU, and 37% in case of CG and approximately half of the memory requirement of SCALE. We measured the performance of FIFO replacement for both regular and partially separated page tables, indicated by *regular PT + FIFO* and *PSPT + FIFO*, respectively. Additionally, we compare the performance of page replacement policies by evaluating the effect of LRU, denoted by *PSPT + LRU*, and Core-Map Count Based replacement, indicated by *PSPT + CMCP*.

The first thing to point out is the fact that there is nothing wrong with regular page tables in case no data movement (and thus no address remapping) is performed by the OS. However, when frequent page faults occur concurrently on several cores, regular page tables hardly scale up to 24 cores,

App.	Policy	Attribute	8 cores	16 cores	24 cores	32 cores	40 cores	48 cores	56 cores
bt.B	FIFO	page faults	2726737	1362879	912466	643175	507325	422293	374839
		remote TLB invalidations	12429404	7363887	5573193	4373695	3803838	3465130	3226009
		dTLB misses	317301578	158902560	104686518	78861340	63265002	52566943	45131883
	LRU	page faults	2081372	1121643	736023	526239	405079	343081	283699
		remote TLB invalidations	36835046	27810383	19186674	13964030	10818576	9064231	7200812
		dTLB misses	329974700	181141377	121038176	90000002	69873462	56684949	48067965
	CMCP	page faults	2095202	1166479	707894	515089	355083	316789	262958
		remote TLB invalidations	8054343	5007407	3492531	2772393	1968787	1932189	1683682
		dTLB misses	303861675	154641090	102907981	77448482	61478878	51527221	43876503
cg.B	FIFO	page faults	1201555	612630	416332	316925	257412	214623	**170332**
		remote TLB invalidations	5135525	2804708	1956586	1518976	1251353	1061759	848976
		dTLB misses	2094329816	1047163487	698202996	523651167	418949006	349143469	299118728
	LRU	page faults	697582	204362	159474	118680	103060	85709	**74393**
		remote TLB invalidations	22972046	10429447	5799486	3472687	2551439	1913195	1536147
		dTLB misses	2102332886	1051392986	700485750	524945408	419223430	348950189	298896012
	CMCP	page faults	974695	507322	355728	273488	219813	169125	**147269**
		remote TLB invalidations	4097411	2270867	1629661	1266941	1024237	788419	689344
		dTLB misses	2092475232	1046394257	697830654	523418261	418753017	348865565	299034762
lu.B	FIFO	page faults	1664098	736180	474095	352133	281916	235222	203914
		remote TLB invalidations	7670041	4370794	3182328	2575556	2166993	1953164	1703195
		dTLB misses	1198077215	599572624	400681210	301074654	241110822	201467566	173098992
	LRU	page faults	1404043	702963	469002	341749	249638	201451	201691
		remote TLB invalidations	184015529	62149332	30745581	19286652	12227868	10137298	7161364
		dTLB misses	1286055611	653339411	431973663	323255046	253339298	209722670	178214335
	CMCP	page faults	849638	534063	415147	260252	172057	153015	159575
		remote TLB invalidations	3791955	2747828	2289613	1476379	1024914	979601	1094896
		dTLB misses	1195314147	598279823	399867708	300469205	240438760	200940292	172782035
SCALE	FIFO	page faults	1689552	845232	563854	171636	116877	96999	83817
		remote TLB invalidations	6612775	3566425	2547823	817612	579835	497952	439276
		dTLB misses	153176016	77193205	52302140	39044538	31526874	26470846	22932556
	LRU	page faults	272450	145358	98365	73234	55315	45500	32988
		remote TLB invalidations	17091293	7262438	4469165	3374882	2674781	2224822	1776893
		dTLB misses	157644315	79764075	54112492	41294510	33055668	27486007	23655615
	CMCP	page faults	698334	256230	137778	92977	73260	61343	62057
		remote TLB invalidations	2522939	985460	545405	382940	312692	269734	281294
		dTLB misses	150999236	75899452	51330254	38831504	31412049	26374264	22871311

Table 1: **Per CPU core average number of page faults, TLB invalidations, and TLB misses for various workloads and page replacement policies as the function of the number of CPU cores utilized by the application.**

resulting in completely unacceptable performance. In fact, one can observe slowdown in most cases when more than 24 cores are utilized.

On the other hand, partially separated page tables provide relative speed-ups (i.e., scalability) similar to the no data movement configuration. Considering page replacement policies, surprisingly, we found that LRU yields lower performance than FIFO, which we will discuss in more detail below. Nevertheless, the key observation with regards to page replacement policies is the superior performance of the Core-Map Count based Replacement policy, which consistently outperforms FIFO, yielding 38%, 25%, 23%, and 13% better results when running on 56 CPU cores for BT (Figure 7a), LU (Figure 7b), CG (Figure 7c), and SCALE (Figure 7d), respectively.

5.5 What is wrong with LRU?

In order to gain a deeper understanding of LRU's behavior we logged various attributes of the execution. Table 1 summarizes the data. We provide per-core average values for the number of page faults, remote TLB invalidations (i.e., TLB invalidation requests coming from other CPU cores), and data TLB misses. As seen, LRU *successfully decreases the number of page faults* compared to FIFO for all benchmarks. We highlighted some of the values for CG to further emphasize the difference. However, it comes at the price of substantial (up to several times) increase in the number of remote TLB invalidations. Contrary to our expectations, the number of dTLB misses isn't increased significantly by

LRU's page scanning mechanism, mainly because there is a large number of TLB misses anyway. Notice that TLB misses do not only stem from TLB invalidations, but simply from the fact that the size of the TLB cache is insufficient for covering the entire address range mapped by the application. Moreover, although it is not included in the table, we also observe up to 8 times increase in CPU cycles spent on synchronization (i.e., locks) for remote TLB invalidation request structures. Altogether, we confirmed that the above mentioned components account for the performance degradation seen in case of LRU. On the other hand, while CMCP also reduces the number of page faults compared to FIFO, supporting the assumption with respect to the importance of pages mapped by multiple CPU cores, it does not introduce any overhead from the above mentioned issues.

It is also worth pointing out that we did experiment with adjusting the frequency of LRU's page scanning mechanism. In principle, the lower the frequency is, the less the TLB invalidation overhead becomes. However, doing so defeats the very purpose of LRU, i.e., decreasing the number of page faults. Eventually, with very low page scanning frequency LRU simply fell back to the behavior of FIFO. Nevertheless, whenever LRU succeeded in decreasing the number of page faults, it always yielded worse performance than FIFO.

5.6 The role of p in CMCP

As we mentioned earlier in Section 3, we provide measurements on the effect of the ratio of prioritized pages for CMCP policy. Figure 9 shows the results. As seen, the ratio of prioritized pages affects performance improvement quite significantly, moreover, the impact is also very workload specific. For instance, CG benefits the most from a low ratio, while in case of LU or SCALE high ratio appears to work better. We adjusted the algorithm's parameter manually in this paper, but determining the optimal value dynamically based on runtime performance feedback (such as page fault frequency) is part of our future work.

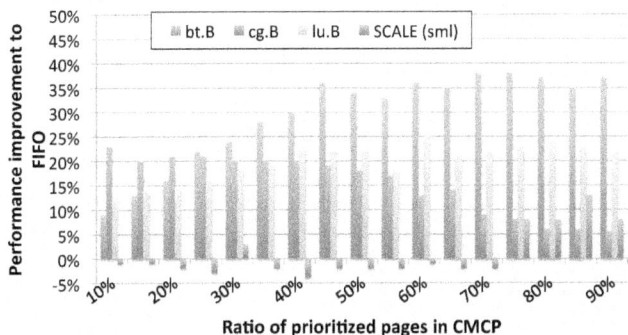

Figure 9: The impact of the ratio of prioritized pages in CMCP.

One could also argue that the number of mapping cores of a given page is dynamic with the time changing which in turn naturally impacts the optimal value of p. Although we believe the applications we consider in this paper exhibit rather static inter-core memory access patterns, a more dynamic solution with periodically rebuilding PSPT could address this issue as well.

5.7 The Impact of Different Page Sizes

In this Section we turn our attention towards the impact of various page sizes (i.e., 4kB, 64kB and 2MB) supported by the Intel® Xeon Phi™. Using larger pages reduces the number of TLB misses and thus can improve performance. However, in case of OS level data movement there are two problems when it comes to larger pages.

First, the usage of larger pages also implies that every time a page is moved to or from the host memory, significantly more data needs to be copied. Second, since with larger pages the granularity of the memory is more coarse grained, the probability of different CPU cores accessing the same page is also increased, and consequently, the price of remote TLB invalidations when the corresponding address is remapped. For example, using 2MB pages is 512x more coarse-grained than the regular 4kB pages, but on the other hand, 64kB pages yield only 16 times more coarse-grained mappings, possibly benefiting more the hierarchical memory scenario. Therefore, the main issue we seek to investigate is how the increased price of the data movement and TLB invalidations compare to the benefits of using larger pages. We are also interested in seeing how the imposed memory constraint influences performance.

We used the C class NPB benchmarks and SCALE with 1.2GB of memory. Figure 10 illustrates the results. Note that we leave the investigation of combining various page replacement policies with different page sizes as future work and we present results only for FIFO replacement in this paper. Nevertheless, for all measurements, we used 56 CPU cores.

As expected, when memory constraint is low, large pages (i.e., 2MB) provide superior performance compared to both 4kB and 64kB pages. However, as we decrease the memory provided, the price of increased data movement quickly outweighs the benefits of fewer TLB misses. Due to their finer granularity, the higher the memory constraint is the more we can benefit from smaller pages. This tendency can be clearly seen in case of BT and LU (Figure 10a and 10b, respectively), where with the decreasing memory first 64kB pages and later 4kB pages prove to be more efficient. On the other hand, we found that for CG and SCALE (Figure 10c and 10d, respectively), 64kB pages consistently outperform 4kB pages even when memory pressure is already considerably high. We believe further increasing the memory pressure would eventually produce the expected effect, but it is yet to be confirmed.

Indeed, the operating system could monitor page fault frequency and adjust page sizes dynamically so that it always provides the highest performance. At the same time, different page sizes could be used for different parts of the address space. Mapping frequently accessed areas with large pages could reduce TLB misses, while data that need to be often moved back and forth could benefit more from smaller page sizes. Exploring these directions is part of our future plans.

6. RELATED WORK

6.1 Operating Systems for Manycores

Operating system organization for manycore systems has been actively researched in recent years. In particular, issues related to scalability over multiple cores have been widely considered.

K42 [12, 20] was a research OS designed from the ground up to be scalable. It's *Clustered Object* model provides a standard way for implementing concurrently accessed objects using distribution and replication, the same principles we applied to page tables. At the time of K42, nevertheless, there were no co-processors or multiple levels of memory hierarchy.

Corey [7], an OS designed for multicore CPUs, argues that applications must control sharing in order to achieve good scalability. Corey proposes several operating system abstractions that allow applications to control inter-core sharing. For example, Corey's *range* abstraction provides means to control whether a memory area is private or shared by certain CPU cores, however, in a Corey range all CPU cores share the same set of page tables, and thus the TLB problem we address cannot be handled by their solution. Moreover, we are also aiming at application transparency.

Barrelfish [28] argues that multiple types of diversity and heterogeneity in manycore computer systems need to be taken into account. It represent detailed system information in an expressive "system knowledge base" accessible to applications and OS subsystems and use this to control tasks such as scheduling and resource allocation. While we explicitly address the Intel® Xeon Phi™ product family in this paper, system knowledge base, as proposed in Barrelfish could be leveraged for placing threads to CPU cores that have low IPI communication cost so that TLB invalidations can be performed more efficiently.

Scalable address spaces in particular have been also the focus of recent research. Clements et. al [9] proposed increasing the concurrency of kernel operations on a shared

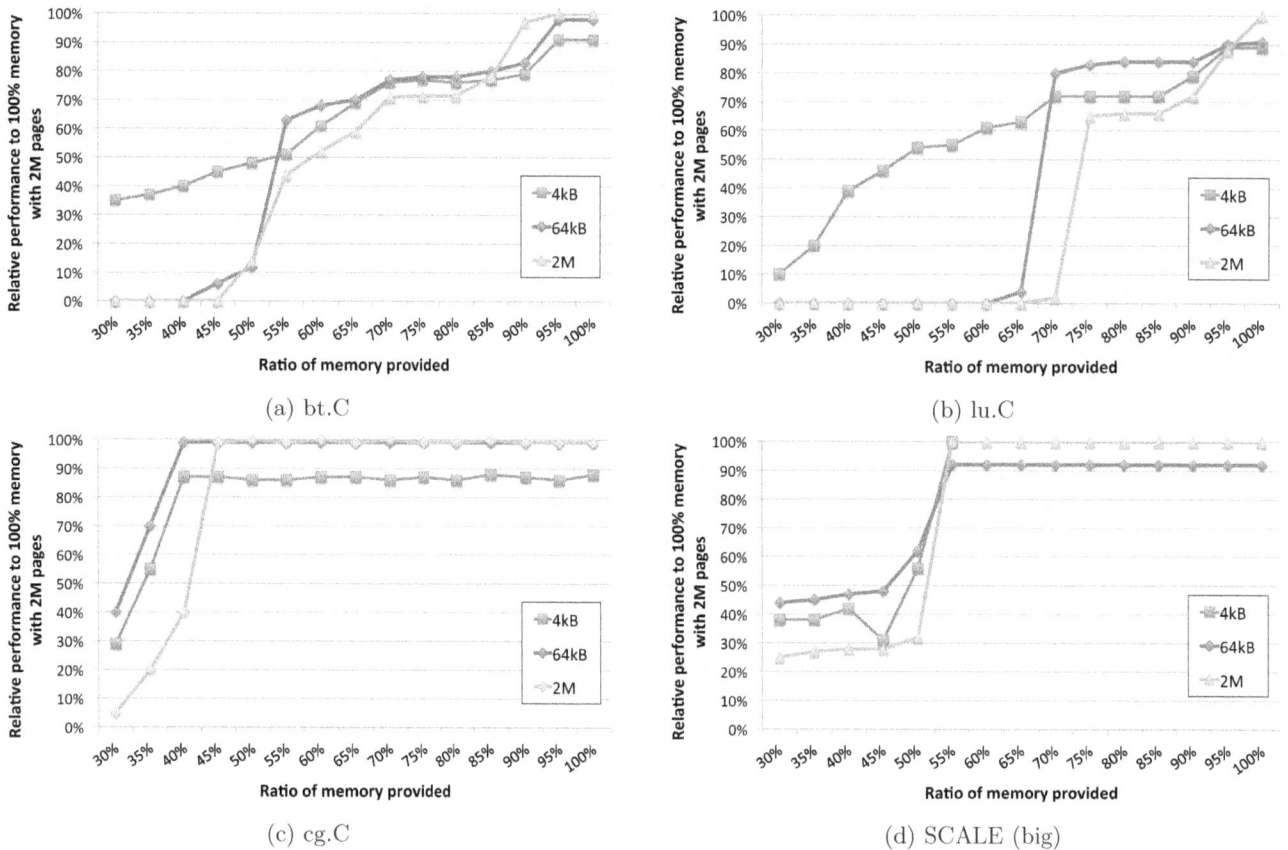

(a) bt.C

(b) lu.C

(c) cg.C

(d) SCALE (big)

Figure 10: The impact of page sizes on relative performance with respect to memory constraint for various benchmarks.

address space by exploiting read-copy-update (RCU) so that operations that mutate the same address space can avoid contention on shared cache lines. Moreover, published at the same time with our previous proposal [14], they also explored the idea of per-core page tables [10], however, neither hierarchical memory nor page replacement policies are considered in their study.

An idea, similar to PSPT, has been discussed by Almaless and Wajsburt [5]. The authors envision replicating page tables in NUMA environments to all memory clusters in order to reduce the cost of address translations (i.e., TLB misses) on CPU cores, which are located far from the otherwise centralized page tables. Although their proposal is similar to ours, they are addressing a very NUMA specific issue, furthermore, they do not provide an actual implementation.

In the context of heterogeneous kernels, IBM's FusedOS [25] also promotes the idea of utilizing different kernel code running on CPU cores dedicated to the application and the OS. However, they do not focus on hierarchical memory systems. GenerOS [32] partitions CPU cores into application core, kernel core and interrupt core, each of which is dedicated to a specified function. Again, the idea of utilizing dedicated cores for system call execution is similar to the utilization of the host machine for offloading system calls from the co-processor.

Villavieja et. al also pointed out the increasing cost of remote TLB invalidations with the number of CPU cores in chip-multiprocessors (CMP) systems [31]. In order to miti-

gate the problem the authors propose a lightweight hardware extension (a two-level TLB architecture that consists of a per-core TLB and a shared, inclusive, second-level TLB) to replace the OS implementation of TLB coherence transactions. While the proposed solution yields promising results, it requires hardware modifications, which limits its applicability. To the contrary, our proposal offers a solution entirely implemented in software.

6.2 Programming Models

Programming models for accelerators (i.e., co-processors) have also been the focus of research in recent years. In case of GPUs, one can spread an algorithm across both CPU and GPU using CUDA [23], OpenCL [19], or the OpenMP [24] accelerator directives. However, controlling data movement between the host and the accelerator is entirely the programmer's responsibility in these models. Nevertheless, a recent announcement by Nvidia reveals *Unified Memory*, a new feature in the upcoming CUDA 6 release [4]. Unified memory will allow the programmer to have a unified view of the host and the device memory on GPUs, eliminating the need to manually orchestrate data movement. Although Nvidia states their mechanism works on the memory page level, no details have been disclosed regarding their page replacement policy.

OpenACC [8] allows parallel programmers to provide directives to the compiler, identifying which areas of code to accelerate. Data movement between accelerator and host memories and data caching is then implicitly managed by the compiler, but as the specification states, the limited device memory size may prohibit offloading of regions of code that operate on very large amounts of data.

Intel provides several execution models for the Xeon Phi™ product family [16]. One of them, the so called *Mine-Your-Ours* (MYO), also referred to as *Virtual Shared Memory*, provides similar features to Nvidia's unified memory, such as transparent shared memory between the host and the co-processor. However, at the time of writing this paper, the main limitation of MYO is that the size of the shared memory area cannot exceed the amount of the physical memory attached to the co-processor. On the contrary, we explicitly address the problem of dealing with larger data sets than the amount of physical memory available on the co-processor card.

Other memory models have been also proposed for GPUs, the *Asymmetric Distributed Shared Memory* (ADSM) maintains a shared logical memory space for CPUs to access objects in the accelerator physical memory but not vice versa. When a method is selected for accelerator execution, its associated data objects are allocated within the shared logical memory space, which is hosted in the accelerator physical memory and transparently accessible by the methods executed on CPUs [13]. While ADSM uses GPU based systems providing transparent access to objects allocated in the co-processor's memory, we are aiming at an approach of the opposite direction over Intel's MIC architecture.

7. CONCLUSION AND FUTURE WORK

Memory management is one of the major challenges when it comes to programming co-processor based heterogeneous architectures. To increase productivity, we have investigated the feasibility of an OS level, application transparent solution targeting the Intel Xeon Phi. Focusing on page replacement algorithms, one of our main findings is that state of the art approaches, such as approximations of the LRU policy, are not well suited for massive many-cores due to their associated cost of obtaining page usage statistics. We emphasize that the problem with LRU on many-core CPUs does not stem from the policy of keeping recently used pages close to the CPU. It is the price of frequently scanning page table entries, which requires a large number of extra TLB invalidations.

Building upon our previous proposal, per-core *Partially Separated Page Tables* (PSPT), in this paper, we have proposed *Core Map Count based Priority* (CMCP) page replacement policy that prioritizes pages based on the number of mapping CPU cores. The main advantage of our approach is the ability to eliminate remote TLB invalidations otherwise necessary for page usage tracking.

We have further evaluated PSPT on various real life applications and demonstrated its scalability to large number of CPU cores. Enhanced with CMCP, we have also shown that we consistently outperform existing page replacement policies by up to 38% when running on 56 cores. Additionally, for the first time, we have provided an implementation of the experimental 64kB page support of the Intel Xeon Phi and concluded that adequate page size is a function of the memory constraint and there is space for 64kB pages in the context of hierarchical memory management. Across various workloads, our system is capable of providing up to 70% of the native performance with physical memory limited to

half, allowing essentially to solve two times larger problems without any need for algorithmic changes.

With respect to future architectures, such as the aforementioned Knights Landing chip, which will replace the PCI Express bus with printed circuit board (PCB) connection between memory hierarchies (rendering the bandwidth significantly higher), we expect to see further performance benefits of our solution. In the future, we intend to dynamically adjust page sizes during runtime in response to memory constraint as well as to integrate such decisions with page replacement policies.

Acknowledgment

This work has been partially supported by the CREST project of the Japan Science and Technology Agency (JST) and by the National Project of MEXT called Feasibility Study on Advanced and Efficient Latency Core Architecture.

We would also like to express our gratitude to Intel Japan for providing early access to the pre-production version of the hardware, as well as for the technical support associated with the Intel® Xeon Phi™ product family.

8. REFERENCES

[1] Intel unveils 72-core x86 Knights Landing CPU for exascale supercomputing. http://www.extremetech.com/extreme/171678-intel-unveils-72-core-x86-knights-landing-cpu-for-exascale-supercomputing.

[2] NASA. NAS Parallel Benchmarks. http://www.nas.nasa.gov/Software/NPB.

[3] RIKEN AICS. Scalable Computing for Advanced Library and Environment. http://scale.aics.riken.jp/.

[4] Unified Memory in CUDA 6. http://devblogs.nvidia.com/parallelforall/unified-memory-in-cuda-6.

[5] ALMALESS, G., AND WAJSBURT, F. Does shared-memory, highly multi-threaded, single-application scale on many-cores? In *Proceedings of the 4th USENIX Workshop on Hot Topics in Parallelism* (2012), HotPar '12.

[6] ARPACI-DUSSEAU, R. H., AND ARPACI-DUSSEAU, A. C. *Operating Systems: Three Easy Pieces.* Arpaci-Dusseau, 2013.

[7] BOYD-WICKIZER, S., CHEN, H., CHEN, R., MAO, Y., KAASHOEK, F., MORRIS, R., PESTEREV, A., STEIN, L., WU, M., DAI, Y., ZHANG, Y., AND ZHANG, Z. Corey: an operating system for many cores. In *Proceedings of the 8th USENIX conference on Operating systems design and implementation* (2008), OSDI'08, pp. 43–57.

[8] CAPS ENTERPRISE AND CRAY INC AND THE PORTLAND GROUP INC AND NVIDIA. The OpenACC Application Programming Interface. Specification, 2011.

[9] CLEMENTS, A. T., KAASHOEK, M. F., AND ZELDOVICH, N. Scalable address spaces using RCU balanced trees. In *Proceedings of the seventeenth international conference on Architectural Support for Programming Languages and Operating Systems* (2012), ASPLOS '12.

[10] CLEMENTS, A. T., KAASHOEK, M. F., AND ZELDOVICH, N. RadixVM: scalable address spaces for multithreaded applications. In *Proceedings of the 8th ACM European Conference on Computer Systems* (2013), EuroSys '13.

[11] DENNING, P. J. Virtual Memory. *ACM Computing Surveys 2* (1970), 153–189.

[12] GAMSA, B., KRIEGER, O., APPAVOO, J., AND STUMM, M. Tornado: maximizing locality and concurrency in a shared memory multiprocessor operating system. In *Proceedings of the third symposium on Operating systems design and implementation* (1999), OSDI '99.

[13] GELADO, I., STONE, J. E., CABEZAS, J., PATEL, S., NAVARRO, N., AND HWU, W.-M. W. An asymmetric distributed shared memory model for heterogeneous parallel systems. In *Proceedings of the fifteenth edition of ASPLOS on Architectural support for programming languages and operating systems* (New York, NY, USA, 2010), ASPLOS '10, ACM, pp. 347–358.

[14] GEROFI, B., SHIMADA, A., HORI, A., AND ISHIKAWA, Y. Partially Separated Page Tables for Efficient Operating System Assisted Hierarchical Memory Management on Heterogeneous Architectures. In *Cluster, Cloud and Grid Computing (CCGrid), 2013 13th IEEE/ACM International Symposium on* (may 2013).

[15] INTEL CORPORATION. Intel Xeon Phi Coprocessor Software Developers Guide, 2012.

[16] INTEL CORPORATION. Knights Corner: Open Source Software Stack, 2012.

[17] JEFFERS, J., AND REINDERS, J. *Intel Xeon Phi Coprocessor High Performance Programming*. Morgan Kaufmann, 2013.

[18] KECKLER, S., DALLY, W., KHAILANY, B., GARLAND, M., AND GLASCO, D. GPUs and the Future of Parallel Computing. *Micro, IEEE 31*, 5 (2011), 7–17.

[19] KHRONOS OPENCL WORKING GROUP. *The OpenCL Specification, version 1.0.29*, 8 December 2008.

[20] KRIEGER, O., AUSLANDER, M., ROSENBURG, B., WISNIEWSKI, R. W., XENIDIS, J., DA SILVA, D., OSTROWSKI, M., APPAVOO, J., BUTRICO, M., MERGEN, M., WATERLAND, A., AND UHLIG, V. K42: building a complete operating system. In *Proceedings of the 1st ACM SIGOPS/EuroSys European Conference on Computer Systems 2006* (2006), EuroSys '06.

[21] MATSUO, Y., SHIMOSAWA, T., AND ISHIKAWA, Y. A File I/O System for Many-core Based Clusters. In *ROSS'12: Runtime and Operating Systems for Supercomputers* (2012).

[22] MAUERER, W. *Professional Linux Kernel Architecture*. Wrox Press Ltd., Birmingham, UK, UK, 2008.

[23] NVIDIA CORP. NVIDIA CUDA Programming Guide 2.2, 2009.

[24] OPENMP ARCHITECTURE REVIEW BOARD. OpenMP Application Program Interface. Specification, 2008.

[25] PARK, Y., VAN HENSBERGEN, E., HILLENBRAND, M., INGLETT, T., ROSENBURG, B., RYU, K. D., AND WISNIEWSKI, R. FusedOS: Fusing LWK Performance with FWK Functionality in a Heterogeneous Environment. In *Computer Architecture and High Performance Computing (SBAC-PAD), 2012 IEEE 24th International Symposium on* (2012), pp. 211–218.

[26] SAHA, B., ZHOU, X., CHEN, H., GAO, Y., YAN, S., RAJAGOPALAN, M., FANG, J., ZHANG, P., RONEN, R., AND MENDELSON, A. Programming model for a heterogeneous x86 platform. In *Proceedings of the 2009 ACM SIGPLAN conference on Programming language design and implementation* (New York, NY, USA, 2009), PLDI '09, ACM, pp. 431–440.

[27] SAINI, S., CHANG, J., HOOD, R., AND JIN, H. A Scalability Study of Columbia using the NAS Parallel Benchmarks. Technical report, NASA Advanced Supercomputing Division, 2006.

[28] SCHÃ¼PBACH, A., PETER, S., BAUMANN, A., ROSCOE, T., BARHAM, P., HARRIS, T., AND ISAACS, R. Embracing diversity in the Barrelfish manycore operating system. In *In Proceedings of the Workshop on Managed Many-Core Systems* (2008).

[29] SI, M., AND ISHIKAWA, Y. Design of Direct Communication Facility for Many-Core based Accelerators. In *CASS'12: The 2nd Workshop on Communication Architecture for Scalable Systems* (2012).

[30] SIVAN TOLEDO. A Survey of Out-of-Core Algorithms in Numerical Linear Algebra, 1999.

[31] VILLAVIEJA, C., KARAKOSTAS, V., VILANOVA, L., ETSION, Y., RAMIREZ, A., MENDELSON, A., NAVARRO, N., CRISTAL, A., AND UNSAL, O. S. DiDi: Mitigating the Performance Impact of TLB Shootdowns Using a Shared TLB Directory. In *Proceedings of the 2011 International Conference on Parallel Architectures and Compilation Techniques* (Washington, DC, USA, 2011), PACT '11, IEEE Computer Society, pp. 340–349.

[32] YUAN, Q., ZHAO, J., CHEN, M., AND SUN, N. GenerOS: An asymmetric operating system kernel for multi-core systems. In *Parallel Distributed Processing (IPDPS), 2010 IEEE International Symposium on* (april 2010), pp. 1 –10.

TOP-PIM: Throughput-Oriented Programmable Processing in Memory

Dong Ping Zhang[1] Nuwan Jayasena[1] Alexander Lyashevsky[1] Joseph L. Greathouse[1]
Lifan Xu[2]* Michael Ignatowski[1]

[1]AMD Research
{Dongping.Zhang, Nuwan.Jayasena, Alexander.Lyashevsky,
Joseph.Greathouse, Mike.Ignatowski}@amd.com

[2]Dept. of Computer and Information Sciences
University of Delaware
xulifan@udel.edu

ABSTRACT

As computation becomes increasingly limited by data movement and energy consumption, exploiting locality throughout the memory hierarchy becomes critical to continued performance scaling. Moving computation closer to memory presents an opportunity to reduce both energy and data movement overheads. We explore the use of 3D die stacking to move memory-intensive computations closer to memory. This approach to processing in memory addresses some drawbacks of prior research on in-memory computing and is commercially viable in the foreseeable future.

Because 3D stacking provides increased bandwidth, we study throughput-oriented computing using programmable GPU compute units across a broad range of benchmarks, including graph and HPC applications. We also introduce a methodology for rapid design space exploration by analytically predicting performance and energy of in-memory processors based on metrics obtained from execution on today's GPU hardware. Our results show that, on average, viable PIM configurations show moderate performance losses (27%) in return for significant energy efficiency improvements (76% reduction in EDP) relative to a representative mainstream GPU at 22nm technology. At 16nm technology, on average, viable PIM configurations are performance competitive with a representative mainstream GPU (7% speedup) and provide even greater energy efficiency improvements (85% reduction in EDP).

Categories and Subject Descriptors

C.1.3 [**Processor Architectures**]: Other Architecture Styles—*heterogeneous (hybrid) systems*

Keywords

Processing in memory, performance modeling and analysis, energy efficiency, GPGPU

---

*Note: Lifan Xu contributed to the application studies during his internship with AMD Research.

1. INTRODUCTION

Processors have steadily become more computationally capable and energy efficient, but improvements in bandwidth, latency and energy consumption of off-chip memory accesses have not kept pace with advances in processor architectures [36, 40]. As a result, the memory system is often a performance bottleneck and accounts for a significant, and increasing, fraction of system level energy consumption [30, 43]. A 64b DRAM access now consumes nearly two orders of magnitude more energy than a double-precision floating point arithmetic operation [4, 15, 27].

Memory system energy consumption is of particular importance for future high-performance computing systems. Sample system goals for the US Department of Energy Exascale efforts include a memory bandwidth of 4 TB/s per node at a system size of 100,000 nodes within a 20 MW power budget [46]. Even with aggressive assumptions about memory and interface technology improvements reducing total DRAM access energy from approximately 60-80 pJ/b for DDR3 [4, 15] to 4 pJ/b[1] [27, 44], sustaining 4 TB/s per node over 100,000 nodes will consume 70% of the entire system's power budget on DRAM accesses alone.

This paper explores the potential of processing in memory (PIM) implemented via 3D die stacking to reduce memory access energy and improve performance. Recent industry trends suggest the imminent adoption of 3D die stacking in mass-produced memory parts [11]. Some vendors have developed DDR3 devices that internally incorporate 3D stacking to increase capacity [5]. Multiple memory vendors are participating in the Hybrid Memory Cube (HMC) consortium aimed at commercializing "memory cubes" consisting of 3D stacked DRAM dies atop a "base" logic die [37]. The Wide I/O JEDEC standard for stacking memory with logic devices aimed at mobile applications was released in early 2012 [1]. A similar JEDEC standard for high-performance applications, High Bandwidth Memory (HBM), was released recently [2]. A number of academic publications have also explored the stacking of DRAM on logic dies [31, 35, 47].

Thermal challenges are a key impediment to stacking memory directly on top of a high-performance processor. Heat generated by the processor reduces the retention time of data in DRAM, requiring the throttling of processor performance and/or increasing memory refresh rate, neither of which is desirable in high-performance systems. In this paper, we explore a system organization where memory is not

---

[1]Note that some predictions are much less optimistic (*e.g.*, 25 pJ/b in 7nm technology [15]).

stacked directly on the main compute processor. Instead, an auxiliary, in-memory processor is incorporated on the base logic die of each memory stack as shown in Figure 1. Memory-intensive code may be offloaded to these in-memory processors to exploit the high bandwidth and low-energy to memory enabled by being stacked directly under the memory. As these in-memory processors are geared towards running memory-intensive code, their compute resources can be optimized for low-energy operation and reduced thermals. As the main compute processor ("host") does not have memory stacked on it, it is not subject to stringent thermal constraints and can support high performance for compute-intensive code. The primary goal of this study is to determine the performance and energy characteristics of such auxiliary, in-memory processors across a wide range of applications.

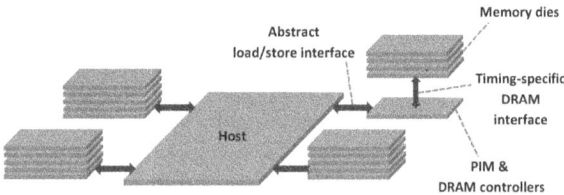

Figure 1: An example system with in-memory processors

Prior research has shown that the most significant performance benefit of stacked DRAM is increased bandwidth [16]. This motivates the incorporation of data-parallel accelerators in the in-memory processors to effectively utilize the available bandwidth. In this study, we focus on GPGPU execution units as the in-memory data-parallel accelerators. The programmability of modern GPUs also enables GPU-accelerated in-memory processors to be utilized over a wide range of applications. Further, the energy efficiency of GPU architectures (in terms of operations/W) also helps reduce thermal concerns for a given level of performance.

Evaluating PIM also presents new simulation challenges. Applications that can best exploit the benefits of PIM are those with large data sets that do not effectively fit into caches. Furthermore, the design space of PIM systems is larger than traditional designs, as both PIM and host configurations must be explored. Slow microarchitectural simulators hinder the ability to execute the necessary applications in a reasonable amount of time, which limits the state space that can be studied. As a result, a fast simulation methodology is crucial for exploring a sufficiently broad spectrum of applications and relevant design points. In order to address this challenge, we propose a methodology that first gathers hardware performance and power statistics during execution on current hardware. This data is then fed into a machine learning (ML) model that predicts the performance and power on future PIM and host hardware configurations.

This paper makes the following primary contributions:

- We explore the viability of GPU-accelerated architectures as in-memory processors and explore their system design space in near-future technology nodes. To our knowledge, this is the first study of using GPUs for in-memory computing in order to accelerate a non-stacked host processor.

- In order to enable rapid design space exploration, we present a simulation methodology that automatically scales performance and power values from existing hardware to future design points and quantify its accuracy.

- We evaluate the energy and performance impact of PIM in near-future technology nodes across a broad range of GPGPU workloads and identify characteristics that make a workload amenable to offload to a throughput-oriented, in-memory accelerator.

The remainder of the paper is organized as follows. Section 2 provides relevant background information. Section 3 describes our proposed system organization with GPU-accelerated in-memory processors. Section 4 describes and characterizes the benchmarks used for our evaluations. Sections 5 and 6 present the performance and power models we have developed for exploring PIM organizations. Section 7 presents and discusses evaluation results. Sections 8 and 9 discuss future directions and related prior work. Finally, Section 10 summarizes our findings and concludes.

2. BACKGROUND AND MOTIVATION

2.1 3D Die Stacking

Vertical stacking of logic and memory dies has been widely discussed in the research literature [12, 28, 31, 32]. We focus on two primary high-level architectural implications of 3D stacking. First, 3D stacking allows multiple implementation technologies to be integrated within a stack, allowing DRAM and logic dies to be coupled together. This is fundamental to our in-memory architecture, in contrast to previous works that try to implement both computation and storage in the same design process. Second, interconnections within a die stack, in the form of through silicon vias (TSV), enable higher bandwidth, lower latency and lower energy communication among the dies within a stack, relative to 2D organizations. The improved bandwidth arises primarily from higher TSV density and the ability to clock these "on-chip" links at higher frequencies than off-chip links with reasonable complexity and energy overheads. TSV pitches of 10-50μm were reported as of 2011 across a variety of vendors, and ITRS roadmaps predict 4-8μm global TSV pitches in the 2015-2018 time frame [7]. Latency and energy benefits arise from the shorter, on-chip vertical distances traversed, and the reduced capacitance compared to off-chip connections and longer wires on 2D organizations. Prior work has estimated that traversal latency of even an extreme case of 20 dies stacked vertically to be on the order of 12ps [32].

2.2 Memory Power

The energy impact of off-chip memory is amplified by the characteristics of today's mainstream DRAM interfaces. Delay/Phase Locked Loops (DLL/PLL) and clocks in high-performance DRAM interfaces such as DDR3 and GDDR5 consume significant energy even when no data is being transferred resulting in high idle power consumption and poor energy proportionality. Prior studies have shown that the effective energy per bit for DDR3 increases by integer factors at low utilization due to interface overheads [33]. Some estimates suggest that 70% or more of the energy per DRAM access is consumed in the DDR3 interface [27, 29]. While mobile DRAM standards (e.g., LPDDR2, LPDDR3) provide lower idle power consumption, they do so at the cost of reduced bandwidth. Emerging memory standards based on high-speed serial links, such as Hybrid Memory Cube (HMC) [37], introduce other interface overheads, including those due to the energy and latency of serialization and de-serialization. The "short reach" SERDES physical interface (PHY) of HMC is expected to consume 5-10 pJ/b out of an expected memory energy budget of 13-20 pJ/b [10, 37]. On the other hand, traversal of a 3D TSV is expected to consume on the order of 30-110 fJ/b [4]. Therefore, there is significant potential to reduce effective memory energy consumption by incorporating die-stacked, in-memory processors and reducing the overheads associated with high-bandwidth, off-chip interfaces.

2.3 GPU Architecture

At a high level, GPU architectures consist of collections of simple execution units (ALUs) operating under a single-instruction, multiple-thread execution model. We base the discussion in this paper on AMD's Graphics Core Next (GCN) GPU core architecture [8]. A simplified overview of a GCN-like GPU is shown in Figure 2. The computing resources are grouped into Compute Units (CU). From a GPGPU perspective, each CU is composed of four 16-wide SIMD units (along with associated register resources), a scalar unit, L1 cache and a shared scratchpad. The off-chip memory (DRAM) is organized as a set of memory channels, each with an associated slice of the L2 cache. The physical address space is striped among the memory channels and the CUs access L2 and DRAM via an on-chip network.

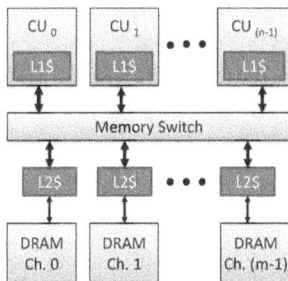

Figure 2: Simplified GPGPU architecture overview

GPUs are highly multi-threaded, with each CU simultaneously running hundreds of threads. This helps them tolerate high-latency operations, such as memory delays; when a thread is stalled due to a long-latency operation, other threads can utilize the available hardware resources. This, in turn, maximizes the computational and memory throughput of GPUs without requiring complex, power-hungry hardware such as out-of-order execution. As such, GPUs can effectively utilize vast amounts of memory bandwidth (consumer GPUs often have 10× or more bandwidth than consumer CPUs). This ability motivates our desire to put GPUs in high-bandwidth in-memory configurations.

2.4 Power and Thermal Considerations

PIM designs raise a number of power-related questions. Like other die-stacked designs [12], PIM can run into thermal constraints because in-memory processor and memory share the same path to the heatsink. Heat from the in-memory processor can raise the temperature of the DRAM,

which places tight bounds on the amount of power PIM can use. The normal operating temperature range for DRAM is considered to be under 85 °C. Any increase in temperature beyond that requires refresh rates to be increased (typically doubled). As such, power estimation is an important aspect of studying PIM and we will factor this consideration into our architecture choices as described in Section 3.2.

3. THROUGHPUT-ORIENTED PIM

In this section, we qualitatively discuss stacked memory organization options and present our architecture with GPU-accelerated in-memory processors.

3.1 Stacked Memory Organization

Anticipated usage scenarios of Wide I/O and HBM, as well as academic studies of 3D stacked memory, predominantly assume one of two organizations: (1) direct 3D stacking of memory on a processor or (2) "2.5D" stacking where processor die(s) and memory stack(s) are mounted side-by-side on a silicon interposer. The first organization provides the benefit of tight coupling between processor and memory but raises thermal challenges. As a result, the thermal envelope of the processor must be constrained to avoid excessively degrading retention time of the stacked DRAM, reducing peak compute performance. The refresh rate of the DRAM may also need to be increased due to heat from the processor, further reducing performance. These constraints can offset a significant fraction of the performance potential of die-stacked memories, especially in high-performance systems. Further, the memory capacity that can be stacked in this organization is limited by the footprint of the processor.

The second organization (2.5D) reduces thermal concerns but incurs the additional cost of an interposer and introduces energy and latency overheads due to all DRAM accesses traversing the interposer. Bandwidth through the interposer may also be lower than that of 3D stacking because it is difficult to have as many wires in the interposer as there are TSVs in the 3D stack, necessitating a reduction in parallel communication channels and bandwidth.

A third alternative, adopted in HMC, is to integrate only the memory controller(s) and other memory support logic on the base dies of the memory stacks. The main processor is not stacked with memory and communicates with memory stacks via board-level or in-package links. This approach avoids thermal and capacity limitations but falls short of the performance and energy benefits of 3D or 2.5D stacking for bandwidth-intensive applications.

The approach we consider, shown in Figure 1, combines desirable aspects of the above three organizations. In-memory processors incorporated on the base logic dies of memory stacks provide the full bandwidth and energy efficiency of true 3D stacking for executing memory-intensive application segments. This alleviates the bandwidth demands on the links between host and memory, enabling board- and package-level interconnects for those links, unlike the more expensive interposer-based solutions required for 2.5D organizations. The host processor does not have stacked memory, thereby avoiding stringent thermal constraints, and can support high performance for compute-intensive code. A similar approach was proposed by Balaprakash et al. in an application-centric study [9]. In this work, we further incorporate realistic hardware area and power constraints. In addition, we analyze a specific processor microarchitecture

(GPU) to determine practical SoC design points and analyze other system bottlenecks beyond memory bandwidth.

3.2 Processor Architecture

Both the host and in-memory processors in our system organization are accelerated processing units (APU). Each APU consists of CPU and GPU cores on the same silicon die. We believe the choice of an APU as the in-memory processor has several benefits. First, the CPU and GPU components support familiar programming models and lower the barrier of using in-memory processors. Second, the programmability allows a broad range of applications to exploit PIM. Third, the use of existing GPU and CPU designs lowers the investment and risk inherent in developing PIM. Finally, the architectural uniformity of the host and in-memory processors ease porting of code to exploit PIM. Porting a subset of an application's routines (*e.g.*, the memory-intensive kernels) to PIM does not require a fundamental rewrite as the same languages, run-time systems and abstractions are supported on both host and in-memory processors. Syntactically, simply annotating the routines that are to be executed using PIM is sufficient. Due to these reasons, we adopt an existing GPU core microarchitecture for PIM. However, to our knowledge, this is the first study to consider a system organization incorporating GPU-accelerated architectures for in-memory computing.

The key programmability challenge in porting applications to our system organization is the distribution of data among multiple memory stacks and ensuring the locality of PIM computation with the associated data. For the purposes of this study, we designed a low-level API that allows programmer control over what data is allocated in a given stack and the ability to dispatch the associated computation to that stack. Further, we study throughput-oriented computations that are natural candidates for effectively utilizing the increased memory bandwidth available to in-memory processors. Consequently, we primarily focus on the GPU execution engines here.

We consider two potential PIM design points geared towards high-performance applications, one in 22nm technology and another in 16nm technology. The relevant hardware configuration parameters are listed in Table 1. The characteristics of these design points were determined based on past GPU architecture scaling trends and publicly available projections of future implementation technologies [7, 14]. As we focus this evaluation on GPU compute aspects, we omit the CPU configuration parameters. We do not include application code execution on the CPU cores of either host or PIM APUs in our evaluations.

As has been the recent trend, we assume host GPU architecture scaling occurs primarily through increasing the number of CUs and not through higher frequencies. We approximate this by holding the CU frequency roughly comparable to today's high-end discrete GPUs over the technology generations studied. The number of host CUs were selected to provide reasonable approximations of possible high-performance APU design points in future technologies. We made no effort to normalize host CU resources across the two configurations (*e.g.*, the host of the 16nm configuration incurs a 33% increase in area and a 34% increase in thermal design power (TDP) attributable to CUs over the 22nm configuration due to doubling of the number of CUs).

Table 1. Host and PIM configurations

	Config. 1	Config. 2
Technology node (nm)	22	16
Host		
Number of CU	32	64
Freq (MHz)	1000	1000
DRAM BW (GB/s)	320	640
DRAM BW/stack (GB/s)	160	160
DRAM capacity per stack (GB)	2	4
Number of DRAM stacks	2	4
Per-stack PIM		
Number of CU	8	12
Freq (MHz)	650	650
DRAM BW per stack (GB/s)	640	640

In-memory processor organizations of the two configurations were selected to fit within the constraints of a DRAM stack. Historically, DRAM die sizes have hovered in the range of 40-80 mm^2 [44]. We assume a logic base die size near the upper end of that range and the CU count of each configuration is selected to not exceed 50% of the logic die's area (including CU support hardware structures, shared caches etc.). The configurations of the in-memory processors were also constrained to not exceed 10W TDP attributable to CUs, caches and support hardware. According to our thermal models, this power level leaves sufficient headroom for other components within the stack while not exceeding 85 °C (and thereby avoiding the need to increase DRAM refresh rates) with commercially viable air-cooling solutions for high-performance systems. Note that these assumptions are more conservative, and result in lower power density, than some previous studies incorporating stacked DRAM [25]. We have also selected conservative operating frequencies for the in-memory processors to reduce dynamic and static power consumption.

We assume the internal CU microarchitecture (including cache hierarchy) does not change significantly from today's high-end GPUs over the period studied as well as between host and PIM implementations. Naturally, this is an unrealistic assumption from a microarchitectural perspective as CU implementations will continue to be refined and improved and variations in cache hierarchy may be desired between host and in-memory processors. However, our focus here is to understand the high-order performance and energy effects of in-memory computation relative to traditional organizations. Therefore, we assume that improvements internal to the processor are likely to benefit both PIM and host implementations in corresponding degrees and defer the evaluation of the impact of microarchitectural evolution to future work.

3.3 Memory Organization

In keeping with recent trends, we assume a memory bandwidth to compute ratio slightly greater than today's high-end GPUs at the 22nm node. While we double the raw bandwidth at the 16nm point, we hold the ratio of bandwidth to compute constant. We loosely model the memory interfaces from host to memory stacks on publicly available data on HMC [3, 37]. Each memory stack provides 160GB/s of bandwidth to the host processor. For PIM configurations, we assume intra-stack memory bandwidth four times greater than externally available bandwidth. We explore the sensitivity to this factor in Section 7.

Figure 1 also identifies the key memory interfaces in our organization. As requests from both the host and PIM must be serviced by the DRAM, the DRAM controllers reside on the logic dies in the memory stacks. Therefore, the interface subject to DRAM timing constraints is the vertical interface between the logic die and the memory dies within each stack. The interface from the host to each memory stack is an abstract, split-transaction, load/store-oriented one.

4. APPLICATIONS

We used 70 kernels from the sources described below for training and validating our ML-based performance prediction model. However, our energy model relies on average power measurements from GPU hardware which is currently only feasible in our framework for kernels with a run time of 1ms or longer. Therefore, we focus our application characterizations (and results discussion in Section 7) on kernels with a run time of 1ms or longer on our AMD Radeon HD 7970 native execution platform.

To provide an overall characterization of the application kernels, we use the following two metrics: sustained bandwidth usage and the number of vector ALU instructions executed per second. Figure 3 shows the kernels discussed in Section 7 in the two-dimensional space of the aforementioned metrics. For applications with multiple kernels, the kernel name is prepended with the application identifiers specified later in this section.

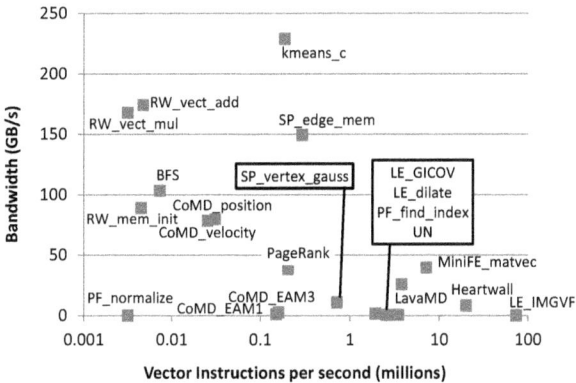

Figure 3: Characteristics of the application kernels

4.1 Graph Applications

We implemented a number of graph applications for this study. *Random walk* (RW) is a GPU implementation based on prior work by Gartner *et al.* [22]. Given a pair of graphs, it first performs random walks on both, then determines and counts the number of matching walks. *Shortest path* (SP) is a GPU implementation based on the prior work by Borgwardt *et al.* [13]. We first convert the input graphs into all pairs of shortest path graphs and compare them by applying a Gaussian kernel on the vertices and edges. *Unordered neighboring* (UN) determines similarities between nodes of two graphs by computing pair-wise similarities between nodes in their neighbor sets. *PageRank* is an algorithm proposed to prioritize web search results. Our implementation is based on recent work by Che *et al.* [17].

4.2 HPC Applications

The Mantevo Project [24] provides a collection of applications designed to mimic the characteristics of widely used high-performance computing algorithms. We study two of these. *MiniFE* represents the characteristics of larger applications modeling fluid and structural dynamics. Sparse matrix-vector multiplications dominate the execution time of the core computation of this benchmark and was chosen due to the importance of sparse matrix operations in HPC workloads. Codesigned Molecular Dynamics (*CoMD*) is a simplified molecular dynamics workflow. *CoMD* implements both Lennard-Jones and Embedded Atom Method (EAM) potential calculations. We use the EAM approach for its relevance for real HPC workloads.

4.3 Adapted Rodinia Benchmarks

Rodinia is a widely used GPGPU benchmark suite intended to be a representative sample covering a wide range of workload characteristics [18]. We use it here to augment the application space covered by the other benchmarks described above. While all Rodinia benchmarks are used in training our performance model, only the benchmarks with at least one kernel with execution time longer than 1 ms that can be obtained by increasing the input data size without algorithmic modifications are presented in our results discussions. The benchmarks that fit this criterion are *Breadth-first search* (BFS), *Heartwall*, *Kmeans*, *Leukocyte* (LE), *particle filter* (PF), and *LavaMD*.

5. PIM PERFORMANCE MODEL AND VALIDATION

Two broad categories of performance models – structural and analytical – are commonly studied in the literature [38]. The former uses simulation techniques to model systems while the latter abstracts design factors of interest into an analytical expression to predict performance. Cycle-accurate simulation is commonly used to evaluate design proposals because it allows researchers to directly model how architectural changes interact with the system. However, these simulators typically run many orders of magnitude slower than native execution and quickly become intractable for long-running workloads. This is especially true for workloads with large data sets and irregular memory access patterns, which are of particular interest for PIM evaluations. Therefore, in this study, we develop an analytical performance modeling framework to study how throughput-oriented PIM systems would perform.

5.1 Performance Model

At a high-level, our simulation framework relies on analyzing an application's behavior on existing GPU hardware to predict the performance of that application on future GPU configurations, including in-memory implementations. The application under test is executed on a real GPU operating at a known configuration (*e.g.*, number of CUs, processor frequency, memory bandwidth). For each GPU kernel invoked, hardware performance counter statistics are gathered, characterizing the application as it runs. This yields both the current performance of the application as well as statistics that indicate how the kernels ran. The statistics gathered from the native execution for each kernel are then fed to an ML-based performance scaling model that predicts the per-

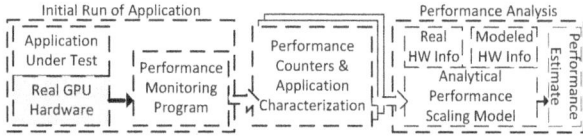

Figure 4: PIM performance modeling framework

formance at other machine configuration points of interest. The overall approach of this methodology is illustrated in Figure 4.

In essence, training kernels are analyzed under different machine configurations to ascertain their sensitivity to metrics such as parallelism, frequency, and memory bandwidth. Hardware performance counters are used to "fingerprint" these training runs. Later, the performance counters from a kernel under analysis will be used to find which training kernel it is most like. This, in turn, enables the model to predict the execution time on a GPU with a different mix of resources. For example, the real GPU used for native execution may be a 1GHz core with 32 CUs and 264GB/s of bandwidth to DRAM. Using the runtime and hardware performance information of an application on this device, our model could, for example, estimate the performance of the same application on a GPU with 8 CUs running at 700MHz with 400GB/s of memory bandwidth.

We use an AMD Radeon HD 7970 GPU for native execution and AMD's CodeXL profiler to collect performance counter metrics from hardware. The specific statistics gathered using performance counters include the number of vector and scalar instructions executed, the number of memory access instructions, the number of local data share accesses, utilization factors of various execution units, cache hit rates and the amount of data accessed from DRAM.

Scaling Assumptions

The key component of the above performance prediction methodology is the model that consumes the data from the native execution and scales the execution time to other hardware configurations. With T_{native} as the measured execution time of an arbitrary kernel on a known, native hardware configuration HW_{native}, the goal of the model is to implement the scaling function m such that:

$$T_{predict} = m(T_{native}, HW_{native}, HW_{predict}, P_{native})$$

where P_{native} is the set of performance counters gathered during native execution, $HW_{predict}$ is the future hardware configuration for which performance is to be predicted, and $T_{predict}$ is the predicted execution time of the same kernel invocation on that future hardware.

In our framework, this model is built on the following assumptions: (1) the detailed microarchitecture of the CUs of $HW_{predict}$ is similar to that of HW_{native} and, therefore, kernel performance is correlated to coarse configuration parameters such as the number of CUs, processor frequency and memory bandwidth; (2) kernels with similar statistics across a broad range of performance counter readings have similar sensitivity to hardware parameters; and (3) the performance impact of varying multiple hardware parameters is separable and the cumulative impact can be approximated by scaling first for the variation of one parameter followed by subsequent scaling for additional parameters.

The rest of this section describes how the ML-based model is constructed off-line using a large amount of training data and how it is used online for performance prediction.

Off-line Learning

Our ML-based performance model is trained using 70 kernels over a discretized 3D grid of 162 operating points that are supported by the native hardware used for our experiments. The dimensions of the grid are the number of CUs (C), CU frequency (f), and memory bandwidth (B). The number of CUs is varied among 32, 16 and 8. The CU frequency is varied from 500 to 1000 MHz in steps of 100 MHz. Memory bandwidth is varied by changing the memory frequency from 500 to 1300 MHz in steps of 100 MHz. Each kernel from the training set is executed at each point on this hardware configuration grid and the kernel execution time and performance counter statistics are obtained. We derive a kernel *feature vector* based on the collected hardware counter statistics at each point in the grid. Once feature vectors are available for all grid points for a given kernel, they are normalized to account for the varying scales used in gathering different metrics. Subsequently, we group the feature vectors of one kernel as a feature array for this kernel.

At each point on the HW configuration grid we also compute a time ratio triplet:

$$(RT_C, RT_f, RT_B) = (\frac{T_{C1}}{T_{C0}}, \frac{T_{f1}}{T_{f0}}, \frac{T_{B1}}{T_{B0}})$$

where each component is a time ratio between neighboring points on the 3D HW grid with other two parameters held constant. For example, RT_C is a time ratio between two neighboring points with different numbers of CUs but with fixed CU frequency and memory bandwidth. Similarly RT_f is a time ratio between two neighboring CU frequency points with fixed number of CUs and memory frequency. And RT_B is a time ratio between two neighboring memory bandwidth points with fixed number of CUs and CU frequency. This results in a 3D time ratio matrix with each element being a vector consisting of these three time ratio components.

Next, we proceed to the key part of the off-line learning process:

- Time ratio matrices are clustered into a predefined number of n clusters (in our implementation, $n = 4$) using the *k-means* algorithm.

- The clustering process produces n centroids, each of which is a time ratio matrix and a corresponding feature array partition. This maps each kernel feature array to a "representative" time ratio matrix.

- Using leave-one-out evaluation to guide the refinement of the clustering, an inner loop is performed:
  - For each test feature vector we use the *k-nearest neighbor* classification with $k = 5$ to find the cluster to which that feature vector belongs.
  - The representative time ratio matrix of the chosen cluster centroid is selected. This matrix is used when performing the prediction because the application under test appears similar to the known applications.
  - The prediction calculation is performed subject to the assumptions described earlier in this section to provide a predicted processing time at each point on the HW configuration grid.

- A relative error is calculated at each point of the grid by comparing predicted time with real measured execution time at that particular hardware configuration.
- The mean of the relative errors is calculated over all feature vectors for the set of time ratio clusters.

To improve the quality of the clustering, this off-line learning process is conducted a sufficiently large number of times to repeat the clustering process with a new set of randomly selected seeds. Each iteration returns one mean relative error. The iteration yielding the minimum error is selected as our learned clusters.

In summary, during the training phase, the above described model "learns" a classification of kernels into different types based on their scaling characteristics and the sensitivity of each type of kernel to individual hardware parameters. As described in the following subsection, this knowledge is then used to predict execution times of new kernels at future design points, resulting in a much more sophisticated model than linearly scaling performance with hardware parameters. Not only is this model sensitive to the fact that some kernels are not affected by some parameters (e.g., memory-bound kernels are insensitive to processor frequency), but it is also able to infer complex interactions between the scaling coefficients of different parameters.

Online Prediction

Once the ML-based performance prediction model is built, performance prediction of new kernels is performed in near-real-time. For an arbitrary application with arbitrary problem sizes running on a known baseline hardware configuration, we collect the performance counter statistics for each kernel invocation and convert the data to a feature vector to be normalized in the same way as the training set. The prediction algorithm is very similar to the body of the off-line inner loop. The normalized feature vector is classified to find a cluster that the new kernel is closest to. Based on that, the representative time ratio matrix is selected and a prediction calculation chain is performed over the selected time ratio matrix based on the baseline (native) HW configuration, the predicted HW configuration and the native execution time. The result is a predicted processing time for the same kernel with the same problem size running on the predicted HW configuration. It is important to note that this model allows performance prediction not just at different hardware configurations, but also for previously unseen kernels.

5.2 Performance Model Validation

The leave-one-out process described for training the model also provides a method for characterizing the prediction accuracy of the model. A kernel that was not used for training the model is executed at a point p in the grid of hardware points described in Section 5.1 and the performance model is used to predict the execution time of that kernel at the other 161 points of the grid. This process is repeated for all possible values of p on the grid for that kernel, resulting in 26,082 ($= 161 * 162$) predictions per kernel. Each of the predicted times are then compared to the measured execution time at the corresponding hardware configuration to calculate the prediction errors. While this does not tell us directly how accurate our estimation is when modeling hardware settings outside our current GPU's range, estima-

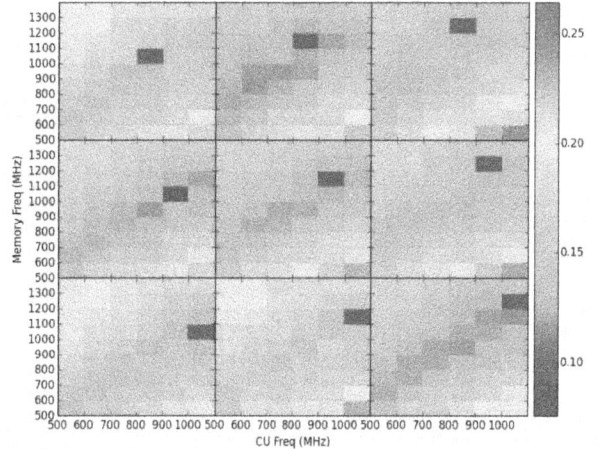

Figure 5: Prediction error (fraction) averaged over all benchmarks for nine native configurations. Purple rectangles are the native configurations and the color scale indicates the different estimation errors when predicting from that native point to other points.

tion mechanisms that have high accuracy in these tests are more likely to be accurate for other design points as well.

Figure 5 shows a subset of the prediction errors of our model determined using the above approach, averaged over all of our benchmarks. Each of the nine tiles in the figure shows the prediction error using a different native execution point p indicated by the dark block. Figure 6 shows the average prediction errors for the kernels discussed in detail in this paper. The dotted line shows the average error (16.1%) across the full set of 70 kernels used in this work.

While our model is intended for near-real-time execution time prediction (after the one-time training overhead), the measured error of our model relative to hardware is competitive with errors observed for detailed simulators that run orders of magnitude slower. For example, Gutierrez *et al.* find 13% to 17% errors in correlating a custom-configured gem5 simulation framework to corresponding real hardware [23], while disabling the hardware features that gem5 couldn't model accurately. Weaver and McKee find errors of 24.6% and 67.6% for integer and floating point SPEC CPU benchmarks between SESC and real hardware [45]. Furthermore, even Yourst's evaluation of a highly-tuned, cycle-accurate simulator, PTLsim, shows 4.3% execution time prediction errors [48].

6. PIM ENERGY MODEL

Much like our performance model, our energy estimates are based on measuring power consumption on existing hardware on a per-kernel basis and projecting to future designs based on technology and system parameters. This power model is similar to the performance model shown in Figure 4. However, in addition to gathering performance counters, it also directly gathers power usage from the hardware.

The first step is to gather dynamic power data from our native execution platform – an AMD Radeon HD 7970 running at a core clock frequency of 1 GHz. AMD GPUs

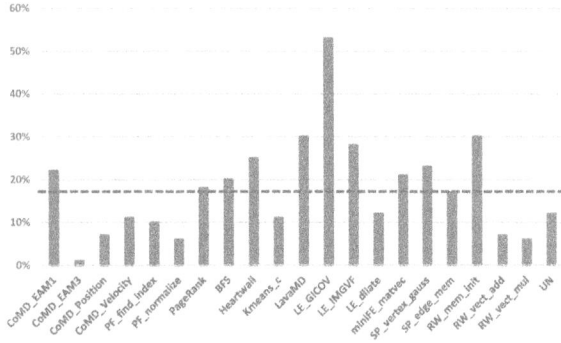

Figure 6: Individual benchmark prediction errors

Table 2. Dynamic power and memory energy estimates

	Baseline	Host		PIM	
Technology (nm)	28	22	16	22	16
Freq (MHz)	1000	1000	1000	650	650
Capacitance scaling	1.00	0.75	0.56	0.75	0.56
Vdd (V)	1.2	1.09	1.03	0.87	0.83
Dynamic CU power scaling	1.00	0.61	0.41	0.25	0.17
Memory energy (pJ/64b)	N/A	522	520	159	155

make chip-wide dynamic and static power available through memory-mapped registers that can be read by the host CPU. A host-side application polls these registers as GPU kernels are executed.

Because dynamic power usage of a chip is influenced by the operations executed on it (rather than just its temperature and voltage), it is important to have multiple dynamic power readings per computational kernel. Since we are able to scale performance only at the granularity of a kernel, we study the average power used over each kernel execution.

The dynamic power values read from the hardware encompass the GPU's die power, but do not include memories on the graphics card, physical interfaces, or other power drains at the periphery of the chip. Accounting for memory energy in our model is described later in this section.

The power values that we gather from existing hardware must be scaled to estimate the power that similar workloads would require on future systems. The two key components of this are scaling to future technologies (and corresponding operating points) and scaling to account for variations in the numbers of CUs.

Scaling to future technologies in our model is based on industry technology scaling projections and the ITRS [14, 7]. Based on those projections, we compute scaling factors for dynamic energy from current 28nm hardware to future design points of interest. Where our desired operating frequency f, as specified in Table 1, differs from those indicated by scaling projections, we adjust V_{dd} based on the relation $f \propto (V_{dd} - V_t)^2/V_{dd}$. Table 2 shows the relevant parameters and dynamic power scaling factors. We compute memory energy for future design points directly from access counts and, therefore, per-access energy from the baseline is not used in our projections.

Table 3. TDP variation normalized for voltage, frequency (MHz), and CU count

Design	CUs	Freq	Normalized TDP/CU
Radeon HD 7770	10	800	1.000
Radeon HD 7870	20	900	1.002
Radeon HD 7970	32	900	0.912
Radeon HD 7970	32	950	0.979

Our model scales design dynamic power (excluding memory and IO) linearly with the number of CUs. This assumes that other on-die resources outside the CUs scale with the number of CUs as well. We show TDP across four AMD GPU implementations from the same generation normalized for operating voltage, frequency and the number of CUs in Table 3. This data shows that TDP scales with CU count to within 10% across these designs and that linear scaling with CU count, therefore, is a reasonable approximation for an analytical model.

We base our static power estimates on the aggressiveness of the target design points for each processor's implementation. For host processors at 1GHz, we assume 30% of TDP as static power. For PIM targeting significantly less aggressive 650MHz operation, we assume 10% of TDP as leakage. We base these off scaled TDP to account for technology, operating point and configuration differences. We use this method instead of scaling the observed static power usage of application runs because static power readings are influenced by temperature, which is difficult to control between runs and may be different for future systems.

Finally, after estimating the power needed to run a computational kernel on a future GPU or PIM, the performance and power estimates are combined to yield energy estimates.

For host memory energy estimation, we assume SERDES power of 5pJ/b, at the low end of the HMC short reach PHY estimates [6]. We assume 7pJ per 64 bits of data for TSV traversal within the stack [4]. For both host and PIM, we assume 2pJ/b for DRAM access itself [27, 29]. We also incorporate factors accounting for wire traversal on the logic die (host or PIM) proportional to the square roots of the corresponding die areas. Table 2 shows the resulting per-access energy for a 64b word. These per access energy estimates are multiplied by dynamically observed access counts (from hardware performance counters) to compute total memory energy estimates. Even though off-chip memory interfaces often have high idle power overheads, we do not account for idle power consumption of host memory interfaces, which introduces a slight bias against the PIM configurations in our energy estimates.

As the objective of our study is to evaluate the energy efficiency of host computation relative to PIM computation, we assume the host is power-gated during PIM execution. Similarly, we assume the PIM logic is power-gated during host execution (aside from the memory access path) and does not contribute to system energy. We defer evaluating concurrent use of host and PIM to future work.

7. EVALUATION

We quantitatively evaluate the PIM architecture design choices described in Section 3 with the set of applications described in Section 4, using our performance and energy models.

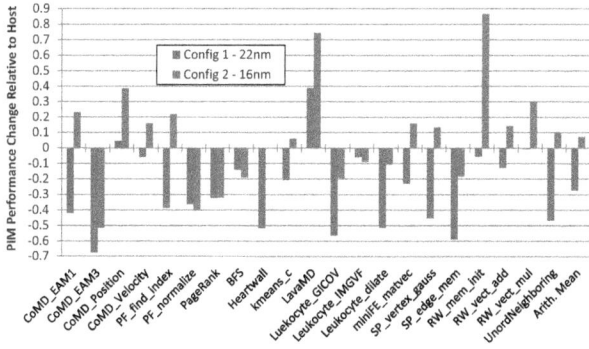

Figure 7: Performance change when executing on PIM, normalized to host performance. Positive values mean higher performance on PIM, while zero implies no performance change.

As discussed in Section 3.2, the characteristics of the design points evaluated here were determined based on past GPU architecture scaling trends and publicly available projections of future implementation technologies [7, 15]. We factored in both prevailing design and technology trends as well as hardware constraints such as area, power, and thermals. We believe this results in a distilled set of realistic design points for both the host and PIM processor implementations.

7.1 Performance Impact

Figure 7 shows the performance of each kernel on PIM normalized to the performance on the corresponding host. This reflects the performance tradeoff of running each kernel on PIM or host at a given technology node based on the configurations described in Table 1. We model each kernel executing on all in-memory processors (i.e., two at 22nm and four at 16nm) in parallel except where noted otherwise later in this section.

As expected, in general, kernels with high compute requirements and low memory demands as characterized by Figure 3 suffer slowdowns on PIM at 22nm. The bandwidth advantages of PIM combined with improved relative PIM compute performance at 16nm (as a result of more CUs within the same 10W-per-stack budget) results in some of these, such as *CoMD_EAM1*, *SP_vertex_gauss* and *UN*, showing performance improvements over host execution. While the limited compute capability of PIM at 22nm results in slowdowns for most kernels, bandwidth-heavy kernels such as *CoMD_position*, *CoMD_velocity*, and *RW_mem_init* show significant performance gains on PIM at 16nm.

Balanced applications with high compute and bandwidth demands, such as *kmeans_c* and *SP_edge_mem* typically perform slower on PIM at 22nm, but gain performance with improved PIM compute capabilities at 16nm.

A number of benchmarks behave counter-intuitively to the characterization in Figure 3. *PF_normalize* and *PageRank* are dominated by synchronization and do not scale to multiple in-memory processors. Therefore, they are constrained to running on a single PIM instance, which results in degraded performance relative to host execution. *LE_IMGVF* does not have sufficient parallelism at the application level to utilize PIM across multiple memory stacks, and is also constrained to run on a single in-memory pro-

cessor. *BFS*, while bandwidth-heavy, is bottlenecked by L1 cache bandwidth due to uncoalesced memory accesses and does not benefit from the improved bandwidth afforded by PIM. Conversely, *LavaMD*, while not bandwidth-intensive, is limited by L2 cache bandwidth and memory latency. As L2 cache bandwidth of GPU architectures are typically correlated to memory system performance (and not processor performance), our model predicts performance benefits for LavaMD from the improved memory system of PIM. *PF_find_index* and *Heartwall* are also L2 bandwidth bound to a lesser extent and is predicted to benefit from high memory system performance of PIM, especially at 16nm. *RW_vect_add* and *RW_vect_mul*, while bandwidth intensive, become constrained by the greatly reduced execution resources available on the 22nm PIM configuration but show speedups over host at the 16nm configuration.

These observations show that while a characterization based on application compute and bandwidth requirements can provide relevant intuitions about computations that may benefit from PIM, deeper analysis and modeling is necessary to fully understand the application characteristics that actually do benefit from the multi-dimensional architectural heterogeneity that exists between PIM and host implementations of even the same underlying microarchitecture.

7.2 Energy Impact

While in-memory processing can help the performance of some applications (especially those that can utilize the added bandwidth), compute-bound applications may see little performance benefit, or even slowdowns, when running their GPGPU computations in memory. Nonetheless, these applications may see energy efficiency benefits.

PIM in our system offers two avenues for these efficiency gains. First, accessing the memory system uses less energy, which directly benefits the energy efficiency of memory-heavy applications. Just as important, however, is the less aggressive processor design used for PIM – they can operate at a much lower frequency and use a less leaky design process while still offering good performance due to their added bandwidth. We found that the in-memory processors in our system always used less energy during our tests.

To quantify the energy impact of our PIM design, we present energy-delay product (EDP) and energy-delay^2 (ED^2) differences between running our benchmarks in memory versus running them on the host. Figure 8 presents the EDP for running the benchmarks on the in-memory processors in 22nm and 16nm designs normalized to the EDP of the host. Figure 9 details the ED^2. In almost all 22nm tests, the PIM's reduced energy yields a better EDP, even for applications that run slower (such as *PF_find_index* and *SP_edge_mem*).

ED^2 more heavily weights performance instead of energy, and Figure 9 shows that, at 22nm, many of the applications that lost performance when moved to PIM are also better run on the host when optimizing ED^2. Nonetheless, at 22nm, PIM is often a more energy-efficient option compared to running on the host.

This trend is further demonstrated at the 16nm design point. In this case, PIM has the benefit, as demonstrated in Section 7.1, of being much more performance competitive with the host. The 16nm node shows that the EDP and ED^2 of PIM is always better than the host, except for the ED^2 of *CoMD_EAM3*. This benchmark is extremely compute intensive, and gains little from in-memory execution.

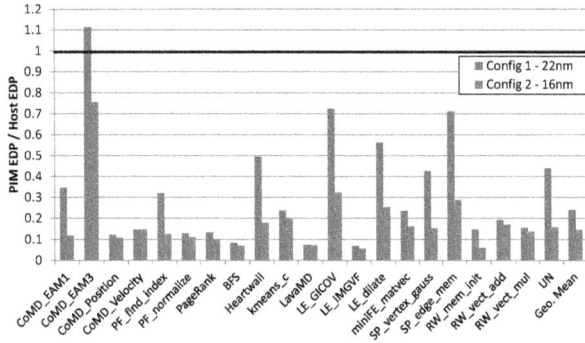

Figure 8: Relative energy delay product

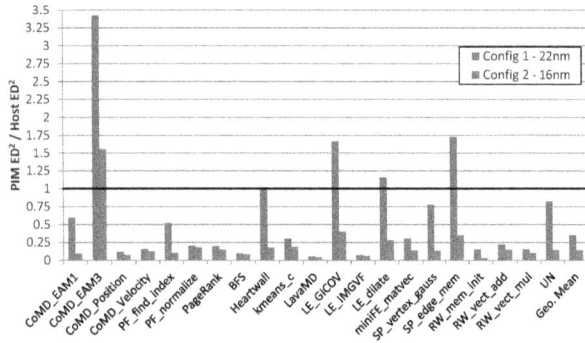

Figure 9: Relative energy-delay^2 (ED^2)

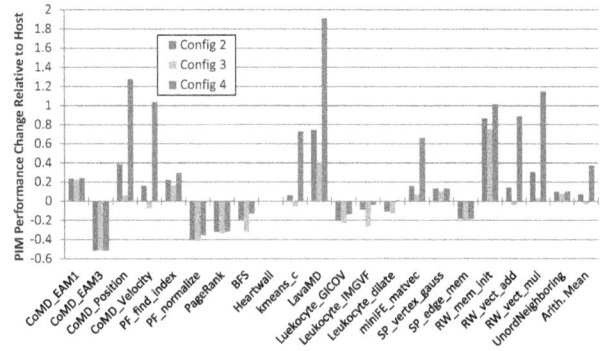

Figure 10: Performance change when executing on PIM, normalized to host performance at 16nm

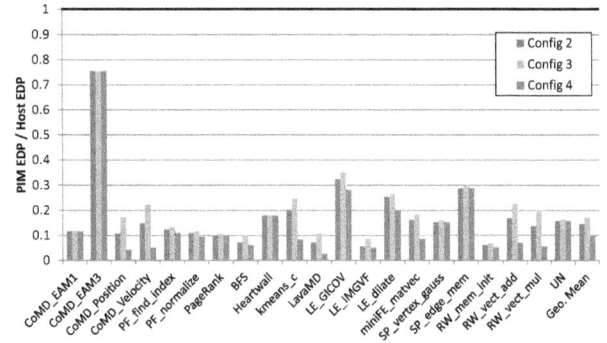

Figure 11: 16nm relative energy delay product

It's worth noting that these energy analyses included core and memory system power, but did not include system power (such as hard disks). These would decrease the energy efficiency benefit of PIM for programs that show a performance loss. However, the difference in power between using the host and PIM was often between 50-70W. As such, the difference when including the rest of the system (which may be blades or diskless HPC servers) will still likely benefit PIM in many cases. Conversely, for applications that run faster on PIM, the energy efficiency benefits when considering the full system may be even greater than reflected in our analyses.

In order to study the sensitivity of the above results to the relative bandwidth ratio between host and PIM, we analyze the two additional configurations described in Table 4. Config 3 is identical to Config 2 but with half the bandwidth for PIM and Config 4 is identical to Config 2 but with half the bandwidth for the host.

Table 4. Configurations to study bandwidth sensitivity

	Config. 3	Config. 4
Technology node (nm)	16	16
Host		
DRAM BW (GB/s)	640	320
DRAM BW/stack (GB/s)	160	80
Per-stack PIM		
DRAM BW per stack (GB/s)	320	640

7.3 Sensitivity to Bandwidth

Figure 10 shows the relative performance change of PIM for Configs 2, 3, and 4 normalized to the corresponding

hosts. Kernels that are heavily compute-limited (e.g., CoMD-_EAM3) are insensitive to the bandwidth variations. However, the reduced bandwidth of Config 3 leads to lower PIM performance for many of the other kernels. Similarly, decreasing the bandwidth of the host in Config 4 results in very significant slowdowns on the host for bandwidth-sensitive kernels.

Figures 11 and 12 show the normalized EDP and ED^2 for Configs 2, 3, and 4. These results show that, even if the in-memory processors were constrained by more pessimistic bandwidth considerations (as in Config 3), the energy benefits of moving the computation into the memory system still hold. Energy efficiency is reduced for these applications because the PIM performance benefits are reduced, but the 3D stacking and less aggressive designs still yield EDP and ED^2 benefits. The more constrained host of Config 4, which reduces the host's performance, again demonstrates this point.

8. FUTURE DIRECTIONS

This work represents a characterization of the tradeoffs of a specific type of processor (the GPU component of an APU) which we believe to be a good fit for in-memory computation. A thorough evaluation of the design space for in-memory processors using 3D die stacking requires a broad exploration encompassing other forms of programmable processors as well as configurable and fixed function processors. Further, this study evaluates the performance and energy efficiency of executing on PIM or host. Other usage models, such as offloading some computations to PIM thereby freeing up the host for other forms of computation, may provide additional benefits and need to be explored.

We have also assumed a generic GPGPU microarchitecture and memory hierarchy for our in-memory processors

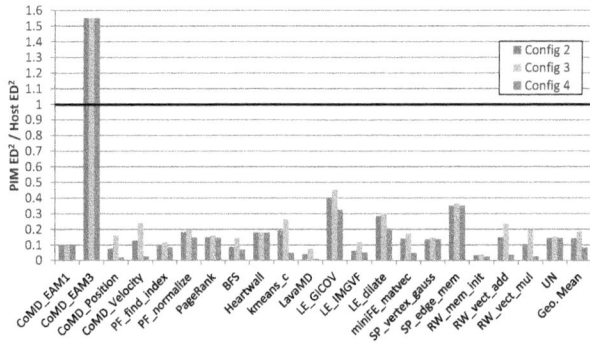

Figure 12: 16nm relative energy-delay^2

in this initial study. Optimization of the architecture and microarchitecture specifically for in-memory processing as well as specialization of communication and synchronization mechanisms present other rich areas for future research. A further area is the impact on host processor architecture if memory-intensive code segments are offloaded to in-memory processors.

As we adopt GPUs and APUs as the PIM processors, augmenting existing programming models (such as OpenCL) with an API to control data placement and compute dispatch suffices for the hardware design space evaluation presented in this paper. However, programmability for future systems with PIM components is a key area that requires further significant research. In particular, more research is needed on high-level abstractions to express application-level locality and data-compute affinity that enable efficient mapping of data and compute to memory stacks without significant programmer effort.

9. RELATED WORK

PIM attracted significant attention in the research community for a short period around the beginning of this century. Many of those efforts focused on one of two approaches. Efforts such as IRAM [21] integrated embedded DRAM on logic chips. However, this approach could not cost-effectively accommodate sufficient memory capacity for mainstream or high-performance systems due to the reduced density of embedded DRAM and the increased cost-per-bit of memory implemented in cutting-edge processor technologies. Efforts such as ActivePages [34], DIVA [20] and FlexRAM [26] integrated logic on memory dies. However, due to the reduced performance of logic implemented in DRAM processes (typically multiple process generations behind contemporary logic processes), such approaches resulted in in-memory processors with very low performance or highly specialized architectures geared only for select operations. This in turn limited the applicability and programmability of such PIM designs which, along with the cost implications of reduced DRAM density due to the presence of compute logic, limited the adoption of such approaches.

Integrating processors and memory using 3D die stacking, as we evaluate in this paper, does not provide as tight a coupling as integration on a single die. However, this approach enables the in-memory processors to be implemented on separate dies using logic processes and do not require significant changes to commodity memory dies geared towards emerging stacked memory standards. Further, as the in-memory

processors are implemented in logic processes, they can be variants of existing processor designs which enable them to easily support familiar programming models while providing sufficient performance to support a broad range of applications. A similar approach has been advocated in a recent FlexRAM retrospective by J. Torrellas [42]. Balaprakash et al. [9] presented a study on HPC application characteristics and an analytical evaluation of their ability to exploit the increased bandwidth available to PIM. While they focused on extrapolating application characteristics to Exascale levels, we emphasize the hardware aspects of PIM in order to determine what PIM design points would result in performance, power, and thermal benefits. We demonstrate that a throughput-oriented processor (GPU) in the memory can effectively utilize the added bandwidth, benefitting a wide range of applications both in and outside of the HPC domain. We demonstrate that, while exascale computing may benefit from PIM, PIM does not require exascale workloads to be useful.

Sampson et al. [41] proposes a 3D stacked processor organization for accelerating 3D ultrasound beamformation. Pugsley et al. propose specialized processors on the base logic layer of HMC-like memory stacks to accelerate MapReduce workloads [39]. Our work differs from these recent efforts in focusing on programmable processors that support well-understood programming models and are broadly applicable across a variety of application domains instead of catering to a specific application domain. Another recent effort, Micron's Automata Processor, incorporates the ability to perform parallel automata processing within the memory arrays on the DRAM dies themselves [19]. However, this is also geared to a specific class of algorithms and further requires a specialized language to program.

10. CONCLUSION

Reducing off-chip data movement is becoming increasingly important for performance and energy efficiency. PIM has the potential to provide significant reductions in off-chip traffic. In this paper, we have presented an architecture for programmable, GPU-accelerated, in-memory processing implemented using 3D die-stacking and an evaluation of the viability of such an architecture. The throughput-oriented nature of GPU architectures is able to efficiently utilize the high bandwidth made available by vertically stacking in-memory processors directly under memory dies while providing the programmability needed to support a broad range of applications. The design points we evaluated were carefully chosen to be within the power and thermal constraints of 3D memory stacks, further establishing the feasibility of GPU-based PIM in near-future technology nodes.

We evaluated the chosen PIM design points using analytical performance and energy models that extrapolate to future design points using data gathered from hardware performance counters during native execution on existing hardware. Our evaluations show that PIM can provide performance and/or energy benefits for a variety of applications spanning a wide spectrum of compute/bandwidth ratios. On average, across the benchmarks evaluated, viable PIM configurations are shown to provide significant improvements in energy efficiency over representative mainstream configurations (76% reductions in EDP) with moderate performance losses (27% slowdown) at the 22nm technology node. At 16nm, viable PIM configurations are shown to provide marginal performance gains (7%) while providing even greater energy efficiency improvements (85% reductions in EDP) on average. While many research areas remain to be explored in the broader context of PIM, our results demonstrate considerable promise in improving overall energy efficiency and performance of memory-limited applications.

11. ACKNOWLEDGEMENTS

We would like to thank Yasuko Eckert and Wei Huang for their input on modeling memory stack thermals. We appreciate the invaluable comments from the anonymous reviewers.

12. REFERENCES

[1] www.jedec.org/standards-documents/docs/jesd229.

[2] www.jedec.org/standards-documents/docs/jesd235.

[3] www.micron.com/products/hybrid-memory-cube.

[4] ITRS interconnect working group, 2012 update. www.itrs.net/links/2012Summer/Interconnect.pptx.

[5] Elpida begins sample shipments of ddr3 sdram (x32) based on tsv stacking technology. www.elpida.com/en/news/2011/06-27.html, 2011.

[6] Initial hybrid memory cube short-reach interconnect specification issued to consortium adopters. Denali Memory Report, August 2012.

[7] International Technology Roadmap for Semiconductors, 2011 Edition. 2012 update.

[8] AMD. White paper: AMD graphics cores next (GCN) architecture. Jun 2012.

[9] P. Balaprakash, D. Buntinas, A. Chan, A. Guha, R. Gupta, S. H. K. Narayanan, A. A. Chien, P. Hovland, and B. Norris. Exascale workload characterization and architecture implications. In Proceedings of the High Performance Computing Symposium, 2013.

[10] R. Balasubramonian. Exploiting 3D-stacked memory devices. IBM Research seminar, October 2012.

[11] B. Black. Die stacking is happening! In 46th IEEE/ACM International Symposium on Microarchitecture Keynote, 2013.

[12] B. Black, M. Annavaram, N. Brekelbaum, J. DeVale, L. Jiang, G. Loh, D. McCauley, P. Morrow, D. Nelson, D. Pantuso, P. Reed, J. Rupley, S. Shankar, J. Shen, and C. Webb. Die stacking 3D microarchitecture. In International Symposium on Microarchitecture, 2006.

[13] K. Borgwardt and H.-P. Kriegel. Shortest-path kernels on graphs. In 5th International Conference on Data Mining, 2005.

[14] S. Borkar. The exascale challenge. Keynote Presentation, 2010 Asia Academic Forum, Nov 2010.

[15] S. Borkar. Exascale computing – a fact or a fiction? Keynote Speech, 27th International Parallel & Distributed Processing Symposium, 2013.

[16] D. Chang, G. Byun, H. Kim, M. Ahn, S. Ryu, N. Kim, and M. Schulte. Reevaluating the latency claims of 3D stacked memories. In 18th Asia and South Pacific Design Automation Conference, 2013.

[17] S. Che, B. M. Beckmann, S. K. Reinhard, and K. Skadron. Pannotia: Understanding irregular GPGPU graph applications. In International Symposium on Workload Characterization, 2013.

[18] S. Che, M. Boyer, J. Meng, D. Tarjan, J. W. Sheaffer, S.-H. Lee, and K. Skadron. Rodinia: A Benchmark Suite for Heterogeneous Computing. In International Symposium on Workload Characterization, 2009.

[19] P. Dlugosch, D. Brown, P. Glendenning, M. Leventhal, and H. Noyes. An efficient and scalable semiconductor architecture for parallel automata processing. To appear in IEEE Transactions on Parallel and Distributed Systems.

[20] J. Draper, J. Chame, M. Hall, C. Steele, T. Barrett, J. LaCoss, J. Granacki, J. Shin, C. Chen, C. W. Kang, I. Kim, and G. Daglikoca. The architecture of the DIVA processing-in-memory chip. In 16th International Conference on Supercomputing, 2002.

[21] B. R. Gaeke, P. Husbands, X. S. Li, L. Oliker, K. A. Yelick, and R. Biswas. Memory-intensive benchmarks: IRAM vs. cache-based machines. In Proceedings of the 16th International Parallel and Distributed Processing Symposium. IEEE Computer Society, 2002.

[22] T. Gartner, P. Flach, and S. Wrobel. On graph kernels: Hardness results and efficient alternatives. In Learning Theory and Kernel Machines, volume 2777, pages 129–143. 2003.

[23] A. Gutierrez, J. Pusdesris, R. Dreslinski, T. Mudge, C. Sudanthi, C. Emmons, and N. Paver. Sources of error in full-system simulation. In International Symposium on Performance Analysis of Systems and Software, 2014.

[24] D. Heroux, M.A.and Doerfler, P. Crozier, J. Willenbring, H. Edwards, A. Williams, M. Rajan, E. Keiter, H. Thornquist, and R. Numrich. Improving performance via mini-applications. Technical report, SAND2009-5574, 2009.

[25] D. Jevdjic, S. Volos, and B. Falsafi. Die-stacked DRAM caches for servers: hit ratio, latency, or bandwidth? have it all with footprint cache. In 40th International Symposium on Computer Architecture, 2013.

[26] Y. Kang, W. Huang, S.-M. Yoo, D. Keen, Z. Ge, V. Lam, P. Pattnaik, and J. Torrellas. FlexRAM: toward an advanced intelligent memory system. In International Conference on Computer Design, 1999.

[27] S. Keckler, W. Dally, B. Khailany, M. Garland, and D. Glasco. GPUs and the future of parallel computing. Micro, IEEE, 31(5):7–17, 2011.

[28] T. Kgil, S. D'Souza, A. Saidi, N. Binkert, R. Dreslinski, T. Mudge, S. Reinhardt, and K. Flautner. PicoServer: using 3D stacking technology to enable a compact energy efficient chip multiprocessor. In 12th International Conference on Architectural Support for Programming Languages and Operating Systems, 2006.

[29] B. C. Lee, E. Ipek, O. Mutlu, and D. Burger. Architecting phase change memory as a scalable DRAM alternative. SIGARCH Computer Architure News, 37(3):2–13, 2009.

[30] C. Lefurgy, K. Rajamani, F. Rawson, W. Felter, M. Kistler, and T. Keller. Energy management for commercial servers. Computer, 36(12):39–48, 2003.

[31] G. Loh. 3D-stacked memory architectures for multi-core processors. In 35th International Symposium on Computer Architecture, 2008.

[32] G. Loi, B. Agrawal, N. Srivastava, S.-C. Lin, T. Sherwood, and K. Banerjee. A thermally-aware performance analysis of vertically integrated (3-D) processor-memory hierarchy. In *43rd Design Automation Conference*, 2006.

[33] K. T. Malladi, B. C. Lee, F. A. Nothaft, C. Kozyrakis, K. Periyathambi, and M. Horowitz. Towards energy-proportional datacenter memory with mobile DRAM. *SIGARCH Computer Architure News*, 40(3):37–48, 2012.

[34] M. Oskin, F. Chong, and T. Sherwood. Active pages: a computation model for intelligent memory. In *25th Annual International Symposium on Computer Architecture*, 1998.

[35] Y. Y. Pan and T. Zhang. Improving VLIW processor performance using three-dimensional (3d) DRAM stacking. In *20th International Conference on Application-specific Systems, Architectures and Processors*, 2009.

[36] D. Patterson. Why latency lags bandwidth, and what it means to computing. Keynote Address, Workshop on High Performance Embedded Computing, 2004.

[37] J. T. Pawlowski. Hybrid memory cube (HMC). In *Hot Chips 23*, 2011.

[38] S. Pllana, I. Brandic, and S. Benkner. Performance modeling and prediction of parallel and distributed computing systems: A survey of the state of the art. In *1st International Conference on Complex, Intelligent and Software Intensive Systems*, 2007.

[39] S. Pugsley, J. Jestes, H. Zhang, R. Balasubramonian, V. Srinivasan, A. Buyuktosunoglu, A. Davis, and F. Li. Ndc: Analyzing the impact of 3d-stacked memory+logic devices on mapreduce workloads. In *International Symposium on Performance Analysis of Systems and Software*, 2014.

[40] B. M. Rogers, A. Krishna, G. B. Bell, K. Vu, X. W. Jiang, and Y. Solihin. Scaling the bandwidth wall: challenges in and avenues for CMP scaling. 36th International Symposium on Computer Architecture, 2009.

[41] R. Sampson, M. Yang, S. Wei, C. Chakrabarti, and T. Wenisch. Sonic millip3De: A massively parallel 3D-stacked accelerator for 3D ultrasound. In *19th International Symposium on High Performance Computer Architecture*, 2013.

[42] J. Torrellas. FlexRAM: Toward an advanced intelligent memory system: A retrospective paper. In *30th International Conference on Computer Design*, 2012.

[43] A. N. Udipi, N. Muralimanohar, N. Chatterjee, R. Balasubramonian, A. Davis, and N. P. Jouppi. Rethinking DRAM design and organization for energy-constrained multi-cores. In *37th International Symposium on Computer Architecture*, 2010.

[44] T. Vogelsang. Understanding the energy consumption of dynamic random access memories. In *43rd International Symposium on Microarchitecture*, 2010.

[45] V. M. Weaver and S. A. McKee. Are cycle accurate simulations a waste of time? In *The Annual Workshop on Duplicating, Deconstructing, and Debunking*, 2008.

[46] A. White. Exascale challenges: Applications, technologies, and co-design. In *From Petascale to Exascale: R&D Challenges for HPC Simulation Environments ASC Exascale Workshop*, March 2011.

[47] D. H. Woo, N. H. Seong, D. Lewis, and H.-H. Lee. An optimized 3D-stacked memory architecture by exploiting excessive, high-density TSV bandwidth. In *IEEE 16th International Symposium on High Performance Computer Architecture*, 2010.

[48] M. Yourst. PTLsim: A cycle accurate full system x86-64 microarchitectural simulator. In *Performance Analysis of Systems Software International Symposium on*, pages 23–34, 2007.

Improving Energy Efficiency of Embedded DRAM Caches for High-end Computing Systems

Sparsh Mittal
Oak Ridge National
Laboratory
mittals@ornl.gov

Jeffrey S. Vetter
Oak Ridge National
Laboratory and
Georgia Institute of
Technology
vetter@computer.org

Dong Li
Oak Ridge National
Laboratory
lid1@ornl.gov

ABSTRACT

The number of cores in a single chip in the nodes of high-end computing systems is on rise, due, in part, to a number of constraints, such as power consumption. With this, the size of the last level cache (LLC) has also increased significantly. Since LLCs built with SRAM consume high leakage power, power consumption of LLCs is becoming a significant fraction of processor power consumption. To address this issue, researchers have used embedded DRAM (eDRAM) LLCs which consume low leakage power. However, eDRAM caches consume a significant amount of energy in the form of refresh energy. In this paper, we propose ESTEEM, an energy saving technique for embedded DRAM caches. ESTEEM uses dynamic cache reconfiguration to turn off a portion of the cache to save both leakage and refresh energy. It logically divides the cache sets into multiple modules and turns off possibly different number of ways in each module. Microarchitectural simulations confirm that ESTEEM is effective in improving performance and energy efficiency and provides better results compared to a recently-proposed eDRAM cache energy saving technique, namely Refrint. For single and dual-core simulations, the average energy saving in memory subsystem (LLC+main memory) with ESTEEM is 25.8% and 32.6% respectively, and the average weighted speedup is 1.09× and 1.22× respectively. Additional experiments confirm that ESTEEM works well for a wide-range of system and algorithm parameters.

Categories and Subject Descriptors

H.4 [**Information Systems Applications**]: Miscellaneous; D.2.8 [**Software Engineering**]: Metrics—*complexity measures, performance measures*

Keywords

Embedded DRAM (eDRAM) cache, low-power, cache reconfiguration, refresh energy saving, leakage energy saving.

HPDC'14, June 23–27, 2014, Vancouver, BC, Canada.
Copyright 2014 ACM 978-1-4503-2749-7/14/06 ...$15.00.
http://dx.doi.org/10.1145/2600212.2600216

1. INTRODUCTION

Managing power consumption of high-end computing systems is extremely important to continue to scale their performance and avoid intolerable operating costs and failure rates [6,13]. The Tianhe-2 supercomputer with largest performance in the top500 list [3] consumes 17 mega-watt power, which is enough to sustain a city of more than 50,000 people: Since the future exascale systems have a 20MW power budget, an exascale machine built with the technology used in modern supercomputers would consume giga-watts of power. Further, for every watt of power dissipated in the computing systems, an additional 0.5 to 1W of power is consumed by the cooling system also [33]. Given such tight power budgets, energy efficiency of current high-end computing systems must be significantly improved to achieve future exascale computing. For these reasons, energy efficiency has now become a first-order constraint in the design of high-end computing systems.

As single-core processor performance becomes power limited, processor designers are using large number of on-chip cores to improve performance. To feed data to these cores and offset the limitations posed by off-chip memory bandwidth, modern processors use large-size last level caches (LLCs) [28]. For example, Intel's Enterprise Xeon processor uses 30 MB LLC [18]. Conventionally, SRAM has been used to design on-chip caches due to its low access-latency. However, SRAM also consumes large leakage power and hence, large last level caches (LLCs) designed with SRAM consume significant fraction of processor power. As an example, leakage power of last level cache accounts for 20% and 30% of the total power in Intel Core 2 Penryn and Intel Xeon Tulsa processors [26]. Further, it has been shown that if large caches are designed with SRAM, they may occupy 90% of the chip-area in upcoming fourth CMOS generation [40] because of the relatively low density of SRAM.

To overcome the limitations of SRAM (i.e., high leakage power and low density), researchers have recently explored alternative device technologies such as non-volatile memory (NVM) and embedded DRAM (eDRAM) for designing on-chip caches. While NVMs, such as STT-RAM (spin transfer torque RAM) and ReRAM (resistive RAM), have the advantage of near-zero leakage energy and high-density, their limited write endurance and high write-latency [36] present a critical bottleneck in enabling their use for on-chip caches. EDRAM has the advantage of low-leakage (nearly 1/8th leakage power consumption compared to SRAM [4]), compatibility with CMOS process, and high write endurance.

These features make them suitable for use as on-chip caches. For this reason, eDRAM has been used to design the LLCs in IBM's Power 7 processor [21] and Blue Gene/L supercomputer chip [19]. Also, Intel's Haswell processor uses 128MB eDRAM L4 cache [25].

A critical limitation of eDRAM cells, however, is that they lose charge over time and, hence, require refresh operations to maintain data integrity. Thus, to avoid failures, an eDRAM cell must be refreshed before its retention period, which is the duration of time for which the cell can retain its state. More precisely, compared to the conventional DRAM, eDRAM uses faster logic transistors with high leakage current and hence, the retention period of eDRAM is in the range of tens of microseconds (e.g. $40\mu s$ [8]), which is nearly a thousand times shorter than that of conventional DRAM, which is in range of 64ms [45]. It has been demonstrated that refresh energy accounts to nearly 70% of the total energy in eDRAM LLCs, while the leakage energy accounts for most of the remaining fraction [4]. With ongoing CMOS scaling, this retention period is expected to reduce further due to increasing leakage and smaller storage capacitance [11], which will increase the overhead of refresh even further. Thus, reducing the refresh energy consumption of eDRAM is extremely important to enable their wide-spread use and also avoid complex cooling solutions (e.g. liquid cooling).

1.1 Contributions

In this paper, we present ESTEEM, an energy saving technique for embedded DRAM caches. ESTEEM uses periodic cache reconfiguration to turn-off a portion of LLC and avoids refreshing it. This leads to saving in both leakage and refresh energy (Section 3). Further, in the active portion of cache, only valid blocks are refreshed. For cache reconfiguration, ESTEEM logically divides the cache-sets into different modules. For example, with 4096 sets and 16 modules, each module has 256 sets. Then, in each module, only the required number of ways are kept active, such that the performance is not affected while largest possible saving in energy is achieved (Section 4). ESTEEM does not require offline profiling or manual tuning of its parameters. Also, its energy saving algorithm runs in software and uses lightweight hardware support. The overhead of ESTEEM is less than 0.1% of the L2 cache size (Section 5).

We perform single and dual-core microarchitectural simulations using an x86-64 simulator and workloads from SPEC06 suite and HPC (high-performance computing) field (Section 6). Also, we compare ESTEEM with a recently proposed technique for saving refresh energy in eDRAM caches, named Refrint polyphase-valid (RPV) ([4], Section 6.2). The experiments have shown that ESTEEM provides better performance and energy efficiency than RPV. For $50\mu s$ retention period and a baseline eDRAM LLC (which periodically refreshes all cache lines), the energy saving achieved using ESTEEM and RPV, for single-core system is 25.82% and 15.93%, respectively. For dual-core system, these values are 32.63% and 14.39%, respectively. ESTEEM also provides higher performance than both baseline and RPV. Experiments with $40\mu s$ retention period show that with lower retention period, the advantage of ESTEEM increases even further. Additional experiments show that ESTEEM works well for a wide range of system and algorithm parameters.

The major contributions of this paper are:

- We propose a dynamic cache reconfiguration technique for saving both leakage and refresh energy in eDRAM caches. Our technique addresses the major challenge that prevents eDRAM to be used as a viable and scalable solution for future high-end computing systems.

- We evaluate our technique with a spectrum of scientific computing applications and over a wide-range of system/algorithm parameters. After detailed comparison with a state-of-the-art energy saving mechanism for eDRAM cache, we demonstrate the effectiveness of our technique.

The remainder of the paper is organized as follows. Section 2 presents the background and related work on eDRAM and power management techniques for caches. Section 3 describes the working of ESTEEM. Section 4 presents the energy saving algorithm of ESTEEM and Section 5 presents its implementation details. Section 6 presents simulation platform, workloads, energy model and evaluation metrics. Section 7 presents the simulation results. Finally, Section 8 presents the conclusion.

2. BACKGROUND AND RELATED WORK

The eDRAM cells are generally of two types, namely the gain cell eDRAM and the 1T1C eDRAM [11]. Both of these cells store data in the form of capacitor. For example, a gain cell utilizes the gate capacitance of its storage transistor and a 1T1C cell utilizes a dedicated capacitor to store its data. In this paper, we assume a gain cell eDRAM as the basis of our study.

Recently, several techniques have been proposed to mitigate the refresh energy in eDRAM devices. Some researchers propose use of error-detection/correction based approaches [39, 45] which allow increasing the refresh period by tolerating some failures. Some researchers propose techniques to detect dead-blocks and avoid refreshing them to save refresh energy [4, 11]. The Smart-Refresh technique [15] avoids refreshing the DRAM rows which are recently read or written. Reohr [38] discusses several approaches for optimizing refresh operations in eDRAM caches, for example, no-refresh, periodic refresh and line-level refresh based on time stamps. In this paper, we use cache-reconfiguration approach to save energy in eDRAM caches.

In literature, several cache reconfiguration techniques have been proposed to save leakage energy in SRAM caches [28]. On the basis of granularity of cache reconfiguration, these techniques can be divided into several categories, such as selective-sets [34], selective-ways [5], hybrid (selective-sets and ways) [30], cache-coloring [29], cache block-level [22–24] etc. ESTEEM uses selective-ways based cache reconfiguration approach, which has low implementation and reconfiguration overhead. Also, unlike selective-sets or cache coloring approach, selective-ways approach does not require a change in set-decoding on cache reconfiguration.

Some cache reconfiguration techniques (e.g. [5, 20]) statically reconfigure the cache and do not allow dynamic reconfiguration. In contrast, ESTEEM uses dynamic cache reconfiguration to easily adapt to intra-application variation in cache demand and provide large energy savings. For SRAM caches, FlexiWay [31] proposes cache reconfiguration at fine-granularity. However, FlexiWay uses complex and higher-overhead scheme for predicting LLC and memory energy, which is likely to be inaccurate due to dynamic behavior of workloads. By comparison, ESTEEM does not require prediction of energy. ESTEEM proposes a novel insight of simultaneously attacking leakage and refresh energy in eDRAM, whereas refresh operations do not happen in SRAM in case of FlexiWay. Also, compared to SRAM, presence of refresh in eDRAM totally changes the relative contribution of dynamic, leakage and refresh energies, thus changing the energy optimization scenario.

To leverage the different features of different memory cells, some researchers have proposed hybrid memory cells. Valero et al. [43] propose a macro-cell that combines SRAM and eDRAM at cell level. They implement an A-way set-associative cache with these macro-cells which consists of one SRAM cell, $A-1$ eDRAM cells and a transistor that acts as a bridge for transferring data between static and dynamic cells. Their approach is suitable for L1 caches but does not work well for lower-level caches. This is because due to filtering of access-stream by L1 cache, the access patterns at lower-level caches are not very predictable.

3. METHODOLOGY

Notations: Let N denote the number of cores. Let S, A, M denote the number of cache sets, cache associativity and number of cache modules, respectively. Let B and G denote the cache-line(block) size and tag size, respectively, which, in this paper, are taken as 512bits (64 byte) and 40 bits, respectively. In this paper, we use the terms 'cache line' and 'cache block', interchangeably.

3.1 Main Idea

Our technique works on the key idea that there exists large intra-application and inter-application variation in the cache requirement of different applications. Thus, by allocating just the right amount of cache to each application, the rest of the cache can be transitioned to low-power state, with minimum performance loss. This leads to reduction in the active-fraction of the cache. This saves both leakage and refresh energy as the inactive area of the cache need not be refreshed and also does not consume leakage energy. Further, in the active portion of the cache, only the valid blocks are refreshed, which further reduces the refresh energy.

To dynamically reconfigure the cache, we use the following approach. It has been shown that the associativity requirement of applications varies across different sets of the cache [31,41]. Conventional way-based reconfiguration techniques (e.g. [5]), turn-off exactly the same number of ways across all the sets. This, however, may lead to loss of flexibility which may lead to performance and/or energy penalty. To address this, we turn-off *possibly different* number of ways in each cache module. This is illustrated in Figure 1. This approach allows fine-grain cache reconfiguration, which also enables achieving a fine-balance between performance loss and energy saving.

To identify the blocks which store dead data (i.e. which are unlikely to be reused) in a low-overhead manner, we use the following observation. The LRU (least recently used) replacement policy works by ordering the cache lines based on their recency (or "age") and evicting the LRU-block on a cache miss. The intuition behind working of LRU is that the older (i.e. least recent or lower in LRU-stack) cache lines are less likely to be reused. Thus, the number of hits are expected to decrease with decreasing recency positions [7]. Hence, the cache ways with less recent positions are suitable

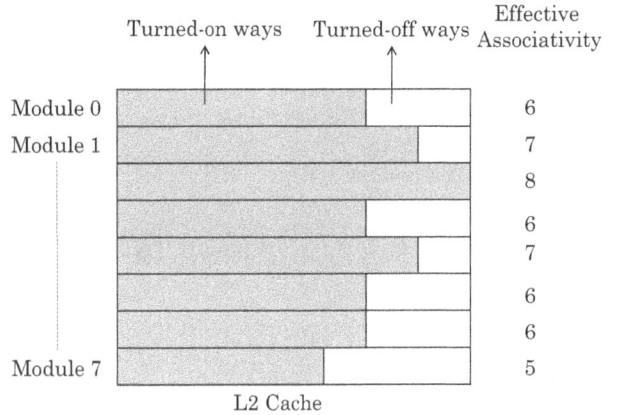

Figure 1: An illustration of ESTEEM approach for an 8-way L2 cache with 8 modules

candidates are turning-off, since turning these ways off leads to minimal impact on performance.

An exception to the above observation happens for the applications which do not show LRU behavior, i.e. for which the hits to the LRU-positions do not decrease monotonically with decreasing recency positions. Examples of such "non-LRU" applications from SPEC2006 suite include omnetpp, xalancbmk etc. [42]. To avoid incurring energy loss for such applications, ESTEEM detects whether in an interval, hits in a cache module show non-LRU pattern. This is detected by noting the hits to different LRU positions and seeing when the number of hits do not decrease monotonically with decreasing LRU-recency position. For such modules, the number of active-ways is not reduced below $A - 1$. In other words, for non-LRU applications, the aggressiveness of cache reconfiguration is reduced.

To decide the exact number of ways to turn-off, we use the following idea: if the total number of hits in all ways of a module are H, then we keep X ($\leq A$) ways turned-on, such that the total hits in X ways are equal to or greater than αH, where $\alpha < 1$ is a parameter. In other words, we keep a number of ways turned-on to cover at least α fraction of cache hits. We show an example to explain this. Assume that for an 8-way cache, the number of hits in different LRU-positions is {10816,4645,2140,501,217,113,63,11}, where the first value shows the hits in MRU (most-recently used) position while the last value shows the hits in the LRU position. Here, we have $H = 18506$. If $\alpha = 0.97$, then we get $X = 4$ since at least 4 ways need to be turned-on to achieve equal to or greater than αH hits. However, if $\alpha = 0.95$, then $X = 3$ and hence, only 3 ways need to be turned-on.

We also use a parameter A_{min}, which shows the minimum number of ways which are always turned-on. The typical values of A_{min} used in this paper are 2, 3 and 4. We do not take $A_{min} = 1$, since keeping only a single-way turned-on makes the LLC a direct-mapped cache, which leads to large performance loss due to increased off-chip accesses.

3.2 Cache Profiling

For making dynamic cache reconfiguration decisions, ESTEEM collects data using dynamic profiling approach. For this purpose, it uses auxiliary tag directory (ATD) [37]. The ATD has the same associativity and replacement policy as the main tag directory (MTD) and uses set-sampling ap-

---
Algorithm 1 ESTEEM Energy Saving Algorithm

1: **INPUT:** nL2Hit[0:M-1][0:A-1] showing the number of hits to different LRU-positions for different modules in last interval; A_{min} showing the minimum number of ways to be always turned-on; α showing the hit threshold.

2: **OUTPUT:** nActiveWay[0:M-1] showing algorithm decision about number of ways to keep turned-on in different modules

3: Let Accumulated_L2Hit[0:M-1][0:A-1] be a variable

4: **for** m=0 to M-1 **do**   ▷ First see, if the module is non-LRU

5:     Let nLRUAnomaly $\leftarrow$0

6:     **for** i=0 to A-2 **do**

7:         **if** nL2Hit[m][i]<nL2Hit[m][i+1] **then**

8:             nLRUAnomaly $\leftarrow$ nLRUAnomaly+1

9:         **end if**

10:     **end for**

11:     **if** nLRUAnomaly $\geq A/4$ **then**

12:         isModuleNonLRU $\leftarrow$ TRUE

13:     **end if**

                                                              ▷ Now decide the number of ways to turn-off

14:     **for** i=0 to A-1 **do**

15:         Accumulated_L2Hit[m][i] $\leftarrow \sum_{j=0}^{i}$ nL2Hit[m][j]

16:     **end for**

17:     totHitsThisModule $\leftarrow$ Accumulated_L2Hit[m][A-1]

18:     **for** i=0 to A-1 **do**

19:         **if** Accumulated_L2Hit[m][i] $\geq (\alpha\times$ totHitsThisModule) **then**

20:             nActiveWay[m] $\leftarrow$ MAX(A_{min}, i+1)

21:             **if** isModuleNonLRU **then**

22:                 nActiveWay[m] $\leftarrow$ MAX(A-1, i+1)

23:             **end if**

24:             Break from for loop

25:         **end if**

26:     **end for**

27: **end for**

        return nActiveWay[0:M-1]
---

proach [35] to keep its overhead small. The ratio of the number of sets in the L2 cache and that in ATD is shown as R_s and its typical values are 32, 64, 128 etc. As an example, for R_s =64, ATD monitors only 1/64 of the sets. We use an ATD, which is embedded in the MTD of the L2 cache. The sets which are monitored are called the leader sets and the remaining sets are called the follower sets. The leader sets do not undergo cache reconfiguration. Profiling information is only collected from the leader sets. The follower sets undergo cache reconfiguration based on the decision of the algorithm. Since the cache-sets are divided into multiple modules, statistics obtained from a leader set count towards the module in which this leader set falls.

4. ENERGY SAVING ALGORITHM

Algorithm 1 shows the energy saving algorithm in ESTEEM, which can be a kernel module. The algorithm runs after every few million cycles (e.g. 10M cycles). The algorithm can be understood as follows. The algorithm first checks whether a module is non-LRU, which is checked by comparing the number of hits at different LRU positions. For each LRU position, the algorithm computes the accumulated hits till that LRU position. The number of ways to keep active can thus be decided by the LRU position, at which total hits are α fraction (e.g. 95%) of the total hits. For a non-LRU module, at most 1 way is turned-off for the reasons explained the previous section. This process is repeated for each of the module.

The overhead of the algorithm is very small. Periodically, a kernel routine is triggered which executes algorithm. The output of the algorithm is the decision about the number of ways to be turned-off in each module, which can be easily implemented using per-way disable bits. Thus, the changes required in the cache and the hardware overhead are very small. The algorithm reads few counters and runs infrequently, so its power overhead is amortized over the length of the phase. The power saving provided by the algorithm easily allow adding small additional hardware within the power-budget. Many processors already use counters for OS or measuring performance [22], which can be leveraged by the algorithm. Modern processors already use write-back buffers, specific instructions, and MSHRs (miss-status holding registers), which handle writing-back of flushed data.

5. IMPLEMENTATION AND OVERHEAD ASSESSMENT

We assume that power-gating of eDRAM is achieved by a suitable circuit-level technique, as proposed by several authors [10, 12, 16, 32]. For each module, we use $A - A_{min}$ control bits which control turning-off or turning-on of the ways in that module.

Cache reconfigurations are handled as follows. When the number of ways is reduced, the clean cache lines in those ways are discarded and the dirty lines are written-back. When the number of ways is increased, the extra ways are simply turned-on and they are subsequently used for storing data. With ESTEEM technique, cache reconfigurations happen only at the end of a large interval and not throughout the execution of the application. Thus, cache line-switching does not lie on the critical access path of the cache. Also, unlike selective-sets approach used in previous works [34], the selective-ways approach used in ESTEEM does not require changing the set-decoding of the cache and hence, ESTEEM does not increase the cache access time. Further, ESTEEM provides fine-grained cache reconfiguration with caches of typical associativity and thus, does not require use of caches of large associativity which have significantly large access time and energy. Also note that ESTEEM does not require tables for offline profiling (as in [44]) or using per-block counters to monitor cache access intensity (as in [22]). Also, it does not require prediction of cache or memory energy (as in [31]) or hits/misses for different cache configurations (as in [30]).

ESTEEM uses counters for recording the number of hits to different LRU positions and execution of algorithm. For nL2Hit and Accumulated_L2Hit, total storage required is $2 \times M \times A$ counters (assuming $A_{min} = 0$ for simplicity) and for nActiveWay, the storage required is M counters. Assuming that each counter takes 40 bits, the total storage overhead of ESTEEM, as a percentage of L2 storage, can be expressed as

$$Overhead = \frac{(2A+1)M \times 40}{SA(B+G)} \times 100 \qquad (1)$$

For a 4MB cache with 16 modules and 16-way set-associativity, the overhead of ESTEEM is found to be 0.06% of the L2 cache size, which is extremely small. For this reason, we ignore the overhead of counters.

6. EXPERIMENTAL METHODOLOGY

6.1 Simulation Platform and Workload

We perform microarchitectural simulation using Sniper x86-64 simulator [9]. The processor has 2GHz frequency. All caches use a line size of 64B. Both L1D and L1I are 32KB, 4-way, LRU caches and have a latency of 2 cycles. The L2 cache is a 16-way, LRU cache with 12 cycle latency. Its size for single and dual-core system is 4MB and 8MB, respectively. L1 caches are private to each core and L2 cache is shared among cores. The latency of main memory is 220 cycles and memory queue contention is also modeled. The main memory bandwidth for single and dual-core system is 10 GB/s and 15GB/s, respectively.

All eDRAM L2 caches have a 4-bank structure. We assume that each bank of L2 cache has dedicated logic to process refresh requests and using pipelining, a line can be refreshed in a single cycle [4]. For eDRAM cells, Barth et al. [8] report a retention period of $40\mu s$ at $105°C$. In this paper, we assume working temperature of $60°C$ and since retention periods are exponentially dependent on temperature [4], we present most of the results with a retention period of 50μ. In Section 7.3, we also present results for a retention period of $40\mu s$.

We use all 29 SPEC2006 benchmarks [17] with *ref* inputs and 5 benchmarks from HPC field (shown as italics in Table 1) [1, 2]. Using these benchmarks, we randomly make 17 dual-core multiprogrammed workloads, such that each benchmark is used only once. These workloads are shown in Table 1.

Table 1: Workloads Used in the Paper

Single-core workloads and their acronyms
As(astar), Bw(bwaves), Bz(bzip2), Cd(cactusADM)
Ca(calculix), Dl(dealII), Ga(gamess), Gc(gcc)
Gm(gemsFDTD), Gk(gobmk), Gr(gromacs), H2(h264ref)
Hm(hmmer), Lb(lbm), Ls(leslie3d), Lq(libquantum)
Mc(mcf), Mi(milc), Nd(namd), Om(omnetpp)
Pe(perlbench), Po(povray), Sj(sjeng), So(soplex)
Sp(sphinx), To(tonto), Wr(wrf), Xa(xalancbmk)
Ze(zeusmp), *Am(amg2013)*, *Co(comd)*, *Lu(lulesh)*
Ne(nekbone), *Xb(xsbench)*

Dual-core workloads and their acronyms
GmDl(gemsFDTD-dealII), AsXb(astar-xsbench)
GcGa(gcc-gamess), BzXa(bzip2-xalancbmk)
LsLb(leslie3d-lbm), GkNe(gobmk-nekbone)
OmGr(omnetpp-gromacs), NdCd(namd-cactusADM)
CaTo(calculix-tonto), SpBw(sphinx-bwaves)
LqPo(libquantum-povray), SjWr(sjeng-wrf)
PeZe(perlbench-zeusmp), HmH2(hmmer-h264ref)
SoMi(soplex-milc), McLu(mcf-lulesh)
CoAm(comd-amg2013)

6.2 Comparison With Other Technique

We compare ESTEEM with Refrint polyphase-valid (RPV) policy [4]. RPV works on the idea that on a read or a write, an eDRAM cache block is automatically refreshed and hence, it need not be refreshed for the duration of one retention period. RPV divides the retention period into a number of phases. Each cache block maintains the information about the phase in which it was last updated. Afterwards, to reduce the number of refresh operations, RPV refreshes the block at the beginning of *this phase* in the next retention period, instead of refreshing at beginning of refresh period itself. Also, RPV only refreshes the valid blocks. We use RPV with four phases, since this has been shown to provide significant energy savings [4].

Agrawal et al. [4] also propose Refrint polyphase-dirty (RPD) policy which eagerly invalidates valid blocks to avoid refreshing them and refreshes only dirty blocks. For applications where the fraction of dirty data is small, RPD policy would aggressively invalidate almost the whole cache which will greatly increase the access to main memory and hence, we do not evaluate this. Further, RPV policy has been shown to perform better than another policy proposed by Agrawal et al., namely the periodic-valid refresh policy [4] and hence, we do not evaluate periodic-valid refresh policy.

6.3 Energy Model

We account for the energy consumption of L2 cache (E_{L2}), main memory (E_{MM}) and energy cost of algorithm (E_{Algo}), since the techniques evaluated here affect the other components only minimally. We use the following notations. LE_{L2}, DE_{L2} and RE_{L2} show the leakage, dynamic and refresh energy consumed in L2 cache, respectively. E_{xyz}^{dyn} and P_{xyz}^{leak} show the dynamic energy per access and leakage energy per second, respectively, in a component xyz (e.g. L2 or MM). For ESTEEM, N_L shows the number of cache blocks which are turned on or off (i.e. undergo state transition); E_χ shows the energy consumed in a single such block transition. F_A, H_{L2} and M_{L2} show the active fraction of cache, number of L2 hits and L2 misses in an interval, respectively. N_R shows the number of cache lines which are refreshed within all refresh-events in an interval. T denotes the time length of an interval (or any time period of measurement) in seconds. A_{MM} shows the number of main memory accesses.

We assume that the L2 leakage energy scales with the active fraction of cache [22,31]. Also, we assume that an L2 miss consumes twice the dynamic energy as that of an L2 hit [29–31]. Thus, we have

$$E = E_{L2} + E_{MM} + E_{Algo} \qquad (2)$$

$$E_{L2} = LE_{L2} + DE_{L2} + RE_{L2} \qquad (3)$$

$$LE_{L2} = P_{L2}^{leak} \times F_A \times T \qquad (4)$$

$$DE_{L2} = E_{L2}^{dyn} \times (2M_{L2} + H_{L2}) \qquad (5)$$

$$RE_{L2} = N_R \times E_{L2}^{dyn} \qquad (6)$$

$$E_{MM} = P_{MM}^{leak} \times T + E_{MM}^{dyn} \times A_{MM} \qquad (7)$$

$$E_{Algo} = E_\chi \times N_L \qquad (8)$$

We ignore the energy overhead of RPV algorithm, thus, for experiments with baseline eDRAM cache and RPV, we have $E_{Algo} = 0$ and $F_A = 1$. Note that F_A for ESTEEM duly takes into account the active area due to leader and follower sets (see Section 3.2).

We use CACTI [27] to obtain the values of E_{L2}^{Dyn} and P_{L2}^{Leak} at 32nm for eDRAM cache. These values are shown in Table 2. Following [4], we assume that for eDRAM cache, the time and energy consumed in refreshing a line is equal to the time and energy to access the line, respectively.

Table 2: Energy values for 16-way eDRAM cache

	E_{L2}^{dyn} (nJ/access)	P_{L2}^{leak} (Watts)
2 MB	0.186	0.096
4 MB	0.212	0.116
8 MB	0.282	0.280
16 MB	0.370	0.456
32 MB	0.467	1.056

E_{MM}^{dyn} and P_{MM}^{leak} are taken as 70 nJ and 0.18 Watt, respectively [23,29,46] and E_χ is taken as 2 pJ [29,30].

6.4 Evaluation Metrics

Our baseline is as an eDRAM cache which periodically refreshes all the cache lines at the given retention period and does not use any refresh-minimization technique. We show the results on the following metrics.

1. Percentage energy saving (as defined above)

2. Weighted speedup (WS) [24,29,31], referred to as relative performance. It is defined as

$$WS = \frac{\displaystyle\sum_{n=0}^{N-1} \frac{\text{IPC}_n(\text{technique})}{\text{IPC}_n(\text{base})}}{N} \qquad (9)$$

Here technique refers to either ESTEEM or RPV.

3. Absolute reduction in number of cache lines refreshed per kilo instructions (RPKI).

For ESTEEM technique, we also show the results on the following metrics:

1. Absolute increase in MPKI (miss-per kilo instructions) [30] due to use of ESTEEM

2. Active ratio (the fraction of active lines averaged over entire execution [22,29])

The decrease in RPKI helps us to evaluate the efficacy of a technique in reducing refresh operations. Active ratio enables us to evaluate the aggressiveness of cache turn-off of ESTEEM and the increase in MPKI helps in evaluating the increase in off-chip traffic. Note that since RPV does not turn-off the cache or cause early invalidation, its ActiveRatio is always 100% and the increase in MPKI is always zero.

The benchmarks were fast-forwarded for 10B instructions. Then, each workload is simulated for 400M instructions. For dual-core system, the benchmark which finished its 400M instructions early was allowed to run, however, its IPC (for computing speedup) was only recorded for the first 400M instructions, following well-established simulation methodology [14,29]. For dual-core system, we have also computed the value of fair speedup [29,31] and found its average value to be close to the weighted speedup. Thus, our technique does not cause unfairness. For the sake of brevity, we omit these results. Across the workloads, speedup (weighted and fair) values are averaged using geometric mean and the remaining metrics are averaged using arithmetic mean, since they can be zero or negative.

7. RESULTS AND ANALYSIS

We now present the results. In Sections 7.1, 7.2 and 7.3, we use the following parameters. The size of L2 cache for single and dual-core systems are 4 and 8 MB, respectively. For ESTEEM, we use the following parameters: $\alpha = 0.97$, $A_{min} = 3$, $R_s = 64$, an interval length of 10M cycles and 8 modules for single-core system and 16 modules for dual-core system.

7.1 Example of working of ESTEEM

To get insights into working of ESTEEM, we first show the cache reconfiguration taking place with ESTEEM for a selected workload (namely h264ref) in Figure 2. Notice

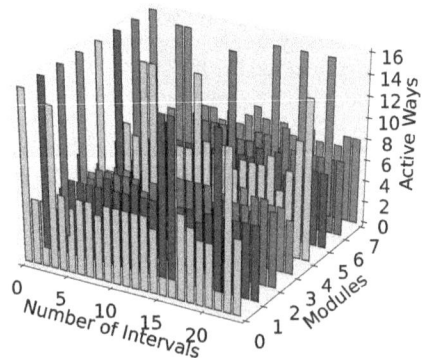

Figure 2: Example of working of ESTEEM for h264ref benchmark. Note that, in any interval, the number of active ways in different modules may be different.

that depending on the cache requirement, the cache active

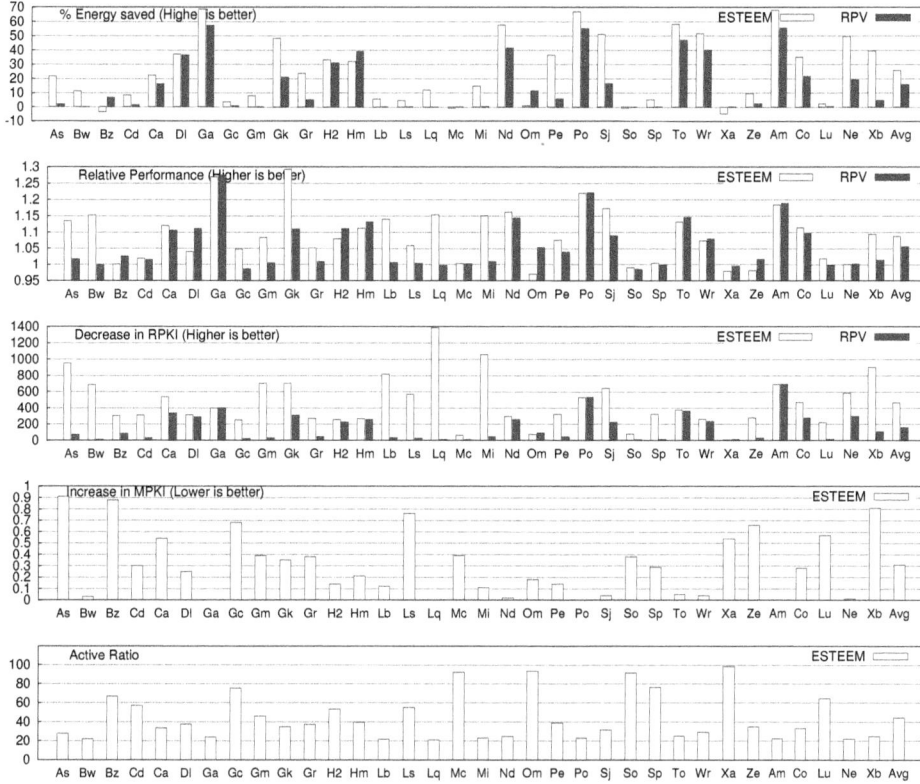

Figure 3: Single-core results for different techniques at 50 µs refresh period.

ratio changes with time (i.e. over different intervals). More importantly, the number of active ways in different modules can possibly be different. This clearly shows the advantage of ESTEEM in exercising fine-grained cache reconfiguration.

7.2 Results with 50µs Retention Period

Figures 3 and 4 show the results for single and dual-core systems, respectively. We now discuss and analyze the results.

For single and dual-core systems, the average saving in memory sub-system energy on using ESTEEM (resp. RPV) are 25.82% (resp. 15.93%) and 32.63% (resp. 14.3%), respectively. Also, the average relative performance on using ESTEEM (resp. RPV) are 1.09× (resp. 1.06×) and 1.22× (resp. 1.09×), respectively. With ESTEEM, for single and dual-core systems, the largest amount of energy saving is seen for gamess (68.7%) and GkNe (77.2%), respectively. The largest improvement in performance is seem for Gk (1.29×) and GkNe (1.48×). The performance is improved despite cache-turnoff due to reduction in refresh operations which offsets the penalty of increased cache misses.

The actual performance/power improvement achieved with ESTEEM depends on interaction of several factors. Turning off large fraction of cache saves large amount of leakage energy and avoids the need of large number of refresh operations. Reduction in refresh operations leads to performance improvement (i.e. reduction in execution time), which further reduces the refresh operations and the refresh and leakage energy consumed in the cache. However, the extra misses and writebacks introduced due to reduced cache size increase the energy consumed in main memory.

RPV saves energy when only a small portion of the cache stores valid data, since in such cases, a large number of refresh operations can be avoided. For some applications, nearly the whole cache stores valid data and hence, the scope for avoiding refresh operations is minimal. Moreover, it has been shown that [22] cache lines typically have a flurry of frequent use when first brought into the cache, and then see a period of "dead time" before they are evicted. Thus, for any cache line, after the last access and before its eviction, RPV does not avoid or minimize refresh operations to the cache line. For these reasons, the effectiveness of RPV in minimizing refresh operations is limited. In contrast, ESTEEM intelligently reduces the active fraction of cache, which intrinsically minimizes the number of cache lines which need to be refreshed.

In general, for dual-core system, the intensity of cache access is higher than that in single-core system. For this reason, the fraction of invalid cache blocks is reduced. Hence, RPV saves smaller percentage of energy in the dual-core system. This is also evident from the smaller value of decrease in RPKI in the case of dual-core system for RPV. For single-core system, the reduction in RPKI on using ESTEEM and RPV are 467 and 161, respectively, and for dual-core system, these values are 511 and 134, respectively. Large reduction in RPKI also reflects in improved performance, since the performance overhead of refresh operations is avoided. Also note that compared to RPV, ESTEEM achieves nearly 4× reduction in RPKI.

Since ESTEEM turns-off a fraction of cache, it also has the advantage of saving leakage energy. With single and dual-core systems, the average active-ratio achieved on us-

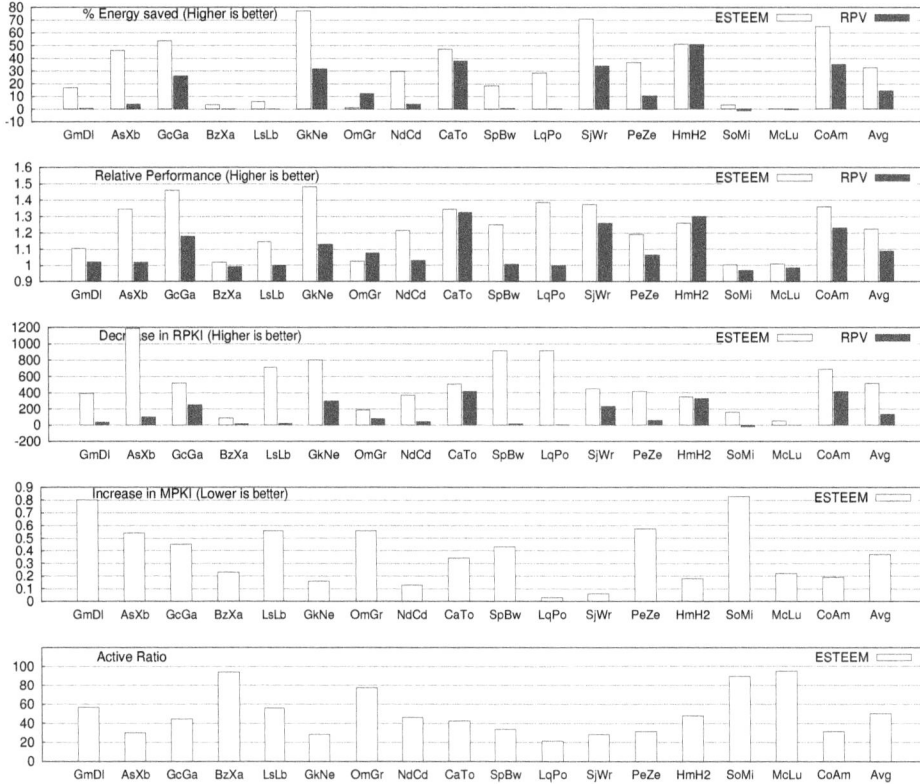

Figure 4: Dual-core results for different techniques at 50μs refresh period.

ing ESTEEM are 44.1% and 50.2%, respectively. For some applications, such as libquantum and milc, the data reuse is very small (i.e. miss-rate is nearly 100%) and thus, the working set size of the application is much smaller compared to the cache size. In such cases, ESTEEM aggressively reduces the cache active fraction and the number of refresh operations and provides large saving in energy.

On using ESTEEM, the average increase in MPKI for single and dual-core system are 0.31 and 0.37, respectively. Thus, the increase in off-chip traffic on using ESTEEM is very small. This is because, by virtue of using dynamic cache reconfiguration, ESTEEM closely adjusts the size of cache in response to intra- and inter-application variation in cache requirement of different applications. Also, it always keeps 3 ways active and keeps as many ways active as required for achieving at least 97% cache hits (assuming the parameters shown above are chosen).

For some single-core workloads, a small loss in performance/energy is seen on using ESTEEM. This is due to either the non-LRU behavior (e.g. omnetpp and xalancbmk) or large application working-set size (e.g. mcf and soplex). Also, in general, the reconfiguration overhead resulting from increased off-chip traffic slightly offsets the energy saving achieved in cache. These overheads can be minimized by increasing the value of α, A_{min} and interval length. We study the effect of these parameters in Section 7.4. The reconfiguration overhead can also be minimized by restricting the maximum number of change in associativity in each interval or detecting and avoiding frequent reconfigurations. This extension of the energy saving algorithm is planned as a future work.

7.3 Results with 40μs Retention Period

Since an increase in temperature and process variations reduce the retention period, we now test ESTEEM and RPV with reduced 40 μs retention period. The results are shown in Figures 5 and 6. In this section, we only comment on the effect of the retention period, compared to the case with 50 μs retention period, since the results can be easily understood based on the above explanation.

With reduced retention period, a large fraction of energy is consumed in the form of refresh energy for the baseline cache. Also, the energy consumption of L2 is increased and hence, it becomes a larger fraction of memory subsystem energy. Furthermore, with reduced retention period, the same number of blocks need to be refreshed within smaller amount of time. These refresh operations also make the cache unavailable, leading to performance loss. Hence, at lower retention period, the scope of and benefits from reducing refresh operations are further increased. This is also reflected in the reduction in RPKI value for both ESTEEM and RPV. For the same reason, both ESTEEM and RPV show larger improvement in performance and energy efficiency. With ESTEEM, the largest improvement in energy saving is seen in gamess (73.6%) and GkNe (83.2%). Also, the largest improvement in performance is seen in gobmk (1.40×) and GcGa (1.72×).

It is clear that a reduction of merely 10μs in retention period can increase refresh energy significantly. Thus, for smaller retention periods, the need of a technique for reducing refresh operations is increased even further. This highlights the importance of our technique.

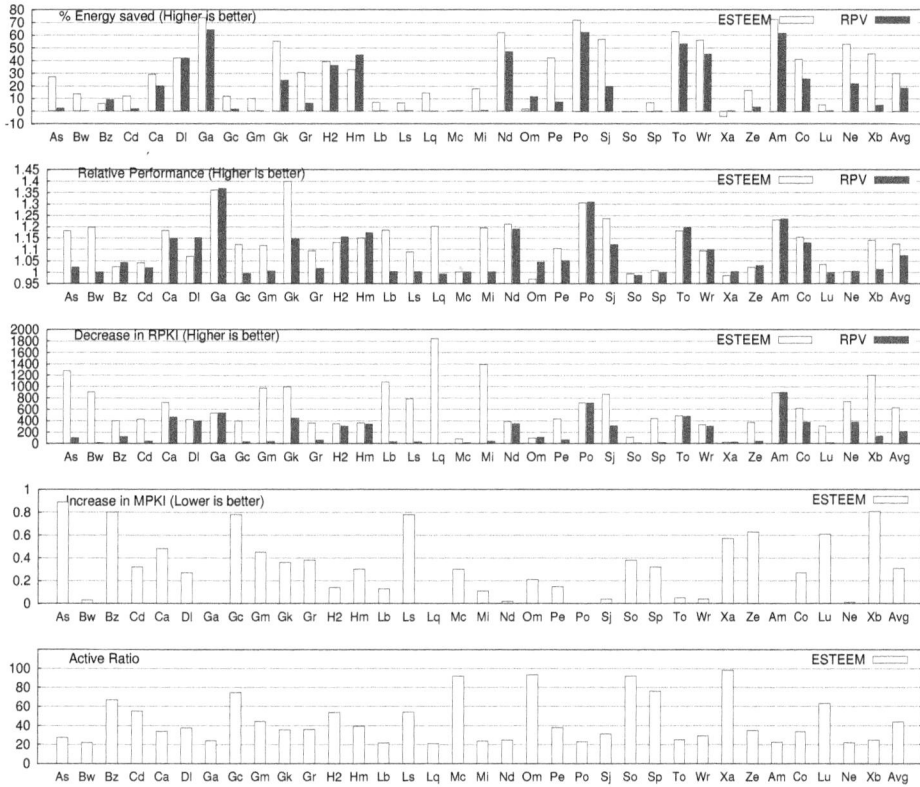

Figure 5: Single-core results for different techniques at $40\mu s$ refresh period.

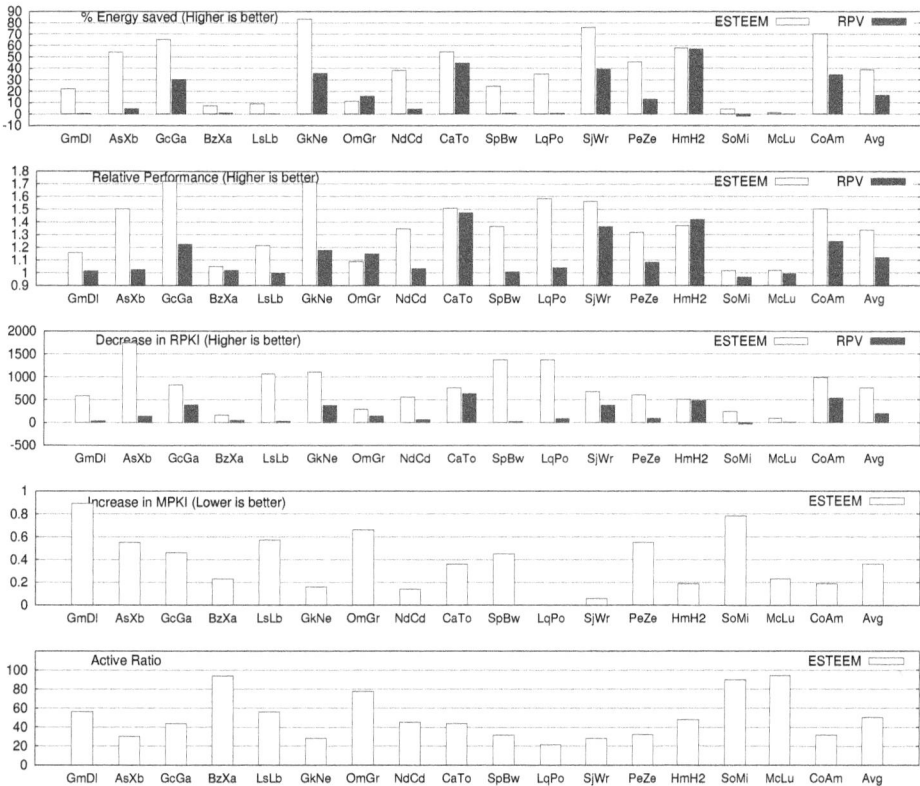

Figure 6: Dual-core results for different techniques at $40\mu s$ refresh period.

Table 3: Parameter sensitivity results for ESTEEM (Rel. Perf. = relative performance, Dec. = decrease, Inc. = increase). Default parameters are shown in the beginning of Section 7.

	% Energy Saving	Rel. Perf.	RPKI Dec.	MPKI Inc.	Active Ratio
Single-core System					
Default	25.82	1.09	467.4	0.31	44.10
A_{min}=2	25.46	1.08	482.4	0.36	41.60
A_{min}=4	25.76	1.09	449.1	0.26	47.00
α=0.95	24.95	1.08	473.9	0.37	42.70
α=0.99	26.56	1.09	458.2	0.24	46.10
2 modules	24.52	1.08	458.5	0.34	44.93
4 modules	25.96	1.09	457.7	0.27	45.20
16 modules	24.87	1.09	478.2	0.37	42.40
32 modules	19.41	1.06	491.0	0.62	38.97
5M interval	24.07	1.09	491.4	0.43	40.40
15M interval	25.82	1.09	456.5	0.27	46.00
R_s =32	25.79	1.09	458.9	0.28	45.80
R_s =128	24.30	1.08	477.7	0.38	42.20
8-way L2	23.68	1.08	397.9	0.20	55.94
32-way L2	24.39	1.08	499.3	0.49	38.27
2MB L2	10.18	1.02	204.4	0.38	48.00
8MB L2	49.42	1.29	1257.3	0.37	41.70
Two-core System					
Default	32.63	1.22	511.9	0.37	50.20
A_{min}=2	32.04	1.22	525.0	0.47	48.50
A_{min}=4	32.44	1.22	495.1	0.31	52.40
α=0.95	32.01	1.23	524.5	0.43	48.10
α=0.99	32.90	1.22	490.9	0.29	53.50
4 modules	31.22	1.19	482.9	0.35	51.40
8 modules	32.15	1.21	497.1	0.35	51.30
32 modules	32.13	1.23	526.1	0.42	47.90
64 modules	28.75	1.21	546.2	0.59	43.69
5M interval	32.41	1.23	543.4	0.49	46.60
15M interval	32.16	1.21	493.5	0.33	52.30
R_s =32	32.69	1.22	500.5	0.35	51.90
R_s =128	32.13	1.23	526.2	0.43	47.90
8-way L2	30.00	1.19	424.7	0.25	60.73
32-way L2	31.91	1.23	541.8	0.56	45.70
4MB L2	8.04	1.06	181.9	0.45	55.70
16MB L2	66.25	2.11	2438.0	0.68	43.70

7.4 Parameter Sensitivity Results

We now focus exclusively on ESTEEM and study its sensitivity for different parameters. The retention period is fixed to $50\mu s$. Each time, we only change one parameter from the default parameters used above. The results are summarized in Table 3. For comparison purposes, the results with default parameters are also shown.

Change in A_{min}: On changing A_{min} (the minimum number of ways which are always kept on) from 3 to 2, the algorithm turns off a larger fraction of cache and hence, the active ratio is reduced and MPKI is increased further. This also reduces the refresh operations further. However, due to increased off-chip accesses, a small reduction in overall saving is achieved. The results on increasing A_{min} to 4 can be similarly understood.

Change in α: On changing α from 0.97 to 0.95, the aggressiveness of cache reconfiguration is increased, as reflected in results on active ratio, MPKI increase and RPKI decrease. However, it also increases the main memory en-

ergy and hence, the overall energy saving is slightly reduced. The opposite is seen on changing α to 0.99.

Change in number of modules (M): We experiment with both smaller and higher number of modules. On reducing the number of modules, both granularity and aggressiveness of reconfiguration is reduced, as reflected from values of MPKI and active ratio. This also reduces the decrease in RPKI and off-chip accesses. The net energy saving and performance depends on the interaction of these parameters. Conversely, on increasing the number of modules, cache can be reconfigured in more fine-grain manner. Thus, the active ratio and RPKI are reduced further, although the off-chip accesses are increased. Using very large number of modules leads to reduced energy savings due to increased overhead of cache reconfiguration.

Change in interval size: On changing the interval size from 10M cycles to 5M cycles, reconfiguration algorithm is more frequently executed. Thus, the active ratio is reduced further, with corresponding reduction in RPKI. However, due to frequent reconfiguration, the overhead of reconfiguration is also increased, as evident from the value of increase in MPKI, which also increases the main memory energy. Hence, the overall energy saving is slightly reduced. The opposite phenomenon is seen on increasing the interval size to 15M cycles and the overall energy saving achieved depends on the interaction of the above mentioned factors.

Change in sampling ratio (R_s): On changing the sampling ratio from 64 to 32, the energy and performance improvement are enhanced. Also, even with the sampling ratio of 128, ESTEEM achieves large improvement in performance and energy efficiency. Thus, a designer can choose a suitable value of sampling ratio to achieve a balance between profiling overhead and the energy saving achieved.

Change in associativity (A): We experiment with both 8-way and 32-way set-associative cache. For 8-way cache, using $A_{min} = 3$ leads to keeping at least 3 out of 8 ways always on. This leads to higher active ratio and smaller increase in MPKI. However, due to this, the aggressiveness of ESTEEM in reducing the refresh operations is also reduced, which leads to smaller energy saving. Conversely, for 32-way cache, using $A_{min} = 3$ leads to keeping only at most 3-ways always on and thus, the active ratio is reduced, although the increase in MPKI is also enhanced. Due to larger fraction of turned-off cache and larger reduction in refresh operations, the energy saving is increased.

Change in cache size: We experiment with both double and half size cache, compared to the cache size used in Section 7.2. On increasing the cache size, the scope for saving both leakage and refresh energy is increased. This is because the applications have fixed working set size and with larger cache size, a large fraction of energy is wasted due to unnecessary refresh operations. Also, for larger cache size, the contribution of L2 cache in memory subsystem energy is also larger. Further, with larger cache size, more cache blocks need to be refreshed in the same amount of time, which significantly degrades the performance. This clearly shows that use of a technique for minimizing refresh energy is inevitable for large-sized last-level caches. From the results, we conclude that ESTEEM provides large energy saving and performance improvement with large cache size, in fact, with double cache size, for dual-core system, 66.25% energy is saved. The opposite trend is seen on reducing the cache size.

The results shown in this section confirm that ESTEEM is effective in saving energy in eDRAM caches and also improves performance. Also, by adjusting α, A_{min} and the interval size, a designer can achieve fine balance between the performance gain and energy saving.

8. CONCLUSION

Embedded DRAM caches present as a promising alternative to SRAM due to their low leakage value, however, addressing their refresh overhead is crucial to enabling their use in designing on-chip caches. In this paper, we presented ESTEEM, a technique for saving both leakage and refresh energy in eDRAM caches. The experimental results have shown that ESTEEM provides significant energy savings, while improving performance. Also, it outperforms a recently-proposed technique for mitigating refresh overhead in eDRAM caches.

Acknowledgements

Support for this work was provided by U.S. Department of Energy, Office of Science, Advanced Scientific Computing Research. The work was performed at the Oak Ridge National Laboratory, which is managed by UT-Battelle, LLC under Contract No. DE-AC05-00OR22725 to the U.S. Government. Accordingly, the U.S. Government retains a non-exclusive, royalty-free license to publish or reproduce the published form of this contribution, or allow others to do so, for U.S. Government purposes.

9. REFERENCES

[1] http://oxbow.ornl.gov/apps.html.

[2] https://github.com/jtramm/XSBench.

[3] Top 500 Supercomputers. www.top500.org, 2013.

[4] A. Agrawal, P. Jain, A. Ansari, and J. Torrellas. Refrint: Intelligent refresh to minimize power in on-chip multiprocessor cache hierarchies. *HPCA*, 2013.

[5] D. H. Albonesi. Selective cache ways: on-demand cache resource allocation. In *MICRO*, pages 248–259, 1999.

[6] C. S. Bae, L. Xia, P. Dinda, and J. Lange. Dynamic adaptive virtual core mapping to improve power, energy, and performance in multi-socket multicores. *HPDC*, pages 247–258, 2012.

[7] A. Bardine, M. Comparetti, P. Foglia, G. Gabrielli, C. Prete, and P. Stenström. Leveraging data promotion for low power D-NUCA caches. In *EUROMICRO Conference on Digital System Design (DSD)*, pages 307–316, 2008.

[8] J. Barth et al. A 500 MHz random cycle, 1.5 ns latency, SOI embedded DRAM macro featuring a three-transistor micro sense amplifier. *IEEE Journal of Solid-State Circuits*, 43(1):86–95, 2008.

[9] T. E. Carlson, W. Heirman, and L. Eeckhout. Sniper: Exploring the level of abstraction for scalable and accurate parallel multi-core simulations. In *SC*, 2011.

[10] M.-T. Chang, P.-T. Huang, and W. Hwang. A 65nm low power 2T1D embedded DRAM with leakage current reduction. In *IEEE International SOC Conference*, pages 207–210, 2007.

[11] M.-T. Chang, P. Rosenfeld, S.-L. Lu, and B. Jacob. Technology Comparison for Large Last-Level Caches (L³Cs): Low-Leakage SRAM, Low Write-Energy STT-RAM, and Refresh-Optimized eDRAM. *HPCA*, 2013.

[12] K. C. Chun, P. Jain, and C. H. Kim. Logic-compatible embedded DRAM design for memory intensive low power systems. In *IEEE International Symposium on Circuits and Systems (ISCAS)*, pages 277–280, 2010.

[13] J. Dongarra et al. The International Exascale Software Project roadmap. *IJHPCA*, 25(1):3–60, 2011.

[14] J. Gaur, M. Chaudhuri, and S. Subramoney. Bypass and insertion algorithms for exclusive last-level caches. *ACM SIGARCH Computer Architecture News*, 39(3):81–92, 2011.

[15] M. Ghosh and H.-H. S. Lee. Smart refresh: An enhanced memory controller design for reducing energy in conventional and 3D Die-Stacked DRAMs. In *40th Annual IEEE/ACM International Symposium on Microarchitecture*, pages 134–145, 2007.

[16] K. Hardee et al. A 0.6 V 205MHz 19.5 ns tRC 16Mb embedded DRAM. In *IEEE International Solid-State Circuits Conference Digest of Technical Papers (ISSCC)*, pages 200–522, 2004.

[17] J. L. Henning. SPEC CPU2006 benchmark descriptions. *ACM SIGARCH Computer Architecture News*, 34(4):1–17, 2006.

[18] Intel. http://ark.intel.com/products/53575/.

[19] S. Iyer, J. Barth Jr, P. Parries, J. Norum, J. Rice, L. Logan, and D. Hoyniak. Embedded DRAM: Technology platform for the Blue Gene/L chip. *IBM Journal of Research and Development*, 49(2.3):333–350, 2005.

[20] X. Jiang et al. ACCESS: Smart scheduling for asymmetric cache CMPs. In *17th International Symposium on High Performance Computer Architecture (HPCA)*, pages 527–538, 2011.

[21] R. Kalla, B. Sinharoy, W. J. Starke, and M. Floyd. Power7: IBM's next-generation server processor. *IEEE Micro*, 30(2):7–15, 2010.

[22] S. Kaxiras, Z. Hu, and M. Martonosi. Cache decay: exploiting generational behavior to reduce cache leakage power. In *ISCA*, pages 240–251, 2001.

[23] S. K. Khaitan and J. D. McCalley. A hardware-based approach for saving cache energy in multicore simulation of power systems. In *IEEE Power and Energy Society General Meeting (PES)*, pages 1–5, 2013.

[24] S. K. Khaitan and J. D. McCalley. Optimizing cache energy efficiency in multicore power system simulations. *Energy Systems*, pages 1–15, 2013.

[25] N. Kurd et al. Haswell: A family of IA 22nm processors. In *IEEE ISSCC*, pages 112–113, 2014.

[26] S. Li, K. Chen, J. H. Ahn, J. B. Brockman, and N. P. Jouppi. CACTI-P: Architecture-level modeling for SRAM-based structures with advanced leakage reduction techniques. In *International Conference on Computer-Aided Design (ICCAD)*, pages 694–701, 2011.

[27] CACTI 5.3. http://quid.hpl.hp.com:9081/cacti/, 2013.

[28] S. Mittal. A survey of architectural techniques for improving cache power efficiency. *Sustainable Computing: Informatics and Systems*, 2013.

[29] S. Mittal, Y. Cao, and Z. Zhang. MASTER: A Multicore Cache Energy Saving Technique using Dynamic Cache Reconfiguration. *IEEE Transactions on VLSI*, 2013.

[30] S. Mittal and Z. Zhang. EnCache: Improving Cache Energy Efficiency Using A Software-Controlled Profiling Cache. In *IEEE International Conference On Electro/Information Technology*, USA, May 2012.

[31] S. Mittal, Z. Zhang, and J. Vetter. FlexiWay: A Cache Energy Saving Technique Using Fine-grained Cache Reconfiguration. In *IEEE International Conference on Computer Design (ICCD)*, pages 100–107, 2013.

[32] F. Morishita et al. A 312-MHz 16-Mb random-cycle embedded DRAM macro with a power-down data retention mode for mobile applications. *IEEE Journal of Solid-State Circuits*, 40(1):204–212, 2005.

[33] C. D. Patel, C. E. Bash, R. Sharma, M. Beitelmal, and R. Friedrich. Smart cooling of data centers. *Pacific RIM/ASME International Electronics Packaging Technical Conference and Exhibition (IPACK03)*, 2003.

[34] M. Powell, S.-H. Yang, B. Falsafi, K. Roy, and T. Vijaykumar. Gated-Vdd: a circuit technique to reduce leakage in deep-submicron cache memories. In *international symposium on Low power electronics and design (ISLPED)*, pages 90 – 95, 2000.

[35] T. Puzak. *Cache Memory Design*. PhD thesis, University of Massachusetts, 1985.

[36] M. K. Qureshi, S. Gurumurthi, and B. Rajendran. Phase change memory: From devices to systems. *Synthesis Lectures on Computer Architecture*, 6(4):1–134, 2011.

[37] M. K. Qureshi and Y. N. Patt. Utility-based cache partitioning: A low-overhead, high-performance, runtime mechanism to partition shared caches. In *MICRO*, pages 423–432, 2006.

[38] W. R. Reohr. Memories: Exploiting them and developing them. In *IEEE International SOC Conference*, pages 303–310, 2006.

[39] P. Reviriego, A. Sánchez-Macian, and J. A. Maestro. Low Power embedded DRAM caches using BCH code partitioning. In *IEEE International On-Line Testing Symposium (IOLTS)*, pages 79–83, 2012.

[40] B. M. Rogers, A. Krishna, G. B. Bell, K. Vu, X. Jiang, and Y. Solihin. Scaling the bandwidth wall: challenges in and avenues for CMP scaling. In *ACM SIGARCH Computer Architecture News*, volume 37, pages 371–382, 2009.

[41] D. Rolán, B. B. Fraguela, and R. Doallo. Adaptive line placement with the set balancing cache. In *MICRO*, pages 529–540, 2009.

[42] A. Samih, A. Krishna, and Y. Solihin. Understanding the limits of capacity sharing in CMP Private Caches. In *HPCA*, 2009.

[43] A. Valero et al. An hybrid eDRAM/SRAM macrocell to implement first-level data caches. In *MICRO*, pages 213–221, 2009.

[44] W. Wang, P. Mishra, and S. Ranka. Dynamic cache reconfiguration and partitioning for energy optimization in real-time multi-core systems. In *DAC*, pages 948–953, 2011.

[45] C. Wilkerson, A. R. Alameldeen, Z. Chishti, W. Wu, D. Somasekhar, and S.-l. Lu. Reducing cache power with low-cost, multi-bit error-correcting codes. *ACM SIGARCH Computer Architecture News*, 38(3):83–93, 2010.

[46] H. Zheng, J. Lin, Z. Zhang, and Z. Zhu. Decoupled DIMM: building high-bandwidth memory system using low-speed DRAM devices. In *ISCA*, pages 255–266, 2009.

Next Generation Job Management Systems for Extreme-Scale Ensemble Computing

Ke Wang
Illinois Institute of Technology
Chicago IL, 60616, USA
kwang22@hawk.iit.edu

Xiaobing Zhou
Illinois Institute of Technology
Chicago IL, 60616, USA
xzhou40@hawk.iit.edu

Hao Chen
Illinois Institute of Technology
Chicago IL, 60616, USA
hchen71@hawk.iit.edu

Michael Lang
Los Alamos National Laboratory
Los Alamos UM, 87544, USA
mlang@lanl.org

Ioan Raicu
Illinois Institute of Technology
Chicago IL, 60616, USA
iraicu@cs.iit.edu

ABSTRACT

With the exponential growth of supercomputers in parallelism, applications are growing more diverse, including traditional large-scale HPC MPI jobs, and ensemble workloads such as finer-grained many-task computing (MTC) applications. Delivering high throughput and low latency for both workloads requires developing a distributed job management system that is magnitudes more scalable than today's centralized ones. In this paper, we present a distributed job launch prototype, SLURM++, which is comprised of multiple controllers with each one managing a partition of SLURM daemons, while ZHT (a distributed key-value store) is used to store the job and resource metadata. We compared SLURM++ with SLURM using micro-benchmarks of different job sizes up to 500 nodes, with excellent results showing 10X higher throughput. We also studied the potential of distributed scheduling through simulations up to millions of nodes.

Categories and Subject Descriptors

D.4.7 [**System Design**]: Organization and Design – *distributed systems*.

Keywords

Job management systems, job launch, scheduling, key-value store.

1. INTRODUCTION

Exascale machines will have billions of concurrent threads of execution [1]. With this extreme magnitude of parallelism, ensemble computing is one way to efficiently use the machines without requiring full-scale jobs. Ensemble computing would combine the traditional HPC workloads that are large-scale applications using MPI [2] as the communication method, with the ensemble workloads that support the investigation of parameter sweeps using many more but smaller-scale coordinated jobs [3]. Given the significant decrease of Mean-Time-To-Failure [4][5] at exascale, ensemble workloads should be resilient because failures affect a smaller part of the machines.

One example of ensemble workloads comes from the MTC [6][7] paradigm. MTC applications have orders of magnitude larger number of jobs/tasks (e.g. billions) with finer granularity in both size (e.g. per-core) and duration (e.g. sub-second to hours) [8] . The tasks do not require strict coordination of processes at job launch as the HPC workloads do. Furthermore, these applications could be data-intensive in nature [9]. Applications that demonstrate characteristics of MTC cover various domains, such as astronomy, bioinformatics, medical imaging and climate modeling [10], and have been run in clusters, grids, supercomputers, and clouds [11].

The job management systems (JMS) for extreme-scale ensemble computing will need to be available and scalable in order to deliver the extremely high throughput and low latency. However, today's batch schedulers (e.g. SLURM [12], Condor [13], PBS [14], SGE [15]) have centralized architecture that is not well suited for the demands, due to both bounded scalability and single-point-of-failure. A popular JMS, SLURM, reported maximum throughput of 500 jobs/sec [16]; however, we will need much higher job scheduling rates (e.g. millions jobs/sec) for next-generation JMS, considering the significant increase of scheduling size and the much finer job granularity. This paper proposes a distributed architecture that supports JMS at extreme-scales.

We implemented a distributed job launch prototype (SLURM++) with multiple controllers participating in allocating resources and launching jobs – an extension to the open source batch scheduler SLURM [12]. We utilized distributed key-value stores (DKVS), specifically ZHT [17], to keep the job and resource metadata. The general use of DKVS in building distributed system services was proposed, and evaluated through simulation in our previous work [18]. We compared SLURM++ with SLURM using micro-benchmarks of different job sizes up to 500 nodes, with excellent results showing 10X higher throughput. In addition, we developed a simulator of SLURM, SimSLURM++, which enables us to study the performance towards exascale with millions of nodes.

2. DISTRIBUTED ARCHITECTURE

The architecture of the next-generation JMS is shown in Figure 1. There will be multiple controllers with each one managing a partition of compute daemons (cd). The controllers are **fully-connected**. In addition, a distributed data storage system is deployed to manage the entire job and resource metadata.

The **partition size** (number of cd a controller manages) is configurable. For a large-scale HPC workload, the partition size could be thousands; for MTC tasks, the partition size could be one which has the 1:1 mapping (millions of controllers and cds at exascale). We can also have heterogeneous partition sizes.

The distributed storage system could be a DKVS. Each controller would be initialized as a DKVS client, which then uses the simple client APIs (e.g. "lookup", "insert", "remove") to communicate with the servers to query and modify the job and resource information, and the system state information transparently.

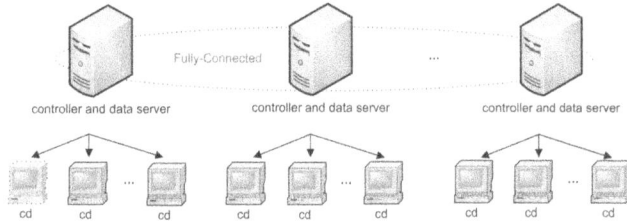

Figure 1: Architecture for distributed JMS; "cd" refers to compute daemon

We propose the **Resource Stealing** technique to balance free "cd" in all the partitions. We implemented a simple **random** resource stealing algorithm. A controller first checks the local free nodes when launching a job. If there are enough available nodes, the controller directly allocates the nodes; otherwise, it allocates whatever resources the partition has, and randomly queries for other partitions (through a "lookup" operation) to steal resources. If the launching controller experiences several failures in a row due to the selected victims have no free nodes, it will release the resources it has already allocated.

One problem of resource stealing technique is the **Resource Conflict** that happens when different controllers try to modify the same resource. We implement the traditional compare and swap atomic instruction [19] as a normal operation in the ZHT. As ZHT serializes requests at one server, this operation guarantees that only one controller could modify a specific resource at one time.

2.1 SLURM++ PROTOTYPE

We developed a distributed job launch prototype, SLURM++, which serves as a core part for JMS. We adopted the open source SLURM [12], and extended it with multiple controllers participating in allocating resources and launching jobs. We used the ZHT DKVS to keep the job and resource metadata.

SLURM++ is directly extended from SLURM. SLURM has a centralized controller (slurmctld) manage all the cds (slurmd). SLURM keeps all the metadata in a centralized local file system. Upon receiving a job, the slurmctld first looks up the global file system to allocate resource. Once a job gets its allocation, it can be launched via a tree-based network rooted at rank-0 slurmd.

In SLURM++, we developed a light-weight distributed controller that can directly talk with slurmds. We utilize the whole slurmd, preserve the hierarchical job launching part unchanged. In addition, each controller is initialized as a ZHT client, and can call the ZHT client APIs to query and modify the job and resource information. Upon receiving all the slurmds' registration messages within a partition, the controller inserts the available nodes to ZHT server. Then, the controllers randomly steal resources from each other when needed. We developed SLURM++ in C. We implemented the controller code, which summed to around 5K lines of code; we put the controller and ZHT directly in the SLURM source file, and named the whole prototype SLURM++. The source code is available at the GitHub website: https://github.com/kwangiit/SLURMPP. SLURM++ has dependencies on Google Protocol Buffer [20], ZHT [17], and SLURM [12].

2.2 SimSLURM++ SIMULATOR

In order to study the scalability of the proposed architecture, we developed a simulator of SLURM++, SimSLURM++, which consists of multiple nodes, and each node has different roles to play (controller, ZHT server, compute daemon). There are two parallel queues in each simulated node: a communication queue for sending and receiving messages, and a processing queue for handling requests locally. The two queues operate in parallel, while within one queue, the requests are processed sequentially.

We followed the simulation work we did before [18][21][22] to build SimSLURM++. SimSLURM++ is a discrete event simulator [23] that was built on top of peersim, a scalable peer-to-peer simulator that offers the framework and functionality of simulating distributed systems. SimSLURM++ is developed in Java, and has about 1500 lines of code, along with the peersim 1.5.0 codebase package. The source code is available at the GitHub website: https://github.com/kwangiit/SimDJL.

3. EVALUATION

We evaluate SLURM++ by comparing it with SLURM using micro-benchmarks containing "sleep 0" jobs on the Kodiak cluster from the Parallel Reconfigurable Observational Environment [24] up to 500 nodes. We used SLURM version 2.6.5, the latest version when we ran experiments. We run SimSLURM++ up to with millions of nodes using real application traces with different configurations on the machine fusion.cs.iit.edu at IIT [18].

3.1 SLURM++ vs SLURM

The micro-benchmark contains independent "sleep 0" HPC jobs that require different number of compute nodes per job. The partition size is configured as 50; at the largest scale (500 nodes), the number of controllers is 10. We will use SLURM++ (M:N) to specify the ratio of the number of controller to the number of slurmds, where M is the number of slurmds and N is the number of controllers, such as SLURM++ (50:1), SLURM++ (1:1).

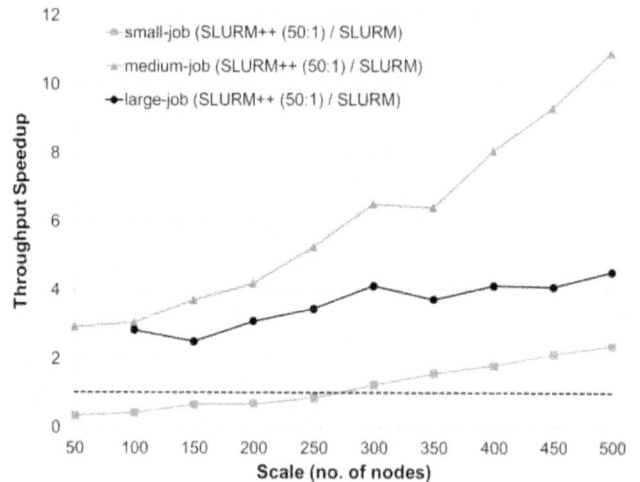

Figure 2: Throughput comparison with different workloads

We conducted experiments with three workloads: small-job workloads (50 jobs per controller, and job size is 1 node), medium-job workloads (50 jobs per controller, and job size is 1-50 nodes), and big-job workloads (20 jobs per controller, and job size is 25-75 nodes). Figure 2 shows that not only does SLURM++ outperform SLURM in nearly all cases, but the performance slowdown due to increasingly larger jobs at large scale is better for SLURM++ by 2X to 11X depending on the job size. The reason that large jobs perform worse than medium jobs is because the larger the jobs are, the more extensively they compete resources. For small jobs, SLURM++'s performance is bounded by SLURM job launching procedure leading to the smallest improvement. Another fact is that as the scale increases, the throughput speedup is also increasing. This indicates that at larger scales, SLURM++ would outperform SLURM even more.

3.2 Evaluation through SimSLURM++

This section presents the evaluation of the scalability of our proposed work through SimSLURM++ towards millions of nodes.

3.2.1 SimSLURM++ HPC Configuration (1024:1)

We configured SLURM++ with 1024:1 mapping. The workload comes from real applications run on the ANL Blue Gene/P machine, during an 8-month period [25]. There are 68,936 jobs. At each scale, we generated a workload with all jobs that preserve the job size distribution of the original workload by applying the job size percentage of the machine size. In addition, we reduced the job duration by 1M times to reduce the job duration granularity to pose significant challenge on launching jobs.

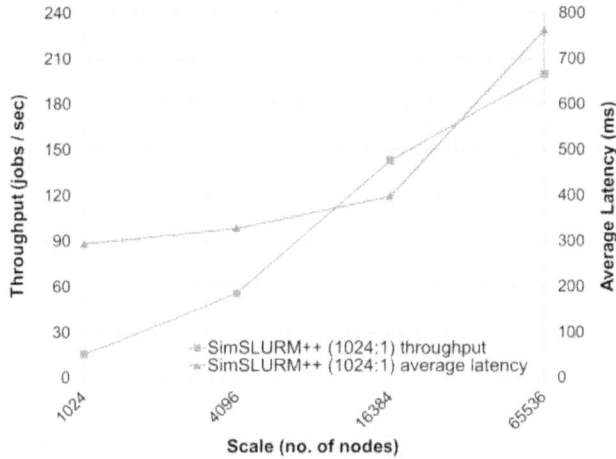

Figure 3: SimSLURM++ (1024:1) throughput and latency

Figure 3 shows the throughput and per-job average latency of SimSLURM++ with HPC configuration. We see that the throughput is increasing with the system scale. This shows that the proposed architecture is scalable. At the meanwhile, the per-job average latency increases moderately from 1024-node to 65536-node.

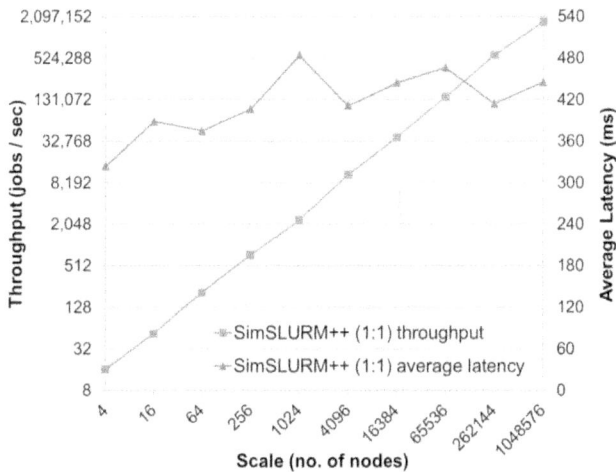

Figure 4: SimSLURM++ (1:1) and latency

3.2.2 SimSLURM++ MTC Configuration (1:1)

We also evaluate SimSLURM++ up to millions of nodes with MTC orientation. The workload is micro-benchmark: each controller handles 10 "sleep 0" jobs, and each job requires 1 or 2 nodes. Figure 4 shows the throughput and per-job average latency of SimSLURM++ with MTC configuration. We see that the throughput is increasing perfectly with the system scale. At 1M-node scale, SimSLURM++ achieves throughput as high as 1.75M jobs/sec, which is very promising. At the same time, the per-job average latency increases trivially from 4-node to 1M-node. These results satisfy the requirements of high throughput and low latency of next-generation JMS for exascale ensemble computing.

4. RELATED WORK

There are other projects that have explored efficient job launch mechanisms. STORM [26] leveraged the hardware collective available in the Quadrics QSNET interconnect to broadcast the binaries to the compute nodes. However, the server is a single-point-of-failure. LIBI/LaunchMON [27] is a scalable bootstrapping service where a tree is used to establish a single process on each compute node. This is a centralized service with no failover or no persistent daemons or state, therefore if a failure occurs they can just re-launch. PMI [28] is the process management layer in MPICH2. It uses a KVS to store job and system information. But the KVS is centralized.

The task execution frameworks that are developed for ensemble MTC workloads are Falkon [29], a centralized task scheduler with the support of hierarchical scheduling, and MATRIX [30][31][32], a distributed task scheduler that uses work stealing [33] for load balancing. Though Falkon can deliver tasks at thousands of task/sec for MTC workloads, it cannot scale to exascale and it lacks support for HPC workloads. Another framework that schedules sub-second tasks for data centers is Sparrow [34]. Though MATRIX and Sparrow have shown great scalability for MTC workloads, neither of them supports HPC workloads.

5. CONCLUSIONS AND FUTURE WORK

Extreme-scale supercomputers require next-generation JMS to be fully distributed that can be much more scalable to deliver jobs with much higher throughput. We have shown that DKVS is a valuable building block to allow scalable job launch. The performance is more preferable (10X) than the centralized production system. Furthermore, our simulation results showed that the distributed architecture resulted in great scalability trends towards extreme-scales supporting both MTC and HPC workloads. In future work, we will explore several techniques, such as caching and distributed monitoring, and MPI applications in both SLURM++ and SimSLURM++ to improve our work. Additions to this work would also include the investigations of distributed power-aware job launch at the core level. Currently, SLURM++ allocates the whole node to a job. In the future, we will over-decompose a node, and launch jobs at the core level in order to save power. Another extension would be to integrate SLURM++ with the MTC task execution fabric, MATRIX [30] (and/or the SimMatrix simulator [35]), and study different job scheduling algorithms for both MTC and HPC workloads [36][37].

6. ACKNOWLEDGMENTS

This work was supported by the U.S. Department of Energy (DOE) contract AC52-06NA25396, and in part by the National Science Foundation (NSF) under award CNS-1042543 (PRObE). We thank Morris Jette and Danny Auble from SchedMD for their help about SLURM, and Tonglin Li for his help with ZHT.

7. REFERENCES

[1] V. Sarkar et al. "ExaScale Software Study: Software Challenges in Extreme Scale Systems", ExaScale Computing Study, DARPA IPTO, 2009.

[2] M. Snir et al. "MPI: The Complete Reference," MIT Press, 1995.

[3] Y. Zhao et al. "Swift: Fast, Reliable, Loosely Coupled Parallel Computation," IEEE Workshop on Scientific Workflows 2007.

[4] D. Zhao et al. "Exploring reliability of exascale systems through simulations." ACM HPC 2013.

[5] I. Raicu et al. "Making a Case for Distributed File Systems at Exascale," ACM Workshop on LSAP, 2011.

[6] I. Raicu. "Many-Task Computing: Bridging the Gap between High Throughput Computing and High Performance Computing", Computer Science Department, University of Chicago, Doctorate Dissertation, March 2009.

[7] M. Wilde et al. "Extreme-scale scripting: Opportunities for large task-parallel applications on petascale computers", Scientific Discovery through Advanced Computing Conference (SciDAC09) 2009.

[8] K. Wang et al. "Modeling Many-Task Computing Workloads on a Petaflop IBM Blue Gene/P Supercomputer." IEEE 27th International Parallel and Distributed Processing Symposium Workshops & PhD Forum (IPDPSW) 2013.

[9] I. Raicu et al. "Towards Data Intensive Many-Task Computing", book chapter in "Data Intensive Distributed Computing: Challenges and Solutions for Large-Scale Information Management", IGI Global Publishers, 2009.

[10] I. Raicu et al. "Middleware Support for Many-Task Computing," Cluster Computing Journal, 2010.

[11] Y. Zhao et al. "Opportunities and Challenges in Running Scientific Workflows on the Cloud", IEEE International Conference on Network-based Distributed Computing and Knowledge Discovery (CyberC) 2011.

[12] M. A. Jette et al. "SLURM: Simple Linux utility for resource management." JSSPP 2003, pages 44–60, June 24, 2003.

[13] D. Thain et al. "Distributed Computing in Practice: The Condor Experience" Concurrency and Computation: Practice and Experience 17 (2-4), pp. 323-356, 2005.

[14] B. Bode et al. "The Portable Batch Scheduler and the Maui Scheduler on Linux Clusters," Usenix, 4th Annual Linux Showcase & Conference, 2000.

[15] W. Gentzsch et al. "Sun Grid Engine: Towards Creating a Compute Power Grid," 1st International Symposium on Cluster Computing and the Grid, 2001.

[16] M. Jette and Danny Auble, "SLURM: Resource Management from the Simple to the Sophisticated", Lawrence Livermore National Laboratory, SLURM User Group Meeting, October 2010.

[17] T. Li et al. "ZHT: A Light-weight Reliable Persistent Dynamic Scalable Zero-hop Distributed Hash Table", IEEE IPDPS, 2013.

[18] K. Wang et al. "Using Simulation to Explore Distributed Key-Value Stores for Extreme-Scale Systems Services," IEEE/ACM Supercomputing/SC 2013.

[19] T. L. Harris et al. "A Practical Multi-Word Compare-and-Swap Operation," In Proceedings of the 16th International Symposium on Distributed Computing, pp 265-279, Springer-Verlag. 2002.

[20] Google. "Google Protocol Buffers," available at http://code.google.com/apis/protocolbuffers/, 2013.

[21] K. Wang et al. "Exploring Design Tradeoffs for Exascale System Services through Simulation." Tech Report, LANL 2013.

[22] K Wang et al. "Centralized and Distributed Job Scheduling System Simulation at Exascale." Tech Report, IIT, 2011.

[23] J. Banks et al. "Discrete-event system simulation - fourth edition." Pearson 2005.

[24] G. Grider. "Parallel Reconfigurable Observational Environment (PRObE)," available from http://www.nmc-probe.org, October 2012.

[25] Available online: http://www.cs.huji.ac.il/labs/parallel/workload/logs.html.

[26] E. Frachtenberg et al. "Storm: Scalable resource management for large-scale parallel computers." IEEE Transactions on Computers, 55(12), 1572-1587, 2006.

[27] J. D. Goehner et al. "LIBI: A Framework for Bootstrapping Extreme Scale Software Systems". Parallel Computing, 2012.

[28] P. Balaji et al. "PMI: A scalable parallel process-management interface for extreme-scale systems". In Recent Advances in the Message Passing Interface (pp. 31-41). Springer Berlin Heidelberg, 2010.

[29] I. Raicu et al. "Falkon: A Fast and Light-weight tasK executiON Framework," IEEE/ACM SC 2007.

[30] K. Wang et al. "MATRIX: MAny-Task computing execution fabRIc at eXascale," tech report, IIT, 2013.

[31] K. Wang et al. "Paving the Road to Exascale with Many-Task Computing." Doctor Showcase, IEEE/ACM SC 2012.

[32] I. Sadooghi et al. "Achieving Efficient Distributed Scheduling with Message Queues in the Cloud for Many-Task Computing and High-Performance Computing." IEEE/ACM CCGrid, 2014.

[33] J. Dinan et al. "Scalable work stealing", IEEE/ACM SC 2009.

[34] K. Ousterhout et al. "Sparrow: Distributed, Low Latency Scheduling," SOSP '13, Farmington, Pennsylvania, USA.

[35] K. Wang et al. "SimMatrix: Simulator for MAny-Task computing execution fabRIc at eXascales," ACM HPC 2013.

[36] K. Ramamurthy et al. "Exploring Distributed HPC Scheduling in MATRIX." Tech Report, IIT, 2013.

[37] X. Zhou et al. "Exploring Distributed Resource Allocation Techniques in the SLURM Job Management System." Tech Report, IIT, 2013.

OpenARC: Open Accelerator Research Compiler for Directive-Based, Efficient Heterogeneous Computing

Seyong Lee
Oak Ridge National Laboratory
Oak Ridge, TN 37831, USA
lees2@ornl.gov

Jeffrey S. Vetter
Oak Ridge National Laboratory
Oak Ridge, TN 37831, USA
Georgia Institute of Technology
Atlanta, GA 30332, USA
vetter@computer.org

ABSTRACT

This paper presents Open Accelerator Research Compiler (OpenARC): an open-source framework that supports the full feature set of OpenACC V1.0 and performs source-to-source transformations, targeting heterogeneous devices, such as NVIDIA GPUs. Combined with its high-level, extensible Intermediate Representation (IR) and rich semantic annotations, OpenARC serves as a powerful research vehicle for prototyping optimization, source-to-source transformations, and instrumentation for debugging, performance analysis, and autotuning. In fact, OpenARC is equipped with various capabilities for advanced analyses and transformations, as well as built-in performance and debugging tools. We explain the overall design and implementation of OpenARC, and we present key analysis techniques necessary to efficiently port OpenACC applications. Porting various OpenACC applications to CUDA GPUs using OpenARC demonstrates that OpenARC performs similarly to a commercial compiler, while serving as a general research framework.

Categories and Subject Descriptors

D.3.4 [**Programming Languages**]: Processors—*code generation, compilers*

Keywords

OpenACC; compiler; source-to-source translation; CUDA; GPU; OpenARC

1. INTRODUCTION

Today's architectures are growing more complex as hardware architects respond to the constraints of energy, density, facilities, and device technology trends [4]. Scalable Heterogeneous Computing (SHC) platforms, enabled by graphics processors, Intel Xeon Phi, etc., are clearly emerging as solutions to these challenges [13]. However, this trend comes at

a cost of portability and productivity: to make use of these platforms, scientists must program and optimize a collection of multiple programming models (e.g., MPI, OpenMP, and CUDA) simultaneously to use these scalable heterogeneous systems. Consequently, the community is rethinking the design of the entire programming system in the hope of solving, or at least mitigating, this challenge.

In this regard, several efforts are investigating directive-based programming models [5, 6, 7, 9, 10] as a solution to this productivity and portability challenge. Among them, OpenACC [10] is the first standardization effort to provide portability across device types and compiler vendors. A major benefit of using directive-based programming models is that they transparently relieve programmers from dealing with complexity of low-level programming languages, such as CUDA or OpenCL, and they also hide most of the complex optimizations that are specific to underlying architectures, such as managing data movement into scratchpad memories.

Conceptually, however, these abstractions must strike a delicate balance. At one extreme, too much abstraction in the models restricts the ability of scientists to debug, port, and tune applications. On the other extreme, too little abstraction results in applications without portability. As a compromise, in many of these programming systems, scientists have added performance-critical hints to inform compilers of various compile-time and runtime optimizations to better utilize the underlying architectural resources, such as cores and specialized memory. In previous work, we investigated existing compilers for GPUs in order to better understand this balance on these emerging programming models; we identified several important issues, such as functionality, scalability, tunability, and debuggability. [8].

The lessons learned from the directive-based programming model study [8], along with observations from a comprehensive study of DOE applications, have motivated us to develop a new research compiler, called OpenARC [1], to allow us to investigate these issues in directive-based, high-level programming models. Here are the main contributions of this paper:

- We present the first open-source compiler that supports *full features* in the OpenACC standard V1.0 [10]. OpenARC has several salient features. First, OpenARC's very high-level IR allows high-level source-to-source translation, offering better readability of the output codes and more enhanced debugging environment than existing OpenACC compilers. Second, mod-

HPDC'14, June 23–27, Vancouver, BC, Canada.
Copyright 2014 ACM 978-1-4503-2749-7/14/06 ...$15.00.
http://dx.doi.org/10.1145/2600212.2600704.

ular design of OpenARC enables clear separation between compiler passes, which communicate with each other through a rich set of annotations. Hence, within OpenARC, we can implement various traceability mechanisms to establish connections between input directive models and output performance.

- The OpenARC framework is shipped with additional types of directives. Combined with built-in tuning tools, these extensions allow programmers to have a fine-grained control over the overall OpenACC-to-GPU translation and optimizations in an abstract manner.

- We design and implement compiler analyses, code transformations, and runtime support for OpenACC-to-GPU translation. We also discuss how traditional parallelization techniques should be adjusted to the OpenACC execution model to preserve the correct program semantics.

- We evaluate thirteen OpenACC programs from various application domains and compare the results against those translated by the PGI-OpenACC compiler. The results show that OpenARC performs similarly to the commercial compiler.

2. OPENARC: OPEN ACCELERATOR RESEARCH COMPILER

OpenARC is the first open-source compiler supporting full features of OpenACC V1.0, which takes C-based OpenACC programs as inputs and generates accelerator-specific output codes. There exist open-source implementations partially supporting OpenACC [11, 12], but they are developed as fast-prototyping tools with limited contexts, while OpenARC supports full research across all OpenACC functionality.

2.1 Extensible Program Representation

Built on top of the Cetus compiler infrastructure [2], OpenARC's program representation inherits several of its predecessor's salient features. OpenARC's IR is implemented in the form of a Java class hierarchy, and it provides an Abstract Syntax Tree (AST)-like syntactic *view* of the input program that makes it easy for compiler-pass writers to analyze and transform the input program. The hierarchical IR class structure provides complete data abstraction such that compiler-pass writers can manipulate the objects only through access functions. OpenARC supports the following important features derived from Cetus.

- *Traversable IR objects.* All OpenARC IR objects extend a base class *Traversable*, which provides the basic functionality to iterate over IR objects. Combined with various built-in iterators (e.g., *BreadthFirst*, *DepthFirst*, *Flat*, etc.), these provide easy traversal and search over the AST-like, n-ary tree structures of the program representation.

- *Rich Annotations.* *Annotation* is a base class type to represent any type of annotations used in OpenARC. By deriving this base class, various types of information, such as comments, directives, raw codes to be inlined, etc., can be added to the OpenARC IRs. An annotation can be associated with any *Annotatable* IR

objects (e.g., OpenMP/OpenACC directives attached to a *ForLoop* statement) or can be stand-alone like a comment statement.

- *Flexible Printing.* The printing functions in each IR class type allow flexible rendering of the program representation, depending on the target languages and translation goals.

As a high-level representation, OpenARC represents program semantics in a language-independent way. The OpenARC class hierarchy, which is more general (abstract) than AST structure, serves as a base vehicle to convey program semantics. The base OpenARC classes can capture semantics common among traditional general-purpose languages, such as Fortran or C/C++, in a generic way. However, traditional general-purpose languages are inherently sequential, and thus the base OpenARC class hierarchy cannot capture other important properties such as concurrency, parallelism, data distribution, etc. Moreover, new parallel programming models such as CUDA and OpenCL introduce new languages features that do not exist in traditional general-purpose languages (e.g., a CUDA kernel function has a mechanism to express the execution configuration for the kernel call).

To address these issues, OpenARC provides two alternative solutions: 1) semantic annotation and 2) class hierarchy extension. The semantic annotation augments existing OpenARC objects with rich semantic information. OpenARC already supports various directives, including OpenMP, OpenACC, and several internal directives, with which OpenARC can capture both task and data parallelisms, data sharing rules, accelerator regions, synchronizations, etc.

The OpenARC class hierarchy extension offers an alternative method to realize richer semantics; it can easily embrace new language constructs. Emerging parallel programming languages, such as X10 and Chapel, support various language constructs to explicitly express data locality, data distributions, etc. Study on extending existing accelerator programming models with these new language constructs may be possible by creating a new IR class or by extending existing classes in OpenARC.

This extensible high-level class hierarchy, with its rich semantic annotation provisions, allows OpenARC to be used as a base framework and starting point for quickly prototyping and exploring the trade-offs in realizing productive programming environment for scalable heterogeneous computing.

2.2 Compiler Analyses

OpenARC exploits various advanced analysis techniques to efficiently port OpenACC applications to a target accelerator. However, some of these techniques cannot be directly applied to the OpenACC translation due to the unique semantics of the OpenACC execution model. This section discusses how to customize general automatic parallelization techniques to the OpenACC context.

2.2.1 Scalar and Array Privatization

Identifying privatizable variables, along with reduction recognition, is one of the most important enabling techniques for automatic parallelization. For this, Cetus provides a general array privatizer, which can detect both scalar and array privatizable variables in a loop nest [2]. If an OpenACC compute region is a perfectly-nested loop, the general privatizer can be directly used to detect OpenACC gang/-worker/vector private variables. However, if the region is not a perfectly nested loop, which may be common in OpenACC *parallel* regions, additional analyses are necessary to identify private variables as follows. 1) If a *parallel* region contains multiple *gang* loops, a variable can be put in the private clause of the region only if the variable is privatizable in all the outermost gang loops contained in the region. 2) The variable should not be *upward-exposed* (used before it is defined) at entry to its enclosing compute region. 3) Variables appearing in any data clauses of the enclosing compute region cannot be privatized unless they are explicitly included in OpenACC *private/firstprivate* clauses (shared by default). 4) Local variables declared in a gang/worker/private loop are private to the enclosing loop, and local variables declared inside a *parallel* region but outside of any work-sharing loop are gang-private by default. A privatization transformation pass should also consider the execution context and a target architecture. For example, the CUDA memory system has several special memories whose visibility and capacity are different; depending on the size and the scope of a private variable, different memory allocation strategies should be applied, which is an important performance tuning subject. For this, OpenARC provides several additional directives and environment variables to control this mapping.

```
#pragma acc parallel \          #pragma acc parallel \
reduction(+gang_num)            reduction(+gang_num)
{ int lnum = 0;                 { int lnum = 0;
  #pragma acc loop gang           #pragma acc loop gang
  for(i=0; i<8; i++) {            for(i=0; i<8; i++) {
                                   }
    lnum = lnum + 1;
  }                              lnum += 8;
  gang_num += lnum;             gang_num += lnum;
} //gang_num will be 8.        } //gang_num will be 64.
      (a) Before IVS                  (b) After IVS
```

Figure 1: Induction Variable Substitution (IVS) Example, which shows IVS can be unsafe depending on the execution modes of OpenACC.

2.2.2 Induction Variable Substitution

The induction variable substitution algorithm is another parallelization-enabling technique, which recognizes an induction form (e.g., $iv = iv + expr$), similar to a reduction form, and converts into a closed form that does not induce data dependence. Cetus provides a powerful induction variable substitution pass that can detect generalized induction variables [2]. However, the traditional substitution algorithm may not be safe in certain OpenACC execution contexts. For example, induction variable substitution may not be applicable to a gang loop in a *parallel* region; in Fig. 1 (a), if the parallel region is executed by eight gangs, the output value of *gang_num* will be 8, since the iterations of the inner gang loop will be partitioned to each gang, and *lnum* is gang-private. However, in Fig. 1 (b), the output value of *gang_num* will be 64, since each gang will redundantly execute the substituted expression ($lnum+ = 8;$). This problem occurs because the code in an OpenACC *par-*

allel region is redundantly executed by a set of participating gangs (i.e., gang-redundant mode) unless work-sharing constructs are encountered. Therefore, the induction substitution algorithm should be applied selectively, depending on the execution modes of OpenACC.

2.2.3 Reduction Recognition and Transformation

Reduction operations are used in many scientific applications, and thus Cetus supports a general reduction variable analyzer that detects additive reduction patterns (e.g., $sum = sum + expr$) in a loop for both scalar and array variables [2]. OpenARC extends the base analyzer to adapt to execution modes in OpenACC; 1) assignment expression outside a loop can be a reduction operation if the expression is executed in a *gang-redundant* mode, meaning that each gang executes the same code redundantly. 2) If a reduction variable recognized in a work-sharing loop is private to the loop, reduction transformation should not be applied to the variable. 3) If an OpenACC *parallel* region is not a loop, additional checking is necessary to make sure that a gang reduction variable is used only for reduction operations within the region.

2.3 OpenARC Directives and Environment Variables

Table 1: Directives Supported by OpenARC

```
#pragma acc accdirective [clause [,] clause]...
#pragma omp ompdirective [clause [,] clause]...
#pragma cetus [clause [,] clause]...
#pragma acc internal [clause [,] clause]...
```

Table 1 shows the list of directives that OpenARC supports; both OpenACC and OpenMP directives are accepted. In OpenARC, however, OpenMP programs are not translated into low-level output codes, such as Pthreads codes; instead, information in the OpenMP directives are used during the OpenACC translation to preserve correct OpenMP multithreading semantics. In addition to these standard directives, OpenARC uses several internal directives; *cetus* annotations are used to convey general analysis outputs generated by various built-in Cetus passes, and *acc internal* directives are used by OpenARC passes to communicate various analysis outputs and configurations specific to the OpenACC translation. Table 2 shows a partial list of the *acc internal* clauses: *kernelConfPt(kernel)* is used by an analysis pass to direct where the translator puts configuration statements for a kernel; *gangconf(list)* is used to generate a multi-dimensional grid when porting to CUDA. These rich set of internal annotations, which can be easily extended to adopt any user-provided directives, are used by internal OpenARC passes to communicate with each other, enabling clear separation between analysis passes and transformation passes. This modular design allows convenient framework for researchers to integrate/debug new compiler passes.

OpenARC environment variables control the program-level behavior of various compiler optimizations, transformations, and execution/tuning configurations. Table 3 shows a partial list of supported OpenARC environment variables; *showInternalAnnotations* controls types of annotations to be included in the output file, varying from nothing to all annotations. This selective annotation printing, combined with

Table 2: A Partial List of OpenARC Internal Clauses

Table 2: A Partial List of OpenARC Internal Clauses

Clause	Description
accglobal(list)	contains global symbols
accexplicitshared (list)	contains symbols that user inserted in data clauses
accreadonly(list)	contains R/O shared symbols
kernelConfPt (kernel)	indicates where to put kernel-configuration statements
gangconf(list)	contains sizes of each gang loop in nested gang loops

other OpenARC-pass-control options (e.g., *AccAnalysisOnly*), provides a simple, but efficient way to trace how OpenARC translates an input OpenACC program to a target device. OpenARC also offers various environment variables to be used for efficient tuning; e.g., *UserDirectiveFile* allows users or external tuning engines to add directives through a separate file, rather than inserting to the source program directly. If *extractTuningParameters* option is on, OpenARC will generate a list of optimizations applicable to a given input program, which can be used to prune the optimization search space that a tuning system should navigate. *genTuning-ConfFiles* generates a set of tuning configurations files based on the information extracted from other tuning-related environment variables. Each tuning configuration file can be used to customize the overall OpenACC translation. Combined with other built-in tuning tools, these environment variables offer powerful building blocks, with which custom tuning system can be easily built.

Table 3: A Partial List of OpenARC Environment Variables

Parameter	Description
AccParallelization	detect parallelizable loops automatically
AccReduction	control reduction variable types (none/scalar/array) to recognize automatically
AccAnalysisOnly	run only selected analysis passes and exit
showInternalAnnotations	control types of annotations to be included in the output file
UserDirectiveFile	specify a file containing user directives
extractTuningParameters	generate a file containing tuning parameters applicable to a given input program
defaultTuningConfFile	specify a file containing default tuning configurations that control tuning configuration generation
genTuningConfFiles	generate tuning configuration files, each of which can be fed to OpenARC compiler

2.4 Overall Compilation Flow

The OpenARC compiler consists of the following major passes, each of which provides one or more checkpoints. Within checkpoints, intermediate results can be saved as output codes with annotations. This is useful for manual debugging or for implementing traceability mechanisms.

Cetus parser calls C preprocessor to handle header files, macro expansion, etc., and converts the preprocessed OpenACC program into internal representations (OpenARC IR).

Input preprocessor parses OpenACC directives and performs initial code transformations for later passes, including selective procedure cloning to enable context-sensitive, interprocedural analyses/transformations.

OpenACC loop-directive preprocessor interprets loop directives, extracts necessary implicit information from the loop constructs and stores them as internal/external annotations, and performs initial loop transformations according to explicit/implicit rules.

OpenACC analysis checks the correctness of the overall OpenACC directives and derives sharing rules for the data not explicitly specified by programmers.

User-directive handler interprets additional annotations provided as a separate file, and stores them into IR.

Optimization pass performs various optimizations such as privatization, reduction recognition, locality analysis, etc. All the optimization results are stored as annotations to inform later transformation passes.

Transformation pass conducts several pre-transformations according to the results passed from the optimization pass.

OpenACC-to-Accelerator translation generates output accelerator codes with post-transformations that are possible only at output codes.

3. EVALUATION

For evaluation, we use thirteen OpenACC programs from diverse application domains, which were manually ported from several OpenMP benchmarks (two NAS Parallel Benchmarks (*EP* and *CG*), three kernel benchmarks (*MATMUL*, *JACOBI* and *SPMUL*), and eight Rodinia Benchmarks [3] (*BACKPROP*, *BFS*, *CFD*, *HOTSPOT*, *KMEANS*, *LUD*, *NW*, *SRAD*)) [8]. The OpenACC programs were translated to output CUDA programs by OpenARC and then compiled using NVCC V5.0 and GCC V4.4.6 . The same OpenACC programs were also ported by the PGI-OpenACC compiler (V13.6). For the programs that don't have manual CUDA versions (*JACOBI*, *SPMUL*, *EP*, and *CG*), locally developed CUDA versions were used. The compiled programs were executed on a platform with Intel Xeon X5660 host CPUs and NVIDIA Tesla M2090 GPU.

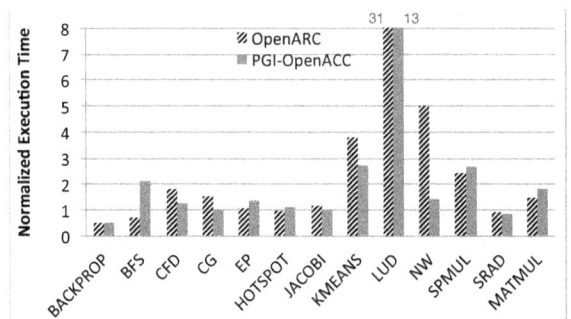

Figure 2: Performance of benchmarks translated by OpenARC and by the PGI-OpenACC compiler. The execution times are normalized to those of manual CUDA versions. Lower is better.

118

Fig. 2 presents the performance of the proposed OpenARC compiler; execution times are normalized to the manual CUDA versions, and thus a normalized value less than one indicates better performance than the manual CUDA versions. The results show that OpenARC performs similarly to the PGI-OpenACC compiler, while our compiler provides much better and extensible environment for program debugging and optimizations. For some benchmarks (e.g., BFS, EP, HOTSPOT, and SPMUL), OpenARC outperforms the PGI-OpenACC compiler, because OpenARC allows more fine-grained control over compiler-specific or GPU-specific features than the PGI-OpenACC compiler. However, the current implementation of OpenARC does not contain some compiler optimizations such as the automatic tiling transformation in the PGI-OpenACC compiler. Research and implementation of various analysis/transformation techniques to enable better utilization of GPUs will be future work.

The figure also indicates that OpenARC and PGI-OpenACC versions perform similarly to the manual CUDA version, except for *LUD*, where OpenARC and PGI-OpenACC perform significantly worse than the manual version. The excellent performance of the CUDA version is due to complex manual optimizations, which partition the whole matrix into many small blocks, and apply different software-caching strategies using complex thread-access patterns. These complex data access patterns to exploit the CUDA shared memory are not expressible in the standard OpenACC model, which motivates research on extending existing directive models to express more architecture-specific features still in high level.

4. CONCLUSIONS

Open Accelerator Research Compiler (OpenARC) is an open-source framework that supports the full feature set of OpenACC V1.0 and serves as a powerful research vehicle for various source-to-source transformation and instrumentation study to address important issues in directive-based, high-level programming models for scalable heterogeneous computing. In this paper, we have provided an overview of the overall design, implementation, and performance of OpenARC. Implementing a reference OpenACC compiler has led us to identify several key analysis techniques required for efficient porting of OpenACC applications. Porting thirteen OpenACC applications from diverse scientific domains shows that OpenARC performs similarly to a commercial compiler, and OpenACC can achieve performance comparable to that of low-level device programming models in many cases.

5. ACKNOWLEDGMENTS

The paper has been authored by Oak Ridge National Laboratory, which is managed by UT-Battelle, LLC under Contract #DE-AC05-00OR22725 to the U.S. Government. Accordingly, the U.S. Government retains a non-exclusive, royalty-free license to publish or reproduce the published form of this contribution, or allow others to do so, for U.S. Government purposes. This research is sponsored by the Office of Advanced Scientific Computing Research in the U.S. Department of Energy.

6. REFERENCES

[1] OpenARC: Open Accelerator Research Compiler. [Online]. Available: `http://ft.ornl.gov/research/openarc`. (accessed April 11, 2014).

[2] H. Bae, L. Bachega, C. Dave, S.-I. Lee, S. Lee, et al. Cetus: A source-to-source compiler infrastructure for multicores. In *Proc. of the 14th Int'l Workshop on Compilers for Parallel Computing (CPC'09)*, page 14 pages, 2009.

[3] S. Che, M. Boyer, J. Meng, D. Tarjan, J. W. Sheaffer, S. ha Lee, and K. Skadron. Rodinia: A benchmark suite for heterogeneous computing. In *Proceedings of the IEEE International Symposium on Workload Characterization (IISWC)*, 2009.

[4] J. Dongarra, P. Beckman, T. Moore, P. Aerts, G. Aloisio, et al. The international exascale software project roadmap. *International Journal of High Performance Computing Applications*, 25(1):3–60, 2011.

[5] T. D. Han and T. S. Abdelrahman. hiCUDA: High-level GPGPU programming. *IEEE Transactions on Parallel and Distributed Systems*, 22(1):78–90, 2011.

[6] HMPP. OpenHMPP directive-based programming model for hybrid computing. [Online]. Available: `http://www.caps-entreprise.com/openhmpp-directives/`, 2009. (accessed April 11, 2014).

[7] S. Lee and R. Eigenmann. OpenMPC: Extended OpenMP programming and tuning for GPUs. In *SC'10: Proceedings of the 2010 ACM/IEEE conference on Supercomputing*. IEEE press, 2010.

[8] S. Lee and J. S. Vetter. Early evaluation of directive-based GPU programming models for productive Exascale computing. In *the International Conference for High Performance Computing, Networking, Storage, and Analysis (SC)*. IEEE press, 2012.

[9] A. Leung, N. Vasilache, B. Meister, M. Baskaran, D. Wohlford, C. Bastoul, and R. Lethin. A mapping path for multi-GPGPU accelerated computers from a portable high level programming abstraction. In *Proceedings of the 3rd Workshop on General-Purpose Computation on Graphics Processing Units*, GPGPU '10, pages 51–61. ACM, 2010.

[10] OpenACC. OpenACC: Directives for Accelerators. [Online]. Available: `http://www.openacc-standard.org`, 2011. (accessed April 11, 2014).

[11] R. Reyes, I. López-Rodríguez, J. Fumero, and F. Sande. accULL: An OpenACC implementation with CUDA and OpenCL support. In *Euro-Par 2012 Parallel Processing*, volume 7484 of *Lecture Notes in Computer Science*, pages 871–882. Springer Berlin Heidelberg, 2012.

[12] X. Tian, R. Xu, Y. Yan, Z. Yun, S. Chandrasekaran, and B. Chapman. Compiling a High-level Directive-Based Programming Model for GPGPUs. *Annual Workshop on Languages and Compilers for High Performance Computing (LCPC)*, 2013.

[13] J. S. Vetter, editor. *Contemporary High Performance Computing: From Petascale Toward Exascale*, volume 1 of *CRC Computational Science Series*. Taylor and Francis, Boca Raton, 1 edition, 2013.

MIC-Check: A Distributed Checkpointing Framework for the Intel Many Integrated Cores Architecture*

Raghunath Rajachandrasekar, Sreeram Potluri, Akshay Venkatesh
Khaled Hamidouche, Md. Wasi-ur-Rahman and Dhabaleswar K.(DK) Panda
The Ohio State University
{rajachan, potluri, akshay, hamidouc, rahmanmd, panda}@cse.ohio-state.edu

ABSTRACT

The advent of many-core architectures like Intel MIC is enabling the design of increasingly capable supercomputers within reasonable power budgets. Fault-tolerance is becoming more important with the increased number of components and the complexity in these heterogeneous clusters. Checkpoint-restart mechanisms have been traditionally used to enhance the dependability of applications, and to enable dynamic task rescheduling in the face of system failures. Naive checkpointing protocols, which are predominantly I/O-intensive, face severe performance bottlenecks on the Xeon Phi architecture due to several inherent and acquired limitations. Consequently, existing checkpointing frameworks are not capable of serving distributed MPI applications that leverage heterogeneous hardware architectures. This paper discusses the I/O limitations on the Xeon Phi system, and describes the architecture and design of a novel distributed checkpointing framework, namely MIC-Check, for HPC applications running on it.

Categories and Subject Descriptors

C.4 [**PERFORMANCE OF SYSTEMS**]: Fault tolerance; D.4.5 [**Reliability**]: Checkpoint/restart

Keywords

Checkpointing, Many Integrated Cores, Xeon Phi, I/O, MPI

1. INTRODUCTION AND MOTIVATION

Many-core architectures are becoming the mainstay of modern system architectures due to the higher compute power they offer at a lower power budget. Many Integrated Core (MIC) architecture [2], from Intel, boasts of several advantages compared to other manycore architectures available today. The first line of products based on the MIC architecture, Xeon Phis [3], pack more than 1Tflops of double precision performance on a single chip. Xeon Phis already power two of the top 10 supercomputers on the Nov'13 Top500 [4] list: Tianhe-2 and Stampede [7].

*This research is supported in part by NSF grants OCI-1148371 and CCF-1213084.

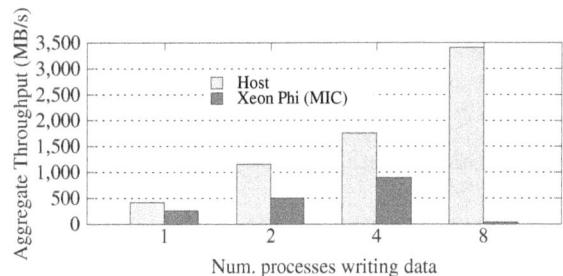

Figure 1: Disparity in I/O performance as seen by processes on the host and MIC

The adoption of MIC-like architectures would also lead to a significant increase in the number of system components in supercomputing installations. Consequently, the Mean time between failures (MTBF) would reduce, and Mean time to repair (MTTR) would increase. A vast majority of current-generation HPC systems and application codes work around system failures using rollback-recovery schemes, also known as Checkpoint-Restart (CR), wherein the parallel processes of an application frequently save a mutually agreed-upon state of their execution as checkpoints in a shared storage medium. In the face of failures, applications rollback their execution to a fault-free state using these snapshots that were saved periodically. Over the years, checkpointing mechanisms have gained notoriety for their colossal I/O demands. While state-of-art parallel file systems are optimized for concurrent accesses from millions of processes, checkpointing overheads continue to dominate application run times, with the time taken to write a single checkpoint taking on the order of tens of minutes. On current HPC systems, checkpointing utilizes 75-80% of the I/O traffic. On future systems, checkpointing activities are predicted to dominate compute time and overwhelm file system resources.

With the Xeon Phi processor, there is a remarkable disparity between the compute and I/O performance capabilities. Figure 1 clearly illustrates the I/O performance of a Xeon Phi (MIC) PCIe-based coprocessor writing data to the Lustre file system on the Stampede supercomputer, by comparing it with that of the Xeon-based system (Host) that is hosting it. In case of the host, the aggregate throughput steadily scales with the number of processes, achieving up to 3.4GB/s with 8 processes, whilst the processes on the coprocessor reach a peak of 893MB/s with 4 processes, after which contention amongst them begins to hurt the aggregate throughput which drops to 41MB/s with 8 processes.

Hence, it is clear that the Xeon Phi coprocessor is not naturally conducive for checkpointing schemes which are I/O-intensive by design. State-of-art checkpointing techniques that alleviate the I/O burden on applications by leveraging multi-level and asynchronous checkpointing schemes will also be subject to the I/O performance penalties on the MIC. It is also not clear how checkpointing will be supported in the variety of usage modes that Xeon Phi offers. In this context, we propose MIC-Check, a novel distributed checkpointing framework for parallel MPI applications that leverage the compute capabilities of the MIC architecture. In this paper, we make the following contributions:

- Detailed insights into the intrinsic and extrinsic I/O limitations on the Xeon Phi coprocessor

- MIC-Check, a novel framework that circumvents the said limitations and provides a scalable checkpointing solution for Xeon Phi clusters

- Support for application and system level checkpointing in the various execution modes of Xeon Phi coprocessor: native, symmetric and offload

- Experimental evaluations of the proposed designs

2. I/O LIMITATIONS ON XEON PHI

The performance of I/O operations is critical to checkpointing protocols, and in reducing the overheads imposed on applications. Figure 1 clearly illustrates the inferior I/O performance of the Xeon Phi coprocessor. This spurs from inherent characteristics of the coprocessor itself, and its interaction with external components like the network infrastructure and the storage subsystem.

2.1 Intrinsic Limitations

The Xeon Phi coprocessor runs an embedded version of Linux with its own Virtual File System (VFS) in the kernel that is very similar to a conventional Linux VFS in terms of functionality. However, it has certain *hot-spots* [1] that hurt checkpointing I/O performance.

(a) When a page involved in an I/O request is not cached by the kernel in its page-cache, the VFS assigns a new page for the data to be cached in memory. While this memory is often sourced from a per-CPU pool of pages, the kernel page allocator is invoked to request a free physical page when the per-CPU pool is depleted. This is a CPU-intensive operation that involves claiming appropriate zone and LRU locks, and identifying physical pages that can be used to replenish the per-CPU pool from which the page was originally requested. The low-frequency processing units on the Xeon Phi, along with reduced cache sizes, reduces the performance of these operations which manifests into the I/O request. **(b)** Copying data to and from user-level buffers is achieved using *copy_from_user* and *copy_to_user* routines that involve page-fault handling. The kernel data-copy routines do not leverage the vector-processing capabilities of the architecture. In addition to polluting caches with data not needed by the kernel, this makes large-sized data-movement really inefficient. **(c)** In order to maintain consistency of the physical pages, each page is associated with a lock bit which indicates the status of its usage. If a lock has been grabbed already, a new thread wanting to read to, or write from, a page gets added to a queue and sent to sleep. When the lock is released, the kernel computes a hash to identify the next thread from the queue that gets to grab the page lock, instead of reading it from memory. However, this becomes expensive on the Xeon Phi, adding to the overheads involved in the VFS page cache management. **(d)** Furthermore, each MIC core is 4-way multi-threaded in the hardware,

		Sandy Bridge	Ivy Bridge
Same Socket	Read from MIC	962 (15%)	3421 (54%)
	Write to MIC	5280 (83%)	6396 (100%)
Different Socket	Read from MIC	370 (6%)	247 (4%)
	Write to MIC	1075 (17%)	1179 (19%)

Table 1: **Network data-transfer throughput to/from the MIC(MB/s)**

and the threads are given control to execute instructions in a round-robin manner. Due to this arbitration, each thread gets to execute a single instruction in every fourth clock cycle. To add to that, the architecture is not capable of branch prediction, speculative or out-of-order execution, which does not bode well for performance.

2.2 Extrinsic Limitations

Although the Xeon Phi coprocessor is an out-of-chip hardware component that communicates with the host system and other system peripherals using the PCIe bus, application processes that execute on the coprocessor have a variety of communication channels to choose from for data movement, either to communicate with other processes, or to read/write data from/to the parallel file system. Table 1 lists the peak bandwidth that is observed on these different paths for the Sandy Bridge and Ivy Bridge architectures. It is clear from these observations that the peak data movement bandwidth to/from a coprocessor heavily relies on the communication path chosen. Specifically, it is apparent that moving data from MIC memory (read from MIC) to the NIC memory and vice versa (write to MIC) incurs significant bandwidth limitations. The proposed checkpointing framework, built on this premise, is designed to leverage the most optimal path for writing the checkpoint snapshots to the parallel file system with the least amount of overhead to the application.

3. PROPOSED ARCHITECTURE

Figure 2 describes the high-level architecture of the MIC-Check framework. It portrays the architecture of one compute node of a supercomputing cluster that employs the Xeon Phi coprocessors on each compute node. With the steady increase in the number of processing cores available on host CPUs, the compute capacity available for applications is aplenty. MIC-Check reserves one of these CPU cores exclusively to a servlet, namely the MIC-Check Proxy (MCP), that progresses checkpointing I/O requests on behalf of the application processes that are residing on the coprocessor. The use of MCP allows the MIC-Check framework to schedule data movement through the most optimal data-movement path. The MCP is exclusively bound to a host processor core on each compute node where the application will be executed. Once bootstrapped by the job-launcher, MCP constantly listens on a known port for incoming SCIF connections.

Step 1. The application links to the MIC-Check I/O interception library (MCI), which can intercept all I/O calls in order to take control of I/O requests from the application. During MPI initialization, the MCI instance associated with each MPI process initiates a SCIF connection with the MCP on its compute node. These connections are persisted for the duration of the job and are terminated only during MPI finalization. If the job is restarting from a failure, the connections are established again before resuming execution.

Step 2. When an application is ready to take a checkpoint, MCI intercepts the *open* call and sends a request to the local MCP. This request also encapsulates metadata of the checkpoint from the application, including the checkpoint path name, size, and more importantly, information about the memory region that was registered

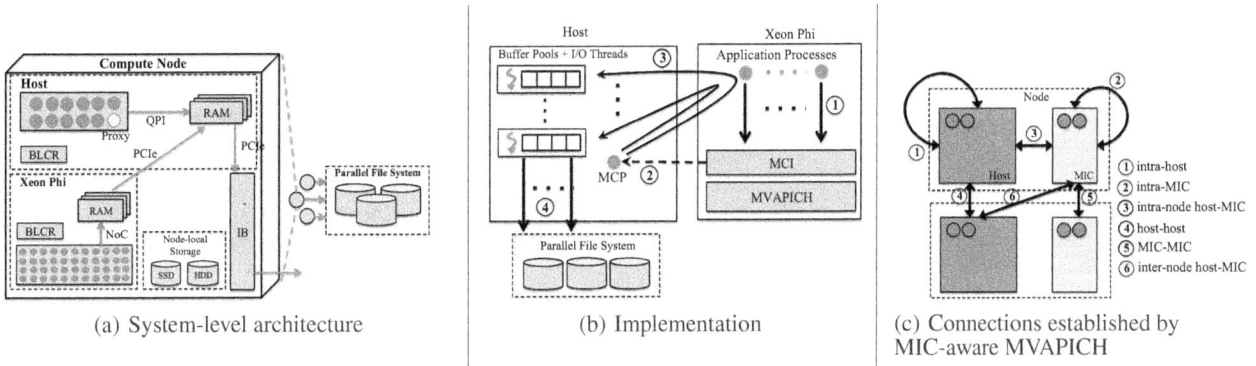

(a) System-level architecture

(b) Implementation

(c) Connections established by MIC-aware MVAPICH

Figure 2: Architecture and Implementation of MIC-Check

with the SCIF-interface, which would give the MCP permissions to read to/write from this region without any involvement from the application processes. Once the application is ready to write the file, MCI intercepts the *write* call and sends a control message to MCP, letting it know that the checkpoint can be read out of the MIC's memory.

Step 3. For each MPI process that connects to the MCP, the MCP spawns a new thread that will progress the I/O on behalf of the client. Each thread also reserves a region of memory to stage data on the host before being written to the underlying file system, and registers this region with the SCIF interface to be able to perform one-sided Remote Memory Access (RMA) operations. On receiving the checkpoint control message from MCI, the MCP initiates a pipelined-RMA protocol using the `scif_readfrom()` routine to asynchronously pull data from the MIC processes' memory, in units of a *pipeline chunk-size*. MCP initiated SCIF reads take advantage of superior Host DMA performance and relieves the application processes from taking part in the checkpoint. The pipelining is achieved by efficiently overlapping the RMA operations with the writes to the parallel file system, using a multiplexed usage of the staging buffers that is available to each thread that is progressing the I/O.

In addition to supporting the application-aware checkpointing paradigm, wherein applications capture the state of their execution in snapshots and write them to persistent storage themselves, MIC-Check also supports the transport system-level checkpointing paradigm. Transparent checkpointing protocols use external libraries, such as BLCR, to record the state of the parallel processes that constitute the application and write them into checkpoint files. The Intel Manycore Platform Software Stack (MPSS), which is the core system software stack needed to run the Xeon Phi coprocessor, has support for BLCR by default. The MIC-aware MVAPICH2 MPI library [6] was enhanced to be able to take transparent distributed checkpoints of an application that natively runs on a set of MICs.

Being able to transparently checkpoint an application involves three stages: a) draining in-flight messages, suspending further message-passing activity between MPI processes, and releasing network resources; b) obtaining a snapshot of the application's execution state and writing it to a globally-visible file system; and c) re-establishing communication channels for MPI processes to resume message-passing activity. Stage (a) is critical with transparent checkpointing as stray messages make the system susceptible to the *Domino effect*. Figure 2(c) illustrates the various communication channels that are setup inside the MVAPICH MPI library with a representative set of MPI processes residing in two compute nodes, both of which have been provisioned with MIC adapters. The en-

hanced MIC-Check MVAPICH library ensures that these additional communication channels established in the presence of a MIC are also flushed and suspended prior to a checkpoint, and re-established after it, in order to preserve the channel consistency. The stage (b) is similar to the application-assisted checkpointing case. However, the I/O operations are no longer intercepted by MCI, as the MPI library already has control over the I/O phase. MIC-Check MVAPICH generates the checkpoint images by itself with help from the BLCR kernel module that is part of the Intel MPSS software stack running on the MIC.

4. EXPERIMENTAL EVALUATION

In this section, we discuss the various experiments that were conducted to evaluate the performance and scalability of the MIC-Check framework. The experiments were conducted on the Stampede [7] supercomputing system at the Texas Advanced Computing Center in Austin.

4.1 Intra-node scalability

The Xeon Phi coprocessor has 61 processing cores that are available for applications to use. However, the degree of parallelism from which applications will benefit will highly depend on their memory requirements, given the limited memory per-core that is available on MIC processors. Figure 3(a) illustrates the performance of MIC-Check, with increasing number of application clients on a single compute node of the Stampede system. An MPI benchmark that measures the aggregate file write-throughput across its processes was used, where each process writes a 256MB file via MCI. The MPI processes in the benchmark, which are run natively on the MIC, each write the checkpoint file to the Lustre parallel file system available on the system. The grey bars represent the aggregate throughput observed by MPI processes on the MIC that directly write to Lustre, and the red bars represent the throughput when MIC-Check progresses the I/O. The former case does not scale at all, with an aggregate throughput of 15.14 MB/s with 1 MPI process, and an aggregate throughput of 21.41 MB/s with 16 MPI processes. While the peak throughput of moving data out of a coprocessor's memory is a mere 962MB/s (as shown in Table 1), this limit is achieved with just 4 MPI processes writing checkpoints. Any more than 4 MPI processes (for the Stampede configuration) will only hurt the throughput significantly. However, the proposed MIC-Check design scales tremendously well, with a throughput of 59.73MB/s when the benchmark is run with 1 process, and a throughput of 731.48MB/s when the benchmark is run with 16 processes on the MIC. With 16 MPI processes on one MIC, the aggregate throughput with MIC-Check was 35 times that of the baseline case. A majority of this benefit comes from efficient usage

123

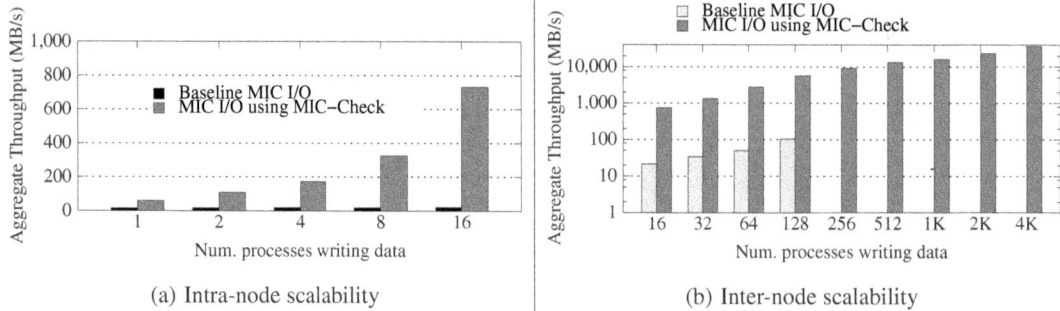

Figure 3: Experimental Evaluation

	Compute Time (s)	Checkpoint Time (s)
Baseline	91.2	44.8
MIC-Check	93.1	1.49

Table 2: Application-level checkpointing of ENZO

of the bandwidth offered by Lustre, and the appropriate use of the SCIF channel to move data from MIC-memory to host memory.

4.2 Inter-node scalability

MIC-Check was designed to be a shared-nothing architecture in order to allow it to scale with the number of nodes. We evaluated the framework's inter-node scaling capacity, the results of which are shown in Figure 3(b). Along the horizontal axis is the number of MPI processes that are writing data to the Lustre file system, and along the vertical axis is the aggregate throughput as observed by the MPI benchmark. The number of processes were varied from 16 to 128 in the baseline case, and from 16 to 4096 in the MIC-Check case, with 16 processes per coprocessor [1]. Since each compute node hosts a MCP to exclusively serve its MPI processes, or those residing on its coprocessor, the only factor that affects the I/O throughput scaling observed by an application will be the file system bandwidth. Unlike the baseline case, even with the MCP serving 16 MIC processes, the checkpointing throughput is not bottle-necked by the InfiniBand bandwidth available to the node (as seen in Figure 3(a)), hence allowing the architecture to scale to higher core counts. At a scale of 128 MPI processes, the throughput with MIC-Check was 54x that of the baseline. At a scale of 4,096 (MIC processes), the MIC-Check framework is able to deliver a throughput of 36.17 GB/s.

4.3 Evaluation with End-Application

ENZO is a complex astrophysics code for multi-scale and multi-physics applications, which has also been ported to run on coprocessors natively [5]. ENZO has inherent capability to save frequent checkpoints of its execution states into files called *data dumps*. For this experiment, we used 128-process runs of the application on the Stampede system. Table 2 shows the total execution time of two ENZO runs - the baseline run in which checkpoints from MIC processes are directly written to Lustre, and the MIC-Check case where data is staged through the host. Both these runs simulate cosmology adiabatic-expansion. A single checkpoint of the application was taken in both these cases, and the time it took for the

checkpoint to be completely persisted into a file is noted in the graph. In both cases, the aggregate checkpoint size was 5.37 GB/s. As observed with benchmark-based evaluation, MIC-Check was able to vastly absorb the checkpointing overhead. The checkpointing time in the baseline case was 44.8s, while that in the MIC-Check case was just 1.49s, giving 30x improvement in checkpointing throughput.

5. SUMMARY AND FUTURE WORK

In this paper, we outline and analyze the intrinsic and extrinsic issues that limit the I/O performance when check-pointing parallel applications on Xeon Phi clusters. We propose MIC-Check, a novel check-pointing framework, that works around these limitations and provides scalable I/O performance on these systems. The proposed check-pointing framework provides a 35x improvement in the aggregate I/O throughput with 16 processes running on a Xeon Phi, and 54x improvement with 4,096 MPI processes running on 256 MICs.

It is yet to be seen how next generation node architectures will address the extrinsic limitations we outlined in this work. Given the light-weight nature of the Linux operating system used on these many-core coprocessors, we expect the impact of intrinsic limitations to be present in next generation MIC products as well. As part of future work, we will study the impact of MIC-Check framework on these next generation architectures and enhance it to suite their characteristics. We are also exploring designs to add support for transparent checkpointing of applications that use the offload mode of execution while sharing data between various compute kernels.

References

[1] Improving File IO performance on Intel Xeon Phi. `http://software.intel.com/en-us/blogs/2014/01/07/improving-file-io-performance-on-intel-xeon-phi`.

[2] Intel MIC Architecture. http://www.intel.com/content/www/us/en/processors/xeon/xeon-phi-detail.html.

[3] XEON-PHI Software Developer's Guide. http://www.intel.com/content/dam/www/public/us/en/documents/product-briefs/xeon-phi-software-developers-guide.pdf.

[4] Top500 Supercomputer List. `http://www.top500.org/lists/2013/11`, November 2013.

[5] K. S. et al. Early Experiences Porting Scientific Applications to the Many Integrated Core (MIC) Platform. In *TACC-Intel Tech. Rep*, 2012.

[6] S. P. et al. MVAPICH-PRISM: A Proxy-based Communication Framework using InfiniBand and SCIF for Intel MIC clusters. In *SC'13*, 2013.

[7] TACC. Stampede Supercomputer. `http://www.top500.org/system/177931`.

---

[1] The contention caused by I/O requests from the baseline experiments on the underlying Lustre file system was enormous enough to affect the other users on the cluster, and hence the authors were requested by TACC staff to limit the baseline testing to 128 processes. This is also the reason why the application-level evaluations were limited to 128 processes.

Communication-Driven Scheduling for Virtual Clusters in Cloud

Haibao Chen
Serv. Comp. Tech.&Sys. Lab
Cluster & Grid Comput. Lab
School of Computers
Huazhong Univ. of Sci.&Tech.
Wuhan, 430074, China
chenhaibao@hust.edu.cn

Song Wu
Serv. Comp. Tech.&Sys. Lab
Cluster & Grid Comput. Lab
School of Computers
Huazhong Univ. of Sci.&Tech.
Wuhan, 430074, China
wusong@hust.edu.cn

Sheng Di
Argonne National Laboratory
9700 S. Cass Avenue
Argonne, IL 60439
INRIA, Grenoble, France
sheng.di@inria.fr

Bingbing Zhou
School of Information Tech.
The University of Sydney
NSW 2006, Australia
bing.zhou@sydney.edu.au

Zhenjiang Xie
Serv. Comp. Tech.&Sys. Lab
Cluster & Grid Comput. Lab
School of Computers
Huazhong Univ. of Sci.&Tech.
Wuhan, 430074, China
xiezhenjiang@hust.edu.cn

Hai Jin, and Xuanhua Shi
Serv. Comp. Tech.&Sys. Lab
Cluster & Grid Comput. Lab
School of Computers
Huazhong Univ. of Sci.&Tech.
Wuhan, 430074, China
hjin@hust.edu.cn

ABSTRACT

Recent research already confirmed the feasibility of running tightly-coupled parallel applications with virtual clusters. However, such types of applications suffer from significant performance degradation, especially as the overcommitment is common in cloud. That is, the number of executable Virtual CPUs (VCPUs) is often larger than that of available Physical CPUs (PCPUs) in the system. The performance degradation mainly results from that the current Virtual Machine Monitors (VMMs) cannot co-schedule (or coordinate at the same time) the VCPUs that host parallel application threads/processes with synchronization requirements.

We introduce a communication-driven scheduling approach for virtual clusters in this paper, which can effectively mitigate the performance degradation of tightly-coupled parallel applications running atop them in overcommitted situation. There are two key contributions. 1) We propose a communication-driven VM scheduling (CVS) algorithm, by which the involved VMM schedulers can autonomously schedule suitable VMs at runtime. 2) We integrate the CVS algorithm into Xen VMM scheduler, and rigorously implement a prototype. We evaluate our design on a real cluster environment, and experiments show that our solution attains better performance for tightly-coupled parallel applications than the state-of-the-art approaches like Credit scheduler of Xen, balance scheduling, and hybrid scheduling.

Categories and Subject Descriptors

D.4.1 [**Operating System**]: process management—*Scheduling*

Keywords

Virtual cluster; Scheduling; Cloud computing

1. INTRODUCTION

Virtualized cloud datacenter, because of its flexibility and cost-effectiveness, is increasingly being explored as an alternative to local clusters by academic and commercial users to run tightly-coupled parallel applications [1]. However, these users still face the performance degradation problem when running such applications in cloud. This problem is mainly due to the fact that current Virtual Machine Monitors (VMMs) do not simultaneously coordinate/schedule Virtual CPUs (VCPUs) that host threads/processes of parallel applications with synchronization requirements.

Despite some works [2, 3, 4] on scheduling in virtualized environment, the focus has so far been primarily on a *single* symmetric multiprocessing (SMP) VM that runs multi-thread application with synchronisation operations, yet there is no existing research about scheduling on virtual clusters hosting tightly-coupled parallel applications. Moreover, in order to maximize cloud resource utilization, overcommitment is a fairly common phenomenon in cloud. For example, recent research from VMware shows that the average VCPU-to-core ratio is 4:1, based on the analysis of 17 real-world datacenters [5]. Such overcommitted situation aggravates the performance degradation problem of parallel applications running in cloud. This paper targets the challenge of how to efficiently schedule virtual cluster hosting parallel applications in overcommitted cloud environment. We introduce a communication-driven approach for scheduling virtual clusters, which can effectively mitigate the performance degradation of tightly-coupled parallel applications running in overcommitted cloud environment.

The rest of this paper is organized as follows. We explain our design motivation in Section 2 followed by the description of our approach in Section 3. Section 4 presents the performance evaluation results. Finally, we conclude the paper in Section 5.

2. DESIGN MOTIVATION

In this section, we analyze the asynchronous scheduling problem and discuss the disadvantage of existing solutions.

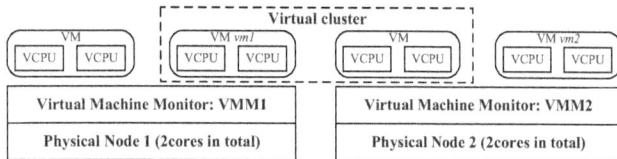

Figure 1: Virtual cluster deployed among two physical nodes. Each VMM carries out scheduling asynchronously without considering the synchronization requirement of VMs belonging to the virtual cluster.

Asynchronous VM scheduling method used by VMMs in multi-core physical nodes is simple to implement and beneficial for high-throughput workloads, yet it is inefficient for virtual cluster running parallel applications that require much coordination among tasks, especially in overcommitted environment. We use Figure 1 to illustrate this problem. In this example, a 4-process tightly-coupled parallel application runs on a virtual cluster, which consists of two 2-VCPU VMs (*vm1* and *vm2*) hosted in two different physical machines (*node1* and *node2*). Suppose Xen is used as the VMM, adopting Credit scheduler (a proportional-share scheduling policy). With the Credit scheduler, VCPUs in all run-queues of PCPUs are scheduled asynchronously on each physical machine. This kind of asynchronous scheduling policy usually cannot take over the lock-holder preemption problem [3], which will vastly increase synchronization latency and potentially block the progress of other VCPUs waiting to acquire the same lock.

Recently, most of existing work (e.g., co-scheduling methods of VMware, hybrid scheduling [3], and dynamic co-scheduling [4]) on VM-based scheduling is only focused on the performance improvement of concurrent workload processing (multi-thread application with synchronization operations) over SMP VM, instead of the parallel applications on virtual clusters. The problem of these approaches is that all VMs inside a virtual cluster are still scheduled asynchronously from the perspective of virtual cluster, which results in the decreased performance of tightly-coupled parallel application running in virtual cluster. As shown in Figure 1, since *VMM1* and *VMM2* make VM scheduling decisions autonomously, the probability of *vm1* and *vm2* (managed by different VMMs) being scheduled simultaneously is very low. That is, the existing scheduling methods for SMP VMs neglect the synchronization requirement among VMs, belonging to the same virtual cluster.

3. OUR APPROACH

We introduce our basic idea in Section 3.1, and propose *communication-driven VM scheduling (CVS)* algorithm and CVS scheduler in this Section 3.2 and 3.3, respectively.

3.1 Basic Idea

Based on experiments in virtualized environment, we find that the inter-VM communication (e.g., the number of received packets) can serve as a signal to detect the coordination demands from the viewpoint of VM-level synchronization. That is, VMMs can make VM scheduling decisions based on this signal to satisfy the coordination demands of VMs belonging to the same virtual cluster.

In order to explore the correlation between the number of packets received by VM and the synchronization requirements, we characterize the number of spinlocks (an indicator of synchronization requirement) and the number of packets via experiments. Four 8-VCPU VMs are used to run a set of MPI programs with 32 processes in parallel. We choose three benchmark programs (called *is*, *ep*, and *lu*) from NPB suite of version 2.4, as they exhibit three typical types of parallel executions: communication intensive application with little computation (*is*); CPU intensive application with little communication (*ep*); and the one that lies in between them (*lu*). For each VM, the number of packets and that of spinlocks are recorded every 120 milliseconds (multiplying the 30ms of Xen Credit scheduler by the number of VMs in this experiment) over 60 seconds.

The analysis of experimental results shows that the average Pearson Correlation Coefficients (PCC) between the number of packets and that of spinlocks in tightly-coupled parallel applications (i.e., *lu* and *is*) are 0.89 and 0.97 respectively, while that value in computation-intensive application (i.e., *ep*) is only 0.17. This implies that the inter-VM communication is a fairly good signal to detect potential synchronization requirements.

3.2 CVS Algorithm

CVS algorithm helps VMMs select and schedule the VM (running tightly-coupled parallel application) with the largest number of received packets counted from the last de-scheduled moment and promotes its priority. The key idea of CVS is based on such an intuition: when running tightly-coupled parallel application in a virtual cluster, the more packets a VM receives during a scheduling period, the more urgent the synchronization requirement of this VM probably is.

Particularly, according to the information of PCPU run-queue, there are three situations that CVS algorithm needs to deal with. If there is no VM that runs tightly-coupled parallel application in the run-queue of PCPU, CVS algorithm will select the VM at the head of run-queue directly, just like the Credit scheduler of Xen does. If there exists only one VM that runs parallel application in the run-queue of PCPU, CVS algorithm will select that VM without any hesitation. When there are more than one VM, which runs tightly-coupled parallel application in the run-queue of PCPU, CVS algorithm will select the VM that receives the largest number of packets counted from the last de-scheduled moment. Further more, if two VMs receive the same number of packets, their remaining CPU shares (e.g., remaining credit values of Xen) will be used to carry out the VM selection, and the more the remaining CPU shares, the higher the priority. If the VMs still cannot be differentiated, CVS algorithm will pick a VM from among all qualified VMs according to their original orders in the run-queue of PCPU.

After CVS algorithm determines which VM should be scheduled for running parallel application, the scheduler of VMM will schedule all VCPUs of the VM simultaneously by sending Inter-Processor Interrupt (IPI) signal to the involved PCPUs on the same physical machine.

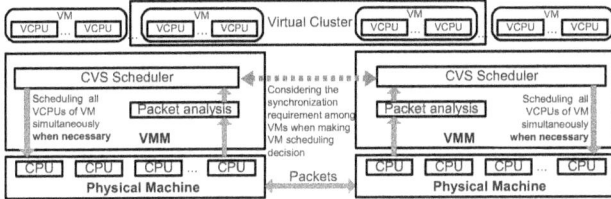

Figure 2: Overview of CVS scheduler. With CVS algorithm, this scheduler takes the synchronization requirement among VMs belonging to the same cluster into consideration when scheduling VMs.

3.3 CVS Scheduler

Based on CVS algorithm, we design and implement our CVS scheduler by extending the Credit scheduler of Xen 3.2, the overview of which is presented by giving an example as shown in Figure 2.

The CVS scheduler monitors the communication states inside each VMM, and dynamically analyzes the statistics of received packets. The monitored communication state is driven by the running parallel application, and we call it *locally visible synchronization requirement information*. With such information, our CVS scheduler can take the synchronization requirement into consideration when scheduling VMs. Meanwhile, CVS scheduler suffers little overheads, because the coordination information demanded (i.e., the statistics of received packets in VM) is implicitly carried in the communication messages. As for the intra-VM scheduling, all VCPUs of each SMP VM can be scheduled at the same time by sending Inter-Processor-Interrupt (IPI) to involved PCPUs when demanded.

4. PERFORMANCE EVALUATION

We first describe our experimental methodology, and then present experimental results in the following sections.

4.1 Experimental Methodology

In order to compare our CVS approach to the state-of-the-art scheduling approaches: **CREDIT**: the default scheduler of Xen, **H**ybrid **S**cheduling (HS), and **B**alance **S**cheduling (BS), we devise a test in this section with some restrictions, e.g., using the given configuration (the size, number, and placement) of virtual clusters, which is split into two parts.

4.2 Fixed Ratio of VCPU to PCPU

In this experiment, we scale the number of physical nodes (each one is equipped with two Intel Xeon E5345 quad-core CPU) from 2 to 32 (2, 4, 8, 16, and 32), and four 4-VCPU VMs are booted up on each physical node. The fixed VCPU-to-PCPU ratio is 2.5:1. Four identical virtual clusters are built using all VMs in the platform, and the four VMs on each physical node belong to them separately. We run *lu* on these four virtual clusters simultaneously for ten times, and record the execution time of *lu* on each virtual cluster. The same test procedures also go to *is* and *ep*, respectively.

Based on Figure 3(a) and 3(b), it is clearly observed that our CVS approach exhibits the best performance and scalability for *lu* and *is*. The performance and scalability of HS

is much better than that of BS. We analyze the key reasons as follows. First, for tightly-coupled parallel applications (e.g., *lu* and *is*), our CVS scheduler outperforms the other three approaches (BS, HS and CREDIT) and scales better because it considers the synchronization requirements of the VMs that belong to the same virtual cluster when making VM scheduling decisions. Second, BS is a probabilistic co-scheduling approach, and the probability of co-scheduling VCPUs of virtual cluster will become lower and lower with increasing number of physical nodes (VMs of virtual cluster). Thus, BS has a slight performance gain over CREDIT when the number of physical nodes is small (e.g., 2), while the performance gain is not clear with large number of nodes. Third, although HS co-schedules all VCPUs of SMP VMs on single physical node, all VMs belonging to the same virtual cluster are still scheduled asynchronously because involved VMMs neglect the synchronization requirements among VMs when making scheduling decision. Therefore, the performance and scalability of HS are between these of CVS and BS.

From Figure 3(c), we can observe that these four approaches have almost the same performance and scalability. The reason is that CVS and HS will gracefully degrade into CREDIT with respect to the CPU intensive applications with little communication (e.g., *ep*).

4.3 Varying Ratios of VCPU-to-PCPU

In this experiment, we dynamically adjust the ratio of VCPU-to-PCPU from 2.5 to 4 by changing the number of VMs hosted on each physical node of platform from 4 to 7. As the configuration of virtual clusters in Section 4.2, VMs on each physical node belong to different virtual clusters separately. Figure 4 presents the average execution time of *lu*, *is*, and *ep* when running on virtual clusters with BS, HS and CVS, respectively.

From Figure 4(a) and 4(b), we can easily observe that our CVS approach has the best performance for *lu* and *is* in scenarios with different ratios of VCPU-to-PCPU, and the performance of HS are between these of CVS and BS. Specifically, the performance of CVS and HS become better with increasing ratio of VCPU-to-PCPU, while the performance gain of BS over CREDIT is not obvious at all. The reasons behind these figures are as follows. First, as the ratio of VCPU-to-PCPU increasing, the probability of co-scheduling VCPUs of virtual cluster using BS approach becomes lower and lower. Therefore, the performance gain over CREDIT is not clear in such situation. Second, HS outperforms BS and CREDIT because it can co-schedule the VCPUs of SMP VM that runs tightly-coupled parallel application. However, it is still worse than our CVS approach due to the fact that involved VMMs with HS neglect the synchronization requirements among VMs when making scheduling decision.

From Figure 4(c), we observe that these four approaches have almost the same performance and scalability for *ep* as the ratio of VCPU-to-PCPU changing, which is due to the same reasons for Figure 3(c) in Section 4.2.

5. CONCLUSIONS AND FUTURE WORK

This paper targets the challenge of how to schedule virtual clusters hosting tightly-coupled parallel applications and mitigate performance degradation in overcommitted cloud environment. We introduce a communication-driven VM schedul-

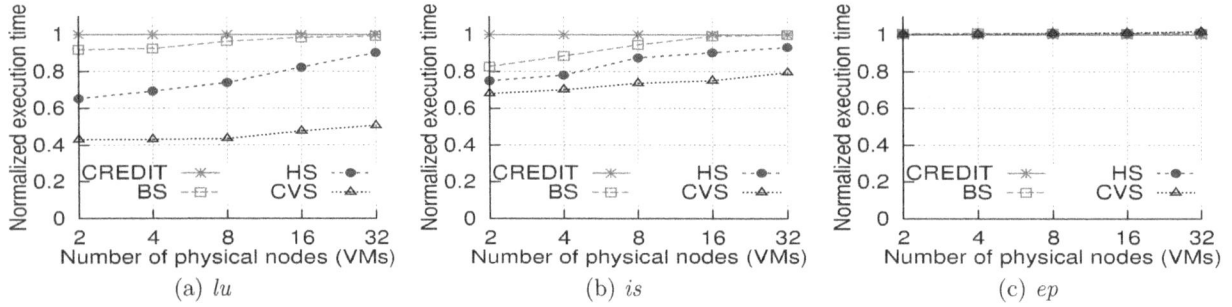

Figure 3: Performance comparison of approaches (CREDIT, BS, HS, and CVS) with fixed ratio of VCPU to PCPU when running benchmarks on 2, 4, 8, 16, and 32 nodes (VMs).

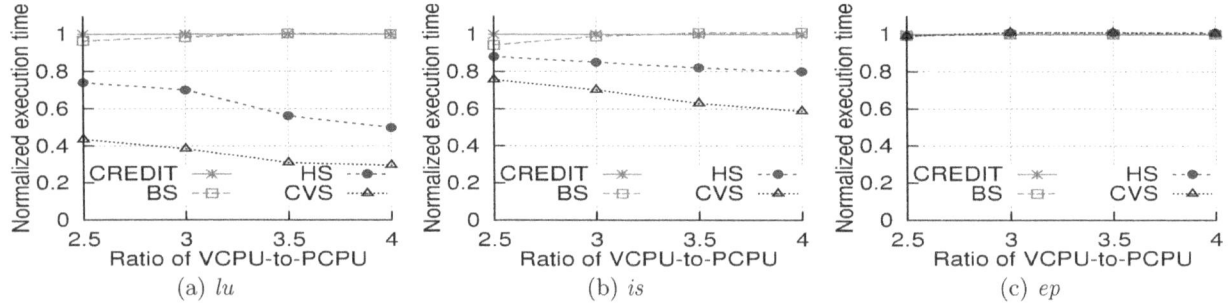

Figure 4: Performance comparison of approaches (CREDIT, BS, HS, and CVS) when running benchmarks with different ratios of VCPU-to-PCPU.

ing (CVS) approach of virtual clusters. This approach is simple to apply in practice. Meanwhile, it allows participating VMMs to act autonomously, thus retaining the independence of VMMs. For tightly-coupled parallel application, our CVS approach improves the application performance significantly in comparison to the state-of-the-art approaches.

Unrestricted simultaneous scheduling of all VCPUs for SMP VM through sending IPIs may cause excessive numbers of preemptions while repeatedly interrupting other VMs, which results in serious performance degradation [6, 7]. To mitigate this problem with unexpected preemptions, we will devise a VM preemption mechanism to enhance our CVS approach. The prerequisite of all co-scheduling algorithms is to know the type of workload running in VMs. That is, the scheduler must understand whether the workload is parallel application or not. Actually, there are at least two alternative ways to do so. The first one is to adopt the inference techniques using gray-box knowledge. The other is to obtain the type information of workload directly from end users, similar to the work in [3, 8]. In this paper we adopt the latter for simplicity. In the future, we will evaluate the former one for comparison.

6. ACKNOWLEDGMENTS

We thank the anonymous reviewers for their insightful comments and suggestions. This work was supported in part by National Science Foundation of China under grant 61232008, National 863 Hi-Tech Research and Development Program under grant 2013AA01A213 and 2013AA01A208, Guangzhou Science and Technology Program under grant 2012Y2-00040, Chinese Universities Scientific Fund under grant 2013TS094, Research Fund for the Doctoral Program of MOE under grant 20110142130005.

7. REFERENCES

[1] Thomas J Hacker and Kanak Mahadik. *Magellan Final Report*. U.S. Department of Energy (DOE), 2011.

[2] Orathai Sukwong and Hyong S Kim. Is co-scheduling too expensive for smp vms? In *Proc. EuroSys*, pages 257–272. ACM, 2011.

[3] Chuliang Weng, Zhigang Wang, Minglu Li, and Xinda Lu. The hybrid scheduling framework for virtual machine systems. In *Proc. VEE*, pages 111–120. ACM, 2009.

[4] Chuliang Weng, Qian Liu, Lei Yu, and Minglu Li. Dynamic adaptive scheduling for virtual machines. In *Proc. HPDC*, pages 239–250, 2011.

[5] Vijayaraghavan Soundararajan and Jennifer M Anderson. The impact of management operations on the virtualized datacenter. In *ACM SIGARCH Computer Architecture News*, volume 38, pages 326–337. ACM, 2010.

[6] Hwanju Kim, Hyeontaek Lim, Jinkyu Jeong, Heeseung Jo, and Joonwon Lee. Task-aware virtual machine scheduling for i/o performance. In *Proc. VEE*, pages 101–110. ACM, 2009.

[7] Hwanju Kim, Sangwook Kim, Jinkyu Jeong, Joonwon Lee, and Seungryoul Maeng. Demand-based coordinated scheduling for smp vms. In *Proc. ASPLOS*, pages 369–380. ACM, 2013.

[8] Cong Xu, Sahan Gamage, Pawan N Rao, Ardalan Kangarlou, Ramana Rao Kompella, and Dongyan Xu. vslicer: latency-aware virtual machine scheduling via differentiated-frequency cpu slicing. In *Proc. HPDC*, pages 3–14. ACM, 2012.

Efficient Task Placement and Routing of Nearest Neighbor Exchanges in Dragonfly Networks

Bogdan Prisacari
IBM Research – Zurich
Säumerstrasse 4
8803 Rüschlikon, Switzerland
bpr@zurich.ibm.com

German Rodriguez
IBM Research – Zurich
Säumerstrasse 4
8803 Rüschlikon, Switzerland
rod@zurich.ibm.com

Philip Heidelberger
IBM Research – Watson
1101 Kitchawan Rd Rte 134
Yorktown Heights, NY 10598
philiph@us.ibm.com

Dong Chen
IBM Research – Watson
1101 Kitchawan Rd Rte 134
Yorktown Heights, NY 10598
chendong@us.ibm.com

Cyriel Minkenberg
IBM Research – Zurich
Säumerstrasse 4
8803 Rüschlikon, Switzerland
sil@zurich.ibm.com

Torsten Hoefler
ETH Zurich
Universitätstrasse 6
8092 Zürich, Switzerland
htor@inf.ethz.ch

ABSTRACT

Dragonflies are recent network designs that are one of the most promising topologies for the Exascale effort due to their scalability and cost. While being able to achieve very high throughput under random uniform all-to-all traffic, this type of network can experience significant performance degradation for other common high performance computing workloads such as stencil (multi-dimensional nearest neighbor) patterns. Often, the lack of peak performance is caused by an insufficient understanding of the interaction between the workload and the network, and an insufficient understanding of how application specific task-to-node mapping strategies can serve as optimization vehicles.

To address these issues, we propose a theoretical performance analysis framework that takes as inputs a network specification and a traffic demand matrix characterizing an arbitrary workload and is able to predict where bottlenecks will occur in the network and what their impact will be on the effective sustainable injection bandwidth. We then focus our analysis on a specific high-interest communication pattern, the multi-dimensional Cartesian nearest neighbor exchange, and provide analytic bounds (owing to bottlenecks in the remote links of the Dragonfly) on its expected performance across a multitude of possible mapping strategies.

Finally, using a comprehensive set of simulations results, we validate the correctness of the theoretical approach and in the process address some misconceptions regarding Dragonfly network behavior and evaluation, (such as the choice of throughput maximization over workload completion time minimization as optimization objective) and the question of whether the standard notion of Dragonfly balance can be extended to workloads other than uniform random traffic.

Categories and Subject Descriptors

C.2.1 [**Computer-Communication Networks**]: Network Architecture and Design; C.4 [**Performance of Systems**]

General Terms

Theory, Performance, Experimentation

Keywords

Dragonfly networks, Stencil computation, Nearest neighbor exchanges, Direct and indirect routing, Cartesian and random task placement

1. INTRODUCTION

High-Performance Computing (HPC) and datacenter networks are continuously growing in scale as larger problems are tackled, with several large scale systems already in use, especially in the HPC space. Technological advances in switch and cabling technology enabled Dragonfly, a new economic and efficient network topology developed independently by IBM (as the interconnection fabric of the PERCS system [2]) and Kim et al. [13]. Dragonfly networks combine high-radix switches and a mix of copper and electrical cables into a hierarchical two-tier topology. Both tiers are logically fully connected, a structure that guarantees low latency and high bisection bandwidth.

Dragonfly networks are scaled in practice to more than 5,200 nodes in Europe's most powerful supercomputer Piz Daint. Their theoretical scalability exceeds tens of thousands of nodes while achieving nearly full bandwidth for random uniform traffic patterns and shortest path routing. However, for deterministic patterns, a common characteristic of scientific applications, the bandwidth depends largely on the routing scheme employed (e.g., indirect random or adaptive) and the task-to-node mapping (e.g., random, blocked, or block-cyclic). The exact tradeoffs between routing and mapping for specific communication patterns are not well understood for Dragonfly topologies.

Cartesian *nearest neighbor exchanges* are very common in scientific computations [12]. They often represent a discretization of a physical system, which is modeled by a set of elements that are arranged in a grid. A typical simulation, e.g., a heat propagation, then solves PDEs and ODEs on this grid to advance the simulated system time. The resulting computational structures are most often Cartesian structures called *stencils*. Stencils combine neighboring values of a grid point to compute its state in the next iteration. A distribution of this scheme requires communication in a Cartesian structure. This pattern is so typical that parallel programming schemes, such as the Message Passing Interface, provide explicit support [9].

Any deterministic traffic pattern may exhibit poor performance if the computation is mapped unfavorably to a Dragonfly [1, 3, 6, 13]. For example, we show in this paper that the completion time for randomly mapped stencil computations can be between 50% to 10 times larger than the best achievable completion time. Several related studies empirically analyzed the impact of routing [6, 13], topology [6] and task mapping [3] to support applications with deterministic communication patterns such as stencil. Those studies report significant improvements for random indirect routing or random task mapping. However, indirect routing reduces the available global network bandwidth by utilizing more links and random task mapping loses communication locality because neighborhoods are spread throughout the system. Both schemes increase the network load and the exact tradeoffs of the routing and mapping selections remain unclear in general.

In this work, we provide a clear set of guidelines how to configure the network for a given workload. For this, we derive a general theoretical model of communication performance of multi-dimensional stencil computations on arbitrary Dragonfly networks considering different domain decompositions and task placements. Our general model allows us to co-design the application decomposition for the class of Cartesian stencil applications with the ideal Dragonfly network configuration.

In summary, we guide the user to select the optimal values of the parameters

- domain decomposition,

- task placement (sparsity and randomization), and

- routing approach.

We also validate our theoretical results against detailed simulations of the targeted scenarios and conclude with a summary of practical recommendations on how to (1) configure an application to run on a Dragonfly network and (2) optimize the design of a Dragonfly network to achieve higher performance for the nearest neighbor exchange.

2. BACKGROUND AND RELATED WORK

Dragonfly topologies are highly scalable high-radix two-level direct networks with a good cost-performance ratio, used for example in the PERCS interconnect [2] and in the Cray Cascade [5] and likely to be one of the options chosen for many of the future Exascale systems.

A dragonfly is a two-level hierarchical network, where fully-connected groups of lower-radix switches at the first level form a virtual high-radix switch. These virtual high-radix switches form another fully-connected graph of groups [13]. The ports that the virtual high-radix switches use to connect to the other virtual switches are distributed across the physical switches that make up the virtual switch.

Dragonflies can be uniquely described by means of three parameters: p, the number of nodes connected to each switch, a, the number of switches in each first level group, and h, the number of channels that each switch uses to connect to switches in other groups. For certain values of these parameters it can be shown that close to ideal throughput can be achieved for uniform traffic.

For the Dragonfly networks studied here, shortest paths between pairs of nodes are unique[1]. The longest possible shortest path is made up of a traversal of a *local* (L) link in the first level group to get to the switch that has a *global* (R) link towards the destination group, a traversal of the R link and a second *local* link traversal in the destination group to get to the switch directly connected to the destination node. Figure 1 illustrates the topological layout of a Dragonfly network and the meaning of the (p, a, h) parameters.

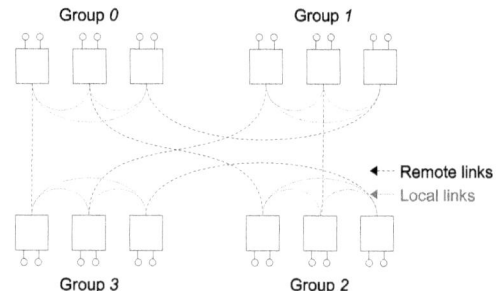

Figure 1: Example of a $(p = 2, a = 3, h = 1)$ Dragonfly topology. Every switch is connected to $p = 2$ nodes, there are $a = 3$ switches in every group and every switch has $h = 1$ links connecting it to switches outside its group.

However, this lack of shortest path diversity can lead to an extreme degradation in performance for certain adversarial traffic patterns [3, 6]. One option to alleviate this degradation is to use Valiant's algorithm [18]. This algorithm routes a packet to a randomly chosen intermediate node first, before routing it to the actual destination. The expectation is that, by using a different random intermediate node for each packet, the original nature of the traffic is shifted towards a uniform random distribution of traffic. However, this is done at the expense of longer paths and results in roughly a doubling of the load for an original traffic that is sufficiently dense (such as originally random uniform traffic [4]).

The longer paths in Valiant routing also have the disadvantage of requiring the use of additional virtual channels to guarantee deadlock freedom. In particular, the Valiant routing variant for dragonflies as described in [13], which we will call *Valiant [Kim:2008]*, requires 3 virtual channels (instead of 2 for shortest paths) for the L links and 2 virtual channels (instead of 1 for shortest path) for the R links, to guarantee deadlock freedom [2]. *Valiant [Kim:2008]* can be described as follows: when a source s in first-level group S sends a message to destination d in first-level group D, an intermediate misroute group is chosen (I). A minimal route (consisting of at most one L and one R hop) is taken to arrive to a switch in group I. Once the packet arrives to this intermediate group I, the packet follows the unique mini-

---

[1]More generally, there may be multiple such shortest paths, especially for networks that are smaller than the maximum possible scale.

mal route from the arriving switch at I to the destination d (requiring at most two L hops and one R hop).

The nearest neighbor exchange (NNE) is a common exchange pattern in many HPC applications. This pattern arises as the result of a decomposition of the domain of a problem into smaller elements. The computation for each element depends on a number of neighboring elements, where the neighborhood definition is dependent on both the specific problem and the specific way of performing the decomposition. In this work, we will consider Cartesian decompositions along a variable number of dimensions, and additionally we will consider that an element only exchanges data with elements with which it shares a (D-1)-dimensional contact plane. We will also make the assumption that the amount of exchanged data needed is proportional to the size of the (D-1)-dimensional contact plane.

A large fraction of HPC applications make use of the multi-dimensional nearest neighbor exchange pattern [12]. Relevant examples are Cactus [8], which uses a grid decomposition to solve Einstein's equations to study astrophysical phenomena, GTC [14] (Gyrokinetic Toroidal Code), which solves the gyrophase-averaged Vlasov-Poisson equations on a 3D toroidal domain, LBMHD [19] (Lattice Boltzmann methods for the problem of magneto-hydrodynamics (MHD)), which uses either a 2D or 3D lattice, or MILC, a 4D lattice QCD code. These represent only a small, but relevant fraction of the many codes which, with variations, rely on efficient nearest neighbor exchanges to achieve performance.

A recent paper [3] analyzed the performance achieved in dragonfly networks when executing such communication patterns with several task-placements and routing schemes (shortest path and Valiant). This work showed how a randomization of the task placement using shortest path routing achieved similar performance to a contiguous task placement using Valiant routing. Another work [11] also explored, for other patterns, the alternative of Valiant routing and of randomized task placement, and concluded that, while randomization improves performance over a naive contiguous placement, the performance achieved is still low when compared to the peak obtained for uniform random traffic, both with direct and indirect routing. Neither of these works studied in detail how the domain decomposition and a structured task placement influences the NNE performance on a dragonfly, and neither has provided a model that is able to predict NNE performance given the topology parameters, the domain decomposition, and the task placement onto a dragonfly.

3. THEORETICAL ANALYSIS

In order to explore the optimization opportunities for multi-dimensional near neighbor communication patterns in Dragonfly networks, we will provide theoretical estimates for the performance of applications executed as a set of concurrent tasks exhibiting arbitrarily shaped Cartesian multi-dimensional nearest neighbor communication patterns and being executed on a system interconnected via arbitrary Dragonfly networks. We will explore different task placement strategies and their effect on network utilization and performance. The end goal is to be able to determine guidelines as to how to map such applications onto the different nodes in the system such that communication performance is maximized.

This section provides the step by step derivation of these guidelines and is fairly technical. The reader that is inter-

ested mainly in the end result should read Section 3.2 where we introduce the main notations and then skip directly to Section 3.5.

3.1 Arbitrary workload performance in Dragonflies

We consider an arbitrary workload given by a traffic demand matrix T, with as many columns and rows as concurrent tasks perform the workload. Each element t_{sd} of the matrix represents the total number of bytes sent by task s to task d. We denote by $\hat{T}$ the normalized traffic demand matrix, where every element $\hat{t}_{sd}$ is the corresponding element in T divided by the total number of bytes sent by source task s.

$$\hat{t}_{sd} = t_{sd} / \sum_d t_{sd} \qquad (1)$$

The goal of this subsection is to formalize the effective injection throughput that will be sustainable at the nodes by estimating the demand that the workload will impose on the network. We will denote this effective injection bandwidth for node n by $B_{\mathrm{P,eff}}^n$. If a link in the network receives more demand than it can sustain, then all sources whose messages periodically use that link will see their effective throughput eventually decreased, to the point at which the demand on the link no longer exceeds its capacity.

The exact distribution of demand to network links will intrinsically be linked to the routing approaches used in the network. Therefore, the routing approach will in turn be a significant factor that will determine the effective performance of the network. For the Dragonfly, we will consider two routing approaches:

1. Dragonfly direct routing, where messages are always sent through the network across shortest paths;

2. Dragonfly indirect routing, where messages are always sent through the network across indirect paths and the indirect paths between any given (source,destination) pair are used evenly via randomization. This includes the case where the source and destination belong to the same group.

Let us consider the entire duration of a workload, or, for ongoing workloads, a large enough amount of time such that all sources inject a statistically significant amount of traffic in the network, i.e., an amount of traffic that roughly obeys the distribution expressed by $\hat{T}$. We define the demand exercised on a given link as being the total number of bytes that need to cross that link in the considered amount of time.

Let us consider a remote link R_{ij} connecting the Dragonfly group G_i to the Dragonfly group G_j, $i \neq j$. The demand $\Delta_{ij}^{\mathrm{R,direct}}$ of that link under the direct routing approach will be equal to the total fraction of traffic sent by sources in G_i that have as a destination any of the tasks in G_j.

$$\Delta_{ij}^{\mathrm{R,direct}} = \sum_{s \in G_i} \sum_{d \in G_j} \hat{t}_{sd} \cdot B_{\mathrm{P,eff}}^s. \qquad (2)$$

The demand $\Delta_{ij}^{\mathrm{R,indirect}}$ of the same link under the indirect routing approach has two distinct components. The first component consists of traffic sent by sources in G_i to any destination outside of G_j and G_i, using G_j as an intermediate routing point. The second component consists of traffic sent by sources anywhere outside of G_i and G_j that is sent to destinations in G_j using G_i as an intermediate routing point.

$$
\begin{aligned}
\Delta_{ij}^{\mathrm{R,indirect}} = &\sum_{p \neq i,j} \sum_{s \in G_i} \sum_{d \in G_p} \hat{t}_{sd} \cdot P(i \xrightarrow{j} p) \cdot B_{\mathrm{P,eff}}^s \\
&+ \sum_{p \neq i,j} \sum_{s \in G_p} \sum_{d \in G_j} \hat{t}_{sd} \cdot P(p \xrightarrow{i} j) \cdot B_{\mathrm{P,eff}}^s
\end{aligned}
\tag{3}
$$

where $P(i \xrightarrow{p} j)$ denotes the probability that the indirect route via group p is chosen when routing from group i to group j.

Concerning the demand imposed on the intra-group links, In contrast to the inter-group network structure, current Dragonfly systems do not exhibit a unique intra-group structure (e.g., the original Dragonfly design uses a standard full mesh, the PERCS interconnect uses a non-uniform (from the bandwidth and latency points of view) full mesh whereas the Cray Cascade interconnect uses a two dimensional Hamming graph). This, coupled to the fact that in practice it is generally the inter-group bottlenecks that determine overall system performance, would make thoroughly analyzing the intra-group demand an unnecessarily complex endeavor. Nonetheless, we will take into account the possibility of bottlenecks shifting inside the groups and will analyze this scenario in detail in Section 4.3.

We will assume that all nodes and switches in the network are identical and thus we can denote by:

- $B_P \rightarrow$ the injection bandwidth available to any node in the network,

- $B_L \rightarrow$ the bandwidth of each local link,

- $B_R \rightarrow$ the bandwidth of each remote link.

We will further make a simplifying assumption that the workload does not induce or is not allowed to induce unfairness in the system, that is, every node will be able to effectively inject the same amount of traffic as any other node. Then, $B_{\mathrm{P,eff}}$ can also be considered uniform across nodes and we can introduce the notion of relative demand δ as being the demand Δ defined above divided by the effective injection bandwidth $B_{\mathrm{P,eff}}$.

$$
\begin{aligned}
\delta_{ij}^{\mathrm{R,direct}} &= \Delta_{ij}^{\mathrm{R,direct}} / B_{\mathrm{P,eff}} \\
\delta_{ij}^{\mathrm{R,indirect}} &= \Delta_{ij}^{\mathrm{R,indirect}} / B_{\mathrm{P,eff}}
\end{aligned}
\tag{4}
$$

Given that the demand Δ on a link cannot exceed the bandwidth of that link, the achievable effective bandwidth is consequently upper bounded by the ratio between a link's bandwidth and the relative demand induced on the link. The throughput limitation that the network imposes on the nodes can thus be formally expressed by Eq. (5) for direct routing and Eq. (6) for indirect routing.

$$
B_{\mathrm{P,eff}}^{\mathrm{direct}} \leq \min\left(B_P, \frac{B_L}{\max\limits_{\mathrm{Llinks}} (\delta^{\mathrm{L,direct}})}, \frac{B_R}{\max\limits_{\mathrm{Rlinks}} (\delta^{\mathrm{R,direct}})} \right)
\tag{5}
$$

$$
B_{\mathrm{P,eff}}^{\mathrm{indirect}} \leq \min\left(B_P, \frac{B_L}{\max\limits_{\mathrm{Llinks}} (\delta^{\mathrm{L,indirect}})}, \frac{B_R}{\max\limits_{\mathrm{Rlinks}} (\delta^{\mathrm{R,indirect}})} \right)
\tag{6}
$$

Eq. (5) and (6) coupled to the load formulations (Eq. (2) and (3)) and to a particular traffic demand matrix allow us to predict network performance for arbitrary workloads in arbitrary dragonflies.

3.2 Formal description of targeted workloads

The workload we focus on in this work are is the multi-dimensional Cartesian nearest neighbor communication. We will assume that the concurrent tasks are solving a problem pertaining to a d-dimensional domain that is intrinsically split (along directions parallel to the coordinate axes) into equally sized d-dimensional elements in a way that is consistent with the domain's structure (e.g., if the domain is larger in one dimension, it will have proportionally more elements along that dimension). The number of elements in each dimension is given by a vector $\alpha \in \mathbb{N}^d$, for a total number of elements $|\alpha| = \Pi_{k=1}^d \alpha_k$. The assignment of the elements to computation tasks is also done along a Cartesian grid, such that the number of tasks in each dimension is given by a different vector $\beta \in \mathbb{N}^d$. Every task will thus be assigned one or several elements, the number of elements per dimension assigned to each task being α divided element by element by β. The total number of tasks is $|\beta| = \Pi_{k=1}^d \beta_k$. Any task can be naturally identified via a d-dimensional vector $x \in \mathbb{N}^d$ such that $0 \leq x_k < \beta_k, \forall 1 \leq k \leq d$. These concepts are illustrated in Fig. 2 for a two-dimensional application domain.

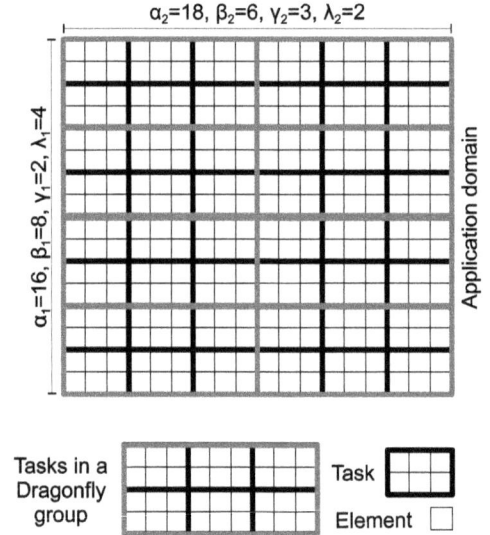

Figure 2: Application domain for a two-dimensional nearest neighbor exchange. The domain admits an intrinsic decomposition into identical elements (the small squares in the figure) along the axes of the Cartesian domain. This decomposition is characterized by the two-dimensional vector α which in the example figure takes the value $\alpha = (16, 18)$. The application is run as a set of concurrent tasks that is each assigned a Cartesian subset of the element grid (the 2×3 rectangles in the figure). Each subset assigned to a task has the same size along every dimension (in the figure, size 2 in the first dimension and size 3 in the second). The sub-decomposition is determined by a second vector β that determines how many tasks there are in each dimension (in the figure, $\beta = (8, 6)$).

132

The inter-task communication pattern considered is the nearest neighbor exchange of distance 1 on the d-dimensional Cartesian grid, where a task that is identified by the vector x communicates with a task identified by the vector y if and only if x and y share $d-1$ coordinates, while the remaining coordinate values x_k and y_k satisfy the relationship $(\beta_k + x_k - y_k) \bmod \beta_k = 1$. We will call two such tasks *neighbors along the k dimension*. We define the function $\nu_{x,y}^k$ which takes a value of 1 if tasks corresponding to x and y are neighbors along the k dimension and 0 otherwise, as follows:

$$\nu_{x,y}^k = \begin{cases} 1 & \text{if } (\beta_k + x_k - y_k) \bmod \beta_k = 1 \\ & \text{and } \forall i \neq k, x_i = y_i \\ 0 & \text{otherwise.} \end{cases} \qquad (7)$$

A very important design choice is the exact manner in which to map the application domain to the network topology. We will consider two task-to-node mapping strategies. The first assumes a regular grouping of tasks in the groups of the Dragonfly. A set of tasks corresponding to a Cartesian application sub-domain is assigned to any given group such that this sub-domain will contain $\gamma \in \mathbb{N}^d$ tasks along each of the d axes. This leads to a total of $|\gamma| = \Pi_{k=1}^d \gamma_k$ tasks in each Dragonfly group. We further define the vector λ in $\mathbb{N}^d$ as the coordinate by coordinate ratio of β and γ: $\forall 1 \leq k \leq d, \lambda_k = \lceil \beta_k/\gamma_k \rceil$. λ will thus represent the d-dimensional decomposition of the application domain into Dragonfly groups. It entails that $|\lambda| = \Pi_{k=1}^d \lambda_k$ Dragonfly groups will be needed to host the entire set of tasks. The second strategy will assume a random placement of tasks within the Dragonfly, keeping however the task count per group to the same $|\gamma|$ value as in the Cartesian case, to allow for fair comparison.

This formalization of the traffic pattern allows us to explore two important performance affecting factors: the shape of the Cartesian intra-group sub-domains (in terms of number of dimensions and ratios between sizes along each dimension) and the level of sparsity (the proportion of nodes used to host the workload in every group). We consider sparse placements as they are becoming more and more common in practice, and are the default strategy in some of the more recent HPC systems [5]. Under a sparse allocation, the higher amount of network resources at the disposal of the application is balanced by an increased probability of interference with other simultaneously running applications. Our model estimates the impact of the placement decision under the assumption that interference from other applications is minimal. The resulting performance metric is a useful baseline for inter-application interference analysis, but the latter is out of the scope of this work.

We will also operate under the assumption that the assignment of tasks to nodes within a group is random (under the constraint that a node will be assigned at most one task), as is the assignment of Cartesian groups of tasks to specific Dragonfly groups. This is a reasonable choice to make as the structure of both the intra-group and inter-group networks is vertex-symmetric. Furthermore, such a placement can prove useful in practice as the randomization has the benefit of disrupting regular patterns that may otherwise cause load imbalance [16].

3.3 Performance evaluation metrics

Two typical metrics are used for evaluating the performance of a fixed-size workload (where a fixed amount of data needs to be exchanged across the network) such as the nearest neighbor exchange. One metric is the completion time, i.e., the time between the moment when the first message enters the network and the moment when the last message is delivered. The second is the average effective throughput, defined as the total number of bytes exchanged divided by the completion time and averaged across the total number of communicating tasks.

Finally, as we are dealing with different shapes of the application domain (as expressed by the α vector) and different ways of partitioning the domain into tasks (as expressed by the β vector), the messages exchanged between tasks will vary in size. Specifically, they will be proportional to the size of the surface separating the communicating tasks. This entails that messages exchanged along the k-th axis, when such an exchange takes place, will have a size μ_k given by

$$\mu_k = \mu \cdot \Pi_{i=1, i \neq k}^d \frac{\alpha_i}{\beta_i} = \mu \cdot \frac{|\alpha|}{|\beta|} \cdot \frac{\beta_k}{\alpha_k}. \qquad (8)$$

3.4 Nearest neighbor communication performance in dragonflies

Two sets of factors determine the theoretical performance of a workload: the $\hat{t}_{sd}$ coefficients of the normalized traffic demand matrix and the $P(i \xrightarrow{p} j)$ routing probabilities in the case of indirect routing. Given the indirect routing assumption stated in 3.1 the value of the latter is

$$P(i \xrightarrow{p} j) = \frac{1}{ah - 1}. \qquad (9)$$

For the nearest neighbor exchange, we compute the traffic matrix as follows. We denote by m_k the proportion of messages (out of a task's entire communication workload) sent to a neighbor along the k-th axis. Due to the way we perform the decomposition of the domain into elements, the way we assign elements to tasks and the way we define the neighborhood of a task (7), it follows that a given task either does not exchange any messages along axis k (when $\beta_k = 1$), or it exchanges messages across two surfaces. If we denote by $\mathbb{1}_{condition}$ the indicator function that takes a value of 1 when the condition is true and a value of 0 otherwise, then the value of this ratio is

$$\begin{aligned} m_k &= \frac{\mu_k \cdot \mathbb{1}_{\beta_k > 1}}{2 \sum_{i=1}^d \mu_i \cdot \mathbb{1}_{\beta_i > 1}} \\ &= \frac{\mu \cdot \frac{|\alpha|}{|\beta|} \cdot \frac{\beta_k}{\alpha_k} \cdot \mathbb{1}_{\beta_k > 1}}{2 \sum_{i=1}^d \mu \cdot \frac{|\alpha|}{|\beta|} \cdot \frac{\beta_i}{\alpha_i} \cdot \mathbb{1}_{\beta_i > 1}} \\ &= \frac{\beta_k \cdot \mathbb{1}_{\beta_k > 1}/\alpha_k}{2 \sum_{i=1}^d \beta_i \cdot \mathbb{1}_{\beta_i > 1}/\alpha_i}. \end{aligned} \qquad (10)$$

These proportions are completely determined by the α and β domain characterization d-dimensional vectors.

Taking into account that if $\beta_k = 2$ for some k, then two tasks that are neighbors along axis k communicate across two surfaces, we obtain:

$$\hat{t}_{sd} = \sum_{i=1}^d m_i \cdot \nu_{s,d}^i \cdot (1 + \mathbb{1}_{\beta_i = 2}) \qquad (11)$$

Cartesian placement.

The case where the tasks assigned to any fixed group form a Cartesian sub-domain is of interest because it allows keeping as much of the communication local as possible. For this strategy, we defined the γ vector characterizing the mapping of tasks to groups. For a fixed γ, we have all the information necessary to compute the demand that the workload induces in the network as described by Eqs. (2) and (3).

Indeed, in the case of direct routing, we would need to estimate the sum of the individual demands induced by sources in a Dragonfly group i sending to destinations in another Dragonfly group j on the remote link connecting the groups. Similarly to how we assigned coordinate vectors to tasks, we can now assign coordinate vectors to groups of Cartesian sub-domains of tasks. A group g will be assigned a coordinate vector x^g in $\mathbb{N}^d$, where every coordinate x_k^g satisfies $0 \le x_k^g < \lambda_k, \forall 1 \le k \le d$. Similarly to the neighborhood relationship for tasks defined by (7) we can define a neighborhood relationship for groups as

$$\tilde{\nu}_{i,j}^k = \begin{cases} 1 & \text{if } (\lambda_k + x_k^i - x_k^j) \bmod \lambda_k = 1 \\ & \text{and } \forall l \neq k, x_l^i = x_l^j \\ 0 & \text{otherwise.} \end{cases} \quad (12)$$

For two neighboring groups along direction k, the traffic exchanged across the common boundary is the aggregate traffic sent to one neighbor along dimension k by all the tasks forming that boundary. Given the shape of the task domain, there are exactly $(1 + \mathbb{1}_{\lambda_k=2}) \cdot |\gamma|/\gamma_k$ tasks on the boundary. Eq. (13) shows the resulting direct routing demand.

$$\begin{aligned} \delta_{ij}^{\text{R,direct}} &= \Delta_{ij}^{\text{R,direct}}/B_{\text{P,eff}} \\ &= \sum_{s \in G_i} \sum_{d \in G_j} \hat{t}_{sd} \\ &= \sum_{k=1}^d (1 + \mathbb{1}_{\lambda_k=2}) \cdot |\gamma|/\gamma_k \cdot m_k \cdot \tilde{\nu}_{i,j}^k \end{aligned} \quad (13)$$

In the case of indirect routing, we start by expressing $\delta^{\text{R,indirect}}$ from Eq. (3) and (4).

$$\begin{aligned} \delta_{ij}^{\text{R,indirect}} &= \sum_{p \neq i,j} \sum_{s \in G_i} \sum_{d \in G_p} \hat{t}_{sd} \cdot P(i \xrightarrow{j} p) \\ &+ \sum_{p \neq i,j} \sum_{s \in G_p} \sum_{d \in G_j} \hat{t}_{sd} \cdot P(p \xrightarrow{i} j) \\ &= \frac{1}{ah-1} \cdot \left(\sum_{p \neq i,j} \sum_{s \in G_i} \sum_{d \in G_p} \hat{t}_{sd} \right. \\ &\qquad \left. + \sum_{p \neq i,j} \sum_{s \in G_p} \sum_{d \in G_j} \hat{t}_{sd} \right) \end{aligned} \quad (14)$$

The two triple sums each evaluate to the same value for reasons that are linked to the symmetry of the communication pattern. Indeed, the amount of traffic sent by tasks in a group i to tasks in all groups $p \neq i,j$ (first triple sum) is equal to the aggregate external nearest neighbor traffic of i minus the traffic that i sends to group j if i and j are neighbors along some dimension. Similarly, the amount of traffic sent by all groups $p \neq i,j$ to tasks in group j (second triple sum) is equal to the aggregate external nearest neighbor traffic received by j minus the traffic that i sends to group j if i and j are neighbors along some dimension. Due to the fact that from the point of view of any individual sub-domain of tasks mapped to a group, the communication

pattern is symmetric (same messages received and sent along each dimension), the two triple sums are equal.

The aggregate nearest neighbor traffic sent (or received) by any group is equal to $2 \sum_{k=1}^d (|\gamma|/\gamma_k \cdot m_k \cdot \mathbb{1}_{\lambda_k>1})$ where the indicator function only serves to take into account the corner case where the intra-group domain would be so large along dimension k that it would completely cover the entire application domain along that direction and thus eliminate any inter-group traffic along that dimension. Eq. (15) shows the resulting indirect routing demand.

$$\begin{aligned} \delta_{i,j}^{\text{R,indirect}} &= (4 \sum_{k=1}^d (|\gamma|/\gamma_k \cdot m_k \cdot \mathbb{1}_{\lambda_k>1}) \\ &- 2\delta_{i,j}^{\text{R,direct}})/(ah-1) \end{aligned} \quad (15)$$

To be able to now derive performance estimations (via Eq. (6)) we maximize the demand. For direct routing, using the fact that Eq. (12) implies that task domains mapped to two groups can only be neighbors in at most one direction and Eq. (13), we obtain the bound in Eq. (16)

$$\max_{i,j}(\delta_{i,j}^{\text{R,direct}}) = \max_k((\mathbb{1}_{\lambda_k>1} + \mathbb{1}_{\lambda_k=2}) \cdot |\gamma|/\gamma_k \cdot m_k) \quad (16)$$

Similarly, Eq. (17) shows the bound obtained when maximizing indirect routing induced demand

$$\max_{i,j}(\delta_{i,j}^{\text{R,indirect}}) = 4 \sum_{k=1}^d (|\gamma|/\gamma_k \cdot m_k \cdot \mathbb{1}_{\lambda_k>1})/(ah-1). \quad (17)$$

As expressed by Eq. (6), maximizing performance is equivalent to minimizing the maximum demand. The previous equations express the maximum demand when the choice of a γ vector defining the mapping of tasks to the system topology has already been made. The same equations can however also be used to reason about what the mapping vectors γ, β themselves should be such that performance is maximized. This can be achieved by shifting the maximization domain to include the domain of possible values for γ and β as well (in addition to the values of k).

Random placement.

The second placement strategy we analyze is one where elements are assigned at random to nodes in the system under the constraints of having at most one element assigned to a given node and exactly 0 or $|\gamma|$ elements per group. This leads to there being exactly $|\lambda|$ groups hosting tasks. This strategy sacrifices communication locality in exchange for more uniform-like traffic that is amenable to direct routing.

Given an arbitrarily chosen group to which tasks are assigned, and given a certain dimension k and direction in which the tasks exchange messages, there will be exactly γ messages that the tasks in the group need to exchange. Due to the placement strategy described above, each of these γ messages have an equal chance to be destined to tasks in each of the $|\lambda|$ groups, including the source group itself. In the case of direct routing, according to Eq. (5), what we are interested in is the expected maximum remote link demand. To estimate it, we note that the problem of assigning messages to destination groups is an instance of the balls-and-bins problem [10], where messages are the balls ($n_{\text{balls}} = |\gamma|$) and the groups are the bins ($n_{\text{bins}} = |\lambda|$) What we are interested in is the expected number of balls that the bin that

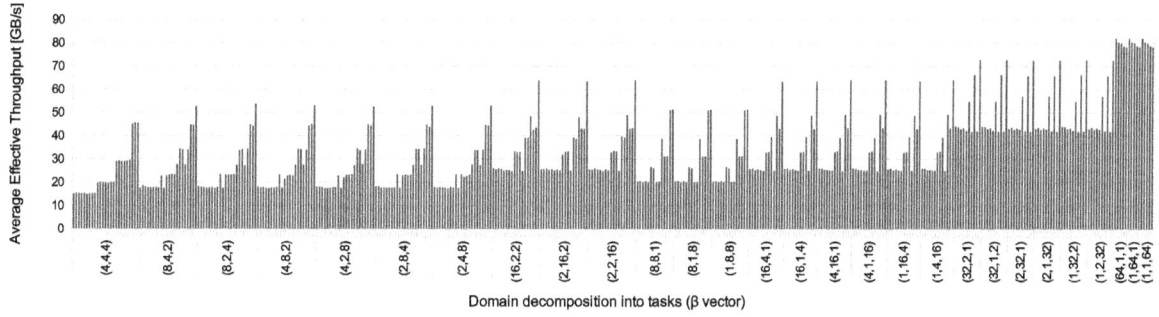

(a) Throughput (higher is better)

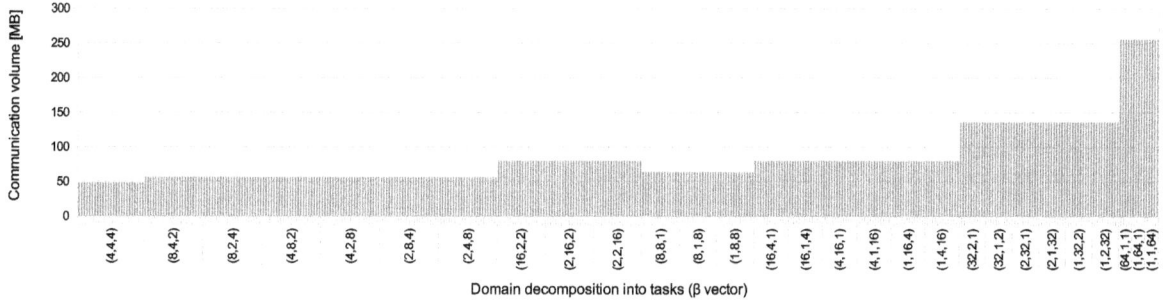

(b) Communication Volume

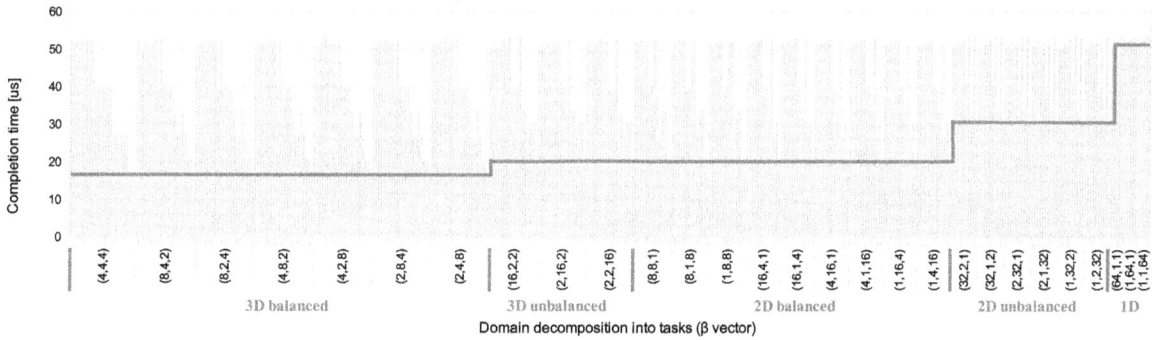

(c) Completion time (lower is better)

Figure 3: Comparison of the measured effective throughput, communication data volume, and completion time for a balanced dragonfly topology under indirect routing for a collection of all possible application domain decompositions into 64 tasks. The x axis of every subfigure shows the β vector defining the decomposition. For a fixed β vector, several task-to-node placement strategies (shown on the charts from denser to sparser left to right) are benchmarked to illustrate the variability of achievable performance. For figure c), the best completion time per domain decomposition is highlighted by means of horizontal lines. This best case performance is shown to be highly correlated with the decomposition type, and as such the same figure shows the clusters of decompositions that share similar characteristics.

has the most balls will have. As proven in [7, 17], for large balls-to-bins ratios, this is given by Eq. (18).

$$\frac{n_{\text{balls}}}{n_{\text{bins}}} \cdot \frac{\log n_{\text{bins}}}{\log \log n_{\text{bins}}} \tag{18}$$

This leads to the expected maximum demand induced by messages exchanged in the chosen direction of the chosen dimension k to be:

$$\frac{|\gamma|}{|\lambda|} \cdot \frac{\log |\lambda|}{\log \log |\lambda|} \cdot m_k. \tag{19}$$

Summing over all dimensions and both directions we obtain

$$\begin{aligned}
\max_{\text{Rlinks}} (\delta^{\text{R,direct}}) &= 2 \sum_{k=1}^{d} \frac{|\gamma|}{|\lambda|} \cdot \frac{\log |\lambda|}{\log \log |\lambda|} \cdot m_k \\
&= \frac{|\gamma|}{|\lambda|} \cdot \frac{\log |\lambda|}{\log \log |\lambda|} \cdot 2 \sum_{k=1}^{d} m_k \\
&= \frac{|\gamma|}{|\lambda|} \cdot \frac{\log |\lambda|}{\log \log |\lambda|}.
\end{aligned} \tag{20}$$

This applies when the ratio of messages to groups is large. Since this is not necessarily the case in several of the configurations we take into account, we can expect the accuracy of

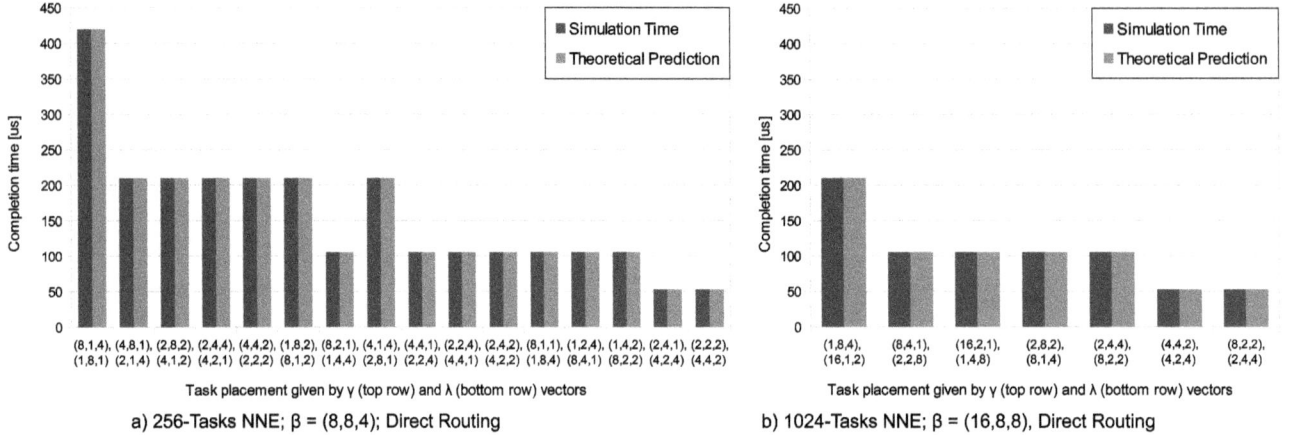

Figure 4: Comparison of the completion time (estimated and measured) for a balanced dragonfly topology under direct routing for a collection of all possible task-placements γ for a 3-dimensional $\beta = (8, 8, 4)$ nearest neighbor exchange of 256 tasks (Figure a)) and a $\beta = (16, 8, 8)$ nearest neighbor exchange of 1024 tasks (Figure b)). The x axis lists the task-placements from least-sparse (each group is fully occupied) to most-sparse (each group contains the minimum number of nodes that still allows for the workload to be scheduled on the Dragonfly system) and within each sparsity level, every possible γ placement whose $|\gamma|$ corresponds to the sparsity level. The first row of the x axis labels defines γ while the second row defines λ.

the random placement model to be somewhat poorer than that of the Cartesian placement model.

Random placement and random indirect routing are two solutions to similar issues arising in Dragonfly networks, each with its advantages and disadvantages. Using the two techniques in conjunction would yield very little benefit beyond the benefits already attainable by employing one or the other separately, and additionally incur the drawbacks of both strategies. Thus, there is little motivation for modeling performance for indirectly routed randomly placed workloads and therefore we will restrict our analysis of randomly placed nearest neighbor exchanges to the direct routing case.

3.5 Summary

In this Section we have introduced a formal performance model for nearest neighbor communication over Dragonfly networks, under i) Cartesian and ii) random task placement and using a) direct or b) *Valiant [Kim:2008]* indirect routing. The results of this analysis are the following.

For Cartesian placement and direct routing, we have shown (Eq. (16) and (5)) that effective injection bandwidth is limited by

$$B_{\text{P,eff}} \leq \frac{B_R}{\max_{k,\gamma,\beta}((\mathbb{1}_{\lambda_k > 1} + \mathbb{1}_{\lambda_k = 2}) \cdot |\gamma|/\gamma_k \cdot m_k)}. \quad (21)$$

By substituting m_k using Eq. (10) we obtain the optimization criterion for this configuration: optimal performance is obtained by minimizing

$$\max_{k,\gamma,\beta} \left[(\mathbb{1}_{\lambda_k > 1} + \mathbb{1}_{\lambda_k = 2}) \cdot \frac{|\gamma|}{\gamma_k} \cdot \frac{\beta_k \cdot \mathbb{1}_{\beta_k > 1}}{\alpha_k} \right]. \quad (22)$$

Strictly speaking this optimizes the performance bound, but we expect it to also optimize performance since the bounds should be tight given our assumption that other limitations on performance are removed.

For Cartesian placement and *Valiant [Kim:2008]* indirect routing, we have shown (Eq. (17) and (6)) that effective

injection bandwidth is limited by

$$B_{\text{P,eff}} \leq \frac{B_R}{\max_{\gamma,\beta}(4 \sum_{k=1}^{d} (|\gamma|/\gamma_k \cdot m_k \cdot \mathbb{1}_{\lambda_k > 1})/(ah - 1))}. \quad (23)$$

By substituting m_k using Eq. (10) we obtain the optimization criterion for this configuration: optimal performance is obtained by minimizing

$$\max_{\gamma,\beta} \left[\sum_{k=1}^{d} \left(\mathbb{1}_{\lambda_k > 1} \cdot \frac{|\gamma|}{\gamma_k} \cdot \frac{\beta_k \cdot \mathbb{1}_{\beta_k > 1}}{\alpha_k} \right) \right]. \quad (24)$$

For random placement and direct routing, we have shown (Eq. (20) and (5)) that effective injection bandwidth is limited by

$$B_{\text{P,eff}} \leq \frac{B_R}{\max_{\gamma,\beta} \left[\frac{|\gamma|}{|\lambda|} \cdot \frac{\log |\lambda|}{\log \log |\lambda|} \right]}. \quad (25)$$

Optimal performance is thus obtained by minimizing

$$\max_{\gamma,\beta} \left[\frac{|\gamma|}{|\lambda|} \cdot \frac{\log |\lambda|}{\log \log |\lambda|} \right]. \quad (26)$$

In all cases, given that the parameter space is not very large, minimization can be achieved by exhaustive exploration.

Thus, the analytical model we introduce has a two-fold use. First, in the context of one of the three routing and placement strategies described, it provides straightforward criteria allowing the selection of the most efficient assignment of domain elements to tasks (β) and assignment of tasks to network nodes (γ, λ). Second, due to its capability to estimate not only the circumstances in which performance is maximized but also actual expected performance, the model allows selecting the (routing, placement) strategy itself. Thus, overall, it allows for the identification of the complete configuration of a workload such that that workload completes in a minimum amount of time.

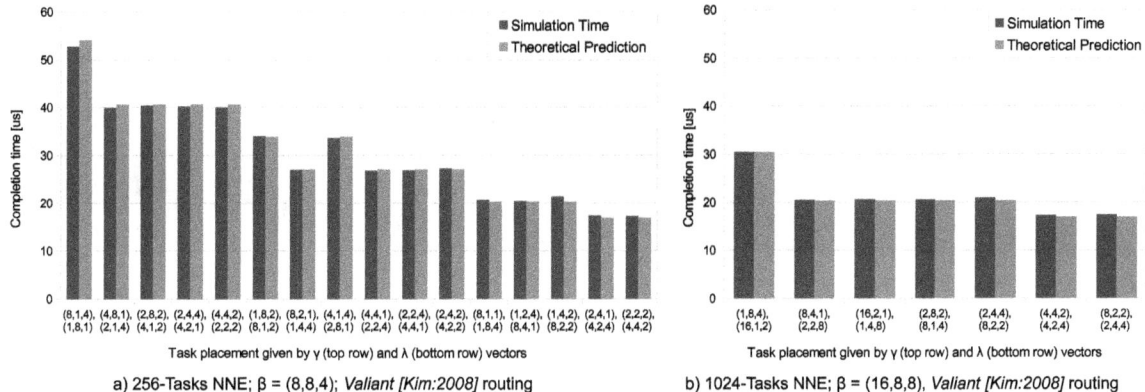

a) 256-Tasks NNE; β = (8,8,4); *Valiant [Kim:2008]* routing

b) 1024-Tasks NNE; β = (16,8,8), *Valiant [Kim:2008]* routing

Figure 5: Comparison of the completion time (estimated and measured) for a balanced dragonfly topology under *Valiant [Kim:2008]* indirect routing for a collection of all possible task-placements γ for a 3-dimensional $\beta = (8, 8, 4)$ nearest neighbor exchange of 256 tasks (Figure a)) and a $\beta = (16, 8, 8)$ nearest neighbor exchange of 1024 tasks (Figure b)). The x axis lists the task-placements from least-sparse (each group is fully occupied) to most-sparse (each group contains the minimum number of nodes that still allows for the workload to be scheduled on the Dragonfly system) and within each sparsity level, every possible γ placement whose $|\gamma|$ corresponds to the sparsity level. The first row of the x axis labels defines γ while the second row defines λ.

4. SIMULATION RESULTS

The results that we present in this section were obtained by means of a simulation framework that is able to accurately model custom networks (including Dragonflies) at a flit level [15]. The simulator is characterized by a high level of customization and modularity, allowing the configuration of the desired model in detail. Given that the parameter space to explore was already very large, we have chosen a fixed representative system scale of 1056 end nodes. Specifically, we have chosen a system interconnected by a balanced $DF(4, 8, 4)$ Dragonfly network, where groups are made up of $a = 8$ switches interconnected in a fully connected mesh and each switch has $p = 4$ nodes attached and $h = 4$ ports towards other groups. The bandwidth of every link was chosen to be 40 Gbit/s. The routing approaches used were direct routing and *Valiant [Kim:2008]*.

The traffic pattern is that of a single, 1D, 2D or 3D, nearest neighbor exchange as described in Section 3.2. The application domain was considered to be made up of 2^{27} elements shaped according to the vector $\alpha = (512, 512, 512)$. The per-element per-neighbor message size was chosen to be 1 KB. This means that if a task shares with a neighboring task a surface made up of E elements, the total amount of data sent by the task to that neighbor will be E KB.

4.1 Optimal application domain to task mapping

We will start by exploring the trade-offs that are associated with the selection of the β vector, expressing the mapping of application domain elements to computational tasks. The selection is done along two dimensions:

1. The total number of tasks.

2. The shape of the element sub-domain assigned to a task. By shape we refer to whether the sub-domain is one, two or three-dimensional as well as to the ratios between the elements of β.

As Eq. (8) shows, the larger the number of tasks the smaller the communication footprint per task will be. Also, regarding the sub-domain shape, similar dimensions of the task sub-domain lead to similar contact surfaces in each dimension, and therefore to more balanced sizes of the messages exchanged along each axis. Given the broad range in which the workload size can vary when choosing different element to task mappings, we will consider for this subsection both the effective completion time of the communication pattern, which is the most relevant performance indicator, and the effective throughput, which is often used as a performance indicator in practice.

We will start by choosing a fixed number of tasks, $|\beta| = 64$, and analyzing all possible domain decompositions. For a given domain decomposition, we will include multiple configurations with respect to parameters such as task-to-node mapping strategy, but we will not analyze them in detail in this subsection. What we will focus on is what performance can be obtained for a fixed domain decomposition (β vector) in the best case. The measured performance is illustrated in Fig. 3; the measured effective throughput is shown in Figure 3a the total volume of exchanged data is shown in Figure 3b and the effective completion time is shown in Figure 3c.

Several conclusions can be drawn from this experiment. First, we notice that there is a clear correlation between the best achievable completion time and the domain decomposition (Figure 3c). Indeed, decompositions that preserve both a higher number of dimensions and a symmetric distribution of tasks across dimensions perform consistently better than decompositions that are at the other end of the spectrum. The completion time of the best decomposition is more than twice as small as the completion time of the worst decomposition, with several performance levels for intermediate decompositions.

Second, the most widely used metric to measure network performance is the throughput that the network can sustain. However, if we were to have based our performance analysis

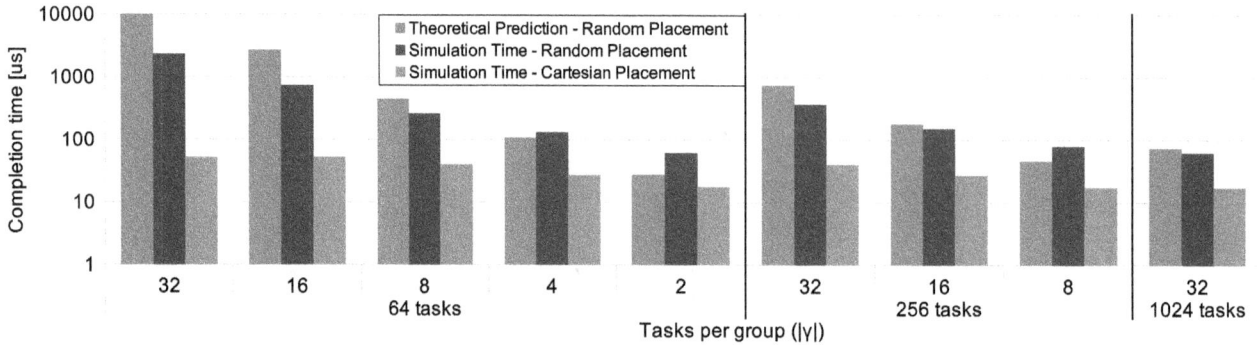

Figure 6: Comparison of the completion time (estimated and measured) for a balanced dragonfly topology under direct routing and random task placement for three 3-dimensional nearest neighbor exchanges ($\beta \in \{(4,4,4),(8,8,4),(16,8,8)\}$). The x axis lists the 3 exchanges from left to right (identifying them by the total number of tasks $|\beta|$), and within each exchange lists several levels of sparsity from least-sparse (each group is fully occupied) to most-sparse (each group contains the minimum number of nodes that still allows for the workload to be scheduled on the Dragonfly system). For each of these configurations, the completion time of the same workload, but this time Cartesian-mapped and indirectly routed, is also shown to allow comparison between the two strategies. The y axis has a logarithmic scale.

on this measure, our conclusions would have been the exact opposite. Indeed, as shown in Figure 3a, judging strictly by maximum achievable throughput, the best decomposition is, by a significant margin, exactly the one that actually takes the longest to complete. Using throughput to measure performance is thus questionable in this context, where the high throughput is actually a direct consequence of the decomposition requiring significantly larger volumes of exchanged data (Figure 3b) to account for the significantly larger contact surfaces between communicating tasks.

Finally, although the correlation between best case completion time and domain decomposition (β choice) is clear, the variability in the performance achieved for a fixed decomposition is extremely high. In fact, it is much higher than the variability across decompositions. This makes the choice of the intra-group task-to-node mapping (γ choice) of the utmost importance.

4.2 Optimal task to network topology mapping and validation of theoretical estimates

Across tested decompositions of the application domain, the best performance was obtained for a domain that is as close to a cube as possible (a β vector with elements as close to equal as possible). Furthermore, from the point of view of the variability induced by the intra-group placement (γ-choice), the different domain decompositions exhibited a similar behavior. Thus, in this subsection we will set the decomposition of the application domain to the decomposition closest to a cube and benchmark all possible intra-group placements (γ choices) under the fixed β vector.

We will consider, instead of the 64 task decomposition, a 256 and a 1024 task decomposition of the same domain to be able to examine the scale dependence of the results we obtain. For the former, we will consider $\beta = (8,8,4)$ while for the latter we will consider $\beta = (16,8,8)$.

For the vector γ, which completely defines a Cartesian task-to-node mapping, we will limit our analysis to values for which the individual elements divide the corresponding β elements. For each choice, we measure the completion time of the workload and compare it against the theoretical pre-

dictions of the model introduced in Section 3. In addition to validating our theoretical framework, by analyzing all possible γ values, we are able to study the impact of the shape of the domains chosen to be mapped to individual groups, as well as the impact of workload sparsity. The measured and predicted performance is shown in Figure 4 for direct routing and in Figure 5 for *Valiant [Kim:2008]* indirect routing.

In order to be able to compare the predicted effective bandwidth induced by remote link bottlenecks to measured performance, for this experiment we consider a high enough bandwidth for the local links, such that the bottleneck does not shift towards them, especially for the sparser mappings.

The main conclusion we can draw from the simulation results is that the theoretical framework is able to accurately capture the behavior of the system. This is particularly true for Cartesian task placements under both direct (Figure 4) and indirect (Figure 5) routing, where the predictions of the model are practically indistinguishable from the measurements. An immediate consequence of this fact is that the model can be used in a standalone fashion not only to select the best configuration to run a particular workload but can also to produce accurate estimates of the absolute performance of arbitrary configurations.

For random task placement (Figure 6), the predictions follow well the evolution of the performance across tested configurations, but the model experiences nonetheless fairly large deviations compared to the absolute measured values. This is due to the fact that the statistical analysis the model is based on in this case relies on the assumption of exchanging a large number of messages relative to the number of occupied Dragonfly groups $|\lambda|$ and this is not always the case in all tested configurations. That being said, the performance trends are captured faithfully and the decision of which configuration suits a particular workload best can still be taken based solely on the model.

Finally, Figure 6 also shows that, for all tested configurations, random task placement with direct routing is consistently outperformed by Cartesian task placement with indirect routing. Indeed, on the configurations that we benchmarked, the former took between 3 and 15 times more time to complete for a fixed β and γ configuration.

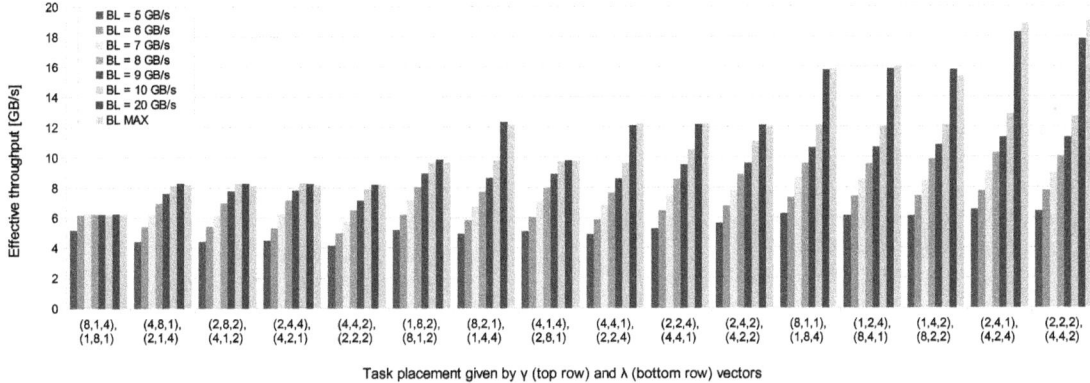

Figure 7: Effective throughput upper bound for nearest neighbor exchange among $|\beta| = 256$ tasks mapped on a 3-dimensional domain of size $\beta = (8, 8, 4)$ for increasingly higher local link bandwidths. The routing used is indirect routing and the placement is Cartesian: the first line of the x axis shows the vector γ while the second line shows the vector λ. By increasing the local link bandwidth, bottlenecks in the local links become less important, up to a point where a balance is reached between the limitations caused by remote links and limitations caused by local links. Further increasing the L link bandwidth will yield practically no further increase of the effective throughput.

4.3 Dragonfly balance for nearest neighbor exchanges

To conclude this section, we revisit the notion of Dragonfly balance in the context of nearest neighbor exchanges. A Dragonfly system is considered balanced if the limitation on effective injection bandwidth imposed by the three system bandwidth parameters B_P, B_L and B_R is the same under uniform random all-to-all traffic. Ensuring this property translates into a set of constraints on what the bandwidth per each type of link should be.

For traffic patterns that do not have a uniform random all-to-all structure and that exhibit poor performance in balanced Dragonfly systems under direct routing, it is generally assumed that a uniform distribution of load in the network can be achieved via indirect routing. It is further assumed that for this new load distribution, the balance of the Dragonfly is similar to that of indirectly routed uniform traffic.

In the case of the nearest neighbor exchange, we study the balance between the local and remote link bandwidth. We look at two extreme cases, one where the bandwidth of the local links is set to a very high value, such that the throughput limitation is the effect of solely a remote link bottleneck, and the other where the dragonfly is balanced for uniform traffic (at 5 GB/s with direct routing). Figure 7 shows that in the latter case, the bottleneck has clearly shifted towards the local links. As such, we benchmarked several L bandwidth values to identify what the tipping point is in terms of bandwidth, and implicitly what the balance of the Dragonfly is when considering nearest neighbor traffic.

We observe that, while for the mapping strategies that exhibit low sparsity, the balance of the system is very close to the uniform traffic balance, as we move toward sparser and more efficient mappings, the local bandwidth required to balance the traffic pattern increases as well, becoming up to a factor of 4 larger in the sparsest case.

4.4 Guidelines for application-network joint configuration and design

In Section 3.5 we have summarized the analytical performance model introduced in this work, which has the ability to i) determine the configuration options that would enable

a Cartesian nearest neighbor exchange to achieve optimum performance on a Dragonfly network and ii) estimate that level of optimum performance. In the current section, we have shown this model to be accurate in both aspects.

Thus, this model can be used in practice as follows. For each of the three routing and placement strategies presented, i.e., Cartesian placement with direct routing, Cartesian placement with indirect routing, and random placement with direct routing, one would use the model (namely Eq. (22), Eq. (24) and Eq. (26) respectively) to determine the configuration of the workload parameters β and γ. Then, one would use these parameters to determine for each (routing,placement) strategy (via Eq. (21), Eq. (23) and Eq. (25) respectively) the expected completion time for the workload, and select the strategy with the lowest one.

Concerning the optimization of the network design, the previous subsection has shown that the generally accepted guidelines for designing balanced, near optimal performance Dragonfly networks [13] (derived for uniform traffic), do not typically hold in the context of Cartesian nearest neighbor exchanges. Indeed, the intra-group aggregate bandwidth should be over-provisioned (relative to the balanced case), for optimal performance by as much as a factor of 4.

5. CONCLUSIONS

In this work we analyze communication workload performance in systems where the interconnect fabric is a Dragonfly network. We introduce a theoretical framework that is able to identify the bottlenecks that appear in the network under arbitrary workloads (specified via their traffic demand matrix), assuming either direct or indirect routing approaches, as well as to determine how those bottlenecks impact the effective injection throughput of the nodes.

With the help of this framework, we analyze Cartesian multi-dimensional nearest neighbor exchanges, a communication pattern that is prevalent in multiple high performance computing applications. Using the resulting theoretical estimates, as well as a wide array of simulations results that validated and augmented the analytical model, we quantify the performance of different nearest neighbor workloads coupled to a variety of mapping strategies. We are able to pinpoint mapping-related performance trends such as the advantages of workload fragmentation and of assigning convex application sub-domains with low surface-to-volume ratios to Dragonfly groups. This enables us to *co-design* application decomposition, routing, and mapping in order to achieve *optimal* overall performance.

Finally, we were able to unveil common misconceptions regarding Dragonfly network design and evaluation. We showed that optimizing for throughput and not workload completion time is often misleading. Furthermore, the notion of system balance that is often cited as a Dragonfly design parameter is not directly applicable to all workloads.

We present a network-application co-design effort between one of the most promising topologies from a scalability and cost point of view, the Dragonfly, and one of the most widely used communication patterns in scientific applications, the Cartesian nearest neighbor exchange. Our theoretical models capture important application and network characteristics and can be solved optimally. We showed substantial performance improvements of up to 10x and expect that our model will soon become a standard technique. For example, a batch system could inform a self-optimizing application about the task mapping and a solver could automatically determine the best decomposition and routing strategy.

6. ACKNOWLEDGMENTS

This work was supported and partially funded by Lawrence Livermore National Laboratory, on behalf of the US Department of Energy, under Lawrence Livermore National Laboratory subcontract number B601996.

7. REFERENCES

[1] M. Alvanos, G. Tanase, M. Farreras, E. Tiotto, J. N. Amaral, and X. Martorell. Improving performance of all-to-all communication through loop scheduling in PGAS environments. In *Proc. of the 27th International Conference on Supercomputing*, ICS '13, pages 457–458, New York, NY, USA, 2013. ACM.

[2] B. Arimilli, R. Arimilli, V. Chung, S. Clark, W. Denzel, B. Drerup, T. Hoefler, J. Joyner, J. Lewis, J. Li, N. Ni, and R. Rajamony. The PERCS High-Performance Interconnect. In *Proc. of the 18th IEEE Symposium on High Performance Interconnects*, HOTI '10, pages 75–82, Washington, DC, USA, 2010. IEEE Computer Society.

[3] A. Bhatele, N. Jain, W. D. Gropp, and L. V. Kale. Avoiding hot-spots on two-level direct networks. In *Proc. of the International Conference for High Performance Computing, Networking, Storage and Analysis*, SC '11, pages 76:1–76:11, New York, NY, USA, 2011. ACM.

[4] W. Dally and B. Towles. *Principles and Practices of Interconnection Networks*. Morgan Kaufmann Publishers Inc., San Francisco, CA, USA, 2003.

[5] G. Faanes, A. Bataineh, D. Roweth, T. Court, E. Froese, B. Alverson, T. Johnson, J. Kopnick, M. Higgins, and J. Reinhard. Cray Cascade: a scalable HPC system based on a Dragonfly network. In *Proc. of the International Conference on High Performance Computing, Networking, Storage and Analysis*, SC '12, pages 103:1–103:9, Los Alamitos, CA, USA, 2012. IEEE Computer Society Press.

[6] M. Garcia, E. Vallejo, R. Beivide, M. Odriozola, C. Camarero, M. Valero, G. Rodriguez, J. Labarta, and C. Minkenberg. On-the-fly adaptive routing in high-radix hierarchical networks. In *Proc. of the 41st International Conference on Parallel Processing (ICPP)*, pages 279–288, 2012.

[7] G. H. Gonnet. Expected length of the longest probe sequence in hash code searching. *J. of the ACM (JACM)*, 28(2):289–304, 1981.

[8] T. Goodale, G. Allen, G. Lanfermann, J. Massó, T. Radke, E. Seidel, and J. Shalf. The Cactus framework and toolkit: Design and applications, 2003.

[9] T. Hoefler, R. Rabenseifner, H. Ritzdorf, B. R. de Supinski, R. Thakur, and J. L. Traeff. The Scalable Process Topology Interface of MPI 2.2. *Concurrency and Computation: Practice and Experience*, 23(4):293–310, Aug. 2010.

[10] N. L. Johnson and S. Kotz. *Urn models and their application: an approach to modern discrete probability theory*. Wiley New York, 1977.

[11] A. Jokanovic, B. Prisacari, G. Rodriguez, and C. Minkenberg. Randomizing task placement does not randomize traffic (enough). In *Proc. of the 7th Interconnection Network Architecture: On-Chip, Multi-Chip*, IMA-OCMC '13, pages 9–12, New York, NY, USA, 2013. ACM.

[12] S. Kamil, J. Shalf, L. Oliker, and D. Skinner. Understanding ultra-scale application communication requirements. *Proc. of the Workload Characterization Symposium*, pages 178–187, Oct. 2005.

[13] J. Kim, W. J. Dally, S. Scott, and D. Abts. Technology-driven, highly-scalable dragonfly topology. *SIGARCH Comput. Archit. News*, 36(3):77–88, June 2008.

[14] Z. Lin, S. Ethier, T. S. Hahm, and W. M. Tang. Size scaling of turbulent transport in magnetically confined plasmas. *Phys. Rev. Lett.*, 88(19):195004–, 2002.

[15] C. Minkenberg, W. Denzel, G. Rodriguez, and R. Birke. End-to-end modeling and simulation of high-performance computing systems. *Springer Proc. in Physics: Use Cases of Discrete Event Simulation: Appliance and Research*, page 201, 2012.

[16] B. Prisacari, G. Rodriguez, M. Garcia, E. Vallejo, R. Beivide, and C. Minkenberg. Performance implications of remote-only load balancing under adversarial traffic in dragonflies. In *Proc. of the 8th International Workshop on Interconnection Network Architecture: On-Chip, Multi-Chip*, INA-OCMC '14, pages 5:1–5:4, New York, NY, USA, 2014. ACM.

[17] M. Raab and A. Steger. Balls into bins - a simple and tight analysis. In *Randomization and Approximation Techniques in Computer Science*, pages 159–170. Springer, 1998.

[18] L. G. Valiant. A scheme for fast parallel communication. *SIAM J. Comput.*, 11(2):350–361, 1982.

[19] S. Williams, J. Carter, L. Oliker, J. Shalf, and K. Yelick. Lattice Boltzmann simulation optimization on leading multicore platforms. In *Proc. of the International Conference on Parallel and Distributed Computing Systems (IPDPS)*, 2008.

Analysis of Dynamic Scheduling Strategies for Matrix Multiplication on Heterogeneous Platforms

Olivier Beaumont
Inria
University of Bordeaux
200 rue de la vieille Tour
33400 Talence, France
olivier.beaumont@inria.fr

Loris Marchal
LIP (CNRS, INRIA, ENS-Lyon, Univ. of Lyon)
46 allée d'Italie
69007 Lyon, France
loris.marchal@ens-lyon.fr

ABSTRACT

The tremendous increase in the size and heterogeneity of supercomputers makes it very difficult to predict the performance of a scheduling algorithm. Therefore, dynamic solutions, where scheduling decisions are made at runtime have overpassed static allocation strategies. The simplicity and efficiency of dynamic schedulers such as Hadoop are a key of the success of the MapReduce framework. Dynamic schedulers such as StarPU, PaRSEC or StarSs are also developed for more constrained computations, e.g. task graphs coming from linear algebra. To make their decisions, these runtime systems make use of some static information, such as the distance of tasks to the critical path or the affinity between tasks and computing resources (CPU, GPU,...) and of dynamic information, such as where input data are actually located. In this paper, we concentrate on two elementary linear algebra kernels, namely the outer product and the matrix multiplication. For each problem, we propose several dynamic strategies that can be used at runtime and we provide an analytic study of their theoretical performance. We prove that the theoretical analysis provides very good estimate of the amount of communications induced by a dynamic strategy and can be used in order to efficiently determine thresholds used in dynamic scheduler, thus enabling to choose among them for a given problem and architecture.

Categories and Subject Descriptors

F.2.0 [**Theory of Computation**]: Analysis of Algorithms and Problem Complexity—*General*

General Terms

Algorithms, Performance

Keywords

Dynamic scheduling, data-aware algorithms, randomized algorithms, performance evaluation, matrix multiplication

HPDC'14, June 23–27, Vancouver, BC, Canada.
Copyright is held by the owner/author(s). Publication rights licensed to ACM.
ACM 978-1-4503-2749-7/14/06 ...$15.00.
http://dx.doi.org/10.1145/2600212.2600223

1. INTRODUCTION

Recently, there has been a very important change in both parallel platforms and parallel applications. On the one hand, computing platforms, either clouds or supercomputers involve more and more computing resources. This scale change poses many problems, mostly related to unpredictability and failures. Due to the size of the platforms, their complex network topologies, the use of heterogeneous resources, NUMA effects, the number of concurrent simultaneous computations and communications, it is impossible to predict exactly the time that a specific task will take. Unpredictability makes it impossible to statically allocate the tasks of a DAG onto the processing resources and dynamic scheduling and allocation strategies are needed. As a consequence, in recent years, there has been a large amount of practical work to develop efficient runtime schedulers. The main characteristics of these schedulers is that they make their decisions at runtime, based on the expected duration of the tasks on the different kind of processing units (CPUs, GPUs,...) and on the expected availability time of the task input data, given their actual locations. Thanks to these information, the scheduler allocates the task to the resource that will finish its processing as soon as possible. Moreover, all these runtime systems also make use of some static information that can be computed from the task graph itself, in order to decide the priority between several ready tasks. This information mostly deals with the estimated critical path as proposed in HEFT [17] for instance.

On the other hand, there has been a dramatic simplification of the application model in many cases, as asserted by the success of the MapReduce framework [8] which has been popularized by Google. It allows users without particular knowledge in parallel algorithms to harness the power of large parallel machines. In MapReduce, a large computation is broken into small tasks that run in parallel on multiple machines, and scales easily to very large clusters of inexpensive commodity computers. MapReduce is a very successful example of dynamic schedulers, as one of its crucial feature is its inherent capability of handling hardware failures and processing capabilities heterogeneity, thus hiding this complexity to the programmer, by relying on on-demand allocations and the on-line detection of nodes that perform poorly (in order to re-assign tasks that slow down the process). As we explained in a previous work [3], MapReduce, although tailored for linear complexity operations (such as text parsing), is now widely used for non linear complexity tasks. In this case, it induces a large replication of the data.

For example, when MapReduce is used to compute the outer product of two vectors a and b, the most common technique is to emit all possible pairs of (a_i, b_j), so that many processors can be used to compute the elementary products. This induces a large replication factor, since MapReduce is not aware of the 2-dimensional nature of the data.

Our goal in this paper is to show how simple data-aware dynamic schedulers can be proven efficient in a specific context. We concentrate here on two elementary kernels, namely the outer product and the matrix multiplication. These kernels do not induce dependencies among their tasks, but because of their massive input data reuse results, a straightforward MapReduce implementations of these kernels would involve a large replication overhead. Indeed, in both cases [3], input vectors or input matrices need to be replicated when the kernel is processed by a large-scale parallel platform, and basic dynamic strategies that allocate tasks at random to processors fail to achieve reasonable communication volumes with respect to known lower bounds.

In the present paper, we first present and study a very simple yet efficient dynamic scheduler for the outer product, that generates a communication volume close to the lower bound. Our main contribution is to analyze the communication volume generated by the dynamic scheduler as a continuous process that can be modeled by an Ordinary Differential Equation (ODE). We prove that the analytic communication volume of the solution of the ODE is close to the actual communication volume as measured using simulations. Moreover, we prove that this analysis of the solution of the ODE can be used in order to optimize a dynamic randomized allocation strategy, for instance, by switching between two strategies when the number of remaining tasks is smaller than a given threshold, that is determined by the theoretical analysis. This simple example attests the practical interest of the theoretical analysis of dynamic schedulers, since it shows that the analytic solution can be used in order to incorporate static knowledge into the scheduler. After presenting our method on the outer product (Section 3), we move to a more common kernel, the matrix multiplication and show how the previous analysis can be extended in Section 4.

2. RELATED WORK

We briefly review previous works related to our study, which deals both with actual runtime schedulers and with their theoretical studies.

2.1 Runtime dynamic schedulers

As mentioned in the introduction, several runtime systems have been recently proposed to schedule applications on parallel systems. Among other successful projects, we may cite StarPU [1], from INRIA Bordeaux (France), DAGuE and PaRSEC [7, 6] from ICL, Univ. of Tennessee Knoxville (USA) StarSs [16] from Barcelona Supercomputing Center (Spain) or KAAPI [10] from INRIA Grenoble (France). Most of these tools enable, to a certain extent, to schedule an application described as a task graph (usually available in the beginning of the computation, but sometimes generated and discovered during the execution itself), onto a parallel platforms. Most of these tools allow to harness complex platforms, such as multicores and hybrid platforms, including GPUs or other accelerators. These runtime systems usually keep track of the occupation of each computing devices and

allocate new tasks on the processing unit that is expected to minimize its completion time. Our goal in this paper in to provide an analysis of such dynamic schedulers for simple operations, that do not involve tasks dependencies but massive data reuse.

2.2 Theoretical studies of dynamic systems

Many studies have proposed to use queuing theory [11] to study the behavior of simple parallel systems and their dynamic evolution. Among many others, Berten et al. [5] propose to use such stochastic models in order to model computing Grids, and Mitzenmacher [14] studies how not-to-date information can lead to bad scheduling decisions in a simple parallel system.

Recently, mean field techniques [9, 4] have been proposed for analyzing such dynamic processes. They give a formal framework to derive a system of ordinary differential equations that is the limit of a Markovian system when the number of objects goes to infinity. Such techniques have been used for the first time in [13] where the author derives differential equations for a system of homogeneous processors who steal a single job when idle.

3. RANDOMIZED DYNAMIC STRATEGIES FOR THE OUTER-PRODUCT

We present here the analysis of a dynamic scheduler for a simple problem from linear algebra, namely the outer-product of two vectors.

3.1 Problem definition

We consider the problem of computing the outer-product ab^t of two large vectors a and b of size N, *i.e.* to compute all values $a_i \times b_j, \forall 1 \leq i, j \leq N$. The computing domain can therefore be seen as a matrix. For granularity reasons, we will consider that a and b are in fact split into N/l blocks of size l and that a basic operation consists in computing the outer product of two (small) vectors of size l.

As stated above, we target heterogeneous platforms consisting of p processors $P_1, \ldots, P_p$, where the speed of processor P_i, *i.e.* the number of outer products of size l vectors that P_k can do in one time unit, is given by s_k. We will also denote by rs_k the relative speed of $rs_k = \frac{s_k}{\sum_i s_i}$. Note that the randomized strategies that we propose are agnostic to processor speeds, but they are demand driven, so that a processor with a twice larger speed will request work twice faster.

In the following, we assume that a master processor coordinates the work distribution: it is aware of which a and b blocks are replicated on the computing nodes and decides which new blocks are sent, as well as which tasks are allocated to the nodes. After completion of their allocated tasks, computing nodes simply report to the master processor, requesting for new tasks.

We will assume throughout the analysis that it is possible to overlap computations and communications. This can be achieved with dynamic strategies by uploading a few blocks in advance at the beginning of the computations and then to request work as soon as the number of blocks to be processed becomes smaller than a given threshold. Determining this threshold would require to introduce a communication model and a topology, what is out of the scope of this paper, and we will assume that the threshold is known. In practice, the number of tasks required to ensure a good overlap has been observed to be small in [12, 15] even though a rigorous algorithm to estimate it is still missing.

As we observed [3], performing a non linear complexity task such as a Divisible Load or a MapReduce operation requires to replicate initial data. Our objective is to minimize the overall amount of communications, *i.e.* the total amount of data (the number of blocks of a and b) sent by the master node initially holding the data, or equivalently by the set of devices holding the data since we are interested in the overall volume only, under the constraint that a perfect load-balancing should be achieved among resources allocated to the outer product computation. Indeed, due to data dependencies, if we were to minimize communications without this load-balancing constraint, the optimal (but very inefficient) solution would consist in making use of a single computing resource so that each data block would be sent exactly once.

3.2 Design of randomized dynamic strategies

As mentioned above, vectors a and b are split into N/l data blocks. In the following, we denote by a_i the ith block of a (rather than the ith element of a) since we always consider elements by blocks. As soon as a processor has received two data blocks a_i and b_j, it can compute the block $M_{i,j} = (ab^t)_{i,j} = a_i b_j^t$. This elementary task is denoted by $T_{i,j}$. All data blocks are initially available at the master node only.

One of the simplest strategy to allocate computational tasks to processors is to distribute tasks at random: whenever a processor is ready, a task $T_{i,j}$ is chosen uniformly at random among all available tasks and is allocated to the processor. The data corresponding to this task that is not yet on the processor, that is one or two of the a_i and b_j blocks are sent by the master. We denote this strategy by RANDOM-OUTER. Another simple option is to allocate tasks in lexicographical order of indices (i, j) rather than randomly. This strategy will be denoted as SORTEDOUTER.

Both previous algorithms are expected to induce a large amount of communications because of data replication. Indeed, in these algorithms, there is no reason why the data sent for the processing of tasks on a given processor P_k may be re-used for upcoming tasks. This is why dynamic data-aware strategies have been introduced. In the runtime systems cited above, such as StarPU, the scheduler is aware of the locality of the data and uses this information when allocating tasks to processors: it is much more beneficial, when allocating a new task on P_k, to take advantage of the a and b data already present on the processor, and to compute for example all possible products $a_i b_j^t$ before sending new blocks of data. We propose such a strategy, denoted DYNAMICOUTER, in Algorithm 1: when a processor P_k receives a new pair of blocks (a_i, b_j), all possible products $a_i b_{j'}^t$ and $a_{i'} b_j^t$ are also allocated to P_k, for all data blocks $a_{i'}$ and $b_{j'}$ that have already been transmitted to P_k in previous steps.

Note that the DYNAMICOUTER scheduler is not computationally expensive: it is sufficient to maintain a set of unknown a and b data (of size $O(N/l)$) for each processor, and to randomly pick an element of this set when allocating new blocks to a processor P_k.

We have compared the performance of previous schedulers through simulations on Figure 1. Processor speeds are chosen uniformly in the interval $[10, 100]$, which means a large

---

Algorithm 1: DYNAMICOUTER strategy.

---

while *there are unprocessed tasks* **do**

Wait for a processor P_k to finish its tasks
$I \leftarrow \{i \text{ such that } P_k \text{ owns } a_i\}$
$J \leftarrow \{j \text{ such that } P_k \text{ owns } b_j\}$
Choose $i \notin I$ and $j \notin J$ uniformly at random
Send a_i and b_j to P_k
Allocate all tasks of $\{T_{i,j}\} \cup \{T_{i,j'}, j' \in J\} \cup \{T_{i',j}, i' \in I\}$ that are not yet processed to P_k and mark them processed

---

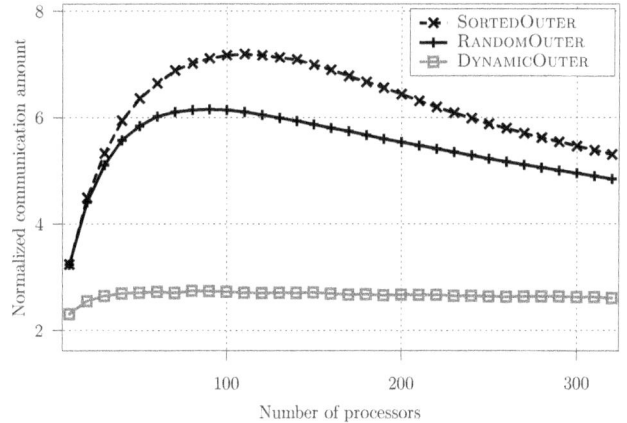

Figure 1: Comparison of random and data-aware dynamic strategies, for vectors of size $N/l = 100$ blocks

degree of heterogeneity. Each point in this figure and the following ones is the average over 10 or more simulations. The standard deviation is always very small, typically smaller than 0.1 for any point, and never impacts the ranking of the strategies. It is thus not depicted for clarity reasons. All communication amounts are normalized with the following lower bound:

$$LB = 2N \sum_k \sqrt{rs_k} = 2N \sum_k \sqrt{\frac{s_k}{\sum_i s_i}},$$

where s_k is the speed of processor P_k and rs_k its relative speed.

Indeed, in a very optimistic setting, each processor is dedicated to computing a "square" area of $M = ab^t$, whose area is proportional to its relative speed, so that all processors finish their work at the same instant. In this situation, the amount of communications for P_k is proportional to the half perimeter of this square of area $N^2 rs_k$. Note that this lower bound is not expected to be achievable (consider for instance the case of 2 heterogeneous processors). The best known static algorithm (based on a complete knowledge of all relative speeds) has an approximation ratio of 7/4 [2]. This algorithm computes an allocation scheme based on the computing speeds of the processors. As outlined in the introduction, such an allocation mechanism is not practical in our context, since our aim is to rely on more dynamic runtime strategies, but can be used as a comparison basis.

As expected, we notice on Figure 1 that data-aware strategies induce significantly less communication than purely random strategies.

Our DYNAMICOUTER allocation scheme suffers some limitation: when the number of remaining blocks to compute is small, the proposed strategy is inefficient as it may send a large number of a and b blocks to a processor P_k before it is able to process one of the last few available tasks. Thus, we propose an improved version DYNAMICOUTER2PHASES in Algorithm 2: when the number of remaining tasks becomes smaller than a given threshold, we switch to the basic randomized strategy: any available task $T_{i,j}$ is allocated to a requesting processor, without taking data locality into account. The corresponding data a_i and b_j are then sent to P_k if needed.

Algorithm 2: DYNAMICOUTER2PHASES strategy.

---

while *the number of processors is larger than the threshold* **do**

  Wait for a processor P_k to finish its tasks
  $I \leftarrow \{i$ such that P_k owns $a_i\}$
  $J \leftarrow \{j$ such that P_k owns $b_j\}$
  Choose $i \notin I$ and $j \notin J$ uniformly at random
  Send a_i and b_j to P_k
  Allocate all tasks of $\{T_{i,j}\} \cup \{T_{i,j'}, j' \in J\} \cup \{T_{i',j}, i' \in I\}$ that are not yet processed to P_k and mark them processed

while *there are unprocessed tasks* **do**

  Wait for a processor P_k to finish its tasks
  Choose randomly an unprocessed task $T_{i,j}$
  if P_k *does not hold* a_i **then** send a_i to P_k
  if P_k *does not hold* b_j **then** send b_j to P_k
  Allocate $T_{i,j}$ to P_k

As illustrated on Figure 2, for a well chosen number of tasks processed in the second phase, this new strategy allows to reduce further the amount of communications. However, this requires to accurately set the threshold, depending on the size of the matrix and the relative speed of the processors. If too many tasks are processed in the second phase, the performance is close to the one of RANDOMOUTER. On the contrary, if too few tasks are processed in the second phase, the behavior becomes close to DYNAMICOUTER. The optimal threshold corresponds here to a few percent of tasks being processed in the second phase. In the following, we present an analysis of the DYNAMICOUTER2PHASES strategy that both allows to predict its performance and to optimally set the threshold, so as to minimize the amount of communications.

3.3 Theoretical analysis of dynamic randomized strategies

In this section, our aim is to provide an analytical model for Algorithm DYNAMICOUTER2PHASES. Analyzing such a strategy is crucial in order to assess the efficiency of runtime dynamic strategies and in order to tune the parameters of dynamic strategies or to choose among different strategies depending on input parameters.

In what follows, we assume that N, the size of vectors a and b, is large and we consider a continuous dynamic process whose behavior is expected to be close to the one of DYNAMICOUTER2PHASES. In what follows, we concentrate on processor P_k whose speed is s_k. At each step, DYNAMICOUTER2PHASES chooses to send one data block of a and one data block of b, so that P_k knows the same number of data

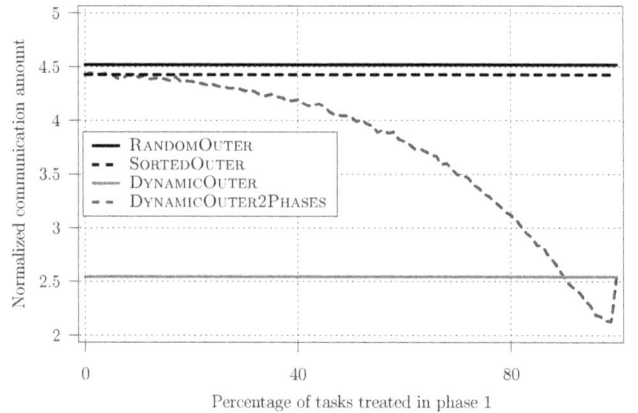

Figure 2: Communication amount of Dynamic-Outer2Phases and comparison to the other schedulers for different thresholds (for a given distribution of computing speeds with 20 processors and $N/l = 100$).

blocks of a and b. As previously, we denote by $M = ab^t$ the result of the outer product and by $T_{i,j}$ the tasks that corresponds to the product of data blocks a_i and b_j

We denote by $x = y/N$ the ratio of elements of a and b that are known by P_k at a given time step of the process and by $t_k(x)$ the corresponding time step. We concentrate on a basic step of DYNAMICOUTER2PHASES during which the fraction of data blocks of both a and b known by P_k goes from x to $x + \delta x$. In fact, since DYNAMICOUTER2PHASES is a discrete process and the ratio known by P_k goes from $x = y/N$ to $x+l/N = y/N+l/N$. Under the assumption that N is large, we assume that we can approximate the randomized discrete process by the continuous process described by the corresponding Ordinary Differential Equation on expected values. The proof of convergence is out of the scope of this paper but we will show that this assumption provides very good results through simulations in Section 3.4.

Let us remark that during the execution of DYNAMIC-OUTER2PHASES, tasks $T_{i,j}$ are greedily computed as soon as a processor knows the corresponding data blocks of a_i and b_j. Therefore, at time $t_k(x)$, all tasks $T_{i,j}$ such that P_k knows data blocks a_i and b_j have been processed and there are x^2N^2/l^2 such tasks. Note also that those tasks may have been processed either by P_k or by another processor P_j since processors compete to process tasks. Indeed, since data blocks of a and b are possibly replicated on several processors, then both P_k and P_ℓ may know at some point both a_i and b_j. In practice, the processor which computes $T_{i,j}$ is the one that learns both a_i and b_j first.

Figure 3 depicts the computational domain during the first phase of DYNAMICOUTER2PHASES from the point of view of a given processor P_k (rows and columns have been reordered for the sake of clarity). The top-left square (in blue) corresponds to value of a and b that are known by P_k, and all corresponding tasks have already been processed (either by P_k or by another processor). The remaining "L"-shaped area (in grey) corresponds to tasks $T_{i,j}$ such that P_k does not hold either the corresponding value of a, or the corresponding value of b, or both. When receiving a new value of a and b (in red), P_k is able to process all the tasks (in red) from the two corresponding row and column. Some elements

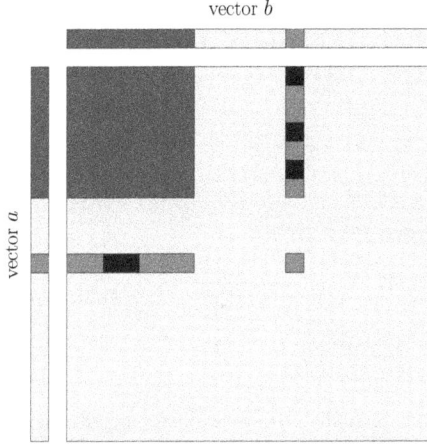

Figure 3: Illustration for the proof of Lemma 1. The top-left blue rectangle represents the data owned by the processor at time $t_k(x)$ (a permutation of the rows and columns has been applied to have it in the upper left corner). The new elements δx are depicted in red, as well as the corresponding available tasks. Note that some tasks (in black) corresponding to the combination of δx with the known elements have already been processed by other processors.

from this row and this column may be already processed (in black).

In what follows, we denote by $g_k(x)$ the fraction of tasks $T_{i,j}$ in the previously described "L"-shaped area that have not been computed yet. We also assume that the distribution of unprocessed tasks in this area is uniform, and we claim that this assumption is valid for a reasonably large number of processors. Our simulations below show that this leads to a very good accuracy.

Based on this remark, we are able to prove the following Lemma

LEMMA 1. $g_k(x) = (1 - x^2)^{\alpha_k}$, where $\alpha_k = \frac{\sum_{i \neq k} s_i}{s_k}$.

PROOF. Let us consider the tasks that have been computed by all processors between $t_k(x)$ and $t_k(x + \delta x)$. As depicted on Figure 3, these tasks can be split into two sets.

- The first set of tasks consists in those that can be newly processed by P_k between $t_k(x)$ and $t_k(x + \delta x)$. P_k has the possibility to combine the $\delta x N$ new elements of a with the xN already known elements of b (and to combine the $\delta x N$ new elements of b with the xN already known elements of a). There is therefore a total of $2\, x\, \delta x\, N^2$ such tasks (at first order). Among those, by definition of g, the expected number of tasks that have not already been processed by other processors is given by $2\, x\, \delta x\, g(x)\, N^2$. Therefore, the expected duration of this step is given by $t_k(x + \delta x) - t_k(x) = \frac{2\, x\, \delta x\, g(x)\, N^2}{s_k}$.

- The second set of tasks consists in those computed by other processors P_i, $i \neq k$. Our assumption states that we are able to overlap communications by computations (by uploading data blocks slightly in advance), so that processors P_i, $i \neq k$ will keep processing tasks

between $t_k(x)$ and $t_k(x + \delta x)$ and will process on expectation $2\, x\, \delta x\, g(x)\, N^2 \frac{\sum_{i \neq k} s_i}{s_k}$ tasks.

Therefore, we are able to estimate how many tasks will be processed between $t_k(x)$ and $t_k(x+\delta x)$ and therefore to compute the evolution (on expectation) of g_k. More specifically, we have

$$g_k(x + \delta x)\, \left(1 - (x + \delta x)^2\right) N^2 =$$

$$g_k(x)\, (1 - x^2)\, N^2 - 2\, x\, \delta x\, g(x)\, N^2 - 2\, x\, \delta x\, g(x)\, N^2 \frac{\sum_{i \neq k} s_i}{s_k},$$

which gives at first order

$$g_k(x + \delta x) - g_k(x) = g_k(x)\, \delta x\, \frac{-2\, x\, \alpha_k}{1 - x^2},$$

where $\alpha_k = \frac{\sum_{i \neq k} s_i}{s_k}$.

Therefore, the evolution of g_k with x is given by the following ordinary differential equation

$$\frac{g_k'(x)}{g_k(x)} = \frac{-2\, x\, \alpha_k}{1 - x^2}$$

where both left and right terms are of the form f'/f, what leads to

$$\ln(g_k(x)) = \alpha_k \ln(1 - x^2) + K$$

and finally to

$$g_k(x) = \exp(K)(1 - x^2)^{\alpha_k},$$

where $exp(K) = 1$ since $g_k(0) = 1$. This achieves the proof of Lemma 1. $\square$

Remember that $t_k(x)$ denotes the time necessary for P_k to know x elements of a and b. Then,

LEMMA 2. $t_k(x) \sum_i s_i = N^2(1 - (1 - x^2)^{\alpha_k + 1})$.

PROOF. We have seen that some of the tasks that could have been processed by P_k (tasks $T_{i,j}$ such that P_k knows both a_i and b_j) have indeed been processed by other processors. In order to prove the lemma, let us denote by $h_k(x)$ the number of such tasks at time $t_k(x)$. Then

$$h_k(x + \delta x) = h_k(x) + 2\, x\, \delta x\, (1 - g_k(x))N^2$$

by definition of g_k so that, using Lemma 1,

$$h_k'(x) = N^2(2x - 2x(1 - x^2)^{\alpha_k})$$

and

$$h_k(x) = N^2\left(x^2 + \frac{(1 - x^2)^{\alpha_k + 1}}{\alpha_k + 1} + K\right)$$

and since $h_k(0) = 0$,

$$h_k(x) = N^2\left(x^2 + \frac{(1 - x^2)^{\alpha_k + 1}}{\alpha_k + 1} - \frac{1}{\alpha_k + 1}\right).$$

Moreover, at time $t_k(x)$, all the tasks that could have been processed by P_k have

- either been processed by P_k and there are exactly $t_k(x)s_k$ such tasks since P_k has been processing all the time in this area,

- or processed by other processors and there are exactly $h_k(x)$ such tasks by definition of h_k.

Therefore,

$$x^2 N^2 = h_k(x) + t_k(x)s_k$$

and finally

$$t_k(x) \sum_i s_i = N^2(1 - (1-x^2)^{\alpha_k+1}),$$

which achieves the proof of Lemma 2. $\square$

Above equations well describe the dynamics of DYNAMIC-OUTER2PHASES as long as it is possible to find blocks of a and b that enable to compute enough unprocessed tasks. On the other hand, at the end, it is better to switch to another algorithm, where unprocessed tasks $T_{i,j}$ are picked up randomly, which possibly requires to send two blocks a_i and b_j. In order to decide when to switch from one strategy to the other, we introduce an additional parameter β.

As presented above, a lower bound on the communication volume received by P_k (if perfect load balancing is achieved) is given by $LB = 2N \sum_k \sqrt{rs_k}$. We will switch from the DYNAMICOUTER to the RANDOMOUTER strategy when the fraction of tasks $x_k^2 N^2$ for which P_k owns the input data is approximately β times what it would have computed optimally, that is, when x_k^2 is close to $\beta \frac{s_k}{\sum_i s_i} = \beta rs_k$, for a value of β that is to be determined. For the sake of the analysis, it is important that we globally define the instant at which we switch to the random strategy, and that it does not depend on the processor P_k. In order to achieve this, we look for x_k^2 as

$$x_k^2 = (\beta rs_k - \alpha rs_k^2)$$

and we search α such that $t_k(x_k)$ does not depend on k at first order in $1/rs_k$, where rs_k is of order $1/p$ and p is the number of processors.

LEMMA 3. If $\alpha = \beta^2/2$, then

$$t_k(x_k) \sum_i s_i = N^2(1 - e^{-\beta}(1 + o(rs_k))).$$

PROOF. Since $t_k(x_k) \sum_i s_i = N^2(1 - (1-x_k^2)^{\alpha_k+1})$, then

$$
\begin{aligned}
t_k(x_k) &= \frac{N^2}{\sum_i s_i}(1 - e^{\frac{1}{rs_k}\ln(1 - \beta rs_k + \alpha rs_k^2)}) \\
&= \frac{N^2}{\sum_i s_i}(1 - e^{\frac{1}{rs_k}(-\beta rs_k + \alpha rs_k^2 - (\beta rs_k)^2/2)}) \\
&\qquad\qquad\qquad\qquad\qquad \text{(at first order)} \\
&= \frac{N^2}{\sum_i s_i}(1 - e^{-\beta}(1 + o(rs_k))).
\end{aligned}
$$

which achieves the proof of Lemma 3. $\square$

One remarkable characteristics of the above result is that it does not depend (at least up to order 2) on k anymore. Otherwise stated, at time $T = \frac{N^2}{\sum_i s_i}(1 - e^\beta)$, each processor P_k has received $\sqrt{(\beta rs_k - \beta^2/2 rs_k^2)N^2} = \sqrt{\beta rs_k}(1 - \beta rs_k/4)N$ data, to be compared with the lower bound on communications for processor P_k: $\sqrt{rs_k}N$.

Using both these results, it is possible to derive the ratio between the overall amount of communication induced by the first phase with respect to the lower bound as a function of β.

LEMMA 4. Let us denote by $\mathcal{V}_{\text{PHASE1}}$ the volume of the communications induced by Phase 1 and by $LB = 2N \sum_k \sqrt{rs_k}$ the lower bound for the communications induced by the whole outer product, then

$$\frac{\mathcal{V}_{\text{PHASE1}}}{LB} \leq \sqrt{\beta} + \frac{\beta^{3/2} \sum_i rs_k^{3/2}}{4 LB} \text{ (at first order)}.$$

PROOF. The proof is obtained by replacing $\mathcal{V}_{\text{PHASE1}}$ by $\sum_k \sqrt{\beta rs_k}(1 - \beta rs_k/4)N$. $\square$

Lemma 4 provides the evaluation of the expected communication volume induced by the first phase of DYNAMIC-OUTER2PHASES with respect to the lower bound. In the following, we will establish a similar result for the second phase in Lemma 5.

LEMMA 5. Let us denote by $\mathcal{V}_{\text{PHASE2}}$ the volume of the communications induced by Phase 1 and by $LB = 2N \sum_k \sqrt{rs_k}$ the lower bound for the communications induced by the whole outer product, then

$$\frac{\mathcal{V}_{\text{PHASE2}}}{LB} \leq e^{-\beta} N \frac{1 - \sqrt{\beta} \sum_k rs_k^{3/2}}{\sum_k rs_k^{1/2}} \text{ (at first order)}.$$

PROOF. During Phase 2, when a processor P_k requests some work, a random task is sent among those that have not been processed yet. This task $T_{i,j}$ induces either the communication of one data block (if either a_i or b_j is already know at P_k) or 2 data blocks (but not 0 by construction).

More precisely, since tasks are sent at random and since P_k knows a fraction $x_k = \sqrt{\beta rs_k}(1 - \beta rs_k/4)$ of the elements of a and b at the end of Phase 1,

- a task induces the communication of one block with probability $\frac{2x_k}{1+x_k}$,

- a task induces the communication of two blocks with probability $\frac{1-x_k}{1+x_k}$.

so that the expected number of communications per task for P_k is

$$\frac{2x_k}{1+x_k} \times 1 + \frac{1-x_k}{1+x_k} \times 2 = \frac{2}{1+x_k}.$$

Moreover, since Phase 2 starts at the same instant on all processors and since processors are continuously processing tasks, P_k processes a fraction rs_k of the $e^{-\beta} N^2$ remaining tasks. The overall communication cost induced by Phase 2 is therefore given (on expectation and at first order) by

$$\mathcal{V}_{\text{PHASE2}} = e^{-\beta} N^2 \left(1 - \sqrt{\beta} \sum_k rs_k^{3/2}\right),$$

which achieves the proof of Lemma 5. $\square$

THEOREM 6. The ratio of the overall volume of communications to the lower bound if we switch between both phases when $e^{-\beta} N^2$ tasks remain to be processed is given by

$$\sqrt{\beta} + \frac{\beta^{3/2} \sum_k rs_k^{3/2}}{4 \sum_k rs_k^{1/2}} + e^{-\beta} N^2 \frac{1 - \sqrt{\beta} \sum_k rs_k^{3/2}}{\sum_k rs_k^{1/2}}.$$

Theorem 6 is a direct consequence of Lemma 4 and Lemma 5. Therefore, in order to minimize the overall amount of communications, we numerically determine the value of β that minimizes the above expression and then switch between Phases 1 and 2 when $e^{-\beta}N^2$ tasks remain to be processed.

3.4 Assessing the validity of the analysis through simulations

We have performed simulations to study the accuracy of the previous theoretical analysis, that is a priori valid only for large values of p and N/l, and to show how it is helpful to compute the threshold for DYNAMICOUTER2PHASES. The simulations have been done using an ad-hoc event based simulation tool, where processors request new tasks as soon as they are available, and tasks are allocated based on the given runtime dynamic strategy. Again, processor speeds are chosen uniformly in the interval $[10, 100]$. This degree of heterogeneity may seem excessive but we show in Section 3.5 that using a different heterogeneity model does not significantly impact the results. The communication amount of each strategy is normalized by the lower bound computed in Section 3.3. Figure 4 presents the results for vectors of 100 blocks and Figure 5 does the same for vectors of 1000 blocks.

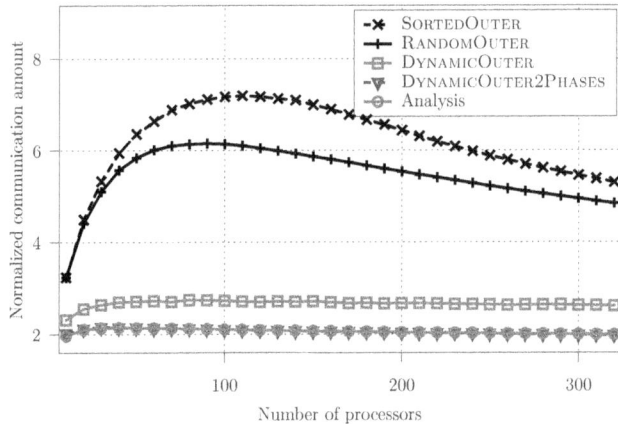

Figure 4: Communication amounts of all outer-product strategies for vectors of size $N/l = 100$ blocks ($(N/l)^2$ tasks).

In both figures, the analysis is extremely close to the performance of DYNAMICOUTER2PHASES (which makes them indistinguishable on the figures) and proves that our analysis succeed to accurately model our dynamic strategy, even for relatively small values of p and N/l. Moreover, we can see in Figure 5 that it is even more crucial to use a data-aware dynamic scheduler when N is large, as the ratio between the communication amount of simple random strategies (RANDOMOUTER and SORTEDOUTER) and dynamic data-aware schedulers (such as DYNAMICOUTER2PHASES) can be very large.

Our second objective is to show that the theoretical analysis that we propose can be used in order to accurately compute the threshold of DYNAMICOUTER2PHASES, i.e., that the β parameter computed earlier is close to the best one. To do this, we compare the communication amount of DYNAMICOUTER2PHASES for various values of the β parameter. Figure 6 shows the results for 20 processors and $N/l = 100$.

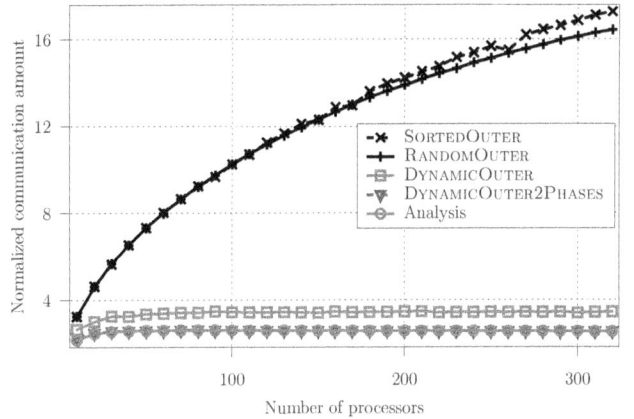

Figure 5: Communication amounts of all outer-product strategies for vectors of size $N/l = 1000$ blocks ($(N/l)^2$ tasks).

This is done for a single and arbitrary distribution of computing speeds, as it would make no sense to compute average values for different distributions since they would lead to different optimal values of β. This explains the irregular performance graph for DYNAMICOUTER2PHASES. This figure shows that in the domain of interest, i.e. for $3 \leq \beta \leq 6$, the analysis correctly fits to the simulations, and that the value of β that minimizes the analysis (here $\beta = 4.17$) lies in the interval of β values that minimize the communication amount of DYNAMICOUTER2PHASES. To compare to Figure 2, this corresponds to 98.5% of the tasks being processed in the first phase.

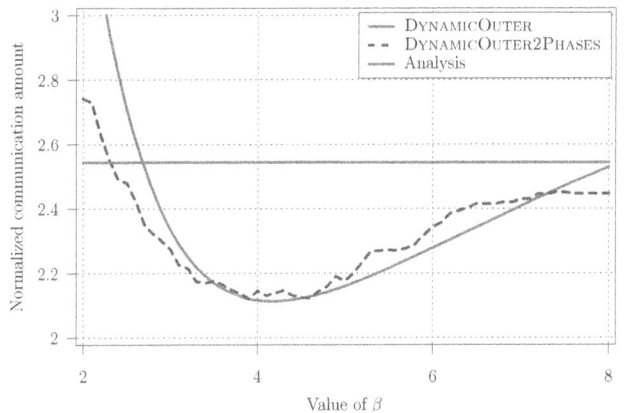

Figure 6: Communication amounts of Dynamic-Outer2Phases and its analysis for varying value of the β parameter which defines the threshold.

3.5 Impact of the heterogeneity

The speed distribution used in the previous experiments (speeds taken in the interval $[10, 100]$) may seem too heterogeneous to reasonably model actual computing platforms, where heterogeneity comes either from the use of a few classes of different processors (new and old machines, processor equipped with accelerators or not, etc.) or from the fact that machines are not dedicated, which implies stochastically variable processor speed. It is natural to ask whether the speed distribution impacts the ranking of the previous heuristics, or the accuracy of our analysis.

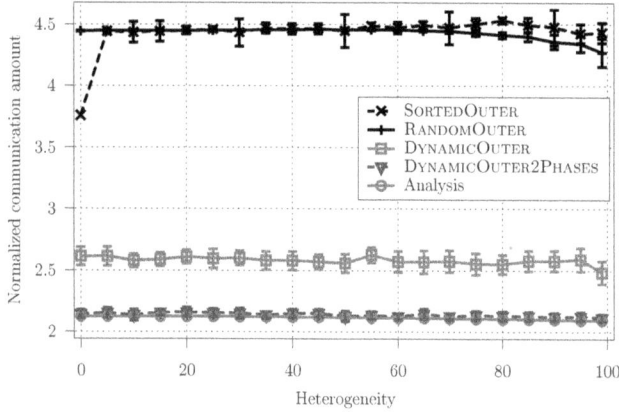

Figure 7: Behavior of the heuristics for outer product for different values of heterogeneity ($p = 20$ processors and $N/l = 100$ blocks). For a given value h of heterogeneity, processor speeds are taken uniformly at random in the interval $[100 - h, 100 + h]$.

Figure 7 presents the behavior of all previous heuristics for a varying range of heterogeneity. A heterogeneity of 0 means perfectly homogeneous computing speeds, while a heterogeneity of 100 means that the ratio between the smallest and the largest speeds is large. In this figure and the following one, error bars represents the standard deviations with 50 tries. We notice that the heterogeneity degree has very little impact on the relative amounts of communication of the studied heuristics.

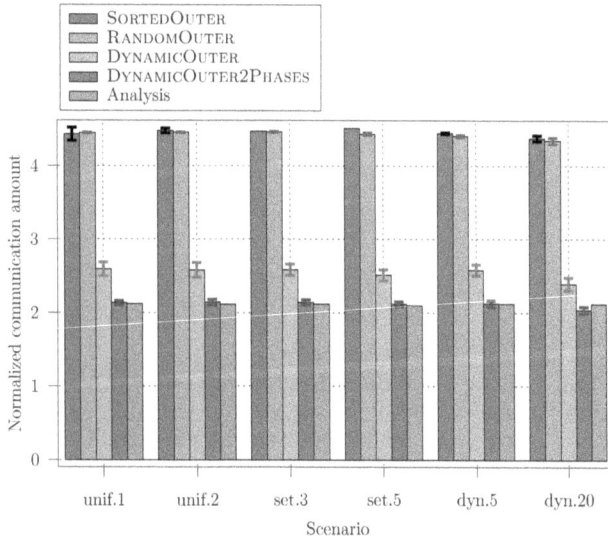

Figure 8: Behavior of the heuristics for outer product for different scenarios of heterogeneity ($p = 20$ processors and $N/l = 100$ blocks).

In Figure 8, we study the same heuristics using different scenarios:

- Scenarios unif.1 and unif.2 corresponds to the previous setting, with speeds taken uniformly at random in intervals $[80, 120]$ (unif.1) and $[50, 150]$ (unif.2).

- Scenarios set.3 and set.5 corresponds to the case when there are a few classes of processors with different speed. The speeds are then taken uniformly from the set of possible speeds: $(80, 100, 150)$ for set.3 or $(40, 80, 100, 150, 200)$ for set.5.

- Scenarios dyn.5 and dyn.20 corresponds to very simple dynamic settings. Each computing speed is first taken uniformly at random in interval $[80, 120]$. Then, after computing a task, a processor sees its computing speed randomly changed by up to 5% (dyn.5) or 20% (dyn.20).

This figure shows that neither the speed distribution nor the dynamic evolution of the speeds notably affect the performance of the heuristics.

3.6 Runtime estimation of β

In order to estimate the β parameter in the DYNAMIC-OUTER2PHASES strategy, it seems necessary to know the processing speed, as β depends on $\sum_k \sqrt{s_k / \sum_i s_i}$. However, we have noticed a very small deviation of β with the speeds. For example, in Figure 6, the value of β computed when assuming homogeneous speeds (4.1705) is very close to the one computed for heterogeneous speeds (4.1679).

For a large range of N/l and p values (namely, p in $[10, 1000]$ and $N/l \in [\max(10, \sqrt{p}), 1000]$), for processor speeds in $[10, 100]$, the optimal value for β goes from 1 to 6.2. However, for fixed values of N/l and p, the deviations among the β values obtained for different speed distributions is at most 0.045 (with 100 tries). Our idea is to approximate β with β_{hom} computed using a homogeneous platform with the same number of processors and with the same matrix size. The relative difference between β_{hom} and the average β of the previous set is always smaller than 5%. Moreover, the error on the communication volume predicted by the analysis when using homogeneous speeds instead of the actual ones is at most 0.1%. These figures are derived with the most heterogeneous speed distribution (speeds in $[10, 100]$) and thus hold for the other distributions of Section 3.5 as well.

This proves that even if our previous analysis ends up with a formula for β that depends on the computing speeds, in practice, only the knowledge of the matrix size and of the number of processors are actually needed to define the threshold β. Our dynamic scheduler DYNAMICOUTER2PHASES is thus totally agnostic to processor speeds.

4. MATRIX MULTIPLICATION

We adapt here the previous dynamic algorithm and its theoretical analysis to a more complex problem: the multiplication of two matrices.

4.1 Notations and dynamic strategies

We first adapt the notations to the problem of computing the product of two matrices $C = AB$. As in the previous section, we consider that all transfers and computations are performed using blocks of size $l \times l$, so that all three matrices are composed of N^2/l^2 blocks and $A_{i,j}$ denotes the block of A on the ith row and the jth column. The basic computation step is a task $T_{i,j,k}$, which corresponds to the update $C_{i,j} \leftarrow$

$C_{i,j} + A_{i,k}B_{k,j}$. To perform such a task, a processor has to receive the input data from A and B (of size $2l^2$), and to send the result (of size $(N/l)^2$) back to the master at the end of the computation. Thus, it results in a total amount of communication of $3\,(N/l)^2$. As previously, in order to minimize the amount of communications, our goal is to take advantage of the blocks of A, B and C that have already been sent to a processor P_u when allocating a new task to P_u. Note that at the end of the computation, all $C_{i,j}$s are sent back to the master that computes in turn the final results by adding the different contributions. This computational load is much smaller than computing the products $T_{i,j,k}$ and we will neglect it in what follows.

As we assume that processors work during the whole process, the load imbalance, *i.e.* the difference between the amount of work processed by P_i and what it should have processed given its speed is at most one block. Thus, a maximal block size l can easily be derived from a maximal load imbalance. The value of l must also be large enough to overlap communications of size $3l^2$ with computations of size l^3. As usual, the block size should also be large enough to benefit from BLAS effect and small enough so as to fit into caches. We assume that the optimal block size l is computed by the runtime environment.

The simple strategies RANDOMOUTER and SORTEDOUTER translate very easily for matrix multiplication into the strategies RANDOMMATRIX and SORTEDMATRIX. We adapt the DYNAMICOUTER strategy into DYNAMICMATRIX as follows. We ensure that at each step, for each processor P_u there exist sets of indices I, J and K such that P_u owns all values $A_{i,k}$, $B_{k,j}$, $C_{i,j}$ for $i \in I$, $j \in J$ and $k \in K$, so that it is able to compute all corresponding tasks $T_{i,j,k}$. When a processor becomes idle, instead of sending a single block of A, B and C, we choose a tuple (i,j,k) of new indices (with $i \notin I$, $j \notin J$ and $k \notin K$) and send to P_u all the data needed to extend the sets I, J, K with (i,j,k). This corresponds to sending $3 \times (2|I|+1)$ data blocks to P_u (note that $|I| = |J| = |K|$). In fact, blocks of C are not send by the master to the processor, but on the contrary will be sent back to the master at the end of the computation; however, this does not change the analysis since we are only interested in the overall volume of communications. Then, processor P_u is allocated all the unprocessed tasks that can be done with the new data. Algorithm 3 details this strategy.

As in the case of the outer product, when the number of remaining blocks to be processed becomes small, RANDOM-MATRIX strategy outperforms the DYNAMICMATRIX strategy. Therefore, we introduce the intermediate DYNAMIC-MATRIX2PHASES strategy that consists into two phases. During Phase 1, the DYNAMICMATRIX strategy is used. Then, when the number of remaining tasks becomes smaller than $e^{-\beta}N^3$ for a value of β that is to be determined, we switch to Phase 2 and use strategy RANDOMMATRIX. As in the case of the outer product, the theoretical analysis proposed in the next section will help us to determine the optimal value of β, *i.e.* the instant when to switch between phases in order to minimize the overall communication volume in the DYNAMICMATRIX2PHASES strategy.

4.2 Theoretical analysis of dynamic randomized strategies

In this section, our aim is to provide an analytical model for Algorithm DYNAMICMATRIX2PHASES similarly to what

---

Algorithm 3: DYNAMICMATRIX strategy.

while *there are unprocessed tasks* **do**

 Wait for a processor P_u to finish its task
 $I \leftarrow \{i$ such that P_u owns $A_{i,k}$ for some $k\}$
 $J \leftarrow \{i$ such that P_u owns $B_{k,j}$ for some $k\}$
 $K \leftarrow \{i$ such that P_u owns $A_{i,k}$ for some $i\}$
 Choose $i \notin I$, $j \notin J$ and $k \notin K$ uniformly at random
 Send the following data blocks to P_u:

 - $A_{i,k'}$ for $k' \in K \cup \{k\}$ and $A_{i',k}$ for $i' \in I \cup \{i\}$

 - $B_{k,j'}$ for $j' \in J \cup \{j\}$ and $B_{k',j}$ for $k' \in K \cup \{k\}$

 - $C_{i,j'}$ for $j' \in J \cup \{j\}$ and $C_{i',j}$ for $i' \in I \cup \{i\}$

 Allocate all tasks $\{T_{i',j',k'}$ with $i' = i$ or $j' = j$ or $k' = k\}$ that are not yet processed to P_u and mark them processed

---

has been done for Algorithm DYNAMICOUTER in Section 3.3. The analysis of both processes is in fact rather similar, so that we will mostly state the corresponding lemmas, the proofs being similar to those presented in Section 3.3.

In what follows, we will assume that N, the size of matrices A, B and C, is large and we will consider a continuous dynamic process whose behavior is expected to be close to the one of DYNAMICMATRIX2PHASES. In what follows, as in Section 3.3, we will concentrate on processor P_k whose speed is s_k and relative speed $rs_k = \frac{s_k}{\sum_i s_i}$. We will also denote by $C = A \times B$ the result of the matrix multiplication. Note that throughout this section, $A_{i,k}$ denotes the *element* of A on the ith row and jth column.

Let us assume that there exist 3 index sets I, J and K such that

- P_k knows all elements $A_{i,k}$, $B_{k,j}$ and $C_{i,j}$ for any $(i,j,k) \in I \times J \times K$.

- I, J and K have size y.

In Algorithm DYNAMICMATRIX2PHASES, at each step, P_k chooses to increase its knowledge by increasing y by l, which requires to receive $(2y+1)l$ elements of each A, B and C. As we did in Section 3.3, we will concentrate on $x = y/N$, and assuming that N is large, we will change the discrete process into a continuous process described by an ordinary differential equation depicting the evolution of expected values and we will rely on extensive simulations to assert that this approximation is valid.

In this context, let us consider that an elementary task $T(i,j,k)$ consists in computing $C_{i,j} \leftarrow C_{i,j} + A_{i,k}B_{k,j}$. There are N^3 such tasks. In what follows, we will denote by $g_k(x)$ the fraction of elementary tasks that have not been computed yet at the instant when P_k knows x^2 elements of A, B and C respectively, in the computational domain that does not include the tasks $T(i,j,k)$ such that $(i,j,k) \in I \times J \times K$ (this domain is equivalent to the "L"-shaped area for the outer product in Section 3.3). The following lemma enables to understand the dynamics of g_k (all proofs are omitted because they are very similar to those of Section 3.3).

LEMMA 7. $g_k(x) = (1 - x^3)^{\alpha_k}$, where $\alpha_k = \frac{\sum_{i \neq k} s_i}{s_k}$.

Let us now denote by $t_k(x)$ the time step such that index sets I, J and K have size x. Then,

LEMMA 8. $t_k(x) \sum_i s_i = 1 - N^2(1 - (1 - x^3)^{\alpha_k + 1})$.

Above equations well describe the dynamics of DYNAMIC-MATRIX2PHASES as long as it is possible to find elements of A, B and C that enable to compute enough unprocessed elementary tasks. On the other hand, as in the case of DYNAMICOUTER2PHASES, at the end, it is better to switch to another algorithm, where unprocessed elementary tasks $T(i, j, k)$ are picked up randomly, what requires possibly to send all three values of $A_{i,k}$, $B_{k,j}$ and $C_{i,j}$. In order to decide when to switch from one strategy to the other, let us introduce the additional parameter β.

As in the outer-product problem, a lower bound on the communication volume received by P_k can be obtained by considering that each processor has a cube of tasks $T_{i,j,k}$ to compute, proportional to its relative speed. The edge-size of this cube is thus $N \sqrt[3]{rs_k}$. To compute all tasks in this cube, P_k needs to receive a square of each matrix, that is $3N^2 rs_k^{2/3}$.

In order to determine when we should switch between Phase 1 and Phase 2, we can observe that if $x_k^3 = \beta rs_k - \beta^2/2rs_k^2$, then

$$t_k(x_k) \sum_i s_i = N^2(1 - e^{-\beta}(1 + o(rs_k))),$$

so that at first order, $t_k(x_k)$ is independent of k. The instant $t = \frac{N^2}{\sum_i s_i}(1 - e^{-\beta})$ is therefore chosen to switch between Phases 1 and 2.

As in the context of the outer product, we need to find the value of β that minimizes the volume of communications. If the switch occurs at time $t = \frac{N^2}{\sum_i s_i}(1 - e^{-\beta})$, then

- the volume of communications during Phase 1 is given by

$$3N^2 \beta^{2/3} \sum_k rs_k^{2/3} - 3N^2 \beta^{5/3} \sum_k rs_k^{5/3},$$

- the volume of communications during Phase 2 is given by

$$e^{-\beta} N^3 \left(1 - \beta^{2/3} \sum_k rs_k^{5/3}\right),$$

so that the total amount of communications with respect to the lower bound $3N^2 \sum rs_k^{2/3}$ is given by

$$\beta^{2/3} - \beta^{5/3} \frac{\sum_k rs_k^{5/3}}{\sum_k rs_k^{2/3}} + \frac{e^{-\beta} N}{\sum_k rs_k^{5/3}} \left(1 - \beta^{2/3} \sum_k rs_k^{5/3}\right).$$

4.3 Simulation Results

We have conducted extensive simulations to compare the performance of the dynamic strategies with the previous analysis. Figure 9 presents the results for matrices of size 40x40 and Figure 10 presents the results for matrices of size 100x100. As in previous simulations, processor speeds are chosen uniformly at random in the interval $[10, 100]$ and all amounts of communications have been normalized using the lower bound $3N^2 \sum_k rs_k^{2/3}$ on communications presented in the previous section.

As for the outer-product problem, we notice that data-aware strategies largely outperform simple strategies, and that DYNAMICMATRIX2PHASES is able to reduce the communication amount even more than DYNAMICMATRIX. When the number of processors is large enough (*i.e.* in our simulation setting, $p \geq 50$), our previous analysis is able to very accurately predict the performance of DYNAMICMATRIX-2PHASES.

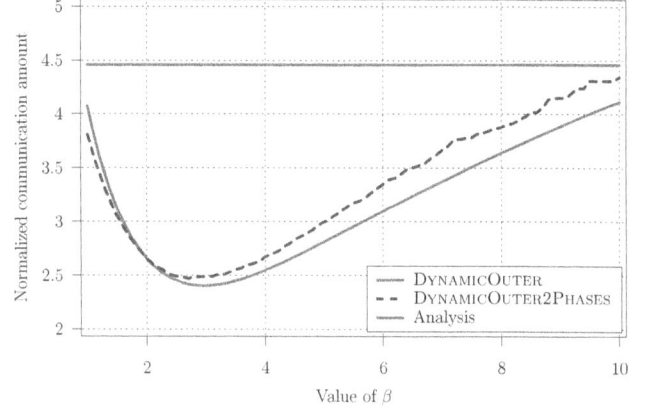

Figure 11: Communication amount of Dynamic-Matrix2Phases and its analysis for varying value of the β parameter which defines the threshold.

We also performed simulations of DYNAMICMATRIX2PHASES with varying values of β to check if the optimal value determined in the theoretical analysis actually minimizes the amount of communications. This is illustrated in Figure 11, for 100 processors, $N/l = 40$ and a fixed distribution of computing speeds. As for the outer product, we notice that the analysis accurately models the amount of communications of DYNAMICMATRIX2PHASES in the range of values of interest of β, and that the optimal value of β for the analysis (2.95) allows to obtain an amount of communications that is close to optimal. This corresponds to 94.7% of the tasks to be processed by the first phase of the algorithm. As for the outer product, we also notice that the value of β given by an analysis which is agnostic to processor speeds and assumes homogeneous speeds is very close to the optimal value (2.92 on this example).

5. CONCLUSION AND PERSPECTIVES

The contributions of this paper follow two directions. First, we have proposed randomized dynamic scheduling strategies for the outer product and the matrix multiplication kernels. We have proved that dynamic scheduling strategies that aim to place tasks on processors such that the induced amount of communications is as small as possible perform well. Second, we have been able to propose an Ordinary Differential Equation (ODE) whose solution describes very well the dynamics of the system. Even more important, we prove that the analysis of the dynamics of the ODE can be used in order to tune parameters and to inject some static knowledge which is useful to increase the efficiency of dynamic strategies.

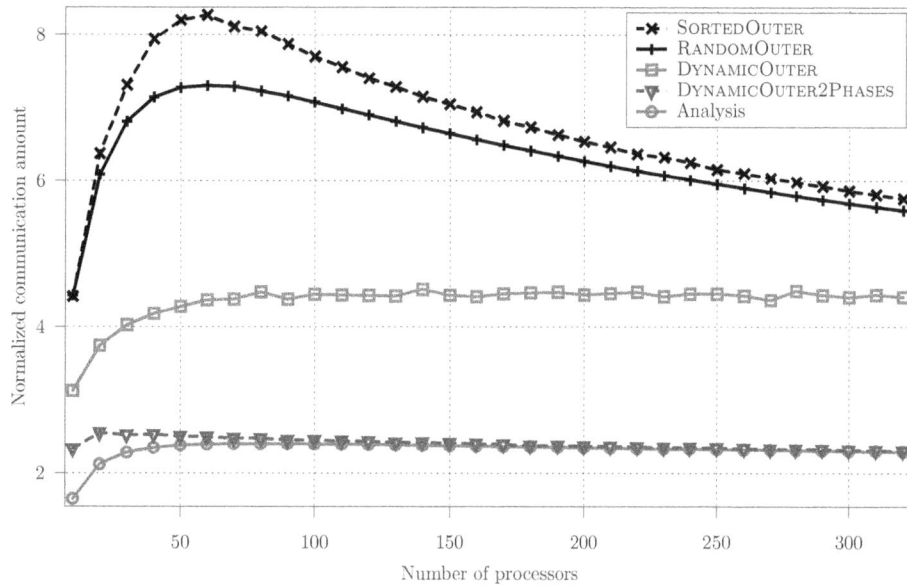

Figure 9: Communication amounts of all strategies for matrices of size $N/l = 40$ blocks ($N^3/l^3 = 64,000$ tasks).

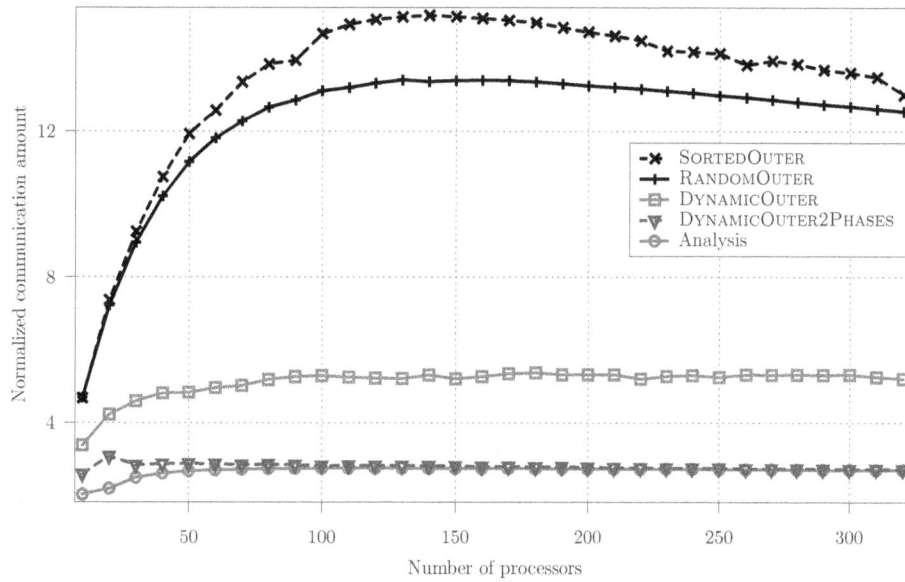

Figure 10: Communication amounts of all strategies for matrices of size $N/l = 100$ blocks ($N^3/l^3 = 1,000,000$ tasks).

A lot remains to be done in this domain, that we consider as crucial given the practical and growing importance of dynamic runtime schedulers. First, it would be of interest to be able to provide analytical models for a larger class of dynamic schedulers even in the case of independent tasks, and to analyze their behavior also in dynamic environments (when the performance of the resources is unknown and varies over time). Then, it would be very useful to extend the analysis to applications involving both data and precedence dependencies. Extending this work to regular dense linear algebra kernels such as Cholesky or QR factorizations would be a promising first step in this direction.

6. ACKNOWLEDGEMENT

This work has been partially supported by the *ANR SOL-HAR* project, funded by the French Research Agency.

7. REFERENCES

[1] C. Augonnet, S. Thibault, R. Namyst, and P.-A. Wacrenier. StarPU: a unified platform for task scheduling on heterogeneous multicore architectures. *Concurrency and Computation: Practice and Experience*, 23(2):187–198, 2011.

[2] O. Beaumont, V. Boudet, F. Rastello, and Y. Robert. Partitioning a square into rectangles: NP-completeness and approximation algorithms. *Algorithmica*, 34(3):217–239, 2002.

[3] O. Beaumont, H. Larcheveque, and L. Marchal. Non linear divisible loads: There is no free lunch. In *International Parallel and Distributed Processing Symposium, 2012*, pages 863–873. IEEE, 2012.

[4] M. Benaim and J.-Y. Le Boudec. A class of mean field interaction models for computer and communication systems. *Performance Evaluation*, 65(11):823–838, 2008.

[5] V. Berten and B. Gaujal. Brokering strategies in computational grids using stochastic prediction models. *Parallel Computing*, 33(4-5):238–249, 2007.

[6] G. Bosilca, A. Bouteiller, A. Danalis, M. Faverge, T. Herault, and J. J. Dongarra. PaRSEC: A programming paradigm exploiting heterogeneity for enhancing scalability. *IEEE Computing in Science and Engineering*, to appear. available online at http://www.netlib.org/utk/people/JackDongarra/PAPERS/ieee_cise_submitted_2.pdf.

[7] G. Bosilca, A. Bouteiller, A. Danalis, T. Herault, P. Lemarinier, and J. Dongarra. DAGuE: A generic distributed DAG engine for high performance computing. *Parallel Computing*, 38(1):37–51, 2012.

[8] J. Dean and S. Ghemawat. MapReduce: Simplified data processing on large clusters. *Communications of the ACM*, 51(1):107–113, 2008.

[9] N. Gast, B. Gaujal, and J.-Y. Le Boudec. Mean field for Markov decision processes: from discrete to continuous optimization. *IEEE Transactions on Automatic Control*, 57(9):2266–2280, 2012.

[10] T. Gautier, X. Besseron, and L. Pigeon. Kaapi: A thread scheduling runtime system for data flow computations on cluster of multi-processors. In *Proceedings of the 2007 International Workshop on Parallel Symbolic Computation*, PASCO '07, pages 15–23, New York, NY, USA, 2007. ACM.

[11] D. Gross, J. F. Shortle, J. M. Thompson, and C. M. Harris. *Fundamentals of Queueing Theory, 4th Edition*. John Wiley and Sons",, 2008.

[12] B. Kreaseck, L. Carter, H. Casanova, and J. Ferrante. Autonomous protocols for bandwidth-centric scheduling of independent-task applications. In *Proceedings of the 17th International Parallel and Distributed Processing Symposium (IPDPS'03)*. IEEE, 2003.

[13] M. Mitzenmacher. Analyses of load stealing models based on differential equations. In *Proceedings of the Tenth Annual ACM Symposium on Parallel Algorithms and Architectures*, SPAA '98, pages 212–221, New York, NY, USA, 1998. ACM.

[14] M. Mitzenmacher. How useful is old information? *IEEE Trans. Parallel Distrib. Syst.*, 11(1):6–20, 2000.

[15] M. Parashar and S. Hariri. *Autonomic computing: concepts, infrastructure, and applications*. CRC press, 2006.

[16] J. Planas, R. M. Badia, E. Ayguadé, and J. Labarta. Hierarchical task-based programming with StarSs. *International Journal of High Performance Computing Applications*, 23(3):284–299, 2009.

[17] H. Topcuoglu, S. Hariri, and M.-y. Wu. Performance-effective and low-complexity task scheduling for heterogeneous computing. *IEEE Transactions on Parallel and Distributed Systems*, 13(3):260–274, 2002.

Design and Evaluation of the GeMTC Framework for GPU-enabled Many-Task Computing

Scott J. Krieder,* Justin M. Wozniak,† Timothy Armstrong,§ Michael Wilde†‡
Daniel S. Katz,‡ Benjamin Grimmer,* Ian T. Foster,§†‡ Ioan Raicu*†
*Department of Computer Science, Illinois Institute of Technology
†Mathematics and Computer Science Division, Argonne National Laboratory
§Department of Computer Science, University of Chicago
‡Computation Institute, University of Chicago & Argonne National Laboratory

ABSTRACT

We present the design and first performance and usability evaluation of GeMTC, a novel execution model and runtime system that enables accelerators to be programmed with many concurrent and independent tasks of potentially short or variable duration. With GeMTC, a broad class of such "many-task" applications can leverage the increasing number of accelerated and hybrid high-end computing systems. GeMTC overcomes the obstacles to using GPUs in a many-task manner by scheduling and launching independent tasks on hardware designed for SIMD-style vector processing. We demonstrate the use of a high-level MTC programming model (the Swift parallel dataflow language) to run tasks on many accelerators and thus provide a high-productivity programming model for the growing number of supercomputers that are accelerator-enabled. While still in an experimental stage, GeMTC can already support tasks of fine (subsecond) granularity and execute concurrent heterogeneous tasks on 86,000 independent GPU warps spanning 2.7M GPU threads on the Blue Waters supercomputer.

Categories and Subject Descriptors

D.1.3 [**Programming Techniques**]: Concurrent Programming

Keywords

Many-task computing; GPGPU; CUDA; Accelerators; Hybrid execution; Workflow; Programming models; Execution models.

1. INTRODUCTION

This work explores methods for, and potential benefits of, applying the increasingly abundant and economical general-purpose graphics processing units (GPGPU) to a broader class of applications. It extends the utility of GPGPU from the class of heavily vectorizable applications to irregularly-structured many-task applications. Such applications are increasingly common, stemming from both problem-solving approaches (i.e., parameter sweeps, simulated annealing or branch-and-bound optimizations, uncertainty quantification) and application domains (climate modeling, rational materials design, molecular dynamics, bioinformatics).

In many-task computing (MTC) [1, 2], tasks may be of short (even subsecond) duration or highly variable (ranging from milliseconds to minutes). Their dependency and data passing characteristics may range from many similar tasks to complex, and possibly dynamically determined, dependency patterns. Tasks typically run to completion: they follow the simple input-process-output model of procedures, rather than retaining state as in web services or MPI processes.

Efficient MTC implementations are now commonplace on clusters, grids, and clouds. In recent years we have extended MTC to applications on homogeneous supercomputers, using tools such as Falkon [3], Swift [4], JETS [5], and Coasters [6]. Other programming models and tools that support MTC include MapReduce, volunteer computing [7], SLURM [8], and Cobalt [9], which allow supercomputer tasks to be subdivided into asynchronous subtasks [10]. All these approaches can benefit from the MTC-enabling accelerator work we describe here. The contributions of this work are as follows:

- Design and implementation of GeMTC, a framework enabling MTC workloads to run efficiently on NVIDIA GPUs.

- Improved dynamic GPU memory management, providing efficient scaling and a 10x improvement over native CUDA dynamic memory management.

- Integration of GeMTC with Swift, enabling a broad class of dataflow-based scientific applications, and improving programmability for both hybrid multicore hosts and extreme scale systems. Work is load balanced among large numbers of GPUs.

- Performance evaluation on synthetic benchmarks and a proxy code representing molecular dynamics simulation workloads.

This paper is organized as follows: Section 2 describes the challenges of many-task computing on GPGPUs. Section 3 describes the GeMTC framework and its underlying architecture. Section 4 describes Swift and its integration as a

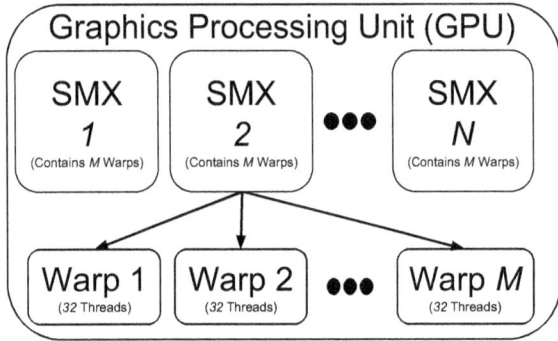

Figure 1: Diagram of GPU architecture hierarchy.

GeMTC programming model. Section 5 presents a performance evaluation, and Section 6 discusses related work. We summarize our contributions in Section 7 and briefly discuss related work.

2. CHALLENGES OF MANY-TASK COMPUTING ON GPGPUS

Our GeMTC work is motivated by the fact that with current mainstream programming models, a significant portion of GPU processing capabilities underutilized by MTC workloads. We advocate sending a larger number of smaller, concurrent, independent tasks to a GPU. The results presented here indicate that this approach enables higher utilization of GPU resources, greater concurrency, and hence higher many-task throughput.

2.1 NVIDIA GPUs and GPGPU Computing.

General-purpose computing on graphics processing units (GPGPU) allows a host CPU to offload a wide variety of computation, not just graphics, to a graphics processing unit (GPU). GPUs are designed for vector parallelism: they contain many lightweight cores designed to support parallel bulk processing of graphics data. GPGPU leverages this parallel architecture for nongraphic computations such as matrix multiplication. In the context of this paper, all references to GPU refer to this GPGPU approach. In addition to application speedup, other benefits to leveraging accelerators include power efficiency (improved Flops/watt) and cost savings (improved Flops/$).

As shown in Figure 1, a NVIDIA GPU (which dominates the GPGPU and HPC marketplace) is comprised of many Streaming Multiprocessors (SMXs). A SMX contains many warps, and each warp provides 32 concurrent threads of execution. All threads within a warp run in a Single Instruction Multiple Thread (SIMT) fashion. As we describe below, GeMTC schedules independent computations on the GPU at the warp level, a level of independent task concurrency not provided by any mainstream GPU programming model.

Our GeMTC work targets the latest generation of NVIDIA GPUs, specifically the Kepler K20X. This device has 14 SMXs with 192 cores per SMX, a maximum of 168 warps, and a total core count of 2,688. MTC workloads that send only single tasks, or small numbers of large tasks, to accelerator devices observe near-serialized performance, and leave a significant portion of device processor capability unused.

Ousterhout et al., [11] make a compelling argument for the pervasive use of tiny tasks in compute clusters. We apply a similar argument to motivate the GeMTC model of running many small independent tasks on accelerators. Driven by this tiny-task motivation, GeMTC provides an architecture for "overdecomposition" [12] of accelerator-resident tasks, which can then be tightly packed into a GPU to maximize efficiency and minimize time to solution. While Swift load balances tasks and applies compiler optimizations in support of overdecomposition, the user must write applications with suitably fine-grained tasks.

2.2 Mainstream GPU Support for MTC

The dominant CUDA and OpenCL GPGPU programming models both provide extensions to traditional programming languages such as C with added API calls to interact with accelerators. CUDA is supported by NVIDIA and works on NVIDIA GPUs. OpenCL is based on an open standard that aims to provide improved portability across a variety of accelerators and other compute devices. OpenACC is a newer pragma-based technology that is gaining momentum. As in OpenMP, OpenACC programmers provide hints to the compiler where they believe a computation would benefit from being offloaded to an accelerator. OpenACC is an open standard and aims to provide the portability of OpenCL while requiring less detailed knowledge of accelerator architecture than is required in CUDA and OpenCL programming. In many cases OpenACC may require significantly less coding, but early measurements (e.g., by Wienke et al. [13]) suggest that OpenACC is not yet capable of delivering equivalent performance.

Concurrent Kernels [14] is a CUDA feature that enables the developer to launch parallel work on a GPU. However, the maximum number of concurrent kernels is limited to 32, far less than the number of 168 independent warps provided by the latest Kepler GPUs. HyperQ and Dynamic Parallelism [15], recent CUDA enhancements introduced by NVIDIA with the Kepler architecture, are a step toward MTC support. HyperQ allows more parallel work to be sent to the GPU, while Dynamic Parallelism allows threads to spawn more threads on the device. The current model of GeMTC and Swift relies on communication between the CPU and GPU to drive tasks to and from the Swift script. If a task sent to GeMTC from Swift was represented by compact code and could be decomposed even further (e.g., loop unrolling) it is possible that GeMTC could utilize Dynamic Parallelism to dynamically launch new tasks and process the parent task with even more improved performance, but we leave that as future work. Most other programming models, however, still treat the GPU as a solution to large vector-oriented SIMD computations and do not adequately support the potential for speedup of many-task applications.

A primary motivation for our work on GeMTC is that none of these mainstream accelerator programming models provides the flexible support for independent concurrent tasks required by many-task applications. In order to effectively utilize an accelerator, MTC applications with complex task dependencies need task results rapidly returned from device to host so that the application can process its dataflow-driven dependencies. To the best of our knowledge, no solution prior to GeMTC offers this capability.

Figure 2(A) illustrates why many-task computing workloads experience low efficiencies through Concurrent Kernels, the best available standard CUDA concurrency model for independent tasks launched by the host. In this model, tasks must be submitted at the same time, and no additional tasks can be submitted until all tasks are complete. With unbalanced task durations, a significant number of GPU processor cores will be underutilized. In addition, to process workflows with complex dependencies, the developer must group tasks into batches and block on batch completion before executing dependent kernels, an inadequate approach for supporting heterogeneous concurrent tasks. Figure 2(B) demonstrates how GeMTC provides support for heterogeneous tasks by treating every warp worker as an independently operating SIMD compute device. Because the warps are operating independently they are able to pick up work immediately rather than block on other warps for completion. Figure 2(C) demonstrates how overdecomposition can be utilized by GeMTC to pack tiny tasks neatly into the GPU, maximizing device core utilization and reducing application time to solution.

3. GEMTC ARCHITECTURE

Given that our target test bed consisted of NVIDIA GPUs and that we wanted to examine the GPU at the finest granularity possible, we opted to implement our framework using CUDA. This decision allowed us to work at the finest granularity possible but limited our evaluation to NVIDIA based hardware. While GeMTC was originally developed on NVIDIA CUDA devices, its architecture is general, and has also been implemented on the Intel Xeon Phi [16]. The Phi, however, represents a different accelerator architecture, meriting separate study, and is not addressed in this paper.

Figure 3 shows a high-level diagram of GeMTC driven by tasks generated by the Swift parallel functional dataflow language (described in Section IV). GeMTC launches a daemon on the GPU that enables independent tasks to be multiplexed onto warp-level GPU workers. A work queue in GPU memory is populated from calls to a C-based API, and GPU workers pick up and execute these tasks. After a worker has completed a computation, the results are placed on an outgoing result queue and returned to the caller.

3.1 Kernel Structure and Task Descriptions

A key element of GeMTC is the daemon launched on the GPU, named the Super Kernel, which enables many hardware level workers (at the warp level) on the GPU. A work queue in GPU memory is populated from calls to a C API, and GPU workers pick up and execute these tasks. After a worker has completed a computation, the results are placed on an outgoing result queue and returned to the caller.

Within traditional GPU programming, a user defined function that runs on the GPU is called a *kernel*. An application may define many GPU kernels, and application logic may be written to execute some or all kernels in parallel. These *concurrent kernels* are a key technology in the GeMTC framework. Once the GeMTC framework is initialized, the *Super Kernel* daemon is started, the memory management system is set up, and calls can begin to Application Kernels (*App-Kernels*). The Super Kernel gathers hardware information from the GPU and dynamically starts the maximum number of workers available on that GPU. A worker consists of a single warp, and therefore the maximum number of workers is equal to the maximum number of warps.

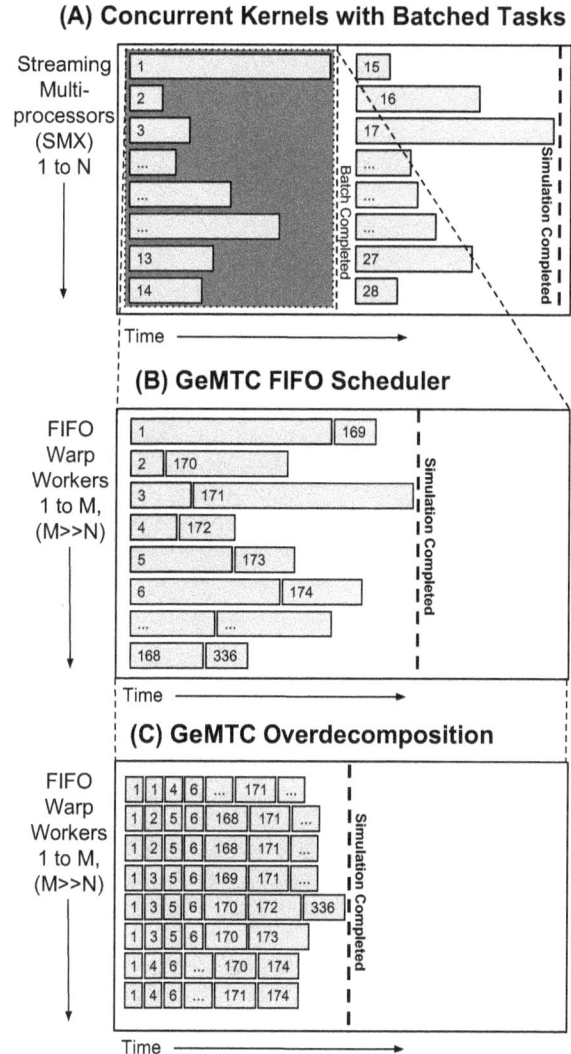

(A) Concurrent Kernels with Batched Tasks

(B) GeMTC FIFO Scheduler

(C) GeMTC Overdecomposition

Figure 2: GeMTC FIFO scheduler processes tasks as soon as they are available, rather than blocking on batches for completion. The warps required to execute cases (B) and (C) are provided by all the streaming multiprocessor's within the shaded area of (A). While the hardware available remains the same, the number of parallel channels is increased for the amount of concurrent parallel work.

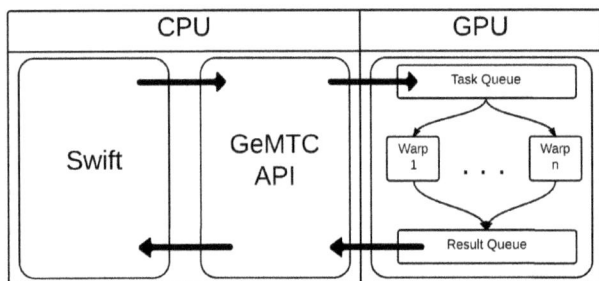

Figure 3: Flow of a task in GeMTC.

```
1    __device__ void MatrixMultiply(void *boxed_input)
2    {
3      //  calibrate for warp size
4      int warp_size = 32;
5      int thread = threadIdx.x % warp_size;
6      //  unbox host parameters
7      float* inputParams = (float*)boxed_input;
8      int matrixWidth = inputParams[0];
9      int matrixSize = matrixWidth * matrixWidth;
10     float *matrixA = inputParams+1;
11     float *matrixB = matrixA + matrixSize;
12     float *matrixOut = matrixA + 2 * matrixSize;
13     //  compute Matrix Multiplication
14     for (unsigned int i = thread; i < matrixWidth;
15        i=i+warp_size){
16       for (unsigned int j = 0; j < matrixWidth; j++) {
17         float sum = 0;
18         for (unsigned int k = 0; k < matrixWidth; k++) {
19   float a = matrixA[i * matrixWidth + k];
20   float b = matrixB[k * matrixWidth + j];
21   sum += a * b;
22         }
23         //  result location from input parameters
24         matrixOut[i * matrixWidth + j ] = sum;
25       }
26     }
27   }
```

Figure 4: GeMTC Mat-Mul AppKernel

Table 1: GeMTC API

API Call	Functionality Provided
gemtc(Setup/Cleanup)	(Start/Stop) GeMTC
gemtc(Push/Poll)	(Submit/Return) Tasks
gemtcMemcpyHostToDevice	Memory Copy
gemtcMemcpyDeviceToHost	Memory Copy
gemtcGPU(Malloc/Free)	(Allocate/Free) Memory

AppKernels are the computations that are executed by a GeMTC worker. The AppKernels are modular in design, and users can quickly contribute to the AppKernel Library by writing their own AppKernels based on pre-existing templates. A major appeal of the GeMTC framework is the decomposition of the GPU programming model. Instead of an application launching hundreds or thousands of threads, which could quickly become more challenging to manage, GeMTC AppKernels are optimized at the warp level, meaning the programmer and AppKernel logic are responsible for managing only 32 threads in a given application. Furthermore, run-time logic can be used to control concurrency of tasks to ensure that GPU cores are kept utilized without exhausting the GPU memory.

The *Task Description* is a C struct that contains relevant information for executing an AppKernel as a task on GeMTC. The Task Description is passed from a client via the GeMTC API (e.g., by Swift) to the GPU and queued with parameters on the device to the input queue or queued with task results on the outgoing result queue.

Figure 4 shows how a sample AppKernel could be written to compute a naive square matrix multiplication through GeMTC. Swift stubs have marshaled AppKernel parameters into a single boxed parameter. Therefore, after calibrating for warp size, the first step is to unbox the parameters. After executing an algorithm optimized for the warp size, the result is stored in a location identified from unboxing the input parameters. The result is then placed on an outgoing result queue, and the warp is ready to pick up new work.

3.2 GeMTC API

The GeMTC API is a C-based API which consists of eight major functions identified in Table 1. Figure 5 uses a simple molecular dynamics (MD) example to demonstrate how a user can leverage the GeMTC API to launch a simulation on the GPU. For the MD example, the user defines the initial universe of molecules as a parameter to the MD function. Once these parameters have been transferred into GPU memory the user pushes the task to the GPU along with all the information needed to create the task description on the device. The push operation contains, as parameters, the four pieces of data necessary to construct the task description; in this case, TaskType = MDLite, TASK_ID is set to a unique integer value (for tracking the task throughout its lifetime), numThreads = 32, and *params = a pointer to device memory where the task parameters are stored.

At this point the user can begin polling for a result. The precompiled MD AppKernel already knows how to pack and unpack the function parameters from memory; and once the function completes, the result is packed into memory and placed on the result queue. When the gemtcPoll function returns a result, the user can then unpack the memory and move to the next operation. The gemtcPoll function does not block on a specific task, and it automatically pops any completed task(s) off the result queue. This strategy is explained in further detail in the Task Bundling subsection. In addition, the example shown in Figure 5 is specific to users leveraging the C API. It is expected that end users will utilize high-level Swift scripts to launch their tasks on GeMTC. The calls described above are implicitly handled by the GeMTC and Swift integration, as explained in further detail in Section 4.

3.3 Queues, Tasks, and Memory Management

GeMTC manages two queues on the device. The *Incoming Work Queue* is populated by calls to the GeMTC API and contains tasks that are ready to execute. The tasks in this queue contain a *TaskDescription* and the necessary parameters to execute the task. Both in-memory queues are configured as circular linked-lists with pointers indicating the front and rear of the queue. When a worker picks up a task, it will dequeue from the front, and any new work is placed at the rear. Figure 6 demonstrates how workers interact with the queues.

```
 1   # include "gemtc.cu"
 2   main(){
 3     //  Start GeMTC
 4     gemtcSetup(QUEUE_SIZE);
 5     //  Allocate device memory
 6     device_params = gemtcGPUMalloc(MALLOC_SIZE);
 7     //  Populate device memory
 8     gemtcMemcpyHostToDevice(device_params,
 9       host_params, MALLOC_SIZE);
10     //  Push a task to the GPU
11     gemtcPush(MD_Lite, NUM_THREADS,
12         TaskID, device_params);
13     //  Poll for completed results
14     gemtcPoll(TaskID, pointer);
15     //  Copy back results
16     gemtcMemcpyDeviceToHost(host_params,
17         pointer, MALLOC_SIZE);
18     //  Free GPU memory
19     gemtcGPUFree(pointer);
20     //  Shutdown GeMTC
21     gemtcCleanup();
22   }
```

Figure 5: Code sample of GeMTC API.

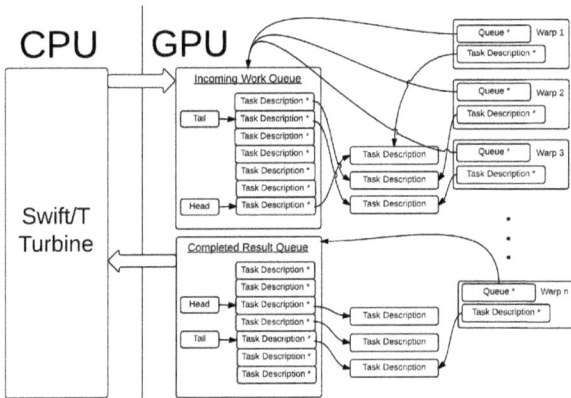

Figure 6: GPU Workers interacting with queues.

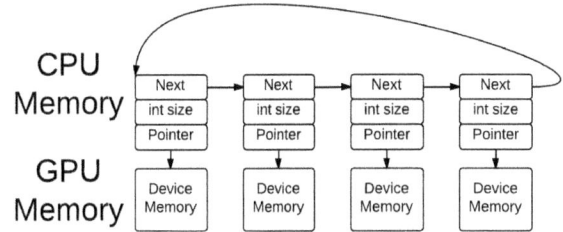

Figure 7: Memory mapping of free memory available to the device.

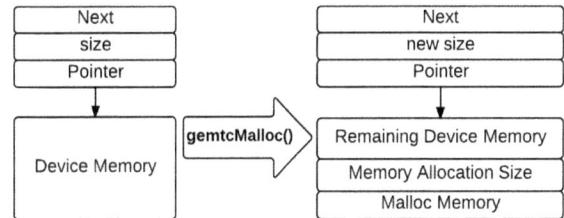

Figure 8: Result of gemtcMalloc on free memory.

The GeMTC framework requires efficient device memory allocation on a per task basis. Each task enqueued requires at least two device allocations: the first for the task itself and the second for parameters and results. The existing CUDA memory management system was not designed for a large number of independent memory allocations. With traditional CUDA programming models the current best practice is to allocate all memory needed by an application at launch time and then manually manage and reuse this memory as needed.

To reduce the large overhead of individual memory allocations for MTC workloads, GeMTC includes a sub-allocator designed to efficiently handle many requests for dynamic allocation. The sub-allocator uses the existing CUDA malloc to allocate large contiguous pieces of device memory, allocating more as needed. Then pointers to these free chunks and their sizes are stored in a circular linked list on the CPU (see Figure 7). This list is ordered by increasing device address to allow for easy memory coalescing of adjacent memory chunks.

When a GeMTC memory allocation request is sent from the host to the GPU, the sub-allocator will traverse the list and select the first chunk of free device memory meeting the allocation requirements. Figure 8 demonstrates how the header is then updated to reflect the remaining free device memory available in that chunk. This operation runs in the same order of time as a single memory copy to the device.

Upon freeing device memory, the header is read to identify the size of the chunk. Then it is added to the list of free memory in the correct location. If there is any free consecutive memory, the chunk is coalesced to provide a single larger contiguous chunk of memory. The operation to free device memory takes roughly the same amount of time as reading the header (i.e., a device memory copy).

Both malloc() and free() within GeMTC's memory management run in $O(n)$, where n is the length of the free memory list. In addition, the size of the list is proportional to the amount of memory fragmentation since each element is recorded as a separate chunk of memory. Because malloc and free both need to write and read to the GPU memory, these operations may scale poorly under workloads with high fragmentation. However, the MTC workloads we examine show no signs of high fragmentation. The original cudaMalloc ran in ~100 microseconds, and our gemtcMalloc runs in ~10 microseconds.

To optimize the GeMTC framework for fine-grained tasks, we have implemented a task-bundling system to reduce the amount of communication between the host and GPU. The main bottleneck for obtaining high task throughput through GeMTC is the latency associated with writing a task to the GPU DRAM memory. This bundling system as shown in Figure 9 creates a buffer of tasks that need to be written to the GPU, and flushes it periodically or when it is full. This

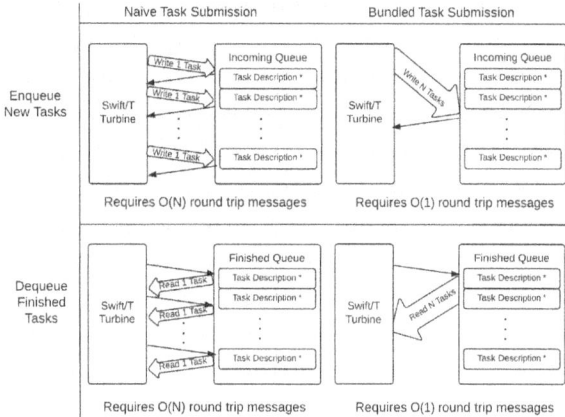

Figure 9: GeMTC implicitly bundles tasks to efficiently utilize PCI bandwidth and latency.

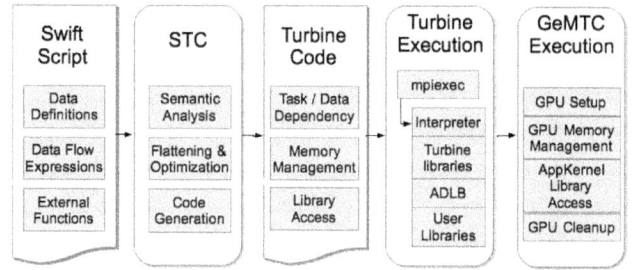

Figure 10: Swift/T stack including GeMTC.

whole buffer can be written to the device in a single copy. Similarly, results of finished tasks can be read from device memory in bulk. The performance improvements of this optimization are substantial. With no bundling (buffer size of one), GeMTC is able to run approximately 6,000 tasks per second on a single GPU. With bundling of 100 task groups, we achieve 22,000 tasks per second, more than a 3x increase in throughput. This optimization allows GeMTC to support many more fine-grained tasks.

4. SWIFT: DATAFLOW EXECUTION AND PROGRAMMING MODEL FOR MTC

Swift [4] is an *implicitly parallel functional dataflow* programming language that is proving increasingly useful to express the higher-level logic of scientific and engineering applications. In this work, we enable Swift to serve as a high-level, high-productivity programming language for hybrid CPU/GPU applications, paving the way for a seamless programming environment for extreme-scale systems composed of hybrid, accelerated nodes.

Many important application classes and programming techniques that are driving the requirements for such extreme-scale systems include branch and bound, stochastic programming, materials by design, and uncertainty quantification. All these classes can be productively expressed as many-task dataflow programs. The dataflow programming model of the Swift parallel scripting language can elegantly express, through implicit parallelism, the massive concurrency demanded by these applications while retaining the productivity benefits of a high-level language. Swift programs can be written with little or no experience in parallel programming, making it a productive language for scientists and engineers to leverage parallel systems.

Swift was originally developed as a scripting language for executing scripts composed from the execution of ordinary application programs on distributed systems such as clusters, grids, and clouds [17]. In this mode, a Swift interpreter, written in Java, executes on a single (possibly multicore) host, and sends work to distributed systems using a variety of "providers" that interface with remote systems.

When using its own resource provisioner [6] Swift is capable of sending approximate 500 tasks per second to a set of resources. When using Falkon [3], Swift achieved over 1,000 tasks per second.

To overcome the limits of this centralized single-node program evaluation model, a new Swift implementation named Swift/T [18] was implemented to achieve extreme scalability. Its innovations are a dataflow engine that provides highly parallel, distributed-memory evaluation; a data store that enables distributed access to memory-resident objects; and a load balancer for scalable low-latency task distribution to systems with millions of cores. While the original Swift language could only specify the execution of application programs as its leaf tasks, and only return files from these tasks, Swift/T enables finer-grained programming of in-memory functions that pass in-memory data objects. Performance (and granularity) has been improved by four orders of magnitude beyond the centralized Swift system, to > 15M tasks/sec (achieved on 128K integer cores of Blue Waters). This enables Swift to express a far broader set of applications, and makes it a productive coordination language for hybrid CPU+accelerator nodes and systems.

GeMTC Integration with Swift

The integration with Swift provides many mutual benefits for both Swift and GeMTC. The four boxes on the left side of Figure 10 show the original Swift/T stack before adding GeMTC support. Users write high-level Swift scripts that are compiled by STC [19] into code which is then executed by Turbine [20]. The final box on the right illustrates how GeMTC fits into the Swift/T stack. Once code has been generated and ready for execution, the Turbine runtime uses the GeMTC API to establish memory for tasks, move tasks into the GPU, and return results from the GPU back to the high level Swift script. Currently each GPU is dedicated to one Swift application. Swift provides logging information for all application runs to allow programmers to pinpoint errors and evaluate safety/reliability issues.

All the GeMTC API calls are managed dynamically within the Turbine worker node of the Swift runtime environment. Thus, the user's Swift application can simply call any function mapped to an AppKernel from the high level Swift program. Figure 11 shows an example of how the user would write a Swift application to utilize a set of GPUs through GeMTC.

Data transfers overlap with ongoing GPU computations implicitly and automatically. And because the GeMTC API calls are handled at the Turbine worker level, the Swift programmer is freed from the burden of writing complex mem-

```
 1 | import gemtc;
 2 | main
 3 | {
 4 |   float input_array[];
 5 |   float result_array[];
 6 |
 7 |   input_array = populate_array(SIZE);
 8 |   result_array = gemtc_mdlite(
 9 |       MD_CONFIGURATIONS, input_array);
10 | }
```

Figure 11: Swift script launching GeMTC.

ory management code for the GPU. Overlapping data transfer with compute is a common way to achieve increased accelerator performance, and the GeMTC + Swift stack provides this functionality automatically.

Integrating GeMTC with Swift allows GeMTC to launch on very large sets of cluster nodes with very low overhead. Swift automatically performs load balancing across all worker CPUs and across nodes, while GeMTC is optimized from the CPU-GPU level down to the GPU warps.

5. PERFORMANCE EVALUATION

This section evaluates the GeMTC framework with a set of AppKernels from the GeMTC AppKernel Library. AppKernels are CUDA device functions that have been tuned to deliver high performance under MTC workloads. AppKernels have been precompiled into the GeMTC framework.

We work with a lightweight molecular dynamics simulation called MDLite. We first evaluate MDLite at the level of a single GPU warp and then over all warps in the GPU. We conclude with an analysis of MDLite over multiple XK7 nodes and examine a set of simple adder benchmarks to highlight throughput and efficiency.

The target test bed for this work is the Blue Waters HPC resource at NCSA. Blue Waters contains ∼20K Cray XE6 CPU based nodes and ∼4K Cray XK7 GPU nodes. While future work aims to address heterogeneous scheduling, this work focuses on the XK7 nodes. Each node contains a single AMD 6276 Interlagos Processor with 8 Bulldozer cores and 16 integer scheduling units. In addition, each node contains 32 GB of memory. Each XK7 node is equipped with a Kepler K20X GPU with 6 GB of memory, 2688 CUDA cores, a peak GPU performance of 1.31 TF (double precision), and a memory bandwidth of 200 GB/s [21].

5.1 Molecular Dynamics

MDLite is a simple molecular dynamics simulation, based on an educational code [22]. The user specifies the number of particles in a "universe" along with their starting positions, the number of dimensions, and a starting mass. MDLite runs a simulation that determines how the potential and kinetic energy in the system changes as the particles change position. MDLite then simulates a particle system with coupled, time-step-discretized differential equations. A MDLite task consists of loading the simulation into GPU memory, running the simulation, and returning the results to Swift. The MDLite workflow may contain dependencies as demonstrated in Figure 12, where simulations exchange data before continuing execution. MDLite is an excellent proxy application for Protlib-2 and InsEnds [23] and demonstrates data movement and fine-grained task execution on accelerators.

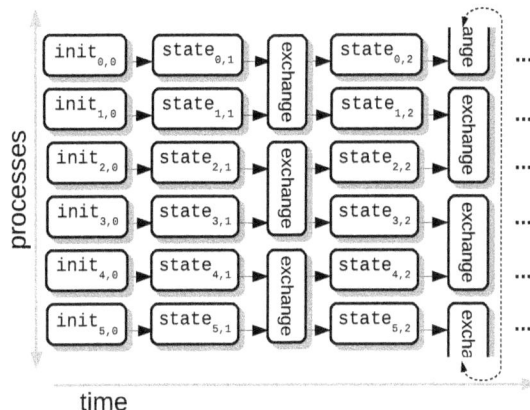

Figure 12: Diagram demonstrating execution model for molecular dynamics with replica exchange. Short simulation segments are run in an ensemble with asynchronous data exchanges [24].

GPU computing traditionally involves managing thousands of threads of execution. First, we scale down to show that it is indeed possible to gain increased performance at a low level using a varied of number of active threads within a single warp. Figure 13 demonstrates that GeMTC is capable of scaling within a single warp. By varying the number of active threads included in a warp computation, we prove that for the right application it could indeed benefit from the 32 threads in a GPU warp. In this figure, 1 thread is a lower bound on performance, and 32 threads are the maximum number of threads available within a single warp. Figure 14 highlights the speedup obtained by varying the level of concurrency for MDLite within a single warp of execution. While the walltime of MDLite successfully decreases as more threads are added, the speedup obtained is significantly less than ideal after 8 threads are active within a single warp. While improved performance could certainly be achieved with added development cycles of fine tuning, we argue for the overdecomposition of large tasks into smaller, easier-to-manage MTC tasks. By identifying the task granularity that observes the best combined performance of walltime and thread utilization, we can run many tasks of that granularity on the GPU.

Scaling an application down to the level of concurrency available within a single warp can provide the highest level of thread utilization for some applications. Next, we evaluate how efficient many of these independent warp workers are when working in parallel across a single GPU.

Figure 15 evaluates a varied number of MDLite simulations running over a K20X GPU. In this experiment a single warp provides a baseline and lower bound on performance. This baseline is achieved by running a single task on a single warp and varying the input vector size from several hundred elements to several thousand. The plot lines in Figure 15 represent active GPU workers in executing the MD application, conveying GeMTC scalability from 1 to the maximum number of GPU workers.

As more workers are added, there is increasingly higher demand on the in-memory queues; specifically, the two locks that keep each queue synchronized become bottlenecks for

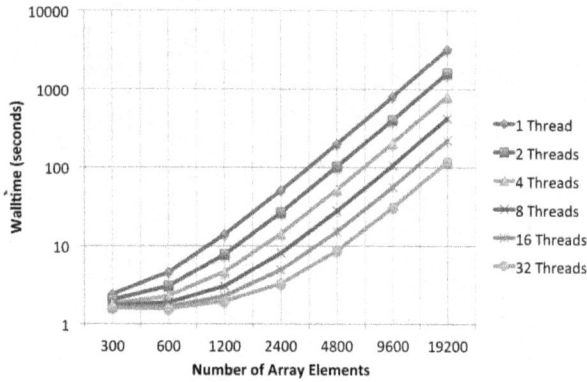

Figure 13: GeMTC scales MD within a single warp and achieves decreased walltime as the level of concurrency within the computation is increased.

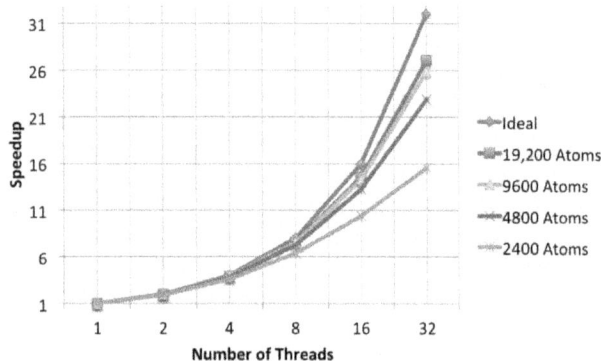

Figure 15: GeMTC utilization on the K20X running MD codes with varied worker counts from 1 to 168.

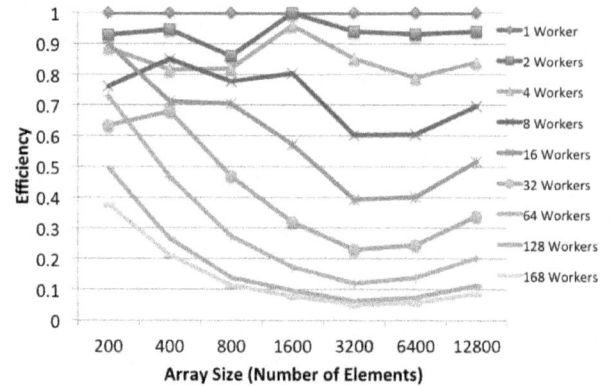

Figure 14: Speedup achieved with varied concurrency (1-32 threads) within a single warp, launching MDLite tasks from 2,500 atoms to 19,200 atoms.

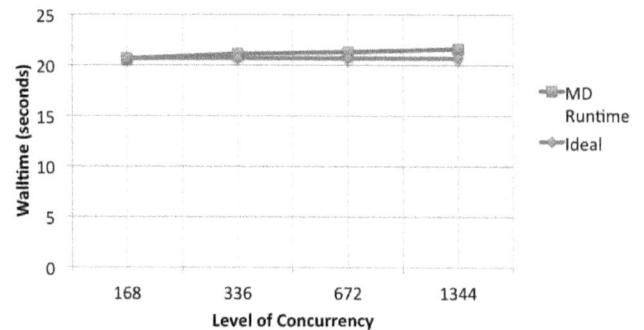

Figure 16: GeMTC and MDLite scaling over 1344 workers on Blue Waters.

the system. We anticipate that implementing a lock-free queueing system on the device will alleviate a significant portion of the latency and provide improved performance; this is left as future work.

We have shown GeMTC is capable of scaling down to manage threads both within a single warp and across multiple warps within a single GPU. Next we highlight how the integration with Swift enables GeMTC to scale across multiple XK7 nodes within Blue Waters. Figure 16 is a multinode scaling experiment where the number of simulations is set equal to the number of workers. At each data point there are two times as many workers as the previous, so we run twice as much work. In an ideal system without any overheads we would expect a flat line demonstrating the ability to conduct the same amount of work at each step. Even after 8 nodes we achieve 96% utilization. Future work aims to evaluate our system at even larger scales on Blue Waters.

5.2 Throughput and Efficiency

Next, we evaluate GeMTC with a simple adder benchmark. The benchmark launches a series of additions on the GPU, for which we have calculated expected runtimes. Af-

terwards, we can easily measure the efficiency and overhead of our system: efficiency = (expected runtime/observed runtime). Expected runtime is calculated during a short calibration phase where kernel runtime is measured with and without our framework.

First, a CPU version of the simple adder is executed through Swift/T on XE6 nodes. The results shown in Figure 17 confirm that Swift/T is highly capable of driving fine-grained work over many nodes on Blue Waters. In particular, tasks with runtimes exceeding 10 ms observe high efficiencies well over 10K processes (where 1 process is running per core) and fits our target duration and scale for the GPU evaluation.

Secondly, we evaluate Swift on a single GPU equipped node to calculate a per node throughput rate for GPU tasks. Figure 18 highlights throughput rates for Swift and GeMTC on a Kepler K20X. In this benchmark the maximum number of available GeMTC workers is enabled (168). Figure 19 demonstrates that Swift + GeMTC is capable of driving a high throughput of fine grain GPU work over many nodes on Blue Waters. As shown in Figure 19 we obtain ~70% of ideal throughput with 10,000-way concurrency. Next, we evaluate GeMTC efficiencies on a single XK7 node with workloads comprising varied task granularities. Figure 20 highlights the single-node efficiency of GeMTC running with

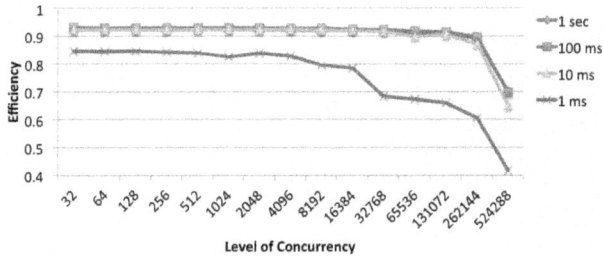

Figure 17: Fine-grained Swift CPU workloads on Blue Waters, demonstrating the ability to drive fine-grained workloads with high efficiency.

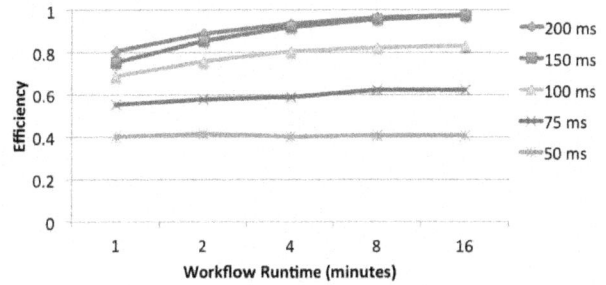

Figure 18: Swift driving GeMTC tasks on a Cray XK7(K20X equipped) node of Blue Waters.

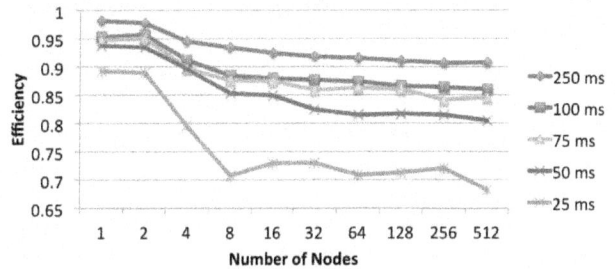

Figure 20: Single-node efficiency on Blue Waters for parallel work with varied task granularities running 168 GPU workers.

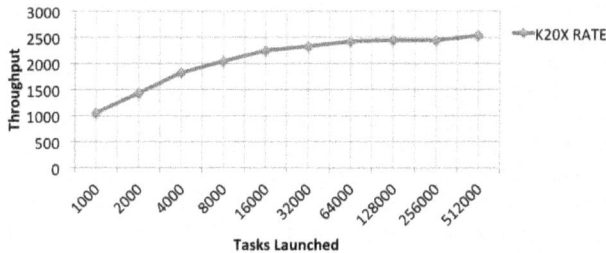

Figure 21: GeMTC + Swift efficiency for varying task granularities up to 512 nodes on Blue Waters with a single GeMTC worker active per node.

168 active workers per GPU. At a single node we continue to observe high efficiencies for tasks with runtimes exceeding ~150ms. In both Figure 19 and Figure 20 the tasks measuring throughput are simple summations with small data parameters (and thus include data movement overhead).

Figure 21 demonstrates an upper bound of GeMTC by launching efficiency workloads on multiple GPU nodes with only a single active GeMTC worker per GPU. We next enable 168 GeMTC warp workers per GPU (the maximum) and evaluate the efficiency of workflows with varied task granularities up to 86k individually operating GPU workers of Blue Waters. After adding 167 additional workers per GPU we do require longer lasting tasks to achieve high efficiency. We attribute this drop in performance to greater worker contention on the device queues and the fact that Swift must now drive 168 times the amount of work per

node. In Figure 22 we observe that tasks exceeding ~1 second achieve high efficiency up to scales of 40K workers. Although we have not yet identified the cause for this drop in performance, we expect that the performance degradation at extreme levels of concurrency comes from the loading of shared libraries from the remote parallel filesystem. In future work we will continue to improve systemwide performance by reducing the reliance on dynamic loadable shared libraries and through larger scale evaluation on all 4K XK7 nodes of Blue Waters.

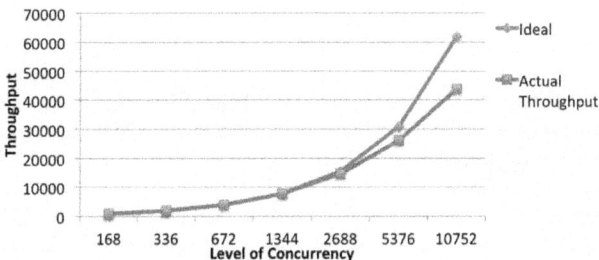

Figure 19: GeMTC + Swift Throughput over 10,000 GPU workers.

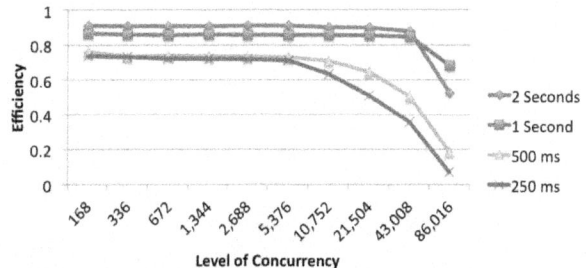

Figure 22: Efficiency for workloads with varied task granularities up to 86K independent warps of Blue Waters. 168 active workers/GPU.

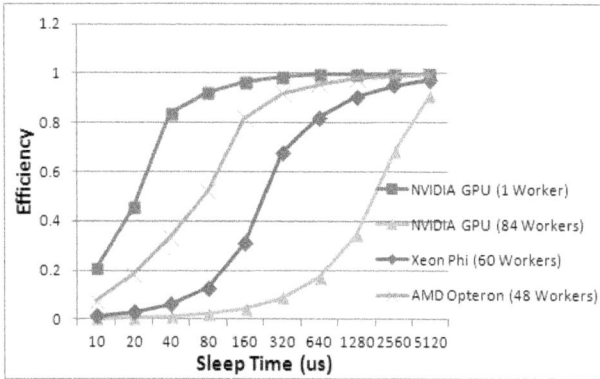

Figure 23: Microbenchmark measuring efficiency for tasks with varied granularities on a variety of hardware: a 1344-core NVIDIA GPU, a 60-core Intel Xeon Phi, and a 48-core AMD Opteron SMP.

5.3 Preliminary MTC Xeon Phi Results

We have also gathered preliminary results for supporting MTC workloads on the Intel Xeon Phi Coprocessor. As shown in Figure 23 we can achieve the same level of efficiency with shorter running tasks (50% shorter) on a Xeon Phi compared with a GTX-680 NVIDIA GPU. We highlight the fact that with GeMTC on its own we observe upwards of 90% efficiency with tasks lasting 5 ms. The AMD Opteron has an even higher level of improved performance. This means that a fully general purpose framework would be capable of launching tasks an order of magnitude faster. We will continue to improve performance to ensure all components of the system can keep up with these task dispatch rates.

6. RELATED WORK

Warp Level Execution. Hong et al. [25] developed and evaluated methods that obtained 9X speedups of breadth-first search in graphs over prior GPU implementations by enabling each warp to run independent threads and even multiple "virtual" threads. While it stopped short of the generalized mechanism for managing independent per-warp tasks presented here, it characterizes the memory access regimes in which many-task programming of accelerators will provide effective speedup, and describes methods for integrating SISD and SIMD code segments within warp-resident tasks that can guide the implementation of GeMTC AppKernels. Chen et al. observed how unbalanced task-based workloads resulted in low utilization of CUDA hardware [26] and multi-GPU systems [27]. While still not a general-purpose solution like GeMTC, our work could benefit from the lock-free queueing system Chen described. While GeMTC is currently optimized for a single GPU per node we believe supporting multi-GPUs on a single node would only require launching additional Swift workers configured to target additional accelerators.

Dataflow on Accelerators. PTask [28], by Rossbach et al. aims to treat GPUs as compute devices from the view of the Operating System. PTask supports the dataflow programming model and provides several scheduling options for tasks including priority, first-available, and data-aware. Unlike Swift, PTask does not support dynamic DAGs. Dandelion

is built on top of PTask and cross compiles .NET code into CUDA code that is then executed on the PTask runtime [29].

Accelerator Virtualization. Virtualization is another technique to decompose hardware. Ravi et al. present a framework to enable GPU sharing amongst GPUs in the cloud [30]. Computing the affinity score allows the authors to determine which applications can benefit from consolidation. Becchi et al. extend the framework to provide additional abstractions for GPU sharing while allowing isolation of concurrent applications [31]. Gupta et al. describe Pegasus [32], which aims to improve GPU utilization through virtualization. The Pegasus project runs at the hypervisor level and promotes GPU sharing across virtual machines, while including a custom DomA scheduler for GPU task scheduling.

Runtime Systems. StarPU [33] is a task-based runtime designed to improve the programmability of accelerators while maintaining efficiencies. StarPU does allow for data dependencies and hints regarding task priorities, but GeMTC provides a finer granularity by leveraging warps as workers. Zhang et al. present GPU-TLS [34], a loop speculative parallelization framework for decomposing large loops into smaller pieces which are then executed in parallel by GPU kernels. Chatterjee et al. describe a runtime [35] that allows different tasks to execute on the same SM in a similar fashion to GeMTC. However, their runtime schedules workers based on the Concurrent Collections (CnC) model and leverages work stealing among SM managed queues to execute tasks. At startup their runtime treats every SM as a single worker, but allows tasks to launch more tasks. Our work could benefit from the idea of additional worker queues to reduce contention. However, our model leverages Swift to manage the dependencies of run-to-completion tasks that are assumed to have already been decomposed to the finest granularity possible. Not only does the Turbine engine within Swift support data dependencies, but the execution of tasks is based on the dataflow model. Added benefits of leveraging Swift include access to the built-in load balancer ADLB, and the ability to easily span multiple nodes. COSMIC [36] is a middleware for multiprocessing on the Intel Xeon Phi. The GeMTC implementation on the Xeon-Phi will benefit greatly from avoiding memory and thread oversubscription, as highlighted in this work.

Alternative Accelerator Programming Methods. Intelligent compilers are another way to avoid low level accelerator development and still gain high performance. If the compiler is able to generate device code and parallel instructions, the developer may opt to write sequential code and benefit from accelerator speedup. OpenMPC [37] is a project that takes OpenMP code and converts it to CUDA, thus enabling many scientific applications already written in OpenMP to take advantage of the accelerator. Other work aims to target accelerators directly from OpenMP [38]. Grophecy [39] attempts to improve the process of migrating codes to the GPU through the analysis of code skeletonization. Grophecy can analyze CPU codes and determine whether they may benefit from being moved to the GPU, saving valuable development cycles. Singe [40] is a Domain Specific Language compiler for combustion chemistry applications. GeMTC could benefit from a Grophecy or Singe-like module for creating warp-optimized AppKernels and vice versa. MPI-ACC [41] aims to provide integrated MPI support for accelerators to allow the programmer to easily execute code on a CPU or GPU.

7. CONCLUSIONS

We have presented GeMTC, a framework for enabling MTC workloads to run efficiently on NVIDIA GPUs. The GeMTC framework encompasses the entire GPU running as a single GPU application similar to a daemon. The GeMTC framework is responsible for receiving work from a host through the use of the C API, and scheduling and running that work on many independent GPU workers. Results are returned through the C API to the host and then to Swift. The GeMTC API enables the framework to closely integrate with parallel scripting systems such as Swift/T. The GeMTC framework simplifies the programming model of the GPU by allowing GPUs to be treated as a collection of independent SIMD workers, enabling a MIMD view of the device. The novel sub-allocator implemented within GeMTC allows for an efficient dynamic allocation of memory once an application is running. In addition GeMTC provides an alternative API call to cudaMalloc, achieving a speedup of roughly 10x. GeMTC has a throughput of roughly 23K tasks per second on a single node. Integration with Swift/T improves programmability of accelerators, while demonstrating the ability to increase scalability to many nodes with many cores in clusters, clouds, grids, and HPC resources.

Our studies suggest that not every workload will achieve increased performance with a fine-grained many-task model on a GPU. Applications that can generate thousands of SIMD threads may prefer to use traditional CUDA programming techniques. GeMTC is currently optimized for executing within environments containing a single GPU per node, such as Blue Waters; but future work aims to address heterogeneous accelerator environments. Under the current configurations, users are required to write their own AppKernels. While a user may use many preexisting AppKernel templates, a system to automatically tune CUDA/C functions to AppKernels would streamline the development process. We leave this for future work.

Future work also includes performance evaluation of diverse application kernels; analysis of the ability of such kernels to effectively utilize concurrent warps; enabling of virtual warps [25] which can both subdivide and span physical warps; support for other accelerators such as the Xeon Phi; and continued performance refinement.

8. ACKNOWLEDGEMENTS

The Blue Waters sustained-petascale computing project is supported by the National Science Foundation (OCI 0725070) and the State of Illinois. Blue Waters is a joint effort of the University of Illinois at Urbana-Champaign and its National Center for Supercomputing Applications. We gratefully acknowledge support from NSF ACI-1148443 (Swift) and DOE DE-SC0005380 (ExM). Work by Katz was supported by NSF while working at the Foundation. Any opinion, finding, and conclusions or recommendations expressed in this material are those of the author(s) and do not necessarily reflect the views of the National Science Foundation. The information, data, or work presented herein was funded in part by the Starr Foundation through its generous donation to Illinois Institute of Technology. The content is solely the responsibility of the authors and does not necessarily represent the official views of the Starr Foundation. The authors also recognize Dustin Shahidehpour and Jeffrey Johnson for their contributions to GeMTC and MDLite.

9. REFERENCES

[1] I. Raicu, Z. Zhang, M. Wilde, I. Foster, P. Beckman, K. Iskra, and B. Clifford, "Toward loosely coupled programming on petascale systems," in *Proc. of 2008 ACM/IEEE Conf. on Supercomputing*, ser. SC '08. Piscataway, NJ: IEEE Press, 2008, pp. 22:1–22:12.

[2] I. Raicu, *Many-task computing: bridging the gap between high-throughput computing and high-performance computing.* ProQuest, 2009.

[3] I. Raicu, Y. Zhao, C. Dumitrescu, I. Foster, and M. Wilde, "Falkon: a Fast and Light-weight tasK executiON framework," in *Proc. of the 2007 ACM/IEEE Conf. on Supercomputing (SC'07)*. New York, NY, USA: ACM, 2007, pp. 43:1–43:12.

[4] M. Wilde, M. Hategan, J. M. Wozniak, B. Clifford, D. S. Katz, and I. Foster, "Swift: A language for distributed parallel scripting," *Parallel Computing*, vol. 37, pp. 633–652, 2011.

[5] J. M. Wozniak, M. Wilde, and D. S. Katz, "JETS: Language and system support for many-parallel-task workflows," *J. Grid Computing*, vol. 11, no. 3, pp. 341–360, 2013.

[6] M. Hategan, J. Wozniak, and K. Maheshwari, "Coasters: uniform resource provisioning and access for scientific computing on clouds and grids," in *Proc. Utility and Cloud Computing*, 2011, pp. 114–121.

[7] D. P. Anderson, "Boinc: A system for public-resource computing and storage," in *Proc of 5th IEEE/ACM Intl. Workshop on Grid Computing*. IEEE, 2004.

[8] A. B. Yoo, M. A. Jette, and M. Grondona, "Slurm: Simple linux utility for resource management," in *Job Scheduling Strategies for Parallel Processing*. Springer, 2003, pp. 44–60.

[9] N. Desai, "Cobalt: an open source platform for hpc system software research," in *Edinburgh BG/L System Software Workshop*, 2005.

[10] IBM, "Sub-block jobs," in *IBM System Blue Gene Solution: Blue Gene/Q System Administration*, 2013, pp. 80–81, Sec. 6.3.

[11] K. Ousterhout, A. Panda, J. Rosen, S. Venkataraman, R. Xin, S. Ratnasamy, S. Shenker, and I. Stoica, "The case for tiny tasks in compute clusters," in *Proc. of the 14th USENIX Conf. on Hot Topics in Operating Systems*. USENIX Association, 2013, pp. 14–14.

[12] L. V. Kale and G. Zheng, "Charm++ and ampi: Adaptive runtime strategies via migratable objects," *Advanced Computational Infrastructures for Parallel and Distributed Applications*, pp. 265–282, 2009.

[13] S. Wienke, P. Springer, C. Terboven, and D. an Mey, "OpenACC - first experiences with real-world applications," in *Euro-Par 2012 Parallel Processing*. Springer, 2012, pp. 859–870.

[14] NVIDIA Inc., "CUDA C Programming Guide PG-02829-001 v5.5, Section 3.2.5, Asynchronous Concurrent Execution," 2013.

[15] NVIDIA Inc. , "CUDA C Programming Guide PG-02829-001 v5.5, Appendix C, Dynamic Parallelism Execution," 2013.

[16] J. Johnson, S. J. Krieder, B. Grimmer, J. M. Wozniak, M. Wilde, and I. Raicu, "Understanding the costs of many-task computing workloads on intel xeon phi

coprocessors," in *2nd Greater Chicago Area System Research Workshop (GCASR)*, 2013.

[17] Y. Zhao, M. Hategan, B. Clifford, I. Foster, G. von Laszewski, V. Nefedova, I. Raicu, T. Stef-Praun, and M. Wilde, "Swift: Fast, reliable, loosely coupled parallel computation," in *Services, 2007 IEEE Congress on*, 2007, pp. 199–206.

[18] J. M. Wozniak, T. G. Armstrong, M. Wilde, D. S. Katz, E. Lusk, and I. T. Foster, "Swift/T: Scalable data flow programming for many-task applications," in *Proc. CCGrid*, 2013.

[19] T. G. Armstrong, J. M. Wozniak, M. Wilde, and I. T. Foster, "Compiler optimization for data-driven task parallelism on distributed memory systems," ANL/MCS-P5030-1013.

[20] J. M. Wozniak, T. G. Armstrong, K. Maheshwari, E. L. Lusk, D. S. Katz, M. Wilde, and I. T. Foster, "Turbine: A distributed-memory dataflow engine for high performance many-task applications," vol. 28, no. 3, pp. 337–366, 2013, fundamenta Informaticae 128(3).

[21] NCSA, "Blue Waters User Portal," 2014, https://bluewaters.ncsa.illinois.edu/hardware-summary.

[22] J. Burkardt, "MD - molecular dynamics," 2013, http://people.sc.fsu.edu/~jburkardt/cpp_src/md/md.html.

[23] A. N. Adhikari, J. Peng, M. Wilde, J. Xu, K. F. Freed, and T. R. Sosnick, "Modeling large regions in proteins: Applications to loops, termini, and folding," *Protein Science*, vol. 21, no. 1, pp. 107–121, 2012.

[24] S. S. Hampton, P. Brenner, A. Wenger, S. Chatterjee, and J. A. Izaguirre, "Biomolecular sampling: Algorithms,test molecules, and metrics," in *New Algorithms for Macromolecular Simulation*, ser. Lecture Notes in Computational Science and Engineering, B. Leimkuhler, C. Chipot, R. Elber, A. Laaksonen, A. Mark, T. Schlick, C. SchÃijtte, and R. Skeel, Eds. Springer-Verlag, New York, 2006, vol. 49, pp. 103–121.

[25] S. Hong, S. K. Kim, T. Oguntebi, and K. Olukotun, "Accelerating CUDA graph algorithms at maximum warp," in *Proc. of the 16th ACM Symp. on Principles and practice of parallel programming*, ser. PPoPP '11. New York, NY, USA: ACM, 2011, pp. 267–276.

[26] L. Chen, O. Villa, S. Krishnamoorthy, and G. R. Gao, "Dynamic load balancing on single-and multi-gpu systems," in *IEEE Intl. Symp. on Parallel & Distributed Processing (IPDPS)*. IEEE, 2010.

[27] L. Chen, O. Villa, and G. R. Gao, "Exploring fine-grained task-based execution on multi-gpu systems," in *2011 IEEE Intl. Conf. on Cluster Computing (CLUSTER)*. IEEE, 2011, pp. 386–394.

[28] C. J. Rossbach, J. Currey, M. Silberstein, B. Ray, and E. Witchel, "Ptask: operating system abstractions to manage GPUs as compute devices," in *Proc. of the Twenty-Third ACM Symp. on Operating Systems Principles*. ACM, 2011, pp. 233–248.

[29] C. J. Rossbach, Y. Yu, J. Currey, J.-P. Martin, and D. Fetterly, "Dandelion: a compiler and runtime for heterogeneous systems," in *Proc. of the Twenty-Fourth ACM Symp. on Operating Systems Principles*. ACM, 2013, pp. 49–68.

[30] V. T. Ravi, M. Becchi, G. Agrawal, and S. Chakradhar, "Supporting GPU sharing in cloud environments with a transparent runtime consolidation framework," in *Proc. of the 20th Intl. Symp. on High performance distributed computing*, ser. HPDC '11. New York, NY, USA: ACM, 2011, pp. 217–228.

[31] M. Becchi, K. Sajjapongse, I. Graves, A. Procter, V. Ravi, and S. Chakradhar, "A virtual memory based runtime to support multi-tenancy in clusters with GPUs," in *Proc. of the 21st Intl. Symp. on High-Performance Parallel and Distributed Computing*. ACM, 2012, pp. 97–108.

[32] V. Gupta, K. Schwan, N. Tolia, V. Talwar, and P. Ranganathan, "Pegasus: coordinated scheduling for virtualized accelerator-based systems," in *Proc. of the 2011 USENIX Annual Technical Conf.*, ser. USENIXATC'11. Berkeley, CA, USA: USENIX Association, 2011, pp. 3–3.

[33] C. Augonnet, S. Thibault, R. Namyst, and P.-A. Wacrenier, "StarPU: a unified platform for task scheduling on heterogeneous multicore architectures," *Concurrency and Computation: Practice and Experience*, vol. 23, no. 2, pp. 187–198, 2011.

[34] C. Zhang, G. Han, and C.-L. Wang, "GPU-TLS: An efficient runtime for speculative loop parallelization on gpus," in *13th IEEE/ACM Intl. Symp. on Cluster, Cloud and Grid Computing (CCGrid)*. IEEE, 2013.

[35] S. Chatterjee, M. Grossman, A. Sbîrlea, and V. Sarkar, "Dynamic task parallelism with a gpu work-stealing runtime system," in *Languages and Compilers for Parallel Computing*. Springer, 2013, pp. 203–217.

[36] S. Cadambi, G. Coviello, C.-H. Li, R. Phull, K. Rao, M. Sankaradass, and S. Chakradhar, "COSMIC: middleware for high performance and reliable multiprocessing on xeon phi coprocessors," in *Proc. of the 22nd Intl. Symp. on High-performance parallel and distributed computing*. ACM, 2013, pp. 215–226.

[37] S. Lee and R. Eigenmann, "OpenMPC: Extended OpenMP for efficient programming and tuning on GPUs," *Intl. J. of Computational Science and Eng.*, 2012.

[38] T. R. Scogland, B. Rountree, W.-c. Feng, and B. R. de Supinski, "Heterogeneous task scheduling for accelerated OpenMP," in *IEEE 26th Intl. Parallel & Distributed Processing Symp. (IPDPS)*. IEEE, 2012.

[39] J. Meng, V. A. Morozov, K. Kumaran, V. Vishwanath, and T. D. Uram, "GROPHECY: GPU performance projection from CPU code skeletons," in *Proc. of 2011 Intl. Conf. for High Performance Computing, Networking, Storage and Analysis*, ser. SC '11. New York, NY, USA: ACM, 2011, pp. 14:1–14:11.

[40] M. Bauer, S. Treichler, and A. Aiken, "Singe: Leveraging Warp Specialization for High Performance on GPUs," in *Proc. of the 19th ACM SIGPLAN Symp. on Principles and Practice of Parallel Programming*, ser. PPoPP '14. New York, NY, USA: ACM, 2014.

[41] A. M. Aji, L. S. Panwar, F. Ji, M. Chabbi, K. Murthy, P. Balaji, K. R. Bisset, J. Dinan, W.-c. Feng, J. Mellor-Crummey *et al.*, "On the efficacy of GPU-integrated MPI for scientific applications," in *Proc. of the 22nd Intl. Symp. on High-Performance Parallel and Distributed Computing*. ACM, 2013.

MROnline: MapReduce Online Performance Tuning

Min Li[†], Liangzhao Zeng[‡], Shicong Meng[‡],
Jian Tan[‡], Li Zhang[‡], Ali R. Butt[†], Nicholas Fuller[‡]
[†] Dept. of Computer Science, Virginia Tech; [‡]IBM TJ Watson Research Center
{limin,butta}@cs.vt.edu, {lzeng,smeng,tanji,zhangli,nfuller}@us.ibm.com

ABSTRACT

MapReduce job parameter tuning is a daunting and time consuming task. The parameter configuration space is huge; there are more than 70 parameters that impact job performance. It is also difficult for users to determine suitable values for the parameters without first having a good understanding of the MapReduce application characteristics. Thus, it is a challenge to systematically explore the parameter space and select a near-optimal configuration. Extant offline tuning approaches are slow and inefficient as they entail multiple test runs and significant human effort.

To this end, we propose an online performance tuning system, MROnline, that monitors a job's execution, tunes associated performance-tuning parameters based on collected statistics, and provides fine-grained control over parameter configuration. MROnline allows each task to have a different configuration, instead of having to use the same configuration for all tasks. Moreover, we design a gray-box based smart hill climbing algorithm that can efficiently converge to a near-optimal configuration with high probability. To improve the search quality and increase convergence speed, we also incorporate a set of MapReduce-specific tuning rules in MROnline. Our results using a real implementation on a representative 19-node cluster show that dynamic performance tuning can effectively improve MapReduce application performance by up to 30% compared to the default configuration used in YARN.

Categories and Subject Descriptors

C.2.4 [**Computer-Communication Networks**]: Distributed Systems —*distributed applications*; D.2.9 [**Software**]: Software Engineering —*software configuration management*

General Terms

Design, Algorithms, Performance, Evaluation.

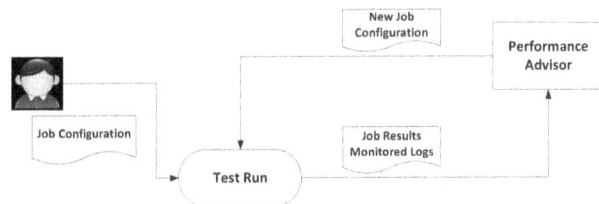

Figure 1: Current offline performance tuning approach used for MapReduce applications.

Keywords

Cloud computing; MapReduce; YARN; Online parameter tuning; Performance tuning; Dynamic parameter configuration; Hill climbing.

1. INTRODUCTION

The use of the MapReduce [3] large-scale data processing framework is growing exponentially as the amount of data created by web search engines, social networks, business web click streams, and academic and scientific research continue to increase at unprecedented rates. While the MapReduce framework enables users to scale up applications easily, writing good MapReduce applications requires specialized system-level skills and extra effort as users also have to provide application-specific job and system configuration parameters. These parameters are crucial and affect performance significantly. For example, consider the configuration parameter $io.sort.mb$ that controls the amount of buffer memory to use when sorting files. Setting $io.sort.mb$ to sub-optimal values can lead to unnecessary I/Os and consequently increase task running time. Moreover, different applications require different values for $io.sort.mb$ depending on the HDFS [8, 11] block size and the map task output size. Similarly, applications vary in demands, e.g., the MapReduce application Grep [9] requires smaller sort space than Terasort [10], as Grep usually outputs much less data than Terasort in the map phase. Recent research such as Starfish [15] shows that MapReduce application performance depends on the size and content of the data set, job characteristics, cluster hardware configuration, and more importantly configuration parameters. The importance of such performance tuning is further highlighted by the observation that a simple web search on the topic yields a long list of best practices and MapReduce tuning guides [1, 2, 16, 17, 31]. These documents show that multiple orders of application performance gains can be achieved when using tuned parameters compared to the default settings.

The challenge is that the MapReduce job parameter tuning is a daunting and time consuming task. This is mainly due to the fact that the parameter configuration space is huge; the number of performance related parameters in Hadoop [8] is more than 70. Moreover, it is difficult for a user to determine the optimal value for a parameter without first having a deep understanding of the application characteristics. The current approach to address this challenge is to use offline performance tuning. As shown in Figure 1, traditional offline tuning first selects a configuration based on default settings or a rough understanding of application characteristics. Next, several test runs of the application are done and profiled to collect data such as job performance counters, and system monitoring logs. The user then feeds the collected data to a performance advisor, or perform manual static analysis, to generate a new configuration. The whole process is then repeated multiple times until a desired performance goal is reached. The selected configuration is then employed for running the application on production clusters.

There are multiple drawbacks of the above traditional performance tuning for MapReduce. First, the process is time consuming as it requires many test runs and each run can only try a single configuration. This is further exacerbated when the application involves long running tasks. Second, the offline approach is not cost effective if the tuning is done for an application that will only run for few times or perhaps just once. Users would rather simply run their applications without tuning, leading to overall inefficient resource utilization. In addition, as shown by Starfish [15], the optimal configuration also depends on the data set and cluster hardware configuration. This implies that users would have to re-adjust the parameters each time they change the input data sets or run the applications on different clusters. Moreover, no one configuration is suitable for all tasks within a job. MapReduce jobs also commonly exhibit data skew [23] that requires different amounts of resources based on the different sizes of data being processed. Finally, the traditional offline tuning statically tunes the parameters once and use the configuration throughout the whole life cycle of a job. However, the job characteristics and cluster utilization are dynamic, and static tuning cannot adapt to such variations and thus cannot avoid performance-degrading cluster hot spots.

In this paper, we mitigate the aforementioned problems by designing an online performance tuning system, MRONLINE. MRONLINE improves single Hadoop job performance via online performance tuning, as well as expedites the performance tuning process by reducing the number of test runs by employing a finer grain online process that tests multiple configurations per run. MRONLINE provides the ability to tune multiple jobs' performance in a multi-tenant environment. Moreover, MRONLINE considers dynamic cluster utilization information to help MapReduce applications avoid hot spots. MRONLINE also does not require any modifications to user programs, which makes it user friendly and encourages quick adoption.

Specifically, this paper makes the following contributions:

- We design and implement a task-level dynamic configuration framework based on YARN [29], the second generation open source MapReduce implementation. MRONLINE enables different configurations for each map and reduce task, which is a key system-level improvement over extant approaches and offers huge optimization opportunities.

- We design a gray-box based smart hill climbing algorithm to systematically search the MapReduce parameter space, which relies on our task-level dynamic configuration framework. We support both aggressive and conservative tuning strategies.

- We propose tuning rules for key parameters, which improve search quality and reduce convergence iterations.

- We evaluate MRONLINE on YARN and present an experimental performance evaluation on a representative 19-node cluster. Our results demonstrate that compared to the default YARN settings, our approach achieves an efficiency improvement of 22% by dynamically tuning the applications. Moreover, for applications that run multiple times, MRONLINE can expedite the test runs and reduce job execution time by up to 30%. Our results show that MRONLINE offers an effective means to improve MapReduce application performance.

The rest of the paper is organized as follows. Section 2 presents an introduction of YARN, the classification of configuration parameters and identifies two use cases that we consider in MRONLINE. Section 3 discusses the system architecture of MRONLINE, followed by an explanation of the task-level dynamic configuration in Section 4. In Section 5, we detail the design of our gray-box based hill climbing algorithm to systematically search for optimal configuration parameters. Section 6 describes the tuning rules for various key job configuration parameters. Section 7 discusses our implementation details. Section 8 demonstrates the effectiveness of MRONLINE versus the default configuration through a series of experiments. Related works are discussed in Section 9, and finally Section 10 concludes the paper.

2. BACKGROUND

In the section, we first describe YARN that serves as an enabler for MRONLINE. Next, we present a classification of the considered configuration parameters, followed by an identification of two specific use cases that we have considered in MRONLINE.

2.1 YARN

MRONLINE is designed and implemented on YARN [29], the latest generation of the publicly available Hadoop platform. We choose YARN as it provides many advantages over prior versions of Hadoop. Hadoop is designed as a monolithic framework, which tightly couples the MapReduce programming model with distributed resource management. This leads to unnecessary/forced use and misuse of the MapReduce programming model when all what users want is to just leverage the large-scale compute resources provided by enterprises and research organizations. For instance, users have been observed to submit map-only applications to simply launch arbitrary processes (not necessarily MapReduce tasks) in Hadoop clusters [29], or submit applications that have map functions implemented as reduce tasks to circumvent limited map quotas [12]. Moreover, Hadoop employs a centralized scheduler for managing tasks of all jobs. This is becoming a performance bottleneck as the number of jobs submitted to a Hadoop cluster grows. Traditional Hadoop implementation also does not support changing the map or reduce slot configurations between different jobs, which precludes dynamically adapting to variations during a job's life-cycle, and consequently reduces system efficiency.

YARN has been designed to address the above limitations. It separates the computational programming models from resource management, and provides support for frameworks other than MapReduce such as Giraph [7, 27], Spark [19, 35], and Storm [28]. In this paper, we focus on tuning parameters of the MapReduce programming model running on top of YARN. However, YARN can be exploited to extend our approach to support performance tuning of other frameworks as well. Another useful feature of YARN is that it delegates application related scheduling to per *application masters* that can employ application-specific resource scheduling, thus providing for higher scalability. For this purpose, YARN manages cluster-wide resources through the use of a new key concept, "container." A container is a resource scheduling unit that encapsulates the number of CPUs, required memory, interconnect bandwidth, etc. for scheduling. Different MapReduce applications can request different-sized containers from YARN as per their needs. For example, an application master is responsible for specifying the number of needed containers, the size of each container, and the mapping between the containers and tasks. MRONLINE leverages the containers to design a task-level configuration framework.

2.2 Parameter Classification

We focus on parameters that impact application performance and are amenable to dynamic configuration. The optimal values of these parameters depend on the application characteristics, the size and the contents of the associated input data and the cluster setup. We classify the considered parameters into three categories based on when the modified value of a parameter can take effect.

The first category includes parameters that are difficult to change after the application has started. The number of mappers, the number of reducers, and slow start (*mapreduce.job.reduce.slowstart.completedmaps*) are three key parameters that fall into this category. Slow start specifies the number of mappers that should be completed before any reducers are launched. Starting the reduce tasks early can help overlap the map tasks execution with the shuffle phase and improve performance. However, starting the reduce tasks too early creates contention for the cluster resources that are also needed by the mappers. The optimal value for the parameter is application specific.

The second category consists of parameters that cannot be changed on the fly for already running tasks, but impact the tasks that will be launched after changes have been made. Examples of such parameters include *io.sort.mb*, the number of virtual cores in a container, the size of memory in a container, and parameters specifying reduce buffer size. Choosing the right values for this category can reduce I/Os and improve the cluster utilization.

The third category consists of parameters that can be changed on the fly and become effective immediately. Parameters such as *mapred.inmemmerge.threshold* and *io.sort.spill.percent* fall into this category. These two parameters control the threshold of when to spill out data from memory onto disks. MRONLINE can even try multiple values within a task for parameters in this category, thus speeding up the tuning process.

MRONLINE currently supports tuning of parameters in the second and third categories. Tuning of parameters in the first category can be done using simulation tools, such as MRPerf [30], and remains a focus of our on-going research.

2.3 Use Cases for MRONLINE

We considered two use cases for designing MRONLINE. The first use case is to expedite test runs by trying multiple task configurations in a single test run. This enables us to reduce the tuning time significantly. The second use case is to improve the performance of applications that are executed only once. MRONLINE employs different strategies for each of these two use cases.

1. Expedited Test Runs Use Case: In this use case, we aggressively and systematically search for different parameter configurations to find optimal values. We first design and implement a task-level configuration framework that enables testing of different parameter configurations in a single test run. We then design a gray-box based smart hill climbing algorithm to find the optimal

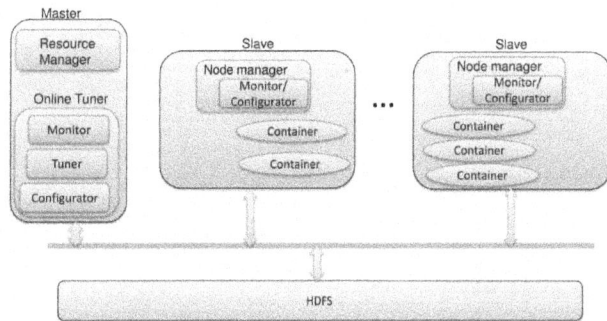

Figure 2: MRONLINE system architecture.

configuration. The quality of the generated solution depends on the number of tasks executed in a single test run. If too few tasks are executed, the configuration quality can be improved by multiple test runs. We also increase the algorithm convergence speed by monitoring and modeling the runtime statistics into the algorithm.

2. Fast Single Run Use Case: In this use case, we improve the application performance in a single run. Here, we conservatively tune the configurations mostly based on the observed runtime statistics. For example, if we observe that too many spills are being written to the disk, we increase the size of the sort buffer. Our main goal in this case is to improve performance of the current task, instead of searching for a desirable configuration that can be used for later runs. This is particularly useful for jobs that run few times or only once. For this use case, a performance boost can be achieved by simply co-executing MRONLINE with target applications.

3. SYSTEM ARCHITECTURE

The overall architecture of MRONLINE is shown in Figure 2. MRONLINE is based on YARN that, unlike the centralized job tracker of earlier versions of Hadoop, has a resource manager that manages cluster resources and the execution cycle of distributed application-specific masters, and tracks node liveness. To support dynamic configuration, MRONLINE modifies the YARN resource manager to support allocation of different-sized containers for different applications. The Node manager, akin to the task tracker of Hadoop, runs on each cluster node and is responsible for managing the containers running locally on the node. However, YARN delegates the task tracking functions to per application components. MRONLINE implements its sub-components within each node manager to leverage existing features such as resource monitoring.

MRONLINE consists of a centralized master component, *online tuner*, which is a daemon that can run on the same machine as the resource manager of YARN or on a dedicated machine. Online tuner controls a number of distributed slave components that run within the node managers on the slave nodes of the YARN cluster.

Online tuner is composed of three components: a *monitor*, a *tuner* and a *dynamic configurator*. The monitor works together with the per-node slave monitors to periodically monitor application statistics. Specifically, the slave monitors gather statistics about the tasks running on the node, as well as the node statistics, and send the information to the centralized monitor. The centralized monitor then aggregates, analyzes and passes the information to the tuner.

The tuner implements the tuning strategies and algorithms, which decide what parameters should be changed and what new values should be assigned. When needed, the tuner generates new configurations for each application and task. Finally, the dy-

API	Description
`List<String> getConfigurableJobParameters(JobID jid)`	Returns the set of configurable parameters for the job with job ID `jid` and associated tasks that are currently running or will run in the future.
`List<String> getConfigurableTaskParameters(JobID jid, TaskID tid)`	Returns the set of configurable parameters for the tasks with job and task IDs `jid` and `tid`, respectively.
`int setJobParameters(JobID jid, Map<String, String> kv)`	Sets the parameters for a job with ID `jid`.
`int setTaskParameters(JobID jid, TaskID tid, Map<String, String> kv)`	Sets the parameters for a task with job and task IDs `jid` and `tid`, respectively.
`int setTaskParameters(JobID jid, Map<String, String> kv)`	Sets the parameters for all the tasks associated with a job with ID `jid`.

Table 1: Key APIs provided by the dynamic configurator of MRONLINE.

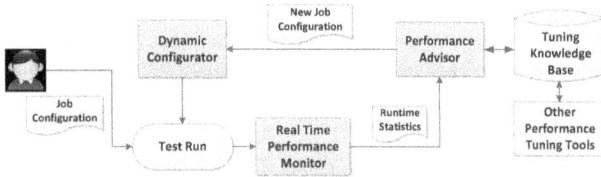

Figure 3: The tuning process used by MRONLINE.

namic configurator takes the newly chosen configurations and distributes the lists of new parameters to the slave configurator components. The slave configurators are responsible for activating the new changes for tasks that are running on their associated nodes.

Figure 3 illustrates the tuning process used by MRONLINE. After storing input data sets in HDFS, a user launches the application using a default configuration or a configuration based on rough understanding of application characteristics. The real-time performance monitor then starts to track runtime statistics including per task information such as task progress rate, CPU and memory utilization, the number of spilled records, I/O utilization and per node resource utilization. This information is periodically sent to the performance advisor that is implemented in the tuner component shown in Figure 2. The performance advisor analyzes and determines new configurations and sends them to the dynamic configurator that then changes the configuration for each task accordingly. The tuning process iterates until a desirable configuration is generated. MRONLINE supports both aggressive and conservative tuning strategies (Section 2). The performance tuning advisor can also be extended to communicate with other performance tuning tools, and the tuning rules can also be stored in a tuning knowledge base to be used across application runs.

4. TASK-LEVEL DYNAMIC CONFIGURATION

We extend YARN to support task-level dynamic configuration. In contrast to traditional YARN applications that use one configuration for executing all of the tasks, MRONLINE enables different configurations for different tasks.

Upon receiving a list of tasks and associated configuration mappings, the dynamic configurator writes per-task configuration files to the working directory of the corresponding application. When the tasks are assigned to containers, the slave configurator on the nodes retrieves the changed configuration files associated with the tasks. The launched tasks then read the changed configuration files, which in turn changes the configuration accordingly. Thus, each task can have a different configuration that can also vary.

Current implementation of YARN supports one fixed container size for all map tasks or all reduce tasks. We extend the resource scheduler to support requests that require different-sized containers. Specifically, we use a hash map data structure to keep track of the different-sized containers requested and corresponding operations such as assignment and release of the containers.

The key APIs supported by the dynamic configurator of MRONLINE are shown in Table 1. The functions $getConfigurableJobParameters$ and $getConfigurableTaskParameters$ return a set of configurable parameters for a specified job or task. The other three functions set the job or task configuration parameters to specified values. The APIs also allow other tuning algorithms, and not just ours, to easily tune the job parameters if needed.

5. GRAY-BOX BASED HILL CLIMBING ALGORITHM

In this section, we present the design of our tuner that systematically searches through the configuration space and finds a desirable configuration given a specific application, data set size and cluster configuration. To this end, we introduce a gray-box based hill climbing algorithm to tune the job parameter configurations for YARN applications. Our approach is inspired by the smart hill climbing algorithm [33] that was developed to provide black-box optimization for configuring web application servers. Our approach has three desirable properties: 1) it provides probabilistic guarantees on the closeness of a determined configuration to the optimal configuration; 2) it effectively tolerates noise in evaluated cost from factors such as resource contention; and 3) it adopts the weighted latin hypercube sampling (LHS) technique that helps improve the sampling quality and increases the convergence speed. Applying LHS in our approach allows us to partition the probability distributions of each parameter value into equal probability intervals, and sample a value from each interval, which leads to higher quality sampling. Moreover, we also consider the system-level monitoring information and apply it to the algorithm to speed up the search process. Thus, our algorithm offers a gray-box based method.

Algorithm 1 shows the details of tuning we have devised in MRONLINE. Our algorithm has two phases, a global search phase and a local search phase. The global search phase aims to find promising local areas to explore through efficient LHS sampling. The local search phase moves or narrows the search neighborhood area determined by any cost improvements compared to the current best configuration, until the size of the neighborhood is smaller than a predefined threshold. The local search phase also uses LHS to search the neighborhood and picks the best configuration.

Algorithm 1 Gray-Box based Hill Climbing.

1: Initialize LHS parameters k, m, n, the threshold of neighborhood size N_t, the shrink factor f and the threshold of global search g.
2: $local\_search = 1, global\_search = 1$
3: config[m] = LHS_sampling(m)
4: C_{cur}=best(config[m])
5: $N_{C_{cur}}$=adjust_neighbor(C_{cur})
6: While $global\_search < g$ do
7:    if $local\_search == 1$ then
8:       while $N_{C_{cur}} > N_t$ do
9:          config[n]=LHS_sampling(n)
10:          C_{candi}=best(config[n])
11:          if($cost(C_{candi}) < cost(C_{cur})$)
12:             C_{cur}=C_{candi}
13:             $N_{c_{cur}}$=adjust_neighbor(C_{cur})
14:          else
15:             $N_{c_{cur}}$=shrink_neighbor(C_{cur})
16:          endif
17:       endwhile
18:       $local\_search = 0$
19:    endif
20:    config[m]=LHS_sampling(m)
21:    C_{candi}=best(config[m])
22:    if($cost(C_{candi}) < cost(C_{cur})$)
23:       $C_{cur} = C_{candi}$
24:       $N_{c_{cur}}$=adjust_neighbor(C_{cur})
25:       $local\_search = 1$
26:    else
27:       $global\_search$++
28:    endif
29: endwhile

The initial value for parameters such as the number of sampled configurations in the global search phase m (set to 24 in our tests), the number of sampled configurations in the local search phase n (16), the threshold of neighborhood size N_t (0.1), and the shrink factor f (0.75) that controls the ratio of the current neighborhood size to the shrunken neighborhood size, are set based on experimentation with the factors along with the theoretical analysis provided by the smart hill climbing algorithm [33]. The LHS interval, k, indicates the granularity of each parameter interval, and is set to 24 in our evaluation.

After the initialization, we enter the global search phase that uses LHS to generate m test configurations. Next, we configure the first m tasks to each use one of the generated configurations. As the tasks execute, the application performance is periodically monitored and the observations are used to estimate the cost of each configuration. We choose the configuration C_{cur} that has lowest estimated cost as the current search point and set the neighborhood size based on C_{cur}. Next, we switch to the local search phase, where we iteratively apply LHS sampling with n sampled configurations on the updated neighborhood with the center point C_{cur}. The dynamic configurator uses the newly calculated configurations to configure the newly launched tasks dynamically and the monitor component then gathers the execution statistics of the launched tasks. A candidate configuration C_{candi} is chosen based on the updated minimum estimated cost. The algorithm compares the estimated costs of a candidate configuration C_{candi} and the current best configuration C_{cur}. If the candidate configuration is better than the current configuration, it implies that there is a high possibility that a better configuration from the neighborhood with center configuration C_{candi} can be obtained. Otherwise, the algorithm shrinks the neighborhood size with the same center point C_{cur} with shrink factor f. The local search phase is then terminated, after the local search finds a local point with a neighborhood size smaller

than a predefined threshold N_t. This implies that the algorithm finds a local optimal point.

After the local search phase, the algorithm enters the global search phase again to find a promising configuration space to analyze. If a point that is better than the current local optimal configuration is found, the system enters the local search phase to refine the search, otherwise the algorithm terminates after a specified number of iterations g (set to 5 in our tests).

There are several challenges we have to address to incorporate the gray-box hill climbing algorithm into MRONLINE.

Mapping Sampled Configurations to Tasks. Our monitor keeps track of the launched tasks and their associated configurations, as well as queued tasks both with and without assigned configurations. Given the fact that the tasks are independent from each other in YARN, when the configurations are generated, our tuning system randomly chooses a task from the queued tasks list and assigns one of the configurations to the task. The configuration is then further adjusted based on the task-related information.

Estimating Cost of Executed Tasks. Equation 1 shows how we estimate the cost of each task. We consider four factors: CPU utilization, memory utilization, ratio of the number of spill records to the number of map output or combiner output records, and ratio of the current task execution time to the maximum task execution time of all the tasks in the job. The goal of this formula is to reduce the task execution time and the number of spill records of all the tasks, while keeping the memory and CPU fully utilized. A caveat to avoid is that over-utilizing resources can create contention between tasks, thus increasing task execution time.

$$y = (1.0 - u_{mem}) + (1.0 - u_{cpu}) + num_{spill}/num_{mapoutput} + T_{task}/T_{maxtask}. \quad (1)$$

Utilizing Tuning Rules to Reduce the Number of Convergence Iterations and Resizing the Neighborhood Size. We consider the statistics collected from the monitor for enhancing search quality, which we detail in Section 6.

Moreover, the dependencies between the parameters are also considered in the algorithm. For example, the memory size of mappers should always be greater than the size of $io.sort.mb$. The parameter $mapreduce.reduce.shuffle.input.buffer.percent$ should always be greater than the parameter $mapreduce.reduce.shuffle.merge.percent$. Since a job with a small number of map tasks can restrict MRONLINE to try out all the parameters listed in Table 2, considering these tuning rules helps us converge to a suitable configuration quickly. In the evaluation section, we quantify how the tuning effectiveness is impacted by the length of a job.

6. TUNING RULES

In this section, we present the guidelines that we incorporate into our gray-box based algorithm (Section 5) for tuning MapReduce setups for the two target use cases identified in Section 2.3. We focus on the CPU and memory related parameters shown in Table 2. Other parameters are tuned using the hill climbing algorithm without using the additional tuning rules.

The tuning rules are aimed at improving the cluster utilization by adjusting containers to meet the task requirements and alleviate over- or under- utilization, as well as to reduce extra I/O traffic by carefully tuning the memory buffer options. The current implementation of MRONLINE provides per-task configuration, and

Configuration Parameters	Default Value
Memory Tuning	
mapreduce.map.memory.mb	1 GB
mapreduce.reduce.memory.mb	1 GB
mapreduce.task.io.sort.mb	100
mapreduce.map.sort.spill.percent	0.8
mapreduce.reduce.shuffle.input.buffer.percent	0.7
mapreduce.reduce.shuffle.merge.percent	0.66
mapreduce.reduce.shuffle.memory.limit.percent	0.25
mapreduce.reduce.merge.inmem.threshold	1000
mapreduce.reduce.input.buffer.percent	0.0
CPU Tuning	
mapreduce.map.cpu.vcores	1
mapreduce.reduce.cpu.vcores	1
mapreduce.task.io.sort.factor	10
mapreduce.reduce.shuffle.parallelcopies	5

Table 2: The key configuration parameters in MRONLINE.

application-wide auto-configuration, e.g., selection of the number of mappers and reducers, remains the focus of our future work.

6.1 Tuning Guidelines for the Considered Use Cases

Expedited Test Runs Use Case: The goal in this case is to reduce the number of test runs and find a near-optimal configuration for YARN applications. To this end, we allow MRONLINE to temporarily yield worse performance than the default configuration as the algorithm searches through the configuration space comprehensively and monitors the changes and their impact. We adopt an aggressive strategy that tries out as many cases as possible using a wave pattern for invoking parameter changes. We first update several tasks with new configurations at once, run and collect data about the tasks, and then adjust the parameter settings in the next wave based on the collected statistics from the previous wave. Moreover, MRONLINE controls the YARN application execution flow by holding off the launching of new tasks until the tasks in the previous wave are finished. This strategy slows down the test run execution, but allows the gray-box search algorithm to find a near-optimal configuration with high confidence.

Fast Single Run Use Case: In this case, we aim to improve performance in a single job run. Here, we adopt a conservative approach. We start the job with default values in the first wave and tune the parameters based on the collected information in the next. Moreover, MRONLINE does not interrupt the application task scheduling sequence, thus minimizing any negative impact of the gray-box algorithm on performance. The slave configurator running on each participating node uses the updated configuration file if available. If the configuration file is not present, the task is launched with the default configuration.

6.2 Memory Tuning

The first part of Table 2 shows parameters that decide the memory allocation of map and reduce tasks and the memory allocation for the sub-phases within these tasks. These parameters should be selected carefully. If the memory is set to too big of a value, it will waste memory resources that can be allocated to other containers, thus reducing overall cluster utilization. In contrast, if the memory is set to too small a value, it will incur resource contention leading to extra disk operations (even out of memory errors), thus degrad-

ing performance. The optimal values depend on the input data size, the map/reduce function, and the output data size.

To tune the memory allocation of map and reduce tasks, we adjust the parameters *mapreduce.map.memory.mb* and *mapreduce.reduce.memory.mb*. For aggressive tuning, we obey the hill climbing algorithm using LHS sampling to try memory options within predefined memory ranges. After we obtain the task execution time and the memory utilization of map or reduce tasks that ran in the previous wave, we adjust memory bounds to help our hill climbing algorithm to narrow down the search space of these two parameters. This is done as follows. If we observe the memory utilization to be beyond 90%, it may cause over-utilization, so we increase the memory lower bounds to the 80th percentile of sampled memory values. We also decrease the memory upper bounds to 80th percentile of sampled memory values if we detect memory under-utilization (50% of memory utilization). When the tasks suffer from data skew and exhibit heterogeneous behavior, MRONLINE keeps track of the 80th percentile value, and adjusts the bounds accordingly. For conservative tuning, we try different memory values only when they have high probabilities to yield better results. For the first wave, we conservatively use default values and collect statistics. We then estimate the memory size needed by the map or reduce tasks using this information. If the memory is underutilized, our hill climbing algorithm tries the lower value with a higher probability; otherwise, it tries the higher value with a higher probability.

The next finer grain level of memory parameter tuning includes three key parameters: *mapreduce.task.io.sort.mb* in the map phase, and *mapReduce.reduce.shuffle.input.buffer.percent* and *mapReduce.reduce.input.buffer.percent* in the reduce phase. These affect performance in that they control the number of spill records written to disks. If enough memory is allocated both in the map and reduce phases, the number of spill records will be minimized. The parameter *mapreduce.tasks.io.sort.mb* should not exceed the memory size of map tasks.

Ideally, the number of spill records in the map phase should equal the number of map output records. The number of spill records in the reduce phase should equal zero. Otherwise, the number of spill records is $3\times$ the number of map output records in the worst case. However, allocating more memory than needed would cause memory contention between the buffers and application logic, which negatively impacts job performance. The optimal memory buffer sizes depend on job and cluster characteristics.

The approach used for tuning the parameter *mapreduce.task.io.sort.mb* is to configure the buffer size based on map output size by continuously monitoring the number of spill records and the size of map outputs. For conservative tuning, the value is set as the default value in the beginning. As the first few map tasks are started, the buffer size is set to the estimated map output size. If the ratio of increased number of spill records to increased map output records is greater than one, we increase the lower bound to 80th percentile of the sampled values, since the current parameter value is not big enough to hold the map or combine outputs. If the ratio is one, MRONLINE decreases the upper bound to 80th percentile of the sampled values. The rule is similar for aggressive tuning, except that before any application statistics are obtained, multiple configurations as determined by the hill climbing algorithm are first tried.

The parameter *mapreduce.map.sort.spill.percent* decides when to spill data out to disks. It enables pipelining between map functions and disk writes. When the parameter *io.sort.mb* is big enough, the value of the parameter *mapreduce.map.sort.spill.percent* should be set to a high value to ensure that disk writes are not triggered. Thus, for both aggressive and conservative tuning, we set the value to 0.99. If spilling extra records is unavoidable, we reset the parameter to its default value.

For tuning buffers in the reduce phase, we calculate the buffer sizes based on the estimated reduce input sizes. Specifically, the input size of each reducer is estimated by monitoring the number of spill records in the reduce phase and the sum of the size of partitions generated by each map output for the corresponding reducer.

The parameter *MapReduce.reduce.input.buffer.percent* decides when to write the merged reduce output to disk. For example, when the reduce function requires only a small amount of memory, the parameter *mapreduce.shuffle.input.buffer.percent* is set equal to the shuffle buffer to avoid any spills written to disks. Specifically, we use the memory utilization statistics from node managers to determine the memory usage of reducers.

The parameter *mapreduce.reduce.shuffle.merge.percent* controls the trigger for memory to disk merge pipelining shuffle and memory-disk merge. It cannot exceed the reduce buffer size. For conservative tuning, the value is initially set as the default value. When the shuffle buffer is big enough to accommodate all the reduce input, the value can be set equal to the shuffle buffer to avoid additional disk I/Os. Otherwise, for safety, the value is set to ($mapreduce.reduce.shuffle.input.buffer.percent -$ 0.04) that has the same value difference with the parameter *mapreduce.reduce.shuffle.input.buffer.percent* as in the default YARN configuration. Finally, we set the parameter *mapreduce.reduce.merge.inmem.threshold* to 0, which makes the merge trigger only based on memory consumption.

6.3 CPU Tuning

Table 2 also lists the key parameters we consider for CPU tuning. YARN supports allocation of different number of CPUs to map and reduce tasks. The parameter *yarn.nodemanager.resource.cpu-vcores* manages the number of CPU virtual cores that can be allocated for containers running in each slave node. If the value is 32, then on a 8-core machine, each virtual core has $1/4$ share of a physical core. Given that the number of physical cores per machine is fixed, a larger value yields smaller share per virtual core. This parameter is not suitable for dynamic tuning.

The parameters *mapreduce.map.cpu.vcores* and *mapreduce.reduce.cpu.vcores* directly control the CPU allocation of map and reduce tasks. The basic tuning rule is to allocate enough CPU resources to map and reduce tasks without sacrificing the cluster utilization. For conservative tuning, we start with the default value of 1, and collect container utilization information from the node manager. If full CPU utilization is observed, we increase the allocation by 1. If the task execution time is reduced and CPU under-utilization is not observed, we continue to increase the virtual core allocation.

The parameter *mapreduce.reduce.shuffle.parallelcopies* determines the concurrent transfers executed by reduce tasks during shuffle. The desirable value depends on the amount of shuffled data. A higher amount leads to a higher number of parallel shuffles. For conservative tuning, starting from the default value, we increase the parameter in increments of 10 until the task execution time is not improved any further.

The parameter *mapreduce.task.io.sort.factor* controls the concurrency of disk to disk merge with a default value of 10. The optimal value depends on the amount of data to be merged. For

conservative tuning, we increase the value by 20 until the task execution time stops showing improvement.

The above discussion introduced all of the guidelines that we have incorporated into MRONLINE for parameter tuning. The provided APIs of the dynamic configurator are flexible, and can be used easily to incorporate additional tuning logic for more parameters as necessary.

7. IMPLEMENTATION

We have implemented MRONLINE on top of Hadoop-2.1.0-beta [8]. The online tuner is implemented as a daemon that extends the AbstractService class within YARN and includes the three components of Section 3 running in dedicated threads. The AbstractService class maintains service state and a list of service state change listeners. Once the service state has been changed, the service state change listeners are informed. The online tuner is implemented by extending CompositeService class within YARN. The CompositeService class consists of a list of AbstractService instances. It has a shutdown hook that allows the child services within the composite service to be shut down gracefully when the Java Virtual Machine (running the YARN instance) is shut down. Leveraging this feature allows us to gracefully shut down the online tuner and its child components as needed.

The monitor periodically gets a job counter for each submitted and running job from YARN through the JobClient interface. It then sends the job identifier and associated job counters to the tuner. The monitor also retrieves the task-level counter and cluster-level information such as the CPU, memory, network I/O, disk I/O from each slave node. The tuner takes the input from the monitor and determines the parameters that have to be changed and the values that should be assigned to these parameters. This is done by using the gray-box hill climbing algorithm and tuning rules described earlier.

After the tuner generates the list of parameters to be changed, it sends the information to the dynamic configurator. The dynamic configurator updates are then communicated to the working directory of corresponding jobs in HDFS through the JobClient interface. The slave configuration thread—that we have implemented in the node manager of YARN—then periodically checks whether per task configuration files are updated, picks up the values and changes the parameters accordingly.

System Overhead: The test runs using aggressive tuning can potentially have longer execution times than compared to the test runs using the default configuration. However, MRONLINE is much more effective than other offline tuning techniques in that we finish the test run in one trial instead of $20 - 40$ trials reported by works such as Gunther [25]. For the fast single run use case, we employ conservative tuning, which does not interfere with the application execution flow and thus have minimal overhead. The design of our monitor is also non-intrusive, since we leverage the JobClient APIs within YARN, which functions periodically in the standard setting as well. The dynamic configurator updates the parameter values, which consumes few resources. Thus, we note that the overall overhead of our system is negligible compared to default YARN.

8. EVALUATION

In this section, we show the effectiveness of our approach on a 19 node cluster. We note that the size of our testbed is in line with those considered by recent related works [15, 25]. We first show the performance improvement achieved for the studied MapReduce applications using the aggressive tuning strategy of MRONLINE. Next, we show that MRONLINE can generate desirable configurations that yield better application performance using conserva-

Benchmark	Input Data	Input Size	Shuffle Size	Output Size	#Map, #Reduce	Job Type
Bigram	Wikipedia	90.5 GB	80.8 GB	27.6 GB	676, 200	Shuffle
Inverted index	Wikipedia	90.5 GB	38 GB	10.3 GB	676, 200	Map
Wordcount	Wikipedia	90.5 GB	30.3 GB	8.6 GB	676, 200	Map
Text search	Wikipedia	90.5 GB	2.3 GB	469 MB	676, 200	Compute
Bigram	Freebase	100.8 GB	84.8 GB	77.8 GB	752, 200	Shuffle
Inverted index	Freebase	100.8 GB	21 GB	11 GB	752, 200	Compute
Wordcount	Freebase	100.8 GB	16.7 GB	9.4 GB	752, 200	Map
Text search	Freebase	100.8 GB	906 MB	229 MB	752, 200	Compute
Terasort	synthetic	100 GB	100 GB	100 GB	752, 200	Shuffle
BBP	N/A	0	252 KB	0	100, 1	Compute

Table 3: The benchmarks used in our tests and their characteristics.

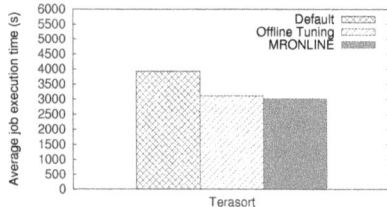

Figure 4: Job execution times under MRON-LINE, offline tuning, and the default YARN configuration for Terasort for the expedited test runs use case.

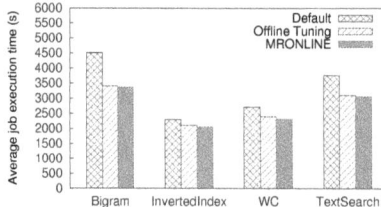

Figure 5: Job execution times under MRON-LINE, offline tuning, and the default YARN configuration using the Wikipedia data set for the expedited test runs use case.

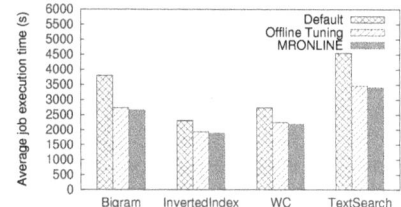

Figure 6: Job execution times under MRON-LINE, offline tuning, and the default YARN configuration using the Freebase data set for the expedited test runs use case.

tive performance tuning as well. Next, we present results to illustrate the impact of job size on the effectiveness of MRONLINE. Finally, we show that MRONLINE can also improve application performance in a multi-tenant environment.

8.1 Methodology

Each node on our 19-node test cluster has two Intel Quad-core Xeon E5462 2.80 GHz CPUs, 12 MB L2 cache, 8 GB memory, a 320 GB Seagate ST3320820AS_P SATA disk, and a 1 $Gbps$ network card. One node works as the master and the rest of the 18 nodes work as slaves. The nodes are arranged in two racks with nine and ten nodes, respectively.

For the expedited test runs use case, we compare MRON-LINE against both the default YARN configuration and a well-regarded offline tuning guide made available by an enterprise cloud provider [2]. For the fast single run use case and multi-tenant tests, we only compare MRONLINE against the default YARN configuration as the offline tuning approach is not capable of tuning and detecting runtime resource utilization hot spots etc. Moreover, since MRONLINE currently does not support the tuning of parameters such as the number of mappers and reducers and application-wide parameters, we use the same values of these parameters for both the offline tuning and MRONLINE. The values used for the default YARN configuration are the ones specified by the Hadoop Wiki [8], with the following changes. We use a block size of 128 MB. The number of virtual cores available for container allocation is 28 (4 for data nodes and node manager daemons), and the memory available for container allocation is 6 GB (2 GB for data nodes and node manager daemons).

Table 3 lists the representative MapReduce applications that we have used in our evaluation. Terasort, word count (WC), text search (Grep), and BBP that is a compute-intensive program that uses Bailey-Borwein-Plouffe to compute exact digits of PI, are available with the Hadoop distribution and serve as standard benchmarks. In addition, we also consider two more applications, *bigram* and *inverted index*. Bigram [26] counts all unique sets of two con-

secutive words in a set of documents. Inverted index [26] generates word to document indexing from a list of documents. We classify the applications into three categories: Map intensive, Shuffle intensive and Compute intensive. Map intensive means that the map phase accounts for the largest part of the execution time (spent mostly doing I/Os). Shuffle intensive jobs spend the largest part of time in the shuffle phase, while compute intensive jobs spend the largest amount of time in the map phase doing computation.

We use two data sets to drive bigram, inverted index, word count and text search. Wikipedia [32] data set has the original size of 45 GB. We concatenate two copies of this data set together to produce a larger data set of 90 GB. Note that this does not change the workload characteristics of the data set. Freebase [18] is an open source 100.8 GB data set released by Google. It is a knowledge graph database for structuring human knowledge, which is used to support the collaborative web based data oriented applications. Finally, the data sets used by Terasort range from 2 GB to 100 GB in size and are generated synthetically using Teragen.

To account for variance in the results due to events such as network, disk I/O congestion, and hardware and file system errors, we repeat each experiment four times. In the following, we report the average results from the multiple runs.

8.2 Performance Improvement for the Expedited Test Runs Use Case

In this experiment, we evaluate the effectiveness of MRONLINE for the expedited test runs use case that employs aggressive tuning. We first run MRONLINE with each of the studied application to generate the best parameter configuration applicable. We then use the configurations to run applications and compare against applications running with the default configuration and with configurations produced using the offline tuning guide [2].

Figure 4 shows the average execution time for Terasort that experiences a 23% improvement in execution time under MRONLINE compared to the default configuration. Figure 5 and Figure 6 show the execution time for the four applications using the Wikipedia and

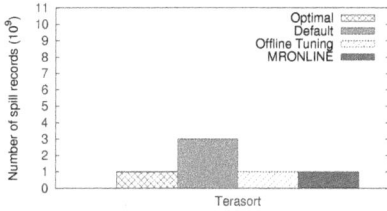

Figure 7: The number of spill records under MRONLINE, offline tuning, and the default YARN configuration for Terasort for the expedited test runs use case.

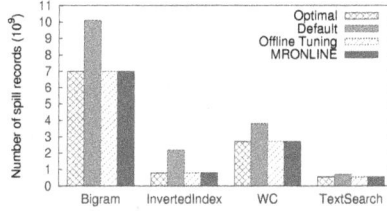

Figure 8: The number of spill records under MRONLINE, offline tuning, and the default YARN configuration using the Wikipedia data set for the expedited test runs use case.

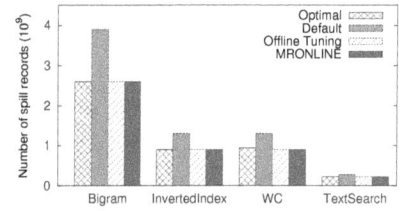

Figure 9: The number of spill records under MRONLINE, offline tuning, and the default YARN configuration using the Freebase data set for the expedited test runs use case.

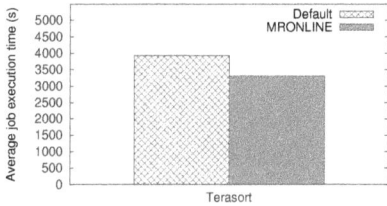

Figure 10: Job execution times under MRON-LINE and the default YARN configuration using Terasort for the fast single run use case.

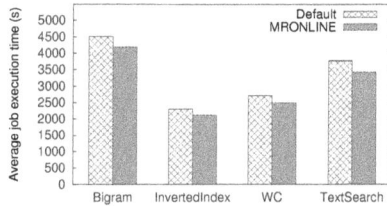

Figure 11: Job execution times under MRON-LINE and the default YARN configuration using the Wikipedia data set for the fast single run use case.

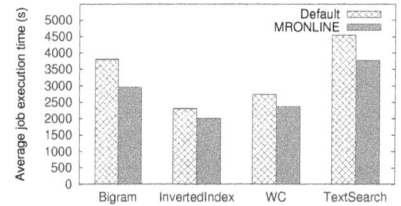

Figure 12: Job execution times under MRON-LINE and the default YARN configuration using the Freebase data set for the fast single run use case.

Freebase data sets, respectively. We observe that for the Wikipedia data set MRONLINE reduces the job execution time by 25%, 11%, 14% and 19% for bigram, inverted index, word count, and text search, respectively. Similarly, the performance enhancement for the Freebase data set under MRONLINE is 30%, 18%, 20%, 25% compared to the default configuration for bigram, inverted index, word count, and text search, respectively. MRONLINE improves the performance mainly due to three factors: 1) it effectively reduces the number of spill records written and read from disks; 2) it increases the resource utilization by tuning the container size for mappers and reducers; and 3) it detects near-optimal values for other performance related parameters. We observe here that compared to the offline tuning guide, MRONLINE yields similar performance. However, MRONLINE is able to finish the gray-box based hill climbing algorithm within a single test run as there are around $600 - 800$ mappers and 200 reducers in these applications. In contrast, the offline guide took us much higher number of runs to determine a suitable configuration to use.

To further understand the effectiveness of MRONLINE, we studied how MRONLINE reduces the number of spill records. Figures 7, 8, and 9 show the number of spill records generated by the map tasks under MRONLINE, the default configuration, and configurations obtained through the offline tuning guide for the studied applications and data sets. In the figures, *Optimal* refers to the number of records generated by a combiner in the map phase or generated by the map function if there is no combiner, and represents the number of spill records that an optimal configuration would produce. We can see that the numbers of spill records are effectively reduced to optimal for all applications by both MRON-LINE and offline tuning. However, MRONLINE also minimizes the number of test runs compared to the offline tuning approach.

8.3 Performance Improvement for the Fast Single Run Use Case

In our next experiment, we compare the job execution time under MRONLINE using the conservative tuning strategy against the

default YARN configuration on the Wikipedia, Freebase and the synthetic data sets. Conservative tuning is beneficial to applications that run once, since the goal is to improve performance and not necessarily find the best configurations. We run the applications under MRONLINE and measure the job execution time. The results are shown in Figures 10, 11 and 12. We observe that MRONLINE is able to improve the performance for all the studied applications and data sets from 8% (for word count using the Wikipedia data set) to up to 22% (for bigram using the Freebase data set). The significant reduction in execution time under MRONLINE is achieved because MRONLINE improves the cluster utilization by adjusting the container size, alleviates the I/O contention by reducing the spill records and searches for the optimal values for other performance related parameters.

This experiment demonstrates that MRONLINE can effectively reduce job execution time for applications that run once or for a few times. For such applications, the users do not need to worry about tuning application parameters before running the jobs and can achieve a speedup automatically by using MRONLINE.

8.4 The Impact of Job Size on the Effectiveness of Parameter Tuning

In our next experiment, we study how the effectiveness of parameter tuning using MRONLINE is affected by job size. To this end, we run Terasort with increasing input data sets ranging from $2\ GB$ to $100\ GB$. The number of reducers is set to about $1/4$ that of the number of mappers. For example, we have 4 reducers and 16 mappers for a job with a size of $2\ GB$, 12 reducers and 46 mappers for another job with a size of $6\ GB$. We execute MRONLINE for a single run of each job to generate an optimal configuration using aggressive tuning. We then use this configuration to run the job again and compare against the default YARN configuration. Figure 13 shows the results, where we can observe that MRONLINE reduces job execution time marginally for jobs with sizes smaller than $10\ GB$. The reason for this is that, for these jobs, MRON-LINE does not have the sufficient number of mappers or reducers

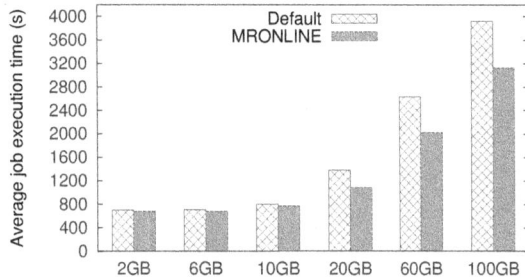

Figure 13: Job execution time under MRONLINE and the default YARN configuration using Terasort with different data set sizes.

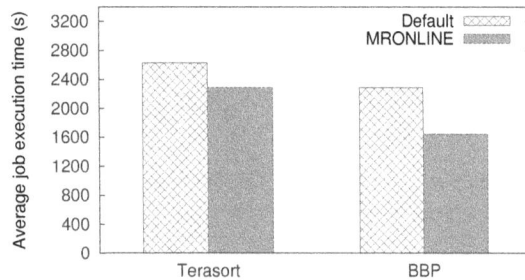

Figure 14: Job execution time for Terasort and BBP.

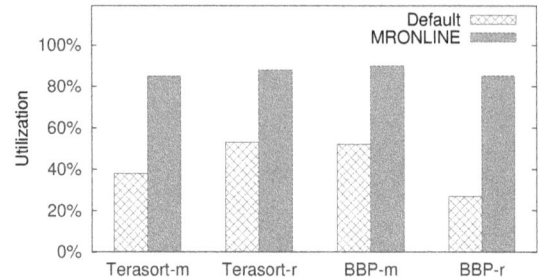

Figure 15: Memory utilization for Terasort and BBP.

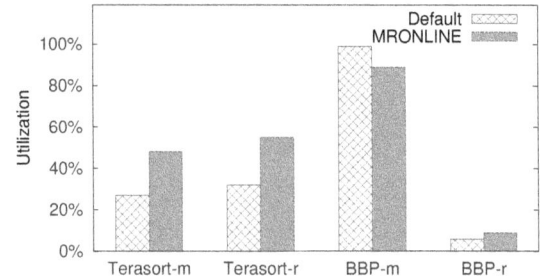

Figure 16: CPU utilization for Terasort and BBP.

to search through the configuration space. Here, jobs finished before MRONLINE can find a good configuration. For jobs that use data sets greater than 20 GB, MRONLINE becomes effective and reduces the job execution time by 21%, 23%, and 20% for job sizes of 20 GB, 60 GB, and 100 GB, respectively. Once MRON-LINE has determined a suitable configuration, increasing the data set size does not further improve performance under MRONLINE. This is because the additional mappers or reducers are unnecessary for MRONLINE as it is able to explore the design space thoroughly using the number available under the 20 GB case.

8.5 MRONLINE Tuning Efficiency in a Multi-tenant Environment

In our next experiment, we demonstrate that MRONLINE is particularly useful in a multi-tenant environment. For this test, we simultaneously run two MapReduce applications, Terasort and BBP, on our cluster using the fair share scheduling algorithm. We configure Terasort with an input data set size of 60 GB with 448 mappers and 200 reducers. BBP is configured to compute 0.5×10^6 digits of PI. We execute MRONLINE with aggressive tuning and produce desirable configurations for the two applications. We compare application characteristics under configurations generated using MRON-LINE to that of the default YARN configuration.

Figure 14 shows the job execution time for Terasort and BBP. We observe that MRONLINE reduces the job execution time by 13% and 28% for Terasort and BBP, respectively. To further understand the performance impact of MRONLINE, we examined the memory and CPU utilization of Terasort and BBP under the two approaches shown in Figure 15 and Figure 16, respectively. In the figures, Terasort-m represents the average utilization of all mappers, while Terasort-r represents the same for all reducers. Similarly, BBP-m and BBP-r show the average utilization for all mappers and reducers, respectively, for BBP. We observe that under the default configuration the memory utilization of both the applications is below

50%. In contrast, MRONLINE improves the memory utilization of the two applications to above 80%, for both map and reduce tasks. For CPU utilization, we see that, with the exception of BBP-m, the utilization is below 25% for all cases under the default configuration. MRONLINE improves the CPU utilization by assigning fewer CPUs to Terasort and BBP-r. Note that the CPU utilization of BBP-m is around 99%. MRONLINE identifies this as CPU over-utilization, and allocates more CPU cores to BBP. Moreover, we note that the number of spill records for Terasort is reduced from 1.8×10^9 under the default configuration to 0.6×10^9 under MRON-LINE. Reducing the number of spill records is beneficial, especially when disk I/O is one of the key performance bottleneck.

This experiment shows that MRONLINE can effectively increase the memory utilization and CPU utilization for Terasort and BBP and thus reduce the job execution time. In other words, in this multi-tenant experiment where CPU is a bottleneck for BBP, MRONLINE successfully identifies idle CPUs and reassign a portion of them to BBP. Thus, we have demonstrated that MRONLINE can mitigate hot spots in the cluster and improve overall system utilization.

9. RELATED WORK

MapReduce Configuration Parameter Tuning: There are several works [13–15] that have focused on MapReduce job configuration tuning in recent years. Herodotos et al. [13–15] proposed a cost based optimization technique to help users identify good job configurations for MapReduce applications. The system consists of a profiler to get concise statistics including data flow information and cost estimation, a what-if engine to reason about the impact of parameter configuration settings, and a cost based optimizer to find good configurations through invocations of the what-if engine. The effectiveness of this approach depends on the accuracy of the what-if engine that uses a mix of simulation and model based estimation. MRONLINE is different from this work in that MRONLINE finds desirable configuration parameters through real test runs on real systems. Additionally, we use task level dynamic configuration to avoid multiple what-if iterations, and unlike such prior approaches are also able to adjust to dynamic cluster runtime status, e.g., network congestion or I/O congestion.

Gunther [25] is another offline tuning method that uses a genetic algorithm to identify good parameter configurations, tries one configuration per test run, and can take $20 - 40$ test runs. In contrast, MRONLINE can perform the tuning in a single job run. Moreover, we use a gray-box based approach that effectively exploits MapReduce runtime statistics, while Gunther is a black-box approach. In addition, we identify two specific use cases where MRONLINE is helpful; aggressive tuning aims to reduce the number of test runs, while conservative tuning can help improve the performance of jobs that only run once. In contrast, Gunther cannot help in either case.

AROMA [24] aims to automate the resource allocation and job configuration for heterogeneous clouds to satisfy SLAs while minimizing cost. AROMA uses a two-phase machine learning and optimization framework based on support vector machine based performance models. The offline phase classifies executed jobs using k-mediod clustering algorithm using CPU, network, and disk utilization patterns, while the online phase captures the resource utilization signature of tested applications. Finally, AROMA finds near optimal resource allocation and configuration parameters based on a pattern matching optimization method. Compared to MRONLINE, AROMA does not support dynamic configuration. Moreover, AROMA has to collect application resource utilization signatures before finding a near optimal configuration. This is not suitable for jobs that run once.

Parameter tuning guides [1, 2, 16, 17, 31] are also proposed by industry and vendors to help MapReduce non-experts to set desirable values for their applications. However, these tuning guides are based on heuristics. The burden is still on the end users to try out multiple parameter combinations, which is time consuming and cumbersome as discussed in Section 1.

MapReduce Performance Tuning: Performance tuning of the MapReduce framework itself [4, 20–22] has also gained a lot of attention from industry and the research community. MANIMAL [20] focuses on the efficiency of query processing of MapReduce framework and utilizes static program analysis techniques on user-defined functions (UDFs) to detect standard query optimization opportunities. To bridge the performance gap of MapReduce and parallel DBMS, Hadoop++ [4] tries to inject optimizations into UDFs, which makes query processing pipeline explicit and present it as a DB style physical query execution plan. This work has a different focus than MRONLINE. SUDO [36] analyzes UDFs to identify beneficial functional properties to optimize data shuffling for MapReduce frameworks by utilizing program analysis techniques. PerfXplain [22] provides a tool for non-expert users to tune MapReduce performance. This tool auto-generates an explanation for the queries comparing two jobs, which can help identify the reasons why inefficient or unexpected behavior happens. However, this work does not provide clear guidelines of what job configuration parameters should be used. Jiang et al. [21] provides a performance study of MapReduce, pinpointing factors that impact MapReduce performance including I/O, indexing, record decoding, grouping schemes and block level scheduling in database context. Although these works share with MRONLINE the goal of improving MapReduce application performance, these systems differ from MRONLINE because of different optimization aspects and different targeted environments. Moreover, to the best of our knowledge, MRONLINE is unique in its focus on YARN-based systems.

Simulation based performance tuning [6, 30] techniques have also been explored. Our own previous work, MRPerf [30], utilizes a simulation methodology to capture various factors that impact Hadoop performance. Similarly, Mumak [6] is designed as a MapReduce simulator for researchers to prototype features and predict their behavior and performance. These projects do not tune configuration parameters as such and only provide means to estimate application performance on given configurations, and thus are complementary to MRONLINE.

Parameter Tuning in Other Areas: A number of search techniques are proposed to find good configuration with high probability [33, 34] in other research areas as well. Recursive random search [34] is a black-box optimization approach that employs a heuristic search algorithm for tuning network parameter configurations. Smart hill climbing, designed for server parameter tuning, is another black-box optimization approach that is designed to improve the recursive random search algorithm. Smart hill climbing adopts a weighted LHS technique to improve the random sampling on the first phase. Moreover, the algorithm learns from past and searches the space using steepest descent direction and improves the search efficiency. The tuning algorithm of MRONLINE is inspired by the smart hill climbing algorithm. However, MRONLINE is unique in its focus on MapReduce, which is a different targeted problem than that addressed by prior works.

iTuned [5] concentrates on tuning database configuration parameters by adaptive sampling and uses an executor to support online experiments through a cycle-stealing paradigm. This approach is not suitable for MapReduce systems. JustRunIt [37] is an experiment based management system for virtualized data centers. It shares with MRONLINE the goal of tuning parameters using actual experiments that are cheaper, simpler and more accurate than performance models or simulations. However, the approach is not simply applicable to MapReduce.

10. CONCLUSION

MapReduce job parameter configuration significantly impacts application performance, yet extant implementations place the burden of tuning the parameters on application programmers. This is not ideal, especially because the application developers may not have the system-level expertise and information needed to select the best configuration. Consequently, the system is utilized inefficiently which leads to degraded application performance. In this paper, we present the design of MRONLINE, a tool that enables task-level dynamic configuration tuning to improve performance of MapReduce applications. MRONLINE expedites the test runs by trying out multiple configurations within a single test run. Given the large MapReduce parameter space, finding a near-optimal configuration in an efficient manner is challenging. To this end, we designed a gray-box based hill climbing algorithm to systematically search through the space and find a desirable configuration. To speedup the convergence iteration of our algorithm, we leverage MapReduce runtime statistics and consider design tuning rules for some of the key parameters. We have implemented MRONLINE on the YARN framework, and our evaluation shows that on a 19-node cluster and across a suite of six representative applications, MRONLINE achieves an average performance improvement of up to 30% compared to the typically used default YARN configurations.

We have focused on key parameters that affect task execution time. In our future work, we plan to investigate tuning of parameters, such as the number of mappers and reducers, which affect the overall application execution time.

11. ACKNOWLEDGMENT

This work was sponsored in part by the NSF under Grants CNS-1016793 and CCF-0746832. Min Li was also supported through an IBM PhD Fellowship. We thank the reviewers for their feedback and appreciate their support for our work. We also thank Minkyong Kim and Krishnaraj K Ravindranathan for the valuable discussions that helped us improve our design.

12. REFERENCES

[1] Cloudera. 7 tips for improving MapReduce performance, 2009. http://blog.cloudera.com/blog/2009/12/7-tips-for-improving-mapreduce-performance/.

[2] Cloudera. Optimizing MapReduce job performance, 2012. http://www.slideshare.net/cloudera/mr-perf.

[3] J. Dean and S. Ghemawat. MapReduce: Simplified data processing on large clusters. In *Proc. USENIX OSDI*, 2004.

[4] J. Dittrich, J.-A. Quiané-Ruiz, A. Jindal, Y. Kargin, V. Setty, and J. Schad. Hadoop++: Making a yellow elephant run like a cheetah (without it even noticing). *Proceedings of the VLDB Endowment*, 3(1-2):515–529, 2010.

[5] S. Duan, V. Thummala, and S. Babu. Tuning database configuration parameters with ituned. *Proceedings of the VLDB Endowment*, 2(1):1246–1257, 2009.

[6] A. S. Foundation. Mumak: MapReduce simulator, 2009. https://issues.apache.org/jira/browse/MAPREDUCE-728.

[7] A. S. Foundation. Apache Giraph, 2013. http://giraph.apache.org/.

[8] A. S. Foundation. Hadoop-2.1.0-Beta, 2013. http://www.trieuvan.com/apache/hadoop/common/hadoop-2.1.0-beta/.

[9] A. S. Foundation. Grep example, 2014. http://wiki.apache.org/hadoop/Grep.

[10] A. S. Foundation. Terasort example, 2014. https://hadoop.apache.org/docs/current/api/org/apache/hadoop/examples/terasort/package-summary.html.

[11] S. Ghemawat, H. Gobioff, and S. Leung. The Google file system. *ACM SIGOPS Operating Systems Review*, 37(5):29–43, 2003.

[12] A. Ghodsi, M. Zaharia, B. Hindman, A. Konwinski, S. Shenker, and I. Stoica. Dominant resource fairness: fair allocation of multiple resource types. In *Proc. USENIX NSDI*, 2011.

[13] H. Herodotou and S. Babu. Profiling, what-if analysis, and cost-based optimization of mapreduce programs. *Proceedings of the VLDB Endowment*, 4(11):1111–1122, 2011.

[14] H. Herodotou, F. Dong, and S. Babu. Mapreduce programming and cost-based optimization? Crossing this chasm with starfish. *Proceedings of the VLDB Endowment*, 4(12):1446–1449, 2011.

[15] H. Herodotou, H. Lim, G. Luo, N. Borisov, L. Dong, F. B. Cetin, and S. Babu. Starfish: A self-tuning system for big data analytics. In *Proc. Conference on Innovative Data System Research*, 2011.

[16] Impetus. Advanced Hadoop tuning and optimizations, 2009. http://www.slideshare.net/ImpetusInfo/ppt-on-advanced-hadoop-tuning-n-optimisation.

[17] Impetus. Hadoop performance tuning, 2012. https://hadoop-toolkit.googlecode.com/files/White paper-HadoopPerformanceTuning.pdf.

[18] G. Inc. Freebase data dumps, 2013. https://developers.google.com/freebase/data.

[19] A. Incubator. Spark: Lightning-fast cluster computing, 2013. http://spark.incubator.apache.org/.

[20] E. Jahani, M. J. Cafarella, and C. Ré. Automatic optimization for mapreduce programs. *Proceedings of the VLDB Endowment*, 4(6):385–396, 2011.

[21] D. Jiang, B. C. Ooi, L. Shi, and S. Wu. The performance of mapreduce: An in-depth study. *Proceedings of the VLDB Endowment*, 3(1-2):472–483, 2010.

[22] N. Khoussainova, M. Balazinska, and D. Suciu. Perfxplain: debugging mapreduce job performance. *Proceedings of the VLDB Endowment*, 5(7):598–609, 2012.

[23] Y. Kwon, M. Balazinska, B. Howe, and J. Rolia. Skewtune: Mitigating skew in mapreduce applications. In *Proc. ACM SIGMOD International Conference on Management of Data*, 2012.

[24] P. Lama and X. Zhou. Aroma: Automated resource allocation and configuration of mapreduce environment in the cloud. In *Proc. ACM International Conference on Autonomic Computing*, 2012.

[25] G. Liao, K. Datta, and T. L. Willke. Gunther: Search-based auto-tuning of mapreduce. In *Proc. Springer Euro-Par*, 2013.

[26] J. Lin and C. Dyer. Cloud9: A hadoop toolkit for working with big data, 2010. http://lintool.github.io/Cloud9/index.html.

[27] G. Malewicz, M. H. Austern, A. J. Bik, J. C. Dehnert, I. Horn, N. Leiser, and G. Czajkowski. Pregel: A system for large-scale graph processing. In *Proc. ACM SIGMOD International Conference on Management of Data*, 2010.

[28] Twitter. Storm: Distributed and fault-tolerant realtime computation, 2013. http://storm-project.net/.

[29] V. K. Vavilapalli, A. C. Murthy, C. Douglas, S. Agarwal, M. Konar, R. Evans, T. Graves, J. Lowe, H. Shah, S. Seth, et al. Apache Hadoop Yarn: Yet another resource negotiator. In *Proc. ACM Symposium on Cloud Computing*, 2013.

[30] G. Wang, A. R. Butt, P. Pandey, and K. Gupta. A simulation approach to evaluating design decisions in mapreduce setups. In *Proc. IEEE MASCOTS*, 2009.

[31] T. White. *Hadoop: The Definitive Guide*. O'Reilly, 2012.

[32] Wikipedia. Wikipedia data dumps, 2014. http://dumps.wikimedia.org/enwiki/latest/.

[33] B. Xi, Z. Liu, M. Raghavachari, C. H. Xia, and L. Zhang. A smart hill-climbing algorithm for application server configuration. In *Proc. ACM International Conference on World Wide Web*, 2004.

[34] T. Ye and S. Kalyanaraman. A recursive random search algorithm for large-scale network parameter configuration. *ACM SIGMETRICS Performance Evaluation Review*, 31(1):196–205, 2003.

[35] M. Zaharia, M. Chowdhury, M. J. Franklin, S. Shenker, and I. Stoica. Spark: Cluster computing with working sets. In *Proc. USENIX Conference on Hot Topics in Cloud Computing*, 2010.

[36] J. Zhang, H. Zhou, R. Chen, X. Fan, Z. Guo, H. Lin, J. Y. Li, W. Lin, J. Zhou, and L. Zhou. Optimizing data shuffling in data-parallel computation by understanding user-defined functions. In *Proc. USENIX NSDI*, 2012.

[37] W. Zheng, R. Bianchini, G. J. Janakiraman, J. R. Santos, and Y. Turner. JustRunIt: Experiment-based management of virtualized data centers. In *Proc. USENIX ATC*, 2009.

Scalable Matrix Inversion Using MapReduce

Jingen Xiang*
SAP
Waterloo, Ontario, Canada
xiangjingen@gmail.com

Huangdong Meng*
University of Toronto
Toronto, Ontario, Canada
mhd0371@gmail.com

Ashraf Aboulnaga*
Qatar Computing Research Institute
Doha, Qatar
aaboulnaga@qf.org.qa

ABSTRACT

Matrix operations are a fundamental building block of many computational tasks in fields as diverse as scientific computing, machine learning, and data mining. Matrix inversion is an important matrix operation, but it is difficult to implement in today's popular parallel dataflow programming systems, such as MapReduce. The reason is that each element in the inverse of a matrix depends on multiple elements in the input matrix, so the computation is not easily partitionable. In this paper, we present a scalable and efficient technique for matrix inversion in MapReduce. Our technique relies on computing the LU decomposition of the input matrix and using that decomposition to compute the required matrix inverse. We present a technique for computing the LU decomposition and the matrix inverse using a pipeline of MapReduce jobs. We also present optimizations of this technique in the context of Hadoop. To the best of our knowledge, our technique is the first matrix inversion technique using MapReduce. We show experimentally that our technique has good scalability, enabling us to invert a $10^5 \times 10^5$ matrix in 5 hours on Amazon EC2. We also show that our technique outperforms ScaLAPACK, a state-of-the-art linear algebra package that uses MPI.

Categories and Subject Descriptors

G.1.3 [**Numerical Linear Algebra**]: Matrix inversion; C.2.4 [**Distributed Systems**]: Distributed applications

Keywords

linear algebra; matrix inversion; analytics; MapReduce; Hadoop

1. INTRODUCTION

Parallel dataflow programming systems like MapReduce [8] and Pregel [21] have become very popular as platforms for scalable, analytical, data intensive computing. These systems offer the scalability and fault tolerance that are required to run in a cloud computing environment, plus simple programming models and easy-to-use programmer interfaces. Rich software ecosystems and large

*Work done at the University of Waterloo.

user communities have developed around these systems, and they are being used for many large-scale computational tasks in diverse scientific, business, and web applications. Due to the success and popularity of MapReduce and similar parallel dataflow systems, they are being used not only for the data intensive tasks for which they were originally designed, but also for computationally intensive tasks that have traditionally been assigned to high-performance computing systems. Therefore, there is significant benefit in developing optimized implementations of computationally intensive tasks using these systems. In this paper, we focus on MapReduce, arguably the most popular parallel dataflow programming system, and we present a technique for matrix inversion in MapReduce.

Matrix operations are a fundamental building block of many computational tasks in diverse fields including physics, bioinformatics, simulation, machine learning, data mining, and many others. In most of these fields, there is a need to scale to large matrices to obtain higher fidelity and better results (e.g., running a simulation on a finer grid, or training a machine learning model with more data). To scale to large matrices, it is important to design efficient parallel algorithms for matrix operations, and using MapReduce is one way to achieve this goal. There has been prior work on implementing matrix operations in MapReduce (e.g., [13]), but that work does not handle matrix inversion even though matrix inversion is a very fundamental matrix operation. Matrix inversion is difficult to implement in MapReduce because each element in the inverse of a matrix depends on multiple elements in the input matrix, so the computation is not easily partitionable as required by the MapReduce programming model. In this paper, we address this problem and design a novel partitionable matrix inversion technique that is suitable for MapReduce. We implement our technique in Hadoop, and develop several optimizations as part of this implementation.

Before we present our technique, we further motivate the importance of matrix inversion by presenting some of its applications in different fields. A key application of matrix inversion is solving systems of linear equations. To solve the equation $\mathbf{A}\mathbf{x} = \mathbf{b}$, where $\mathbf{A}$ is an $n \times n$ matrix, and $\mathbf{x}$ and $\mathbf{b}$ are both vectors with n elements, one can multiply both sides of the equation on the left by the the matrix inverse $\mathbf{A}^{-1}$, to get $\mathbf{x} = \mathbf{A}^{-1}\mathbf{b}$.

Matrix inversion is also related to finding eigenvalues and eigenvectors, which is a central problem in many physics and engineering applications. The eigenvalues and eigenvectors of an $n \times n$ matrix can be computed using the inverse iteration method. This method assumes that there is an approximate eigenvalue μ and an approximate eigenvector $\mathbf{v}_0$ for matrix $\mathbf{A}$. The method uses an iteration step to compute an increasingly accurate eigenvector, $\mathbf{v}_{k+1} = \frac{(\mathbf{A} - \mu \mathbf{I}_n)^{-1} \mathbf{v}_k}{||(\mathbf{A} - \mu \mathbf{I}_n)^{-1} \mathbf{v}_k||}$, where I_n is an $n \times n$ identity matrix. At any step in the iteration, the current eigenvalue can be computed as

$\lambda = \frac{\mathbf{v}^T \mathbf{A} \mathbf{v}}{\mathbf{v}^T \mathbf{v}}$, for real-valued $\mathbf{A}$ and $\mathbf{v}$. The efficiency of this iterative method relies on the ability to efficiently invert matrix $\mathbf{A} - \mu \mathbf{I}_n$.

Matrix inversion is also widely used in computed tomography (CT). In CT, the relationship between the original image of the material ($\mathbf{S}$) and the image ($\mathbf{T}$) detected by the detector can be written as: $\mathbf{T} = \mathbf{MS}$, where $\mathbf{M}$ is the projection matrix [28]. In order to reconstruct the original image, we can simply invert the projection matrix and calculate the product of $\mathbf{M}^{-1}$ and $\mathbf{T}$. As the accuracy of the detector increases, the number of image pixels increases and hence the order of the projection matrix ($\mathbf{M}$) also increases, motivating the need for scalable matrix inversion techniques. Image reconstruction using matrix inversion can also be found in other fields such as astrophysics [30].

In bioinformatics, matrix inversion is used to solve the problem of protein structure prediction [22]. A scalable matrix inversion technique would enable novel insights into the evolutionary dynamics of sequence variation and protein folding.

These are but a few of the numerous applications that rely on matrix inversion. In some cases, it may be possible to avoid matrix inversion by using alternate numerical methods (e.g., pseudo-Newton methods for convex optimization), but it is clear that a scalable and efficient matrix inversion technique such as the one we present would be highly useful in many applications.

The fact that our technique uses MapReduce and Hadoop has several advantages. First, our technique benefits from the scalability and fault tolerance of MapReduce. Second, our technique is part of the rich and popular software ecosystem of Hadoop that includes many systems and libraries such as HDFS, Pig, Mahout, Zookeeper, Cassandra, etc. Thus, our matrix inversion technique can easily be integrated with other parts of this ecosystem as needed. Finally, it is important to note that matrix inversion is often not a standalone activity, but rather one component of a rich data analysis workflow. These days, such a workflow is quite likely implemented in Hadoop, so the input matrix to be inverted would be generated by a MapReduce job and stored in HDFS, and the inverse matrix produced as output also needs to be stored in HDFS to be consumed by another MapReduce job. Therefore, while it may be possible to implement matrix inversion using other parallelization platforms such as MPI, a MapReduce matrix inversion technique that can be used as a pluggable component in complex Hadoop data analysis workflows is highly desirable. It may be possible to switch between MapReduce and MPI to perform scalable matrix inversion in these workflows, but staying within MapReduce is certainly more convenient.

Our goal is not to demonstrate that MapReduce is fundamentally superior to MPI or other parallelization platforms. As a matter of fact, some of the optimizations that we propose can be implemented in MPI. Instead, our goal is to provide a novel and powerful matrix inversion implementation that can be used in MapReduce systems, and to demonstrate the judicious mathematical manipulation and careful systems engineering behind this implementation. We experimentally demonstrate by comparing to ScaLAPACK [4] that we do not lose performance by using MapReduce, especially for large matrices (Section 7.5).

Our matrix inversion technique relies on computing the LU decomposition of the input matrix and using that decomposition to compute the required matrix inverse. We chose to use LU decomposition for matrix inversion since it enables us to partition the computation in a way that is suitable for MapReduce. In particular, we developed a technique for computing the LU decomposition of the input matrix using subtasks that do not communicate among each other except through intermediate results, which exactly matches the way mappers and reducers communicate in the

MapReduce computational model. In addition, our LU decomposition technique is carefully designed to partition the computation into subtasks that require the same amount of computation, which ensures that the load among the mappers and reducers is balanced and no map or reduce task can hold up the computation. Our LU decomposition technique is implemented as a pipeline of MapReduce jobs, where the number of jobs in the pipeline and the data movement between the jobs can be precisely determined before the start of the computation.

We also developed a MapReduce technique for computing the inverse of the input matrix from its LU decomposition, and optimizations to improve numerical accuracy and performance in the context of Hadoop.

Note that the crux of our technique is partitioning the computation required for matrix inversion into independent subtasks. Such partitioning is required for any cluster computing framework. Thus, while this paper focuses on MapReduce, our technique can be used as a basis for implementing matrix inversion in other cluster computing systems such as Spark [34] or DryadLINQ [33]. We leave this point as a direction for future work.

The contributions of this paper are as follows:

- The choice of LU decomposition for matrix inversion in order to enable a MapReduce implementation.

- An algorithm for computing the LU decomposition that partitions the computation into independent subtasks.

- An implementation of the proposed algorithms as a pipeline of MapReduce jobs. The source code of this implementation is available on GitHub [31].

- Optimizations of this implementation to improve numerical accuracy, I/O performance, and memory locality.

- An extensive experimental evaluation on Amazon EC2.

The rest of the paper is organized as follows. In Section 2, we present some basic matrix inversion algorithms on a single node. In Section 3, we present related work. Our algorithm is introduced in Section 4, and our implementation in Section 5. We describe optimizations of the implementation in Section 6. We present an experimental evaluation in Section 7. Section 8 concludes.

2. MATRIX INVERSION PRELIMINARIES

For any matrix $\mathbf{A}$, let $[\mathbf{A}]_{ij}$ denote its element of the i-th row and the j-th column, and denote by $[\mathbf{A}]_{[x_1...x_2][y_1...y_2]}$ the block defined by the beginning row x_1 (inclusive) and the ending row x_2 (exclusive), and by the beginning column y_1 (inclusive) and the ending column y_2 (exclusive).

A square matrix $\mathbf{A}$ is a matrix with the same number of rows and columns. The number of rows and columns n is called the *order* of the matrix. The inverse of $\mathbf{A}$ is another square matrix, denoted by $\mathbf{A}^{-1}$, such that $\mathbf{A}\mathbf{A}^{-1} = \mathbf{A}^{-1}\mathbf{A} = \mathbf{I}_n$, where $\mathbf{I}_n$ is the identity matrix of order n. A square matrix $\mathbf{A}$ is invertible if and only if $\mathbf{A}$ is non-singular, that is, $\mathbf{A}$ is of full rank n. The rank of a matrix is the number of rows (or columns) in the largest collection of linearly independent rows (or columns) of a matrix. Therefore a square matrix is invertible if and only if there are no linearly dependent rows (or columns) in this matrix.

The inverse of a matrix can be computed using many methods [23], such as Gauss-Jordan elimination, LU decomposition (also called LU factorization) [19], Singular Value Decomposition (SVD) [27], and QR decomposition [7]. In order to clarify our choice of matrix inversion method for MapReduce, we briefly discuss the different methods. We will show that most of these methods are not easily parallelizable in a MapReduce setting, and justify our choice of LU decomposition. A more detailed discussion can be found in [29].

Gauss-Jordan elimination is a classical and well-known method to calculate the inverse of a matrix [23]. This method has two different variants: row elimination and column elimination. They are quite similar so we only discuss the method using row elimination. The method first concatenates the matrix $\mathbf{A}$ and the identity matrix $\mathbf{I}_n$ into a new matrix $[\mathbf{A}|\mathbf{I}_n]$. Then, using elementary row operations which include row switching, row multiplication, and row addition, the method transforms the left side to the identity matrix, which leaves the right side as the inverse of matrix $\mathbf{A}$. Specifically,

$$[\mathbf{A}|\mathbf{I}_n] \xrightarrow{\text{row operations}} [\mathbf{U}|\mathbf{B}] \xrightarrow{\text{row operations}} [\mathbf{I_n}|\mathbf{A^{-1}}] \qquad (1)$$

where $\mathbf{U}$ is an upper triangular matrix (nonzero elements only on the diagonal and above). The Gauss-Jordan elimination method first converts the matrix $\mathbf{A}$ into an upper triangular matrix in n steps using linear operations on the rows of the matrix as follows. In the first step, the first row is multiplied by a constant such that the first element in this row equals to 1, and the first row times a constant is subtracted from the i-th $(1 < i \leq n)$ row of $[\mathbf{A}|\mathbf{I}_n]$ such that the first element in the i-th $(1 < i \leq n)$ row is 0. In the k-th step, the k-th row is multiplied by a constant such that the k-th element in this row equals to 1, and the k-th row times a constant is subtracted from the i-th $(k < i \leq n)$ row of $[\mathbf{A}|\mathbf{I}_n]$ such that the k-th element in the i-th $(k < i \leq n)$ row is 0. If the k-th element of the k-th row is already 0 or close to 0 before the subtraction, we first swap the k-th row with any row below k where the k-th element is not 0. This is called *pivoting*, and it improves numerical accuracy. After $n - 1$ steps, the left part of matrix $[\mathbf{A}|\mathbf{I}_n]$ is converted into an upper triangular matrix.

Next, the method converts the upper triangular matrix into an identity matrix using row operations similar to the ones described in the previous paragraph. This requires n steps, and it also converts the right part into the inverse of matrix $\mathbf{A}$. The Gauss-Jordan method uses n^3 multiplication operations and n^3 addition operations to invert an $n \times n$ matrix, which is as efficient as, if not better than, any other method. However, due to the large number of steps that depend on each other in a sequential fashion, this method is difficult to parallelize in MapReduce since it would require a large number of MapReduce jobs that are executed sequentially. For example, Quintana et al. [25] propose a parallel (not MapReduce) matrix inversion algorithm based on Gauss-Jordan elimination, but this method requires n iterations so a MapReduce implementation would require a pipeline of n MapReduce jobs. A main contribution of our paper is reducing this number to around n/n_b jobs (details in Section 4).

The LU decomposition method, also called LU factorization, first decomposes the original matrix into a product of two matrices $\mathbf{A} = \mathbf{LU}$, where $\mathbf{L}$ is a lower triangular matrix that has nonzero elements only on the diagonal and below, and $\mathbf{U}$ is an upper triangular matrix that has nonzero elements only on the diagonal and above. Since the inverse of a triangular matrix is easy to compute using back substitution (described in Section 4), we compute the inverse of $\mathbf{A}$ as $\mathbf{U}^{-1}\mathbf{L}^{-1}$. The LU decomposition method uses the same number of multiplication and addition operations as the Gauss-Jordan method. However the LU decomposition method is much easier to parallelize because the LU decomposition can be implemented using a recursive block method. Therefore, in this paper, we use the LU decomposition method (details in Section 4).

Instead of decomposing matrix $\mathbf{A}$ into the product of two matrices, the SVD decomposition method [23] decomposes matrix $\mathbf{A}$ into the product of three matrices, $\mathbf{A} = \mathbf{UWV}^T$ ($\mathbf{V}^T$ is the transpose of matrix $\mathbf{V}$). $\mathbf{W}$ is a diagonal matrix with only positive or zero elements. $\mathbf{U}$ and $\mathbf{V}$ are both orthogonal matrices (i.e., $\mathbf{UU}^T = \mathbf{VV}^T = \mathbf{I}_n$), such that the inverse of $\mathbf{A}$ can be given by $\mathbf{A}^{-1} = \mathbf{VW}^{-1}\mathbf{U}^T$, where the inverse of diagonal matrix $\mathbf{W}$ is easily obtained by $[\mathbf{W}^{-1}]_{ii} = 1/[\mathbf{W}]_{ii}$ in running time $O(n)$. The SVD method needs frequent row exchanges, which means that the computation cannot be partitioned into independent subtasks, so it is not suitable for MapReduce.

The QR decomposition first decomposes the original matrix $\mathbf{A}$ into a product of an orthogonal matrix $\mathbf{Q}$ and an upper triangular matrix $\mathbf{R}$, i.e., $\mathbf{A} = \mathbf{QR}$ and $\mathbf{A}^{-1} = \mathbf{R}^{-1}\mathbf{Q}^T$. One way to compute the QR decomposition is using the Gram-Schmidt process [23]. This effectively decomposes the matrix but requires computing a sequence of n vectors where each vector relies on all previous vectors (i.e., n steps are required). Thus, the QR decomposition method is not easy to parallelize in MapReduce.

To recap: There are multiple ways to compute the inverse of a matrix. Many of these ways use an optimal number of multiplication and addition operations, but are not easy to parallelize. In this paper we use LU decomposition since it uses the optimal number of operations and is easy to parallelize. LU decomposition can also be used with pivoting to improve numerical accuracy.

3. RELATED WORK

Several software packages have been developed that support matrix inversion, such as LINPACK [10], LAPACK [2], and ScaLA-PACK [4]. The LINPACK package is written in Fortran and designed for supercomputers. The LAPACK package is developed from LINPACK and is designed to run efficiently on shared-memory vector supercomputers. ScaLAPACK is a software package that tries to provide a high-performance linear algebra library for parallel distributed memory machines instead of shared-memory in LA-PACK. This package provides some routines for matrix inversion (see Section 7.5 for details). However, this package does not provide any fault tolerance, while our algorithm provides fault tolerance through the use of MapReduce. In addition, we show that the scalability of ScaLAPACK is not as good as our algorithm.

Parallel algorithms for inverting some special matrices also appear in the literature. Lau, Kumar, and Venkatesh [17] propose algorithms for parallel inversion of sparse symmetric positive matrices on SIMD and MIMD parallel computing platforms. It is not a surprise that these algorithms perform better than general algorithms that do not take into account any special properties of the input matrix. For symmetric positive definite matrices (not necessarily sparse), Bientinesi, Gunter, and Geijn [3] present a parallel matrix inversion algorithm based on the Cholesky factorization for symmetric matrices. Their implementation is based on the Formal Linear Algebra Methodology Environment (FLAME). The implementation shows good performance and scalability, but it does not work for general matrices and is not suitable for large clusters.

The most important step in our matrix inversion technique is LU decomposition. This decomposition has been investigated by many researchers. Agullo et al. [1] have shown that the LU decomposition in double precision arithmetic can reach a throughput of 500 Gflops. That work uses powerful CPUs, GPUs, and large memory. Although this method can solve the LU decomposition problem very efficiently, it is a centralized method that is not suitable for MapReduce. Moreover, it needs special hardware (GPUs) and large memory.

Zheng et al. [36] present an implementation of LU decomposition on a multi-core digital signal processor that does pre-fetching and pre-shuffling in MapReduce [26]. The algorithm is very simple and only runs row operations in reduce tasks, using the LU decomposition algorithm on a single node. That is, one reduce task computes one row as in lines 10–12 in Algorithm 1, so that the method needs n MapReduce tasks to decompose an $n \times n$ matrix, which represents very poor scalability.

Matrix inversion using LU decomposition has been investigated recently by Dongarra et al. [9], where a tile data layout [1] is used to compute the LU decomposition and the upper triangular matrix inversion. In that paper, a run time environment called QUARK is used to dynamically schedule numerical kernels on the available processing units in order to reduce the synchronization required between different CPU cores. The algorithm is suitable for multi-core architectures with shared memory and it achieves better performance than other numerical libraries, such as LAPACK and ScaLAPACK. However, this algorithm is not suitable for a distributed environment, since it relies on large shared memory. Hence, its scalability is limited.

Zhang and Yang [35] investigate I/O optimization for big array analytics. They improve the performance of a broad range of big array operations by increasing sharing opportunities. Our technique also optimizes I/O for big matrices (Section 6.2). However, our technique mainly focuses on reusing the data in memory as many times as possible to reduce the need for reading data from disk.

To the best of our knowledge, there are no matrix inversion algorithms using MapReduce, although there are several software systems for other matrix operations using MapReduce. One of these systems is SystemML [13], which provides a high-level language for expressing some matrix operations such as matrix multiplication, division, and transpose, but not matrix inversion. SystemML provides MapReduce implementations of these operations, and it achieves good scalability and fault tolerance. A MapReduce implementation of matrix factorization using distributed stochastic gradient descent is described in [12], and is extended to Spark in [18]. These works do not help in solving the matrix inversion problem.

Two other systems that support matrix operations are the MADlib library [15] and MadLINQ [24]. MADlib does not use MapReduce but instead focuses on parallel analytics inside relational database systems. MADlib includes a conjugate gradient method to solve linear equations, but it does not support parallel matrix inversion. MadLINQ provides a programming model for matrix operations and an execution framework based on DryadLINQ [33], but it does not directly address matrix inversion.

4. MATRIX INVERSION USING LU DECOMPOSITION

As discussed in Section 2, LU decomposition is the fundamental step in our solution to the matrix inversion problem. In this section, we show how we compute the lower triangular matrix $\mathbf{L}$ and the upper triangular matrix $\mathbf{U}$ in both single node and parallel settings.

4.1 LU Decomposition on a Single Node

The LU decomposition algorithm on a single node is widely studied. It has two variants: with and without pivoting. Since pivoting can significantly improve numerical accuracy, we only discuss the algorithm with pivoting (in Algorithm 1, the row having the maximum j-th element among rows j to n is selected in the j-th loop). Although this algorithm can be found in many references (e.g., [14] and [23]), we present it here for completeness.

Algorithm 1 LU decomposition on a single node.

1: **function** LUDecomposition($\mathbf{A}$)
2: **for** i = 1 **to** n **do**
3:     j = {j | $[\mathbf{A}]_{ji}$ = max($[\mathbf{A}]_{ii}, [\mathbf{A}]_{i+1i}, ..., [\mathbf{A}]_{ni}$)}
4:     Add j to $\mathbf{P}$
5:     Swap i-th row with j-th row if $i \neq j$
6:     **for** j = i + 1 **to** n **do**
7:         $[\mathbf{A}]_{ji} = [\mathbf{A}]_{ji}/[\mathbf{A}]_{ii}$
8:     **end for**
9:     **for** j = i + 1 **to** n **do**
10:         **for** k = i + 1 **to** n **do**
11:             $[\mathbf{A}]_{jk} = [\mathbf{A}]_{jk} - [\mathbf{A}]_{ji} \times [\mathbf{A}]_{ik}$
12:         **end for**
13:     **end for**
14: **end for**
15: **return** $(\mathbf{A}, \mathbf{P})$ /* i.e., **return** (L, U, P) */

Let $a_{ij} = [\mathbf{A}]_{ij}, l_{ij} = [\mathbf{L}]_{ij}$, and $u_{ij} = [\mathbf{U}]_{ij}$. The LU decomposition $\mathbf{A} = \mathbf{L}\mathbf{U}$ can be presented as follows (the blank elements in the $\mathbf{L}$ and $\mathbf{U}$ matrices are zeros):

$$
\begin{pmatrix}
a_{11} & a_{12} & ... & a_{1n} \\
a_{21} & a_{22} & ... & a_{2n} \\
a_{31} & a_{32} & ... & a_{3n} \\
... & & & \\
a_{n1} & a_{n2} & ... & a_{nn}
\end{pmatrix} = \tag{2}
$$

$$
\begin{pmatrix}
l_{11} & & & \\
l_{12} & l_{22} & & \\
l_{13} & l_{23} & l_{33} & \\
... & & & \\
l_{n1} & l_{2n} & ... & l_{nn}
\end{pmatrix}
\begin{pmatrix}
u_{11} & u_{12} & ... & u_{1n} \\
 & u_{22} & ... & u_{2n} \\
 & & u_{33} & ... \\
 & & & ... \\
 & & & u_{nn}
\end{pmatrix}
$$

This matrix multiplication can be viewed as a system of linear equations. Since the difference between the number of unknown arguments (l_{ij} and u_{ij}) and the number of equations is n, there are n free arguments that can be set to any value. Generally, these n free arguments are chosen to be l_{ii} or u_{ii} ($i = 1, ..., n$) and they are all set to be 1.0. In our work, we set all l_{ii} to 1.0. The other remaining unknown arguments can be derived using the following equations:

$$
u_{ij} = a_{ij} - \sum_{k=1}^{j-1} l_{jk} u_{kj}
$$

$$
l_{ij} = \frac{1}{u_{jj}} (a_{ij} - \sum_{k=1}^{j-1} l_{ik} u_{kj}) \tag{3}
$$

In order to improve numerical accuracy, the rows of the original matrix $\mathbf{A}$ are permuted, and we decompose the pivoted (i.e., permuted) matrix $\mathbf{PA}$ instead of the original one. That is, we find $\mathbf{L}$ and $\mathbf{U}$ such that $\mathbf{PA} = \mathbf{LU}$. The permutation matrix $\mathbf{P}$ is a square binary matrix, in each row and column of which there is exactly one entry that is 1, and 0's elsewhere. Multiplying this matrix into $\mathbf{A}$ will permute the rows or columns of $\mathbf{A}$. It should be noted that pivoting in LU decomposition does not affect the final inverse of matrix $\mathbf{A}$ because we can apply the permutation matrix $\mathbf{P}$ to the product of the inverses of $\mathbf{L}$ and $\mathbf{U}$. That is, we can compute $\mathbf{U}^{-1}\mathbf{L}^{-1}\mathbf{P}$ to obtain the inverse of original matrix $\mathbf{A}$ since $\mathbf{U}^{-1}\mathbf{L}^{-1}\mathbf{PA} = \mathbf{I}_n$. Computing $\mathbf{U}^{-1}\mathbf{L}^{-1}\mathbf{P}$ is equivalent to permuting the columns in $\mathbf{U}^{-1}\mathbf{L}^{-1}$ according to $\mathbf{P}$. The pseudocode of LU decomposition with pivoting is shown in Algorithm 1.

In this algorithm, the result lower triangular matrix and upper triangular matrix are stored in place of the input matrix $\mathbf{A}$. That is,

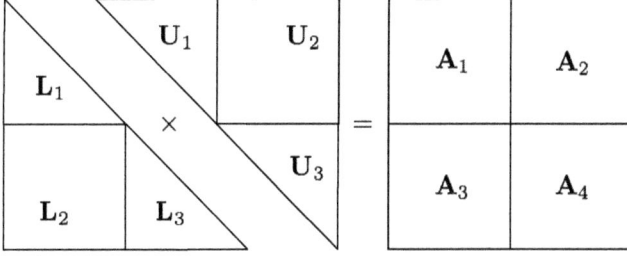

Figure 1: Block method for LU decomposition.

at the end of the algorithm, the lower triangle of $\mathbf{A}$ will be replaced with the lower triangle of $\mathbf{L}$ (excluding the diagonal elements of $\mathbf{L}$, which are all set to 1.0 and do not need to be stored), and the upper triangle of $\mathbf{A}$ will be replaced with the upper triangle of $\mathbf{U}$.

Since there is only one nonzero element in each row or column of the permutation matrix $\mathbf{P}$, the permutation of rows can be stored in an array $\mathbf{S}$, where $[\mathbf{S}]_i$ indicates the permuted row number for the i-th row of $\mathbf{A}$.

After decomposing $\mathbf{A}$ into $\mathbf{L}$ and $\mathbf{U}$, we need to invert $\mathbf{L}$ and $\mathbf{U}$ separately. The inverse of a lower triangular matrix is given by

$$[\mathbf{L}^{-1}]_{ij} = \begin{cases} 0 & \text{for } i < j \\ \frac{1}{[\mathbf{L}]_{ii}} & \text{for } i = j \\ -\frac{1}{[\mathbf{L}]_{ii}} \sum_{k=j}^{i-1} [\mathbf{L}]_{ik}[\mathbf{L}^{-1}]_{kj} & \text{for } i > j \end{cases} \quad (4)$$

The inverse of the upper triangular matrix can be computed similarly. In fact, in our implementation, we invert the upper triangular matrix $\mathbf{U}$ by computing the inverse of $\mathbf{U}^T$, which is a lower triangular matrix, as an optimization (details in Section 5).

4.2 Block Method for Parallel LU Decomposition

The classical LU algorithm is not suitable for parallelization in MapReduce, so we use a block method instead to compute the LU decomposition in parallel. Block methods have been used before for LU decomposition. For example, the tile LU algorithm [1] splits the matrix into square submatrices and updates these submatrices one-by-one. Our block method splits the input matrix as illustrated in Figure 1. In this method, the lower triangular matrix $\mathbf{L}$ and the upper triangular matrix $\mathbf{U}$ are both split into three submatrices, while the original matrix $\mathbf{A}$ is split into four submatrices. These smaller matrices satisfy the following equations:

$$\begin{aligned} \mathbf{L}_1\mathbf{U}_1 &= \mathbf{P}_1\mathbf{A}_1 \\ \mathbf{L}_1\mathbf{U}_2 &= \mathbf{P}_1\mathbf{A}_2 \\ \mathbf{L}_2'\mathbf{U}_1 &= \mathbf{A}_3 \\ \mathbf{L}_3\mathbf{U}_3 &= \mathbf{P}_2(\mathbf{A}_4 - \mathbf{L}_2'\mathbf{U}_2) \\ \mathbf{L}_2 &= \mathbf{P}_2\mathbf{L}_2' \end{aligned} \quad (5)$$

where both $\mathbf{P}_1$ and $\mathbf{P}_2$ are permutations of rows. The entire LU decomposition can be represented as

$$\mathbf{LU} = \begin{pmatrix} \mathbf{P}_1 & \\ & \mathbf{P}_2 \end{pmatrix} \mathbf{A} = \mathbf{PA}$$

where $\mathbf{P}$ is also a permutation of rows obtained by augmenting $\mathbf{P}_1$ and $\mathbf{P}_2$.

This method partitions an LU decomposition into two smaller LU decompositions and two linear equations which can easily be computed in parallel, as we explain next. The logical order of computing the L and U blocks on the left-hand-side of Equation 5 is as

follows: First, $\mathbf{L}_1$ and $\mathbf{U}_1$ are computed from $\mathbf{A}_1$. Then, $\mathbf{L}_2'$ and $\mathbf{U}_2$ are computed from $\mathbf{L}_1$, $\mathbf{U}_1$, $\mathbf{A}_2$, and $\mathbf{A}_3$. Third, $\mathbf{L}_3$ and $\mathbf{U}_3$ are computed from $\mathbf{A}_4 - \mathbf{L}_2'\mathbf{U}_2$. Finally, $\mathbf{L}_2$ is computed from $\mathbf{L}_2'$ and $\mathbf{P}_2$.

First, let us examine the computation of $\mathbf{L}_1$ and $\mathbf{U}_1$. If submatrix $\mathbf{A}_1$ is small enough, e.g., order of 10^3 or less, it can be decomposed into $\mathbf{L}_1$ and $\mathbf{U}_1$ on a single node very efficiently (about 1 second on a typical modern computer). In our MapReduce implementation, we decompose such small matrices in the MapReduce master node using Algorithm 1.

If submatrix $\mathbf{A}_1$ is not small enough, we can recursively partition it into smaller submatrices as in Figure 1 until the final submatrix is small enough to decompose on a single node. Note that while this is conceptually a recursive computation, the number of partitioning steps (i.e., the depth of recursion) can be precomputed at the start of the matrix inversion process, so that the computation is implemented by a predefined pipeline of MapReduce jobs. In this pipeline, the input matrix is read only once and the partitioned matrix is written only once, as described in Section 5.2.

After obtaining $\mathbf{L}_1$ and $\mathbf{U}_1$, the elements of $\mathbf{L}_2'$ and $\mathbf{U}_2$ can be computed using the following two equations (for simplicity, we present the equations without pivoting since pivoting does not increase the computational complexity):

$$\begin{aligned} [\mathbf{L}_2']_{ij} &= \frac{1}{[\mathbf{U}_1]_{ii}} \left([\mathbf{A}_3]_{ij} - \sum_{k=1}^{i-1} [\mathbf{L}_2']_{ik}[\mathbf{U}_1]_{kj} \right) \\ [\mathbf{U}_2]_{ij} &= \frac{1}{[\mathbf{L}_1]_{ii}} \left([\mathbf{A}_2]_{ij} - \sum_{k=1}^{i-1} [\mathbf{L}_1]_{ik}[\mathbf{U}_2]_{kj} \right) \end{aligned} \quad (6)$$

From these equations, it is clear that the elements in one row of $\mathbf{L}_2'$ are independent of the elements in other rows. Similarly, the elements in one column of $\mathbf{U}_2$ are independent of the elements in other columns. Therefore, each row of $\mathbf{L}_2'$ and each column of $\mathbf{U}_2$ can be computed independently, so we can parallelize the computation of $\mathbf{L}_2'$ and $\mathbf{U}_2$. In MapReduce, we can use one map function (multiple copies of which are executed in parallel in multiple map tasks) to compute $\mathbf{L}_2'$ and $\mathbf{U}_2$ in parallel. We use the reduce function of the same MapReduce job to compute $\mathbf{A}_4 - \mathbf{L}_2'\mathbf{U}_2$ in parallel in the reduce tasks.

After obtaining $\mathbf{A}_4 - \mathbf{L}_2'\mathbf{U}_2$, we decompose it into $\mathbf{L}_3$ and $\mathbf{U}_3$. If $\mathbf{A}_4 - \mathbf{L}_2'\mathbf{U}_2$ is small enough, $\mathbf{L}_3$ and $\mathbf{U}_3$ are computed on the MapReduce master node using Algorithm 1. Otherwise, $\mathbf{A}_4 - \mathbf{L}_2'\mathbf{U}_2$ is further partitioned and the computation proceeds recursively. As with $\mathbf{A}_1$, the number of partitioning steps can be precomputed and the recursive computation can be implemented by a predefined pipeline of MapReduce jobs. One difference between $\mathbf{A}_1$ and $\mathbf{A}_4 - \mathbf{L}_2'\mathbf{U}_2$ is that $\mathbf{A}_1$ can be read from the input matrix and completely partitioned into as many pieces as necessary before the LU decomposition starts, while $\mathbf{A}_4 - \mathbf{L}_2'\mathbf{U}_2$ can be computed and partitioned only after $\mathbf{L}_2'$ and $\mathbf{U}_2$ are computed. Note that while $\mathbf{A}_1$ and $\mathbf{A}_4 - \mathbf{L}_2'\mathbf{U}_2$ may need additional partitioning, $\mathbf{A}_2$ and $\mathbf{A}_3$ never need additional partitioning due to the easily parallelizable nature of computing $\mathbf{L}_2'$ and $\mathbf{U}_2$ using Equation 6.

The pseudocode of block LU decomposition is shown in Algorithm 2. In this algorithm, at the end of the block decomposition, the permutation matrix $\mathbf{P}$ is obtained by augmenting $\mathbf{P}_1$ and $\mathbf{P}_2$. The lower triangular matrix $\mathbf{L}$ is obtained by augmenting $\mathbf{L}_1$, $\mathbf{L}_2'$ permuted by $\mathbf{P}_2$, and $\mathbf{L}_3$. The upper triangular matrix $\mathbf{U}$ is obtained by augmenting $\mathbf{U}_1$, $\mathbf{U}_2$, and $\mathbf{U}_3$ (Figure 1).

Algorithm 2 Block LU decomposition.

1: **function** BlockLUDecom($\mathbf{A}$)
2:   **if** A is small enough **then**
3:     $(\mathbf{L}, \mathbf{U}, \mathbf{P}) = $ LUDecompoistion($\mathbf{A}$)
4:   **else**
5:     Partition $\mathbf{A}$ into $\mathbf{A}_1, \mathbf{A}_2, \mathbf{A}_3, \mathbf{A}_4$
6:     $(\mathbf{L}_1, \mathbf{U}_1, \mathbf{P}_1) = $ BlockLUDecom($\mathbf{A}_1$)
7:     Compute $\mathbf{U}_2$ from $\mathbf{A}_2$, $\mathbf{U}_1$ and $\mathbf{P}_1$
8:     Compute $\mathbf{L}_2'$ from $\mathbf{A}_3$ and $\mathbf{U}_1$
9:     Compute $\mathbf{B} = \mathbf{A}_4 - \mathbf{L}_2' \mathbf{U}_2$
10:     $(\mathbf{L}_3, \mathbf{U}_3, \mathbf{P}_2) = $ BlockLUDecom($\mathbf{B}$)
11:     $\mathbf{P} = $ Combination of $\mathbf{P}_1$ and $\mathbf{P}_2$
12:     $\mathbf{L} = $ Combination of $\mathbf{L}_1, \mathbf{L}_2', \mathbf{L}_3$, and $\mathbf{P}_2$
13:     $\mathbf{U} = $ Combination of $\mathbf{U}_1, \mathbf{U}_2$ and $\mathbf{U}_3$
14:   **end if**
15: **return** $(\mathbf{L}, \mathbf{U}, \mathbf{P})$

It should be noted that the MapReduce implementation of block LU decomposition consists of a pipeline of MapReduce jobs. MapReduce implementations of other matrix inversion methods such as Gauss-Jordan elimination or QR decomposition would also consist of pipelines of MapReduce jobs. However, a key advantage of block LU decomposition, and the main reason we chose it over other matrix inversion methods, is that the number of iteration steps (i.e., the number of MapReduce jobs in the pipeline) can be reduced by LU decomposing small matrices on one computer (the MapReduce master node). If n_b is the maximum order of a matrix that can be LU decomposed on a single computer in a few seconds, then block LU decomposition would require around n/n_b iterations (modulo rounding if n is not a power of 2 and is not divisible by n_b). In contrast, we were unable to reduce the number of iterations required by other methods such as Gauss-Jordan elimination or QR decomposition below n. The reason is that the computation in these other methods proceeds one vector at a time, and we have n vectors, while the computation in block LU decomposition proceeds on block at a time, and we have around n/n_b blocks.

To quantify the difference in the number of iterations, consider that in our experiments we use $n_b = 3200$. For this n_b, inverting a matrix with $n = 10^5$ requires 32 iterations using block LU decomposition as opposed to 10^5 iterations using, say, QR decomposition.

4.3 Computing the Matrix Inverse

After obtaining the lower triangular matrix $\mathbf{L}$ and the upper triangular matrix $\mathbf{U}$, we can compute the inverses of these two matrices using Equation 4. Inspecting this equation, we can see that a column of the matrix inverse is independent of other columns of the inverse. Therefore, the columns can be computed independently in parallel. After computing the inverses of $\mathbf{L}$ and $\mathbf{U}$, the inverse of the original matrix can be obtained by multiplying $\mathbf{U}^{-1}$ by $\mathbf{L}^{-1}$, which can also be done in parallel, and then permuting the resulting matrix according to array $\mathbf{S}$ (recall that $\mathbf{S}$ is a compact representation of $\mathbf{P}$). That is, $[\mathbf{A}^{-1}]_{[\mathbf{S}]_i j} = \sum_{k=1}^{n} [\mathbf{U}^{-1}]_{ik} [\mathbf{L}^{-1}]_{kj}$.

5. IMPLEMENTATION IN MAPREDUCE

In this section, we discuss the implementation of our algorithm in MapReduce. This implementation is available on GitHub [31]. It involves several steps: (1) We use the master compute node to create some control files in HDFS, which are used as input files for the mappers of all MapReduce jobs. (2) We launch a MapReduce job to recursively partition the input matrix $\mathbf{A}$. (3) We launch a series of MapReduce jobs to compute $\mathbf{L}_2'$, $\mathbf{U}_2$, and $\mathbf{B} = \mathbf{A}_4 -$

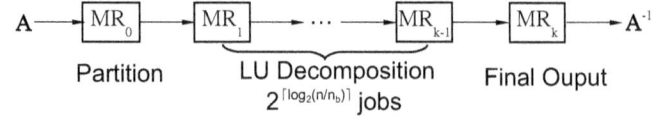

Figure 2: MapReduce pipeline for matrix inversion.

$\mathbf{L}_2' \mathbf{U}_2$ for the different partitions of $\mathbf{A}$ as in Algorithm 2. Matrices $\mathbf{L}_1$, $\mathbf{U}_1$, $\mathbf{L}_3$, and $\mathbf{U}_3$ are computed in the master nodes of these MapReduce jobs if they are small enough (line 3 in Algorithm 2). Otherwise, they are computed by other MapReduce jobs assigned by the master node (line 15 in Algorithm 2). (4) We launch a final MapReduce job to produce the final output by computing $\mathbf{U}^{-1}$, $\mathbf{L}^{-1}$ and $\mathbf{A}^{-1} = \mathbf{U}^{-1} \mathbf{L}^{-1} \mathbf{P}$.

The number of MapReduce jobs required to compute the LU decomposition (Step 3) depends on the order n of matrix $\mathbf{A}$, and on the bound value n_b. Recall that n_b is the order of the largest matrix that can be LU decomposed on a single node (in our case the MapReduce master node). The number of MapReduce jobs is given by $2^{\lceil \log_2 \frac{n}{n_b} \rceil}$. Thus, we have a pipeline of MapReduce jobs as shown in Figure 2. For typical values of n and n_b, the number of MapReduce jobs in this pipeline is small enough that coordination and bookkeeping overheads are minimal. In our experiments, the maximum number of MapReduce jobs in any pipeline was 33.

The bound value should be set so that the time to LU decompose a matrix of order n_b on the master node is approximately equal to the constant time required to launch a MapReduce job. If the running time to decompose a matrix of order n_b on the master node is significantly less than the launch time of a MapReduce job, there will be more MapReduce jobs than necessary and we can increase n_b to reduce the number of MapReduce jobs and also reduce the total running time of LU decomposition. On the other hand, if the running time on the master node is significantly larger than the launch time of a job, the LU decomposition on the master node becomes the bottleneck and we can improve performance by reducing n_b so that we partition the matrix into smaller submatrices. Based on this reasoning and measurements conducted in our experimental environment, we set n_b to 3200 in our experiments.

In our implementation, we use the Java data type **double** (64 bits) for the input matrix and all our calculations. This data type provided sufficient numerical accuracy in all our experiments. We leave a deeper investigation of numerical stability for future work.

Next, we discuss the steps of the implementation. For the purpose of this discussion, Figure 3 shows an example of how the input matrix is partitioned, and Figure 4 shows the HDFS directory structure used by our implementation. HDFS directory "Root" is the work directory, and file "a.txt" in "Root" is the input matrix.

5.1 Input Files on MapReduce

In the first step, the master compute node controlling the entire workflow creates m_0 files in HDFS, where m_0 is the number of compute nodes. These files are used as input files for all launched MapReduce jobs and they are stored in "Root/MapInput/" (purple labels in Figure 4). The purpose of these files is provide an identifier for each mapper, so that the mapper can determine its role based on this identifier. Each file contains one integer: the first file A.0 contains 0, the second file A.1 contains 1, ..., and the last file A.$m_0 - 1$ contains $m_0 - 1$. The mappers use these files to control the computation, and they produce the output required for inverting the input matrix by writing directly to HDFS.

5.2 Data Partitioning and I/O Efficiency

In this section, we discuss how the input matrix is partitioned for LU decomposition and how the different partitions flow through the

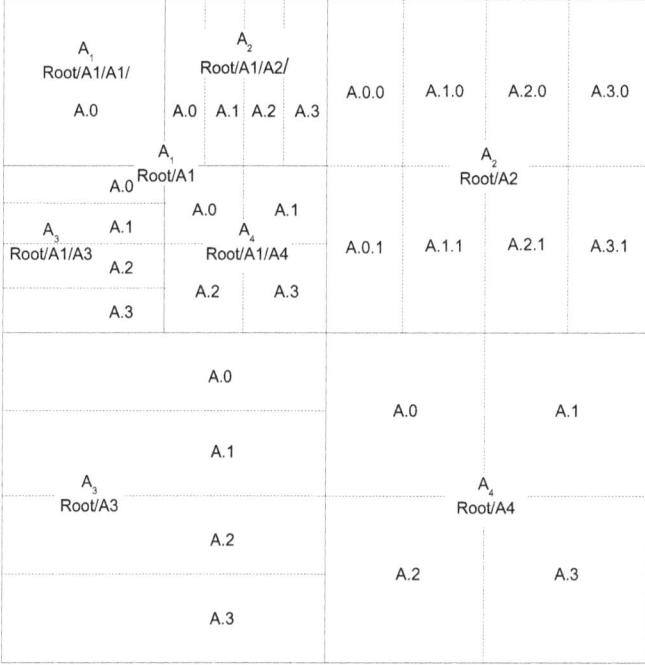

Figure 3: Matrix partitioning for LU decomposition.

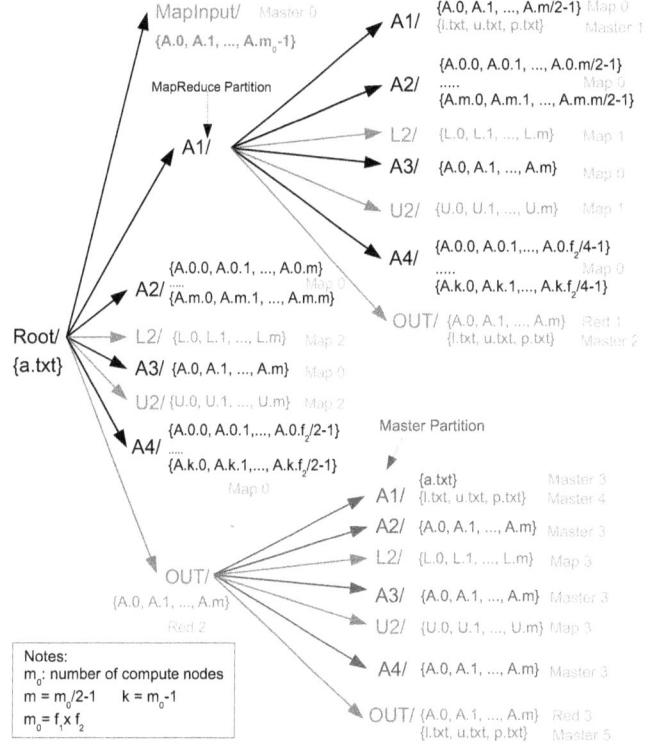

Figure 4: HDFS directory structure used by implementation.

MapReduce pipeline. We also discuss how the input, intermediate, and output data files are stored in HDFS to improve I/O efficiency. In Figure 4, the green labels indicate which process produces each result or intermediate data file. For example "Map 0" means that the result is produced by the mappers in the first MapReduce job, and "Master 0" means that the result is produced by the master node of that job. Therefore, these labels also represent the computation process of the LU decomposition.

We launch a MapReduce job to partition matrix $\mathbf{A}$. This is a map-only job where the mappers do all the work and the reduce function does nothing. This is the only partitioning job, and it recursively partitions $\mathbf{A}$ into as many submatrices as needed, according to the depth of recursion implied by n and n_b. The mappers of this job read their input files from "Root/MapInput/". The integer read by each mapper tells that mapper which rows of the input matrix in the HDFS file "Root/a.txt" to read and partition. In order to improve I/O performance, each map function reads an equal number of consecutive rows from this file to increase I/O sequentiality. Worker j (the mapper assigned input file "Root/MapInput/A.j") reads rows $r_1 = \frac{nj}{m_0}$ to $r_2 = r_1 + \frac{n}{m_0}$ (exclusively). Each block is written to "Root/A1" and "Root/A2" if the block is in the first half of $\mathbf{A}$. Otherwise it is written to "Root/A3" and "Root/A4".

In order to improve I/O efficiency while reading submatrices from disk in subsequent MapReduce jobs, each submatrix, whether $\mathbf{A}_1$, $\mathbf{A}_2$, $\mathbf{A}_3$, or $\mathbf{A}_4$, is split into multiple parts, each of which is stored in a separate file. This ensures that there will never be multiple mappers that simultaneously read the same file. For example, $\mathbf{A}_3$ is stored in $\frac{m_0}{2}$ files because we use only half the compute nodes to compute $\mathbf{L}_2'$ using $\mathbf{A}_3$, while the other half are used to compute $\mathbf{U}_2$ using $\mathbf{A}_2$ (details later). Therefore, $m = \frac{m_0}{2} - 1$ in Figure 4. This approach also ensures that no two mappers write data into the same file, thereby eliminating the need for synchronization between mappers and improving I/O efficiency. Mappers and reducers in subsequent jobs also write their data into independent files, so synchronization on file writes is never required and

I/O efficiency is maintained. The separate files written by worker nodes are shown in Figure 4, for example, "L2/L.1".

In Figure 3, which shows an example of matrix $\mathbf{A}$ partitioned by four mappers, the square blocks surrounded by solid lines are submatrices, while the rectangular blocks divided by dashed lines are separate files storing these submatrices. In Figure 4, the black labels within braces are the file names of partitioned submatrices. The value f_2 is the maximum factor of m_0 less than $\sqrt{m_0}$ (see the discussion in Section 6.2). The depth d of the directory structure equals the depth of data partitioning given by $\lceil \log_2 \frac{n}{n_b} \rceil$ (that depth is 2 in Figure 4). The pseudocode of the data partitioning algorithm for LU decomposition is given in Algorithm 3. This listing shows one map function partitioning the block of data in rows r_1 to r_2.

Partitioning submatrix $\mathbf{B} = \mathbf{A}_4 - \mathbf{L}_2'\mathbf{U}_2$ is handled differently from the input matrix. This submatrix is produced by m_0 reducers of a MapReduce job and stored in m_0 files. These files are not read simultaneously by many mappers or reducers, so instead of materializing the data partitions of $\mathbf{B}$ after this submatrix is produced, we only record the indices of the beginning and ending row, and the beginning and ending column, of each partition in this submatrix. We also record the names of the files storing this data. Using this approach, the files in "Root/OUT/A1", "Root/OUT/A2", "Root/OUT/A3", and "Root/OUT/A4" (indicated by blue labels in Figure 4) are very small (in general, less than 1 KB). The running time to partition $\mathbf{A}_4 - \mathbf{L}_2'\mathbf{U}_2$ with such a method is quite short (less than 1 second). Therefore, it is not necessary to launch a MapReduce task to partition this matrix. In our implementation, we partition this matrix in the master node.

5.3 LU Decomposition Using MapReduce

After partitioning $\mathbf{A}$, we use Algorithm 2 to compute the LU decomposition. Since $\mathbf{A}$ has been partitioned, line 5 is ignored, and $\mathbf{A}_1$, $\mathbf{A}_2$, $\mathbf{A}_3$, and $\mathbf{A}_4$ are read from HDFS files. We launch one

Algorithm 3 Data partitioning for LU decomposition.

1: **function** Partition($\mathbf{A}$, r_1, r_2, n, n_b, m, f_1, f_2, "path")
2: /* $\mathbf{A}$ is the original matrix. r_1 is the index of the beginning row to be saved by this function and r_2 is the index of the ending row. n is the order of the matrix. n_b is the bound value for data partitioning. m is the number of map workers partitioning the current submatrix (e.g., the submatrix in the directory Root/A1 shown in Figure 3), f_1 and f_2 indicate that $\mathbf{A}_4$ is partitioned to $f_1 \times f_2$ blocks according to the optimization in Section 6.2. */
3:   **if** $n < n_b$ **then**
4:     /* Save A1*/
5:     Save $[\mathbf{A}]_{[r_1 \ldots r_2][0 \ldots n]}$ to "path/A1/A.$\frac{r_1 m}{n}$"
6:   **else**
7:     **if** $r_1 < \frac{n}{2}$ **then**
8:       Partition($\mathbf{A}$, r_1, r_2, $\frac{n}{2}$, n_b, $\frac{m}{2}$, f_1, f_2, "path/A1")
9:       /* Save A2 */
10:       **for** $i = 0$ to m - 1 **do**
11:         Save $[\mathbf{A}]_{[r_1 \ldots r_2][\frac{n}{2} \ldots n]}$ to "path/A2/A.i.$\frac{r_1 m}{n}$"
12:       **end for**
13:     **else**
14:       /* Save A3 */
15:       **for** $i = 0$ to $\frac{(r_2 - r_1)m}{2n} - 1$ **do**
16:         $k = \frac{(2r_1 - n)m}{4n} + i$
17:         Save $[\mathbf{A}]_{[r_1 \ldots r_1 + \frac{2m(i+1)}{n}][0 \ldots \frac{n}{2}]}$ to "path/A3/A.k"
18:       **end for**
19:       /* Save A4 */
20:       **for** $j = 0$ to $f_2 - 1$ **do**
21:         $l = (\frac{2r_1 f_1}{n} - f_1)f_2 + j$
22:         **for** $i = 0$ to $\frac{2(r_2 - r_1)f_1}{n} - 1$ **do**
23:           Save $[\mathbf{A}]_{[r_1 \ldots r_1 + \frac{(i+1)n}{2f_1}][\frac{n}{2} \ldots \frac{n}{2} + \frac{(j+1)n}{2f_2}]}$ to "path/A4/A.l.i"
24:         **end for**
25:       **end for**
26:     **end if**
27: **end if**

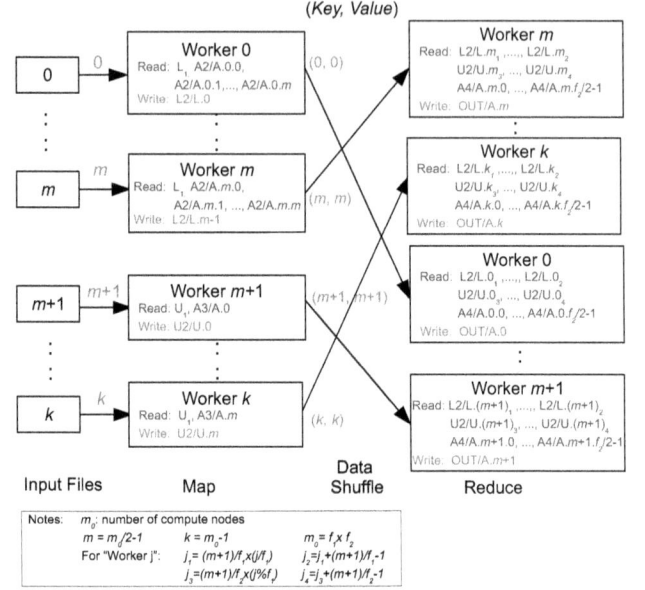

Figure 5: MapReduce job to compute $\mathbf{L}_2'$, $\mathbf{U}_2$, and $\mathbf{A}_4 - \mathbf{L}_2'\mathbf{U}_2$.

Algorithm	Write	Read	Transfer	Mults	Adds
Our Algorithm	$\frac{3}{2}n^2$	$(l+3)n^2$	$(l+3)n^2$	$\frac{1}{3}n^3$	$\frac{1}{3}n^3$
ScaLAPCK	n^2	n^2	$\frac{2}{3}m_0 n^2$	$\frac{1}{3}n^3$	$\frac{1}{3}n^3$

Table 1: Time complexity of our LU decomposition algorithm, in comparison with the ScaLAPACK algorithm, for $n \times n$ matrix on m_0 compute nodes, where $m_0 = f_1 \times f_2$ and $l = \frac{1}{4}(m_0 + 2f_1 + 2f_2)$.

MapReduce job for lines 7–9 of this algorithm. One MapReduce job is sufficient regardless of the size of the input block. The map function of this job computes $\mathbf{L}_2'$ and $\mathbf{U}_2$, while the reduce function computes $\mathbf{A}_4 - \mathbf{L}_2'\mathbf{U}_2$ (red labels in Figure 4). In our implementation, we use half of the mappers to compute $\mathbf{L}_2'$ and the other half to compute $\mathbf{U}_2$, since computing $\mathbf{L}_2'$ has the same computational complexity as computing $\mathbf{U}_2$. Each mapper reads an input file from the directory "Root/MapInput/". If the value in this file is $\leq m = \frac{m_0}{2} - 1$, the mapper computes part of $\mathbf{L}_2'$. Otherwise it computes part of $\mathbf{U}_2$. This is illustrated in Figure 5.

If worker j is computing part of $\mathbf{L}_2'$, this worker is assigned the file "A.j". The worker reads $\mathbf{L}_1$ from HDFS directory "Root/A1" and $\mathbf{A}_{2.j}$ from files "Root/A2/A.j.0, Root/A2/A.j.1, ..., Root/A.j.m", and computes one part of $\mathbf{L}_2'$, which is written to "Root/L2/L.j".

Each mapper in this MapReduce job emits one (*key, value*) pair containing (j, j), where j is the value read by the mapper from its input file. These (*key, value*) pairs are used to control which part of $\mathbf{A}_4 - \mathbf{L}_2'\mathbf{U}_2$ each reducer should compute. In our implementation, we use block wrap for matrix multiplication (Section 6.2), so worker j computes the j-th block of $\mathbf{A}_4 - \mathbf{L}_2'\mathbf{U}_2$. The detailed files read and written are shown in Figure 5. It should be noted

that after obtaining $\mathbf{L}_2'$ and $\mathbf{P}_2$, $\mathbf{L}_2$ can be easily obtained by permuting $\mathbf{L}_2'$ based on the permutation matrix $\mathbf{P}_2$. Therefore in our implementation, $\mathbf{L}_2$ is constructed only as it is read from HDFS.

The time complexity of our LU decomposition is shown in Table 1. We also present the time complexity of the algorithm used in ScaLAPACK (which we compare to in Section 7.5). Since the data in MapReduce is stored in a distributed environment, the amount of data transferred is one of the main bottlenecks. Therefore, we also show the total data transfer in this table. In our algorithm, all data is written to HDFS, which means that the amount of data read from HDFS is the same as the amount of data transferred between compute nodes. In the MPI implementation of ScaLAPACK, the data is read only once (better than our algorithm), but large amounts of data are transferred over the network between the master and workers (worse than our algorithm).

5.4 Triangular Matrix Inversion and Final Output

One MapReduce job is used to compute the inverses of the triangular matrices $\mathbf{L}$ and $\mathbf{U}$ and the product of their inverses. In the map phase, the inverses of the triangular matrices are computed using Equation 4. Half of the mappers compute the inverse of $\mathbf{L}$ and the other half compute the inverse of $\mathbf{U}$. In order to balance load, the i-th node is used to compute the $(k \times m_0 + i)$-th column of $\mathbf{L}^{-1}$ if i is less than $\frac{n}{2}$. If $i \geq \frac{n}{2}$, the node computes the $(k \times \frac{n}{m_0} + i - \frac{n}{2})$-th row of $\mathbf{U}^{-1}$, where k is an integer ($0 \leq k < \frac{n-i}{m_0}$ for $i < \frac{n}{2}$ or $0 \leq k < \frac{3n-2i}{2m_0}$ for $i \geq \frac{n}{2}$). Thus, each mapper computes an equal number of non-contiguous columns of $\mathbf{L}^{-1}$, which is designed to ensure balanced load. For example, if there are 4 map-

Algorithm	Write	Read	Transfer	Mults	Adds
Our Algorithm	$2n^2$	ln^2	$(l+2)n^2$	$\frac{2}{3}n^3$	$\frac{2}{3}n^3$
ScaLAPCK	n^2	$m_0 n^2$	$m_0 n^2$	$\frac{2}{3}n^3$	$\frac{2}{3}n^3$

Table 2: Time complexity of our triangular matrix inversion and final matrix inversion, in comparison with the ScaLA-PACK algorithm, for $n \times n$ matrix on m_0 compute nodes, where $m_0 = f_1 \times f_2$ and $l = \frac{1}{2}(m_0 + f_1 + f_2)$.

pers, *Mapper0* computes columns $0, 4, 8, 12, \ldots$, *Mapper1* computes columns $1, 5, 9, 13, \ldots$, and so on.

In the reduce phase, the product of these two inverses $\mathbf{U}^{-1}\mathbf{L}^{-1}$ is computed. Each reducer reads a number of columns of $\mathbf{L}^{-1}$ and a number of rows of $\mathbf{U}^{-1}$, and multiples these two parts. In order to reduce read I/O, block wrap is used for matrix multiplication (Section 6.2). In order to balance load, instead of partitioning the final matrix into $f_1 \times f_2$ blocks (see Section 6.2), each of which contains consecutive rows and consecutive columns, the matrix is partitioned into grid blocks, each of which contains discrete rows and discrete columns. Worker j computes the product of row $\frac{m_0}{f_1} k_1 + j_1$ of $\mathbf{U}^{-1}$ and column $\frac{m_0}{f_2} k_2 + j_2$ of $\mathbf{L}^{-1}$, where $j_1 = \frac{j}{f_1}$, $j_2 = j \bmod f_1$. Here k_1 is any of the non-negative integers that satisfy $\frac{m_0}{f_1} k_1 + j < m_0$, and k_2 is any of the non-negative integers that satisfy $\frac{m_0}{f_2} k_2 + j < m_0$. As in the implementation of LU decomposition, all outputs, $\mathbf{L}^{-1}$, $\mathbf{U}^{-1}$ and $\mathbf{A}^{-1} = \mathbf{U}^{-1}\mathbf{L}^{-1}\mathbf{P}$, are written to HDFS. The map function only emits integers (j, j) to control the reduce tasks, and does not emit outputs. Table 2 shows the time complexity and data transfer of our matrix inversion algorithm, and the corresponding values in ScaLAPACK.

6. OPTIMIZATIONS OF THE MAPREDUCE IMPLEMENTATION

In this section, we present optimizations that we use to improve the performance of our implementation. Two of these optimizations aim to reduce read and write I/O, namely storing intermediate data in separate files (Section 6.1) and block wrap (Section 6.2). A third optimization aims to improve memory access locality (Section 6.3).

6.1 Storing Intermediate Data in Separate Files

In order to reduce the amount read and write I/O in different MapReduce jobs, we do not combine the results, such as $\mathbf{L}_1$, $\mathbf{L}_2$, and $\mathbf{L}_3$, in any stage. The results are located in many different files as shown in Section 5. Algorithm 2 writes all outputs into HDFS as separate files and skips lines 11–13. The total number of files for the final lower triangular or upper triangular matrix is $N(d) = 2^d + \frac{m_0}{2}(2^d - 1)$, where m_0 is the number of compute nodes, and d is the recursive depth that is constrained by the matrix order n, i.e., $d = \lceil \log_2 \frac{n}{n_b} \rceil$. For example, given a square matrix $\mathbf{A}$ with $n = 2^{15}$, $n_b = 2^{11} = 2048$, and $m_0 = 64$, the recursive depth d is 4 and the final lower triangular matrix $\mathbf{L}$ is stored in $N(d) = 496$ files. In our implementation, these files are read into memory recursively.

Because combining intermediate files can only happen on one compute node, such as the master node, and other compute nodes have to wait until combination is completed, combining intermediate files significantly increases the running time, and this optimization significantly improves performance, as shown in Section 7.3.

6.2 Block Wrap for Matrix Multiplication

Our algorithm requires multiplying two matrices at different stages, for example $\mathbf{L}_2'$ and $\mathbf{U}_2$, or $\mathbf{U}^{-1}$ and $\mathbf{L}^{-1}$. A simple and easy-to-implement way to multiply two matrices while reducing the amount of data read is to use the block method for matrix mul-

tiplication. In general, in order to compute $\mathbf{L}_2'\mathbf{U}_2$, each compute node can read a number of rows, e.g., i-th to j-th rows, of $\mathbf{L}_2'$ and the entire matrix $\mathbf{U}_2$. This compute node can then compute the i-th to j-th rows of $\mathbf{L}_2'\mathbf{U}_2$. If the number of compute nodes is m_0, the amount of data read in each node is $(1 + \frac{1}{m_0})n^2$ and the total data read is $(m_0 + 1)n^2$.

There is a better method to multiply two matrices, called the *block wrap* method [6], which reduces the amount of data read. In this method, $\mathbf{L}_2'$ is divided into f_1 blocks, each of which contains $\frac{n}{f_1}$ consecutive rows, while $\mathbf{U}_2$ is divided into f_2 blocks, each of which contains $\frac{n}{f_2}$ consecutive columns. Using this partitioning, every block of $\mathbf{L}_2'$ will need to be multiplied by every block of $\mathbf{U}_2$, and the final matrix is partitioned into $f_1 \times f_2$ blocks. Each of these blocks is computed by one compute node. That is, each compute node reads $\frac{n}{f_1}$ rows of $\mathbf{L}_2'$ and $\frac{n}{f_2}$ columns of $\mathbf{U}_2$ (one block from each matrix) and computes the product of these two block. f_1 and f_2 are chosen so that $m_0 = f_1 \times f_2$. The data read in each compute node is $(\frac{1}{f_1} + \frac{1}{f_2})n^2$, and the total data is $(f_1 + f_2)n^2$, which is significantly less than $(m_0 + 1)n^2$. In order to obtain the minimum data read, we compute f_1 and f_2 from n such that $|f_1 - f_2|$ is as small as possible. That is, we choose $f_2 \le f_1$, and there is no other factor of m_0 between f_1 and f_2. For example, given 64 nodes, in the naive algorithm each node reads data of size $\frac{65}{64}n^2$, and the total data read for all 64 nodes is $65n^2$. Using the block wrap method and $f_1 = f_2 = 8$, each node reads data of size $\frac{1}{4}n^2$, and the total data read for all nodes is $16n^2$, much better than the naive algorithm.

6.3 Storing Transposed U Matrices

In general, matrices $\mathbf{L}_2'$ and $\mathbf{U}_2$ are linearized in row-major order both in memory and in HDFS. The product of $\mathbf{L}_2'$ and $\mathbf{U}_2$ is computed as follows:

$$[\mathbf{L}_2'\mathbf{U}_2]_{ij} = \sum_{k=1}^{n} [\mathbf{L}_2']_{ik} \times [\mathbf{U}_2]_{kj} \qquad (7)$$

However, when the order of the matrices n is large, each read of an element from $\mathbf{U}_2$ will access a separate memory page, potentially generating a TLB miss and a cache miss. If a page can hold k data items, this access pattern can generate up to $n^3 + \frac{k+1}{k}n^2$ misses for data read and matrix multiplication.

In our implementation, the upper triangular matrix is always stored in a transposed fashion, i.e., we store $\mathbf{U}^T$ instead of $\mathbf{U}$. The product of $\mathbf{L}_2'$ and $\mathbf{U}_2^T$ can be computed as follows:

$$[\mathbf{L}_2'\mathbf{U}_2]_{ij} = \sum_{k=1}^{n} [\mathbf{L}_2']_{ik} \times [\mathbf{U}_2^T]_{jk} \qquad (8)$$

The number of misses can be reduced to $\frac{n^3}{k} + \frac{2n^2}{k}$, which is significantly less than the unoptimized implementation and can substantially improve performance.

7. EXPERIMENTAL EVALUATION

In this section, we present an experimental evaluation of our technique. We study the scalability of our algorithm and implementation, the impact of our proposed optimizations, and we compare to a state-of-the-art alternative, namely ScaLAPACK.

7.1 Experimental Environment

We implemented our algorithm on Hadoop 1.1.1, the latest stable version at the time the work was done. All experiments were

Matrix	Order	Elements (Billion)	Text (GB)	Binary (GB)	Number of Jobs
M_1	20480	0.42	8	3.2	9
M_2	32768	1.07	20	8	17
M_3	40960	1.68	40	16	17
M_4	102400	10.49	200	80	33
M_5	16384	0.26	5	2	9

Table 3: Five matrices used for the experiments.

performed on medium instances of Amazon's Elastic Compute Cloud (EC2) [11], except for the largest matrix M_4, for which large instances were used. Each medium instance has 3.7 GB of memory and 1 virtual core with 2 EC2 compute unit, where each EC2 compute unit has performance similar to a 2007-era 1.0–1.2 GHz AMD Opteron or Xeon processor.

We use five matrices in our experiments. We were not able to find large, real-world, public benchmark matrices for which matrix inversion is required, so all of our test matrices were randomly generated using the Random class in Java. Note that the performance of our algorithm depends on the order of the input matrix and not on the data values in this matrix, so performance is not expected to change if we use real-world matrices instead of synthetic ones.

Details about the matrices used are shown in Table 3, which shows the order of each matrix, the number of elements (data type double), the size of the matrix in text format, and the size in binary format. Recall that the bound value n_b used in our experiments is 3200. Table 3 shows, for this value of n_b, the total number of MapReduce jobs required for inverting each matrix. The matrices are stored in HDFS with the default replication factor of 3.

7.2 Algorithm Scalability

In this section, we investigate the scalability of our proposed algorithm, focusing on strong scalability. The running time versus the number of EC2 instances for three matrices is shown in Figure 6. One ideal scalability line (i.e., running time proportional to 1 over the number of nodes) has been over-plotted on this figure in order to demonstrate the scalability of our algorithm. We can see that our algorithm has very good strong scalability, with a minor deviation from ideal scalability when the number of nodes is high. This deviation is due to the constant launch time of MapReduce jobs, since our algorithm uses multiple MapReduce jobs. However, we also note that the number of MapReduce jobs is proportional to the matrix order n, while the running time is proportional to n^3. Therefore we can expect that the larger the matrix, the better the algorithm scalability, which can be seen in Figure 6.

We investigated improving scalability by using systems that support iterative MapReduce computations, such as HaLoop [5]. However, we found that HaLoop and similar systems do not reduce the launch time of MapReduce jobs. HaLoop maintains intermediate state between MapReduce jobs, which is not useful for our algorithm. There are techniques for reducing the overhead of launching MapReduce jobs, such as having pools of worker processes that are reused by map and reduce tasks. These techniques can definitely benefit our work, but they do not require any changes to the matrix inversion MapReduce pipeline. Specifically, our analysis of how finely to decompose the computation holds even under faster job launching.

In order to verify the correctness of our implementation and check whether the data type double is precise enough, we compute $I_n - MM^{-1}$ for matrices M_1, M_2, M_3, and M_5. We find that every element in the computed matrices is less than 10^{-5}, which validates our implementation and shows that the data type double is sufficiently precise.

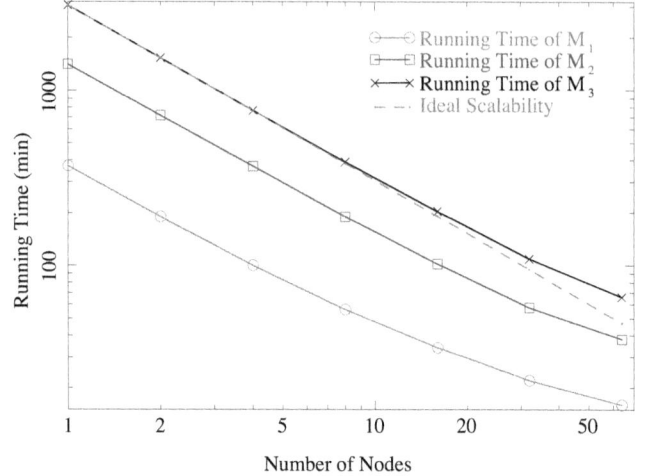

Figure 6: The scalability of our algorithm, in comparison with ideal scalability (purple line), which is defined as $T(n) = T(1)/n$, where $T(n)$ is the running time on n medium EC2 instances.

The largest matrix M_4 is used to further test the scalability limits of our algorithm (Section 7.4), and the smallest matrix M_5 is used to evaluate our optimizations in the next section.

7.3 Evaluating the Optimizations

Our first proposed optimization is storing intermediate data in separate files. Without this optimization, we combine all separate files of L and U in each MapReduce job in our iterative MapReduce process. The combination happens in the master node and the combined file is written by that node into HDFS. Since the combination is a serial process done on one node, it takes a constant time to combine the files independent of the number of the compute nodes. Therefore, we can expect that the benefit of keeping separate intermediate files increases as the number of compute nodes increases, since the running time gets smaller and the overhead of combination remains constant.

To validate this expectation, we conduct an experiment with matrix M_5 in which we compare the time taken by our optimized algorithm to the time taken by the algorithm that combines L and U files at each step. The ratio of the unoptimized running time to the optimized running time for 4–64 nodes is shown in Figure 7. The figure shows the unoptimized version to be close to 30% slower in some cases, demonstrating the importance of this optimization.

As mentioned in Section 6.2, the block wrap method can significantly reduce read I/O, thereby improving performance. In this section, we use matrix M_5 to evaluate the effect of using block wrap on performance. As before, we measure the running time without this optimization on 4–64 compute nodes and compare this to the running time with the optimization. The improvement is shown in Figure 7. The figure shows that the larger the number of compute nodes, the larger the improvement in performance.

We did not systematically evaluate the third optimization (transpose storing) in our experiments. It is a simple and intuitive optimization, and our experience is that it greatly improves the performance of our algorithm, by a factor of 2–3.

7.4 Scaling to a Very Large Matrix

In this section, we study the ability of our algorithm to invert a very large matrix, namely M_4, which is a matrix of order 102400. We measure the running time on 128 Amazon EC2 large instances, each of which has two medium CPU cores, for a total of 256

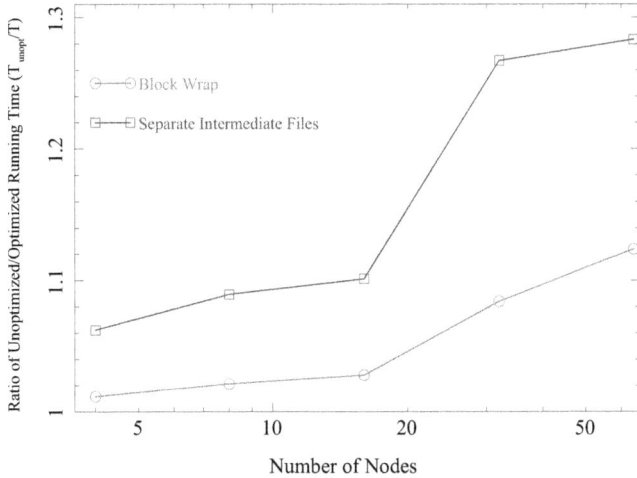

Figure 7: The running time of the optimized algorithm compared to the algorithm without the separate intermediate files optimization (blue), and without the block wrap optimization (red).

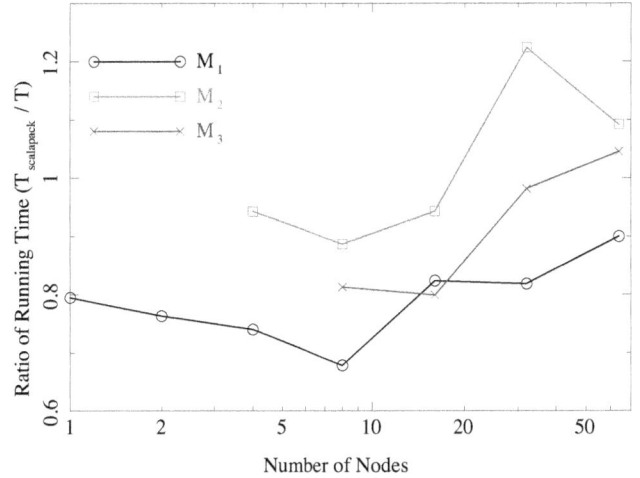

Figure 8: The ratio of the running time of ScaLAPACK to the running time of our algorithm.

medium CPU cores. A medium CPU core has performance similar to two 2007-era 1.0–1.2 GHz AMD Opteron or Xeon processors.

We executed two runs of our algorithm to invert this large matrix. In the first run, it took about 8 hours to solve the problem. During this run, one mapper computing the inverse of a triangular matrix failed and this mapper did not restart until one of the other mappers finished. This increased the running time. However, this failure recovery is a good demonstration of the benefit of using a fault tolerant framework like MapReduce for large scale problems. In the second run, there were no failures and it took about 5 hours to invert the matrix.

The large matrix is about 80 GB in size in binary representation. Our algorithm on the EC2 large instances writes more than 500 GB of data and reads more than 20 TB of data in the 33 MapReduce jobs required to invert the matrix.

We also used 64 medium EC2 instances to invert this matrix. It took about 15 hours in this case to invert the matrix. Analyzing the scalability of the medium instances compared to the large instances, we see that the medium instances show better scalability, based on a simple calculation as follows. Assume for simplicity that each medium instance core has similar compute performance to a large instance core. When we used 128 large EC2 instances we were using 256 cores, whereas when we used 64 medium instances, we were using 64 cores. Thus, we have four times as many cores when using large instances. Therefore, if our algorithm has ideal scalability, the running time in large instances should be $15/4 = 3.8$ hours (four times the cores should result in $\frac{1}{4}$ the running time). However, the running time we observed on large instances (5 hours) is longer than this time that assumes ideal scalability. There are two possible reasons related to EC2 for the running time being longer than expected. The first reason is that we found that the performance variance between different large EC2 instances is high, even though the instances are supposed to have similar performance. The second reason is that the data read speed on some large instances is less than the speed on the medium instances. We found that the speed of copying files between large instances is around 30–60 MB/s, while the speed of copying files between medium instances is around 60 MB/s. The main point of the experiment is that we are able to scale to such large scales in terms of both input size and number of nodes, and that this scalability holds in different runs on different cluster sizes, even in the presence of failures.

7.5 Comparison to ScaLAPACK

ScaLAPACK is a popular library of high-performance linear algebra routines for distributed memory message passing computers and clusters. ScaLAPACK is an extension of LAPACK [2], and it has been shown to have good scalability and performance. More details about ScaLAPACK can be found in [4]. In this section, we compare our matrix inversion technique to ScaLAPACK, to see how we stack up against a state-of-the-art competitor.

In this experiment, the package libscalapack-mpi-dev in Ubuntu is used. The version of MPI used is MPICH [20]. The drive routines PDGETRF and PDGETRI in ScaLAPACK are used to compute the LU decomposition and the triangular matrix inverse respectively. In order to reduce the data transfer between compute nodes in ScaLAPACK, we use an optimization similar to our *block wrap* optimization. In particular, we set the process grid to $f_1 \times f_2$, where $m_0 = f_1 \times f_2$ is the number of compute nodes, $f_1 < f_2$, and there is no factor of m_0 between f_1 and f_2, which means that the matrix is partitioned into $f_1 \times f_2$. The matrix is first partitioned into blocks of dimension 128×128, since we found that this size provides the best performance in our experiments. Next, these blocks are assigned to the process grid. In order to improve load balancing, the blocks are assigned as follows: the block in row $f_1 \times m_1 + i$ and column $f_2 \times m_2 + j$ is assigned to the $(f_2 \times j + i)$-th compute node, where m, n, i and j are integers that are constrained by following inequalities: $f_1 \times m_1 + i < \frac{n}{128}$, $f_2 \times m_2 + j < \frac{n}{128}$, $i < f_1$, and $j < f_2$, where n is the order of the matrix. In our ScaLAPACK implementation, all intermediate data is stored in memory, such that the matrix is read only once and written only once.

The ratio of the running time of ScaLAPACK to the running time of our algorithm on medium EC2 nodes for matrices $\mathbf{M}_1$ to $\mathbf{M}_3$ is shown in Figure 8. The figure shows that for these small matrices, there is a slight performance penalty for using our algorithm compared to ScaLAPACK. We expect ScaLAPACK to perform well since it is a highly optimized state-of-the-art library. The point of Figure 8 is to show that the performance of our MapReduce matrix inversion algorithm is comparable to ScaLAPACK. The advantages of using the popular and widely deployed MapReduce framework, such as scalability, fault tolerance, ease of programming, and rich software ecosystem, do not come at a high cost in terms of performance.

Figure 8 shows that our algorithm approaches or outperforms ScaLAPACK for larger matrices and a larger number of nodes. That is, our algorithm has better scalability than ScaLAPACK. To better demonstrate the scalability of our algorithm compared to ScaLAPACK, we run another experiment in which we use ScaLAPACK on 128 large EC2 instances (256 CPU cores) and 64 medium EC2 instances (64 CPU cores) to compute the inverse of the largest matrix, M_4. These are the same cluster sizes that we used with our algorithm for this matrix in the previous section. ScaLAPACK took 8 hours on the large instances and more than 48 hours on the medium instances to invert matrix M_4, both of which are significantly longer than our results reported in Section 7.4 (5 hours on large instances and 15 hours on medium instances). It should be noted that the running time of our algorithm on the large instances with a failure (8 hours) is similar to the running time of ScaLAPACK without failure. Thus, while our algorithm may have a small performance penalty compared to ScaLAPACK at low scale, it has better scalability and performance than ScaLAPACK at high scale.

The reason that our algorithm is better than ScaLAPACK at high scale is that ScaLAPACK transfers large amounts of data over the network (Tables 1 and 2). At low scale, the network can accommodate the required bandwidth, but it becomes a bottleneck at high scale. In addition, MapReduce scheduling is more effective than ScaLAPACK at keeping the workers busy. The scalability of ScaLAPACK scheduling is not an issue at low scale, but it is a limitation at high scale.

8. CONCLUSIONS AND FUTURE WORK

We presented a scalable and fault tolerant algorithm for matrix inversion using MapReduce. Our algorithm relies on recursive block LU decomposition to partition the computation in a way that is suitable for parallelization in a cluster environment using MapReduce. The algorithm uses a pipeline of MapReduce jobs to partition the input matrix, compute the LU decomposition of this matrix, and compute the inverse of the input matrix from its LU decomposition. We implemented this algorithm in Hadoop, and presented optimizations to improve its I/O efficiency and memory locality. Our experimental evaluation on Amazon EC2 shows that our algorithm has better scalability than the state-of-the-art ScaLAPACK package, inverting a large matrix of order 102400 in 5 hours on 128 Amazon EC2 large instances.

Many of the lessons and techniques in this paper may be applicable to matrix operations other than matrix inversion, such as finding eigenvalues or principal component analysis. For example, we have identified LU decomposition from among different matrix decompositions as suitable for MapReduce. The block computation style in Algorithm 2 may be useful for other matrix operations. Other matrix operations may also benefit from the matrix partitioning style in Figure 3 and Algorithm 3, and the corresponding file layout in Figure 4. The scheduling of tasks into MapReduce jobs and the optimizations in Section 6 may also be useful.

One promising direction for future work is to implement our matrix inversion technique on the Spark system [34]. In our implementation using Hadoop, all intermediate data, such as L_1 and U_1, is written to HDFS files by one MapReduce job and read from these HDFS files by the next MapReduce job in the pipeline. Therefore, the amount of read I/O in our algorithm is much larger than other algorithms that keep intermediate data in memory, such as the MPI implementation of ScaLAPACK (see Table 1). In Hadoop, it is not easy to keep intermediate data in memory and still preserve fault tolerance. On the other hand, Spark provides parallel data structures that allow users to explicitly keep data in memory with fault tolerance. Therefore, we expect that implementing our algorithm in Spark would improve performance by reducing read I/O. What is promising is that our technique would need minimal changes (if any) in order to be implemented on Spark, and the scalability of our technique would be even better on Spark than it is on Hadoop.

A relatively recent development in the Hadoop ecosystem is the use of resource managers such as Hadoop YARN [32] and Mesos [16]. These resource managers make it easier to run MPI-based packages such as ScaLAPACK alongside MapReduce on the same cluster. Thus, it would be interesting to investigate the conditions under which to use ScaLAPACK or MapReduce for matrix inversion, and to implement a system to adaptively choose the best matrix inversion technique for an input matrix. An important question would be if the performance benefit obtained from ScaLAPACK is high enough to warrant the administrative overhead and programming complexity of installing and operating two frameworks (MPI and MapReduce) on the same cluster.

9. REFERENCES

[1] E. Agullo, C. Augonnet, J. Dongarra, M. Faverge, J. Langou, H. Ltaief, and S. Tomov. LU factorization for accelerator-based systems. In *Proc. ACS/IEEE Int. Conf. on Comp. Systems and Applications (AICCSA)*, 2011.

[2] E. Anderson, Z. Bai, J. Dongarra, A. Greenbaum, A. McKenney, J. Du Croz, S. Hammerling, J. Demmel, C. Bischof, and D. Sorensen. LAPACK: a portable linear algebra library for high-performance computers. In *Proc. Conf. on Supercomputing (SC)*, 1990.

[3] P. Bientinesi, B. Gunter, and R. A. v. d. Geijn. Families of algorithms related to the inversion of a symmetric positive definite matrix. *ACM Trans. Mathematics Software*, 35(1):3:1–3:22, 2008.

[4] L. S. Blackford, J. Choi, A. Cleary, E. D'Azevedo, J. Demmel, I. Dhillon, J. Dongarra, S. Hammarling, G. Henry, A. Petitet, K. Stanley, D. Walker, and R. C. Whaley. *ScaLAPACK Users' Guide*. Society for Industrial and Applied Mathematics, 1997.

[5] Y. Bu, B. Howe, M. Balazinska, and M. D. Ernst. HaLoop: efficient iterative data processing on large clusters. *Proc. VLDB Endow. (PVLDB)*, 3(1-2):285–296, 2010.

[6] K. Dackland, E. Elmroth, B. Kågström, and C. V. Loan. Design and evaluation of parallel block algorithms: LU factorization on an IBM 3090 VF/600J. In *Proc. SIAM Conf. on Parallel Proc. for Scientific Computing*, 1991.

[7] B. De Schutter and B. De Moor. The QR decomposition and the singular value decomposition in the symmetrized max-plus algebra. In *Proc. European Control Conf. (ECC)*, 1997.

[8] J. Dean and S. Ghemawat. MapReduce: simplified data processing on large clusters. *Comm. ACM*, 51(1):107–113, 2008.

[9] J. Dongarra, M. Faverge, H. Ltaief, and P. Luszczek. High performance matrix inversion based on LU factorization for multicore architectures. In *Proc. ACM Int. Workshop on Many Task Computing on Grids and Supercomputers*, 2011.

[10] J. J. Dongarra, P. Luszczek, and A. Petitet. The LINPACK benchmark: Past, present, and future. *Concurrency and Computation: Practice and Experience*, 15:2003–2016, 2003.

[11] Amazon Elastic Compute Cloud (Amazon EC2). http://aws.amazon.com/ec2/.

[12] R. Gemulla, E. Nijkamp, P. J. Haas, and Y. Sismanis. Large-scale matrix factorization with distributed stochastic gradient descent. In *Proc. ACM SIGKDD Int. Conf. on Knowledge Discovery and Data Mining*, 2011.

[13] A. Ghoting, R. Krishnamurthy, E. Pednault, B. Reinwald, V. Sindhwani, S. Tatikonda, Y. Tian, and S. Vaithyanathan. SystemML: Declarative machine learning on MapReduce. In *Proc. IEEE Int. Conf. on Data Engineering (ICDE)*, 2011.

[14] G. H. Golub and C. F. Van Loan. *Matrix computations*. Johns Hopkins University Press, third edition, 1996.

[15] J. M. Hellerstein, C. Ré, F. Schoppmann, D. Z. Wang, E. Fratkin, A. Gorajek, K. S. Ng, C. Welton, X. Feng, K. Li, and A. Kumar. The MADlib analytics library: or MAD skills, the SQL. *Proc. VLDB Endow. (PVLDB)*, 5(12):1700–1711, 2012.

[16] B. Hindman, A. Konwinski, M. Zaharia, A. Ghodsi, A. D. Joseph, R. Katz, S. Shenker, and I. Stoica. Mesos: A platform for fine-grained resource sharing in the data center. In *Proc. USENIX Conf. on Networked Systems Design and Implementation (NSDI)*, 2011.

[17] K. K. Lau, M. Kumar, and S. Venkatesh. Parallel matrix inversion techniques. In *Proc. IEEE Int. Conf. on Algorithms and Architectures for Parallel Processing*, 1996.

[18] B. Li, S. Tata, and Y. Sismanis. Sparkler: Supporting large-scale matrix factorization. In *Proc. Int. Conf. on Extending Database Technology (EDBT)*, 2013.

[19] S. Lupke. LU-decomposition on a massively parallel transputer system. In *Proc. Int. Conf. on Parallel Architectures and Languages*, 1993.

[20] E. Lusk, N. Doss, and A. Skjellum. A high-performance, portable implementation of the MPI message passing interface standard. *Parallel Computing*, 22:789–828, 1996.

[21] G. Malewicz, M. H. Austern, A. J. Bik, J. C. Dehnert, I. Horn, N. Leiser, and G. Czajkowski. Pregel: a system for large-scale graph processing. In *Proc. ACM SIGMOD Int. Conf. on Management of Data*, 2010.

[22] D. Marks, L. Colwell, R. Sheridan, T. Hopf, A. Pagnani, R. Zecchina, and C. Sander. Protein 3d structure computed from evolutionary sequence variation. *PLoS One*, 6(12):e28766–e28766, 2011.

[23] W. H. Press, S. A. Teukolsky, W. T. Vetterling, and B. P. Flannery. *Numerical Recipes: The Art of Scientific Computing*. Cambridge University Press, third edition, 2007.

[24] Z. Qian, X. Chen, N. Kang, M. Chen, Y. Yu, T. Moscibroda, and Z. Zhang. MadLINQ: Large-scale distributed matrix computation for the cloud. In *Proc. ACM European Conf. on Computer Systems (EuroSys)*, 2012.

[25] E. S. Quintana, G. Quintana, X. Sun, and R. vande Geijn. A note on parallel matrix inversion. *SIAM J. Sci. Comput.*, 22(5):1762–1771, 2000.

[26] S. Seo, I. Jang, K. Woo, I. Kim, J.-S. Kim, and S. Maeng. HPMR: Prefetching and pre-shuffling in shared MapReduce computation environment. In *Proc. IEEE Int. Conf. on Cluster Computing and Workshops*, 2009.

[27] M. Wall, A. Rechtsteiner, and L. Rocha. Singular value decomposition and principal component analysis. In *A Practical Approach to Microarray Data Analysis*. Springer, 2003.

[28] R. J. Warp, D. J. Godfrey, and J. T. Dobbins III. Applications of matrix inversion tomosynthesis. *Physics of Medical Imaging*, 3977:376–383, 2000.

[29] J. Xiang. Scalable scientific computing algorithms using MapReduce. Master's thesis, University of Waterloo, 2013.

[30] J. Xiang, S. N. Zhang, and Y. Yao. Probing the spatial distribution of the interstellar dust medium by high angular resolution X-ray halos of point sources. *The Astrophysical J.*, 628:769–779, 2005.

[31] J. Xinag, H. Meng, and A. Aboulnaga. Source code of "Scalable Matrix Inversion Using MapReduce". https://github.com/JingenXiang/MatrixInversion.

[32] Apache Hadoop NextGen MapReduce (YARN). http://hadoop.apache.org/docs/r2.3.0/hadoop-yarn/hadoop-yarn-site/YARN.html.

[33] Y. Yu, M. Isard, D. Fetterly, M. Budiu, U. Erlingsson, P. K. Gunda, and J. Currey. DryadLINQ: a system for general-purpose distributed data-parallel computing using a high-level language. In *Proc. Symp. on Operating Systems Design and Implementation (OSDI)*, 2008.

[34] M. Zaharia, M. Chowdhury, T. Das, A. Dave, J. Ma, M. McCauley, M. J. Franklin, S. Shenker, and I. Stoica. Resilient distributed datasets: a fault-tolerant abstraction for in-memory cluster computing. In *Proc. USENIX Conf. on Networked Systems Design and Implementation (NSDI)*, 2012.

[35] Y. Zhang and J. Yang. Optimizing I/O for big array analytics. *Proc. VLDB Endow. (PVLDB)*, 5(8):764–775, 2012.

[36] Q. Zheng, X. Wu, M. Fang, H. Wang, S. Wang, and X. Wang. Application of HPMR in parallel matrix computation. *Comp. Engineering*, 36(08):49–52, 2010.

Supporting Correlation Analysis on Scientific Datasets in Parallel and Distributed Settings

Yu Su
Computer Science and
Engineering
The Ohio State University
Columbus, OH 43210
su1@cse.ohio-state.edu

Gagan Agrawal
Computer Science and
Engineering
The Ohio State University
Columbus, OH 43210
agrawal@cse.ohio-
state.edu

Jonathan Woodring
Los Alamos National
Laboratory
Los Alamos, NM 87544
woodring@lanl.gov

Ayan Biswas
Computer Science and
Engineering
The Ohio State University
Columbus, OH 43210
biswas.36@osu.edu

Han-Wei Shen
Computer Science and
Engineering
The Ohio State University
Columbus, OH 43210
hwshen@cse.ohio-
state.edu

ABSTRACT

With growing computational capabilities of parallel machines, scientific simulations are being performed at finer spatial and temporal scales, leading to a data explosion. Careful analysis of this data holds much promise for future scientific discoveries. Particularly, *correlation analysis*, which focuses on studying the potential relationships among multiple variables, is becoming a useful method for scientific analysis. This paper focuses on the problem of correlation analysis across large-scale simulation datasets, including 1) accelerating this analysis with the use of bitmap indexing as a representative summary of the data, 2) developing efficient algorithms for parallel execution, 3) performing analysis in distributed environments, i.e., for cases where different attributes are stored in geographically distributed repositories, and 4) combining sampling with correlation analysis. These algorithms have been implemented in a system that provides a high-level API for specification of the analyses, including allowing correlation analysis on specified value-based and dimension-based subsets of the data, and supports interactive and incremental analysis. We have extensively evaluated our framework for efficiency, and have also carried out case studies with domain scientists to establish how it can aid data-driven discovery process.

Categories and Subject Descriptors

I.3.1 [**Computing Methodologies**]: HARDWARE ARCHITECTURE—*Parallel Processing*; H.3.1 [**Information Systems**]: CONTENT ANALYSIS AND INDEXING—*Indexing Methods*; H.1.1

[**Information Systems**]: SYSTEMS AND INFORMATION THEORY—*Information Theory*

Keywords

Big Data; Correlation Analysis; Indexing; Parallel Processing

1. INTRODUCTION

As science has become increasingly data-driven, and as data volumes and velocities are increasing, scientific advances in many areas will only be feasible if critical "big-data" problems are addressed. One of the key challenges being faced by data-intensive science efforts is that while the dataset sizes continue to grow rapidly, disk speeds, and both inter-cluster and wide-area bandwidths are not coping up. Thus, data movement is increasingly becoming the bottleneck.

There is often a need for complex analyses over datasets generated by scientific simulations. Such analyses can be classified into two categories: *individual variable analysis* and *correlation analysis*. Individual variable analysis involves analysis over each variable or attribute independently, and can take the form of data subsetting, data aggregation, data mining or visualization. Much of the existing work, especially in data visualization, has focused on individual variable analysis. However, more recently, several efforts [4, 26] have focused on studying the relationship among multiple variables and making interesting scientific discoveries based on such analysis.

This paper focuses on the problem of correlation analysis on massive scientific datasets in parallel and distributed settings. The "big data" problem of data movements being the constraint becomes even more severe for correlation analysis, because of several reasons. Even if different data files are stored on the same server, correlation calculation has a large memory cost and the entire calculation process is extremely time-consuming. Parallelizing such analysis is also hard, because of the possibility of large-scale data movement. Moreover, besides addressing the algorithmic challenges, there is a need for a system that can offer a high-level interface for such analysis. For example, in many cases, scientists may only be interested in performing correlation analysis over (*value-based* and/or *dimension-based*) subsets of the data, and a structured query interface is needed for such analysis. Because scientific datasets are stored in formats like NetCDF or HDF5, and not in a database, support for such subsetting (especially, value-based subsetting) is not (efficiently) available.

Yet another problem arises from the fact that different variables may be stored in different servers. For example, consider Earth System Grid Federation (ESGF). Each *data node* can choose to download a subset of data available in the entire grid, and thus, it is possible that different attributes may be stored at different sites. Because of the volume of data, it is not feasible to simply download the data to be analyzed at one site, and a more intelligent approach is needed.

In our work, we propose a set of algorithms and a system for correlation analysis in parallel and distributed settings, starting from a high-level API, and with support for incremental and interactive analysis. From an algorithmic side, we present a series of methods for correlation analysis using bitmap indexing [8, 30, 31]. Bitmap indices, one of the popular indexing methods, preserve both the value distribution and the spatial locality of the data, and thus can be treated as a summary or profile of the original dataset, though much smaller in size. Moreover, because bitmap indices can help support basic database-like operations, e.g., data subsetting [8, 21], they do not have to be built exclusively for correlation analysis. Because of the data reduction associated with bitmap indices, the novel correlation calculation algorithms we have developed can incur much smaller network data transfer and memory accesses costs compared with the traditional method. We have designed two different indexing methods, which are *dynamic* and *static* indexing, to improve the efficiency. It turns out that bitmap indices or *bitvectors* also can help reduce the amount of communication during the computation of correlations in a parallel environment. We have developed two different partitioning methods, dimension-based partitioning and value-based partitioning, to perform parallel correlation analysis with bitvectors. These methods are also extended to a distributed setting, where datasets corresponding to different variables may be stored at geographically distributed locations.

Finally, with the help of bitmap indexing, we are able to generate *accurate* samples, which are then used to perform correlation analysis more efficiently. This allows us to trade some of the accuracy for improved response time. We have developed algorithms to use bitvectors for sampling and support correlation analysis based on these samples.

The algorithms we have developed have been incorporated in a flexible correlation analysis system, which also has several other desirable properties. First, correlation analysis is offered from a high-level API, where users can conveniently express *dimension-based* and *value-based* subsetting conditions (using an SQL-like syntax). These subsetting conditions are also supported on scientific datasets using bitmap indices. Moreover, we support *incremental* analysis. Users can add additional constraints on the top of the subset used for the last round of analysis. Finally, users can also perform an *undo* operation, which will allow them to build on top of not the most recent result, but an earlier result (and possibly further specialize on those subsets). With the help of bitmap indexing, we only need to keep track of bitvectors during the interactive querying process to support these features.

We have extensively evaluated our system. We compare the correlation analysis efficiency between the traditional method and our method in a stand-alone environment, and show that our dynamic indexing method can achieve a speedup from 1.78x to 3.61x and static indexing method can achieve a speedup from 11.4x to 15.35x. We show the scalability of the parallel method and compare the efficiency between two different partitioning methods. Next, we show that in an environment where computing resources and the data are geographically distributed, our method can further improve the efficiency compared with the traditional by 1.87x to 2.96x. We also show that if correlation analysis is performed over samples of the

data (e.g., 25%), we can achieve a significant speedup (1.69x) with only a small accuracy loss (3.42%). Besides efficiency evaluation, we have also demonstrated the efficacy of the system, by case studies involving domain scientists at the Los Alamos National Laboratory, establishing how that our system is able to aid the data-driven discovery process.

2. MOTIVATING QUERIES AND PROPOSED SYSTEM INTERFACE

This section first introduces the popular correlation metrics, whose computations we are supporting. Next, we explain the query interface and the functionality we are intending to provide.

2.1 Correlation Metrics

This subsection introduces several correlation metrics from information theory [10, 24, 25, 5] that have lately been used in scientific data analysis.

2-D Histogram: In statistics, a histogram is a graphical representation of the distribution of the data, or in other words, an estimate of the probability distribution of a continuous variable. A 2-D histogram reflects the value distribution of one variable regarding to the value changes of another, and is a useful metric to indicate the value distribution relationship between variables.

Information Entropy: In information theory, the information content of a random variable can be quantified by Shannon's entropy [12]. Constant data (easily predictable) have low entropy, while apparently random data (uniform probability) have high entropy. Although entropy is normally applied to single variable, it can also be used to indicate correlations among variables (an example will be shown in Section 6).

Mutual Information: Mutual information is the metric for computing the dependence between two random variables, and shows the amount of shared information between two variables in the number of bits. If the mutual information is low, then the two variables are independent. Conversely if mutual information is high, one variable provides information about the other. Equation 1 shows the expression to calculate the mutual information. Here, we index the data in the variables or attributes A and B by j and k separately, and use x_j and y_k to represent each distinct value. N_A and N_B represent the number of distinct values of each attribute, and three probability distribution functions, P_A, P_B and P_{AB}, capture the probability of having each distinct value for A, for B, and for a pair of values of A and B, respectively.

$$I = \sum_{j=1}^{N_A} \sum_{k=1}^{N_B} P_{AB}(x_j, y_k) \times \log\left(\frac{P_{AB}(x_j, y_k)}{P_A(x_j)P_B(y_k)}\right) \quad (1)$$

2.2 Query Interface and Desired Functionality

We now show the functionality and the interface we intend to support, through an example shown in Figure 1. In the first step, the users are asked to input variable names for correlation analysis. In this example, users want to perform correlation analysis over ocean temperature (*TEMP*), salinity (*SALT*), and flow velocity (*UVEL*). In the following steps, users are able to input different queries that specify subsets of the data they want to perform correlation analysis on. Particularly, in the example shown, users want to first see the correlations among *TEMP*, *SALT* and *UVEL* when the ocean temperature is between 0 and 1 and the depth of the ocean is below 50 meters. After the query is submitted, the system is able to calculate different correlation metrics among the variables directly and return the results (histogram, entropy, mutual information) as the output. Users are able to see the correlations and may be interested in further analysis, For example, a user may find that the mutual information between *TEMP* and *SALT* is much higher than

- Please enter variable names which you want to perform correlation queries:
- TEMP SALT UVEL
- Please enter your query:
- SELECT TEMP FROM POP WHERE TEMP>0 AND TEMP<1 AND depth_t<50;
- **Entropy: TEMP: 2.29, SALT: 2.66, UVEL: 3.05;**
- **Mutual Information: TEMP→SALT: 0.15, TEMP→UVEL: 0.036;**
- **Histogram: (Value Distribution of SALT, UVEL based on TEMP);**
- Please enter your query:
- SELECT SALT FROM POP WHERE SALT<0.0346;
- **Entropy: TEMP: 2.28, SALT: 2.53, UVEL: 3.06;**
- **Mutual Information: TEMP→UVEL: 0.039, SALT→UVEL: 0.33;**
- **Histogram: (Value Distribution of UVEL based on TEMP and SALT);**
- Please enter your query:
- UNDO
- **Entropy: TEMP: 2.29, SALT: 2.66, UVEL: 3.05;**
- **Mutual Information: TEMP→SALT: 0.15, TEMP→UVEL: 0.036;**
- **Histogram: (Value Distribution of SALT, UVEL based on TEMP);**
- Please enter your query:
- SELECT SALT FROM POP WHERE SALT>=0.0346;
- **Entropy: TEMP: 2.22, SALT: 1.58, UVEL: 2.64;**
- **Mutual Information: TEMP→UVEL: 0.31, SALT→UVEL: 0.21;**
- **Histogram: (Value Distribution of UVEL based on TEMP and SALT);**
- ......

Figure 1: Example Showing Supported Query Interface

that between *TEMP* and *UVEL*, which means *TEMP* and *SALT* are high correlated for this data subset.

Then, in the next step, they may want to further explore a subset of values for *SALT*, i.e., further specialize on the previous query to generate more specific correlations. This is supported efficiently through *incremental analysis*, which we will describe later. If users are not satisfied with the current result, our approach supports an *undo* operation to go back to previous step. In this case, the system goes back to the second-last query. Thus, a new query can now specialize on top of the second-last query, and not the last query.

3. ALGORITHMS FOR CORRELATION ANALYSIS

This section describes correlation analysis algorithms we have developed. We start with a simple algorithm, explain its limitations, and then introduce bitmap indexing. We show a series of methods based on bitmap indexing, and then describe methods for execution in parallel and distributed settings.

3.1 Initial Method

A default algorithm that can be used for calculating any of the correlation metrics we listed comprises four steps. First, we need to load the entire data for the variables involved, say, variables A and B, into the memory. Next, if the correlation required is for certain subsets of the data, we take a pass through the data for the variables A and B to generate the data subsets based on queries. As a next step, we generate *joint bins* for A and B, i.e., first divide data for A and B into bins based on values, and thus generate (A_1, A_2, …, A_m) and (B_1, B_2, …, B_n), and then generate joint bins based on individual bins and the dataset, which are $(A_1, B_1) \rightarrow count_0$, $(A_1, B_2) \rightarrow count_1$, …, $(A_m, B_n) \rightarrow count_{mn}$, where $count_i$ is the number of elements located within the joint bin i. Finally, these counts are used to calculate the correlation metrics.

As one can see, the algorithm has a very high memory requirement. If the data corresponding to the two attributes cannot fit in memory, we need to orchestrate complex data movements, which can be very expensive.

3.2 Bitmap Indexing

To speed up the above method, we consider indexing methods that have been proposed in the literature. Broadly, indexing provides an efficient way to support value-based queries and has been extensively researched and used in the context of relational databases. Bitmap indexing, which utilizes the fast bitwise operations supported by the computer hardware, has been shown to be an efficient approach, and has been widely used in scientific data management [20, 30]. In particular, recent work has shown that bitmap indexing can help support efficient querying of scientific datasets stored in native formats [8, 21].

ID	Value	e_0	e_1	e_2	e_3	i_0	i_1
		=1	=2	=3	=4	[1, 2]	[3, 4]
0	4	0	0	0	1	0	1
1	1	1	0	0	0	1	0
2	2	0	1	0	0	1	0
3	2	0	1	0	0	1	0
4	3	0	0	1	0	0	1
5	4	0	0	0	1	0	1
6	3	0	0	1	0	0	1
7	1	1	0	0	0	1	0
Dataset		Low Level Indices				High Level Indices	

Figure 2: An Example of Bitmap Indexing

Figure 2 shows an example of a bitmap index. In this simple example, the dataset contains a total of 8 elements with 4 distinct values. The *low-level* bitmap indices contain 4 bitvectors, where each bitvector corresponds to one value. The number of bits within each bitvector is the same as total number of elements in the dataset. In each bitvector, a bit is set to 1 if the value for the corresponding data element's attribute is equal to the *bitvector value*, i.e., the particular distinct value for which this vector is created. The *high-level* indices can be generated based on either the value intervals or value ranges. From Figure 2, we can see two *high-level* indices are built based on value intervals.

This simple example only contains integer values. Bitmap indexing also has been shown to be an efficient method for floating-point values [32]. For such datasets, instead of building a bitvector for each distinct value, we can first group a set of values together (*binning*) and build bitvectors for these bins. This way, the total number of bitvectors is kept at a manageable level.

From the example we can also see that the number of bits within each level of bitmap indices is $n \times m$, where n is the total number of elements and m is the total number of bitvectors. This can result in sizes even greater than the size of the original dataset, causing high time and space overheads for index creation, storage, and query processing. To solve this problem, *run-length compression* algorithms such as Byte-aligned Bitmap Code (BBC) [2] and Word-Aligned Hybrid (WAH) [31, 13] have been developed to reduce the bitmap size. The main idea of these approaches is that for long sequences of 0s and 1s within each bitvector, an encoding is used to count the number of continuous 0s or 1s. Such encoded counts are stored, requiring less space. Another property of the run-length compression methods is that it supports fast bitwise operations without decompressing the data.

3.3 Advanced Algorithm Using (Dynamic) Bitmap Indexing

We now describe an efficient method for computing correlations, which we refer to as *dynamic* bitmap indexing based method. This method requires single-variable indices (one bitmap index over one variable).

Correlation calculation between the variables A and B using bitmap indexing is shown in Figure 3. This method assumes that bitmaps have been constructed for each of the variables or attributes involved. The algorithm involves three steps. First, we directly find

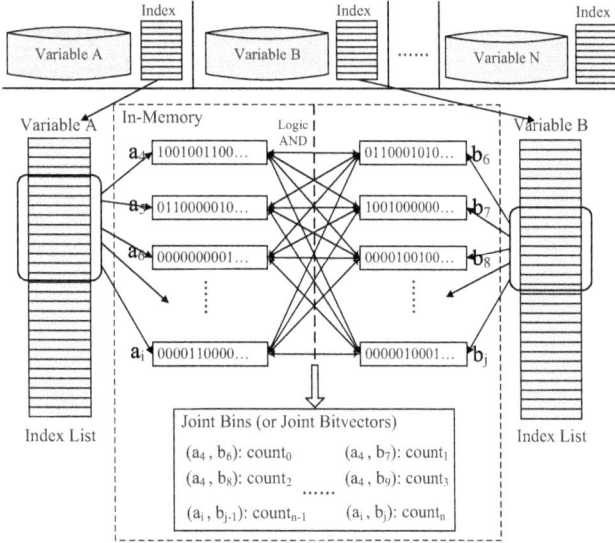

Figure 3: Dynamic Indexing based Correlation Computation

ID	A Value	B Value	jb$_0$ A[1,3] B[2,4]	jb$_1$ A[1,3] B[5,7]	jb$_2$ A[1,3] B[8,10]	jb$_3$ A[4,6] B[2,4]	jb$_4$ A[4,6] B[5,7]	jb$_5$ A[4,6] B[8,10]
0	4	3	0	0	0	1	0	0
1	1	2	1	0	0	0	0	0
2	4	5	0	0	0	0	1	0
3	1	9	0	0	1	0	0	0
4	2	3	1	0	0	0	0	0
5	6	10	0	0	0	0	0	1
6	5	3	0	0	0	1	0	0
7	4	7	0	0	0	0	1	0
8	1	9	0	0	1	0	0	0
9	2	5	0	1	0	0	0	0
Dataset			Multi-Variables Bitmap Indices					

Figure 4: Static Indexing

the subsets of bitvectors of the dataset for A (a_4 to a_i, in the example) and B (b_6 to b_j, in the example), which satisfy the current query and load them into the memory. Note that both *dimension-based* and *value-based* subsetting can be easily supported on bitmap indices, as they simply involve choosing certain rows and columns respectively from the bitvectors. In the second step, we generate *joint bins* for A and B. Because individual bins have been generated during the index generation phase and stored in the form of bitvectors, we only need to perform logic AND operations between bitvectors of A and B for this step. The total complexity of this step is $m \times n$, where m and n are the number of bitvectors (used in query) of A and B. In the final step, we calculate different correlation metrics based on the joint bins, just like the original method.

If we compare the indexing based method with the original method, we find that there are at least three advantages of using bitmap indices. First, our method only needs to load the indices (which are much smaller in size) instead of loading the dataset into the memory. Compared with the original method, we have much smaller memory requirements and the time to load data is also reduced. Second, data filtering, especially for a value-based filtering condition, is very costly with the original method, as one needs to examine each element. However, our method achieves this step by simply loading the bitvectors that satisfy the current value-based condition. Finally, a key step of calculating correlation metrics is to generate joint bins. Without indexing support, the joint bins have to be generated by scanning through each element in the data subset. However, with the help of bitmap indexing, the joint bins is based on logic AND operations, and is much simpler.

One issue, however, is the cost of creating bitmap index on the data, which can be expensive. However, in many cases, an index may be created for a variety of reasons, like supporting data subsetting [21] or sampling [22].

3.4 Using Static Bitmap Indexing

A further optimization of the above method is based on the following motivation. Within most of the scientific datasets, some variables are highly correlated while others are not. Meanwhile scientists also have preferences on correlation analysis over specific variable set. Static indexing, which builds multi-variable indices (i.e., one bitmap index over multiple variables) involves higher upfront cost and storage, but can be used to answer queries for specific combination of variables efficiently.

Specifically, we note that the (dynamic) indexing based method described above still requires bitwise operations between the datasets of variables A and B to generate the joint bins. The purpose of static indexing is to further reduce the cost of bitwise operations by generating a more involved index, over multiple variables, as shown in Figure 4. During the bitmap index generation phase, instead of generating two separate bins (A and B), we perform binning based on value subranges of both A and B (i.e., $A \cdot B$), and generate joint bitvectors based on the joint bins. In this example, the total number of joint bitvectors generated is 6. During the query process, we directly load the subset of joint bitvectors that satisfy the current query conditions into memory and generate joint bins by simply performing 1-bits counting operations over each bitvector. Based on that, the probability distribution of A, and B and $A \cdot B$ are generated and different correlation metrics are calculated. Moreover, static index can also be directly used to further calculate correlations between the current variable set and other variable or variable set, which is more efficient than dynamic indexing method

If we compare static indexing with dynamic indexing, static indexing method has larger index generation and storage costs, but the advantage is that for each query, we can directly find the subsets of joint bitvectors and calculate correlation metrics efficiently based on that. In comparison, with dynamic indexing, there is a need to perform bitwise operations between the bitvectors for different variables for each query. Hence, static indexing is more suitable for the cases where we know that certain variables are highly correlated, and/or it is known that the users will like to perform frequent correlation analysis on these variables.

3.5 Hierarchical Bitmap Indexing

Combining the benefits of both dynamic and static indexing, we have developed a hierarchical bitmap indexing framework to answer correlation analysis for scientific datasets. An example of this process is shown in Figure 5, where 11 variables are involved.

The entire process contains four steps. First, we build one bitmap index for each variable. These indices can be used for both individual data subsetting, as well as correlation analysis using dynamic indexing. Second, a simple clustering algorithm is applied over all variables to find and group those highly correlated variable pairs. In this step, an initial or approximate correlation values between each variable pair is calculated and each pair whose correlation results is larger than a certain threshold is clustered into one group. From the figures, we can see that Var_1 and Var_2 are clustered into one group, and Var_5 and Var_6 are clustered into another. In this step, users are also able to manually build up groups if they want to perform frequent correlation analysis between certain variables, e.g., Var_9 and Var_{10}. After clustering, in the third step, static indices, as described earlier, are built over those clusters that contain two variables. These indices can be used to process frequent queries

194

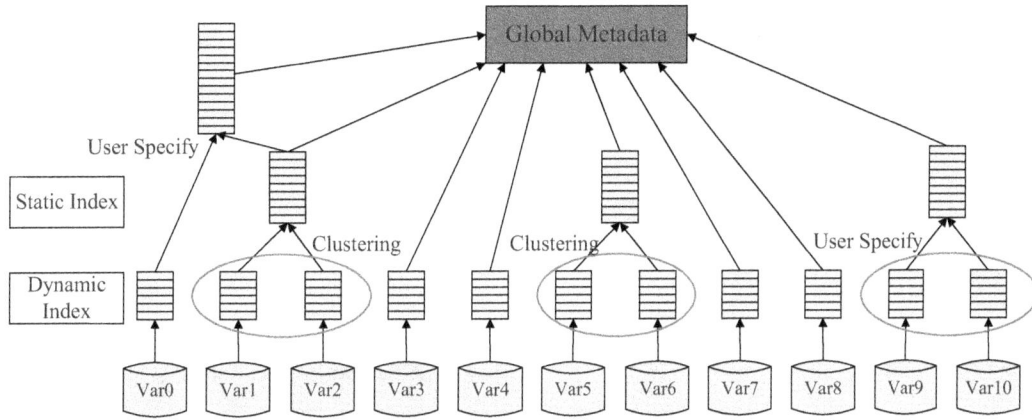

Figure 5: Hierarchical Bitmap Indexing

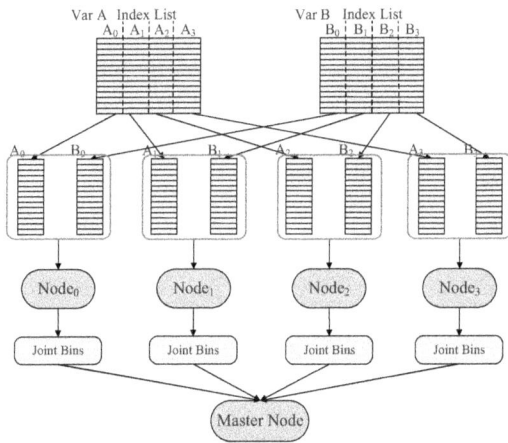

Figure 6: Dimension-based Partitioning Method

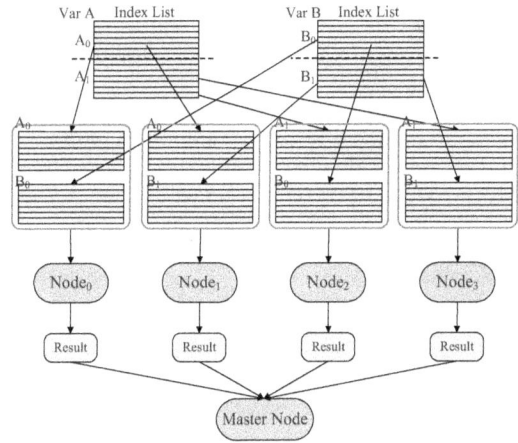

Figure 7: Value-based Partitioning Method

more efficiently. Moreover, our framework is flexible enough that if users want to add another variable into an existing cluster (support correlation analysis between one variable and one variable set), we can simply perform bitwise operations between the index of the single variable and static multi-variable index to generate a larger static index, such as the one involving Var_0, Var_1 and Var_2 in this figure. Finally, a global metadata is maintained to keep track of the entire hierarchy. When the system receives a query, the system can automatically find the right indexing method by looking up the global metadata.

3.6 Parallel Correlation Analysis

Our bitmap based sequential methods are the basis for the parallel and distributed algorithms we have developed. This section describes two parallelization methods (*dim-based partitioning* and *value-based partitioning*). We assume that the dynamic indexing method is being used - parallelizing the method based on static indexing is similar but also simpler.

Dim-based partitioning (referring to dimension-based partitioning) is the more straight-forward way of parallelization. Figure 6 shows the process of calculating correlation information between two variables in parallel using the *dim-based partitioning* method. The bitvectors for both variables A and B are first partitioned into 4 sub-index lists (A_0, A_1, A_2, and A_3; and B_0, B_1, B_2, and B_3) based on the dimensions. Each sub-index list corresponds to one data sub-block of the original dataset. Suppose there are 4 worker

nodes ($Node_0$, $Node_1$, $Node_2$, and $Node_3$) in the parallel environment. Each node will be assigned with one sub-index of A (A_i) and one sub-index of B (B_i). For each correlation query, the bitwise operations between sub-index of A and B will be performed in parallel to generate the joint bins for data sub-blocks. After that, the joint bins will be sent to the master node, and the master node will calculate different correlation metrics based on that.

The advantage of this method is that it supports efficient indexing generation and analysis of each individual variable. In fact, during the index generation phase, instead of generating index-lists for the entire variable, the sub-index lists can be directly generated in parallel by different nodes. If subsetting conditions on individual variables are involved, they can also be easily applied. However, this method has a significant limitation during the stage when the correlations are computed. For several important correlation metrics such as the mutual information, the correlation results cannot be simply computed by taking counts from the sub-blocks of the data. Thus, each worker node must send the joint bins to the master node, which adds a large load on the network. Finally, master node has to perform an expensive global combination operation to calculate the metrics.

In view of this, we have designed a *value-based partitioning* method to support efficient parallel correlation analysis, as shown in Figure 7. Instead of generating sub-index lists based on dimensions, this method generates sub-index lists based on the partition of bitvectors (values). For example, suppose the total number of

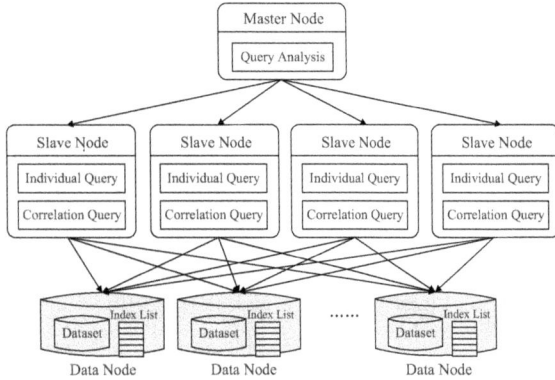

Figure 8: Correlation Analysis in a Distributed Environment

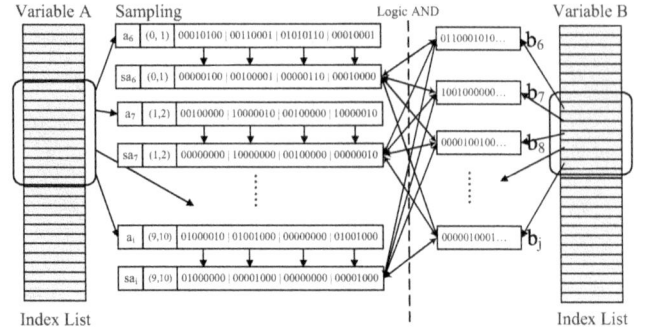

Figure 9: Sampling Using Bitvectors and Correlation Analysis

bitvectors for the variables A and B is 14 each. After partitioning, each sub-index list (A_0 and A_1; and B_0 and B_1) will have 7 bitvectors each. Now, each of the 4 worker nodes can be assigned a pair of sub-index, i.e., four sets (A_i, B_j) are created, where each of i and j can be 0 or 1.

Now, each worker node can perform bitwise operations on the pair that is assigned to it, generate joint bins, and calculate the correlation metrics results directly in parallel. The results of each worker nodes will be sent to the master node and master node only needs to combine the partial results together, which has very low cost. We can see that though there is some replication of data, the total number of bitwise operations for each worker node remains almost the same. Compared with the *dim-based partitioning* method, it has a very low network transfer cost and correlation calculation cost. The only disadvantage is that during the index generation phase, each worker node needs to scan the entire data block to generate indices for corresponding value sub-range.

3.7 Correlation Analysis in a Distributed Environment

Our bitvector based approach also forms the basis for correlation computations on datasets that are spread over geographically distributed repositories. The key advantage of our approach lies in the use of bitmaps as a space efficient summary of original dataset, which is also sufficient for calculating correlation metrics.

We further assume the following. The data over which correlations need to be computed are across multiple repositories, each of which could hold different variables or different dimensional partitions. We assume that bitvectors have been generated and stored within each repository together with the dataset, and further, they can be subset within the repository. We assume that no computational cycles are available at each repository, and thus, correlation computations can only be performed in a compute cluster. Figure 8 shows the environment.

The correlation query that needs to be processed is initially submitted to the master node. The master node decides how the computation and downloading of the data will be divided among the worker nodes. Accordingly, subsets of available bitvectors are downloaded from the data repositories. Subsequently, the rest of the processing is just like parallel computation of bitvectors, which we have already discussed. The key advantage of the approach is that the amount of data downloaded from the repositories is significantly smaller, leading to overall reduction in the time required for computing the correlations.

3.8 Correlation Analysis over Samples

As dataset sizes are growing rapidly, analyzing the entire dataset is often not feasible. It turns out that an added benefit of bitvectors

is that they allow sampling to be performed, in a fashion that value distribution is preserved in the sample.

We describe index-based sampling method and its application to correlation analysis using an example, which is shown in Figure 9. In this example, we still want to generate the correlation results between variable A and variable B. Instead of correlation analysis over all data elements, we want to perform correlation analysis over only 50% of the data. Bitvectors of variable A and B that satisfy the current query are selected and loaded into the memory. From the figure, we can see that this small dataset contains 32 elements, so each bitvector has 32 bits. The bitvectors of A are $a_6(0, 1)$, $a_7(1, 2)$, $a_8(2, 3)$, ..., $a_i(9, 10)$, and the bitvectors of B are b_6, b_7, b_8, ..., b_j.

Though one can sample data corresponding to each variable and then perform correlation computation, obtaining representative samples for each variable (preserving the value-distributions) can be expensive in practice. Thus, we select only one variable, which is the variable with a smaller number of bitvectors, and generate samples based on it. This allows sampling to be efficient, and yet, we get a favorable reduction in the computation time, while preserving accuracy, for the correlation computation step. The bitvector based sampling we perform on each variable is as follows. Our goal is to preserve distribution of values in each spatial region. For this purpose, we divide bitmap indices into *spatial sectors*. In the figure, we can see that the variable A is selected as the variable for sampling, and every selected bitvector of A is divided into 4 sectors, such that there are 8 bits within each sector.

After creating these sectors, sampling is applied within each sector for each bitvector. Particularly, within each bitvector, a desired fraction (sampling rate) of bits that are 1 are chosen. This ensures that the value distribution within each sector is maintained. In Figure 9, we are generating 50% samples out of original dataset. We can see that sa_6, sa_7, ..., sa_i are identifiers of data records that are in the sample generated, and only half of bits that have the value 1 are picked. For example, after sampling, the number of bits 1 in the sample bitvector sa_6 is 6, which is only half of that in original bitvector a_6. After that, the bitwise operations are performed between the sampled bitvectors of A and the original bitvectors of B, following the same steps as in the dynamic indexing method based on the entire data. This method still reduces the time spent on creating joint bins and computing correlations, as we will show through experimental results.

4. PUTTING IT TOGETHER: SYSTEM OVERVIEW

The approach and algorithms discussed in the previous section have been put together in an interactive system. The system supports a high-level query interface, and can provide incremental analysis by maintaining bitvectors for the last several queries.

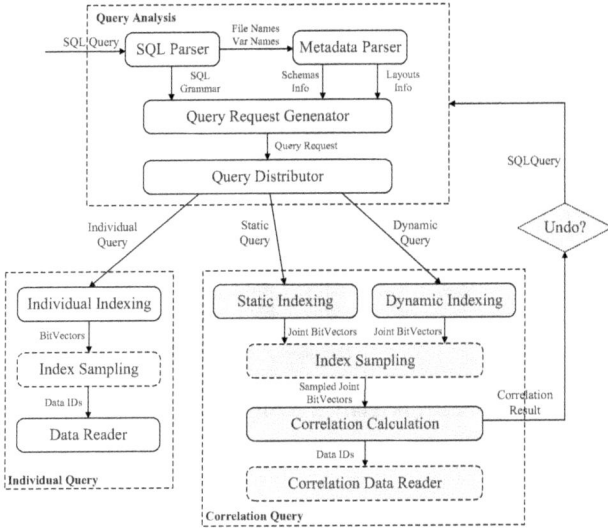

Figure 10: System Overview

Figure 10 shows a high-level overview of our system, which can be divided into three modules: *Query Analysis Module*, *Individual Query Module* and *Correlation Query Module*. The *Query Analysis Module* takes structured queries (using an SQL-like syntax) as the input, generates internal query requests by parsing the query and analyzing the corresponding metadata. *Individual Query Module* supports flexible data subsetting and sampling over each variable [22, 23]. *Correlation Query Analysis* supports the interactive correlation queries among multiple variables, which is the main contribution of this work. It contains five components:

1) Indexing Service: The bitmap indexing services, irrespective of whether they are static or dynamic indexing, take the query request as the input, perform indexing operations and generate joint bins across the variables involved as the output. The joint bins are used in the *Correlation Calculation* module to compute different correlation metrics.

2) Sampling Service: Sampling is used when the entire dataset cannot be analyzed in a timely fashion. This module performs data sampling directly over the bitvectors and outputs only a small sample of the data (in the form of *sampled joint bitvectors*). Then, the correlation calculation is performed based on this sample. As we described in Section 3.8, bitvector based sampling can generate "accurate" samples, and thus they provide the flexibility of accelerating correlation analysis with only a small sacrifice in the accuracy.

3) Correlation Calculation: This component calculates different correlation metrics (histogram, entropy, mutual information) based on the joint bitvectors (bins). One feature that is supported in our current implementation and has not been discussed so far is the use of *multi-level* indexing. A multi-level index uses a coarse-grained binning at the high-level level and a fine-grained binning at the lower-level. Subsequently, low-level bitvectors can be used to generate more accurate calculation of the correlations, though with additional time cost. In contrast, high-level bitvectors provide much faster response time, but generate correlation information in a coarse level.

4) Support for Incremental Analysis and "Undo": Two important features of the system for supporting interactive analysis are - incremental analysis and an "Undo" operation. After users have seen results on a particular subset of data, they can further specialize in the query by adding another condition. Users can also do an "Undo" to step back to the earlier results, and specify additional

conditions for incremental analysis on top of them. This functionality is supported efficiently by keeping the query bitvectors at each step (or a certain k previous steps). On one hand, new subsetting conditions can be applied on top of the bitvectors stored from the previous steps. At the same time, because the size of bitvectors is much smaller than the dataset, we can store bitvectors from the last several steps without very high overheads.

5) Data Reader: Our system also allows users to view the actual data. Suppose during interactive correlation analysis, users specify a subset of data that turns out to be intriguing. Because our system records the bitvectors corresponding to this subset, users can obtain the original data corresponding to this subset efficiently.

5. EXPERIMENTAL RESULTS

In this section, we report results from a number of experiments conducted to evaluate our correlation analysis approach and algorithms. We designed experiments with the following goals: (1) We compare the correlation analysis efficiency among the original *no indexing*, *dynamic indexing*, and *static indexing* methods in a sequential environment, and show that correlation analysis with the help of bitmap indexing can improve the efficiency. (2) We show the scalability of our parallel indexing method with the increasing number of nodes and compare the *value-based partitioning* method with the *dim-based partitioning* method. (3) We show that in an environment where data is stored on geographically distributed repositories, our method is able to speed up the correlation analysis process compared to a simple method that does not use any indexing. (4) We show that if correlation analysis is performed over samples, and not the entire dataset, what kind of speedup we can achieve and how much accuracy is lost.

The dataset we used here is generated by the Parallel Ocean Program (POP) [15], which is an ocean circulation model. The simulation we used has a grid resolution of approximately 10 km (horizontally), and vertically it has a grid spacing close to 10 m near the surface, increasing up to 250 m in the deep ocean. POP generates 1.4 GB output for each variable per time-slice. The total number of variables in the dataset is 26, and each variable is modeled with either two dimensions (longitude and latitude) or three dimensions (longitude, latitude, and depth). The data is stored in the NetCDF format. The size of bitmap indices ranges from 12.1% to 26.8% compared to the size of its corresponding variable. The total number of bitvectors of each variable is from 203 to 431, and the bitvectors generation time ranges from 112 to 187 seconds for each variable per time-slice, depending on the value ranges of variables. For bigger data size, parallel index generation can be applied to improve the efficiency. Also index generation can be treated as a preprocessing step, since once these indices have been calculated, they can be used for a variety of queries, not limited to correlation analysis (for example, subsetting [21] and sampling [22]). We chose the same binning scales for the *no indexing*, *dynamic indexing* and *static indexing* methods so that the correlation results of all methods are same. All of our experiments were conducted on the Glenn cluster from Ohio Supercomputing Center, where every node has 8 cores, 2.6 GHz AMD Opteron(TM) processors, with 64 GB RAM and 1.9 TB local disk space.

5.1 Efficiency Improvement Using Bitmap Indexing

The experiments in this subsection compare the correlation analysis time among the original or the *no indexing* method, the *dynamic indexing* method, and the *static indexing* method. Two variables were chosen and we calculate entropy of each variable and the 2D histogram and the mutual information between them.

Figure 11 shows the correlation analysis time among these three methods based on different queries. We selected 1000 queries with different dimension-based and value-based subsetting conditions,

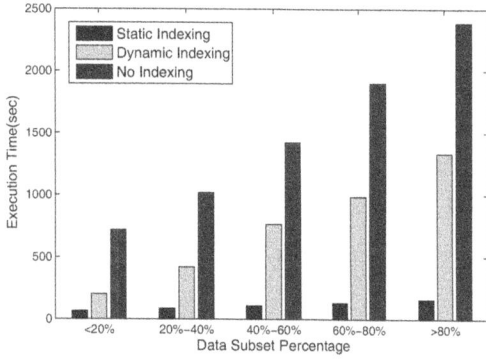

Figure 11: Comparison of Correlation Analysis Time with Queries with Different Subsetting Levels

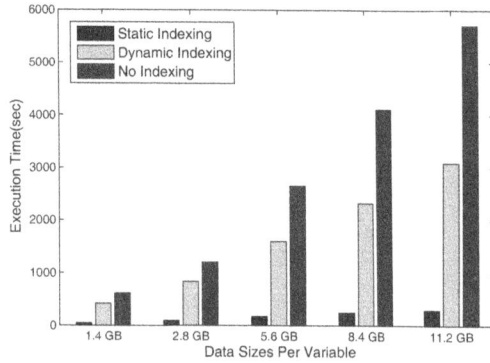

Figure 12: Comparison of Correlation Analysis Time with Queries with Different Dataset Sizes

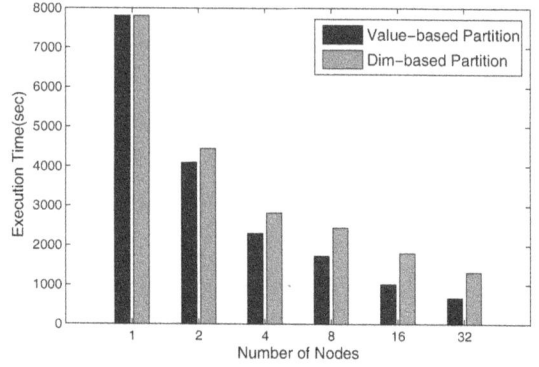

Figure 13: Parallel Correlation Analysis - Varying Number of Nodes

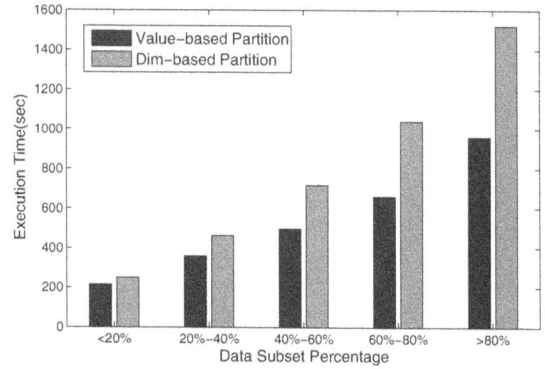

Figure 14: Parallel Correlation Analysis - Queries with Different Subsetting Levels

and then divide them into five categories based on data subsetting percentage (<20%, 20%-40%, 40%-60%, 60%-80%, >80%). Each variable is 5.6 GB (4 timestamps merged together) in size. The time cost of the original or the *no indexing method* includes the data loading time, the data filtering time (where subsetting conditions are applied), the joint bins generation time, and finally, the correlation metrics calculation time. Without indexing support, the entire datasets for the two variables involved have to be loaded into the memory, and subsequently, filtering conditions are applied to examine each data element. The joint bins are generated by binning over each element within the data subset, which is also time consuming.

The time cost of *dynamic indexing* includes bitvectors subset loading time, bitwise operation time to generate joint bins, and the correlation metrics calculation time. Compared with *no indexing method*, *dynamic indexing* method has much lower data loading time, as the size of the bitvectors is much smaller than the size of the data block, and only a subset of bitvectors that satisfy the current query conditions need to be loaded into the memory. Moreover, the joint bins are generated based on fast bitwise operations. This is reflected in the experiments, and from the figure, we can see that, irrespective of the data subsetting percentage, the *dynamic indexing* method always achieves better efficiency than the *no indexing method*. The speedup factor varies from 1.78x to 3.61x, becoming smaller as data subset percentage increases. This is because the larger the subsetting percentage is, a larger fraction of bitvectors have to be loaded into the memory, and more bitwise operations need to be performed. The time cost of the *static indexing* method includes only the joint bitvectors loading time and the

correlation metrics calculation time. Compared with *no indexing* method, the speedup is from 11.4x to 15.35x.

Figure 12 shows the correlation analysis time among three methods over different sizes of the data. Here the correlation metrics calculation is over the entire data blocks of two variables, without any subsetting. The size of the dataset for each variable ranges from 1.4 GB to 11.2 GB. From the figure we can see that even without data subsetting, for all different cases, both *dynamic indexing* and *static indexing* methods perform well, with their advantage even increasing as the dataset sizes increase. This is because our indexing based methods require less memory.

5.2 Scalability of Parallel Indexing

The experiments in this subsection show the speedup of parallel correlation analysis using multiple nodes. During this evaluation, we also compare the efficiency of *value-based partitioning* method with the *dim-based partitioning* method. Correlation analysis is performed over two variables, and the data sizes for each is 28 GB (20 timestamps merged together). We use between 1 and 32 nodes for our experiments, and because the method is memory-intensive, only 1 core per node is used.

Figure 13 shows the scalability of our parallel correlation analysis method with different number of nodes. The X axis shows number of nodes (from 1 to 32) used. The correlation calculation here is over the entire data blocks (all elements), i.e., no subsetting condition is involved. From the figure we can see that both *value-based partitioning* and *dim-based partitioning* methods show good speedup as number of nodes increases. For the *value-based partitioning* method, the speedup using 2, 4, 8, 16, and 32 nodes is 1.87x, 3.4x, 4.53x, 7.68x, and 11.79x, respectively. For *dim-based*

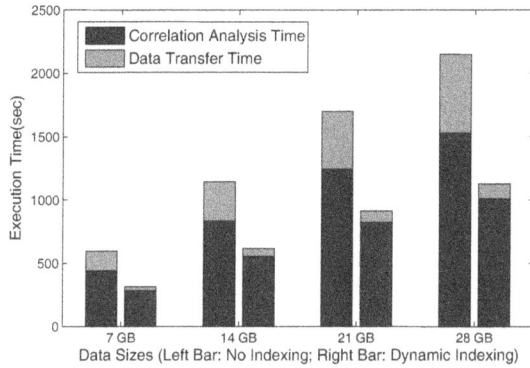

Figure 15: Distributed Analysis - Data Downloaded from a "Local" Data Server with 1 Gb/sec Bandwidth

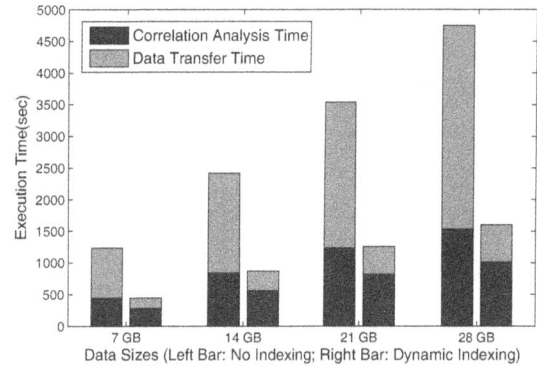

Figure 16: Distributed Analysis - Data Downloaded from a "Remote" Data Server with 200 Mb/sec Bandwidth

partitioning method, the speedup using 2, 4, 8, 16, and 32 nodes is 1.73x, 2.77x, 3.18x, 4.32x, and 5.96x, respectively. The reason for higher efficiency of *value-based partitioning* is because the master node is a bottleneck for *dim-based partitioning*. Note that the speedups for *value-based partitioning* are still not close to linear. This is because different bitvectors can have different number of 1s, which leads to different amounts of time for the bitvector operations.

Figure 14 shows the efficiency of both partitioning methods with different queries, which are then classified with respect to the subsetting percentage involved. The number of nodes here is 16. From the figure we can see that for both methods, the execution time increases as data subset percentage increases, as we expect. However, if we compare the two partitioning methods, we can see that the relative improvement from the *value-based partitioning* method becomes more significant than the *dim-based partitioning* method as data subsetting percentage increases (relative improvement ranges between 1.17x to 1.58x). The reason is that as data subsetting percentage increases, the number of joint bins generated by each process also increases, which imposes a more significant network overhead for the *dim-based partitioning* method.

5.3 Efficiency Improvement in Distributed Environment

The experiments in this subsection analyze the efficiency of performing correlation analysis in a distributed environment, where data is stored over geographically separated data servers, and analysis is performed over a single cluster. In such a case, without bitmap indexing, datasets corresponding to variables involved need to be downloaded to the cluster used for the computations. Instead, if the indices have been generated and stored together with the dataset, only the index files need to be downloaded to the cluster. In our experiment, we use 16 compute nodes for parallel correlation calculation. We use a *local* data server (1 Gb/sec bandwidth connection to the compute-cluster) and a *remote* data server (200 Mb/sec bandwidth connection to the compute-cluster) in separate sets of experiments.

Figure 15 compares the total time between the *dynamic indexing* method and the *no indexing* method using local data server. The data size of each variable ranges from 7 GB to 28 GB. No subsetting is involved. The total execution time with either of the methods can be divided into two parts: the network data transfer time and the parallel correlation analysis time. As expected, our method reduces the data transfer time, because only bitvectors are being downloaded, and not the full dataset. For parallel correlation analysis, to make a fair comparison, both methods used *value-based partitioning*, i.e., without indexing, the full dataset is partitioned

on the basis of the values. While partitioning bitvectors based on values is trivial, there is a processing cost associated with partitioning the dataset based on values. We do not report the extra value partitioning time for the *no indexing* method. We can see that our method is still able to achieve much better efficiency than the *no indexing* method, because our method has much smaller memory data loading cost and the computation costs for joint bins are also lower. The overall improvement ranges from 1.87x to 1.91x.

Figure 16 compares the total time between the *dynamic indexing* method and the *no indexing* method using a remote data server, with lower (200 Mb/sec) bandwidth. From the figure, we can see that while the parallel correlation analysis time of both methods is similar (as in the previous experiment), our method further improves the efficiency by saving the data transfer time. The overall speedup ranges from 2.78x to 2.96x.

It should be further noted that our experiments did not include any data subsetting. If correlation queries involve any subsetting condition, the size of the bitvectors involved can be reduced further. In comparison, a data repository without any indexing support may not allow any subsetting, and users may have to download all the data for each variable being analyzed.

5.4 Efficiency and Accuracy Comparison with Sampling

Our last set of experiments compares the efficiency and accuracy of performing correlation analysis with different sampling levels (sampling applied to bitvectors). We selected 10 variables (each has three dimensions with 1.4 GB in size) from the POP dataset, and calculated the mutual information between each distinct pair of them. The total number of such pairs is 45. Dynamic indexing is used in these experiments.

Figure 17 shows the efficiency of calculating mutual information for 45 variable pairs with different samples. The X axis shows different sample percentages (100%, 50%, 25%, 10%, 5%, 1%) compared with original data size, and the Y axis shows the entire correlation analysis time. Overall, we can see that the entire analysis efficiency greatly improves as sample size becomes smaller. Compared with correlation analysis over the original dataset (100%), the speedup using 50%, 25%, 10% 5%, and 1% samples is 1.34x, 1.69x, 2.17x, 2.93x, and 6.84x, respectively. While the steps for constructing joint bins and calculating the metrics are accelerated by almost the same factor as the sampling level, the cost of reading the original bitvectors remains almost the same, and an additional cost of sampling is introduced.

Figure 18 shows the accuracy of mutual information results using different sampling levels. Here we generated 45 mutual information results (45 pairs) for each sampling level. We compute

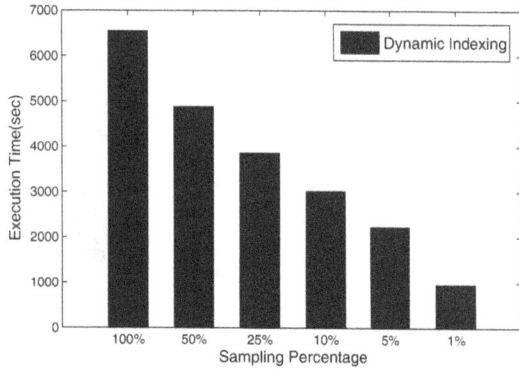

Figure 17: Efficiency Comparison with Different Sampling Levels

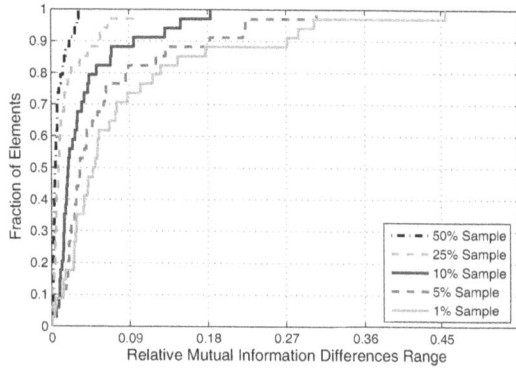

Figure 18: Cumulative Frequency Plot to Show Accuracy Comparison with Different Sampling Levels

the relative value differences using expression $(original\_result - sample\_result)/original\_result$ for each pair. Then, we use a *Cumulative Frequency Plot* (CFP) to represent the relative mutual information differences for all pairs. In CFP, a point (x, y) indicates that the fraction y of all calculated relative value differences are less than x. Because the value differences should be as small as possible, it implies that a method with the curve to the left has a better accuracy than the method with the curve to the right. From the figure we can see that the accuracy using 50% samples is very close to the original dataset, as errors are very close to 0 for almost all points. Not surprisingly, accuracy becomes worse as sparser samples are taken. If we calculate the average accuracy lost based on the CFP, we find that the average accuracy loss with 50%, 25%, 10%, 5% and 1% sample is 1.53%, 3.42%, 7.91%, 12.57%, and 18.32%, respectively. Because our bitvector based sampling method preserves distribution of values, reasonably high accuracies are maintained even with a small sample of data. Overall, our sampling method provides a way to accelerate the computations while obtaining reasonably accurate results. Sampling can also provide a way to further reduce the data transfer volumes when the data is stored in geographically distributed servers. In fact, as our previous work has shown [22], bitmap indexing can be used to perform server-side sampling of the data.

6. CASE STUDIES DEMONSTRATING EFFICACY OF TOOL

All results presented in the previous section focused on demonstrating the efficiency of the methods. In this section, our goal is to demonstrate how the tool is useful to the scientists. Particularly, we

show that the ability to compute correlations over various subsets through an intuitive and high-level query interface makes our tools extremely valuable for scientific discoveries.

The studies were conducted at the Los Alamos National Laboratory (LANL), using datasets generated from the POP simulation. Among the two scientists, one is a physical chemist interested in studying bio-geochemistry data, such as the production ("PROD") and sinking ("FLUX-IN") of Silicate (SiO2), Calcium Carbonate (CaCO3), and Particulate Organic Carbon (POC), as well as Oxygen (O2) production ("PROD") and consumption ("CONSUMP"). The second scientist focused on studying the relationship between Temperature (TEMP) and Salinity (SALT), which are the two basic elements of the ocean data. Using our system, they are able to explore different correlations over different areas or value ranges by submitting different queries, and our system returns correlation metrics results (histogram, entropy, and mutual information) as the output.

Figure 19 shows different correlation results our system presented to the scientists. The description below focuses on showing (in intuitive terms) the observations that can be made from the data.

Subfigure 19(a) shows the histogram of $SALT$ based on different value ranges of $TEMP$. Let us first look at the $SALT$ value along the X axis. Here we define p as the value on the X axis where the curve has the highest Y value. When $TEMP < 5$, the p value of $SALT$ is around 0.0349. However, as the temperature increases, the salinity decreases. When $TEMP >= 5$ and $TEMP < 10$, the p value decreases to 0.0342. After that, the salinity increases as the temperature increases. When $TEMP >= 10$ and $TEMP < 15$, the p value increases to 0.0345, and then when $TEMP >= 15$, the p value of $SALT$ increases to 0.035. Thus, salinity is high when the temperature is either low or high. After talking to the scientists, we find that this is because on one hand, the deeper into the ocean, the colder the water gets, and the water also gets denser, which implies a higher salinity. On the other hand, the surface salinity also increases in areas close to the equator, because of hotter air. This happens because water evaporates faster, leaving more salt to a smaller amount of water. Moreover, if we look at the Y axis, we are able to see the diversity of the salinity within different temperature ranges. For example, when $TEMP < 5$, over 23% of the data elements' value is around 0.035. However, when $TEMP >= 15$, only around 6% of the data elements' value is around 0.035.

Subfigure 19(b) shows the histogram of $SALT$ based on different areas of the ocean (dimension subsets). From the figure we can see that the p value of $SALT$ within the Atlantic Ocean and the Mediterranean Sea areas is larger than the p value within the Pacific Ocean and the Indian Ocean, which reflects the actual features of these areas.

Subfigure 19(c) shows the histogram of $SALT$ based on different value ranges of $TEMP$ inside the Mediterranean Sea. This figure is used to show that our system is able to perform correlation analysis over flexible combinations of dimension subsets and value subsets. From the figure we can see that although the value subrange of $TEMP$ is the same as in subfigure 19(a), the relationship between $TEMP$ and $SALT$ has changed: particularly, now salinity increases as the temperature increases. This is because this area is warm.

Subfigure 19(d) shows the histogram of sink volumes of Silicate $SiO2\_FLUX\_IN$ based on different sink volumes of Calcium Carbonate $CaCO3\_FLUX\_IN$. We can see that the p value of $CaCO3\_FLUX\_IN$ increases as $SiO2\_FLUX\_IN$ increases. This is because more sinks of Silicate implies more plankton in this area, and more plankton implies more Calcium Carbonate generated and more sinks of Calcium Carbonate. Hence, 2D histogram is able to help scientists find different value distributions of one variable based on value changes of another.

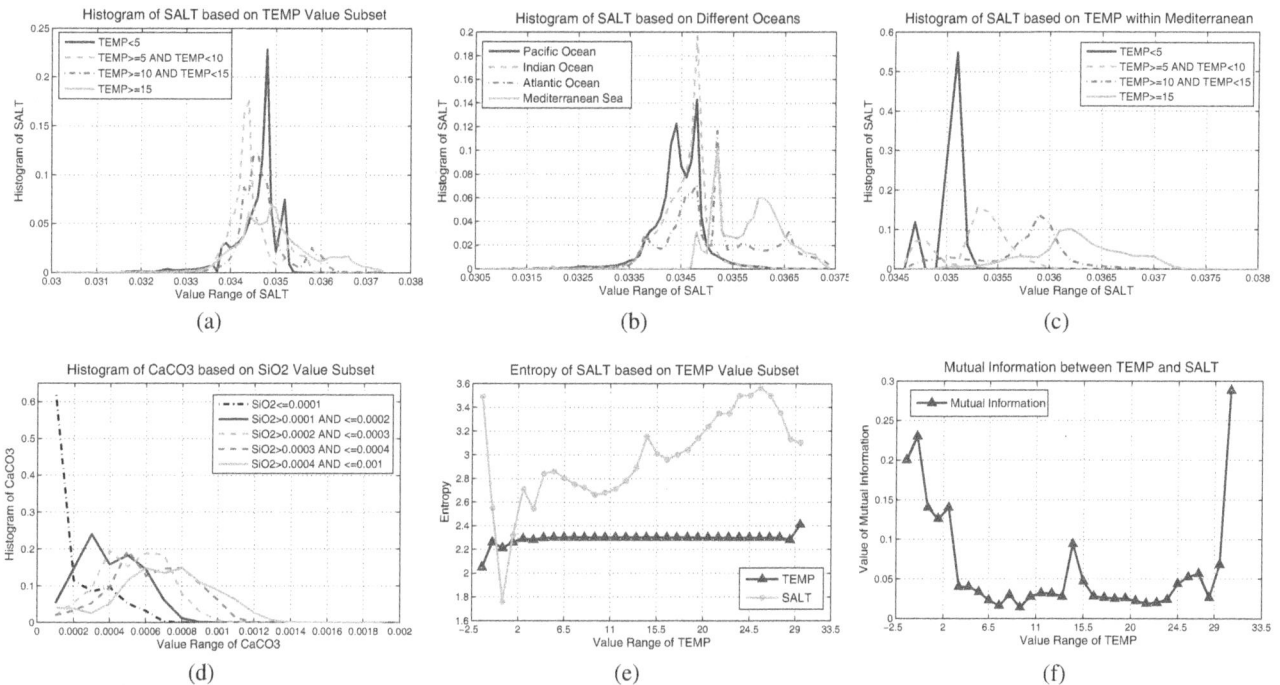

Figure 19: Correlation Metrics Results over Data Subsets

Subfigure 19(e) shows an example of using entropy for correlation analysis. The goal here is to see the changes of entropies of $SALT$ with respect to the different value subsets of $TEMP$. A total of 30 queries are submitted and each query specifies a $TEMP$ subset with similar value intervals, which makes the entropy values of $TEMP$ similar. From the figure we can see that while the entropy values of $TEMP$ are similar, the entropy values of $SALT$ have large differences. When the $TEMP$ value is around one centigrade, entropy of $SALT$ is the lowest, and it increases as the $TEMP$ value increases. In another word, the value of salinity is more constant and predicable as temperature is around one centigrade, whereas one sees a diversity of salinity values as the temperature increases.

Finally, subfigure 19(f) shows the mutual information between $TEMP$ and $SALT$ based on the value distribution of $TEMP$. From the figure, we can see that mutual information between $TEMP$ and $SALT$ is high when the temperature values are either low or high. This implies that $TEMP$ and $SALT$ are highly correlated within these two value ranges. For the other value ranges, where the mutual information is close to 0, correlation is very small between the two variables.

Overall, the representative results above show that correlation analysis over flexible subsets of data can help scientists confirm known facts, and even make new observations.

7. RELATED WORK

Our work has some similarities to a number of efforts from high performance data management area, as well as visualization.

Closely related to our work, Fastbit [30] and FastQuery [8] apply bitmap indexing and parallel indexing to support efficient value-based subsetting (for individual variables). Our work builds on top of these, but is unique in applying bitvectors for correlation analysis. There has also been a growing trend towards building database-like functionality on top of native storage of the data. Ex-

amples include the NoDB approach [1] and automatic data virtualization [28]. Our work is an example of this approach, but, again, unique in its focus on correlation analysis. In recent years, many Array DBMSs, including SciDB [6] and RasDaMan [3] have been designed, and are gaining popularity. None of these systems have provided support for correlation analysis across variables.

In scientific data analysis, much of the recent focus has been on in-situ analysis, with ADIOS project providing a mature implementation of this approach [16]. DIRAQ [17] provides a parallel in-situ, in network data encoding and reorganization technique that enables the transformation of simulation output into a query-efficient form. In the future, we will like to develop methods for in-situ correlation analysis. Other tools for scientific data analysis include OPeNDAP [9], which provides data virtualization through a data access protocol and data representation. SciHadoop [7] and SciMATE [27] integrate map-reduce and its variant with scientific library to enable map-reduce tasks over scientific data. Scientific Data Manager (SDM) [19] employs the Metadata Management System (MDMS) and provides a programming model to abstract low-level parallel I/O operations for complex scientific processing. FASM [18] utilizes statistical metadata with various subsetting schemes to perform efficient analyses on large datasets. None of these efforts have considered correlation analysis.

Analysis of multiple variables and their relationships in scientific simulation outputs has been an ongoing topic of research. In a very recent work, Biswas et al. [4] have presented an information theoretic framework for exploring multivariate datasets in a "top-down" manner, where they divide the variables into groups based on their information overlap, and then identify representative variables from each group to conduct further relationship analysis. Wang et al. [26] used information theory for exploring the causal relationship among the variables of a time-varying multivariate dataset. In an earlier work, Jänicke et al. [14] applied the dimensionality reduction on the high dimensional data where each dimension was analogous to a variable in the multivariate context. Another well-known multivariate exploration technique was developed by Di Yang et al. [33]. They use a Nugget Management System (NMS), where the nuggets represent the information that the users are interested in. Several authors have surveyed existing multivariate data analysis techniques [29, 11]. Almost none of these efforts have focused on scalability limitations, especially, what happens when the data does not fit into memory, or if the data is stored in geographically distributed repositories. Parallelization of the methods is another challenge that has not been addressed.

8. CONCLUSIONS

While the potential of data-driven discoveries for scientific advances is being increasingly recognized, several trends are making interactive and efficient data analysis hard. On one hand, the amount of data generated by scientific simulation (or instruments) is rapidly increasing. On the other hand, computing environments are becoming more and more constrained with respect to data movement (at all levels).

This paper has focused on the problem of correlation analysis in parallel and distributed settings. We have developed a series of techniques, with the main underlying idea that bitmap indices can serve as a concise and representative summary of the original dataset, allowing computation of the correlation metrics more efficiently. Our algorithms have been incorporated in a system that offers a high-level API, where users can interactively choose subsets of the data to be analyzed, and sampling can be combined with correlation analysis. We have extensively evaluated our system and shown the efficiency improvement using our method. We also conducted a user-evaluation with domain scientists and demonstrated how our system is able to aid the data-driven discovery process.

9. ACKNOWLEDGMENTS

This work was partially funded by the Department of Energy (DOE) Office of Science (OSC) Advanced Scientific Computing Research (ASCR) and also partially funded by NSF award ACI-1339757 to the Ohio State University.

10. REFERENCES

[1] Ioannis Alagiannis, Renata Borovica, Miguel Branco, Stratos Idreos, and Anastasia Ailamaki. NoDB: efficient query execution on raw data files. In *Proceedings of the 2012 ACM SIGMOD International Conference on Management of Data*, pages 241–252, 2012.

[2] G. Antoshenkov. Byte-aligned bitmap compression. In *Data Compression Conference, 1995. DCC'95. Proceedings*, page 476. IEEE, 1995.

[3] P. Baumann, A. Dehmel, P. Furtado, R. Ritsch, and N. Widmann. The Multidimensional Database System RasDaMan. In *Proceedings of the 1998 ACM SIGMOD International Conference on Management of Data*, pages 575–577, 1998.

[4] Ayan Biswas, Soumya Dutta, Han-Wei Shen, and Jonathan Woodring. An information-aware framework for exploring multivariate data sets. *IEEE Transactions on Visualization and Computer Graphics*, 19(12):2683–2692, 2013.

[5] Udeepta D Bordoloi and H-W Shen. View selection for volume rendering. In *Visualization, 2005. VIS 05. IEEE*, pages 487–494. IEEE, 2005.

[6] Paul G. Brown. Overview of SciDB: large scale array storage, processing and analysis. In *Proceedings of the 2010 ACM SIGMOD International Conference on Management of Data*, pages 963–968, 2010.

[7] J. Buck, N. Watkins, J. LeFevre, K. Ioannidou, C. Maltzahn, N. Polyzotis, and S. Brandt. Scihadoop: Array-based query processing in hadoop. In *SC*, 2011.

[8] J. Chou, K. Wu, O. Rübel, M.H.J.Q. Prabhat, B. Austin, E.W. Bethel, R.D. Ryne, and A. Shoshani. Parallel index and query for large scale data analysis. In *SC*, 2011.

[9] P. Cornillon, J. Gallagher, and T. Sgouros. Opendap: Accessing data in a distributed, heterogeneous environment. *Data Science Journal*, 2(0):164–174, 2003.

[10] Thomas M Cover and Joy A Thomas. *Elements of information theory*. John Wiley & Sons, 2012.

[11] M.C.F. de Oliveira and H. Levkowitz. From visual data exploration to visual data mining: a survey. *Visualization and Computer Graphics, IEEE Transactions on*, 9(3):378–394, 2003.

[12] Stefan Gumhold. Maximum entropy light source placement. In *Visualization, 2002. VIS 2002. IEEE*, pages 275–282. IEEE, 2002.

[13] Gheorghi Guzun, Guadalupe Canahuate, David Chiu, and Jason Sawin. A tunable compression framework for bitmap indices. In *Proceedings of the 30th international conference on data engineering (ICDE)*. IEEE, 2014.

[14] H. Jänicke, M. Bottinger, and G. Scheuermann. Brushing of attribute clouds for the visualization of multivariate data. *Visualization and Computer Graphics, IEEE Transactions on*, 14(6):1459–1466, 2008.

[15] PW Jones, PH Worley, Y. Yoshida, JB White III, and J. Levesque. Practical performance portability in the parallel ocean program (pop). *Concurrency and Computation: Practice and Experience*, 17(10):1317–1327, 2005.

[16] Scott Klasky, Hasan Abbasi, Jeremy Logan, Manish Parashar, Karsten Schwan, Arie Shoshani, Matthew Wolf, Sean Ahern, Ilkay Altintas, Wes Bethel, et al. In situ data processing for extreme-scale computing. In *Proc. Conf. Scientific Discovery through Advanced Computing Program (SciDACÂŠ11)*, 2011.

[17] Sriram Lakshminarasimhan, David A Boyuka, Saurabh V Pendse, Xiaocheng Zou, John Jenkins, Venkatram Vishwanath, Michael E Papka, and Nagiza F Samatova. Scalable in situ scientific data encoding for analytical query processing. In *Proceedings of the 22nd international symposium on High-performance parallel and distributed computing*, pages 1–12. ACM, 2013.

[18] Jialin Liu and Yong Chen. Fast data analysis with integrated statistical metadata in scientific datasets. In *2013 IEEE International Conference on Cluster Computing (CLUSTER)*, pages 1–8. IEEE, 2013.

[19] B. Ludäscher, I. Altintas, C. Berkley, D. Higgins, E. Jaeger, M. Jones, E.A. Lee, J. Tao, and Y. Zhao. Scientific workflow management and the kepler system. *Concurrency and Computation: Practice and Experience*, 18(10):1039–1065, 2006.

[20] P. O'Neil and D. Quass. Improved query performance with variant indexes. In *ACM Sigmod Record*, volume 26, pages 38–49. ACM, 1997.

[21] Y. Su, G. Agrawal, and J. Woodring. Indexing and parallel query processing support for visualizing climate datasets. In *2012 41th IEEE/ACM International Conference on Parallel Processing (ICPP)*, pages 249–258. IEEE, 2012.

[22] Yu Su, Gagan Agrawal, Jonathan Woodring, Kary Myers, Joanne Wendelberger, and James Ahrens. Taming massive distributed datasets: data sampling using bitmap indices. In *Proceedings of the 22nd international symposium on High-performance parallel and distributed computing*, pages 13–24. ACM, 2013.

[23] Yu Su, Yi Wang, Gagan Agrawal, and Rajkumar Kettimuthu. Sdquery dsi: integrating data management support with a wide area data transfer protocol. In *Proceedings of SC13: International Conference for High Performance Computing, Networking, Storage and Analysis*, page 47. ACM, 2013.

[24] Pere-Pau Vázquez, Miquel Feixas, Mateu Sbert, and Wolfgang Heidrich. Automatic view selection using viewpoint entropy and its application to image-based modelling. In *Computer Graphics Forum*, volume 22, pages 689–700. Wiley Online Library, 2003.

[25] Ivan Viola, Miquel Feixas, Mateu Sbert, and Meister Eduard Groller. Importance-driven focus of attention. *Visualization and Computer Graphics, IEEE Transactions on*, 12(5):933–940, 2006.

[26] Chaoli Wang, Hongfeng Yu, Ray W Grout, Kwan-Liu Ma, and Jacqueline H Chen. Analyzing information transfer in time-varying multivariate data. In *Pacific Visualization Symposium (PacificVis), 2011 IEEE*, pages 99–106. IEEE, 2011.

[27] Yi Wang, Wei Jiang, and Gagan Agrawal. Scimate: A novel mapreduce-like framework for multiple scientific data formats. In *Cluster, Cloud and Grid Computing (CCGrid), 2012 12th IEEE/ACM International Symposium on*, pages 443–450. IEEE, 2012.

[28] Li Weng, Gagan Agrawal, Umit Catalyurek, Tahsin Kurc, Sivaramakrishnan Narayanan, and Joel Saltz. An Approach for Automatic Data Virtualization. In *Proceedings of the Conference on High Performance Distributed Computing (HPDC)*, June 2004.

[29] Pak Chung Wong and R. Daniel Bergeron. 30 years of multidimensional multivariate visualization. In *Scientific Visualization, Overviews, Methodologies, and Techniques*, pages 3–33, Washington, DC, USA, 1997. IEEE Computer Society.

[30] K. Wu, W. Koegler, J. Chen, and A. Shoshani. Using bitmap index for interactive exploration of large datasets. In *15th International Conference on Scientific and Statistical Database Management*, pages 65–74. IEEE, 2003.

[31] K. Wu, E.J. Otoo, and A. Shoshani. Compressing bitmap indexes for faster search operations. In *Scientific and Statistical Database Management, 2002. Proceedings. 14th International Conference on*, pages 99–108. IEEE, 2002.

[32] K. Wu, K. Stockinger, and A. Shoshani. Breaking the curse of cardinality on bitmap indexes. In *Scientific and Statistical Database Management*, pages 348–365. Springer, 2008.

[33] Di Yang, E.A. Rundensteiner, and M.O. Ward. Analysis guided visual exploration of multivariate data. In *Visual Analytics Science and Technology, 2007. VAST 2007. IEEE Symposium on*, pages 83–90, 2007.

A Methodology for Evaluating the Impact of Data Compression on Climate Simulation Data

Allison H. Baker
National Center for
Atmospheric Research
Boulder, CO
abaker@ucar.edu

Haiying Xu
National Center for
Atmospheric Research
Boulder, CO
haiyingx@ucar.edu

John M. Dennis
National Center for
Atmospheric Research
Boulder, CO
dennis@ucar.edu

Michael N. Levy
National Center for
Atmospheric Research
Boulder, CO
mlevy@ucar.edu

Doug Nychka
National Center for
Atmospheric Research
Boulder, CO
nychka@ucar.edu

Sheri A. Mickelson
National Center for
Atmospheric Research
Boulder, CO
mickelso@ucar.edu

ABSTRACT

High-resolution climate simulations require tremendous computing resources and can generate massive datasets. At present, preserving the data from these simulations consumes vast storage resources at institutions such as the National Center for Atmospheric Research (NCAR). The historical data generation trends are economically unsustainable, and storage resources are already beginning to limit science objectives. To mitigate this problem, we investigate the use of data compression techniques on climate simulation data from the Community Earth System Model. Ultimately, to convince climate scientists to compress their simulation data, we must be able to demonstrate that the reconstructed data reveals the same mean climate as the original data, and this paper is a first step toward that goal. To that end, we develop an approach for verifying the climate data and use it to evaluate several compression algorithms. We find that the diversity of the climate data requires the individual treatment of variables, and, in doing so, the reconstructed data can fall within the natural variability of the system, while achieving compression rates of up to 5:1.

Categories and Subject Descriptors

E.4 [**Coding and Information Theory**]: Data compaction and compression; H.3.m [**Information and Storage Retrieval**]: Miscellaneous; D.2.4 [**Software and Program Verification**]: Validation

Keywords

data compression, high performance computing

1. INTRODUCTION

The Community Earth System Model (CESM) is an important and widely-used earth system model whose development is centered at the National Center for Atmospheric Research. Model simulations from CESM, which we will refer to as data, are used by scientists around the world as well as by the Intergovernmental Panel on Climate Change (IPCC). To illustrate the potential size of a data set, we note that a recent high-resolution CESM simulation generated on the order of one terabyte of data per compute day (corresponding to half a terabyte of data per simulation year) [17]. CESM simulation data are written to "history files" in time slices at pre-defined sampling rates that vary by variable and model component (e.g., the ocean, the atmosphere, the land, etc.). The history files are in NetCDF format and are used for post-processing analysis. The files contain floating-point data that are truncated from double- to single-precision at the time they are written. Furthermore, in practice, climate scientists are often forced to save variables to history files less frequently than they wish due to storage considerations, and a low sampling rate results in even more data loss (see, e.g., [11]). Despite the fact that the simulation data in the history files has already been subjected to these two lossy processes, climate scientists have resisted applying compression algorithms to the history files. Our goal is to develop a suite of quality metrics that can assess whether or not the loss of information due to the application of lossy data compression is detectable within the context of climate data analysis. In other words, are the complete dataset and the reconstructed dataset (that has undergone lossy compression) statistically distinguishable? We focus on lossy compression as it provides a bigger advantage in terms of data reduction. Note that CESM also writes 'restart files" in full-precision (8-byte floating-point) that are used to continue a stopped simulation (i.e., checkpointing). We do not consider compressing restart files at this time, but will examine lossless techniques for these data in the future (as done in [12] for multi-physics simulations).

We are initially focusing on using compression as a means of reducing online and archive storage requirements, ie. "disk-compression" [12], as opposed to reducing the required I/O bandwidth of our application. Therefore, we examine compression with the intention of integrating it into a post-processing step that converts the CESM time-slice data history files to time series data files for each variable. It is well known that losslessly compressing floating-point scientific data is difficult (see, e.g., [14, 1, 12, 11]), primarily due to the almost random (highly entropic) nature of the floating-point data. In particular, the significands of the floating point numbers often look random after the first several digits, depending on the type of data and whether the number of digits that are physically significant is less than the precision used by the model and the precision of the input data. Furthermore, while compression techniques have been studied extensively in areas such as image, video, and audio files, compression of scientific data has only received attention relatively recently. In addition, the metrics typical used to evaluate whether a lossy compression technique is acceptable for image compression may be quite different than what is required to verify scientific simulation data (see, e.g., [15]). Therefore, while performance metrics (such as compression speed and compression ratio) and average error metrics (such as peak signal-to-noise-ratio and root mean squared error) are of interest, of foremost importance is accurately accessing the impact of data compression on climate simulation data. In practical terms, if the reconstructed and the original climate simulation data are indistinguishable during the post-processing analysis, which includes both visualization and analytics, then the effects of compression fit within the natural variability of the system and applying compression is certainly a reasonable thing to do. In summary, we make the following key contributions:

- development of a thorough approach for the verification of climate data that has undergone compression and decompression, and

- evaluation of several existing compression techniques on CESM data, and

- demonstration that climate data compressed by as much as 5:1 can be reconstructed to be statistically indistinguishable from the original

This paper is organized as follows. We discuss related work in Section 2. In Section 3, we describe the attributes of compression methods that were chosen for our study. Our verification methodology is presented in Section 4, and results from compressing the CESM data are given in Section 5. We give concluding remarks in Section 6.

2. RELATED WORK

A number of lossless and lossy compression techniques have been proposed that have potential value for climate data. We give a brief overview of some of these approaches and discuss the metrics used to evaluate the lossy methods.

2.1 Lossless Methods

Traditional general-purpose lossless compression techniques (i.e., methods that exactly preserve the data), such as *gzip*, *bzip2*, and *lmza*, for example, are relatively ineffective on most scientific data and have motivated the development of more recent lossless approaches such as [14, 2, 16, 6]. In [14], the *fpzip* algorithm is presented, with a focus on lossless online compression to reduce bandwidth requirements for scientific data. This method uses predicative coding and can also be used in a lossy manner (by truncating a specified

number of least significant bits when the floating-point values to be compressed are converted to integers). Burscher's lossless *FPC* method [2, 3] aims to simultaneously obtain both a good compression ratio and fast compression and decompression speeds with a predictive coding method that targets 64-bit values. However, his results show that the FPC method (as well as some other lossless methods) does not achieve good compression ratios on datasets with a large amount of randomness. An interesting alternative approach for lossless compression is the ISOBAR-compress method (In-Situ Orthogonal Byte Aggregation Scheme) [16]. *ISOBAR* is a preconditioner that operates on the data to be compressed in a manner that makes it more amenable to compression. Another preconditioner-type method is developed in [6] and applies binary masks to the dataset before the compression step. In addition, in [7], the lossless compression technique *MAFISC* is presented and evaluated on climate data from the German Weather Service (GWS) and CMIP5 [10]. *MAFISC* essentially acts as a preconditioner as well by applying multiple filters to the data before a standard compression method is used. *MAFISC* slightly improves upon the standard lossless method *lmza*, compressing the GWS data by about fifty percent.

2.2 Lossy Methods

Because of the inherent randomness in scientific data, a lossy technique (i.e., the reconstructed data will differ from the original) is typically needed to achieve useful compression rates. Recently, lossy techniques such as those in [21, 11, 1, 20, 12, 8, 9, 18] are being actively developed and applied to scientific datasets. As mentioned previously, *fpzip* [14] can be used in a lossy fashion, and *fpzip* is compared to the commercial software APAX (APplications AXceleration) [20] in [12]. Like *fpzip*, *APAX* also uses predictive encoding, but the two methods differ in their quantization method. The *fpzip* scheme results in a bounded relative error, while APAX bounds the absolute error. It is notable that in [12], the authors attempt to evaluate the impact of the compression by a 'physics-based' approach that specifically tailors a metric(s) for each of three different physics codes. The work by Iverson et. al in [9] is novel as well in that it achieves very good compression ratios on scientific data on unstructured grids by modeling the grid data as a graph and taking advantage of locality. The error metrics used in their study are the maximum pointwise error, the root mean squared error (RMSE) and the peak signal-to-noise ratio (PSNR). In [21], the main objective is to reduce the transfer time for large climate (more specifically, ocean) datasets. The authors use a JPEG2000 compression scheme (wavelet-based) and prefer to evaluate the error with a maximum pointwise error metric, rather than the RMSE. This wavelet-based compression also requires grid information, and the ocean data is compressed with a commercial JPEG2000 package in multiple 2-D slices after a quantization pre-processing step. The lossy *ISABELA* method in [11] appears attractive because it compresses data locally by first preconditioning the data to increase smoothness and then approximating with B-splines or wavelets. A threshold relative error is defined, and the quality is measured with a normalized RMSE and the Pearson correlation coefficient. Bicer et. al in [1] develop a new lossy compression approach, called *CC* ("Climate Compression"), that they apply to the GCRM (global cloud-resolving model) climate dataset. Their compression method is a type of delta compression that takes advantage of spatial and temporal neighbor information and can also be used in a lossless manner. They emphasize integrating compression into a data processing or simulation application, and there is little discussion of validation beyond indicating the number of least significant bits that are dropped. In [8], the authors look at compressing climate data from the European climate model ECHAM using *GRIB2, APAX*, and *MAFISC*. *GRIB2* [5] is essentially a bit-oriented file format standard defined by the World Meteorological Organization that results in lossy data compression from the format conversion. These *GRIB2* files can then be further compressed with a standard compression method, typically JPEG2000 (see [8] or [18] for further description). The metrics for comparison in [8] are compression speed, compression ratio, number of bits of precision, and a so-called signal-to-residual ratio (SRR), which is the ratio between the standard deviation of the data and the standard deviation of the point-wise error in the reconstructed data. Finally, we note that in [18], Sullivan explores finding a suitable compression technique for meteorological data, detailing existing compression software options and highlighting the difficulties in meeting all of a user's requirements.

Although compression of simulation data from a climate model has been explored in [8], [21], and [1], the verification of the resulting reconstructed climate dataset has not been sufficiently addressed for our purposes. While quantifying the maximum pointwise error (or number of significant digits) or average error results in useful information, our goal of incorporating compression into the CESM workflow requires a more comprehensive analysis strategy. To our knowledge, the only work on compressing scientific data that, similar to our effort, emphasizes data verification is that of Laney et. al [12], where specific application-based metrics are developed for several physics codes at Livermore National Laboratory.

3. SELECTION OF ALGORITHMS

3.1 Criteria

We considered several factors similar to Sullivan's study of meteorological data in [18] to choose and evaluate compression algorithms. First, climate models typically contain a large and diverse set of variables. Some variables may have small ranges, while others are quite large, and the magnitudes may be quite different for each variable even within a particular component. For example, in the community atmosphere model (CAM), the sulfur dioxide variable (SO2) has a maximum value of $\mathcal{O}(10^{-8})$, whereas the maximum cloud condensation concentration at $S = 0.1\%$ (CCN3) is $\mathcal{O}(10^3)$. Some variables are smoother than others, and many missing or special values exist. For example, the value of sea-surface temperature in the ocean model component (POP2) for a land point is undefined and set to 10^{35}. Therefore, we need a compression algorithm that can handle different types of data, and ideally one that can be either lossy and lossless and allows specification of error or compression rates. This flexibility is important because our intent is to customize the compression for each variable individually. Second, because compression will eventually be integrated into the I/O package of CESM, the software must be robust and sharable with a diverse user community. Third, achieving good compression ratios while maintaining the integrity of the reconstructed data is critical. Therefore, the compres-

sion software for CESM datasets should ideally possess the following attributes:

1. open source or freely available (i.e., no intellectual property restrictions);

2. permits lossy and lossless modes;

3. allows the specification of error or compression rate for a variable;

4. handles both 32- and 64-bit data;

5. does not require grid information; and

6. can accommodate special or missing values.

Items 2-6 are necessary due to the variety of data generated by CESM, and the first item is highly desirable because of the size of the CESM user community.

3.2 Algorithms

With the above selection criteria in mind, we chose several algorithms from those described in Section 2 to evaluate with CESM: *fpzip, ISABELA, APAX*, and *GRIB2* (with JPEG2000 compression). We briefly describe each of these algorithms in more detail and list some of their properties in Table 1. Note that all algorithms chosen have a lossy mode and do not require grid information, but none of the algorithms satisfy all of the desired requirements. Most do not accomodate special or missing values, but we hope that capability could be added.

3.2.1 fpzip

fpzip [14] can perform in both lossy and lossless mode, and in lossy mode the amount of compression achieved is affected by the number of least significant bits truncated. In particular, one can specify the number of bits of precision to retain, which must be a multiple of 8 (i.e., 8, 16, 24, or 32, the latter of which is lossless for single-precision data). Recent results on real physics applications are encouraging [12].

3.2.2 ISABELA

ISABELA [11] is aimed at compressing data that is potentially noisy and enabling random access to that compressed data. This method pre-sorts spatial data so that it is relatively smooth before applying a curve-fitting approximation, such as a B-spline or wavelet. A window size within which to sort as well as the desired per-point relative error must be specified by the user. (We use the recommended window size of 1024.) Because *ISABELA* is a local method, a subset of the data (instead of the entire dataset) can be decoded, which is potentially useful for post-processing analysis tasks. As expected for a wavelet method, it can be sensitive to data at the boundaries of a window, but the results shown in [11] are good.

3.2.3 GRIB2 with JPEG2000 compression

We selected *GRIB2* [5] for further investigation because of its wide acceptance in the meteorological community. Unfortunately, it is non-trivial to use as the compression parameters that control the bits of precision (and indirectly the compression rate) have to be customized for each variable according to the variable's magnitude, which will be discussed further in Section 5. Also, the encoding itself into

Table 1: Algorithm properties.

Method	lossless mode	special values	freely avail.	fixed quality	fixed CR	32- & 64-bit
GRIB2 + jpeg2000	N	Y	Y	N	N	N
APAX	Y[1]	N	N	Y	Y	Y
fpzip	Y	N	Y	N	N	Y
ISABELA	N	N	Y	N	N	Y

the *GRIB2* format is lossy, and, therefore, lossless is not an option even if one uses lossless JPEG2000 compression.

3.2.4 APAX

Because both [12] and [8] show good results for Samplify's *APAX* compressor, we were curious to apply it CESM data, despite its being a commercial product. Also, *APAX* is the only method that allows for the specification of fixed compression rates (with varying quality), which is very useful in practice. Another nice feature is the *APAX* profiler tool that illustrates the quality of the reconstructed data and recommends encoding rates. In fact, *APAX* is the only method where the user can specify a fixed quality mode (with varying compression rates). All three previous methods require the much more effort and tuning on the user's part to achieve a fixed quality.

4. VERIFICATION PROCESS

In this section, we describe metrics to characterize the original data, to quantify the difference (i.e., error) between the reconstructed and original data, and to evaluate the reconstructed data in the context of an ensemble of CESM runs with slight perturbations. In the following discussion, denote the original spatial dataset X as $X = \{x_1, x_2, \ldots, x_N\}$, with x_i a scalar, and the reconstructed dataset $\tilde{X}$ by $\tilde{X} = \{\tilde{x_1}, \tilde{x_2}, \ldots, \tilde{x_N}\}$. We denote the range of X by R_X (i.e., $R_X = x_{max} - x_{min}$). Note that although climate data is both spatial and temporal, we are considering a single temporal step for this preliminary analysis.

4.1 Characterizing the Original Data

First, characterizing the original data is important for gaining insight into what types of compression schemes will or will not be effective for a particular variable. We employ several standard metrics for characterizing X: the minimum (x_{min}) and maximum (x_{max}) values, the mean (μ_X), and the standard deviation (σ_X). We also measure how well lossless compression works on data from a particular variable. We use the lossless compression scheme that is part of the NetCDF-4 library (zlib) and to compress our original file, F_{orig}, which results in the losslessly compressed file F_{comp}. The compression ratio (CR) is defined as the ratio of the size of the compressed file to that of the original file (c.f. [9, 18]):

$$\mathrm{CR}(F) = \frac{\mathrm{filesize}(F_{comp})}{\mathrm{filesize}(F_{orig})}. \qquad (1)$$

[1] Lossless mode is not supported for 64-bit data.

If the CR for the NetCDF-4 lossless compression for a particular variable is close to one, then lossless compression is not effective.

4.2 The Original and Reconstructed Data

Second, we characterize the difference between the original and reconstructed datasets via measures of pointwise error, average error, and correlation. The pointwise error at point i between the original and the reconstructed data is denoted by e_i, where $e_i = x_i - \tilde{x}_i$. The maximum absolute pointwise error, or maximum norm, is denoted by e_{max} and its magnitude indicates the minimum precision that has been achieved. Because our simulation data varies quite a bit in magnitude, depending on the variable, we define the normalized maximum pointwise error as

$$e_{nmax} = \frac{\max_{i=1:N} |e_i|}{R_X}, \qquad (2)$$

which facilitates comparisons of error between variable types. We decide whether or not e_{nmax} is an acceptable size based on our ensemble results described in Section 4.3. To evaluate the average error in the reconstructed data, we evaluate the popular root mean squared error (RMSE):

$$\mathrm{rmse} = \sqrt{\frac{1}{N} \sum_{i=1}^{N} (e_i)^2}. \qquad (3)$$

Again, due to the diversity of variables, we prefer the *normalized* RMSE (NRMSE) measure:

$$\mathrm{nrmse} = \frac{RMSE}{R_X}. \qquad (4)$$

Looking at the pointwise error in combination with the average error for a large dataset is important as the average error could be quite small despite a relatively large error at one or more points. We note that another commonly used average error metric for evaluating compression schemes, particularly in visualization, is the peak signal-to-noise ratio (PSNR). The PSNR evaluates the size of the RMSE relative to the peak size of the signal (see. e.g., [15, 9]), but we do not report on the PSNR as it conveys the same type of error information as the NRMSE.

To evaluate the correlation between the values of a particular variable in the original and reconstructed datasets, we utilize the Pearson correlation coefficient (ρ):

$$\rho = \frac{\mathrm{cov}(X, \tilde{X})}{\sigma_X \sigma_{\tilde{X}}}, \qquad (5)$$

where $\mathrm{cov}(X, \tilde{X})$ is the covariance. This coefficient indicates the strength of the linear relationship between the variables, where $\rho \in [-1, 1]$ and $\rho = 1$ indicates a perfect positive correlation. For context, the APAX profiler recommends that the correlation coefficient be .99999 (or better) between the original and reconstructed data. We currently use .99999 as the acceptance threshold for our tests.

4.3 Data in the Context of an Ensemble

Finally, we evaluate the reconstructed data in the context of the new CESM port-verification tool (CESM-PVT) [13], which we describe briefly in this section. The purpose of the CESM-PVT is to determine whether a change in CESM that does *not* result in bit-for-bit agreement with the previous result is statistically distinguishable (i.e., is it "climate-changing" or not). The motivation for developing this tool was to create a straightforward way to verify the CESM code after porting it to a new machine architecture. Although running a CESM simulation on a new machine will not give the same bit-for-bit results as on the original "trusted" machine, the results should not be climate-changing. Previous to the development of the CESM-PVT, CESM was evaluated on a new architecture by comparing the results of a single 500-year simulation run on each of the two architectures. The previous methodology for comparing the two long runs was resource intensive and not entirely rigorous because of its use of subjective evaluations.

The CESM-PVT uses the following approach. First, an ensemble $E = \{E_1, E_2, \dots, E_{101}\}$ consisting of 101 one-year climate simulations is run with annual averages of output for a selected grid resolution on a "trusted" machine. These 101 simulations differ only in a random perturbation of the initial atmospheric temperature condition of $\mathcal{O}(10^{-14})$. Such a perturbation should not be climate-changing over a one-year timeframe. Due to the nonlinear properties of this model, the trajectories of the ensemble members will rapidly diverge, but the statistical properties of the ensemble members are expected to be the same. Then, for each ensemble member m, the mean and standard deviation are calculated at every grid point x_i in the sub-ensemble $\{E \setminus m\}$ (consisting of the remaining 100 members) for each variable X and are denoted by $\bar{x}_i^{E \setminus m}$ and $\sigma_{x_i}^{E \setminus m}$, respectively. The Z-score that compares the value of x_i of ensemble member m (x_i^m) to sub-ensemble $\{E \setminus m\}$ is

$$Z_{x_i}^m = \frac{x_i^m - \bar{x}_i^{E \setminus m}}{\sigma_{x_i}^{E \setminus m}} \qquad (6)$$

Therefore, the root mean squared Z-score for dataset X of ensemble m is given by

$$\mathrm{RMSZ}_X^m = \sqrt{\frac{1}{N_X} \sum_i \left(Z_{x_i}^m\right)^2}, \qquad (7)$$

where N_X is the total number of grid points in X. This process, applied to each ensemble member in E, results in a distribution of 101 RMSZ scores for each output variable. In addition, global means of each of the variables are calculated.

The second step in the verification is to run a small number (generally three is sufficient) of randomly selected ensemble runs on the new architecture. The global means from the new runs are compared against the global mean of ensemble E in order to detect whether there has been a range shift (which would indicate a changed climate). In addition, we calculate the RMSZ scores for the variables in the new ensemble runs and check whether or not they fall within the z-score distribution from E.

If a variable's RMSZ score falls within the distribution, then that variable is considered to have "passed". A subject of future work is determining which variables are "critical" and *must* pass and which variables may be allowed to fall outside of the distribution (by some specified amount). At present, because the ensemble runs are one-year in length, only the output variables from the atmospheric model are evaluated, as the atmosphere model will be affected by feedback sooner than the ocean or ice models, for example.

One can also imagine that even on the benchmark machine, a non-bit-for-bit change in CESM could be the result of compiling the code with different compiler options (or a different compiler) [4], of making an incremental improvement to the code, or of redesigning an algorithm such that the order of operations is affected in parallel. It makes sense to eventually apply the CESM-PVT to these scenarios as well. For our purposes in evaluating the reconstructed data after compression, we employ the CESM-PVT in a slightly different way. We verify a compression utility by requiring that if we choose three members at random from ensemble E, denoted by index m, and apply the compression/decompression to each m, then the RMSZ score of the reconstructed result must at minimum fall within the distribution of the RMSZ values from the ensemble E, as with the CESM-PVT test. More stringently, though, we also require the difference between the original and reconstructed RMSZ score to be "small" as compared to the range of the ensemble RMSZ scores. For the variables we test in the next section, the range of RMSZ scores is $\mathcal{O}(1)$ (and is less than two, in most cases), and we require the difference between the two RMSZ values to be less that $1/10$ for the reconstructed data to pass this test.

$$|RMSZ_X^m - RMSZ_{\tilde{X}}^m| \leq \frac{1}{10} \qquad (8)$$

When the reconstructed RMSZ score satisfies the CESM-PVT requirements of lying within the distribution, this shows that the impact of the compression on the solution is on par with that of a bit perturbation on the initial conditions. However, when the difference between the original and reconstructed values satisfy (8), then this implies that the distribution itself is essentially unchanged (statistically indistinguishable) by replacing the original data with the reconstructed data.

Additionally, we use the CESM-PVT to evaluate whether the compression utility has added any bias to the climate data. First, we compress and decompress all 101 members of ensemble E, resulting in the new reconstructed ensemble $\tilde{E}$. Next, for each ensemble member m in $\tilde{E}$, we calculate the RMSZ score of the reconstructed ensemble in the same manner as before with equations (6) and (7), substituting $\tilde{E}$ for E. Then, for each variable, we compare the 101 RMSZ scores of ensembles $\tilde{E}$ and E via a simple linear regression plot. An accurate reconstruction will yield a strong linear relationship, and we can estimate the standard deviation for the fit. For an unbiased reconstruction, the fitted line would have a slope of 1 and an intercept of 0, otherwise we have introduced bias. Therefore, a simple scatterplot of slope versus intercept that contains each compression method with its 95% confidence region (indicated by a rectangle) allows us to evaluate which methods have introduced bias. This plot will be clarified in the next section with data for several variables (Figure 4). The degree of uncertainty for each compression method is quite important. For example, if the line of best fit has a slope of (nearly) one and small uncertainty, but a non-zero intercept, then bias has been introduced uniformly, and this will be detected by the RMSZ ensemble test. On the other hand, if the uncertainty is relatively large, then even if the slope is close to one, the RMSZ ensemble test may not have caught the bias error (depending on the random samples chosen). Therefore we evaluate the distance between the ideal and worst case values for the slope, s_I

and s_{WC}, respectively, based on the 95% confidence region. We require that this distance be less than .05 for the method to be acceptable for compression:

$$|s_I - s_{WC}| \leq .05. \qquad (9)$$

This criteria may be stricter than necessary, and we plan to explore the detection of bias further in subsequent work.

Finally, to evaluate whether the normalized maximum pointwise error, e_{nmax}, between the original and reconstructed data is reasonable, we extend the CESM-PVT to include a distribution of the maximum pointwise error. To do this, we follow a procedure similar to that for building the distribution of RMSZ scores. In particular, for each ensemble member m, at each grid point x_i, we calculate the maximum pointwise error between ensemble m and that grid point in all members of the sub-ensemble $\{E \setminus m\}$. The maximum pointwise error for member m is then the maximum of the maximum pointwise error over all grid points. Therefore, for the variable in dataset X of ensemble m, the normalized maximum pointwise error is given by

$$E_{nmax}^{m_X} = \frac{\max_i(\max_{n \in E \setminus m} |x_i^m - x_i^n|)}{R_X^m}, \qquad (10)$$

where R_X^m indicates the range of X for ensemble member m. Following this procedure for all 101 ensemble members creates a distribution that then can be used to determine whether or not the value of e_{nmax} (between the original and reconstructed data) falls within the variability of the ensemble. The acceptance criteria for this test is similar to that for the RMSZ ensemble test. We choose three ensemble members at random, and at minimum, the value of e_{nmax} for those must certainly be smaller than the range between the maximum and minimum values of $E_{nmax}^{m_X}$, which is noted bu $R_{E_{nmax}^X}$. However, we additionally require that the maximum pointwise error between the original and reconstructed datasets to be an order of magnitude less than that range so that replacing the original data with the reconstructed data would have little effect on the ensemble distribution:

$$\frac{e_{nmax}}{R_{E_{nmax}^X}} \leq \frac{1}{10}. \qquad (11)$$

Note that we are careful not to include any special values (such as the 10^{35} mentioned in Section 3.1) when calculating our metrics.

5. EXPERIMENTAL RESULTS

In this section, we explain the experiments that we performed on various datasets from CESM. We detail the results and apply the metrics outlined in Section 4.

5.1 Preliminaries

The results in this work were obtained from the 1.1 release version of CESM, using an active CAM5 atmosphere and CLM land model. We concentrate on the CAM history files, which contain a total of 83 two-dimensional and 87 three-dimensional variables, that are currently supported by the CESM-PVT. This spectral-element version of CAM uses a $ne = 30$ resolution, which corresponds to a 1-degree global grid, containing a total of 48,602 horizontal grid-points and 30 vertical levels.

We apply the four lossy methods described in Section 3.2 to the 170 CAM variables. For *fpzip*, we use two different

Table 2: Characteristics of the datasets for variables U, FSDSC, Z3, and CCN3.

Variable	units	x_{min}	x_{max}	μ_X	σ_X	CR
U	m/s	-2.56e1	5.45e1	6.39e0	1.22e1	.75
FSDSC	W/m^2	1.24e2	3.26e2	2.43e2	4.83e1	.66
Z3	m	4.12e1	3.77e4	1.12e4	1.01e4	.58
CCN3	$\#/cm3$	3.37e-5	1.24e3	2.66e1	5.57e1	.71

levels of precision: 16- and 24-bit precision, which we denote as fpzip-16 and fpzip-24. We apply the B-spline variant of *ISABELA* with three different per-point relative error values: 1.0, 0.5, 0.1. The three options are called ISA-1.0, ISA-0.5, and ISA-0.1, respectively. As noted previously, applying *GRIB2* with JPEG2000 compression requires variable-level customization to achieve reasonable results due to the diversity (e.g., magnitude and range) of variables in CAM, and, therefore, we only show one result, which we denote by GRIB2. Finally, we evaluate the *APAX* compressor using the fixed compression rates 2, 4 and 5, which we refer to as APAX-2, APAX-4, and APAX-5, respectively.

Datasets from several CAM variables will be presented in more detail: geopotential height above sea level (Z3), clear sky downwelling solar flux at surface (FSDSC), cloud condensation nuclei concentration at S=0.1% (CCN3), and zonal wind (U). Note that FSDSC is a 2D field and the rest are 3D. We selected these variables to represent the differing effects of compression on climate variables, and the characteristics described in Section 4.1 are given in Table 2. Note that "CR" in the table indicates the compression ratio for the lossless method from NetCDF-4, and the "units" column indicates the scientific units for the variable.

5.2 The Original and Reconstructed Data

We first compare the original and reconstructed data as described in Section 4.2. The two box plots in Figure 1 demonstrate how the datasets of all 170 variables respond to the four compression methods and the variants within each method. In the left plot, the y-axis indicates the normalized maximum pointwise error between the original and reconstructed data, and in the right plot, the y-axis is the NRMSE, as given in (4). The x-axis lists the compression methods evaluated, with the rectangle in each column indicating the range of the lower to upper quartiles and the red line denoting the median. The "whiskers" extending from the top and bottom of the rectangles denote the full range

Table 3: NRMS errors (and compression ratio CR) between the original and reconstructed datasets for U, FSDSC, Z3, and CCN3.

Comp. Method	U	FSDSC	Z3	CCN3
		NRMSE (CR)		
GRIB2	3.6e-4 (.10)	1.4e-4 (.22)	7.8e-8 (.32)	2.3e-8 (.37)
APAX-2	5.8e-7 (.50)	8.3e-7 (.50)	7.0e-8 (.50)	1.6e-7 (.50)
APAX-4	1.4e-4 (.25)	2.1e-4 (.26)	2.0e-5 (.25)	4.1e-5 (.25)
APAX-5	4.3e-4 (.20)	5.4e-4 (.21)	5.1e-5 (.19)	9.9e-5 (.20)
fpzip-24	2.2e-6 (.39)	1.8e-5 (.34)	5.1e-6 (.19)	6.5e-7 (.36)
fpzip-16	5.7e-4 (.15)	4.6e-3 (.10)	1.2e-3 (.04)	1.7e-4 (.12)
ISA-0.1	8.7e-5 (.57)	4.1e-4 (.37)	3.8e-5 (.39)	2.8e-5 (.37)
ISA-0.5	2.7e-4 (.44)	9.1e-4 (.36)	9.8e-5 (.37)	1.2e-4 (.38)
ISA-1.0	3.7e-4 (.41)	1.1e-3 (.36)	1.5e-4 (.36)	2.0e-4 (.37)

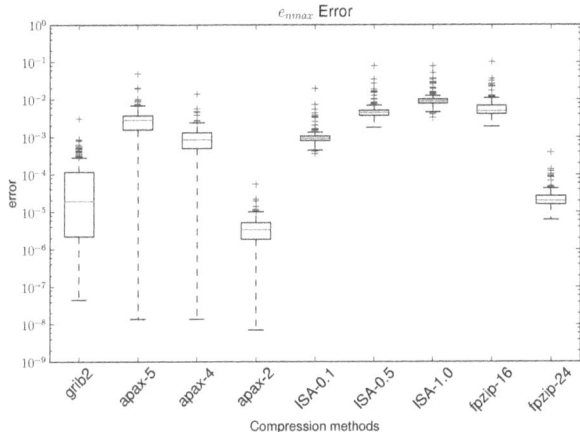

(a) Normalized maximum pointwise error.

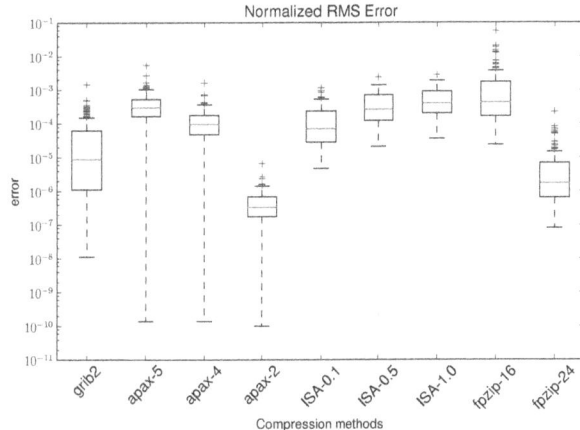

(b) Normalized RMSE.

Figure 1: Normalized maximum pointwise and normalized RMS errors for all 170 variable datasets.

Table 4: Maximum relative pointwise errors (and compression ratio) between the original and reconstructed datasets for U, FSDSC, Z3, and CCN3.

Comp. Method	U	FSDSC e_{nmax} (CR)	Z3	CCN3
GRIB2	6.2e-4 (.10)	2.5e-4 (.22)	1.6e-7 (.32)	4.9e-8 (.37)
APAX-2	3.3e-6 (.50)	4.7e-6 (.50)	3.3e-6 (.50)	2.9e-6 (.50)
APAX-4	9.0e-4 (.25)	1.1e-3 (.26)	8.3e-4 (.25)	7.5e-4 (.25)
APAX-5	2.7e-3 (.20)	2.7e-3 (.21)	3.1e-3 (.19)	1.9e-3 (.20)
fpzip-24	1.2e-5 (.39)	3.9e-5 (.34)	3.3e-6 (.19)	2.4e-5 (.36)
fpzip-16	3.1e-3 (.15)	9.9e-3 (.10)	6.8e-3 (.04)	5.3e-3 (.12)
ISA-0.1	6.4e-4 (.57)	1.6e-3 (.37)	9.8e-4 (.39)	8.7e-4 (.37)
ISA-0.5	2.9e-3 (.44)	7.6e-3 (.36)	4.9e-3 (.37)	3.9e-3 (.38)
ISA-1.0	4.9e-3 (.41)	1.5e-2 (.36)	9.9e-3 (.36)	7.9e-3 (.37)

of the distribution (i.e., the maximum and minimum). As expected, these two error metrics vary quite a lot between the 170 variables. For example, if we consider the APAX-4 method, the NRMSE ranges from $\mathcal{O}(10^{-3})$ to $\mathcal{O}(10^{-10})$. Also, the methods with higher levels of compression clearly result in higher errors, as expected. These plots suggest that to achieve a fixed quality on our diverse set of CESM variables, treating the variables individually in terms of choosing a compression method is required. (We note that because *APAX* offers both a profiler and a fixed quality mode, this task is considerably simpler for *APAX* than for the other methods.) In fact, some variables may need to be compressed with a lossless variant to achieve acceptable quality, but we do not include lossless results in this figure as *ISABELA* and *GRIB2* cannot be run losslessly.

Now we take a closer look at the datasets for variables U, Z3, FSDSC, and CCN3 to better illustrate the effects of the various compression methods. Tables 3 and 4 show the average and pointwise error metrics, NRMS and e_{nmax}, respectively, between the original and reconstructed datasets, as well as the compression ratio. The effectiveness of the different compression techniques on the datasets for a particular variable varies quite a bit, as does the effectiveness of a single method across variable datasets. For example, *ISABELA* is clearly not doing as well as the other methods in terms of both the average and pointwise errors, reflecting perhaps

on *ISABELA*'s focus on enabling random access. Also the difference between the three *ISABELA* variants is small for all four variables because the amount of storage needed for the sort index is a higher percentage of the total for single-precision data (we would expect *ISABELA* to obtain better compression ratios on double-precision data). Note that the *APAX* methods are operating at a fixed compression rate, which is convenient in practice. Z3 generally compresses the most (i.e., has the smallest compression ratios), as with the lossless compression in Table 2. The method providing the lowest compression ratios overall is fpzip-16, but the errors are also the largest. GRIB2 performs well in terms of obtaining good compression ratios and small errors. For example, comparing GRIB2 with fpzip-24 on CCN3 indicates that, for a similar CR, the GRIB2 errors are about three orders of magnitude smaller. Similarly for U, GRIB2 yields smaller errors and a smaller CR than fpzip-16. Finally we note that for these variables, the NRMSE and e_{nmax} roughly correlate; the NRMSE tends to be an order of magnitude smaller.

While the focus of this manuscript is on the quality of the compressed data, performance of the methods cannot be ignored, particularly given the volume of climate data that will be compressed. Table 5 lists the time to compress and reconstruct the datasets for variables U and FSDSC, as well as the achieved compression ratio, for all the methods. The (*) by some of the CR values for variable FSDSC indicates that the reconstructed data from that method was not of sufficient quality to pass test metrics. The time to compress and reconstruct our data depends on the variable, and variable U took more time to compress than FSDSC. The *APAX* method is clearly the fastest of the methods, sometimes by a couple orders of magnitude.

5.3 Comparing to an Ensemble

By simply comparing the original data to the reconstructed data with standard metrics, as done in Section 5.2, it is difficult to evaluate the effectiveness of the methods relative to each other (as well as the quality of the reconstructed data). Therefore, we now look at the reconstructed data in the context of the CESM-PVT ensemble, as described in Section 4.3. First, the four plots in Figure 2, one for each variable, show the distribution of the RMSZ scores for the 101

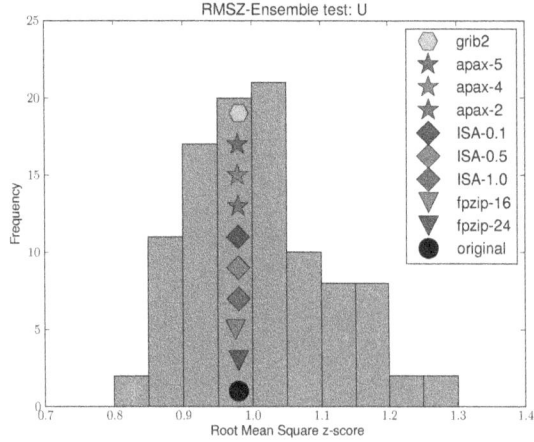

(a) Variable U (zonal wind).

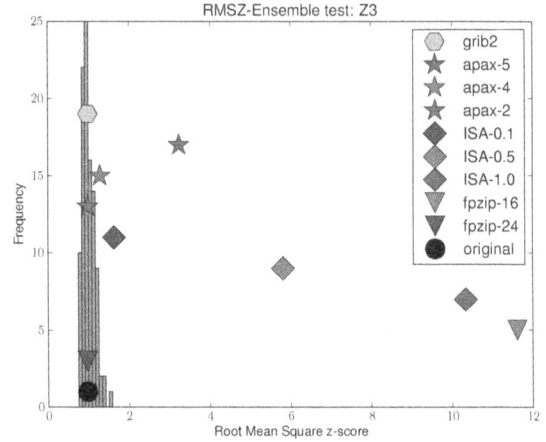

(b) Variable Z3 (geopotential height above sea level).

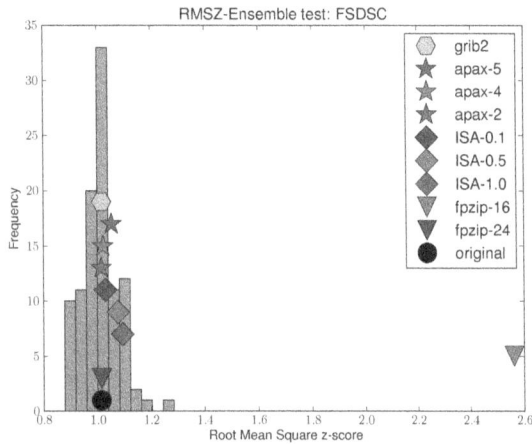

(c) Variable FSDSC (clear sky downwelling solar flux at surface).

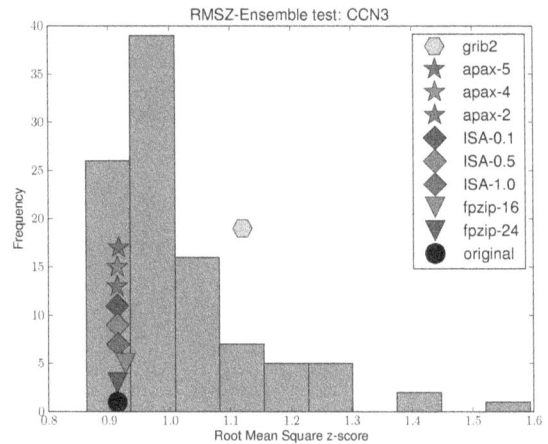

(d) Variable CCN3 (CCN concentration at S=0.1%).

Figure 2: Ensemble plots for variables U, Z3, FSDSC, and CNN3 with results off all data compression methods indicated.

Table 5: Compression and reconstruction timings (in seconds) and compression ratios (CR) for variables U (3D) and FSDSC (2D).

Comp. Method	U comp.	U reconst.	CR	FSDSC comp.	FSDSC reconst.	CR
GRIB2	0.284	0.264	0.10	0.020	0.017	0.22
APAX-2	0.068	0.044	0.50	0.002	0.001	0.50
APAX-4	0.062	0.042	0.25	0.002	0.001	0.26
APAX-5	0.059	0.042	0.20	0.002	0.001	0.21(*)
fpzip-24	0.123	0.114	0.39	0.004	0.004	0.34
fpzip-16	0.101	0.097	0.15	0.003	0.003	0.10(*)
ISA-0.1	4.016	0.508	0.57	0.053	0.016	0.39
ISA-0.5	2.455	0.530	0.44	0.042	0.016	0.36(*)
ISA-1.0	1.852	0.478	0.41	0.042	0.016	0.35(*)

ensemble runs. The different markers indicate the RMSZ scores from one of the reconstructed members, whose original RMSZ score is indicated by the black circle. Note that the y-axis value (frequency) is not relevant for the markers; they are stacked for aesthetic reasons. Recall that the goal of using the CESM-PVT tests is to ensure that the reconstructed data falls not only within the original distribution, but is also quite close, e.g. equation (8), to the original value. Theses plots show that in terms of obtaining a similar RMSZ value with the reconstructed data, all compression methods do well for the variable U and most do well for FSDSC. These two variables both have a small range, and, because U represents wind speed, it typically varies quite smoothly. The *ISABELA* methods and fpzip-16 are the worst performers for FSDSC. Interestingly, from the NRMSE result in Table 3, the results for *APAX* and *ISABELA* for FDSDC are similar, but Figure 2 shows that the ISA-0.5 and ISA-1.0 RMSZ scores are much further away from the original for FSDSC. Also fpzip-16 has a similar NRMSE to that of ISA-1.0, but this plot shows that it does very poorly in the ensemble test. All of the methods perform the worst on variable Z3, despite its obtaining the lowest compression ratios in Tables 3 and 4. The dataset for this variable has quite a large standard deviation (Table 2), and though the lossless method obtained the best CR, the lossy methods have difficulties. Finally, all methods do reasonably well with CCN3, except for GRIB2. CCN3 has quite a large range, and we find that GRIB2 does not perform well on such variables in terms of the RMSZ score of the reconstructed data, something which is not apparent for GRIB2 and CCN3 from Tables 3 and 4.

Next, we evaluate e_{nmax} in the context of the CESM-PVT ensemble, as described in Section 4.3, to determine whether the normalized maximum pointwise error between the original and reconstructed data (Table 4) is acceptable. Figure 3 displays four box plots, one for each variable. In each box plot, the y-axis indicates the value of e_{nmax} (note that the range shown for the y-axis varies for each plot). The leftmost column on the x-axis shows the distribution of the ensemble as calculated by equation (10). The rectangle indicates the range of the lower to upper quartiles, with the red line denoting the median. The whiskers extending from the top and bottom of the rectangle denote the full range of the distribution. The remaining columns represent the values of e_{nmax}, as calculated by equation (2), between the original ensemble member and the reconstructed data for each compression method. The plots in this figure show that all methods do quite well on the dataset for variable U in terms of the pointwise error. For FSDSC, the *ISABELA* methods show some larger errors, and several methods have some difficulty with Z3. For CCN3, we again see that GRIB2 does much worse than the other methods.

Finally, we use the ensemble to evaluate whether the compression process has introduced bias into the reconstructed datasets. The four plots in Figure 4 show the slope-versus-intercept data described in Section 4.3. A 95% confidence region is shown for each compression method. Note that both the y-axis and x-axis ranges are quite different for each subplot in the figure. Also, the sizes of the uncertainty regions vary quite a lot between the compression methods for a particular variable. A larger uncertainty in the estimation implies that all ensemble members are responding differently to the compression process. We have chosen 95% as a useful level of confidence and are evaluating the slope based on Equation 9. For U, it appears that most of the compression methods are introducing bias because the rectangles do not contain (1,0). However, the scale of the x-axis shows that the amount of bias added is so small that it is insignificant to us. FSDSC is similar in that we only see one rectangle containing the origin, but four of the other methods are acceptable because their uncertainty is within our tolerance. For CCN3, *GRIB2* does much worse that the other methods and is not shown on the plot (its slope ranges from .93 to .97). Variable Z3 has some significant outliers as well.

5.4 Customizing by Variable

We now explore customizing each of the four compression methods by variable to perform optimally in terms of quality and CR on each variable's dataset. To begin, Table 6 summarizes the results of the compression methods on the datasets for all the variables with our four metric tests. For each method, we indicate how many variables (out of 170 total) "passed" each of the tests, according to the criteria defined in the previous section. The second column, labeled "ρ", is the Pearson correlation coefficient value test.

Table 6: Number of passes for all compression methods on 170 variables.

| Comp. Method | | Number of passes | | | |
	ρ	RMSZ ens.	E_{rmax} ens.	bias	all
GRIB2	167	163	170	124	121
APAX-2	170	170	170	146	146
APAX-4	167	163	165	126	122
APAX-5	130	152	160	111	85
fpzip-24	170	164	170	167	163
fpzip-16	122	129	138	126	113
ISA-0.1	168	160	164	160	152
ISA-0.5	140	154	145	161	123
ISA-1.0	63	154	112	161	43

Table 7: Results from customizing each compression method by variable and forming a hybrid method.

	GRIB2	*ISABELA*	*fpzip*	*APAX*	NC
avg. CR	0.37	0.42	0.18	0.29	0.61
best CR	0.03	0.20	0.02	0.06	0.07
worst CR	0.86	0.77	0.68	0.80	0.86
avg. ρ	.9999999	.9999991	.9999995	.9999991	1.0
avg. nrmse	5.73e-5	3.22e-4	2.35e-4	2.61e-4	0.0
avg. e_{nmax}	1.01e-4	5.56e-3	2.76e-3	1.83e-3	0.0

The third column, "RMSZ ens.", contains the results of the RMSZ ensemble test, and the fourth and fifth columns are the E_{nmax} ensemble and bias tests, respectively. The rightmost column indicates the number of variables that pass all four tests in columns 2-5. As expected, methods with higher compression rates generally have fewer test passes. Because none of the methods has perfect passing rate, we will need to use a lossless method on some of the variables.

Based on the per-variable test results for the compression methods, we now construct the best "hybrid" option for each of our four methods. In particular, we choose the variant of each method (i.e., level of compression) for each variable that yields the best CR and passes all of our tests, choosing a lossless variant if necessary. For example, if fpzip-16 is not of acceptable quality for variable Z3 (i.e., does not pass all four tests in Table 6), then we evaluate fpzip-24. If fpzip-24 is not acceptable, then we use fpzip's lossless compression option (fpzip-32). We expect this selection process to be more sophisticated in the future. Note that because *ISABELA* and

Table 8: Number of variables (out of 170 total) that each variant of each compression method uses to form the hybrid method results in Table 7.

Method	Variant	Number of Variables
GRIB2	GRIB2	121
	NetCDF-4	49
ISABELA	ISA-1.0	43
	ISA-0.5	80
	ISA-0.1	29
	NetCDF-4	18
fpzip	fpzip-16	113
	fpzip-24	50
	fpzip-32	7
APAX	APAX-5	85
	APAX-4	37
	APAX-2	24
	NetCDF-4	24

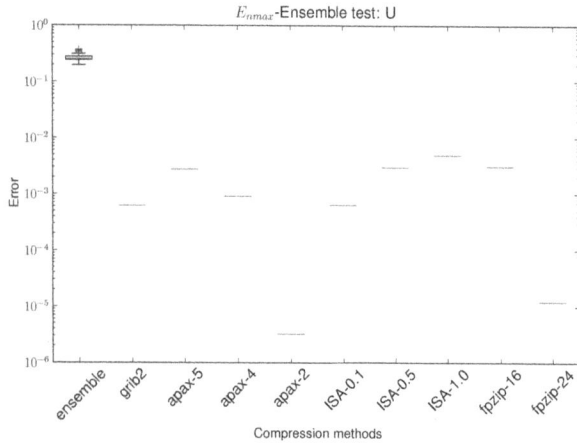

(a) Variable U

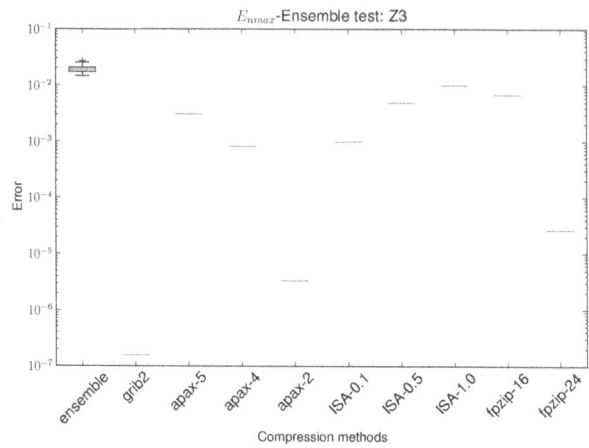

(b) Variable Z3

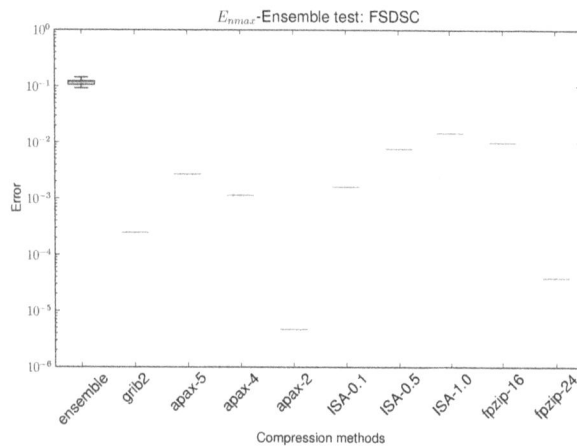

(c) Variable FSDSC

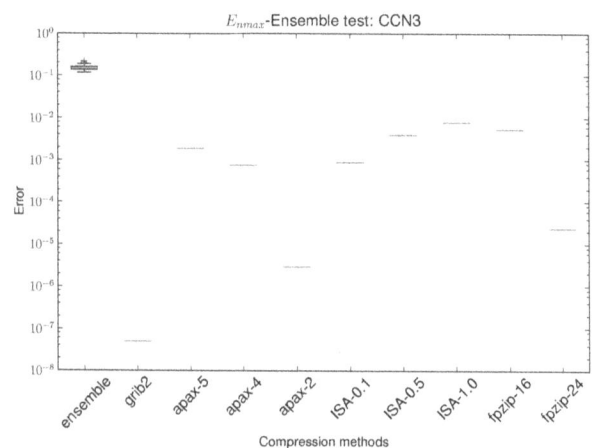

(d) Variable CCN3

Figure 3: Ensemble plot for E_{nmax} with all data compression methods indicated.

GRIB2 cannot be lossless, we use NetCDF4 compression for any variable that requires lossless treatment. The results of this customization for each of the four methods are listed in Table 7, which gives statistics that compare the original and reconstructed datasets. For comparison, the right-most column, labeled "NC", indicates lossless NetCDF4 compression on all variables. The first three rows list the average, best, and worst compression ratios, respectively, over all 170 variables. The fourth, fifth, and sixth rows list the average Pearson correlation coefficient, nrmse, and e_{nmax} values, respectively. To illustrate the composition of the four hybrid methods in Table 7, Table 8 indicates the number of variables used by each variant of each method (summing to 170).

Note that because *GRIB2* requires a compression parameter for each variable that indicates bits of precision, we have essentially already undergone this customization process for *GRIB2* in the results shown. (Though at this point, we do select lossless compression if needed.) When we initially ran *GRIB2*, we selected the same decimal scale factor (D), which is used to achieve desired precision, for each variable, and our initial results for *GRIB2* were quite poor. The results did improve by specifying a D for each variable that

depended on the magnitude (and range) of that variable. However, we were only able to achieve the more competitive results presented here for *GRIB2* by using the RMSZ ensemble test as a guide for choosing an optimal D.

The hybrid method results in Table 7, particularly the average compression ratio, indicate that *fpzip*, followed by *APAX*, performed the best on this climate data while maintaining an acceptable level of quality. In choosing a method to continue forward, we recall Table 1 and consider several factors. Both *APAX* and *fpzip* are lacking support for special values, but we assume that could be either easily incorporated into the algorithm or handled through our pre- and post-processing. It is noteworthy that the method with the best compression rate, *fpzip*, is also freely available. However, we also note that the fastest method, *APAX*, has some attractive features that are quite useful in practice, such as fixed compression mode, fixed quality mode, and the inclusion of a profiler. Also, we have not yet tried fixed compression rates 6 and 7 for *APAX*, which, given that 85 variables were able to use APAX-5, may lower the average CR for *APAX*. The biggest drawback for *APAX* is the fact that it's a commercial product. On the other hand, the biggest draw-

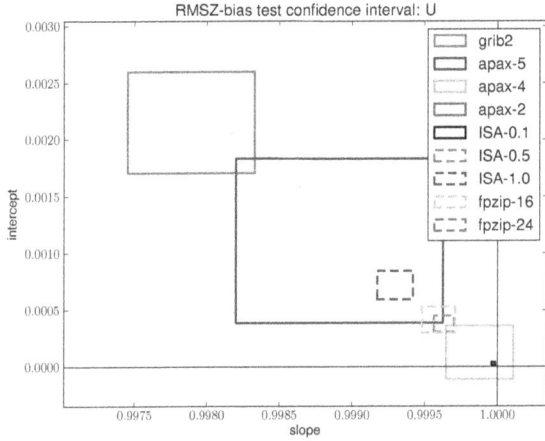

(a) Variable U

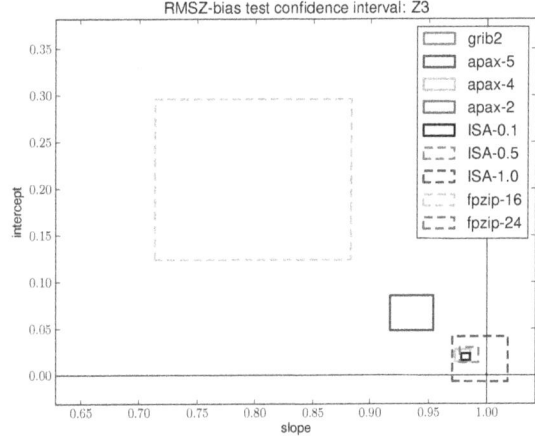

(b) Variable Z3

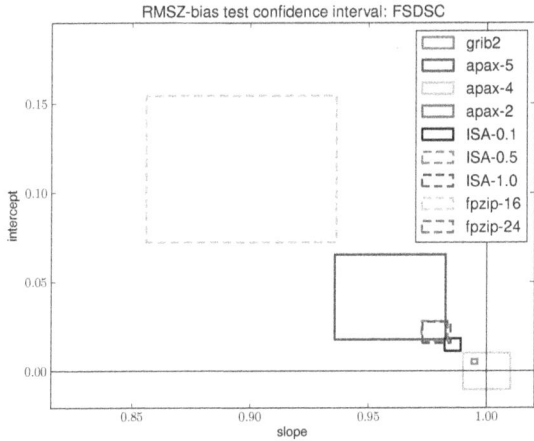

(c) Variable FSDSC

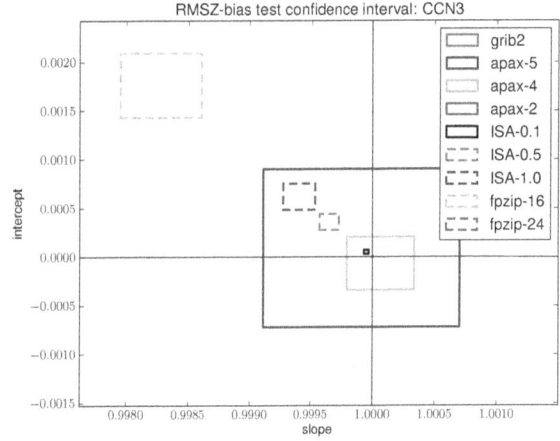

(d) Variable CCN3

Figure 4: Bias plots for variables U, Z3, FSDSC, and CCN3 with all data compression methods indicated.

back for *fpzip* is the restriction that the precision specification be a multiple of 8, leaving less room for customization.

6. CONCLUDING REMARKS

The disparity between the rapidly decreasing cost to compute floating-point operations and the more slowly decreasing cost of data storage is problematic for the data-intensive earth system modeling community. The rising relative cost of storing the output data from climate simulations can no longer be ignored, and the length and size of certain large-scale climate simulations are already being constrained by disk storage limitations. The use of lossy data compression could enable the simulation of longer time periods or more frequent output for a fixed on-line storage cost. This paper presents a preliminary, but thorough, study of several state-of-the-art compression techniques on data from CESM. These compression techniques are evaluated based on the development of a more comprehensive set of verification metrics than are used in a typical data compression study. Our metrics serve to ensure that the reconstructed data is indistinguishable from the natural variability of the system. We show that individually addressing the compres-

sion needs of each climate variable's dataset is a necessity, given the diversity of data in a climate model, and our preliminary effort at this achieved compression rates of up to 5:1. While decisions about "correctness" are specific to an application domain, our methodology is certainly applicable to other domain scientists working with model simulation data.

In subsequent work, we will fine tune the variable-by-variable customization needed to obtain maximum compression while ensuring that our reconstructed data is virtually indistinguishable from the original in terms of the post-processing data analysis that occurs. This customization will be investigated in close collaboration with climate scientists who can provide valuable insight into variable attributes and analysis. We plan to extend our verification metrics to evaluate the impact of compression on global energy budget calculations as well as on field gradients. In addition, because climate scientists visualize subsets of their simulation data as part of the post-processing analysis workflow, it is important that the reconstructed data produces quality images. We intend to utilize the structural similarity (SSIM) index [19], a recent and meaningful metric of image quality, as it relates to human perception. Finally, exploring different grid resolutions, particularly finer ones, is critical.

7. ACKNOWLEDGMENTS

Special thanks to Steve Sullivan and Kevin Paul.

8. ADDITIONAL AUTHORS

Jim Edwards (NCAR, email::jedwards@ucar.edu) and Mariana Vertenstein (NCAR, email::mvertens@ucar.edu) and Al Wegener (Samplify, email:awegener@samplify.com) .

9. REFERENCES

[1] T. Bicer, J. Yin, D. Chiu, G. Agrawal, and K. Schuchardt. Integrating online compression to accelerate large-scale data analytics applications. *Parallel and Distributed Processing Symposium, International*, 0:1205–1216, 2013.

[2] M. Burtscher and P. Ratanaworabhan. High throughput compression of double-precision floating-point data. In *Data Compression Conference*, pages 293–302, 2007.

[3] M. Burtscher and P. Ratanaworabhan. FPC: A high-speed compressor for double-precision floating-point data. In *IEEE Transactions on Computers*, volume 58, pages 18–31, January 2009.

[4] M. J. Corden and D. Kreitzer. Consistency of floating-point results using the Intel® compiler or Why doesn't my application always give the same answer? Technical report, Software Solutions Group, Intel Corporation, 2012.

[5] C. F. Day, C. Sanders, J. Clochard, J. Hennessy, and S. Elliott. Guide to the WMO table driven code form used for the representation and exchange of regularly spaced data in binary form, November 2007. http://www.wmo.int/pages/prog/www/WMOCodes /Guides/GRIB/GRIB2_062006.pdf.

[6] L. A. B. Gomez and F. Cappello. Improving floating point compression through binary masks. In *IEEE BigData*, Santa Barbara, CA, 2013.

[7] N. Hübbe and J. Kunkel. *Computer Science - Research and Development*, chapter Reducing the HPC-datastorage footprint with MAFISC - multidimensional adaptive filtering improved scientfic data compression. Springer, Hamburg, Berlin, Heidelberg, 2012.

[8] N. Hübbe, A. Wegener, J. M. Kunkel, Y. Ling, and T. Ludwig. Evaluating lossy compression on climate data. In *Proceedings of the International Supercomputing Conference (ISC '13)*, pages 343–356, 2013.

[9] J. Iverson, C. Kamath, and G. Karypis. Fast and effective lossy compression algorithms for scientific datasets. In *Proceedings of the 18th International Conference on Parallel Processing*, Euro-Par'12, pages 843–856, Berlin, Heidelberg, 2012.

[10] K.E.Taylor, R. Stouffer, and G. Meehl. An overview of CMIP5 and the experiment design. *Bulletin of the American Meteorical Society*, 93:485–498, 2012.

[11] S. Lakshminarasimhan, N. Shah, S. Ethier, S. Klasky, R. Latham, R. Ross, and N. F. Samatova. Compressing the incompressible with ISABELA: In-situ reduction of spatio-temporal data. In *Proceedings of the 17th International cCnference on Parallel Processing*, Euro-Par'11, Bordeaux, France, Aug 29 - Sep 2 2011.

[12] D. Laney, S. Langer, C. Weber, P. Lindstrom, and A. Wegener. Assessing the effects of data compression in simulations using physically motivated metrics. In *Supercomputing 2013 (SC'13)*, 2013.

[13] M. Levy, A. H. Baker, J. Anderson, J. M. Dennis, J. Edwards, A. Mai, D. Nychka, J. Tribbia, S. Vadlamani, M. Vertenstein, D. Williamson, and H. Xu. A new verification tool for the Community Earth System Model. *In preparation*, 2014.

[14] P. Lindstrom and M. Isenburg. Fast and efficient compression of floating-point data. *IEEE Transactions on Visualization and Computer Graphics*, 12:1245–1250, 2006.

[15] K. Sayood. *Introduction to Data Compression*. Morgan Kaufmann, fourth edition, 2012.

[16] E. R. Schendel, Y. Jin, N. Sha, J. Chen, C. Chang, S.-H. Ku, S. Ethier, S. Klasky, R. Latham, R. Ross, and N. F. Samatova. ISOBAR preconditioner for effective and high-throughput lossless data compression. In *IEEE 28th International Conference on Data Engineering (ICDE)*, 2012.

[17] J. Small, J. Bacmeister, D. Bailey, A. H. Baker, F. Bryan, J. Caron, J. Dennis, E. Munoz, J. Edwards, M. Holland, D. Lawrence, A. Mai, T. Scheitlin, B. Tomas, J. Tribbia, M. Vertenstein, and Y. Tseng. A new high-resolution global climate simulation using Community Atmosphere Model version 5 and an eddy-resolving ocean model. *In preparation*, 2014.

[18] S. Sullivan. Wavelet compression for floating point data - Sengcom. Technical report, University Corporation for Atmospheric Research, 2012. http://www.unidata.ucar.edu/software/netcdf/ papers/sengcom.pdf.

[19] Z. Wang, A. C. Bovik, H. R. Sheikh, and E. P. Simoncelli. Image quality assessment: From error visibility to structural similarity. *IEEE Transactions on Image Processing*, 13(4):600–612, 2004.

[20] A. Wegener. Adaptive compression and decompression of bandlimited signals. US Patent 7009533, March 2006. http://www.patentlens/patentlens/patent/US_7009533.

[21] J. Woodring, S. M. Mniszewski, C. M. Brislawn, D. E. DeMarle, and J. P. Ahrens. Revisting wavelet compression for large-scale climate data using JPEG2000 and ensuring data precision. In D. Rogers and C. T. Silva, editors, *IEEE Symposium on Large Data Analysis and Visualization (LDAV)*, pages 31–38. IEEE, 2011.

Computation and Communication Efficient Graph Processing with Distributed Immutable View

Rong Chen†, Xin Ding†, Peng Wang†, Haibo Chen†, Binyu Zang†, Haibing Guan§
Shanghai Key Laboratory of Scalable Computing and Systems
†Institute of Parallel and Distributed Systems, Shanghai Jiao Tong University
§Department of Computer Science, Shanghai Jiao Tong University
{rongchen, dingxin, peng-wp, haibochen, byzang, hbguan}@sjtu.edu.cn

ABSTRACT

Cyclops is a new vertex-oriented graph-parallel framework for writing distributed graph analytics. Unlike existing distributed graph computation models, Cyclops retains simplicity and computation-efficiency by synchronously computing over a *distributed immutable view*, which grants a vertex with read-only access to all its neighboring vertices. The view is provided via read-only replication of vertices for edges spanning machines during a graph cut. Cyclops follows a centralized computation model by assigning a master vertex to update and propagate the value to its replicas unidirectionally in each iteration, which can significantly reduce messages and avoid contention on replicas. Being aware of the pervasively available multicore-based clusters, Cyclops is further extended with a hierarchical processing model, which aggregates messages and replicas in a single multicore machine and transparently decomposes each worker into multiple threads on-demand for different stages of computation.

We have implemented Cyclops based on an open-source Pregel clone called Hama. Our evaluation using a set of graph algorithms on an in-house multicore cluster shows that Cyclops outperforms Hama from 2.06X to 8.69X and 5.95X to 23.04X using hash-based and Metis partition algorithms accordingly, due to the elimination of contention on messages and hierarchical optimization for the multicore-based clusters. Cyclops (written in Java) also has comparable performance with PowerGraph (written in C++) despite the language difference, due to the significantly lower number of messages and avoided contention.

Categories and Subject Descriptors

D.1.3 [**Programming Techniques**]: Concurrent Programming—
Distributed programming

Keywords

Graph-parallel Computation; Distributed Processing

HPDC'14, June 23–27, Vancouver, BC, Canada.
Copyright 2014 ACM 978-1-4503-2749-7/14/06 ...$15.00.
http://dx.doi.org/10.1145/2600212.2600233 .

1. INTRODUCTION

Graph-structured computation has become increasingly popular due to its emerging adoption in a wide range of areas including social computation, web search, natural language processing and recommendation systems. With the continually increasing scale and complexity of graph dataset, it is vital to effectively express and efficiently process large-scale graph dataset, while allowing users to trivially write graph-processing programs and reason about the correctness.

The strong desire of efficient and expressive programming models for graph-structured computation has recently driven the development of several graph-parallel programming models and runtime such as Pregel [24] and its open-source alternatives [2, 1, 30], GraphLab [23, 22] and a hybrid approach called PowerGraph [12]. Basically, they encapsulate computation as vertex-oriented programs, but follow different approaches in interactions between vertices, i.e., synchronous message passing [24] vs. asynchronous shared memory [23].

As a large graph inevitably needs to be partitioned among multiple machines, we believe the following three properties are critical to a graph processing system: 1) expressiveness and programmer-friendliness so that it is not difficult to write and reason about a graph algorithm, even if it is distributed; 2) computation-efficiency so that the computation overhead is small; 3) communication-efficiency so that there won't be large amount of messages among machines and heavy contentions among messages. However, none of the above graph engines hold all the three properties. Pregel and its variants are easy to program but not computation and communication efficient as they lack support of dynamic computation and incur a lot of redundant messages. GraphLab is harder to program due to its asynchronous programming model and there is non-trivial overhead due to distributed vertex scheduling and locking. PowerGraph, which performs the best among these graph systems, requires extensive messages among machines due to distributing computation among replicated vertices.

In this paper, we describe Cyclops, a vertex-oriented graph-parallel model for distributed environment. Cyclops departs from the BSP (bulk synchronous parallel) model [32] in providing synchronous computation, but additionally introduces a key abstraction called *distributed immutable view* that provides a shared-memory abstraction to graph algorithms. To provide such a view, Cyclops replicates vertices for inter-partition edges across a partitioned graph in a cluster and only grants the master vertex with write access, whose updates will be propagated to its replicas unidirectionally at the end of each superstep (i.e., iteration). To provide computation efficiency, Cyclops grants a vertex with read-only access to all its neighbors using shared memory. As a result, a programmer can easily write a distributed graph algorithm with local semantics.

Unlike prior work (e.g., PowerGraph [12]) that distributes computation among multiple replicas of a vertex, Cyclops follows a centralized computation model such that only a master vertex does the computation and sends messages to its replicas. This is based on our evaluation that many real graphs [27, 15] do not exhibit extremely high skewed power-law distribution such that one machine cannot accommodate the computation over one vertex. Hence, it may not always be worthwhile to distribute graph computation for a single vertex among multiple machines, which causes excessive message exchanges (usually more than 5X than Cyclops, section 6.12). In contrast, there is only one unidirectional message from the replica master to each of its replicas in Cyclops, and thus there is no contention in receiving messages.

Further, being aware of the hierarchical parallelism and locality in a multicore-based cluster, Cyclops is extended with a hierarchical processing model that transparently decomposes each worker into several threads on-demand in a superstep, which is hard or impossible on the general BSP model. This significantly reduces the amount of replicas and messages within a single machine, and fully harnesses the CPU and network resources.

We have implemented Cyclops based on Hama [2], a popular open-source clone of Pregel. Cyclops mostly retains the programming interface and fault tolerance model of Hama so that most existing graph algorithms for Hama can be trivially ported to Cyclops. Our evaluation results using a set of popular graph algorithms such as *PageRank* [5], *Alternating Least Squares*, *Single Source Shortest Path*, and *Community Detection*, show that Cyclops outperforms Hama ranging from 2.06X to 8.69X on a 6-machine cluster (each machine having 12 cores and 64 GB memory) using the default hash-based graph partition algorithm. When integrating a better graph partition algorithm (i.e., Metis [20]), Cyclops achieves a significantly larger speedup over Hama, ranging from 5.95X to 23.04X. We further show that Cyclops performs comparably with PowerGraph for *PageRank* on different graphs, despite the fact that Cyclops is based on a worse baseline (execution deficiency due to managed runtime, poor object serialization and inferior RPC library). The reason is that PowerGraph has 5.5X messages compared to Cyclops.

In summary, this paper makes the following contributions:

- The *distributed immutable view* abstraction that allows efficient graph computation and distributed activation (Section 3).

- An optimization that exploits the hierarchical parallelism and locality of multicore clusters (Section 5).

- An implementation based on Hama (Section 4) and a thorough evaluation on Cyclops that confirms the efficiency and effectiveness of Cyclops (Section 6).

The rest of the paper is organized as follows. Section 2 presents an overview of BSP, and discusses issues with prior graph computation models. Section 3 describes the graph computation model of Cyclops and its overall execution flow. Section 4 describes system implementation of Cyclops, followed by the hierarchical optimization in section 5. Section 6 presents the performance evaluation results. Section 7 describes the remaining related work. Finally, we conclude the paper with a brief discussion on future work in section 8.

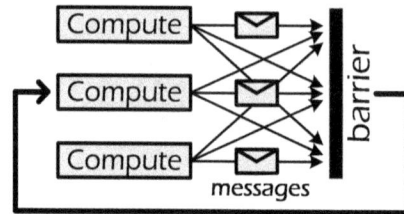

Figure 1: *The execution flow of BSP model*

2. BACKGROUND AND MOTIVATION

This section first briefly introduces the *Bulk Synchronous Parallel* (BSP) model and the Pregel framework. Then, we examine issues with other graph programming models like GraphLab and PowerGraph.

2.1 Pregel and BSP

Pregel [24] and its open-source clones [2, 1] are built on the *Bulk Synchronous Parallel* (BSP) [32] programming model and use pure message passing to exchange updates among vertices. The Pregel framework mostly only requires programmers to provide a *compute* function for each vertex to implement a graph algorithm. Figure 1 uses a flow chart to illustrate an outline of the BSP model, which expresses the program as a sequence of *supersteps*. In each superstep, each vertex receives messages in the previous superstep from its neighbors, updates its local value using the user-defined *compute* function and sends messages to its neighbors. There is a global barrier between two consecutive supersteps where messages are aggregated and delivered to vertices. Figure 2 illustrates the pseudo-code of the *PageRank* algorithm using the BSP model. The *compute* function sums up the ranks of incoming vertices through the received messages, and sets it as the new rank of current vertex. The new rank will also be sent to its neighboring vertices by messages until a global convergence estimated by a distributed aggregator is reached or the number of supersteps exceeds a threshold.

```
public void compute(Iterator msgs) {
  double sum = 0, value;

  while (msgs.hasNext())
    sum += msgs.next();
  value = 0.15 / numVertices + 0.85 * sum;
  setValue(value);

  double error = getGlobalError();
  if (error > epsilon)
    sendMessageToNeighbors(value / numEdges);
  else
    voteToHalt();
}
```

Figure 2: *The compute function of PageRank using the BSP model*

2.2 Issues with the BSP model

Though the BSP model has been successfully shown by Pregel to be a simple and effective alternative to handle large-scale graph processing applications, it also comes with some deficiencies in performance and accuracy. In the following, we will use the *PageRank*, the original example in the Pregel paper, on GoogleWeb dataset [27] as an example to illustrate potential issues with performance and accuracy.

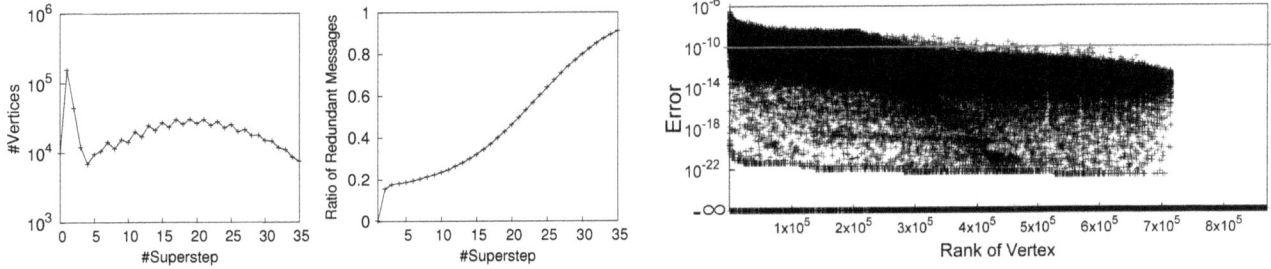

Figure 3: *(1) Number of vertices converged in each superstep. (2) Ratio of redundant messages in each superstep. (3) Distribution of vertices error (The left ones are with higher page rank values).*

2.2.1 Computation Efficiency

The BSP model described in *PageRank* proactively pushes values by message passing in each superstep. However, some algorithms like *PageRank* are essentially pull-mode algorithm [1], where a vertex needs to collect all values from its neighboring vertices to compute the new rank. The algorithm shown in Figure 2 actually relies on the programmer to ask the framework to proactively fetch messages before the computation can continue. This unfortunately requires all neighboring vertices of a non-convergent vertex to be alive just to send (redundant) messages, even if the neighbors have converged in a very early superstep.

For many pull-mode algorithms, however, the convergence of vertices is usually asymmetric, where a majority of vertices converge in the first few iterations. Consequently, a large fraction of time is wasted to repeatedly compute over converged vertices and send messages with the same values. Figure 3(1) shows the number of vertices converged in each superstep for *PageRank* algorithm on GoogleWeb [27]. In the BSP model, about 20% vertices converge after the first two supersteps, and the majority of the vertices converge in less than 16 supersteps.

2.2.2 Communication Efficiency

The BSP model focuses on parallelizing computation using bulk synchronization, which avoids potential contention on sharing vertices. However, the communication overhead dominates the execution time in distributed environment. For example, The *PageRank* spends more than 50% execution time on sending and parsing messages in our test environment. Figure 3(2) also shows that the ratio of messages with the same value in each superstep. After 14 supersteps, there are more than 30% redundant messages in each superstep.

The communication in the BSP model allows multiple vertices to simultaneously send updates to a single vertex, which may results in contention in the receiving end. Even if the updates from the same machine can be combined, the contention from different machines is still inevitable. Further, the combiner should only be used for commutative and associative operations. Figure 4 provides an example of the communication cost for each iteration on partitioned graph for vertex 1 in different models. In the BSP model, the message enqueue operation should be protected by a *lock*. Usually, a system may use a global queue for all vertices to improve the locality of enqueue operations on batched messages, thus a *global* lock would significantly degrade the performance of communication.

2.2.3 Convergence Detection

The termination condition of a BSP job depends on all vertices converging to an error bound and voting to halt, which means that the update of value is less than an *epsilon* defined by user. For pull-mode algorithms written in BSP, since all vertices must be alive in each superstep, the system cannot detect convergence through liveness of vertices. Hence, an application usually uses a distributed aggregator to estimate the global error (the average error of live vertices), and relies on it to determine whether to terminate the job or not.

However, there are several issues with such a convergence detection approach. First, the aggregator adds extra overhead to each superstep, since it has to apply an *aggregation* function to live vertices and gather results to the master. This may easily become a scalability bottleneck. Second, the global error is a relatively coarse-grained parameter, and thus a user cannot exactly control the proportion of converged vertices. Specifically, an algorithm using the same global error bound may get a diverse proportion of convergence with different dataset. For example, the proportion of converged vertices of the *PageRank* algorithm on Google Web and Amazon dataset [27] with the same error ($e = 10^{-10}$) is 94.9% and 87.7% respectively, according to our evaluation. Finally, as all vertices are alive in each superstep, the converged vertices may be still repeatedly computed and contribute little or even zero impact to the accumulated global error. The excessive number of converged vertices not only wastes a large number of computation and network resources, but also falsely converges some important vertices with still large error values.

Figure 3(3) shows the final errors of all vertices when the global error ($e = 10^{-10}$) is reached. The vertices are sorted by their rank values (a lower rank means a higher rank value), which means the importance of vertex. The vertices above the red line mean that they are still not converged yet. All non-converged vertices reside centrally on the upper-left corner, which is the important area due to their high rank values. A large number of vertices are with zero error values, which sink to the bottom of the figure. Hence, using global error convergence detection may cause significant accuracy issues in graph computation.

2.3 Issues with Other Models

GraphLab follows an asynchronous distributed shared memory programming model by allowing a vertex to directly read and update the values of its neighbors, which may result in relatively efficient convergence [4]. However, programmers need to understand the consistency model, and the execution on GraphLab is non-deterministic in essence, making it hard to debug and diagnose correctness and performance bugs. Further, the performance overhead due to distributed vertex scheduling and locking for consistency may reduce the improvement from the elimination of the global barrier and allowing direct vertex access using shared mem-

---

[1] Informally, in a pull-mode algorithm, a vertex will proactively fetch values from its neighboring vertices to compute; a push-mode algorithm instead lets a vertex passively wait for messages from its neighboring vertices and only become active to compute upon receiving a message.

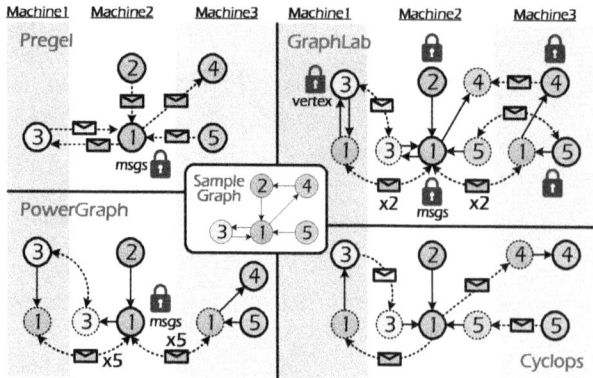

Figure 4: *An example of communication cost in different models*

```
public void compute() {
    double sum = 0, value, last = getValue();

    Iterator *edges = getInEdgesIterator();
    while (edges.hasNext())
        sum += edges.next().vertex.getMessage();
    value = 0.15 / numVertices + 0.85 * sum;
    setValue(value);

    double error = Math.abs(value - last);
    if (error > epsilon)
        activateNeighbors(value / numEdges);
    voteToHalt();
}
```

Figure 5: *The compute function of PageRank in Cyclops*

ory. As shown in Figure 4, to compute over vertex 1, it first *locks* itself and then asks all its neighboring vertices (may through replicas) to be *locked* using distributed vertex locks before computation. Finally, GraphLab enforces all operations on vertices in a pure local fashion, thus it requires to create duplicate replicas for each edge spanning machines and demands bidirectional messages (i.e., sending update from master to replicas and activation from replicas to master). In Figure 4, the edge from vertex 1 to vertex 4 appears in both machines and incurs two replicas. The replica 4 implements local activation for vertex 1, while the replica 1 implements local access for vertex 4. Due to bidirectional communication, vertex 1 may receive multiple activation messages from its replicas. Hence, there may be contention on vertex 1 and it requires a *lock* to coordinate message receiving.

PowerGraph [12] abstracts computation as *Gather*, *Apply* and *Scatter* (GAS), in which a vertex collects messages from its replicas, computes its new value and sends the new value to all its replicas, and ask all its replicas to activate their neighboring vertices. As shown in Figure 4, it takes three rounds of bidirectional message passing between a master and its replicas in each iteration to support the GAS model. The major benefit is that this can decompose the computation of an extremely skewed vertex in natural graphs to multiple machines. However, the bidirectional message passing between a master and replicas also results in contention when multiple replicas send messages to the master in the Gather and Scatter phase. Further, the GAS model requires about 5 messages for each replica of the vertex in one iteration (2 for Gather, 1 for Apply and 2 for Scatter), which significantly degrades the performance.

3. DISTRIBUTED IMMUTABLE VIEW

Being aware of the deficiency with prior systems, we describe Cyclops, a synchronous graph processing model that departs from the BSP model implemented in Pregel, and combines the best features from both GraphLab and PowerGraph. From GraphLab, Cyclops borrows direct memory access through vertex replicas to avoid redundant computation and messages. From PowerGraph, Cyclops borrows distributed activation to avoid duplicate replicas and bidirectional communication.

At the heart of Cyclops is the *distributed immutable view* abstraction, which presents a graph application with the view of the entire graph right before the beginning of each superstep. Unlike Pregel that requires message passing to push updates to neighboring vertices, the view grants a vertex with read-only access to its neighboring vertices through shared memory, thus providing local semantics to programmers. The immutable view abstraction still retains the synchronous and deterministic nature of the BSP model. Unlike GraphLab that limits replicas to single purpose (i.e., access

or activation), the replicas in distributed immutable view also bear the task of distributed activation of vertices, thus avoiding the messages from replicas to its master. Hereby, *distributed immutable view* only requires one round one-way message from master to its replicas, and thus is immune from contention among messages.

In the rest of this section, we will use the *PageRank* algorithm as a running example and describe the programming interface, graph organization, vertex computation, message passing and execution model in Cyclops.

3.1 Programming Interface

Cyclops mostly retains the programming interface of BSP implemented in Pregel (see Figure 2). The key difference is that instead of using message passing to receive updates from its neighboring vertices, Cyclops relies on shared memory access to directly read the values from its neighboring vertices. Further, Cyclops uses a local error detection scheme instead of using the average error from all vertices, thus a vertex will deactivate itself by default and only become active again upon receiving activation signal.

Figure 5 shows an example implementation of the *compute* function of *PageRank* in Cyclops. In contrast to the implementation in Figure 2, the iterator of messages is no longer necessary, but instead the application directly reads values from neighboring vertices provided by the *distributed immutable view*. Hence, Cyclops no longer requires keeping all vertices alive for sending messages. Further, it no longer relies on the global error but instead uses the local error to decide whether to activate neighboring vertices. By default, a vertex will deactivate itself and only become active again upon receiving activation signal at the end of each superstep.

3.2 Graph Organization

The program state in the BSP model is modeled as a directed graph, which is split into multiple partitions and assigned to multiple workers. Each worker is in charge of running the *compute* function on local vertices in parallel. Since a graph is partitioned, the communication between vertices is performed by message passing.

Similarly, the graph in Cyclops is also split and assigned to workers. However, to provide a *distributed immutable view* for each vertex, Cyclops maintains a read-only replica of each vertex for edges spanning machines during a graph cut. This makes sure that there is always a read-only memory reference for a partitioned graph in each machine. In each superstep, only the master vertex may be scheduled to execute the *compute* function, while replicas are just one-way synchronized by its master vertex at the end of each superstep.

Figure 6 shows a sample graph with six vertices, which is split and assigned to three workers. In the BSP model (Part A), for example, the worker 2 would run the *compute* function on vertex 3

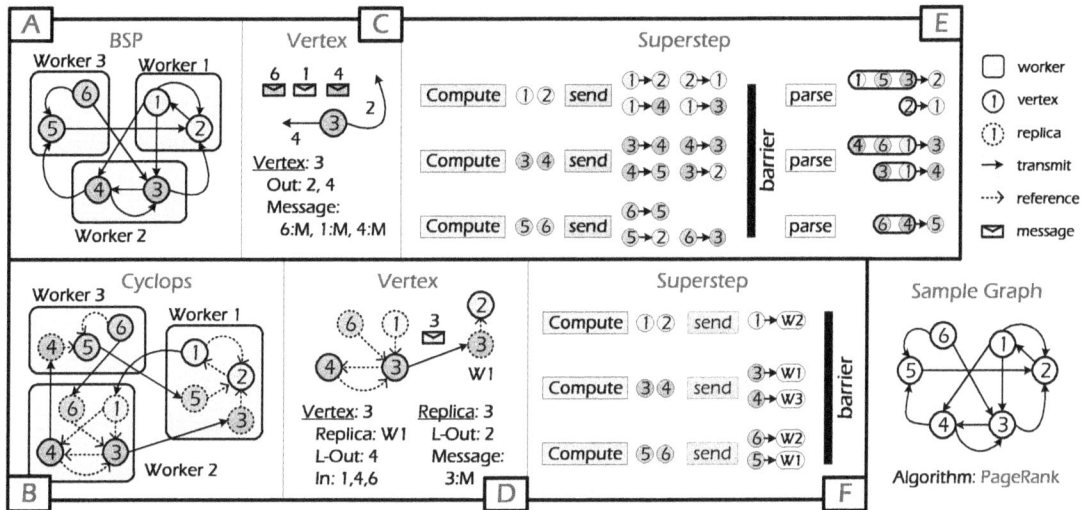

Figure 6: *An example of PageRank algorithm on Pregel and Cyclops for a simple graph. The symbol Out and In mean out-edges and in-edges, and the L-Out represents out-edges to local vertices. The message from vertex X is label as X:M.*

with messages from vertices 1, 4 and 6, and send two messages to vertices 2 and 4. In contrast, the *compute* function on vertex 3 in Cyclops (Part B) may directly read data from vertex 4 and replicas 1 and 6, and synchronize data with replica 3 in worker 1.

3.3 Vertex Computation

Vertex computation in the BSP model is presented in the form of user-defined *compute* functions. The *compute* function can be executed in parallel, as it is only allowed to inspect and modify the data of the current vertex, including the value and edges. In addition, all external information is obtained by messages as parameters, which should be sent in the previous superstep. Accordingly, the messages sent by the *compute* function will arrive before the forthcoming superstep.

Rather than using message passing, Cyclops provides a *distributed immutable view* of the previous superstep to each vertex like the *scope* in GraphLab [22]. However, the immutable view is synchronous, and thus the *compute* function can freely access it in read-only mode without worrying about consistency issues. Based on the immutable view, Cyclops naturally implements dynamic computation to support pull-mode algorithms. The *compute* function can directly access values of neighbors, even if they have converged and are inactive.

As shown in Figure 6, vertex 3 in the BSP model (Part C) maintains information (*e.g.,* the unique identifier) of outgoing neighbors (vertices 2 and 4) for sending messages, and messages from incoming neighbors (vertices 1, 4 and 6). In Cyclops (Part D), the references of incoming neighbors (vertices 1, 4 and 6) are stored to in-edges of vertex 3, which provide an immutable view to the *compute* function on vertex 3. Note that the references of vertices 1 and 6 are pointed to the replicas, since they are the remote vertices. The rest edges of vertex 3 are used to activate local vertices and synchronize with its replicas.

3.4 Message Passing

In the BSP model, message passing is used both to transfer data and to activate vertices. It results in the contention on message enqueue, and a large number of redundant computation and message passing for converged vertices in pull-mode algorithms.

In Cyclops, *the data movement between adjacent vertices is decoupled from message passing* as data transfer between them is

performed by shared memory access. Cyclops uses a *distributed* approach to implement vertex activation by using a master vertex to send activation requests together with values to propagate to its replicas. As the remote worker with outgoing neighbors of current vertex must have a replica of vertex, each vertex and its replicas are responsible for activating its local outgoing neighbors.

The only message required in Cyclops is used to synchronize replicas with their master vertices in each superstep. It guarantees each replica only receiving at most one message, thus there is no protection mechanisms in message passing of Cyclops. For the sample graph in Figure 4, all messages could be served in parallel in Cyclops.

In Figure 6, the out-edges of vertex 3 in the BSP model (Part C) are used to send message to outgoing neighbors (vertices 2 and 4) regardless of whether they are in local or remote workers. In Cyclops (Part D), vertex 3 maintains the location (worker 1) of replica for synchronization. The local out-edges to vertices 4 and 2 maintained in vertex 3 and its replica are used for distributed activation.

3.5 Execution Model

The BSP execution model uses a separate ingress phase to load and split a directed graph from the underlying file system. The input graph is split by a distributed graph partitioning heuristic (*e.g.,* random hashing, Metis [20]) into multiple partitions and assigned to workers. The execution phase of the BSP model presents as a single loop of *supersteps*. Each superstep consists of four sequential operations: message parsing (PRS), vertex computation (CMP), message sending (SND) and global barrier (SYN). At the beginning of each superstep, while there are messages or vertices alive, the worker parses messages received in the last superstep and uses them to activate vertices. After that, all active vertices execute user-defined *compute* function, and send messages to neighbors. A vertex deactivates itself by voting to halt. Before entering the global barrier, all messages sent in current superstep should be transmitted to destination.

Cyclops follows a similar execution model. Each worker executes the *compute* function on active master vertices, which pulls data from neighbors through shared memory access. The modification on non-converged vertices results in synchronization messages from master to replicas. Because the messages are directly used to update replicas and activate local neighbors in parallel by receiv-

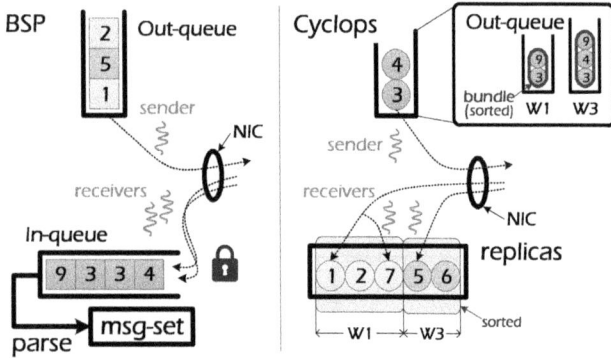

Figure 7: *An example of communication in BSP and Cyclops*

ing threads, Cyclops does not require the message parsing before vertex computation.

Figure 6 illustrates four consecutive operations intercepted from two connected supersteps. The two execution flows are similar (Part E and F), except for messages. The workers in the BSP model send and parse messages from vertices to its outgoing neighbors (*e.g.*, from vertex 3 to vertices 2 and 4). In contrary, the worker in Cyclops only sends the messages and update the replicas (*e.g.*, vertex 3 to replica 3).

3.6 Fault Tolerance

The fault tolerance mechanism used in Pregel is based on checkpoint and restore. After each global barrier, workers can save the states of their graph partition to underlying storage layer (e.g., HDFS). The necessary state consists of superstep count, vertex values, edge values and messages. This is much simpler than an asynchronous shared memory system like GraphLab, which requires an eventual consistent checkpoint algorithm [8]. Cyclops follows a similar mechanism used in Pregel, except that workers does not require to save the replicas and messages.

4. IMPLEMENTATION ISSUES

We have implemented Cyclops and its optimizations based on Apache Hama [2], a popular clone of Pregel implemented in Java. Cyclops adds around 2,800 SLOCs to Hama. Cyclops is mostly compatible with the interfaces and graph processing in Hama. However, there are a few differences to support the *distributed immutable view* in Cyclops.

4.1 Message Passing

Hama splits the vertex computation and message passing to avoid interference. As shown in Figure 4, all messages are cached in a global out-queue before sending. To improve the network utilization, Hama combines the messages sent to the same vertex if possible, and bundles the messages sent to the same worker in one package. Further, Hama uses a global in-queue to temporally store all messages to exploit locality of enqueue operations, and parses messages to each vertex at the beginning of next superstep. The enqueue operations from multiple receiving threads should be *serialized* to avoid contention.

In Cyclops model, the replica only receives at most one message, thus we optimize message passing to directly update replicas in parallel by multiple receiving threads. The message combining and parsing are no longer necessary. To further improve the locality, Cyclops groups replicas according to the location of its master, and sorts replicas within group at graph ingress. Cyclops uses multiple sub-queues to separately cache messages sent to different workers, and sorts the messages in bundle before sending.

4.2 Graph Partition

Cyclops is orthogonal to the graph partition algorithms and the default partition algorithm (i.e., hash partition) can be used directly without changes to Cyclops. However, as the graph partition quality may affect the amount of replicas in Cyclops, using a better partition algorithm may generate a balanced edge-cut. This may evenly assign vertices to workers and reduce the number of inter-partition edges, thus reduces the amount of replicas and replica synchronization messages. Hence, we additionally implement the Metis [20] partition algorithm that tries to minimize inter-partition edges and balance the vertices among partitions. In section 6.6, we will show that this may result in significant performance boost.

4.3 Graph Ingress

The in-memory graph organization is slightly different from that in Hama due to the need for creating replicas, adding in-edges and local out-edges for all vertices to maintain the *distributed immutable view* for the *compute* function. To avoid unnecessary burden for programmer, Cyclops maintains compatibility of the input file format with Hama, but instead reuses the ingress phase to load and split graph.

In addition to the ingress phase in Hama, Cyclops adds its own ingress phase to create replicas and add in-edges and local out-edges. This is done by letting each vertex to send a message to its out-edges. Each vertex will create a replica for the sending vertex upon receiving a remote message when such a replica is not created yet. It will further create an in-edge from the replica and a local out-edge for the replica to itself. This is essentially a superstep in Hama.

4.4 Convergence Detection

Cyclops supports the original global aggregation based convergence detection. However, as we discussed in section 2.2.3, using such a global error to indicate whether the graph processing have converged may cause accuracy problems. Hence, we further add a fine-grained convergence detection scheme by counting the proportion of converged vertices, which is more suitable for the dynamic computation nature of many graph algorithms.

5. HIERARCHICAL GRAPH PROCESSING WITH CYCLOPS

With the prevalence of multicore-based clusters, the two-level hierarchical organization raises new challenges and opportunities to design and implement an efficient large-scale graph processing framework. To our knowledge, Pregel and its open-source clones like Hama currently are oblivious to the underlying hardware topology and use a uniform way to manage all workers.

Inspired by the hierarchical-BSP model [6], we apply a hierarchical design to exploit such parallelism and locality, which is called CyclopsMT. CyclopsMT uses a three-level scheme to organize tasks: the main task in superstep (level 0) is first partitioned into machines in cluster (level 1), and the worker in each machine further partitions the task to multiple threads running on multicore hardware (level 2). At any time, only the last-level threads perform tasks. Their parents, i.e., the workers in higher levels, just wait until all their child threads finish their tasks. Note that, CyclopsMT still preserves the synchronous and deterministic computation nature in Cyclops, as all threads sharing the same parent synchronize with each other at the end of each superstep.

However, it is non-trivial to parallelize tasks in each superstep using multi-thread for BSP model. This is because the message operations in each superstep have *poor locality* and *heavy contention*.

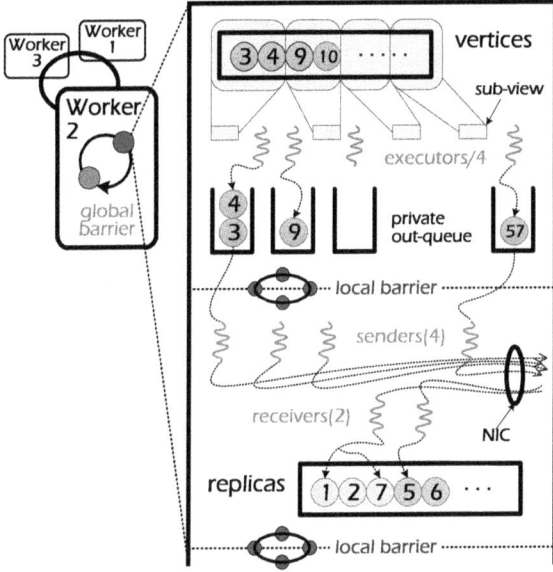

Figure 8: *The architecture of hierarchical Cyclops (CyclopsMT)*

Table 1: *A collection of real-world graphs.*

Algorithm	Graph	$|V|$	$|E|$
PageRank	Amazon	403,394	3,387,388
	GoogleWeb(GWeb)	875,713	5,105,039
	LiveJournal(LJournal)	4,847,571	69,993,773
	Wiki	5,716,808	130,160,392
ALS	SYN-GL	110,000	2,729,572
CD	DBLP	317,080	1,049,866
SSSP	RoadCA	1,965,206	5,533,214

For message parsing, trivially splitting received messages to multiple threads may result in heavy contention on destination vertices, especially when a large number of messages are delivered to the same vertex. For message sending, using a separate queue to buffer messages for each thread is harmful to message batching and aggregation.

In Cyclops, fortunately, the data movement between vertices is decoupled from message passing, and thus the messages are only sent from master vertices to their replicas and there are no duplicate replicas in the destination. This opens opportunities of parallelizing each superstep in Cyclops. Hence, CyclopsMT adopts a *split* design to parallelize computation on master vertex and message passing to replicas in each superstep, and to exploit the locality of communication and synchronization without contention.

Figure 5 illustrates how CyclopsMT parallelizes all operations in a superstep. For vertex computation, all vertices are evenly mapped to multiple threads and are executed fully in parallel. The vertex activation requests in the *compute* function are treated differently. The remote activation is delayed to message sending during replica synchronization, while the local activation is performed immediately by setting the corresponding incoming edge of destination vertex, which is a *lock-free* operation.

In the message sending phase, all updated vertices with replicas need to send synchronization messages. The remote activation requests will be combined with synchronization messages. Since there are no duplicate messages sent to the same destination replica, message combination is no longer required. *Private* out-queues are used to reduce the contention on underlying network hardware.

In the message receiving phase, multiple message receivers are launched to exploit the parallelism. Because there are no duplicate messages sent to the same replica, the update operation on replica is *lock-free* and *non-blocking*. However, with the growing number of threads within one worker, too many message receivers would result in heavy contention on underlying network hardware. The improvement is also devoured by the workload imbalance of message receivers.

CyclopsMT support separately configure the parallelism of vertex computation and message passing according to different behavior of algorithm and workloads. In Figure 5, CyclopsMT launches

4 working threads to compute master vertices in parallel, and 2 message receivers to receive messages and update replicas.

Finally, with the growing number of participants, the performance overhead of global barrier rapidly increases. Hierarchical design in CyclopsMT provides a natural solution to reduce the overhead. The main thread represented as the whole worker performs distributed protocol of a global barrier, and the rest of threads wait on a local barrier. The hierarchical barrier reduces the number of messages and the latency of communication.

6. EVALUATION

This section evaluates Cyclops and its optimizations against the baseline system Hama using four typical graph algorithms: *PageRank* (PR), *Alternating Least Squares* (ALS), *Community Detection* (CD) and *Single Source Shortest Path* (SSSP). The first three are pull-mode algorithms, while the fourth one is a push-mode algorithm.

6.1 Overview of Tested Graph Algorithms

PageRank [5] (PR): It is a widely-used and well-studied graph algorithm. A web page's rank is computed as a weighted sum of all its incoming neighbors' rank value. In graph-parallel models, each vertex receives messages from all its incoming neighbors to compute its new rank and send the new value to all its outgoing neighbors. Since a vertex needs to gather data from all its neighbors, PageRank is a typical pull-mode algorithm.

Alternating Least Squares (ALS): It was used by Zhou et.al [36] to do recommendation in Netflix. The input to ALS is a sparse users by movies matrix R, where each entry contains the movie rating of each user. This algorithm uses U * R to simulate the ranking value. It iteratively refines U and V by computing the least square solution with the other fixed. ALS can easily fit into the graph computation framework if we consider the input matrix as a graph connecting users with movies [12].

Community Detection (CD): It is a simple community detection application based on label propagation [36]. Each vertex has a label value, which is assigned with the most frequent labels in its neighbors. Vertices with the same label are considered as a community.

Single Source Shortest Path (SSSP): It is a typical push-mode application. A vertex will not do computation unless messages arrive to wake it up. A vertex uses only the incoming messages to update its value. After that, it can go to sleep. We use the SSSP algorithm to show that even the push-mode applications has no redundant vertex computation and message passing, Cyclops and CyclopsMT still outperforms Hama through the elimination of contention on communication and exploiting the parallelism and locality of multicore-based cluster.

All these algorithms can be trivially written/ported to Cyclops due to its synchronous nature with local semantics exported to the *compute* function. It requires 8 and 7 SLOCs to adapt the existing Hama implementation of PR and SSSP to Cyclops. We implement ALS and CD to both Hama and Cyclops and the code difference between Hama and Cyclops is only 10 and 6 SLOCs accordingly.

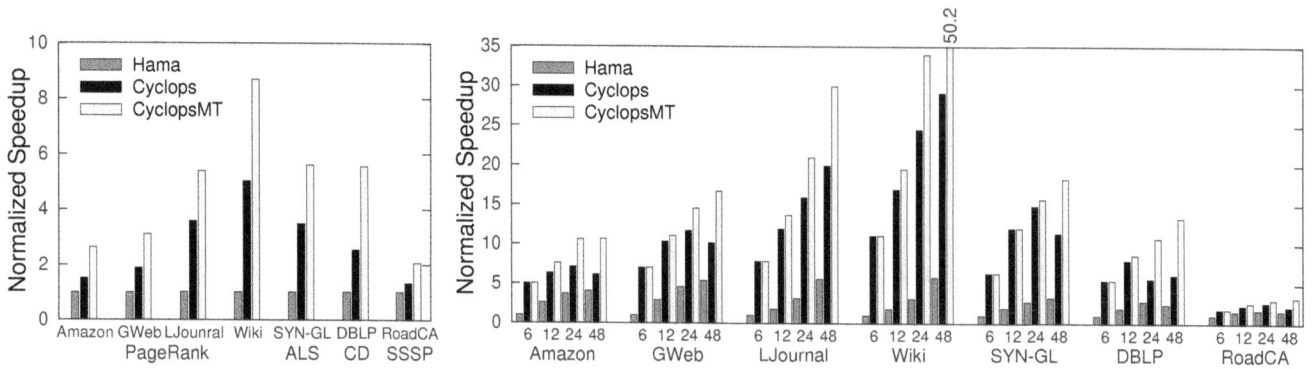

Figure 9: *(1)The speedup of Cyclops and CyclopsMT over Hama using 48 workers for a variety of dataset. (2)The scalability of Cyclops and CyclopsMT over Hama using 6, 12, 24 and 48 workers for a variety of dataset (Speedup is normalized against Hama with 6 workers).*

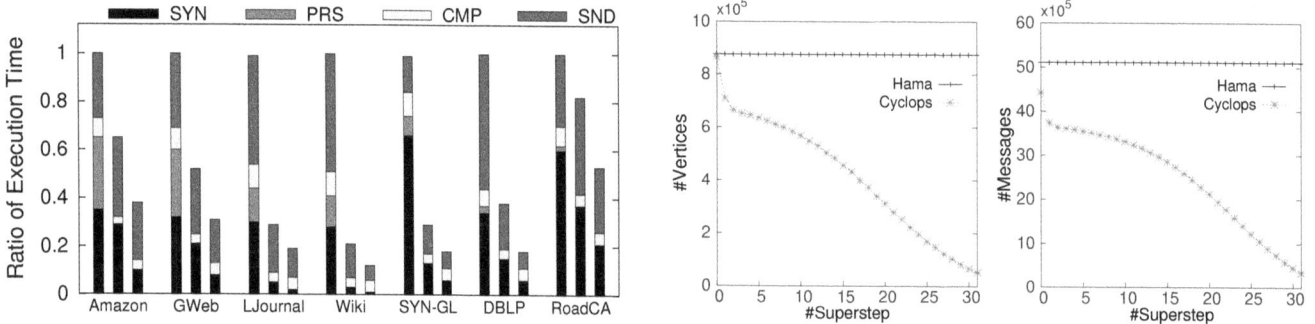

Figure 10: *(1) The breakdown of execution time on Hama, Cyclops and CyclopsMT using 48 workers with different benchmarks. (2) The number of active vertices in each superstep on Hama and Cyclops for PageRank algorithm with GWeb dataset. (3) The number of messages in each superstep on Hama and Cyclops for PageRank algorithm with GWeb dataset.*

6.2 Experimental Setup

All experiments are performed on an in-house 6-machine multicore cluster. Each machine has a 12-core AMD Opteron 6168 CPU, 64GB RAM, 2x1TB Hard Drivers and 1 GigE network ports. We run HDFS on the same cluster for underlying storage layer, and use a graph ingress phase to load the graph to main memory before doing graph computation.

Table 1 lists a collection of large graphs used in our experiments. Most of them are from Stanford Large Network Dataset Collection [27]. The Wiki dataset is from [15]. The dataset for the ALS algorithm is synthetically generated by tools provided from that used in the Gonzalez et al. [12]. The SSSP algorithm requires the input graph to be directed and weighted. Since the RoadCA graph is not originally weighted, we synthetically assign a weight value to each edge, where the weight is generated based on a log-normal distribution ($\mu = 0.4, \sigma = 1.2$) from the Facebook user interaction graph [34].

6.3 Overall Performance

Figure 9 summarizes the normalized performance of Cyclops and CyclopsMT compared to Hama with different configurations. Note that we evenly distribute workers in each machine, and run 8 threads at most on a single machine for CyclopsMT because JVM doesn't scale well on large-scale multicore platforms and the JVM itself will create a number of auxiliary threads. The number of workers shown in figure for CyclopsMT is equal to the total number of threads.

As shown in Figure 9(1), Cyclops and CyclopsMT outperforms Hama in all algorithms over different datasets with 48 workers. For PR, the speedup increases with the growing size of input graph.

The largest speedup of Cyclops and CyclopsMT comes from Wiki (our biggest graph), which is 5.03X and 8.69X accordingly. The speedup of Cyclops and CyclopsMT is also remarkable for ALS with SYN-GL (3.48X and 5.60X) and CD with DBLP (2.55X and 5.54X). For SSSP with RoadCA, the performance improvement is relative small (1.33X and 2.06X). This is because SSSP is a typical push-mode algorithm, and thus there are no redundant vertex computation and message passing.

Figure 9(2) compares the scalability of Cyclops and CyclopsMT compared to Hama with different workers from 6 to 48. With the growing of workers, the number of edges spanning machines rapidly increases, which results in the amplification of the number of messages. Hence, the time spent on message passing in several applications significantly degrades the performance of Hama and Cyclops. However, due to exploiting the locality of messages and using hierarchical barrier, CyclopsMT reduces the performance degradation in communication. Further, for applications whose performance are dominated by vertex computation, the scalability is still quite good, including PR with most graphs, ALS and CD. For the performance of application dominated by communication, the growth of speedup appears slightly slowdown, including PR with Amazon and SSSP with RoadCA.

6.4 Performance Breakdown

In this section, we categorize the source of performance speedup through a breakdown of execution time and the number of active vertices and messages in each superstep.

Figure 10(1) shows the ratio of execution time breakdown of benchmarks on Hama, Cyclops and CyclopsMT using 48 workers with different benchmarks. The result is normalized to Hama, and the labels SYN, PRS, CMP and SND correspond to synchro-

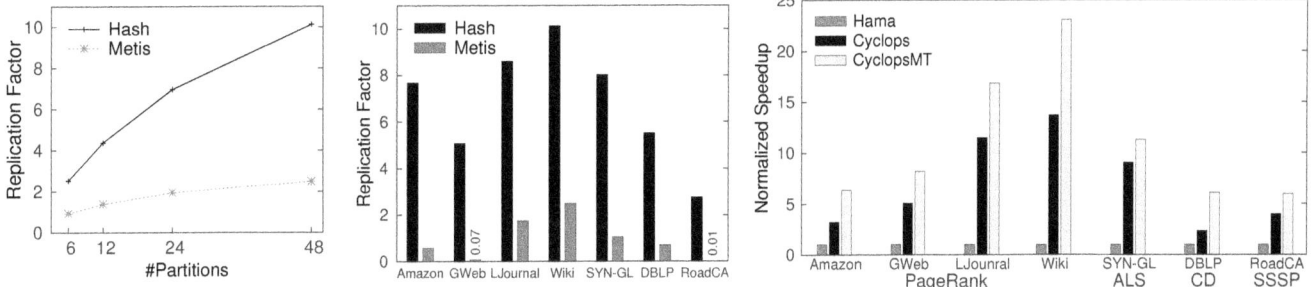

Figure 11: *(1) The replication factor on Wiki dataset using different partitions. (2) The replication factor for a variety of dataset using 48 partitions. (3) The performance of Hama, Cyclops and CyclopsMT with Metis partition using 48 workers for a variety of dataset. Speedup is normalized against Hama under Metis partition.*

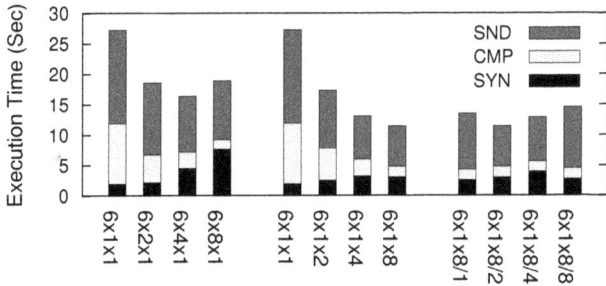

Figure 12: *The breakdown of execution time on CyclopsMT for PageRank with GWeb dataset using different configurations. The labels under histogram are the configuration, and the symbol of 'MxWxT/R' corresponds to #machines, #workers, #threads and #receivers.*

nization, message parsing, vertex computation and message sending accordingly. Cyclops and CyclopsMT significantly outperform Hama for pull-mode applications because of two major benefits. The first is from the elimination of redundant computation and message passing for converged vertices, which efficiently improves the performance of pull-mode applications. The second exploits the parallelism and locality of message passing, through the elimination of the contention in message parsing. The significant improvement in SYN phase also benefits from the load balance in each superstep. CyclopsMT further reduces the number of replicates and messages within a single machine, and improves the synchronization among workers by the hierarchical barrier. For SSSP, Cyclops and CyclopsMT achieves modest speedup to Hama through optimized message passing and efficient vertex access through shared memory.

Figure 10(2) and (3) show the number of active vertices and messages in each superstep for PageRank algorithm on GWeb. The number of active messages and messages decides vertex computation time and message passing time respectively. Compared to Hama, Cyclops significantly reduces the number of active vertices and messages as expected.

6.5 Improvement of CyclopsMT

To illustrate the effect of hierarchical Cyclops (CyclopsMT) on multicore-based clusters, we evaluate the PR algorithm on GWeb dataset with different configurations of CyclopsMT. In Figure 12, the configuration labeled 6xWx1 correspond to Cyclops, which launch W single thread workers on each machine. With the increase of workers, the workload of vertex computation is constant, but the number of messages increases because of the growing number of

replicas. Cyclops can efficiently parallelize the vertex computation and message parsing, thus the execution time of computation (CMP) rapidly decreases and the communication time(SND) is stable. Further, the overhead of synchronization (SYN) increases with the growing number of participants, which results performance degradation when the number of workers exceeds 24. The configuration labeled 6x1xT correspond to CyclopsMT, which launch 1 worker with T threads on each machine. Because of the fixed number of worker, the overhead of communication and synchronization are also stable. The performance improvement mainly comes from vertex computation. The only contention in CyclopsMT is from the underlying hardware. Too many receiving threads would contend on CPU and network resources, thus CyclopsMT provides separate configuration to control interference. The best performance is from configuration labeled 6x1x8/2, which only launches 2 receiving threads for communication.

6.6 Impact of Graph Partitioning Algorithms

In all prior evaluation, we simply use the naive hash-based graph partitioning algorithm, which may result in an excessive amount of edges being cut. To study the impact of graph partition algorithm on Hama and Cyclops, we compare the performance using two graph partitioning methods (*e.g.*, Hash-based and Metis [20]) with all algorithms on different datasets. Figure 11(1) depicts the average number of replicas for different number of partitions for Wiki dataset and Figure 11(2) shows the average number of replicas for different datasets on 48 partitions, using the hash-based and Metis partition algorithms. With the increase of partitions, the average number of replicas under the hash-based partition algorithm rapidly approaches the average number of edges per vertex. In contrast, Metis significantly reduces the average number of replicas.

In Figure 11(3), Cyclops and CyclopsMT using Metis significantly outperform their counterparts using hash-based partitions. However, Hama does not obviously benefit from the Metis partition algorithm, because the Metis partition algorithm only tries to minimize the total number of edges spanning machines while trying to balance vertices, and the vertices may be a little bit out of balance. In Cyclops, as the number of converged vertices rapidly increases along with graph computation, the degree and impact of imbalance for vertices will be decreased. However, Hama will remain imbalanced along all of its execution.

6.7 Ingress Time

The input graph is loaded from a text file stored in a distributed file-system (HDFS). The graph processing runtime then splits the file into multiple blocks and generates in-memory data structures by all workers in parallel. Each worker reads vertex from a block and sends vertices to their target workers according to the graph

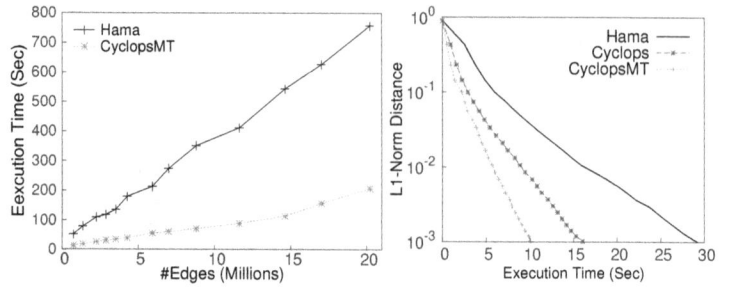

Graph	LD (sec) H / C	REP (sec) H / C	INIT (sec) H / C	TOT (sec) H / C
Amazon	6.2 / 5.9	0.0 / 2.5	1.7 / 1.5	7.9 / 9.9
Gweb	7.1 / 6.8	0.0 / 2.8	2.6 / 1.9	9.7 / 11.4
Ljounral	27.1 / 31.0	0.0 / 44.7	17.9 / 9.2	45.0 / 84.9
Wiki	46.7 / 46.7	0.0 / 62.2	33.4 / 20.4	80.0 / 129.3
SYN-GL	4.2 / 4.0	0.0 / 2.6	2.4 / 1.8	6.6 / 8.4
DBLP	4.1 / 4.1	0.0 / 1.5	1.3 / 0.9	5.4 / 6.5
RoadCA	6.4 / 6.2	0.0 / 3.9	0.9 / 0.6	7.3 / 10.7

Figure 13: *(1)The execution time of graph ingress. H represents Hama, and C represents Cyclops (2)The scalability of Cyclops with ALS benchmark. (3)The L1-Norm distance of Hama, Cyclops and CyclopsMT on PageRank algorithm with GWeb dataset.*

Table 2: *The memory behavior of Hama, Cyclops and CyclopsMT on PageRank algorithm with Wiki dataset.*

Configuration	Max Cap (GB)	Max Usage (GB)	Young GC Num	Young GC Sec	Full GC Num	Full GC Sec
Hama/48	1.7	1.5	132	45.7	69	18.7
Lyra/48	4.0	3.0	45	62.9	15	13.9
LyraMT/6x8	12.6/8	11.0/8	268/8	67.8/8	32/8	2.52/8

Table 3: *Message passing micro-benchmark results.*

#Message	Hama (sec) SND	Hama (sec) PRS	Hama (sec) TOT	PowerGraph (sec) SND	PowerGraph (sec) PRS	PowerGraph (sec) TOT	Cyclops (sec)
5M	9.7	0.4	10.1	0.7	0.1	0.8	1.0
25M	56.4	1.9	58.3	3.4	0.2	3.6	5.6
50M	183.4	3.8	187.2	6.9	0.4	7.3	9.6

partition algorithm. Finally, each worker initializes its own vertices. Cyclops requires an additional phase to create replicas and refine vertices.

Figure 13(1) shows the breakdown of ingress time using 48 workers with different input graphs. We split the ingress time into graph loading (LD), vertex replication(REP) and vertex initialization (INIT). The overhead of ingress time in Cyclops is mainly from the vertex replication phase, and the rest portion of time is close to Hama. The time spent on vertex replication depends on the size of graph, and the increase of time is still modest. Nevertheless, this is a one-time cost as a loaded graph will usually be processed multiple times.

6.8 Scale with Graph Size

To show how CyclopsMT scales with graph size, Figure 13(2) illustrates the execution time of ALS algorithm on dataset with a varying number of edges from 0.34M to 20.2M using 48 workers. The execution time only increases from 9.6 (for 0.34M) to 207.7 (for 20.2M) seconds, indicating that the performance of CyclopsMT scales well with the growing size of input graph.

6.9 Convergence Speed

To evaluate the convergence speed of Cyclops and CyclopsMT compared to Hama, we evaluate the L1-Norm distance to the final result as the execution time goes by. The final result is collected offline, and the partial result of applications on Cyclops, CyclopsMT and Hama are dumped after each superstep. In Figure 13(3), both Cyclops and CyclopsMT significantly accelerate the convergence of PageRank on GWeb dataset compared to Hama.

6.10 Memory Consumption

As Cyclops needs some replicas for vertices to maintain the *distributed immutable view*, an intuitive impression is that Cyclops may significantly increase the memory consumption. To compare the memory behavior of Cyclops and Hama, we use *jStat* to evaluate the memory usage and the times of the garbage collection (GC) execution. Note that we configure the Hama and Cyclops are configured using Concurrent Mark-Sweep (CMS) collector as

GC. The partition algorithm is the hash-based partition instead of Metis, which should be a worst case of memory consumption for Cyclops.

Table 6.9 illustrates the memory behavior per worker of Hama, Cyclops and CyclopsMT using 48 workers for the PageRank algorithm. The input graph is Wiki, and CyclopsMT is configured as 1 worker per machine with 8 threads. The maximum memory spaces allocated to Cyclops is larger than that in Hama. However, The number of Young and Full GC in Cyclops is actually less than Hama due to the elimination of redundant messages, which occupies a large number of memory in each superstep. CyclopsMT overall consumes much less memory per work than Cyclops and Hama, since it shares replicas among threads, and replaces the usage of internal message with memory reference.

6.11 Communication Efficiency

We demonstrate the benefits of unidirectional communication of Cyclops by comparing the results of the message passing microbenchmark using three different implementations. The microbenchmark launches five workers to concurrently send messages to update the element of an array in master worker. Each message is a pair of index and value. The first implementation used by Hama is based on Apache Hadoop RPC lib. It uses a global queue to serially buffer messages from multiple senders, and uses an additional message parsing phase to update values to array. The second implementation used by PowerGraph is based on C++ Boost RPC lib, and it adopts the same method to send and parse messages. The last implementation used by Cyclops is also based on Apache Hadoop RPC lib, but it directly updates the messages from multiple senders to array without protection. As shown in Table 6.10, there is one order of magnitude performance slowdown between the implementations on Hama and PowerGraph, even using the same method. However, the implementation used by Cyclops has slightly better performance than PowerGraph, even if Cyclops uses a much worse RPC library as that in Hama, due to significantly less messages (see next section).

6.12 Comparing with PowerGraph

Since PowerGraph [12] is the well-known distributed graph processing system, readers might be interested in how the performance of Cyclops compares to that of PowerGraph, even if PowerGraph

Table 4: *A comparison between CyclopsMT and PowerGraph.*

DataSet	Hash-based Partition								Heuristic Parirition		
	Execution Time(s)		AVG #Replicas	#Messages(M)	Msg/Rep	CMP			Execution Time(s)		AVG #Replicas
	Cyclops : PG	Net	Cyclops : PG	Cyclops : PG	Cyclops : PG	Cyclops			Cyclops : PG	Net	Cyclops : PG
Amazon	10.5 : 14.8	+41%	3.86 : 3.77	38 : 192	1.0 : 5.2	11%			4.9 : 7.8	+59%	0.24 : 0.40
GWeb	11.4 : 15.2	+33%	2.44 : 2.57	38 : 212	1.0 : 5.3	15%			4.9 : 6.5	+33%	0.04 : 0.82
Ljournal	97.1 : 72.9	-25%	2.69 : 2.62	353 : 1873	1.0 : 5.4	25%			53.0 : 49.1	-8%	0.64 : 1.18
Wiki	75.6 : 61.9	-18%	2.51 : 2.60	218 : 1366	1.0 : 6.2	39%			59.9 : 43.2	-28%	0.93 : 1.08

was *written in C++*. We use the bulk synchronous version as opponent, since it has the best performance among three variants of PowerGraph. We use the CyclopsMT for comparison as PowerGraph is essentially multithreaded.

Table 6.10 summarizes the comparison between Cyclops and PowerGraph for PageRank algorithms with different datasets and graph partition algorithms. For comparison under hash-based graph partition, the similar hash functions are used to partition graphs based on vertex and edge for Cyclops and PowerGraph accordingly. Though the average number of replicas in Cyclops and PowerGraph are close, each vertex sends 5 messages in each superstep in PowerGraph, of which 3 are used in Gather and Apply phases and the other 2 are used in Scatter phase. Cyclops only requires at most 1 message for vertex in one iteration. Due to the improvement in communication, Cyclops outperforms PowerGraph on Amazon and GWeb datasets. However, for LJournal and Wiki datasets, the performance is affected more by vertex computation, which takes more than 25% and 39% of execution time in Cyclops, respectively. The improvement from communication is not enough to overcome the performance gap between languages.

For heuristic graph partitioning, Cyclops uses Metis algorithm and PowerGraph uses Coordinated Greedy algorithm to partition graphs. We did not use the same partition algorithm as the former tries to minimize edges to cut while the latter tries to minimize vertices to cut. As the average numbers of replicas are still comparable, the results are similar to that of hash-based partition.

7. RELATED WORK

Large-scale graph processing: The emergence of social network and web search have stimulated the development of a number of large-scale graph processing. MapReduce [11] and its relatives [17, 7] have been shown to effectively process web graphs by ranking pages [5] and other graph-related algorithms [25, 35]. Based on MapReduce and its relatives, there have been several systems such as PEGASUS [19], Presto [33], HADI [18] and MadLinq [29] that extend such platforms for graph processing. However, the iterative nature and cross-computation dependence in typical graph algorithms may result in suboptimal performance for large-scale graph processing [22, 21, 12] on such platforms.

Piccolo [26] uses a distributed key-value table abstraction to allow computation on different machines to access shared and mutable states. Unlike Piccolo, the immutable view abstraction provides just read-only access to distributed shared graph views and thus is immune to possible data races and does not have to worry about consistency issues. Trinity [31] in an on-going research project that supports online graph processing, which, however, has to confront users from the consistency models. It also proposes to restrict message passing by buffering and aggregating messages in memory. However, it still requires message passing to access the cached messages. Kineograph [10] aims at online graph processing by using an epoch commit protocol on periodic snapshots, which may

be beneficial for extending Cyclops to support incremental graph processing.

Bulk synchronous parallel: Since its first invention by Valiant [32], there have been a number of BSP library implementations, including BSPlib [16] and Greep BSP library [13]. There have also been several extensions to the BSP model, including the hierarchical BSP model [6], which is similar to the hierarchical processing optimization in Cyclops.

Graph Replication and Partition: Parallel BGL [14] distributes graphs by using a property map to store values corresponding to a vertex. It introduces the ghost cell, which allows a vertex to access values through the put/get interfaces to the property map. However, the ghost cell in parallel BGL is write accessible and an application-specific resolver is required to arbitrate and combine messages, which may cause consistency issues and incur burdens to programmers. In contrast, the immutable view provided in Cyclops allows read-only replication of vertices and is with clearer semantics and potentially better scalability due to elimination of frequent coherence messages. Pujol et al. [28] describe an online partition scheme that tries to minimize replicas of vertices through joint partition and replication. This can benefit Cyclops from reducing requires replicas without comprising load balancing. The Surfer [9] captures the network unevenness in cloud environments during graph partitioning by accounting both the machine topology graph and data graph. Such an integrated partitioning may improve performance of Cyclops running in cloud environments.

8. CONCLUSION AND FUTURE WORK

This paper identified issues with existing graph computation models and presented Cyclops, a synchronous vertex-oriented graph processing system that is easy to program and provide efficient vertex computation, yet with significantly less messages than prior systems. We showed that Cyclops performed comparably with PowerGraph despite the language difference due to less messages. A release of Cyclops is available at: `http://ipads.se.sjtu.edu.cn/projects/cyclops/cyclops-snapshot-0.1.tar.gz`

Cyclops currently has no support for topology mutation of graph yet, as its baseline system (i.e., Hama) does not have such a feature yet. We plan to add such support in our future work. Further, we currently evaluated Cyclops only in a small-scale in-house cluster. We plan to study its performance in a larger scale cluster using Amazon EC2-like cloud platforms. In addition, Some features of efficient software and hardware, such as zero-copy protocol in Ibis [3] and RDMA in Infiniband, can also benefit Cyclops. We will consider them in future work.

9. ACKNOWLEDGMENTS

We thank the anonymous reviewers for their insightful comments. This work is supported in part Doctoral Fund of Ministry of Education of China (Grant No. 20130073120040), the Program for New Century Excellent Talents in University of Ministry of Education of China, Shanghai Science and Technology Development Funds (No. 12QA1401700), a foundation for the Author of National Excellent Doctoral Dissertation of PR China, China National Natural Science Foundation (No. 61003002) and Singapore NRF (CREATE E2S2).

10. REFERENCES

[1] Apache. The Apache Giraph Project. http://giraph.apache.org/.

[2] Apache. The Apache Hama Project. http://hama.apache.org/.

[3] H. E. Bal, J. Maassen, R. V. van Nieuwpoort, N. Drost, R. Kemp, T. van Kessel, N. Palmer, G. Wrzesinska, T. Kielmann, K. van Reeuwijk, et al. Real-world distributed computer with ibis. *Computer*, 43(8):54–62, 2010.

[4] D. P. Bertsekas and J. N. Tsitsiklis. *Parallel and distributed computation: numerical methods*. Prentice-Hall, Inc., Upper Saddle River, NJ, USA, 1989.

[5] S. Brin and L. Page. The anatomy of a large-scale hypertextual web search engine. In *WWW*, pages 107–117, 1998.

[6] H. Cha and D. Lee. H-bsp: A hierarchical bsp computation model. *J. Supercomput.*, 18(2):179–200, 2001.

[7] R. Chaiken, B. Jenkins, P. Larson, B. Ramsey, D. Shakib, S. Weaver, and J. Zhou. SCOPE: easy and efficient parallel processing of massive data sets. *VLDB Endowment*, 1(2):1265–1276, 2008.

[8] K. Chandy and L. Lamport. Distributed snapshots: determining global states of distributed systems. *ACM TOCS*, 3(1):63–75, 1985.

[9] R. Chen, M. Yang, X. Weng, B. Choi, B. He, and X. Li. Improving large graph processing on partitioned graphs in the cloud. In *ACM SOCC*, 2012.

[10] R. Cheng, J. Hong, A. Kyrola, Y. Miao, X. Weng, M. Wu, F. Yang, L. Zhou, F. Zhao, and E. Chen. Kineograph: taking the pulse of a fast-changing and connected world. In *EuroSys*, pages 85–98, 2012.

[11] J. Dean and S. Ghemawat. Mapreduce: simplified data processing on large clusters. *Commun. ACM*, 51(1):107–113, Jan. 2008.

[12] J. Gonzalez, Y. Low, H. Gu, D. Bickson, and C. Guestrin. PowerGraph: Distributed graph-parallel computation on natural graphs. In *OSDI*, 2012.

[13] M. Goudreau, K. Lang, S. Rao, T. Suel, and T. Tsantilas. Portable and efficient parallel computing using the bsp model. *IEEE Trans. Computers*, 48(7):670–689, 1999.

[14] D. Gregor and A. Lumsdaine. The Parallel BGL: A generic library for distributed graph computations. *Parallel Object-Oriented Scientific Computing (POOSC)*, 2005.

[15] H. Haselgrove. Wikipedia page-to-page link database. http://haselgrove.id.au/wikipedia.htm, 2010.

[16] J. Hill, B. McColl, D. Stefanescu, M. Goudreau, K. Lang, S. Rao, T. Suel, T. Tsantilas, and R. Bisseling. BSPlib: The BSP programming library. *Parallel Computing*, 24(14):1947–1980, 1998.

[17] M. Isard, M. Budiu, Y. Yu, A. Birrell, and D. Fetterly. Dryad: distributed data-parallel programs from sequential building blocks. In *EuroSys*, pages 59–72, 2007.

[18] U. Kang, C. Tsourakakis, A. Appel, C. Faloutsos, and J. Leskovec. HADI: Fast diameter estimation and mining in massive graphs with Hadoop. *ACM TKDD*, 5:8:1–8:24, 2011.

[19] U. Kang, C. E. Tsourakakis, and C. Faloutsos. PEGASUS: A Peta-Scale Graph Mining System Implementation and Observations. In *ICDM*, pages 229–238, 2009.

[20] G. Karypis and V. Kumar. Parallel multilevel k-way partitioning scheme for irregular graphs. In *Int. Conf. Supercomputing*, 1996.

[21] A. Kyrola, G. Blelloch, and C. Guestrin. GraphChi: Large-scale graph computation on just a PC. In *OSDI*, 2012.

[22] Y. Low, D. Bickson, J. Gonzalez, C. Guestrin, A. Kyrola, and J. M. Hellerstein. Distributed GraphLab: a framework for machine learning and data mining in the cloud. *VLDB Endow.*, 5(8):716–727, 2012.

[23] Y. Low, J. Gonzalez, A. Kyrola, D. Bickson, C. Guestrin, and J. M. Hellerstein. GraphLab: A New Parallel Framework for Machine Learning. In *Conf. on Uncertainty in Artificial Intelligence*, Catalina Island, California, 2010.

[24] G. Malewicz, M. H. Austern, A. J. Bik, J. C. Dehnert, I. Horn, N. Leiser, and G. Czajkowski. Pregel: a system for large-scale graph processing. In *SIGMOD*, pages 135–146, 2010.

[25] B. Panda, J. Herbach, S. Basu, and R. Bayardo. PLANET: massively parallel learning of tree ensembles with MapReduce. *VLDB Endowment*, 2(2):1426–1437, 2009.

[26] R. Power and J. Li. Piccolo: building fast, distributed programs with partitioned tables. In *OSDI*, pages 1–14, 2010.

[27] S. N. A. Project. Stanford large network dataset collection. http://snap.stanford.edu/data/.

[28] J. Pujol, V. Erramilli, G. Siganos, X. Yang, N. Laoutaris, P. Chhabra, and P. Rodriguez. The little engine (s) that could: scaling online social networks. In *ACM SIGCOMM*, pages 375–386, 2010.

[29] Z. Qian, X. Chen, N. Kang, M. Chen, Y. Yu, T. Moscibroda, and Z. Zhang. MadLINQ: large-scale distributed matrix computation for the cloud. In *EuroSys*, pages 197–210, 2012.

[30] S. Salihoglu and J. Widom. GPS: A Graph Processing System. http://infolab.stanford.edu/gps/, 2012.

[31] B. Shao, H. Wang, and Y. Li. The trinity graph engine. Technical Report 161291, Microsoft Research, 2012.

[32] L. G. Valiant. A bridging model for parallel computation. *Commun. ACM*, 33(8):103–111, Aug. 1990.

[33] S. Venkataraman, E. Bodzsar, I. Roy, A. AuYoung, and R. S. Schreiber. Presto: distributed machine learning and graph processing with sparse matrices. In *Proc. EuroSys*, pages 197–210. ACM, 2013.

[34] C. Wilson, B. Boe, A. Sala, K. P. Puttaswamy, and B. Y. Zhao. User interactions in social networks and their implications. In *EuroSys*, pages 205–218, 2009.

[35] J. Ye, J. Chow, J. Chen, and Z. Zheng. Stochastic gradient boosted distributed decision trees. In *ACM CIKM*, pages 2061–2064, 2009.

[36] Y. Zhou, D. Wilkinson, R. Schreiber, and R. Pan. Large-scale parallel collaborative filtering for the netflix prize. In *Int. Conf. on Algorithmic Aspects in Information and Management*, pages 337–348, 2008.

Seraph: an Efficient, Low-cost System for Concurrent Graph Processing

Jilong Xue, Zhi Yang, Zhi Qu, Shian Hou and Yafei Dai
Department of Computer Science, Peking University
Beijing, China
{xjl, yangzhi, quzhi, hsa, dyf}@net.pku.edu.cn

ABSTRACT

Graph processing systems have been widely used in enterprises like online social networks to process their daily jobs. With the fast growing of social applications, they have to efficiently handle massive concurrent jobs. However, due to the inherent design for single job, existing systems incur great inefficiency in memory use and fault tolerance. Motivated by this, in this paper we introduce Seraph, a graph processing system that enables efficient job-level parallelism. Seraph is designed based on a decoupled data model, which allows multiple concurrent jobs to share graph structure data in memory. Seraph adopts a copy-on-write semantic to isolate the graph mutation of concurrent jobs, and a lazy snapshot protocol to generate consistent graph snapshots for jobs submitted at different time. Moreover, Seraph adopts an incremental checkpoint/regeneration model which can tremendously reduce the overhead of checkpointing. We have implemented Seraph, and the evaluation results show that Seraph significantly outperforms popular systems (such as Giraph and Spark) in both memory usage and job completion time, when executing concurrent graph jobs.

Categories and Subject Descriptors

C.4 [**Computer Systems Organization**]: Performance of systems; H.3.4 [**Information Storage and Retrieval**]: Systems and Software—*Distributed systems*

Keywords

Graph processing; Concurrent jobs; Graph sharing; Fast recovery

1. INTRODUCTION

Due to the increasing need to process and analyze large volumes of graph-structured data (e.g., social networks and web graphs), there has been a significant recent interest in parallel frameworks for processing graphs, such as Pregel [19], GraphLab [18], Power-Graph [13], GPS [27], Giraph [11] and Grace [25]. These systems allow users to easily process large-scale graph data based on certain computation models (e.g., BSP [32] model).

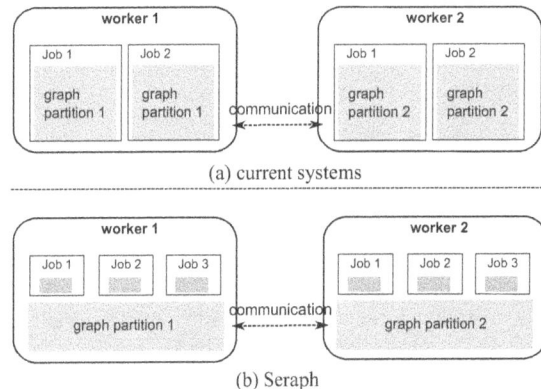

Figure 1: The manner of executing concurrent jobs for (a) existing graph systems and (b) Seraph

Recently, online social networks begin to leverage these graph systems to process their daily computation and analytics [28]. For example, Facebook [10] uses Apache Giraph [11] to process various graph algorithms across their many products, including typical algorithms such as label propagation, variants of Pagerank, k-means clustering, etc. With a large number of emerging applications running on the same graph platform of social networks, it easily generates jobs overlapping in time (i.e., concurrent jobs). Our measurements on a large Chinese social network's computing cluster confirm that more than 83.4% of time has at least two graph jobs executed concurrently.

Although existing systems can process single graph job efficiently, they incur high cost when handling multiple concurrent jobs. Specifically, existing systems do not allow multiple jobs to share the graph data in memory. In particular, these systems usually tightly combine graph structure and job-specific vertex value together. As a result, each individual job needs to maintain a separate graph data in memory, introducing inefficient use of memory, as illustrated in Figure 1(a). Moreover, to tolerate failures, multiple concurrent jobs have to periodically checkpoint the large volume of memory data into disk, which significantly incurs I/O bottleneck and delays the computation.

In this paper, we try to solve these problems through decoupling the data model and computing logics in current systems. First, through decoupling graph structure data and job-specific data, concurrent jobs can share one graph structure and thus greatly save the memory occupation. Second, through decoupling the computation into more specific processes, we only need to checkpoint a small amount of necessary data which can be used to recover the whole computation states.

Based on this decoupled model, we propose a new graph processing system, called Seraph, which can efficiently execute multiple concurrent graph jobs. Seraph enables multiple jobs to share the same graph structure data in memory, as illustrated in Figure 1(b). Each job running in Seraph only needs to maintain a small amount of job-specific data.

To maximize job-level parallelism, Seraph incorporates three new features: First, it adopts a "copy-on-write" semantic to isolate the graph mutations from concurrent jobs: once a job needs to modify the graph structure, Seraph copies the corresponding local region and applies the mutations, without affecting other jobs. Second, Seraph uses a *lazy snapshot protocol* to maintain the continuous graph updates and generates consistent snapshot for each new submitted job. Finally, Seraph implements an efficient fault tolerant mechanism, which uses *delta-graph checkpointing* and *state regeneration* to efficiently tolerate both job-level and worker-level failures.

We have implemented Seraph system in Java based on our design. Seraph adopts the master-slave architecture. Each Seraph instance can load a graph and execute one or more jobs concurrently on it. Graph mutation is allowed for each job during computation and system guarantees the isolation. If there is no job running, Seraph will enter hibernate mode to save memory occupation. In addition, to avoid the aggressive resource competition, Seraph implements a job scheduler to control the execution progress and message flow of each concurrent job.

We evaluate the overall performance of Seraph by comparing it with popular systems, including Giraph (graph-parallel system) and Spark (shared memory data-parallel system). Our experiments show that Seraph could reduce 67.1% memory usage and 58.1% average job execution time, as compared with Giraph. When failure occurs, the recovery of Seraph is more than 4× faster than Giraph. Compared with Spark, we shows that Seraph is nearly 6× faster than Spark when executing graph algorithms, and can reduce memory usage of Spark by 14×.

This paper is organized as follows. Section 2 describes the background and our observation on graph computation. In Section 3, we introduce the design of Seraph. The graph sharing and lightweight fault tolerance are introduced in Section 4 and Section 5 respectively. We describe implementation details in Section 6. Section 7 evaluates the performance of Seraph through comparing with Giraph and Spark. We then describe related work in Section 8 and conclude in Section 9.

2. BACKGROUND

In this section, we first introduce the practice usage of graph computing system in online social network, and then reveal the inefficiency of existing systems through measuring the real workload. Finally, we address the inherent inefficiency through abstracting the data model of current systems.

2.1 Graph Computation in Practice

Recently, several popular graph-parallel computation systems, such as Pregel [19], Giraph [11] and PowerGraph [13], have been widely used in the enterprises like online social networks (e.g., Facebook [10] and Renren [26]). Typically, these systems are deployed as an open platform in a company, and used to process large number of daily graph jobs across different products. These jobs include friend recommendation, advertisements, variants of Pagerank, spam detection, kinds of graph analysis, label propagation, clustering even some third-party developer's jobs [28].

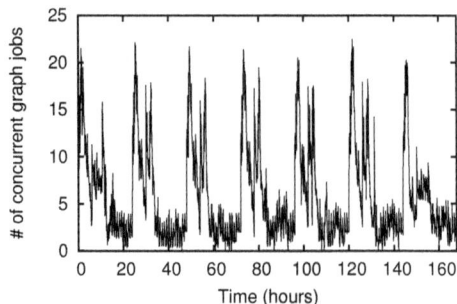

Figure 2: One week's workload of graph computation in real social network cluster

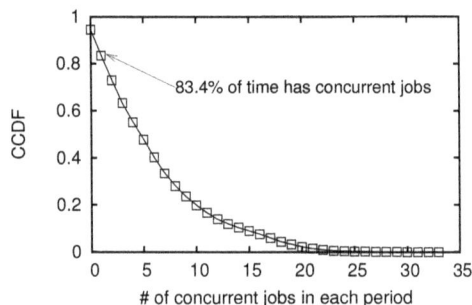

Figure 3: The distribution of graph jobs running on one social network's computing cluster

With increasing number of jobs running on the same platform of social networks, it easily generates jobs overlapping in time (i.e., concurrency). To demonstrate this scenario, we collect one month job execution logs from a large Chinese social network. Figure 2 depicts one week's workload (number of jobs at each time) of graph computation from Nov 1, 2013. The stable distribution shows that a significant number of jobs are executed concurrently every day. At peak time, there are more than 20 jobs submitted to the platform. We also depict the complementary cumulative distribution of the number of concurrent jobs in each time period (one second) in Figure 3. As it shows, more than 83.4% of time has at least two jobs executed concurrently. The average number of concurrent jobs is 8.7.

However, the existing graph processing systems are all designed for single job execution, which are much inefficient when processing multiple concurrent jobs. The inefficiencies mainly fall in two aspects: *inefficient use of memory* and *high cost of fault tolerance*.

Inefficient memory use: For most existing graph-parallel systems, one vital cost of job execution is to maintain the large graph data in main memory. Taking Giraph[1] as an example, Figure 4 shows the memory usage of Giraph job when running Pagerank algorithm on various graph datasets [1, 2]. From the figure we see that the graph data occupies majority of memory as compared with vertex values and messages (job-specific data), and its proportions are varying from 71% to 83% for different datasets. Due to the heavy memory cost of graph computation, it is hard to execute many concurrent graph jobs in a resource-limited cluster. For ex-

---

[1]Giraph is one of most popular open source graph computing system, which is currently used in Facebook.

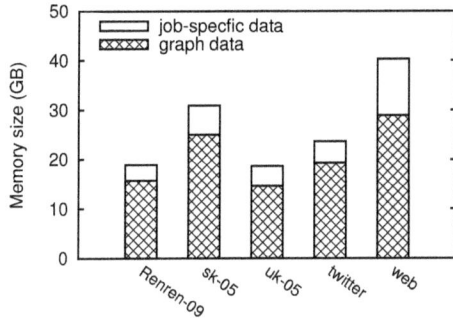

Figure 4: The memory usage of Giraph

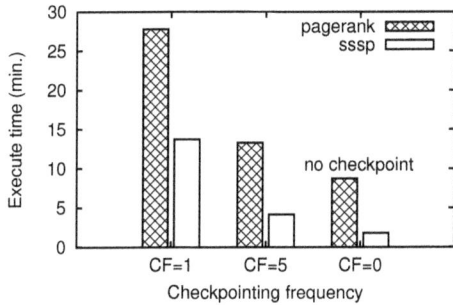

Figure 5: The latency incurred by checkpoint mechanism

ample, in our experiments, a powerful HPC cluster with 16 nodes (each with 64GB memory), could only support at most 4 concurrent Giraph jobs over a graph with 1 thousand million vertices.

Notice that almost all concurrent jobs are executed on same underlying graph. For example, most graph computations and analytics in Facebook are executed on a same friendship graph [28]. Thus, the graph structure data is duplicated in memory when running concurrent jobs. The memory usage can be reduced by allowing multiple parallel jobs to share graph data in memory. To do so, we need to decouple the graph structure data from the job-specific data and resolve conflicts when graph mutations occur. We will address the graph sharing functionality in Section 4.

High fault tolerance cost: The existing graph systems, such as Pregel, Giraph, GraphLab and PowerGraph, rely on checkpointing and rollback-recovery to achieve fault tolerance [19, 11, 18, 13]. When failures occur, program rollbacks to the latest checkpoint and continues the computation. Each checkpoint needs to store all the data required by computation in that step.

However, for existing graph systems, the computation in each superstep takes all the data (graph data and other computation states) as program input, leading to a high cost of checkpointing. First, the checkpoint size is very large. All the graph, vertex states and exchanging data should be saved in a persistent storage. In Giraph, running a single Pagerank job on a 100 gigabytes graph with checkpointing at each superstep, the total data saved in HDFS are more than 9 terabytes, which is really a heavy cost for real cluster.

Second, saving the large checkpoints involves a great executing latency. Figure 5 shows the execution time of running Pagerank and SSSP algorithm on a 25 million vertices graph with different checkpointing frequency (CF). As the figure shows, the total overhead of execution time is increased by 218.8% due to check-

pointing when CF=1, and 52.7% when CF=5 for Pagerank. Similar result is showed for SSSP. The heavy cost of checkpointing makes most users prefer to disable the fault tolerance mechanism.

In section 5, we will propose delta-graph checkpointing and state-regeneration mechanisms to address these checkpoint overheads.

2.2 Data Model of Graph Computation

To fundamentally address the inherent reason that cause the problems of existing systems, we abstract the data model of current graph computations. Although most of these systems use different computation models, e.g., BSP model for Pregel [19], and GAS model for PowerGraph [13], they are similar from the perspective of data management. Specifically, we find that existing systems are based on the same abstracted data model, as showed in Figure 6.

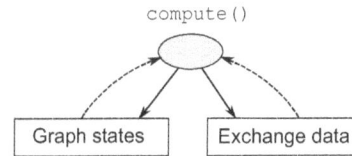

Figure 6: Data model of graph computation

In this model, the graph states are composed of two parts: graph structure and associated vertex values on the graph. The graph structure, simply denoted as *graph*, is made up of vertices and edges. The *values* are commonly associated with vertices. During the computation, there will be some exchanging data (e.g., *messages*) generated to assist the computation. For example, the exchanging data in Pregel is message data [19], and in GraphLab is replicas of vertices [18]. In this model, The computation is realized through executing user-defined program `compute()` on each vertex. In each superstep, the computation takes both the graph states and exchange data as input, and updates both of them during the execution. The computation of a graph algorithm continuously mutates the graph states until some termination condition is satisfied.

However, this tightly-coupled model inherently causes the inefficiency of existing systems when running concurrent jobs (the problems of memory inefficiency and high fault-tolerance cost). In this model, since the graph states combine graph structure and *job-specific* vertex value together, the system do not allow concurrent jobs (running on same graph) to share one common in-memory graph, leading to a high memory waste. Meanwhile, for fault tolerance, the system has to checkpoint a large amount of graph computation state, including graph structure, vertex state and the exchanging data. leading to a high checkpoint/recovery cost.

3. SERAPH DESIGN

To avoid the high memory usage and fault tolerance cost, we first present a novel fine-granularity data model to support graph computing. Based on this model, we then propose an efficient, low-cost graph computing system.

3.1 Decoupled Model

Essentially, the high cost of memory use and fault tolerance are both caused by the tightly-coupled model in Figure 6. As we have explained, the graph structure and vertex states are tightly-coupled, making it impossible to share the graph data over concurrent jobs. Moreover, the tightly coupled computing program requires the system to record all in-memory data, leading to a high checkpoint cost.

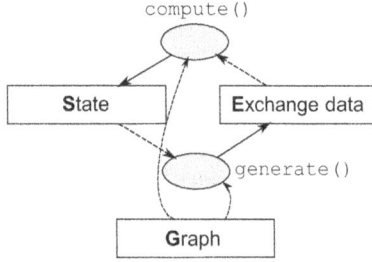

Figure 7: Data model of graph computation

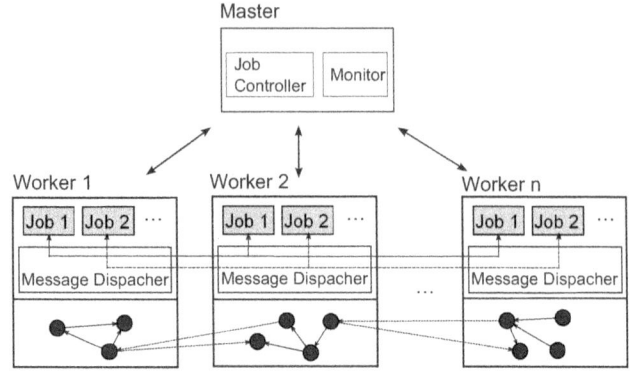

Figure 8: The system architecture of Seraph

To efficiently avoid these costs, we propose a novel fine granularity data model for the graph computation, called **GES** (Graph-Exchange-State) model. In GES model, a graph computation program is based on three types of data: **graph, exchanging information** and **state**. The graph **G** is commonly static data describing the graph structure and some inherent graph properties, such as edge weight. It can be expressed as a tuple of vertices set, edges set and optional weights, i.e., $\mathbf{G} = (V, E, W)$. The state data $\mathbb{S}$ is set of vertex values associated with each vertex, which are used to record the current state of a program. The exchanging data $\mathbb{E}$ is used to share the states among vertices.

Generally, a graph computation can be described as a series of transformations or updates between these three parts of data, as illustrated in Figure 7. The following functions shows the dependence between these data.

$$\mathbb{S} \leftarrow f_c(\mathbf{G}, \mathbb{E}) \qquad (1)$$

$$\mathbb{E} \leftarrow f_g(\mathbf{G}, \mathbb{S}) \qquad (2)$$

In each superstep, the function f_c takes the exchanging data $\mathbb{E}$ (messages) as input and compute the new state $\mathbb{S}$. And the function f_g takes the state $\mathbb{S}$ as input to generate exchanging data for next superstep. Taking the Pagerank algorithm as an example, the algorithm is executed through several iterations (supersteps). Within a superstep, each vertex first does a computation which takes received messages from other vertices as input and updates its own new value (**state**). Then based on the new value, generates and sends its impacts (**exchanging data**) to its outgoing neighbors. Based on GES model, the computation in each superstep can be described as,

$$s_i \leftarrow \alpha \sum m_{ji} + (1 - \alpha) / N \qquad (3)$$

$$m_{ij} \leftarrow s_i / |e_i|, \forall j \in e_i \qquad (4)$$

where s_i is the state of vertex i, m_{ij} is the message from vertex i to j and e_i is neighbor set of vertex i.

The GES model has two major advantages: First, it decouples data into the job-specific data (i.e., states and exchanging data) and static data (i.e., graph), thus enabling the job-level parallelism on a shared graph, i.e., multiple jobs jointly use one graph dataset in memory. This can greatly reduce the memory occupation due to the fact that the size of graph data is very large, as compared with job-specific data. In particular, suppose that an algorithm working on a graph with N_v vertices and N_e undirected edges, the total memory size of the *graph* structure is $O(N_v + 2N_e)$. The states data is associated with each vertex, so the total space for states data is $O(N_v)$. The worst case of the memory usage for exchanging data is that each vertex obtains all the state of their neighbors. In this case, the memory space for exchanging data is $O(N_e)$. As N_e

is usually much larger than N_v (i.e., $N_e \gg N_v$), we see that graph structure occupies at least $2/3$ of the total memory usage.

Second, the GES model decouples the computation program into two separated processes: *compute* and *generate*. With this decoupling, exchanging data in any superstep can be generated by state data in previous step according to the GES model. Thus, to recover a job in case of failures, we only need to checkpoint the small amount of *state* data, which makes the checkpoint very low-cost.

3.2 System Overview

To implement the GES model, we design *Seraph*, a graph computation system that can support parallel jobs running on a shared in-memory graph. Figure 8 shows the high-level architecture of a Seraph. A Seraph cluster includes a single master (with a backup master to tolerate failures) and several workers. The master controls the execution of multiple jobs, and each worker executes part of individual jobs.

The master is mainly responsible for controlling the execution of multiple jobs and monitoring the state of workers. Specifically, *job controller* receives job submissions and dispatches jobs to workers holding the corresponding data. It also controls the job progress, including startup, superstep coordination and termination. The master also checkpoints the states of each job for fault-tolerance.

Several workers execute jobs and maintains its portion of the graph in memory. To share graph among multiple jobs, Seraph implements a graph manager to decouple global graph structure data from job-specific data (e.g., vertex value), and only maintains one graph data in memory. The graph manager is also responsible for graph updating and snapshot maintaining. We shall detail these functions in the Section 4.

At startup, a worker registers with the master, and periodically sends a heartbeat to demonstrate its continued availability. When a job is dispatched to a worker, a new executor is created and invoked. The executor is a generic component that performs computation in a superstep. It loops through all vertices and call user defined external programs.

The computation on each vertex is simply separated into two sub functions: `compute()` to updates the new vertex value, and `generate()` to generate messages to neighbors for next superstep. Through this decoupling, the value and message in runtime memory can be generated separately. Based on this characterises, we design a lightweight fault tolerant mechanism. We detail the design of its key components in Section 5.

230

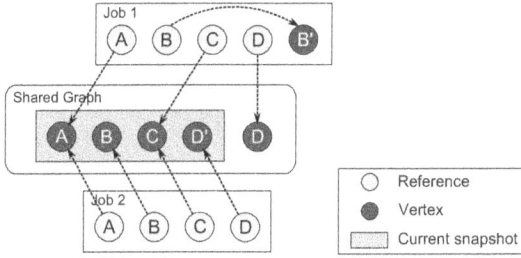

Figure 9: Illustration of graph mutation and graph update in Seraph

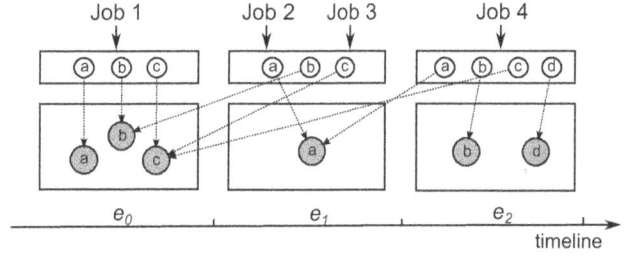

Figure 10: Illustration of lazy snapshot generation in Seraph

4. GRAPH SHARING

The unique feature of Seraph is that concurrent jobs could share graph structure data to avoid memory waste. Specifically, Seraph only stores and maintains one graph data in memory. Instead of executing on a separate graph, each individual of the concurrent jobs uses the same shared graph by creating a reference to it. Then each job creates its own job-specific data (vertex states and exchanging data) in local memory space.

To efficiently support graph sharing, we have to address some conflicts caused by the graph sharing. First, the local graph mutations must be isolated. Some graph algorithms may modify the graph structure during the computation (e.g., a K-core algorithm may delete some edges or vertices in each superstep). Without isolation, the mutations would interfere other jobs due to using a common graph data. Second, we should maintain a proper graph snapshot for each individual job according to its submission time. For example, the global updates of the underlying graph (e.g., the arrival of new vertices or edges) should be only visible to the jobs submitted later than the updates. In this section, we show how Seraph achieves these requirements.

4.1 Graph Mutation

To isolate the graph mutation for each job, Seraph adopts a "copy-on-write" semantic to isolate the local mutations of individual job. In particular, when the algorithm (i.e., a job) needs to modify the edge list of a vertex, it first creates a `delta graph` object in local space and copies the corresponding edge list to it. Then the mutations are applied on that local copy. Meanwhile, the job changes its reference of this vertex to the one in local graph. The original vertex (and edge list) is still used by other jobs. This method only copies mutated vertices for the corresponding job, thus incurring little memory overhead. After job got finished, these copied vertices in local memory will be released.

Figure 9 illustrates the example of graph mutation. Job 1 needs to modify vertex B's edges (the modification may be add or delete operation). It first copies the vertex B to local memory space, noted as vertex B', then modifies it locally and change the reference of B to B'. After this, the later mutations on this vertex will be directly applied on the local data. Since jobs only mutate little part of graph during the computation, the copy-on-write is efficient way with little extra replication cost. Note that this kind of mutation is not applied on the shared graph, so it is transparent to other jobs.

4.2 Graph Update

Different from graph mutation caused by running jobs, graph update are caused by the changing of underlying graph (e.g., the new arrival of edges and vertics). Seraph guarantees that a new submitted job can see all previous changes on the shared graph. Formally,

when an update is committed at time t, it should be visible (or invisible) to jobs submitted after (or before) t.

Seraph achieves the above requirement through a snapshot mechanism. Graph managers at individual workers collaboratively maintain graph snapshot. When an update arrives, Seraph incrementally creates a new snapshot as the up-to-date snapshot. When a job is submitted, it refers to the latest snapshot of graph. The mechanism of generating a consistent snapshot will be addressed in following subsection.

Figure 9 illustrates the update/snapshot process. When job 1 is submitted, it is executed on the graph snapshot $\{A, B, C, D\}$. During job 1's execution, graph has been updated on vertex D. Since job 1 still uses vertex D, Seraph copies a new vertex D' from D and applies the update. Hence, a new snapshot $\{A, B, C\} \cup D'$ is formed. Later, job 2 is submitted, and it just refers to this new snapshot. Note that when job 1 finished (the number of reference on D will be zero), the vertex D will be released by graph manager.

4.3 Consistent Snapshot

A consistent snapshot of graph is critical for the computation in Seraph. Notice that the shared graph in Seraph is partitioned and maintained by multiple workers. The update on any portion of graph may incur inconsistence for the graph. An algorithm running on inconsistent graph would incur incorrect results or even runtime errors, e.g., sending messages to non-existed vertices or counting deleted edges.

However, existing methods for generating consistence are too costly for Seraph. First, to implement the consistence in a distributed system, it needs to assign a global timestamp [5, 17] or sequence number [6] on each update unit (e.g., edge in graph system). However, assigning a timestamp on each edge will double the memory occupation of graph data. Moreover, it needs a complex distributed algorithm to generate snapshot, such as Chandy-Lamport algorithm [4]. In fact, the traditional mechanism provides a consistence at any moment, which is unnecessary in our system. Seraph only needs a consistent snapshot of graph when a new job is submitted. This relaxed requirement enables us to design more low-cost snapshot protocol.

Therefore, we present a *lazy snapshot protocol*, where a global consistent snapshot of graph is generated only when a new job is submitted. Our idea is packaging the updates in batch, so as to save the memory of storing timestamps. In Seraph, each update is sequentially appended into the master node. When a new job is submitted, the master will notify each worker's graph manager to step into a new epoch, and package all local buffered updates into a transaction and dispatch each update to corresponding workers, as illustrated in Figure 10. Here, we define that all the updated vertices in epoch n compose a *delta-graph* Δ_n. A transaction is updated through a two phases commit protocol. In the

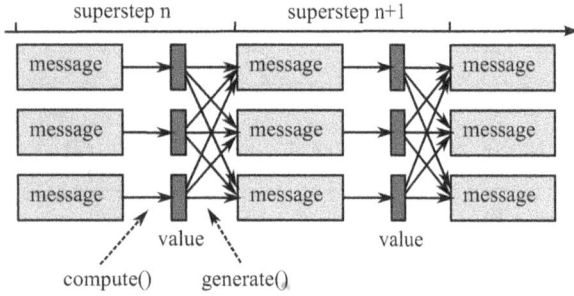

Figure 11: The data transformation and computation model of Seraph

first phase, master dispatchs updates to workers and receives acknowledgements from all workers. The worker node just caches but not applies the updates. In second phase, master sends confirm messages to each worker and worker nodes apply updates to graph. When a transaction is successfully submitted, all the pending jobs can be dispatched to workers and begin their computation.

5. LIGHTWEIGHT FAULT TOLERANCE

Current graph processing systems rely on checkpoint/rollback-recovery to achieve fault tolerance [19, 11, 18, 13]. For example, in Pregel or Giraph, user can optionally choose to set checkpoint at the end of each superstep, and the program will roll back to the latest checkpoint when failures occur. However, existing graph computation systems need to checkpoint all the values, messages and graph data into persistent storage, incurring a heavy checkpoint cost and long checkpoint delay.

In contrast, Seraph is able to make lightweight fault tolerance based on the decoupled data model. Through sharing the graph, Seraph only needs to keep one graph copy to tolerate failures of multi-jobs. Also, we propose a delta-checkpointing mechanism to checkpoint the graph incrementally. Further, through decoupling computation model, Seraph can recover messages from previous values, and thus prune the checkpointing traffic caused by the messages. In the following, we will introduce all of these designs in details.

5.1 Computation model

Seraph's computation model is derived from the Pregel. In general, the graph computation consists of several supersteps, in each of which a vertex can collect messages and execute user-defined functions. In Pregel, all these actions are coupled in a user implemented function: `compute()`. This vertex-centric approach can express the behavior of a broad set of graph algorithms [35].

However, according to the GES model in section 3.1, a better way to express the behavior of graph computation is separating the `compute()` function into two individual functions: `compute()` and `generate()`. Here, the new `compute` interface is to compute new values based on received messages from last superstep, and `generate` interface is to generate the messages for the next superstep according to the new values. Figure 11 shows the data transformation and computation model of Seraph. To show how our model can easily express typical graph algorithms, Figure 12 illustrates the "compute-generate" implementation of Pagerank, SSSP and Wcc algorithms.

After this separation, Seraph can use the `generate` function to regenerate message data based on the value data of last step.

Specifically, for Pregel model, if superstep i fails, the system recoveries through rerunning the `compute` function:

$$V_i \leftarrow compute(M_i, V_{i-1})$$

where M_i and V_{i-1} are the messages and values checkpointed in last superstep. However, by adding the `generate` interface, the recovery process changes as:

$$M_i \leftarrow generate(V_{i-1})$$
$$V_i \leftarrow compute(M_i, V_{i-1})$$

Thus, we only need to checkpoint a small amount of value data (e.g., V_{i-1}) at each step to reduce checkpoint cost, since the size of message data is often much larger than that of value data.

5.2 Delta graph checkpointing

After checkpointing values for each job, Seraph can recover the job-specific data (including message and value data), so as to tolerate any job-level failures. Now, we begin to look at how Seraph recovers the shared graph data when a worker fails. Notice that each job is running on a different snapshot of graph. When failures occur, Seraph need to recover the corresponding graph snapshot for each job.

Recall that once a new job is submitted at epoch e_i, there will be a *Delta-graph* generated, denoted as Δ_i (see Figure 10). Graph snapshot in epoch e_n can be generated though the graph snapshot in epoch e_{n-1} and delta-graph in e_n:

$$G_n = G_{n-1} \oplus \Delta_n \qquad (5)$$

where the operation "$\oplus$" has the following definition: for graph or delta-graph G_1 and G_2,

$$S_{G_1 \oplus G_2} = (S_{G_1} \setminus S_{G_2}) \cup S_{G_2} \qquad (6)$$

where S_G means the set of vertices in graph G.

Thus, when the underlying graph is changed in epoch e_n, Seraph only checkpoint the delta graph Δ_n. In Seraph, the worker will checkpoint the delta-graph at the beginning of each epoch. When failures occur, Seraph can easily reconstruct the corresponding snapshot for each individual job through each delta graph. The delta-graph is quite small compared with the whole graph data, thus the incremental checkpointing significantly reduce the checkpoint cost.

5.3 Failure Recovery

The failures in Seraph are classed into two kinds: job failure and worker failure. For job failure, since the graph is decoupled with job, only the values and messages associated with the job will be lost. Seraph will restart the job on each worker, and roll back to last superstep of failure step. By running `generate()` function on that superstep to regenerate the lost message, Seraph can quickly recover from failure.

When a worker fails, the graph partition on that worker will be lost. Seraph assigns the graph partition to a standby worker and construct underlying graph according to the checkpointed delta-graphs, as well as the specific snapshot for each running job. After that, the graph jobs restart and continue the computation from the failed step.

6. SERAPH IMPLEMENTATION

We have fully implemented Seraph in Java. The communication between the workers in Seraph is based on Apache MINA [20]. Like Giraph, the underlying persistent storage is using Hadoop

Pagerank	SSSP	Wcc

```
//compute
compute(Msgs):
  sum = 0;
  for (m:Msgs)
    sum += m;
  setValue(sum*0.85 + 0.15);

//generate message
generate(value):
  sendMsgToNbrs(value/#nbrs);
```

```
//compute
compute(Msgs):
  for (m:Msgs)
    minValue = Min(minValue, m);
  setValue(minValue);

//generate message
generate(value):
  if (changed(value))
    sendMsgToNbrs(value + 1);
```

```
//compute
compute(Msgs):
  for (m:Msgs)
    maxValue = Max(maxValue, m);
  setValue(value);

//generate message
generate(value):
  if (changed(value))
    sendMsgToNbrs(value);
```

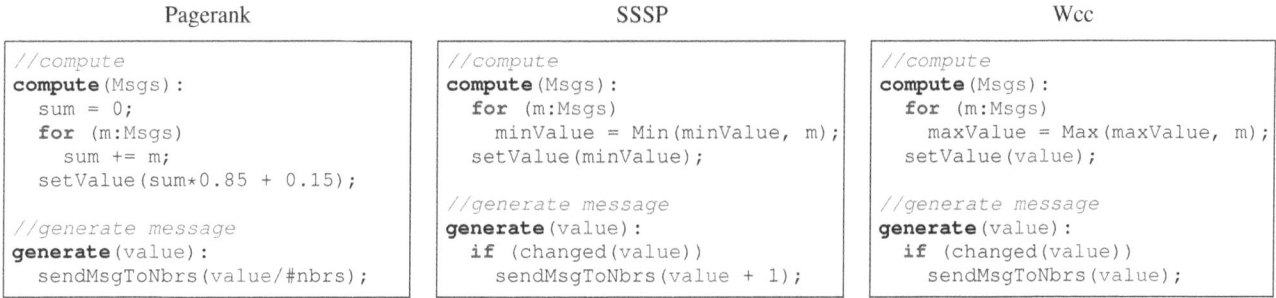

Figure 12: The example of implementations of graph algorithms based on compute-generate model

HDFS [30], and all the checkpointing data are stored in HDFS. Seraph only loads a single copy of graph into main memory to support multiple concurrent jobs. In the following, we give the specific implementation details of graph management and job scheduling.

6.1 Graph Management

Graph sharing: We have introduced the design of graph sharing in section 4, now we explain how Seraph implements this mechanism through decoupling graph and job-specific data.

In existing systems (e.g., Giraph), a graph in memory is stored as a set of `Vertex` objects. Each `Vertex` object includes vertex value, message queue and an adjacency list storing neighbor edges. Notice that the edge list is unique to all jobs and could be very large (e.g., Facebook users have an average number of 190 neighbors [31]). Thus, Seraph extracts edge list from `Vertex` object and forms a new global `graph` set containing each vertex's edge list. After this change, each job only needs to make a reference to this unique graph object to get the graph structure. The reference pointing to the edge list of each vertex, which is far smaller than a whole edge list.

Hibernate mode: Different from existing systems, Seraph is an online running platform due to supporting the updates on graph. However, in the case of no jobs running, the memory used for storing the graph is wasted. To overcome this problem, we implement a hibernate mode for Seraph.

Once the system is idle for a period (e.g., longer than a certain threshold), Seraph allows all the workers to hibernate. Each worker will make a checkpoint of the full graph (instead of delta-graph). This graph will be considered as the new initial graph G_0, and all the old G_0 and previous delta graphs on HDFS will be deleted. After that, the memory storing graph will be reclaimed. In the hibernate mode, all graph updates will be cached on master node. When a new job arrives, master will wake up all the workers and apply the cached updates to the graph maintained by them. Note that the checkpoint is serialized in disk, so the waking up process is much faster than reloading the raw graph data from HDFS.

6.2 Job Scheduling

Parallel job execution can improve the system throughput due to full resource utilization (e.g., network and CPU). However, aggressive resource competition might increases job execution time. To avoid this, Seraph implements a *job scheduler* to control job execution. The scheduler assigns each job a priority based on its submission order, e.g., job submitted earlier has a higher priority. The

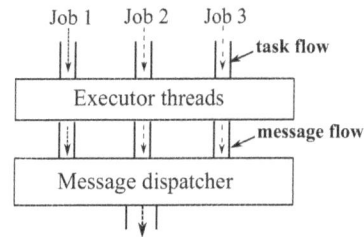

Figure 13: Two level flow control model for job scheduling in Seraph

higher priority job gains resource access firstly, whereas the lower priority job gains access once the resource is not used by the higher one. Hence, Seraph can guarantee that early jobs are finished as quickly as possible, meanwhile, job submitted later can exploit the idle resource. The job scheduler is implemented through performing flow control at two levels: controlling job execution and controlling the message dispatch, as shown in Figure 13.

Execution controlling. In Seraph, job's execution is through performing each vertex's `compute()` and `generate()` operations. We package a bunch of vertices' operations of a job and the job ID into a `task` package, which composes the minimum execution unit in Seraph. Thus, each job is executed through submitting their tasks to executing threads pool. The submission rate of each job is customized based on the priority. Currently, the flow rate r of each job is set as inverse ratio to its priority level p, which is $r = 1/(p - p_h + 1)$, where the p_h is the highest priority among current running jobs.

Message dispatcher. Message dispatcher uses a priority queue to buffer messages from all jobs. In each step, Seraph fetches messages from the head of queue (i.e., the message of highest priority job), and send them to the corresponding worker. Meanwhile, Seraph assigns each job a different threshold to control the max buffer size it can use, which is similarly setting as the inverse ratio to its priority. When a job achieves the maximum buffer size, its incoming flow path will be blocked and executor will be paused. This avoids the low-priority jobs to aggressively compete for bandwidth with high-priority jobs.

7. EXPERIMENTS AND EVALUATIONS

Our experiments deploy Seraph on a cluster with 16 machines. Each machine has 64GB of memory and 2.6GHz AMD Opteron

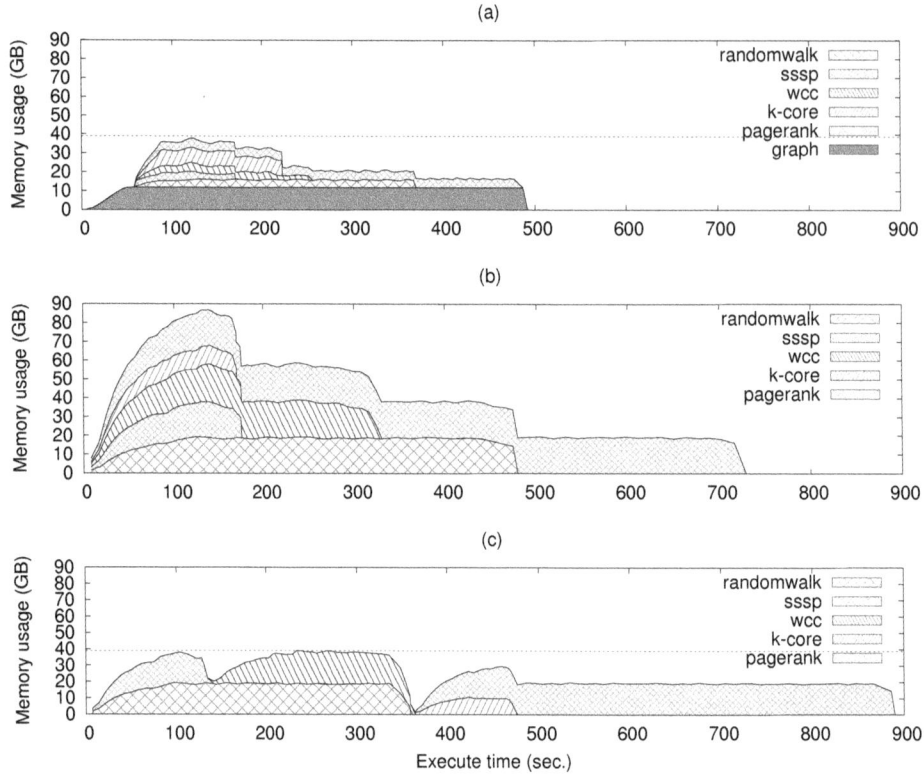

Figure 14: The memory usage for 5 parallel graph jobs on: (a) Seraph with maximum memory resource of 40GB, (b) Giraph with unlimited memory (heap usage is 87GB) and (c) Giraph with same limitation of maximum 40GB memory

4180 Processor (12 cores). All these machines are connected by a gigabit switch. We use one machine as the master and other 15 machines as workers.

We take some popular graph algorithms as benchmarks to e-valuate Seraph's performance, including Pagerank, random walk, Weakly connected component (Wcc), Single source shortest path and K-core. All these algorithms have different characteristics in resource usage. For example, PageRank is network-intensive, where-as random walk is computation-intensive. Among them, K-core is the only one which mutates graph structure during the computation. In our following experiments, we set PageRank's max iter-ation steps to 20. For random walk, we set 100 walkers for each vertex and the length of walk is 10 steps. For k-core, we set $k = 5$.

We run the benchmarks on a graph from history snapshot of Ren-ren network, one of the largest online social network of China. The snapshot graph totally contains more than 25 million vertices (user-s) and 1.4 billion relational edges.

7.1 Comparison with Giraph

We first examine the performance of Seraph through comparing it with other graph-parallel computing systems. We choose the lat-est version of Apache Giraph (version 1.0.0), one of the most popu-lar open-source Pregel implementation, as an comparison baseline. In this section, we first compare their computational efficiency (in-cluding memory usage and execution time), and then compare their fault-tolerance performance.

7.1.1 Computational Efficiency

To compare their computational efficiency for concurrent jobs, we first run all the five different jobs (random walk, SSSP, WCC, K-core and PageRank) simultaneously. Note that we only need to run a single Seraph instance to execute these jobs due to its graph-sharing feature. In contrast, to use Giraph executing jobs in a par-allel manner, each job needs to initiate a Giraph instance.

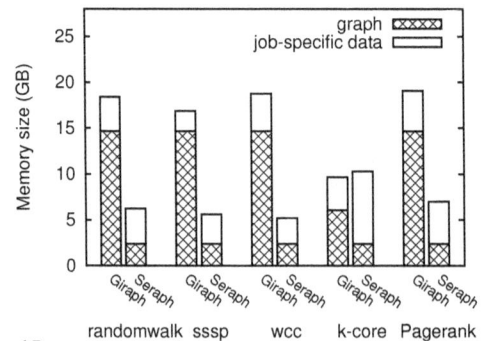

Figure 15: The memory usage for individual jobs in Giraph and Seraph

Memory usage: Figure 14(a) and 14(b) show the memory usage during the execution of Seraph and Giraph, respectively. Seraph first loads the underlying graph, which occupies 11.86GB memo-ry. Then, Seraph executes multiple jobs in parallel over the shared graph. The peak memory usage of Seraph during the execution is

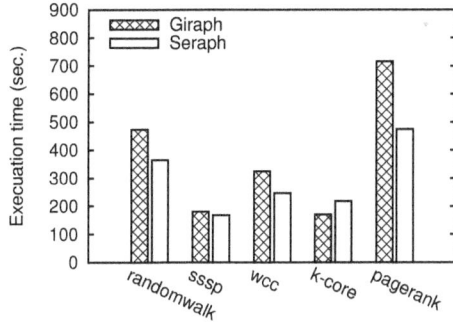

Figure 16: The execution time for concurrent jobs with sufficient memory, the peak memory usage of Seraph and Giraph are 37.8GB and 87GB, respectively

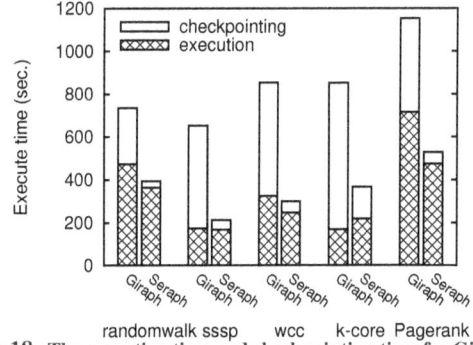

Figure 18: The execution time and checkpointing time for Giraph and Seraph

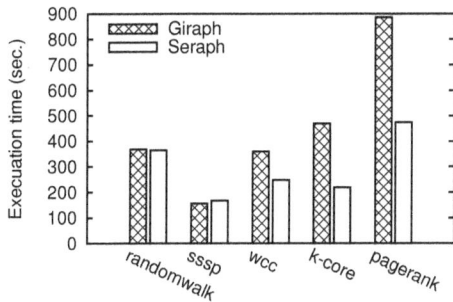

Figure 17: The comparison of execution time for each job executed with limited memory, both set maximum memory as 40GB

37.8GB. Note that the K-core algorithm occupies more job-specific memory than others, because its graph mutation operations incur copy-on-write data in its local memory space.

For Giraph, each job has to work on a separate graph in the memory, so the total memory usage is much larger than that of Seraph. From Figure 14(b) we see that the total memory rapidly increases with the number of parallel jobs, and its peak memory occupation is about 87GB. Notice that K-core occupies less memory than other jobs, which is different from its behavior in Seraph. This is because that the algorithm can mutate its separate graph (e.g., deletes some vertices) directly.

Figure 15 shows the memory occupation for each individual jobs, which includes memory occupation of graph data and job-specific data (e.g., states and messages). Since the graph data is shared among five jobs in Seraph, we consider that each job has 1/5 graph memory. On average, Seraph reduce about 67.1% memory usage than Giraph for each job except K-core. K-core in Seraph incurs little more memory usage than Giraph due to the part of copy-and-mutated graph in its local memory space.

Execution time: We first compare the execution time of Giraph and Seraph with both running 5 jobs in parallel, i.e., the case in Figure 14(a) and (b). In this case, Seraph can reduces the memory usage of Giraph by half, but still outperforms Giraph in terms of execution time, as shown in Figure 16, Although Seraph increases the execution time of K-core due to copy-on-write operations, Seraph reduces the overall execution time of five jobs by 28% than Giraph. The reduction is mainly brought by the job scheduling mechanism which avoids aggressive resource competition.

Next, we limit the peak memory usage of Giraph equal to that of Seraph (e.g., 40GB). With this limitation, Giraph can only execute two jobs in parallel, with others pending until the resource is available. Figure 14(c) shows the memory usage of Giraph in this case. We see that the wcc, K-core and pagerank job needs to be pending for a period, increasing the total execution time.

Given the same memory limitation, Figure 17 shows the execution time of individual jobs executed in Giraph and Seraph, respectively. Note that the execution time includes the job pending time. We see that Seraph executes jobs much faster than Giraph. On average, it reduces the individual job completion time by 24.9%, as compared with Giraph. In term of the total completion time of five jobs, Seraph brings a reduction of 46.4% as compared with Giraph.

7.1.2 Fault Tolerance

We now compare Seraph with Girpah in the fault-tolerant performance. Seraph checkpoints the vertex values at the end of each superstep. Due to heavy checkpoint cost, Giraph requires to set the checkpoint frequency (i.e., the number of supersteps for every checkpoints), which is a tradeoff between the execution delay and recovery time. Frequent checkpoint reduces the recovery time, but will delay the execution due to checkpoint cost. Based on the experience of [7], we set the checkpoint frequency as 5 for Giraph.

Checkpointing cost: Making checkpoint will delay the job's execution due to writing state data into disk. We evaluate this cost of checkpointing for both Giraph and Seraph. In our experiments, Giraph makes checkpoint every 5 supersteps, whereas Seraph makes checkpoint every superstep. Figure 18 shows the total completion time (including execution time and checkpointing time) of each job for both Giraph and Seraph. Overall, the total job completion time of Seraph is reduced by 58.1% than that of Giraph. As shown in the figure, the checkpointing in Giraph accounts for a significant part of total job completion time, e.g., 57.8% for the five jobs on average. In contrast, checkpointing time in Seraph occupy only 19.3% on average, even though Seraph checkpoints every step.

Note that the K-core in Seraph spends more time on the checkpointing than other jobs because Seraph uses the *delta-graph checkpointing* for K-core due to it mutates graph in each superstep. To evaluate the overhead of delta-graph checkpointing, we collect each superstep's checkpoint size in HDFS for both Giraph and Seraph. For Giraph, each checkpoint needs to save the whole graph data and other job-specific data. However, Seraph's *delta-graph checkpointing* only needs to checkpoint the changed part of graph in each superstep. Figure 19 depicts the cumulative checkpoint size of K-core in each superstep. According to the figure, each superstep's

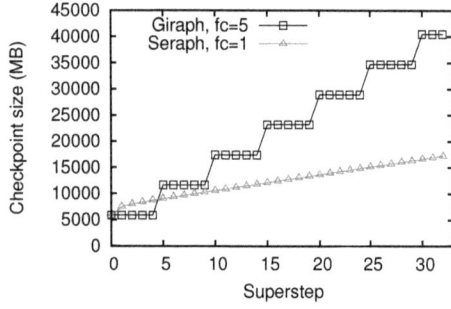

Figure 19: Cumulative checkpointing size of K-core job, Giraph checkpoints every 5 superstep and Serpah checkpoints at every supersteps

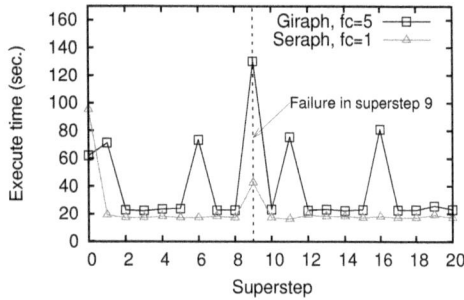

Figure 20: Illustration of checkpointing time and recovery time running Pagerank jobs, Giraph checkpoints every 5 superstep and Serpah checkpoints at every supersteps

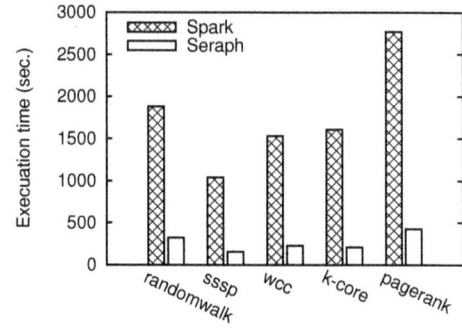

Figure 21: The comparison of execution time of graph algorithms for Spark and Seraph

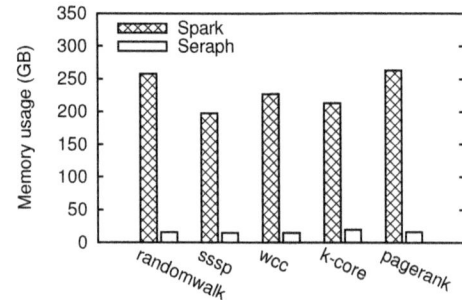

Figure 22: The comparison of memory usage of graph algorithms for Spark and Seraph

checkpoint size of Giraph is about 5.8GB. However, Seraph averagely just checkpoints 522MB in each superstep. After the job finished, the size of total checkpoint of Giraph is 2.35× that of Seraph.

Recovery time: We intentionally generate a failure to a running job (e.g., pagerank), and test the recovery time for both Giraph and Seraph. For fairness, we let failure occurs in superstep 9, which is the average number between two checkpoint (superstep 6 and 11) for Giraph. Figure 20 illustrates the checkpointing time and recovery time when runing Pagerank jobs on Giraph and Searph, respectively. Since Seraph checkpoints every superstep, it can recover from the last superstep. For Giraph, it checkpoints every 5 steps, thus has to roll back to the latest checkpoint in superstep 6. From figure we see that the recovery time for Seraph is reduced about 76.4% compared with Giraph.

7.2 Comparison with Spark

In this section, we compare the performance of Seraph with popular in-memory data-parallel system, Spark [36]. Spark is a data-parallel system which shares in-memory data through RDD (Resilient Distributed Dataset) and tolerate failures using lineage. Spark can also compute graph algorithms. Spark puts all data in memory and naturally separates each of dataset using RDD, and the RDD can be shared during the computation.

We have implemented all the five graph algorithms in Spark. For each implementation, we use three separated RDDs to repersent the graph, vertex states and exchanging data. To achieve the best performance of Spark, we partition each RDD through the operation `partitionBy()` to ensure the data with same key can be co-located in same worker. The graph RDD in each job is set as `persist()` to share for each iterations, except for K-core algorithm. Note that K-core needs to mutate the graph in each iteration.

In our experiments, we use the latest version of Spark (0.8.1) which is deployed on the same cluster as Seraph. We let Spark use all the cores of our cluster (the total number of cores is 192).

Execution time: First, we compare the execution time of Spark and Seraph. Figure 21 shows the execution time of each job. We see that Seraph significantly outperforms Spark. Seraph is more than 6× faster than Spark in terms of average execution time. To understand why Spark is slow, we analyze the time consumption of each operation in Spark. We find the most time-consuming operation in each jobs is *join* of two RDDs. Take the example of Pagerank execution, Spark separates the graph (*links*) and values (*ranks*) to share the graph for later iteration's use. However, in each iteration, it needs to join this two datasets before computation. In contrast, Seraph separates these data but with an explicit connection using reference, which can avoid the overhead of joining.

Memory usage: Spark is an in-memory system which put all datasets (RDD) in main memory by default. To test the memory usage for Spark, we give Spark sufficient memory (each worker with 40GB) when executes each job, and we monitor the usage of memory on each worker using Ganglia[2].

Figure 22 depicts the average memory usage comparison for Spark and Seraph. As the figure shows, Spark uses an order of magnitude larger memory than Seraph. On average, the memory usage

---
[2]Ganglia is a distributed monitoring system for high-performance computing systems

of Spark is more than $14\times$ larger than that of Seraph. The major reason of large memory occupation in Spark is that Spark will allocate new RDD for each mutation, since RDD is immutable. However, most graph algorithms usually just mutates a little part of the whole dataset, such as the value RDDs in SSSP and Wcc algorithm, and the graph RDD in k-core algorithm. Thus, there are many duplication in Spark. However, Seraph only mutate the changed data which avoids the overhead.

8. RELATED WORK

Seraph is based on a primitive idea in our previous workshop paper [37], with significantly redesigning the system based on decoupled data model and adding lightweight fault tolerance, lazy snapshot protocol and other optimizations. This section summarizes the recent studies on the efforts of processing large graph.

Graph-parallel computing systems: Recently, several projects have been developed for processing large graphs on parallel machines or multi-cores, such as Pregel [19], Giraph [11], GPS [27], GraphLab [18] and PowerGraph [13]. These systems are based on BSP model [32] to implement a vertex-centric computation. There are other systems try to optimize the graph computation. Sedge [35] aims to minimize the inter-machine communication by graph partitioning, and Mizan [16] implements dynamic load balancing mechanism to solve the straggler problem. Other type of graph computation systems targets multi-core environment, such as Grace [25] and Galois [21]. However, all of them suffer the problems of memory inefficient and high fault tolerant cost when executing multiple jobs in a parallel manner, as we explained in Section 2.

Graph database and online graph processing system: Some graph storage and management systems are proposed to manage and support efficient queries on the continuously updated graph structure data. Neo4j [12] is a highly scalable, robust (fully ACID) native graph database, and HyperGraphDB [15] is another graph database based on a powerful knowledge management formalism known as directed hypergraphs. They both only support some simple graph traversals and relational-style queries. Due to they focus on the transaction maintaining, they are not suitable for batched graph computations.

Another class of graph systems is online graph processing systems, which can manage continuous incoming graph, support online querying and execute offline graph processing on it. Trinity [29] is a graph engine that supports both online query processing and offline analytic on large graphs. However, Trinity cannot address the problems of concurrent job execution, such as inefficient memory use, and mutation conflicts on a shared graph.

Another online graph system is Kineograph [6], which takes a stream of incoming data to construct a continuously changing graph. It also supports some graph-mining algorithms to extract timely insights from the fast-changing graph structure. Similar with Seraph, they both enable to capture the changing graph through constructing new snapshot continuously. However, Kineograph focuses on reducing the computation latency through incremental computing, without considering the case of concurrent jobs.

In-memory data parallel computation systems: A bunch of in-memory data parallel computing system are proposed to process large scale data. Spark [36] is a general-purpose and fault-tolerant data-flow abstraction which focuses on the in-memory data sharing through RDD and the fault tolerant using lineage. Same with Seraph, Spark implements very low cost fault tolerance through recomputing on history dataset. However, the dataset in Spark (RD-

D) is inherently immutable, which incurs many inefficiency when computing graph algorithms. For example, SSSP only mutates a little part of vertex values in most supersteps, however Spark has to create a new RDD in each step, leading to a significant duplication. This problem also exist in GraphX [34], which is another graph computing framework built on the top of Spark engine. Furthermore, both Spark and GraphX can only share RDD or RDG for the operations in inner job, and do not allow them to share the underlying graph structure data at the job level.

There are also some systems allow memory-sharing. Piccolo [24] allows computation running on different machines to share distributed, mutable data via a key-value table interface. However, it has not isolated the job mutations when multiple graph jobs sharing the graph. Piccolo uses Chandy-Lamport (CL) distributed snapshot algorithm [4] to perform checkpointing. However, the cost is high due to checkpointing all in-memory data for graph jobs. Other class of in-memory data sharing systems includes Twister [9] and HaLoop [3], which are based on iterative MapReduce [8]. What's more, Presto [33] is a distributed system that extends R, which can shares sparse structured data (e.g., sparse matrices) to multiple cores. However, these frameworks only perform data sharing inner the jobs.

Other memory shared systems, such as distributed shared memory (DSM) systems [22], in-memory key-value stores like RAM-Cloud [23], and in-memory file system Tacyon [14], can share in-memory data to different jobs. However, compared with Seraph, they don't provide high-level programming model or specific interface for graph computation. For example, Tacyon provides the operations on files like other disk-based file systems. In addition, all these systems implement fault tolerance through checkpointing all in-memory data, which is highly expensive. In contrast, Seraph combines checkpointing and re-computation to implement a very low cost fault tolerance.

9. CONCLUSION AND FUTURE WORK

This paper introduces Seraph, a large scale graph processing system that can support parallel jobs running on a shared graph. The basic idea of Seraph is decoupling the data model of current graph computation, which allows multiple concurrent jobs to share graph structure data in memory. Seraph adopts a copy-on-write semantic to isolate the graph mutation of concurrent jobs, and a lazy snapshot protocol to generate consistent graph snapshots for jobs submitted at different time. Moreover, Seraph adopts an incremental checkpoint/regeneration model which can tremendously reduce the overhead of checkpointing.

In the future, we shall study the load balance mechanism given the multiple jobs sharing the same graph, i.e., how to migrate data by taking into account the different loads of jobs on each worker. We also attempt to make Seraph a real-time graph processing platform, where the system keeps up with continuous updates on the graph, and performs incremental graph computation for multiple jobs running on the platform.

Acknowledgement

We would like to thank the anonymous reviewers for their comments. This work was supported by the National High Technology Research and Development Program ("863" Program) of China (Grant No.2013AA013203), the National Basic Research Program of China (Grant No. 2011CB302305), and the State Key Program of National Natural Science of China (Grant No. 61232004). Zhi Yang is the corresponding author of this paper.

10. REFERENCES

[1] P. Boldi, M. Rosa, M. Santini, and S. Vigna. Layered label propagation: A multiresolution coordinate-free ordering for compressing social networks. In *Proceedings of the 20th international conference on World Wide Web*. ACM Press, 2011.

[2] P. Boldi and S. Vigna. The WebGraph framework I: Compression techniques. In *WWW 2004*, pages 595–601, Manhattan, USA, 2004. ACM Press.

[3] Y. Bu, B. Howe, M. Balazinska, and M. D. Ernst. Haloop: Efficient iterative data processing on large clusters. *Proc. VLDB Endow.*, 3(1-2):285–296, Sept. 2010.

[4] K. M. Chandy and L. Lamport. Distributed snapshots: Determining global states of distributed systems. *ACM Trans. Comput. Syst.*, 3(1):63–75, Feb. 1985.

[5] F. Chang, J. Dean, S. Ghemawat, W. C. Hsieh, D. A. Wallach, M. Burrows, T. Chandra, A. Fikes, and R. E. Gruber. Bigtable: A distributed storage system for structured data. In *OSDI '06*, 2006.

[6] R. Cheng, J. Hong, A. Kyrola, Y. Miao, X. Weng, M. Wu, F. Yang, L. Zhou, F. Zhao, and E. Chen. Kineograph: Taking the pulse of a fast-changing and connected world. In *EuroSys '12*, 2012.

[7] J. T. Daly. A higher order estimate of the optimum checkpoint interval for restart dumps. *Future Gener. Comput. Syst.*, 22(3):303–312, Feb. 2006.

[8] J. Dean and S. Ghemawat. Mapreduce: Simplified data processing on large clusters. *Commun. ACM*, 51(1):107–113, Jan. 2008.

[9] J. Ekanayake, H. Li, B. Zhang, T. Gunarathne, S.-H. Bae, J. Qiu, and G. Fox. Twister: A runtime for iterative mapreduce. In *Proceedings of the 19th ACM International Symposium on High Performance Distributed Computing*, HPDC '10, 2010.

[10] http://www.facebook.com.

[11] http://giraph.apache.org/.

[12] http://neo4j.org.

[13] J. E. Gonzalez, Y. Low, H. Gu, D. Bickson, and C. Guestrin. Powergraph: Distributed graph-parallel computation on natural graphs. In *OSDI '12*, October 2012.

[14] L. Haoyuan, G. Ali, Z. Matei, B. Eric, S. Scott, and I. Stoica. Tachyon: Memory throughput i/o for cluster computing frameworks. In *7th Workshop on Large-Scale Distributed Systems and Middleware*, LADIS '13, 2013.

[15] B. Iordanov. Hypergraphdb: A generalized graph database. In *Proceedings of the 2010 International Conference on Web-age Information Management*, WAIM '10, 2010.

[16] Z. Khayyat, K. Awara, A. Alonazi, H. Jamjoom, D. Williams, and P. Kalnis. Mizan: A system for dynamic load balancing in large-scale graph processing. In *EuroSys '13*, 2013.

[17] A. Lakshman and P. Malik. Cassandra: A decentralized structured storage system. *SIGOPS Oper. Syst. Rev.*, 44(2):35–40, Apr. 2010.

[18] Y. Low, J. Gonzalez, A. Kyrola, D. Bickson, C. Guestrin, and J. M. Hellerstein. Graphlab: A new parallel framework for machine learning. In *Conference on Uncertainty in Artificial Intelligence (UAI)*, July 2010.

[19] G. Malewicz, M. H. Austern, A. J. Bik, J. C. Dehnert, I. Horn, N. Leiser, and G. Czajkowski. Pregel: A system for large-scale graph processing. In *SIGMOD '10*, 2010.

[20] http://mina.apache.org/.

[21] D. Nguyen, A. Lenharth, and K. Pingali. A lightweight infrastructure for graph analytics. In *Proceedings of ACM Symposium on Operating Systems Principles*, SOSP '13, 2013.

[22] B. Nitzberg and V. Lo. Distributed shared memory: A survey of issues and algorithms. *Computer*, 24(8):52–60, Aug. 1991.

[23] J. Ousterhout, P. Agrawal, D. Erickson, C. Kozyrakis, J. Leverich, D. Mazières, S. Mitra, A. Narayanan, G. Parulkar, M. Rosenblum, S. M. Rumble, E. Stratmann, and R. Stutsman. The case for ramclouds: Scalable high-performance storage entirely in dram. *SIGOPS Oper. Syst. Rev.*, 43(4):92–105, Jan. 2010.

[24] R. Power and J. Li. Piccolo: Building fast, distributed programs with partitioned tables. In *Proceedings of the 9th USENIX Conference on Operating Systems Design and Implementation*, OSDI '10, 2010.

[25] V. Prabhakaran, M. Wu, X. Weng, F. McSherry, L. Zhou, and M. Haridasan. Managing large graphs on multi-cores with graph awareness. In *Proceedings of the 2012 USENIX Conference on Annual Technical Conference*, USENIX ATC '12, 2012.

[26] http://www.renren.com.

[27] S. Salihoglu and J. Widom. Gps: A graph processing system. In *Scientific and Statistical Database Management*. Stanford InfoLab, July 2013.

[28] http://www.facebook.com/notes/facebook-engineering/scaling-apache-giraph-to-a-trillion-edges/10151617006153920.

[29] B. Shao, H. Wang, and Y. Li. Trinity: A distributed graph engine on a memory cloud. In *Proceedings of the 2013 ACM SIGMOD International Conference on Management of Data*, SIGMOD '13, 2013.

[30] K. Shvachko, H. Kuang, S. Radia, and R. Chansler. The hadoop distributed file system. In *Proceedings of the 2010 IEEE 26th Symposium on Mass Storage Systems and Technologies*, MSST '10, 2010.

[31] J. Ugander, B. Karrer, L. Backstrom, and C. Marlow. The anatomy of the facebook social graph. *CoRR*, abs/1111.4503, 2011.

[32] L. G. Valiant. A bridging model for parallel computation. *Commun. ACM*, 33(8):103–111, Aug. 1990.

[33] S. Venkataraman, E. Bodzsar, I. Roy, A. AuYoung, and R. S. Schreiber. Presto: Distributed machine learning and graph processing with sparse matrices. In *EuroSys '13*, 2013.

[34] R. S. Xin, J. E. Gonzalez, M. J. Franklin, and I. Stoica. Graphx: A resilient distributed graph system on spark. In *First International Workshop on Graph Data Management Experiences and Systems*, GRADES '13, 2013.

[35] S. Yang, X. Yan, B. Zong, and A. Khan. Towards effective partition management for large graphs. In *Proceedings of the 2012 ACM SIGMOD International Conference on Management of Data*, SIGMOD '12, 2012.

[36] M. Zaharia, M. Chowdhury, T. Das, A. Dave, J. Ma, M. McCauley, M. J. Franklin, S. Shenker, and I. Stoica. Resilient distributed datasets: A fault-tolerant abstraction for in-memory cluster computing. In *NSDI '12*, 2012.

[37] Y. Zhi, X. Jilong, Q. Zhi, H. Shian, and D. Yafei. Seraph: An efficient system for parallel processing on a shared graph. In *7th Workshop on Large-Scale Distributed Systems and Middleware*, LADIS '13, 2013.

CuSha: Vertex-Centric Graph Processing on GPUs

Farzad Khorasani   Keval Vora   Rajiv Gupta   Laxmi N. Bhuyan

Computer Science and Engineering Department
University of California Riverside, CA, USA
{fkhor001, kvora001, gupta, bhuyan}@cs.ucr.edu

ABSTRACT

Vertex-centric graph processing is employed by many popular algorithms (e.g., PageRank) due to its simplicity and efficient use of asynchronous parallelism. The high compute power provided by SIMT architecture presents an opportunity for accelerating these algorithms using GPUs. Prior works of graph processing on a GPU employ *Compressed Sparse Row* (CSR) form for its space-efficiency; however, CSR suffers from irregular memory accesses and GPU underutilization that limit its performance. In this paper, we present **CuSha**, a CUDA-based graph processing framework that overcomes the above obstacle via use of two novel graph representations: *G-Shards* and *Concatenated Windows* (CW). *G-Shards* uses a concept recently introduced for non-GPU systems that organizes a graph into autonomous sets of ordered edges called *shards*. CuSha's mapping of GPU hardware resources on to shards allows fully coalesced memory accesses. CW is a novel representation that enhances the use of shards to achieve higher GPU utilization for processing *sparse graphs*. Finally, CuSha fully utilizes the GPU power by processing multiple shards in parallel on GPU's streaming multiprocessors. For ease of programming, CuSha allows the user to define the vertex-centric computation and plug it into its framework for parallel processing of large graphs. Our experiments show that CuSha provides significant speedups over the state-of-the-art CSR-based virtual warp-centric method for processing graphs on GPUs.

Categories and Subject Descriptors

D.1.3 [**Programming Techniques**]: Concurrent Programming—*Parallel Programming*

General Terms

Algorithms, Performance

Keywords

GPU, Graph Representation, G-Shards, Concatenated Windows, Coalesced Memory Accesses

1. INTRODUCTION

The need for efficient large scale graph processing has grown due to the importance of applications involving graph mining and graph analytics. However, using GPUs for efficient graph processing remains a challenging open problem. Even though GPUs provide a massive amount of parallelism with the potential to outperform CPUs, the SIMD architecture demands repetitive processing patterns on regular data which is contrary to the irregular nature of graphs. This leads to the problems of irregular memory accesses and underutilization of GPUs; thus limiting the performance of graph algorithms on GPUs.

Existing graph processing techniques [10, 12, 21] primarily rely on the Compressed Sparse Row (CSR) representation of graphs because CSR consumes minimal storage space. However, accesses involving a node's neighbors lead to poor locality causing large amounts of random input-dependent memory references, popularly known as *non-coalesced accesses*. Also, these techniques are inherently fraught with GPU underutilization caused by workload imbalance resulting from mapping of irregular graphs to the GPU's symmetric hardware architecture.

In this paper we present **CuSha**[1], a framework for processing graphs on GPUs, that overcomes the drawbacks associated with the CSR representation. We recognize and explore the potential of a recently introduced representation for efficient disk based graph processing, known as *shards* [14]. Shards distribute graph data in a manner that places edges and vertices required by a subset of computation contiguously in memory. *G-Shards* adapts the shard based representation to efficiently process graphs on GPUs. In G-Shards each shard becomes a workload for a GPU thread block and multiple thread blocks are processed in parallel. Within each block, entries of a shard (representing edges) are processed in parallel by the threads. By mapping shards to blocks in this manner, we leverage the parallelism in the computation involving both vertices and edges. Even though G-Shards provides better locality, it is sensitive to the nature of input graphs. For large sparse graphs – large real world graphs are often sparse – the workloads assigned to warps inside a block become too small causing threads within the block to remain idle leading to GPU underutilization. To efficiently process sparse graphs, we propose a modification of G-Shards called *Concatenated Windows* (CW). CW representation concatenates multiple computation windows from shards so that GPU threads are highly utilized.

---

[1]Available at *http://farkhor.github.io/CuSha*.

We have developed a CUDA based prototype of the *CuSha* graph processing framework that internally makes use of G-Shards and CW representations. CuSha relies on an iterative vertex-centric model where a given compute function is iteratively applied to each vertex in the graph until a convergence condition is met. This allows developers to easily program graph applications using CuSha – programmer provides simple processing functions which deal with a vertex and its neighbors and the framework automatically parallelizes the computation over the entire input graph. As opposed to the Bulk Synchronous Parallel (BSP) model [26], CuSha provides asynchronous execution that lets updated vertex values to be visible during the same iteration; hence enabling faster convergence for iterative graph algorithms.

The key contributions of this work are as follows:

- We recognize the potential of shards and introduce an effective mapping of shards to various GPU subcomponents via the *G-Shards* representation. On average, our approach improves memory load and store efficiency by nearly 26% and 52% respectively.

- We propose *Concatenated Windows*, an extension built upon G-Shards to leverage better locality. On average, for large sparse graphs, CW improves GPU utilization by 57%.

- We implemented *CuSha*, a vertex-centric framework that internally uses G-Shards and Concatenated Windows to represent graphs. CuSha allows non-expert developers to quickly implement graph algorithms on GPUs without worrying about the inner details related to parallelization and synchronization.

- We demonstrate that *CuSha* outperforms state-of-the-art warp-centric algorithm [12] across wide range of benchmarks and large real world input graphs. For *PageRank*, average speedup of 7.21x is observed across the input graphs.

The rest of the paper is organized as follows. Section 2 overviews and evaluates state-of-the-art CSR-based virtual warp-centric method using several graph applications and large real world graphs. Section 3 presents the graph representations we proposed (G-Shards and Concatenated Windows) to overcome drawbacks of CSR. Section 4 presents details of the CuSha framework including the iterative execution model and the easy to use programming interface. Experimental evaluation is presented in Section 5. Sections 6 and 7 present related work and conclusion.

2. MOTIVATION: LIMITATIONS OF CSR

Representing graphs in memory to efficiently process them on GPUs has been a challenging task. Consider examples of some real world graphs shown in Table 1 whose degree distribution is shown in Figure 1. As we can see, these graphs are usually sparse and their sizes are large involving processing over millions of vertices and edges. The latter makes it infeasible to store the graph in the space inefficient *adjacency matrix* representation. Hence, prior graph processing approaches [22, 8, 4] primarily rely on the *Compressed Sparse Row* (CSR) representation because of its compact nature. For any given vertex, the CSR representation allows fast access to its incoming/outgoing edges along with the addresses of source/destination vertices at the other end of these edges. The representation mainly consists of 4 arrays:

Graph	Edges	Vertices
LiveJournal [17]	68 993 773	4 847 571
Pokec [25]	30 622 564	1 632 803
HiggsTwitter [7]	14 855 875	456 631
RoadNetCA [17]	5 533 214	1 971 281
WebGoogle [17]	5 105 039	916 428
Amazon0312 [16]	3 200 440	400 727

Table 1: Real-world graphs used in the experiments.

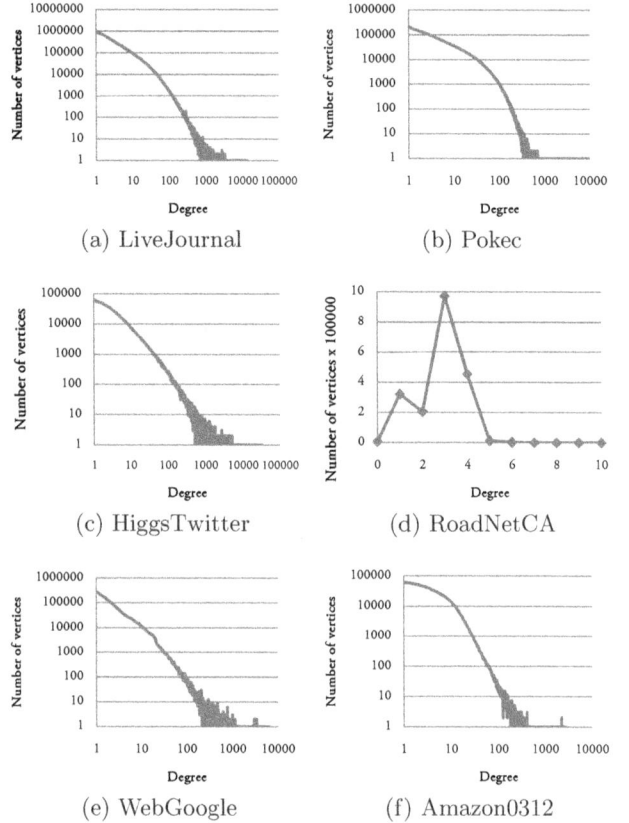

(a) LiveJournal   (b) Pokec

(c) HiggsTwitter   (d) RoadNetCA

(e) WebGoogle   (f) Amazon0312

Figure 1: Degree distribution for graph vertices.

- *VertexValues*: $VertexValues[i]$ $(0 \le i < n)$ represents the value of vertex v_i.

- *SrcIndxs*: $SrcIndxs[i]$ $(0 \le i < m)$ represents for edge e_i, the index of the source vertex in *VertexValues*. The incoming edges for a given vertex are stored in consecutive locations of this array.

- *InEdgeIdxs*: $InEdgeIdxs[n] = m$. $InEdgeIdxs[i]$ $(0 \le i < n)$ represents the starting index of a sub-array E_i of *SrcIndxs*. The end of this sub-array E_i can be determined by the entry at $i + 1$. E_i combined with *SrcIndxs* represents the incoming edges for node n_i.

- *EdgeValues*: $EdgeValues[i]$ $(0 \le i < m)$ represents the value of the edge e_i.

The neighborhood of vertex n_i can be determined by looking at locations of *VertexValues* which are represented by the sub-array starting at $SrcIndxs[InEdgeIndxs[i]]$ and ending at $SrcIndxs[InEdgeIndxs[i + 1]]$ and the edge weights can be determined by the sub-array of *EdgeValues* starting at $InEdgeIndxs[i]$ and ending at $InEdgeIndxs[i+1]$. Figure 2

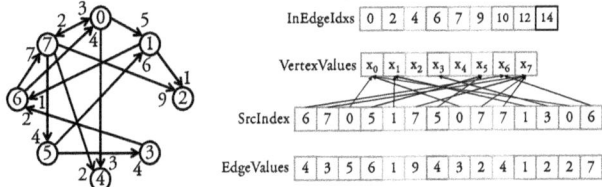

(a) Example graph. (b) CSR representation of the graph.

Figure 2: An example graph and its CSR representation.

Application Name	Global Memory Accesses	Warp Execution
Breadth-First-Search (BFS)	12.8%-15.8%	27.8%-38.5%
Single Source Shortest Path (SSSP)	14.0%-19.6%	29.7%-39.4%
PageRank (PR)[23]	10.4%-14.0%	25.3%-38.0%
Connected Components (CC)	12.7%-20.6%	29.9%-35.5%
Single Source Widest Path (SSWP)	14.5%-20.0%	29.7%-38.4%
Neural Network (NN)[3]	13.5%-17.8%	28.2%-37.4%
Heat Simulation (HS)	14.5%-18.1%	27.6%-36.3%
Circuit Simulation (CS)	12.0%-18.8%	28.4%-35.5%

Table 2: CSR-based Virtual Warp-Centric method [12] for graphs in Table 1: Minimum and maximum efficiency of global memory accesses and warp execution across all iterations between all graphs.

shows an example of a graph and its CSR representation using its incoming edges. As we can see, the neighborhood of vertex 2 (shown in green) is represented by *VertexValues*[1] and *VertexValues*[7] and the sub-array *EdgeValues*[4:5].

To process graphs on GPUs, Virtual Warp-Centric technique [12] has been shown to perform better than other techniques like [10]. Here, the physical warp is broken into 2, 4, 8 or 16 smaller virtual warps to control the trade-off between GPU underutilization and path divergence. Processing is done iteratively such that each iteration is performed by a separate GPU kernel call. In each iteration, a virtual warp handles the computation of a set of vertices. For each vertex, threads within the virtual warp process the vertex neighbors in parallel; each of its incoming edges is read and processed by a separate thread in the virtual warp. Then, parallel reduction technique [11] is used to calculate the new vertex value. Even though Virtual Warp-Centric method achieves faster graph processing compared to other techniques, its performance is limited by two major phenomena: high *non-coalesced memory accesses*; and high *GPU underutilization & intra-warp path divergence*. We elaborate upon these drawbacks next.

Non-Coalesced Accesses: As discussed, *SrcIndxs*[i] and *SrcIndxs*[i + 1] represent non-consecutive indices in *VertexValues* array. Hence, parallel reading of these values by threads in a virtual warp leads to random non-coalesced memory accesses requiring multiple inefficient memory transactions. Note that a major portion of graph processing is reading these vertex structures over and over again, making the problem very significant. Table 2 shows the average efficiency of memory accesses for different applications. Global memory access efficiency essentially tells how well coalesced global accesses are. Such low percentages of efficiency indicates that a great number of accesses were fulfilled using greater than minimal number of transactions due to poor locality of data of interest.

Underutilization & Intra-warp Divergence: Graph processing is highly sensitive to the degrees of vertices in the input graph. Processing of a low-degree vertex causes threads within the virtual warp to remain idle, leading to GPU underutilization. If we select a smaller virtual warp size to decrease underutilization, different amounts of computation load for threads inside the physical warp cause intra-warp path divergence. Figure 1 shows that real world graphs have a mix of low and high degree vertices. Table 2 shows that the warp execution efficiency is quite low for eight graph applications on different input graphs. High intra-warp divergence and GPU underutilization limit warp execution efficiency; thus, degrading the overall performance of the GPU kernel.

In conclusion, even though CSR representation is a popular choice because of its space-efficiency, high frequency of non-coalesced memory accesses because of poor locality and path divergence because of variable degree distribution of real graphs, significantly limit its performance while processing graphs on GPUs. In addition, the user is always trapped in a trade-off between intra-warp path divergence and GPU underutilization which has a different best configuration for different graphs. This motivates the need to explore novel graph representations that are GPU friendly and allow faster processing.

3. CUSHA GRAPH REPRESENTATIONS

In this section we discuss two graph representations that result in improved coalescence in memory accesses and high GPU utilization and hence achieve higher performance.

3.1 G-Shards

Representing a graph with shards has been shown to improve I/O performance for disk based graph processing on a shared memory system [14]. Since shards allow contiguous placement of the graph data required by a subset of computations, G-Shards uses the shard concept to secure benefits from coalesced accesses.

G-Shards presents a graph G as a set of shards where each shard is an ordered list of incoming edges and each edge $e = (u, v)$ in the shard is represented by a 4-tuple:

- *SrcIndex*: Index of the source vertex u
- *SrcValue*: Content of source vertex u
- *EdgeValue*: Content or weight of the edge e
- *DestIndex*: Index of the destination vertex v

The set of shards used to represent a graph G exhibit the following properties:

- *Partitioned*: V is partitioned into disjoint sets of vertices and each set is represented by a shard such that it stores all the edges whose destination is in that set.
- *Ordered*: The edges in a shard are listed based on increasing order of their *SrcIndex*.

Figure 3(a) shows G-Shards representation for the graph shown in Figure 2(a). We divide the vertex-set into two groups so that *Shard-0* has the list of edges whose destination is between 0 to 3 and *Shard-1* has the list of edges whose

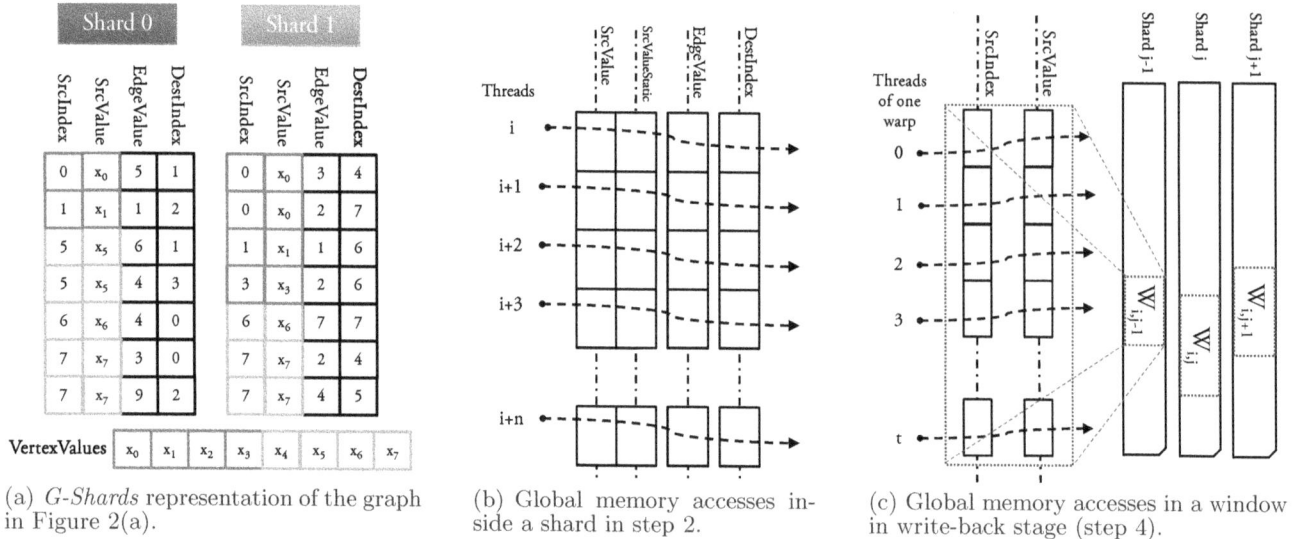

(a) *G-Shards* representation of the graph in Figure 2(a).

(b) Global memory accesses inside a shard in step 2.

(c) Global memory accesses in a window in write-back stage (step 4).

Figure 3: G-Shards representation providing coalesced memory accesses.

destination is between 4 to 7. Note that within *Shard-0* (and *Shard-1*), the edges are sorted based on *SrcIndex*.

To facilitate efficient processing of graphs on GPU using shards, G-Shards also maintains a separate array named *VertexValues* which allows quick access to values of vertices. Throughout the computation. *VertexValues[i]* represents the most updated value of vertex v_i.

Each shard is processed by a block in the GPU in 4 steps. In step 1, the threads fetch the updated vertex values from the *VertexValues* array to the shared memory of the block. Consecutive threads of the block read consecutive elements of *VertexValues* array; hence load requests coalesce into minimum number of transactions. In step 2, using the fetched values, block threads process edges inside the shard in parallel. Figure 3(b) shows consecutive threads of the block read consecutive shard entries residing in global memory thus providing coalesced global memory loads. In step 3, the threads write back the newly computed values to the *VertexValues* array. This step is done in a similar manner as step 1 except that reads are replaced by writes. Thus, global memory stores in this step, similar to global loads in step 1, are satisfied by minimum number of write transactions in memory controller. Step 4 (write-back stage) performs the remaining task which is to propagate computed results to other shards *SrvValue* array. To have coalesced global memory accesses in write-back stage as well, we assign each warp in the block to update necessary SrvValue elements in one shard. Because of aforementioned *Ordered* property of shards, elements in one shard that need to be read and written by another shard are arranged contiguously. Figure 3(c) shows consecutive threads inside a warp read consecutive *SrcIndex* elements inside another shard and write to consecutive *SrcValue* elements; therefore memory accesses are coalesced.

Thus, we observe that shard processing by threads of a block on GPU involves fully coalesced global memory reads and writes during all steps. Accesses to *VertexValues* in steps 1 and 3, reading shard elements in step 2, and updating regions of other shards in step 4 all become coalesced.

Each shard region whose elements need to be accessed and updated together by another shard is called a computation window. A computation window W_{ij}, is the set of entries in shard j that are involved during processing of shard i such that, each edge in W_{ij} has *SrcIndex* in the range of vertex indices associated with shard i. This means that the source vertices of all the edges in W_{ij} belong to the vertex-range a to b if shard i represents edges whose destination vertices belong to the same range a to b. As an example, different colors for entries in Figure 3(a) distinguish different computation windows; the windows W_{0j} are represented in red (first two elements of shard-0 and first four elements of shard-1) and windows W_{1j} are represented in green for $0 \leq j < 2$. Intuitively, for a constant k, if number of shards is p, the collection of edges in windows W_{kj}, $0 \leq j < p$, completely represents the sub-graph induced over the subset of vertices associated with shard k.

3.2 Concatenated Windows (CW)

G-Shards representation on GPU provides coalesced global memory accesses to neighbor's contents which was not achievable by CSR. However, the performance can be limited by various characteristics of input graphs. First, imbalanced shard sizes can cause inter-block divergence. We found that this effect is insignificant because of the abundance of shards to be processed that keeps the Streaming Multiprocessors busy. Second, unbalanced window sizes can cause intra-block/inter-warp divergence; however, due to similar reason, we conclude that its impact is insignificant too. Finally, sparse graphs lead to small window sizes which cause GPU underutilization. This is mainly because most of the threads within the warp are idle when entries for the computation window are being processed by other threads. This makes G-Shards representation on GPUs sensitive to window sizes; in particular, smaller window sizes lead to inefficient write-back of updated values in the windows.

Next we show that the window size is mainly determined by the size of the input graph, its sparsity, and the number of vertices assigned to shards. Let us consider a graph $G = (V, E)$ to be represented by $|S|$ shards. The average shard size (the number of edges in the shard) is $\frac{|E|}{|S|}$. Since each shard has at most $|S|$ windows (one for each shard), the average window size becomes $\frac{|E|}{|S|^2}$. Assuming that a shard

242

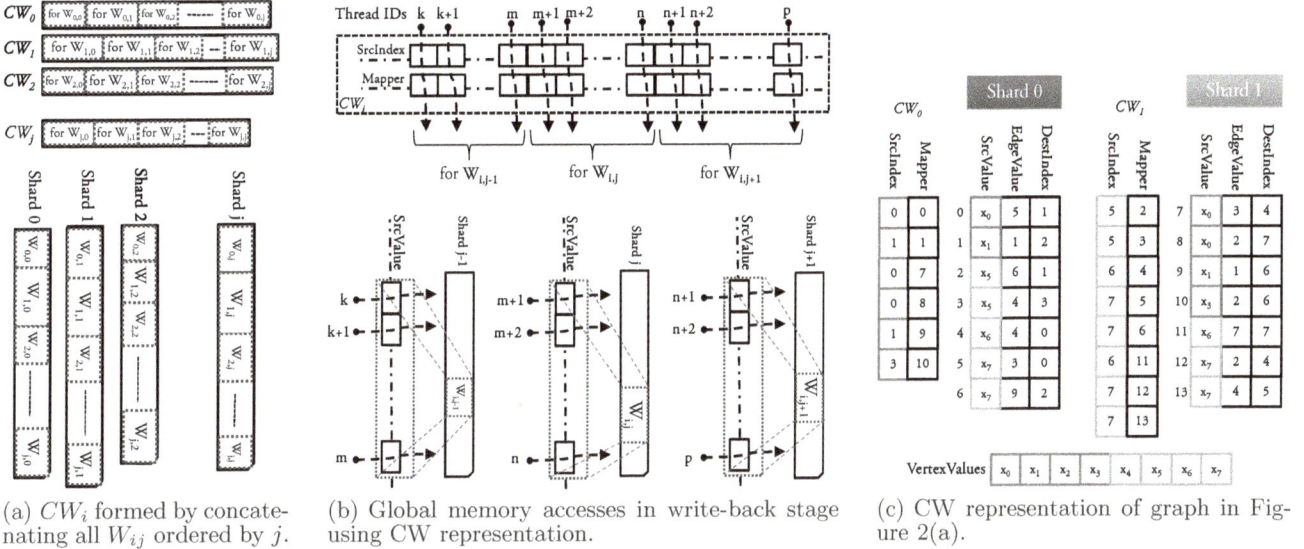

(a) CW_i formed by concatenating all W_{ij} ordered by j.

(b) Global memory accesses in write-back stage using CW representation.

(c) CW representation of graph in Figure 2(a).

Figure 4: Concatenated Windows Representation and its Avoidance of GPU underutilization in presence of small windows.

is assigned at most $|N|$ vertices, $|S| = \lceil \frac{|V|}{|N|} \rceil$. Hence, the average window size is approximately $\frac{|E||N|^2}{|V|^2}$. Thus, the windows become smaller as the graph becomes sparser. Also, the quadratic term in the denominator indicates that the windows rapidly become smaller as the number of vertices in the graph increases.

We develop the *Concatenated Windows* representation to address the above issue. To avoid GPU underutilization induced by large sparse graphs, CW collocates computation windows. For a given shard i, a Concatenated Window CW_i is defined as a list of *SrcIndex* elements of all computation windows W_{ij}, ordered by j, as shown in Figure 4(a). Here, we retain the original representation of shards, but separate out the *SrcIndex* entries to order them differently. *SrcIndex* entries for shard i in CW representation can be created by concatenating *SrcIndex* in all W_{ij} in G-Shards representation. Hence, a directed graph is represented as a set of shards, each of them associated with a separate *SrcIndex* array. Each shard is an ordered list of incoming edges where each edge is now represented by a 3-tuple: *SrcValue*, *EdgeValue*, and *DestIndex*. The set of shards is *Partitioned* and *Ordered* as described in the previous section. Note that by separating out *SrcIndex* array from the rest of the shard, we break the association between *SrcIndex* and *SrcValue* entries which is required to write-back the updated values. Therefore, to facilitate fast access of *SrcValue* entries using *SrcIndex* entries, we use an additional *Mapper* array.

Processing graphs using Concatenated Windows, similar to G-Shards representation, takes 4 steps with a difference in 4th step (write-back stage). As Figure 4(b) shows, a thread is assigned to every entry of *SrcIndex*. Using the entries in *SrcIndex* and *Mapper* arrays, the thread updates corresponding *SrcValue* entries in the shard. By concatenating small windows to form a larger set, consecutive threads within the block continuously process consecutive entries, thus improving GPU utilization for large sparse graphs.

Figure 4(c) shows the Concatenated Windows representation for the graph shown in Figure 2(a). As we can see, the *SrcIndex* columns are separately ordered compared to the rest of the shards. There are six entries in *SrcIndex*

(shown in red) associated with *Shard-0* representing values from CW_0. The first two entries come from W_{00} and the rest come from W_{01}. The eight entries in *SrcIndex* (shown in green) are associated with *Shard-1* and represent values from CW_1. The first five come from W_{10} and the rest come from W_{11}.

By retaining the basic representation of G-Shards, we leverage the locality of data required by each computation set. By changing the ordering of the *SrcIndex* column using Concatenated Windows, we benefit from higher utilization of threads in warps, thus achieving best of both worlds.

4. CUSHA FRAMEWORK

In this section we first describe how CuSha executes iterative parallel graph algorithms. Then we show that CuSha makes various applications easy to program.

Iterative parallel graph processing in CuSha. The parallel execution framework of CuSha implements iterative parallel graph processing where each iteration performs three phases: *gather/read*, *update/compute* and *scatter/write*. CuSha's computational model is largely based on the *read-compute-write* iterative processing mechanism where the *compute* phase is further split into two phases.

Figure 5 shows the pseudo-code for iterative processing. The host continuously launches new GPU kernels until the algorithm converges to a stable solution. At the end of each iteration, the host and the device implicitly synchronize using a *cudaMemcpy* that copies *is_converged* back to CPU-side (line 29). After each iteration, the CPU determines whether or not the next iteration should be performed by launching another GPU kernel.

Each shard is completely processed by one GPU block. For each shard, a *values_updated* flag resides in the shared memory and indicates whether or not the values were updated. It is initially set to false (line 5) by one of the threads in the block. Appropriate *Vertex*, *Edge* and *StaticVertex* structures are initialized where the *StaticVertex* structure refers to properties of the vertex that remain constant throughout the execution.

```
0.  is_converged = false;
1.  while (!is_converged) {
2.    is_converged = true;
3.    parallel-for shard s in shards {
4.      shared Vertex local_vertices[N];
5.      shared values_updated = false;
6.      offset = s.ID * N;
7.      Vertices = VertexValues+offset;
        /* 1st stage */
8.      parallel-for vertex index v in s {
9.        init_compute( local_vertices+v,
          Vertices+v );
10.     }
11.     synchronize; //synchronizes block threads
        /* 2nd stage */
12.     parallel-for edge index e in s {
13.       compute( s.SrcValue+e, s.SrcValueStatic+e,
            s.EdgeValue+e,
            local_vertices+s.DestIndex[e]-offset );
14.     }
15.     synchronize; //synchronizes block threads
        /* 3rd stage */
16.     parallel-for vertex index v in s {
17.       if ( update_condition
            ( local_vertices+v, Vertices+v ) ) {
18.         Vertices[v] = local_vertices[v];
19.         values_updated = true;
20.       }
21.     }
22.     synchronize; //synchronizes block threads
        /* 4th stage */
23.     if( values_updated ) {
24.       w = window_set_from_all_shards(s);
          //Windows in all the shards for shard-k
25.       write_back( local_vertices, w );
26.       is_converged = false;
27.     }
28.   }
29.   barrier;
30. }
```

Figure 5: Graph processing procedure in CuSha.

In the *first stage*, consecutive threads initialize *local_vertices* array from consecutive *VertexValues* array elements in the global memory (line 9) thus providing fully coalesced memory accesses.

The *second stage* mainly involves invoking the *compute* method with the appropriate parameters for shards. Global memory access pattern in this stage is depicted in Figure 3(b). Since multiple threads can simultaneously modify the same shared memory location, the user-provided *compute* function must be *atomic* with respect to updating the destination vertex. Note that the atomic operation will be inexpensive mainly because it is a shared memory update and hence, only can affect other threads inside the same streaming multiprocessor, leaving the threads in other streaming multiprocessors unaffected. Furthermore, the lock contention is low because of the size of shards, allowing these operations to be performed almost independently with respect to each other. Also, since the order of these invocations is nondeterministic, the compute function must be both, *commutative* and *associative*.

In the *third stage*, the threads invoke the *update_condition* method (lines 17 - 19). If a true value is returned by this method, the threads update the contents of *VertexValues* and *values_updated* is set. Note that the *update_condition* method can also be used to perform computations unique to each vertex. In this case, the computation logic can be split across the *compute* and *update_condition* methods such that

```
0.  typedef struct Edge { unsigned int Weight; } Edge;
1.  typedef struct Vertex { unsigned int Dist; } Vertex;
2.  __device__ void init_compute(
      Vertex* local_V, Veretx* V ) {
3.    local_V->Dist = V->Dist;
4.  }
5.  __device__ void compute(
      Vertex* SrcV, StaticVertex* SrcV_static,
      Edge* E, Vertex* local_V) {
6.    if (SrcV->Dist != INF)
7.      atomicMin ( &(local_V->Dist),
          SrcV->Dist + E->Weight );
8.  }
9.  __device__ bool update_condition(
      Vertex* local_V, Vertex* V ) {
10.   return ( local_V->Dist < V->Dist );
11. }
```

Figure 6: SSSP implementation in CuSha.

the *compute* method mainly leverages edge-level parallelism and the *update_condition* method leverages vertex-level parallelism.

In the *last stage*, if *values_updated* flag is set, windows in all the shards are updated with newly computed values (line 25) and one of the threads inside the block sets the *is_converged* flag. With G-Shards representation, the threads of a block are grouped into warps which iterate through the corresponding windows in all the shards (Figure 3(c)). As we discussed in Section 3.2, although the accesses are coalesced in this case, the technique is susceptible to GPU underutilization when windows are small. With CW representation, the threads of a block read the *SrcIndex* and *Mapper* array and appropriately update the windows in all shards (Figure 4(b)). Even though the memory accesses are not fully coalesced in this case, it requires the same number of memory transactions as in G-Shards representation with the added benefit of utilizing all threads.

Selecting shard size. As we know, processing graphs using G-Shards and CW representations is sensitive to window sizes which, in turn, is dependent on the size of shards. Hence, during initialization, CuSha determines the number of vertices assigned to shards for each input graph using average window size formula: $\frac{|E||N|^2}{|V|^2}$ derived in Section 3.2. From the architecture standpoint, $|N|$ is limited by the size of shared memory; to achieve maximum theoretical occupancy and to fully utilize the SM resources, $|N|$ is dependent on the number of blocks residing on a single SM. For example, if a SM has 48KB shared memory and we wish to have two blocks residing in it at the same time, each block can be assigned up to 24KB of shared memory. Assuming that vertex value is 4 bytes, $|N|$ can at most be 6K. Similarly, with four blocks on one SM, $|N|$ can at most be 3K. Choosing the largest value for $|N|$ (6K in the above example) and hence, having a block with a lot of threads increases the likelihood of conflicts during atomic operations due to limited number of shared memory lock indices. Hence, for a given input graph, CuSha first calculates $|N|$ by assuming the average window size to be 32 (equal to the warp size). Then, it determines block size to be the nearest value to the calculated $|N|$ that utilizes all available shared memory quota for the block on the SM. This allows CuSha to generate the set of shards that is best suited for each input graph.

Programming applications using CuSha. The above computational model enables users to easily implement a

Benchmark	typedef struct Vertex { }Vertex;	typedef struct StaticVertex { }StaticVertex;	typedef struct Edge { }Edge;	__device__ void init_compute(Vertex* local_V, Veretx* V){}	__device__ void compute(Vertex* SrcV, StaticVertex* SrcV_static, Edge* E,Vertex* local_V){}	__device__ bool update_condition(Vertex* local_V, Vertex* V){}
BFS	unsigned int Level;			local_V->Level =V->Level;	if(SrcV->Level!=INF) atomicMin(&(local_V->Level) ,SrcV->Level+1);	return(local_V->Level < V->Level);
SSSP	unsigned int Dist;		unsigned int Weight;	local_V->Dist =V->Dist;	if(SrcV->Dist!=INF) atomicMin(&(local_V->Dist) ,SrcV->Dist+E->Weight);	return(local_V->Dist < V->Dist);
PR	float Rank;	unsigned int NbrsNum;		local_V->Rank =0;	unsigned int nbrsNum= SrcV_static->NbrsNum; if(nbrsNum!=0)atomicAdd (&(local_V->rank), SrcV->Rank/nbrsNum);	local_V->rank= (1-DAMPING_FACTOR)+local_V ->rank*DAMPING_FACTOR; return(fabs(local_V-> rank-V->rank)>TOLERANCE);
CC	unsigned int Cmpnent;			local_V->Cmpnent = V->Cmpnent;	atomicMin(&(local_V->Cmpnent) ,SrcV->Cmpnent);	return(local_V->Cmpnent < V->Cmpnent);
SSWP	unsigned int BWidth;		unsigned int Width;	local_V->BWidth =V->BWidth;	if(SrcV->BWidth!=0) atomicMax(&(local_V->BWidth) ,min(SrcV->BWidth,E->Width));	return(local_V->BWidth > V->BWidth);
NN	float x;		float Weight;	local_V->x =0;	atomicAdd(&(local_V->x) ,SrcV->x*E->weight);	local_V->x= tanh(local_V->x); return(fabs(local_V->x - V->x)>TOLERANCE);
HS	float Q; float Q_new;		float coeff;	local_V->Q=V->Q; local_V->Q_new =local_V->Q;	atomicAdd(&(local_V->Q_new) ,(SrcV->Q-local_V->Q) *E->coeff);	bool B=fabs(local_V->Q- local_V->Q_new)>TOLERANCE; if(B) local_V->Q= local_V->Q_new; return B;
CS	float V; float GsumOrA;		float G;	local_V->V=0; local_V-> GsumOrA=0;	float G=E->G; atomicAdd(&(local_V->V) ,SrcV->V*G); atomicAdd(&(local_V ->GsumOrA),G);	if(V->GsumOrA){ local_V-> GsumOrA=1; local_V->V=V->V; return false;} else if(local_V->GsumOrA){ local_V->V /= local_V->GsumOrA; local_V-> GsumOrA=0; return(fabs(local_V->V-V->V)>TOLERANCE);} else return false;

Table 3: Implementation of various benchmarks in CuSha.

wide range of graph processing algorithms. As an example, let us consider the implementation of Single Source Shortest Path (SSSP) algorithm. The vertex-centric approach for SSSP is to iteratively compute the value for each vertex based on the minimum sum of its neighbor's value and the corresponding edge weight. Figure 6 presents the structure of a vertex and the functions required to compute SSSP on a graph. Every vertex holds an integer (initially set to a very large number representing ∞) standing for the shortest distance from the source (line 0). Source vertex value is set to 0. At the beginning of each iteration, the *init_compute* method loads the most updated vertex values into the block's shared memory. The *compute* function sets the distance of a vertex by atomically choosing the minimum of the calculated distances. The *update_condition* signals the caller to execute the next iteration if the new distance of the vertex is smaller than its old value. As we can see, the user only has to provide the *init_compute*, *compute*, and *update_condition* methods along with the *required structures*; hence making it easier to code graph processing algorithms using CuSha. Also, the commonalities among various algorithms allow users to quickly implement different algorithms by simply modifying the existing ones. Table 3 presents 8 graph processing al-

gorithms we implemented using CuSha alongside variables for structures and instructions for three functions used by these algorithms. Note that having arrays of structure in older generations of CUDA devices could limit the effective bandwidth due to strided distribution of elements. However, simultaneous accesses to structure elements alongside the introduction of global L2 cache in newer CUDA-enabled GPUs significantly diminishes the impact of strided accesses.

5. EXPERIMENTAL EVALUATION

In this section, we evaluate the performance of our CuSha framework using the eight graph applications listed in Table 2 and six publicly available [15] real-world graphs listed in Table 1. The graphs cover a broad range of sizes and sparsity and come from different real-world origins. *LiveJournal* and *Pokec* are directed social networks which represent friendship among the users. *HiggsTweet* is a social relationship graph among twitter users involved in tweeting about the discovery of Higgs particle. *RoadNetCA* is the California road network in which the roads are represented by edges and the vertices represent the intersections. *WebGoogle* is a graph released by Google in which vertices represent web pages and the directed edges are hyperlinks

		BFS	SSSP	PR	CC	SSWP	NN	HS	CS
LiveJournal	CuSha-CW	166	346	709	190	531	203	386	855
	CuSha-GS	170	414	885	195	683	197	465	929
	VWC-CSR	280-420	770-1075	2814-3503	264-396	1346-1954	3872-6568	458-647	984-1423
Pokec	CuSha-CW	70	143	255	103	137	3202	246	186
	CuSha-GS	63	138	267	86	134	3278	244	175
	VWC-CSR	125-172	283-357	1539-3246	109-135	310-375	678-827	313-385	190-246
HiggsTwitter	CuSha-CW	59	130	345	72	94	246	150	96
	CuSha-GS	61	127	375	71	89	246	143	89
	VWC-CSR	76-241	175-556	682-2750	67-164	113-325	224-713	112-319	70-171
RoadNetCA	CuSha-CW	286	384	54	435	1026	247	43	2472
	CuSha-GS	432	647	122	897	1905	328	41	2521
	VWC-CSR	655-5727	710-6731	103-521	747-5665	2071-15500	308-1984	76-253	4634-31792
WebGoogle	CuSha-CW	28	41	69	29	74	115	84	98
	CuSha-GS	27	42	73	26	77	125	83	116
	VWC-CSR	100-138	138-208	181-306	63-123	247-373	133-196	148-213	159-197
Amazon0312	CuSha-CW	19	36	44	17	44	40	47	504
	CuSha-GS	24	45	46	18	52	49	55	509
	VWC-CSR	35-53	80-117	87-157	17-55	79-121	48-83	67-117	621-940

Table 4: CuSha-CW, CuSha-GS, and VWC-CSR running times on different algorithms and inputs. Reported times include host-device data transfers and are in milliseconds.

	CuSha-GS over VWC-CSR	CuSha-CW over VWC-CSR
Averages Across Input Graphs		
BFS	1.94x−4.96x	2.09x−6.12x
SSSP	1.91x−4.59x	2.16x−5.96x
PR	2.66x−5.88x	3.08x−7.21x
CC	1.28x−3.32x	1.36x−4.34x
SSWP	1.90x−4.11x	2.19x−5.46x
NN	1.42x−3.07x	1.51x−3.47x
HS	1.42x−3.01x	1.45x−3.02x
CS	1.23x−3.50x	1.27x−3.58x
Averages Across Benchmarks		
LiveJournal	1.66x−2.36x	1.92x−2.72x
Pokec	2.40x−3.63x	2.34x−3.58x
HiggsTwitter	1.14x−3.59x	1.14x−3.61x
RoadNetCA	1.34x−8.64x	1.92x−12.99x
WebGoogle	2.41x−3.71x	2.45x−3.74x
Amazon0312	1.37x−2.40x	1.57x−2.73x

Table 5: Speedup Ranges of CuSha-GS and CuSha-CW over VWC-CSR Configurations.

	CuSha-GS over MTCPU-CSR	CuSha-CW over MTCPU-CSR
Averages Across Input Graphs		
BFS	2.41x−10.41x	2.61x−11.38x
SSSP	2.61x−12.34x	2.99x−14.27x
PR	5.34x−24.45x	6.46x−28.98x
CC	1.66x−7.46x	1.72x−7.74x
SSWP	2.59x−11.74x	3.03x−13.85x
NN	1.82x−19.17x	1.97x−19.59x
HS	1.74x−7.07x	1.80x−7.30x
CS	2.39x−11.06x	2.49x−11.55x
Averages Across Benchmarks		
LiveJournal	4.1x−26.63x	4.74x−29.25x
Pokec	3.26x−15.19x	3.2x−14.89x
HiggsTwitter	1.23x−5.30x	1.23x−5.34x
RoadNetCA	1.95x−9.79x	2.95x−14.29x
WebGoogle	1.95x−9.79x	2.95x−14.29x
Amazon0312	1.65x−6.27x	1.88x−7.20x

Table 6: Speedup Ranges of CuSha-GS and CuSha-CW over MTCPU-CSR Configurations.

connecting those pages. *Amazon0312* is Amazon's product co-purchasing network collected on March 2, 2003. In this graph, vertices are products and an edge between vertices indicates that the two products were frequently co-purchased.

The experiments were performed on a system with Nvidia GeForce GTX780 which has 12 SMX multiprocessors and 3 GB GDDR5 RAM. On the host side, there is an Intel Core i7-3930K Sandy Bridge CPU with 12 cores (hyper-threading enabled) operating at 3.2 GHz clock frequency. PCI Express 3.0 lanes operating at 16x speed transfer data between the host DDR3 RAM (CPU side) and the device RAM (GPU side). The benchmarks were evaluated using CUDA 5.5 on Ubuntu 12.04, Kernel v3.5.0-45. All the programs were compiled with the highest optimization level flag (-O3).

5.1 Performance Analysis

To evaluate the effectiveness of graph processing on CuSha we compare the performance of following techniques:

- **CuSha-GS**: This is our Cusha framework when using G-Shards representation;

- **CuSha-CW**: This is our CuSha framework when using CW representation;

- **VWC-CSR**: This is *virtual warp-centric* [12] technique using CSR representation. We considered virtual warp sizes of 2, 4, 8, 16, and 32; and

- **MTCPU-CSR**: This is the multi-threaded CPU implementation using the CSR representation built using pthreads such that each thread is assigned to a group of vertices that are adjacent to each other in the CSR representation. We considered the runs with 1, 2, 4, 8, 16, 32, 64, and 128 threads on the 12-core host processor with hyper-threading enabled.

Speedups. Table 4 shows raw processing time (including host-device data transfers) of CuSha-CW, CuSha-GS, and VWC-CSR. These times are presented as ranges (min - max) because VWC-CSR is run for several configurations as its performance varies with chosen virtual warp sizes. From this table we can get the speedups of CuSha over VWC-CSR. When averaging speedups across all benchmarks and inputs, CuSha-GS provides speedups in range of 1.72x -

4.05x while CuSha-CW provides speedups in range of 1.89x - 4.89x over VWC-CSR. Table 5 shows the speedup ranges separately for each benchmark when averaged across all inputs and then separately for each input graph when averaged over all benchmarks. We observe that CuSha outperforms VWC-CSR across all benchmarks and all inputs with maximum improvements observed for PageRank (PR) program and RoadNetCA input graph. We also observe that both G-Shards and Concatenated Windows contribute substantially to the resulting speedups. For example, for PageRank, maximum speedup observed using CuSha-GS is 5.88x and this increases to 7.21x when CuSha-CW is used.

Results in Table 6 demonstrate CuSha's substantial performance improvements over MTCPU-CSR. The maximum speedups correspond to the single-threaded CPU implementation while the minimums correspond to use of best number of CPU threads. Best configuration varies from one benchmark and graph combination to another. When averaging speedups across all benchmarks and inputs, CuSha-GS provides speedups in range of 2.57x - 12.96x while CuSha-CW provides speedups in range of 2.88x - 14.33x over MTCPU-CSR. Highest speedups were observed for PageRank program and the largest input graph *LiveJournal*.

Data transfer times between the host and the device have been included in the results reported in Table 5 and Table 6.

	CuSha-CW	CuSha-GS	Best VWC-CSR
LiveJournal	929.1 M	692.2 M	272.4 M
Pokec	1009.9 M	942.2 M	269.7 M
HiggsTwitter	378.8 M	323.9 M	208.8 M
RoadNetCA	19.9 M	13.0 M	8.5 M
WebGoogle	242.7 M	243.1 M	52.5 M
Amazon0312	208.8 M	149.4 M	89.8 M

Table 7: Traversed Edges Per Second (TEPS) for BFS with CuSha-CW, CuSha-GS, and VWC-CSR using the best configuration for each graph.

TEPS data for BFS traversal. Table 7 shows number of Traversed Edges Per Second (TEPS) in BFS for CuSha-CW, CuSha-GS, and VWC-CSR with the best performance handpicked by running it with different virtual warp sizes. As the table shows, CuSha can be up to 5 times better than the best VWC-CSR. CuSha provides performance gain over VWC-CSR by eliminating non-coalesced accesses and thread divergence, which will be further explored in this section.

Figure 7 shows the number of vertices updated during BFS traversal iteration by iteration over time for CuSha-CW and CuSha-GS, and for VWC-CSR with the warp size exhibiting best performance. Processing with CuSha-CW and CuSha-GS usually includes more iterations than VWC-CSR because G-Shards and CW contain more than one version of vertex values; unlike CSR that only stores one version of it. On the other hand, iterations take much less time with G-Shards and CW because of the GPU-friendly representation. Faster iterations in G-Shards and CW result in much quicker convergence of BFS in all the graphs.

Global memory and warp execution efficiency. The speedups of CuSha over VWC-CSR observed can be explained by studying the improvements in global memory accesses and warp execution efficiencies. As we had shown earlier, these efficiencies are quite low for VWC-CSR. Figure 8 compares the average global memory store efficiency,

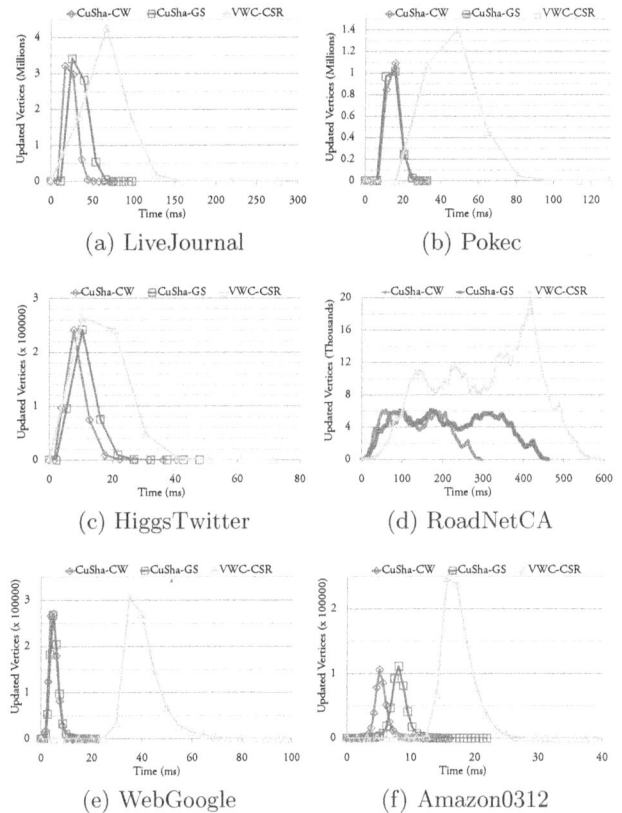

(a) LiveJournal   (b) Pokec

(c) HiggsTwitter   (d) RoadNetCA

(e) WebGoogle   (f) Amazon0312

Figure 7: BFS traversal for CuSha-CW and CuSha-GS, and for VWC-CSR with the best handpicked virtual warp size. Each point stands for an iteration.

the average global memory load efficiency, and the average warp execution efficiency of VWC-CSR with best configuration, CuSha-GS, and CuSha-CW while processing *LiveJournal* graph.

The global memory store efficiency is the ratio of the global memory store throughput achieved by the program to the global memory store throughput that is actually needed by the program. It indicates how well the threads within a kernel write to the global memory: a high value shows that more store operations are fulfilled with coalesced writes. The average of this value across all kernel iterations during a run is the average global memory store efficiency. As we can see, VWC-CSR has a very low average global memory store efficiency (1.93% on average) because when the warp needs to update the vertex content, only one thread inside the virtual warp is active and writing to memory. On the other hand, CuSha-GS and CuSha-CW have a much higher average global memory store (27.64% for G-Shards and 25.06% for CW) because updates to vertex contents are done in parallel by multiple threads.

The global memory load efficiency indicates the ratio of achieved global memory load throughput to required load throughput. Compared to CuSha, VWC-CSR achieves lower global memory load efficiency (28.18% on average) mainly because of non-coalesced accesses. CuSha-GS and CuSha-CW achieve 80.15% and 77.59% global memory load efficiency on average, respectively. For both CuSha-GS and CuSha-CW, the average global memory load is higher than store mainly because of the heavy, but coalesced, memory reads of shard entries.

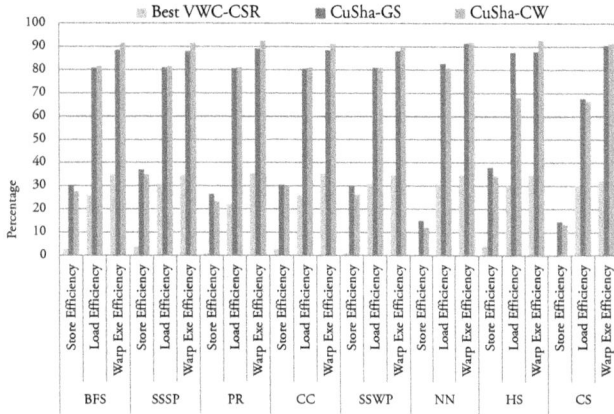

Figure 8: Average profiled efficiencies of CuSha-GS and CuSha-CW vs. best VWC-CSR configuration on *LiveJournal* graph.

Finally, the warp execution efficiency is defined as the ratio of the average active threads in a warp to the maximum possible active threads in a warp per multiprocessor. It indicates how well GPU hardware resources are utilized. Figure 8 shows that the VWC-CSR has a much lower warp execution efficiency (34.48% on average) compared to CuSha (88.90% for G-Shards and 91.57% for CW on average) mainly due to the impact of different number of neighbors in VWC-CSR. Since CuSha organizes graph edges in large shards, this effect is heavily reduced.

Memory occupied by different graph representations. Next we evaluate the cost of using G-Shards and CW representations in terms of increased memory requirement and copying time over CSR.

Figure 9 shows minimum, average, and maximum space consumed by CSR, G-Shards, and CW representations for each input graph, across all benchmarks and normalized with respect to the CSR average for each benchmark. G-Shards and CW take 2.09x and 2.58x more space, on average, than CSR. G-Shards representation adds an overhead of about $(|E| - |V|) \times size\_of(Vertex) + |E| \times size\_of(index)$ bytes over CSR. For CW, this overhead increases by $|E| \times size\_of(index)$ bytes. Even though the overhead is input dependent, technological advancements allow us to leverage reasonably large RAM on the GPU which can easily fit most real world graphs. If graphs do not fit in the GPU RAM, a multi-streamed procedure should be incorporated to overlap computation and data transfer.

Figure 10 breaks the total time, taken by all the benchmarks on *LiveJournal* input, down into the time taken by: 1) H2D copy - time to copy graph from CPU side memory to GPU global memory; 2) GPU Computation - time to process the graph on GPU; and 3) D2H copy - time to copy the results back from GPU global memory to CPU side memory. We can see that CuSha takes more H2D copy time compared to VWC-CSR mainly because of the space overheads involved in using G-Shards and CW. However, computation friendly representations of G-Shards and CW allow faster processing, which in turn significantly improves the overall performance. D2H copy only involves the final vertex values and hence, is negligible. Also, CuSha-CW takes more time to copy compared to CuSha-GS because of the additional mapper array.

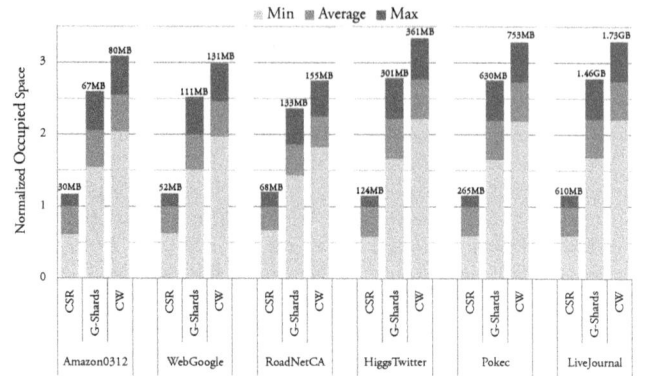

Figure 9: Memory occupied by each graph using CSR, G-Shards, and CW representations over all benchmarks – values are normalized with respect to CSR average. Numbers in the figure are maximums in each case.

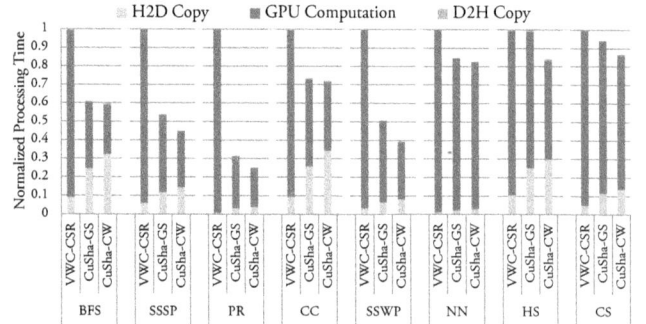

Figure 10: Time breakdown: device-to-host copy time, GPU execution time, and host-to-device copy back time on LiveJournal. VWC-CSR has the best configuration.

5.2 Sensitivity Analysis of CW

In this section we study the sensitivity of CuSha-CW across different input graph characteristics. To create the graphs used in this study we use the SNAP graph library [2] and the RMAT [5] model that generates scale free graphs which resemble the characteristics of real-world graphs such as power-law graphs.

Figure 12 shows the total running time normalized with respect to the shortest time for SSSP on CuSha with nine synthetically-created RMAT graphs across range of different *sizes* and *sparsities*. It confirms the sensitivity of G-Shards representation to the graph size, the graph sparsity, and the number of vertices assigned to a shard ($|N|$). We discuss each of these parameters with the help of Figure 11 which shows the distribution of window sizes in different scenarios.

Graph size: Increasing the number of edges and vertices in the graph causes the frequency of small windows to increase (see Figure 11(a)). This makes the G-Shards representation more vulnerable to graph size compared to CW. This can be seen in Figure 12: processing time with G-Shards more than doubles from 67_8 graph with $|N| = 3k$ to 134_16 graph with $|N| = 3k$ while with CW it increases by 1.6x.

Sparsity: Figure 11(b) shows that by increasing graph sparsity, the number of windows with size close to zero increases.

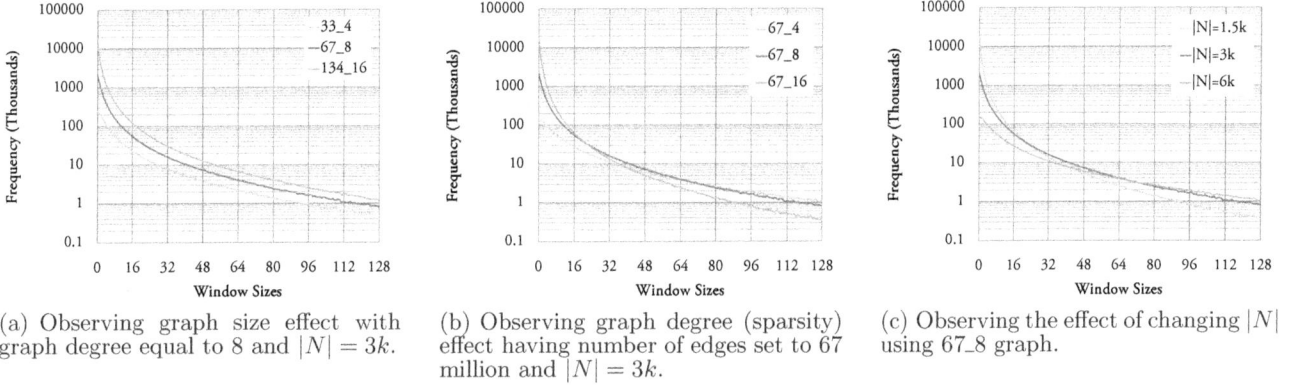

(a) Observing graph size effect with graph degree equal to 8 and $|N| = 3k$.

(b) Observing graph degree (sparsity) effect having number of edges set to 67 million and $|N| = 3k$.

(c) Observing the effect of changing $|N|$ using 67_8 graph.

Figure 11: Frequency of window sizes (from 0 to 128) having different RMAT input graphs. $|N|$ is the number of vertices assigned to a shard. A i_j graph has around i million edges and j million vertices.

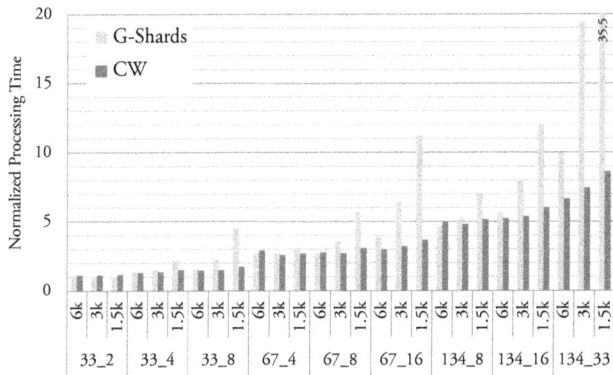

Figure 12: Normalized CuSha running time configured to use G-Shards and CW against RMAT graphs having different shard sizes in SSSP benchmark. In the figure, a i_j graph has around i million edges and j million vertices. Numbers close to x axis are number of vertices assigned to a shard.

G-Shards representation is more sensitive to small sized windows compared to CW, i.e., as graphs become sparser, the performance of G-Shards degrades rapidly compared to CW. In Figure 12, the G-Shards processing time doubles from 67_4 graph with $|N| = 3k$ to 67_16 graph with $|N| = 3k$ while CW processing time increases only slightly.

Vertices assigned to shard ($|N|$): Larger $|N|$ reduces the number of shards and increases their size. As a result, larger $|N|$ increases the size of windows as shown in Figure 11(c). Hence, while processing very sparse graphs using G-Shards, it is crucial to have a large value for $|N|$. Comparatively, CW is not heavily impacted when $|N|$ is small as shown with the biggest and sparsest graphs in Figure 12.

We further compared CW sensitivity with VWC-CSR's. Figure 13 presents the speedup of CW over VWC-CSR on RMAT graphs. It shows that with increasing size and sparsity of the RMAT graph, CW's superiority over VWC-CSR increases. It also reveals the performance change of VWC-CSR method when different warp sizes are employed. It is evident from the figure that different graphs with different characteristics require different configuration of VWC-CSR for best performance.

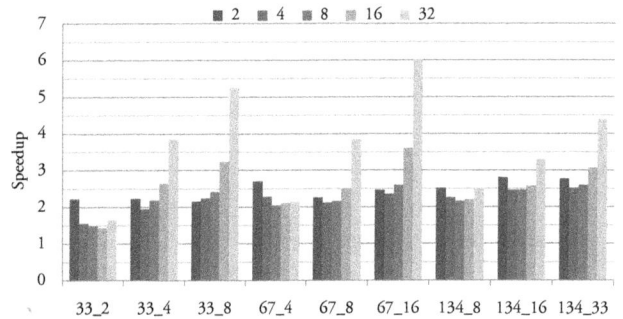

Figure 13: CW speedups over VWC-CSR with virtual warp sizes 2, 4, 8, 16, and 32 against RMAT graphs in SSSP benchmark. CW has $|N| = 3k$. In figure above, a i_j graph has around i million edges and j million vertices.

6. RELATED WORK

Using GPUs for high performance graph processing was first introduced in [10]. Since then CSR has been the most popular representation to store graphs on GPU. Even though efforts have been spent to minimize path divergence as in [12] and minimize load imbalance as in [21], the CSR representation inherently suffers from poor locality [18].

Apart from having virtual warps, [12] offers *deferring outliers* and *dynamic workload distribution* techniques in order to reduce intra-warp divergence and achieve a balanced load for different warps. However, the improvements achieved by these two methods are limited because of the heavyweight atomic operations on global memory. The technique presented in [28] tries to balance the load in graphs represented in CSR by reorganizing the vertices and putting them in three bins. Based on the size of these bins, appropriate number of GPU threads are assigned to process these bins, hence providing a balanced workload distribution.

In [9], TOTEM abstracts away development complexity and reduces communication overhead for processing graphs by message aggregation in a heterogeneous many-core system. Another hybrid CPU-GPU method that improves the efficiency of BFS is presented in [13]. During the initial phases when there are fewer number of vertices to be processed, the CPU performs the computation. Later, when the number of vertices to be processed becomes larger, the computation is moved onto the GPU. Authors also propose a read-queue hybrid technique that switches the processing scheme based on the size of next level in BFS. [1], [21] and [19] are various multi-core CPU and GPU works that employ queues to handle vertices that should be explored in the next level. The technique presented in [21] efficiently computes the prefix sum for scatter offset in parallel to produce global computation frontier queues. Even though using frontiers is still susceptible to input-dependent non-coalesced memory accesses, the GPU underutilization is eliminated by this technique. CuSha is a framework that supports a broader range of graph algorithms compared to such problem-specific queue-based solutions for BFS.

Medusa [30] is a generalized GPU-based graph processing framework that focuses on abstractions for easy programming and scaling to multiple GPUs. CuSha primarily focuses on exploring new graph representations to allow faster graph processing. Apart from CSR, various other graph representations have been proposed that are typically beneficial for targeted applications. For instance, [20] introduces a novel idea of using sparse bit vectors, a structure similar to linked list. However, this representation is highly space inefficient and is only beneficial for morph algorithms when data access patterns exhibit spatial locality.

Dymaxion [6] is an API to improve memory access patterns on GPUs. It uses two fundamental techniques to leverage high memory coalescing:

- **Data restructuring:** Although this method is effective and quite common [24], its use in Dymaxion is limited to predictable data patterns, such as transformation of two-dimensional matrices from row-major order to column-major order or vice versa.

- **Memory remapping:** Allows efficient accessing of data elements via an intermediate mapping function. It is similar to CuSha's CW method.

In [29], authors present *data reordering* and *job swapping* techniques to remove GPU memory access irregularities. *Data reordering*, similar to *data restructuring*, repositions elements of an array to minimize required global memory transactions. In *job swapping*, threads exchange work in order to achieve more coalesced memory accesses. It is usually done using reference redirection, which is similar to *memory remapping*. Despite their benefits for applications with regular chunkable input data, irregular and unpredictable dependency between real-world graph elements makes it costly to employ these techniques for graph applications.

Recently, Wu et al. classified and analyzed few fundamental methods to minimize non-coalesced memory accesses in [27]. CuSha employs three of these techniques:

- **Duplication:** Vertices and destination indices are duplicated for edges.
- **Reordering:** Edges within the shards are sorted based on their source indices.
- **Sharing:** Irregular memory accesses are confined to fast shared memory in the GPU.

7. CONCLUSION

In this paper, we first recognized the use of shards for efficient graph processing on GPUs through coalesced memory accesses and introduced G-Shards: a graph represen-

tation that effectively maps shards to various GPU subcomponents. We also proposed a novel representation named Concatenated Windows to eliminate GPU underutilization for very large and sparse graphs. Finally, we built CuSha, a framework to enable users to easily define vertex-centric algorithms for processing large graphs on GPU. CuSha internally relies on both G-Shards and Concatenated Windows and exposes necessary functions to be provided by the users. CuSha achieves substantial speedups over the finetuned state-of-the-art virtual warp-centric method. We believe that increasing amount of shared memory per SM along with performance enhancements of shared memory atomic operations in upcoming CUDA devices will further enhance the superiority of our two newly introduced representations.

8. ACKNOWLEDGMENTS

We thank the reviewers for their detailed feedback for improving the paper.

This work is supported by National Science Foundation grants CCF-1157377 and CCF-0905509 to the University of California Riverside.

9. REFERENCES

[1] V. Agarwal, F. Petrini, D. Pasetto, and D. A. Bader. Scalable graph exploration on multicore processors. In *SC*, pages 1–11, 2010.

[2] D. A. Bader and K. Madduri. Snap, small-world network analysis and partitioning: An open-source parallel graph framework for the exploration of large-scale networks. In *IPDPS*, pages 1–12, 2008.

[3] A. Bakhoda, G. Yuan, W. Fung, H. Wong, and T. Aamodt. Analyzing cuda workloads using a detailed gpu simulator. In *ISPASS*, pages 163–174, 2009.

[4] J. Barnat, P. Bauch, L. Brim, and M. Ceska. Computing strongly connected components in parallel on cuda. In *IPDPS*, pages 544–555, 2011.

[5] D. Chakrabarti, Y. Zhan, and C. Faloutsos. R-mat: A recursive model for graph mining. In *In SDM*, 2004.

[6] S. Che, J. Sheaffer, and K. Skadron. Dymaxion: Optimizing memory access patterns for heterogeneous systems. In *SC*, pages 1–11, 2011.

[7] M. De Domenico, A. Lima, P. Mougel, and M. Musolesi. The anatomy of a scientific rumor. *Scientific Reports*, 2013.

[8] A. Gharaibeh, L. Beltrão Costa, E. Santos-Neto, and M. Ripeanu. A yoke of oxen and a thousand chickens for heavy lifting graph processing. In *PACT*, pages 345–354, 2012.

[9] A. Gharaibeh, L. Beltrão Costa, E. Santos-Neto, and M. Ripeanu. Efficient Large-Scale Graph Processing on Hybrid CPU and GPU Systems. In *CoRR*, 2013.

[10] P. Harish and P. J. Narayanan. Accelerating large graph algorithms on the gpu using cuda. In *HiPC*, pages 197–208, 2007.

[11] M. Harris et al. Optimizing parallel reduction in cuda. *NVIDIA Developer Technology*, 2, 2007.

[12] S. Hong, S. K. Kim, T. Oguntebi, and K. Olukotun. Accelerating cuda graph algorithms at maximum warp. In *PPoPP*, pages 267–276, 2011.

[13] S. Hong, T. Oguntebi, and K. Olukotun. Efficient parallel graph exploration on multi-core cpu and gpu. In *PACT*, 2011.

[14] A. Kyrola, G. Blelloch, and C. Guestrin. Graphchi: Large-scale graph computation on just a pc. In *OSDI*, pages 31–46, 2012.

[15] J. Leskovec. Stanford large network dataset collection. *http://snap.stanford.edu/data/index.html*, 2011.

[16] J. Leskovec, L. A. Adamic, and B. A. Huberman. The dynamics of viral marketing. *ACM Trans. Web*, 1(1), May 2007.

[17] J. Leskovec, K. J. Lang, A. Dasgupta, and M. W. Mahoney. Community structure in large networks: Natural cluster sizes and the absence of large well-defined clusters. *CoRR*, abs/0810.1355, 2008.

[18] A. Lumsdaine, D. Gregor, B. Hendrickson, and J. Berry. Challenges in parallel graph processing. *Parallel Processing Letters*, 17(01):5–20, 2007.

[19] L. Luo, M. Wong, and W.-m. Hwu. An effective gpu implementation of breadth-first search. In *DAC*, pages 52–55, 2010.

[20] M. Mendez-Lojo, M. Burtscher, and K. Pingali. A gpu implementation of inclusion-based points-to analysis. In *PPoPP*, pages 107–116, 2012.

[21] D. Merrill, M. Garland, and A. Grimshaw. Scalable gpu graph traversal. In *PPoPP*, pages 117–128, 2012.

[22] R. Nasre, M. Burtscher, and K. Pingali. Morph algorithms on gpus. In *PPoPP*, pages 147–156, 2013.

[23] L. Page, S. Brin, R. Motwani, and T. Winograd. The pagerank citation ranking: Bringing order to the web. Technical Report 1999-66, Stanford InfoLab, 1999.

[24] M. Samadi, A. Hormati, M. Mehrara, J. Lee, and S. Mahlke. Adaptive input-aware compilation for graphics engines. In *PLDI*, pages 13–22, 2012.

[25] L. Takac and M. Zabovsky. Data analysis in public social networks. In *International Scientific Conference and International Workshop Present Day Trends of Innovations*, 2012.

[26] L. G. Valiant. A bridging model for parallel computation. *Commun. ACM*, 33(8):103–111, 1990.

[27] B. Wu, Z. Zhao, E. Z. Zhang, Y. Jiang, and X. Shen. Complexity analysis and algorithm design for reorganizing data to minimize non-coalesced memory accesses on gpu. In *PPoPP*, pages 57–68, 2013.

[28] T. Wu, B. Wang, Y. Shan, F. Yan, Y. Wang, and N. Xu. Efficient pagerank and spmv computation on amd gpus. In *ICPP*, pages 81–89, 2010.

[29] E. Z. Zhang, Y. Jiang, Z. Guo, K. Tian, and X. Shen. On-the-fly elimination of dynamic irregularities for gpu computing. In *ASPLOS*, pages 369–380, 2011.

[30] J. Zhong, and B. He. Medusa: Simplified Graph Processing on GPUs. In *IEEE Transactions on Parallel and Distributed Systems*, 2013.

APPENDIX

A. VIRTUAL WARP-CENTRIC METHOD

Figure 14 shows the pseudo-code for Virtual Warp-Centric (VWC) method. Similar to CuSha, it performs each iteration of the vertex-centric algorithm in a single GPU kernel call. During the kernel, the GPU assigns one virtual warp

```
0.  is_converged = false;
1.  while (!is_converged) {
2.    is_converged = true;
3.    parallel-for virtual warp VW{
4.      allVWs = blockDim / VW.size;
5.      shared Vertex old_V[allVWs];
6.      shared Vertex local_V[allVWs];
7.      shared Vertex outcome[blockDim];
8.      shared unsigned int edges_start[allVWs];
9.      shared unsigned int nbrs_size[allVWs];
10.     if ( virtual_lane_ID == 0 ) {
11.       edges_start[VW.ID] = InEdgeIdxs[VW.ID];
12.       nbrs_size[VW.ID] = InEdgeIdxs[VW.ID+1]
            - edges_start[VW.ID];
13.       old_V[offset] = VertexValues[VW.ID];
14.       InitCompute( local_V+offset,
            old_V+offset );
15.     }
16.     parallel-for Nbr in neighbors of vertex
          with index VW.ID{
17.       edge_index = Nbr+edges_start[VW.ID];
18.       Nbr_index = SrcIndex[edge_index];
19.       Compute( VertexValues+Nbr_index,
            VertexValuesStatic+Nbr_index,
            EdgeValues+edge_index, outcome+Nbr );
20.       ParallelReduction(outcome,nbrs_size[VW.ID],
            local_V+offset,Nbr);
21.     }
22.     if ( virtual_lane_ID == 0 &&
          UpdateCondition ( local_V+offset,
          old_V+offset ) ) {
23.       VertexValues[VW.ID]=local_V[offset];
24.       is_converged = false;
25.     }
26.   }
27.   barrier;
28. }
```

Figure 14: Graph processing procedure in virtual warp-centric method using CSR representation.

to process a single vertex (line 3). One virtual lane within the virtual warp retrieves the starting address for the incoming edges array and the number of neighbors and then, calls the *InitCompute* function (lines 10-15). Next, the threads within the virtual warp are assigned to process the neighbors (line 16) using the *Compute* function (line 19). Parallel reduction [11] computes the final value of the vertex assigned to the virtual warp (line 20). Finally, one virtual lane in the virtual warp performs the *UpdateCondition* function and updates the source vertex, if necessary (lines 22-25).

Our implementation of VWC requires only one thread inside the virtual warp to perform the Single Instruction Single Data (SISD) phases as opposed to [12] in which all the threads execute these phases. Therefore, it avoids possible bank conflicts and serialization of write instructions in the shared and global memory respectively.

Improving Parallel I/O Autotuning with Performance Modeling

Babak Behzad
Univ. of Illinois at
Urbana-Champaign

Surendra Byna
Lawrence Berkeley Laboratory

Stefan M. Wild
Argonne National Laboratory

Prabhat
Lawrence Berkeley Laboratory

Marc Snir
Argonne National Laboratory

ABSTRACT

Various layers of the parallel I/O subsystem offer tunable parameters for improving I/O performance on large-scale computers. However, searching through a large parameter space is challenging. We are working towards an autotuning framework for determining the parallel I/O parameters that can achieve good I/O performance for different data write patterns. In this paper, we characterize parallel I/O and discuss the development of predictive models for use in effectively reducing the parameter space. Applying our technique on tuning an I/O kernel derived from a large-scale simulation code shows that the search time can be reduced from 12 hours to 2 hours, while achieving 54X I/O performance speedup.

Keywords

Parallel I/O, Autotuning, Performance Optimization, Performance Modeling

1. INTRODUCTION

Achieving efficient parallel I/O in high-performance computing (HPC) applications is a nontrivial task because of the complex interdependencies between the multiple layers of I/O middleware and storage hardware. Each I/O middleware layer offers a set of tunable parameters. However, the configuration of these parameters to obtain the best possible I/O performance depends on diverse factors, such as the I/O application, storage hardware, problem size, and number of processors. HPC application developers, typically experts in their scientific domains, do not have the time or expertise to explore the intricacies of I/O systems. Their resorting to using default I/O parameters often results in poor performance. As the complexity and concurrency of future HPC systems grow, we expect that so too will obstacles to achieving high-performance I/O.

We have recently developed a parallel I/O autotuning framework [2] with the ambitious goal of hiding the complexity of the I/O stack from scientific application developers. The autotuning framework uses a genetic algorithm (GA) to search through a large set of possible parameters. After constructing a random initial population, the GA produces new generations of populations by applying mutation and crossover operations. The GA thus determines values for the tunable parameters that result in good I/O performance. The dynamic library of our autotuner applies the selected parameter values by intercepting the data write calls. Our current implementation of the tuner, called "H5Tuner," is capable of intercepting the write calls of the HDF5 library and applying tunable parameters from HDF5, MPI-IO, and parallel-file systems (i.e., Lustre and GPFS).

While we consistently demonstrated I/O write speeds between 2X and 100X in our previous work [2], the overhead of the GA approach was significant. For example, running the GA for fifteen generations with a population of forty members typically takes about twelve hours. This overhead is considerable; it severely limits the general-purpose applicability of such an autotuning framework.

In this paper, we significantly reduce the search time by using empirical models of the I/O performance. We characterize performance of a typical parallel I/O subsystem with multiple levels of data movement and develop performance prediction models. Existing models for predicting parallel I/O performance (see, e.g., [8, 6, 7]) often aim for highly accurate predictions of I/O performance and are relatively complex. Many of these models have limited applicability, being restricted to specific systems or I/O kernels. We take a two-step approach: the first step crafts an empirical model that effectively reduces the search space of interest and the second step searches in this small parameter space.

Our paper makes the following technical contributions: We develop an approach to construct automatically an I/O performance model. We then use the model to reduce the search space for good I/O configurations and we demonstrate the applicability of the autotuning framework to scientific I/O kernels with various problem sizes.

2. EMPIRICAL PERFORMANCE MODELS

We have tested our autotuning framework on Hopper system located at the National Energy Research Scientific Computing Center (NERSC). Hopper is a Cray XE6 system containing 6,384 twenty-four core nodes with 32GB of memory per node. We used a Lustre file system of Hopper with 156 OSTs and a peak bandwidth of about 35GB/s for storing data. We used Cray's MPI library v6.0.1, HDF5 v1.8.11, and H5Part v1.6.6 for compiling the I/O kernels.

We examined the VPIC-IO I/O kernel in our study. This kernel is extracted from a particle physics simulation (VPIC [3, 4]). The kernel mimics exact I/O operations of the real application configuration.

We denote the independent variables/parameters (e.g., the stripe count of Lustre) in our model by $\mathbf{x} = [x_1, \cdots, x_{n_x}]$ and the scalar-valued output/dependent variable (e.g., the write time) associated with the configuration $\mathbf{x}$ by $y(\mathbf{x})$. In our setting, this output depends on the state of the system and can be viewed as stochastic. By y^j we denote a particular measurement of the output at a specific $\mathbf{x}^j$. Hence, collected data is of the form $\{(\mathbf{x}^j, y^j) : j = 1, \ldots, n_y\}$, where the $\mathbf{x}^j$ need not be distinct (which occurs if replicated measurements are conducted at a particular $\mathbf{x}^j$).

We consider smooth, nonlinear models, which can be written as linear combinations of n_b nonlinear basis functions ϕ,

$$m(\mathbf{x}; \beta) = \sum_{k=1}^{n_b} \beta_k \phi_k(\mathbf{x}). \tag{1}$$

Once a basis ϕ has been selected, the hyperparameters β can be selected by standard regression-/optimization-based approaches. For example, since these models are linear in β, a common approach is to employ

$$\hat{\beta} = \arg \min_{\beta} \sum_{j=1}^{n_y} \left(m(\mathbf{x}^j; \beta) - y^j \right)^2, \tag{2}$$

which corresponds to the maximum likelihood estimator for β under the assumption that y is Gaussian.

There can be many choices of basis functions; for simplicity, we focus on terms that are low-degree polynomials in either the parameter, x_i, or the inverse of the parameter, $\frac{1}{x_i}$. In particular, we consider terms of the form

$$\left\{ \prod_{i=1}^{n_x} (x_i)^{p_i} : p_i \in \{-1, 0, 1\}, i = 1, \ldots, n_x \right\}. \tag{3}$$

We could have expanded our set to include terms that could better account for differences in scale (e.g., $x_1 \log(x_2)$) or higher degree polynomials (e.g., $\frac{x_1^2 x_2}{x_3^2}$), but found that the set (3) was sufficiently rich for our purposes.

Since one of our goals in building a model of the form (2) was simplicity of the model, we desired to incorporate only a handful of basis terms, n_b, from the set (3). Each term in (3) can be defined by the integer vector $\mathbf{p} \in \{-1, 0, 1\}^{n_x}$. We let $\hat{m}(\mathbf{x}; \mathbf{P})$ denote the model prediction at $\mathbf{x}$ resulting from selecting a basis defined by $\mathbf{P} = \{\mathbf{p}^1, \cdots, \mathbf{p}^{n_b}\}$ and using the coefficients defined by (2). Given an initially empty set $\mathbf{P}$, we follow a greedy procedure (also known as a *forward* model selection approach) of adding to $\mathbf{P}$ the $\mathbf{p}$ that most reduces the prediction error. Formally, this means we determine the $\mathbf{p}$ that solves

$$\min_{\mathbf{p} \in \{-1,0,1\}^{n_x}} \sum_{j=1}^{n_y} \left(\frac{\hat{m}(\mathbf{x}^j; \mathbf{P} \cup \mathbf{p}) - y^j}{y^j} \right)^2. \tag{4}$$

After updating $\mathbf{P}$, this procedure can be repeated until: (i) we have reached a desired limit on the number of terms to include, (ii) we have exhausted the set in (3), or (iii) additional terms lead to negligible reductions of the prediction error (which, under certain regularity assumptions can be interpreted as the terms not being statistically significant). In

Parameter	Tested Values	# of Values
c, stripe count	1,2,4,8,16,32,64,96,128,156	10
s, stripe size (MB)	1,2,4,8,16,32,64,96,128	9

Table 1: Training configurations (90 in total) tested as part of the single-node experiment.

our experiments, we always terminated the approach based on (i), reaching an upper limit to the number of model terms.

Before proceeding, we note that in (4) we are using a relative error metric that is slightly different from the usual least-squares error criterion (e.g., as used in (2)). We made this choice in order to bias our model terms toward smaller values of the output y. In the context of I/O models for optimization, we are less interested in accurately predicting large times than we are small times. An alternative approach to building models based on a bias toward high-performing configurations is discussed in [1].

Here, we consider models that could be employed in tuning for multiple file sizes simultaneously. Consequently we will have $n_x = 4$ independent variables, $\mathbf{x} = (c, s, a, f)$, and there are $3^{n_x} = 81$ possible terms in the set (3).

Experimentally, we ran tests using VPIC-IO and different file sizes (i.e., different core counts). The training set for each of the VPIC-IO experiments and their file sizes are shown in Table 2. We have chosen to decrease the size of the training set as the core counts (and hence file sizes) increase because of the corresponding increase in computational resources required. The way that these training sets are chosen is done in a systematic and automatic manner: For example, for the 2048-core experiments for stripe count, out of the 10 values shown in Table 1, 3 were chosen to cover the space: [16, 32, 256]. We chose 4 values (in MB) for stripe size, [1, 4, 16, 64], and 5 values for the number of aggregators, [16, 32, 48, 64, 80]. This leads to 60 configurations used for training our model. Since 2048 cores on at least needs 85 nodes on Hopper, and we follow the one-aggregator-per-node rule, 80 is the maximum value of the aggregators.

# of cores	file size (GB)	training set size
128	32	216
256	64	120
512	128	72
1024	256	60
2048	512	60

Table 2: Breakdown of training set for the parallel I/O model.

Using the above approach on the entire training data set, we obtain a six-term basis of $\{1, f, \frac{f}{a}, \frac{a}{c}, \frac{cs}{a}, \frac{cf}{a}\}$. However, inspection of this basis shows that any resulting model is necessarily monotone in s: if the coefficient for $\frac{cs}{a}$ is positive, the write times are increasing in s, otherwise the write times are non-increasing in s. Consequently, we made the decision to include a seventh term. The term with a factor $\frac{1}{s}$ that best solved (4) given the other six terms was determined to be $\frac{a}{s}$. Therefore, our seven-term model is of the form

$$m(\mathbf{x}) = \beta_1 + \beta_2 f + \beta_3 \frac{f}{a} + \beta_4 \frac{a}{c} + \beta_5 \frac{a}{s} + \beta_6 \frac{cs}{a} + \beta_7 \frac{cf}{a}, \tag{5}$$

with a fit to the data yielding $\hat{\beta} = [-20.65, 0.11, 4.17, 27.13, 4.50, 0.0038, 0.01]$.

In the next section we will analyze this model's ability

to perform space reduction and optimization for a variety of I/O tuning tasks. Before proceeding to this study, we note that the model (5) includes both actionable parameters (c, s, a) as well as an ancillary parameter (f) determined from an input. In the context of model-based optimization, we could use this new model in a minimization for any file size for which the model is deemed reliable,

$$m^*(f) \equiv \min_{(c,s,a) \in \Omega} m(c, s, a, f). \qquad (6)$$

We also note that the application considered here is a weak-scaling application (i.e., the number of processors used to run the application is directly proportional to the file size). Therefore, there was no need to use the number of processors (p) as another parameter in the model. If instead, the file size is fixed as we scale the number of processors, p, should also be an independent variable in the model.

3. APPLYING PERFORMANCE MODELS

We show the process of using the empirical model in our I/O autotuning framework in Figure 1. The three steps of the autotuning process are: *pruning, exploration,* and *refitting.* In the pruning step, for a given I/O kernel and problem size, the framework predicts the I/O cost for all combinations of tunable parameters and selects the top twenty configurations with the least I/O cost. In the exploration step, the framework executes the I/O kernel with the selected twenty configurations to determine their empirical (rather than predicted) performance. The framework then refits the model with the newly collected write time data included. In the simplest case, which we use in this paper, the autotuning system runs the top ten configurations with the refitted model and returns the best-performing configuration to the user. One can use this configuration for future executions of the application at varying levels of concurrency.

The selection of the best performing configurations from the model-predicted write times and the number of iterations of refitting are controllable by the user of our framework. While we used the top twenty configurations, which proved to be effective in our tests, if a user prefers to select a different number of best-predicted configurations or wishes to refit the model iteratively, the user can configure the framework with simple settings.

4. EXPERIMENTAL RESULTS

In this section, we present the I/O write time results for the VPIC-IO kernel at different scales. We first compare the performance of our autotuning framework using the empirical models with that of the previous framework using GAs [2]. We then evaluate the effectiveness of the model-based framework on a variety of problem settings.

To develop the model, we ran various training configurations. The number of configurations for each scale is shown in Table 2. The total time to run all the configurations of VPIC-IO at the specified number of processors was 16.5 hours. Note that this training cost is a *one-time expense* for the performance model. The resulting model is used for predicting write times across different concurrencies. Once the model is formed, the incremental time spent in the pruning, exploration, and refitting steps is minimal. For example, the exploration step of the VPIC-IO kernel using 2048 cores took 31 minutes. In contrast, our GA-based tuning process,

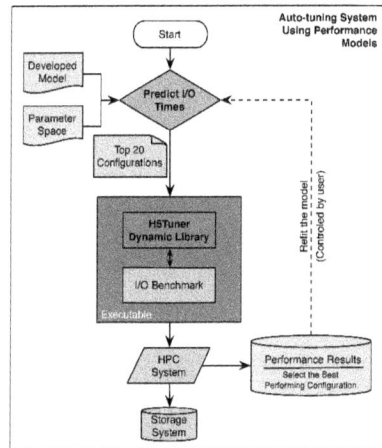

Figure 1: Design of our new autotuning system making use of performance models.

which tested roughly 400 configurations for the VPIC-IO kernel (running at 2048 cores), ran for 12 hours.

To summarize, the GA-based approach has a high run-time overhead associated with every kernel and scale level. The empirical-model-based approach has a one-time cost associated with fitting a model for a specific kernel, but can thereafter be used to predict times for any number of processors, with a fractional cost for refitting.

We now evaluate the framework with a large space of 640 configurations for the VPIC-IO kernel running on 512 cores. Figure 2 shows the twenty selected configurations with the least predicted write times for the original space along with the actual time it took to run them on the platform. The autotuning framework found configurations that achieve an approximately 1.4X speedup of write time performance by using the larger configuration/search space. The new configurations use larger stripe counts, stripe sizes, and numbers of aggregators. In this 512-core VPIC-IO experiment, the number of nodes used is equal to 22 (i.e., 512 divided by 24 cores per node). It has been suggested by some studies that using one aggregator per node achieves the best write times. We observe that all of the top-ten configurations use more aggregators than the number of nodes. Further analysis is needed to characterize the reasons for such behavior.

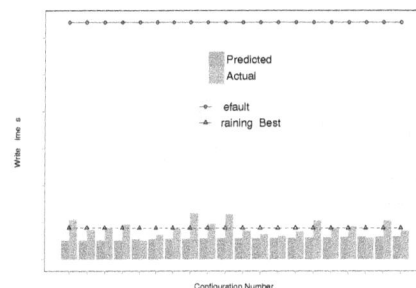

Figure 2: Comparison of the write times of the top-twenty configurations for VPIC-IO on 512 cores.

We tested the autotuning framework to tune the VPIC-IO kernel on a different number of processors (2048 cores). We compare the performance of the selected top-twenty configurations (from a space of 640 input configurations) and the best ten configurations (after the refitting process), respectively, in Figure 3. In this test, we observe that the tuned parameters values differ for I/O kernels running at different number of processors. Among the configurations, the number of aggregators is again larger than the number of nodes (85 for the 2048-core test) in many cases. Although the accuracy of predicted write times is lower than the 512-core experiment, the best configuration achieves a 27X speedup over the default configuration.

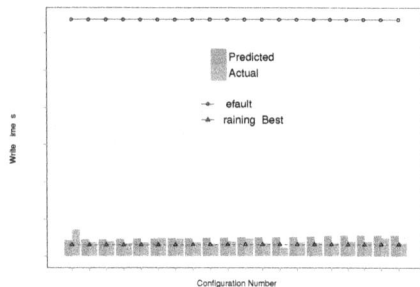

Figure 3: Comparison of the write times of the top-twenty configurations for VPIC-IO on 2048 cores.

We evaluate the model developed using the training configurations at smaller scales (see Table 2) in order to tune the I/O kernel running at 8192 cores. Note that we did not use any configurations from the 8192-core runs in training the model. The 8192-core runs use 342 nodes of Hopper and produce roughly 2TB of data. We used a configuration/search space of 1080 configurations for the model.

We show the I/O cost of the selected top-twenty configurations after the pruning and exploration steps in Figure 4. We observe significant performance improvement. The speedups over the default I/O configurations on Hopper at a concurrency of 8192 cores are on the order of 54X for VPIC-IO.

Table 3 summarizes the achieved speedups for the VPIC-IO kernel running at different concurrencies. The table also shows the size of the data written to the file system and the I/O bandwidth achieved. Overall, the tuned configurations achieve speedups ranging from 3.5X to 50X, which is consistent with exploring the search space using GAs. The time to traverse the search space after training was reduced from 12 hours to a maximum of two hours. In most cases, exploring the top-twenty configurations took one hour, resulting in significant improvements to overall parallel I/O performance.

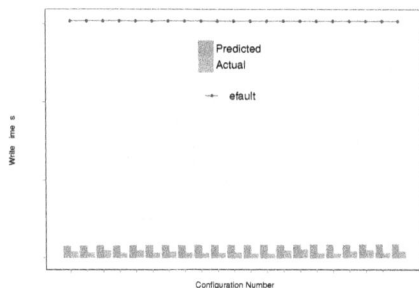

Figure 4: Comparison of the write times of the top-twenty configurations for VPIC-IO on 8192 cores.

# cores	I/O Kernel	File Size (GB)	Actual B.W. (MB/s)	Default B.W. (MB/s)	Speed-up
128	VPIC	32	2074.65	471.75	4.40
512	VPIC	128	5185.4	408.6	12.69
1024	VPIC	256	6181.75	336.6	18.37
2048	VPIC	512	11422.28	412.19	27.71
8192	VPIC	2048	18857.3	345.27	54.62

Table 3: Speedups of VPIC-IO with our autotuning framework.

5. CONCLUSION AND FUTURE WORK

This paper has presented an important development in our work on autotuning parallel I/O. We have dramatically reduced the run time for our framework from *12 hours to 2 hours* by incorporating an empirical performance model. The model accounts for major parameters pertaining to parallel I/O operations on a production supercomputing platform. We fit the model with a relatively small training set of application runs. The model was then used to predict configurations with high levels of I/O performance on two applications and at varying levels of concurrency.

Our current approach of determining a training set is based on a batch execution model. Namely, we precompute a training set with a space-filling design in advance, and evaluate the training set in a single batch job. We could have opted for an adaptive, "sequential design of experiments" approach (see, e.g., [5]), where each configuration is based on the results of the previous runs. This has the potential to further reduce the size of the training set.

Acknowledgment

This work was supported by the Office of Advanced Scientific Computing Research, Office of Science, U.S. Department of Energy, under contract numbers DE-AC02-05CH11231 and DE-AC02-06CH11357. This research used resources of the National Energy Research Scientific Computing Center.

6. REFERENCES

[1] P. Balaprakash, R. Gramacy, and S. M. Wild. Active-learning-based surrogate models for empirical performance tuning. CLUSTER '13, pages 1–8, 2013.

[2] B. Behzad, L. Huong Vu Thanh, J. Huchette, S. Byna, Prabhat, R. Aydt, Q. Koziol, and M. Snir. Taming parallel I/O complexity with auto-tuning. SC '13, 2013.

[3] K. J. Bowers, B. J. Albright, L. Yin, B. Bergen, and T. J. T. Kwan. Ultrahigh performance three-dimensional electromagnetic relativistic kinetic plasma simulation. *Physics of Plasmas*, 15(5):7, 2008.

[4] S. Byna, A. Uselton, Prabhat, D. Knaak, , and Y. He. Trillion particles, 120,000 cores, and 350 TBs: Lessons learned from a hero I/O run on Hopper. In *CUG'13*, 2013.

[5] R. B. Gramacy and H. K. H. Lee. Adaptive design and analysis of supercomputer experiments. *Technometrics*, 51(2):130–145, 2009.

[6] H. Shan, J. Shalf, and K. Antypas. Characterizing and predicting the I/O performance of HPC applications using a parameterized synthetic benchmark. In *SC' 08*. ACM/IEEE, 2008.

[7] E. Smirni, C. L. Elford, D. A. Reed, and A. A. Chien. Performance modeling of a parallel I/O system: An application driven approach. In *PPSC*. SIAM, 1997.

[8] H. You, Q. Liu, Z. Li, and S. Moore. The design of an auto-tuning I/O framework on Cray XT5 system. In *CUG'11*, Fairbanks, Alaska, May 2011.

SLAM: Scalable Locality-Aware Middleware for I/O in Scientific Analysis and Visualization

Jiangling Yin, Jun Wang, Xuhong Zhang,
Junyao Zhang
EECS, University of Central Florida
Orlando, Florida 32826
{jyin,jwang,xzhang,Junyao}@eecs.ucf.edu

Wu-chun Feng
Department of Computer Science
Virginia Tech
Virginia Tech, Blacksburg, VA 2406
wfeng@vt.edu

ABSTRACT

Whereas traditional scientific applications are computationally intensive, recent applications require more data-intensive analysis and visualization. As the computational power and size of compute clusters continue to increase, the I/O read rates and associated network cost for these data-intensive applications create a serious performance bottleneck when faced with the massive data sets of today's "big data" era.

In this paper, we present "Scalable Locality-Aware Middleware" (SLAM) for scientific data analysis applications. SLAM leverages a distributed file system (DFS) to provide scalable data access for scientific applications. To reduce data movement and enforce data-process locality, a data-centric scheduler (DC-scheduler) is proposed to enable scientific applications to read data locally from a DFS. We prototype our proposed SLAM system along with the Hadoop distributed file system (HDFS) on two well-known scientific applications. We find in our experiments that SLAM can greatly reduce I/O cost and double the overall performance, as compared to existing approaches.

Keywords

MPI/POSIX I/O; HDFS; Parallel BLAST; ParaView

1. INTRODUCTION

Modern technological advances have led to scientific instruments and computer simulations that create or collect extremely large and diverse datasets. To readily analyze and interpret this data, many scientific analysis/visualization applications have been designed. For instance, gene analysis tools such as parallel BLAST have been developed to help researchers to better understand the functionality of biological entities and processes [5]. Also, visualization applications such as ParaView [1] can interpret and graphically represent raw simulation/scientific data. These applications are developed with MPI programming model, in which the shared dataset is stored in a network accessible storage system like NFS, PVFS, or Lustre, and transferred to a parallel

HPDC'14, June 23–27, Vancouver, BC, Canada.
Copyright is held by the owner/author(s). Publication rights licensed to ACM.
ACM 978-1-4503-2749-7/14/06 ...$15.00.
http://dx.doi.org/10.1145/2600212.2600709.

MPI process during execution. However, in today's big data era, rapidly growing data sets are too heavyweight to be moved efficiently over the network due to limited resources.

Distributed file systems, constructed from machines with locally attached disks, can scale with the problem size and number of nodes as needed. For instance, the Hadoop system employs a DFS for MapReduce applications and allows map tasks to access data locally. As the number of cluster nodes increases, the Hadoop system can scale-out, expanding storage and launching MapReduce tasks on the additional nodes. Compared to the MPI programming model,however, the MapReduce programming model lacks the flexibility and efficiency to implement the complex algorithms executed in scientific applications such as parallel BLAST [5], FLASH physics, or visualization applications.

In this paper, we propose "Scalable Locality-Aware Middleware" (SLAM), which allows scientific analysis applications to benefit from data-locality exploitation with the use of HDFS, while also maintaining the flexibility and efficiency of the MPI programming model. SLAM employs a process-to-data mapping scheduler (DC-scheduler) to transform a compute-centric mapping into a data-centric one so that a computational process always accesses data from a local or nearby computation node. We realize a SLAM prototype system using mpiBLAST and ParaView to demonstrate the efficiency of SLAM. In our work, SLAM runs on the Hadoop distributed file system (HDFS). Our experiments show that the I/O cost of data movement is highly reduced when S-LAM is incorporated.

2. SLAM DESIGN AND IMPLEMENTATION

The objective of SLAM is to allow scientific analysis programs to benefit from data locality exploitation in HDFS. Since the data is distributed in advance within HDFS, the default task assignment may not allow parallel processes to fully benefit from local data access without considering data distribution. Thus, we need to intercept the original tasks scheduled and re-assign the tasks so as to achieve maximum efficiency on a parallel system with a high degree of data locality and load balancing.

SLAM system consists of two important parts: a data centric load-balanced scheduler called DC-scheduler and a translation I/O layer called SLAM-I/O. The DC-scheduler determines which specific data fragment is assigned to each node to process, thus minimizing the number of fragments pulled over the network. The SLAM-I/O will allow parallel MPI processes to directly access fragments treated as chunks in HDFS from local hard drive, which is part of the entire HDFS storage.

2.1 SLAM-I/O: A Translation Layer

Current scientific parallel applications are mainly developed with the MPI model, which employs either MPI or POSIX-I/O to run on a network file system or a network-attached parallel file system. SLAM uses HDFS to replace these file systems, which entails handling the I/O compatibility issues between MPI-based programs and HDFS.

We implement a translation layer, SLAM-I/O, to handle the incompatible I/O semantics. The basic idea is to transparently transform high-level I/O operations of parallel applications to standard HDFS I/O calls. We elaborate how SLAM-I/O works as follows. SLAM-I/O first connects to the HDFS server using hdfsConnect() and mounts HDFS as a local directory at the corresponding compute node. Hence each cluster node works as one client to HDFS. Any I/O operations of parallel applications that work in the mounted directory are intercepted by the layer and redirected to HDFS. Finally, the correspondent hdfs I/O calls are triggered to execute specific I/O functions *e.g.* open /read /write /close.

In the experiments to follow, we prototype SLAM-I/O using FUSE, a framework for running stackable file systems in a non-privileged mode. An I/O call from application to Hadoop file system is illustrated in Figure 1. Firstly, the Hadoop file system is mounted on all participating cluster nodes through the SLAM-I/O layer. Then the I/O operations of scientific applications are passed through a virtual file system (VFS), taken over by SLAM-I/O through FUSE and then forwarded to HDFS.

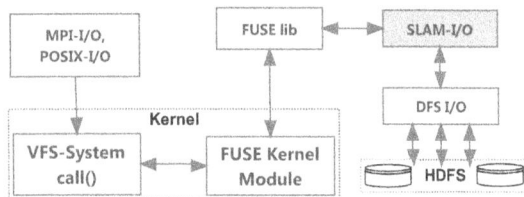

Figure 1: The I/O call in our prototype. A FUSE kernel module redirects file system calls from parallel I/O to SLAM-I/O. SLAM-I/O wraps HDFS clients and translates the I/O call to DFS I/O.

2.2 A Data Centric Load-balanced Scheduler

Scalability and high performance in data intensive scientific applications relies on data locality and load balance. However, heterogeneity issues exist that could potentially result in load imbalance. For instance, in parallel gene data processing, the global database is formatted into many fragments, and the data processing job is divided into a list of tasks corresponding to the database fragments. On the other hand, HDFS random chunk placement algorithm may distribute database fragments unevenly within the cluster, leaving some nodes with more data than others.

We implement a fragment location monitor as a background daemon to report unassigned fragment locations to the DC-scheduler. At any point of time, DC-scheduler always tries to launch a *local task* of the requesting process, that is, a task with its corresponding fragment available on the node of the requesting process. In practice, a high degree

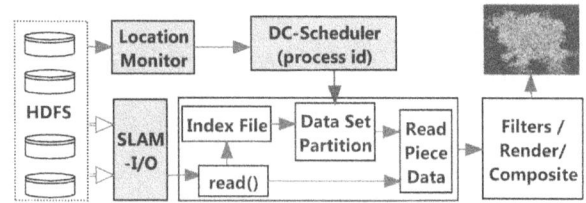

Figure 2: Proposed SLAM for ParaView. The DC-scheduler assigns data processing tasks to MPI processes such that each MPI process could read the needed data locally.

of data locality could often be achieved as each fragment has three physical copies in HDFS, leaving three different node candidates available for scheduling.

Upon an incoming data processing job, the DC-scheduler invokes the location monitor to report the physical location of all target fragments. If a process from a specific node requests a task, the scheduler assigns a task to the process using the following procedure. First, if local tasks exist on the requesting node, the scheduler will evaluate which local task should be assigned to the requesting process in order to make other parallel processes achieve locality as much as possible. Second, if no local task exists on the node, the scheduler will assign a task to the requesting process by comparing all unassigned tasks in order to make other parallel processes achieve locality. The node will then pull the corresponding fragment over the network.

Since mpiBLAST adopts a master-slave architecture, the DC-scheduler could be directly incorporated into the master process, which performs dynamic scheduling according to which nodes are idle at any given time.

2.3 ParaView with SLAM

We show how SLAM is implemented in Paraview in this section. ParaView employs reader modules on data server processes to interpret data from files. To process a dataset, the data servers running in parallel will call the reader to read a meta-file, which points to a series of data files. Then, each data server will compute a designated fragment of the data assignment according to the number of data files, number of parallel servers, and server rank. Data servers will read the data in parallel from the shared storage and then filter/render.

In order to achieve locality computation for ParaView, the default task assignments need to be intercepted to use our proposed DC-scheduler to assign tasks for each data server at run time. Specifically, we illustrate the SLAM framework organization for ParaView in Figure 2.

Our proposed DC-scheduler strategy in Section 2.2 is very suitable for applications with dynamic scheduling algorithms, such as mpiBLAST, in which scheduling is determined by which nodes are idle at any given time. However, since the data assignment in ParaView uses a static data partitioning method, the work allocation is determined beforehand; no process works as a central scheduler. For this kind of scheduling, we adopt a round-robin request order for all data servers. Until the task set is empty, the data server process with a specific process ID can get all the data pieces assigned to it. The data servers will read the data in parallel and then filter/render.

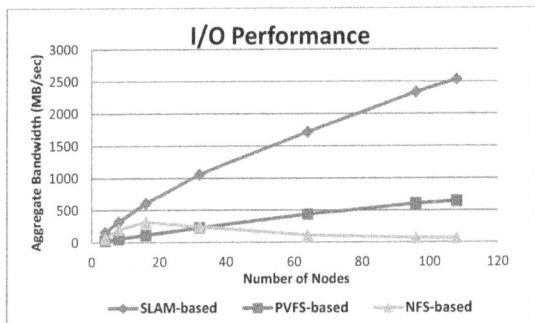

Figure 3: Read bandwidth comparison of NFS, PVFS and SLAM based BLAST schemes.

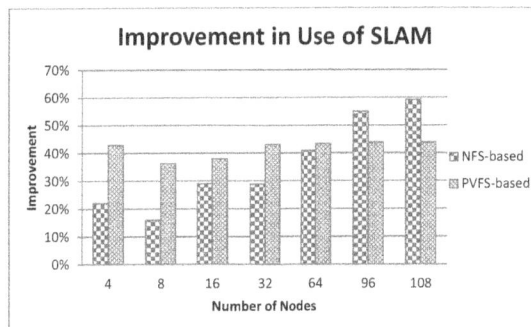

Figure 4: Performance gain of BLAST execution time when searching the *nt* database using SLAM, compared to NFS and PVFS-based.

3. EXPERIMENTS AND ANALYSIS

3.1 Experimental Setup

We conducted comprehensive testing on our proposed middleware SLAM on Marmot. *Marmot* is a cluster of the PRObE on-site project [4] and housed at CMU in Pittsburgh. The system has 128 nodes / 256 cores and each node in the cluster has dual 1.6GHz AMD Opteron processors, 16GB of memory, Gigabit Ethernet, and a 2TB Western Digital SATA disk drive.

In our experiment, MPICH [1.4.1] is installed as parallel programming framework on all compute nodes running CENTOS55-64 with kernel 2.6. We chose Hadoop 0.20.203 as the distributed file system, which is configured as follows: one node for the NameNode/JobTracker, one node for the secondary NameNode, and other compute nodes as the DataNode/TaskTracker. For comparison to SLAM, we run experiments with two conventional file systems—NFS and PVFS2. We choose NFS as it is the default shared file system on most clusters. Additionally, we installed PVFS2 version [2.8.2] with default setting on the cluster nodes.

3.2 Evaluating Parallel BLAST with SLAM

To make comparison with the open source parallel BLAST, we deploy mpiBLAST version [1.6.0] on all the nodes in the clusters. Equipped with our SLAM-I/O layer at each cluster node, HDFS can be mounted as a local directory and used as shared storage for parallel BLAST. BLAST itself can then run on HDFS without recompilation. For clarity, we labeled them as NFS-based, PVFS-based and SLAM-based BLAST. During the experiments, we mount NFS, HDFS and PVFS2 as local file systems at each node if a BLAST process is running on that node.

We select nucleotide sequence database *nt* as our experimental database. The *nt* database contains the GenBank, EMB L, D, and PDB sequences. At the time when we performed experiments, the *nt* database contained 17,611,492 sequences with a total raw size of about 45 GB. The input queries to search against the *nt* database are randomly chosen from *nt* and revised, which guarantees that we find some close matches in the database. We used the same input query in all running cases and fixed the query size to be 50 KB with 100 sequences, which generated a same output result in the amount of around 5.8 MB. The *nt* database was partitioned into 200 fragments.

To test scalability we collected results of aggregated read bandwidth for an increasing number of nodes as illustrated in Figure 3. The bandwidth is based on the total read time and overall amount of data processing. We find SLAM to be a scalable system, since the read bandwidth greatly increases as the number of nodes increase. However, the NFS and PVFS based BLAST schemes have a considerably lower overall bandwidth, and as the number of nodes increases, they do not achieve the same bandwidth increase. This indicates a large data movement overhead exists in NFS and PVFS over the network that bars them from being efficiently scalable.

When running parallel BLAST on a 108-node configuration system, we found the total program execution time with NFS, PVFS and SLAM based BLAST to be 589.4, 379.7 and 240.1 seconds, respectively. We calculate the performance gain as Equation 1, where $T_{\text{SLAM-based}}$ denotes the overall execution time of parallel BLAST based on SLAM and $T_{\text{NFS/PVFS-based}}$ is the overall execution time of mpiBLAST based on NFS or PVFS.

$$improvement = 1 - \frac{T_{\text{SLAM-based}}}{T_{\text{NFS/PVFS-based}}}. \quad (1)$$

As seen from Figure 4, we conclude that SLAM-based BLAST could reduce overall execution latency by 15% to 30% for small-sized clusters with less than 32 nodes as compared to NFS-based BLAST. Given an increasing cluster size, SLAM reduces overall execution time by a greater percentage, reaching 60% for a 108-node cluster setting. This indicates that NFS-based setting is not scaling well. In comparison to PVFS-based BLAST, SLAM runs consistently faster by about 40% for all cluster settings.

3.3 Evaluating ParaView with SLAM

To test the performance of ParaView with SLAM, ParaView [3.14] was installed on all nodes in the cluster. To enable off-screen rendering, ParaView made use of Mesa 3D graphics library version [7.7.1]. The DC-scheduler is implemented with VTK MultiBlock datasets reader for data task assignment. A multi-block dataset is a series of sub datasets, together they represent an assembly of parts or a collection of meshes.

For our test data we use the Macromolecular datasets that was obtained from a Protein Data Bank containing a repository of atomic coordinates, information describing proteins and biological macromolecules. The processed output of

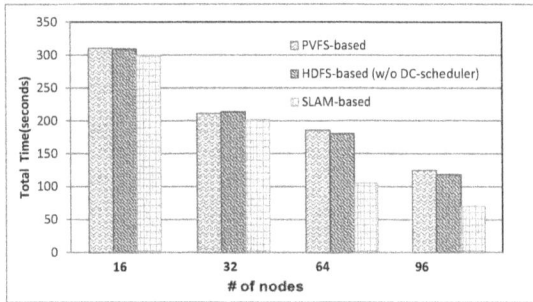

Figure 5: Execution time of PVFS, HDFS and S-LAM based ParaView.

these protein datasets are polygonal images, and ParaView is used to process and display such structures. In our test, we take each dataset as a time step and convert it to a subset of ParaView's MultiBlock file with extension ".vtu". Due to the need to download multiple datasets to the test system, we duplicate some datasets with a little revision and save them as new datasets in "binary" mode. For each rendering 96 subsets from 960 datasets were selected. As a result, our test set was approximately 40 GB in total size and 3.8 GB per rendering step. We use a python script to setup the visualization environment and needed filters to create a reproducible test. The script was submitted to the ParaView server via the provided pvbatch utility to produce a test run on a given node count.

Figure 5 illustrates the overall execution time of a ParaView analysis for an increasing number of nodes with the use of PVFS, HDFS and SLAM. With a small cluster size, the total time of the ParaView experiment did not greatly differ because the available network bandwidth is sufficient to deliver the data needed by the computational processes and there is no network contention. At 64 nodes however, the SLAM based ParaView shows it's strength in large clusters seeing a major reduction in total time when compared with the PVFS and HDFS based ParaView, being nearly 100 seconds quicker in execution for a total execution time of 110 seconds. In a 96 node cluster, the difference between SLAM and the other filesystems is lessened, but still a great improvement is observed with SLAM based ParaView executing in 70 seconds, a reduction almost twice over PVFS and HDFS based ParaView.

4. RELATED WORK

The data locality [7] or in-situ computation is a desirable technique to improve I/O performance. VisIO [6] obtains a linear scalability of I/O bandwidth for ultra-scale visualization but requires hard coding effort to rewrite the ParaView read methods. Janine *et. al.* [2] develop a platform which realizes efficient data movement between in-situ and in-transit computations that perform on large-scale scientific simulations. The Hadoop Distributed File System (HDFS) is an open source community response to the Google File System (GFS), specifically for the use of MapReduce style workloads [3]. Dryad and Spark are two other frameworks to support data locality computation. The idea behind these frameworks is that it is faster and more efficient to send the compute executables to the stored data and process in-situ rather than to pull the data needed from storage. Different

from these approaches, our SLAM uses an I/O middleware to allow existing MPI-based parallel applications to achieve scalable data access with an underlying distributed file system.

5. CONCLUSIONS

In this paper, we developed a scalable locality-aware middleware to dramatically improve the I/O performance of scientific analysis applications. A SLAM-I/O layer is implemented to allow traditional MPI or POSIX based applications to run using Hadoop distributed file system. To exploit data-task locality computation, we proposed a novel data-centric load-balancing scheduler. The scheduler is independent of specific applications and could be adopted for other MPI-based programs that benefit from some form of data locality computation. By conducting experiments over two real scientific application, we found that SLAM can greatly reduce the I/O cost and double the overall execution performance as compared with existing schemes.

6. ACKNOWLEDGMENTS

This work is supported in part by the US National Science Foundation Grant CNS-1115665, CCF-1337244 and National Science Foundation Early Career Award 0953946.

This work is conducted at a PRObE staging cluster-128-node Marmot cluster, which is supported in part by the National Science Foundation under awards CNS-1042537 and CNS-1042543 (PRObE).

7. REFERENCES

[1] J. Ahrens, B. Geveci, and C. Law. Paraview: An end-user tool for large data visualization. *The Visualization Handbook*, 717:731, 2005.

[2] J. C. Bennett, H. Abbasi, P.-T. Bremer, R. Grout, A. Gyulassy, T. Jin, S. Klasky, H. Kolla, M. Parashar, V. Pascucci, P. Pebay, D. Thompson, H. Yu, F. Zhang, and J. Chen. Combining in-situ and in-transit processing to enable extreme-scale scientific analysis. In *Proceedings of the International Conference on High Performance Computing, Networking, Storage and Analysis*, SC '12, pages 49:1–49:9, Los Alamitos, CA, USA, 2012. IEEE Computer Society Press.

[3] J. Dean and S. Ghemawat. Mapreduce: simplified data processing on large clusters. *Communications of the ACM*, 51(1):107–113, 2008.

[4] G. Gibson, G. Grider, A. Jacobson, and W. Lloyd. Probe: A thousand-node experimental cluster for computer systems research. volume 38, June 2013.

[5] H. Lin, X. Ma, W. Feng, and N. F. Samatova. Coordinating computation and i/o in massively parallel sequence search. *IEEE Trans. Parallel Distrib. Syst.*, 22(4):529–543, Apr. 2011.

[6] C. Mitchell, J. Ahrens, and J. Wang. Visio: Enabling interactive visualization of ultra-scale, time series data via high-bandwidth distributed i/o systems. In *IPDPS, 2011 IEEE International*, pages 68–79, May.

[7] S. Sehrish, G. Mackey, J. Wang, and J. Bent. Mrap: A novel mapreduce-based framework to support hpc analytics applications with access patterns. In *Proceedings of the 19th ACM International Symposium on High Performance Distributed Computing*, HPDC '10, pages 107–118, New York, NY, USA, 2010. ACM.

SOR-HDFS: A SEDA-based Approach to Maximize Overlapping in RDMA-Enhanced HDFS *

Nusrat S. Islam, Xiaoyi Lu, Md. W. Rahman, and Dhabaleswar K. (DK) Panda
Department of Computer Science and Engineering
The Ohio State University
{islamn, luxi, rahmanmd, panda}@cse.ohio-state.edu

ABSTRACT

In this paper, we propose *SOR-HDFS*, a SEDA (Staged Event-Driven Architecture)-based approach to improve the performance of HDFS `Write` operation. This design not only incorporates RDMA-based communication over InfiniBand but also maximizes overlapping among different stages of data transfer and I/O. Performance evaluations show that, the new design improves the aggregated write throughput of Enhanced DFSIO benchmark in Intel HiBench by up to 64% and reduces the job execution time by 37% compared to IPoIB (IP over InfiniBand). Compared to the previous best RDMA-enhanced design [4], the improvements in throughput and execution time are 30% and 20%, respectively. Our design can also improve the performance of HBase `Put` operation by up to 53% over IPoIB and 29% compared to the previous best RDMA-enhanced HDFS. To the best of our knowledge, this is the first design of SEDA-based HDFS in the literature.

Categories and Subject Descriptors

C.4 [**PERFORMANCE OF SYSTEMS**]: Design studies

Keywords

Big Data; HDFS; Storage; Clusters and Networks

1. INTRODUCTION

As a distributed file system, HDFS operations are communication intensive. Since the map tasks usually read data in the local storage, most of the communication intensive part is in HDFS `Write` operation and the objective of this paper is to propose a new architecture for HDFS `Write` that can maximize the throughput. During HDFS `Write`, a data block is transferred as packets from clients to DataNodes. Each packet goes through processing

---

*This research is supported in part by National Science Foundation grants #OCI-0926691, #OCI-1148371 and #CCF-1213084. It used the Extreme Science and Engineering Discovery Environment (XSEDE), which is supported by National Science Foundation grant number OCI-1053575.

and replication; finally, it is stored inside the DataNode. As illustrated in Figure 1(a), default HDFS adopts the One-Block-One-Thread (OBOT) architecture to process data sequentially. Since HDFS is primarily designed for MapReduce jobs running on commodity servers that usually have larger sizes (64MB+) of blocks to be transferred and stored on low-speed interconnects and disks, the choice of OBOT design is a good trade-off between simplicity and performance for default Hadoop.

Authors in [5] have identified the performance bottlenecks of HDFS. RDMA-enhanced HDFS designs [3, 4] have improved the Write performance with pipelined and parallel replication schemes, respectively. These designs keep the default OBOT architecture intact and the major improvements come from the reduction of communication time. However, due to the sequential data processing feature in the default OBOT architecture, the incoming data packets should wait for the I/O stage of the previous packet to be completed before they are read and processed. This phenomenon is more obvious in RDMA-enhanced HDFS than the default one, since the performance bottleneck moves from data transmission to data persistence. This indicates that we need to choose a higher-throughput architecture for RDMA-enhanced HDFS to maximize overlapping among various stages.

Staged Event-Driven Architecture (SEDA) [7] is one of the most commonly used high-throughput design approach for Internet services in distributed computing area. It decomposes a complex processing logic into a set of stages connected by queues. HDFS Write operation also consists of several stages as demonstrated in Figure 1(a). But the sequential execution of these stages limits HDFS from fully utilizing the hardware capabilities (such as RDMA) and obtain peak performance. These issues lead us to the following broad questions and design challenges: **1.** How can we re-design HDFS to maximize overlapping among different stages of HDFS Write operation? **2.** Can we adopt high-throughput SEDA-based approach to achieve maximum overlapping? **3.** How much performance improvement can we obtain with the SEDA-based approach using RDMA for communication? **4.** Can we guarantee performance benefits across different HPC clusters with different configurations using the proposed design?

Figure 1(b) shows an outline of our proposed approach. SEDA-based HDFS can perform the stages of packet read, processing, replication, and I/O in an overlapped manner not only among different blocks but also for the same block.

In this paper, we propose a SEDA-based approach for HDFS Write operation. The proposed approach not only incorporates RDMA-based communication but also re-designs the internal software architecture from OBOT to SEDA for exploiting maximum overlapping among different stages of HDFS operations. Performance evaluations show that, the new design can improve the ag-

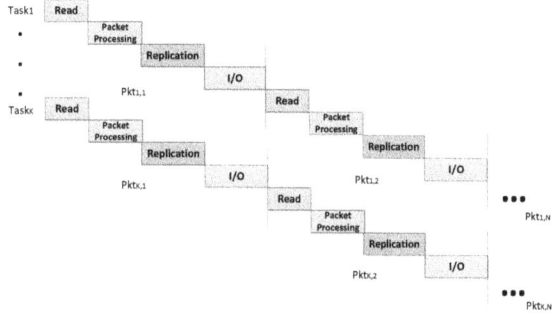

(a) Sequential Data Processing in Default HDFS (One-Block-One-Thread (OBOT) Architecture)

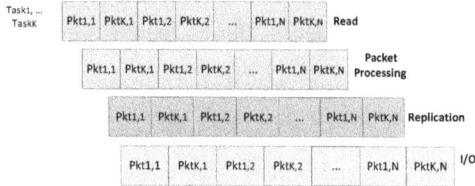

(b) Overlapped Data Processing in Proposed HDFS (Staged Event-Driven Architecture (SEDA))

Figure 1: Default vs. Proposed HDFS Architecture

gregated write throughput of Enhanced DFSIO benchmark in Intel HiBench by up to 64% and reduce the job execution time by 37% compared to IPoIB. Compared to the previous best RDMA-enhanced design, the improvements in throughput and execution time are 30% and 20%, respectively. Our design can also improve the performance of HBase `Put` operation by up to 53% over IPoIB and 29% compared to RDMA-enhanced HDFS.

2. PROPOSED DESIGN

In this section, we describe the architecture and design-details of SOR-HDFS.

2.1 Architectural Overview

The primary goal of SOR-HDFS is to exploit maximum overlapping in HDFS write with a SEDA-based architecture. In our design, we have divided the operations of HDFS write and replication into four stages: (1) Read, (2) Packet Processing, (3) Replication, and (4) I/O. After data is received via RDMA, the data is first read into a Java I/O stream. The received packet is then replicated after some processing operations. The data packet is also written to the disk file. In the default architecture of HDFS, all these stages are handled sequentially by a single thread per block. Whereas, in the proposed design of SOR-HDFS, each of the stages is handled by different thread pools and thus the operations among different stages can overlap at packet level also.

2.2 Design of SOR-HDFS

In this section, we discuss different stages of SOR-HDFS.

Read Stage: Figure 2 shows the architecture of the Read stage. This stage consists of an RDMA-based receiver that receives data in an RDMA Connection object. The Connection object supports multiple end-points. Each DFSClient connects to one of the end-points. This stage also has a pool of buffers that can be used for data received at any end-point in a Round-Robin manner. In our

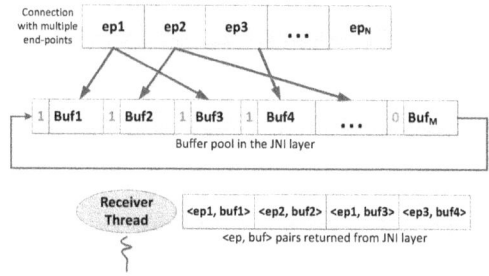

Figure 2: Read stage

previous design [4], we had a single buffer per end-point and this is well-suited with the default architecture. But with the SEDA-based approach, while one packet is in the I/O phase, many other packets may arrive at the receiver from the same DFSClient that keeps on sending packets back to back. Each of the buffers has an associated flag bit to indicate whether the buffer is free or not. When data comes to an end-point, it is assigned a free buffer. The RDMA-based receiver thread returns the buffer pointer of each received packet to the Packet Processing stage.

Packet Processing Stage: The Read stage returns the <end-point, bufferId> tuple for each packet and passes it to the Packet Processing stage. This stage has a pool of worker threads that wait on a Process Request Queue (PRQ). The Process Request Controller (PRC) is responsible for choosing free worker threads from the pool and assigning them to the incoming packets. When a worker thread gets the header for a block, the PRC assigns it for that particular block and passes all the subsequent data packets belonging to this block, to that particular worker thread. In this way, the sequence of packets within a block is maintained by the PRC.

Replication Stage: This stage consists of a pool of threads that replicate the data packets via an RDMA Connection object that supports multiple end-points. The pool of replicator threads wait on a Replication Request Queue (RRQ). RRQ gets data from the worker threads. The Replication Request Controller (RRC) finds out a free thread from the pool and assigns it to replicate a block. This stage also has a Responder thread that receives acknowledgements coming to different end-points of the RDMA Connection.

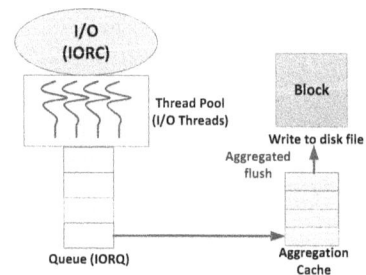

Figure 3: I/O stage

I/O Stage: Figure 3 shows the architecture of the I/O stage of SOR-HDFS. This stage consists of a pool of I/O threads. The worker threads in the Packet Processing stage aggregate multiple data packets into the aggregation cache and puts an I/O request in the I/O Request Queue (IORQ). The I/O Request Controller

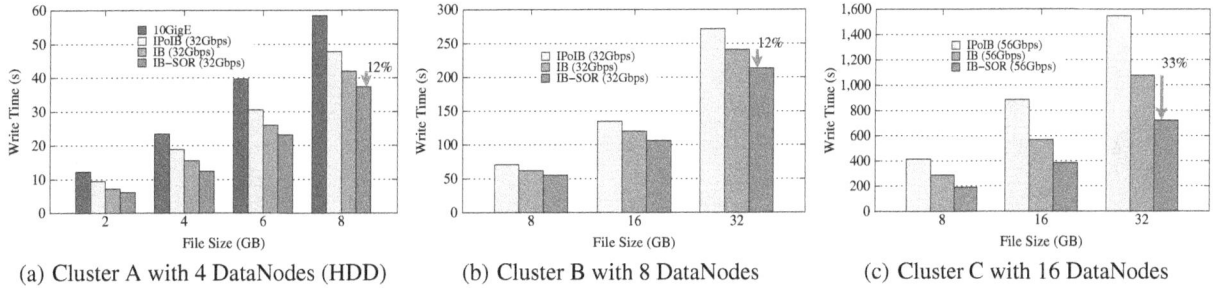

| (a) Cluster A with 4 DataNodes (HDD) | (b) Cluster B with 8 DataNodes | (c) Cluster C with 16 DataNodes |

Figure 4: Write time evaluation using HDFS microbenchmark (SWL)

(IORC) assigns the incoming requests to appropriate I/O threads such that data is written sequentially. The I/O threads flush the aggregated data from the cache to the disk file.

Design of DFSClient: In the pipelined replication technique, the DFSClient sends data to the first DataNode and packets are sent back to back over RDMA. In order to efficiently handle this type of pipelined data transfer, the SOR-HDFS design has a single RDMA Connection with multiple end-point support. DFSClient can dynamically create an end-point with respect to a DataNode and then cache it for subsequent data transfers. The client side also maintains a pool of buffers (Java Direct Buffer) that are used in a Round-Robin manner to send data in a non-blocking fashion.

In parallel replication, there is no replication stage in the DataNode and DFSClient directly writes all the replicas in parallel.

SOR-HDFS provides overalpping among data read, processing, replication, and I/O phases for the same block. The proposed design also preserves overlapping among communication and other phases of HDFS write via back to back data transfer. In this way, in addition to providing task-level parallelism, SOR-HDFS achieves overlapping among various stages of the same block.

3. PERFORMANCE EVALUATION

In this section, we present the detailed performance evaluations of SOR-HDFS design using well-known Hadoop benchmarks and HBase and compare the performance with those of the default architecture over various interconnects, protocols and storage systems. In all our experiments, we used Hadoop1.2.1 and JDK1.7. The HDFS replication factor was set to three with pipelined replication. For experiments with HBase, we used HBase-0.94.14 and YCSB-0.1.4.

3.1 Experimental Setup

We used three different clusters for our evaluations:

1. Intel Westmere Cluster (Cluster A): Xeon Dual quad-core processor (2.67 GHz), NetEffect NE020 10Gb Accelerated Ethernet Adapter (iWARP RNIC), 24 GB RAM, 1TB HDD, 300GB OCZ VeloDrive PCIe SSD. **2.** SDSC Gordon [1] (Cluster B) and **3.** TACC Stampede [6] (Cluster C)

In the figures presented in this section, we have mentioned IB and IB-SOR to indicate the RDMA-enhanced design (HDFSoIB) and SOR-HDFS, respectively. IPoIB QDR is denoted by IPoIB (32Gbps) and IPoIB FDR by IPoIB (56Gbps).

3.2 Parameter Tuning of SOR-HDFS Threads

RDMA connection creation is more expensive than that of Socket. So we have used a single connection i.e. a single receiver thread that minimizes the connection creation overhead. The number of replicator threads is related to the NIC bandwidth of the DataN-

odes. In order to find out the optimal number of replicator threads, we ran the OSU-Multi-Pair-Bandwidth (inter-node) test in OSU-MPI-Microbenchmark over IB and selected the number of concurrent processes that can utilize the network bandwidth most efficiently. In this way, we have used four replicator threads on Cluster A and B and eight on Cluster C (has IPoIB FDR). The number of I/O threads is determined by the maximum disk bandwidth through IOzone write test. Based on these experiments, for Cluster A (HDD nodes), we have selected two I/O threads for SOR-HDFS. The optimal number of I/O threads in Cluster C is one, whereas, in Cluster B we can use up to eight I/O threads (storage in Cluster B is SSD). In our experiments, we tuned the number of the worker threads while keeping the other thread-counts fixed (as determined from the above-mentioned experiments) and found that in all the three clusters, 16 is the optimal number.

3.3 Evaluation using HDFS Microbenchmark

In this section, we have evaluated our design using the HDFS microbenchmark of Sequential Write Latency (SWL) [2]. Figure 4(a) shows the performance of our design on Cluster A. On HDD DataNodes, SOR-HDFS reduces the latency of SWL benchmark by 25% over IPoIB (32Gbps) and 12% compared to the previous best RDMA-based design of HDFS for 20 GB file size. We have also performed microbenchmark level evaluations on Cluster B (cluster size 8) and Cluster C (cluster size 16). On Cluster B, our design improves the performance of SWL by 22% over IPoIB (32Gbps) and 12% over HDFSoIB (32Gbps). On Cluster C, our design shows a benefit of up to 57% over IPoIB (56Gbps) and 33% compared to HDFSoIB (56Gbps).

3.4 Evaluation using MapReduce benchmarks

In these set of experiments, we evaluate our design with the Enhanced DFSIO benchmark of Intel HiBench on three different Clusters. In Cluster A, we perform Enhanced DFSIO test on four SSD DataNodes and vary the file size from 8 to 32 GB. As observed from Figure 5(a), our design increases the aggregated write throughput of Enhanced DFSIO by 37% over IPoIB (32Gbps) and 17% over HDFSoIB (32Gbps) in Cluster A. SOR-HDFS can also reduce the execution time of Enhanced DFSIO by 15% over IPoIB (32Gbps) and 8% over HDFSoIB (32Gbps). Figure 5(b) shows the aggregated write throughput for three different cluster sizes in Cluster B. In this experiment, we varied the cluster size from 8 to 32 DataNodes and the data size was varied from 32 GB (in 8 nodes) to 128 GB (in 32 nodes). SOR-HDFS achieves an improvement of up to 47% over IPoIB (32Gbps) and 20% over HDFSoIB (32Gbps) in aggregated write throughput. The execution time is also reduced by up to 9% compared to that of HDFSoIB (32Gbps). Figure 5(c) shows the aggregated write throughput for three dif-

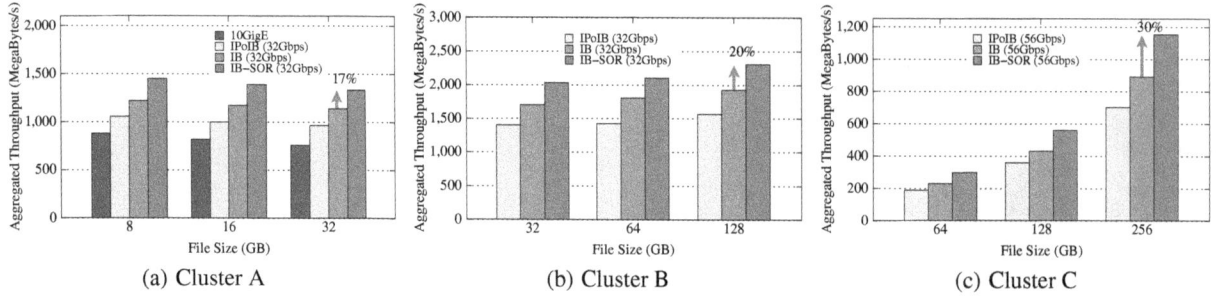

| (a) Cluster A | (b) Cluster B | (c) Cluster C |

Figure 5: Enhanced DFSIO throughput evaluation of Intel HiBench

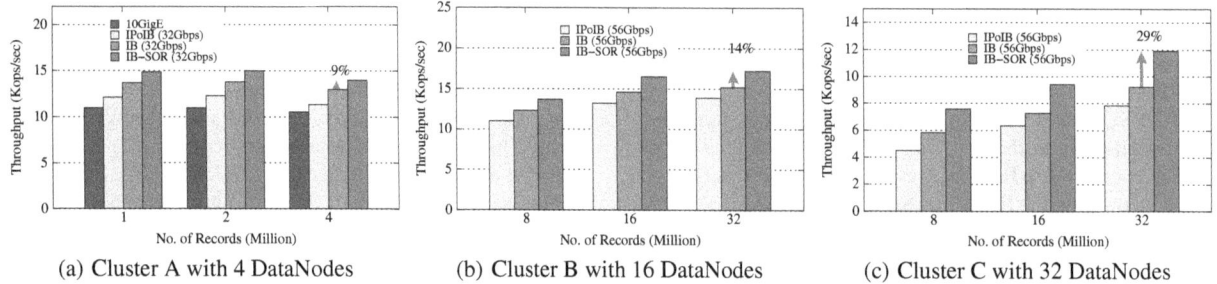

| (a) Cluster A with 4 DataNodes | (b) Cluster B with 16 DataNodes | (c) Cluster C with 32 DataNodes |

Figure 6: Evaluation of HBase Put throughput

ferent cluster sizes in Cluster C. In this experiment, we varied the cluster size from 16 to 64 DataNodes and the data size was varied from 64 GB (in 16 nodes) to 256 GB in (64 nodes). SOR-HDFS achieves an improvement of up to 64% over IPoIB (56Gbps) and 30% over HDFSoIB (56Gbps) in aggregated write throughput. The execution time is also reduced by up to 22% compared to that of HDFSoIB (56Gbps).

3.5 Evaluation using HBase

In this section, we evaluate the performance of HBase Put operation by running HBase on top of SOR-HDFS. For this experiment, we have used the YCSB benchmark. During flush, HBase writes the MemStore to HDFS as an HFile instance. HBase also stores the HLogs into HDFS. Therefore, we load the data from workload A in YCSB on different clusters. In Cluster A, we run the YCSB load experiment in four DataNodes. As shown in Figure 6(a), our design achieves an improvement of 23% over IPoIB (32Gbps) and 9% over HDFSoIB (32Gbps) in HBase Put throughput. We performed tests with the YCSB benchmark on Cluster B and C also. As observed from Figures 6(b) and 6(c), our design achieves a performance gain of up to 25% over IPoIB (32Gbps) and 14% over HDFSoIB (32Gbps) in Cluster B; the benefit is up to 53% over IPoIB (56Gbps) and 29% over HDFSoIB (56Gbps) in Cluster C.

The overlapping among different stages of data write, proper utilization of disk and network bandwidth as well as RDMA-based communication lead to large performance benefits for SOR-HDFS. SOR-HDFS also shows better improvements in throughput compared to latency. This is because of the SEDA-architecture which is particularly designed to maximize throughput.

4. CONCLUSION AND FUTURE WORK

In this paper, we proposed SOR-HDFS, a new HDFS design that maximizes overlapping among different phases of HDFS write op-

eration by leveraging the event-driven principle in SEDA architecture. Performance evaluations show that, our design can achieve a performance gain of up to 64% over IPoIB and 30% over HDFSoIB for the Enhanced DFSIO benchmark of Intel HiBench. SOR-HDFS also improves HBase Put operation throughput by up to 53% over IPoIB and 29% compared to HDFSoIB. As a future work, we would like to evaluate the impact of SEDA-based approach on other HDFS operations also.

References

[1] Gordon at San Diego Supercomputer Center. http://www.sdsc.edu/us/resources/gordon/.

[2] N. S. Islam, X. Lu, M. W. Rahman, J. Jose, H. Wang, and D. K. Panda. A Micro-benchmark Suite for Evaluating HDFS Operations on Modern Clusters. In *The Proceedings of 2nd Workshop on Big Data Benchmarking (WBDB)*, India, 2012.

[3] N. S. Islam, X. Lu, M. W. Rahman, and D. K. Panda. Can Parallel Replication Benefit Hadoop Distributed File System for High Performance Interconnects? In *The Proceedings of IEEE 21st Annual Symposium on High-Performance Interconnects (HOTI)*, San Jose, CA, 2013.

[4] N. S. Islam, M. W. Rahman, J. Jose, R. Rajachandrasekar, H. Wang, H. Subramoni, C. Murthy, and D. K. Panda. High Performance RDMA-based Design of HDFS over InfiniBand. In *The Proceedings of The International Conference for High Performance Computing, Networking, Storage and Analysis (SC)*, Salt Lake City, 2012.

[5] J. Shafer, S. Rixner, and A. L. Cox. The Hadoop Distributed Filesystem: Balancing Portability and Performance. In *The Proceedings of the Internation Symposium on Performance Analysis of Systems and Software (ISPASS'10)*, White Plains, NY, 2010.

[6] Stampede at Texas Advanced Computing Center. http://www.tacc.utexas.edu/resources/hpc/stampede.

[7] M. Welsh, D. Culler, and E. Brewer. SEDA: An Architecture for Well-Conditioned, Scalable Internet Services. In *Proceedings of the 18th ACM Symposium on Operating Systems Principles (SOSP)*, Banff, Alberta, Canada, 2001.

Squirrel: Scatter Hoarding VM Image Contents on IaaS Compute Nodes

Kaveh Razavi
Dept. of Computer Science
VU University Amsterdam
The Netherlands
k.razavi@vu.nl

Ana Ion
Dept. of Computer Science
VU University Amsterdam
The Netherlands
a.ion@student.vu.nl

Thilo Kielmann
Dept. of Computer Science
VU University Amsterdam
The Netherlands
thilo.kielmann@vu.nl

ABSTRACT

In IaaS clouds, virtual machines are booted on demand from user-provided disk images. Both the number of virtual machine images (VMIs) and their large size (GBs), challenge storage and network transfer solutions, and lead to perceivably slow VM startup times. In previous work, we proposed using small VMI caches ($O(100\,\text{MB})$) that contain those parts of a VMI that are actually needed for booting. Here, we present Squirrel, a fully replicated storage architecture that exploits deduplication, compression, and snapshots from the ZFS file system, and lets us keep large quantities of VMI caches on all compute nodes of a data center with modest storage requirements. (Much like rodents cache precious food in many distributed places.) Our evaluation shows that we can store VMI caches for all 600+ community images of Windows Azure, worth 16.4 TB of raw data, within 10 GB of disk space and 60 MB of main memory on each compute node of our DAS-4 cluster. Extrapolation to several thousands of images predicts the scalability of our approach.

Categories and Subject Descriptors

D.4.2 [**Storage Management**]: Storage hierarchies;
E.4 [**Coding and Information Theory**]: Data compaction and compression

General Terms

System Design, Experimentation

Keywords

VM Images, Caching, Deduplication, Compression

1. INTRODUCTION

With the advent of public Infrastructure-as-a-Service (IaaS) clouds, like Amazon EC2 or Windows Azure, the use of virtualized operating systems, "virtual machines", has gained

widespread use. The promise of elastic computing is instantaneous creation of virtual machines, according to the needs of an application or web service. In practice, however, users face VM startup times of several minutes, along with high variability, depending on the actual system load [16, 21]. One important factor contributing to VM startup time is the transfer of the VM image (VMI) from a storage node, via the data center network, to the selected compute node [35].

The simplest VMI transfer technique copies the whole VMI, typically several GBs, to the selected compute node's disk, from where the VM will boot. State of the art is to use Copy-on-Write (CoW) images on the compute nodes, which means accessing the VMI over a network file system and reading only those parts that are needed at boot time, while directing write operations to a local CoW image.

In our recent work [34], we proposed to put a VMI cache in between VMI and CoW image, preferably on the compute node's local disk. As with CoW images, the compute node mounts the VMI and reads it on demand. The difference is that VMI caches are populated with the data read from the VMI in a Copy-on-Read (CoR) fashion. As soon as the VM is booted, the VMI cache contains the boot working set. The next time the compute node needs to boot from the same VMI, it finds a warmed-up cache and can boot the VM without further network transfers, both speeding up the VM boot process, and lowering the traffic pressure on the data center network.

While the VMI caching mechanism overcomes scalability problems of VM startup, it introduces a new set of challenges for avoiding cold caches. Traditional solutions to this problem include cache replacement policies (e.g. LRU [32]) as well as cache-aware VM scheduling. In this work, we take a radically different approach: We propose a fully replicated design, storing *all* VMI caches of a data center on *all* its compute nodes. We show that this is both possible and scalable. We term this approach *scatter hoarding* in analogy to the technique of creating a large number of small hoards (caches) by which squirrels store their food reserves.[1] We describe our implementation of such a design, named *Squirrel*, and thoroughly evaluate its important properties.

The contributions of this paper are as follows:

1. We study the effects of deduplication when combined with compression on both VMIs and VMI caches (Section 2). To the best of our knowledge, this is the first study of its kind. We show that smaller block sizes do

---

[1] http://en.wikipedia.org/wiki/Hoarding_(animal_behavior)

not necessarily yield better overall compression ratios. More importantly, we show that storing caches of *all* VMIs of a data center is feasible with modest storage requirements on the compute nodes.

2. Backed by these observations, we devise a new, fully replicated storage architecture aimed at storing the caches of *all* VMIs of a data center on *all* the compute nodes. We present Squirrel, our implementation of such a design, based on VMI caches and the ZFS file system [4] (Section 3).

3. We evaluate Squirrel using the set of the 600+ community images from Windows Azure[2] to show its desirable properties (Section 4).

Our evaluation shows that that VMI caches have higher cross-similarity than their associated VMIs. This is because VMI diversity mostly comes from installed software, while boot working set diversity (i.e. VMI caches) comes from only a few OS distributions. Better cross-similarity of VMI caches means that they add fewer hashes to a deduplicated storage on average, making their storage more scalable. For our Windows Azure dataset, worth 16.4 TB of raw data, Squirrel only requires 10 GB of disk space and 60 MB of main memory on each compute node of our DAS-4 cluster. Extrapolating these storage requirements shows that Squirrel can scale to thousands of VMI caches with modest disk and memory requirements on current or near-future compute node hardware. Further, we show that, with proper parameter tuning, booting from a deduplicated and compressed file system can be as fast as a normal file system, despite earlier reports [26, 44].

After our evaluation, we discuss related work on VMI storage and transfer in Section 5, and we conclude in Section 6.

2. BACKGROUND

There are essentially two main ideas behind the work presented in this paper: (1.) using VMI caches and (2.) applying deduplication combined with compression to these VMI caches. In Section 2.1, we briefly explain how VMI caches operate. In Section 2.2, we discuss the effects of deduplication and compression on VMI caches. We then hint at the possible effectiveness of compressing VMI caches when applying these techniques.

2.1 VMI cache chaining

Figure 1 (top diagram) shows the internal operation of CoW. A compute node mounts the base VMI and reads from it on demand. Write operations are saved on the CoW image, keeping the base VMI clean. CoW saves the need for copying the entire VMI before booting can begin. This significantly reduces both the VM startup time, and the load on network and storage servers. One drawback with CoW is, however, the need to transfer the boot working set every time a new VM starts up.

In our previous work [34], we showed that transferring the boot working set at scale results in scalability problems. More specifically, when starting one VM from a single VMI on many nodes, the data center network becomes the scalability bottleneck, and when starting VMs from different VMI sources, the storage nodes become the scalability bottleneck.

[2]More precisely, there were 607 images in November 2013.

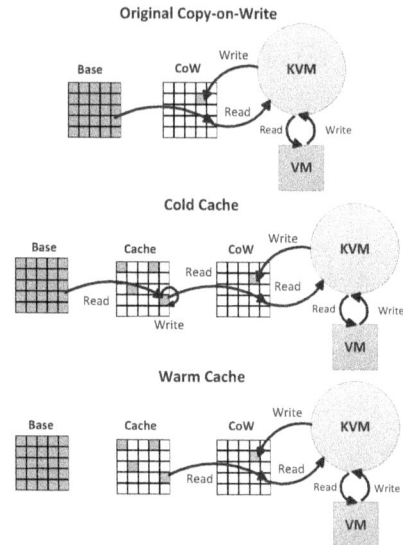

Figure 1: The introduction of VMI caches.

The former scenario is common for high-performance computing applications (e.g., parameter sweeps) as well as autoscaling systems (e.g., [13]). The latter is more common in large-scale, multi-user IaaS clouds with concurrent VM startups by different users.

To address these scalability problems, we introduced VMI caches, a mechanism that allows us to quickly boot a VM by storing the boot working set of a VMI on or near the compute node, avoiding the use of the data center network or the disks at the storage nodes at boot time. Typically, this boot working set is only a small fraction ($O(100\,\text{MB})$) of the original VMI, usually several GBs. The VMI caches are chained in between traditional CoW images and VMIs.

Figure 1 (middle) shows how VMI chaining operates with VMI caches, in contrast to the original CoW architecture. When a node boots from a particular VMI for the first time, the VMI cache is still empty ("cold"). With a cold cache, before handing the reads from the base VMI to the VM process, we write them to the VMI cache. This process is called copy-on-read (CoR), and we showed that it is possible to perform CoR with competitive performance compared to the original CoW architecture [34]. Once the caches are warm (shown at the bottom of Figure 1), the system does not need to read from the base VMI anymore during the boot process.

As mentioned, CoW images typically reside on compute nodes, and VMIs on storage nodes. In principle, VMI caches can reside on any storage medium in between CoW images and base VMIs. The candidates are the disks at compute nodes or the memory of storage nodes. While each candidate has its benefits, we showed in [34] that storing VMI caches on the disks at compute nodes is the preferable option for most scenarios. In this paper, we are looking at efficiently storing our VMI caches on the disks of the compute nodes.

2.2 Compression efficiency

In this section, we analyze the trade-offs involved in compressing the contents present in VMIs and VMI caches. Although the focus here is on VMI caches, the results with

VMIs are also provided for additional insight. In Section 4, we provide information on our VMI repository as well as the data set used in the figures presented in this section.

We use compression ratio as a metric for compression efficiency. If, for a given set of VMIs or VMI caches, the set of unique blocks is defined as U, and the set of nonzero blocks is defined as N, compression ratio for deduplication (i.e., the deduplication ratio) is defined in [12] as:

$$\text{Deduplication ratio} = \frac{|N|}{|U|},$$

where $||$ is the cardinality of a set. The compression ratio for content compression is defined as:

$$\text{Compression ratio} = \frac{\sum\limits^{i \in U} \frac{size(compress(i))}{size(i)}}{|U|},$$

where *compress* is the compression routine (e.g., gzip).

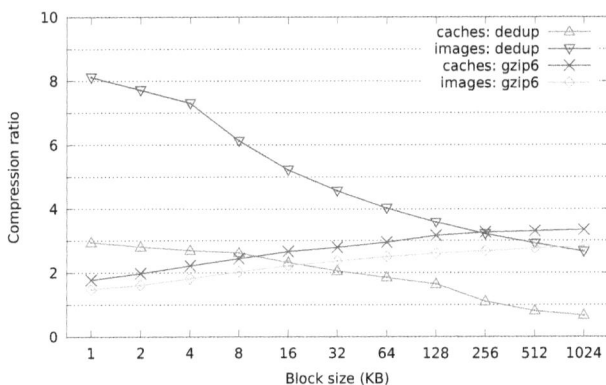

Figure 2: Compression ratio of VMIs and caches with dedup and gzip6

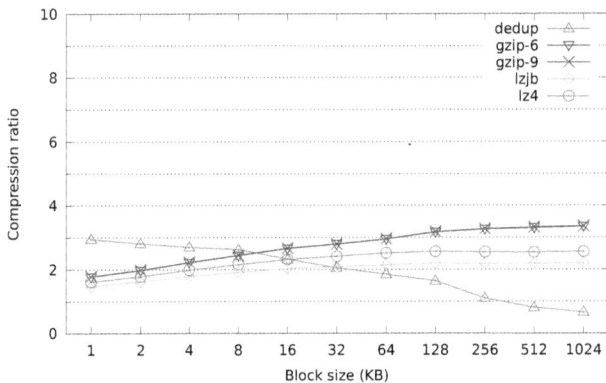

Figure 3: Compression ratio of VMI caches with different routines.

Figure 2 shows the compression ratio with deduplication and gzip6 compression. When decreasing the block size[3], we can see two conflicting trends: Deduplication ratio starts increasing, and gzip's compression ratio starts decreasing. As numerous VMI deduplication studies [18, 19, 26, 44] have pointed out, the reasons for higher deduplication ratio with smaller block sizes are (1.) the fact that small differences

[3]In this paper, we study the trends when making block size smaller. Thus, it is natural to read the figures, that have block size on the horizontal axis, from right to left.

in otherwise similar larger blocks do not result in different hashes for the whole block, and that (2.) similar data with different alignments have a better chance of producing the same hash (i.e., deduplicating). Larger block sizes have better compression (with e.g., gzip) because the chance of finding similar duplicate strings within the block increases. We have also measured cache compression ratios for gzip9, lz4, and lzjb algorithms shown in Figure 3. gzip9 is compressing almost the same as gzip6 with higher CPU cost. lz4 and lzjb are faster compression algorithms than gzip6, but with lower compression ratios. As we will show in Section 4.2.3, since the extra CPU cycles for decompression do not lead to performance degradation, we decided to continue with gzip6. The results for VMIs are the same and omitted for the sake of brevity.

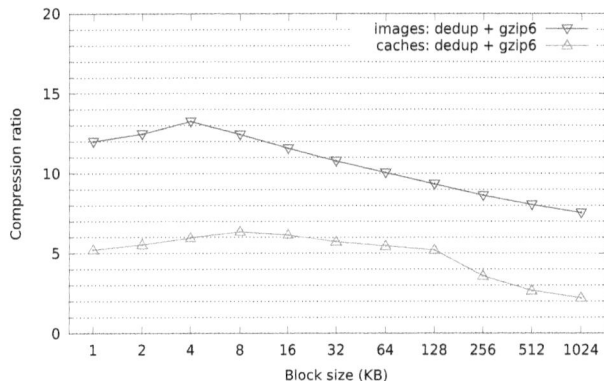

Figure 4: Combined compression ratio of VMIs and caches.

Because of the conflicting trends in compression efficiency for deduplication and compression, there exists an optimization point, after which lowering the block size will result in lower storage efficiency. We define combined compression ratio (CCR) as a metric that considers the effects of both compression techniques combined, and is calculated as:

$$\text{CCR} = \text{deduplication ratio} \times \text{compression ratio}$$

Figure 4 shows the CCRs for VMIs and caches. Despite common understanding, the smaller block sizes do not necessarily result in better compression ratios when considering both deduplication and compression. This is an important finding, not only because of storage efficiency, but also because smaller block sizes consume more memory for deduplication tables as we will show in Section 4.2.2. For VMIs, when reducing the block size, the CCR steadily increases up until 4 KB and then starts to decrease. For caches, the CCR does not show much improvement when reducing the block size after 128 KB, and starts to decrease after 8 KB. Note that while VMIs have better combined compression ratios than caches, we will show in Section 4.3 that storing them at compute nodes is neither efficient nor scalable.

2.3 Summary and discussion

We have highlighted the essential background work in this section. We briefly looked at our enabling mechanism, VMI caches, in Section 2.1. We then looked at compression opportunities for VMI caches in Section 2.2.

Table 1 shows the storage reduction as we apply different storage techniques to our VMI repository. With block size

Original	Nonzero	Caches (Nonzero)	Caches/CCR
16.4 TB	1.4 TB	78.5 GB	15.1 GB

Table 1: Attained storage efficiency with 128 KB block size.

of 128 KB (default in the ZFS file system), if the file system supports sparse files, the original 16.4 TB raw data reduces to 1.4 TB. Our VMI caches reduce that to 78.5 GB, and if compression and deduplication are applied, we get to a modest 15.1 GB of disk resources. This indicates that our claim of storing all VMI caches on compute nodes is feasible. It allows us to deploy fully replicated storage architecture for VMI caches. In Sections 4.2 and 4.3, we show that our approach is not only efficient, but also scalable to thousands of VMI caches.

3. SYSTEM ARCHITECTURE

In this section, we will first discuss the architecture of Squirrel, a fully replicated VMI caching system that is aimed at caching *all* VMIs on *all* compute nodes. We then describe how certain operations such as *register*, *boot*, and *deregister* are implemented using VMI caches, and the ZFS file system that provides us with inline compression and deduplication as well as snapshot versioning. Further, we will explain how VMI caches are propagated if some of the compute nodes are not online during the *register* operation.

3.1 Squirrel

Mainstream in today's IaaS cloud architectures are the following assumptions: (1.) There is an explicit separation between compute nodes and storage nodes. (2.) Compute nodes use all their resources to run VMs. (3.) Storage nodes provide a high performance, high volume, and fault-tolerant storage space for the running VMs on compute nodes.

Mainstream in current VMI distribution engines is the assumption that data transfer between storage nodes and compute nodes, or between compute nodes (i.e. peer-to-peer systems) is coming for free. Violating the second and third assumptions of cloud architectures, VMI transfers, an administration overhead, become a burden on storage nodes and/or consume network bandwidth available on compute nodes, making the running VMs prone to network SLA violations.

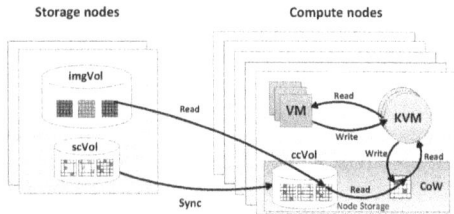

Figure 5: Squirrel architecture diagram.

Squirrel's architecture, depicted in Figure 5, is aimed at eradicating network I/O during VM startup for all VMIs of an IaaS cloud by using modest storage resources at compute nodes. We assume that there exists an off-the-shelf parallel file system that manages the storage nodes. In a typical scenario, the VMIs are stored on top of this parallel file system and are accessed by compute nodes during VM startup.

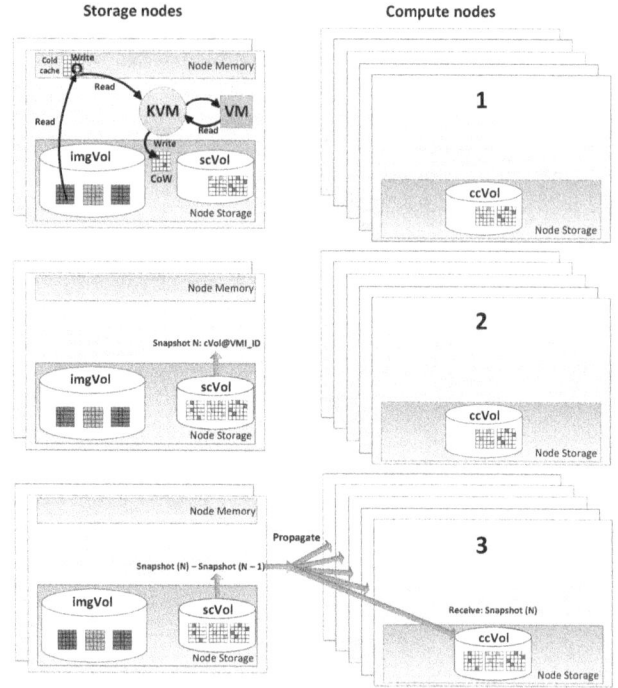

Figure 6: Squirrel VMI registration workflow.

Squirrel adds a cache volume, called *cVolume*, backed by the ZFS file system, next to the VMIs. The cVolume at the storage nodes, called *scVolume*, stores deduplicated and compressed VMI caches for all the VMIs currently registered to the system. At each compute node, Squirrel controls one cVolume, named *ccVolume*. In a stable state, the ccVolumes are in sync with the scVolume. We will explain how we exploit ZFS snapshots to bring the ccVolumes at lagging compute nodes (e.g. due to possible failures or down times) back in sync with the scVolume in Section 3.5.

We will now discuss how Squirrel implements the main VMI operations; namely *register*, *boot*, and *deregister*.

3.2 Register

We assume that the IaaS provider already has a mechanism for users to upload their VMIs to the storage nodes. For example, Amazon EC2 [2] provides **ec2_upload_bundle** [3] for this purpose, or OpenNebula [23] provides its users with the **oneimage create** command that uploads the VM image during the registration process.

Figure 6 shows Squirrel's workflow for image registration. With the VMI accessible, Squirrel first boots the VMI for the first time in one of the storage nodes to create the cache. In our previous work [34], we have shown that this takes no longer than a normal VM boot. In Section 4.2.3, we show that on average the VMs in our dataset boot in less than 20 seconds. Once the cache is created, Squirrel destroys the VM, and moves the cache from memory to the scVolume. Next, Squirrel creates a snapshot of the scVolume for this newly added VMI cache. ZFS snapshots are cheap in terms of storage as long as they do not reference data that no longer exists (i.e., deregistered VMIs). They are also cheap in terms of creation time since they are read-only. Finally, Squirrel propagates the VMI cache by sending the diff between this snapshot and the previous snapshot from the storage node to all online compute nodes. The diff is generated using ZFS incremental snapshot-send functionality. Transferring the diff (i.e., the new cache) from one node to many others is a common scenario in scalable data transfer, and has been extensively studied in the literature [8, 31, 38, 40]. With a simple IP multicast approach, transferring a diff of $O(100\,\text{MB})$, does not take more than a couple of seconds even on a commodity 1 GbE.

In total, the image registration workflow does not take more than a minute. Given that the actual VMI upload takes significantly longer, we consider Squirrel's registration workflow, which is an infrequent operation and not in the critical path for booting VMs, to be a modest price to pay for all the benefits that it delivers. These benefits are discussed in Section 4.

3.3 Boot

Booting a VM from a VMI in Squirrel is depicted in Figure 7. Squirrel chains an empty copy-on-write image on the local storage to the requested VMI cache on the ccVolume. The VMI cache on the ccVolume is chained to the original VMI, which is backed by the cloud storage and mounted on the compute node(s). During VM boot, all VM reads (of all possible VMIs) will be handled by the ccVolume. All VM writes will go to the copy-on-write image.

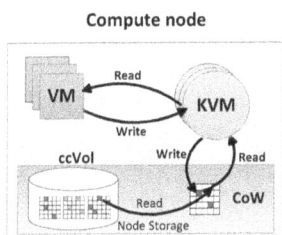

Figure 7: Booting a VM with Squirrel's ccVolume.

3.4 Deregister

VMI deregistration is as simple as deleting the original VMI and its associated cache on the scVolume. The more important background operation that keeps the cVolumes sustainable, while providing a window for offline propagation, is called garbage collection in Squirrel.

Squirrel implements garbage collection by keeping only the snapshots that are taken in the last n days, and the latest snapshot regardless of its creation time. n is a configurable variable that defines the offline propagation window, for when compute nodes miss a new cache, as well as the amount of time that dead references (i.e. unregistered VMI caches) remain in the system. Squirrel runs garbage collection as a daily cron job on all Squirrel cVolumes.

Note that Squirrel is not creating snapshots when deleting caches for the sake of simplicity. The information about unregistered VMIs will propagate to ccVolumes as soon as there is a new registered VMI (i.e., a new snapshot).

3.5 Offline propagation

With the increasing number of commodity servers in data centers, the likelihood of node failure increases. If a set of compute nodes are offline during the last stage of Squir-

rel's VMI registration or during deregistration, their ccVolumes become stale. To overcome this problem, each compute node, upon boot, queries for a diff between the latest snapshot available locally at its ccVolume, and the latest snapshot available at the scVolume. Two scenarios are likely to happen: (1.) The node has not been offline for more than n days. In this case, the incremental snapshot will succeed and the compute node receives the latest snapshot. (2.) The node has been offline for more than n days, or the node is a new addition to the compute node pool. In this case, the incremental snapshot fails, and Squirrel needs to replicate the entire scVolume. The second scenario however, does not happen often with a large enough n, and even if it does, as we show in Sections 2.2 and 4.3, the size of cVolumes never exceeds a few tens of GBs (same order as a single VMI).

One question that is likely to arise is why Squirrel uses snapshots to keep the ccVolumes in sync with scVolume, rather than simply using the rsync [37] utility for this purpose. The answer to this question is twofold. First, rsync is a many-to-one operation, and can easily create a bottleneck at the storage nodes. The ZFS incremental snapshot can be streamed using any conventional peer-to-peer or multicasting approach. Second, using rsync on-demand could potentially avoid the bottleneck, but it translates to VM booting delay for the first time. Further, with commodity networks (e.g., 1 GbE) booting on-demand at scale with a cold cache can introduce network bottlenecks as we have shown in [34].

4. EVALUATION

We evaluate different aspects of Squirrel's cVolumes in this section. Namely, in Section 4.2, we evaluate the storage requirements and effects on boot time for Squirrel's cVolumes, in Section 4.3, we evaluate the scalability of cVolumes to large numbers of VMI caches, and we analyze network transfers with Squirrel in Section 4.4.

For all the experiments of this section, we have used up to 68 standard nodes of the DAS-4/VU cluster [11]. Each standard DAS-4/VU node is equipped with dual quad-core Intel E5620 CPUs, running at 2.4 GHz, 24 GB of memory, and two Western Digital SATA 3.0 Gbps/7200 RPM/1 TB disks in software RAID-0 fashion. The nodes are connected using a commodity 1 Gb/s Ethernet and a premium QDR InfiniBand providing a theoretical peak of 32 Gb/s.

At the time of writing this paper, DAS-4/VU nodes are running CentOS 6.4 Linux. XFS is used as the local file system, and we have used a native ZFS installation [41] to run cVolumes as images on top of the XFS file system. It is possible to run ZFS directly on the disk(s), but we decided not to change the configuration of local disks on the nodes, as they are shared by many users.

We use the 600+ community images of Windows Azure as test case for our experiments. We provide detailed information about our VMI repository in Section 4.1. To generate the data for Figures 2, 3, 4, and 12, we submitted simple MapReduce jobs to Hadoop [5] running on a subset of the DAS-4/VU nodes for analyzing our data set. For Figures 8, 9, 10, and 13, we used the statistics of the ZFS file system for our analysis. The "real" data points in Figures 14, and 16 are also reported by ZFS.

4.1 Dataset information

The VMIs in our dataset are consisting of Linux-based operating systems, that are registered by the users of Win-

Table 2: OS diversity in Windows Azure and Amazon EC2.

OS distribution	Windows Azure	Amazon EC2
Ubuntu	579	5720
RedHat/CentOS	17	847
OpenSuse/Suse Ent.	5	8
Debian	3	30
Windows	0	531
Unidentified Linux	3	2654
Total	607	9871

dows Azure. Table 2 shows the number of VMIs for each OS found in our dataset and, for comparison, in Amazon EC2[4], the largest existing IaaS provider. The numbers reported by Amazon EC2 are for all the regions combined, so the numbers per region are likely to be smaller. We have provided extrapolations to thousands of VMI caches based on our dataset in Section 4.3.2.

The community VMIs of Windows Azure do not include Windows distributions, likely due to licensing reasons. If we had Windows in the mix, the boot working sets of different Windows distributions would have deduplicated with each other, thus adding a constant factor to Squirrel's storage requirements.

4.2 Cache volume efficiency

In this section, we analyze the effects of compressing and deduplicating the contents of VMIs and VMI caches in ZFS volumes. We first look at disk and memory requirements, and then we move on to booting performance from ccVolumes. In the end, we will summarize our findings.

4.2.1 Disk

To verify our findings with respect to combined compression ratio presented in Section 2.2, we stored once the VMI repository, and once the corresponding VMI caches in the ZFS file system and measured the respective disk consumption. Figure 8 shows the disk consumption for VMIs and caches with varying block size. To our surprise, when lowering block size, the point which results in worse CCR happens sooner than what we measured in Figure 4 (16 KB for images and 32 KB for caches). We suspected this is due to the fact that the deduplication table itself also needs to be written to the disk, resulting in even lower compression efficiency for small block sizes. Figure 9 measures this overhead with varying block size. The overhead of storing deduplication tables on the disk is indeed considerable with decreasing block size and this verifies our theory.

4.2.2 Memory

As discussed in Section 2, deduplication, albeit effective in compressing VMI contents, comes at the cost of the need to keep a deduplication table in memory for fast access to data blocks on disk. We have established in the previous section that smaller block sizes may lead to better compression ratios, but resulting in bigger deduplication tables. Figure 10 measures the amount of memory consumed by a cVolume with varying block size. For VMI caches, the memory consumption is below 100 MB for block size of 32 KB and

[4]These numbers were reported by Amazon EC2 in their web console in October 2013

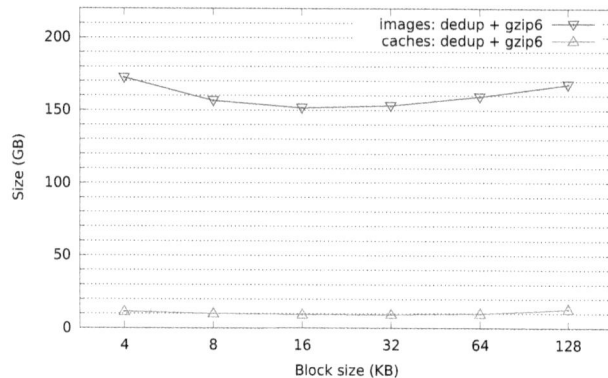

Figure 8: Disk consumption with deduplication and compression.

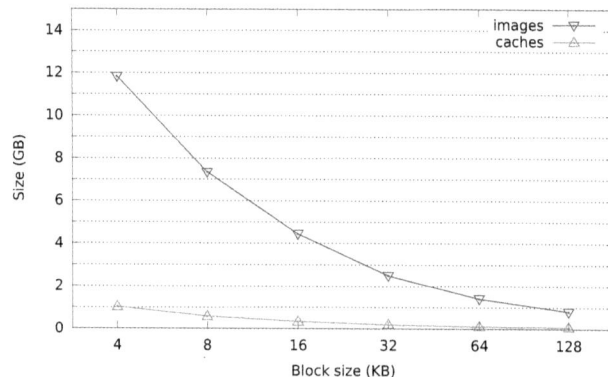

Figure 9: Deduplication table size on disk.

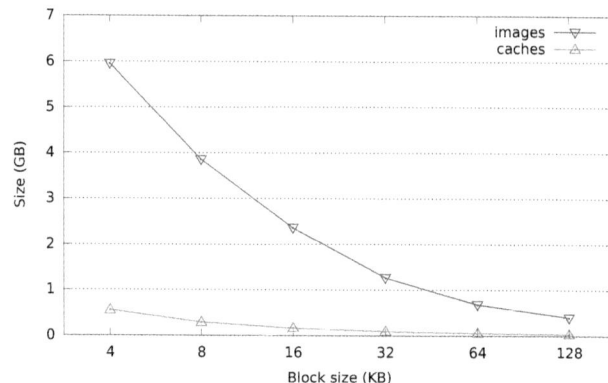

Figure 10: Memory consumption for deduplication tables.

above, and remains relatively small for smaller block sizes. For VMIs however, the memory consumption increases at an alarming rate when reducing the block size. We will explain this behavior further in Section 4.3.1.

4.2.3 Boot time

Deduplication generally slows down reading data from disk due to two reasons. First, each access needs a lookup in the deduplication table. Second, as shown in [14], as data is being deduplicated, adjacent data blocks will end up scattered on the disk. This effect results in random access patterns when reading a chunk in a file that consists of mul-

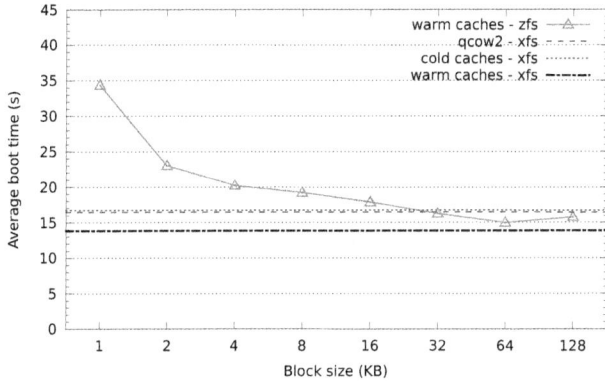

Figure 11: Performance of booting from deduplicated and compressed VMI caches.

tiple sequential data blocks, and conventional disks do not handle random accesses well.

As we reduce the block size, the deduplication table grows in size, resulting in slower lookups. Further, data blocks get even more scattered on the disk as the number of possible hashes increase. Figure 11 shows the effect of varying block size on VM boot performance from a warm cache. For this experiment, we have measured the average boot time of the VMs in our VMI repository when stored on cVolumes with different block sizes. For reference, we have also included the average boot time when booting: (1.) from the local file system, (2.) and creating the cold cache, (3.) from a warm cache stored on the local file system.

Booting from a warm cache increases the booting performance on average by 16% when compared to booting from the VMI stored on the local disk (baseline). To explain this speed up, we need to look at the operation of QCOW2 [22]. Without a VMI cache, each time a VM boots, there are a number of read requests from the CoW image to the VMI. These requests, that are in the form of *(offset, num_sectors)*, usually read from scattered locations around the disk depending on the file system layout of the root partition of the VMI (look at Figure 1 of [36]). Assuming the default cluster size of QCOW2 (64 KB or 128 sectors), when booting from a warm cache, the read requests from the CoW image to the cache image, although usually smaller than 128 sectors, translate to *(offset, 128)* due to the way QCOW2 operates. The Linux page cache, running on the host, caches these sectors. Incidentally, these cached sectors will be needed in a near future, mostly because these other sectors are also part of the boot working set as they are in the warm cache. The end result is a free boost in performance due to reading a large part of the boot working set from the page cache rather than the disk. One could say that Squirrel VMI caches are getting similar effects to prefetching [29] for free.

This boost in performance masks the deduplication and compression overhead for block sizes that are equal and bigger than 32 KB. Also, 128 KB cVolume boots slower than 64 KB cVolume despite the trend. The reason is most likely the default QCOW2 cluster size of 64 KB, which results in read sizes of 64 KB from the KVM process to the cVolume.

4.2.4 Summary

To summarize our findings, we showed in Section 2.2 that smaller block sizes than 64 KB do not yield considerable stor-

age efficiency. In this section, we showed that both disk and memory requirements for the deduplication tables of cVolumes are fairly modest as long as the block size is not too small. We then measured that the cVolume with block size of 64 KB has the best booting performance. Even with deduplication and gzip compression, the average booting performance of Squirrel's cVolume is about 10% better than when the VMI is available *locally* on the compute node. To conclude, the block size of 64 KB is optimal for cVolumes. However, when necessary, we will report on other block sizes in the rest of this section.

4.3 Scalability

Scalability is the most important requirement for a system such as Squirrel that argues for storing *all* the VMI caches in its cVolumes. To demonstrate that Squirrel is scalable, we will first show in Section 4.3.1 that VMI caches share more similarity among each other, than their associated VMIs. We will then extrapolate the disk and memory consumption of cVolumes using standard extrapolation techniques in Section 4.3.2. At the end, we will iterate over the findings of this section.

4.3.1 Cross-similarity of caches

We form the theory that caches share a lot more contents with each other than their associated VMIs. VMI caches usually contain the operating system kernel, boot loader, and some standard services (i.e., a boot working set), whereas VMIs contain a significant amount of libraries and user-level software on top, that may or may not be used during a VM life time. The rationale behind our theory is that the boot working set does not differ much across many VMI caches, unlike the user-level software that shows more variability across different VMIs.

The reason behind better similarity in the boot working set, is related to the fact that VMIs, although different from each other, still are based on a certain number of distributions (e.g., Ubuntu, Debian, CentOS, etc.), and boot working sets of VMIs (i.e., VMI caches) from the same distributions are likely to show high similarity.

If our theory is correct, it shows the scalability of our cVolumes. To prove the theory, we have defined a new metric, called *cross-similarity*. Cross-similarity measures data block sharing across files and is defined as:

$$\text{Cross-similarity} = \frac{\sum\limits_{i \in U} repetition_i}{\sum\limits_{i \in I} |U_i|},$$

where U is the set of all unique blocks, I is the set of all VMIs, U_i is the set of unique blocks in VMI i, and *repetition* of a data block is defined as the number of times a data block appears across "different" files, or 0 if it has never been repeated. In extreme cases, cross-similarity is 1 if the images are the same, and 0 if they share no single data block.

Figure 12 measures the cross-similarity of VMIs and caches. This figure shows that:

1. VMIs do not exhibit a good similarity across each other, whereas caches show a strong cross-similarity, effectively proving the theory discussed earlier.

2. As a result, with high similarity, a new VMI cache, on average, introduces only a few hashes to cVolumes, making Squirrel's cVolumes scalable.

271

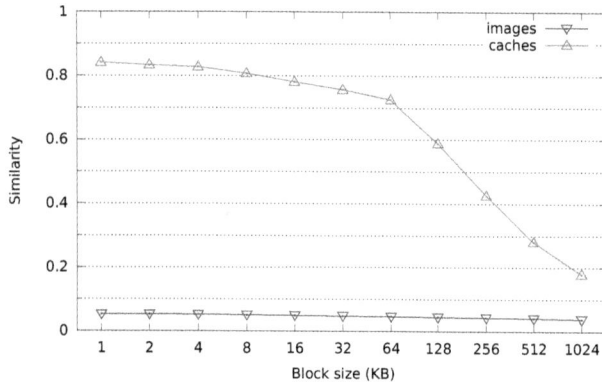

Figure 12: Cross-similarity of VMIs and caches.

3. With smaller block sizes, the similarity increases for caches, but not considerably with block sizes that are smaller than 64 K. This is yet another reason that argues in favor of choosing 64 KB block size for cVolumes.

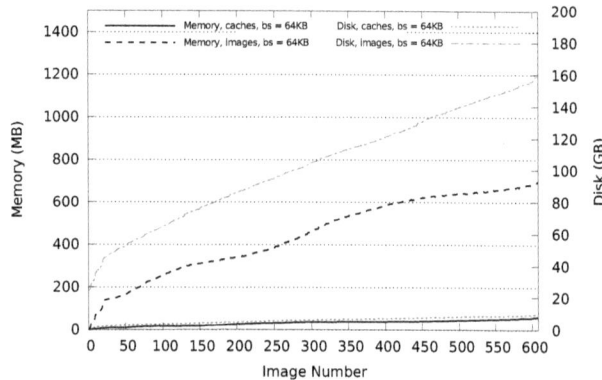

Figure 13: Resource consumption of ZFS when iteratively adding VMIs or caches.

To verify our theory in practice, we added VMI caches iteratively to a ZFS file system with 64 KB block size, and measured the memory and disk consumption when each VMI cache was added to the system. We repeated the same experiment with VMIs. Figure 13 shows the results for both memory and disk. The slopes for VMIs look much steeper than for caches. This means that each VMI is adding relatively more hashes to file system than its associated VMI cache. We use the resource consumption trends for VMI caches as a basis for the extrapolations in the following.

4.3.2 Extrapolations

To understand the extent of Squirrel's cVolume scalability, we need to extrapolate their resource consumption. We will use the disk consumption trend when adding new VMI caches as a basis for extrapolation. We then extend our extrapolation for memory as well.

Disk.

To extrapolate the disk consumption, we need to find a curve that fits the current data points well, and still has a relatively low error when predicting the future. We devised the following approach, common in machine learning,

for finding the best fitting curve: (1.) We fed half of our data points to our curve fitting program [10], and asked for the two best non-polynomial fits as well as linear regression (the simplest curve). (2.) We measured root-mean-square error (RMSE) of the three candidate curves for *all* the data points. (3.) We then used the curve type with the lowest RMSE to find the best parameters that fit all the data points. (4.) The resulting curve is then used for extrapolation. The two functions with the best scores with the first half of our data points were Morgan-Mercer-Flodin (MMF) and Hoerl curves:

$$MMF(x) = \frac{a \times b + c \times x^d}{b + x^d}$$

$$hoerl(x) = a \times b^x \times x^c$$

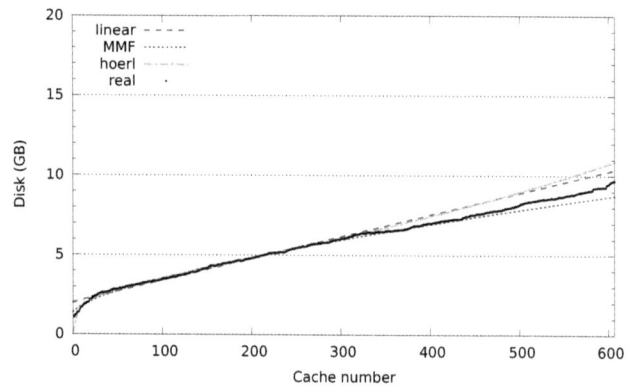

Figure 14: Disk consumption curve-fitting quality (BS = 64 KB).

Figure 14 shows the fitted curves when training with half of the data points. Visually, all curves seem to have a close estimate. MMF seems to be underestimating, while Hoerl and linear regression seem to be overestimating. To find the best fit, we need to calculate the RMSE with all our data points as explained earlier.

Table 3 shows the RMSE of the curves for various block sizes. According to the table, the linear regression has the lowest RMSE and is thus the winner.

Table 3: RMSE of various curves that estimate disk consumption.

Block size	Linear	MMF	Hoerl
128 KB	0.04	0.04	0.08
64 KB	0.03	0.04	0.04
32 KB	0.02	0.04	0.04
16 KB	0.02	0.05	0.03

With linear regression producing a good fit, this time we trained it with all our available data points. Figure 15 shows the resulting extrapolations for different block sizes. With the chosen 64 KB block size for cVolumes, we can store 1200+ caches in about 18 GB of disk space. The extrapolation in Figure 15 continues till 3000 VMI caches, but after 1200 (the vertical line in Figure 15) our curve fitting approach does not guarantee a small RMSE.

Memory.

We repeated the same exercise to extrapolate the memory consumption. MMF and Hoerl functions won good scores for

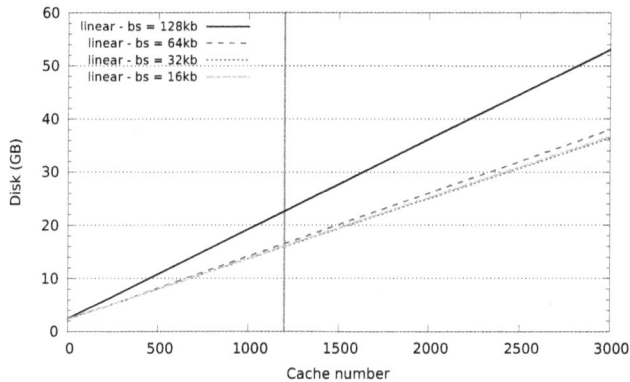

Figure 15: Extrapolation of disk consumption.

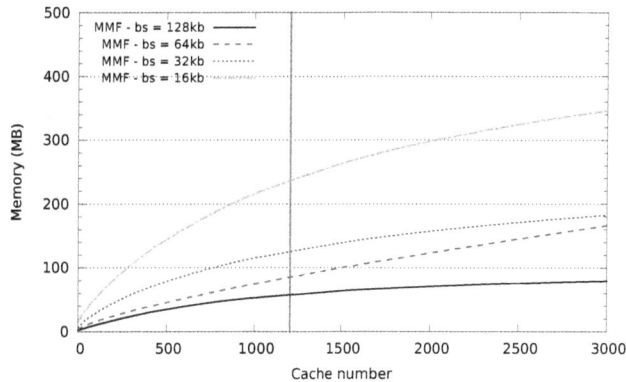

Figure 17: Extrapolation of memory consumption.

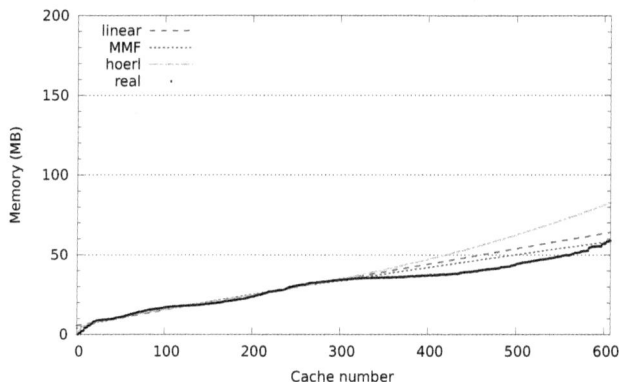

Figure 16: Memory consumption curve-fitting quality (BS = 64 KB).

that cVolumes require modest disk and memory resources in such a scale, for example 18 GB disk and 85 MB memory for storing 1200+ VMI caches.

4.4 Network transfer size

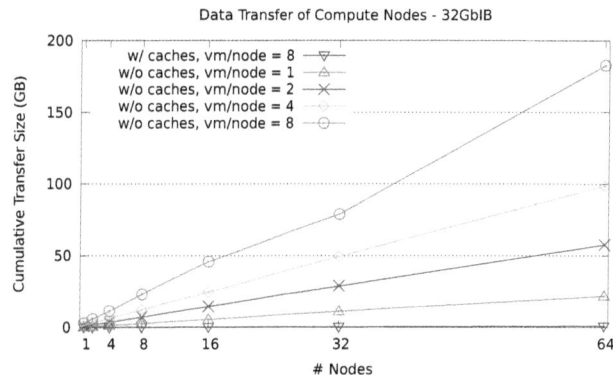

Figure 18: Network transfer size with scaling the number of nodes and the number of VMs per node.

memory consumption as well. Figure 16 shows the curves when trained with half of our data points. Visually, this time all three curves have a small overestimation, with MMF having the smallest. Looking at RMSEs in Table 4, except for 16 KB block size, MMF seems to estimate memory consumption the best, and specifically with 64 KB.

Table 4: RMSE of various curves that estimate memory consumption.

Block size	Linear	MMF	Hoerl
128 KB	0.21	0.14	0.15
64 KB	0.20	0.02	0.95
32 KB	0.44	0.26	1.03
16 KB	0.61	1.13	0.28

We then trained MMF with all our data points for memory consumption. Figure 17 shows the extrapolations with different block sizes. According to the extrapolation for 64 KB block size, Squirrel cVolumes only consume about 85 MB of memory for the deduplicating 1200+ VMI caches; a very modest requirement.

4.3.3 Summary

In Section 4.3.1, we have shown that VMI caches have a very good cross-similarity. This entails that adding new VMI caches to cVolumes does not result in too many new hashes on average, and makes our cVolumes scalable. We then extrapolated resource consumption for Squirrel's cVolumes beyond caching 1000 VMIs in Section 4.3.2, and showed

In this section, we will look at the amount of network transfers of compute nodes when starting VMs at scale. We assigned 64 of DAS-4/VU nodes as compute nodes, and 4 nodes as storage nodes. On the storage nodes, we ran glusterfs, an off-the-shelf parallel file system. We configured glusterfs with two levels of striping and two levels of replication, to have a good random access performance (over four disks), and fault tolerance (tolerating one disk failure in each of the two groups). We measured the amount of network transfers at compute nodes once with Squirrel and once without any caching. Since Squirrel is the first system that caches all the bits that are needed for all VMI startups, the amount of network transfers of all previous VMI distribution systems will be in between the results shown.

Figure 18 shows the aggregated amount of network transfers for VM startup at compute nodes.[5] We are scaling the number of compute nodes, and the number of VMs per compute node. At each node, each VM is booting from a different VMI. Without Squirrel, the amount of network

---

[5]Results shown are for Infiniband. Results for 1 GbE are omitted for brevity as they are essentially the time despite a little smaller per-packet overhead.

transfers increase as there are more VMs starting up in the cluster. In the extreme case, with 512 VMs (64 nodes times 8 VMs), the aggregated transfer at compute nodes is about 180 GB, happening in a relatively short period of time, and disturbing any existing VM that is using the network. With Squirrel, however, compute nodes do not need to do any network I/O, even when executing 8 VMs on each node from different VMI sources.

4.5 Summary

We have evaluated the effects of placing Squirrel's VMI caches on all compute nodes of a data center using the set of 600+ community images from Windows Azure. All tests have shown a block size of 64 KB to be a sweet spot at which disk and memory consumption is acceptably low while boot times are not slowed down by using a compressed and deduplicated file system instead of a plain XFS volume. With block size of 64 KB, Squirrel's cVolumes only consume 10 GB of disk space, and 60 MB of memory for storing VMI caches for *all* Windows Azure community VMIs. Further, the average booting time over Squirrel's cVolumes, even though they are compressed and deduplicated, is reduced by 10%, compared to when the VMIs are available *locally* at compute nodes, due to the caching effect explained in Section 4.2.3.

We have extrapolated our results to larger numbers of VMI caches to be stored, and identified the need for 18 GB disk and 85 MB memory for storing 1214 VMI caches. Given current hardware, these amounts are very modest, if not to say negligible. We consider it likely that in the near to midterm future, even storing several thousand VMI caches per node can be sustained by available node hardware.

To complete our evaluation, we measured the network traffic necessary for concurrently booting up to 512 VMs on 64 nodes, comparing Squirrel to the absence of VMI caches. Here, Squirrel showed the need for zero network traffic, and hence no interference at all with other user network traffic.

5. RELATED WORK

We distinguish related work to Squirrel in three distinct, but overlapping categories: (1.) Systems that implement some sort of VMI caching or storage on the compute nodes. (2.) Systems that focus on scalable distribution of VMI contents. (3.) Systems that perform deduplication and/or compression for efficient VMI storage. We will discuss each category separately, and make comparisons to Squirrel or discuss how Squirrel complements an existing system.

5.1 Storing VMI contents on compute nodes

There are a number of systems that aim at minimizing the amount of network transfers by means of caching VMI contents. OpenStack's [17] Glance API server has the ability to cache VMIs. It is possible to run the Glance API server on many compute nodes to have cached VMIs on many locations. Compared to Squirrel, Glance API servers cannot cache many multi-GB VMIs.

The Liquid file system [44] is designed for VMI distribution and has an architecture similar to Squirrel. Liquid keeps a cache of deduplicated VMI contents on each compute node. The caches transfer data among each other and from storage nodes as necessary. Squirrel is different from Liquid in two important aspects: (1.) Squirrel's VMI caches are isolated from each other: The VMI blocks needed for starting one VM do not evict boot working set blocks of dif-

ferent VMIs. (2.) Squirrel's ccVolumes are fully replicated. They do not need to transfer data between each other over the network, reducing the variations in network bandwidth observed by other VMs.

VMThunder [42] is a VMI distribution engine that provides scalable, on-demand P2P streaming, and a per-VMI caching functionality similar to that of Squirrel. The evaluation in [42], however, does not consider the case with many VMIs, common in today's data centers. Compression mechanisms, absent in VMThunder, are necessary for scaling the caches to large numbers of VMIs.

Nicolae et al. [28] stripe VMI chunks across the disks of many compute nodes. During VM boot, if a chunk is required and missing, it is fetched from a peer that has that chunk. They further improve their approach in [29] by means of prefetching the chunks required for VM startup. The access-pattern knowledge used in prefetching is retrieved from the peers that boot a little faster. BlobSeer [27], the file system that they have built upon, also keeps a cache of the most recently accessed chunks, very much like Liquid. Our comparison with Liquid holds here as well.

VDN [33] is a network hierarchy-aware system for transferring VMIs to compute nodes. Each VMI is divided into chunks and each compute node has a cache for these chunks. When booting a new VM, the compute node fetches the VMI chunks that it lacks in its local cache from its peers in a network topology-aware fashion. Squirrel solves the problem that VDN is addressing by efficiently storing all VMI caches in its ccVolumes.

Ming et al. [43] suggest that simply using NFS to transfer VMIs is sub-optimal. By adding a module to NFS to cache a number of NFS requests at the compute nodes or a proxy, they improve the VM booting process with a warm cache. They further improve the performance of the virtual disk by doing copy-on-write in an NFS proxy that is running inside the VM [7]. In contrast, Squirrel's VMI caches provide a clean caching abstraction at VMI-level. This makes it possible to perform resource accounting per VMI. Further, Squirrel's ccVolumes persistently store all the blocks needed for booting from all VMIs.

In general, Squirrel's cVolumes can be used as a replacement to improve the caching strategy used by the systems discussed in this section.

5.2 Scalable distribution of VMI contents

There is an increasing demand for scalable VM startup as cloud computing is being adopted for computationally demanding areas, such as high-performance computing. A number of studies have looked at scalable startup of VMs:

5.2.1 Peer-to-peer approaches

Peer-to-peer networking is a common technique for transferring a single VMI to many compute nodes [8, 31, 40]. The main issue so far has been the considerable delay of startup time in order of tens of minutes. This is because the complete VMI needs to be present before starting the VM. VMTorrent [36] combines on-demand access with peer-to-peer streaming to reduce this delay significantly.

While peer-to-peer transfer is a good match to scalable content transfer in slower networks, it uses substantial network resources to deliver the VMI to the compute nodes. Squirrel, in contrast, caches all data blocks of all VMIs needed for booting, and can save large amounts of network transfers as we have shown in Section 4.4.

LANTorrent [30], from the Nimbus project, combines simultaneous VMI requests and builds a pipeline for streaming complete VMIs from the storage node to all requesting compute nodes. This is very adequate for applications or services starting up with many VMs at the same time. For small, private clouds, where all nodes are connected to a single network switch, this chaining maximizes the throughput. LANTorrent, however, introduces startup delay, as it needs to transfer the multi-GB VMI through the network, most of which never gets accessed during the life of a VM. LANTorrent, however, is a good candidate to transfer our small VMI caches to Squirrel's ccVolumes during VMI registration.

5.2.2 IP Multicasting

IP multicasting is another approach for scalable data transfer from one-to-many nodes. Here, we will discuss related work that use multicast as a mechanism to deliver VMIs.

Schmidt et al. [38] use Unionfs, a stacked file system used for VMIs. The base VMI that contains a big chunk of the final VMI, remains constant among different VMIs. By caching the base VMI on the compute nodes and transferring the rest using multicast, they achieve short startup delays. Squirrel only relies on multicast for offline transfer of VMI caches as part of VMI registration. Further, the read-only nature of VMI caches can relax the requirement for a stacked file system. VMI caches can be created for any type of image in any state. The user-customized part can be transferred in the form of a copy-on-write image to the compute nodes that recurses to the cache image if necessary.

Haizea [39] is a lease-management architecture that combines leasing VMs for batch execution. Haizea addresses the problem of scalable deployment by means of multicasting the complete VMI to the compute nodes and caching it there. Squirrel can be used alongside Haizea to reduce the deployment time significantly, and remove the burden of cache management from Haizea.

Multicasting has been used for cloning the VM state as well. SnowFlock [20] can start many stateful worker VMs in less than one second. It introduces *VMFork* and *VM descriptor* primitives that fork child VMs that are in the same state as the parent VM when they start. SnowFlock achieves good performance by multicasting the requested data to all workers and uses a set of avoidance heuristics at child VMs to reduce the amount of memory traffic from the parent to the children. While efficient, SnowFlock introduces change in all layers of the system, at the VMM, and the VM, down to the application. VMScatter [9] is a similar system, but less intrusive, and also less efficient in terms of scale.

5.3 Compressing VMI contents

Squirrel's cVolumes store VMI caches efficiently by exploiting deduplication and compression techniques in an off-the-shelf ZFS file system [4]. There is a strong body of research on deduplication of VMIs.

Jin et al. [19] performed a detailed study on the effectiveness of deduplicating VMIs. From their findings, the fact that fixed-size chunking works equally well (or sometimes even better) when compared to variable-sized chunking is relevant to our choice of using ZFS that employs fixed-size chunking. Their results have been independently verified over a large VMI repository in [18]. Jin et al. also report

similar numbers to ours when looking at similarity between different VMIs. In Section 4.3, we showed that VMI caches show a much better similarity among each other than VMIs, a fact that makes Squirrel's cVolumes scalable.

LiveDFS [26] is a file system aimed at VMI deduplication. Compared with ZFS, LiveDFS' deduplication tables consume less memory, making LiveDFS suitable for deployment on commodity servers. Squirrel's VMI caches, however, have a high cross-similarity, and as a result they only need modest memory requirement for deduplication. We thus decided to use ZFS, which is of commercial quality.

Deduplication of disk content has been used to improve the effectiveness of the page cache. Content-based block caching [24] improves the overall system performance by reducing redundancy of the page cache, and avoiding some of the writes on disk that have the same content. Garces-Erice et al. [15] use a similar approach to improve the performance of the page cache in storage servers that serve IaaS compute nodes. Their approach makes sure that data blocks that are shared between many VMIs are less likely to be evicted from the page cache. In our previous work with VMI caches [34], we also made better use of storage servers' memory by storing VMI caches in a *ramfs*. With Squirrel, however, we are storing all the important blocks at compute nodes in order to completely eradicate the VM startup load on storage nodes.

VMFlock [1] is a cross-cloud co-migration system that transfers a set of VMIs, from one cloud to another. VMFlock uses deduplication opportunities among the set of VMIs to be migrated, as well as the VMIs already available in the destination cloud, to significantly reduce the amount of data that needs to be transferred between clouds. VMI caches are generally small ($O(100\,\text{MB})$), but due to their high cross-similarity, the information that each new one adds to Squirrel's cVolume (i.e., cVolume diff) is even smaller ($O(10\,\text{MB})$). Similar to VMFlock, we only need to transfer a cVolume diff, instead of the whole VMI cache.

Coriolis [6] is a deduplication management system that tries to efficiently cluster VMIs based on their similarity. The grouping of VMIs with similar content results in high deduplication ratio within a VMI cluster that can be stored on separate locations. Similar to Coriolis, Rangoli [25] tries to find similar files to maximize the amount space reclamation when migrating a set of files. The scalability of Squirrel's cVolumes gives us the luxury of storing all VMI caches, without worrying about space reclamation.

6. CONCLUSIONS

The promise of elastic cloud computing is instantaneous availability of virtual machines (VMs). In practice, however, users often have to wait several or even a few tens of minutes until they can actually use their requested VMs. An important factor of this delay is the actual VM boot process that is slowed down by the need to transfer bulky, multi-GB virtual machine images (VMIs) from storage nodes to the selected compute nodes.

In previous work [34], we proposed using a VMI cache on the compute nodes that contains the boot working set, removing the need for network transfers while booting VMs. We showed that VMI caches resolve scalability problems of VM startup. Whereas VMI caches work well, they need to be present and "warm" before a VM starts up.

This work is based on the observation that the many existing VMIs are mostly user customizations of only a few types of operating systems and OS distributions. We have shown that VMI caches (the boot working sets) have high cross-similarity among each other, hence lending themselves well for deduplication-based storage. Combined with compression, the storage of *all* VMI caches on compute nodes becomes possible. Thus, instead of studying cache replacement policies and/or cache-aware VM scheduling, we propose a fully replicated storage design for caching *all* VMIs of an IaaS cloud on *all* the compute nodes.

We have presented Squirrel, a concrete implementation of this design using VMI caches and the ZFS file system. Squirrel can store large amounts of VMI caches within a deduplicated and compressed file system, on the local disks of all compute nodes. We name this approach *scatter hoarding* after the rodent approach for creating many, small food caches.

Our evaluation using all 600+ community images from Windows Azure shows that Squirrel is able to store VMI caches for the overall 16.4 TB of VMIs within 10 GB of disk and 60 MB of main memory, on all compute nodes. We consider these requirements to be rather negligible on current hardware. We have then extrapolated these requirements to the storage needs for thousands of VMI caches and found confirmation that our approach indeed scales to such large numbers on current or near-future hardware.

To summarize, Squirrel completely removes the need for network transfers towards compute nodes when booting virtual machines, either from storage nodes or from other compute nodes. Hence, Squirrel enables large-scale, public IaaS clouds to provide dynamic VM startup purely within the time it takes to boot the virtual OS itself, which is typically tens of seconds, rather than within several minutes as it is common today. This advantage especially helps for dynamic scaling of (e.g., web) applications, helping to close the gap towards truly elastic computing infrastructures.

Acknowledgments

This work is partially funded by the FP7 Programme of the European Commission in the context of the Contrail project under Grant Agreement FP7-ICT-257438, and by the Dutch public-private research community COMMIT/. The authors would like to thank Kees Verstoep for providing excellent support on the DAS-4 clusters, and HPDC's anonymous reviewers for providing valuable feedback on the earlier version of this paper.

7. REFERENCES

[1] S. Al-Kiswany, D. Subhraveti, P. Sarkar, and M. Ripeanu. VMFlock: Virtual Machine Co-migration for the Cloud. In *Proceedings of the 20th International Symposium on High Performance Distributed Computing*, HPDC '11, pages 159–170, 2011.

[2] Amazon Elastic Compute Cloud. http://aws.amazon.com/ec2/, 2006. [Online; accessed 22-01-2014].

[3] ec2_upload_bundle. http://docs.aws.amazon.com/AWSEC2/latest/CommandLineReference/CLTRG-ami-upload-bundle.html, 2006. [Online; accessed 22-01-2014].

[4] J. Bonwick and B. Moore. ZFS: The Last Word in File Systems. *The SNIA Software Developers' Conference*, 2008.

[5] D. Borthakur. *The Hadoop Distributed File System: Architecture and Design*. The Apache Software Foundation, 2007.

[6] D. Campello, C. Crespo, A. Verma, R. Rangaswami, and P. Jayachandran. Coriolis: Scalable VM Clustering in Clouds. In *Presented as part of the 10th International Conference on Autonomic Computing*, pages 101–105, 2013.

[7] V. Chadha and R. J. Figueiredo. ROW-FS: a user-level virtualized redirect-on-write distributed file system for wide area applications. In *Proceedings of the 14th international conference on High performance computing*, HiPC '07, pages 21–34, 2007.

[8] Z. Chen, Y. Zhao, X. Miao, Y. Chen, and Q. Wang. Rapid Provisioning of Cloud Infrastructure Leveraging Peer-to-Peer Networks. In *Proceedings of the 2009 29th IEEE International Conference on Distributed Computing Systems Workshops*, ICDCSW '09, pages 324–329, 2009.

[9] L. Cui, J. Li, B. Li, J. Huai, C. Ho, T. Wo, H. Al-Aqrabi, and L. Liu. VMScatter: Migrate Virtual Machines to Many Hosts. In *Proceedings of the 9th ACM SIGPLAN/SIGOPS International Conference on Virtual Execution Environments*, VEE '13, pages 63–72, 2013.

[10] CurveExpert Professional. http://www.curveexpert.net/products/curveexpert-professional. [Online; accessed 24-01-2014].

[11] DAS-4 clusters. http://www.cs.vu.nl/das4/clusters.shtml. [Online; accessed 24-01-2014].

[12] M. Dutch. Understanding data deduplication ratios. *SNIA Data Management Forum*, 2008.

[13] H. Fernandez, G. Pierre, and T. Kielmann. Autoscaling Web Applications in Heterogeneous Cloud Infrastructures. In *Proceedings of the IEEE International Conference on Cloud Engineering (IC2E)*, Mar. 2014.

[14] L. Garces-Erice and S. Rooney. Scaling OS Streaming Through Minimizing Cache Redundancy. In *Proceedings of the 2011 31st International Conference on Distributed Computing Systems Workshops*, ICDCSW '11, pages 47–53, 2011.

[15] L. Garces-Erice and S. Rooney. Scaling OS Streaming through Minimizing Cache Redundancy. In *31st International Conference on Distributed Computing Systems Workshops (ICDCSW)*, pages 47–53, 2011.

[16] A. Iosup, S. Ostermann, N. Yigitbasi, R. Prodan, T. Fahringer, and D. Epema. Performance Analysis of Cloud Computing Services for Many-Tasks Scientific Computing. *IEEE Transactions on Parallel and Distributed Systems*, 2010.

[17] K. Jackson. *OpenStack Cloud Computing Cookbook*. Packt Publishing, 2012.

[18] K. R. Jayaram, C. Peng, Z. Zhang, M. Kim, H. Chen, and H. Lei. An Empirical Analysis of Similarity in Virtual Machine Images. In *Proceedings of the Middleware 2011 Industry Track Workshop*, number 6 in Middleware '11, pages 6:1–6:6, 2011.

[19] K. Jin and E. L. Miller. The Effectiveness of Deduplication on Virtual Machine Disk Images. In *Proceedings of SYSTOR 2009: The Israeli*

Experimental Systems Conference, number 7 in SYSTOR '09, pages 7:1–7:12, 2009.

[20] H. A. Lagar-Cavilla, J. A. Whitney, A. M. Scannell, P. Patchin, S. M. Rumble, E. de Lara, M. Brudno, and M. Satyanarayanan. SnowFlock: rapid virtual machine cloning for cloud computing. In *Proceedings of the 4th ACM European conference on Computer systems*, EuroSys '09, pages 1–12, 2009.

[21] M. Mao and M. Humphrey. A Performance Study on the VM Startup Time in the Cloud. In *5th International IEEE Conference on Cloud Computing*, CLOUD '12, pages 423–430, 2012.

[22] M. McLoughlin. The QCOW2 Image Format. `http://people.gnome.org/~markmc/qcow-image-format.html`, 2008. [Online; accessed 24-01-2014].

[23] D. Milojičić, I. Llorente, and R. S. Montero. OpenNebula: A Cloud Management Tool. *IEEE Internet Computing*, 15(2):11–14, 2011.

[24] C. B. Morrey and D. Grunwald. Content-Based Block Caching. In *23rd IEEE, 14th NASA Goddard Conference on Mass Storage Systems and Technologies*, MSST '06, 2006.

[25] P. Nagesh and A. Kathpal. Rangoli: Space Management in Deduplication Environments. In *Proceedings of the 6th International Systems and Storage Conference*, SYSTOR '13, 2013.

[26] C.-H. Ng, M. Ma, T.-Y. Wong, P. P. C. Lee, and J. C. S. Lui. Live Deduplication Storage of Virtual Machine Images in an Open-source Cloud. In *Proceedings of the 12th ACM/IFIP/USENIX International Conference on Middleware*, Middleware '11, pages 81–100, 2011.

[27] B. Nicolae, G. Antoniu, L. Bougé, D. Moise, and A. Carpen-Amarie. BlobSeer: Next-generation data management for large scale infrastructures. *Journal of Parallel and Distributed Computing*, 71(2):169–184, 2011.

[28] B. Nicolae, J. Bresnahan, K. Keahey, and G. Antoniu. Going Back and Forth: Efficient Multideployment and Multisnapshotting on Clouds. In *Proceedings of the 20th International Symposium on High Performance Distributed Computing (HPDC '11)*, pages 147–158, 2011.

[29] B. Nicolae, F. Cappello, and G. Antoniu. Optimizing multi-deployment on clouds by means of self-adaptive prefetching. In *Proceedings of the 17th international conference on Parallel processing - Volume Part I*, Euro-Par '11, pages 503–513, 2011.

[30] Nimbus Project. LANTorrent. `http://www.nimbusproject.org/docs/current/admin/reference.html#lantorrent`, 2010. [Online; accessed 27-01-2014].

[31] C. M. O'Donnell. Using BitTorrent to distribute virtual machine images for classes. In *Proceedings of the 36th annual ACM SIGUCCS fall conference: moving mountains, blazing trails*, SIGUCCS '08, pages 287–290, 2008.

[32] E. J. O'Neil, P. E. O'Neil, and G. Weikum. The LRU-K Page Replacement Algorithm for Database Disk Buffering. In *Proceedings of the 1993 ACM SIGMOD International Conference on Management of Data*, SIGMOD '93, pages 297–306, 1993.

[33] C. Peng, M. Kim, Z. Zhang, and H. Lei. VDN: Virtual machine image distribution network for cloud data centers. In *29th Conference on Computer Communications*, INFOCOM '10, pages 181–189, 2012.

[34] K. Razavi and T. Kielmann. Scalable Virtual Machine Deployment Using VM Image Caches. In *Proceedings of the International Conference on High Performance Computing, Networking, Storage and Analysis*, number 65 in SC '13, 2013.

[35] K. Razavi, L. M. Razorea, and T. Kielmann. Reducing VM Startup Time and Storage Costs by VM Image Content Consolidation. In *1st Workshop on Dependability and Interoperability In Heterogeneous Clouds*, Euro-Par 2013: Parallel Processing Workshops, 2013.

[36] J. Reich, O. Laadan, E. Brosh, A. Sherman, V. Misra, J. Nieh, and D. Rubenstein. VMTorrent: scalable P2P virtual machine streaming. In *Proceedings of the 8th international conference on Emerging networking experiments and technologies*, CoNEXT '12, pages 289–300, 2012.

[37] rsync. `http://rsync.samba.org`. [Online; accessed 22-01-2014].

[38] M. Schmidt, N. Fallenbeck, M. Smith, and B. Freisleben. Efficient Distribution of Virtual Machines for Cloud Computing. In *18th Euromicro International Conference on Parallel, Distributed and Network-Based Processing (PDP)*, PDP '10, pages 567–574, 2010.

[39] B. Sotomayor, K. Keahey, and I. Foster. Combining Batch Execution and Leasing Using Virtual Machines. In *Proceedings of the 17th International Symposium on High Performance Distributed Computing*, HPDC '08, pages 87–96, 2008.

[40] R. Wartel, T. Cass, B. Moreira, E. Roche, M. Guijarro, S. Goasguen, and U. Schwickerath. Image Distribution Mechanisms in Large Scale Cloud Providers. In *2010 IEEE Second International Conference on Cloud Computing Technology and Science*, CloudCom '10, pages 112–117, 2010.

[41] ZFS on Linux. `http://zfsonlinux.org`. [Online; accessed 24-01-2014].

[42] Z. Zhang, Z. Li, K. Wu, D. Li, H. Li, Y. Peng, and X. Lu. VMThunder: Fast Provisioning of Large-Scale Virtual Machine Clusters. *IEEE Transactions on Parallel and Distributed Systems*, 99, 2014.

[43] M. Zhao, J. Zhang, and R. Figueiredo. Distributed File System Support for Virtual Machines in Grid Computing. In *Proceedings of the 13th IEEE International Symposium on High Performance Distributed Computing*, HPDC '04, pages 202–211, 2004.

[44] X. Zhao, Y. Zhang, Y. Wu, K. Chen, J. Jiang, and K. Li. Liquid: A Scalable Deduplication File System for Virtual Machine Images. *IEEE Transaction on Parallel and Distributed Systems*, 2013.

Exploiting Redundancy for Cost-Effective, Time-Constrained Execution of HPC Applications on Amazon EC2

Aniruddha Marathe
Rachel Harris
David K. Lowenthal
Dept. of Computer Science
The University of Arizona

Bronis R. de Supinski
Barry Rountree
Martin Schulz
Lawrence Livermore
National Laboratory

ABSTRACT

The use of clouds to execute high-performance computing (HPC) applications has greatly increased recently. Clouds provide several potential advantages over traditional supercomputers and in-house clusters. The most popular cloud is currently Amazon EC2, which provides a fixed-cost option (called *on-demand*) and a variable-cost, auction-based option (called the *spot market*). The spot market trades lower cost for potential interruptions that necessitate checkpointing; if the market price exceeds the bid price, a node is taken away from the user without warning.

We explore techniques to maximize performance per dollar given a time constraint within which an application must complete. Specifically, we design and implement multiple techniques to reduce expected cost by exploiting redundancy in the EC2 spot market. We then design an adaptive algorithm that selects a scheduling algorithm and determines the bid price. We show that our adaptive algorithm executes programs up to $7x$ cheaper than using the on-demand market and up to 44% cheaper than the best non-redundant, spot-market algorithm.

Categories and Subject Descriptors

C.4 [**Computer Systems Organization**]: Performance of Systems

Keywords

Cloud; Cost; Resource Provisioning; Fault-tolerance

1. INTRODUCTION

Traditionally, high-performance computing (HPC) users execute scientific applications on dedicated HPC clusters hosted by national laboratories, companies or universities, typically managed through some kind of block allocation or grant mechanism. However, recently the use of cloud resources to execute HPC applications is becoming a popular alternative, due to factors such as machine availability and lower wait queue time. Success stories of scientific applications at HPC scale on the cloud have appeared in the popular press [13]. Unlike standard HPC clusters, however, cloud resources come with variable usage costs for individual users. Cloud resource providers, such as Amazon EC2, offer several *pay-as-you-go* offerings for purchasing cloud resources, which presents a complex optimization problem: What is the most cost effective strategy to execute a given high-performance computing application?

Often, HPC users simply execute their applications on EC2 in the *on-demand market*, which provides dedicated access to a set of machines for a fixed cost per unit time. However, if the application completes before the deadline by which the user requires the results, a second market, the *EC2 auction ("spot") market*, can result in lower cost. While the spot market can provide resources at low cost, jobs are terminated immediately if the current spot price exceeds the bid price. Thus, applications must checkpoint periodically to use the resources productively. Overall, the spot market requires two key decisions: (1) how much to bid; and (2) when to checkpoint.

We explore algorithms to determine the bid price and when to schedule checkpoints for HPC applications that execute on EC2. The algorithms attempt to minimize total user cost while honoring a user-specified application time bound. In one of our key contributions, our algorithms exploit redundancy across multiple groups of EC2 resources, so-called *zones*, to obtain higher availability. We show that, despite higher up-front cost, redundancy often results in lower total application cost because of less frequent downtimes and therefore lower checkpoint frequency.

Each algorithm has its strengths and weaknesses, which leads us to an adaptive algorithm that automatically selects from the algorithms based on current conditions. Our adaptive algorithm uses past spot price behavior to determine an effective algorithm along with an effective bid price. We also consider a relatively simple but often effective scheme that simply bids an excessively large amount, which avoids termination at the risk of higher cost.

We make the following contributions in the paper.

- We show that on the EC2 spot market, checkpoint-insertion algorithms using redundancy typically result in lower cost than their non-redundant counterparts.

- We analyze and categorize situations in which the different algorithms perform well.

- We develop an adaptive approach that automatically selects an algorithm based only on past spot price behavior.

Our evaluation revealed several insights. Compared to the naive approach of using on-demand, our adaptive scheme yields up to 7x lower cost. In addition, our adaptive scheme executes programs up to 44% cheaper than the best-case existing non-redundant algorithms that use the spot market. In comparison to an approach in which a user simply bids a large amount in order to avoid job termination, our adaptive scheme provides a significant advantage in avoiding situations in which the cost is much larger than simply using the on-demand market.

The paper is organized as follows: Section 2 provides the necessary background, and Section 3 describes how we exploit redundancy. We describe our algorithms in Section 4, the experimental setup in Section 5, and the experimental results in Section 6. These results motivate the need for an adaptive policy, which is described and evaluated in Section 7. We then describe related work in Section 8 and conclude in Section 9.

2. OVERVIEW

In this section we first describe the mechanics of the EC2 spot market and define the problem of selecting a fault-tolerance mechanism for time-constrained runs. Next, we describe why our work on the spot market on Amazon EC2 is relevant, in general, to clouds. Finally, we describe our system model.

2.1 EC2 Spot Market

The standard offering from Amazon EC2, known as *on-demand* pricing, guarantees resource availability for an hour of use at a fixed rate. At the end of every hour, the contract between the user and the cloud provider is renewed, and resource usage is granted for the next hour. Alternatively, EC2 auctions unused resources, which Amazon denotes the *spot market*. Spot prices can be significantly less than their on-demand counterparts for high-end EC2 resources. Popular HPC offerings such as Cluster Compute Eight Extra Large (CC2) instances are as much as eight times less expensive on the spot market as their corresponding on-demand prices. On the spot market, the user selects a *bid price*, and EC2 grants the resource if the bid is higher than the (EC2-maintained and demand-based) spot price. However, the system terminates the resource *immediately* and without warning if the spot price moves above the bid.

The spot market employs the following set of rules:

- Hour-boundary pricing: The user is charged for the hour based on the spot price (*not the bid price*) at the start of the hour. Spot price movements within the user's bid price do not affect the rate for that hour.

- Partial-hour usage: Partial-hour resource usage due to abrupt termination by EC2 is not charged to the user.

- Fixed bid: Once a spot request is submitted, the user cannot alter the bid. To change the bid, the user must cancel the spot request and submit a new request.

- Abrupt termination: EC2 does not notify the user before terminating a resource.

- Uncertain wait time: The user does not acquire a resource when the spot price is larger than the bid price.

To exploit low spot market prices for running tightly coupled HPC applications, one must use fault-tolerance techniques. Generally, HPC applications use checkpointing for such situations, which has a tradeoff between the overhead of checkpoints and how much computation is lost when a failure occurs. Previous work in this area focuses on predicting failures by analyzing real-time spot price data (see Section 8).

Running applications on the spot market does not provide a guaranteed completion time. Many scientific HPC applications must complete within a user-defined time bound in order to be useful. The bound depends upon context (e.g., "finish the weather prediction for tomorrow before the evening newscast at 7pm"). Typically, the deadline is further from the current time than the application takes to complete assuming uninterrupted execution. The difference between the deadline and the earliest possible completion time is *slack*. Given non-zero slack, the spot market can be used. However, the application then requires an algorithm to schedule checkpoints that minimizes the total cost.

2.2 Relevance to General Clouds

Our research on Amazon EC2 is relevant and applicable to the cloud in general. Amazon EC2 has become a popular platform for running scientific applications cost-effectively in recent years. In the HPC arena, Amazon EC2 has been evolving to provide top-of-the-line, HPC-grade compute resources securing a high ranking in the well-known Top-500 supercomputer list [15]. Stories of hero-type runs on EC2 frequently appear in the news [13]. Recent success stories on running scientific applications on the spot market present an attractive performance-per-dollar trade-off compared to existing, institution-owned HPC clusters [14]. A recent study shows that Amazon EC2 is significantly larger in compute capacity than their competition *combined* [4]. Consequently, the problem of selling unused capacity during sluggish demand is much more important to Amazon than other providers and will continue to exist for current and future cloud providers. Note also that our work, while targeted towards MPI applications in this paper, is in no way dependent on MPI.

Amazon's spot price mechanism is, in our view, not likely to change in the future. The objective behind the way Amazon's spot market has been structured is two-fold. One goal is to attract a sufficient number of users at a significantly discounted price compared to on-demand, so that the operating costs of already running unused instances is recovered. The second goal is to prevent users from monopolizing resources through the spot market, which would decrease Amazon's profit. The discounted nature of spot prices satisfies the first objective. On the other hand, Amazon provides no guarantees on instance up time via abrupt termination along with a fixed bid price, which accomplishes the second objective. Work by Ben-Yehuda et al. [1] on statistically analyzing the

Term	Description
t_c	Checkpoint cost
t_r	Restart cost
B	User's bid price
S	Spot price
C	Total uninterrupted computation time
C_r	Remaining computation time
D	User-defined time bound (deadline)
P	Progress made
T	Current time
T_r	Remaining time
T_u	Instance up-time
T_l	Slack time
T_s	Scheduled checkpoint time

Table 1: System model variables.

spot prices concluded that the spot prices are not purely based on user bid or resource supply, and hence users may not be able to make well-informed predictions of the spot prices over a long period of time.

Modifications to the spot market are full of practical problems. For example, instead of abrupt termination, the user could be provided with a notification beforehand. Another modification could be to notify the user about an out-of-bid situation and charge at a higher rate for a shorter billing cycle (less than one hour), allowing for a checkpoint before termination. Briefly, such schemes generally are undesirable to Amazon, because they could lead to fewer users using the (higher profit-generating) on-demand market. Appendix A discusses in detail the ramifications of such modifications.

2.3 System Model

Next, we present definitions for our underlying system model of both the Amazon EC2 spot market and checkpoint scheduling mechanisms. EC2 offers top-of-the-line HPC compute clusters, labeled *CC2 instances*, with node performance competitive to computing resources found on traditional dedicated HPC clusters at universities or national laboratories. In this paper, based on our previous experience as well as that of other groups [11], we use the spot market to run only CC2 instances and ignore other inferior clusters.

The user specifies an *experiment* as a configuration of a number of nodes, problem size, execution time and job completion deadline. We denote as C the (user-provided) execution time for the given number of nodes and problem size, i.e., the time to execute the application under the EC2 on-demand option with no system interruptions. The user also provides the deadline, which we denote as D, which is the time span in which the job *must* complete ($D \geq C$). We denote the *slack* between the deadline and the given execution time as T_l ($T_l = D - C$).

Let B be the user's bid price, which is the maximum amount the user is willing to pay per hour, and let S be the spot price. When S exceeds B, the currently running spot instance is terminated. Similarly, when S becomes less than or equal to B, a currently submitted spot instance is initiated. We assume constant checkpoint and restart costs for a configuration denoted by t_c and t_r respectively. Variable T_s denotes the time at which a checkpoint is initiated. Table 1 summarizes the variables in our model.

Figure 1 provides an example. The x-axis shows the progression of time and the y-axis shows price per hour. Plot

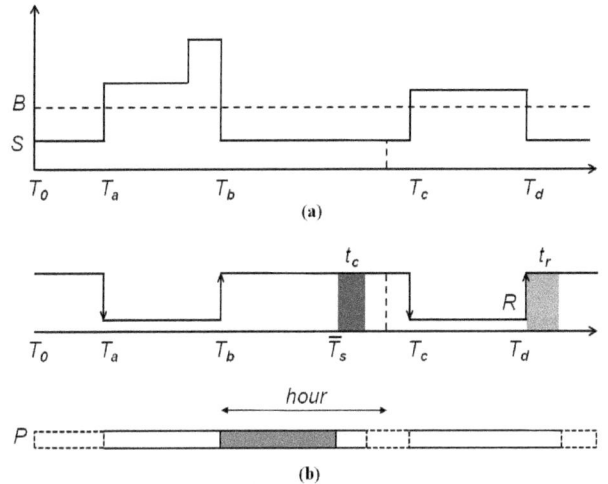

Figure 1: Spot price movements and state transitions: (a) spot price movements and progress; (b) instance states and checkpoint-restart costs.

(a) shows a scenario on the spot market with a user bid of B and movement over time of spot price S. Plot (b) shows the state transitions of the instance corresponding to the spot price movements relative to B. The instance starts at T_0 because $S < B$. At time T_a, $S > B$, so the instance is terminated. When S is again less than B at time T_b, the instance is re-initiated. The application restarts from its initial state since no checkpoint was taken (so its state was lost at T_a). The user schedules a checkpoint at $\overline{T_s}$ where the system takes t_c time to checkpoint (shown in dark grey). Termination again occurs at T_c, as does instance re-initiation at T_d. However, the application restarts from the checkpoint taken at $\overline{T_s}$. The restart operation R takes t_r time (shown in light grey). The user is charged the value of S at T_b for the first hour. Net application progress, denoted by P, is shown by the grey horizontal bar at the bottom of plot (b). Dotted boxes denote speculative progress that is not committed by a checkpoint. Empty boxes denote no computational progress due to a checkpoint, a restart, or system downtime.

3. EXPLOITING REDUNDANCY

EC2 auctions computational resources at different data centers (known as *availability zones*) at independent bid prices. For applications with significant slack and low checkpoint cost, bidding in a single zone results in low cost while still meeting the deadline. However, for applications with little slack or high checkpoint cost, or during times of spot price volatility, bidding only in a single zone can incur:

- Low system availability while the spot price is high;

- High checkpoint overhead; or,

- High rollback costs.

For such situations, the user could simply increase the bid. However, this choice does not guarantee high system availability at *low cost*, due to the nature of spot price movements (see Section 6). Thus, we introduce redundancy as an alternate, complementary fault-tolerance mechanism.

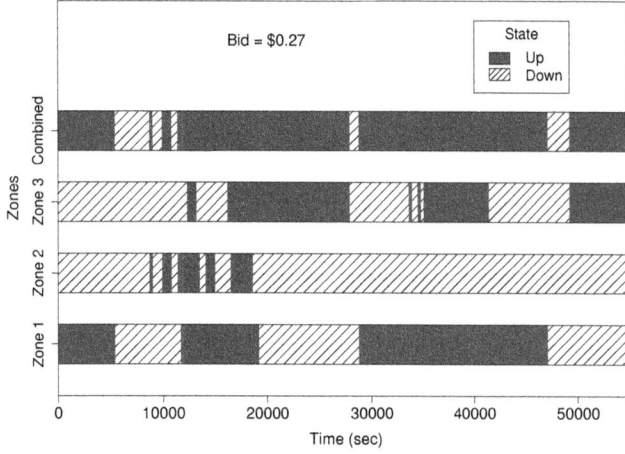

Figure 2: Availability for the three CC2 zones in the US-East region and the combined availability during a 15 hour period on December 19, 2012.

3.1 Redundancy in Independent Zones

Figure 2 shows an example of three CC2 zones in the US-East region. The solid portions show when the zones are up, and the textured portions when they are down. The top bar shows the combined up time; i.e., the times that at least one zone is up. Clearly, redundancy demonstrates potential for significantly increased up time in situations where individual zones have volatility.

However, for redundancy to be a viable solution, the movements in spot prices in different EC2 zones must be sufficiently independent. To investigate the interdependence of prices in different zones, we employed a *Vector Auto-Regression*, using the Akaike criteria to determine the optimal number of lags. As expected, each zone has a strong dependency on its own price history. Though there is some statistical significance in the dependencies across zones, the size of the effect is consistently 1-2 orders of magnitude smaller than within a zone. This difference of magnitude in same-zone vs. across-zone lagged price effects indicates an opportunity for computational arbitrage.

3.2 General Algorithm to Determine Checkpoints with Redundant Zones

In order to use the spot market efficiently across multiple zones, we need new algorithms to determine when to checkpoint. These algorithms lead to a set of policies to optimize use of spot market resources.

We start with the base algorithm that Algorithm 1 shows and extend it in the following section. The base algorithm alone extends prior work in two ways: first, it guarantees completion within the user time bound D; and second, it allows use of multiple zones. Our algorithm takes several parameters as input—the number of zones (degree of redundancy), $N \geq 1$; the bid and spot prices (B and S_i); and the checkpoint and restart costs (t_c and t_r) — and determines when to initiate checkpoints.

A zone is considered *up* when a spot instance is requested, and $B \geq S$ for the zone. Each zone runs a separate MPI application in its entirety with a fixed number of (user-specified) virtual machine instances. In the algorithm, $Instance_i$ refers to the application executing on zone i ($\forall i \in N$). Based on the conditions on the spot market and the remaining time

---

Algorithm 1 Algorithm framework to schedule checkpoints. Inputs are number of zones, N, bid and spot prices (B and S_i), and checkpoint and restart costs (t_c and t_r). $Instance_i$ is initially down ($\forall i, 1 \leq i \leq N$).

1: **while** T_r != 0 && C_r != 0 **do**
2:   **for** i = 1 to N **do**
3:     **if** $Instance_i$ is up and $B < S_i$ **then**
4:       $Instance_i \leftarrow$ down;
5:     **else if** $Instance_i$ is down and $B \geq S_i$ **then**
6:       $Instance_i \leftarrow$ waiting;
7:     **end if**
8:   **end for**
9:   $T_r \leftarrow D - T$
10:   $C_r \leftarrow C - P$
11:   **if** ($T_r == C - P + t_c + t_r$) **then**
12:     /* switch to on-demand to meet deadline */
13:     Checkpoint();
14:     RestartOnDemand(); /* single zone */
15:   **else**
16:     **if** ($\exists i \in N \mid Instance_i$ is up) **then**
17:       **if** ($CheckpointCondition()$) **then**
18:         $P \leftarrow$ Checkpoint();
19:         **for** i = 1 to N **do**
20:           **if** $Instance_i$ is waiting **then**
21:             $Instance_i \leftarrow$ up;
22:             RestartFromRecentCheckpoint();
23:             ScheduleNextCheckpoint();
24:           **end if**
25:         **end for**
26:       **end if**
27:     **else**
28:       /* No zone is up */
29:       **for** i = 1 to N **do**
30:         **if** $Instance_i$ is waiting **then**
31:           $Instance_i \leftarrow$ up;
32:           RestartFromPreviousCheckpoint();
33:           ScheduleNextCheckpoint();
34:         **end if**
35:       **end for**
36:     **end if**
37:   **end if**
38:   Compute(); /* run on all zones that are up */
39: **end while**

T_r, the algorithm chooses between on-demand and the spot market and selects N if the spot market is chosen. We assume that the algorithm monitors application progress, P, through an interface; e.g. `MPI_Pcontrol` is often used to indicate iteration completion in iterative MPI applications. Because the algorithm continuously monitors T_r, it can potentially handle changes in the input parameters such as the deadline D (modified by the user during application runtime) or variation in application performance (which affects P).

Lines 2-8 update the state of $Instance_i$ based on B and S_i. Lines 9 and 10 update the current T_r and C_r respectively. Line 11 ensures that the deadline D will be met by using on-demand market if the remaining time is equal to the remaining computation plus migration overhead (i.e, a checkpoint and a restart). If at least one zone is up and $CheckpointCondition()$ is true, then lines 16-18 take

Algorithm 2 $ScheduleNextCheckpoint()$ for Markov-Daly policy.

1: $ScheduleNextCheckpoint()$
2: {
3:   $E[T_u] \leftarrow$ expected_uptime$(B, i \in N)$;
4:   $T_s \leftarrow T +$ opt_ckpt$(E[T_u], t_c)$;
5: }

---

a checkpoint, update progress and line 23 schedules a new checkpoint.

To avoid checkpoint and restart overheads every time a zone is re-started, we introduce *waiting* state. Lines 5-6 mark a zone that is eligible to run as waiting ($B \geq S_i$; but no spot instance is requested on the zone). Thus, the zone can receive a checkpoint from another zone before starting. A running zone that takes a checkpoint at line 18 restarts waiting zones (lines 19-22) from that checkpoint by requesting a spot instance on the zone and marks them as running. If no zone is running, lines 29-33 restart all waiting zones from a previous checkpoint, the zones are marked as running, and the next checkpoint is scheduled. The algorithm is generic and can accept any $CheckpointCondition()$ and $ScheduleNextCheckpoint()$. We define each policy, as described in the next section, by these two functions.

4. REDUNDANCY-BASED POLICIES

In this section we describe our policies that exploit redundancy. In turn, we describe our *Periodic*, *Markov-Daly*, *Edge*, and *Threshold* checkpointing policies.

4.1 Periodic policy — checkpointing at hour boundaries

Given N zones, $ScheduleNextCheckpoint()$ (see Algorithm 1) schedules a checkpoint at regular intervals (at the end of every hour in this paper) such that the checkpoint *completes* within the hour boundary ($T_s = hour - t_c$) [18]. The user is charged S at the end of each hour, as long as $B > S$ throughout the hour. Function $CheckpointCondition()$ returns *true* when $T = T_s$.

4.2 Markov-Daly policy — predicting up time

Building on previous work [2] to predict up time for single zone cases (and without considering checkpointing), we use a variant of the Chapman-Kolmogorov equation to get the expected up time of a zone using the zone's price history. Algorithm 2 shows the basic idea behind $ScheduleNextCheckpoint()$: first, calculate the expected uptime given a bid price; then, use that expected up time to determine the optimal checkpoint frequency. The Markov model produces the expected up time. We then use Daly's equation [3], a well-known tool to calculate optimal checkpoint frequency to safeguard against hardware failures, to obtain the optimal checkpoint frequency. As with *Periodic*, $CheckpointCondition()$ simply checks if $T = T_s$. We calculate $E[T_u]$ for each zone on line 3 of Algorithm 2. For zones with *independent* price movements (see Section 3), the combined $E[T_u]$ is the sum of $E[T_u]$ of individual zones. Thus, $E[T_u]$ for the replication-based scheme is necessarily larger than with individual zones. We combine $E[T_u]$ and t_c as input to Daly's equation to calculate the optimal checkpoint

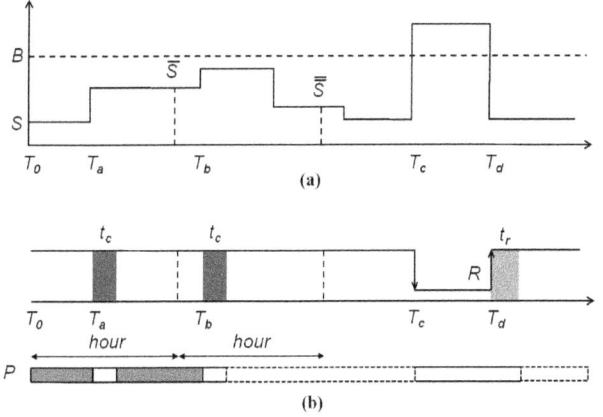

Figure 3: Rising Edge checkpoint policy. Part (a) shows user bid and spot price movements; Part (b) shows instance states, checkpoint-restart events and costs, and net progress.

frequency, which decreases as N increases. The Appendix fully details our Markov approach.

4.3 Rising Edge policy — reacting to rising price

This algorithm (referred to as *Edge* hereafter) sets $CheckpointCondition()$ from Algorithm 1 to *true* whenever an upward movement occurs in the spot price S in an executing zone [18]. The upward movement indicates that $S > B$ might occur soon. Hence by taking a checkpoint, progress is saved. Function $ScheduleNextCheckpoint()$ is a no-op, because the checkpoint decision is made instantaneously based solely on current values of B and S. Figure 3 shows the steps involved in the *Edge* policy. For a zone with relatively stable spot prices, the *Edge* policy saves checkpoint costs compared to periodic checkpointing, but can lose substantial progress if the spot price increases sharply.

4.4 Threshold checkpoint scheduling policy — reducing cost of Edge policy

Previous work on scheduling checkpoints in a single zone [7] describes an algorithm that is an outgrowth with the *Edge* policy. The algorithm operates on two thresholds. $CheckpointCondition()$ is set to true if either of the following two conditions is true in an executing zone. First, a price threshold $PriceThresh$ is calculated as the average of minimum spot price S_{min} and B. The first condition is *true* when S shows a rising edge and $PriceThresh \leq S$. Second, a time threshold $TimeThesh$ is calculated as the probabilistic average up time of a zone. Another variable, execution time at B, equals the up time at bid price B since the most recent restart or checkpoint. The second condition is *true* when $TimeThresh$ is less than execution time at B. $ScheduleNextCheckpoint()$ schedules an immediate checkpoint if either condition is true.

5. SIMULATION SETUP

This section describes our assumptions about the working environment, applications and checkpointing policies. We make the following assumptions about experiment configurations to evaluate policies presented in the paper.

- The problem size and number of MPI tasks are fixed for an experiment.

- Bid prices for all nodes in a zone are identical.

- Checkpoints are stored onto an I/O server that runs in an on-demand instance as long as spot instances are running.

HPC users typically run MPI applications on the spot market along with one or more I/O instances through the on-demand option with persistent storage (e.g., EBS volumes on EC2) attached [9]. A typical I/O server setup (non-CC2) at the on-demand price costs only a fraction of the total cost of running a tightly coupled MPI application at scale. Hence, we ignore the cost of running such I/O server setup in our experiments. A sophisticated multi-I/O server setup has been discussed elsewhere and is beyond the scope of this work [9].

Recovery costs for an MPI application on the spot market include instance queuing delay, which is the time between the submission of the spot request ($S \leq B$) to the time when the instance is accessible. Previous studies have shown that Amazon EC2 instances incur a measurable boot time on the on-demand option (order of several minutes in the worst-case) [11]. We measured the queuing delay on the spot market for CC2 instances by submitting spot instance requests at 7:00 AM and 7:00 PM every day for two months with the bid price equal to the instantaneous spot price. We measured the time between the submission of the spot request to the time when the instance was available for login by attempting to establish an SSH connection to the instance every ten seconds after the instance became "*running*". We observed an average queuing delay of 299.6 seconds with best-case and worst-case delays of 143 seconds and 880 seconds, respectively. The queuing delay on the spot market contributes to an added penalty to application recovery cost.

Another major factor contributing to checkpoint costs originates from inferior network bandwidth on the cloud. We confirm previous findings that showed that when using system-level checkpointing, MPI benchmarks from the NAS benchmark suite showed up to 200 seconds of overhead for small problem sizes at up to 64 tasks [5]. Due to limited funds, we could not perform extensive runs on EC2 to measure checkpoint costs for real applications with large working sets. Previous work shows that real applications spend a significant portion of the hour in checkpoint and restart operations (up to tens of minutes) [9] and we therefore assume checkpoint and restart overheads compatible with the range of existing studies of 300 to 900 seconds. For simplicity, we also assume checkpoint and restart costs are equal. Although resource acquisition on the spot market involves variable delay even in perfect conditions ($S \leq B$), our assumptions about fixed restart costs do not negatively affect the correctness of our work.

For the purpose of simulation, we assume an uninterrupted application execution time of 20 hours. We choose slack values of 15% to 50% (3 to 10 hours). We use the spot price history of CC2 instances with Linux of over 12 months (between December 2012 to January 2014). The state of spot prices in all zones is sampled at a 5-minute interval for all three zones. Spot price movements within a 5-minute interval (although present) are rare and hence the loss in precision does not affect the key findings in our work. We observe several low, moderate and high spot price volatility windows in our 12-month data. However, for representative results, we use low spot price volatility and high spot price volatility windows for evaluation of our policies over different spot price behaviors. For low spot price volatility window, we use the spot price data for March 2013 with average spot price of $0.30 and a variance of less than 0.01 in each zone. Similarly, for the high spot price volatility window, we use the spot price data for January 2013 with average spot prices between $0.70 to $1.12 and a variance of up to 2.02 in each zone. We run 80 experiments over partially overlapping chunks in each spot price window. To build the system state for *Markov-Daly* policies, we use a price history size of 2 days and we assume bid prices between $0.27 to $3.07 in steps of $0.20. We use bid prices larger than $2.40 to avoid failures due to occasional spot price spikes of up to $3.00.

6. EVALUATION OF POLICIES

We now show the effectiveness of the various policies discussed in Section 4. Figure 4 compares different single-zone checkpointing policies with the *best-case* redundancy-based policy. The comparison is shown for low and high volatility windows as well as low and high slack values; in addition, the checkpoint cost is fixed at 300 seconds. For each single-zone checkpoint policy, we merge the results from all three individual zones (each of which could be selected by a user) to generate one boxplot. Similarly, due to space limitations and consistency, we pick the best-case redundancy-based policy for each experiment, though our redundancy-based policies perform fairly similarly (with *Markov-Daly* performing slightly better than others). We observed diminishing returns with $N \leq 2$ zones for redundancy, and so we do not include this case in our evaluation. The x-axis shows checkpoint scheduling policies, and the y-axis shows the total cost per instance in dollars. The boxplot shows the variation in cost of execution at different slack values (denoted T_l) for low (top) and high (bottom) volatility windows. For plots (a) and (c), $T_l = 15\%$ of computation time, and for plots (b) and (d), $T_l = 50\%$. Due to limited space, we do not show the boxplots for high checkpoint cost (900 seconds). We summarize which policies have lowest cost in Table 2 (low checkpoint costs) and Table 3 (high checkpoint costs).

We make several observations from the boxplots. First, at low T_l (plots (a) and (c)), spot price volatility determines if single-zone or redundancy-based policy results in the least cost. In general, low volatility results in higher availability (uptime) per zone at low bid. For time-constrained execution, higher availability on the spot market results in lower overall costs due to lower use of the (expensive) on-demand option. In the case of low volatility (plot (a)), *Periodic* is superior due to low checkpoint cost (which in our implementation of *Periodic* is incurred hourly) as well as infrequent restarts (because with low volatility, there are fewer failures). This is true even at low bids. On the other hand, for high volatility, redundancy generally results in lower cost (plot (c)). This is because of (1) lower checkpoint overhead and (2) higher combined system availability at a lower bid. For example, in the case of low T_l with high volatility (plot (c)), the best-case redundancy-based policy results in 23.9% lower costs than *Periodic*, which is the best-case existing single-zone policy in this case.

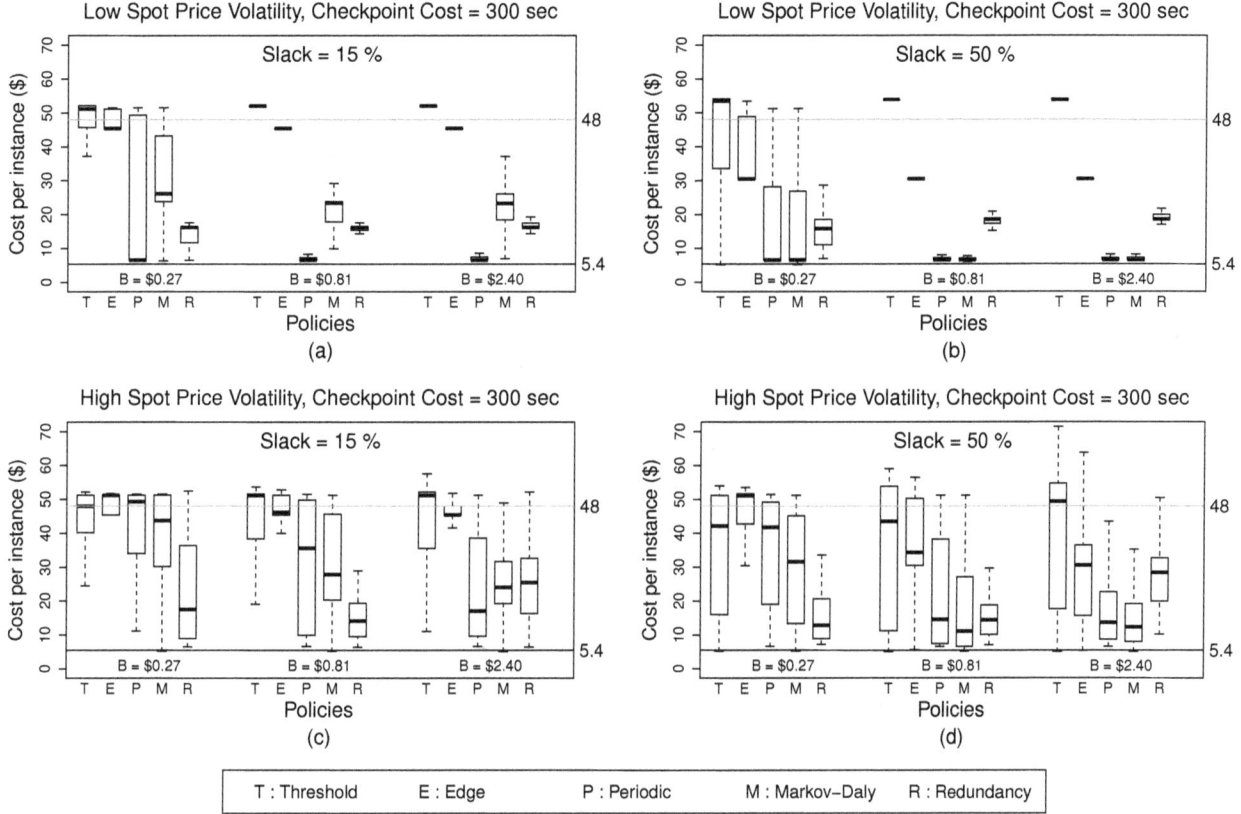

Figure 4: Comparison of single-zone checkpoint and best-case redundancy-based policies for checkpoint cost = 300 seconds at B = \$0.27, \$0.81 and \$2.40. The comparison is shown for two data-sets: low volatility (top row) and high volatility (bottom row). A horizontal grey line at \$48.00 shows the cost at on-demand rate (\$2.40/hr), and a horizontal black line at \$5.40 shows reference cost at lowest spot price (\$0.27/hr). Protocol abbreviations are Threshold, Rising Edge, Periodic, Single-Zone Markov-Daly, and Redundancy-based (best-case)

Second, at a high T_l (plots (b) and (d)), single-zone policies generally show lower costs than redundancy-based policies because a single zone has a sufficiently high probability of executing solely on the spot market at a low bid price. Again, low or high volatility influences the cost difference between single-zone and redundancy-based policies. In case of low volatility (plot (b)), *Periodic* and single-zone *Markov-Daly* show lower median costs (confirming prior results for *Periodic* [18]). For high volatility (plot (d)), the best-case redundancy-based policy shows median costs similar to single-zone policies. In this case, median costs depend on particular price movements in individual experiments.

Third, redundancy generally shows better median costs at lower bid prices ($B \leq \$0.81$) due to the lower possibility of paying for all three zones at a higher combined availability. Higher T_l results in lower worst-case costs but does not significantly affect the median costs of redundancy-based policies. This is because the checkpoint/restart overhead is already low and system availability is already high, so there is little added benefit from additional slack. As mentioned earlier, Table 2 summarizes the results for low checkpoint costs.

Table 3 summarizes the best policies for configurations with large checkpoint costs (900 seconds). For low and high volatility windows with low T_l, the best-case redundancy-based policy yields the lowest median-costs. (up to 56% better than the best single-zone policy). For high T_l, low spot price volatility results in single-zone *Periodic* as well as *Markov-Daly* yielding the lowest median costs; this is due to their low checkpoint frequency when slack is high. For high spot price volatility and high T_l, *Markov-Daly* yields the lowest median costs. We observe that *Edge* and *Threshold* policies result in high median costs due to high recovery costs resulting from inadequate checkpointing at low bid prices. This confirms prior results [8]. Hence, we exclude *Edge* and *Threshold* in all further evaluation.

Spot price volatility	Slack	
	15%	50%
Low	Periodic (bid = \$0.81)	Periodic/Markov-Daly (bid = \$0.81)
High	Redundancy (bid = \$0.81)	Markov-Daly (bid = \$0.81)

Table 2: Optimal policies for the experiments with $t_c = 300$ seconds, low (15%) and high (50%) slack for low and high spot price volatility windows.

285

Spot price volatility	Slack	
	15%	50%
Low	Redundancy (Bid = \$0.27)	Periodic/Markov-Daly (Bid = \$0.81)
High	Redundancy (Bid = \$0.81)	Markov-Daly (Bid = \$2.40)

Table 3: Optimal policies for the experiments with $t_c = 900$ seconds, low (15%) and high (50%) slack and low and high spot price volatility windows.

Summary.

The critical point here is that for different experiment configurations and bid prices, different protocols result in the best costs. Spot price volatility also influences the median costs. In addition, the boxplots above show only a small subset of the permutations of bid price, checkpoint policy and number of zones from which the user can select. Note that in general single-zone *Periodic* shows better median costs at $B = \$0.81$, whereas, higher bid prices result in better costs for single-zone *Markov-Daly*. Higher bid prices (after a sweet-spot) generally increase the median cost for redundancy-based policies as a result of paying more for additional zones. These factors motivate an adaptive mechanism to select the most appropriate policy given past and current conditions on the spot market. In the next section, we design, implement, and evaluate such a mechanism.

7. ADAPTIVE POLICY

As we showed in Section 6, the best choice of policy changes depending on the condition of the spot market. This section first explains our design and implementation of an "adaptive policy" (denoted *Adaptive* hereafter) that can switch checkpoint or redundancy-based policies dynamically depending on spot market conditions. Next, we evaluate *Adaptive*, which shows that we achieve two broad results. The first is that *Adaptive* typically results in a policy that is as good or nearly as good as the best policy from Section 4. The second is that *Adaptive* in general *avoids* choosing a policy that leads to high cost.

7.1 Description

The optimal algorithm for time-constrained execution of an experiment depends on two fixed parameters (the slack (T_l) and the checkpoint cost (t_c)), and three variables (bid price (B), number of zones used (N), and the policy used). It also depends on changes in the spot price (S). From a user perspective, the problem of selecting the correct policy to optimize cost while completing in the time-bound is nontrivial. Furthermore, the best policy changes over time depending on S. Finally, the values of B and N need to be chosen; the algorithms in the previous subsection do not indicate how to choose them. In this section we describe our novel *Adaptive* checkpoint scheduling scheme, which chooses an effective policy as well as B and N.

Adaptive works as follows. First, it boot-straps by reading the spot price history prior to the experiment start time to load the "current state". At each 5-minute step, *Adaptive* simulates cost and computation for each permutation of B, N, and policy; B is chosen in a range of \$0.27 to \$3.07 (the upper bound covers occasional spikes) in steps of \$0.20 and N is 1, 2, or 3. During an experiment, *Adaptive* selects a new

permutation, if any of the following is true: (1) the current zone has been terminated due to $S > B$; (2) the billing hour has ended; or (3) the new policy does not change the running zone or B in the current billing hour.

A new configuration is chosen at run-time as follows. To guarantee completion by the user's deadline, *Adaptive* considers the following inequality:

$$C_r - T_r \times \frac{P}{T} > 0 \qquad (1)$$

where, C_r is the remaining computation, T_r is the remaining time to meet the deadline, and $\frac{P}{T}$ denotes the current rate of progress (see Table 1). *Adaptive* evaluates $\frac{P}{T}$ for each permutation of B, N, and policy. For a permutation, if the left hand side of the inequality is positive, then a switch to on-demand will occur; otherwise, only spot market will be used at the current rate of progress (assuming for the moment that there is no cost to checkpoint and restart during the switch to on-demand). To select the least-cost policy, *Adaptive* estimates, for each permutation, (1) the time on the spot market before the switch to on-demand and (2) the remaining time on on-demand (using Inequality (1)). It is straightforward to estimate the total remaining cost based on the current rate of expenditure on the spot market and the fixed rate of \$2.40 for on-demand. Then, *Adaptive* chooses the permutation with the least predicted remaining cost. To add checkpoint and restart costs, we merely place their sum as a term on the left-hand side of Inequality (1).

7.2 Evaluation

We show the effectiveness of *Adaptive* with two experiments. First, we evaluate the cost-effectiveness of *Adaptive* against existing protocols. Second, we compare *Adaptive* to a simple but often effective policy called *Large-bid* [8].

7.2.1 Comparison to Single-Zone and Redundancy-Based Protocols

Figure 5 compares *Adaptive* with best-case single-zone checkpointing policies (*Periodic* and *Markov-Daly*) as well as the best-case redundancy-based policy. As in the previous subsection, we merge the boxplots of single-zone checkpoint policies from each zone for a fair comparison. We observe that $B = \$0.81$ generally results in better median costs compared to other bid prices. Hence, we choose the bid price of \$0.81 to compare best-case costs of policies (see Figure 4).

The key point is that *Adaptive* is always at least competitive with the *best* of the other three algorithms, and which is best (and worst) changes with spot price and slack. Therefore, *Adaptive* avoids situations that would lead to large costs to the user. In the case of low volatility (plots (a), (b), (c) and (d)), *Adaptive* quickly converges to the best-case single-zone or redundancy-based policy for different T_l and t_c values, resulting in similar median as well as worst-case costs. Specifically, low T_l values (plots (a) and (b)) result in median costs of *Adaptive* that are comparable to existing policies, but show a smaller range of second and third quartile costs (and so have low variance). Higher checkpoint costs ($t_c = 900$ sec) (plot (b)) result in median cost for *Adaptive* that is up to 44.2% lower than the best-case median cost across all bid prices for the existing single-zone policy (which, in this case, is *Periodic*). Note that the comparison is between *Adaptive* and the *best-case* existing policy—and a user will not in general be able to determine the best-case

Low Spot Price Volatility

High Spot Price Volatility

P : Periodic   M : Markov–Daly   R : Redundancy   A : Adaptive

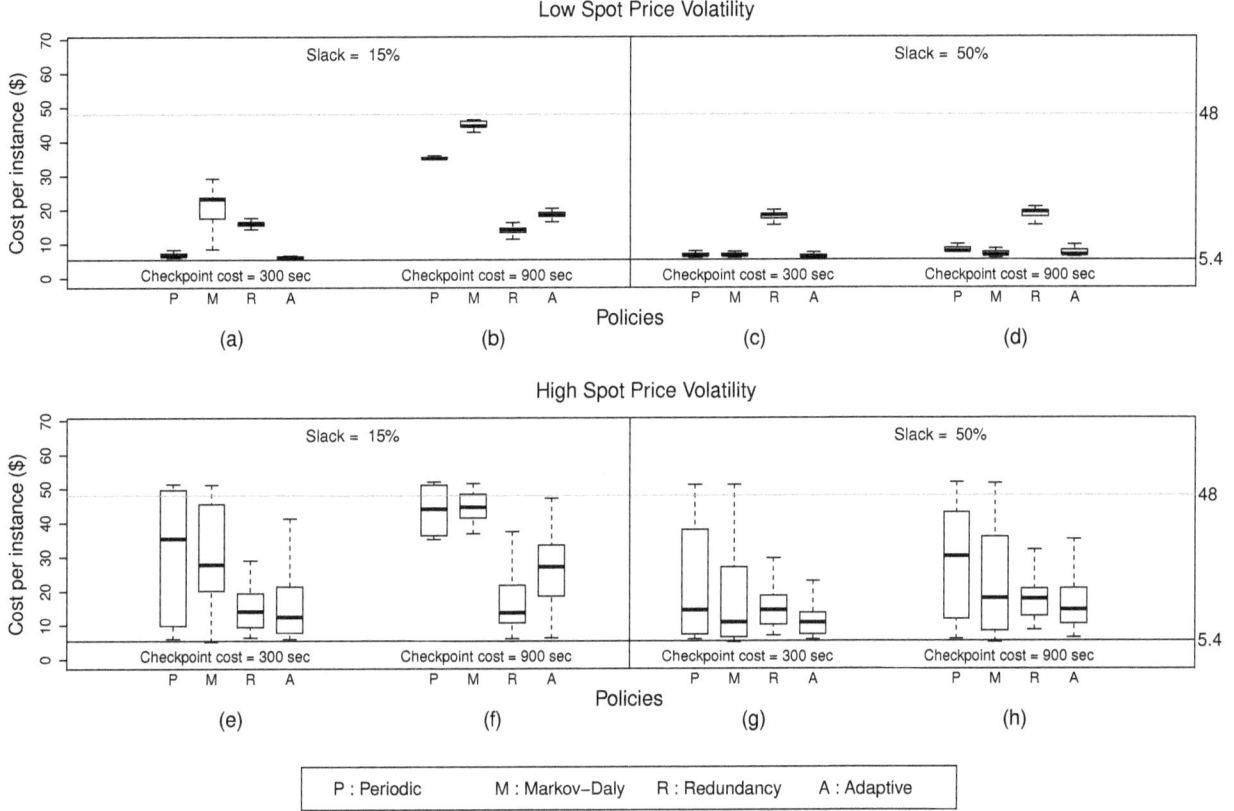

Figure 5: Comparison of **A**daptive policy with other policies: **P**eriodic, Single-zone **M**arkov-Daly and **R**edundancy-based (best-case). Results for different spot price volatility windows are shown (low at the top and high at the bottom). A horizontal grey line at \$48.00 shows the cost at on-demand rate (\$2.40/hr) and a horizontal black line at \$5.40 shows reference cost at lowest spot price (\$0.27/hr).

policy. For higher T_l values (plots (c) and (d)), the median costs of *Adaptive* are comparable to single-zone policies, but again the range of the second and third quartile costs is smaller.

With high volatility (plots (e), (f), (g) and (h)), the overall costs for *Adaptive* are strongly influenced by the amount of slack T_l. For low T_l (plots (e) and (f)), the median costs for *Adaptive* are magnified by checkpoint/restart costs. Specifically, choosing the policy that has high availability at low amortized checkpoint/restart overhead results in lower costs. Plot (e) shows that median costs for *Adaptive* are as good as the median costs for best-case redundancy-based policies. Higher checkpoint cost ($t_c = 900$ seconds) (plot (f)) magnifies errors, if they occur, when an incorrect policy is chosen near execution start (before there is enough information for *Adaptive* to make a good choice). This error results in higher checkpoint/restart overhead (in terms of both checkpoint frequency and cost), which inversely affects the amount of slack available on the spot market. Thus, for high checkpoint costs ($t_c = 900$ seconds) and low slack ($T_l = 15\%$) for both low and high volatility windows, *Adaptive* shows higher median costs compared to best-case costs for redundancy-based policies.

For high T_l (plots (g) and (h)), *Adaptive* yields better costs, because a switch to on-demand to compensate for errors near the start of execution is not necessary (due to larger slack). Although *Adaptive* does not guarantee a total

cost of less than the cost via on-demand, the upper bound on the cost is a function of the slack and (user-configurable) maximum bid price, which also applies to individual policies except *Periodic*. However, due to the way the algorithms select the policy with least predicted cost, total cost never exceeds 20% above the on-demand cost for our experiments involving 12-month data. This cost is much less than the other policies.

7.2.2 Comparison to Large-Bid

Our final comparison is *Adaptive* to *Large-bid* [8]. In *Large-bid*, the user submits a large B but maintains a second, smaller value, L, for cost control. Variable B is chosen such that it is extremely unlikely that it is ever smaller than S (e.g., $B = \$100$; the largest S we have observed in the 12-months data is \$20.02). With large bid, the user has no control over the cost of execution on the spot market; a price spike can result in a large expense. The motivation behind *Large-bid* is that, in general, the spot price remains significantly lower than the on-demand price. Variable L provides limited control of the cost of execution with *Large-bid*. If S moves above L, the spot instance is allowed to run for the on-going hour. If S remains larger than L near the end of the hour, a checkpoint is taken followed by a manual termination of the instance. The instance is restarted as soon as S moves below L. *Large-bid* is a strictly single zone policy. Since *Large-bid* does not provide an upper bound on

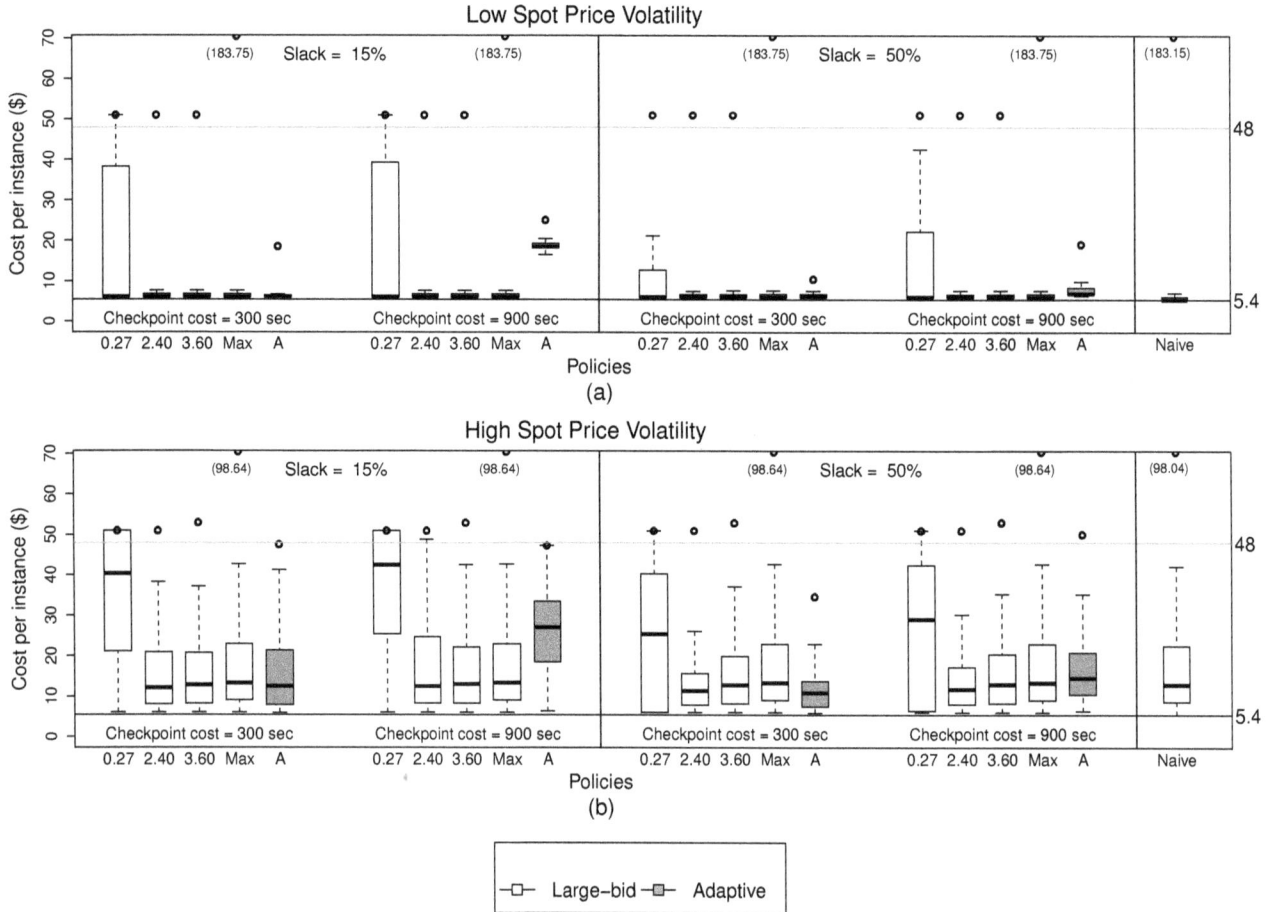

Figure 6: Comparison of *Large-bid* with *Adaptive*. Spot price volatility is low (top) and high (bottom). The user-defined threshold L is on the x-axis and the y-axis shows *Cost per Instance* in \$. The horizontal grey line at \$48.00 shows the cost at on-demand rate (\$2.40/hr) and a horizontal black line at \$5.40 shows reference cost at lowest spot price (\$0.27/hr). Circles denote maximum cost incurred.

the cost, we do not consider *Large-bid* as a candidate policy for *Adaptive*.

Figure 6 compares *Large-bid* with *Adaptive*. The user threshold is set from a low price of \$0.27 to a high price of \$20.02 (denoted as *Max* in the figure). As can be seen, in most cases *Adaptive* results in better worst-case costs than *Large-bid*. On the other hand, *Large-bid* sometimes results in lower median costs than *Adaptive* at different user thresholds for different spot price behavior and experiment configurations.

There are two key advantages of *Adaptive* over *Large-bid*. First, *Adaptive* does not incur large costs— typically well below on-demand. On the other hand, *Large-bid* offers no control over the periodic cost on the spot market until *after* the user pays a high periodic cost. For low volatility window (plot (a)), *Adaptive* results in similar median costs, but better worst-case costs than *Large-bid*. The worst-case costs for *Large-bid* are as high as *3.8x* the on-demand costs (the worst-case cost of \$183.75 results due to a spike in the spot price of \$20.02 between March 13th to March 14th, 2013). For high volatility window (plot (b)), *Adaptive* typically results in better median and worst-case costs than several *Large-bid* threshold values (except for the case where $T_l = 15\%$ and $t_c = 900$ seconds). The worst-case costs are

as high as *2.0x* the on-demand costs (for *Max* threshold). We observe that for moderately volatile prices in a zone, *Large-bid* switches to on-demand to meet the time-bound *after* paying a high cost on the spot market. *Adaptive* predicts the optimal bid price and guarantees a *bounded* cost while completing within the time bound. Also, regardless of slack and checkpoint costs, *Adaptive* results in comparable median cost and lower worst-case cost.

Second, *Adaptive* does not have any user-chosen thresholds. In *Large-bid*, a low threshold (L = \$0.27) results in lower worst-case cost, but higher median costs. Using higher threshold values for *Large-bid* allows more resistance to checkpoint cost and slack, but increases worst-case cost. Thus, the "sweet-spot" value of the threshold depends on future spot prices that are unknown to the user. In contrast, *Adaptive* handles this implicitly, with no input from the user. Importantly, when no threshold is used (labeled *Naive* in the figure), the worst case *Large-bid* cost is larger than the worst-case cost for *Adaptive*. Moreover, without a threshold, reaching this worst-case cost in a given experiment is more likely, even for a situation with moderate spot price volatility.

7.3 Summary

Adaptive shows median costs competitive to best-case median costs for existing single-zone policies. Choosing the policy with least predicted cost for high spot price volatility is non-trivial at low slack (T_l). An error in making this choice is magnified by higher checkpoint/restart costs (t_c). Even for high spot price volatility, *Adaptive* results in median costs better than existing single-zone policies and competitive to best-case costs for redundancy-based policies for a configuration with low T_l and high t_c. For other configurations, *Adaptive* results in median costs similar to the best-case median costs of the other three policies. Unlike *Large-bid*, *Adaptive* chooses the user bid and the policy with the least predicted cost resulting in a *bounded* cost, even with high spot price volatility.

8. RELATED WORK

The problem of optimizing cost of running HPC applications on the cloud has been an active area of research. Previous work focuses on predicting spot price movements for selecting the optimal bid price and fault-tolerance technique on the EC2 spot market. Machine learning approaches to predict future spot prices apply well-known statistical models to study spot price distribution [6, 1, 10]. Chohan et. al employ a Markov model to predict instance up time [2] for MapReduce-type applications.

There exists a large body of work on exploring bid price prediction and fault-tolerance strategies. Yi et. al present cost-performance trade-offs of different checkpoint scheduling policies on the spot market [18]. The study shows two things: that the frequency of checkpointing directly affects total execution time of the application, and that the frequency of checkpointing affects the time to recover from failure. Therefore, the choice of frequency also affects total cost of execution, as higher overhead or higher recovery time both contribute to monetary cost. Yi et. al and Voorsluys et. al extend the preceding work to explore cost-effectiveness of different cost-aware checkpointing schemes coupled with task migration and duplication on to different resource types [17, 16]. Since we address tightly coupled HPC applications running on HPC-grade CC2 instances, addressing their work is beyond the scope this paper. Jung et. al present an improved *Edge* algorithm to efficiently schedule checkpoints [7]. Another scheme presented by Khatua et. al presents the large-bid approach for cost-effective runs on the spot market [8]. We address both schemes in our evaluation. Our work differs from previous work in two ways: (1) we evaluate redundancy as the first-class fault-tolerance mechanism at different bid prices, and (2) our work provides guarantee on job completion times.

Previous work on optimizing cost of time-constrained execution on the spot market predicts optimal bid prices for each hourly billing cycle [12, 19] with a fixed, hourly checkpoint frequency. Work by Tang et. al [12] focuses on optimizing cost or performance with time or cost constraints, respectively. Their work does not guarantee a strict deadline and cannot be directly applied to tightly coupled HPC applications. Work by Zafer et. al [19] addresses the problem of running loosely coupled applications and does not predict optimal checkpoint frequency. Our *Adaptive* checkpoint scheduling scheme solves the problem of running tightly coupled HPC applications with a guaranteed completion time and predicts the optimal bid price, number of zones and optimal checkpoint frequency for each billing cycle.

9. CONCLUSION

This paper focused on exploiting redundancy for cost-effective execution on the spot market. The user provides an execution time bound, and our *Adaptive* algorithm chooses a bid price and a checkpoint-insertion algorithm that results in meeting the bound at low cost. We found that in comparison to *Large-bid*, *Adaptive* has bounded costs and avoids worst cases in which the user is charged an exceedingly large amount (e.g., more than using the on-demand market). Overall, we believe that our *Adaptive* scheme is a step towards more practical, cost-effective use of the spot market.

APPENDIX
A. SPOT MARKET MODIFICATIONS

In this appendix we explain in detail the ramifications of modifications to the spot market mechanism. First, instead of abrupt termination, the user could be provided with a notification that the spot price is about to change and the instance may be terminated. In this case, the user could take a checkpoint and save application state just before termination. However, we argue that such a window would not always be sufficiently large to save the state of an HPC application with a large working set over a large number of tasks (the checkpoint costs also involve bottleneck at the I/O server–*ten* minutes). On the other hand, a window of notification sufficiently large to save a checkpoint would work against the principle of the spot market in which prices change within ten minutes.

Second, the user could be allowed to adjust the user bid at run time to retain spot instances at high spot prices. However, there are several problems with such a provision. First, spot prices primarily consist of spikes that are difficult to predict (from our study), thus necessitating the use of a fault-tolerance mechanism. Second, a scheme in which the user follows the spot price essentially becomes a "large-bid" policy described in Section 7, which is inferior in worst-case costs. Third, for long periods of time where spot prices are predictable, the provision may enable the user to utilize the spot market at a much cheaper cost, disrupting the balance between the spot and on-demand markets. This would lower Amazon's overall profit.

Third, when the spot price is about to rise over the user bid price, Amazon could offer the user a significantly higher rate for shorter billing cycles (e.g. 5-minute cycle), during which the application state could be saved. Such an enhancement seems better for the user since the user could pay more to avoid the need to employ fault tolerance. It also seems better for Amazon, who could attract more users who would like to avoid the need for fault tolerance. However, we find the following issues with the provision. First, it would be difficult to apply pricing at such a short billing granularity and hard to predict (for both the user and Amazon) how long it will take to save the application state. Second, the price for the short billing cycle would likely be variable, since longer uninterrupted runs for the user could mean more "value" associated with the checkpoint. Third, such a scheme would work against the second objective of the spot market–of keeping the users from hogging low-cost resources for a long time. Fourth, it would also work against free partial-hour usage, which is attractive for users with short-lived burst requests. We argue that the above reasons would prevent Amazon from making such provisions in the spot market mechanism.

B. MARKOV MODEL DETAILS

For completeness, we provide the basic idea behind the Markov model. We calculate the expected up time of the instance at a bid price B as follows: $PROB$ denotes a $1 \times N$ probability matrix for N different spot prices in the price history. $TRANS$ is an $N \times N$ transition matrix in which the element at (n, m) represents the probability of spot price moving from n to m, $\forall\ n, m \in N$ (i.e. n^{th} row to m^{th} column). For a step size of 5 minutes, we predict the state of $PROB$ for the next step as shown in Equation 2. We choose step size of 5 minutes because spot price movements do not occur in such duration in most cases (from our price history of 12 months).

$$\forall j \in N, PROB_j^{k+1} = \sum_{i=1}^{N} [PROB_j^k \times TRANS_{i,j} \times I(i)] \quad (2)$$

$$I(i) = \begin{cases} 1, & \text{if } P_i \leq B \\ 0, & \text{otherwise} \end{cases}$$

Expected up time $E[T_u]$ is calculated as a weighted average over $k=1$ to Th steps as shown in Equation 3. Intuitively, the equation calculates a weighted average of zone up-time over each step with conditional probability of zone being terminated at the end of each step (note that the condition is reversed for $I(i)$ [not shown]). Th is the minimum value at which the expected up time does not change at seconds granularity over multiple iterations.

$$E[T_u] = \sum_{k=1}^{Th} k \times \left[\sum_{i=1}^{N} PROB_i^k \times I(i) \right] \quad (3)$$

Acknowledgments

Part of this work was performed under the auspices of the U.S. Department of Energy by Lawrence Livermore National Laboratory under Contract DE-AC52-07NA27344 (LLNL-CONF-652718). We also thank Amazon for a grant for time on EC2. Finally, we thank the anonymous reviewers for comments that improved the quality of this paper.

C. REFERENCES

[1] O. A. Ben-Yehuda, M. Ben-Yehuda, A. Schuster, and D. Tsafrir. Deconstructing Amazon EC2 spot instance pricing. In *IEEE International Conference on Cloud Computing Technology and Science*, pages 304–311, 2011.

[2] N. Chohan, C. Castillo, M. Spreitzer, M. Steinder, A. Tantawi, and C. Krintz. See spot run: using spot instances for mapreduce workflows. In *USENIX Hot Topics in Cloud Computing*, pages 7–7, 2010.

[3] J. T. Daly. A higher order estimate of the optimum checkpoint interval for restart dumps. *Future Gener. Comput. Syst.*, pages 303–312, Feb. 2006.

[4] Gartner Inc. Toolkit: Comparison Matrix for Cloud Infrastructure as a Service Providers, 2013. https://www.gartner.com/doc/2575815, 2013.

[5] J. Hursey, J. M. Squyres, T. I. Mattox, and A. Lumsdaine. The design and implementation of checkpoint/restart process fault tolerance for Open MPI. In *IEEE International Parallel and Distributed Processing Symposium*, 2007.

[6] B. Javadi, R. K. Thulasiramy, and R. Buyya. Statistical modeling of spot instance prices in public cloud environments. In *Proceedings of the 2011 Fourth IEEE International Conference on Utility and Cloud Computing*, pages 219–228, 2011.

[7] D. Jung, S. Chin, K. Chung, H. Yu, and J. Gil. An efficient checkpointing scheme using price history of spot instances in cloud computing environment. In *Proceedings of the 8th IFIP International Conference on Network and Parallel Computing*, 2011.

[8] S. Khatua and N. Mukherjee. Application-centric resource provisioning for Amazon EC2 spot instances. In *International Conference on Parallel Processing*, pages 267–278, 2013.

[9] M. Liu, Y. Jin, J. Zhai, Y. Zhai, Q. Shi, X. Ma, and W. Chen. ACIC: Automatic Cloud I/O Configurator for HPC applications. In *International Conference for High Performance Computing, Networking, Storage and Analysis, SC'13, Denver, CO*, page 38, 2013.

[10] M. Mazzucco and M. Dumas. Achieving performance and availability guarantees with spot instances. In *IEEE International Conference on High Performance Computing and Communications*, pages 296–303, 2011.

[11] S. Niu, J. Zhai, X. Ma, X. Tang, and W. Chen. Cost-effective cloud HPC resource provisioning by building semi-elastic virtual clusters. In *ACM/IEEE Supercomputing*, page 12, 2013.

[12] S. Tang, J. Yuan, and X.-Y. Li. Towards optimal bidding strategy for Amazon EC2 cloud spot instance. In *IEEE International Conference on Cloud Computing*, pages 91–98, 2012.

[13] A. Technica. $4,829-per-hour supercomputer built on Amazon cloud to fuel cancer research. http://arstechnica.com/business/news/2012/04/4829-per-hour-supercomputer-built-on-amazon-cloud-to-fuel-cancer-research.ars, 2012.

[14] A. Technica. 18 hours, $33K, and 156,314 cores: Amazon cloud HPC hits a "petaflop". http://arstechnica.com/information-technology/2013/11/18-hours-33k-and-156314-cores-amazon-cloud-hpc-hits-a-petaflop/, 2013.

[15] TOP500. Top500 List - November 2013. http://top500.org/list/2013/11/, 2013.

[16] W. Voorsluys and R. Buyya. Reliable provisioning of spot instances for compute-intensive applications. In *IEEE Int'l Conference on Advanced Information Networking and Applications*, pages 542–549, 2012.

[17] S. Yi, A. Andrzejak, and D. Kondo. Monetary cost-aware checkpointing and migration on Amazon cloud spot instances. *IEEE Transactions on Services Computing*, 2011.

[18] S. Yi, D. Kondo, and A. Andrzejak. Reducing costs of spot instances via checkpointing in the Amazon Elastic Compute Cloud. In *IEEE International Conference on Cloud Computing*, pages 236–243, 2010.

[19] M. Zafer, Y. Song, and K.-W. Lee. Optimal bids for spot VMs in a cloud for deadline constrained jobs. In *IEEE International Conference on Cloud Computing*, pages 75–82, 2012.

Domino: An Incremental Computing Framework in Cloud with Eventual Synchronization

Dong Dai, Yong Chen
Dept. of Computer Science
Texas Tech University
dong.dai@ttu.edu,
yong.chen@ttu.edu

Dries Kimpe, Rob Ross
Mathematics and Computer
Science Division
Argonne National Laboratory
dkimpe@mcs.anl.gov,
rross@mcs.anl.gov

Xuehai Zhou
Computer Science College
University of Science and
Technology of China
xhzhou@ustc.edu

ABSTRACT

In recent years, more and more applications in cloud have needed to process large-scale on-line data sets that evolve over time as entries are added or modified. Several programming frameworks, such as Percolator and Oolong, are proposed for such incremental data processing and can achieve efficient updates with an event-driven abstraction. However, these frameworks are inherently asynchronous, leaving the heavy burden of managing synchronization to applications developers. Such a limitation significantly restricts their usability. In this paper, we introduce a trigger-based incremental computing framework, called Domino, with a flexible synchronization mechanism and runtime optimizations to coordinate parallel triggers efficiently. With this new framework, both synchronous and asynchronous applications can be seamlessly developed. Use cases and current evaluation results confirm that the new Domino programming model delivers sufficient performance and is easy to use in large-scale distributed computing.

Categories and Subject Descriptors

D.4.7 [**OPERATING SYSTEMS**]: Organization and Design—*Distributed systems*

Keywords

Cloud Computing, Incremental Computing, MapReduce

1. INTRODUCTION

Continuous data streams are of increasing importance to real-world analysis today. In order to process these data streams, incremental approaches are often more efficient. Popular batch-processing programming models, like Dryad and MapReduce, provide only shallow support for incremental processing. Although there are extensions based on

the batch-processing models to support incremental applications [5, 4], it is hard to eliminate the unnecessary processing on unchanged data and difficult to choose the right time to process new data streams, since such models are not aware of incremental streams.

In order to address these challenges, event-driven models have emerged in cloud computing [6, 7]. Event-driven applications are triggered by external data streams to process new updates. Most event-driven abstractions are designed and implemented based on triggers or observers to handle data updates, like Percolator [7] and Oolong [6]. In a distributed environment, these triggers/observers will run concurrently on different servers. Synchronization of these concurrent triggers/observers then becomes an important issue. However, most of them consider themselves as pure asynchronous frameworks without providing any synchronization mechanisms [6], or just provide write transactions to keep data consistency instead of synchronizing different executions [7]. This drawback has significantly limited their usability.

In this paper, we present Domino, a *trigger-based incremental programming framework with a flexible synchronization mechanism* to address these issues. To our best knowledge, Domino is the first system that provides flexible synchronization based on a trigger-based distributed programming model: it supports both *natural* asynchronization, which is brought by the trigger-based model inherently, and new *wait-free* eventual synchronization. Hence, it can support a broad range of applications including most MapReduce applications and asynchronous algorithms.

2. MOTIVATION

Many Cloud applications usually contain iterative procedures. Among different iterations, accumulation is used to gather partial results from last iteration, which usually leads to a global synchronization. How to handle these synchronizations could be very complex and challenging in any event-driven computing models. Figure 1 shows an example that an accumulation needs to synchronously gather partial results from four triggers. The most straightforward way is using distributed locks to enforce the triggers wait until all of them finished, as Fig. 1(a) shows. However, the challenge is that in the incremental computing scenario, we do not know how many updates will be there. As shown in Fig. 1(a), the first *Sync* could already generate correct accumulation results because C and D will not execute in the future, but distributed locks require waiting until trigger

C and D finish. Another possible solution is using a *time window*, which defines a fixed waiting time (t_w) and makes the accumulation progress each t_w as Fig. 1(b) shows. However, choosing t_w itself would be a challenge for developers. Moreover, it still faces the problem of not knowing when the synchronization should return.

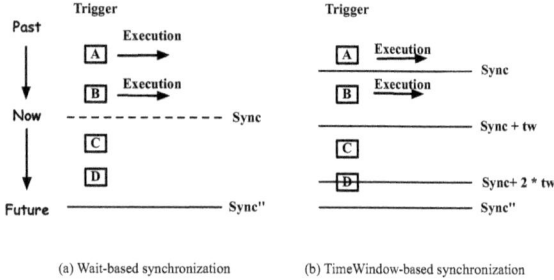

(a) Wait-based synchronization   (b) TimeWindow-based synchronization

Figure 1: Synchronization in incremental scenario.

Our goal is to develop a programming model for incremental applications with a synchronization mechanism that avoids unnecessarily waiting for the uncertain future trigger executions, and frees developers from choosing synchronization intervals or managing the return.

3. DOMINO MODEL

In Domino, we abstract all data sets as *sparse tables*. The continuous data streams can be viewed as *insert* or *update* on tables. This table-based data model is similar to the Bigtable data model and has been proven to be capable of describing most of the data sets in cloud applications. Similarly, the sparse tables in Domino also provides concept of column-family, which gathers all the similar columns and is guaranteed to be stored on the same server. Besides, each cell in the sparse table contain multiple versions of data.

Based on *sparse tables* data model, the Domino programming model consists of three components: events, conditions, and actions. An *event* is generated from the continuous external data streams, which could be any operations on the sparse tables. To detect the events, applications need to declare which columns, column-families, or tables they are monitoring. A *condition* is used to filter events in order to control the execution of *actions*. It is a user-defined function that returns *true* or *false* to denote whether current event should be processed or not. One of the most important uses of conditions is to stop an iterative execution of triggers. An *action* is the real logic of a user's application. It consumes the events and writes the results back persistently. Actions always run on the server where event is fired. This locality of action execution significantly improves the performance and reduces the possibility of network congestion.

Combing these three parts, we form a *trigger*, which is the core concept of Domino: all the applications in Domino are written as a series of triggers. One trigger maybe run at different servers concurrently. Each run is called a *trigger instance*. Domino has three types of triggers: plain triggers, asynchronous accumulator triggers, and synchronous accumulator triggers.

Plain trigger is the simplest case. It responds to new data streams and executes independently in different servers in parallel. Other two triggers are both used to accumulate partial results from other triggers. For each accumulator

trigger, Domino runtime will automatically create a table with only one column-family (*partial-results*). This new table is invisible to other applications so that it avoids misbehaviors from shared users. The *asynchronous accumulator trigger* represents the natural asynchronous semantic: partial results arrive and activate the execution of accumulator trigger without any coordination. The *synchronous accumulator trigger* provides a self-managed eventual synchronization mechanism between different triggers. The eventual synchronization avoids unnecessary global blocking and helps the applications make progress. It is also simpler to use because developers do not need to explicitly set up global locks or barriers.

Based on the concepts and definitions of Domino, we demonstrate the implementation of incremental PageRank algorithm, which iteratively calculates the priority of web pages based on links to them. Table *WebRepo* (Table. 1) shows the whole web repository with url as row key. Column *Meta:Rank* column stores current PageRank value, *Meta:OutEdges* represents all the out edges of current page, *Cot:En* stores the actual contents of a page.

Table 1: WebRepo Table

RowKey	Meta:Rank	Meta:OutEdges	Cot:En
url_1	1.0	$url_{11}, url_{12}, ...$	...
url_2	1.0	$url_{112}, url_{21}, ...$	...
...	...	... , ...	...

Incremental PageRank needs two triggers to work. The first trigger is a plain trigger monitoring on the *Meta* column-family in Table 1: whenever the *OutEdges* or *Rank* value changes, it will execute to calculate all the outgoing edges' weights of the that page. Those updates are written to the second trigger, which is a synchronous accumulator trigger. It accumulates all the incoming edges' weights to form a new PageRank value for that page, which will be written into the *Meta:Rank* column of Table 1 and activate the next round execution. To stop iterations, we can check whether the new PageRank value is close enough to the old one as a condition in the first trigger. This incremental version of PageRank needs strong synchronization during accumulating. Based on our Domino abstraction, developers can easily set accumulator trigger as a synchronous trigger, which will execute in an efficient wait-free way.

4. DESIGN AND IMPLEMENTATION

Domino was tightly integrated with HBase [1] in the current implementation. However, it can work well with other distributed storage systems as long as they support the sparse table data model with version capacity and persistence guarantee. The Domino instance runs along with the HBase instance on each server. There is one TriggerMaster node performing trigger management and collocated on the HMaster node. Other nodes, namely TriggerWorkers, run on these nodes along with the HRegionServer. The major components of Domino include event detector, trigger manager, scheduler, and gathered I/O.

Event detector detects updates on *sparse table*. It intercepts the core execution path of Write-Ahead-Log (WAL) appending in HBase. It will build an event object containing the information collected from the logs and send it to the local event queue. Events queue manages all the local fired event objects. Inside this queue, events are ordered by their keys. A key is a vector consisting of the monitored table name, column-family, and column. Since different triggers are allowed to monitor on the same dataset, a fired event may cause multiplex triggers to execute. There is a consumer waiting on each event queue. Whenever an event is appended, it will be notified and send this event to the corresponding trigger actions. The event then will be processed by the user-defined action function. For execution, each action function is attached to a preallocated thread. All action threads are managed by the action thread pool component.

Gathered I/O component encapsulates all the data accesses in action functions into a delegate to accelerate I/O accesses. *Gathered input* is for accumulator triggers only: the Domino framework will automatically collect all the accumulated partial results while processing accumulating events. The gathered inputs contain all the columns' values with the proper id_p and id_r number (described later) in the *partial-results* column-family. For accumulator triggers with wait-free eventual synchronization, the proper versions refer to less than or equal to the fired data versions; for other accumulator triggers, they would be the latest value based on timestamps. *Gathered output* is general for all triggers. It is a per-server component: in each trigger, all the data is written into in-memory cache first instead of the HBase tables. Domino combines cached writes and flushes them later according to their initial order of calling the append method.

Eventual synchronization integrated with accumulator triggers concepts plays a critical role to guarantee the final result will be eventually synchronized and overwrite incomplete results with the asynchronous partial results. The eventual synchronization in Domino includes two parts: the accumulator triggers and the version management. For each accumulator trigger, Domino implicitly creates an invisible HBase table as Fig.2 shows. It contains a predefined column-family named *partial-results*, which is automatically monitored by the newly created accumulator trigger instance. Just like the other table, all writes to accumulator triggers should contain a row key (r_i), column indicator (c_j), and value with different versions (v). All the accumulator triggers execute in the same way except that the synchronous accumulation triggers need to choose data with the right version while accumulating. This strategy makes sure that the partial results from stragglers can also be accumulated with the right data in a synchronous way.

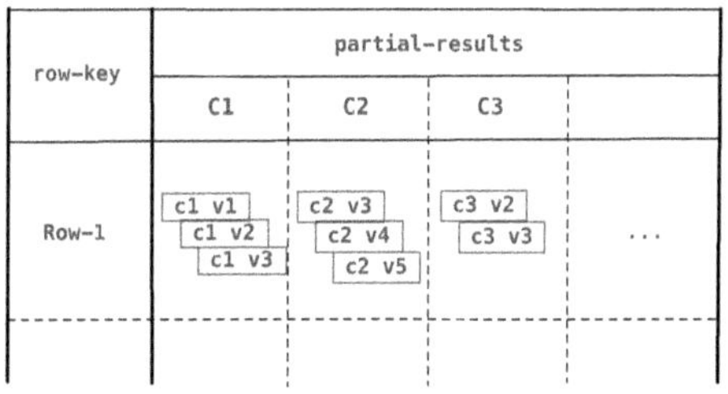

Figure 2: Invisible table for accumulator trigger.

To describe the executions of incremental applications, we categorize them into three types: iterative only, incremental only, and both iterative and incremental applications. In iterative only applications, each trigger simply writes into dataset monitored by itself and causes itself to run again. In this case, we can use a auto-increase index (id_r) to dis-

tinguish different execution rounds. In incremental only applications, triggers are activated only by external inputs. The id_r will remain the same, whereas external inputs are changing. We can use another index (id_p) to trace the inputs. For executions of both iterative and incremental, both the id_r and id_p change.

The sparse table in Domino stores multi-version data for each cell, which allows us to trace the executions status $(id_r$ and $id_p)$ to restrict the data access. First, we initialize id_r and id_p for each execution based on the version values stored with the data that triggers the execution. Each time a trigger execution writes into HBase, the Domino framework will merge its id_r and id_p into a version number $(id_p : id_r)$ and write into HBase table. If this data activates another trigger execution, then the new execution will automatically read this version number, parse it into id_p and id_r, and set its new id_r^n equal to id_r+1. The id_p changes only if external inputs are written into a data cell, then Domino read the newest id_p, set a new $id_p'=id_p+1$, and initialize id_r equal to 0 for the new input. With these versions, Domino restricts the execution of accumulator triggers and makes sure they only read data with right version. In this way, Domino guarantees that when the last intermediate values are updated in the *partial-results* column family, the accumulator trigger action will read the same inputs as a strict synchronization action does and eventually return the correct results.

5. EVALUATIONS

The evaluation of the Domino system was based mainly on a 12-node cluster. We also evaluated Domino on the Amazon EC2 platform using up to 64 m1.medium nodes.

The Domino framework supports a large range of applications. In this section, we evaluate two typical applications: WordCount and PageRank. All evaluations were run on our local 12-node cluster. Since Percolator is not public, we can not make direct comparisons with it. In this evaluation, we mimic the behavior of Percolator based on open source software stacks currently accessible. Specifically, we use HBase Coprocessor to mimic the observers of Percolator and use the combination of Omid [2] and ZooKeeper [3] to simulate the transactions and distributed locks.

The most critical performance measurement of incremental applications is how fast they can absorb the new inputs. The faster the external data streams come, the higher the pressure that is placed on the underlying infrastructure. For different evaluations, we created a large number of static input datasets and different changing data sets. These changing datasets were written into the underlying HBase storage system as fast as possible. We also ran the MapReduce applications as a comparison. Running MapReduce on the smaller changing datasets shows the best performance MapReduce can achieve because they only process the updated data. Running MapReduce on the whole dataset shows the baseline performance and also represents the response time that current batch-based frameworks can achieve in incremental scenarios.

In the following evaluation figures, Domino indicates the Domino performance; MR(1R) means one round of MapReduce for iterative applications; MR(FR) means the whole execution time (full round) for iterative applications; MapReduce(Whole) means the execution time of applying MapReduce on the whole data set; MapReduce means that MapReduce was executed on the changing data sets; and Mimic(P) represents our mimic Percolator.

Figure 3 shows the performance of WordCount with different data sizes. We can see that Domino achieves slightly better performance than MapReduce running only on the changed dataset. The Mimic Percolator version does not scale well because it does not provide the *gethered I/O* optimization, so during execution, it issues too many small writes to HBase. Compared with the MapReduce running on the whole dataset, Domino clearly has much better performance. Although in WordCount we can deploy MapReduce only on the changed dataset to obtain right results, the frequency of running MapReduce is hard to decide and difficult to manage with different stream speeds. Domino, on the other hand, provides an easy way to run it in incremental situations, and it achieves sufficient performance.

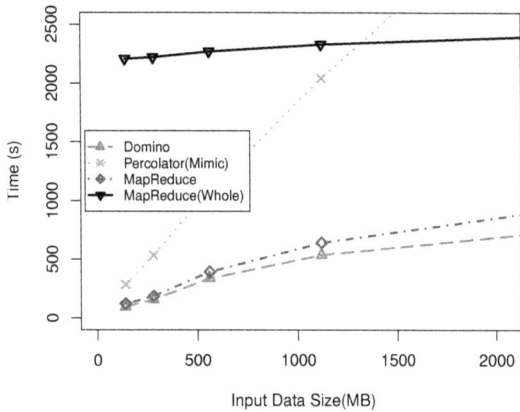

Figure 3: WordCount under different sizes.

The synchronous PageRank application runs on a synthetic web repository with increasing input size. PageRank is iterative, so in order to compare different implementations fairly, the MapReduce version needs to run enough times to make sure convergence of every page is met. Therefore, we also show the execution time of one MapReduce iteration (MR(R1)) in the result as a hint. The Mimic-Percolator does not support synchronous accumulation in its design. In this evaluation, therefore, we mimic such supports by setting up a time window to wait until the lock is released and continue to accumulate.

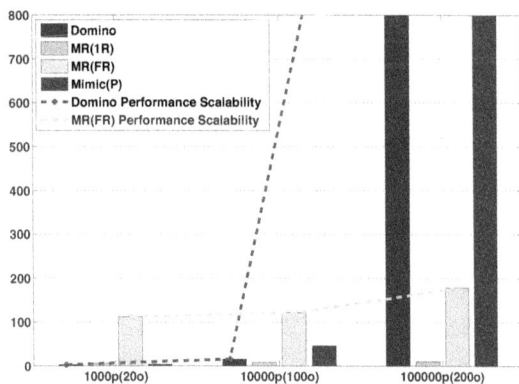

Figure 4: PageRank under different changing sets.

Figure 4 shows the execution time for different changing sets. We labeled each input data set in the x-axis of Fig. 4: p means the page number and o means the out-edges of each page. We can see that the Domino significantly outperforms the MapReduce in first two cases. Because of the fixed time window, which applications in our Mimic Percolator system have to wait for accumulating, the Mimic(P) is much slower than our Domino implementation, but it still outperforms MapReduce at these input data sets. However, we can also observe that while the input size increasing, the MapReduce execution time is increasing much more slowly than that of Domino and Mimic Percolator. But note that the MapReduce performance here is actually the upper bound of what MapReduce can achieve: it does not contain any processing on existing data. Furthermore, the burst new inputs in this evaluation are rare in real-world applications. Continuous small updates are the normal cases, where Domino outperforms MapReduce considerably.

6. CONCLUSION

In this study, based on existing event-driven programming models, we proposed Domino, a trigger-based incremental programming model with wait-free eventual synchronization for cloud applications. We introduced the necessity of synchronization in an incremental processing framework, and we presented a novel design and implementation of this wait-free synchronization (eventual synchronization). The current use cases and experimental results have confirmed the efficiency and benefits. The design and development experiences of Domino can help the community better support incremental processing of cloud applications.

Acknowledgment

This work was supported in part by the National Science Foundation under grant CNS-1162488 and by the U.S. Department of Energy, Office of Science, under Contract No. DE-AC02-06CH11357.

7. REFERENCES

[1] Hbase project. In *http://hbase.apache.org*.
[2] Omid project. In *https://github.com/yahoo/omid*.
[3] Zookeeper project. In *http://zookeeper.apache.org/*.
[4] BHATOTIA, P., WIEDER, A., RODRIGUES, R., ACAR, U., AND PASQUIN, R. Incoop: Mapreduce for incremental computations. In *Proceedings of the 2nd ACM Symposium on Cloud Computing* (2011), ACM.
[5] EKANAYAKE, J., LI, H., ZHANG, B., GUNARATHNE, T., BAE, S., QIU, J., AND FOX, G. Twister: a runtime for iterative mapreduce. In *Proceedings of the 19th ACM International Symposium on High Performance Distributed Computing* (2010), ACM.
[6] MITCHELL, C., POWER, R., AND LI, J. Oolong: asynchronous distributed applications made easy. In *Proceedings of the Asia-Pacific Workshop on Systems* (2012), ACM, p. 11.
[7] PENG, D., AND DABEK, F. Large-scale incremental processing using distributed transactions and notifications. In *Proceedings of the 9th USENIX conference on Operating systems design and implementation* (2010), USENIX Association.

Glasswing: Accelerating MapReduce on Multi-core and Many-core Clusters

Ismail El-Helw
Department of Computer
Science, Vrije Universiteit
Amsterdam, The Netherlands
ielhelw@cs.vu.nl

Rutger Hofman
Department of Computer
Science, Vrije Universiteit
Amsterdam, The Netherlands
rutger@cs.vu.nl

Henri E. Bal
Department of Computer
Science, Vrije Universiteit
Amsterdam, The Netherlands
bal@cs.vu.nl

ABSTRACT

The impact and significance of parallel computing techniques is continuously increasing given the current trend of incorporating more cores in new processor designs. However, many Big Data systems fail to exploit the abundant computational power of multi-core CPUs and GPUs to their full potential. We present Glasswing, a scalable MapReduce framework that employs a configurable mixture of coarse- and fine-grained parallelism to achieve high performance on multi-core CPUs and GPUs. We experimentally evaluated the performance of five MapReduce applications and show that Glasswing outperforms Hadoop on a 64-node multi-core CPU cluster by a factor between 1.8 and 4, and by a factor from 20 to 30 on a 16-node GPU cluster.

Categories and Subject Descriptors

D.1.3 [**Software**]: PROGRAMMING TECHNIQUES—*Concurrent Programming, Distributed programming*; D.3.3 [**Software**]: PROGRAMMING LANGUAGES—*Frameworks*

General Terms

Design, Experimentation, Measurement, Performance

Keywords

MapReduce, Heterogeneous, OpenCL, Scalability

1. INTRODUCTION

MapReduce is a programming model designed to cater for large data center computations and data mining applications [4]. It relieves developers from managing the complexity of concurrency, communication and fault tolerance. The original MapReduce design followed a simple scale-out methodology and was designed to use a massive number of primitive low-end commodity machines [4]. However, several aspects of MapReduce need to be revisited to exploit current hardware trends. Single and dual core machines are becoming a rare commodity. Therefore, improved concurrency and task granularity control is needed to cater for the new many-core

architectures. Additionally, usage of accelerators such as GPUs should be treated as a mainstream feature and not an exception. This is especially vital for machine learning algorithms and scientific applications that benefit from the massive computational capability of GPUs.

In response to the new hardware trends, multiple studies [3, 13, 16] investigated the benefits of running MapReduce on multi-core processors. Similarly, several attempts were made to accelerate MapReduce applications using GPUs [1, 5, 6, 7, 8, 9, 15] and other accelerators [2, 10, 11, 12, 14]. However, all of these efforts suffer from at least one of the following limitations: (i) focusing on accelerating specific applications instead of providing a generic framework for developing new ones; (ii) enforcing that all input, intermediate or output data reside in memory which limits its applicability to tiny problems; (iii) restricting developers to use GPUs only which is unsuitable for many I/O-bound applications; (iv) limiting data representation to arrays of primitive types thereby hindering application development.

In this paper we present Glasswing, a high-performance MapReduce framework that excels at exploiting the computational power of multi-core CPUs and GPUs. Glasswing leverages OpenCL to facilitate the development of application-specific map and reduce functions and allows for fine-grained parallelism. Additionally, it provides its services to developers through a unified API that is consistent with the MapReduce abstraction. Unlike previous work, Glasswing was designed to manage out-of-core data set sizes and does not place limitations on data representation or the choice of compute device to be used. An experimental evaluation of five MapReduce applications with varying properties shows that Glasswing significantly improves job performance compared to Hadoop, a popular MapReduce framework.

The remainder of this paper is organized as follows. Section 2 presents the design of Glasswing and Section 3 evaluates its contributions. Finally, Section 4 concludes.

2. GLASSWING DESIGN

The Glasswing framework is composed of a pipeline and an accompanying set of APIs. The pipeline is responsible for managing the execution and monitoring the progress of a given MapReduce application. The Glasswing framework offers its services to user applications through the Glasswing API which is composed of two components: an OpenCL API and a Configuration API. The OpenCL API provides several utilities that facilitate the development of the map and reduce functions in OpenCL. The Configuration API allows developers to specify the input and configuration of their applications. In this section, we present the design and implementation of each of these components.

```
void map(MapInput,MapOutput)
void reduce(ReduceInput,ReduceOutput)
```
Map utility methods:
```
bool MapInput_hasMore(MapInput)
MapRecord MapInput_nextValue(MapInput)
void emit_intermediate(Key,Value,MapOutput)
```
Reduce utility methods:
```
bool ReduceInput_hasMore(ReduceInput)
ReduceRecord ReduceInput_nextValue(ReduceInput)
void emit(Value,ReduceOutput)
```

Table 1: Glasswing OpenCL API.

2.1 Glasswing Pipeline

Each cluster node in a Glasswing deployment runs an instance of the pipeline. The Glasswing pipeline coordinates between all the activities involved in the MapReduce work-flow. The pipeline notifies a user application when it is ready to read a new input split, stages data, and invokes mappers and reducers. Furthermore, it handles the partitioning, delivery and storage of intermediate data between participating cluster nodes. Similarly, it manages the delivery of intermediate data to reducers and the storage of produced final data. A key aspect that sets Glasswing apart from other frameworks is the pipeline's ability to perform all of its activities concurrently. For instance, an input split can be processed by a mapper while the following input split is being read from the file system. Therefore, the pipeline reduces a job's execution time by overlapping independent coarse-grained operations.

2.2 Glasswing OpenCL API

Applications utilizing Glasswing must implement their map and reduce functions in OpenCL. The Glasswing OpenCL API gives user applications an environment that closely resembles the MapReduce programming model. It implements kernel functions that serve as the entry points to the OpenCL code base and is responsible for invoking the user-defined map and reduce functions. Additionally, the API is responsible for delivering input records and handling output to and from the user functions.

A simplified version of the Glasswing OpenCL API is presented in Table 1. The map() and reduce() functions implemented by users must adhere to the function signatures shown in the table. The MapInput and ReduceInput parameters provide iterators to records to be processed. MapInput_hasMore() and ReduceInput_hasMore() can be used to check whether all input data have been consumed. MapInput_nextValue() and ReduceInput_nextValue() fetch the next available input record. The function emit_intermediate() can be used by map() to inform the framework that a new key/value pair was produced. Similarly, emit() can be used by reduce() to inform the framework of a new final value. Like standard MapReduce, Glasswing allows the user to implement a combiner function that has an interface similar to reduce(). Combiner functions operate over values associated with a given key and can perform aggregations to decrease the volume of intermediate data. Glasswing invokes the combiner after the completion of every map() invocation.

The Glasswing OpenCL API provides several methods to enable fine-grained workload division across threads. The default method does not involve any thread collaboration. Each thread is allocated a set of input records which it will process sequentially. A more advanced form involves the collaboration of multiple threads over a single input record. This form is beneficial to applications where the processing of each record is computationally expensive and parallelizable. Applications can use OpenCL's work-item and task group information to create their own workload division schemes.

2.3 Glasswing Configuration API

The Glasswing Configuration API provides applications with an extensible object-oriented API that facilitates their development. It defines an input interface that can be extended by user applications to implement their own file format handling. The role of this class is to read input files and divide them into input records to be processed by the mapper kernels. Additionally, the framework provides an application base class to extend by user applications, that is also used to specify configuration parameters. For instance, users can select compute devices, and control the number of threads for mappers and reducers. Applications can also use this API to specify their memory demands. The following section discusses the key configuration properties.

Device Selection and Code Compilation

Employing the Configuration API, applications can select the compute device to be used for the map() and reduce() functions separately. The OpenCL code is compiled at runtime to apply optimizations specific to the selected compute device.

OpenCL Kernel Shaping

Glasswing is responsible for invoking OpenCL kernels and managing synchronization. However, it delegates the responsibility of shaping the kernel invocations to the application. Each application implements a map and a reduce shaper. These methods are queried by the pipeline before each kernel invocation to specify the number of OpenCL threads to execute on a given input set. This flexibility allows applications to fine-tune work granularity. Additionally, it establishes a direct relation between an application definition and its OpenCL code. Therefore, an application may choose to customize and optimize its map and reduce functions further based on its shaping policy.

Memory Allocations

OpenCL does not support dynamic memory allocation from within kernels. Therefore, all allocations need to be made prior to the invocation of the kernels from the host code. To comply with the buffer allocation limits of OpenCL, a Glasswing application implements a set of functions that describe its resource requirements. Given an input buffer size, applications need to specify the maximum number of keys and values that map() may produce. Additionally, the application must inform the framework of the maximum aggregate space to be used by all keys and values. Given this information, Glasswing can allocate the necessary buffer pools and delegate their management to the Glasswing framework. Application developers must provide an upper-bound estimate when provided with the input buffer size.

For example, consider the Word Count application that reports the frequency of word occurrences. Since words are separated by a non-word character, the worst case is a chain of one-character words. Therefore, if the input buffer size is N, the maximum number of keys and values is $\lceil N/2 \rceil$. The space needed to hold all keys does not exceed the input buffer size. The aggregate space required to hold all generated values is the value type size multiplied by the number of values. Since Word Count uses a 4-byte integer data type for its values, the maximum value space is $2N$ bytes.

Scratch Memory

Using the Configuration API, users can specify additional scratch memory to be allocated in OpenCL's global and local memory regions. For example, applications may improve performance by caching data structures in local memory to avoid the high latency of global memory. Global scratch memory may be required to

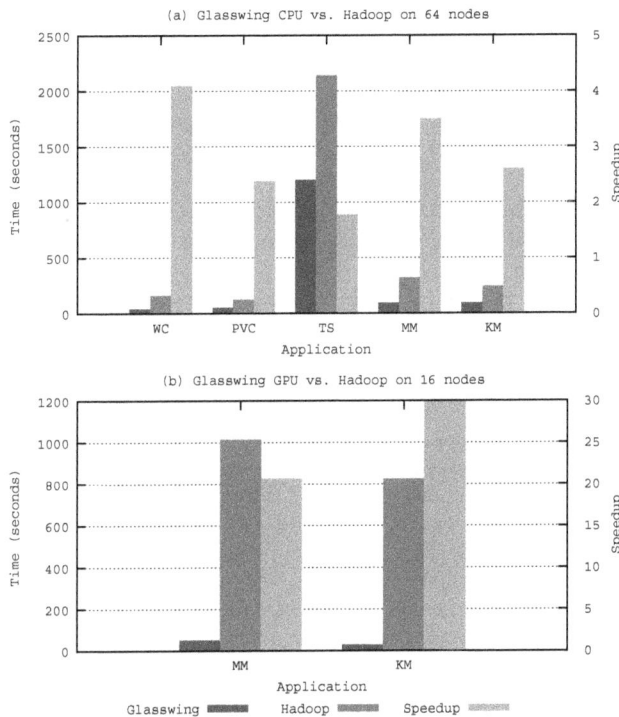

Figure 1: Performance comparison between Glasswing and Hadoop (a) on 64 nodes without GPUs and (b) on 16 nodes with GPU acceleration. Speedup of Glasswing is normalized over Hadoop's job completion time for the same cluster size.

Application	Data Set
Word Count	87GB English Wikipedia dump.
Page View Count	143GB of Wikipedia web server logs.
TeraSort	2TB generated using Hadoop's teragen application.
Matrix Multiply	Two square matrices of size 32768^2.
K-Means Clustering	1024^3 points, 8192 centers in 4 dimensions.

Table 2: Description of data sets used in evaluation.

preserve state across multiple kernel invocations for one key. In OpenCL, all memory regions lose their state between kernel invocations except the global region. Since Glasswing targets applications that process massive amounts of data that generally use multiple kernel invocations, providing persistent storage is crucial. An obvious user of global scratch memory is the reduce() function. Since the MapReduce model assumes that all values associated with a given key are processed by the same reducer, reducer state must be preserved across calls for the same key.

MapReduce applications often use configuration data that is broadcast to all worker nodes to modify or fine-tune their behavior. Therefore, Glasswing allows applications to allocate a persistent read-only configuration buffer.

3. EVALUATION

The following subsections test and validate the contributions of Glasswing. First, we present Glasswing's performance and compare it to Hadoop. Finally, we evaluate the performance of Glasswing under different resource limitations on Amazon's EC2 cloud.

Performance Comparison

In order to compare the performance of Glasswing and Hadoop we conducted experiments on the VU Amsterdam cluster of DAS4, a compute cluster running CentOS Linux. Each node is equipped with a dual quad-core Intel Xeon 2.4GHz CPU, 24GB of memory and two 1TB disks configured with software RAID0. The nodes have hyperthreading enabled, so in many cases they can run 16 processes fully in parallel. Additionally, 16 nodes have an NVidia GTX480 GPU. All cluster nodes are connected via Gigabit Ethernet and QDR InfiniBand. Glasswing was configured to use AMD's OpenCL SDK 2.7 for the CPU executions and NVidia's OpenCL SDK that comes bundled with CUDA 5.0 for the GPUs. We used Hadoop stable version 1.0.0 and instrumented Glasswing to use HDFS as its file system for comparison fairness.

We evaluated the performance of Glasswing with a spectrum of MapReduce applications of varying compute and data intensities, implemented and carefully performance-tuned in both Glasswing and Hadoop. These applications can be divided into two groups: a data-intensive group consisting of Word Count (*WC*), Page View Count (*PVC*) and TeraSort (*TS*), and a compute-intensive group including Matrix Multiply (*MM*) and K-Means Clustering (*KM*). The input data sets used for evaluation are described in Table 2.

Figure 1 (a) presents the job completion time of five applications on 64 cluster nodes, with Glasswing on the CPU. Glasswing outperforms Hadoop for all five applications. A deeper analysis shows that Glasswing particularly excels when there is higher potential for overlapping concurrent operations such as file reads and computation. This observation is further illustrated by the speedup of Glasswing over Hadoop on the same cluster setup. Speedup numbers are shown on the right Y-axis. For example, Glasswing outperforms Hadoop by a factor of 4 in the case of *WC* as it performs more operations per input record compared to the more data-intensive *PVC* and *TS*. In contrast, *KM* has the highest compute intensity but it exhibits a speedup of 2.6x as its computation pipeline stage is dominant.

One of the primary benefits of Glasswing is its ability to exploit the powerful processing capabilities of GPUs. Figure 1 (b) presents the execution times of the two compute-intensive applications running over Glasswing and Hadoop on 16 nodes. In this case, Glasswing uses a GPU per cluster node to accelerate the processing of the map and reduce kernels. As shown in the figure, the relative performance difference between Glasswing and Hadoop increases further and reaches speedups of 20x and 30x for *MM* and *KM* respectively.

The results presented in this section confirm our hypothesis that MapReduce applications are prime candidates for exposure to fine-grained parallelism through a generic API. This can be attributed to the data-parallel nature of the MapReduce model. Additionally, compute-intensive applications can further improve their performance when accelerated with GPUs.

Resource Utilization Efficiency

To evaluate the performance of Glasswing under different resource limitations we tested it on a variety of Amazon EC2 instance types. These experiments used Amazon's Simple Storage Service (S3) for storing input and output data which incurs additional I/O overhead due to the remote file accesses. Figure 2 displays single node job completion times of *KM* and *WC* on several EC2 instance types for smaller data set sizes. Specifically, *KM* used a total of 4×1024^2 points and *WC* uses 16GB of the Wikipedia dump. The m1 and m3 instance types use successive generations of Intel Xeon with m3 being the latest E5-2670 processors. The m1-large, m1-xlarge, m3-xlarge and m3-2xlarge instance types provide 2, 4, 4, and 8

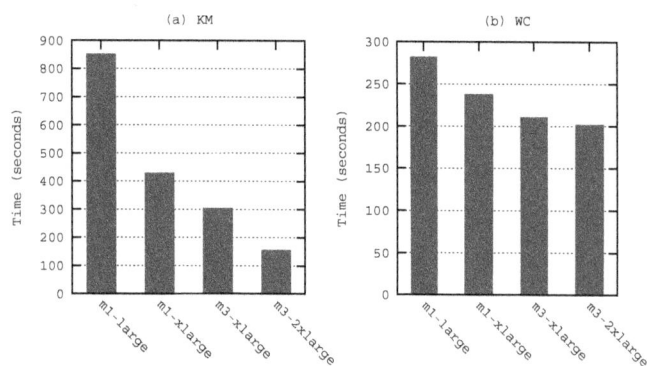

Figure 2: Performance of Glasswing on different EC2 instance types.

virtual cores respectively. Moreover, the instances include 7.5GB, 15GB, 15GB, and 30GB of memory in the same order.

Since *KM* is compute-intensive it scales well with larger instance types which contain more or faster virtual CPU cores. However, *WC* scales less as the main bottleneck in its execution is reading the input data from S3. Therefore, the number of cores and the availability of excess RAM do not contribute as significantly to its performance.

4. CONCLUSION

Glasswing is a high-performance MapReduce framework that is capable of improving the utilization of modern processors. It allows for a combination of coarse-grained and fine-grained parallelism without sacrificing the programming model's abstractions or scalability. A study of five applications revealed that Glasswing exhibits superior performance compared to Hadoop. In addition to Glasswing's clear performance advantage for compute-intensive applications, its architecture boosts data-intensive ones as well.

5. ACKNOWLEDGMENTS

This work was partially funded by the Netherlands Organization for Scientific Research (NWO).

6. REFERENCES

[1] L. Chen and G. Agrawal. Optimizing MapReduce for GPUs with effective shared memory usage. In *Proceedings of the 21st international symposium on High-Performance Parallel and Distributed Computing*, HPDC '12, pages 199–210, New York, NY, USA, 2012. ACM.

[2] L. Chen, X. Huo, and G. Agrawal. Accelerating MapReduce on a coupled CPU-GPU architecture. In *Proceedings of the International Conference on High Performance Computing, Networking, Storage and Analysis*, SC '12, pages 25:1–25:11, Los Alamitos, CA, USA, 2012. IEEE Computer Society Press.

[3] R. Chen, H. Chen, and B. Zang. Tiled-MapReduce: optimizing resource usages of data-parallel applications on multicore with tiling. In *Proceedings of the 19th international conference on Parallel architectures and compilation techniques*, PACT '10, pages 523–534, New York, NY, USA, 2010. ACM.

[4] J. Dean and S. Ghemawat. MapReduce: simplified data processing on large clusters. In *Proceedings of the 6th conference on Symposium on Opearting Systems Design &*

Implementation - Volume 6, OSDI'04, pages 10–10, Berkeley, CA, USA, 2004. USENIX Association.

[5] R. Farivar, A. Verma, E. Chan, and R. Campbell. MITHRA: Multiple data independent tasks on a heterogeneous resource architecture. In *Cluster Computing and Workshops, 2009. CLUSTER '09. IEEE International Conference on*, pages 1–10, 31 2009-Sept. 4 2009.

[6] M. Grossman, M. Breternitz, and V. Sarkar. HadoopCL: MapReduce on Distributed Heterogeneous Platforms Through Seamless Integration of Hadoop and OpenCL. In *Proceedings of the 2013 IEEE 27th International Symposium on Parallel and Distributed Processing Workshops and PhD Forum*, IPDPSW '13, pages 1918–1927, Washington, DC, USA, 2013. IEEE Computer Society.

[7] B. He, W. Fang, Q. Luo, N. K. Govindaraju, and T. Wang. Mars: a MapReduce framework on graphics processors. In *Proceedings of the 17th international conference on Parallel architectures and compilation techniques*, PACT '08, pages 260–269, New York, NY, USA, 2008. ACM.

[8] C. Hong, D. Chen, W. Chen, W. Zheng, and H. Lin. MapCG: writing parallel program portable between CPU and GPU. In *Proceedings of the 19th international conference on Parallel architectures and compilation techniques*, PACT '10, pages 217–226, New York, NY, USA, 2010. ACM.

[9] F. Ji and X. Ma. Using Shared Memory to Accelerate MapReduce on Graphics Processing Units. In *Parallel Distributed Processing Symposium (IPDPS), 2011 IEEE International*, pages 805–816, May 2011.

[10] M. D. Linderman, J. D. Collins, H. Wang, and T. H. Meng. Merge: a programming model for heterogeneous multi-core systems. *SIGPLAN Not.*, 43(3):287–296, Mar. 2008.

[11] A. Papagiannis and D. Nikolopoulos. Rearchitecting MapReduce for Heterogeneous Multicore Processors with Explicitly Managed Memories. In *Parallel Processing (ICPP), 2010 39th International Conference on*, pages 121–130, Sept. 2010.

[12] M. Rafique, B. Rose, A. Butt, and D. Nikolopoulos. CellMR: A framework for supporting mapreduce on asymmetric cell-based clusters. In *Parallel Distributed Processing, 2009. IPDPS 2009. IEEE International Symposium on*, pages 1–12, May 2009.

[13] C. Ranger, R. Raghuraman, A. Penmetsa, G. Bradski, and C. Kozyrakis. Evaluating MapReduce for Multi-core and Multiprocessor Systems. In *High Performance Computer Architecture, 2007. HPCA 2007. IEEE 13th International Symposium on*, pages 13–24, Feb. 2007.

[14] Y. Shan, B. Wang, J. Yan, Y. Wang, N. Xu, and H. Yang. FPMR: MapReduce framework on FPGA. In *Proceedings of the 18th annual ACM/SIGDA international symposium on Field programmable gate arrays*, FPGA '10, pages 93–102, New York, NY, USA, 2010. ACM.

[15] J. Stuart and J. Owens. Multi-GPU MapReduce on GPU Clusters. In *Parallel Distributed Processing Symposium (IPDPS), 2011 IEEE International*, pages 1068–1079, May 2011.

[16] J. Talbot, R. M. Yoo, and C. Kozyrakis. Phoenix++: modular MapReduce for shared-memory systems. In *Proceedings of the second international workshop on MapReduce and its applications*, MapReduce '11, pages 9–16, New York, NY, USA, 2011. ACM.

CBL: Exploiting Community based Locality for Efficient Content Search in Online Social Networks

Hanhua Chen
Serv. Comp. Tech.&Sys. Lab
Cluster & Grid Comput. Lab
School of Computers
Huazhong Univ. of Sci.&Tech.
Wuhan, 430074, China
chen@hust.edu.cn

Fan Zhang
Serv. Comp. Tech.&Sys. Lab
Cluster & Grid Comput. Lab
School of Computers
Huazhong Univ. of Sci.&Tech.
Wuhan, 430074, China
zhangf@hust.edu.cn

Hai Jin
Serv. Comp. Tech.&Sys. Lab
Cluster & Grid Comput. Lab
School of Computers
Huazhong Univ. of Sci.&Tech.
Wuhan, 430074, China
hjin@hust.edu.cn

ABSTRACT

Retrieving relevant data for users in online social network (OSN) systems is a challenging problem. Cassandra, a storage system used by popular OSN systems, such as Facebook and Twitter, relies on a DHT-based scheme to randomly partition the personal data of users among servers across multiple data centers. Although DHT is highly scalable for hosting a large number of users (personal data), it leads to costly inter-server communications across data centers due to the complex interconnection and interaction among OSN users. In this paper, we explore how to retrieve the OSN content in a cost-effective way by retaining the simple and robust nature of OSNs. Our approach exploits a simple, yet powerful principle called Community-Based Locality (CBL), which posits that if a user has an one-hop neighbor within a particular community, it is very likely that the user has other one-hop neighbors inside the same community. We demonstrate the existence of community-based locality in diverse traces of popular OSN systems such as Facebook, Orkut, Flickr, Youtube, and Livejournal.

Based on the observation, we design a CBL-based algorithm to build the content index in OSN systems. By partitioning and indexing the relevant data of users within a community on the same server in the data center, the CBL-based index avoids a significant amount of inter-server communications during searching, making retrieving relevant data for a user in large-scale OSNs efficient. In addition, by using CBL-based scheme we can provide much shorter query latency and balanced loads. We conduct comprehensive trace-driven simulations to evaluate the performance of the proposed scheme. Results show that our scheme significantly reduces the network traffic by 73% compared with existing schemes.

Categories and Subject Descriptors

C.2.4 [**Computer Networks**]: Distributed Systems

HPDC'14, June 23–27, Vancouver, BC, Canada.
Copyright 2014 ACM 978-1-4503-2749-7/14/06 ...$15.00.
http://dx.doi.org/10.1145/2600212.2600707.

Keywords

Community-based locality, Online social networks

1. INTRODUCTION

Since the emergence of the Online Social Network (OSN) systems, such as Facebook and MySpace, hundreds of millions of users have started to use OSNs for communication, interaction and content sharing through social links. Different from traditional web information sharing applications, the unique feature of OSNs is that the most relevant information is a user's own data and the content from his/her friends [3]. A traditional Web search engine provides a common view for all the users. In contrast, OSN users pay more attentions to their privacy. For example, Facebook limits the visibility of a user's events among his/her friends by default. Views in OSN searching are formed on a per-user basis, since different users see different neighbors (in this paper, we use the terms neighbor and friend interchangeably). Previous wisdom for web search is to collect the pages into a centralized repository and build the index for searching. However, it is difficult, if not impossible, to build an OSN search engine using existing indexing schemes due to the feature of per-user view.

Currently, popular OSNs commonly utilize scalable Key-Value distributed stores [9, 1], which leverage the de facto underlying consistent hashing mechanism. Based on the Key-Value store mechanism, it is difficult to provide keyword-based content search. Due to the de-facto random partition strategy of consistent hashing, friends of a user are assigned to different random servers across the data centers. A simple query processing within a user's neighbors typically needs to contact a large number of servers across the data center. Suppose we have a number of N users in the system, each having a number of M neighbors. If each user issues a number of R search queries, the system needs to process a total number of $N \times M \times R$ query messages. This incurs a large amount of inter-server traffic across the data center. The problem becomes particularly acute under heavy data center loads.

A second scheme maintains a centralized inverted index for the entire search system. Due to the per-user view, the search process has two steps. In the first step, it performs query processing like a traditional Web search engine. After all the matched documents identified, the search system further filters the results which are not accessible for the user. Assume S_N is the set of intermediate results achieved in the first step while S_M is the set of documents which a user is allowed to access. The final results returned to the user should be $S_N \cap S_M$. By sorting the set of S_M before searching, the computing complexity of the extra intersection operation can be reduced to $O(|S_N| \log(|S_M|))$. The operation, however, can be prohibitively inefficient [5] due to the fact that S_N is potentially extremely large in real world OSNs. Building a common-view based global index of all the OSN users' data is neither necessary nor efficient.

Our design philosophy departs from the existing work in such a way that we seek to retain the simple and robust nature of OSNs. Based on the analysis of real-world traces from popular OSN systems, we identify a powerful principle: if a user has an one-hop neighbor in a particular community, it is very likely that the user has other one-hop neighbors inside the same community. We name this principle as Community-Based Locality (CBL). That is to say the OSNs participants are self-organized into communities within which the interconnections of users are dense, but between which they are sparser. We build a mathematical model to formally define and justify the intuition. Using the model, we explore several popular real-world OSN systems, including Facebook, Orkut, Flickr, Youtube, and Livejournal. Results demonstrate the existence of community-based locality in popular OSN systems.

Based on the observation that the most relevant data for a user in OSNs is his/her own data and that of his/her direct neighbors, we propose a CBL-based scheme for content indexing in OSN systems. In CBL-based scheme, the content generated by the users from the same community is stored and indexed in the same server. Thus, the content retrieval operations, which are related to the data one-hop away, can be handled locally. We further proposed a weighted community structure model to balance the loads among servers by dividing similar number of users into different partitions. We conduct comprehensive simulations using real-world traces to evaluate the performance of our design. Results show that CBL-based indexing scheme significantly reduces the network traffic by 73% compared to existing designs.

The rest of the paper is organized as follows. In Section 2, we review the related work. In Section 3 we present the principle of community-based locality. In Section 4, we propose the CBL-based content indexing scheme. Section 5 evaluates the performance of CBL-based indexing scheme. Section 6 concludes the paper with future work.

2. RELATED WORK

An OSN search engine should realize keyword-based content search as well as enforcing access control. Existing indexing techniques for OSN content searching can be classified into two types: federated searching [4] and centralized index with access filtering [5].

A federated search engine maintains a local index for the content generated by each user [4], where an inverted index can be easily implemented atop popular OSN Key-Value stores following the widely used column family data model [6]. When a user issues a query, the search engine broadcasts the query messages to all his/her neighbors and performs a search in their local indices. All the matched documents will be returned for ranking. Such a scheme is simple and effective. It however introduces a large amount of inter-server communication cost during searching because the system needs to contact all the neighbors of a user to guarantee the

search quality, even though the vast majority of the neighbors have no matched results.

A second scheme maintains a centralized inverted index for the entire search system. The search process has two steps. In the first step, it performs query processing like a traditional Web search engine. After all the matched documents identified, the search system further filters the results which are not accessible for the user. The problem is that the extra intersection operation on the set of matched intermediate results and the set of the visible documents for the user is prohibitively inefficient [5]. Another problem of such a scheme is that the failure of the centralized index server can paralyze the entire search engine.

3. COMMUNITY-BASED LOCALITY

In this section, we conduct an empirical study on large-scale traces from popular OSN systems. At first, we use a formal mathematical model [7] to measure the principle of community-based locality in OSNs. We leverage a heuristic algorithm to obtain a good community division. At last, we measure the community-based locality in diverse OSN systems using the traces from real-world systems.

3.1 CBL Model

In our model, an OSN is viewed as a graph $G = (E, V)$ representing the inter-connection between participants, where vertices V represent participants and edges E represent social links among participants. We use the following adjacency matrix A with Boolean entries a_{ij} to represent the active social links of any two participants, where e_{ij} is the social link between the ith participant and the jth participant.

$$a_{ij} = \begin{cases} 1 & \text{if}(e_{ij} \in E) \\ 0 & \text{if}(e_{ij} \notin E) \end{cases} \quad (1)$$

Suppose the social graph is partitioned into a set of r communities $\{C_i, 1 \le i \le r\}$. We use an $r \times r$ symmetrical matrix whose elements c_{mn} represents the fraction of all edges in the graph that link vertices in community C_m to vertices in community C_n,

$$c_{mn} = \frac{\sum_{v_i \in C_m} \sum_{v_j \in C_n} a_{ij}}{\sum_{v_i \in V} \sum_{v_j \in V} a_{ij}} \quad (2)$$

The diagonal elements c_{kk} quantifies the fraction of edges that fall within community C_k,

$$c_{kk} = \frac{\sum_{v_i \in C_k} \sum_{v_j \in C_k} a_{ij}}{\sum_{v_i \in V} \sum_{v_j \in V} a_{ij}} \quad (3)$$

Let δ_i be the fraction of all the ends of edges that are attached to vertices in C_i. We can calculate δ_i straightforward by noting that $\delta_i = \sum_{1 \le j \le r} c_{ij}$. If the ends of edges are connected together randomly, the expected fraction/probability of the resulting edges that connect vertices within C_i is δ_i^2.

We use the following equation [10] to measure the strength of community-based locality,

Algorithm 1 Achieve CBL

FindingBestQ(Γ_0)
```
1:  Γ ← Γ₀; Γ_best ← Γ₀, Q ← Q_Γ₀;
2:    repeat
3:        ΔQ* ← 0;
4:        for ( each pair(C_i, C_j) within Γ ) do
5:            calculate ΔQ_ij ← Q_ij − Q;
6:            /* Q_ij is value after merging C_i and C_j */
7:            if(ΔQ_ij > ΔQ*) then
8:                ΔQ* ← ΔQ_ij;
9:                i* ← i; j* ← j;
10:               /* ΔQ_max ← max{ΔQ_ij}; */
11:           end if
12:       end for
13:       if(ΔQ* > 0) then
14:           Γ ← join_community(C_i*, C_j*);
15:           Q ← Q + ΔQ*;
16:       end if
17:   until(ΔQ* < 0)
18:   return(Γ);
```

$$Q = \sum_k \left(c_{kk} - \delta_k^2 \right) \qquad (4)$$

Here, $c_{kk} - \delta_k^2$ is the fraction of the edges that fall within community C_k minus the expected value of the same quantity if edges fall at random. The larger the deviation is with community C_k, the more distinct the community-based locality feature is with community C_k. By summing up the deviations of all the communities in the given community division, Q quantifies the strength of community-based locality of the entire network. It is not difficult to see that, if a particular division gives not more within-community edges than would be expected by random chance, this model will obtain the minimum value $Q = 0$. Values other than 0 indicate deviations from randomness.

Hence, by optimizing the division to obtain the maximum value of Q, we can achieve the underlying strength of the community-based locality. It is clear that a high value of Q represents a distinct community-based locality feature of an OSN. The community division of a given OSN can be achieved by optimizing divisions over all the possible combinations to obtain the maximal Q. However, exhaustive optimization of Q is costly.

As aforementioned, performing an exhaustive search over all possible divisions to obtain the global optimal value of Q takes at least an exponential amount of time. The optimizing speed is critically important in designing a practical algorithm, since existing popular OSNs have hundreds of millions of active users. In this paper, we design a "greedy" optimization algorithm (Algorithm 1), which is believed to perform fast over large-scale networks. The algorithm starts with an initial state Γ_0 in which each vertex is a single-member community. At each step, the pair that results in the greatest increase in Q merge as a new community. By repeatedly joining communities together in pairs, the greedy algorithm achieves the best Q value fast.

3.2 Measurement

We have collected a number of traces from popular online social network systems including Facebook, Flickr, Orkut, Youtube, and Livejournal. The networks vary from 400,000 nodes Orkut graph to 1.1 million nodes Facebook graph. On top of each trace we collected, we run the algorithm 1 pre-

sented in Section 3.1 to optimize the division of communities until the maximum Q is obtained. We present the results in Table 1. Results show that all the OSNs achieve high best Q values as expected. Among all the OSN systems, Facebook has the strongest feature of community-based locality with a maximum Q value of 0.59. We further examine the division that archives the best Q. The third column in Table 1 presents the numbers of communities discovered in the network based on the traces we collected. It shows that the OSNs are divided into hundreds or thousands of different communities. We will look into the communities in more details and try to investigate what these communities are, and how they are important to the structure of the entire systems. Before showing that, we first take a closer look at the optimizing steps of Q.

Figure 1 demonstrates the optimizing process of the fast heuristic algorithm obtaining the best Q using the different traces presented in Table 1. Each curve shows the whole Q optimizing process from the beginning to the end for an OSN trace. It is clear that each optimizing curve consists of several sub-curves. It is not difficult to see that the gradients of each sub-curve change in a similar way: the slope is very high at the beginning and then the slope drops while the curve becomes flat. The whole curve changes periodically until they reach a max value of Q. The process well resembles the situation of mountain climbing, *i.e.*, steep and flat in the course, and finally reaching the summit. We analyze this result and find that each sub-curve represents a merging procedure of a huge community. When forming each huge community the greedy algorithm performs efficiently at the beginning while the optimizing efficiency decreases in the end. Although we get a large number of communities for each network shown in Table 1, the majority of the users continue to merge into a few huge communities to achieve a best Q. Some others are commonly with a small number of nodes. According to our experiments with other networks, we find the typical Q value of a network with a strong feature of community-based locality falls in the range of 0.4 to 0.7. In this study, for almost all the traces we evaluated, we obtained high values of Q, revealing that strong community-based locality exist in these OSN systems.

Although the interaction social graph traces we collected contain more than one million nodes, it is difficult, if not impossible, to use this trace to represent the complete OSN system. To demonstrate our findings in this study based on the traces is valid, it is important to study the properties in different scales. It matters how the properties change when the scale of a network changes. For investigation, we conduct the evaluation experiment on top of 11 different traces of Facebook with different scales. The scale of the traces varies from 10K nodes to 1.1 million nodes.

Figure 2 plots the curves of the optimizing process on all of the 11 traces. The results show that when the scale

Table 1: Statistics of Optimal Divisions

Data Sets	Max Q	♯ of Communities
Facebook	0.59	560
Orkut	0.48	272
Youtube	0.52	4,173
Flickr	0.51	5,392
LiveJournal	0.47	704

of Facebook topology changes from $10K$ nodes to 1.1 million nodes, the best Q values are quite steady within the range of $[0.57, 0.66]$ with very slight difference. The results show that communities in different scales all have a strong property of community-based locality.

4. CONTENT INDEXING USING COMMUNITY BASED LOCALITY

4.1 Overview

Based on the above observation of the community-based locality in popular OSN systems, we propose a community based index scheme to efficiently support content searching over OSNs. The basic idea of our scheme is to partition and index user data based on the principle of community structure we identified in OSNs. Intuitively, by placing and indexing the data of users within the same community in a same server, we can effectively reduce the inter-server communication cost for OSN content indexing. Furthermore, since the relevant information in OSN is the content from his/her friends [3], the community-based index can allow search queries to be resolved locally on the server, avoiding a large amount of inter-server communication during searching. The difficulty here is that the sizes of the communities can be very different while the amount of content generated by different users are also quite different, making the above community structure model not applicable to OSN content indexing. Thus, partitioning the users using the straightforward community structure model defined above will lead to serious unbalance of loads.

To address the problem, the basic idea is to adjust the community structure optimizing algorithm to achieve the communities with similarly sizes. However, the amount of content generated by different users may be quite different. We collected a large scale trace from Wikipedia using the same ID of the Facebook users. We estimate the distribution of the volume of different Facebook users, by analyzing the volume of the content generated by a user, which can be obtained by crawling the his/her notes, his status, et al. Totally, we crawl ten thousand Facebook users' information. The fitting result reveals a zipf's distribution of $y = 978166.574x^{-1.02}$ for the volume of user generated data.

Due to the high skewed data volume distribution, it is necessary to model the community structure based on a weighted graph model. Taking the diverse volumes into consideration, we adapt the community structure proposed in Eq.(4) and designed a new algorithm called *Weighted Modularity Optimization* (WMO) to achieve the load balance among of all the servers.

4.2 Weighted Modularity Optimization for Balancing Loads

Assume the OSN system has a total number of U users, where a user u_i needs the storage cost of w_i. If we have a number of p homogeneous servers, in order to reach the load balance, after we partition all the data, the difference of each pair of servers' storage cost should be smaller than a pre-determined parameter e.

$$
\begin{cases}
\displaystyle\sum_{i=1}^{p} \sum_{k \in P_i} w_k = \sum_{k=1}^{U} w_k \\
\left| \displaystyle\sum_{k \in P_i} w_k - \sum_{k \in P_j} w_k \right| \le e \quad (\forall i \ne j, 1 \le i, j \le p)
\end{cases}
\tag{5}
$$

After a simple transformation, we can get a simplified constraint condition as shown in Eq.(6),

$$
\sum_{k \in P_i} w_k \le \frac{\displaystyle\sum_{k=1}^{U} w_k + e}{p} \quad (1 \le i \le p)
\tag{6}
$$

It is not difficult to see that if we get a balanced partition, each server's data volume will have an upper limit S_{max} determined by the system scale and the total volume of the user generated data in the system.

Following the model of community structure defined in Section 3.1, we adapt the unweighed graph based model and view the OSN as a weighted graph $G = (E, V)$ by assigning each edge a weight which quantifies the sum of the storage cost of the users represented as the edge's two ends. Formally, for the edge e_{ij}, its weight is computed by adding the weights value of the connected two nodes $w_{ij} = w_{ji} = w_i + w_j$.

Suppose the weighted graph of the social network is partitioned into a set of r communities $\{C_i, 1 \le i \le r\}$. We use an $r \times r$ symmetrical matrix whose elements c_{mn} represents the fraction of all the weight of the edges in the graph that link vertices in community C_m to those of C_n,

$$
c'_{mn} = \frac{\displaystyle\sum_{v_i \in C_m} \sum_{v_j \in C_n} a_{ij} w_{ij}}{\displaystyle\sum_{v_i \in V} \sum_{v_j \in V} a_{ij} w_{ij}}
\tag{7}
$$

Accordingly, the diagonal elements c'_{kk} quantifies the fraction of weight of edges that fall within community C_k,

$$
c'_{kk} = \frac{\displaystyle\sum_{v_i \in C_k} \sum_{v_j \in C_k} a_{ij} w_{ij}}{\displaystyle\sum_{v_i \in V} \sum_{v_j \in V} a_{ij} w_{ij}}
\tag{8}
$$

Thus the fraction of the weight of the edges that are attached to vertices in C_i can be computed by $\xi_i = \displaystyle\sum_{1 \le j \le r} c'_{ij}$.

It is not difficult to see that if the ends of edges are connected together randomly, the expected fraction of the resulting weight of the edges that connect vertices within C_i is ξ_i^2.

Finally we can achieve the following equation to measure the OSN modularity for weighted graph.

$$
Q' = \sum_k (c'_{kk} - \xi_k^2)
\tag{9}
$$

Based on the weighted modularity model defined in Eq.(9), we propose the WMO algorithm. The algorithm performs in two steps.

Initially, we regard each node in the network as an independent community and perform Algorithm 1. Then, for

Algorithm 2 Partition into servers

PartitionintoServers(Γ_0)

1: $\Gamma \leftarrow \Gamma_0$; $\Gamma_{best} \leftarrow \Gamma_0$, $S_{max} \leftarrow \dfrac{\sum w_k + e}{p}$;
2:   **repeat**
3:     $C \leftarrow F(\Gamma)$ /*partition algorithm*/
4:     sort C_i by $\sum\limits_{k \in C_i} w_k$ in descending sequence
5:     **for**(each $C_i \in C$) **do**
6:       **if**($\sum\limits_{k \in C_i} w_k \leq S_{max}$) **then**
7:         **for**(each $P_j \in P$)
8:           **if**($C_i \neq \emptyset \wedge (|P_j| + \sum\limits_{k \in C_i} w_k < S_{max})$)
9:           **then**
10:             $P_j \leftarrow P_j \cup C_i$
11:             $C_i \leftarrow \emptyset$
12:           **end if**
13:         **end for**
14:       **end if**
15:     **end for**
16:     $\Gamma \leftarrow \bigcup \{C_i\}$
17:   **until**($\Gamma = \emptyset$);
18:   **return**(Γ);

each node i, if there is a community C which does not contain i itself but contains another node in C which connects to i, we attempt to move i from its original community to C and calculate the gain of the modularity $\Delta Q'$. If there is not such a move which achieves positive $\Delta Q'$, we remain i in its original community; otherwise, we move i into the community C_j which achieves the maximum $\Delta Q'$. We loop this process until no nodes in the network can be further moved in this way. In this way, we may get some small communities. We make each community seem as a virtual node. The virtual nodes constitute a new weighted graph. The weights of the newly formed virtual edges are the sum of the weights of the edges between nodes in the corresponding two communities. Formally, $e'_{ij} = \sum\limits_{v_k \in C_i} \sum\limits_{v_t \in C_j} a_{kt} w_{kt}$. Repeat the above step until we can not make any more changes, i.e, the modularity reaches the maximum value. It is clear that the communities we achieve can not ensure the load balanced if we straightforwardly put the communities into servers.

In the second step, we initially sort the communities achieved above in an descending order of the sum of all users' data volume within a community. Each time we find the server with the current largest remaining capacity, S_{max}. If the largest community's storage cost is less than S_{max}, we put all the users' data of this community in this server. Otherwise, we merge all the nodes in these remaining communities as a new weighted network. By repeating the steps above, we partition the newly obtained weighted graph into smaller communities. The process continues until all the nodes are put in the servers. We detail the pseudo code of the WMO scheme in Algorithm 2.

4.3 Indexing with Replication

It is clear that although the community-based data replacement mechanism can remain the user data as local as possible, there are still some friends outside the same community. Cross-community interconnection will incur extra inter-server communication cost during searching. An effec-

tive way is to leverage replication strategy to further improve the operation locality. Here we further examine two approaches: replica copy strategy (CS) and replica non-copy Strategy (NCS).

Replica copy strategy. Using the above algorithm, we can successfully partitioned all users into different communities and each user belongs to only one community. For simplicity, before building the community based index, we first classify the community-based data (CBD) into two types: the community's all members' data (CMD) and the replication data (RD) of users who do not belong to the given community but have social links with users in that community. Based on the CBD of a community inside a single server, we build an inverted index called community based index (CBI). The recall of the keyword search results is guaranteed because each server's CBD contains all the friends' data of each user in the given server. That is to say, for each user in the server, all the data that he/she has permission to access is stored inside the local server.

We use the notation S to denote the intermediate matched result set using CBI, and the notation N to denote the intermediate matched result set using global index. The advantages of the search using CBI are twofold: 1). the quantity of the set S is commonly several orders of magnitude smaller than that of N when we perform a keyword search; 2). the CBI based index takes good advantages of the locality of the data for a user (a user's all friends' data and his/her own data). It is obvious that our data placement strategy can avoid a large amounts of inter-server communications while guarantee the recall of the search results. Furthermore, when we obtain the final results by performing the intersection operation, our scheme is much cost efficient due to the much smaller size of the intermediate results.

Replica non-copy strategy. It is clear that the CS consumes extra storage cost due to data replication. The volume of the storage cost is determined by the density of interconnections between different servers. This means a better community partition result will lead to less storage cost. If the storage volume is limited, the CS may not be an advisable choice. Here we propose an alternative choice called NCS, where we do not copy the RD to local server and the CBI is built only based on the CMD. Therefore when a user U submits a keyword search, the system needs to check not only the local server's CBI, but also those friends whose data is not indexed in the same server. It is clear that the NCS strategy does not consume extra storage cost but will cause inter-server communication cost and increase search latency. Above all, whether to choose CS or NCS is a tradeoff between storage cost and search latency as well as the inter-server communication cost.

5. RESULTS

In this section, we evaluate the performance of our design using trace-driven simulations. At first, we present the data sets we use in the evaluation. Next, we describe the details of the simulation setups. Then we introduce the metrics used to compare our design with existing schemes. In the evaluation, we use Cassandra [9] as the underlying data stores. We simulate the proposed summary index scheme, and examine the performance improvement of our design against existing schemes. In the simulation, we use the Facebook traces. Since there has been no standard data set for evaluating the performance of content-based OSN search, we built

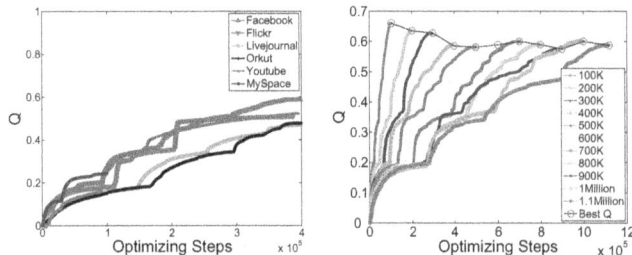

Figure 1: Optimizing procedure   Figure 2: Optimizing with different scales   Figure 3: Search Traffic   Figure 4: Load Balance

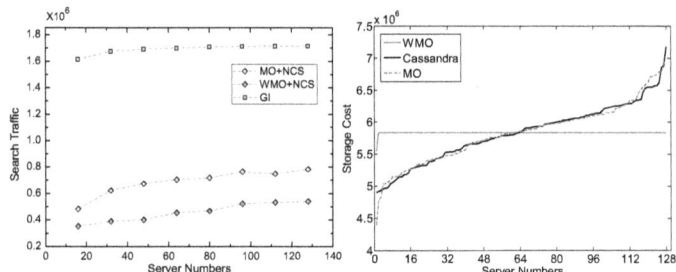

one based on the TREC WT10G Web corpus [8] provided by the National Institute of Standards and Technology (NIST), which is a large test set widely used for performance evaluation in Web search area. We evaluate our design using the MSN query logs from Microsoft.

We simulate our system using ns-2, which has been widely used in simulating large-scale systems deployed in data centers [2]. In order to better represent real-world OSN systems, we consider both the underlying physical data center networks and the logical OSN social graph. To simulate the underlying data center networks, we generate a fat-tree network [11] with rich configuration information, including bandwidth capacity, latency, and so forth.

Our design considers both the user-perceived service quality and the system efficiency. The quality focuses on the search latency, while the efficiency focuses on the network traffic in the data center.

Figure 3 illustrates the traffic of search with MO and WMO algorithms separately with NCS approach. Since using CS approach will not cause traffic cost during searching, we do not need to examine MO+CS and WMO+CS strategies. The results show that the WMO algorithm consumes 33% less communication cost than the MO algorithm when using NCS approach. The GI consumes scheme [5] 350% more communication cost than our WMO algorithm. The search traffic of the MO scheme is 0.6880×10^6 and the search traffic of the GI is 1.6914×10^6. The average search traffic of our WMO scheme is 0.4580×10^6. Our scheme significantly reduce the search traffic of GI by 73%. Figure 4 shows that our WMO-based index can achieve satisfactory load balance compare to the GI scheme and the straightforward MO-based index scheme.

6. CONCLUSION AND FUTURE WORK

In this work, we identify the community based locality (CBL), an unique feature of OSN systems, using large scale traces of diverse popular OSN systems. Based on this observation, we propose a novel CBL-based algorithm to build the content index for keyword search. Our scheme can avoid a large amount of inter-server communications as well as significantly reducing the latency during search. We also achieve good load balance for content indexing. The comprehensive trace-driven simulation results show that our scheme greatly outperforms existing schemes. In the next step, we will examine our scheme under more dynamical environments where the servers and interconnections may change frequently.

7. ACKNOWLEDGEMENTS

This paper is supported by NSFC fund (No.61370233), Foundation for the Author of National Excellent Doctoral Dissertation of PR China (No.201345), Ministry of Education and China Mobile Communications Corporation (MoE-CMCC) Research Founding (No.MCM20130382), Research Fund for the Doctoral Program of Higher Education of China (No.20110142120080), and Fundamental Research Funds for the Central Universities (No.2014YQ014, No.2014TS150 and No.2013TS095).

8. REFERENCES

[1] Hbase. http://hbase.apache.org/, 2013.

[2] M. Alizadeh, A. Greenberg, D. A. Maltz, J. Padhye, P. Patel, B. Prabhakar, and S. Sengupta. Data center tcp (dctcp). In *SIGCOMM*, 2010.

[3] F. Benevenuto, T. Rodrigues, M. Cha, and V. A. F. Almeida. Characterizing user behavior in online social networks. In *IMC*, pages 49–62, 2009.

[4] T. A. Bjørklund, M. Gotz, and J. Gehrke. Search in social networks with access control. In *KEYS*.

[5] T. A. Bjørklund, M. Götz, and J. Gehrke. Workload-aware indexing for keyword search in social networks. In *CIKM*, pages 535–544, 2011.

[6] F. Chang, J. Dean, S. Ghemawat, W. C. Hsieh, D. A. Wallach, M. Burrows, T. Chandra, A. Fikes, and R. E. Gruber. Bigtable: A distributed storage system for structured data. In *OSDI*, 2006.

[7] H. Chen, H. Jin, N. Jin, and T. Gu. "minimizing inter-server communications by exploiting self-similarity in online social networks. In *Proceedings of the 20th IEEE International Conference on Network Protocols (ICNP)*, 2012.

[8] D. Hawking. Overview of the TREC-9 web track. In *TREC*, 2000.

[9] A. Lakshman and P. Malik. Cassandra: a decentralized structured storage system. *ACM SIGOPS Operating Systems Review*, 44(2):35–40, 2010.

[10] M. Newman. Fast algorithm for detecting community structure in networks. *Physical Review E*, 69:066133, 2004.

[11] R. Niranjan Mysore, A. Pamboris, N. Farrington, N. Huang, P. Miri, S. Radhakrishnan, V. Subramanya, and A. Vahdat. Portland: a scalable fault-tolerant layer 2 data center network fabric. In *ACM SIGCOMM*, 2009.

Data Filtering for Scalable High-dimensional k-NN Search on Multicore Systems

Xiaoxin Tang[1], Steven Mills[2], David Eyers[2], Kai-Cheung Leung[2],
Zhiyi Huang[2], Minyi Guo[1]

[1]Shanghai Key Laboratory of Scalable Computing and Systems, Shanghai Jiao Tong University, China
[2]Department of Computer Science, University of Otago, New Zealand

ABSTRACT

K Nearest Neighbors (k-NN) search is a widely used category of algorithms with applications in domains such as computer vision and machine learning. With the rapidly increasing amount of data available, and their high dimensionality, k-NN algorithms scale poorly on multicore systems because they hit a memory wall. In this paper, we propose a novel data filtering strategy, named Subspace Clustering for Filtering (SCF), for k-NN search algorithms on multicore platforms. By excluding unlikely features in k-NN search, this strategy can reduce memory footprint as well as computation. Experimental results on four k-NN algorithms show that SCF can improve their performance on two modern multicore platforms with insignificant loss of search precision.

Categories and Subject Descriptors

I.0 [**Computing Methodologies**]: GENERAL

General Terms

Performance

Keywords

K Nearest Neighbors; High-Dimensional Space; Memory Wall; Multicore Systems; Subspace Clustering for Filtering.

1. INTRODUCTION

Similarity search is one of the applications that demands efficient parallel algorithms on multicore systems. Through finding similar items within a known database, existing knowledge can be used for predicting unknown information. Many domains, such as computer vision [14], bioinformatics [3], data analysis [5], handwriting recognition [16], and many other statistical classification tasks, rely on similarity search and demand high-performance algorithms, especially under the pressure of *big data* [10]. For example, the large amount of available images makes image-matching [13] from computer vision a very interesting and challenging problem.

K Nearest Neighbors (k-NN) search is one frequently used category of algorithms for solving similarity search problems. Here,

we take the concept "feature" to represent one data item in the database. In general, a feature f can be defined as a D dimensional vector—we later refer to its components as e_1 through e_D. The database X is defined as a set of N such features: $X = \{f_1, f_2, \ldots, f_N\}$. The similarity is often measured by Euclidean Distance (ED). Based on these definitions, the k-NN problem can be formally described as: given a query feature q, find k reference features in X that have the shortest (Euclidean) distances to q.

In general, most algorithms need two types of data structures: index data and feature data, both of which are frequently visited during k-NN search. The index structure is used for finding reference features—called candidate features—that are most likely to be the k nearest neighbors. To decide whether a candidate feature is one of the k nearest neighbors, the feature data will be visited in order to evaluate their similarity. The feature data structure is a matrix and can consume up to $O(ND)$ memory space.

As image-matching applications are becoming more and more popular, the size of typical feature sets X is increasing. The dimensionality of features is also high: e.g. SIFT [9] features have 128 dimensions. When both N and D are very large, which is often the case of problems like image matching, the feature structure can consume up to several dozens of megabytes for a single image. In this case, many available algorithms do not work efficiently on multicore systems [13] due to memory latency and bandwidth limitations (also known as the *memory wall*), as the data structure is not small enough to fit in the last-level cache.

In this paper, we propose a novel *data filtering* strategy for high-dimensional k-NN search on multicore systems. Instead of finding the likely candidates, our data filtering strategy excludes those unlikely features based on distance estimation. The data filtering strategy has two advantages. First, it reduces computation and the number of memory accesses by replacing high-dimensional distance calculation with simple distance estimation. Second, its index structure for filtering has a very small memory footprint and thus reduces the effect of memory wall.

This paper is organized as follows: Section 2 presents the SCF method. Section 3 shows performance results of SCF that is applied to four k-NN algorithms on multicore systems. Section 4 discusses the related work. Finally, Section 5 draws conclusions of this paper.

2. THE DATA FILTERING STRATEGY

In this section, the following Squared Euclidean Distance (SED) is used to measure the similarity between two features:

$$SED(f_i, f_j) = \|f_i - f_j\| = \sum_{m=1}^{D} (f_i[m] - f_j[m])^2. \quad (1)$$

The square root in ED is not used in the SED, which can reduce the computation without changing the search results.

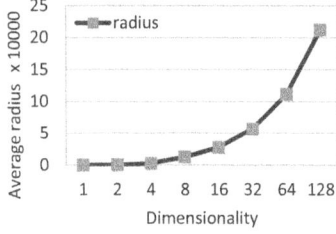

(a) Average radius of a random dataset.

	e_1	e_2	e_3	e_4
q	0	0	0	0
A	-4	2	3	4
B	-2	2	1	0
C	2	-3	0	1
D	4	-3	4	3
g_1	-3	2	2	2
g_2	3	-3	2	2

(b) A 4-dimensional case.

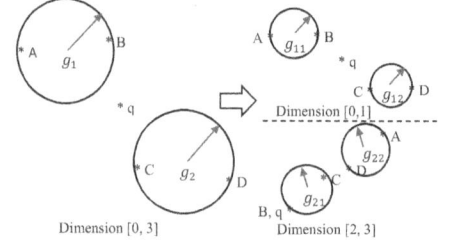

(c) From a full-space clustering to subspace clustering.

Figure 1: Challenges of using clustering for distance estimation in high-dimensional space. (a) The left figure shows the average radius of a randomly generated dataset. This dataset contains 10,000 features, which are divided into 32 groups. Each element of the features is uniformly distributed in the range of $[1, 128]$. (b) The table in the middle gives a simple 4-dimensional example. (c) The right figure shows our subspace clustering method.

2.1 A case study: brute-force search

Here we use the brute-force k-NN search to demonstrate how our data filtering strategy works. To find the k-NN of a given query feature, brute-force search first calculates all the distances between the query feature and all reference features in the database. It uses a max-heap of size k to accumulate the features with the smallest distances. After all of the distances are pushed onto the heap, the k-NN results can be collected from it. This algorithm is very computation-intensive as it will cost[1] $O(ND)$ to calculate the distances and $O(N \log k)$ to find the k-NNs. Distance calculation will dominate the time as $\log k$ is very small for small k while D can be large for high-dimensional problems. It also has a large memory footprint as it needs to scan the whole database for each query.

Since k is usually much smaller than the size of the database X, many distance calculations are not necessary as most features are far away from the query feature. If we can exclude those features that are unlikely to be a k-NN using simple distance estimation, we can reduce the computation as well as the memory footprint.

2.2 Distance estimation through clustering

The key issue now is how to estimate the distances accurately and efficiently. Clustering is a traditional method that is used to estimate the distances to a group of features. In this paper, we use the k-means algorithm of the FLANN library [11] for subspace clustering in our distance estimation. Though better clustering methods may be used, they do not affect our general approach.

After clustering, each reference feature will be assigned to the group whose group center is the closest to that reference feature. Then, these group centers will represent the features within their corresponding groups. However, when the dimensionality becomes large, the features are sparsely distributed in the space and the radius of each group becomes large as well. For example, Figure 1a gives the average radius of the groups generated from random dataset with variable dimensionality. As we can see, the radius of the groups grows quickly with the increasing dimensionality. When the radius is large, clustering-based distance estimation becomes less accurate.

Consider a simple 4-dimensional case as an example, which is given in Figure 1b. Here, q is the query feature; A, B, C and D are four reference features. After clustering on the reference features based on the all four dimensions, A and B are put into the same group with the center g_1, and C and D are put into the other group with the center g_2. The left side of Figure 1c illustrates the

---

[1] Big-O notation usually denotes asymptotic effects, but we will use it as shorthand for proportionality without simplified expressions.

clustering result (it is simplified with circles as it is hard to draw 4-dimensional space). If we use this clustering result to estimate distances between the query and the reference features, then $\|g_1 - q\|$ will represent $\|A - q\|$ and $\|B - q\|$ while $\|g_2 - q\|$ will represent $\|C - q\|$ and $\|D - q\|$. As $\|g_1 - q\| = 21$ and $\|g_2 - q\| = 26$, the order of the reference features based on the distance estimation is A, B, C, D. However, their real distances are $\|A - q\| = 52$, $\|B - q\| = 8$, $\|C - q\| = 15$ and $\|D - q\| = 43$, and the right order should be B, C, D, A. If $k = 1$, the results based on this distance estimation will have 0% accuracy, while in the case of $k = 2$, the accuracy is only 50%.

From the above example we can see that clustering within high-dimensional spaces has two problems. First, it is so coarse-grained that it is not able to tell the differences between features within the same group. For example, it cannot tell that B is much closer to q than A. Second, it could present incorrect results easily as a closer group center does not mean all features in that group are closer to the query. For example, though group g_1 is closer to q than group g_2, feature C in g_2 has a smaller distance to q than A of group g_1. The reason is that the radius of each group could be very large, and thus can obscure the differences between groups.

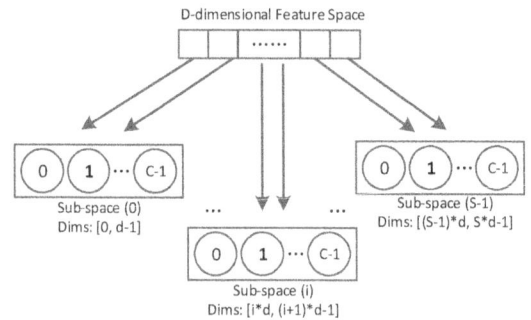

Figure 2: The basic structure for SCF method. It contains S subspaces. All features are divided into different groups by using the corresponding dimensions within each subspace.

2.3 Subspace Clustering for Filtering

Based on the above analysis, we propose the following Subspace Clustering for Filtering (SCF) method. As Figure 2 shows, the data structure of SCF is a multi-level cover of the feature space. Instead of using all the dimensions for clustering, SCF divides the whole space into S subspaces, each of which may contain $\lfloor \frac{D}{S} \rfloor$ dimen-

Algorithm 1: Build the SCF index.

$d \leftarrow \lfloor \frac{D}{S} \rfloor$;
for $i \leftarrow 0$ **to** $S - 1$ **do**
  Based on dimensions $[i \times d, (i + 1) \times d)$, use a clustering method (e.g. k-means) to divide X into C groups;
  for $j \leftarrow 0$ **to** $N - 1$ **do**
    $\beta[j][i] \leftarrow$ group ID that feature j belongs to;
  for $j \leftarrow 0$ **to** $C - 1$ **do**
    $\theta[i][j] \leftarrow$ center of group j;
    $\gamma[i][j] \leftarrow$ radius of group j;
return β, θ and γ;

Table 1: PSEDs between q and the group centers in the example.

	g_{11}	g_{12}	g_{21}	g_{22}
q	13	18	0.5	24.5

Algorithm 2: Calculation of partial distances between the query feature and the center of each group in each subspace

$d \leftarrow \lfloor \frac{D}{S} \rfloor$;
$\delta[S][C] \leftarrow 0$;
for $i \leftarrow 0$ **to** $S - 1$ **do**
  for $j \leftarrow 0$ **to** $C - 1$ **do**
    $l \leftarrow i \times d$;
    $u \leftarrow (i + 1) \times d - 1$;
    $\delta[i][j] \leftarrow PSED_{[l,u]}(q, \theta[i][j])$
return δ;

Algorithm 3: $SCF\_Estimation(q, r_t)$

$ESED \leftarrow 0$;
for $i \leftarrow 0$ **to** $S - 1$ **do**
  $ESED \leftarrow ESED + \delta[i][\beta[t][i]]$;
return $ESED$

sions. The remainder of $\frac{D}{S}$ can either be treated as an additional subspace, or these dimensions can be distributed to the other subspaces. Then, within each subspace, we use the aforementioned k-means clustering method to divide the features into C different groups where each group may contain $\frac{N}{C}$ features on average.

The SCF-based distance estimation depends on two data structures: the SCF index and a matrix of partial distances for the query feature. The SCF index is created based on the clustering results in the subspaces. The detailed algorithm for creating SCF index is shown in Algorithm 1. β, θ and γ in the algorithm are three matrixes that represent the SCF index. Each element β_{ij} ($i \in [0, N)$, $j \in [0, S)$) in the index represents the group ID of the ith feature of X within the jth subspace. θ_{jt} ($t \in [0, C)$) represents the center point of the tth group in the jth subspace. Similarly, γ_{jt} is used to represent the radius of the tth group in the jth subspace.

The matrix of partial distances for the query feature is created by Algorithm 2. It is represented by the matrix δ in the algorithm. The matrix gives the Partial SED (PSED) between the query feature and the center of each group in each subspace. It can be defined as:

$$PSED_{l,u}(f_i, f_j) = \sum_{m=l}^{u} (f_i[m] - f_j[m])^2 \qquad (2)$$

where $1 \leq l \leq u \leq D$, and $[l, u]$ bound the dimensions used to form a subspace.

Algorithm 3 shows the steps for distance estimation. The PSED between the query and the center of a group is used to estimate the PSED between the query and the reference features of that group. For each reference feature, the sum of all estimated PSEDs in every subspace is used as the Estimated SED (ESED) between the query and the reference feature.

Table (1) shows the matrix for the PSEDs of the previous example, where $g_{11} = (-3, 2, \cdot, \cdot)$, $g_{12} = (3, -3, \cdot, \cdot)$, $g_{21} = (\cdot, \cdot, 0.5, 0.5)$, and $g_{22} = (\cdot, \cdot, 3.5, 3.5)$. Thus, in the right side of Figure 1c, the ESED of each reference features are:

$$\|A - q\|_{\text{est}} = \|g_{11} - q\|_{\text{psed}} + \|g_{22} - q\|_{\text{psed}} = 37.5,$$
$$\|B - q\|_{\text{est}} = \|g_{11} - q\|_{\text{psed}} + \|g_{21} - q\|_{\text{psed}} = 13.5,$$
$$\|C - q\|_{\text{est}} = \|g_{12} - q\|_{\text{psed}} + \|g_{21} - q\|_{\text{psed}} = 18.5,$$
$$\|D - q\|_{\text{est}} = \|g_{12} - q\|_{\text{psed}} + \|g_{22} - q\|_{\text{psed}} = 42.5.$$

They result in the estimated order B, C, A, D, which is closer to the real order of B, C, D, A than that estimated based on the original full-space clustering.

It is worth noting that the overhead of Algorithm 1 is a one-off cost, which will be relatively minor when amortized over many queries. Also note that by adjusting S and C in the above algorithms, we can change the estimation accuracy of SCF. Usually when S and C are increasing, the estimation accuracy can be improved. Since this paper focuses on performance and due to the limited space here, we do not give further discussions on how to maintain a high estimation accuracy. However, the real accuracy achieved by our method is given in the experimental section.

2.4 Space complexity analyses

As shown in the above algorithms, SCF uses small index structures. Since there are S subspaces and each one has C groups, it takes $O(SC\frac{D}{S}) = O(CD)$ memory space to store all the group centers (θ) and $O(SC)$ memory space to store radius of each group (γ). Then, it takes $O(NS)$ memory space to store group IDs (β) for all reference features. During runtime, it will cost $O(SC)$ memory space to store the PSEDs (δ) for each query feature. Overall, the total memory used is $O(CD + SC + NS + SC)$ for SCF method. As N is the dominant one among all parameters, the space complexity for SCF can be reduced to $O(NS)$. Since S is much smaller than D (8 versus 128 in our implementation for SIFT dataset), the index structure of SCF is more likely to fit into the shared cache. For example, when $N = 20000$, the brute-force algorithm needs to access up to 10 MiB memory (each element of the feature is float number) while the SCF structure only needs around 160 KiB (group ID is represented by one byte). Therefore, SCF can better utilize the shared cache and requires significantly fewer memory accesses compared to the brute-force algorithm.

3. EVALUATION

In this section, we evaluate the performance of our SCF method when it is applied to four k-NN algorithms: Brute-force (BF), Randomized KD-Trees (RKD), Hierarchical k-means (Kmeans) and Random Ball Cover (RBC). The first three algorithms (BF, RKD and Kmeans) are chosen from the FLANN [11] library, which is also contained in OpenCV [2] to provide fast approximate k-NN search functionality. RBC is a state-of-the-art algorithm on parallel platforms [4] and is well optimized to reduce scalability problems when running on multicore systems. As the BF algorithm is the most computation- and memory-intensive algorithm, we use it to show that the SCF method can effectively reduce computation and

Table 2: Filtering rate (FR) and lost precision (LP) after applying SCF on each algorithm and dataset.

Dataset Algs	SIFT		Random		Madelon		HAR		Digits	
	FR	LP	FR	LP	FR	LP	FR	LP	FR	SP
BF_SCF	96.87%	3.23%	89.53%	3.76%	67.75%	0.58%	89.21%	0%	96.64%	3.51%
RKD_SCF	82.99%	2.83%	84.48%	3.54%	20.22%	0.08%	76.88%	3.81%	66.84%	3.05%
Kmeans_SCF	77.66%	3.49%	87.43%	2.96%	48.39%	0%	34.5%	3.38%	47.38%	3.64%
RBC_SCF	87.81%	2.72%	85.75%	2.14%	48.87%	0%	68.38%	3.97%	81.24%	4.61%

Table 3: Overview of each test dataset.

Name	Ref	Query	Dim
SIFT	25271	7481	128
Random	25000	7500	128
Madelon	2000	1800	500
HAR	7352	2947	560
Digits	3823	1797	64

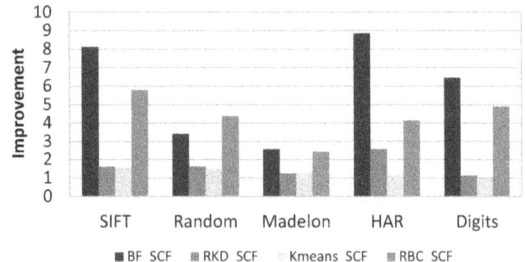

Figure 3: Performance improvement of sequential execution after applying SCF to each algorithm on AMD64 machine.

memory footprint. However, we will also demonstrate that the filtering method is very effective when applied to other optimized algorithms such as RBC.

The datasets listed in Table (3) are used to evaluate the performance of the above algorithms. In the table, "SIFT" represents features generated by the SIFT [9] algorithm, which is commonly used in computer vision. "Random" contains features that are randomly generated and evenly distributed in the feature space (a hypercube with sides of length 128). The "Digits", "Madelon" and "HAR" datasets are selected from the UCI Machine Learning Repository [1]. In Table (3), the "Ref" column indicates the number of reference features while the "Query" column lists the number of query features used in the experiment. The "Dim" column specifies the dimensionality of the datasets.

Two multicore platforms are used in our evaluation:

- AMD64: AMD Opteron Processor 6276, 16 cores × 4 @ 2.3 GHz, 16 MiB L3 shared cache, 64GiB DDR3 (1333 MHz) memory;

- MIC: Intel Xeon Phi Coprocessor 5110P, 60 cores @ 1.0 GHz, 30 MiB L2 shared cache, 8 GiB GDDR5 (5.5 GHz) memory.

The g++-4.4 compiler is used on the AMD64 machine and icc-14.0 is used for the code generation for the Xeon Phi.

3.1 Performance of sequential execution

In this section, we evaluate the performance after applying SCF to the aforementioned four algorithms under sequential execution. The results are collected from running the algorithms on a single core of AMD64. As shown in Table (2), two metrics are used to evaluate the performance and precision of SCF. The first one is Filtering Rate (FR), which represents the percentage of features that can be filtered by SCF. Thus, the higher the FR, the more computation and memory accesses it reduces, which leads to better performance. The second one LP, indicates the lost precision compared with the original k-NN results. For example, the LP of RBC_SCF is the number of k-NN that are not in the k-NN results of the original RBC, divided by the total number of k-NN of the original RBC in each test. From the table we can see that SCF can successfully maintain a LP of under 5%.

Though LP is very small in Table (2), FR varies across different datasets and algorithms. This is because different algorithms have different search precisions on different datasets. For example, RKD can find the k-NN of "Madelon" efficiently, which leads to a lower FR (20.22%). In this case most features the original RKD

has found are good candidates that SCF cannot exclude. Similarly, Kmeans processes "HAR" well, and thus SCF achieves a lower FR (34.5%). SCF works well on BF and RBC in most cases as both algorithms are highly dependent on exhaustive search of the feature space, which is very suitable for applying SCF.

Figure 3 gives the performance improvement on a single core of AMD64 after applying SCF to each algorithm. As we can see, SCF can improve the performance by up to $8.85\times$ for BF (in the "HAR" case) and up to $5.78\times$ for RBC ("SIFT"). This can be explained by the exhaustive search in both algorithms benefiting greatly from SCF. Though FR for RKD and Kmeans is high for some datasets, their performance improvement is not as good as BF and RBC. This is because both RKD and Kmeans spend a lot of time searching their complex index structures to get a small number of good candidates. Since the number of candidates for filtering is small, SCF has a smaller effect on these two algorithms, even though FR is high. However, on average, SCF can still improve the performance of RKD by 33% and that of Kmeans by 19%. Moreover, on multicore platforms, RKD and Kmeans will benefit more from SCF due to reduced memory accesses, as we demonstrate later.

3.2 Performance of parallel execution

Although the computing power is increasing on multicore machines, memory latency and bandwidth are often the bottleneck that leads to poor performance. We will show that, after applying our SCF method, the scalability of the k-NN algorithms on multicore machines is greatly improved. Here, all algorithms are parallelized by using OpenMP and the suffix "_SCF" means that SCF is applied to the corresponding algorithm. The improvements are calculated by comparing with the original algorithm. For example, the improvement for BF is calculated as the execution time of the parallelized original BF divided by the time of the parallelized BF_SCF.

Table 4: Parallel performance improvement of BF_SCF over the original BF algorithm on each platform and dataset.

Platform	SIFT	Random	Madelon	HAR	Digits
AMD64	15.54×	5.04×	2.66×	9.43×	4.13×
MIC	3.23×	2.11×	1.43×	2.97×	1.33×

(a) Scalability on AMD64.

(b) Performance improvement on AMD64.

(c) Performance counters on AMD64.

(d) Scalability on MIC.

(e) Performance improvement on MIC.

(f) Performance counters on MIC.

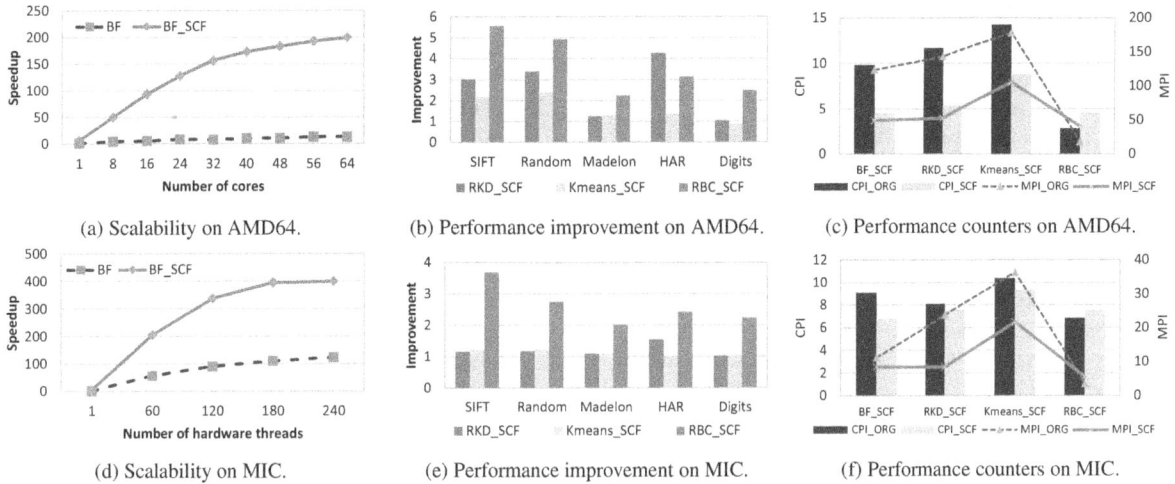

Figure 4: Performance statistics of SCF.

3.2.1 Performance improvement of the BF_SCF

Table (4) lists the parallel performance improvement of BF_SCF on AMD64 and the MIC machines. Compared with their sequential performance shown in Figure 3, the BF_SCF search has the most improvement. For the case of the SIFT dataset on AMD64, its improvement is $15.54\times$ (64 cores), which is much better than the $8.11\times$ on a single core. Figure 4a explains why the parallel BF_SCF is able to get more performance gain than its sequential counterpart. The speedup curves in the figure show the good scalability of BF_SCF, while the original BF's speedup curves become flat after 32 cores. On the AMD64 machine, the BF hits the memory wall much earlier than when all cores are used.

This result shows that for an embarrassingly parallel algorithm like BF, the memory wall becomes one of the most serious bottlenecks, which is supported by our statistics collected from performance monitoring counters. However, after applying SCF, its scalability has been significantly improved. For example, the speedup against the original sequential BF has been improved from $12.84\times$ to $199.63\times$ on AMD64 when all cores available are used. On the MIC platform, the scalability of the original BF is better because MIC has much better memory bandwidth. Moreover, since MIC has four hardware threads in each core, it can efficiently hide the memory latency through overlapping computation and memory access. In this case, the memory wall problem in the original BF is greatly relieved and it has reasonable scalability on MIC, as shown in Figure 4d. However, BF_SCF still has much better performance than the original BF, as can be seen in the other series on that figure.

3.2.2 Performance improvement of other algorithms

Figures 4b and 4e show the performance improvement of other k-NN algorithms on parallel platforms. This compares the original algorithm running across all cores to the SCF version. The performance improvement of RBC_SCF is very similar to that of its sequential counterpart ($5.64\times$ versus $5.54\times$ on AMD64 in the best cases). Since this algorithm has already been optimized for multicore platforms, it scales well on parallel platforms and does not suffer from the memory wall. This shows that SCF is very cache-efficient and has little impact on the performance of those algorithms that already have good cache utilization. On AMD64, RKD_SCF and Kmeans_SCF get their best performance improvement of $4.25\times$ and $2.39\times$, which is much better than their sequential improvement ($2.55\times$ and $1.53\times$).

However, for the "Madelon" and "Digits" datasets, neither the RKD_SCF nor Kmeans_SCF algorithms have more of a performance improvement than their sequential counterparts do. The reason is that both datasets are quite small (3.8 MiB for "Madelon" and 0.88 MiB for "Digits") so that they can fit in the last-level cache and are less likely to hit the memory wall. Moreover, due to the lower dimensionality, RKD and Kmeans perform efficiently on "Digits" anyway. Thus, fewer features can be filtered by SCF. Nonetheless, in most cases SCF can significantly improve performance in these algorithms on AMD64.

Since MIC has a higher memory bandwidth, the memory wall problem is relieved for the k-NN algorithms. This is due to its usage of the GDDR5 memory and a larger shared L2 cache that provides very high memory throughput. The performance improvement of most algorithms after applying SCF is quite similar to their sequential counterparts, which means they scale well on this new platform.

We note that the current evaluation code does not contain low-level optimizations specific to the architecture, and thus its computing ability may not be fully utilized. For example, the Vector Processing Unit (VPU) in Xeon Phi contributes most to the platform's peak computing power. If the VPUs are fully utilized, the memory latency may again become the bottleneck. We will explore this in our future work.

3.2.3 Performance monitoring counter statistics

Figure 4c and 4f are provided to verify our previous observations and analyses. In the figures, Cycles Per Instruction (CPI) is used to evaluate the computing efficiency while Misses Per Instruction (MPI) is used to represent intensity of the last-level cache misses per instruction. For AMD64, the CPIs have a very close relationship with the MPIs as they grow and drop in the same pattern. That means that the CPIs are mainly affected by the memory wall. However, for MIC, CPI is not significantly influenced by MPI, which demonstrates that the Xeon Phi can provide enough memory bandwidth for these algorithms.

In summary, SCF is general enough to improve the performance of existing k-NN algorithms on different datasets by reducing both computation and memory accesses. Both memory-intensive and computation-intensive k-NN algorithms can benefit from our proposed method.

4. RELATED WORK

As far as we know, this is the first effort on optimization of approximate k-NN algorithms on multicore systems that addresses both performance and precision.

Garcia *et al.* [6] first used the GPU to implement the brute-force algorithm. However, as implementing efficient max-heaps on GPU is very difficult, it becomes very slow in searching for the smallest distances, especially when the required number of results (k-NN) is larger than 2 [13]. Designing other multicore-friendly approximate algorithms has been a recent trend for accelerating k-NN search (e.g. RBC [4]). Although they have achieved very good performance on multicore platforms, they still incur a great deal of unnecessary computation, which can be reduced with our data filtering mechanism.

The Vector Approximation (VA) [15] and Vector Quantization (VQ) [12] approaches share a similar idea of using small structures to represent data and estimate distances. However, they are designed to reduce disk I/O overhead. While VA uses one dimension and VQ uses full dimensions to build the index, our method can choose any number of dimensions to better balance time complexity and estimation accuracy. Location Sensitive Hashing (LSH) [3] uses special hash functions so that features that are close to each other will get the same hash value. However, developing an appropriate hash function can be a very complex undertaking [4].

The Xeon Phi is a new coprocessor with the Intel Many Integrated Core (MIC) architecture. Currently, many researchers are exploring this new architecture. For example, Alexander *et al.* have implemented the famous Linpack Benchmark on Xeon Phi [7], and Liu *et al.* have designed efficient sparse matrix-vector multiplication on this new architecture [8]. As far as we know, our work is the first effort evaluating the performance of k-NN algorithms on Xeon Phi.

5. CONCLUSIONS

Traditional k-NN algorithms run into serious bottlenecks caused by the memory wall on multicore systems. In this paper, we propose a data filtering strategy that tries to reduce the computation- and memory-intensive distance calculation. We propose the Subspace Clustering for Filtering (SCF) method, which can accurately estimate similarity. Experimental results show that SCF is general enough to significantly improve the performance of several k-NN algorithms on multicore platforms.

In the future, we intend to further explore how to improve our method so that it can efficiently utilize the massive computing ability and memory bandwidth of new hardware such as next generation GPUs and the Xeon Phi.

Acknowledgment

We thank the anonymous reviewers for their valuable comments. Xiaoxin Tang would like to thank the University of Otago for hosting his PhD internship during the course of this research. This work was partially supported by the Program for Changjiang Scholars and Innovative Research Team in University (IRT1158, PCSIRT) China, NSFC (Grant No. 61272099, 61261160502) and by the Scientific Innovation Act of STCSM (No. 13511504200).

6. REFERENCES

[1] K. Bache and M. Lichman. UCI machine learning repository, 2013.

[2] G. Bradski and A. Kaehler. *Learning OpenCV: Computer vision with the OpenCV library*. O'Reilly Media, Incorporated, 2008.

[3] J. Buhler. Efficient large-scale sequence comparison by locality-sensitive hashing. *Bioinformatics*, 17(5):419–428, 2001.

[4] L. Cayton. Accelerating nearest neighbour search on manycore systems. In *IEEE Int. Parallel and Distributed Processing Symposium (IPDPS)*, 2012.

[5] D. L. Donoho et al. High-dimensional data analysis: The curses and blessings of dimensionality. *AMS Math Challenges Lecture*, pages 1–32, 2000.

[6] V. Garcia, E. Debreuve, F. Nielsen, and M. Barlaud. K-nearest neighbor search: Fast GPU-based implementations and application to high-dimensional feature matching. In *Image Processing (ICIP), 2010 17th IEEE International Conference on*, pages 3757–3760, 2010.

[7] A. Heinecke, K. Vaidyanathan, M. Smelyanskiy, A. Kobotov, R. Dubtsov, G. Henry, A. G. Shet, G. Chrysos, and P. Dubey. Design and implementation of the Linpack benchmark for single and multi-node systems based on Intel Xeon Phi coprocessor. *Parallel and Distributed Processing Symposium, International*, 0:126–137, 2013.

[8] X. Liu, M. Smelyanskiy, E. Chow, and P. Dubey. Efficient sparse matrix-vector multiplication on x86-based many-core processors. In *Proceedings of the 27th international ACM conference on International conference on supercomputing*, ICS '13, pages 273–282, New York, NY, USA, 2013. ACM.

[9] D. Lowe. Object recognition from local scale-invariant features. In *Computer Vision The Proceedings of the Seventh IEEE International Conference on*, volume 2, pages 1150–1157 vol.2, 1999.

[10] J. Manyika, M. Chui, B. Brown, J. Bughin, R. Dobbs, C. Roxburgh, and A. H. Byers. Big data: The next frontier for innovation, competition, and productivity. Technical report, McKinsey Global Institute, 2011.

[11] M. Muja and D. G. Lowe. Fast approximate nearest neighbors with automatic algorithm configuration. In *International Conference on Computer Vision Theory and Application VISSAPP'09)*, pages 331–340. INSTICC Press, 2009.

[12] S. Ramaswamy and K. Rose. Adaptive cluster distance bounding for high-dimensional indexing. *Knowledge and Data Engineering, IEEE Transactions on*, 23(6):815–830, 2011.

[13] X. Tang, S. Mills, D. Eyers, K.-C. Leung, Z. Huang, and M. Guo. Performance bottlenecks in manycore systems: A case study on large scale feature matching within image collections. In *Proceedings of the 15th IEEE International Conference on High Performance Computing and Communications*, 2013. to appear.

[14] A. Torralba, R. Fergus, and W. T. Freeman. 80 million tiny images: A large data set for nonparametric object and scene recognition. *Pattern Analysis and Machine Intelligence, IEEE Transactions on*, 30(11):1958–1970, 2008.

[15] R. Weber and K. Böhm. Trading quality for time with nearest-neighbor search. In C. Zaniolo, P. Lockemann, M. Scholl, and T. Grust, editors, *Advances in Database Technology (EDBT)*, volume 1777 of *Lecture Notes in Computer Science*, pages 21–35. Springer Berlin Heidelberg, 2000.

[16] C. Zanchettin, B. L. D. Bezerra, and W. W. Azevedo. A KNN-SVN hybrid model for cursive handwriting recognition. In *Proceedings of the International Joint Conference on Neural Networks*, 2012.

Bobolang - A Language for Parallel Streaming Applications

Zbyněk Falt   David Bednárek   Martin Kruliš

Jakub Yaghob   Filip Zavoral

Charles University in Prague, Faculty of Mathematics and Physics
Czech Republic
{falt,bednarek,krulis,yaghob,zavoral}@ksi.mff.cuni.cz

ABSTRACT

At present time, the programmers may choose from a number of streaming languages. They cover various aspects of the development process of streaming applications; however, specification of complex or runtime-dependent parts of the applications still remains a great challenge. We have analysed a large amount of requirements raised by the development of multiple data streaming parallel applications and proposed a novel language called Bobolang. It contains syntactic and semantic features which allow the programmer to naturally solve most of the problems, which we met in the design of streaming applications. The language is used to specify the structure of the whole application as well as the inner structure of each operator. Thanks to the properties of the language, Bobolang can create an optimized evaluation plan which is capable of making the best use of the available hardware resources. The language has been employed in several practical problems and it has proven itself to be a very powerful tool for the development of data-intensive parallel applications.

Keywords

Bobolang, Bobox, streaming systems, language, parallel

1. INTRODUCTION

Streaming systems represent a specific domain in the data processing systems. Number of such systems exists [12, 11, 13, 4, 3, 10, 1], while each is designed for specific purpose, different hardware architecture, or different programming language. These systems operate with data streams, which are basically unidirectional flows of structured tuples. Streams are processed by operators (also denoted as functions, kernels, or filters) which may have multiple inputs and outputs. These operators transform data from the input streams by performing their built-in functionalities and pass their results into the output streams. A streaming application is typically represented by an oriented graph, where

HPDC'14, June 23–27, 2014, Vancouver, BC, Canada.
Copyright is held by the owner/author(s). Publication rights licensed to ACM.
ACM 978-1-4503-2749-7/14/06 ...$15.00.
http://dx.doi.org/10.1145/2600212.2600711.

the vertices are operators and the edges prescribe the data flow between them. In the remaining of this paper, we will refer to the graph as to the *execution plan*.

In streaming systems, we distinguish two types of parallelism – *inter-operator* (among the operators) and *intra-operator* (within one operator). The *inter-operator parallelism* (i.e., when independent operators are processed concurrently) can be achieved naturally if there are enough data fragments to keep multiple operators occupied. The *intra-operator parallelism* (i.e., parallelism within a single operator) cannot be achieved automatically at the streaming system level, since the operators are usually treated as black boxes. However, in some cases, we can decompose an operator into multiple sub-operators which substitute its functionality. This decomposition modifies the structure of the execution plan (replacing one vertex by a subgraph), which may increase the level of inter-operator parallelism. In the rest of the paper, we use the term *intra-operator parallelization* as a process of operator decomposition.

In this paper, we propose a new language for operator decomposition description called Bobolang. The programmer has only to implement strictly serial sub-operators (that cannot be decomposed any further) and specify the schema of the sub-operators composition. Moreover, Bobolang contains language constructs which allows some operators to be replicated automatically. The interpreter of Bobolang performs the real decomposition and operator replication, thus exploits the inter-operator parallelism to the limits of the host system hardware configuration.

The paper is organized as follows. The Bobolang language is described in Section 2. In Section 3, we evaluate Bobolang on practical examples. Related work is collected in Section 4 and Section 5 concludes the paper.

2. THE BOBOLANG LANGUAGE

Bobolang is a language designed for formal description of execution plans in an easy and intuitive way. The execution environment provides basic operators and data types implemented and compiled natively in the underlying systems (e.g., in C++) and the Bobolang code specifies which operators are used in the execution plan, how they are interconnected, and what data types are passed over the connections. Furthermore, Bobolang allows the programmer to create composite operators from the existing ones and to specify operator templates. A definition of a new operator is illustrated in the following example:

```
operator new_operator(int)->(int,int) {
    split_op(int)->(int),(int) split;
    filter_op(int)->(int,int) filter1, filter2;
    join_op(int,int),(int,int)->(int,int) join;

    input -> split;
    split[0] -> filter1 -> [0]join;
    split[1] -> filter2 -> [1]join;
    join -> output;
}
```

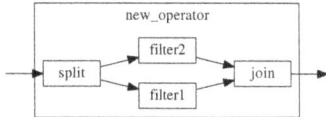

Figure 1: Internal structure of the `new_operator`.

The first line declares a new operator called `new_operator`. The operator has one input (a stream of integers) and one output (a stream of integer pairs). The body of the operator has two parts. The first part contains a list of sub-operators from which the operator is composed of. This part has similar syntax as definition of variables in C++, i.e., each sub-operator specifies its type including its input/output data descriptor followed by the local identifier of the operator.

The second part specifies the connections between operators. Statement `op1 -> op2` defines the connection of `op1` output to `op2` input. The corresponding input and output must have the same data type descriptor. The syntax allows creating chains, so the `op1 -> op2 -> op3;` statement is just a shorthand expression for `op1 -> op2;` and `op2 -> op3;`.

In addition to explicitly defined sub-operators, each body implicitly contains two special sub-operators – `input` and `output`. These sub-operators represent the input and the output of the operator `new_operator`.

Operators may have multiple inputs or outputs. The inputs/outputs are indexed by consecutive numbers starting with zero. The index of an output is written in brackets as a suffix of the identifier of the operator, the index of an input is written analogically as a prefix. If an operator has only one input/output, the index may be omitted. Note that the `(int),(int)` denotes two streams of integers, whereas `(int,int)` denotes one stream of integer pairs.

The resulting internal structure of the `new_operator` is depicted in Figure 1.

2.1 Multiplication of Inputs and Outputs

In order to easily apply schemas like the one depicted in Figure 2, the Bobolang language introduces multiplication of inputs and outputs. By default, each input/output is single. The multiplied input/output can be specified by an asterisk suffix. The following operator has multiplicated output:

```
broadcast(int)->(int)* bcast;
```

Bobolang allows to connect single or multiplicated output to single or multiplicated input which leads to four possible combinations:

1. *single output to single input* – the target sub-operator is automatically replicated according to the number of

replicas of the source sub-operator and the corresponding replicas get connected. This is demonstrated in the following example on operators `op2` and `op3`.

2. *multiplicated output to single input* – the target sub-operator is automatically replicated. Each output is connected to the input of the corresponding replica of the target. This situation usually fits the data dispatching/broadcasting scenario (see `op1` and `op2` operators).

3. *single output to multiplicated input* – only one replica of the target sub-operator is created and its each input is connected to the output of the corresponding source. This situation is usually described as data consolidation and illustrated on operators `op4` and `op5`.

4. *multiplicated output to multiplicated input* – the target sub-operator is automatically replicated according to the number of replicas of the source sub-operator and each side has as many inputs/outputs as there are replicas. The connections are made so that each source replica has a connection to all target replicas, thus each target replica is connected with all source replicas. This situation is depicted in the following example as the connection between `op3` and `op4`.

When a sub-operator is automatically replicated due to multiplicated input/output, every replica is assigned its own unique RID which might be essential for implementation of some operators, such as the `parallel_merge` in Section 3.1. Current implementation of the Bobolang interpreter tries to keep the number of replicas same as the number of threads in the system; however, we plan to address this issues in future, since it may not yield to optimal results.

The following Bobolang code demonstrates the described behaviour. The instantiated execution plan is depicted in Figure 2.

```
operator new_operator(int)->(int) {
    sub_operator(int)->(int)* op1;
    sub_operator(int)->(int) op2;
    sub_operator(int)->(int)* op3;
    sub_operator(int)*->(int) op4;
    sub_operator(int)*->(int) op5;

    input -> op1 -> op2 -> op3;
    op3 -> op4 -> op5 -> output;
}
```

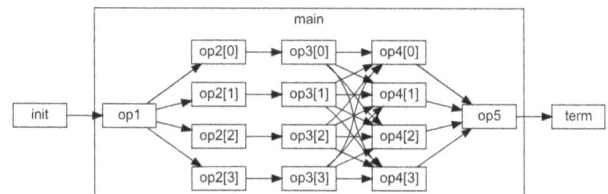

Figure 2: An example of execution plan with multiplicated inputs/outputs.

In this section, we have presented the fundamental principles of the Bobolang language. Besides these properties, there are several features of lower importance such as support of semi-automatic parallelization, parameter passing to sub-operators, `typedef` keyword, named inputs/outputs, template operators, possibility of the specification of the whole execution plan not only operators, etc. These features make the Bobolang language more user friendly; however, they are beyond the scope of this paper. More detailed description of the language syntax is available in the technical documentation of the project[1].

3. EVALUATION

In this section, we present examples of parallel algorithms and their implementation created in Bobolang. We will focus solely on the top-level source code of these algorithms to present Bobolang features and expressive power. More details and benchmark results can be found in the cited papers.

We have also utilized the Bobolang language on various practical and more complex problems. For instance, the framework was successfully used in the implementation of parallel SPARQL engine [7]. However, these experimental results are beyond the scope of this paper.

3.1 Parallel Sorting

Parallel sort algorithms are subjected to an intensive research, since the sorting operation is essential for many areas of data processing. In this example, we use an idea that is often employed in parallel and external sorting – the merging of sorted sequences. We split the input stream into several sub-streams and sort each one independently using efficient single-threaded in memory algorithm. Afterwards, the streams are merged into one final stream.

The key part of this algorithm is the merging phase. We introduced a `parallel_merge` operator [6] which is able to perform the merging operation in parallel without significant serial bottleneck. The source code of the parallel sort algorithm can be expressed in a very compact form in Bobolang:

```
operator parallel_sort(T)->(T) {
    dispatch(T)->(T)* disp;
    single_threaded_sort(T)->(T) sort;
    broadcast(T)->(T)* bcast;
    parallel_merge(T)*->(T) merge;
    consolidate(T)*->(T) cons;

    input -> disp -> sort -> bcast -> merge;
    merge -> cons -> output;
}
```

An instance of the operator for four worker threads is shown in Figure 3.

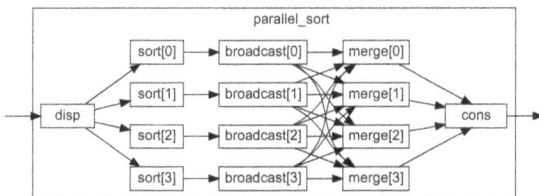

Figure 3: Parallel sort operator

The details about the implementation of the `parallel_merge` and the `single_threaded_sort` operators, as well as

experiments which test the scalability of the algorithm, can be found in previous work [6].

3.2 Parallel Merge-Join

Merge join is one of the most important database operations, especially in combination with an efficient scalable sorting algorithm. The general idea of the algorithm is to preprocess the input packets, so that they can be joined independently in parallel. There are several technical issues which complicate the implementation of all auxiliary sub-operators. Fortunately, we have been able to implement a very scalable and skewness resistant parallel merge join algorithm [8]. We present the Bobolang part of its source code in the following:

```
operator parallel_join(L),(R)->(O) {
    preprocess(L),(R)->(L),(R) prep;
    broadcast(L)->(L)* lbcast;
    broadcast(R)->(R)* rbcast;
    merge_join(L),(R)->(out_type) join;
    consolidate(out_type)*->(out_type) cons;

    input[0] -> [0]prep[0] -> lbcast;
    input[1] -> [1]prep[1] -> rbcast;
    lbcast -> [0]join;
    rbcast -> [1]join;
    join -> cons -> output;
}
```

An instance of the operator using four worker threads is depicted in Figure 4.

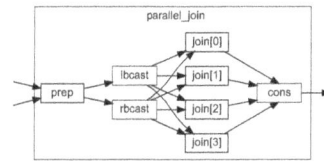

Figure 4: Parallel merge join operator

The detailed description of the `preprocess` and the `merge_join` operator as well as several other benchmarks which shows the quality of the algorithm can be found in previous work [8].

4. RELATED WORK

Contemporary streaming languages basically differ in their focus. Each one is designed with a particular intent which significantly influences their syntax and semantics. In this section, we provide a comparison of the Bobolang language to other languages from the domain of streaming systems.

The languages Brook [2, 3], StreamC/KernelC [5], and StreaMIT [12] are intended for the development of efficient streaming applications. They introduce a language based on the C/C++ syntax, which allows the programmer to implement the operators and as well as to specify their mutual interconnections. The compiler exploits the streaming nature of the application to perform specific analyses and optimizations designed to increase the performance with a particular emphasis on concurrent execution. The compiler also creates a static mapping of the operators to the execution units such as CPUs, GPUs, or FPGAs. The X Language [9] is another example of modern streaming language which has syntax similar to Bobolang.

---

[1]http://www.ksi.mff.cuni.cz/bobox/

The main difference between these languages and Bobolang is that they lack support for constructions such as multiplication of inputs/outputs (see Section 2.1). The absence of this feature makes the execution plans static.

On the other hand, Bobolang is not designed to be used in systems, which employ static scheduling. Furthermore, making the execution plans portable to heterogeneous hardware platforms such as GPUs, Xeon Phi cards, or FPGAs will be a challenging task.

5. CONCLUSION

In this paper, we have introduced the Bobolang language, designed to make the specification of execution plans for streaming systems simple, programmer friendly, and human readable. The language was designed with strong emphasis on concurrent execution and scalability, thus it naturally integrates some functionality that the regular streaming languages and frameworks do not possess. It contains syntactic and semantic features which make the intra-operator parallelization semiautomatic and more intuitive for the programmer.

In the future work, we would like to enhance the language with a support for distributed systems and massively parallel accelerators (especially GPUs), so the developer would be able to specify some important details like the distribution of the sub-operators among the system nodes or its suitability for GPU offloading. Additionally, we want to address the issues of work scheduling under various system configurations and workloads to better determine the number of replicas for each operator.

6. ACKNOWLEDGEMENTS

The authors would like to thank the Grant Agency of Charles University (GAUK), project no. 277911, and Czech Science Foundation (GACR), project no. P103-13-08195S which supported this paper. This work was also supported by project SVV-2014-260100.

7. REFERENCES

[1] D. Bednarek, J. Dokulil, J. Yaghob, and F. Zavoral. Bobox: Parallelization Framework for Data Processing. In *Advances in Information Technology and Applied Computing*, 2012.

[2] I. Buck. Brook: A streaming programming language, 2001.

[3] I. Buck, T. Foley, D. Horn, J. Sugerman, K. Fatahalian, M. Houston, and P. Hanrahan. Brook for GPUs: Stream Computing on Graphics Hardware. *ACM Transcations on Graphics*, 23:777–786, 2004.

[4] C. Consel, H. Hamdi, L. Réveillère, L. Singaravelu, H. Yu, and C. Pu. Spidle: a DSL approach to specifying streaming applications. In *Proceedings of the 2nd international conference on Generative programming and component engineering*, pages 1–17, New York, NY, USA, 2003. Springer-Verlag.

[5] A. Das, W. J. Dally, and P. Mattson. Compiling for stream processing. In *Proceedings of the 15th international conference on Parallel architectures and compilation techniques*, pages 33–42, New York, NY, USA, 2006. ACM.

[6] Z. Falt, J. Bulanek, and J. Yaghob. On Parallel Sorting of Data Streams. In *ADBIS 2012 - 16th East European Conference in Advances in Databases and Information Systems*, 2012.

[7] Z. Falt, M. Cermak, J. Dokulil, and F. Zavoral. Parallel SPARQL Query Processing Using Bobox. *International Journal On Advances in Intelligent Systems*, 5(3 and 4):302–314, 2012.

[8] Z. Falt, M. Cermak, and F. Zavoral. Highly Scalable Sort-Merge Join Algorithm for RDF Querying. In *Proceedings of the 2nd International Conference on Data Management Technologies and Applications*, 2013.

[9] M. Franklin, E. Tyson, J. Buckley, P. Crowley, and J. Maschmeyer. Auto-pipe and the X language: A pipeline design tool and description language. In *20th International Parallel and Distributed Processing Symposium*. IEEE, 2006.

[10] U. J. Kapasi, W. J. Dally, S. Rixner, J. D. Owens, and B. Khailany. Programmable stream processors. *IEEE Computer*, 36:282–288, 2003.

[11] W. R. Mark, R. Steven, G. Kurt, A. Mark, and J. Kilgard. Cg: A system for programming graphics hardware in a c-like language. *ACM Transactions on Graphics*, 22:896–907, 2003.

[12] W. Thies, M. Karczmarek, and S. Amarasinghe. StreamIt: A language for streaming applications. In *Compiler Construction*, pages 179–196. Springer, 2002.

[13] D. Zhang, Z.-Z. Li, H. Song, and L. Liu. A programming model for an embedded media processing architecture. In *Embedded Computer Systems: Architectures, Modeling, and Simulation*, pages 251–261. Springer, 2005.

A Scalable Distributed Skip List for Range Queries

Sarwar Alam
Dept. of Computer Science
University of British Columbia
Vancouver, BC, Canada
sarwar@cs.ubc.ca

Humaira Kamal
Dept. of Computer Science
University of British Columbia
Vancouver, BC, Canada
kamal@cs.ubc.ca

Alan Wagner
Dept. of Computer Science
University of British Columbia
Vancouver, BC, Canada
wagner@cs.ubc.ca

ABSTRACT

In this paper we present a distributed, message passing implementation of a dynamic dictionary structure for range queries. The structure is based on a distributed fine-grain implementation of skip lists that can scale across a cluster of multicore machines. Our implementation makes use of the unique features of Fine-Grain MPI and introduces novel algorithms and techniques to achieve scalable performance on a cluster of multicore machines. Unlike concurrent data structures the distributed skip list operations are deterministic and atomic. Range-queries are implemented in a way that parallelizes the operation and takes advantage of the recursive properties of the skip list structure. We report on the performance of the skip list for range-queries, on a medium sized cluster with two hundred cores.

Categories and Subject Descriptors

E.1 [**Data Structures**]: Distributed Data Structures; D.1.3 [**Programming Techniques**]: Concurrent Programming—*Distributed programming*; H.3.4 [**Information Storage and Retrieval**]: Systems and Software—*Distributed systems*

Keywords

Fine-Grain MPI; performance; message-passing; multicore; range-query; skip list; concurrency; data structure.

1. INTRODUCTION

Key-value stores have emerged as an important data storage structure in today's large scale distributed systems. Typically these have been designed for reliability and disk-based storage, however, more recently the demand to process real-time streaming data has lead to the use of in-memory key-value storage. Key-value stores are based on hashing which provides a simple technique for distributing the data but not as efficient for range queries which are better suited for ordered structures such as a sorted list. There are systems designed to extend key-value stores to efficiently process range-queries in the case of disk-based systems [8]. As well, there is recent work on key-value stores for in-memory structures [12], but these have not

been extended to range queries. In this paper we present a novel implementation of a fully-distributed, in-memory, skip list data structure and augment the structure to support range-queries.

A Skip list is a common data structure used to implement ordered dictionaries [14]. A skip list probabilistically achieves $O(\log N)$ time for FIND, INSERT and DELETE operations. A nice property of skip lists is it consists of a hierarchy of lists with a list of all the items on level 0 with each subsequent level a sublist of the list below it. A sublist on level i can be viewed as a list of shortcuts to the list on level $i - 1$. In addition to FIND, INSERT and DELETE one can augment these queries with a range query operation that can take advantage of the ordering of the keys to output the result in a single operation. In this paper we will consider range queries over multi-dimensional keys where one or more ranges can be specified. For example "4.[2,8].3.[1,3]" is a range query over four dimensions searching for records exactly matching the first and third dimensions in the range specified in the second and fourth dimensions.

As an example as to why these type of data structures are useful for highly dynamic applications consider the following graph application[1]. For the graph, one can store the edges of the graph, lexicographical sorted by node i and then j, inside a skip list. The structure can be searched and updated by traversing the links, but more importantly the graph can be fully dynamic with nodes and edges continuously being inserted or deleted. The incoming data could be the arrival and departure time of airline flights with the system supporting queries that can find flights within a given temporal or spatial range. The advantage of our implementation of skip lists is that it is fully distributed efficiently making use of both multicore and multiple machines to scale across hundreds and potentially thousands of cores. In addition the service has been designed to adapt to the data and machine, to overlap computation with communication and load-balance the structure across the machines.

A crucial element of our design is the use of Fine-Grain MPI [11] (FG-MPI). FG-MPI extends MPI and makes it possible to express and exploit finer-grain, function-level concurrency and parallelism by allowing for multiple MPI processes inside an OS-process. This effectively decouples the process structure of the application from that of the underlying system now making it possible to have thousands and millions of MPI processes. As a result it is now possible to have the process structure match the application rather than tying the structure tightly to the underlying machine. The result is a "process-oriented" design of a skip list that is similar to concurrent data structures in object-oriented languages. However concurrent data structures, like those in Java, are built on top of a shared memory programing model. There are several implementations of skip lists using locks or lock-free techniques [9, 10], however,

---

[1] TAO [6] by Facebook was introduced to solve a similar problem on social graphs.

these implementations are targeted towards exploiting parallelism on multicore machines. They do not easily scale outside a single machine and do not scale to larger clusters where communication is by message-passing and there is not the support for shared memory. Our process-oriented design makes it possible to seamlessly distribute processes between cores inside a single machine and between machines and relies only on message passing.

The contributions and properties of our system are as follows. (a) Introduces a novel process-oriented implementation of skip lists. Unlike concurrent skip list structures, the system is deterministic and in essence acts like a pipeline with service requests flowing in and results flowing out. Range queries in the structure are automatically split over the extent of the range and computed in parallel. (b) The skip list operations are atomic, and have a non-overtaking property that makes it possible to use shortcuts [2] as an optimization to trade off consistency semantics for performance. Using this guarantee it is possible to support total ordering, sequential consistency, and, when shortcuts are used, no-consistency. (c) The list is dynamically load-balanced by controlling the granularity (number of items per process), the number of MPI processes per OS-process (core), and the allocation of list processes from the free process service. (d) We achieve scalable performance on a medium sized cluster of over 200 cores.

2. OVERVIEW

Our design of the distributed skip list is based on a novel message passing approach where each node of the skip list is implemented as a user-level process. Each of these processes may hold one or more list data items and communication among the skip list nodes is through messages. An example of a small skip list is shown in Figure 1. Each node consists of a tower of pointers to the other

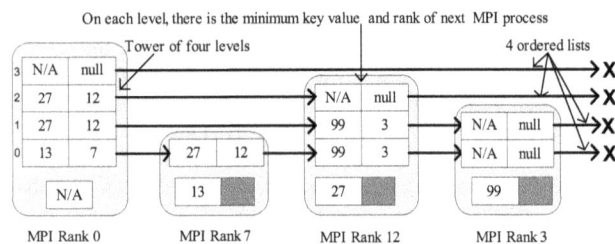

Figure 1: An example of a skip list where one or more data items are stored at each process.

nodes along with the key-value pair(s) that it stores. The root node in the skip list is configured to have the highest tower height and sentinel values are used to denote the left and right ends of the lists at each level. As shown in Figure 1, each node in the skip list is an MPI process which is identified by its MPI process rank[2]. In our implementation an MPI process rank is used in the same way a pointer to a memory address is used in a sequential implementation. Requests to perform an operation is through messages that are passed from process to process along the list.

One difference in our distributed process implementation and that of a sequential skip list implementation is that at every level we store the minimum key of the next successor process. For example, level 2 at process 0 stores the key 27, which is the key at process 12. The advantage to storing the minimum key at the predecessor is that requests do not need to query the next process to determine

---

[2] All processes in an MPI program with N processes are assigned a rank from 0 to $N-1$. In MPI, process rank is used as the source and destination of messages.

whether or not to forward the request. This significantly reduces the amount of messaging, but more importantly, it is now possible for requests to propagate asynchronously rather than the query-response type of handshaking needed when the minimum value is not available. The added overhead for storing the minimum key decreases with increasing granularity as we store multiple key-value pairs per process.

Our design approach requires a system that can support large numbers of small processes with low messaging and synchronization overheads. Fine-Grain MPI is such a system that extends the execution model of MPI to support large-scale, fine-grain concurrency.

2.1 Fine-Grain MPI

FG-MPI, which extends the MPICH2 middleware [4], decouples the notion of an MPI process from that of an OS process and makes it possible to have multiple MPI processes inside an OS process. MPI processes inside an OS process execute concurrently in an interleaved manner as non-preemptive threads (coroutines) and they cooperate with each other in the progression of the MPI requests. Because of the lightweight nature of coroutines it is possible to support thousands of processes inside an OS process and millions of processes across cores and machines in a cluster environment.

An FG-MPI execution, $[P, O, M]$, can be described in terms of P, the number of MPI processes per OS process[3], O, the number of OS processes per machine and M, the number of machines. A typical MPI execution is of the form $[1, O, M]$ where N, the total number of MPI processes as given by the "-n" flag of MPI's mpiexec command, equals $O \times M$. In FG-MPI, a "-nfg" flag was added to mpiexec enabling one to specify $P > 1$, where $N = P \times O \times M$.

We take a service-oriented approach [2] to the design of the system where the skip list has a service interface that interacts with other processes through message passing. Each OS process is configured to have an application process, a manager process and one or more processes that are either free or a skip list process. Application processes send requests to the skip list service and receive back responses. The manager processes are part of the free process service and they service requests for the allocation and de-allocation of free processes.

At start-up, the skip list service consists of the skip list root process, application processes, and one manager process per OS process. All of the remaining processes are configured to be free processes. These free processes are all blocked on a receive call and FG-MPI's runtime scheduler [11] ensures that they remain on a blocked queue and do not add any overhead while blocked. Skip list processes make free node requests to the co-located manager process which cooperates with the other managers to find a free process. Once a free process is found, it is converted into a skip list process by sending a message to it. Unlike in a usual MPI environment, we can co-locate multiple processes together and take advantage of the FG-MPI scheduler to execute the co-located processes that can make progress. The number of co-located processes in an OS process can be flexibly adjusted along with the number of key-value pairs that each skip list process stores. Tuning these parameters allow us to maximize the opportunity for parallelism, while reducing the amount of messaging. This is typically not possible in MPI without resorting to threads and relying on the operating system do the scheduling, which is unaware of the interactions between the MPI processes.

---

[3] We refer to these P MPI processes as *co-located* processes sharing a single address space. The terms *process*, *fine-grain process* and *MPI process* are used interchangeably. The term "OS process" is used to refer to an operating-system process.

3. SKIP LIST DESIGN

As shown in Figure 1, each skip list node is a process comprising of (a) a *tower* of `<key,rank>` pairs where each key is the minimum key (`min-key`) of the skip list process with that rank, (b) key (or list of keys in the multi-key case), and (c) the associated data. Operation requests are atomic. Each list process blocks waiting for a request to perform an operation and processes do not accept another request until it has completed sending all messages needed to locally complete the operation. Request messages contain the key information along with the process rank of the application node making the request. Request messages may alter nodes (INSERT, DELETE) and can mutate (RANGE-QUERY) as they traverse the skip list.

In the case of FIND, an application process initiates the request which traverses the list being forwarded either to the next process in the list at a given level or dropping down and forwarded to the next process on a lower level. Once it reaches the process holding the value (or failure) the process responds back to application process that initiated the request. INSERT and DELETE are implemented in a similar manner, however, in these cases the towers themselves have to be modified as the request travels along skip list. INSERT and DELETE also uses the free process service to allocate and de-allocate new list processes.

The RANGE-QUERY operation differs from FIND in that, when necessary, it splits the request. As a result, as the RANGE-QUERY traverses the list and splits, more of the query is done in parallel. By design, skip lists adapt to the distribution of the data and similarly our range queries will split more in dense areas of the key space thus providing the added parallelism where it is needed.

In the multi-key per node case, the number of returned key-values depends on the distribution of the data and may vary from one to the number of keys in the range. Each split partitions the range and each new request records the start and end of its part. The application re-assembles the parts and the query is complete when the application detects that the original range is complete.

The skip list has the following properties. Since the skip list may consist of hundreds and thousands of processes it was important to ensure freedom from deadlock and this was achieved by handling requests atomically and ensuring that all requests are only performed in the forward direction. The system was also designed with a non-overtaking property. The non-overtaking property ensured that given two requests r_i and r_j, if message r_i is before message r_j in the skip list, then r_i is always before r_j for the duration of the operation associated with r_i and r_j. Given the non-overtaking property the list can be configured for *total order*, where all requests go to the head, *sequential consistency*, where a hold-back queue is used to ensure that the operations by a process are completed in the order they were issued, and *no-consistency*, where the application and the list use shortcuts.

3.1 Experiments

The test setup consisted of a cluster with 25 machines connected by a 10GigE Ethernet interconnection network. Each of the machines in the cluster is a quad-core, dual socket (8 cores per machine) Intel Xeon® X5550, 64-bit machine, running at 2.67 GHz. All machines have 12 GB of memory and run Linux kernel 2.6.18-308.16.1.el5. All experiments were of the form $[P = 100, O = 8, M]$ with M ranging from 2 to 25.

In the experiments each OS process is configured with one application process that generates requests to the skip list. We vary the list size from 2^{20} (over 1 million) to 2^{24} key-values. INSERT operations are used to randomly insert items until the list is full. Once the list is full we generate requests as specified for the work-load and measure the system throughput (operations per second). Due to space limitations we report only our experiments on single-dimensional range queries.

Figure 2 shows the scaling behavior of range queries for three different sized range queries. The largest size query returns 1% of the list, which is a large portion of the skip list and is an extreme type of query. Recall that the range-query is automatically split as it traverses the list and each process with any portion of the result replies to the application. Therefore as the number of cores increases we go from having fewer and larger replies (i.e. returned messages) to having more and smaller replies. Figure 2 reports throughput with respect to (a) the number of operations, (b) the number of returned messages, and normalizes the performance across query types by giving (c) the number of returned key-values per second.

As expected, as the size of the range of a query increases, the operations per second that we can send to the skip list decreases. This is because application processes have to wait longer for all replies to return before it can send a new range query. However, as we can see in Figure 2(c), for larger queries we can return more key-values from the service, which is because a single range query operation sweeps through the service generating key-value results as opposed to having multiple separate FIND queries for each result. Figure 2(b) shows the number of returned messages all the application processes receive per second. All three range query sizes do scale with respect to the number of returned messages they can receive.

4. RELATED WORK

A skip list is a well-known data structure that has been frequently implemented as a concurrent data structure [9, 10]. Unlike the work on concurrent data structures our implementation does not depend on shared memory and does not have the non-determinism inherent in lock-based designs. There are some similarities in the design, for example, the notion of atomic actions, consistency, and techniques such as hand-over-hand access and forward-only traversal. Another significant difference is that the list elements are active processes where the data structure has control over the operations, not the application processes as in the case of concurrent data structures.

Our coarsening of the skip list by having each process store a set of keys is similar to Leaplists [5], a concurrent data structure where each node stores multiple keys. Unlike Leaplists, which used transactional memory, in our case the multiple keys helped to reduce the amount of messaging and provided a way to better adjust the amount of concurrency to the characteristics of the machine.

As previously mentioned hash-based key-value stores are an important data structure in distributed computing environments. Our implementation is focused on in-memory data structures and support for multi-dimensional range queries. SD-Rtree [7], RAQ [13] and SkipTree [1] are distributed tree data structures that support multi-dimensional range queries. Our implementation has the advantage of creating query splits automatically based on the probabilistic nature of the skip list tower creation. Where there is dense data, there are more towers and hence more opportunity for parallel access.

Pastry [15] and Skip Webs [3] are designed for peer-to-peer systems. Although these systems are based on message passing they are optimized for coarse-grain access to large data. Our distributed skip list is built with a focus on scalability and low-latency for in-memory access to data rather than large blocks of data residing on disk. As well, as expected, distributed storage systems are designed for availability and reliability, which we do not consider at present.

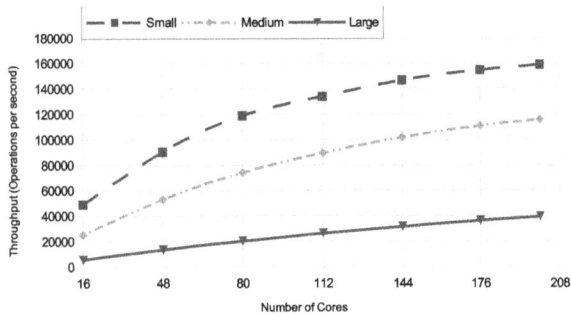

(a) Operations per second

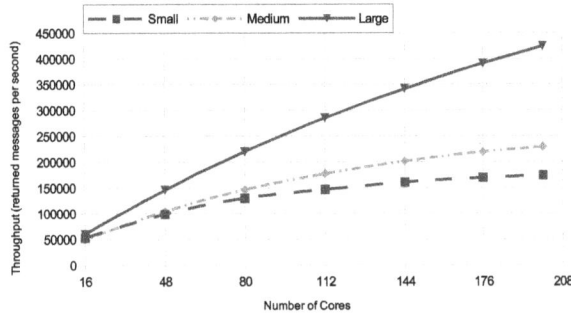

(b) Number of returned messages per second

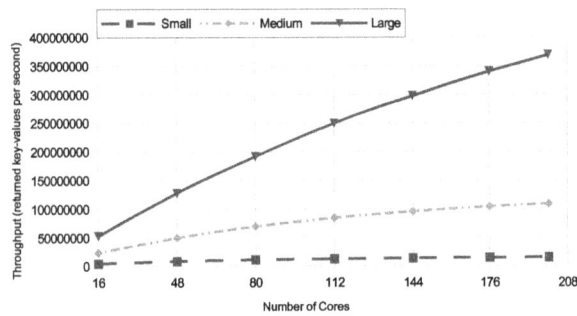

(c) Number of returned key-values per second

Figure 2: Scaling behavior of RANGE-QUERY with three fixed size range queries: Small = 100, Medium = 1000 and Large = 10000 key-value results per operation. Workload uses 100% RANGE-QUERY operations. Semantics used is no-consistency. Configuration: List size grows from 2^{20} to 2^{24}, MPI process per OS process, $P = 100$.

5. CONCLUSIONS

In this paper we presented and evaluated the design of a novel distributed message-passing implementation of a skip list to support range queries. We showed that the operations can be implemented atomically and that there is an interesting ordering property whereby operations cannot overtake one another. This property makes it possible to reason about operations deterministically and made it possible to implement total ordering and sequential consistency semantics. The experiments demonstrated the ability to scale to an ordered skip list with over a million data items with up to 20,000 MPI processes executing on 200 cores.

Acknowledgements

We gratefully acknowledge NSERC Canada and Mitacs Inc. for their support of this research. We thank Edward Soo for help on the airline application. FG-MPI is available for download.

6. REFERENCES

[1] S. Alaei, M. Ghodsi, and M. Toossi. Skiptree: A new scalable distributed data structure on multidimensional data supporting range-queries. *Computer Communications*, 33(1):73–82, 2010.

[2] S. Alam, H. Kamal, and A. Wagner. Service Oriented Programming in MPI. In *Communicating Process Architectures 2013*, pages 93–112. Open Channel Publishing Ltd., England, August 2013.

[3] L. Arge, D. Eppstein, and M. T. Goodrich. Skip-webs: efficient distributed data structures for multi-dimensional data sets. In M. K. Aguilera and J. Aspnes, editors, *PODC*, pages 69–76. ACM, 2005.

[4] Argonne National Laboratory. MPICH2: A high performance and portable implementation of MPI standard. Available from http://www.mcs.anl.gov/research/projects/mpich2/index.php.

[5] H. Avni, N. Shavit, and A. Suissa. Leaplist: lessons learned in designing tm-supported range queries. In *Proceedings of the 2013 ACM symposium on Principles of distributed computing*, PODC '13, pages 299–308, New York, NY, USA, 2013. ACM.

[6] N. Bronson et al. TAO: Facebook's Distributed Data Store for the Social Graph. *USENIX Annual Technical Conference (ATC)*, 2013.

[7] C. du Mouza, W. Litwin, and P. Rigaux. SD-Rtree: A scalable distributed Rtree. In *Data Engineering, 2007. ICDE 2007. IEEE 23rd International Conference on*, pages 296–305, 2007.

[8] R. Escriva, B. Wong, and E. G. Sirer. HyperDex: A distributed, searchable key-value store. In *Proc. of ACM SIGCOMM 2012 Conference on Applications, Technologies, Architectures, and Protocols for Computer Communication*, pages 25–36, 2012.

[9] M. Fomitchev and E. Ruppert. Lock-free linked lists and skip lists. In *Proceedings of the twenty-third annual ACM symposium on Principles of distributed computing*, PODC '04, pages 50–59, New York, NY, USA, 2004. ACM.

[10] M. Herlihy, Y. Lev, V. Luchangco, and N. Shavit. A provably correct scalable concurrent skip list. In *Conference On Principles of Distributed Systems (OPODIS)*. Citeseer, 2006.

[11] H. Kamal and A. Wagner. An integrated fine-grain runtime system for MPI. *Computing*, 96(4):293–309, 2014.

[12] H. Lim, D. Han, D. G. Andersen, and M. Kaminsky. MICA: A holistic approach to fast in-memory key-value storage. In *11th USENIX Symposium on Networked Systems Design and Implementation (NSDI 14)*, pages 429–444, Seattle, WA, Apr. 2014. USENIX Association.

[13] H. Nazerzadeh and M. Ghodsi. Raq: A range-queriable distributed data structure (extended version. In *In Proceeding of Sofsem 2005, 31st Annual Conference on Current Trends in Theory and Practice of Informatics, LNCS 3381*, pages 264–272. Citeseer, 2005.

[14] W. Pugh. Skip lists: a probabilistic alternative to balanced trees. *Commun. ACM*, 33:668–676, June 1990.

[15] A. Rowstron and P. Druschel. Pastry: Scalable, decentralized object location, and routing for large-scale peer-to-peer systems. In *Middleware 2001*, pages 329–350. Springer, 2001.

Author Index